THE
PAPER

THE PAPER

The Life and Death of the
New York Herald Tribune

RICHARD KLUGER

with the assistance of Phyllis Kluger

Alfred A. Knopf New York 1986

THIS IS A BORZOI BOOK
PUBLISHED BY ALFRED A. KNOPF, INC.

Grateful acknowledgment is made to Simon & Schuster, Inc., for
permission to reprint a cartoon from The Best of H. T. Webster, by H. T.
Webster. Copyright 1953 by New York Herald Tribune, Inc. Copyright
renewed 1981 by I. H. T. Cooperation.

Illustration credits appear on page 803.

Library of Congress Cataloging-in-Publication Data
Kluger, Richard.
    The paper: the life and death of the New York
herald tribune.
    Bibliography: p.
    Includes index.
    1. New York herald tribune. I. Kluger, Phyllis.
II. Title.
PN4899.N42N355   1986   071'.471   86-45276
ISBN 0-394-50877-7

Manufactured in the United States of America
FIRST EDITION

TO THE PRESERVATION of the First Amendment of the Constitution of the United States, which asserts: "Congress shall make no law respecting an establishment of religion, or prohibiting the free exercise thereof; or abridging the freedom of speech or of the press; or the right of the people peaceably to assemble, and to petition the Government for a redress of grievances." If this singular blessing were not long and well established, it is uncertain as of this writing whether the American people would now authorize its creation.

Contents

PART THREE 1941–1958

PART FOUR 1958–1966

Illustrations follow page 310

THE
PAPER

October 10, 1945: A Prelim

From the moment, two weeks earlier, when he had abandoned his banker's gray and dark blue suits for officer's dress at the naval base in San Francisco, he had been treated like royalty. They wined and dined him at every stop, admirals and generals and a flock of attentive staff people, and showed him what sights there were—the POW compound for the Japanese on Guam, the world's largest landing field on Tinian with its eight runways, the stark topography of Iwo Jima, where the devastation of war had denuded the island of vegetation. And now, for the last leg of his transpacific tour, they had provided him the services of his older son, Whitelaw, a navy lieutenant with a distinguished record as a pilot. If he had had any doubts of his national standing or that of the newspaper he owned, such a display of solicitude was reassuring to Ogden Mills Reid.

Still a handsome man in his sixty-fourth year—and thirty-third as president and editor of the *New York Herald Tribune*—he had begun to show the ravages of disease and alcohol, but there had been little diminution of his great natural dignity. The broad shoulders of the athlete he had been in his youth and the trim build he had never lost gave him the appearance of height beyond his six feet. The noble head was high-domed, almost hairless now except on the sides, and his features conspired to produce a somewhat craggy aspect: the long, straight nose, the full lips, the good jaw, the fine dark brown eyes, large and wide-set, with their hint of melancholy. The patrician's bearing was unmistakable; he moved slowly but left a sizable wake.

He watched with pride how his boy "Whitie" deftly handled the controls of the four-engined navy Privateer, the patrol craft he had flown ahead of the fleet during its steady westward advance across the Pacific in the lately concluded hostilities. A boyish blond whippet even at thirty-two, Whitie Reid had his father's amiable and undemonstrative disposition and former easy grace of movement. But the face, with the strong cheekbones and the pale blue eyes that seemed to look through whatever they beheld, were his mother's. Whitie would run the *Tribune* someday soon enough, his father supposed, but the lad had been in no great hurry for the prize; he was too discreet, too respectful, too nice for that. In its 104 years of life, astonishingly, there had been only three real rulers of the paper: Ogden, Ogden's father, and Horace Greeley.

The skies thickened as they neared the coast of Japan. Weather reports indicated typhoon conditions were accumulating. Atsugi airfield on Tokyo Bay radioed that visibility there was only a mile and the ceiling was five hundred feet. But Whitie Reid could not deny his father a display of airmanship in what had otherwise been a routine four-hour flight. As Ogden sat in the front dorsal turret, calmly catching up on back issues of the *Tribune*, his son took the heavy aircraft through the overcast, guiding by the shoreline of the great bay, brought it roaring in low over the water, buzzed the field, and put down neatly on the runway. In his own quiet way, Whitie Reid had moxie.

Ogden Reid toured the vanquished enemy capital with Wilbur Forrest, his companion on the trip and assistant editor of the *Tribune*, and found Tokyo a wilderness of fire damage. At U.S. Army headquarters, they presented Reid with a Japanese officer's pistol as a souvenir, and at a luncheon with General Douglas MacArthur, commander of the occupying forces, the Occidental potentate favored him and Bill Forrest with a forceful fifteen-minute lecture on the need for Mr. Truman's government to stand taller against the Soviets, who were eager for the Americans to get out of Japan and leave it to their tender ministrations.

They went for a relaxing weekend to the Fujiya Hotel, a hot springs resort with its luxurious appointments intact, in the mountains about two hours out of Yokohama, where they were joined by Frank Kelley, a *Tribune* foreign correspondent stationed in Japan, and an army lieutenant serving them as equerry. After dinner, their host, a U.S. major in charge of the resort, informed them that it was time to return to their rooms, exchange their uniforms for terry-cloth robes provided in the closet, and go for a sauna and a swim. "Good idea," said Ogden, and led the way. When they had been steaming on wood benches for a time, a comely young Japanese woman delivered a tray of scotch and glasses and a bucket of ice, adding considerably to the sociability of the occasion. As the time came to quit the sauna for the pool, the rest of them, well heated inside and out, went hesitantly and not without flinching; Ogden Reid, as befit the former captain of the Yale swimming and water polo teams, plunged right in, stroked happily for several laps, and emerged to pronounce it a glorious, bracing experience.

On dry land, he was less sure of his bearings. His sense of time, for one thing, was notoriously delinquent. It was often as if he dwelled in a world set off from other people's. As they waited for him in the hotel lobby the next day, and waited and waited, Forrest said to Kelley, "He's probably up in the room, and I'll tell you what he's probably doing—he's checking his cigars, he's checking his wallet, he's checking his fly—and don't quote me but he's probably checking the legs on all the chairs."

It was not said unkindly. Bill Forrest had been Ogden Reid's confidant for nearly fifteen years now—some *Tribune* staff people called the stocky, bronchial-sounding Forrest the owner's bootlicker and some called him his nursemaid, but neither characterization quite caught the nuanced relationship. Forrest genuinely liked the man, for all the indignities the job imposed along with the honors and delegated power.

Just why Ogden Reid had won the goodwill of his staff was hard to explain to outsiders. On the face of it, he was not an especially admirable figure: he was neither dynamic nor politic nor generous nor even very personable, although his big hearty laugh would occasionally boom across the city room or down at Bleeck's; indeed, he was nearly inarticulate. Bill Forrest was there to speak for him and write his letters and memos. Ogden Reid, to be blunt about it as few ever were at the time, was practically dysfunctional as the editor and head of one of the great newspapers of the world—and had been for nearly twenty years now. Yet his very nonfeasance had its uses; they liked him for what he was not. For all his inherited wealth and the high social standing it brought him, he was not a stuffed shirt. His shyness, common in rich men wary of why they are befriended, did not prevent him from appearing nightly in the city room and asking, almost as litany, "Anything unusual in the news tonight, gentlemen?" And he drank with them at Bleeck's, although he often needed Bill Forrest or one of the other editors to identify the help by name. Ogden Reid was not a smart man, which was not to say he was dumb; there was just nothing quick or deep or penetrating about his intellect. But he was an aristocrat, and aristocrats were not required to be smart. Besides, his wife had enough brains for both of them.

What Ogden Reid was not, most of all, was an autocrat. There was none of the flamboyant arrogance of W. R. Hearst or other lords of the press. He ruled instead with a light hand, deferring to the able professionals who manned the paper and submerging what personality he had within the institution itself. He had, to be sure, enormous pride in the *Herald Tribune*—in its literate writing, its fairness and objectivity in reporting the news, its standing as guardian of the conscience of the Republican Party, of American liberties and the fruits of the free-enterprise system. The truth was that he thought of his newspaper not so much as a family property but as a public trust, a national treasure, not to be compromised on the altar of profits. If you had accused him of noblesse oblige, he would not have argued the charge but taken it, rather, as a commendation. The *Herald Tribune* may have been Ogden Reid's personal property, but it was more important by far than anyone connected with it, himself included. What mattered most was that it should endure in ink-stained immortality beyond the life spans of those who created it new every morning. The owner performed his role as The Owner. He embodied traditions and sustained standards; his staff operated. It was an atmosphere that attracted and held competent men and women. Other newspapers were larger and paid better, but in terms of individual fulfillment, there was none better to work on.

There was one other thing about him that not only deflected the sort of resentment American hired hands feel is their birthright against their employer —especially one like him who had had the operation handed to him on the silveriest of platters—but actually endeared him to them in a perverse way. Ogden Reid was a drunk.

Everyone at the paper knew it. It had been going on for as long as anyone could remember. There had been a few vain efforts to cure him of it, but as the years passed, he seemed to work less and drink more. He drank a lot, and he drank everything. At Bleeck's he might start with a scotch and follow with the house drink, a "rye gag" (defined officially as "an old-fashioned without the garbage in it"), and then turn to the reporter or editor nearest him, ask what the fellow was drinking, and order two of whatever it was—one for each of them —and on into the night. He was not a mean drunk or a loud one and never made a spectacle of himself, except for falling down one time in the city room, and then no one knew which would be worse, to pick him up or leave him there; they turned away and left him, and those who watched out of the corners of their eyes reported that on hoisting himself upright, Ogden appeared grateful for having been ignored.

One unfortunate effect of his alcoholism was to curtail his outreach to the men and councils of power and to leave his newspaper something of a headless wonder. Nobody knew why a man who had so much to live for habitually drank himself into oblivion. Those on the paper who bothered to theorize suggested that as the overindulged son of overbearing parents with unfulfillable expectations of him, he had been driven into a marriage with an ambitious woman who, longing for him to prove his mettle on his own, managed in the long run only to disable him further. Whatever the cause, Ogden Reid retreated deeper into his own world as his life lengthened. He took refuge in his large corner office with his father's portrait behind him, in his homes—the big townhouse on East Eighty-fourth Street, a few doors from Fifth Avenue; the family estate at Purchase in Westchester; Camp Wild Air, carved with rough-hewn elegance from the wilderness on the shore of Upper St. Regis Lake in the Adirondacks, and Flyway, the hunting lodge with its boggy surround in southeastern Virginia near the Carolina border—and his clubs, athletic or nautical or cultural but always social, including the Knickerbocker, New York Yacht, Lotos, Apawamis, Union, Brook, Century, Union League, Army and Navy, City, Pilgrims, Riding, and Players. Others were delegated to run the family philanthropy, which happened to be a famous old newspaper.

He was on best behavior during the trip to the Orient, where he had never been before, and Bill Forrest monitored him extra dutifully as their pace quickened and their agenda grew more serious. They spoke earnestly about freedom of the press to Japanese publishers, flew over the ruins of Nagasaki and on to Korea, where officials were less than sanguine about the prospects of self-government after forty years under the Japanese heel. The China portion of their tour was climaxed by an overnight visit with Generalissimo and Madame Chiang Kai-shek in Chungking, where they heard about the rise of Maoist power. There were still more meetings with officials, U.S. military and native, in the Philippines, the very archipelago that Reid's father had maneuvered, as the pivotal member of the Spanish-American War treaty commission, into Yankee hands, and a commemorative visit to the way stations of the Bataan death march, one of the atrocities that Japan could never pay for dearly enough.

By the time they touched down again on American soil, they had logged 30,000 air miles over seven weeks. No reporters waited at the airport to interview him about his reflections on what he had seen and heard. Instead, Ogden Reid was greeted by a long takeout headlined "The Trib's Mrs. Reid" in *Time* magazine's "Press" section. Pegged to the paper's just concluded annual forum on current problems that drew three days of overflow crowds to the grand ballroom of the Waldorf-Astoria, the article noted the blue-ribbon roster of speakers, including Secretary of State James F. Byrnes, Army Chief of Staff George C. Marshall, and war-hero generals Jonathan Wainwright and Claire Chennault, on hand to discuss the theme "Responsibility of Victory," and called the unique national assemblage the brainchild of "tiny, self-assured" Helen Reid. It went on to paint her as a dynamic executive who kept two secretaries and two phone lines clicking all day and used her lunch hour to sell advertisers on the pulling power of her paper. She took pains to describe herself as Ogden's "first mate," but it was she whom they wrote about, she whom they had featured in a two-parter titled "Queen Helen" in *The Saturday Evening Post* the year before—it was always Helen and never Ogden. It was not entirely fair.

For one thing, his wife reigned over the *Tribune* at Ogden's sufferance. They had made a good team. Her activism, liberality, and alertness to new ideas were the perfect complement to his passivity and conservatism and his hold on the paper's traditions and the values of its readership among the better social classes. If he had not confined her primary spheres of influence to the advertising department, promotional events like the forum at the Waldorf, and soft-news areas like women's features and the arts, dear driving Helen might have made rather a mess of things.

More to the point, why was nobody writing about how far the paper had come under his stewardship? The *New York Tribune* was selling hardly more than 25,000 copies a day in 1912 when Ogden took over after two decades of his father's absentee management; it was surviving at all only because of cash subsidies from his mother's inherited fortune. Under his editorship the process of rejuvenation had begun, under him the *Tribune* had bought out the *Herald* in 1924, under him the seamless amalgamation had flourished. There had been seven morning newspapers in New York when he had taken over, and now only two were left—and the two others that had since arisen, the racy tabloid *News* and *Mirror,* could hardly be dignified as *news*papers. It was under his name, his standards, his steadfastness that the paper had risen to a greatness it had not known since its early years of eminence under Greeley—and the world had become a vastly more complicated place, and the nation a colossus, in the intervening generations.

The achievement was undeniable. The newspaper Ogden Reid came home to in November of 1945 was about to post pre-tax profits of more than two million dollars for the third year in a row; it had never been more prosperous. Finally they would be able to put in badly needed press units. And the Paris edition, resumed the previous December after a four-and-a-half-year shutdown during the Nazi occupation, was going great guns—it would return a profit of $200,000 for the calendar year. That spring, the *Tribune*—few people bothered any longer to call it by both its names, and those less reverential than the paper's old guard were coming to call it just "the Trib"—had been awarded the Ayer Cup, emblematic of excellence in newspaper typography and layout, for the sixth time since the competition had been inaugurated in 1931, more than any other paper; graphically, esthetically, the *Tribune* had been repeatedly judged the best-looking daily in America. And in quality of content, it had only one serious rival if all factors were considered: the range and depth of news coverage, including local, national, foreign, financial, cultural, and sports; the literacy and clarity of its writing; the thoughtfulness of its editorial page; and the soundness and care of its editing. Other papers may have matched or excelled it in given departments. The *Chicago Daily News,* for example, had a tradition of strong foreign coverage and bright writing, but its very inland location did not require it to do what the *Herald Tribune* did every day in covering developments in the nation's financial and cultural capital. The Washington papers, the *Post, Times-Herald,* and *Star,* did well covering government news but not much else. The *Chicago Tribune* and *Los Angeles Times* were great thick sheets but blatantly boosterish and parochial in their approach to news selection and hopelessly retrogressive in their editorial columns. The Baltimore *Sun* was a distinguished paper in many ways but rather colorless in its post-Mencken era and typographically antiquarian. The *Post-Dispatch* in St. Louis had a noteworthy editorial page and often lively quality in other departments in the Pulitzer tradition, but it was inescapably a regional paper. All things considered, there was only one other great national newspaper in America at the end of 1945, and you could get quite an argument, especially within journalistic circles, which was then the better one —the *Herald Tribune* or *The New York Times.* *

In terms of financial health, the contest was not so close. In sales, the *Tribune* at war's end had 63 percent of the *Times*'s daily circulation and 70 percent of its Sunday edition—respectable figures but hardly neck and neck. The *Tribune,* in fact, ranked only sixth in circulation among New York's nine citywide papers, ahead of just three evening entries, the *Sun,* the *Post,* and *PM.* But its advertising revenues, based on claims of high-income readership that was especially strong in the most affluent suburbs, had climbed to 85 percent of the *Times*'s total that year, and it was being heavily used by the carriage-trade department stores. Editorially, there was no denying the *Times*'s lead in strictly quantitative terms—neither the *Tribune* nor any other American paper approached it for the range or depth of its compendious news product. It was thick, solid, comprehensive, and reliable. And it was dull. Almost defiantly so. Its dullness to the eye and the intellect was nearly a concomitant of its solidity. The *Tribune* was a serious paper, too, but it had verve and was easier to read. The *Times* had no editorial writer with the bite and edge of the *Tribune*'s Walter Millis. Or war correspondent with the dash and grit of Homer Bigart. Or critic in the arts like the brilliantly knowledgeable Virgil Thomson. Or commentator on global events like the philosophical and sometimes profound Walter Lippmann. Or sportswriter like this new fellow, Walter (Red) Smith, whom Reid's doughty sports editor, Stanley Woodward, had just imported to the staff from Philadelphia. Or a passionate expert on food like Clementine Paddleford. Or comics of the sedate and homey sort the *Tribune* carried to lighten the often grim daily news load. Or a daily crossword puzzle, the delight of train commuters, which the *Times* considered beneath its dignity. Nor did the *Times* run any public-affairs event comparable to the *Tribune*'s annual forum, broadcast across America over all four major radio networks. Nor did it sell any of its own features to newspapers outside its prime circulation area as the Herald Tribune Syndicate did in making national figures of the likes of Lippmann and Jay Darling, the two-time Pulitzer Prize–winning cartoonist who signed his work "Ding." Nor did it have an edition in Europe; the *Tribune* was the only American paper that did.

As he returned home, then, from his Pacific adventure and began what was to prove the last year of his life, Ogden Reid, for all his limitations, deserved

---

* Alone among American newspapers, the *Times,* when cited in books and periodicals, usually has its city of publication as well as its name italicized. This form is generally assumed to have evolved as a means of distinguishing it from *The Times* of London, with which it has never been associated except in an occasional joint editorial project. In this book, the name of the city in which a paper was published is italicized when it was a formal part of its name; the same rule has been followed for the word "The" when the full, formal name of a paper is given. But "The" was never part of the official name of the *New York Herald Tribune,* for example. In the short form of newspaper names—e.g., the *Times*—the "The" has been lowercased. In quoted material, however, the original form of newspaper names has been retained.

credit for having skippered his craft ably, no matter whose hands were actually on the wheel. His taste and sensibility ever reassured the crew during the choppy voyage. The *New York Herald Tribune,* a marriage of two newspapers that, in their nineteenth-century youth, had done more than any others to create modern American journalism, was now at its apex of power and prestige. What follows is the story of how it arrived there and then, just twenty-one years later —its influence still felt in every newsroom in the nation—was gone.

PART ONE

1835-1900

Fame is a vapor; popularity an accident, riches take wings; the only earthly certainty is oblivion; no man can foresee what a day may bring forth; while those who cheer to-day will often curse to-morrow; and yet I cherish the hope that the journal I projected and established will live and flourish long after I shall have mouldered into forgotten dust, being guided by a larger wisdom, a more unerring sagacity to discern the right, though not by a more unfaltering readiness to embrace and defend it at whatever personal cost. . . .

—HORACE GREELEY, Recollections of a Busy Life (1868)

1

The Righteous
and the Wrathful

Seen even from the rear, his is the most conspicuous figure in Broadway's midday throng as, swaying and rocking at high velocity, the twin tails of his very long, very loose, very worn white coat flying out behind him, he proceeds like a bent hoop, appearing to occupy both sides of the street at the same time. The footwear propelling him is not fashionable. Large, heavy, and coarse, his boots are mud-spattered like the trouser bottoms that have worked their way out of hiding and now bunch atop the boots. At a glance one might take him for an elder rustic, come to the city to sell a load of turnips and cabbage.

Inspected from the front, he is larger and younger than his stoop and gait suggest, but not a whit more stylish. The suit, rumpled beyond redemption, nevertheless reveals itself as untattered, essentially clean, and of good quality. Like its owner's cravat, it seems to have been donned by inadvertence and almost certainly without reference to a mirror. Standing still and upright, this paragon of disarray would measure an inch or two below six feet and carry perhaps 145 pounds on his long legs. But he has rarely stood still in his entire forty years of life; his stoop is less a product of age than of occupation. For a quarter of a century, he has bent over a printer's stone or typecase or editor's desk, and whatever pliancy his backbone may have possessed at birth has long since eroded. There is, too, the weight it has had to bear of that enormous head, covered at the moment with a wilted white hat. The head is twenty-three and one-half inches in circumference, and phrenologists who have studied it say the brain within is *very* large, and in all the right places. The face this head wears is round and pale, the bottom half rimmed with an absurd fringe of whisker, flaxen once but whitening now like the sprigs of hair that steal out from beneath the hat and straggle down his neck. It is the deep-set blue eyes, though, beaming and beneficent, that lend the countenance its look of youthful good humor. Behind the round, full forehead, rising into a high and stately dome, he contemplates this evening's principal labor: an editorial that first honors and then dismembers the archbishop for his latest volley on public education.

His person is as heavily freighted as his mind. Scraps fill his pockets, notes to himself after a morning at home with the newspapers and his correspondence. One arm bears a bundle of material to dispatch, letters written, books and manuscripts to return, implements to exchange; the other arm wields a fat umbrella. If Horace Greeley did not most emphatically exist, Charles Dickens, his almost exact contemporary, would have had to invent him. Indeed, Greeley on the go resembles no one so much as Cruikshank's rendering of Mr. Pickwick. Mr. Greeley you would perhaps not take for a gentleman, but you would never mistake him for a common man. In fact, he is at this very instant among the most celebrated and influential of his countrymen and, arguably, the most widely and fervently read writer in the land.

The City Hall clock says 12:17 as he lurches past it across the little park. His destination is just to the east—a squat, five-story, dry-goods box occupying the south end of the triangular block bounded by Park Row, Nassau Street, and Spruce. Its label is in five-foot-high letters placarded above the roofline, proclaiming that here is published the TRIBUNE. He had not chosen the name idly. Like the tribunes of ancient Rome, he would serve the common people in the defense and promulgation of their rights. No other newspaper in the city seemed so disposed. Its great, clattering, six-mouthed press in the low-ceilinged basement is now disgorging nearly 20,000 copies of the *Tribune* every evening but Saturday. Its eight densely packed pages, arranged in six wide columns of small but neat and elegant type, contain enough reading matter to fill an amply margined book of 400 pages. The press is run by steam, of course, in the best modern manner—a far cry from the hand-cranked model he had operated in his Vermont apprenticeship; that one produced hardly 200 sheets an hour, each impression requiring nine separate operations and wearying his young bones. The type is still set by hand—an entire generation will pass before machines assume that most exacting of the printer's functions—and the paper is folded the same way. The folders, though, are so adept it is hard to conceive of a machine that will beat them; each copy requires six folds, and the fastest men can do thirty copies a minute. The *Weekly Tribune* run is approaching 50,000 copies, making it probably the most widely circulated journal in America. It has surpassed the unspeakable Bennett's weekly edition, though Bennett's daily *Herald* is still running well ahead of the *Tribune*. But Bennett, after all, had a six-year head start, and much of the material on which he has built his circulation was aimed, as the *Tribune* had never been, at arousing the lowest instincts of the masses. Will the *Tribune* lose that advantage in appealing to the educated when little Raymond's mannerly entry, *The New-York Daily Times,* with a lush bankroll of more than $100,000 behind it, appears shortly? Is there enough business for them all—the six-penny papers catering to the counting-houses; the low-minded but readable *Sun,* at a penny still the largest seller in town, and now a *Times* directed to conservative readers who thought Bennett's sheet had no principles and his own too many of the wrong sort?

He is, by nature, an optimist, so the prospect of intensified rivalry does not daunt Greeley as he turns the corner onto Nassau and rolls into his headquarters like a fleet admiral taking the deck of his flagship. New York is booming as never before. Its population now, in the first year of the second half of the nineteenth century, has passed half a million, by a wide margin the largest in the Western Hemisphere, and shows no signs of letting up. The Croton aqueduct that he has so ardently championed is at last fully functional, measurably improving public health conditions, and the underground sewer system will shortly become a reality, along with Central Park, another vital civic amenity he has passionately urged while there was still time and room. The harbor has never been more crowded, and the Erie Railroad's steel tendrils are now adding hundreds of new miles of feeder lines into and out of the city annually. In the twenty years since his arrival, New York has become the grand emporium of the New World— one of the busiest bazaars on earth. Destiny, Horace Greeley has long been sure, favors America, and New York, which he partially adjudges a Sodom-by-the-sea, is just as surely fate's darling.

For all his interest in public sanitation, he is oblivious to the condition of the *Tribune*'s staircase, rated by connoisseurs of filth as among the dirtiest in creation. The dingy door to the third floor, inscribed "Editorial Rooms of the New York Tribune, H. Greeley," is no more inviting, but the usual assemblage of unsolicited visitors awaits him within. He navigates the narrow entrance passageway and pauses at the first of the two small closed rooms to his left, from which emerges the soft, rapid sibilance of a proofreading team, one member reciting aloud from the original penned copy to his silently scrutinizing partner. There were two spelling errors in that morning's edition, The Editor advises, thrusting open the door and filing his charge in a high, soft, but distinctly querulous voice. One of the errors was a misspelled name, and nothing depresses him more than getting a name wrong; it undermines confidence in everything else in the paper. An excuse is tendered—the culprit was a new man, working late, and the offending piece was one of the last to be set. The explanation is not acceptable. The Editor marches on.

The main editorial room, a long but skinny apartment, is lightly inhabited at this hour. Only the shipping news editor and his staff are astir, compiling tomorrow's list of two hundred sailings and arrivals, to be supplemented by excerpts from no fewer than two dozen ships' logs. Over there at his desk against the wall is the round, imperturbable Ripley, whom The Editor greets with a nod and a "Ripley"—Greeley, the consummate democrat, is not much of one for "Mistering." He has just approved raising Ripley's salary to twenty-five a week, not much, some would say, for drudging through the mountain of new books, journals, and miscellaneous literary fare from both sides of the Atlantic that rises fresh each morning on his desk top. But George Ripley, forty-nine, of Harvard College (1823), of Harvard Divinity School (1826), of the Brook Farm Association, of the Boston transcendentalists' *Dial* magazine, is now in the fourth year of the thirty-one he will spend as literary editor of the *Tribune,* and he does not view his occupation as drudgery. He is, incomparably, the most knowledgeable and skillful critic of any employed by an American daily journal. He does not merely fashion book notices; he produces a large quantity of meaty reviews, serious yet popularly accessible evaluations of an astonishing variety of contemporary works. Highly learned, he presides in splendid vigilance over the dignity of the language and its use, but he is not a pedant; his gravest fault, if any, is a tendency to be too lenient on his subjects. Unofficially, he is the office watchdog over the *Tribune*'s standard of prose; a misused word discovered by him has been known to cost the malefactor a week's suspension from the staff.

The Editor's carpeted private office just off the main room is anything but; it is not even his alone. Within, a vast bookshelf filled with reference works serves as the paper's library, open to the staff day and night. Of the two desks, his is plainly the unoccupied one near the window with its splendid view of City Hall. Its green felt surface, shelving, drawers, and cubbyholes might appear to a stranger as a monument to confusion; but in the spillage of manuscripts, proof sheets, exchange papers, books, journals, letters, circulars, scraps bearing messages, and a pair of scissors tied to a strap so it will not be swallowed up forever in the rummage, Greeley sees only genial disorder: the very aspect he himself presents to the world. Atop the highest shelf of all sits a bronze bust, garlanded in dust, of Henry Clay, the noblest politician of his time, in The Editor's estimate. In addition to all the paper summonses, he is awaited by the usual assortment of callers without appointment. He will see and dispose of them all in his fashion, some attentively, some with a yawn, some while studying his mail and messages. Among them are an inventor wishing publicity for a device he has lately perfected; a Cincinnati litterateur wishing him to appear at the lecture series there on his tour next winter (for the usual share of the house); an upstate minister wishing to make his acquaintance and to seek his advice on their mutual crusade for temperance; a councilman wishing to take issue with him on the matter of awarding streetcar franchises; an admirer wishing to borrow money (and unaware that Greeley's days as the softest touch in town are long past); a scholar with a suggestion for improving *The Whig Almanac,* shortly to be renamed *The Tribune Almanac,* nonpartisanship being thought likely to improve its salability.

Across the room from this congregation sits the *Tribune*'s second-in-command, his desk in perfect order, conducting real business in brisk, marginally civil tones; Charles A. Dana is a managing editor who manages. His flowing beard adds massiveness to his authoritative manner. In the interstices of the afternoon, he edits the foreign correspondence. Just now he is examining the latest offering from the new London correspondent, a chap Dana himself has recruited; with magisterial contempt, Karl Marx, an exiled German editor opposed to the Prussian regime, writes of the benightedness of tsarist Russia and the hardly less lamentable imperialism of Her Majesty's government in Parliament. A witness to and sympathizer with the crushed continental revolutions of '48, Dana reads with approval. Mr. Marx will remain more or less a *Tribune* regular for the rest of the decade.

By four o'clock The Editor has dealt with the preliminaries of the day and disappears for a vegetarian dinner at Windust's, a few doors away from the *Tribune* building. By the time he returns, the editorial rooms are bathed in gaslight and the pace of activity has noticeably quickened. His is a nocturnal business: 70 percent of the paper's contents will be set between nightfall and midnight. Seven reporters, all shirtsleeved and mustached, scribble away at their little desks, fifty or so words to a page, and penmanship counts. All are paid at space rates, so the editors must guard against a tendency to windiness. This fellow here writes of the day's session of the Common Council, that one on a gathering of the Tammany sachems, that one over there on a lecture about the great adventure unfolding in California. Inkstands and pastepots are everywhere. Rusty pen points and bits of blotting paper litter the floor. A tin jar of ice water sits in a corner. Pipe smoke sweetens and thickens the air. The copy box rattles every now and then up the wooden pipe, bearing its freshly composed cargo to the fourth-floor composing room, where three dozen printers labor in eerie silence at an average rate of seventy lines an hour (all to be disassembled the same way, letter by letter, and replaced each in its case the next morning). Ottarson, the city editor, who rose to that eminence from devil to apprentice printer to journeyman to reporter, activates a bell up in the shop and grunts a few instructions into the metal speaking tube, specifying the setting order of the copy just transmitted. Visitors, mostly supplicants for precious space in print, come and go. Messengers from the telegraph office arrive more urgently by horse cab. A report on a just concluded debate in the Congress has been wired from Washington; Dana devours it. The downtown apple woman circulates among the desks, peddling her wares unimpeded. All is orderly as the work speeds ahead without excessive displays of energy or verbal outburst.

Bolt upright at his desk, his nearsighted eyes augmented by thick spectacles, The Editor composes the lead editorial. Filled with his sprawling scrawl, all but undecipherable outside the office, leaves of foolscap fly from beneath his beautifully shaped hand, so remarkably white that the ink staining his thumb, index, and middle fingers has become nearly indelible. He writes without pause, seemingly without thought—for he has done all his thinking long before the act of composition. Archbishop Hughes has issued a letter unfavorable to the efficacy of public education upon the souls of Catholic children. Greeley is distressed, especially since, as he acknowledges at the outset of his leader, the cleric holds "a spiritual power among us greater than that of any other living man." His fiat could remove 50,000 children from the common schools and rekindle the fires of theological rancor, best left to the dead European past. The Editor, knowing the combustible nature of the material at hand, is not shrill; he despises the demagogic. But he will not withhold plain words, forcefully expressed. "Now when the Archbishop charges our system of Republican Liberty with putting 'God and the Devil, truth and falsehood, on the same level,'" The Editor charges, "he surely misconceives that system." He marshals his argument point by roman-numeral point, culminating at VIII with:

> . . . He would have Religion form a part of every child's education. Very good—we concur in that view. But it is one thing to assume that each child should be taught Religion, and quite another to maintain that Religious dogmas should be taught in *common schools.* We desire and intend that our own children shall be taught Religion; we do *not* desire that it shall be taught them in Common Schools. For this we shall take them to Church, to Sunday School, to Bible Class, or wherever else they may be taught by those who we believe will teach them Divine Truth in its purity.

Intermittently he bounds up the stairs, two at a time when inspiration prods, to make a change or insertion; when the latter, he takes pains to remove as many words as he adds so that an entire section will not have to be laboriously reset to indulge him.

He reads the completed essay. It will do. He titles it "The Archbishop's Letter" and at the extreme right of the not quite full last line adds "H.G." In rural areas and settlements along the great western lakes where the weekly edition is the only regularly read newspaper, some folks think "H.G." authors the *Tribune* in its entirety. He does not go to great lengths to disabuse them of this notion.

The City Hall clock, illuminated now, shows half past eleven. Dana will linger till the paper locks up at midnight; Ottarson, till three, awaiting any late news and preparing the reporters' assignments for the morrow. Greeley exchanges final words with his deputy, who, with the pressure of the workday abated, is a charming conversationalist. Dana is respectful but makes no show of veneration. The Editor, for his part, instructs largely by indirection, leaving his full oracular meaning to be intuited. The system works well.

Homeward, his perpetual bundle in place with fresh contents sifted from the desk-top debris for his pre-office attention in the morning, Greeley is only slightly more bent than upon his arrival. A waiting cabbie bears him away to his modest house on Nineteenth Street, between Broadway and Fourth Avenue: Horace Greeley in momentary repose. Greeley, the very embodiment of his countrymen's collective virtues and hopeless contradictions. He idealizes rural life, which he has abandoned, and excoriates city life, upon which he thrives. In attaining material success and fame, he aspires most of all to righteousness. He believes, that is, not merely in doing well by doing good—he insists upon it. In ideology, he is a radical conservative; no other description will serve. He favors a society based on sound, solid institutions, but they must be made to work humanely as well as profitably. He wishes the laboring man well, wars on his degradation, demands that he be given opportunity to work and rise in the world and practice thrift and form alliances and learn skills and economy—yet Greeley is equally all for the capitalist and *his* self-aggrandizement in a marketplace free but insulated from foreign marauders. He favors government that spends less and does more than at present. In his almost childlike optimism and inclination to oversimplify, he is certain all problems can be solved by reason, goodwill, hard work, and development of the West. Meanwhile, he bears all the world's woes and infirmities on his shoulders and ponders how next to instruct it in their alleviation.

II

He came of struggling but not destitute farm folk in south-central New Hampshire. His mother had lost her first two babies and cherished this new frail one all the more. She made him her constant companion and confidant from the moment he was old enough to talk. She read to him, crooned to him, instructed him, filled him with family, ancestral, and regional lore. By age three he could read; by five he was reading everything his mother could obtain—the Bible, Shakespeare, a miscellany of classics, whatever newspapers found their way to the little town of Amherst. At school he could outspell his masters and had easily outread them. At nine he was conversant with the great issues of the day, approving (not without reservation) the Missouri Compromise. He was, in short, a prodigy.

Genius, or its close approximation, was not in large supply in the neighborhood, and so the local people offered to finance Horace's education, at nearby Phillips Exeter Academy and then at college. This neighborly generosity precipitated a crisis in the Greeley home. Pride decided. There was, furthermore, the added consideration that the boy, however brainy, was needed to help his father farm their eighty stony acres. Forever after, Horace would profess gladness that he had been "indebted for schooling to none but those of whom I had a right to ask and expect it."

Formal and, as had been offered, superior education might well have made him more analytical and better able to appreciate opposing points of view— never his strength when later occupying his editorial throne. On the other hand, his parents' denial to him of higher learning spared him the constricting classical curriculum; instead of such dry fare, the lad feasted omnivorously on whatever he came upon. Great curiosity and openness to social, cultural, and technological developments of his age became a Greeley hallmark. Owing nothing, not even thanks, to his neighbors had the further effect of deepening the independence of his character, perhaps his greatest strength through long years of trial, temptation, and obloquy. Finally, if he had gone on to college and learned all about becoming a gentleman, he would likely have turned into a far different Horace Greeley from the one history remembers; the printer's trade, however ennobling or artful a craft, was at bottom hard manual labor.

His adult social agenda had detectable origins in his childhood. His father's hard luck and marginal competence at farming were made worse by his fondness for liquor; for the rest of his life, Horace was a teetotaler and worked tirelessly for the temperance movement. Bankruptcies and foreclosures were said to be common in the area because local laborers and manufacturers could not compete with cheap goods flooding New England from the mother country. The protective tariff, nurturing native industry and the American worker with it, would also become a mainstay of the Greeley political creed—and there was nothing abstract about his abiding fervor on the subject.

When the family started over in Vermont, Horace helped his father drive the team and clear the woods and make the charcoal, but their fortunes did not improve much. When he was fifteen, the rest of the family went farther west, clear to the other end of New York State, where relatives in Erie County held out hope to them of fruitful land and better times. But their lanky book lover they left behind. Horace's future, they all saw, was not in working the soil. He was apprenticed to the printshop in East Poultney, a tiny hamlet set on a picture-book hillside a few miles east of the New York border; its main product was an indifferent little weekly called the *Northern Spectator.* Horace received forty dollars a year, board, clothing of a sort, and the grounding that stood him so well in the profession he would shortly pioneer.

The *Spectator* was a shaky enterprise. The town was too small, really, to support its own newspaper; civic pride sustained it more than anything else. East Poultney was an upright, decent community, and while not close to the center of things, it kept up. There was, for example, the weekly lyceum held in the brick schoolhouse, and no one participated more avidly in it than the apprentice printer. They treated him as an adult and listened to him with respect since so much of what he said made sense. It was as if Horace Greeley could barely wait to escape childhood; so far as he could remember, he would write later, he never played a game of ball in his life. Nor was he much at dancing, flirting, or the other social graces. In a way, he was a ward of the whole town, but practically speaking, he was self-taught, self-motivated, self-sufficient, and not surprisingly, rather full of himself.

His superiors came and went at the *Spectator* office; the job paid a poor living. But it suited the apprentice fine: the less he was monitored, the more it fell his lot to do. He began to write articles as well as set them, proof them, and print them, and continued to read everything he could get his hands on, mining the local library and poring over every word in the exchange papers that came in. By the time he rejoined his family four years later and got work on the paper in Erie, he was a journeyman printer and both student and shaper of the language.

Reunion with his family was short-lived. Although his work in Erie was more than satisfactory, slow business forced retrenchment and Horace was let go. He had had enough of economic and geographic backwaters; he would make his way now onto the great stage. It is true that he knew no one there, had never been in a real city in his life actually, came without capital—the twenty-five dollars with which he left Erie had shrunk to ten by the time he journeyed east over the canal and down the Hudson by boat—and without letters of recommendation, which he might readily have obtained had he known the ropes. But it cannot be said that Horace Greeley came to New York in 1831, his twentieth year, ill equipped for the challenge. He had a skill and was no stranger to hard labor, and he was as earnest as he was callow.

What he beheld on arriving was a vast concourse of strangers, in Jacksonian din, generating an incessant clatter upon filthy streets clogged with traffic pulsing east and west between the two rivers as Manhattan turned into one of the great ports of the world. What the world beheld, in its turn, was a pale beanpole of an overgrown boy, with pants too short for his lank frame and an excessive growth of almost white-blond hair. When he presented himself for a position at *The Journal of Commerce,* its editor took him for a runaway apprentice and urged him to repent. Horace's was not a figure to inspire confidence. The only job he could find was one nobody else wanted—setting the type for a miniature, two-column, annotated edition of the Bible, a task so ill paid and exacting that he had to put in twelve to fourteen hours a day, often working by candlelight, to earn five or six dollars a week. But he loved the Bible, as literature as well as spiritual revelation, and no doubt there were moments when he felt there was something providential in his having been assigned to this trial of faith and conscientiousness as the ticket of entry to his personal promised land.

He performed creditably and found better work after that. His fellow printers liked him, teased him—they called him "the Ghost" for his extreme paleness of complexion and matching hair—and exploited his innocence, borrowing from him and repaying casually if at all. He was often so involved in his work that he would forget whether he had taken his meals. Such dedication was not lost on his employers. But he was not content to drudge for others. Horace served as a journeyman for just fourteen months before setting up his own shop in partnership with the young foreman at his last place of employment. Between them they had $150 in capital, a supply of type purchased on credit, a promise to serve as printers of a sheet called the *Bank Note Reporter,* then circulating among the business houses, and an opportunity to make history.

For a year and a half or so, a recent medical school graduate named Horatio David Sheppard had been obsessed by the simple but radical notion that since you could sell almost anything on the streets of New York for a penny—boys peddling spice cakes for that price soon depleted their supply, he noted—why not sell a daily newspaper for that price too? Such a publication would contrast utterly with the journalistic staple of the day, the large-sized six-penny papers that primarily served the banking and mercantile houses and were solemn things: a column of news, generally political; a column at most of business and shipping intelligence; a half-column editorial, usually partisan, often intemperate, and on frequent occasions devoted to attacking the character of the editor of a rival sheet; and all the rest advertisements, mostly for recently arrived wares. Who among the general public, in an age when the average daily salary was about eighty-five cents, would hand over six of them for that? Even at Sheppard's suggested price of a penny, who would be interested? The answer, of course, was to create a different sort of paper, one that might appeal to the masses: so striking a departure that it would have amounted to an almost wholly new literary form.

Printed material, from its fifteenth-century origins until the American revolutionary era, had been primarily luxury goods for the ruling classes of church, state, aristocracy, and, with the great post-Renaissance discoveries that opened the world's waterways, merchant princes and their minions. The cost of building and operating presses, the expense and fragility of type, and the scarcity of paper all conspired to place printed work beyond the reach of the multitudes, who, at any rate, were largely illiterate. Monarchy and Europe's rigid class system were hardly to be served by broadening opportunities for education. Only with the rise of representative government and its evolving impulse to ease the degradation of the masses did the press begin to emerge as a discrete and economically viable entity. The development was most perceptible in Great Britain and its colonies, where the Crown still exercised close supervision over what emerged from the printshops, but books, pamphlets, and broadsides started to pass into the possession of others than the dominant class. *News*papers, as such, remained unconceived, if not inconceivable, and totally impractical. What regularly published sheets there were tended to be literary periodicals, perhaps occasionally dabbling in genteel social satire, like *The Spectator*, but hardly subversive to the ruling order.

The colonial press in British America was a bit more free-spirited, and an occasional misguided zealot like Peter Zenger might take the Crown to task for insufficient regard for the rights of the colonists. But such instances were aberrant and massively, punitively discouraged. The few journals that thrived, like the Franklin brothers' *New England Courant* and then Ben's *Pennsylvania Gazette*, were pleasant miscellanies; what "news" they chronicled was of an official nature—decrees, speeches, proclamations, texts of laws or court opinions. Timeliness, in an age when wind and horsepower were the engines of transportation, was not thought of as a determinant of what was new. If the fleetest ships took six weeks to sail from England to New York, "news" was, by definition, whatever had not been known before; when the events had occurred, usually months and often years ago, was beside the point. Nor were strictly local happenings, except now and then in the coastal cities, deemed worthy of recording in print; people knew of them firsthand or by word of mouth. Why consume costly paper and press time to memorialize such trivia? Opinion, moreover, on matters of public or official policy was rarely sanctioned and even more infrequently risked. The colonial press, if it wished to survive, remained neutral; it was permitted no opinions of its own that might conflict with government.

It is too much to claim that the Stamp Act of 1765 created, at a stroke, a distinctly American press, but from that time forth printers in the British colonies ceased being supplicants for royal approval. A Crown tax of a half-penny per two-sided copy of a colonial journal and a full penny for a four-pager, with additional stiff fees for each advertisement run, was the first of the onerous measures passed by Parliament, and the papers themselves, their survival now threatened more by compliance than defiance, put out a drumbeat of dissent. Resentment turned into insubordination, and colonial assemblies were yoked in a movement that swept up into a revolution. No American publication was successfully prosecuted for failing to obey the Stamp Acts.

If the Revolution stirred a truly American press, it did not greatly advance the idea of the *news*paper. Journals passionately devoted to the cause of freedom, of which Isaiah Thomas's *Massachusetts Spy* was perhaps the leading example, subordinated all else to that end. They were primarily action-oriented tracts, and they could not survive the conclusion of hostilities. The papers that sprang up in the Federalist period were less exclamatory, but they, too, had a mission: the nation had to be organized or anarchy would be loosed. Political and economic stability commanded the highest loyalty of the press, which not only did not protest the secrecy of the deliberations in Philadelphia in 1787 while the Constitution was being forged but devoted large quantities of its space to promoting its ratification; the *Federalist* papers document that crusade in behalf of constitutional democracy. Still, the papers were primarily polemical and became more so with the rise of the party system. Press freedom under the Bill of Rights created the most active, most numerous, and most abusive papers the world had ever seen—George Washington did not escape their sting, and Thomas Jefferson was bespattered as few chief magistrates have been since—but "news" as an orderly and ordering presentation of contemporary events remained unborn.

Political debate grew more heated and widespread as the nineteenth century opened, but partisanship alone was not enough to sustain papers. They required advertising, even as merchants required a printed medium to display their wares, especially in the burgeoning port cities.

Commercial interests, furthermore, had a particularly large stake in an effective central government, comity among the states, and the internal development of the vast hinterland with its boundless promise of prosperity for the infant American nation. The party press and the mercantile element were thus closely allied, considering their goals complementary if not identical. The eleven weeklies published in New York City in 1800 were dependent, for the most part, on commercial interests and trimmed their editorial sails accordingly. Their editors were less journalists than clerks or secretaries, exercising little discretion in what materials they set in type. Their patrons and readers resided mostly in the business community, which governed their political outlook. The very names of the papers that were spawned—the *Commercial Advertiser,* the *New York Advertiser, The Journal of Commerce*—announced their contents and purpose.

By the third decade of the century, however, changes of large social consequence were in the making. Print technology had not essentially advanced since Gutenberg's time, but the arrival of steam power altered that. In 1825, the *New York Advertiser* became the first paper in the city to install a steam-driven press; it was capable of printing 2,000 sheets an hour, an astonishing leap. Steamboats, similarly, sharply reduced the time of seagoing travel. Railroads were developing, the electromagnetic telegraph was only a dozen or so years distant, the problems created by time and distance were being annihilated by human ingenuity, and the notion of what was "news" altered sharply. As papers became cheaper to print, they proliferated, and competition among them intensified. The more enterprising began to go after the news actively now, instead of waiting for it to reach them in its own sweet time. News ships were sent out into New York Harbor to meet incoming vessels and obtain the latest intelligence from overseas. Express riders and then railways hurried news of the federal government up from Washington. Improved mails brought word of events in outlying communities.

As technology was reshaping the time frame of news, politics was about to broaden its contents no less drastically. Until then, works of history, literature, and philosophy and such periodicals as deserved attention beyond a glance were concerned, for the most part, with the lives and deeds of great men, with great events and profound ideas. The daily lives and concerns of the masses were not dignified by print. But in Jacksonian America, a new spirit arose in the common man, who was encouraged to believe that his life, his voice, his vote were of some importance. He was learning to read and insisting on being educated beyond that, for upon his muscles and brains together would a new civilization be built out of the wilderness of the New World. These heightened expectations, irrepressible once released, suggested a rich new subject for a new literary form with a potentially large new readership—society itself, and the collective and individual acts of its members, in humble as well as high places, to be chronicled in a more appealing way than the six-penny press wanted or knew how to undertake. When Horatio David Sheppard, having exhausted all other possibilities, approached Horace Greeley and his partner and asked them to print a cheap paper that he felt could not fail to sell at least twice or three times as many copies as the 5,000 a day sold by the *Courier and Enquirer,* the largest of the city's six-pennies, history was on his side.

Greeley was interested but cautious. True, his capital had not been solicited, but young Dr. Sheppard's bankroll was small, and his knowledge of editing even slimmer. It would not do for the fledgling firm of Greeley & Co. to be associated with a failure at the outset, particularly one that left a stack of unpaid bills. Greeley calculated that a cheap paper might go, especially if hawked for cash by boys on the streets in the novel way Sheppard proposed instead of by annual subscription price as the six-pennies were sold, but he felt that two cents was the ideal price, not one. Sheppard yielded, and the New York *Morning Post* appeared on the streets on the first of January 1833.

It was not a good day to launch a noble experiment. A snowstorm had emptied the streets, and the intrepid newsboys wandered lucklessly in search of customers. The city remained snowbound for days. Far worse, the newspaper itself had little beyond price to recommend it. A readership lay in wait, but Sheppard did not know how to reach it. His circulation never rose higher than a few hundred. At the beginning of the second week, he cut his price to a penny but did not enliven the contents. By its third Wednesday, the *Morning Post* was dead.

Its legacy was not dormant long. The following September, a young New York printer named Benjamin Day, only a year older than Greeley, issued the first number of his *Sun,* charged a penny for it, and scored an almost instant success. Within months it had the largest circulation in America.

In every way, the *Sun* differed from the six-penny papers. They were printed on a huge sheet, some reaching five feet in width, as if physical dimension were the measure of their virtue; the *Sun* was tidily printed on four little pages, ten inches deep, each divided into three columns. The "blanket sheets," as they came to be ridiculed, reported on politics, money matters, and shipping news; the *Sun* had next to nothing on these subjects. Instead, it featured a variety of breezy items, mostly local and about the tragicomedy of the daily life of ordinary citizens. Its staple was the coarse humor of the police courts, where drunkenness and domestic tribulation provided grist for a flippant style of writing. Thieves and streetwalkers and arsonists also paraded across the *Sun*'s small pages, along with fiction and poetry, sketches of city life, reports of curiosities, monstrosities, and other rumored sensations. Of editorial commentary and other forms of profundity, there was none, not in the early stages of a newspaper life that would span 117 years. Its criterion for inclusion was anything that was interesting regardless of its importance—precisely the opposite standard from that of the somber six-pennies. Newsboys paid seven cents to its publisher for each ten copies they carried out to the streets. In a year, they were selling 10,000 copies daily; in two years, 15,000.

Horace Greeley did not think a great deal of the *Sun.* It was cheap in more ways than one and had an unprofessional, helter-skelter air about it, for all its sprightliness. Yes, it dealt with humanity in a way that the elitist commercial papers had not, but to the highly moral young man from rural New England, it exploited rather than ennobled it. And there were serious as well as trifling matters for a daily paper to treat in an instructive and engaging fashion.

A man who concurred in that judgment soon paid a visit to Horace Greeley's printshop. James Gordon Bennett's reputation as a clever writer preceded him.

A gaunt, cross-eyed Scotsman a few inches taller and sixteen years older than Greeley, Bennett had produced for the *Courier* highly informed and often irreverent reportage out of Washington on the administration of John Quincy Adams—a kind of personalized, somewhat flamboyant, but authoritative writing that had not been seen before—and then fell in and out of favor with the Jackson crowd. There was something moody and quarrelsome about him, they said, even while conceding his talents. Would Greeley be interested, Bennett asked, in forming a partnership with him to publish a new penny paper, a really professional one, now that the *Sun* had proven there was a market for a cheap daily? He flashed a fifty-dollar bill and a few smaller ones, noting that his own resources were limited but that he was rich in experience.

Made cautious by the short-lived venture with Sheppard, Greeley declined and urged his visitor to try the large shop that was job-printing the *Sun*. Bennett had wanted a partner, not merely a printer, and deciding that, anyway, he did not much like the looks of this pasty-faced cherub with the Dresden-doll blue eyes, took his leave. The name of the paper he wished to launch, James Gordon Bennett had told Horace Greeley, was the *New York Morning Herald*.

III

Greeley & Co. prospered as job printers, thanks in part to work it did for the New York state lottery. But Horace's ambition was to be an editor and publisher in his own right, not merely a collaborator. Printing his own publication in his own shop would give him the advantage of reduced costs, and performing most of the editorial functions himself would further improve his chances for success. All he needed was the right idea.

He had been in the city only two and a half years when in March 1834 Greeley & Co. issued the first number of a weekly intended "to combine the useful with the agreeable—substantial information with pleasing interest—the instruction of the mind with the improvement of the heart." It was called *The New-Yorker*. Issued each Saturday evening, it consisted of sixteen packed but handsomely printed pages nine by twelve inches in size and divided into three columns—a lot of reading matter for three dollars a year. What subscribers received for their money was a hybrid of literary selections and political digest with some editorials, usually a substantial leader and one or two shorter comments, on the larger social issues of the day. It was a somewhat odd mixture, but what was truly extraordinary about *The New-Yorker* was the quality of its contents, from beginning to end. That it could be conceived, edited, and in large measure written by a man of twenty-three, who had worked previously only on two small and very provincial papers and since arriving in New York been closeted at his mechanical labors in the shop, almost defied belief.

It had a pleasingly modest, straightforward tone throughout. The literary department was distinguished by the excellence of its selections, some original but most taken from other publications—pirated, we would call it now—and duly credited, as was the custom then. Its reviews, some by Greeley himself and the rest farmed out, had spirit and bite without arrogance—James Fenimore Cooper's *The Pathfinder,* for example, was given respectful attention based on the author's earlier achievement but was not spared rebuke for a somewhat lackluster performance judged by his own previous attainments. Most of all, Greeley knew—as posterity would confirm—which works were worth his space. *The New-Yorker* was an avid admirer of Wordsworth and Melville, and when Alexis de Tocqueville's *Democracy in America* appeared, the editor varied his usual format of leading the magazine with literary selections and opened instead with a commendatory essay-review, quoting liberally from the Frenchman's masterwork.

The political section was still more important. It established itself at once as the most accurate, objective collection of political intelligence regularly published in the nation. Through his own enterprise, a growing circle of contacts, and a careful sifting of a great many exchange papers, Greeley monitored the proceedings of Congress, state legislatures, and the New York City Council, explaining and summarizing them deftly. The paper excelled at covering nominations and elections, with more complete statistical and tabular matter than was anywhere else available in a single publication. Before long, the editor of *The New-Yorker* was a walking political encyclopedia.

But it was his editorials above all that put Greeley's stamp on the magazine. At first he indulged himself by running a number of his own poems, which showed a certain verbal virtuosity but seemed labored. He soon concluded where his true gift lay: in writing simple, forceful prose on a wide range of social issues. He discussed "The Interests of Labor," "The Science of Agriculture," "The March of Humbug," usury laws and capital punishment and the need for registering voters and American relations with France and the relief of the poor and the treatment of the Indians. One Fourth of July he wrote with passion against the tyranny of orthodoxy he saw everywhere around him afflicting free thought and discussion. And he wrote with unmistakable disapproval on the subject that would win him his widest fame throughout the Union—and the hatred of the South—slavery. There was restraint in his first antislavery piece, appearing in July 1834, just three months after *The New-Yorker*'s debut, and it illustrated a tenet he held to until the Civil War itself: however gross an iniquity he thought human bondage to be, he did not propose its abolition on American soil. After all, the drafters of the Constitution, in their infinite vision, had permitted the practice, and "why should not even the existing evils of one section be left to the correction of its own wisdom and virtue, when pointed out by the unerring finger of experience?"

Starting with a subscription list of a few hundred, *The New-Yorker* attracted a circulation of 2,500 within its first six months and 4,500 by the close of its first year. The magazine had been mentioned admiringly in some three hundred papers and periodicals throughout the country, and its editor was suddenly established as a literary figure, political sage, and social commentator. There was no other publication comparable to his of such size and such intellectual accomplishment. The only blot on this happy picture was that *The New-Yorker,* for all Greeley's prodigious efforts, was losing money—$3,000 the first year and, despite attaining the level of 7,000 subscribers, $2,000 the second year. Although sustained by its editor's talents and industry and his partner's indulgence, the magazine was threatening to bankrupt the firm that produced it. Pyrrhic triumphs were not at all what Horace Greeley had had in mind.

IV

Greeley, when he said no to James Gordon Bennett, became the latest in a long line of people who had disappointed and embittered the Scot. A graceless, homely man about to turn forty, riddled with cynicism and on the edge of active misanthropy, Bennett had somehow kept his faith in himself. Three earlier attempts at newspaper proprietorship had quickly foundered. But he proceeded now, against great odds, with one final effort. In the spring of 1835, he rented a basement apartment on Wall Street, stretched a few pine boards between a set of flour barrels for a desk, and began single-handedly to produce the first genuine *news*paper in the United States. More than any other man, he invented and refined the art of reportage. As a conceptualizer of what "news" was and how it might be rendered in a daily publication, there had been no one like him, and his match would not appear again until Joseph Pulitzer arrived in New York nearly half a century later.

There were dark, cold spaces in his past that Bennett himself never chose to explain. At an early age, he had become severely disaffected from his origins. Born in 1795 in a Scottish hamlet among a people notable for their poverty, piety, and industry, he found himself perplexed by a double religious ethic that threatened to smother him before he could escape the bondage of childhood. On one side of him stood the Church of Scotland, chilling and obdurate, and on the other, his own heritage of Catholicism, drilling him endlessly in its liturgies and imbuing him with contempt rather than faith.

He went to seminary in Aberdeen and enjoyed a mind-opening curriculum. Besides four years of church doctrine, he studied history, logic, French, geography, bookkeeping, and some science, and all but embraced literature as his new god. He consumed Byron, Burns, Boswell, Smollett, Sir Walter Scott, and the *Edinburgh Review* and joined and wrote for the literary club. Whatever possibility had remained of his taking vows was gone now; he saw the Catholic Church as obsessed by ritual and haunted by superstition, an anti-progressive authority from which he fled at the first opportunity. What he fled to is not known; between his nineteenth and twenty-fourth years, James Gordon Bennett's life is a mystery. All that is known for certain is that he accumulated few earthly goods and was much moved by the autobiography of Benjamin Franklin. Attracted by that exemplary life among a self-possessed people, so much freer from the strictures of caste and faith than inhabitants of the Old World, he sailed for America without a trade to offer or a fixed destination in mind.

Lean, hungry, ascetic, he wandered the streets of Boston, enthralled by its historic monuments, but its orderliness, even tightness, of living pattern was no great departure from the life he had abandoned. His literary bent won him a clerk's position at Wells & Lilly, prominent booksellers and publishers, where he serviced Boston's social and cultural elite and, in the process, managed to sample the merchandise generously. Customer relations was not his strength, however—he lacked graces, and his ungainly figure and gruff, undiminished burr were not calculated to please. Whether by choice or command, he was transferred to the back rooms, where he served as a proofreader and picked up the rudiments of the publishing trade. Soon, though, the familiar sense of entrapment closed in, and he made his way to New York.

Here Bennett found easy acceptance; here, he decided, he would try to make his mark. But before he had much opportunity to do so, a fortuitous meeting on the waterfront with the owner of the Charleston *Courier,* probably the most accomplished newspaper then published in America, led him South. He would spend only ten months in South Carolina, but they would confirm his writing skill, introduce him to the mechanics of newspapering, and tilt his social views to a position the polar opposite of Horace Greeley's.

Charleston's beauty, climate, and grace charmed him. It was the heyday of John Calhoun, and the region's pride in its convictions about states' rights and a society built on white supremacy and black servitude swayed him. The worst abominations of slavery were shielded from him, out in the low-country plantations where the cotton kingdom was flourishing; in Charleston, the lash was not seen and its victims wore livery. At the paper he encountered men of cultivation who wrote with the style and confidence befitting the freshly minted gentry who made up much of the *Courier*'s clientele. Bennett himself, with his linguistic gifts, was assigned to do translations from the French and Spanish papers that reached Charleston harbor from Havana and other Caribbean ports. The *Courier* thus served in the United States as a primary source of news from large areas of the Old World and the New. Bennett was becoming a cosmopolitan.

But wherever he went in Charleston, Bennett was the perpetual outsider, stern, direct, sometimes savagely cynical. Incapable of endearing himself to others, he saw advancement eluding him. He would have to rely on ability to earn what personality could not.

Back in New York, he struggled for the next decade to survive in the jungle of journalism. It was an unruly, primitive place, inhabited by creatures of prey who knew no law beyond self-interest. The "reading public" was at best an inchoate entity, and the prospect of edifying it held little conceivable profit; the press was there, rather, to propagandize, to merchandise wares and politicians. Newspapers were numerous and debt-ridden, none achieving sales of more than a few thousand. Their tiny staffs were poorly paid and easily persuaded by their willful patrons. Editors tended to be lazy, uncultivated men—William Cullen Bryant, arriving on the *Evening Post* in 1826, was the only authentic man of letters among them—and newsgathering was, accordingly, a casual act and too often corrupt, especially in the financial area, where promoters and speculators were always eager for a hearing and printed puffery was duly rewarded. Ironically, nothing was more highly valued than moralizing pieces, which James Gordon Bennett was not willing to provide. In a world where hacks were readily available to do as they were bid, Bennett had to grub for piecework. Slowly, and never far from destitution, he became known for reliability and persistence in a field where sloth, drunkenness, and corruptibility were common. He accepted political partisanship as one of the working conditions of his trade—there simply was no independent press—and began to cultivate connections among lower echelons of the Tammany Democratic apparatus. Working within those prescribed limits, he nevertheless managed to broaden the bounds and animate the contents of journalism as a literary form and, in so doing, demonstrate a social utility that would allow his calling the dignity of labeling itself a profession.

Bennett's advance was spurred by his link to Mordecai Noah, a self-promoter who ran a Tammany sheet called the *National Advocate* until a quarrel severed his quasi-official tie to the party and he offered his following a new paper, the New York *Enquirer.* Noah assigned Bennett to write some light, bright sketches; one of the first, titled "Shaking Hands," was a witty dissertation on that "troublesome civility" which, as indiscriminately practiced in the United States, often threatened bodily harm. In its place, Bennett offered customs of other cultures (e.g., greeters might place leaves on each other's heads, as New Guineans were wont to, or mush noses in the manner of Laplanders). The article attracted so much attention, both admiring and disapproving, that Noah was forced to recognize that superior writing might actually improve the fortunes of his newspaper.

The editor went so far as to commission Bennett to go to Washington and report on whatever he fancied, and Bennett found endless subjects just awaiting a caustic observer with a modicum of knowledge of how the national government operated. In the late stages of the laconic administration of John Quincy Adams, the capital was a growing but still small place, with no more than 3,000 dwellings and so relaxed an air that it was possible, if one had nothing better to do, to observe the President skinny-dipping in the Potomac. With characteristic doggedness, Bennett got to know the place inside out, lingering in the Senate and House galleries, visiting cabinet and congressional offices, attending functions at the White House, brooding over bills and reports at the Library of Congress. In a style barbed, picturesque, and openly partisan—he found Adams a dull, cold subject and much preferred the rambunctious, up-and-coming Jacksonian crowd—Bennett began to send letters back to the *Enquirer* of a kind no American newspaper had run before. He analyzed the hidden jockeying in the legislative process, skewered the grandiloquence of congressional and other orators, pitied the President for his tireless handshaking feats—his sole triumph, to the eyes of Bennett, who showed no compassion for his foes—and described the social scenery with gleeful hyperbole, as in his rendering of a party at Secretary of State Henry Clay's residence:

> ... Do you see that lady at the Northwest corner of the second cotillion? She dresses elaborately. Every pin has its place, every hair its locality. The caputography of her head would puzzle a corps of engineers—her smiles rise, brighten, decay and disappear with as much preconcert as a drama. She is half *belle,* half *bleu.* Some show their skill in dancing; others drawl through the cotillion with the greatest nonchalance. Dresses are found of all kinds, the French, the English, the Anglo-French, the classical, the picturesque and the no-style. Did you ever see something half-way between Egyptian mummers and *en-bon-point,* arrayed in a style that would make a fellow imagine that a rainbow had been hauled down from the clouds and made up into a dress by some outlandish French milliner?

His sentences had a cadence, his paragraphs a structure, his metaphors a facility and flamboyance that stamped their author as unique. His identity was unknown to appreciative *Enquirer* readers since the pieces were unsigned, but Bennett won recognition within the trade and among his not always grateful subjects in the capital as the first real Washington reporter.

With the ascension of Andrew Jackson, Bennett had his first taste of personal power. He consorted with the Democrats, sought and gloried in their confidences—he had not, after all, ever received much material reward for his labors—and used these heroes of popular sovereignty even as they used him. He was never servile, but their interests generally coincided with his. When Bennett undertook an extensive piece of investigative reportage, examining the award of postmasterships to assess the charge that Jackson's patronage practices constituted a "spoils system," the results not surprisingly exonerated the President. Bennett was welcomed around Washington as he never had been elsewhere, and moved easily about the off-season political circuit in Saratoga, where society and government summered, and Albany, where the governor of the most populous state, Jackson advocate Martin Van Buren, would resign shortly to become Secretary of State. Bennett found in Van Buren an intelligence, wit, and charm that he himself could manage only on paper and angled his way close to the Dutchman, whom he saw as Old Hickory's prospective heir.

In 1829, the *Enquirer* was taken over by the New York *Courier,* under the editorial command of a handsome, bumptious young West Point graduate named James Webb, son of one of George Washington's leading aides-de-camp. The resulting amalgam became at once the ranking journal of the city, and Bennett, its most valuable asset. He was named associate editor and allowed to rove where he chose when activity was slow in Washington. In the summer of 1830, the *Courier and Enquirer* prominently billed his planned coverage of a murder trial in Salem, Massachusetts, that had stirred the town as nothing since the witchcraft proceedings in the seventeenth century. What he produced instead was the fiercest outcry for liberty of the press since the storm over the Alien and Sedition Acts at the turn of the century.

On trial were the alleged killers of a retired sea captain, found slain in his bed; Daniel Webster, pre-eminent attorney of his time, had joined the state prosecutorial team, and a corps of perhaps a dozen reporters was on hand for what promised to be a grand and gory show. Not eager to have the dignity of the commonwealth tainted, the attorney general of Massachusetts lectured the reporters on proper courtroom decorum and laid down a series of restrictive regulations on what they might write. Bennett, with friends in high places and as the disdainful representative of New York's leading paper, rose up in anger. "It is an old, worm-eaten, Gothic dogma of the Courts," he wrote in an indictment that was read in Salem three days later, "to consider the publicity given to every event by the Press, as destructive to the interests of law and justice." If it were true, he added, that the publication of facts or even rumors served to undermine the operations of justice, then "the more utterly ignorant a man is, the fitter he is to sit as a juror." He was fed up with people who belittled and degraded the press, Bennett thundered, concluding:

> The honesty, the purity, the integrity of legal practice and decisions throughout this country, are more indebted to the American Press, than to the whole tribe of lawyers and judges, who issue their decrees. *The Press* is *the living Jury of the Nation.*

The Massachusetts authorities responded, in their fury, by forbidding the reporters to take notes for articles to be transmitted out of state before the trial was over. Bennett reported that as well, and thereafter the focus of the event was not the guilt or innocence of the accused but whether the press was in contempt of court by informing the people of its proceedings. Bennett was laying claim for the press as a coequal, if unelected, fourth branch of government, ventilating the other three with a mandate from the Founding Fathers. That the press should first set its own house in order was a rebuttal that the thrust of Bennett's own work was beginning to correct.

The limits of a reporter's power were bitterly brought home to him the next year when in support of the Jacksonians' opposition to the United States Bank, termed "this hydra of corruption" by the President, Bennett investigated the far-flung operations of the bank, concluded it was venal, and, citing names, dates, places, and misdeeds, wrote a scalding series of articles that he persuaded Webb to carry in the *Courier* over a period of two months. Then, with no explanation other than that he had exhausted the subject, Bennett was ordered to halt his attack. But it had gone on long enough to further secure his position with Jackson's people and emboldened him to play the kingmaker's role in the Democrats' nomination for governor of New York. He relished, almost flaunted, what he supposed was his personal influence. Not long before the presidential election in 1832, Webb switched the *Courier*'s support from Jackson to Clay, so stunning a blow that a congressional committee explored the matter and discovered that the United States Bank had bought off Bennett's financially troubled publisher with loans totaling $53,000, initiated while his attacks against its corrupting power were appearing in print. Vindicated but disgusted, Bennett decided to strike out on his own; the timing seemed perfect. His capital was minimal, but with his closeness to a national administration almost certain to be returned to power, he was confident he could attract what backing he needed to sustain the venture.

He named his paper the *Globe* and announced it with the back of his hand for rivals already in the field:

> For years past the public has *been cloyed with immense sheets—bunglingly made up—without concert of action or individuality of character.* . . . I shall give my readers the cream of foreign and domestic events. . . .

He would candidly "aid the great cause of Jackson and Democracy" during the campaign but afterward widen its variety of material so that his paper would be a welcome visitor at both the tea table and the countinghouse.

It was not Bennett's first attempt as publisher. Seven years earlier, he had been handed control of a dying Sunday weekly for practically nothing and invited to breathe it back to life. But he had too little money, credit, and time to turn the trick, and after a month gave it up. This time he was a somebody. His prospects appeared bright—until the election was over and his readers, conceiving the *Globe* to be hardly more than another partisan sheet to bolster the Jackson campaign, slipped away fast. Bennett's resources again proved inadequate to see him through, and no help was forthcoming from a party that, reconfirmed in power, had its pick of solicitous publishers.

Broke, and doubly embittered, Bennett had to return to piecework—essays, sketches, stories, poems, any sort of assignment he could coax out of those smaller papers willing to deal with him. Webb, once his champion, now turned on his former associate editor, attacking him in print, and Bennett's fortunes fell further. He thought he saw deliverance when word reached him that for a few dollars he could obtain control of a small, troubled Philadelphia daily, the *Pennsylvanian.* A new city might change his luck, and surely Jackson's people would rally to him as a Democratic counterweight to the Philadelphia-based United States Bank in its own lair. But he miscalculated both the enmity toward him by the unforgiving bank and the gratitude felt for him in Washington. When he appealed for funding to the clique surrounding Van Buren, now Vice President, he was refused. Distraught, he sent off a pitiable letter to an intimate of the Vice President that read in part:

> . . . after nearly ten years . . . working night and day for the cause of Mr. Van Buren and his friends; surrounded, too, as I have been, with those who were continually talking against him, and poisoning me to his prejudice, and the treatment which I

have received from him and his friends this last year, and up to this moment, is as superlatively heartless . . . as it is possible to conceive or imagine. . . .

He had wanted to have it both ways: the spiritual and material backing of politicians while retaining functional independence of them. He returned to New York, a three-time loser as a publisher, down at the heels, and perceived to be as dangerous as he was talented with a pen. He applied for work to the new, prospering *Sun*; he thought he knew how to turn the spirited little daily into something beyond a sensation-mongering gossip sheet. The offer was declined. Realizing finally that if he were ever to direct a newspaper of his own, it must be entirely independent of political partisanship, he resolved to make one final effort. His resources were as slender as they had ever been, however, and he needed a trustworthy ally, one who would defer to him. A partner with a printshop would be ideal.

When Horace Greeley, too, rejected him, Bennett, with almost truculent defiance of a world that refused to embrace him, did it by himself.

V

In the way that most great conceptions are said to be simple at their core, James Gordon Bennett fashioned his *New York Herald* upon an idea that was both obvious and novel. Appearing for the first time on May 6, 1835, the four-page sheet, somewhat larger than the *Sun* but much smaller than the six-penny blankets, was directed, according to its proprietor, at readers in all stations of life, "the journeyman and his employer—the clerk and his principal." The *Herald* would present reading matter of such interest that it would bridge their common humanity. It promised to be "the organ of no faction or coterie"; its creator had invested his heart in causes too often in the past to risk having it shattered a final time. While small, his paper would compensate with "industry, good taste, brevity, variety, point, piquancy, and cheapness."

With the first and last of these ingredients there could be no quibbling. Bennett priced his paper at the same penny the *Sun* cost, but he offered much more reading matter. And he offered something neither the *Sun* nor any other paper in the city could: himself and his professionalism. He knew more about the techniques of reporting than his contemporaries, and he poured himself into the effort now, with his last five hundred dollars and the shreds of his reputation on the line. He went out after the news everywhere: the stock exchange, City Hall, the police courts, the docks, the coffeehouses, reporting with the same doggedness he had brought with him to Washington a decade earlier, infiltrating, persisting, asking questions no one else did and not going away until he had his answers. And now he was unpurchasable by favors or access to power; he had known those and come at last to see they were no different in essence from more blatant forms of bribery.

His skills, unleashed in a frenzy of nonstop workdays, at once asserted their superiority over his rivals'. Where the *Sun* offered brief, smirking police reports, the *Herald* played it straight but carried far more of them with details of the demimonde and domestic dramas played out in startling numbers throughout the city. Bennett's paper contrasted itself even more sharply with his competitors at the other end of the market; he covered financial news with an accuracy, clarity, and candor unknown in the six-penny press. Over the years Bennett had trained himself in political economy, first immersing himself in the work of his fellow Scotsman Adam Smith, and his familiarity with banking practices and market forces made him a highly informed interrogator on his Wall Street rounds. Under the chaste heading "Money Markets," he turned out a daily piece that members of the financial community could ignore only at their peril. In his first piece, he set the tone: "This uncommon rise in the stock market is not produced by accident." He advised his readers on the effects of interest rates, the money supply, the chicanery of manipulators, and a dozen other factors largely shrouded from the general public and often poorly understood by market players and plungers themselves. In a time when many editors, especially those on the commercial papers, were known to be stock speculators, Bennett denied himself the temptation totally, as he did alcohol, tobacco, churchgoing, and what he regarded as other pollutants of body and soul. And he never betrayed a confidence; his sources trusted him, but if they used him ill, he was too shrewd to fall for the ruse a second time. The *Herald,* moreover, carried the most authentic and thorough list of market prices published anywhere; for these alone it commanded universal attention in financial circles. Between his expanded police coverage and Wall Street intelligence, Bennett forged a two-edged sword to smite his leading foes. The *Sun* and its lesser imitator, the *Transcript,* did not circulate among the downtown financial crowd, he told potential advertisers, while the *Courier and Enquirer, The Journal of Commerce,* and their ilk "are never seen in the crowd." Only the *Herald* was designed to reach all.

Beyond its reportorial initiatives was the *Herald*'s—which is to say Bennett's—writing. The format may have been sedate, with tiny headings in an age when display headlines were still unknown and without typographic ornament, except on the rarest of occasions when it broke out with a woodcut illustration, but the *Herald*'s prose was as good as its editor's promise: it sparkled. In place of the casual, discursive English that filled most papers on both sides of the Atlantic, Bennett perfected the kind of fresh, pointed prose practiced in the French press at its best. Every paragraph had to do its work to compel reader interest. And the *Herald*'s language flouted the pruderies of the age; it called a leg a leg instead of "a limb" and spoke openly of pants and petticoats. Reward, in the form of circulation, was swift.

Toward the close of its first year of publication, the *Herald* provoked a sensation that established it beyond question as the leading *news*paper in the city and the nation. When a beautiful twenty-year-old prostitute named Ellen Jewett was found hacked to death and partially burned in her bed in a house of ill fame on Thomas Street, about six blocks from City Hall, Bennett at first simply gave a more detailed account than other papers of the lurid crime (e.g., "the bone was cleft to the extent of three inches") and all but convicted the chief suspect, an eighteen-year-old Wall Street clerk who had spent part of the evening with her and whose cloak was found in the dead girl's quarters. But then the editor seemed to sense he was on to something especially promising. Here was an occasion not only to whet readers' morbid curiosity but to lift the curtain on a forbidden aspect of the city's life, to explore the sociology of sin and report it more graphically and honestly than convention had permitted. He *developed* the story—exploited it for sales, without a doubt—but in the very act of follow-through, of continuous investigation and revelation, broke new journalistic ground. Bennett went to the scene of the crime the next day, "said to be one of the most splendid establishments devoted to infamous intercourse that the city can show," and to his mingled horror and delight, discovered the corpse had not yet been removed. The sight may have been "ghastly," as he assured readers, but he left them with a different emotional reaction as well: ". . . the perfect figure, the exquisite limbs, the fine face, the full arms, the beautiful bust, all surpassed in every respect the Venus de Medici. . . . For a few moments I was lost in admiration of this extraordinary sight." He went on to describe the room, "elegant but wild and extravagant in its ornaments," and, in subsequent articles, what manner of life she had led, her intellect and refinement, how she paraded Wall Street in her splendid green dress, her passion for seducing nice young men, particularly those who resisted her charms, how she became the star attraction of the house, "giving grace to its licentiousness." He got hold of her letters to and from customers and suitors and ran excerpts, noting that there was not an unchaste word on the beautifully embossed paper she preferred. He went again and interviewed the madam of the house and used her own words to turn, in best detective style, suspicion upon her and away from the accused young clerk. When the *Sun* charged that bachelor Bennett was in cahoots with the defense and had himself been a bawdy-house customer, perhaps even at the very house where the victim had offered her services, he turned the canard into a self-deprecating triumph. The only time he had visited such a place, long ago in his youth, he wrote, ". . . the girls told me, 'You're too ugly a rascal to come among us,'" and a colleague was told, "Never bring that homely scoundrel to our house; the sight of him gives us the ague." He kept milking the story, in short, right through the trial, which ended with the acquittal of the accused, the *Herald*'s circulation at 15,000 copies a day, and Bennett's name as the best known, if most notorious, of any journalist in the country.

While the *Sun* remained ahead of the *Herald* in circulation, Bennett's far more substantial paper ran well ahead in advertising. And with no real margin of safety in his own bank account, he decided early on to put his advertising accounts on a cash-only basis. Newspaper and periodical customers had long been extreme laggards in paying for both subscriptions and advertising—an indication, to Bennett's thinking, of the low esteem in which the press was held by the public. With a winner finally in his hands, Bennett would no longer countenance such practices. At the same time, he recognized—indeed, insisted upon—the news value of advertising and ended the common practice of carrying ads that ran with unvarying copy in every edition for a charge of thirty or forty dollars a year. In the *Herald* an ad could stand unchanged for no longer than two weeks; eventually, Bennett would rule that the copy had to be altered every day. He wanted his paper read, and columns of dead matter would not advance that end. But in all other regards, he was exceedingly liberal about what his advertisers could say in print. The *Herald* operated on the doctrine of *caveat emptor*, welcoming purveyors of any and all quack nostrums, promises to teach readers to play the piano in six easy lessons, abortionists to service the needy. And its "Personals" columns bulged with tales of intrigue: dates and times of assignations that their participants could not more easily or safely communicate, loveless women looking for husbands, forlorn mothers looking for lost children, unvirtuous women none too subtly looking for customers. Determined to succeed now, knowing that he could not remain independent of political or other vested interests unless he built his paper to a level of prosperity unknown before in the American press, Bennett was impatient with readers finicky about his advertising policies. To one who complained about ads for a certain Dr. Brandreth's remarkably efficacious pills, Bennett shot back in June 1836:

> Send us more advertisements than Dr. Brandreth does—give us higher prices—we'll cut Dr. Brandreth dead—or at least curtail his space. Business is business—money is money. . . . We permit no blockhead to interfere with our business.

Success may not have done much to improve Bennett's personality, but it decisively enhanced the quality of his newspaper. Confident that he had built a solid enough following to risk increasing the *Herald*'s price to two cents, Bennett promptly employed the added revenues in an ongoing series of improvements. He enlisted a staff, installed a bureau in Washington and expanded coverage from there, and on a trip to Europe assembled a network of correspondents writing exclusively for him and making the *Herald* the first American paper to offer systematic foreign coverage. He began a weekly edition and a news digest in the daily. He improved local news by doing more with shipping and sporting events and compartmentalizing reports from the courts and municipal offices. Nothing better illustrated Bennett's capacity now for separating his personal piques, phobias, and hatreds, amply evident in the *Herald*'s editorials, from the interests of his readers than the paper's coverage of religious news. His editorial denunciations of "the rotting fiber of professional churchmen" did not prevent him from ordering the paper to start carrying regular reports on the sermons of those same loathsome clerics—reports that the editor insisted be courteous and accurate—and extensive coverage of religious meetings, assemblies, and conventions with a nice impartiality toward all sects. Principle and expediency coincided as the *Herald* forged a new standard of journalistic objectivity.

Perhaps Bennett's most daring and impudent novelty was his assault on the citadels of society. Never himself granted admission to the drawing rooms of the city's elite, which he considered mercantile in origin and therefore *arriviste*, pretentious, exhibitionist, synthetic, and fit prey for his pen, Bennett began featuring accounts of major social events, rendered in a happy style midway between lampoon and sycophancy. Such previously unheard-of effrontery reached a high point when the March 2, 1840, issue of the *Herald* burst forth with its front page devoted almost wholly to a report headed "Grand Fancy Dress Ball, at Brevoort Hall" with the subheading "Blaze of Beauty—Brilliant Display of Dress, Taste and Elegance—Immense Sensation in the Fashionable World," accompanied by a layout plan of the first two floors of the hosts' mansion on Fifth Avenue at Ninth Street. Identifying the guests by their initials to mute the shock of exposure to public scrutiny (and no doubt to forestall violent reaction by offended subjects), the *Herald* reporter, who had donned knight's armor for the job, disclosed that "Catharine of Aragon wore a real tiara of diamonds"; Mrs. J. W. O—'s dress, black velvet studded with silver stars, cost over $800; a man costumed as a Chinese mandarin ate (with chopsticks), danced, and spoke "*à la Chinoise,* to the delight of the ladies"; another man, intending to cavort as a bloodhound, "burst his dog skin breeches putting them on," while the most amusing Mr. W— E—, a six-footer dressed as a little schoolgirl, "had on a short white frock and pantalettes." Interspersed were an account of a fistfight, a snatch of dialogue from an attempted seduction, the carryings-on of a Miss B—y, "long a beautiful belle," who broke many hearts at the ball and then eloped the next day with a gentleman from South Carolina who had not attended, and a sensual, almost tactile, description of "Mrs. L—n as a Virgin of the Sun."

Such visions awakened awe, envy, and fascination among the larger run of mankind barred from the Brevoorts' door—and sold a great many papers for James Gordon Bennett, who was redefining the meaning of "news."

Sprung from the doldrums inflicted by so many years of anonymous, unrewarded virtuosity in a profession that scarcely existed before his entry into it, Bennett displayed immodesty that knew no bounds. "Shakespeare is the great genius of the drama," he wrote in 1837, "Scott of the novel, Milton and Byron of the poem—and I mean to be the genius of the newspaper press." His sin was not high aspiration but advertising it. His ambition ran beyond art toward power, of a sort no other journalist had been brash enough to articulate or skilled enough to dream of; Bennett asked, not at all rhetorically:

What is to prevent a daily newspaper from being made the greatest organ of social life? Books have had their day—the theatres have had their day—the temple of religion has had its day. A newspaper can be made to take the lead of all these in the great movements of human thought and . . . civilization. A newspaper can send more souls to Heaven, and save more from Hell, than all the churches and chapels in New York—besides making money at the same time. . . .

Perhaps it has always been an occupational hazard for the masters of the press to believe their own notices. Even the astute Bennett, in all probability, did not appreciate the true nature of the social impact his paper was creating. Newspapers have saved only a limited number of souls and not scored notably more successes in leading "great movements of human thought." What they can do at their best is to inform, a function urgently needed at the time Bennett's *Herald* appeared. His adopted city, setting the pattern for increasingly urbanized life in nineteenth-century America, presented in its vastness and impersonal rush for sustenance what latter-day commentators would characterize as a panorama of travail. For all its teeming streets, New York induced loneliness, anxiety, and sorrow over life's oppressions as well as delight in its variety of pleasures. Family, church, and neighborhood ties that bound men and women in other places and earlier times were of less importance to the new city dweller, caught up with occupational, logistical, fraternal, cultural, and political concerns. It was these new urbanites the *Herald* and its progeny served. Adrift in the urban vortex, people craved a sense of belonging, and Bennett was supplying the links. His varied, comprehensive, often provocative fare helped to alleviate solitude, to reassure readers of the universality of their tribulations, to bring hope that adversity was not insurmountable—and to demonstrate that, however small a fraction of it, they were an integral part of the human drama enacted each day within a community so large and so diverse that they could not have perceived it without reading the *New York Herald*. Within four years of its founding, the *Herald*'s circulation surpassed *The Times* of London's.

2

Instructing
the Nation

The editor of *The New-Yorker* was in the habit of collecting the mail himself at the post office each morning.

This practice, while revealing an eagerness to move the day's business along, had its drawbacks. Not the most orderly of men, Horace Greeley sometimes failed to direct each piece of correspondence toward its swift and proper disposition. To tell the truth, there were times when he forgot about the mail altogether, like the brisk spring morning he tucked the day's letters into his overcoat pocket upon leaving the post office, and then hung up the coat for the summer. It was not that Greeley was absentminded; the problem, rather, was the opposite. The large head was overstimulated by the play of events in a far-flung society that he took *in toto* for his subject. Although subscription payments grew in delinquency—or gathered unopened in his coat pocket—and deficits unaccountably accumulated, the editor could not be distracted from his mission. He persisted even as his partners, more caught up than the editor in material matters, began to come and go; he had seven different ones in five years. A fire destroyed his office, his books and papers and statistical records all went up in the blaze, and he began again, having to skip only one issue. His life, for all its cliff-edge uncertainty, was consuming and full. It became fuller in 1836 when he married a pretty young schoolteacher with a headful of dark curls and lively thoughts—about everything but politics, which left her indifferent even if it obsessed him. Mary Cheney, known as Molly, was a painfully neat homemaker who pried Horace out of himself, persuaded him to share her delight in dancing, and presided with verve over the regular Friday-night literary gatherings at the snug, if hardly fashionable, Greeley residence.

The financial panic of 1837 snuffed out that short, gay season of youth and hope. Subscriptions dropped by 3,000, and many who paid used wildcat currency. There was no financial cushion to absorb the blow. The magazine was too steadfastly intellectual to attract any large following and Greeley had been too indulgent of freeloading subscribers, imploring them politely in print to help him meet his bills instead of ruthlessly cutting them from the list. He was too easy, too affable, too ready to tackle the world's problems at the expense of his own. To keep *The New-Yorker* alive, he had to hand over his firm's printing business, the only profitable part, to his partner, borrow a thousand dollars at steep interest, and curtail the quadrilles and socializing upon moving to a smaller apartment befitting his reduced circumstances. Times were bad—the worst in memory; hunger and joblessness were rampant in the city, and while Greeley did what he could to relieve the desperation among his neighbors in the Sixth Ward, his own plight deepened.

Relief came in the wake of the election returns that sorry year. Democrats were widely rebuked at the polls, and nowhere more sharply than in New York, where the Whigs, emerging now as a full-dress conservative party in opposition to the Jackson–Van Buren regime, took decisive control of the state legislature. Successor to the loosely defined and structured National Republican Party with its remnants of the old Federalist camp, the Whig coalition reached out to the new business class of tradesmen and entrepreneurs who hungered for the return of stable economic conditions. The nation, Whiggery argued, needed more positive initiatives from government, a more ready supply of capital to spur manufacturing, less political cant, and prosperity for all.

Horace Greeley's infatuation with the Whigs defied, on the face of it, the logic of all his prior leanings. But there was much about his political creed that seemed inconsistent or even self-contradictory. He was living, he was sure, in the century and the homeland of the common man, who, by educating himself in "useful knowledge" and struggling to overcome adversity, would achieve his individual fulfillment—even if it took collectivist programs to advance that end. His hatred of inherited privilege and his preference for inalienable rights that were mankind's universal heritage from a merciful God should have made him, almost by definition, a staunch Jacksonian. But he was highly ambivalent toward mass man. He himself had risen above—though perhaps not very far above —the commonness and poverty of his origins; for those who would not do likewise, who would not acquire knowledge to match their freedom, who would not discipline their wayward impulses and labor mightily to advance, he had only contempt. They were a rabble, a blind multitude, prey to a demagoguery he found the Jacksonians all too adept at exercising. He feared a tyrannizing majority, licensed to wage class warfare that could end only in social chaos. In the Whigs he found a more congenial crowd, wary of radical tampering with the nation's institutions—even as he himself was of endorsing, for example, the outright abolition of slavery instead of merely halting its spread—but eager to make them work better in a climate of moral decency and benevolent patriotism. Let the unemployed move to the unoccupied West and, with a modest subsidy from their government, realize the fruits of America's heaven-sent liberty. If the Whigs tended a bit toward the patrician, Horace Greeley could not hold that against them; was he not himself one of nature's noblemen?

Up to his small office late in 1837 climbed the large, florid figure of an Albany newspaperman who had just succeeded in making himself master of the state political landscape. In less than a decade, Thurlow Weed had moved from Rochester, where he had converted a weekly into a small daily, to the state capital, where he had bought the Albany *Evening Journal,* got himself elected to the legislature, and taken on and tamed the resident political power brokers. A robust, genial man who enjoyed hearty talk over a meal of oysters and wine, Weed was never too busy to do a friend a favor or overly scrupulous about how it was repaid. He was shrewd, manipulative, and resolute, a man who played politics to win and not to enshrine high principles. Somewhat coarse-grained, he had precisely the ingredients required to shape an effective party mechanism out of the disparate elements of New York Whiggery; the money crowd rallied to his leadership. With the legislature under control by his party for the first time, he moved now to consolidate his gains and put a Whig in the governor's mansion in the 1838 elections. Weed's candidate was William H. Seward, a little red-haired lawyer with a beak nose and a silver tongue. Some said Seward was Weed's creature, but Greeley rated him a humane progressive, unswerving in his antislavery faith, with charm to match his ambition. Weed wanted an editor for a campaign weekly that would help put Seward over; he had enough contributions in hand from big Whigs to subsidize the venture and offered Horace Greeley, upon whom he had never laid eyes before, a wage of one thousand dollars to take on the job for one year. His finances close to desperate, Greeley accepted before the night was over.

Calling itself *The Jeffersonian,* the party sheet first appeared in mid-February of 1838 and showed Greeley's stamp. It was written to convince readers, not to batter them into submission with propaganda. The editor dashed back and forth all year, running his magazine in the city and putting out *The Jeffersonian* from Albany, where he also covered proceedings of the legislature for Weed's *Evening Journal* and became transfixed by his political legerdemain. The campaign paper reached a circulation of 15,000; its serious contents were credited with enhancing Seward's stature and contributing to his 10,000-vote victory in the fall.

The triumph left Greeley heady but hardly richer. He was offered no post in the new administration and found himself grubbing for survival money of twelve dollars a week as a contributing editor to the weekly *New York Whig.* Domestically, his life was still bleaker. The Greeleys' first child, a son, had been born dead, and the cruel surgical procedure to try to save it made Molly an invalid for six months. A second conception ended in miscarriage in the winter of 1839, further weakening her. Even so, Greeley returned to Albany that winter, staying during the week and coming home for weekends. The schedule could not have brought much comfort to his wife; the best that could be said was that it enabled him to earn twenty-five dollars a week writing for Weed's paper and more from stringing for Whig papers in New York, Boston, and Harrisburg, Pennsylvania—money badly needed to care for Molly as he himself could not or would not.

Weighted by financial worries, Greeley, like Bennett, started dreaming of salvation in the form of a cheap daily paper. The principal difference between their dreams was that Bennett turned away from the politicians and Greeley turned directly to them. He had remained on close terms with Weed and Seward, but they viewed him as a somewhat volatile and unreliable adjutant; his reformist zeal inevitably conflicted with the stratagems of Albany's realistic rulers. Still, "Greeley the Horace," as Bennett's paper teasingly tagged him, had his uses. He was a one-man intelligence service and welcome for dinner at the governor's. But he declined further invitations after accepting the first; Seward seemed indifferent to his plight and lent his dream of a penny Whig daily in the city no encouragement. Greeley's real reward was nearness to power. He watched and savored the behind-the-scenes maneuvering as the presidential election year of 1840 unfolded and Thurlow Weed moved to extend his sway to the White House.

His chosen instrument was William Henry Harrison, hero of the close army victory in 1811 over marauding Indians at the Tippecanoe River in Indiana. If the Democrats had ascended to power with Jackson, a retired general-hero, why not use another one to wrest it from them? Persuaded that Harrison had a better chance to dethrone Jackson's successor, Martin Van Buren, than did Henry Clay, his own *beau idéal* among politicians, Greeley functioned as an agent for Weed's kingmaking ploys. When the Whigs' conclave chose "Tippecanoe," Greeley, the kingmaker's exalted errand boy, was not forgotten.

In a campaign marked by more bunkum and ballyhoo than any presidential race yet, the Democrats slandered Harrison as an imbecilic dotard who was a bad general in his prime and had, since his retirement to a log home in Ohio, been passing his last years guzzling hard cider. To counter, the Whigs put Greeley back to work for the party. *The Log Cabin,* a four-page paper issued sixteen times during the campaign for fifty cents a subscription, was a lot less sedate in its arguments and presentation than *The Jeffersonian* had been. It was full of woodcuts of Harrison slaying Injuns on the frontier, words and music for campaign songs, sloganeering—"Tippecanoe and Tyler Too" passed into American political folklore before the dust settled in November—and a level of rhetoric that Greeley had not practiced before but dispensed now with joyous abandon. *The Log Cabin* proved remarkably popular; its circulation rose to more than 80,000 and turned a modest profit for Greeley. Harrison, boosted by songs and cheers and rallies and torchlight parades, won handily—only to fall ill at his inauguration and die a month later.

These events decisively affected Greeley's career. Politically partisan journalism, he concluded, could pay off; *The New-Yorker*'s brainy, literate, almost astringent approach never could. In the immediate post-election euphoria, Greeley again took up his dream of a penny Whig daily in New York. The market, upon casual examination, appeared flooded; there were already thirty newspapers circulating in the city, a dozen dailies and the rest weeklies; the *Herald* and the *Sun,* in terms of circulation and renown, were the goliaths of the American press. Neither of the two successful cheap dailies, though, had any marked political identification, and to the extent they disclosed an affiliation from time to time, it was with the Democrats. But with the Whigs suddenly in command of the state and national political scene, Greeley projected a substantial readership for an avowedly Whig daily selling for a penny. He himself at thirty was young but experienced, full of energy and connections to men of means and power, and had won literary standing through *The New-Yorker,* however untamed a dog it had proven financially, and become well known politically by his bravura performance editing *The Log Cabin.* And most prominent, perhaps, of all the factors favorable to him was the public repugnance that had coalesced during that election year toward the editor of the *Herald.*

Bennett's misanthropy, which at first had seemed to have about it the calculated quality of mere attention-getting, edged toward the pathological even as his success mounted. Whether from delusions of invulnerability or a compulsion to exorcise regularly the demons harbored within him from all those past slights and grudges and shows of ingratitude, the fact is that the *Herald,* immensely more readable than any other journal ever issued in America, was likely to spew forth at any time editorial invective offensive to wide segments of the reading public. It was stridently disrespectful of the church and its leaders and blasphemously so of Roman Catholicism, with its allegedly slavish adherents among the Irish rabble, arriving in the city then in rising numbers:

> . . . We have no objection to the doctrine of Transsubstantiation being tolerated for a few years to come. We may for a while indulge ourselves in the delicious luxury of creating and eating our Divinity. A peculiar taste of this kind, like smoking tobacco or drinking whiskey, cannot be given up all at once. The ancient Egyptians . . . had not discovered the art, as we Catholics have done, of making a God out of bread, and of adoring and eating him at one and the same moment. . . .
>
> If we must have a Pope, let us have a Pope of our own—an American Pope, an intellectual, intelligent, and moral Pope,—not such a decrepit, licentious, stupid, Italian blockhead as the College of Cardinals at Rome condescends to give the Christian world of Europe.

No doubt Bennett's contempt enhanced his following among anti-church and anti-Irish readers, but it won him thundering reproofs from the pulpits of the city. So did the relish with which the *Herald* reported on illicit sexual episodes and battened on scandal, with or without names.

Bennett's outbursts were directed, depending on the day, against deceitful politicians, venal Wall Streeters, society poseurs, and anyone who ever said an unkind word about the *Herald* or its proprietor. His most reckless attacks he reserved for his rivals, incompetents to a man. The *Sun* he called "a small, decrepit, dying penny paper, owned and controlled by a set of woolly-headed and thick-lipped Negroes." Bryant of the *Evening Post* was a villain for stirring up the labor masses. Webb of the *Courier and Enquirer* he charged twice with stock manipulating—and earned, on both occasions, a public beating, which Bennett duly wrote up. His lowest blow was struck against Park Benjamin, a cripple, who in 1839 had launched the *Evening Signal,* not a robust entry; Bennett wrote that Benjamin's misfortune was "a curse by the Almighty."

He was guilty as well of egregious tastelessness in writing about himself. Having applied his dubious charms to a comely piano teacher who unaccountably reciprocated, Bennett wrote on his own front page:

> . . . I am going to be married to one of the most splendid women in intellect, in heart, in soul, in property, in person, in manner, that I have yet seen in the course of my interesting pilgrimage through human life. . . . I must give the world a pattern of happy wedded life, with all the charities that spring from a nuptial love.

It went on and on. Bennett in love was, if possible, more unpleasant than Bennett angry.

This behavior finally brought on, in the spring of 1840, what came to be known as "the moral war" against him. It called for the boycott of the *Herald* by its readers and advertisers and for the ostracism of its owner, now being variously termed by the city and national press "an obscene vagabond" whose "reckless depravity" had turned his paper into a purveyor of "moral leprosy." Efforts were made to root out the *Herald* from every home, club, hotel, coffeehouse, and other gathering place that wished to be perceived as decent, and advertisers were threatened with a sharp loss of patronage. Bennett tried to shrug it off, blaming the massed attack upon him on the jealousy of outdistanced rivals—no doubt a major factor. But the drive took its toll; the *Herald* lost nearly a quarter of its readership and a no less painful part of its advertising revenues. Bennett, paranoia rising, responded that he was being called scoundrel by those stimulated by

> the worst men in society—by speculators—by pick-pockets—by six penny editors— by miserable hypocrites, whose crimes and immoralities I have exposed, and shall continue to expose, as long as the God of Heaven gives me a soul to think, and a hand to execute.

But the damage had been done, by and to him. Without conceding anything, he curbed his excesses, and the *Herald* went on in time to new heights of prosperity. But Bennett himself would never overcome his reputation as the bad boy of American journalism. His personal standing among his contemporaries may be judged by the outcome of the libel suit he brought against a paper that wrote that the son his new wife bore him in the first year of their marriage had been fathered by someone else. The issue was never in doubt, but the Bennetts were awarded damages of only $250. Yet however unsympathetic to the man himself, people continued to read his paper.

With the leading journal of the city under a cloud, the *Sun* still a small sheet but popular, and all the rest grouped far behind, Horace Greeley marshaled his assets—youth, energy, brains, talent, experience, connections, a thousand dollars in cash, another thousand in type and equipment, a thousand on loan from a prominent Whig businessman and more available if need be—and decided they would suffice. His daily newspaper emerged on April 10, 1841, under leaden skies, as the city held a funeral procession to mark the passing of William Henry Harrison, briefest President of the United States.

II

From the start it was steeped in propriety and politics. Both were essential in positioning the *Tribune* on a level above and beyond the *Herald*.

It was to be a moral, devotedly civic sheet, uplifting and instructive, without allusion to metaphysics. It was to be a paper every member of the family so inclined could read without sullying mind or soul or taste. When it covered crime, it did not, as both the *Herald* and the *Sun* appeared to, celebrate waywardness; the *Tribune* left out, or overlooked, the details of depravity. It was acceptable to report on antisocial and immoral incidents but in a disapproving context and vocabulary. But if a certain resulting dryness marked much of the other contents in the *Tribune*'s early stages, there was nothing bland or antiseptic about its political personality.

"My leading idea," Greeley wrote in his memoirs, "was the establishment of a journal removed alike from servile partisanship on the one hand and from gagged, mincing neutrality on the other." So fierce and intolerant was party spirit in America, he went on, that the unaligned editor was inhibited from saying his piece on vital topics, whereas the partisan journal was not allowed to diverge from the dictates of its party.

> . . . I believed there was a happy medium between those extremes,—a position from which a journalist might openly and heartily advocate the principles and commend the measures of that party to which his convictions allied him, yet frankly dissent from its course on a particular question, and even denounce its candidates if they were shown to be deficient in capacity or (far worse) in integrity.

What is most notable about this retrospective statement of creed and others Greeley issued on the founding of his paper is that he said so little about how it would gather and present the news, as if those functions were entirely second-ary to the *Tribune*'s responsibility to instruct, to monitor, and to persuade. One had the sense that the news, *all* the news, was there largely to serve his higher purposes, to allow him to make a point. This partisanship was manifest in the very first issue; indeed, it almost overwhelmed the rest of it. Much of the front page was given over to the six-week-old text of an opinion by the attorney general of New York, rendered to the governor, on the conduct of a criminal courts judge, Robert H. Morris, a Democrat, while investigating alleged ir-regularities in the city's tobacco-inspection practices. The chief object of the probe was a Whig, whose papers Morris had taken in "midnight seizures" for use in the course of his inquisition and subsequently handed over to the newspa-pers. Only when the reader reached the editorial on the second page was the full significance of this malfeasance of office apparent. Governor Seward, a Whig, had removed Morris from office, a man whose

> acts were high-handed, as contrary to every principle of Civil Liberty and enlight-ened jurisprudence as a Judge's acts could be. . . . Can it be possible that Robert H. Morris is about to be chosen Mayor of New-York over an opponent of blameless life and unsullied integrity? It cannot—it must not be! Freemen! vindicate the security of your homes and the inviolability of your ideals! The hour approaches!

In case anyone somehow missed the point, a second editorial, headed "Plain Talk to Whigs," stressed that the *Tribune* was the only authentic, true-blue Whig entry among the cheap papers—and some of the six-penny sheets thought to be in the Whig camp were at best sometime loyalists.

Throughout its early years, partisanship skewed the *Tribune*'s news selec-tion and reporting, and its editorials were too full of attitudinizing. Bawdy houses, when cited at all, were said to be run and countenanced only by Demo-crats. The paper did not always print both sides of political debates. Dispatches from Washington, especially those written over the years by Greeley himself, were often blatantly partisan. A *Tribune* account of a meeting of Tammany Democrats was as likely as not to wind up like this:

> . . . and then a string of resolutions was brought forward, so long that the first one was forgotten before the reader got within hailing distance of the last one. . . . Their substance, deeply hidden under the catch-words of State Rights, Rights of the Laboring Classes, Opposition to Monopoly, &c. &c., was, in plain English, that the party had been without the spoils long enough and it was now time that they should go to work in good earnest to help the Whigs.

Reportage in keeping with Greeley's affinities went beyond politics to his social judgments as well. The tendency was noted in an article in the *North American Review* by James Parton, later to become a Greeley biographer. The *Tribune* editor took issue with Parton, who in defense cited a strike then being waged by New York street-railway conductors and said the reader could learn more about the pressing subject from the *Herald* than any other paper. "Well," Greeley offered, "I don't want to encourage these lawless proceedings."

"Exactly," returned Parton. "I could not ask a better case in point." A newspaper's role was not to represent one side or the other, he added—merely to give *all* the news. Greeley could have been no fonder of that instruction than of a remark in Parton's article that "an editorial is a man speaking to men, but the news is Providence speaking to men." For all James Gordon Bennett's sardonic ax-grinding, it was a precept he understood far better than Horace Greeley. The latter, though, might have countered that Providence is far less open to persuasion—and far less in need of it—than mankind.

Politicized as it was, the *Tribune* was hardly a campaign organ. It was a serious, literate paper, offering far more intelligence on a wider variety of subjects than any other New York paper but Bennett's. By the end of its first week, it was selling 2,000 copies a day; the total rose by five hundred a week before settling around the 10,000 mark. But it was still running in the red. "I was not made for a publisher," Greeley conceded, noting that "indeed, no man was ever qualified at once to edit and to publish a daily paper." The solution was a member of the bar in good standing, the well-connected Thomas McElrath, who had been a principal of the publishing firm above whose premises Greeley had first worked as a printer on coming to the city. He had married into wealth and was a solidly respected attorney with lines out to Seward's camp. After watching the creditable quality of Greeley's paper for four months, he bought a 50 percent share of the enterprise for $2,000 and joined it as the full-time publisher. "From that hour on," the most unbusinesslike editor remembered, "my load was palpably lightened."

McElrath stayed sixteen years, long enough to assure the financial solidity of the paper. Not especially brilliant or energetic, he was a close calculator and strict disciplinarian, roles foreign to Greeley. McElrath had two other virtues in the editor's eyes. The *Tribune* never really adapted itself to the political and commercial atmosphere of its city, which was Democratic and inordinately concerned with profit; he was Whig and devoted to social justice. The *Tribune*'s new constituency proved to lie well beyond the banks of the Hudson. McElrath's equal billing at the top of the first page—the logotype read "New-York Tribune" and under it in small letters "By Greeley & McElrath"—served to reassure city merchants that the editor was no mere moralizing visionary and to increase their advertising patronage, grudging until then. His other virtue was even more liberating to Greeley, a man who would not count the cost of his words or write to please. McElrath never once indicated to Greeley that the editor's "anti-Slavery, anti-Hanging, Socialist, and other frequent aberrations from the straight and narrow path of Whig partisanship were injuries to our common interests" nor "did he even *look* grieved at anything I did." As a trade-off or unspoken bargain, perhaps, Greeley was less than fastidious about censoring quack-medicine advertising in the *Tribune,* explaining lamely when pressed that the management was not qualified to judge the therapeutic value of such merchandise but hoped to educate its readers to distinguish the spurious from the efficacious. Similarly, the paper paid no or very little heed to the theater, which Greeley regarded as a locus of licentiousness—in truth, many prostitutes sold their wares in or around theaters, and more than an occasional male spectator retired to convenient chambers during the intermission or after the performance for a bit of dalliance—but it did not refuse theatrical advertising. Greeley was not the first man charged with hypocrisy as the price of survival; the evidence suggests, however, that it pained him more than most.

Hardly in McElrath's category as essential but nonetheless vital to the *Tribune*'s early success was Greeley's first editorial assistant, a twenty-one-year-old graduate from the college at Burlington, Vermont, who had shown up at *The New-Yorker* office not long before the *Tribune* was launched and asked to make himself useful without pay while he tried to find employment someplace that could afford him. Henry Jarvis Raymond, a small, black-bearded fellow with a face once described as "no bigger than a snuff-box," proved so handy at the magazine, especially with Greeley caught up in the election campaign, that the editor reluctantly parted with eight dollars a week to retain his services when a paying job materialized elsewhere. "Abler and stronger men I may have met; a cleverer, readier, more generally efficient journalist I never saw," Greeley said of him. Raymond distinguished himself in reporting on the trial of one John Colt, brother of the inventor of the Colt six-shooter, who had been charged with murdering a printer over a trifling debt and, after his conviction, cheated the gallows by taking his own life with a knife three hours before the scheduled execution. Among Raymond's skills was a kind of long shorthand that enabled him to take down remarkably faithful accounts of public meetings and lectures. At least one prominent speaker used Raymond's rendering of his scientific lectures as the text for a book based on them. In addition, the young journalist was a competent book reviewer, editorial writer, and rewriter of paragraphs clipped from exchange papers. And Greeley exploited him to the hilt. Even with the paper turning a profit, the first assistant was paid the same eight dollars he had been receiving on *The New-Yorker.* Only when Raymond fell ill and Greeley badly missed his services did he visit his aide in his room, inquiring in passing when the patient might next be seen at the *Tribune.* "Never, at the salary you paid me!" Raymond was quoted by his biographer as having said, whereupon Greeley met the requested increase to twenty a week. Raymond's case was the first in a pattern that would mark the entire history of the paper: it attracted young men of extraordinary talent and underpaid them, forcing all but a handful of the most devoted to go elsewhere. Raymond remained with Greeley for three years, then joined the *Courier and Enquirer;* seven years after that, he began *The New-York Daily Times.*

When the *Tribune* was half a year old, Greeley made a move that solved the problem of *The New-Yorker*'s everlasting deficit and turned it into an asset that allowed his whole enterprise to prosper. He merged the magazine with a weekly edition of the *Tribune* launched in September; two months later, he also merged the remnants of *The Log Cabin,* which he had sustained for a year after the 1840 election as a break-even Whig propaganda organ. The amalgam worked at once.

The *Weekly Tribune* outstripped Bennett's comparable edition and future entries in the field by the *Times* and the *World* for precisely the same reasons Greeley's paper did not find New York its natural habitat. An inveterate moralizer in a city whose god was expediency, Greeley had never shucked his rural roots and values. Out in the country, on the farms, in the small towns of New England and New York state and the frontier communities along the Great Lakes, there was his natural constituency, and his words rang out along the back roads and waterways with a palpable earnestness that made for grand reading in places where not much printed material was readily available. A daily paper would have taken too long to reach them and been too costly; a weekly nicely digesting major events and offering additional useful intelligence, especially in matters of agronomy, was ideal. Mostly, though, they wanted to read what "Old Horace" had to say to them that week. The *Herald,* far more metropolitan in tone and scornful in voice, lacked that appeal.

Greeley pushed the weekly's circulation hard, offering such premiums as strawberry plants and gold pens to spur local solicitors. Bulk sales of a hundred to "Tribune Clubs" enabled individual subscribers to receive the paper for just two dollars annually. Within a year, the *Weekly Tribune* had a subscription list of 15,000; within a decade, 50,000. So far and well did it travel that Ralph Waldo Emerson reported on his return from a lecture tour that Greeley's weekly was educating the West at two dollars per capita per annum—a good deal less, actually, if anyone could have calculated through how many hands each issue of the paper passed. Not a bad bargain.

III

"No other public teacher lives so wholly in the present as the Editor," Horace Greeley once wrote of his vocation. He expected oblivion, not immortality, to be the sure fate of his daily works. Even so, there were to him two kinds of successful editors. The first, an utterer of "silken and smooth sayings," knew how to condemn vice without discomfiting the vicious, to champion liberty without offending the practitioners of slavery, to support labor without exposing the devices by which it was plundered. "Thus sidling dextrously between somewhere and nowhere," the able editor might glide respectably through his career "and lie down to his long rest with the non-achievements of his life emblazoned on the very whitest marble, surmounting and glorifying his dust."

But there was another, sterner path. This one, Greeley asserted, demanded "an ear ever open to the plaints of the wronged and the suffering, though they can never repay advocacy, and those who mainly support newspapers will be annoyed and often exposed by it." Also needed were a tuned ear and "a heart as sensitive to oppression . . . in the next street as . . . in Brazil or Japan."

To observe life neutrally, coolly, imperturbably was not Horace Greeley's idea of newspapering. It went beyond, to bettering, to uplifting. Not to do so was to squander the franchise, to become a mere profit-gatherer, and what was exalted about that? Without a doubt he treated the columns of the *Tribune* as his personal pulpit; many mocked him for it, but none doubted the sincerity of his passion. It was the making of the paper.

His moral outrage had greatly intensified in the years of financial travail immediately preceding the start-up of the *Tribune.* He had been especially moved by the squalor and despair afflicting his Sixth Ward neighbors in the terrible New York winter of 1837–38, when business had been paralyzed and joblessness widespread. His fellow citizens were starving and freezing to death. As a member of one of the visiting committees that tried to raise funds and relieve the most extreme cases of destitution, he saw pathetic sights he could never forget: a family burrowing into an earthen cellar beneath a stable, hoping to ward off cold, vermin, and famine; widows and their children surviving in an attic on three dollars a week produced by their apple stand, and such other scenes of sorrow as to leave a pitying heart intent on remedying them. The afflicted were not beggars, content to lie idle and useless and take whatever alms were flung their way; they had been able-bodied laborers before being reduced in spirit and energy, and they wanted nothing more than the chance to work and improve their lot. That, Greeley decided, was the essential and inalienable right society owed its every member. He called it "the great, the all-embracing Reform of our age," one that sought to lift the laboring class "not out of labor, by any means . . . but out of ignorance, inefficiency, dependence, and want" and place it "in a position of partnership and recognized mutual helpfulness with the suppliers of the Capital which they render fruitful and efficient." He was unstinting in his egalitarianism. The man who had only his labor to barter for wages or bread, Greeley cautioned, was forced to look up to the buyer of his sole commodity as a benefactor, as his master; he could not stand "on a recognized footing of reciprocal benefaction." His longing for equality of the spirit, though not of possessions, and the dignity it imbued led the young editor down the pathway to socialism—of a benign and voluntary sort, to be sure, but one that even in its pre-Marxist form aroused uneasiness when planted in American soil.

Greeley was converted to the socialist banner for the better part of a decade, one that coincided with the *Tribune*'s formative years. The effect on the paper's fortunes was mixed: it marked Greeley from the first as a controversialist and radical reformer if not quite a revolutionary. Detractors were divided over whether he was imbecilic or just impractical; admirers saw a prophet bent on justice and read him as scripture.

Greeley's socialism was highly programmatic. Its architect was a French *philosophe,* a poor clerk named Charles Fourier, who had worked for thirty years in taciturn obscurity thinking up a system of industrial household communities, or "associations," based on the principle of joint stock investment. In his dogmatic, almost algebraic prose, Fourier depicted society as nothing more than organized rapacity and urged its most sorely used victims, laborers suffering under repulsive conditions that individually they could never overcome, to pitch in together in a common household and workshop of four or five hundred families occupying some 2,000 acres, to be made productive by their joint efforts and for their mutual fulfillment. Fourier died in 1837, but his message was brought back to America by a privately educated young gentleman about Greeley's age named Albert Brisbane, who had studied with Hegel and other European philosophers and believed such socialist experiments had a far greater chance to take root and succeed in his native America than in tradition-bound Europe. Brisbane set out to convert the new continent. He lectured on Fourierism, wrote articles and pamphlets, published a magazine he called *The Future* and asked Greeley's firm to print it, having sensed a kindred spirit in editorials he read on problems of the laboring class in *The New-Yorker.* Greeley, in turn, was dazzled by the remedial, formulaic content of Fourierism as broadcast by its American apostle and made it, with modifications for domestic consumption, a principal plank of the *Tribune* platform.

At first Brisbane did the work by purchase of a column on the front page of the paper. The articles, signed "B.," ran every day for a time and then three times a week over a period of more than two years starting in March 1842. Meant to persuade, they inevitably fatigued readers and became the most skippable portion of the paper. Greeley himself, though, began to pick up the slack, editorializing on the topic when a suitable point of departure occurred to him. He was less doctrinaire in his approach—"I accept, unreservedly, the views of no man, dead or living," he would write, and recognized that Fourier was in many respects an "erratic, mistaken visionary"—but his social creed borrowed freely from the Frenchman's teachings. He believed, and so itemized them, that (1) society pays more for the support of able-bodied paupers than it would cost to eliminate them; (2) "they babble idly and libel Providence who talk of surplus Labor, or the inadequacy of Capital to supply employment to all who need it"; (3) labor is inefficient because of bad management, which provides inadequate tools, machinery, and power to operate it; (4) inefficiency in production is paralleled by waste in consumption ("A thousand cooks are required, and a thousand fires maintained, to prepare badly the food for a township; when a dozen fires and a hundred cooks might do it far better, and with vast saving in quantity as well as improvement in quality"); (5) youth should be instructed in industrial and other "useful arts" as well as in letters in order to improve the productivity of labor; (6) isolation is the enemy of efficiency and progress; (7) collective effort is the workman's sole hope of betterment; and (8) "Association" in the form of self-sufficient communities is the only practicable means for the masses to take matters into their own hands and become masters of their fate.

With Brisbane's articles gone, Greeley throughout 1845 sustained the call for reform by articles as well as editorials on the working and living conditions of labor in New York. A series on the depressed wages of pieceworkers reported that seamstresses on the job from sunrise to midnight earned only seventy-five cents a week and that the most skilled makers of boys' caps did only slightly better: twenty-five cents a day running between fifteen and eighteen hours. He lamented the conditions of almshouses, with fifty or more in a room, and called for the city, with 60,000 of its inhabitants jobless, to take the lead in establishing an enclave two miles square with workshops and power sources "affording employment in some shape to every one who have any capacity or physical ability to labor." And when a convention was held in New York of like-minded reformers, featuring representatives of Brook Farm in Roxbury, Massachusetts, among the earliest of the Association experiments in America and notable for the presence of cultivated, even scholarly individuals in its ranks, the *Tribune* reported its proceedings in detail. From the *Herald* came a classical Bennett-esque appraisal:

> The philosophers of the *Tribune* are eternally harping on the misery, destitution and terrible sufferings of the poor of this city and throughout the country. There is nothing more ridiculous than all of these tirades about this fancied distress. . . . [Poverty arises] out of indolence, licentiousness or drunkenness.

Rather than receding, as *Tribune* publisher McElrath would have much preferred, Greeley's pet social program became the subject of intensified debate, climaxing in a series of twelve articles each in the *Tribune* and the *Courier and Enquirer* over a six-month period starting late in 1846.

None of the idealistic communities patterned after Fourierism and its variants was a large success in America; even Brook Farm, for all its enlightened membership, could not compensate for its lack of capital and agricultural skill and struggled on only five or six years. Lacking a practical working model, Greeley turned to less institutionalized programs to ease the plight of labor: a strong protective tariff to create more jobs in domestic manufacturing; homesteading the West,* where surplus Eastern labor could migrate, and, especially, checking the territorial reach of slavery, against which free labor could not compete economically.

Among the legacies of the *Tribune*'s campaign for socialist reform were two members of the Brook Farm experiment who became invaluable editors on the paper—Charles Dana and George Ripley—and Greeley's adoption in 1849 of

---

* Many who know nothing else about him believe Greeley to be the coiner of the phrase "Go West, young man," but they are misinformed. The attribution, like so much about Greeley, a skillful self-promoter, has passed into folklore; it is correct enough in spirit if not fact. Writing in *The New-Yorker,* Greeley had urged, rather less pithily than the more familiar form puts it, "If you have no family or friends to aid you, and no prospect opened to you there, turn your face to the Great West and there build up a home and fortune." The short version is attributed by some sources to John Babson Lane Soule, who first used it in the Terre Haute *Express* in 1851. Greeley, believing city life to be morally degrading for those on its economic fringe, invoked the phrase—and often the sentiment—but did not coin it.

Fourierist terminology in rechristening his company the Tribune Association and making available in it one hundred shares at $1,000 each to any staff members able and inclined to buy. It proved little more than a gesture; only about a dozen men on the editorial side and a few on the mechanical side actually bought in as Greeley and McElrath reduced their share of the ownership. The principals sold off to outsiders as well, and by the end of Greeley's tenure, one-third of the stock was held by non-staff members. The *Tribune,* despite Greeley's good intentions, never truly became a cooperative.

IV

Greeley's benevolence was matched by his courage. Sometimes it was direct physical menace he withstood. Early in the *Tribune*'s second year, for example, the paper had carried detailed, dispassionate reports on the election-day rowdyism of the notorious Mike Walsh's "Spartan Band" of Irish toughs, marauding through the city's bloodiest battleground, the Sixth Ward. The *Tribune* accounts so incensed Walsh that he sent word to Greeley that if there were no retractions, the newspaper's premises would be attacked. The editor, untrained in the arts of self-defense, did not hesitate. Plans were made to repulse any invaders with scalding water drawn from the steam pipes and brickbats heaved from the roof. The attack did not materialize; the articles were not retracted.

In December 1842, Greeley displayed a different kind of fortitude in a confrontation with America's most eminent man of letters, James Fenimore Cooper. The legal heart of the controversy was strikingly similar to the one in the trial of Peter Zenger more than a century earlier—was truth an acceptable defense against the charge of libel?—and Greeley, like Zenger's lawyer, appealed beyond the narrow confines of repressive law. It cost him $200, cheap enough for a place of honor in his field.

The appearance in 1841 of Cooper's *The Deerslayer,* culminating volume of his interrupted "Leather-Stocking" saga, had helped to restore the novelist's sagging reputation. Yale-educated scion of a frontier patrician family from New York's midstate lake country, Cooper was a model of democratic profession and aristocratic condescension. By the time he left for a seven-year stay in Europe in 1826, he was the lion of New York letters. His ambivalence toward his homeland intensified while he was abroad, where he challenged anti-American cultural biases but himself took on heavier airs as a prince of the American Eden. On his return, he was shocked by the effects of Jacksonian democracy. Gone were the innocence and decorum that his own works had conveyed against a romanticized backdrop of unspoiled nature; in their place, he found a brawling people, rank with vulgarity, stupidity, dishonesty, and cruelty—and he was quick to portray them thus. His shrill, intemperate tone found favor with neither reviewers nor readers, and Cooper's disposition soured accordingly.

In such a mood, he struck at his neighbors in Cooperstown (named for his family) by reclaiming title to an untillable acre of land on the shore of Otsego Lake that for forty years had provided a prime recreation spot for the public. This churlish act, abruptly and unapologetically announced in a local paper, drew a loud civic outcry, duly reported in a rival Whig paper in terms unflattering to Cooper. The novelist sued the offending editor for libel and eventually a whole string of editors, including Thurlow Weed and his Albany *Evening Journal,* for reprinting and embellishing the defamatory account. When Cooper used a thinly disguised version of the ruckus, featuring a handsome Mr. Effingham as his alter ego, for three chapters in his 1838 novel *Home As Found,* a battle with the press ensued. James Webb's review of it in the *Courier and Enquirer* was representative, charging that Cooper had "basely and meanly devoted his talents to catering for the gross appetite which unfortunately exists in Europe, for everything calculated to bring the customs, manners, and habits of Americans into disrepute." Concurring in Greeley's *New-Yorker* was a piece by Park Benjamin, who was soon to strike out as a publisher on his own. Benjamin scalded Cooper: "He is as proud of blackguarding as a fish-woman is of Billingsgate," he wrote, adding that the author had exploited the novelistic form with which he had become a favorite of the American public "to asperse, vilify, and abuse that public. . . . The superlative dolt!"

Cooper sued Webb—and later Benjamin and everyone else in sight who joined in the criticism—and when a Cooperstown grand jury returned an indictment against him, *The New-Yorker,* probably in the person of Greeley himself, struck back by underscoring the real issue involved in what was coming to be known as "the Effingham libels." Did an author subject himself, as distinguished from his creation, to personal criticism by submitting a work to the public? Not necessarily, Greeley's magazine answered itself. "But if he makes his work the channel of disparaging remarks upon others—whether individuals or in masses —is not the case essentially altered?" More unsympathetically still, it lamented Cooper's resort to the courts to exact retribution:

> . . . [H]e who lives by his pen should regard that as his appropriate weapon. To carry a controversy from the press into the law is to acknowledge either his own incompetency to wield his proper implement or the superiority of the courts of judicature to the high court of Public Opinion in which he is by right a practitioner.

Upstate judges and juries took a less sporting view of the question. The press's privilege to criticize artistic works was countenanced, said the judge in the suit against Benjamin, by a single test of the critic: "Has he or has he not confined himself in this Review, to the Author, and not traveled beyond the record to assail the private character of the *man*?" Evidence about that private character was disallowed in all the Effingham trials; all that could be considered was the fact of publication and the scope of the printed comment. Cooper won all the cases, although the juries awarded low damages.

The stakes rose in 1840 when Cooper got around to suing Weed for $10,000 for failing to retract his reprint of the original Cooperstown fracas three years earlier. The trial was postponed for six months when Weed claimed to have forgotten the date set for it, and after he failed to show up for the rescheduled trial on the ground that his wife and daughter were seriously ill, Cooper pressed his advantage. Weed was given till the next day to appear. When he sent word that he would not desert his ailing family, Cooper gained the verdict and $400 in damages. Weed's unsigned account of the event, appearing in his own paper and later in the *Tribune* in shortened form, noted that his spokesman in court had appealed to Cooper's humanity in asking him to permit the trial to be delayed, "[b]ut that appeal of course was an unavailing one"; the meager award, under the circumstances, constituted "a severe and mortifying rebuke to Cooper, who had everything his own way." Weed then drove home his lance: "The value of Mr. Cooper's character, therefore, has been judicially ascertained. It is worth exactly four hundred dollars." For reprinting Weed's words, Greeley was sued by Cooper, who demanded $3,000.

The trial was held at Ballston, midway between Albany and Saratoga Springs, on Friday, December 9, 1842. Greeley went without a lawyer—did not even consult with one. Part of the reason, no doubt, was that Cooper had taken to representing himself at some of the Effingham trials, and, as no mean man of letters himself, the thirty-one-year-old Greeley could likewise stand up for himself. "Greeley has prepared a speech and is anxious to deliver it," Cooper wrote to his wife the night before. "His friends advise him to retract, but he must have his speech. We shall try his case to-morrow and shall be home to a tea-dinner on Saturday: with a clear verdict of from $200 to $400."

In his clear, piping voice Greeley flatly denied that he had, as charged, "falsely, wickedly, and maliciously" published articles subjecting the plaintiff to ignominy. For one thing, "indignation is not malice." If you saw a powerful man beating up a feeble one, you would naturally be indignant, but nobody could justly impute malice to your indignation. For a second thing, Greeley argued, the jury ought to consider his occupation as a public journalist, obliged by duty "to speak out in reprehension of injustice, oppression and wrong, when another citizen may innocently forbear. To this end, the Freedom of the Press is carefully guarded by our Federal and State Constitutions."

But such freedom did not, of course, provide Greeley or any journalist with immunity from the consequences of what he unjustly published. No one had restrained him from printing Weed's account. The issue was whether the article was fair and truthful. "I read it, believed its statement of facts, and thereupon formed the opinion that its strictures on Mr. Cooper's conduct were warranted by the facts." When Cooper later offered his version of the facts, Greeley published them as well but repeated his opinion that the author's conduct against Weed had not been honorable or magnanimous. Now it was not part of his case, he told the jury, to prove that his opinion was the sound and correct one: "It is enough that it *was* my opinion, [and] in this Free Land I had a right to cherish an opinion and express it."

Cooper scorned Greeley's argument, mocked Weed's excuse of family illness for not having appeared at his own trial—contagion must have been conveniently virulent in the Weed household just then—and waxed hot on the arrogance of the press. The judge agreed, telling the jury that the only question at law was whether Greeley had published the offensive piece; the truth of its character evaluation was irrelevant. Thus instructed, the jury complied with a $200 judgment against the editor. Greeley left the court, hurried by sleigh down to Troy, and took the first steamboat down the Hudson, arriving at his office the next morning and working straight through until 11 p.m. on his account of the case. It ran to eleven and a quarter columns and, under the title "Cooperage of the Tribune," filled most of the December 12 issue of the paper. By his estimate, it was the best single day's work of his career.

Greeley's account of his own trial stands as a classic of American reportage. It was not impartial, certainly, but it was not tendentious, and he gave Cooper his due—and more, so much more that it set the whole city to laughter and, for having tweaked his tormentor so ably, drove Cooper to file a new libel suit against him. One of Greeley's sinning passages read:

> . . . we did not enjoy Fenimore's talk . . . of Weed's family and of Weed himself as a man so paltry that he would pretend sickness in his family as an excuse to keep away from Court, and resort to trick after trick to put off his case for a day or two —it seemed to us, considering the present relations of the parties, most ungen— There we go again! We mean to say that the whole of this part of Mr. Cooper's speech grated upon our feelings rather harshly. We believe *that* isn't a libel. (This talking with a gag in our mouth is rather awkward at first, but we'll get the hang of it in time. . . .)

He went on to confess he had found "a good deal of fun" in the zesty combat; in fact, "we rather like the idea of being (for our means) so munificent a patron of American literature; and we are glad to do anything for one of the most creditable (of old) of our authors." Nevertheless, the result of the Cooper libel suits was that the power of the press "to rebuke wrong and to exert a salutary influence upon the Public Morals is fearfully impaired." He did not see how any paper could exist, acting worthily and usefully, in the state of New York under its current laws without subjecting itself daily to innumerable unjust and crushing prosecutions and indictments for libel as interpreted by the courts.

"But the Liberty of the Press has often been compelled to appeal from the Bench to the People," he asserted. "It will do so now," and no cunning wrongdoer should suppose himself "permanently shielded, by this misapplication of this law of Libel, from fearless exposure to public scrutiny and indignation by the eagle gaze of an unfettered Press."

The words rang with a historic resonance: 107 years earlier, Peter Zenger stood accused of seditious libels for running articles in his New York *Weekly Journal* that, often in satiric or cryptic form but nonetheless unmistakably, denounced the oppressive policies of the royal governor and endorsed the virtues of representative government in the colonies. As soon as Zenger's celebrated attorney, eighty-year-old Andrew Hamilton of Philadelphia, conceded publication of the offensive material, the Crown attorney moved for a verdict for the king, "for supposing the libels were true, they are not the less libelous for that; nay, indeed, the law says their being true is an aggravation of the crime." Hamilton began to argue that the published words must be found false, scandalous, and seditious to be criminal "or else we are not guilty." But the royal bench, as the upstate New York judges were still ruling in the Cooper cases, declared: "You cannot be admitted, Mr. Hamilton, to give the truth of a libel in evidence." At which point, Hamilton turned to the jury and delivered a passionate address that concluded:

> . . . the question before the court and you gentlemen of the jury is not of small nor private concern; it is not the cause of the poor printer, nor of New York, alone. No! It may, in its consequences, affect every freedom that lives under a British government on the main of America. It is the best cause. It is the cause of liberty . . . the liberty both of exposing and opposing arbitrary power by speaking and writing Truth.

The judge's charge notwithstanding in both cases, Zenger fared better at the jury's hands than Greeley. But the latter turned for reinforcement in his fight against the indefatigably litigious Cooper to a leading member of the New York bar—William Seward, the former governor and future Senator and Secretary of State. Seward succeeded in legal maneuvers and delays that left the case instigated by Greeley's "Cooperage of the Tribune" still unresolved by the time of Cooper's death in 1851. And before long, the New York statutes were revised to take a more generous view of truth as a complete defense to the claim of libel.

In his volume of memoirs, *Recollections of a Busy Life,* issued twenty-six years after the court had gone against him in the Cooper case, Greeley wrote that he did not hold with those who contended editors considered themselves privileged characters who claim immunity to charges of criminal libel. Quite the opposite. "What I claim and insist on is . . . [*t*]*hat the editor shall be protected by the nature and exigencies of his calling to the same extent, and in the same degree, that other men are protected by the exigencies, the requirements, of THEIR calling . . .* " (Greeley's italics). The difference, of course, which Greeley did not acknowledge as integral to the antagonism that journalists have earned as the price for keeping liberty's vigil, is that their calling exercises a judgmental function toward everyone else's calling. It is a peculiar power, one that only rarely earns the public gratitude. Those who, as James Fenimore Cooper did, find the press intrusive or oppressive, are quick to denounce it. But if the press at its worst can tyrannize, so at its best can it liberate. Both capabilities are implicit in the old saw that the pen is mightier than the sword. The blows of the latter, though, are generally mortal; the pen can only mortify. Greeley understood the difference.

V

Among the most enlightened and open-minded men of his time, he could also be dogmatic and orthodox. The result was a potpourri of philosophical inconsistencies and contradictions that undermined Greeley's effectiveness as both logician and polemicist. This proneness to ambivalence was amply revealed in his confounding attitude and behavior toward feminism, of which he might have been supposed an advocate on the strength of—if nothing else—his employment in 1844 of Sarah Margaret Fuller as the first woman to serve as a regular editorial staff member on a prominent American newspaper.

At first encounter she was so phenomenally homely—the giraffe neck, the fluttery eyes, the thin and stringy hair, the nasal voice—as to appear almost physically repellent. But there was a pliancy and animation to her features and a compelling energy to her speech that sprang from a mind second to none. Margaret Fuller was probably the best-instructed woman in the United States —both her blessing and her dilemma; the nation did not know how to accommodate such a creature.

The eldest of nine children brought up near Boston by a passive mother and a dictatorial father, who was a lawyer and four-term member of the United States House of Representatives, Margaret underwent as rigorous a course of instruction as any son of wealth and culture had available to him at the time —except that there was no college open to her. Private lessons and voracious self-instruction honed her precocious intellect; they also overloaded a charged and passionate nature that left her prey to excruciating headaches throughout much of her life. Politics behind him, her father moved the family to a farm far enough from the city to leave Margaret feeling intellectually marooned and functionless. She devoted herself to teaching her younger siblings, and when her father was inconsiderate enough to die without a sizable estate, she was obliged to teach at a girls' academy for several years and did very well at it, so well that in time she was invited to conduct a series of informal seminars—"conversations" she simply called them—at the home of one of the doyennes of Boston society. Attended by women of intellectual as well as social aspiration, Margaret Fuller's salons were celebrated and mocked, but they won her eventual entry, and on equal terms, to the mostly male Boston literary-cultural circle of, among others, Channing, Alcott, Thoreau, and Emerson. Sometimes arrogant and abrasive, sometimes wonderfully satiric, she wielded a formidable intellect that dared to range beyond the decorous and allowable thought of her time and place. Attracted by transcendentalism, the reigning philosophical movement, she served as the managing editor of its distinguished magazine, *The Dial,* and engaged in a passionate love-hate relationship, however virginal and cerebral, with the great Emerson. Then, too tightly cloistered by all this, she shocked proper Boston by accepting Horace Greeley's offer to come to vulgar New York and dirty her hands in the employ of a mere newspaper.

The city melted her reputation as a stone woman. For twenty months she gloried in the richness and variety of New York's teeming life that could not be found, as she wrote afterward, in twenty years spent in any other part of the country. To acclimate and comfort her, the Greeleys invited her to live in their spacious home at Forty-ninth Street and "the Third Avenue," still a countrified location but connected to the city core by hourly coach. Wearing what Greeley called her characteristic expression of "grave thoughtfulness," she loved to haunt the piazza that ran the length of the house and roam over the shrub-strewn lawn to the gravel path down the steep bank of the East River, where sailboats rounded a rocky point and, with the quirky current, glided by in a sidelong way that seemed to her a private greeting. "The beauty here, seen by moonlight, is truly transporting," she wrote friends at home.

But Fuller had not come to contemplate nature. Her articles, running in the *Tribune* two or three times a week, were identified by a large asterisk at the end and a style too often turgid and embarrassingly self-conscious. There was no denying the force or authority of the intellect behind them, though. She hurled herself into the task, seeking by her critical essays to promote a national litera-ture "as wide and full as our rivers, flowery, luxuriant and impassioned as our vast prairies, rooted in strength as the rocks on which the Puritan fathers landed." While her first piece was full of praise for a new volume of Emerson's essays, she was by no means indulgently generous to her subjects. Longfellow she gored for shallowness of culture and Poe, whose tales she admired, had failed to realize his promise as a poet, she felt, because his imagination "rarely expresses itself in pronounced forms, but rather in a sweep of images thronging and distant like a procession of moonlight clouds on the horizon. . . ."

Her work was journalistic as well as literary. In relishing the wide, free rush of New York life, she regretted the speed of it and what it did to those caught in its underside. Among the sketches to which she brought a tenderly humane sensibility was one titled "Woman in Poverty," about an encounter with an old laundress whose dignity and propriety struck her full force. Fuller inquired why in the depths of winter she delivered her heavy baskets through the slippery streets and was told by her subject that she could not afford an errand boy but did not begrudge her fate; she was glad, at her age, to have enough work to keep body and soul together and would not, at any rate, have to wait long to rejoin the shades of her husband and children, from whom she had long been sepa-rated. Duty had kept this unprepossessing figure upright, wrote Fuller, through a life of incessant toil and bereavement and not warped her character. Why, only lately she had taken in a poor, homeless girl who had been dying in a hospital and nursed her through the last weeks of her life.

Such vignettes also demonstrated the feminism of which she was an outspoken advocate in her own day and which would make her a saint and a martyr to the suffragist movement that bloomed later in her century and the women's liberation cause that sprang up two-thirds through the next one. In 1845 Greeley published her book *Woman in the Nineteenth Century,* the outgrowth of an article she had written for *The Dial.* In it, she decried the benign neglect of women's intellectual powers and the social and legal customs that doomed them to second-class citizenship. She was especially eloquent in opposing the view of matrimony that defines a wife as the property of her husband rather than as forming a whole with him. Probably more out of respect than in jest, Greeley refused to open doors for her in his home in view of her insistence on equality of treatment for women.

Having savored New York as the point where American and European interests converged, she bid farewell to the city in a memorable article appearing in the August 1, 1846, issue of the *Tribune* and headed for the Old World "to behold the wonders of art, and the temples of old religion. But I shall see no forms of beauty and majesty beyond what my Country is capable of producing in myriad variety, if she has but the soul to will it. . . ." In Europe she mingled with such figures as Carlyle, George Sand, and the Brownings and sent back to Greeley letters of her conversations with the celebrated that he published and made her, in effect, the first more or less regular female foreign correspondent for any American paper.

Her legend was burnished by her activities in Italy, where Fuller joined with Mazzini and the cause of Italian republicanism, part of the revolutionary wave that swept over Europe in 1848. She sent the *Tribune* accounts of the fighting she witnessed in the siege of Rome and worked long and heroically in a hospital there attending war casualties. Among the republican ranks she met and married a man ten years her junior, an impoverished *marchese* of limited intellectual powers, and had a son by him. After Mazzini's movement was suppressed, her little family sought to survive in Florence while she tried to write an account of what she had witnessed. Poverty drove them to book passage for America, where whisperers wondered if the couple had ever been joined in holy matrimony. When their ship foundered on rocks off Fire Island, within sight of its destination, some of the passengers and crew made it ashore safely. Margaret, clinging to her husband and infant in the disintegrating forecastle for twelve hours in the hope of rescue, did not. She was forty years old. Greeley said she was "the loftiest, bravest soul that has yet irradiated the form of an American woman"; him she had called "the most disinterestedly generous person I have ever known."

And yet, he was incapable of interpolating between this specific instance of transcendent womanhood and the generic capacity of her sex to stand in coequal citizenship with men. Greeley's position on women's rights, notwithstanding the courtesies of full coverage of the topic in the *Tribune,* was more reactionary than radical.

He damned the suffrage movement by faint praise. It was easy to sneer at the demands of female reformers, he editorialized, but "when a sincere republican is asked to say in sober earnest" the reason women are denied full voting rights, "he must answer, None at all." True, he might think it unwise of women to make the demand and that the great majority want no such thing, preferring "to devote their time to the discharge of home duties and the enjoyment of home delights," but finally it had to be acceded to because it was "the assertion of a natural right." But when he chaired the committee on suffrage at the 1867 New York state constitutional convention and cordially introduced his friends Susan B. Anthony and Elizabeth Cady Stanton to the panel, accession was not in him. He remarked in a thoroughly unsympathetic manner that he doubted one woman in ten craved the ballot—a statistic he must have gleaned by divine revelation—and did nothing to advance the cause.

He was still more opposed to lenient divorce laws, although he conceded that wives were known to be bullied and brutalized by their husbands, even as husbands were scolded and henpecked by their wives. That he could not distinguish between the two conditions was evidenced in his most extensive remarks on the subject, a debate with the social reformer Robert Dale Owen printed in the *Tribune* in 1860. For allowing divorce on grounds other than adultery, the only one Greeley accepted in accordance with the teachings of Jesus, the editor denounced Owen's adopted state of Indiana as "a paradise of free love." Owen replied that Greeley failed to recognize that husbands have "the command of torments, legally permitted, far beyond those of the lash. . . . There is not a womanly instinct he cannot outrage." Never mind, insisted Greeley; marriage was a solemn contract for life, not merely during pleasure, and if the partners were intended to be true to each other "only so long as they shall each find constancy the dictate of their several inclinations, there can be no such crime as adultery." He prescribed separation as preferable to a marriage of ceaseless strife, which Owen had called the real immorality of indissoluble unions. Owen scoffed at a bond sustained by separation as a contradiction in terms, one resulting in law-condemned celibates who, "unable to marry . . . may do worse." Greeley then embraced the Catholic position that "the divine end of marriage . . . is parentage" and that no worthy mother would "seek to marry another while the father of her children is still living. I do not think she could look those children in the eye with all a mother's conscious purity and dignity while realizing that their father and her husband, both living, are different men."

Would he have said the same for men? Possibly. He was never accused of philandering throughout the course of his thirty-six-year marriage, which was notable for the long stretches he spent away from home and the sorrow that followed from the fact that seven of the nine children Horace and Molly Greeley conceived ended in miscarriage, stillbirth, or death in infancy. Parentage may indeed have been the divine end they both sought in marriage, but it proved as elusive for them as happiness together. That others might have valued the latter end as the higher divinity, he could not comprehend. If Margaret Fuller had reached the shore instead of dying just short of it, she might have altered his convictions on the subject.

VI

Not until the escalating conflict in Vietnam some 120 years later would the American people again be as divided over the justification for going to war as they were at the outbreak of hostilities with Mexico in 1846. The division was nowhere more clearly illustrated than in the opposing attitudes toward it in Bennett's *Herald,* then in its twelfth year of publication, and Greeley's *Tribune,* entering its sixth. Their opposition was less interesting for what it said of the clashing political stances of each than for the way it dramatized their differing conceptions of what was most essential in the life of a newspaper.

For James Gordon Bennett, the American war with Mexico was the occasion for demonstrating enterprise and expertise in the coverage of some damned exciting news, news the nation couldn't wait to read about, and so he did his best to speed along the word. For Horace Greeley, it was a matter for moral outrage.

The slave power had openly begun casting covetous eyes on Texas and the Mexican territory almost as soon as John Tyler of Virginia, a Whig of dubious allegiance, succeeded Harrison as President. The election of Democrat James Polk, a Tennessee expansionist, in 1844 left little doubt about the direction of American jingoism as steered by the masters of the cotton kingdom. Bennett, acutely tuned to the course of events, established a courier system between New York and New Orleans in 1845. He meant to be first in publishing news from the trouble spot and would not content himself with accepting official statements by the government. The *Herald*'s couriers were so efficient that they outsped the carriers of the U.S. mail, a forbidden practice in the eyes of the Postmaster General, who ordered it ended. But Bennett, sympathetic with Southern anxieties over the growing power of the far more populous North in Congress, saw the inevitable and did his best to stir it into being. "The multitude cry aloud for war," he editorialized in August 1845; Americans were "restless, fidgety, discontented, anxious for excitement."

The outbreak of combat found the *Herald* ready and eager for action. It was the only New York paper to assign a reporter to the scene—in fact the only American paper to do so except two in New Orleans, the closest sizable city to the battleground. With the cooperation of the *Ledger* in Philadelphia and the *Sun* in Baltimore, Bennett re-established his courier system and tied it to Samuel

Morse's new electromagnetic telegraph. The system was still mostly primitive
—by news boat across the Gulf of Mexico to New Orleans, by fast horses
overland to the North, by wire only for the last lap from Philadelphia—but it
outstripped the rest of the American press by days and provided the government
in Washington with its first word on the distant encounters. Bennett had infected his charges with the newsman's hunger, and his paper gave matchless
play to the battle reports and the casualty lists and the political repercussions
on the home front. The *Herald*'s was a rooting interest, little affected by the
merits of the war: news sold papers, and no paper was newsier than his.

The *Tribune,* as anxious for sales, would not glorify what it believed to be
immoral. "People of the United States! your rulers are precipitating you into a
fathomless abyss of crime and calamity," Greeley shouted. "Why sleep you
thoughtless on its verge?" Polk he called "the Father of Lies" for claiming
Mexico had imposed the war while "we are a meek, unoffending, ill-used people." The *Tribune* was hardly the only paper to cry out against the war as
slavocracy's adventurism—many Whig journals joined in the denunciation—
but none matched it for unequivocation or the loudness of its prose. Bennett was
quick to brand Greeley a traitor, and Webb's *Courier* tried to incite a mob
against him for subverting the national interest, but the *Tribune*'s editor had a
higher definition of patriotism than blind allegiance to wrongheadedness. " 'Our
Country, Right or Wrong,' is a maxim as foolish as Heaven-daring," he wrote.
"If your country be wrong . . . it is madness, it is idiocy, to wish to struggle for
her success in the wrong; for such success can only be more calamitous than
failure, since it increases our Nation's guilt."

As Zachary Taylor's troops posted victory upon victory and swept down on
Mexico City, Greeley's killjoy lamentations were harder to sustain, yet he never
stinted. Of the impending prospect of slavery's establishment in the territories
seized from Mexico, he wrote that Congress might have such power but it had
no more *right* to do so than to legalize "Polygamy, Dueling, Counterfeiting,
Cannibalism or any other iniquity condemned by and gradually receding before
the moral and religious sentiment of the civilized and Christian world." He
called for peace at any price—"Sign anything, ratify anything, pay anything to
end the guilt, the bloodshed, the shame"—and while he hailed the valor of
American fighting men, he greeted a congressional proposal for life benefits for
those disabled in the Mexican conflict by crying:

> Uncle Sam! you bedazzled old hedge-hog! don't you see "glory" is cheap as dirt,
> only you never get done paying for it! Forty years hence, your boys will be still paying
> taxes to support the debt you are now piling up, and the cripples and other pensioners
> you are now manufacturing. How much more of this will satisfy you?

He much preferred using his columns to promote opponents of the death penalty
than proponents of unjustifiable carnage. Bennett, unbothered by such scruples,
scooped him at every turn, even in reporting the peace treaty.

VII

If Bennett's fulfillment was to ride alongside the current of history, expertly charting its course, detailing its eddies, thrilling to its stretches of whitewater, Greeley's ambition was to harness the stream and direct it. The newspaper in his hands was primarily an instrument to shape public opinion, not reflect it. Thus, he had both ready means and a divine end, and they were yoked by his own skills with a pen. Had he true mastery of that instrument, it might have been different with him, for, as he put it,

> . . . to write nobly, excellently, is a far loftier achievement than to rule, to conquer, or to kill, and . . . the truly great author looks down on the little strifes and agitations of mankind from an eminence which monarchs can but feebly emulate, and the ages can scarcely wear away.

Perhaps he knew the seeds of true greatness as a writer were not within him; perhaps he knew he had neither the patience to climb to that eminence nor the serenity to render the outlook indelibly if he ever reached it. But the unsettling fact of Horace Greeley's professional life was that personal ambition chronically distracted him. As the *Tribune* grew in circulation and influence, so did its editor's yen for laurels. It was not enough for him that he commanded a growing, if invisible, constituency of readers who provided assurance that his voice would be heard in the councils of party and government. More than influence he wanted power, power to direct the unruly body politic; he wanted office to validate his espousal of a higher moral order than party hackery could or would conceive; he was ever readier to translate conviction into action—if only they would hand him a scepter. Some attributed this yearning to runaway ego, some to messianic compulsion. More charitably, one may impute the impulse to Greeley's view of the journalist as public servant; it was no trick to sit back like Bennett and wisecrack or sharpshoot at passing events and men; the true civic spirit drives a newsman into the arena.

Whatever its genesis, his political ambition was blatant. If preferment had come to him unsought, he might have coolly weighed his prior commitments and gratefully declined to serve. But he was a constant suitor for office, basing his hopes on Weed and Seward, who for more than twenty years were masters of the New York political landscape. He was more useful to them than they ever proved to him. As the eloquent editor of a rising newspaper that reached, through its weekly edition, throughout the Empire State, Greeley was a lively fish on the hook, to be fed enough line to thrash about picturesquely until reeled in tightly during campaign season.

His hopes for office had been first inflamed by his involvement through his party sheets in the successful Whig campaigns for the New York governorship

in 1838 and the presidency two years later. That the party had provided him with
the means to broaden his reputation he never considered adequate compensation. In 1843 he was handed a sop—the Whig nomination to become state
printer, not likely to be approved by a Democratic legislature. The following
year he let Weed know of his interest in the lieutenant governor's place on the
state ticket. The Albany Whig leader nimbly sidestepped; Greeley's principles
may have been admirable, but many of them, like his prominent advocacy of
Fourierism and temperance, were political liabilities, and his calls for reforming
the political process by rigorous monitoring of the patronage and registration
systems were a bone in Weed's throat. And as the Mexican War came on and
proved the fulfillment of jingoist dreams, Greeley's pacifism seemed more and
more ill-considered.

But Weed dared not snub him outright. The perfect opportunity to reward
him cheaply arose in 1848 when the congressional seat representing the city
above Fourteenth Street fell vacant after disclosure that the Democrat holding
it had been elected by the import of paupers from the Blackwells Island alms-
house in the East River. The unexpired term would last for only the final three
months of the Thirtieth Congress, and since the Whigs had already designated
their candidate for the seat for the ensuing full term, Greeley's reward was of
limited duration. On election day, Zachary Taylor of Louisiana, most of whose
policies Greeley abhorred, took the White House for the Whigs, and the *Tribune*'s editor rode the bandwagon into office with nearly 60 percent of the vote.
It would be his only term in public office, and quite a spectacle it was.

He went to Washington with a dual purpose: to represent the people of his
district in an exemplary manner and to let his readers know from the inside what
sort of cockpit Congress could be. He achieved the first by tireless performance
of his duty, never missing a session of the House or of the committees on which
he served. The result was utter futility. But his daily reports back to the *Tribune*
on the buffetings he endured were indeed revealing, if self-serving, dispatches
from the very Seat of Corruption. Inevitably, they made him into something of
a tattletale, hardly an endearing role for a novice politician to take. In all ways,
he was impolitic; he waded into the fray, unloosing his arrows in every direction.

One of his first acts was to introduce a major land-reform bill, providing that
any landless citizen could claim 160 acres of the public domain so long as he
would settle on it and improve it, and would have seven years to buy it at the
government's price of $1.25 per acre. When a Western member of the House
wondered aloud why New York should busy herself about the disposal of public
lands far beyond the Hudson, Greeley answered that his interest was stimulated
by the fact that he represented more landless men than any other member on
the floor. The disarming riposte worked no wonders; his bill was put aside.

So were his subsequent proposals to outlaw the franking privilege, which he
felt diminished the influence of newspapers and hurt efforts to cut the postal
rates; force the Congress not to adjourn for a long Christmas–New Year's
holiday; deduct the pay of congressmen for sessions they did not attend; change

the name of the United States of America to "Columbia"; abolish the slave trade in the District of Columbia (he drafted the preamble to the bill); deny the army's request for $38,000 for recruitment because he alleged it went mainly to shanghai drunks off the streets; abolish flogging and grog rations in the navy, reduce its list of warrant officers, and halt promotions into higher ranks already filled with idle officers; and amend the abuse by congressmen of the mileage allowance they collected for their travel to and from the Capitol. It was this last proposal that assured his crowning by acclamation as the least popular man in Congress.

The law allowed each congressman eight dollars per twenty miles "by the usually traveled road," but on inspecting figures provided him by the House Sergeant at Arms, Greeley thought the sums excessive. He put a reporter to work calculating the shortest route between each congressman's home and Washington, using post office routes as the basis. The resulting overcharge came to $73,492.60 for the previous term. Only twelve congressmen were innocent of abuse; a first-termer from Illinois, Abraham Lincoln, was paid $676.80 more than he should have been, according to Greeley's figures. Before bringing any of it up in the House, he aired the dirty linen in the *Tribune*.

The exposé was a national sensation and set tempers boiling in the House all the more because papers everywhere echoed the *Tribune*'s call for reform. When Greeley was finally allowed the floor after being called fifteen species of scoundrel, he lamely explained that the article never said his colleagues had done anything illegal; it was the law that had to be altered. The vilification continued. They tarred him for trying to besmirch the reputation of Congress, seeking publicity, editing his newspaper from the House floor, and behaving generally as a preposterous ass. When he had had enough, Greeley stood and said:

> ... I knew very well—I knew from the first—what a low, contemptible, demagoguing business this of attempting to save the public money always is. It is not a task for gentlemen—it is esteemed rather disreputable even for editors. Your gentlemanly work is spending—lavishly—distributing—taking. Savings are always such vulgar, beggarly, two-penny affairs—there is a sorry and stingy look about them most repugnant to all gentlemanly instincts. ... Ah! Mr. Chairman, *I* was not rocked in the cradle of gentility!

They needled him to the end of the lame-duck session, threatened to expel him, did nothing about curbing the mileage abuse, but still he did not relent. His report on the bedlam of the final session of the term, ending at five in the morning, was one of his most graphic and damning. It detailed the use of arrogant procedural expedients to assure the payment of $250 bonuses—to which Greeley was opposed—to congressional aides as "the free liquor and trimmings provided by the expectants of the bounty had for hours stood open to all comers in a convenient sideroom, and a great many had already taken too much."

If he had made a spectacle of himself, Congress had done no less. Greeley attended the inauguration ball for General Taylor and then came home. No congressman had ever served his constituents more faithfully nor any editor, his readers. But practically speaking, Greeley's political career was put to rest, though his ambition lived on undiminished. "He martyrizes himself five or six times daily," Senator-elect Seward wrote Weed from Washington. Greeley was too much the reformer to abide the endless compromises that are the essence of effective politics. Anyone who witnessed the editor of the *Tribune* perform in that shirttail session of Congress and predicted he would run for President of the United States two dozen years later and attract 44 percent of the popular vote would have been committed to the madhouse on the spot. The most ludicrous of politicians, he remained the unelected tribune of the people.

3

The Crusader

By its second decade the *New York Tribune* was no longer a one-man band. Greeley's warmth of heart, wealth of ideas, and dynamic character drew gifted young men to his newspaper. But those who stayed often did so despite the editor, not because of him.

Without a doubt Horace Greeley could be the most generous and sympathetic of men. Yet his true concern seemed to be for the generality of mankind, not the individuals with whom he had daily contact. He was not unsociable—he loved to hear or tell a good story as much as any man—but he had few close friends off the *Tribune* staff and none on it.* He was thoroughly au courant with events, personalities, topics, and books of the day, yet he was curiously abstracted much of the time, caught up in himself and his thoughts. He rarely

---

* Unlikeliest of Greeley's good friends was Phineas Taylor Barnum, the showman, who had published an abolitionist paper in Connecticut in his salad days and shared with the *Tribune*'s editor an array of social concerns and a remarkable gift for self-promotion. Greeley frequently visited at Barnum's home in the city, where a desk much to the editor's taste was set aside for him to write at; there, too, he met with politicians and office seekers. Barnum tried in vain to get his friend to shuck his heavy boots in favor of carpet slippers, but Greeley did occasionally shed his coat in favor of one of his host's dressing gowns. It was perhaps not entirely coincidental that when, in 1850, Barnum imported soprano Jenny Lind for an American concert tour as the successor sensation to the retired two-foot midget General Tom Thumb, the *Tribune* greeted her arrival warmly and reported on her generously; Bennett's *Herald* took issue with the ticket prices Barnum charged and much else about the tour.

found time to flatter, and never to coddle, and if he had an admiring word to pass along, it was as likely as not to be tied to a querulous or cautionary one. He was a perfectionist and not a little afflicted with egomania as success and fame flowed to him. His stance, though, so plainly on the side of the angels, and the transparency of his earnestness were an irresistible lure to idealistic enlistees. Even more than idealism, they brought skilled pens with them. Greeley was a rare judge of writing talent. E. L. Godkin, who was to edit *The Nation* and the *New York Evening Post,* would remark that selection for the *Tribune* staff gave young writers "a patent of literary nobility"—a distinction that the paper continued to confer throughout almost its entire life. By the mid-1850s, Greeley had assembled the most brilliant staff yet to serve on an American newspaper.

As Greeley was the *Tribune*'s wagon master, Charles Anderson Dana served as its linchpin. For fifteen years beginning in 1847, Dana kept the vehicle on course, all the while coping with his superior's flamboyant and often volatile personality, so different from his own direct, concise, virile one. They shared New Hampshire as a birthplace—Dana was eight years younger—and a broad, general intelligence along with a passion for social justice. On those grounds their valuable union endured as long as it did, cemented by mutual respect and large quantities of forbearance by the adjutant. Bitterness followed their parting.

Dana's family, like Greeley's, moved to western New York, and Charles as a boy learned much of the world while clerking for his uncle's dry-goods store in Buffalo, a thriving community after the Erie Canal opened it and the western hinterlands to access from the sea. When he had exhausted the learning facilities there, he entered Harvard at the age of twenty and stayed two years until failing eyesight and poverty forced his resignation. For the next five years, he was a leading member of the Brook Farm social experiment in communal living, a magnet for the highminded, literate, and impoverished.

Among the nonresidents with whom he became acquainted there was Horace Greeley. Correspondence between them survives from as early as 1842, when the editor was already promoting in the *Tribune* the sort of communal democracy Dana was practicing in Roxbury. While supportive of Brook Farm, Greeley was dubious of its prospects. He did not deny the desirability of the sort of community Dana described to him—"actuated solely by a true Christianity or a genuine manfulness," disposed to bear others' burdens and happily suffer for the indolent and unthankful—yet he questioned the likelihood of bringing the world "speedily to this frame of mind." He thought it "adapted only to angelic natures," he wrote Dana, "and that the entrance of one serpent would be as fatal as in Eden of old." Fourierism, "by having a rampart of exact justice behind that of philanthropy," seemed a more rational, practicable hope to Greeley.

When the farm and the fervor nourishing it petered out, Dana spent a year in Boston on a sheet called the *Daily Chronotype,* which paid him a munificent four dollars a week. Appealing to Greeley for a spot, he was accepted at once and did not take long to make his mark as a highly versatile craftsman who read his fond but somewhat intemperate taskmaster like an open book. The new-comer wrote in a firm, economical style—Greeley provided quite enough flights of rhetoric when at full propulsion—and his skills as a linguist proved especially useful in culling and translating the foreign news. He worked dutifully directing the city staff, but as events in Europe heated up, his eye was drawn there to the revolutionary movements beginning to challenge monarchy and autocracy. Liberty was on the march, and Greeley reluctantly let him go to report its progress in weekly letters for the *Tribune*. It is doubtful if any other American paper carried a more thoughtful, truthful, or colorful rendition of the European uprisings of 1848.

For the task he brought with him wide-open eyes and a compassionate heart, each contributing to the freshness of style with which he described the turmoil in the streets of Berlin, the rampant beggary in Paris, the fragile base of England's majesty with its "feudal aristocracy monopolizing the soil" and its "moneyed aristocracy monopolizing the materials and implements of industry . . ." The American journalist "regards nothing with indifference," Dana wrote in the *Tribune* two years later in an essay that might well have been describing his European reporting, but "carries with him a degree of genuine sympathy in the event and its actors which renders him an excellent observer and reporter. He is no dull analyzer, and sees the thing before he attempts to speculate on its philosophy and consequences . . . [H]is enthusiasm—of which he has a large stock—concentrates itself upon persons and deeds and makes him almost a part of the occurrence he describes. His element is action and his method rapidity."

Here was the nub of a debate on the fundamental value system of journalism that had hardly been framed before then and that has been going on ever since: Are objectivity and neutrality interchangeable concepts in journalism, or should the skillful journalist, observing intently, conclude judgmentally—provided he is independent and not predisposed to the outcome he reports? The purist school that gathered strength toward the end of the nineteenth century held that journalism more closely approximated a profession the more faithfully it approached the clinical in its reporting. The reporter's sympathies and enthusiasm, according to this regimen, are to be curtailed well short of the printed page. The countervailing argument, advanced with renewed vigor most prominently by Dana's *Tribune* progeny more than a century after his first pronouncement on the issue, holds there to be no such animal as objective truth—only imperfect versions of it glimpsed prismatically by countless observers; therefore, why pretend to a serene and sterile account when journalistic honesty resides in him who "regards nothing with indifference"? The mood of the assemblage (not merely its size or location), the intonation of the speaker's words (not only their substance), their motivations, intended effects, and likely consequences (not simply their declaration)—all are the proper business of the astute reporter. Consider this snatch of Dana's description of the first appearance of Louis Napoleon before the French Assembly:

> . . . He was instantly the sole object of attention to every person in the House
> except the unlucky orator who happened to be in the tribune; even the elegant and
> massive lorgnette of ivory that President Marast wields with such consummate
> skill was gracefully levelled upon him. He bore the quizzing with calmness and
> courage. He was dressed in black with a bad-looking mustache—at least that was
> the verdict of the ladies in the gallery. He is rather undersized and seemed worn
> with dissipation. . . .

Subjective judgments abound here, but, discounting the arguably libelous implication of the last four words in the passage, was Dana merely embroidering the
scene before him or capturing it more graphically, arrestingly, and authentically
than "facts" alone could have transmitted? Without a doubt, the grant of such
discretion to the eyes and pen of the beholder bestows a power open to abuse
and requiring close oversight by editors. Is it certain, however, that the denial
of such a license assures the reading public a purer distillation of truth? What
are the ideal dimensions and parameters of "the news"? Are sensibility and
nuance a part of reporters' tools or ought their dispatches to be limited to
demonstrable, undeniable phenomena?

Dana, so adept at portraiture, did not try to hide his point of view in an
age when the sin of his profession was in not having one. Abuse arose when
the correspondent's opinions became so strong as to blind him to the plain import of unfolding events. In Dana's case, his sympathy for social radicalism
grew with the toll of injustice he encountered, but he was hardly unaware of
the cost of upheaval. "The struggle for freedom may be terrible," he wrote on
his return from Europe in 1849, "but the stagnation of oppression is more
so."

Greeley promoted him to second-in-command. And command he did, somewhat peremptorily at times and with a nice brevity. The delegation of authority
worked because of Dana's incontrovertible skills and the social agenda he shared
with Greeley; both were Whigs, Free-Soilers (as opponents of slavery's extension into the Union's newly added territories were called), and protectionists in
trade, and both sympathized mightily with the downtrodden. Dana, though,
was the far more sensitive of the two to injustices closer to home. The corporate
minute books of the Tribune Association show him repeatedly speaking up for
fairer wages for his charges. At a meeting of the directors in 1855, for example,
he noted that the *Tribune*'s mechanical department was the best paid in town
while "intellectual labor was but poorly paid for." It was Dana, not Greeley,
who governed the newswriting policies of the paper in its day-to-day operations;
witness his resolution presented to the May 1, 1852, board meeting that "no puffs
or announcements of any private establishment or business, shall be admitted
into the editorial columns of The Tribune, except with the word 'Advertisement'
over the same; from this rule are excepted statements which are news and
regular criticisms or editorial comments, which in no case are to be paid for.
Speeches and reports which the editor shall judge to be of sufficient public

interest may be published without the word advertisement." Such were the soft edges of journalistic principle in that day on the most self-righteous newspaper in New York.

Dana, too, was more philosophical than Greeley about the nature of their trade, and more articulate. Few more instructive reflections on American journalism have ever been offered than Dana's essay "The Newspaper Press," published in the *Tribune* in 1850. In contrast to European practitioners, preoccupied with the rules of rhetoric and wedded to a style smacking more of the scholar's study than the mood and tempo of the street, the American journalist-editorialist, according to Dana,

> does not seek to make elaborate essays; his ambition lies not in fine writing; he spends no long hours in polishing the turns of his periods. All that presupposes a certain degree of leisure and perhaps a kind of taste to which he is a stranger. At any rate, he has too many things to look after, too many subjects to discuss, too large a round of affairs to understand and write about, to cultivate with assiduity the mere perfumeries and pigeon-wings of his profession. From necessity, he had rather be brief and pointed than elegant and classical; his best triumph as a writer is an occasional felicity, which is, after all, often an accident. . . .

Such an appraisal would seem to have held the press, if not a captive of the headlong pace of American life and the impatience of its people with heavy thoughts, at least a willing accomplice. For Dana, this was a thoroughly positive development. He was drawing the distinction between an elitist press, serving Europe's class-ridden societies, and one more consciously vernacular that served a dynamic young society's nation-building process by helping destroy social barriers and promote wholesale accessibility. The American press, proliferating at a pace unknown elsewhere, exalted the common man and made him the world's best-informed and most opinionated citizen. That it may also have helped make him at times the most unmanageable and cynical of democrats did not detract from its usefulness.

Chief among the other men of intellect and cultivation who gravitated to the *Tribune* under Greeley and Dana were William H. Fry, a musicologist and composer of the opera *Leonora,* who would slowly pace about the paper's premises, thinking out the sledgehammer editorials with which he demolished perpetrators of villainy; Richard Hildreth, whose six-volume economic history of the United States was completed shortly before he joined the staff in 1854; James S. Pike, who abandoned a successful career as a Maine businessman to become the *Tribune*'s fearless Washington commentator, much unloved by capital Democrats; Solon Robinson, a returnee from the Indiana frontier, whose crop reports and market estimates were as invaluable to rural readers as his expert advice, offered with rough wit, on the evolving science of agronomy; George Ripley, the patriarch of Brook Farm, who lent a paternal air to the paper and much encouragement to the literary output of his young nation; and Bayard Taylor, the natty little travel writer with delicate features and curling beard, whom some thought a better voyager than journalist but whose globe-trotting reports held great appeal for homebound *Tribune* readers over a career that outlasted all of Greeley's other lieutenants.

It was Taylor, aspiring to greatness as a poet and having to settle for literary distinction as a lyric translator of Goethe's *Faust,* who produced one of the most notable early *Tribune* exclusives. After reporting from California in 1849 on the gold rush for five dollars a letter and doubling as solicitor there at 25 percent commission for subscriptions to a special California edition of the paper, Taylor was granted leave in 1852 for what was expected to be a nine-month trip to witness the excavation of Nineveh and travel up the Nile. In the latter stages of his journey, he received word to stand by on the chance that the *Tribune* might succeed in getting him assigned to Commodore Matthew C. Perry's fleet, about to embark on its mission to negotiate—or force, if necessary—the opening of Japan to Western trade. Taylor waited around Constantinople for a month and was on the point of leaving when a letter arrived from New York enclosing money to cover his travel costs to the coast of China, across the entire vast Asian land mass. Perry said he would be glad to see him if Taylor was on hand when the American fleet arrived, but declined to promise he would allow him aboard for the fateful mission to Japan. Taylor, the most gamely peripatetic journalist of his day, unhesitantly made the journey and his rendezvous with Perry, onetime pursuer of pirates in the West Indies and a leading advocate of steam-powered warships. He found the commodore "a blunt, honest old fellow . . . well-disposed towards me," and, outfitted in a blue coat with big gilt buttons, "a gilt anchor on front of my cap, and a terrible sword by my side," Taylor was taken on board the flagship *Susquehanna* as master's mate. No other representative of the American press went along.

The rules of the service forbade him from writing a line for publication, he was told, and required him to surrender his journal to the Navy Department at the end of the cruise. "But I shall have little difficulty, through Commodore Perry's aid, in reclaiming it and publishing a history of the expedition," he wrote to his mother. In this hope, however, he was badly mistaken. The Navy Department never did return Taylor's detailed journal to him, and the only extensive published account of the Perry expedition was the commodore's own. But Taylor had prevailed upon Perry to let him write letters to the *Tribune* provided they passed under the commodore's eye. His accounts, thus circumscribed, were still enough to drive James Gordon Bennett into a paroxysm of envy. When Taylor finally returned home after a voyage of nearly 15,000 miles via the Cape of Good Hope, he was greeted as a celebrity and his lecture appearances around the country regularly outdrew those of, among other prominent literary orators of the age, Greeley and Emerson.

II

For all the solidity of the supporting timber with which it was being built, the *Tribune* relied for its foundation upon the vigor of its editorials. Others besides Greeley now emulated his upright, downright, forthright style and added variations of their own. In the 1850s, the *Tribune* editorials were institutionalized on a separate page, consuming from one-fifth to one-quarter of the entire space unoccupied by advertisements. They were the pride and showcase of the paper and became, by the skill with which they were composed and the attention they commanded, the national prototype.

The attention paid to newspaper editorials before the arrival of radio and television should not be judged in terms of the wan latter-day "think pieces" that too often seem confected solely to record management's proprietary interests on a page otherwise usefully devoted to syndicated columns and letters from readers. Greeley's America was different from ours: younger, smaller, simpler, less connected. The newspaper was the only real mass medium of the age and, after the Bible and the clergy, its chief instructor in the ways of the world. Greeley's repertoire of subject matter, settled upon early, was one long reprise of reformist pleading: the streets must be cleaner, the milk purer, the tariff higher, the jobless put to work, the wide West opened, harbors and roads improved and all the rivers bridged; every child must attend schools adequately supported by taxes and there must be evening schools for those unable to attend by day and normal schools to train teachers. Not even cutthroats should hang, and first offenders should be jailed separately from hardened criminals, and debtors' prisons should be abolished, along with corruption in office, rigged elections, the spread of slavery, and the sale of liquor, which brutalizes the ignorant, the wayward, and the hopeless. It was a radical Christianity, impelled by a universal love and augmented by ample servings of Old Testament rage to smite the irredeemable. Surfeited with principle, neutral about nothing, Horace Greeley became the reading public's leading oracle.

His editorials were not written to analyze or discuss; they were weapons, rather, in a ceaseless war to improve society. He wrote to convince and incite, to win votes and voices for specific political positions and moral stances. Behind the force of his advocacy was no power of originality; he was a champion, not a leader or creator, of causes. Nor was his a disciplined mind, adept at perceiving issues from all sides before passing judgment. He judged and then bent the case to his mold. His method appealed to a young nation in ferment. His tone was elevated but hardly exalted; his conviction, beyond doubting. Above all, his message was accessible. Dana may have best explained Greeley's great knack as an editorialist in his 1850 essay on the press, although he did not specifically allude to his chief in noting, "Many a quill-driver will turn off indefinite lengths of correct and even elegant English, not deficient in sense either, who can not achieve a dozen lines such as every body shall read and nobody forget the point of."

Greeley lifted the American newspaper editorial to the level of a legitimate literary form. It is worth pausing a moment to anatomize his technique. Consider by way of example the thirteen-paragraph piece titled "Street-Cleaning" that ran in the *Tribune* on Thursday morning, June 1, 1854. Since the principal means of conveyance at that time was the undiapered horse, the problem was anything but cosmetic. In most of his best work, Greeley marched directly up on his subject and made plain at the earliest possible point the seriousness of the issue at hand; thus, this one began:

> The People of this City eminently need and ardently desire Clean Streets; they pay enough to secure them; yet they suffer immensely in purse and person, in health and comfort, for the want of them. It is a moderate estimate that One Thousand Lives and One Million dollars' worth of property are annually sacrificed in this City through the excessive filthiness of our streets.
> Why is this? . . .

Having provoked attention, he then set about at once to explain the nature of the problem, using its ironical quality to underscore why it was so intolerable. Hardly an acre of the city—by which he meant Manhattan Island—was more than half a mile from navigable water, by which means "all the fertilizing matter that can be swept from under our feet for the next century" could readily be transported to meet the needs of "the hungry soil of Long Island"; other adjacent areas had a similar requirement "for manures, and [are] ready to reward generously their application." In controlled and majestic cadence, his compacted fury poured forth, intensifying phrase by phrase:

> . . . And yet we die here each summer of fevers, cholera, and other diseases which faithful Street-Cleaning would obviate or greatly modify, until despair has become a current faith, and thousands virtually concede that, though New-York can build Steamships by the score, Oceanic Canals, Panama Railroads, and, if need be, Overland Pacific Railroads, she must always remain the filthiest and most noisome city of Christendom. And the conviction is very general that the vital reason for this is not that Street-Cleaning is essentially difficult, or more difficult here than elsewhere, but that *our functionaries in charge of the streets can aggrandize and enrich themselves rather by SLIGHTING their work than by faithfully DOING it.* We believe this is the mournful truth. [Italics Greeley's.] . . .

The details of this alleged scandal, prominently involving the Commissioner of Streets and Lamps and tolerated by the mayor and his camp, were presented chapter and verse in subdued recitation until, with renewed but more lethal irony, the writer noted "a serious discrepancy" between the street-cleaning contractors' understanding of their duties and the public's: "The People and the Council supposed they were to sweep the streets; *their* understanding, on the contrary, seemed to be that they were to sweep only the Treasury." At specific issue was the contractual provision that the streets were to be swept twice weekly if weather permitted; if it did not, however, the pay was not reduced. Gorge rising once more but with language tightly modulated, the editorial decried the lunacy of the arrangement:

> . . . Of course, no man of common sagacity could expect that the streets would be cleaned under such a specification, since every week in which the contractor could plead rain, or snow, or mud, as an excuse for doing nothing, would give him a pull at the City Treasury for just nothing at all. . . . The temptation to collusion between Commissioner and Contractors to enrich themselves and rob the City would be very strong. . . .

A sensible compromise had been proposed: in weeks when weather interfered, the contractors would receive half-pay to cover the cost of removing garbage and ashes and maintaining their teams of horses. "Yet this indispensable necessary, this indisputably mercifully just requisition, was voted down by the Board of Councilmen, and so stands to this day unadopted." Meanwhile the peril to the public health remained. The closing paragraph skewered this exemplary case of municipal malfeasance, misfeasance, and nonfeasance by noting:

> . . . if our citizens should miss Street-Cleaning before their doors, they will undoubtedly find any amount of it in their tax-bills. It is a nice thing for a hungry and seedy politician to have full swing at a purse of $300,000, to spend it at his discretion; and if [the commissioner in question] should lose anything, or fail to serve his friends, by his present control of Street-Cleaning, he will show himself more honest or less adroit than most men would be in his position. . . .

This is the high rhetoric of Greeleyesque outrage, reviling by barb, understatement, and direct frontal assault. The output of verbal energy swells and ebbs with the undulations of his dialectic, and the vocabulary grows more or less picturesque, the constructions more or less parallel, as the indictment is leveled, explicated, and finally held aloft on the knight's trusty lance. Greeley did not deal in glancing blows; he aimed only to unhorse, preferably to gore.

Greeley at his editorial best dwelled on public policy; at his worst, on personal invective. For a man professionally given to passing judgment on others, he himself was exceedingly thin-skinned and prone to confuse rebuttal of his positions and beliefs with assault on his character. He was quick to label those who disputed him as liars or worse. More detachment would have greatly enhanced his stature, but he seemed incapable of distancing himself from encounters that were the verbal equivalent of a barroom brawl. The tendency made him an easy mark, especially for Bennett's *Herald,* which specialized in short, often cynical paragraphs on an editorial page that bore little resemblance to the *Tribune*'s.

Greeley may have reached his sardonic high—or low—point in dispensing personal abuse in an editorial he titled "Judgment on the Satanic Press," published in the issue of December 15, 1853. For five years, Bennett's lawyers had stalled off a libel trial brought against him by Edward P. Fry, the proprietor of a New York theater he had refurbished for the presentation of opera and other musical productions. Fry had taken pains to improve both the caliber of artistry on display at his theater by importing talent and the behavior of his clientele by banning the sale of liquor on the premises. When he declined to advertise in the *Herald* or hand out passes to any of its representatives or have his printing done in its shop, Bennett began the most blatant sort of character assassination and charged, among other things, that the theater and its environs were crawling with prostitutes. Fry sued to end the economic harassment and finally prevailed; the jury awarded him $10,000 in damages—a very substantial sum in that day —plus some $7,000 in expenses and court costs. The *Herald* distorted its coverage of the trial, omitting the most damaging testimony against its owner and continuing to attack Fry until the case went to the jury. Greeley, gleeful at the outcome, began his editorial thus:

> When we gave, a few months since, apropos to something, a review of The Satanic Press, with the Life and Adventures of its Editor, James Gordon Bennett, we mentioned that among other marks of public distinction which he had received were seven horsewhippings in public, not counting sundry "cuts," cuffings and kickings, and having his jaws forced open and his throat spat into. We are reminded by a good authority that we have done Mr. Bennett injustice in limiting the number of such marks of public distinction received by him: it was not simply seven horse-whippings he received, but nine. . . .

It went on to rehearse the case and commend Fry for his courage in withstanding the assaults by Bennett, who, "[s]worn to do him all the evil that bloated power and unchecked villainy could compass . . . frothed, steamed and reeked. . . ." Bennett's abuses had run unchecked for too long, Greeley declared, but:

> The tide is now turned. The ruffian has got his deserts. The low-mouthed, blatant, witless, brutal scoundrel is condemned—condemned, too, by THE PEOPLE. . . .
> The Jury, indeed, have entitled themselves to the lasting gratitude of the community. They have proved that Justice, when perseveringly pursued, can be obtained even against a libeler fortified behind a fortress of gold and silver, and wielding a greater engine of intimidation than the history of this country has hitherto known.

One senses, even at a remove of generations, that some of Greeley's most sulfuric epithets may have been intended less to preach probity than to sell newspapers.

III

Horace Greeley never denied Henry Raymond's usefulness to him in the early days of the *Tribune.* There was the time, for example, when his speed and accuracy as a reporter enabled the paper to score a clear beat on a major speech delivered in Boston by Daniel Webster. While the great orator was speaking, a small crew of *Tribune* printers bearing type cases took possession of a state-room on the overnight steamer plying Long Island Sound. Little Raymond darted from the lecture hall, eluding fellow correspondents, and made directly for the *Tribune*'s floating composing room, where he speedily turned out page after page of copy so that by the time the ship docked at dawn, the story was all set up and on the press within an hour. "Clever but careless" was the nitpicking Greeley's contemporary judgment of his young assistant, whom he faulted for being rather a passionless technician and a political reactionary—but useful nonetheless.

When Raymond decided he was being overused and underpaid, he set out on a path that would, within a decade, place him nearly on a par with Bennett as Greeley's principal rival for leadership of the New York press. His admirers found him well-spoken and tactful, his detractors called him crafty, but all agreed he had brains and pluck to go with his industry. On the *Courier and Enquirer,* he rose to managing editor and sparked that leading but lackluster six-penny sheet. His six-month debate in print with Greeley over the merits of Fourierist socialism won Raymond wide regard as a defender of capitalism and a disputationist more than able to hold his own against the *Tribune* editor. He spoke as well as he wrote, and when he, too, succumbed to political ambition, he was taken up by the Whig powers as the volatile Greeley never would be. Raymond at least was not out to reform the world. Articulate, orthodox, reli-able, he went into the New York State Assembly in 1849 and within two years, at the age of thirty, was chosen its Speaker.

Whether he had overstepped his authority in trying to improve the *Courier* or failed to sympathize with the political ambitions of his boss, James Watson Webb, was not clear—both reasons may have applied—but Raymond left the paper to concentrate on politics. His departure from journalism proved brief. The growing prosperity of the *Herald* and the *Tribune* suggested to Raymond that there was room for another low-priced daily, one directed at intelligent conservatives who found Bennett's sensationalism and Greeley's reformism to be offensive. Word circulated that the *Tribune,* with far less advertising support from the city merchants than the *Herald,* had posted a profit of $60,000 in 1850, and while the surviving minute books of the Tribune Association suggest that the net was only a bit more than half that figure, the marketplace looked attractive enough for several Whig bankers in Albany to join forces with Ray-mond and promise to raise what he needed to start up his paper. On a European vacation over the summer of 1851, Raymond drafted his prospectus for the new venture. He would call it *The New-York Daily Times,* even though seven previ-ous entries with that name had been established starting in 1813 and all had foundered. No doubt he hoped to model his paper after *The Times* of London, the nonpareil of journalistic authority and decorum, and replicate its influence. He promised his backers he would publish "at once the best and the cheapest daily family newspaper in The United States," and given Raymond's acumen as both journalist and politician, they had no great trouble in accumulating $110,000 to launch the *Times*.

No American paper had ever been so amply funded from the first. The war chest allowed Raymond to buy a new Hoe "Lightning" press, hire a large enough staff—including three editors, a dozen compositors, and several pressmen lured from the *Tribune*—and try out his new paper for a week in the city's better residential neighborhoods. His first issue, on September 18, 1851, announced itself not as partisan but strictly pragmatic in policy: "We shall be *conservative* in all cases where we think conservatism essential to the public good, and we shall be *radical* in every thing which may seem to us to require radical treatment and radical reform." But lest there be any doubt that his paper would be of far more subdued coloration and therefore sounder than Greeley's, Raymond wrote:

> . . . We do not believe that every thing in society is exactly right or exactly wrong; what is good we desire to preserve and improve; what is evil, to exterminate and reform. . . . [W]e shall . . . seek to be tempered and measured in all our language. *We do not mean to write as if we were in a passion* unless that shall really be the case, and we shall *make it a point to get into a passion as rarely as possible.* There are very few things in this world which it is worth while to get angry about, and they are just the things that anger will not improve. [Italics Raymond's.]

As intended, the *Times* displayed none of the bite or brilliance of the *Herald* or the combative zest of the *Tribune*. And there was no way to confuse its appeal with that of the chatty little *Sun*, still prosperous but stuck to a kind of backstairs disreputability that kept it beyond arm's length from the educated and prosperous. The *Times* exhibited from the beginning precisely the qualities that have sustained it since: prudence, good manners, and industry in the gathering, editing, and presentation of the news. Stylishness tended, as Bennett all too distressingly demonstrated, to veer into flamboyance and distortion; partisanship, as Greeley revealed, too often invited telling omissions or reportage tainted by polemics. The *Times* was straightforward and impersonal in tone, serving readers who did not want or need their news cosmeticized. It placed heavy stress, from the first issue, upon foreign news; its columns throughout were marked by an almost unrelieved seriousness that was matched by a grim grayness in its typography.

Like the *Tribune* a decade earlier, the *Times* found a readership almost at once. Greeley vainly tried to prevent newsboys who carried his paper from handling the *Times*, just as the *Sun* had tried, somewhat more aggressively, to put a crimp in the *Tribune*'s distribution when it began. But within ten days of its start-up, the *Times* claimed a daily circulation in excess of 10,000 copies, taken largely by "business men at their stores" and "the most respectable families in town." After a year, Raymond reported sales at well above 20,000, close to the *Tribune*'s total for its daily edition but in no way imperiling the large and growing circulation of its weekly. His warmest acceptance, Raymond continued to boast, was among "the best portion of our citizens," who preferred the *Times* because it did not "pander to any special taste, least of all to any low or degrading appetite." Raymond lost no time in branding the *Herald* "the recognized organ of quack doctors," and advertisers flocked to his new standard as they never had to the *Tribune,* whose reformist tub-thumping displeased the business community. Profits, however, did not flow so swiftly. The printing plant, sizable staff, telegraph costs, and promotional expenses ate into the rapidly growing revenues, and five years would pass before the *Times* was solidly in the black.

Greeley surveyed Raymond's handiwork and announced that it appeared to be "conducted with the most policy and least principle of any paper ever started"—an aphoristic dismissal of its carefully discursive and rarely incisive editorial stands. But its editorials were not the main dish of the *Times,* any more than were those of the *Herald,* and Greeley's denigration of them had the flavor of sour grapes as he watched his former assistant scramble up toward his level of professional eminence.

More galling still was the rapidity with which the *Times* appeared to replace Greeley's paper as the favorite of New York Whigs despite all his work for and devotion to the party. After Seward entered the Senate, for example, in 1849, he would often send copies of his speeches to the *Tribune* for publication and distribution to other New York papers—a symbol, however token, of mutual esteem between Greeley and his party's principal New York officeholder. Within a year and a half, Seward's speeches were going to Raymond first instead. The shift in preference was compounded in the spring of 1853 when the legislature in Albany passed a bill requiring the weekly publication of reports on business transacted by the New York City banks; the reports, along with a brief summary, were to be run at the banks' expense in one of the city's morning papers. The bill was originated in the Assembly, of which Raymond had only recently been the leader, and the selection of the paper in which the bank reports were to be advertised was placed in the hands of the superintendent of the state's Bank Department, a friend of Raymond and a charter shareholder in the *Times.* When Raymond's paper was chosen as recipient of this large weekly plum, Greeley seethed still more. Nor did Raymond hesitate to vaunt his success over his erstwhile employer. The *Times* appeared to balk at distributing the summary of the weekly bank reports to other papers that wished, as the *Tribune* did, to run it without charge as news. This withholding of what was, after all, public information for its own advantage prompted Greeley to complain about the *Times*'s tactics to the state banking superintendent:

> . . . The consequence is, that I and others are put to a serious expense to collect these [reports], which the official paper might give us without expense or trouble. I have a most insolent and scoundrelly letter from your favorite, Raymond, offering to send me these [reports] at his own convenience if I will credit them to the *Times* . . . and talking of his willingness to *grant favors* to those who prove worthy of them, but not

to be *"kicked into benevolence,"* etc. *All this insolence of this little villain is founded on your injustice.* I have not written to him; I have asked no favor of him; and I shall not answer him. . . .

To Weed, still leader of New York Whiggery, Greeley sent a copy of Raymond's letter and noted, ". . . see the insolence with which the little viper talks to me."

Greeley's "little villain" label stuck to Raymond ever after, but Greeley conceded privately that his new rival had taken away several thousand of the *Tribune*'s daily subscribers and caused yet more damage to its advertising revenues. Something had to be done to meet the challenge. Toward the close of the *Times*'s second year, the *Tribune* installed new, more legible type and enlarged its page size so that it was carrying a full one-third more reading matter than before. Readership responded, and when Greeley's voice led the antislavery outcry greeting congressional passage of the Kansas-Nebraska bill in the spring of 1854, a still heavier influx of readers followed. But advertising did not, and in view of its higher expenses for paper and production, the *Tribune* faced intensified financial pressure. Publisher McElrath pushed the resistant Greeley to raise the price of the paper from two cents to three; the editor finally agreed, provided the *Herald,* long priced at two cents, and the *Times,* which had raised its price from a penny to two at the end of its first year, went along. Bennett agreed, but Raymond declined—as his successor proprietors would decline to accommodate the inheritors of Greeley's and Bennett's papers a century later —and the *Tribune* was forced to reduce its page size as an economy move.

To rile Greeley still further, his overtures for the gubernatorial nomination that fall found no favor with the leadership of the decaying Whig cause. Weed wanted no part of such a candidacy; at the least, it would imperil William Seward's re-election to the Senate, and Seward was still Weed's meal ticket. Greeley's renewed call for prohibition of alcohol, stirred by Maine's recent passage of such a statute, made him as much of a liability as an asset at the polls to Weed, who now found him, as Greeley himself put it, neither useful nor ornamental. Greeley, not quite groveling but apparently famished for honors, said the lieutenant governorship would do as well. Weed in fact put his name forward for the post, but when a prohibitionist acceptable to the rising Know-Nothing movement, whose nativist biases Greeley deplored, won the top spot on the Whig ticket, politics decreed that second place could not also be given to a dry. The party's nomination for lieutenant governor went to none other than Henry Raymond. The *Times* editor outran the ticket and won handily.

Gloom enveloped Greeley. A few days after the election results were certified he wrote a long, bitterly reproachful letter to Seward, who was positioning himself to run for President in 1856. Greeley complained that he had labored hard and long for the party starting in 1838, when he edited *The Jeffersonian,* which had helped put Seward in the governor's mansion, but had never been rewarded with its favors. He had put great effort into helping General Harrison get elected: "I asked nothing, expected nothing; but you, Governor Seward, ought to have asked that I be postmaster of New York." The passing years, he went on, brought no improvement in his political prospects, and then came the just concluded campaign year when he would have liked the nomination for governor or lieutenant—"my running would have helped the ticket and helped my paper"—but he was not only rejected but humiliated:

> . . . No other name could have been put upon the ticket so bitterly humbling to me as that which was selected. The nomination given to Raymond—the fight left me. . . .
> Governor Seward, I know that some of your most cherished friends think me a great obstacle to your advancement. . . . I trust I shall never be found in opposition to you; I have no further wish but to glide out of the newspaper world as quietly and as speedily as possible, join my family in Europe, and if possible, stay there quite a time,—long enough to cool my fevered brain and renovate my overtasked energies. . . .

And so he dissociated himself from Seward and Weed, his allies of many years. Yet though his ambitions for office may have been shattered, and his struggle for primacy among the newspapers of New York had drained his energies, the chapter in which he would make his most important political and social mark on American history was just beginning.

IV

Among the events most firmly imprinted in his memory when Horace Greeley was an impressionable apprentice on the weekly newspaper in East Poultney, Vermont, was the community's response to the arrival of a runaway slave from nearby New York state.

New York's emancipation law said that born slaves could be held in bondage until their twenty-eighth birthday—an unsatisfactory arrangement to the young bondsman who fled to Vermont and was given work and shelter in Greeley's adopted village. One day the fugitive's owner was reported en route, and the town green was swiftly filled with men and boys contemplating appropriate action. The result was "a speedy disappearance of the chattel, and the return of his master, disconsolate and niggerless, to the place whence he came." The rescue had been instinctive and impromptu, little complicated by antipathy to the South and this unwelcome outreach of its peculiar institution. "Our people hated injustice and oppression," Greeley wrote in his memoirs, "and acted as if they couldn't help it."

He did not need wholesale evidence of its barbarity to adopt a lifelong loathing of human bondage. The very idea of it appalled him. Probably because of it, he traveled little in the South, assuming he knew all he needed to know of the region and the attitudes of its masters. Blacks to him were not noble savages whose salvation would be assured by emancipation; nor were they the white man's equal after having been long victimized by systematic exploitation. But if taught and trained, he argued, their industrial capabilities could be developed and they would stand as good a chance to win economic self-sufficiency as whites. But this prospect of black betterment was precisely what poor whites in the South, whose skin was their only badge of honor, and Northern laborers, sweating out their wages, feared most: masses of coloreds to compete with them and drive them farther down the economic ladder. Such antipathy Greeley would neither acknowledge nor approve. Whites enjoyed civil rights regardless of their native endowments or acquired abilities, and the black man was entitled to no less. "We hold it unjust and cruel to aggravate his natural disabilities by legal or social degradations," he wrote in May 1853. He insisted that "Man's inalienable right to equality under the laws is not at all invalidated by his intellectual deficiencies, but rather fortified and hallowed by them. . . ."

Yet he did not push for the abolition of slavery where it was already in place. In time, he argued, non-slaveholding whites would recognize that they were as much the victims of the South's oppressive system as the bondsman—and when they demanded and won their right to economic improvement, slavery would wither. It was a delusion he never abandoned. What he was certain of, though, was that any effort by the rest of the nation to stamp out the system in the South by imposed abolition would tear the Union apart. His most passionate words were directed not against the existing iniquities of the South but against their expansion into territories not yet incorporated into the nation. It was a distinction without a difference to the rulers of the South; those who this year opposed the extension of slavery into fresh areas would next year probably demand its being outlawed in the heart of Dixie. But unless slavery were held in check, Greeley's dream of economic nationalism would be forever thwarted. Every element in his ardently argued editorial program would be subverted by the South's territorial ambitions. How could the country be internally developed if slave labor were permitted side by side with free labor? Supply and demand would depress wages hopelessly, small farms would never prosper, local industry would never take root, and low tariffs favored by slave-rich planters who imported most of their food and supplies would doom native manufacturers to unfair competition from abroad. Greeley wanted an America that would soon become its own chief market, not primarily a supplier of high-bulk, low-cost commodities to the Old World in a colonial pattern that would sentence the nation to continued economic dependency. "Free Soil and Free Labor" was Greeley's war cry, and he sounded it in full voice until his newspaper became the most influential of any in the United States throughout the painful prelude to and the still more agonizing course of civil war.

Until late in 1853, he often couched his argument in partisan terms. Slavery was the world's most serious obstacle to democratic progress, and the Democratic Party, which by and large espoused it, was therefore a diabolical political engine; its very name was a misnomer that deceived innocents throughout the North. Greeley habitually referred to it as "Sham Democracy" in pushing the Whig cause in *Tribune* editorials aimed especially at farmers and mechanics who were the backbone of the *Weekly Tribune* readership. When Democrat Franklin Pierce defeated Winfield Scott for the presidency in 1852 and Clay and Webster, the Whigs' foremost statesmen, died soon thereafter, Greeley's party was left leaderless and growing terminally dispirited. It split into irreconcilable factions—*"cotton"* proslavery Whigs and "conscience" antislavery Whigs were the most prominent among the subspecies—and Greeley went in search of a political party where economic nationalism was understood to be advanced in inverse ratio to the spread of King Cotton. When Senator Stephen A. Douglas of Illinois moved at the end of 1853 to open the Nebraska Territory to slaveholders, Greeley at once saw that the uneasy truce imposed upon the nation by the Compromises of 1820 and 1850 was mortally endangered. From that moment forward, Greeley acted to convert what had been primarily a political war into a moral one.

Douglas's Kansas-Nebraska bill sought to apply the principle of popular sovereignty: the settlers themselves would decide, both when they applied for territorial status and later when they attained statehood, on the legality of slavery within their sovereign borders. Greeley saw in this plan only the plottings of those he leaped to label "doughfaces," Northern Democrats, like Douglas and President Pierce, of essentially Southern inclinations. The principle of "squatter sovereignty" was a sham, he argued, for it begged the question of whether slaveholders would be permitted to bring their chattels into the territory *before* any vote was taken. If so, Free-Soilers could be bullied and beaten by an influx of residents from adjacent slave states and the best land snatched up by planters who would push small farmers into the backlands as effectively as they had done all over the South.

Throughout the five-month course of the congressional debate over Douglas's bill, Greeley's *Tribune* mobilized the soul of antislavery sentiment throughout the North and West. In the most eloquent editorials of his career, he wrote that believers in American liberty and justice could no longer indulge in the luxury of complacency; if it were not halted now, the slavocracy would suffocate freedom and deny the nation the chance to fulfill its destiny as a land where every man could one day hope to enjoy the fruits of his labor. But the *Tribune*'s campaign against the Kansas-Nebraska bill was not limited to editorials. It sprouted a feature column called "Facts of Slavery" that dwelled on the most brutalizing aspects of the system. Under alternate headings like "A Scene of Cruelty and Bloodshed" and "The Shame of Virginia" and "Mechanics Bought and Sold," accounts were given of the sexual abuse, torture, and murder of slaves, who were portrayed as universally seeking escape—and when they did flee, were pursued remorselessly by bloodhounds with dripping jaws. The articles were made up into pamphlets and distributed for six dollars per hundred.

Greeley intensified his efforts as antislavery lecturer and everywhere spread the
message that the North ought no longer to be blackmailed by the South's threats
of secession every time its demands were not granted. A few weeks before
Congress acted on Douglas's bill, Greeley wrote:

> . . . [L]et us have a fair understanding all around that the North regards the Union
> as of no special, peculiar advantage to her and can do without it much better than
> the South can, and we shall have fewer secession capers. . . . [T]his [understanding]
> would be found after a little to exert a decidedly sedative, tranquillizing effect on the
> too susceptible nerves of our too excitable Southern brethren. Instead of bolting the
> door in alarm . . . in case the South shall hereafter threaten to walk out of the Union,
> we would hold it politely open and suggest to the departing the policy of minding
> his eye and buttoning his coat well under his chin preparatory to facing the rough
> weather outside. . . .

The *Tribune* would sound this refrain repeatedly during the ensuing seven years:
The Union was no boon conferred on the needy North by the gracious South;
if there was any dependency, it ran in the other direction. Such a contention may
have stoked Greeley's rhetoric, but it failed to perceive both the strength and
the desperation of the planters.

As the South moved toward the apex of its power in the immediate antebellum years, it possessed nearly four million slaves to do its drudgery. Cotton was
blooming as never before. And the federal government had proven pliable to
Southern interests. Eleven of the first fourteen Presidents had come from the
slave states, as had almost two-thirds of the Justices of the Supreme Court,
Attorneys General, Speakers of the House, and foreign ministers. The Southerners claimed to have built a uniquely admirable civilization, one whose produce
served as the nation's collateral in foreign markets. But theirs was also a
uniquely vulnerable society whose economic system was notable mostly for its
waste and extravagance. A resentful, subversive labor force tilled poorly, and
the land eroded rapidly. Each new expansion of the cotton kingdom, furthermore, required massive infusions of capital for seed, supplies, and slaves. Provided mostly by Northern and British financiers, the capital had to be repaid;
this steady siphoning of the South's profits prevented it from ever accumulating
enough wealth to supply its own needs, and so it kept overpaying and going
increasingly into debt with nothing to show for it but growing numbers of
blacks. Their slaves were the root of their power as men, the source of their
increasingly inflated pride, and so they sought to continue adding to their
hegemony because that was the only way to keep the whole gaudy construction
from breaking down. Southern spokesmen performed with brilliance and determination on the national political level until their certainty shaded over into an
arrogance that at last provoked people like Horace Greeley beyond endurance.
The South would have its own way—or it would go its own way. Only the latter
alternative was acceptable to Greeley after Douglas introduced his damnable
bill.

But in his endorsement of peaceable secession as preferable to enforced union of North and South, he was playing poker against an opponent who had to stake all on the outcome, and Greeley believed the slave power could be bluffed into submission. It was the same misreading of intransigence he had made in championing settlement of the West by homesteading grants to alleviate the plight of sweated free labor. He had clearly perceived the injustices visited upon the American workingman, free and slave alike, and he saw, more dimly, how their fates were entwined. Yet his flawed reading of the character of their two sets of masters—the planters of the South and industrialists of the North —led him to escapist solutions that only compounded the problem. It was not the slaveholders' dependence on outside capital that imperiled their economic survival as much as it was their pathological need for dominion over the black man. On the other side of the same false coin, Greeley saw the free laborer as victimized not by the greed of aggressive employers but by their own status as inadequately trained dependents without the gumption to direct their own fate. To Greeley every worker was an independent contractor and an entrepreneur-in-the-making, whether as a small farmer if his government would stake him to the spread or as a mechanic in joint venture with fellow journeymen or in any sort of undertaking that provided a man dignity and fulfillment by a route of his own choice. That some laborers might be suited to be only jobholders, needing direction and a fair wage for their survival, was as inadmissible to Greeley as the possibility that some capitalists were not to be brought to dealing fairly with their hired hands by sweet reason alone. And in neither case would he subscribe to the application of force—namely, the abolition of slavery in the South and the application of collective bargaining by trade unions in the North —as an acceptable means of social readjustment. Each was too radical, and Horace Greeley, at the core of his reformist soul, would not risk unbalancing the established order to win a paradise on earth.

His solution, then, to the profound grievances of the common man, both white and black, rested upon proper use of the vast American interior: That virgin land had to be placed forever beyond the grasp of the slavocracy and reserved first of all for the use of free laborers who had been victimized by an imperfectly adjusted industrial mechanism. That many such victims were not suited to working the soil, that such dislocations took capital and often great hardiness, that militant trade unions using the compacted might of their membership might far more readily win a decent standard of living than mass emigration to the West—these practicalities did not concern Horace Greeley. Yet who could doubt his concern for the workingman? Had not the printers of New York, forming a union of their own in 1850, elected the former journeyman who founded the *Tribune* as their first president? Did he not voluntarily pay his printers the best going wage in the trade? All employers would come in time to see that their enlightened self-interest dictated a similar generosity of spirit.

When Congress, despite the full fury of the *Tribune*'s denunciation, passed the Kansas-Nebraska bill, Greeley was too spent at first to do more than issue a plaintive call for its repeal. But by midsummer of 1854, he knew that a far broader strategy was required to halt the advance west by the slave states. To rally the nation's antislavery forces became his consuming task. His mechanisms were two: a new political coalition born from the ashes of the Whig Party and the full propagandizing power of the *Tribune* with its reach all the way across the free soil of the Union.

Contrary to his reputation for rashness, Greeley now moved cautiously and expertly in the political arena. He was in the forefront but not alone in issuing the call for a convention, held at Saratoga in August 1854, of New York "conscience" Whigs, Free-Soilers, abolitionists, prohibitionists, disaffected Democrats, and antislavery elements of the nativist Know-Nothing movement who had grown bolder as the Irish immigration and other Catholic newcomers fueled fears of Papist influence. What united them all was determination to immunize the Nebraska Territory—and all other territories—from slavery. High on the agenda was a decision whether to put up a slate of candidates, using the same party label adopted by similar fusion movements in Michigan, Wisconsin, and several other states: Republican. Greeley, under heavy pressure from Weed, who feared that the new party would strip away the radical element from his ebbing Whigs and cost him control of the legislature and Seward's Senate seat with it, urged a wait-and-see policy. Anxious not to frighten off conservatives, furthermore, the convention declined to call for repeal of the harsh 1850 fugitive slave law; it contented itself instead with endorsing "anti-Nebraska" men in every congressional district in the state (twenty-nine out of thirty-one would win that fall) and the swift colonization of Kansas by Northern settlers.

His own ambition for office utterly frustrated, Greeley declared his political independence of Weed and Seward and worked tirelessly during the next two years to build the Republican Party into a national power. His watchword was harmony. He sought allies among both capital and labor; business, he argued, could not tolerate a climate of chronic uncertainty over the slavery question. All who favored a vigorous national economy ought to rally to the antislavery standard, and the white worker had no less a vested interest in restricting the spread of black bondsmen. As the Republicans geared to field a national ticket in the 1856 presidential contest, Greeley steered the party away from such avowed antislavery contenders as Seward and Salmon P. Chase of Ohio, who would have given it a radical tinge, and instead embraced explorer and soldier of fortune John C. Frémont, a young Lochinvar who had won fame as an adventurer in California. At the first national Republican convention, Greeley buried the hatchet temporarily with Henry Raymond, who delivered the keynote address, and himself played a major role on the platform committee. Bennett's *Herald* denounced the newly minted Republican platform for "niggerizing," which the *Tribune* denied by insisting the Northern white laborer was the chief intended beneficiary of the party's program, not the South's slaves, whom it had no intention of freeing.

So ardently did the *Tribune* support Frémont's cause that its office became a virtual national Republican headquarters during the campaign, issuing among other broadsides a pamphlet instructing party speakers how best to orate in the candidate's behalf. Its partisanship was the high point of the paper's increasingly shrill anthem to "Free Soil and Free Labor." It had played the "Bleeding Kansas" theme for all it was worth, starting with a call early in 1855 for a massive migration to the new territory, under resolute leaders and abundantly funded, to save it from the "Cossacks of civilization." Greeley himself was a member of a New York City committee devoted to supplying guns to the New England Emigrant Aid Company, and his newspaper trumpeted the antislavery drive not only on the editorial page but in articles, letters, poems, fiction, and dispatches from its own Kansas correspondent, who reported he was "hunted like a wild beast" by proslavery ruffians from across the Missouri border. No Northern settler was motivated by any but the highest of principles, according to the *Tribune*'s pages, or ever committed an ignoble act; even the Free-Soilers' occasional atrocities were excused as self-defense. Civil disobedience, peaceably manifested, was urged against "bogus" laws enacted by a pro-Southern territorial legislature that Greeley painted as a puppet of the Pierce administration, itself the plaything of Southern Democrats bent on having Kansas for their own. When Lawrence, Kansas, was burned by proslavery raiders, the *Tribune* wrote:

> . . . a few bare and tottering chimneys, a charred and blackened waste, now mark the site hallowed to all eyes as that where the free sons of the North have for two years confronted the myrmidons of Border Ruffianism, intent on the transformation of Kansas into a breeding-ground and fortress of Human Slavery.

The "devastation and butchery" there had been consummated "in the name and by the authority of the Federal Union," and President Pierce had been "sprinkled from head to foot with the blood of the Free-State men of Kansas, and his whole person illuminated . . . with the blaze of their burning houses." Acts of peace preservation by federal troops went unnoted. Nor was the *Tribune*'s agitation limited to lopsided reporting and lurid propaganda. The paper sponsored a "Kansas Fund" to aid the antislavery settlers, collecting more than $20,000 for the cause, and promoted mass meetings to urge the formation of Kansas committees everywhere to swell the tide of emigration. Even the *Tribune* advertising columns heavily featured announcements of printed material on the subject.

The conspicuousness of Greeley's efforts could not escape attention in the South. He was steadily attacked in the proslavery press and by Southern leaders such as Sam Houston, who, in one of the milder epithets directed against Greeley, denounced his "sneaking villainy," though a less furtive personality would have been hard to conjure. His very blatancy had caught up with him earlier in 1856 when he went to Washington to cover Congress himself and use its deliberations as the departure point for his overriding mission. That winter the House was locked in a fierce debate over the choice of a Speaker; the nominees' stand on the Kansas issue was the point of contention. Greeley had backed as compromise choice a breakaway Democrat from Massachusetts, Nathaniel Banks, an antislavery man with nativist leanings. Banks led the voting for weeks but could not attract the last few votes needed for a majority. Finally, Representative Albert Rust of Arkansas proposed that Banks withdraw from the race along with all the other contenders and new names be entered. Greeley, who had worked intensely but maladroitly behind the scenes to bring about Banks's election, wrote of this proposal with a characteristic lack of circumspection:

> I have had some acquaintance with human degradation; yet it did seem to me to-day that Rust's resolution in the House was a more discreditable proposition than I had ever known gravely submitted to a legislative body.

The next day, Rust lay in wait for the *Tribune* editor after the House adjourned. A larger, far stronger man, he hovered until Greeley was alone in front of the Capitol and, after confirming Greeley's identity, inquired, "Are you a noncombatant?" Greeley later wrote that he had replied, "This is according to circumstances." Rust's version was that he had asked, "Would you resent an insult?" and that Greeley answered, "I don't know, sir," in a highly provocative tone. Whatever was said, Rust delivered a series of blows to the right side of Greeley's head while the stunned editor's hands were still in his overcoat pockets. The assailant retreated only to strike again near Greeley's hotel, this time producing a heavy cane and directing a severe blow at his victim's head; instead, it caught Greeley's upraised left arm and bruised it badly. Then Rust slipped away into an accompanying crowd of Southerners. Greeley pressed no charges but returned to his room and, head and arm wrapped in compresses, wrote up the incident for the *Tribune,* noting that he had come to Washington half expecting not to leave it alive,

> . . . for my business here is to unmask hypocrisy, defeat treachery and rebuke meanness, and these are not dainty employments even in smoother times than ours. But I shall stay here just as long as I think proper, using great plainness of speech. . . . I shall carry no weapons and engage in no brawls; but if ruffians waylay and assail me I shall certainly not run, and, so far as able, I shall defend myself.

Beyond the abuse that he seemed almost to invite, Greeley endured political, professional, and personal blows that would have thoroughly intimidated all but the most willful of men. His infant Republican Party grew rapidly in strength but lost badly to James Buchanan in the 1856 presidential election. Graver still to the fortunes of the antislavery faction was the *Dred Scott* decision of the Supreme Court the following year when two Northern Justices joined their five Southern brethren to strike down the principle of squatter sovereignty in Union territories as it applied to slaveholding; no citizen and his property, living or inanimate, could be barred from American soil except in states where slavery was already forbidden by statute, the high court ruled. Greeley's lament knew no bounds; the political system was conspiring on the side of iniquity. The

Tribune itself, furthermore, suffered in the economic panic of that year as advertising and subscriptions fell off and its publisher and stout financial pillar, Thomas McElrath, went into bankruptcy, leaving the paper a debt of $20,000 and its credit standing impaired. Greeley's prime tormentor, James Gordon Bennett, lost no opportunity to remark on the *Tribune*'s fiscal woes and to impugn its editor's integrity by, for example, repeatedly charging him with misuse of funds gathered for charitable causes. Citing outside income earned by Greeley on his lecture tours and by subeditors Dana and Ripley from writing and editing books as evidence of the *Tribune*'s imminent fiscal ruin, the *Herald* editor observed that "nigger worship is nearly at its close . . . anti-slavery agitation is going down, and . . . whenever it becomes defunct, the *Tribune*'s nigger circulation will collapse." He mocked extremists on both sides of the battle—of whom "Massa Greeley" was among the most deplorable—and noted that the *Herald* had long been "the only Northern journal that has unfailingly vindicated the constitutional rights of the South." His severest scorn Bennett reserved for the *Tribune*'s advocacy journalism; it had never been an objective purveyor of news per se, he charged, and now it had become the prime agent provocateur against slave power. In this regard, it must be noted that Bennett practiced what he preached. Even at the height of antebellum hysteria, the *Herald* did a far better job than any other paper, North or South, at separating commentary from reporting. When the *Tribune,* for example, was characterizing John Brown as a saint sprung from the Book of Revelation after his raid at Harpers Ferry in October 1859, the *Herald,* which editorially viewed the act as demented, ran a detailed objective account and followed up with interviews in depth with Brown and his followers, rendered with meticulous neutrality.

Greeley's family life brought him no balm. In 1853 he bought a run-down farm just east of the village of Chappaqua some thirty-five miles north of the city and, reasoning it would be a more healthful place to raise his children, set about to restore it by the most modern methods of agronomy. He experimented with the latest thing in farm mechanics, a steam-driven tractor, introduced subsoil plowing and planned reforestation, and built a stone barn for $6,000. Yet Greeley was almost never in Chappaqua except on Saturdays, and then only when his lecture schedule relented. Thus marooned, Mary Greeley, whether broken in health or only seeming so to herself, turned still further into a thin-lipped scold with an explosive temper. Her aimless domestic efforts made the home a madhouse in which Greeley found scant refuge and to which few guests repaired. Still, he kept pouring money into the farm and going into debt to do so. But whether he traveled the lecture circuit away from New York as much as one-third of the year primarily for the money itself or for the celebrity that attended his appearances or to propagandize for the cause in far-flung places—or to get away from Molly—can only be conjectured; probably all those combined to drive him at a frenetic pace the year long. He was away lecturing in February 1857 when word reached him that his six-year-old son, Raphael, had come down with a serious case of the croup. Greeley, who had been heartbroken when in 1849 cholera claimed his first son, Arthur, hurried home but arrived an hour after the child had died. There were to be no other sons; two daughters survived him.

For all his travails and despite the fact that for much of the time he left the paper in the hands of Dana and his lieutenants, Greeley's *Tribune* surged ahead throughout its second decade; the daily more than tripled in circulation between 1850 and 1860 and the weekly more than quadrupled. As antislavery ferment boiled toward its tragic denouement, the *Tribune* was issuing 55,000 copies a day, just behind the *Sun*'s 60,000 and a more than respectable third to the *Herald*'s 77,000; the *Times,* with neither militancy nor style to animate it, trailed with 35,000. The *Weekly Tribune* was selling more than 200,000 copies by then and, given the scarcity of other reading matter in the largely rural and frontier communities where it was most attentively read, Greeley could reasonably claim a collective readership of some one and a half million Americans. None of his countrymen attracted a larger congregation.

At the apex of his influence, the editor of the *Tribune* played a prominent part in the event that finally tumbled the nation from its long high-wire balancing act on the slavery issue and into terrible fratricidal strife: the election of the first Republican President, Abraham Lincoln.

During his abbreviated tenure in Congress, Greeley had met the lanky Illinoisian, then a first-term representative, and had not been smitten. Their mutually exasperating relationship did not really begin until ten years later when Lincoln waged his spirited but losing fight for Stephen Douglas's Senate seat. As Republicans, Lincoln and his followers had expected strong support from Greeley's weekly edition, which sold some 10,000 copies in Illinois. But the *Tribune* was playing for higher stakes than a single senatorial seat. The Supreme Court, in its *Dred Scott* ruling, had dealt what appeared to be a fatal blow to the Free-Soil movement, but it had also left Douglas out on a very shaky limb. The keystone of his Kansas-Nebraska Act, allowing settlers in a territory to determine for themselves whether slavery was permissible, had been knocked away by the Justices, and Douglas was left to suggest lamely that the ruling could be circumvented by local authorities who had only to fail to enforce slaveholders' claims on their bondsmen in territories designated as free soil by their settlers. Greeley attacked such an extralegal remedy, arguing that the federal government was not so feeble as all that. But when Douglas soon after disavowed the constitution passed by a wholly proslavery legislature meeting in Lecompton, Kansas, as a travesty of the popular sovereignty he had championed, Greeley ended his attacks on the Little Giant. If a wedge could be driven between the Northern and Southern wings of the Democratic Party, Greeley saw, the way would be open for a Republican triumph in 1860. The *Tribune* therefore had kind words for Douglas in his memorable campaign against Lincoln—words that Greeley assured Illinois Republicans would prove the kiss of death but nonetheless infuriated the Lincoln camp. Switching then to tepid praise for Lincoln, Greeley failed to avoid the lasting displeasure of

Illinois Republicans, who accused him of undue meddling in their politics.

The rift had not healed when Lincoln appeared at the Cooper Union in New York at the end of February in 1860 to deliver what amounted to a declaration of his availability for the presidency. The *Tribune* was generous in its appraisal of the speech, noting editorially that "Mr. Lincoln is one of Nature's orators, using his rare powers solely and effectively to elucidate and to convince, though their inevitable effect is to delight and electrify as well." But Greeley doubted that Lincoln was presidential timber, rating him at best a contender for second place on the ticket; a conservative border-state man, authentically antislavery but impossible to be mistaken for an abolitionist, was the Republicans' safest and strongest bet, Greeley reasoned. Above all, he sought to deny the nomination to the party's most prominent and outspoken antislavery man, William Seward, once the object of his keenest loyalty. At the Republican convention in Chicago, Greeley was everywhere on the scene, arguing that Seward, whom he claimed personally to favor, was incapable of carrying the nation in November. Partly as a result of Greeley's maneuvers, the way was opened to Lincoln's nomination. And when, as Greeley had hoped and worked to achieve, the Democrats split and left Douglas with only half a party behind his candidacy, Lincoln was on his way to the White House—and the country, to war.

As well as he had succeeded in mobilizing public opinion in the North, Greeley failed utterly now to defuse tempers in the South. The courses open to the nation upon Lincoln's election were compromise, peaceful secession, or war. The first and last were equally obnoxious to the *Tribune*. The Crittenden Compromise, formulated late in 1860 as a constitutional amendment, would have extended the Missouri Compromise line between free soil and slave to the West Coast, negating the *Dred Scott* ruling, and alleviated the most inhumane aspects of the fugitive slave law while tightly prohibiting renewal of the slave trade. The measure, backed by Weed and other Northern pragmatists, was unacceptable to Greeley, who wrote to the President-elect, lest he throw his support to the proposal, that "another nasty compromise . . . will so thoroughly disgrace and humiliate us that we can never again raise our heads." On the other hand, as he had editorialized the day after Lincoln's election: "War is a hideous necessity at best—and a civil conflict, a war of estranged and embittered countrymen—is the most hideous of all wars."

Greeley's solution was for Lincoln to stand fast and let the South secede if it so chose—a step he was sure it would not take if invited rather than coerced to. "We hope," he wrote on November 9, "never to live in a republic whereof one section is pinned to the other by bayonets." Over the next two months, the *Tribune* carefully spelled out the conditions under which secession might be decently accomplished. Southern hotheads were not to be allowed to harangue their fellow citizens "with rancor, prejudice, and misrepresentation"; the proposition had to be discussed freely and openly. The decision would have to be made by a referendum carried out democratically "beyond any shadow of doubt." And if the verdict were to favor splitting the federal government, the transaction had to be arranged peacefully through negotiations carried out in Washington between statesmen of the two regions. Always Greeley was for sweet reason; always he was sure the South would come to its senses and not veer off on the road to self-destruction. Lincoln, praying for the same outcome but Greeley's temperamental opposite, looked on from Springfield with growing distress as the influential *Tribune* held open the door to peaceable disunion; the Constitution prohibited it. Lincoln's Union was indissoluble even if Greeley's was not. When the governor of South Carolina, the first Southern state to secede, cited the *Tribune* editorial stand in justifying the break, Lincoln's adamancy appeared all the more prophetic.

As the other cotton states followed South Carolina early in 1861, Greeley cried out that they were not playing by his rules, that the fire-eaters had wrested the reins from the South's pauperized majority and that their departure was illegal. Suddenly—belatedly—before him was the imminent prospect of the new Confederacy spreading its power west and south, to the Caribbean and Mexico and perhaps beyond that, reopening the slave trade, dealing with foreign nations, and malevolently restricting the growth and prosperity of the Union. Now the *Tribune* thundered:

> . . . Stand firm! No compromise; no surrender of principle! No cowardly reversal of the great verdict of the sixth of November. Let us have the question of questions settled now and for all time! There can never be another opportunity as good as the present. Let us know once for all whether the slave power is really stronger than the Union. . . .

This newly confrontational language, while unquestionably approved by Greeley, was almost certainly the product of Charles Dana's pen. Greeley's managing editor had long been the more radical of the two, and now he came to the fore, confident that the moral strength of the South had been drained away and that if war came, it would be brief. Without his superior's ambition for office —even now Greeley hoped to sit in Lincoln's Cabinet as Postmaster General or to take Seward's place in the Senate—Dana saw scant need for restraint in putting forward his bold views. His nerves were steadier than Greeley's, his vision less distracted, his capacity to carry the paper's work load larger than his employer's, and Greeley, who was frequently away from the office, was more and more inclined to delegate authority to his trusted aide.

Lincoln welcomed the *Tribune*'s new militancy no more than he had its invitation to orderly Southern departure. If the Union temporized, took the secessionist votes for noisy rhetoric in the absence of overt acts of war, disaster might yet be avoided. But he would not chastise Greeley, whose support was so essential, especially in view of the hostility intensifying toward him in New York, the commercial colossus of the North: the city's voters had opposed him in the election nearly two to one; Bennett's *Herald* had openly called upon him not to take office as the only measure that could avoid war; the *Sun* had proposed a constitutional amendment sanctioning secession; and Fernando Wood, mayor of the city that handled one-third of the nation's exports and two-thirds of its imports, proposed that New York break away from the Union and become an open, neutral port—anything to avoid bloodshed and the disruption of trade.

Greeley, for his part, dealt with Lincoln before Fort Sumter as if the *Tribune* were a sovereign power. Although the paper had backed his candidacy fully once he had the party's nomination, portraying him as a man of the people in the Jacksonian mold, Greeley lacked faith in his ability to master the ever-deepening crisis. He feared that Lincoln was in the hands of advisers too shrewd and manipulative for him—men like Seward and Chase, whom he had named to the State and Treasury posts in his Cabinet—and saw himself as a counterbalancing mentor. When the private train bearing the President-elect toward Washington rolled into the little town of Girard in westernmost Pennsylvania, Greeley scrambled aboard briefly to pay his respects, but in so offhand a fashion that witnesses judged his unceremoniousness as bordering on the impertinent. He was more disheveled than usual, his coat collar turned in and partly standing up, his pockets stuffed with papers and magazines, his hat perched jauntily on back of his large head, and a pair of blue blankets over his arm, as he waited for Lincoln to approach him rather than taking the initiative himself. And when Mrs. Lincoln was presented to him, the editor's broad-brimmed hat did not leave his head. Nor would it have, in all likelihood, if she had been Queen Victoria. That Lincoln took no umbrage was testified to three weeks later when Greeley sat just behind him at the inauguration ceremonies, expecting an assassin's bullet to fly in their direction at any moment. The inaugural address, in Greeley's estimate, demonstrated that the nation still lived "with a Man at the head of it." In the *Herald,* Bennett called it a "crude performance," revealing nothing more than "[a] resolve to procrastinate," and soon afterward was actually proposing vigilante action to depose the new administration. In another man, such a proposal would have qualified as treason; in Bennett, who knew no loyalty beyond self-interest, it was merely a typical outburst.

When hostilities began a month afterward in Charleston harbor, the *Tribune* was unequivocating. "Fort Sumter is lost," it declared, "but Freedom is saved. . . . We are at war. Let us cease mere fending off and strike home. The territorial integrity and the political unity of the nation are to be preserved at whatever cost. . . ." Angry crowds, meanwhile, milled outside the *Herald* office, where the Stars and Stripes were hastily and prominently hung out, followed by an editorial denouncing the rebellion and ending Bennett's long flirtation with the rulers of the South.

Before a month was out, Greeley, through Dana, was calling for prompt action by Union forces to nip the rebel army in the bud. By the beginning of June, the exhortation "Onward" grew louder still, and by month's end, the head of the *Tribune* editorial columns was bristling daily with

> The Nation's war-cry—Forward to Richmond! Forward to Richmond! The Rebel Congress must not be allowed to meet there on July 20th! By that date the place must be held by the National army!

Copies of the demand for action were seen throughout the White House. Not one to be stampeded easily, Lincoln nevertheless approved within days thereafter the decision to make the first major strike of the war at Manassas Junction in the Virginia countryside barely thirty miles from the capital. The resulting disaster of Bull Run disclosed the foolhardiness of precipitous assault with green troops. A disconsolate Greeley found himself as prominent a target of rebuke as the War Department. Bennett and Raymond, among many others, lit into him for impetuosity. Displaying the emotional instability that would mark his behavior throughout the war, Greeley responded in print:

> I wish to be distinctly understood as not seeking to be relieved for any responsibility for urging the advance of the Union army in Virginia, though the precise phrase, "Forward to Richmond," was not mine, and I would have preferred not to reiterate it. Henceforth I bar all criticism in these columns on army movements. Now let the wolves howl on! . . .

It was a craven disclaimer. Greeley had injured himself chopping wood at Chappaqua and been out of the *Tribune* office recuperating for a number of weeks while the call to arms was being sounded by Dana, but he saw the paper regularly and retained the title and full responsibility as its editor; to try to excuse himself as he did, after the fact, only made matters worse. In a frenzy of contrition and despair, he wrote to Lincoln a week later to ask if the President felt that the rebels could still be beaten and, if not, "if our recent disaster is fatal . . . [i]f the Union is irrevocably gone," to urge an armistice of a month or two or three or four, "better still for a year. . . . Send me word what to do. . . . If it is best for the country and for mankind that we make peace with the rebels at once, and on their own terms, do not shrink even from that."

The stoical Lincoln did not answer the hysterical Greeley on that occasion, and soon the editor calmed himself and for the time being honored his pledge not to second-guess the government's management of the war. Greeley's restraint pleased the President. And when the editor maneuvered later in the year through a Lincoln intimate to try to obtain advance word on administration policies, the President seized the chance to use the *Tribune* covertly as his mouthpiece to launch what a later generation of Washington political players would call "trial balloons." The arrangement suited both their purposes. "Having him firmly behind me," Lincoln wrote of Greeley, "will be as helpful to me as an army of one hundred thousand men."

4

Trampling Out
the Vintage

T he American newspaper came into its own as a habitual form of literature during the Civil War when the life of the nation was daily imperiled
and the slaughter of its young manhood was news that no one could
ignore. The event was so overwhelming, the battles so large and bloody, the
seemingly endless agony so traumatizing, that the very conception of what a
newspaper was underwent revolutionary changes. The message it bore was
urgent now, almost all the time. Advertisements that once filled part or all of
the first several pages were subordinated to the news. The structure of news
stories altered with the development of the modern "lead," replacing the old,
leisurely form of narrative, usually offered in chronological order so that the
reader had to wait till the end for the principal news. No longer were dispatches
on a breaking story run in the sequence received; they would be reshaped, when
time allowed, to transmit the essence of the news as clearly and swiftly as
possible. The telegraph, less than two decades old, became an essential tool of
the trade, no longer a novelty or luxury, and new printing techniques, especially
the introduction of stereotyping, which allowed semicircular plates to be fitted
together onto revolving presses, greatly improved the speed and efficiency of
production to meet the increased demand for papers. Most of all, the war
enhanced the stature of the reporter.

No war before it had been covered so closely or exhaustively. The battlefields
and combatants were accessible to the special correspondents—"specials," they

were called for short—hired in unprecedented numbers by the papers and provided with whatever equipment and funds were required to hurry the news back to their home offices. What the specials could not witness for themselves on foot or horseback they could reconstruct with the help of generals, eager to publicize triumphs or explain away defeats, and line soldiers, among whom they could freely circulate. Censorship was lax and erratic, by and large, slowing down telegraph transmission of disastrous news but not suppressing it for long. Competition among the newsmen was intense; the first paper to receive word of battle results, especially in New York, could sell tens of thousands of extras within hours.

Among the most instructive accounts of the ordeal routinely undergone by Civil War correspondents was a letter by the *Tribune*'s Charles A. Page, sent to his New York office while he was recuperating from sunstroke. A clerk in the Treasury Department in his prewar days, Page primarily covered the campaigns in Virginia, scene of the war's heaviest fighting. Constant danger, "without the soldier's glory," was his only regular companion as he roamed the parched wastes of the Old Dominion in midsummer, he wrote, under a brass sky "heated to a white fervor" by a pitiless sun. Grit coated his mouth whenever he opened it during his endless rides while he boiled, panted, and thirsted, but:

> Pooh, man! You forget that you are a "special," and therefore not supposed to be subject to the laws which govern other mortals. You are a Salamander. . . . You are Hercules. . . . Be jolly. Ride your ten, fifteen hours; your twenty, thirty, forty, fifty miles. Fatigue is your normal condition. Sleeplessness, ditto.

It was likely to be well after dark when he finally halted to eat and drink; then, longing for a cake of soap, he would squat like a toad before a campfire and, taking stubby pencil in hand and battling smoke in his eyes and ashes on his dingy notepaper, begin to compose. His brain was fuzzed, no part of him without its special pain and torment, but write he must, "and when you are done, do not read it over, or you will throw it into the fire." At dawn he might awaken to find his horse gone or his saddlebags stolen, and if he was lucky enough to be on hand when the mail arrived, he experienced the exquisite misery, along with other "specials," of reading his paper and seeing how his dispatches had been botched. The *Herald* man swore oaths loud and deep at being rewritten. The *Times* man groaned at finding something he described as "impudent" appearing in print as "important." And the *Tribune* man, even discounting such routine manglings, learned that his account of that week-ago engagement had induced grief in the general's tent. But on he rode until exhaustion, rebel fire, or reassignment brought respite.

For massive outlay of money, energy, and manpower, no American paper came close to the *Herald* in war coverage. Bennett, nearly sixty-six at the outbreak of hostilities, enlarged and revamped his staff and drove it at a frantic pace. He steeped himself in the campaigns of Caesar and Hannibal, of Napoleon and Wellington and Frederick the Great, and ordered his editors to accumulate background data on military tactics, on the nation's forts and harbors and railroad routes and roadways, on population density, topography, agriculture and manufacturing, so that a vast pool of relevant information would be readily on hand when war news broke. A special Southern desk, exploiting the paper's long-standing cordial relations with the slave states, was established, and hard-to-get Confederate papers found their way to the office, further assuring the *Herald*'s leadership in coverage. At one point the paper was able to demonstrate its virtuosity by running in a single edition what it claimed to be the entire roster of the rebel army. Bennett kept at least two dozen correspondents in the field throughout the conflict. Their instructions were simple: get as much accurate information as you can by personal observation and forward it with the utmost dispatch regardless of expense, labor, or danger; artfulness was not necessary —the home office would supply that on the rewrite bank. Hospitals were systematically canvassed after a battle to obtain lists of casualties, usually more accurate and always more promptly compiled than the official tally; publishing such vital information as a public service kept the *Herald* at twelve pages a day throughout the war. Messages from the wounded were also solicited when possible and forwarded to the paper, where a crew of letter-writers passed them on to the nearest of kin—a compassionate service to the public and a sure stimulus to circulation. There was no rigid scrutiny of the field men's expense accounts, no inquiries about why a horse was ridden to death, no grumbling about the cost of chartering a coach or steamboat or train. The only time Bennett was known to have balked about a payment was the result of a tardy dispatch by a rider whose mount fell in combat, costing the *Herald* a scoop; "a horse that couldn't beat the *World,*" the old Scotsman was heard to grouch, "isn't worth paying for." But pay he did for the paper's extraordinary enterprise. According to Bennett's gifted managing editor, Frederic Hudson, the *Herald* spent the then vast sum of $525,000 on its war coverage. By way of comparison, the *Tribune*'s annual outlay for its entire editorial department, including travel and telegraph expenses, was running at the rate of just under $50,000 shortly before the war began. Pieces from the war zone that captured Bennett's favor earned bonuses for their authors of two and three times the going rate. Staff motivation nearly matched the misery and the peril of field conditions.

The *Herald* established its edge in battle coverage right at Bull Run, where most other papers' correspondents mistook the Confederate fallback for a general retreat and, like Raymond, who himself covered the war's first action for the *Times,* prematurely proclaimed a great Union triumph. Not the *Herald*'s Henry Villard, a twenty-six-year-old, Bavarian-born reporter whose unsympathetic assessment of his editor-in-chief's editorial policies was an early and classic instance of the divergence in social values between the proprietors of newspapers and their hired editorial hands—a schism that has given the American daily press a split personality and probably saved its soul.

Immigrating at eighteen after a dispute with his family over politics, Villard soon found a model for his republican ideals while covering the Lincoln-Douglas debates for the leading New York German-language paper. Thereafter as the Associated Press correspondent in Springfield, Illinois, he came to know and admire Lincoln for his simplicity of manner and rare good sense, and upon Lincoln's victory in 1860, was engaged to cover the President-elect for the *Herald*—but only after satisfying himself that his reports did not have to hew to the paper's almost brutally anti-Lincoln editorial line. Bennett honored his bargain to the letter, and the *Herald* ran fair and even friendly news reports on Lincoln while its editorial page continued to savage him. Villard followed Lincoln to Washington for the inaugural, and with the onset of war in plain view, Bennett summoned his young reporter to New York to carry a message to the new President.

Villard rode the train up from the capital full of curiosity about the notorious character for whom he worked. He viewed Bennett's editorials as shameful and the *Herald* as sneakily sympathetic to the South's rebellion. At the office, though, he received a disarming invitation to join Bennett and his twenty-year-old son, James, Jr., for dinner at his farmhouse in Washington Heights. He studied Bennett's tall, slender figure and light, curly hair as they rode uptown through Central Park, admiring the intelligence that played across a face made forbidding by its uncoordinated eyes. The sinister look, the reporter soon discovered, was more than skin-deep. "Intercourse with him, indeed, quickly revealed his hard, cold, utterly selfish nature," Villard later wrote of the encounter, "and incapacity to appreciate high and noble aims." Bennett wanted him to assure Lincoln that the *Herald* would henceforth support his efforts to suppress the rebellion—under increasing threat of mob violence for suspected treason, the paper now had little choice—and asked in return only that his son's sailing yacht be accepted as a gift by the government for the revenue service and the lad be commissioned as a naval officer. The transaction was made, but the *Herald* editorials hectored almost every policy decision by Lincoln until the war's end; its news coverage, however, remained evenhanded.

Villard was not a picturesque writer; he stressed accuracy most of all, a quality little in evidence in the stories of the reporters eager to wire home an account of the first Union advance of the war across Bull Run at Manassas Junction that first July of the war. Villard, as green as the others at covering warfare, did not rush his judgment, and when the tide of battle turned late in the afternoon, he was on hand to witness the debacle. After the Union lines broke, Confederate cavalry pursued and an orderly retreat became a panic-stricken traffic jam on the road back to Washington. Even as the *Times* was receiving Raymond's story and heading it "Crushing Rebellion" and the *Herald* was setting up with an Associated Press account headed "Brilliant Union Victory," Villard guided his horse off the main road and across a countryside swarming with thousands of men in blue tossing away their arms and knapsacks and blankets and mounting horses and mules unhitched from every available supply wagon to speed their flight. So frenzied was the rout that Villard had to dismount at several points and thread his way, horse in tow, through the tangled mass back to the capital and an unmonitored telegraph line. Hungry and exhausted from following the grim spectacle for eighteen hours, he arrived in Washington at seven in the morning and at once put on the wire a short account that the *Herald* hurried into print—the first inkling of the truth to reach New York readers. The full, utterly disheartening report with which he followed that evening caused Bennett, still anxious about having his paper closed down for traitorous leanings, to shorten and soften its portrayal of the pandemonium. Even so, Villard's was the first generally faithful appraisal of Bull Run to circulate throughout the North.

Villard's performance may have set the *Herald*'s standard for accuracy in war reporting, but it was not a mark frequently met. The paper gave its highest priority to speed, as if the basic lesson from which it had so profited at Bull Run had been lost on the teacher. It substituted quantity for quality of reportage, shuttling relays of reporters back and forth from the battlefronts and relying on the expertise assembled in the home office to structure and embellish. It was systematic enough, but the truth often failed to catch up with the paper's speeding presses. Frank Chapman, the *Herald*'s ace man in the West and composer of more than his share of purple prose, scored a clear beat, for example, in reporting the results at Shiloh in the spring of 1862, but it essentially missed the real outcome of the battle and was both false and obsequious in its report on General Ulysses S. Grant, whose dilatory conduct contributed to the Union setback. Chapman described Grant as at one point having ordered his troops to countercharge, "himself leading, as he brandished his sword and waved them on to the crowning victory, while cannon balls were falling like hail around him." There were too many other *Herald* accounts of crowning victories that never occurred, scenes like the naval encounter off Port Hudson near New Orleans reported with datelines that *Herald* men were unable to justify by their presence, sensations like the *Herald* disclosure that the Confederate army had opened the dams on the Chickahominy River to flood the countryside at the Union rear—a revelation without basis in fact. Under war conditions, mistakes were inevitable, but in its zeal to excel, the *Herald* unnecessarily victimized itself and its readers and negated its many undeniable reportorial achievements. Its shortcomings were caustically summarized by George Alfred Townsend, one of the war's ablest correspondents, who switched from the *Herald* to the *World* after determining how his talents might best be utilized. Too many of the *Herald* field men, he wrote, were "uneducated, flimsy-headed, often middle-aged, misplaced people, who had mysteriously gotten on a newspaper. They were capable of plenty of endurance, and would ride up and down, and talk with great confidence, and be familiar with everybody, and then not know how to relate what they saw." Whenever a battle started up, a *Herald* man would rush for New York with early reports that resulted in imagined maneuvers and forced crossings of "creeks running the wrong way." Instead of deploying a few well-equipped and suitable young men who would be allowed to function independently, gain the confidence of the general officers, and thereby "make the reputation of the newspaper with their own, the work was all cut up. . . ."

The *Tribune*, with fewer resources and a far smaller contingent in the field, followed the course Townsend prescribed and produced, man for man, the best reporting of the war. Better equipped, better mannered, treated as individuals and not merely as interchangeable parts in an implacably grinding news machine like Bennett's, the *Tribune* "specials" were far less concerned with scoring beats than getting it right. After a year on the *Herald,* Villard switched to the *Tribune,* where he found the Republican air more congenial and his plain, factual reports, stressing policy and strategy over color and emotion, more highly prized. The difference between the *Herald*'s coverage, with its field men strongly dictated to by its editors in New York, and the *Tribune*'s, far more reliant on the judgment and integrity of correspondents on the scene, was well illustrated by Villard's reaction to a letter from the *Tribune* managing editor, Sidney Howard Gay, urging him to ingratiate himself with the commanding general by showing him dispatches and inviting his comment and amplification. Such a step could not be taken, Villard replied, "without degrading me to a mere mouthpiece of him, as which my self-respect and conception of professional dignity will never allow me to serve."

Nor were the *Tribune* men inclined to bathe their battle scenes with lotions of false heroics. Less able and confident reporters regularly resorted to stereotypes of boldly advancing battle lines, dashing cavalry charges, and orderly troops burning to be led against the foe. Charles Page spoke for the *Tribune* correspondents as a whole in observing:

> . . . Writers who indulge in the use of such phrases, know nothing of armies, or rather state what they do not know. . . . The man who affects any of this fine frenzy is a coward. Let it be understood that troops never "rush frantically to the front" for the love of the thing—at least not after they have been in one fight. After that, they are sure to know better.

For all its admirable restraint, the *Tribune* was far from casual in its pursuit of battle news. Managing editor Gay, unhappy with the pace of coverage of the Peninsula campaign in the spring of 1862, berated one of his men for a report that arrived eight days after the battle: "Of course it was useless. . . . The *Herald* is constantly ahead of us with Yorktown news," obliging the *Tribune* to copy from it. "I pray you," Gay exhorted in words that constitute a model directive from editor to reporter, "remember ye *Tribune* is a *daily news*-paper—or meant to be—& not a historical record of past events. Correspondents to be of any value must be prompt, fresh, & full of facts. . . ."

On rare occasions one of Gay's correspondents not only fulfilled those requirements but also produced a piece of writing good enough to qualify for the annals of battlefield literature. Of these, none surpassed the feat of George Washburn Smalley, covering the events near Sharpsburg, Maryland, at a creek called Antietam in early September 1862.

A graduate of Yale College and Harvard Law School, Smalley decided in his late twenties to abandon his State Street legal practice and Beacon Hill home in Boston and, with a letter of introduction to Charles Dana, take up the antislavery cause as a member of the *Tribune* staff. Stationed in Washington when Lee's army crossed the Potomac some eighty miles above the capital and advanced into Maryland, Smalley caught wind of reports that George B. McClellan was about to lead his troops in pursuit of the Confederate forces. The young *Tribune* man, expecting to be gone no more than a day or two, took only his toothbrush and a mackintosh with him; the trip lasted six weeks.

Correspondents were not authorized to travel in the midst of Union forces on the move, so Smalley joined up as a voluntary aide-de-camp to one of McClellan's corps commanders and, before the campaign was over, underwent a baptism of fire that made him an overnight veteran lucky to be alive. He observed the compact, square-chested McClellan closely during the preliminary battles; that the commander of the Army of the Potomac was exceedingly deliberate in approach and followed the course of action with a singular air of detachment bothered Smalley far less than his irresolution once the fight had been joined. McClellan, he later wrote, "had it not in him to do anything at once, or to do it once for all," and many a young Yankee in blue died unnecessarily as a result, Smalley judged.

After McClellan's army won a bloody, unnecessary victory at South Mountain, he might have followed up swiftly and caught Lee's not fully redeployed ranks, but a wrong road was taken and time and advantage were squandered. Then Smalley learned that one of McClellan's most aggressive commanders, General Joseph Hooker, was to make a probe into Lee's left flank and rode to join his staff, not one of whom knew Smalley or asked who he was or why he was there. Trailing Hooker's unorthodox style of reconnaissance in force, Smalley found a leader who was everything McClellan was not. Hooker's outriders made contact with Lee's men at dusk; a major battle was in store. Smalley slept on the ground that night, his horse's bridle wrapped around his arm; at 4 a.m. he awoke to ride close to Hooker while chronicling the largest clash of armies the world had witnessed in half a century.

"Fighting Joe" Hooker rode carelessly while on the march, but once the bullets began to fly, he sat straight up in his bright blue uniform, his ruddy face and white horse a tempting target to rebel sharpshooters, and issued orders "like the sound of the first cannon shot." Smalley saw him gather up his brigades and divisions and hurl them straight at the enemy, scattering his staff men to prod the troops forward and then riding alone on the firing line. How much his men dreaded as well as loved Hooker, Smalley discovered when the general, badly needing an officer to carry a command for him and finding none, turned to the

Tribune man. "Who are you?" he asked. Smalley told him. "Will you take an order for me?" Certainly, said the correspondent. And off he dashed, only to be questioned at the delivery end; Smalley recorded the exchange in his memoirs:

> "Who are you?"
> "The order is General Hooker's."
> "It must come to me from a staff officer or from my brigade commander."
> "Very good. I will report to General Hooker that you decline to obey."
> "Oh, for God's sake don't do that! The Rebels are too many for us but I had rather face them than Hooker."

On his return, Hooker sent him out again with orders, and again and again as the tide of battle swept back and forth indecisively but was marked by firmness of will among the Union forces not demonstrated in any previous major battle. Smalley had two horses shot out from under him and his jacket torn by an enemy shell, but he did not abandon the front line until after Hooker was wounded in the foot and forced to retire to the rear. McClellan had fresh troops to spare but would not commit them to take full advantage of the momentum generated by Hooker's forces.

Still exhilarated, Smalley gathered up the notes of the other *Tribune* men on the scene, borrowed one of their horses, and set out to find the nearest telegraph operator. He had thought arrangements would have been made by the Union command to wire word of the outcome to Washington, but the nearest line was in Frederick, Maryland, thirty miles east. Sleeping in the saddle part of the way, he arrived at three in the morning to find no operator on duty. Smalley wrapped his blanket around him and dozed in the entrance-way of the telegraph office till seven, when he was able to transmit a 1,200-word synopsis of the two days of combat. Unknown to him, his report was routed directly to Washington, where the government had had no prior word on the course of the battle and was in no hurry to forward it to the *Tribune*. Smalley decided to try to reach New York in time to get his full story into the following day's paper, but no one seemed to know when the next train would come through Frederick for Baltimore, and his request to charter a special train was met by silence from the War Department. Finally, a mixed civilian-military train came through, landing him in Baltimore late in the afternoon just ten minutes before an express to New York was due. The faster way would have been to put his full report on the telegraph, but the Baltimore operator would make him no promises, so Smalley took the surer route. Un-washed, unshaven, almost benumbed from his heroic efforts, he stood in the crowded, swaying railroad coach under one of the dim lanterns at either end of the car and, out of composite dog-eared notes from the *Tribune* men and his own fresh memories enhanced by proximity to the high command, com-posed an 8,000-word article that began:

BATTLEFIELD OF SHARPSBURG.

Wednesday evening, Sept, 17, 1862

Fierce and desperate battle between 200,000 men has raged since daylight, yet night closes on an uncertain field. It is the greatest fight since Waterloo—all over the field contested with an obstinacy equal even to Waterloo. If not wholly a victory to-night, I believe it is the prelude to a victory to-morrow. But what can be foretold of the future of a fight in which from 5 in the morning till 7 at night the best troops of the continent have fought without decisive result?

He sketched the pre-battle scene with graphic menace:

. . . Broken and wooded ground behind the sheltering hills concealed the Rebel masses. What from our front looked like only a narrow summit fringed with woods was a broad table-land of forest and ravine; cover for troops everywhere, nowhere easy access for an enemy. The smoothly sloping surface in front and the sweeping crescent of slowly mingling lines was only a delusion. It was all a Rebel stronghold beyond.

He presented the Union strategy of battle and charted its early success, driving the enemy back into a thicket:

But out of those gloomy woods came suddenly and heavily terrible volleys— volleys which smote, and bent, and broke in a moment that eager front, and hurled them swiftly back for half the distance they had won. . . . Closing up their shattered lines, they came slowly away—a regiment where a brigade had been, hardly a brigade where a whole division had been, victorious. . . . In ten minutes the fortune of the day seemed to have changed—it was the Rebels now who were advancing, pouring out of the woods in endless lines, sweeping through the corn-field from which their comrades had just fled. . . .

In its immediacy, force of narrative, and assemblage of deftly compacted detail, Smalley's article was not simply a report *about* something; it was a thing with a life of its own. And it did not spare the horror or purvey vainglory. Of that gorily contested acre of corn he wrote:

The field and its ghastly harvest which the reaper had gathered in those fatal hours remained finally with us. Four times it had been lost and won. The dead are strewn so thickly that as you ride over it you cannot guide your horse's steps too carefully. Pale and bloody faces are everywhere upturned. They are sad and terrible, but there is nothing which makes one's heart beat so quickly as the imploring look of sorely wounded men who beckon wearily for help which you cannot stop to give.

His train from Baltimore arrived in Jersey City at 6 a.m. and when his ferry reached New York, a waiting cab hurried Smalley and his copy to Nassau Street, where a crew of printers stood by to rush out a *Tribune* extra by a few minutes after eight. The *Evening Post* under Bryant, least hateful of Greeley's rivals, commended the six-column report, even as the *Tribune* itself had done in an accompanying editorial. But neither paper mentioned the name of the correspondent.

II

Starting his third decade as founder, editor, and spiritual overseer of the *Tribune*, Horace Greeley ought ideally to have been a bulwark of serene resolve against the storm that broke over his beloved country. In fact, the emotional volatility that was his nature was unsuited to the long ordeal of intramural war between the outnumbered South and the outgeneraled North. In his defense, it should perhaps be said that the inconstancy his paper displayed toward Lincoln's guidance of the Union was an almost perfect reflection of the alternating waves of hope and despair that swept over the North as the killing continued at a horrendous rate.

Although he had promised after Bull Run not to question the government's conduct at arms, Greeley lost patience with McClellan's leadership as 1862 arrived with no real sign of improving fortunes for the Union cause. The rebellion was an established fact and could be suppressed only by bold confrontation and conquest; swift, hard, mortal blows might have brought the South to its senses, but there were none. Greeley saw politics behind McClellan's overcaution, suspecting the young general of ambitions for the Democratic presidential nomination in 1864 on the strength of a stalemated war; his political victory would then foretell a suit for peace on terms highly favorable to the Confederacy. The war, moreover, was dissipating the Union's financial resources at the rate of two to three million dollars a day, Greeley argued, and so McClellan's waiting game was only playing into the rebels' hands.

Greeley's depression and dismay may have contributed largely to his decision late in March 1862 to amputate his strong right arm, Charles Dana. Without citing a reason, or at least none that was ever recorded or communicated to outsiders, Greeley told the *Tribune* trustees that either he or Dana would have to leave the paper, and promptly; they chose Dana. But the manner in which they directed his dismissal—with note taken of "his many noble and endearing qualities" and the award of six months' salary as severance pay—hardly suggests heinous behavior on the managing editor's part. Dana was stunned by the decision, especially since, as he wrote to a friend, the relationship between him and Greeley, however intermittently stormy in the past, had "of late been more confidential and friendly than ever."

Upon years of reflection, Dana would conclude that "the real explanation was that while he was for peace I was for war, and that as long as I stayed on the *Tribune* there was a spirit there which was not his spirit—that he did not like." Their doctrinal differences on the proper conduct of the antislavery crusade were undeniable. To Dana, the toleration of slavery could not be countenanced when it included submission, under any circumstances, to dismemberment of the Union. War was less of a crime against humanity than tacit

surrender to the forces of a benighted aristocracy; the United States was a republic and a democracy, not a pawn of slave masters. At every opportunity he
drove home the point to Greeley and, when Greeley did not object, through the
Tribune's editorial columns. It was as if Dana were Greeley's more wrathful,
less politic self; to Greeley, the political process was a hallowed contest in which
each side may have stated its extreme position at the outset but God-given
reason would eventually arbitrate. Yet the South's intransigence together with
Dana's confrontational response drove Greeley from wishful miscalculation of
his enemy's pliancy to reluctant approval of force to gain what civility could not.
Thus his passive acquiescence in Dana's "Forward to Richmond" editorial
campaign. But when resort to arms appeared to be no surer a solution, he was
quick to try to distance himself from that policy—and now, in the early spring
of 1862, from its principal proponent within his own ranks. Beyond that, there
was a classic antagonism of dispositions between the two men: Dana, brisk,
orderly, unwavering, expeditious; Greeley, rhetorical, impulsive, manipulative,
egotistical. That Dana had long flirted with insubordination and mastered it was
testimony not of craven character but rather the opposite; Greeley clearly
recognized in him a man of both talent and principle and granted him editorial
hegemony—until he finally came to feel that continued tolerance of so powerful
a satellite would fatally disturb his own future orbit.

But it was done badly. Dana, nearly forty-three, with a wife and children
to support, was exorcised from Greeley's soul without warning or explanation.
Rising prices and expenses had cut into the paper's profits, so when Dana sold
his stock in it, he received $10,000 less than it would have fetched the year before
—a small fortune in that era. Two days after having sent word to the trustees
that he wanted Dana out, Greeley appeared before them and claimed it was "a
damned lie" he had issued them an ultimatum and said he would be glad to have
Dana stay on as an editorial writer. But he never went manfully to Dana to
explain the alleged mix-up or anything else; Dana not unreasonably concluded
that "he is glad to have me out." And soon afterward, according to the paper's
corporate minutes, Greeley urged the trustees to consider reneging on the
severance-pay promise because "there were evidences that Mr. Dana was making war upon the *Tribune*"; a committee was formed to inquire into an interview
Dana had had with Bennett and disclosures he had apparently made about the
sale of the *Tribune* stock that had resulted in an attack on the paper. Dana,
replying to the trustees' inquiry, said it was incredible that they would contemplate going back on their word to him and insisted that the charges made were
frivolous, irrelevant, and untrue; the trustees rated his response "uncivil" but
apparently did not cancel the promised payments. The entire dispute, at any
rate, hardly shattered Dana's career. Recognized by Lincoln's camp as an
unswerving patriot, he was installed within months as the Assistant Secretary
of War; after Appomattox, his journalistic star would climb to its zenith—and
he would make Greeley and the *Tribune* pay for having discarded him.

Dana's dismissal liberated Greeley to pursue an unhampered editorial course, which increasingly sought to achieve by an act of state—namely, the emancipation of the slaves—what was not being gained on the battlefield. Indeed, the Union's military reverses led Greeley to the spiritual conclusion that the Lord would not smile on the North's armies unless their commander-in-chief embraced emancipation as an article of faith. More and more, Greeley saw the struggle as a contest between light and darkness, with the nation's moral regeneration or its death as the only possible outcomes. Freeing the slaves by edict, moreover, could bring as many as 400,000 black men into the Union ranks, useful for combat or in whatever other way Lincoln's generals saw fit.

The President that spring still harbored a less radical solution. He asked Congress to appropriate four hundred dollars in compensation to the owner of each emancipated slave if the secession ended and also proposed the support of efforts to recolonize the freed blacks in Africa. Greeley, at his scornful best, dismissed the whole idea and suggested instead that the wiser and less expensive course would be to colonize the Southerners inasmuch as they had been so anxious to civilize the Africans. Congress was no more sympathetic with the President's concessionary stance and, faced with the need to clarify the status of slaves in areas of the secessionist states that had come under Union military control, passed several acts directing its field officers to confiscate rebel property, human and other. Throughout the summer of 1862, Greeley's editorials called for a more sweeping proclamation by the President, outlawing bondage in law if not in fact; military conditions demanded nothing less. The culminating editorial in this campaign was his August open letter to Lincoln titled "The Prayer of Twenty Millions," in which Greeley took for himself the role of spokesman for the entire Northern body politic; at the very least, he wrote, the Union's generals ought faithfully to enforce the confiscation bills passed by Congress, for to continue to disregard them, as inconvenient as they might prove under wartime conditions, was to overlook the very cause of the rebellion they were sworn to put down. The *Tribune*'s national stature was such that Lincoln felt obliged to respond to Greeley's passionate imploring; the President's cause was no less passionate:

> My paramount object in this struggle is to save the Union, and is not either to save or to destroy slavery. If I could save the Union without freeing any slaves, I would do it; and if I could do it by freeing all the slaves, I would do it; and if I could save it by freeing some and leaving others alone, I would also do that. . . .

The unequivocal declaration of his priorities masked the decision Lincoln had already reached but was uncertain of when he could implement: he would proclaim all secessionists stripped of their human chattel, but to do so without a major Union success on the battlefield would appear an empty gesture, rhetoric without sovereign power behind it. Within a fortnight, Lee had been repulsed at Antietam and driven back across the Potomac. Lincoln's historic proclamation followed shortly; the Thirteenth Amendment, outlawing human bondage, gave his edict constitutional legitimacy less than a year after the war ended. If

Greeley deserved blame for hastening the disaster at Bull Run, he was not less entitled to credit for spurring Lincoln's boldest humanitarian act in an earlier season than the Great Emancipator may have intended. No other organ of public opinion, certainly, was capable of having exercised such suasion. "GOD BLESS ABRAHAM LINCOLN!" the *Tribune* exclaimed in hailing the step as "the beginning of the end of the rebellion; the beginning of the new life in the nation."

Other acts of government also buoyed Greeley. Congress, without the seceded slave states to block the way, had now passed a homesteading act and a strong protective tariff, long cherished goals of the editor. But without victory and peace, they were of little more practical meaning than freeing the slaves. And the news did not improve on the war front. Republican reversals at the polls in November, increasing the possibility of a Democratic takeover of the Union two years hence, were followed the next month by the North's defeat at Fredericksburg. At year's end, Greeley was gamely predicting that the Emancipation Proclamation, to go into effect the first of January 1863, would drain the South's resistance within three months—six at most—and peace would soon follow. In truth, he was an anxious, discouraged man at the dawn of the war's pivotal year.

When successive changes of the Union's military command, endorsed heartily by Greeley as presaging an imminent turn of battlefield fortune, failed to work any more miracles than had the emancipation of the slaves, his veneer of bravado peeled away to reveal the old doomsaying accommodationist of the days just after Bull Run. Following Hooker's catastrophe at Chancellorsville in May, *Tribune* readers began to be told that there was no such thing as a good war or a bad peace; hostilities should be pressed for three more months and if no breakthroughs were achieved, perhaps the moment was at hand to sue for peace on the best terms that could be arranged—even if that meant prolonging slavery. Greeley himself put out feelers to Copperhead Democrats to advance the prospect of a negotiated peace through the offices of the French minister. For his troubles, he was denounced by Secretary of State Seward and his principal press ally, Henry Raymond, as a meddling defeatist; the *Times* called for endurance to fight for however long it took at whatever cost for justice to prevail. More than faintheartedness, though, colored Greeley's picture of the situation. Everywhere he looked he saw gloomy portents: a President apparently incapable of inspiring his people or selecting competent military leadership, a Cabinet of men who were his enemies or whom he did not much respect, rival editors who would destroy the Union en route to saving it—and the rumored possibility that Great Britain, with so many Southern sympathizers, was on the verge of granting diplomatic recognition to the Confederacy and thereby stiffening both its will and its diminished credit standing. By midyear Lee was across the Mason-Dixon line into Pennsylvania; unless he was thrown back for good, unless Grant's bold stroke down the Mississippi to capture Vicksburg succeeded, disaster for the Union might lie just ahead.

The results at Gettysburg and Vicksburg, coming in quick succession, summoned Greeley back from despondency—and much of the Union with him. If victory had not come, the new draft law due to go into effect in mid-July might have inspired mutiny throughout the North. As it was, resistance to conscription was largely limited to violence in New York City, with Greeley and his paper as prime targets.

The *Tribune* had endorsed a controversial provision of the draft bill allowing would-be conscripts to be exempted for a $300 payment to the government—as unambiguous a piece of class legislation as it would be possible to conceive. Greeley argued that the bill had the double virtue of weeding out those who would prove poor fighting men and raising money for the hard-pressed United States Treasury. Both points were plainly valid but in no way addressed themselves to the justice of the act. Since the most willing soldiers had presumably already stepped forward for service voluntarily, the draft had to be left with a pool of reluctant conscripts, rich and poor together; the government's bill let the wealthy buy their way out of service, equating their money with the lives of the less well-off. Such a definition of patriotism, added to the *Tribune*'s traditional antislavery and more recent emancipationist policies, fueled the anger of the mob of young laborers, many of them new immigrants and some from the criminal element, who were not eager to serve as cannon fodder. As they began boiling through the streets of New York for three days, burning, looting, lynching blacks on lampposts, and clubbing known abolitionists to the ground, his associates urged the *Tribune* editor to fortify the premises. "No," Greeley reportedly replied, "do not bring a musket into the building. Let them strike the first blow. All my life I have worked for the workingmen; if they would now burn my office and hang me, why, let them do it."

Rival papers afterward spread the story that Greeley had cowered under a table in a nearby restaurant while the mob rampaged through Printing-House Square and stormed his office; in truth, friends took him to an early and protracted dinner, trying to keep the conspicuous editor out of harm's way until the threat had passed. Some five thousand rioters surged toward the paper, bellowing the likes of "Down with the *Tribune*! Down with the old white coat what counts a nayger as good as an Irishman!" and chanting, "We'll hang Horace Greeley to a sour-apple tree!" The editor, insisting he wanted to be at his desk at the moment of ultimate peril, left the restaurant and headed for his office on the streets behind the paper. But the approaching tumult was so ugly that Greeley let himself be persuaded to take a carriage home with its shades drawn. By the time he returned to the *Tribune* later that evening with cannon and musketry in tow, he found windows shattered all over the building, downstairs counters torn up, furniture broken, gas burners twisted off, and scorched spots on the floor where the mob had tried to torch the place before the police subdued it. All but three of the paper's staff of a hundred and fifty had scrambled for safety via the roof; among the trio who stayed at their posts was George Washburn Smalley, home from the war. The paper was out on schedule the next morning, devoting its entire front page to the rioting, the worst to afflict an American city until the uprising in the

Watts section of Los Angeles 102 years later—when race and injustice would again provide the spark.

III

The sheer logistics of bearing battle reports from the front to a telegraph sending station gave the *Tribune* more than its share of Civil War heroes. Among the most resourceful was A. Homer Byington, the editor of a weekly in Norwalk, Connecticut, before joining Greeley's sheet and promptly scoring perhaps the biggest news scoop of the war.

Approaching to within a dozen miles of Gettysburg from the east, Byington discovered that Confederate cavalrymen had cut down a five-mile stretch of telegraph line paralleling the train track. As the guns began to echo across the Pennsylvania hills, Byington left the early stages of coverage to other *Tribune* men on the scene and instead bent his efforts on finding the local telegraph operator at a nearby hotel. After instructing the fellow to go home to retrieve his battery and sounder and extracting a pledge from him for his exclusive services for the next two days, Byington assembled a repair crew, commandeered giant spools of wire from a warehouse, rented a handcar from railroad officials, and spent the first day of the battle of Gettysburg restringing the downed telegraph line. The next day he was a reportorial whirlwind, and as dusk fell and relays of *Herald* riders had to travel fifty miles to Lancaster to wire home the news, the *Tribune* received the first comprehensive report on the war's pivotal battle over Byington's private line.

A yet more heroic courier, whose daring finally cost him his grim scoop but won a tall friend in the White House, was young Henry Ebenezer Wing, a veteran of Fredericksburg, where he had lost two fingers of his left hand. The neophyte among the *Tribune* team (headed by Byington) that covered the battle of the Wilderness in March 1864, Wing showed up for duty wearing what the snappy *Tribune* correspondent was expected to sport: a buckskin jacket, riding breeches of Irish corduroy, new calfskin boots, and the finest kid gloves. Selected to carry back to Washington a report on the first day's terrible carnage in the smoky forest, Wing stopped at General Grant's headquarters to ask if there was any message for the White House. Consumed by the fate of his army locked in deadly embrace with an enemy that had the advantage of familiarity with the shrouded terrain, Grant growled, "Just tell them that things are going swimmingly here." The young reporter's face registered his dismay; was this the only word that was to be relayed to his anxious commander and the waiting North? Grant thought the better of it and caught up with Wing in the doorway. "Well, if you see the President," he said, "tell him from me that whatever happens, there will be no turning back."

Armed with directions and the names of a few sympathizers along the route, Wing set out on horseback at 4:30 in the morning across a countryside teeming with Confederate guerrillas and roving bands of cavalry irregulars. His first contact urged him to shed his finery for a suit of butternut homespun, worn brogans, and an old wool hat appropriate to a backwoodsman if he did not want to be seized as a Union agent. And a good thing, for he was soon stopped by a band of Mosby's raiders who accepted his story that he was carrying word of Lee's great victory in the Wilderness to Confederate agents in Washington and insisted on accompanying him part of the way north. Alas, they reined up at an inn where Wing had stayed a few days before the battle and the secessionist keeper now recognized him. Only a frantic breakaway prevented his capture. He plunged into the nearby Rappahannock, missing the ford and, along with his horse, having to swim for his life. Furious pursuit and warnings sent out in advance of his route forced Wing to proceed on foot, following railroad tracks where possible, dodging in and out of thickets, hiding in brush aswarm with insects while a detachment of rebel cavalry rested only feet away. Near Manassas and the sight of Union camps, he was captured and tossed into a cattle pen, only to slip away at dusk and complete his twenty-four-mile trek at Union Mills, twenty miles from Washington. The telegraph agent, though, said he was authorized to send only military messages. Calculating quickly, Wing thought perhaps that Charles Dana, now in the War Department, might possess enough residual feeling for the *Tribune* to pass along his news. Back came a message instead from Dana's superior, Secretary of War Edwin M. Stanton, commanding Wing to send his news and message from Grant at once or be arrested as a spy. Wing declined and surrendered to the operator. A few minutes later, a second message arrived from Washington:

> This is the President. Mr. Stanton tells me you have news from the Army. Will you give it to me? We are anxious here in Washington to learn developments at the front.   A. LINCOLN.

The cheeky young newsman replied that "my news is for the *Tribune*" but "I will be glad to tell you all I know if you will see that a message goes forward tonight to my paper." The President agreed; Wing at once dictated the highlights of his report, which Lincoln sent on but got *Tribune* managing editor Gay to share with the Associated Press, thereby destroying the exclusivity Wing's efforts had nearly won for his paper. Brought to Washington by special train, Wing appeared like a bedraggled scarecrow before a middle-of-the-night gathering of the Cabinet to present a first-person battle report. Only when the others had retired did Wing give the President Grant's pledge of dogged advance. Lincoln, his long search for a resolute commander at last over, bent down and kissed the youth on the forehead. Next time he returned to Washington with battle news, Lincoln added, Wing should come directly to the White House.

The occasion came just three weeks later when Wing brought back grave word from Cold Harbor. This time the reporter confided in Lincoln how appalled he was by the mayhem, by the jealousies of squabbling commanders, by the pain of wandering the battlefield after the guns had ceased and looking for dead and dying men he knew from his native Connecticut so he might send messages back to their families. He badly wanted to quit and go home; Lincoln told Wing that he shared his sentiments to the full yet he supposed both of them had their duty to do until the end was at hand. And so Wing stayed on the *Tribune* throughout the final year of the war, and it was he who, having arranged with one of Grant's subordinates to signal him on the favorable outcome of the private surrender talks with Lee by mopping his forehead three times as the generals emerged, flashed the world its first word of the peace reached at Appomattox Court House.

No *Tribune* men, and few on any other paper, paid a dearer or more protracted price for their devotion to duty than Albert Deane Richardson, a highly skilled reporter who had smuggled coded dispatches out of New Orleans in the months just preceding the war, and an associate named Junius Henri Browne, who joined him north of Vicksburg at the beginning of May 1863 as reporters scrambled to catch up with Grant's sudden move against the rebel stronghold that blocked passage up or down the Mississippi.

Richardson, a thirty-year-old native of Massachusetts with a wife and three daughters, had learned they could reach Grant's camp without resort to a three-day, seventy-five-mile ride through swampy bayous by instead hopping a steam-powered Union supply tug camouflaged with hay barges lashed to the side. The only problem was that the nine-hour voyage downriver would take them directly under rebel guns twice where the river S-turned at Vicksburg. Sipping Catawba wine while sprawled on a couch of hay bales, the two *Tribune* men and a third reporter from the New York *World* enjoyed the spring fragrances from the moss-draped shoreline until a bright moon rose into a cloudless night sky and left their craft an easy target for Confederate gunners as it chuff-chuffed lazily downstream. The tug was just a few minutes short of successfully running the gauntlet of fire when a shell found the boiler, killed the captain, and showered sparks onto the hay bales. Richardson was the first one over the side of the floating inferno. A Confederate yawl retrieved the three newsmen, who spent two days in the Vicksburg city jail while waiting to be exchanged and file the ripping yarn with their papers. But Grant's operations in the vicinity, they were advised, had curtailed normal exchange procedures; they would have to be sent to Richmond, where they could no doubt expect passage home on the first truce boat.

A two-week trip on rickety trains across the South landed them in a converted tobacco warehouse known as Libby Prison, reserved for Union officers and civilians, in the Confederate capital. They were able to supplement their diet of bread and salt pork with fresh produce bought for them by their guards; newspapers and pipe tobacco were also available, so the hardship of their internment was bearable during the ten-day wait for the first truce ship to sail up the James. But when it came, only the *World* reporter was on the list of those authorized for release. Back in New York, he went at once to the *Tribune* to advise Sidney Gay of his correspondents' plight. Gay promptly wrote the White House, and the War Department exerted effort to obtain Richardson's and Browne's freedom, but the Confederate Commissioner of Exchange was adamant, at first charging that the reporters were particularly obnoxious noncombatants and later confiding that it was the *Tribune* itself, that virulent antislavery scourge, that was the target of Confederate vengeance.

Their confinement grew more oppressive with the summer heat, and Browne was riven with fever as their strength and hope waned. In September the two men were transferred to nearby Castle Thunder, a holding pen for common prisoners who, lowlife though they were, joined the *Tribune* men in an elaborate escape plan involving bribed guards, smuggled Confederate uniforms, forged identification papers, and tunneling under the prison walls from a subterranean storage room. Last-minute confusion over a bribe payment thwarted the plan and did their case no good when the reporters hired a Richmond attorney to petition the Confederate Secretary of War for their release. Instead, they won an unappealable sentence of confinement until the war's end and transfer in January 1864 to a prison in Salisbury, North Carolina.

A four-story brick cotton factory with six outbuildings on a four-acre plot, their new jail resembled a small New England college. Holding only six hundred prisoners, it offered a courtyard where fresh air and well water were available, as well as eggs and fresh vegetables from the countryside and access to a 2,000-volume library owned by a compassionate townsman. Imprisonment once more seemed tolerable until shattering word came that Richardson's wife had died of measles and that one of his daughters had followed her to the grave a week later. By that fall, in the wake of Stanton's ruling against continued exchange of prisoners in order further to drain the South's depleted manpower resources, Salisbury prison's population had increased more than tenfold. Men had to burrow under the foundations and into the courtyard earth to keep warm; malnutrition and disease were rampant, and the death rate ran at 13 percent. The *Tribune* men were placed in charge of the medical arrangements, allowing them considerable freedom of movement among the prison buildings, and, under increasingly desperate circumstances, were able in December 1864—twenty months after they had been fished out of the Mississippi—to walk nonchalantly past the night shift of guards in one of the buildings used as a Confederate hospital and reach freedom.

To reach safety entailed a further twenty-seven-day ordeal that surpassed anything they had yet endured. Weak, scantily clad against the midwinter weather, ever wary of search parties, often not knowing whom to trust or where to turn, they rode when they could and hobbled when they could not up and over the Blue Ridge into Tennessee—a total of some 340 miles—until they at last reached the Union lines near Knoxville. Richardson wired the paper: "Out of the jaws of Death; out of the gates of Hell." From Cincinnati they sent back a full account of their extraordinary travail. On the way home, they stopped off in Washington to plead with Stanton that his draconian policy against exchanging prisoners was dooming thousands of captured Union soldiers to certain death. They carried their plea to the public, and in a few weeks the policy was reversed.

Richardson remained on the *Tribune* staff for four years after the war until he was shot while in the paper's counting room by a man who accused him of sexual intimacy with his former wife. The fatally wounded reporter was removed to the Astor House, where, thanks in part to Greeley's intercession, the Reverend Henry Ward Beecher performed a deathbed marriage ceremony for Richardson and his assailant's former wife. His intention, Greeley explained to a *Herald* reporter, was to assure that Richardson's orphaned daughters would have a mother; his reward was to be accused of fostering free love—than which, by the lights of the *Tribune*'s founder, there was no more shameful sin.

IV

The singular goal of Horace Greeley's last years was to bind up the deep wounds of war so that the reunited American nation might begin to realize the full measure of its grand destiny. Toward that end he projected himself onto the public stage on two prominent occasions as a performer rather than a commentator. The first incident, occurring in the summer of 1864, revealed that even at his most clumsily duplicitous, Greeley was well-intentioned; the second, two years after the war had closed, demonstrated that even at his most disinterestedly magnanimous, he was likely to be vilified as misguided and self-seeking.

Continued Union misfortune on the battlefield had induced a fresh and deepening depression in Greeley as the presidential election year of 1864 lengthened. He had largely written off Lincoln as a mediocrity; the war had become a bloodbath, and there was no end of it in sight. The Republicans seemed likely, in his view, to lose in the fall election, and the Democrats likely to negotiate a peace that would mean the Union dead had died in vain. Any terms that could be obtained in advance of such an eventuality were therefore likely to be preferable.

In such a frame of mind, Greeley received word in July that a three-man Confederate mission was standing by in Canada fully empowered to talk peace with Union officials. Subsequent evidence has indicated that the Confederate ambassadors had actually been dispatched to undermine the Union war effort by encouraging elements in both parties who were most eager to end the fighting —especially the so-called Peace Democrats. To the impetuous Greeley, consideration of such Southern motives was beside the point, which was, as Greeley wrote to Lincoln upon learning of this reported Confederate initiative, that "our bleeding, bankrupt, almost dying country . . . longs for peace." He said he feared that Lincoln did not realize how greatly the people wanted the war to be over and that a frank statement of acceptable settlement terms might stave off insurrection in the North. His own list of acceptable terms, Greeley added, consisted of restoration of the Union, abolition of slavery, unqualified amnesty for the secessionists, and a federal payment of $400 million to former slaveholders for the confiscation of their property. Lincoln wrote back not only indicating full openness to peace overtures but also instructing Greeley himself to proceed to Niagara Falls, where the Confederate delegation was lodged on the Canadian side, and to determine if their emissaries were empowered to offer a peace that included an end to the secession and the abandonment of slavery, "whatever else it embraces"; if so, Greeley should bring them directly to the White House. When Greeley answered that he had not intended to seek a negotiator's role for himself, Lincoln told his captious critic, "I not only intend a sincere effort for peace, [b]ut I intend that you shall be a personal witness that it is made."

No doubt mindful of the appealing role of peace instigator that history might assign him, Greeley went to Niagara Falls. But apparently so anxious was he to place no impediment in the way of negotiations that Greeley made no mention to the Confederate agents of the two indispensable conditions of a settlement that Lincoln had put down. The door to the White House that Greeley held open to them dismayed rather than pleased the Southerners, whose true purpose had been to fuel anti-war sympathies among Union voters, and so they said they lacked credentials to carry on formal negotiations—only an informal exchange between civilians had been anticipated—but such could be obtained if they were granted safe passage to Richmond. Lincoln thereupon sent John Hay, one of his personal secretaries, to Niagara Falls with a "To Whom It May Concern" letter granting the Confederates safe passage and reiterating his receptivity to peace terms so long as they included the two essential ones he had instructed Greeley to convey. Seeing their opportunity, the rebel agents issued a flamboyant statement accusing Lincoln of going back on his word—Greeley had mentioned no preconditions—and of a wish to continue inflicting undue misery on the peoples of both North and South. So ended the last fleeting hope for a peace won at the bargaining table.

But the recriminations were bitter and lasting. Greeley, stung by charges by Raymond of the *Times* and Bryant of the *Post* that he had been used as a cat's-paw in Southern treachery that undermined Lincoln, and by Bennett, who branded his pet target in the trade a "nincompoop," defended himself in a fashion that essentially reinforced the Southern charges. The President should have dispensed with preliminary conditions to peace talks, he insisted, thereby tacitly conceding his own bad faith in transmitting Lincoln's offer to negotiate. When the *Times* called for public disclosure of the original exchange of letters between Greeley and Lincoln to reveal where the fault lay, the President agreed provided only that several of Greeley's defeatist passages, sure to demoralize the public in view of the editor's stature, be deleted; Greeley said the texts had to be disclosed in their entirety or not at all. Lincoln then invited him to the White

House to thrash out the matter, but Greeley feared he would be stepping into an enemy camp and declined. Before long the *Tribune* was lashing Lincoln over the alleged lost opportunity for peacemaking and urging him to invite a fresh one—or, if none were forthcoming, to agree to a one-year armistice during which a full-dress peace conference could be undertaken. Such a step would have been tantamount, of course, to a reprieve to the South's diminishing capacity to wage war. Lincoln, who had once prized the support of the *Tribune* editor so highly, had had enough of him. "He is not truthful," the President now said of him within the Cabinet room but refrained from public repudiation.

Although he had favored Chase or Frémont for the Republican nomination, Greeley bowed to the inevitable and supported Lincoln's re-election drive wholeheartedly; the alternative—George McClellan in the White House—was unthinkable to him. And he fully endorsed the tenor of Lincoln's second inaugural address—"with malice toward none" in a Confederacy now on its knees and awaiting Grant's coup de grace. When surrender came within a month, Greeley editorialized at once for blanket clemency. In an editorial titled "Magnanimity in Triumph," he wrote:

> We plead against passions certain at this moment to be fierce and intolerant; but on our side are the Ages and the voice of History. We plead for the restoration of the Union, against a policy which would afford a momentary gratification at the cost of years of perilous hate and bitterness.

He cried out against the *Times*'s proposal to hang Jefferson Davis, president of the fallen Confederacy, and spare all other rebels, because "a single Confederate led out to execution would be evermore enshrined in a million hearts as a conspicuous hero and martyr." As to the blacks, "so lately the slaves, destined still to be the neighbors, and we trust at no distant day the fellow-citizens of the Southern Whites," Greeley was sure they, too, would call out now, could their voice be heard, "on the side of Clemency—of Humanity" toward their former masters.

Lincoln's murder several days later released a tidal wave of abuse against Greeley and his pleas for forgiveness of an enemy that displayed its lack of contrition by slaying the President. But he would not waver before hostility as he had in storms just past. Proclaiming a policy of "Universal Amnesty and Impartial Suffrage"—meaning Southern whites should be fully exonerated for their rebellion provided they granted the ballot and rights that flowed from it to their former bondsmen—Greeley seemed almost to have taken for himself the role of spiritual successor to the fallen Lincoln, whom he proclaimed in death, as he had not in life, a figure of towering patience, compassion, and humanity. Behind the words he bannered were, as so often, political considerations. Assured of a monolothic black vote in the South, the Republicans could retain national power; without it, they were likely to yield to resurgent Democrats whose ranks would be swollen by the return to citizenship in good standing of Southern whites. But Greeley's powers as a psychologist of the South had not improved. The pacified rebels would not further humiliate themselves by voluntarily extending their hands to the people they had so long brutalized; oppressive black codes and Southern rejection of the Fourteenth Amendment brought on a radical reconstruction that was to perpetuate the nation's emotional schism for generations. Still Greeley would not abandon his effort at reconciliation.

He thought he saw an opportunity to dramatize his plea when Jefferson Davis's wife turned to him, as she had to others, to ease the plight of her husband, who had been languishing in jail for two years awaiting a trial for treason that could never be conducted impartially. Davis had been a reluctant secessionist, in Greeley's view, and it was unfair to keep him in judicial limbo simply because he was, with Robert E. Lee, the most prominent embodiment of the late rebellion. After satisfying himself that Davis had not been involved in the plot that took Lincoln's life or in prisoner-of-war atrocities, Greeley enlisted a New York attorney to obtain the captive's release on bail and offered his name, if needed, as an endorser of the bail bond. The offer was accepted— the other signers were a representative of Commodore Cornelius Vanderbilt, perhaps the North's most prominent industrialist, and Gerrit Smith, a veteran leader of the antislavery movement and ally of John Brown—and Greeley appeared at the federal district courthouse in Richmond on May 13, 1867, to affix his name to the humane document. Asked if he had any objection to being introduced to the object of his charity, Greeley said no and, wearing an expression at first somewhat startled and then revealing a measure of satisfaction at having been able to perform the symbolic good deed, extended his hand. Afterward he went to address an appreciative and racially mixed audience, whites in the center section and blacks in the side aisles, at a large African church in the former Confederate capital. He regretted the South's enactment of its black codes, which he said had had the appearance to the North of an effort to revive the war. And he said that the ignorant and degraded condition of Southern blacks was no reason to deprive them of equal rights and liberties "so long as ignorance or degradation is no bar to citizenship as to white men." At the conclusion, in words that perfectly reflected his life's remaining mission, he called on Americans of all parties, races, and factions "to bury the dead past in mutual and hearty good will . . . and exalt the glory of our long-distracted and bleeding, but henceforth reunited, magnificent country."

For his troubles, massive obloquy once more descended on the editor of the *Tribune.* Reports were widespread that he had exhibited warmth toward Davis at their meeting. The gesture was widely characterized as an attention-seeking stunt. *The Nation,* the most influential political periodical in the country, called the act "simply detestable." The *Tribune*'s circulation and advertising fell off markedly. Sales of the recently issued second volume of Greeley's hasty history of the Civil War, *The American Conflict,* plummeted. And the Union League Club, of which Greeley was a member, scheduled a meeting to discuss the propriety of his bonding Davis and invited the editor to attend. He replied to the club's committee in a letter he published in the paper:

I do not recognize you as capable of judging, or even fully comprehending me. You evidently regard me as a weak sentimentalist, misled by maudlin philosophy. I arraign you as narrow-minded blockheads, who would like to be useful to a great and good cause, but don't know how. . . .

. . . So long as any man was seeking to overthrow our Government, he was my enemy; from the hour in which he laid down his arms, he was my formerly erring countryman. . . .

On reflection, the Union League decided to drop the matter.

His conduct at Niagara Falls and its aftermath had been Greeley at his most execrable: dogmatic, petulant, vituperative; his behavior in connection with Davis was Greeley at his most admirable: staunch, candid, chivalrous, dreaming of a world that never was but might yet be.

V

A strange device appeared as the centerpiece of the logotype at the top of the first page of the *New York Tribune* on April 10, 1866, the twenty-fifth anniversary of the paper's founding, and remained there ever after—a banner unique among the newspapers of the world. It is there still atop the *International Herald Tribune.* Staff members over the years came to call the odd little drawing "the dingbat," which Webster's defines as meaning, among other choices, "thing, object, or contrivance." A contrivance it surely was: in the middle of the crudely drawn tableau is a clock reading twelve minutes past six—no one knows why (conceivably it was the moment of Horace Greeley's birth); to the left, Father Time sits in brooding contemplation of antiquity, represented by the ruin of a Greek temple, a man and his ox plowing, a caravan of six camels passing before two pyramids, and an hourglass; to the right, a sort of Americanized Joan of Arc, arms outstretched beneath a backwards-billowing Old Glory, welcomes modernity in the form of a chugging railroad train, factories with smoking chimneys, an updated plow, and an industrial cogwheel (over which the incautious heroine is about to trip); atop the clock, ready to take off into the boundless American future, is an eagle—all for no extra cost. It was a baroque snapshot of time arrested, an allegorical hieroglyph of the newspaper's function to render history on the run.

The installation of the dingbat was a signpost that a new era had begun. The *Tribune* was no longer Greeley's personal instrument. After a quarter of a century, he felt as much imprisoned as enlarged by it. He devoted more time now to writing books, including his memoirs, and pursuing the chimera of elective office. He ran for Congress in 1866 and lost, sought the gubernatorial nomination in 1868 and did not get it, ran for state comptroller in 1869 and lost. He seemed an increasingly lonely figure, a man who had outlived his time; at fifty-five he was not precisely ancient, but he had pursued his ends with such unremitting intensity that a weariness of body and mind had set in. With his grandfatherly spectacles and corona of white hair and whiskers that surrounded his cherubic features like an untidy halo, he had become almost an icon of homespun virtue, whose likeness now adorned the steel engravings and fob watches that the *Tribune* gave away as premiums to new subscribers.

The time had come to pour new wine into an aging bottle. Sidney Gay, second-in-command, was in declining health at fifty; never a robust figure, especially in comparison with his predecessor, Dana, he left now, and a fresh generation of talent began to flow through the door. Of these newcomers, the youngest, most gifted, and most flawed in character was John Russell Young, who, his slight, boyish figure notwithstanding, was given the managing editor's reins, amid wide astonishment, at the age of twenty-six.

Starting in the proofroom at the Philadelphia *Press* when he was fifteen, Young learned his trade so well that he rose to managing editor by the time he was twenty-two. Associated during the war with Philadelphia banker Jay Cooke, he came to New York to assist that financier's effort to sell half a million dollars in bonds to pay for the Union military machine. During that time, he submitted a number of editorials to the *Tribune* phrased with a sort of incisive truculence not unlike Greeley's; the editor took note, and a friendship ensued. The opportunistic Young ingratiated himself, and perhaps seeing in the gifted young man the son that heaven had denied him, Greeley brought him onto the paper and gave him license to clean house.

Despite his youth, or possibly because of it, he ran the office like a strict military commander. Deadwood was disposed of along with those who did not suit his style, like Amos Cummings, the knowledgeable, high-strung city editor, dismissed for use of profanity; in their place he did not hesitate to install friends and acquaintances, many from Philadelphia, among them his brother, whom he made head of the *Tribune*'s Washington bureau. The paper itself became, if anything, more austere in appearance; its veteran mechanical superintendent, Thomas N. Rooker, prided himself on the neatness of its typography and the efficiency of its production staff. The multiple-deck headlines that adorned the front page during the war were gone, replaced by sedate label headings never more than a single column wide. But the writing in the paper took on a new verve and energy. The basic reporting, reflecting less of Greeley's reformist zeal in its choice of subject and prominence of play, grew more fact-laden and less elaborate—what one of the *Tribune*'s more illustrious postwar recruits, Lincoln's former secretary John Hay, tagged "the Grocer's Bill style." But wide stylistic latitude was granted to feature writers and correspondents like George Smalley, established in London as chief of European correspondence; William Winter, beginning a career that would last into the twentieth century as the first real drama critic on an American paper; and Mark Twain, contributing pieces that would become famous when bound up with others under his name and issued as *Innocents Abroad*. But it was the editorial page that especially sparkled with eloquence and humor in the hands of Young and such new arrivals as John R. G. Hassard, one of the wittiest stylists ever to write for the paper. Greeley's touch was still in evidence, of course, as he moved somewhat to the left politically in his ultimate endorsement of a radical reconstruction of the South and to the right economically, calling for harder money and less government spending than favored by the administrations of Andrew Johnson and U. S. Grant. He continued to flay the special objects of his scorn, like William Seward, whose proposal to buy Alaska from Russia he condemned as extravagant nonsense and an affront to Britain and its dominion over adjacent Canada. Young's own stylistic elegance and strong-willed judgments, though, more and more came to dominate the page. He was a master at barbed characterizations of public figures —his Grant, for example, was "that sashed and girded sphinx"—and lucid if slightly sardonic summaries of views other than his own, as in noting of Greeley, ". . . [h]is dislike of slavery, when you sifted it down, was rather an earnest of sympathy with the white man who was undersold in his labor than sentiment for the negro." He took the paper, in Greeley's absence but with the long leash the editor had awarded him, into steadily more extravagant positions, growing intemperate finally in his calls for Johnson's impeachment—a stand Greeley had resisted on the ground that the President would do himself in—and urging on Grant a frankly imperialist policy with regard to the Caribbean and even Canada.

The net effect of this precocious leadership was tonic for the *Tribune*. Its gross revenues in 1868 passed the million-dollar mark for the first time, the paper was more talked about in positive ways than previously in the postwar period, and the bonding of Jefferson Davis receded from memory. But John Russell Young, for all his virtues and energy, was something of an intriguer and too ambitious for his own and the *Tribune*'s good.

Not content with the power he exercised as helmsman of one of the nation's most influential papers, he became a secret backer of and prime fund-raiser for two new Philadelphia papers, the *Star* and the *Post*. The latter he made his special clandestine project, arranging for it to receive copies of the *Tribune*'s Associated Press dispatches when the fledgling Philadelphia paper was denied membership in the wire service—in blatant circumvention of the AP rules. Young's maneuvers were disclosed in April 1869 when the New York *Sun*, taken over the year before by Charles Dana, who apparently was eager to snipe at his former employer, ran a four-column, front-page exposé based on a batch of purloined personal letters of Young. His bitterness not well disguised, Dana opened by describing how Young had arrived at the *Tribune* with a small carpetbag, a straw hat, a large nose, "two restless eyes, and a head phrenologically well developed in the region of secretiveness and rather low in the vicinity of cautiousness." The rascal crept up the stairs and soon "dug himself a rifle-pit in the affections of Mr. G." But it was Young's own words that did him in. Possibly obtained through the intercession of Amos Cummings, the resourceful city editor whom Young had fired from the *Tribune* and who now worked for

Dana, Young's letters told a tawdry tale of his efforts to raise money for his struggling Philadelphia papers by such means as peddling the *Tribune*'s influence to ambitious Pennsylvania politicians whose national careers could be advanced by a powerful word from New York. Young's contempt for a number of *Tribune* veterans whom he called "old fogies," like Samuel Sinclair, McElrath's successor as publisher, and mechanical chief Rooker, whom he called "an eye-sore," was amply drawn along with self-indicting remarks about his part in smuggling Associated Press material to Philadelphia. Young, badly shaken, called the disclosure "a dastardly assault" and blustered about filing a massive libel suit against the *Sun;* he did not deny authorship of the letters but claimed their content had been criminally distorted. His abuse of the authority Greeley had handed him was undeniable, however, and when he gave his resignation in to the founder, who was a model of kindness throughout his protégé's public discomfiture, it was accepted. Young's meteoric career, while not entirely snuffed out, had reached its premature zenith before he was thirty.

Power at the *Tribune* passed almost at once to a tall, slender figure whom Greeley had hired six months earlier and installed as chief editorial writer and a counterweight to Young, whose positions may have come to seem as excessive to him as Dana's had at the beginning of the decade. Whitelaw Reid was thirty-one when he joined the paper. His sway there would last forty-four years.

While he shared most of Greeley's political creed, Reid was his polar opposite in temperament and personality. His long, handsome face ended in a little chin beard, and he wore his lengthy hair in the "rebel" style bespeaking his origins in southern Ohio, where Southern manners had long predominated. Smooth and groomed where Greeley was brusque and disheveled, Reid had armed himself with culture and grace to face the world. His politesse made him welcome in clubs and salons and the city's elegant circles where the indecorous Greeley was deemed unacceptable. But Reid also built around him a wall of reserve that repulsed familiarity and invited little of the personal loyalty and affection that Greeley's open, spontaneous, palpably human personality could evoke. Passionless and calculating, in the better sense of the word, Reid was nevertheless far more loyal to Greeley than Young had been.

Of stern Calvinist parentage, he was raised on a farm but was extremely well educated for a rural boy. His uncle, a doctor of divinity, ran a private academy near the Reids' homestead in Xenia, Ohio, where Whitelaw was heavily exposed to the literary classics. A model of applied intellect, he made a brilliant academic record at Miami University and then, after teaching briefly, took control with his brother of the newspaper in Xenia. But Whitelaw Reid was cut out for the wider world and soon joined the Cincinnati *Gazette,* among the best papers in the West, covering the state legislature and rising to city editor. The high drama of civil conflict was too great, though, to keep a young man deskbound, and Reid, writing under the demure pen name "Agate," a printer's designation for small type, became one of the leading correspondents of the war. Highly critical of the Union's military operations, which he found inadequate and wasteful in training and bumbling and laggard in execution, he attracted national attention with his 19,000-word account of the confusion and near-rout of Union forces at Pittsburg Landing in Tennessee, better known as the battle of Shiloh, in April 1862. Where other reporters hurried back with accounts that sought to salvage some glory for the North from the encounter, Reid did massive interviewing among soldiers of all ranks and drew a dark picture of Grant caught napping in bivouac and the resulting turmoil. The article was reprinted in many papers, including the *New York Tribune,* and earned its author promotion to Washington, the nation's news center for the duration of the war. He operated there at will for the *Gazette* and met the powerful national figures of the day, Greeley among them, establishing ties that would serve him well throughout the remainder of his career. After a postwar fling as a carpetbag planter in the Deep South that ended in respectable failure, Reid returned North and, while serving as the star writer and one-twelfth owner of the *Gazette,* resisted and then yielded to recruitment by Greeley, who promised his own imminent retirement and the prospect of a leading role for Reid in the *Tribune*'s future.

Assigned the odd title of "First Writing Editor," Reid worked in uneasy harness with John Russell Young for half a year before the latter's humiliation and departure. A surviving note from Reid, prompted by changes made in an editorial of his at Young's command, advised the managing editor that he felt he had faithfully followed Greeley's instructions in drafting the piece and that while he did not want to fight over it, it would have been nice of Young to have told him directly about the revisions rather than letting him learn about them through office channels. With Young out, Reid succeeded to the managing-editorship in everything but name.

He was an efficient administrator, good at delegating authority and granting his charges breathing space. Under him the paper also exhibited considerable investigative enterprise. While the *Times* was drawing acclaim for its exposure of the monumental graft extracted from the city treasury by the Tweed Ring, the *Tribune* was recording much more than its accustomed share of exclusives. It bared fraudulent practices by the Port of New York health officer and by Grant appointees in the New York Custom House. Its reporters undertook such daring ventures as going incognito to expose inhumane conditions at the Bloomingdale Asylum, breaking up a gang of river pirates, and traveling as far afield as South Carolina to examine allegations of corruption and abuses in the Reconstruction government. Most sensationally, it yanked away the cloak of secrecy surrounding the Senate's treaty negotiations with Great Britain over reparations for her complicity in the damage done to Union shipping by Confederate forces. In printing the complete text of the treaty before it was ratified—other papers copied it verbatim, including typographical errors—the *Tribune* aroused the wrath of the Senate, which commanded the detention on its premises of the two correspondents responsible until they agreed to disclose the identity of their informant. Other than to indicate that their source was neither anyone in the Senate nor any of the officials concerned on either side, the *Tribune* men held fast, enduring spacious quarters, the best of food, the company of friends, and double pay until the end of the congressional term. "If the government can't keep its own secrets," the paper editorialized, "we do not propose to undertake the contract." In foreign coverage, Reid scored a still greater success in granting Smalley liberal use of the new transatlantic cable for coordinating reports from the efficient and courageous band of continental correspondents he had enlisted to cover the Franco-Prussian War. The paper spent $125,000 on the costly cables, but its front-paged exclusives gave the *Tribune* the fastest and most complete coverage in the English-speaking world.

With the new generation firmly and ably in command of his own paper, Greeley endured a final assault from each of his two principal rivals before he and they all died within a short period and put to rest the first great epoch of American journalism.

Henry Raymond, the youngest of the three, was the first to go. But not before delivering a stiff lecture in print to Greeley in 1868. Raymond's political stature had soared for a time near the end of the war when he played an important role in Andrew Johnson's nomination for Vice President and served as Republican national chairman and a member of the House of Representatives. But in his capacity as a leading champion of Johnson's moderate Reconstruction policies, Raymond was badly outmaneuvered and outvoted by the Radicals and finally abandoned politics to concentrate his energies on the *Times*. Having earned journalistic distinction for nonpartisanship in the presentation of the news and balanced editorial commentary devoid of invective, he could not resist belaboring Greeley for a *Tribune* editorial in which the governor of Connecticut had been accused of being a liar—that was the precise word—for allegedly misstating certain government expenditures. In an editorial titled "Good Manners in Journalism," Raymond objected that such language was used "only by the coarsest, lowest, and most ignorant people" and had no place in respectable newspapers "because it is indecent. It shocks the taste, the sense of propriety of every man." He added:

> . . . There are people who relish obscenity and profanity, just as there are people who enjoy prize-fights, dog-fights, or cock-fights, or any other low and brutalizing exhibition; but it is not always proper or decent to pander to such tastes, and the number of American newspapers which adopt it as their standard of manners and propriety is much less than it once was.
>
> We see no reason why the language of a newspaper should be very different from the language of decent society, from the language used by gentlemen in their daily intercourse. . . .

Greeley accepted the rebuke "with due meekness" but noted that the *Times*, in seeking to purify the public dialogue, had not addressed the no less serious question of whether the honorable gent had in fact lied. Raymond, no doubt having given up trying to reform his erstwhile mentor, went to his grave the next year at forty-nine.

Bennett, Greeley's senior rival, had long since passed beyond being lectured to by anyone on good journalistic manners. He had turned over active management of the *Herald* to his son and namesake shortly after the war and lingered in mysterious seclusion at his Washington Heights farmhouse along the Hudson and his city place on Fifth Avenue, keeping in regular touch with the office by telegraph. Rarely now was seen that long, narrow head with its clustering white hair, powerful jaw, and roving eye that cast arrowlike looks at a world that had never loved him. The junior Bennett, brought up mostly by his mother in Paris, where she had fled with the boy to escape the abuse that her husband seemed deliberately to invite, was a spoiled, high-spirited, and pathologically self-centered young man. Although a spectacular wastrel, he nevertheless retained his father's approval because he was proving as readily acceptable to high society as Bennett himself had been roundly rejected by it. The playboy showed flashes of journalistic initiative when he was not indulging himself in capricious command. To perk up profits, he launched a sister paper to the *Herald* in the evening field; called the *Telegram,* it was printed on pink paper and lacked almost all the saving graces and none of the excesses of its famous sibling. James Jr. was not blessed with his father's writing skills but knew a well-turned line when he saw one. It was he who hired Mark Twain away from the *Tribune* as a regular correspondent and put him to work in the American West; many of the pieces that were collected in *Roughing It* first ran in the *Herald.* More famously still, it was Bennett the Younger who in 1870 commissioned free lance Henry Morton Stanley to try to find the Scottish missionary-physician David Livingstone in Africa.

The elder Bennett loosed his parting salvo at Greeley the same year Raymond did—1868—declaring, "[H]e is the source in his party of all extreme tendencies—all those desperate efforts to remodel the nation in accordance with extravagant and misty theory—those ridiculous vagaries of a dreaming enthusiast, who fancies he is a politician and a statesman." Bennett lived four more years to the age of seventy-six, long enough to suffer the pain of seeing that misty extremist, Horace Greeley, nominated for President of the United States against Grant, one of the few political figures whom Bennett did not entirely disdain. At the end, Bennett heaved his frail frame back into the bosom of the Catholic faith he had reviled since his youth; no one in his family, no friend or *Herald* retainer, was at his bedside when he died—only a priest. In his prime, he would have savored the irony.

The *Tribune* saluted him in death as a splendid collector of the news but said that in developing the capacities of journalism, he had degraded its character. In time, it was true, the *Herald* had acquired decency but never principle. Having pronounced this sentence, Greeley would manage to survive the proprietor of "The Satanic" by less than half a year.

VI

The most perverse reward fate dealt him was undoubtedly the last one. Having sought every elective office but dogcatcher and, save for his consolation-prize three-month display of impolitics in Congress, failed utterly, even Horace Greeley could not have confected a more improbable consummation than being nominated for the American presidency—with the endorsement, moreover, of the party he had spent a career defaming. Yet under the circumstances, no event could have put a more fitting seal on the bittersweet life of one of the nation's truly fabulous characters.

For one thing, there was the man from whom he was trying to wrest the job. The contrast between them could not have been sharper. Ulysses Grant, even to the eyes of many who supported him, was a cigar-puffing, whiskey-quaffing war hero masquerading as a statesman, an incompetent caught in the clutches of conniving politicians. Greeley did not smoke, had long striven for the prohibition of alcohol, was a pacifist, and felt there was nothing he did not know about the intrigues of politics and the righteousness required to disperse them. Under Grant, he charged, the civil service had turned into a mockery of the name; bribes changed hands routinely, and the subversion of public trust by his appointees—most prominently in New York, where the conservative Republican faction Greeley ardently opposed had been repeatedly rewarded—had stained the national morality. To eradicate the effects of this cynical coterie in power, a rump movement of liberal Republicans coalesced, beginning in 1870; among its principal movers were leading newspaper publishers and editors from Western and border states. It was not entirely unnatural, therefore, that when the breakaway faction convened in Cincinnati in the spring of 1872 to seek a champion to dislodge the smoky, bibulous sphinx in the White House, they would select a journalist renowned as a reformer and idealist. Horace Greeley was "Old Honesty," the embodiment of journalistic integrity, up-from-poverty enterprise, and popular wisdom. The white hat and rimmed spectacles that adorned his campaign literature had become practically a trademark of his nationally familiar, homespun personality.

Beyond fame itself was his postwar conduct that had gone far to disarm the South's former hatred of him. His continuous call for amnesty and reconciliation of the sections, his symbolic bailing of the deposed Confederate president, and his admission that misrule by occupying Radical Reconstructionists had done as much as Southern intractability to delay the healing of regional differences earned him the endorsement of the recuperating Democratic Party. In the West, where the transcontinental rail link had just been forged, his ardent support for development had long made him a popular figure. In his native New England, his exhortations for thrift, hard work, and morality fit like an old shoe.

In industrial New York and Pennsylvania his crusade to protect American industrialism from cheap foreign competition was as useful to him as his endorsement of farmers everywhere as the truest noblemen in Uncle Sam's Eden. And next to that whiskered, stripe-pantsed geezer, was there a more expansive, embraceable relative in the American family than old Uncle Horace?

The opposition's campaign went far to shred that kindly avuncular image. The cruelty of American politics was not unknown to Horace Greeley, but he was unprepared for the savagery of men in power vowed not to yield it. They portrayed him as a ludicrous figure, awkward, boorish, meddlesome, temperamentally unfit to govern. William Cullen Bryant of the *Evening Post,* his only surviving rival for literary distinction among the journalists of the age, dealt him the unkindest cut in rebuking the impudence of his candidacy with the remark that the President of the United States, whatever his other qualities, ought at least to be a gentleman. Thomas Nast, the nineteenth-century genius of graphic invective, portrayed him in *Harper's Weekly* as reaching across Lincoln's grave to shake hands with John Wilkes Booth; rumors abounded that if elected, Greeley would urge pensions for veterans of the late Confederate army and federal repayment of the debts of the fallen Confederacy. Businessmen were told that his hard-money philosophy and other misguided policies would destabilize the burgeoning economy; not coincidentally, Grant's campaign chest overflowed with ten times the contributions that Greeley's Liberal Republican and Democratic fusion attracted. Even those like Dana, who endorsed him with patronizing mockery, were heard to speak of him as "Old Chappaquack." The epithets and charges flew so thickly that the famously thin-skinned candidate confided at one point during the ordeal that he was no longer sure whether he was running for the presidency or the penitentiary.

Added to the mountainous abuse was his wife's failing health. She had returned from Europe with their daughters in midsummer and looked a wraith; her teeth were gone, her body was disfigured by virulent rheumatism, and her mental state matched her physical decay. Long an embarrassment to him, Molly dying became an unbearable encumbrance to whatever chance he retained of fulfilling his misplaced ambition for political power. If she had arranged it by design, she could not have more surely repaid him for all those years of neglect. But he was doggedly dutiful at the end, staying up with her through the long painful nights, contracting insomnia, sliding ever deeper into hopelessness.

And yet he forbore magnificently. He did not lash back at his defamers as had been his wont. The *Tribune,* which he had left totally in Reid's hands, was likewise a model of decorum. His speeches were the best he ever delivered, calling on the nation for a "New Departure" from strife and hatred, for a restoration of honesty to government, for the development of the hinterland in a fashion to benefit the deserving families who worked it and not just railroad tycoons, speculators, and grafters like those revealed by Dana's timely exposure in the *Sun* that September of the Crédit Mobilier with its crooked hand deep inside the pockets of the Grant circle.

But the odds against him were too long. Mary Greeley's death at the end of October was an omen of the outcome at the polls the week following. His liberal supporters were disorganized, and too many of them had never warmed to his antique ways. Democrats stayed home massively on election day, especially in the South, where memories of him as an antislavery firebrand would not die. And the outpouring of support for Grant in the financial community and establishment circles everywhere was overwhelming. Grant drew 55.6 percent of the popular vote to Greeley's 43.8 percent.

Mud-spattered, grief-stricken, humiliated, broken in body and spirit, he returned tearfully to the *Tribune* and in a welter of self-reproach asked forgiveness for the foolhardy judgment that had permitted him to seek the nation's highest office. The outcome had no doubt gravely damaged the standing of the paper, so hopelessly out of favor now with the ruling sector of the party and the community. The trustees nevertheless asked him to resume his duties at the paper and voted him full pay, by then $10,000 a year, for the months he had been away campaigning. But it was plain that he could not retake the helm, not in that state and at that age, and guide the ship through the rising gale. Nor were his young replacements eager to yield command to the old captain; they had done well enough without him. Fine to welcome him home in the storm: let him be useful, contributing what gems of wisdom his pen was yet capable of yielding. A cosmetic restoration was not, though, what the founder appeared to have in mind. With eloquent brevity and directness, he announced his return at the head of the *Tribune* editorial page:

> The undersigned resumes his Editorship of the *Tribune* which he relinquished upon embarking in another line of business six months ago. Henceforth, it shall be his endeavor to make this a thoroughly independent journal treating all parties and political movements with judicial fairness and candor, but courting the favor and deprecating the wrath of no one.   HORACE GREELEY
> November 7, 1872

Whether out of pique over this development or in misconceived celebration of it, Greeley's juniors on the paper, in the person of John Hassard but with the knowledge of many including adjutant Whitelaw Reid, inserted in the same issue of the paper a short editorial titled "Crumbs of Comfort." Jocular in intention at a moment when such therapy was badly needed, the squib misfired. It began by noting that for the past dozen years the *Tribune* had been a kind of hiring hall for those "indisposed to work for a living" but nonetheless eager for a place at the federal trough. But since the editor no longer had "any credit with the appointing powers," the piece gaily went on, the office would at last be freed of "blatherskates and political beggars" and of the "red-nosed politicians who had cheated at the caucus and fought at the polls." No longer would the editor have to hasten to Washington to push one cause or quash another. "At last we shall be let alone to mind our own affairs and manage our own newspaper without being called aside every hour to help lazy people whom we don't know and . . . benefit people who don't deserve assistance."

Greeley had not been shown the piece in advance; perhaps Reid feared that his dark mood would not enable him to endorse its sentiment until he encountered it as an accomplished fact in print. But such a reason, or any other, was inadequate to meet the objection that the article read as if Greeley and none other had composed it with transparent bitterness. The *Times* at once denounced the item as unseemly, quoting it at length and remarking:

> And this is the man who, intoxicated with the flattery of the base wretches who had been swarming about him, imagined he had amassed enough "political capital" by his humiliating office brokerage to be elected President of the United States, and who, now that he is contemptuously put aside by the people, appears at the old stand, and hawks his own virtues with unabated vigor. Has he not even yet discovered that the people are not fools, or will nothing shake his faith in that most delusive of all the shams he has publicly supported—himself?

Other papers without the enmity of the *Times* also seized upon the piece to deliver its putative author a final blow, but Whitelaw Reid, who was responsible for the publication of "Crumbs of Comfort" as Greeley had been for Dana's "Forward to Richmond" campaign eleven years prior, would not concede his error. If he had written it himself to drive the distraught Greeley to his wits' end, he could not have succeeded better. Greeley at once wrote out a short, fierce disclaimer, saying he had never seen "Crumbs of Comfort" before it was printed and labeling it "a monstrous fable based on some other experience than that of any editor of this journal," and sent it directly to Tom Rooker in the composing room to make sure it appeared in the next day's issue.

Reid now compounded his inexcusable mistake in permitting the offensive piece to be published in the first place by the unforgivable decision to suppress Greeley's disclaimer. He told friends he feared the staff would mutiny if he ran the old man's overwrought note; if so, the bunch of them were as insensitive as he. What is most difficult to understand about his conduct at this delicate moment is that Reid had behaved with almost exemplary loyalty to Greeley since joining the paper, and unless his deft handling of Greeley's cause at the Liberal Republican convention that spring is to be attributed solely to a wish to have him transferred for good from the editorial rooms of the *Tribune* to the precincts of the White House—or anywhere else on earth—Whitelaw Reid acted at the end in an uncharacteristic, and surely ungrateful, manner to his patron. If Greeley had been unfit to resume the editorship, there would have been more seemly ways to accomplish his early removal.

"I don't go to the office any more," Greeley told a friend, according to the *Sun,* reporting the episode three weeks afterward. "I have no business there." Within ten days, then, he had lost his wife, the presidency, and the *Tribune.* And then his mind; in the terminology of the age, it was diagnosed as "acute mania" and said to be manifested by inflammation of the lining of the brain. He was removed to a private asylum near Pleasantville, not far from his country home, and lingered only briefly. Death came on November 29, 1872, at the age of sixty-one. Grant rode in his funeral procession. The *Tribune* paid his burial expenses.

At the beginning of the year, when his name had begun to be prominently mentioned as a possible presidential nominee in the anti-Grant Republican camp, Greeley was favorably compared with Benjamin Franklin. There were many superficial similarities. Both were poor boys who taught themselves to be printers and writers; both were of a philosophical bent but dwelled primarily on practical virtues and solutions, finding in politics the hope that social man could conduct himself without reference to brute force. Greeley, though, lacked Franklin's intellect; too often he arrived at a righteous position and stuck to it without having delved deeply enough to justify it. This cultural deficiency had the unfortunate effect of making him most stubborn on subjects about which he knew least. Nor was his mind as original as Franklin's or his character as composed.

Yet he merits posterity's esteem for pioneering in the process that turned the newspaper into a powerful form of folk art and creator of popular culture. The *Tribune* as literature transmitted an authentic vision of life in its manifold aspects, rendered in elevated yet not inaccessible language. Its beauty consisted not only in its rhetorical force and stylistic grace but in its ambition: to forge a shared frame of communal reference essential to the nation-building process and, beyond that, to project a more perfect union of lives in which reasonableness and loving-kindness would triumph over ignorance and greed. Greeley wore himself out in the struggle to win dignity for the degraded and instill decency in the hearts of all. For him there was no better way to spend a life, no better end in publishing a newspaper.

James Gordon Bennett, on the other hand, conducted his paper as a form of industrial art; the more amply, efficiently, and divertingly it informed, so would it prosper. If society did not know enough to benefit from the wares he manufactured, surely he was not to blame. His achievement was not less than Greeley's; had he reverenced his fellow man more and mocked him less, Bennett's would have been the more striking life's work.

5

Midas
Touches

Although he had created an institution in the *Tribune* that became less and less a personal manifestation of its founder toward the close of his thirty-one-year rule, Horace Greeley remained the heart and soul of his paper, and its survival without him was by no means certain. Avowed Republicans who composed the core of its readership had abandoned it in sizable numbers when Greeley defied orthodoxy for a final time by opposing the party incumbent in the White House: would even Greeley's most loyal admirers stick with the paper after he was gone? *Tribune* revenues were off, an aura of defeat and death clung to it, and Greeley's heir apparent was publicly charged by the *Sun,* in a detailed account of the "Crumbs of Comfort" episode, with having betrayed him.

Financial control of the paper was dispersed among several dozen stockholders, over whom Greeley, with just six of the one hundred outstanding shares at the time of his death, was by no means dominant. Whitelaw Reid, with the backing of the younger element on the editorial staff, commanded less than one-fifth of the stock, which had a market value of $10,000 per share. But Reid was not the kind of magnetic fellow to attract the financial backing of outsiders unfamiliar with his strengths. He had not been in New York many years and had labored dutifully in the shadow of his conspicuous employer. His credentials as a journalist were solid and his administrative skills formidable, but his was not a shaping talent nor was his contribution indispensable. While he had a number of friends with money, their aggregate wealth was not placed freely at his disposal, and so, lacking strong personal, financial, or political sponsorship, Reid prepared to clear out of the *Tribune* when, within two weeks of Greeley's demise, the old guard designated its choice for his successor: the retiring Vice President of the United States.

On the face of it, Schuyler Colfax had ideal credentials to take up Greeley's mantle. A northern Indiana newspaperman who had pioneered in the creation of the Republican Party, he had long been acquainted with Greeley and frequently corresponded with him. His seven-year term in the House of Representatives was crowned by six years in the Speakership during the tumultuous postwar era, and he had served four years with Grant. Who could be better to return the *Tribune* to the happy center of the Republican mainstream? Samuel Sinclair, the paper's publisher and, with twenty shares, its largest single stockholder, wrote to him in November after Greeley's estrangement and the onset of his illness to ask whether Colfax might be interested in becoming the editor of the *Tribune*. The idea attracted him, but it presented problems as well that would have to be worked out.

Once his name began to circulate as Greeley's possible successor, however, Colfax's not inconsiderable liabilities were also cited. Nicknamed "the Smiler" in knowing political circles, he had a reputation as a somewhat unctuous, waffling personality. As Vice President, he emitted contradictory signals regarding his political future, first indicating that he would retire after Grant's first term and then hinting of his interest in succeeding to the White House—jockeying that caused the President to drop him from the 1872 ticket. In September he was tarred by disclosures linking him, along with many another Grant Republican, to the Crédit Mobilier scandal enriching stockholders in a transcontinental-railroad-building scheme that had bilked the federal treasury. Although he denied any wrongdoing, Colfax was ruined as an active political figure thereafter; he became, willy-nilly, precisely the sort of corruptible figure Greeley's reform campaign had aimed at, and so in terms of both manner and character, his selection would have been a refutation of everything Greeley had been and had stood for. Many of the best journalists in New York, even some who had found Greeley less than totally endearing, said as much in print or out loud.

Still, Sinclair preferred him to Reid as someone likely to shore up the *Tribune*'s tottering position. With the cooperation of such *Tribune* veterans and stockholders as financial editor George Snow, literary editor George Ripley, and mechanical superintendent Thomas Rooker, all of whom may well have disapproved heartily of Reid's behavior toward their fallen leader, Sinclair rounded up controlling interest in the paper and sold it in December to a leading New York industrialist and power in the regular Republican organization, William Orton. A shrewd, energetic, hardheaded lawyer, Orton had made his mark in New York ward politics before serving with distinction as the U.S. Commissioner of Internal Revenue—a performance that won him appointment to the presidency of the fast-rising Western Union Telegraph Company. Orton and other Republican leaders saw an opportunity to regain a valuable trophy for the party in the availability of the *Tribune* as proffered by Sinclair and his group, and fifty-one shares were purchased in his name for $510,000. Tentative agreement was reached with Colfax to take Greeley's post; he was to have a two-year contract at an annual salary of $15,000 along with a one-year option to buy a dozen shares of the paper at the inside price of $100,000. But, at the brink, Colfax hesitated. The appointment would have meant uprooting himself from his home in South Bend, Indiana, and leading a far more hectic style of life, one he was not sure either he or his wife really wanted. And there was the disturbing other matter about which he wrote his wife in connection with Orton: "He wants me to be editor, but I must find out who is the moneyed man behind him. If some railroad king, and he wants it for railroad interests, I will not go in."

Although a successful businessman, Orton had not accumulated the kind of fortune that could easily part with the half million dollars that control of the *Tribune* cost. Newspapers, furthermore, were a risky investment in that era— so different in this regard from the late twentieth century, when papers have commonly become legalized regional monopolies of immense value, despite the rise of television. Besides, the *Tribune*'s competitive position was unattractive; the *Times,* in the afterglow of its Tweed Ring revelations, had surpassed it in circulation, and the *Sun* was ascendant under Dana, as was the *Herald* under Bennett the Younger, basking in the acclaim that his brainstorm of dispatching Stanley to Africa to find Livingstone had won in the form of heightened readership. The reading public was too fickle to justify investing in a newspaper strictly for the return; nor did advertising revenues, at a time when large-scale manufacturing, brand-name products, and department-store merchandising were barely on the horizon, warrant tying up so much capital. Some other motive, even beyond party politics, had to have inspired Orton's investment, as Colfax surmised—someone seeking either self-aggrandizement or self-protection, possibly both. Jay Gould was such a man with precisely such motives at that moment in his guileful career.

All the existing literature agrees that Gould was the hidden figure behind the transfer of *Tribune* ownership after Greeley's death, but nowhere is there any specific corroborative documentation—not in anyone's source notes or in the surviving *Tribune* records or in Gould's papers or in the archives of the Reid family, which held title to the paper for three generations. Typical of the references is the account of Colfax's 1886 biographer, O. J. Hollister, who wrote that when Colfax asked for a three-day postponement of his decision to accept the *Tribune* editorship so that he might discuss the matter fully with his reluctant wife, Orton withdrew the offer; then Hollister adds: "Within a week Mr. Reid had somehow displaced Mr. Orton in Mr. Gould's good graces. Gould found Orton's collateral unsatisfactory; Orton's friends failed to come to his assistance. . . ." No sources are supplied for these statements.

The circumstantial evidence, on the other hand, is considerable. Gould had lately been reviled in the press as a pitiless operator for his killing in the gold market in 1869, with its ruinous effects on many a speculator, and for his still more notorious manipulations of the securities of the Erie Railroad. To have a voice, especially one as venerable and righteous as the *Tribune*'s, on his side to counteract the public outcry against him—and to assist in his future financial scheming—was probably an irresistible lure to Gould. He was in the midst, moreover, of a twenty-year campaign to capture control of Western Union; it is not unlikely that he sought to advance his cause by serving the political purposes of its president, Orton, in the form of a loan to capture the *Tribune* for the New York Republican regulars. Whatever the motives on all sides, the *Tribune* records show only that, in late December, Orton sold control of the paper to Whitelaw Reid. Historians on the subject are unanimous, without providing evidence, that Reid paid for his shares largely if not entirely with money borrowed from Gould. Reid extracted an ironclad five-year contract for his services as editor, but the fact that the financier could have called in his loan at any time is indicated by a remark Reid made in a letter in 1874 replying to a friend who had heard rumors that his controlling interest in the *Tribune* was imperiled. "The 'controlling interest' is locked up in my safe. I have . . . absolute control of it. . . . There is a possibility, of course, of my needing a great deal of money suddenly, someday, to hold on [but] I see no present danger." Reid did not deny the widespread reports of Gould's unseen hand despite ample provocation; Dana's *Sun,* which made him a special object of its editorial sniping, repeatedly called Reid Gould's "stool pigeon" and "hireling" and spoke of the *Tribune* as a "stock jobbing organ." Extensive research into the Gould-Reid relationship yielded the author of this book only two thin but revealing rays of illumination, both involving Whitelaw Reid's papers in the Library of Congress. Among these are several notes from Gould's personal secretary (also financial surrogate and bodyguard), Giovanni P. Morosini, to Reid requesting the *Tribune*'s coverage of events involving his daughter. One, dated June 20, 1879, calls attention to a school commencement and concludes, "As my oldest daughter will play the principal part I would like a true report of the Performance." The following April, Morosini wrote Reid about a concert in which one of his daughters was performing and added:

> I would like to have yourself there and any of your friends you may wish to bring with you. Mr. Gould Mrs. G. and great many [sic] Wall St. people will be there. Please send me word, how many tickets to send & oblige. . . .

The tone of the invitation, an unlikely high point on Reid's social calendar, has the distinct ring of a command performance. The editor's reluctance to comply is testified to by two follow-up notes from Morosini expressing chagrin that he had not heard back from Reid. A yet more telling clue that Reid found his alliance with Gould an unwelcome necessity was provided by Harry W. Baehr, who, in preparing his 1936 book, *The New York Tribune Since the Civil War,* consulted with Whitelaw Reid's official biographer, Royal Cortissoz, the paper's art critic for more than half a century and so close to the Reids as nearly to qualify as a family retainer. After being granted full access to Reid's papers for his fawning two-volume biography, Cortissoz sifted through them on instructions from Reid's widow, and before they were sent to the Library of Congress, he removed all documents relating to (1) Reid's premarital relationship with the feminist lecturer Anna Dickinson and (2) Reid's business relationship to Gould. That relationship ended when Reid married the daughter of one of the wealthiest men in the nation in 1881 and, as what Baehr understood from Cortissoz to have been a condition of the union, the unsavory Gould's claim against Reid's stock was bought out. No mention of these arrangements, of course, was included in Cortissoz's biography; indeed, neither Gould's name nor that of the shamelessly outspoken Miss Dickinson was cited at all. Baehr's creditable book told less than he knew about the subject, but he, too, had had the full cooperation of the Reid family.

Reid, at any rate, made his bargain with the devil, though the *Tribune* had denounced Gould for reprehensible conduct only a few months earlier. If the former proprietor never measured the cost of his words, the new one was obliged to. And it is a fact that Jay Gould's behavior was not criticized in the paper for the nine years he likely held a lien upon its controlling interest. Greeley's brand of fearless advocacy and disinterested denunciation had been fatally compromised to advance his successor's ambition.

Having won his prize, Reid moved boldly to protect it. Almost his first step was to proceed with long-held plans to build a new home befitting the *Tribune*'s national reputation. What better way to demonstrate its permanence and allay rumors of its shaky condition than to put up the biggest building in New York? He hired Richard Morris Hunt, perhaps the leading architect in the nation, to design it on the same site as the old building while the staff moved to rented quarters nearby for the two years that the construction consumed. When it was done, the *Tribune* had the fanciest home of any newspaper in America. Its Florentine campanile of a tower soared 260 feet above City Hall Park; only the spire of Trinity Church at the western end of Wall Street rose higher. A morale-boosting landmark, it also proved a good investment; rentals in the centrally located structure helped quickly liquidate the mortgage and thereafter supplemented the paper's modest profits. Most appealing of all from the standpoint of staff members was the beer saloon located in the basement, where a decent meal could be procured. Plainly the *Tribune*'s advocacy of prohibition was at an end.

The new quarters, however, did not dispel the leisurely, literary spirit among the companionable editorial staff, most of which remained after Reid's takeover. He took pains, though, to clean up the administrative mess that the departed Samuel Sinclair had left behind and get the business side running more smoothly. New, faster presses allowed the forms to remain open until three in the morning to accommodate late-breaking news. Among the distinguished new correspondents were Henry James, writing from Paris; William Dean Howells, contributing from Boston; and Bret Harte, from here and there. The *Tribune* without its founder was alive and well enough to ride out the economic storms that blew in 1873 and reduced it to an only marginally profitable operation for several years thereafter. To cut costs, Reid imposed salary reductions, ranging from 5 percent on incomes of $1,000 or under to 25 percent on those of $6,500 or more, rather than fire anyone. He was less beneficent where his production department was concerned. Claiming that the introduction of larger type and more generous spacing had made the compositor's job less onerous, Reid demanded that his printers accept a pay cut amounting to 25 percent, well below union scale, and desist from the practice of setting "bogus," make-work that duplicated material the paper received already set from composing rooms at other papers. Resentful of the haughty manner of the new proprietor, so different from the founder, who had been a printer himself, the *Tribune* shop walked out and was replaced by a scab crew pledged to a no-strike contract. Reid saved the paper perhaps 20 percent on its composition payroll but won it fifteen years of labor strife that effectively demolished its reputation as a champion of the workingman.

The resurrection of its all but vanished strength within the Republican Party coincided with the dark dealings behind the disputed presidential election in 1876 of Rutherford B. Hayes, Reid's fellow Ohioan, who ran on a Greeleyesque platform of amnesty for the South and civil service reform. Although the *Tribune* had endorsed his opponent, the progressive and candid Democrat Samuel J. Tilden, in his successful contest for governor of New York two years earlier, thereby further distancing the paper from the party it had helped establish, Reid found Hayes an acceptable presidential candidate and bid for reconciliation by supporting him. Hayes proved responsive to the *Tribune*'s Cabinet suggestions and appeared to be otherwise justifying Reid's faith in him. Still, he held office despite Tilden's victory in the popular vote and amid continuing reports of attempted bribery for the electoral votes that had given him the presidency. Tilden waited in the wings, a ceaseless claimant to the title allegedly filched from him, and cast a shadow across the Hayes administration. The *Tribune* lifted that shadow. Its feat was the result of one of the finest pieces of detective work in the annals of American investigative journalism.

Late in 1877, the Democratic-controlled House appointed a committee to get to the bottom of the rumors surrounding the Hayes election. Among the materials subpoenaed were hundreds of coded telegrams to and from Tilden's residence at 15 Gramercy Park in New York, where his nephew purportedly operated out of a basement office in December 1876, trying to negotiate the purchase of votes of contested electors in Oregon, Florida, and South Carolina. The code, in a complex double cipher, was beyond the powers of the House committee members, who directed that the documents be returned to Western Union. Through the intercession of Republican Representatives, Hayes administration members, and party officials, nearly six hundred of the messages found their way to the *Tribune* tower, where Reid set two of his cleverest men to translating the gibberish. It proved a formidable challenge.

The messages seemed completely disjointed, as if the words had been shaken in a bag, drawn out blindly, and set down as chance dictated. When patience and diligence were applied to the reconstruction of even the shorter messages, several alternatives seemed to make grammatical sense but were still meaningless because of too many blind proper nouns that were obviously code names. Key words or terms like "Republican," "Democrat," "returning board," or "elector" never appeared nor did any numbers, although there were many names of foreign countries and cities and American rivers. The *Tribune* cryptographers attacked the puzzle separately through the summer of 1878, financial writer William M. Grosvenor working at his home in Englewood, New Jersey, and editorial writer–music critic John Hassard at his city home on Eighteenth Street, so their approaches would not be influenced by each other.

Vacationing that August at Saratoga, Reid ran into Tilden, advised him that the paper had in its possession all the coded telegrams that had gone between his home and Florida, and laughingly asked him to provide the key since his staff detectives could not make head or tail of them. Tilden smiled—"blushed, innocent as a baby," Reid later wrote of the incident—and passed on. But the next day he sought Reid out and declared fervently that he had never received the coded messages, did not believe they had been delivered to his house, and up to that very moment had never laid eyes on a single one of them.

But someone working in his interest knew all about them, and the key to unlocking their meaning began to turn when the *Tribune* investigators finally hit upon the fact that all the messages, which for the most part contained twenty to fifty words, though some ran to more than a hundred, were of a word length divisible by five. That could not be an accident. In seeking the proper transposition, Grosvenor and Hassard assumed that the keys would vary with the length of the message. They then set down a number of messages of the same length in a grid, listing the text of each vertically in a separate column in its original nonsense word order, and began to look for patterns of meaning that applied uniformly across the board. Their only systematic method was an inductive one; they fit together little groups of words, trying every conceivable combination of two or three and then verifying the experiment by comparing the grouping with words in the corresponding position in the other columns. Making sense of even the smallest groups when so many of the words had obviously coded meanings would have been impossible without the help of historical knowledge obtained from newspapers published in the state capitals at the time official boards met to resolve conflicts over which electors ought to be certified. Thus, if the decoders knew from their reading of the Tallahassee newspaper that the Florida canvassing board had met the same day as the one on which a message was sent containing the dispersed words "adjourned," "until," and "tomorrow," and the only plausible subject for the grouping was the coded word "London," they concluded with some confidence that "London" meant "the state canvassing board." And the more fragments that were fitted together, the easier it became to figure out where the remaining words ought to go—and the easier in context to unpuzzle the coded words. Some words, though, after much agonizing trial and error, still seemed to elude meaning when placed in their proper sequence until the *Tribune* men observed that they all fell at the end of the messages and were "nulls," words that in fact had no meaning and were included just to pad out the telegram so its length would be divisible by five. Keys were thus uncovered for messages of ten, fifteen, twenty, twenty-five, and thirty words; longer messages were decipherable by applying shorter sequences to their components (e.g., forty-word messages made sense when the key for the sequence of twenty-word messages was applied to each half). To make matters more confusing, the key was sometimes reversed for messages of the same length, but that trick, too, was in time figured out, and in context the code names presented little difficulty: "Russia" was Tilden, "Greece" was Hayes, "Ithaca" meant Democrats, and "Havana," Republicans.

The whole damning scheme was spelled out in the October 7, 1878, issue of the *Tribune* under an exceedingly rare two-column heading, "THE CAPTURED CIPHER TELEGRAMS." The detective work, explained with clarity and expanded upon with illustrations at every point, was utterly convincing. Subsequent issues carried the texts of the messages, which formed so powerful an indictment that the congressional committee which had abandoned its investigation of the alleged scandal was reconvened and the principal players, including Tilden's nephew, were summoned and confronted with the *Tribune* findings. Although they all argued for Tilden's ignorance of their efforts on his behalf, they also conceded the accuracy of the decodings, and the game was clearly up.

As a piece of journalistic ingenuity, the Tilden disclosures showed even more enterprise than the *Times* had seven years earlier in its Tweed Ring exposure, the source of which simply marched through the front door with the incriminating data. The *Tribune* investigation was hardly disinterested, however; it is doubtful that so much effort would have been expended if the pinching shoe had been found on the other foot. By thus humiliating the Democrats and displaying them in acts every bit as venal as those that had plagued the Grant administration, the *Tribune* had helped mightily to exorcise lingering Republican guilt. Whitelaw Reid was welcomed into the highest party councils now as Greeley had never been, and the *Tribune*'s power as a party organ—and therefore as a national institution—was in large part restored.

By decade's end, Reid was comfortable with his own and his newspaper's standing. He launched a Sunday edition of the *Tribune* in 1879, a sixteen-page assortment of news, features, and literary material that helped compensate for the sagging revenues of the regular weekly edition. It was a sign of the paper's orthodoxy, not to say piety, that it had been the last of the major New York papers to issue a Sunday edition. Its circulation, stabilized at about 30,000, gradually edged its way up, but the *Tribune* lagged well behind all the other important papers in town except the *Post.* Still, Reid was unconcerned. His paper was earning over $100,000 a year, and with the establishment of the Sunday edition, its format and news presentation were fixed in a mold that would not change perceptibly for the next twenty years. Its stubborn editorial and typographical conservatism Reid wore as a badge of honor. The next major innovation in the field, he declared in an 1879 speech before the Editorial Associations of New York and Ohio, would be "the story better told; better brains employed in the telling." A renewal of scandal-mongering by his gener-ally estimable competitors was unthinkable, he said, for "there is not an Editor in New York who does not know that fortune that awaits the man there who is willing to make a daily paper as disreputable and vile as a hundred and fifty thousand readers would be willing to buy." No, the masses would not be so pandered to. His own program was to issue an ever more intelligently written paper for a like-minded readership. His own image reflected the gravity of this intention. An introverted bachelor of forty-two, wedded only to his paper, manners polished to a stiffness that repulsed casual advance toward him, he had a decided fragility to his appearance. The hair was still long, though brushed back now, but the forehead was higher, the cheekbones more prominent, only the hint of an imperial beard anchoring the bottom of the face, and the shoulders were inclined to droop slightly in a way that made him look doubly careworn at moments of fatigue. In fact, though, he was in his vigorous prime, and the ascent to the White House of his old and good Ohio friend James A. Garfield made him, for a short season, among the most influential of his countrymen. It was at this timely juncture that Reid solidified his position professionally, socially, and politically by marrying into one of the great American fortunes.

Elisabeth Mills, whom he met at her family's 6,000-acre fiefdom outside San Francisco, was twenty years younger than Reid. No beauty, she was generously described as possessing "a modest demeanor" but notable charm, intelligence, and character—no doubt important considerations to the *Tribune*'s editor-owner, who was said to have been attracted to her almost at once. He could hardly have been repelled, however, by the achievements of her father, Darius Ogden Mills. With the help of relatives, Mills had built a modest career and solid credit rating at a small Buffalo bank, but when gold was discovered in Califor-nia, an uncharacteristic boldness seized him, and he made his way west by an arduous journey via Panama. Selling supplies to the gold-seekers, he made $40,000 within a year, returned east for more capital and better supply lines, then went back to Sacramento and became, in the decade between 1850 and 1860, the most successful banker in the state. In passing, he invested in the Southern Pacific Railroad and the mining operation popularly known as the Comstock Lode. In time, he opened an investment house in New York, and his life and business operations thereafter straddled both coasts. At his death in 1910, his fortune was estimated at between fifty and sixty million dollars. Beyond the vastness of this accumulation, D. O. Mills's career was distinguished by several exceedingly attractive traits. For one thing, in the robber-baron age he made his money honestly and not at the expense of others. He acted decisively with judgment and foresight so unerring as to approach genius. For a man of such accomplishments, furthermore, he had an extraordinarily subdued manner about him. With the gentleness and refinement of a scholar, he chose his words carefully and, while he had strong, well-considered opinions on many subjects, did not feel duty-bound to impress them on the world. His habitual somber dress, consisting of a black sack suit and high flat derby that exaggerated his six-foot height, was brightened only by a pearl pin fixed to his black four-in-hand. Finally, he was a generous early donor to such institutions as the University of California, the Metropolitan Museum of Art, and the New York Botanical Gardens, and he was the imaginative founding benefactor of a training school for male nurses and a chain of hotels for indigent men. And his daughter Lizzie was the light of his life.

It was therefore with some misgivings that he heard Whitelaw Reid, after a short courtship carried on largely by a chaste transcontinental correspondence, ask for his daughter's hand. Mills was but twelve years older than the suitor. Reid's impeccable courtliness and high rank in his field no doubt went far to exempt him from the category of fortune hunter, but there was the unseemly connection with Gould, precisely the kind of vicious manipulator Mills loathed, that would have to be attended to if Reid was to be admitted to the family. And so it was done. The wedding was held at the Mills home on Fifth Avenue in April 1881, and the longevity of the *Tribune* was thus assured. But in their very availability to it, the Mills millions turned the paper into a hereditary possession to be sustained as a public duty rather than developed as a profit-making opportunity. In that loss of dynamism were planted the seeds of its doom.

II

As Whitelaw Reid began to settle into his new life of luxury and comfort and his newspaper into its freshly oiled groove of respectability, only *The New York Times* among his chief rivals trudged through the closing decades of the nineteenth century at so stolid a pace. Under Henry Raymond's successor, George Jones, a businessman turned publisher with little transfusion of printer's ink in the process, the *Times* remained civic-spirited, reliable, and colorless. A grave-looking gent with gold-rimmed spectacles and a lush beard, Jones was a ponderous man running a ponderous paper.

Not so Charles Dana and James Gordon Bennett the Younger. For fifteen years their two papers warred for supremacy in circulation and editorial brilliance among the New York dailies. But as journalists, the two could not really be spoken of in the same breath.

With Greeley, Raymond, and the elder Bennett in their graves, Dana had clear claim at being the most accomplished journalist in the nation. When he took over the *Sun* in 1868, its circulation was around 40,000; ten years later, it was nearly 100,000 higher and in seesaw rivalry with the *Herald* for the lead among major New York papers. In a way the *Sun* was still the same small four-page sheet it had always been, but Dana aimed at enticing readers into consuming every word of it. A driving taskmaster who regularly logged a seventy-two-hour workweek, a perfectionist grammarian who was said to have dismissed a man for writing "None are," he insisted that every piece, whether on crime or society scandal or a leading event of the day, be carried off with zest. To be amusing whenever possible was highly desirable; to be interesting always was essential. News to Dana was no mere orderly recital of election results, legislative sessions, gyrating stock prices, and bodily dismemberments. Almost anything in life could be fascinating grist for his press: why a child sat crying on the curb, exactly how much a presidential candidate weighed, the idiosyncrasies of the City Hall clock, the seamy reasons behind a vendetta in Mulberry Bend. News was anything new: the latest slang expression or style of whiskers, a just developed strain of apple, a strange four-master in the harbor. This freshness of outlook, tuned to the unexamined in what was familiar in life and to the delight or shock in what was unexpected, was lastingly expressed by Dana's city editor, John B. Bogart, who remarked apropos the *Sun*'s philosophy, "Whan a dog bites a man, that is not news, because it happens so often. But if a man bites a dog, that is news." What the *Sun* lacked was bulk in its news diet and seriousness and consistency in its editorial positions. As he aged, Dana deepened into disillusion, and his sardonic pen too often dabbled in the frivolous when confronting profound issues; his influence waned accordingly. But he was almost never dull.

By remaining comprehensive as well as lively, the *Herald* sustained its lead in the industrious gathering and brisk presentation of the news. And under the lash of its founder's son and namesake, it grew richer than it had ever been as rising national prosperity swelled its revenues, especially from advertising. Whether the *Herald* prospered to the extent it did—one million dollars in profits in good years, of which there were many, in the last quarter of the century—because of or despite its temperamentally volatile owner is arguable.

Hovered over in three languages by an adoration of nursemaids, isolated from others his age and privately taught, indulged in every whim, James Gordon Bennett, Jr., grew into a swaggering, precociously dissolute lout who rarely stifled an impulse. He drank, wenched, yachted, and played polo with spectacular gusto, and when, late at night, he took it into his pickled brain to bound into the nearest Bennett coach and drive the team through the dark at a frothing pace, careening wildly around corners, thundering over bridges, bowling aside anything in his way, stripping off his clothing as the wayward vehicle flew along and caterwauling at the moon, no one afterward told him to behave.

Unlike his father, young James proved irresistible to proper New York society. As high-spirited as the *pater* was glum, with a fluency in French that made him an international sophisticate, a dashing sportsman who had been admitted to the New York Yacht Club at sixteen, younger than any member before him, Jimmy Bennett would serve as Exhibit A in any treatise on the fluidity of the American caste system: in a single generation the central figure of the family was lifted from pariah to grandee. The lad's looks and bearing helped considerably. Tall and straight-backed, with chilly blue eyes and a hussar's tawny, upturned mustache to light his long, bony face, he dressed elegantly, talked bawdily, and marched about with a hauteur that took the finest drawing rooms of the city by storm.

Handed the *Herald* at twenty-six without having been trained for the task, relying presumably on genetic equipment and his father's off-the-premises but nearby presence to monitor his excesses and deficiencies, he ruled the paper more attentively than anyone had supposed possible—and more was the pity. Modern psychology would doubtless have analyzed his bizarre managerial technique as a form of perverse compensation for a well-concealed inferiority complex common in those who are given a position of high responsibility they have in no way earned. Whatever the nature of his disorder, the new lord of the *Herald* was an aloof autocrat who ruled by caprice and fear. "I want you fellows to remember," he once told a group of his executives, "that I am the only reader of this paper. I am the only one to be pleased. If I want it to be turned upside down, it must be turned upside down. I want one feature article a day. If I say the feature is to be black beetles, black beetles it's going to be." His arbitrariness was matched only by his self-indulgence. Though he had no talent as a writer, he wrote when it pleased him to—editorials, usually, that he ordered set in larger-than-usual type and importantly leaded out. When unduly exhilarated or in his cups—the two conditions were generally simultaneous—he would appear in the office after dinner, likely as not in formal attire and trailing a retinue, and make alterations that tickled him but grieved the craftsmen who were his hirelings. One night he ordered up the editorial proofs and scrawled in the sentence "This is the last dying kick of the Tammany anaconda!"—his notion of a trenchant political thrust. It was pointed out to him politely that anacondas have never been known to kick. "That's the fun of it," said Bennett. "I want it in, and I'll have it in."

"Suppose," suggested Joseph Ignatius Constantine Clarke, the night editor, "you say 'squirm'?"

"Hmm," pondered the potentate. "Squirm, squirm. Yes, squirm is disagreeable, but I want to give Tammany a kick, so I'll stick to 'kick.' " And he followed the proof to the composing room to be sure the change was made.

Fearful of a palace revolution at any moment, he oversaw the staff in a manner ideally calculated to precipitate one. Spies were installed in all departments, evaluation reports of one's colleagues were regularly required, and the more nearly indispensable a man was said to be, the more likely Bennett was to fire or demote him. Loyalty was tested by ordeal; valuable personnel might at any time be sent halfway around the world on a fool's errand and expected to comply happily. "I can hire all the brains I need for twenty-five dollars a week," he said with characteristic contempt for the men who kept his pockets lined with gold. His ingratitude for the feats of virtuosity performed by *Herald* staff members knew no bounds. The classic instance was his attitude toward Henry Stanley, who had undergone lengthy and excruciating agonies and demonstrated undiluted heroism in his trek through remotest Africa to find Livingstone—an event that almost by itself had restored the *Herald*'s flagging reputation. When Stanley was jealously sniped at for his bastard birth, casual soldiering in the Civil War, and alleged counterfeiting of documents that proved his claims to have met and been befriended by the British missionary, Bennett backed him inconstantly, then less and less, carping all the while that it was he who had thought up the idea in the first place, he who had sponsored the expedition, he who deserved credit and praise for it and received little of either. Yet he fully recognized the promotional value of the feat and funded the reporter-explorer's return to Africa, where Stanley won new glory by crossing the continent from east to west, tracing the Congo River from source to mouth, and on the way christening the largest peak in view Mount Gordon Bennett. More molehill than mountain, the current owner of the name repaid the gesture by raging against Stanley even as his legend grew. Bennett's obsessive envy crested twenty years after the Livingstone adventure when rumor reached him that Stanley was mistreating his wife, daughter of a politically prominent Briton, and he sent his ace correspondent to investigate at a Tyrolean resort where the couple was vacationing. Believing the *Herald* man's arrival to be a step by Bennett toward long-overdue reconciliation, Stanley waxed expansive for several days in an effort to provide the reporter with ample material for his presumed interview piece. "Mr. Stanley," the poor reporter burst out at last, "do you beat your wife?"

"My God," said the explorer, comprehension chasing rage from his burning dark eyes, "I used to have to do that myself."

For all his pride, then, the younger Bennett was too small a man to appreciate the distinction between patron and artist, too egomaniacal an impresario to yield top billing to his acts.

Even so, his paper grew in fame and fortune. For Bennett was also capable of responsible behavior, such as contributing to the regular post-luncheon editorial conference to plan the next day's paper. At its best under him, the *Herald* could mount such prodigious performances as its scoop on the Custer massacre of 1876 scored by its Dakota Territory correspondents, who filed 50,000 words in a twenty-four-hour period at a cost of $3,000. When hot news was involved, money was no object to Bennett; no other paper spent so freely for the commodity basic to the trade. At its worst under Bennett, the *Herald* could foist on the public an issue like the one of Monday, November 9, 1874, probably inspired by a particularly slow news Sunday; the entire front page was filled with a saga headed:

AWFUL CALAMITY

———

The Wild Animals Broken Loose from Central Park.

———

Terrible Scenes of Mutilation.

———

A Shocking Sabbath Carnival of Death.

———

Awful Combats Between the Beasts and the Citizens.

———

The Killed and Wounded.

Complete with the names and species of the casualties, both man and beast, the story did not reveal until the end that it was totally invented to show how much havoc could be wrought among city dwellers if a zookeeper got careless. It made for gripping prose, but the stunt, which Bennett neither invented nor objected to, could only have undermined the public confidence in journalism as an honorable profession.

Bennett's own honor was irretrievably lost on New Year's Eve of 1876 when, an aging bachelor of thirty-four, he attended a party at the Manhattan home of his fiancée's parents. His notion of high jinks had previously strained society's tolerance, as on the day he rode one of his polo ponies into the reading room at the Newport Casino; on this particular festive evening he exceeded the limits of permissible buffoonery by relieving himself—either in the fireplace or the grand piano, accounts differ—in the presence of mixed company. Bennett was ushered unceremoniously out the front door, his fiancée called off their engagement, and a few days later, upon leaving the Union Club, Bennett was horse-whipped by the young lady's brother until the snow ran red with his blood. Male socialites did not entirely snub him, but he was not invited thereafter to gatherings attended by women; the editor-owner of the world's most profitable newspaper was, in the eyes of decent society, not yet housebroken. Bennett soon packed up and returned to Paris, where he had been raised, and stayed there more than forty years: the most infamous American expatriate in the French capital. He had been in residence there ten years when his high life went a bit stale, so he started up a Paris edition of his New York paper—a perfectly absurd notion to amuse a self-indulgent man; it is still there nearly a century later.

In exile, Bennett used the *Herald*'s profits to live like royalty. In addition to his father's old house and his own place in New York, he maintained more or less sumptuous residences in Paris, Versailles, the Riviera, and Scotland (for hunting and communing with ancestral ghosts) and plied the Mediterranean on veritable floating palaces, attended by a court of titled has-beens and sycophantic poseurs. Out of sight, though, Bennett was never out of mind at the *Herald.*

A ranking official was on duty at the paper twenty-four hours a day to receive any messages that might be sent by the Commodore, as Bennett now styled himself in honor of his transatlantic exploits as a yachtsman. All the New York papers were sent to him regularly, and he kept the cable humming with instructions and complaints. Editors might be summoned to him on the first available boat, and by the time they showed up, Bennett had often as not forgotten the pretext for the summons.

Yet in his own terrifying way, he cared deeply about the paper. When he named Edward T. Flynn managing editor in 1882, Bennett wrote a detailed letter of instructions to the appointee, who had done well for him at the *Telegram,* the *Herald*'s raffish younger sibling. He wanted the local part of the paper to be "enterprising, lively and thoroughly condensed," Bennett ordered, and pains should be taken with the Wall Street coverage so as "not to let the paper be used either by the writers themselves or by outsiders who may influence them for this purpose." A splinter off the old block. Throughout the paper he wanted "all the points of the day's news without the verbiage," then added:

> . . . Never, however, spare expense or space when the news justifies it. Whenever there is an important piece of news I want the *Herald* to have the fullest and best account of it. Another point which I think you understand is letting a thing drop the moment public interest in it begins to flag. The instant you see a sensation is dead drop it and start in on something new.

And when he said black beetles, black beetles it still had to be. To stress the point, he would cross the ocean once a year, career through the office, and clean house in his hit-or-miss fashion.

III

In the fall of 1883 a New York clergyman named Kemlo slashed his wife to death, cut his own throat, and, as if to take no chances that he had bungled the job, leaped to his doom from their fourth-floor apartment. The gory details and the murderer's profession guaranteed prominent play of the story in the city's press, but one paper gave its coverage a graphic twist that cried out for more attention than the others. The *World,* bought the previous May by a gangling thirty-seven-year-old newcomer from St. Louis with a bulbous head and poor eyesight, accompanied its account with a drawing of the Kemlo apartment and labeled it with letters that, when explained by the caption, left little to the imagination: "A – Door stained with blood; B – Window stained with blood from which Kemlo jumped; C – Bed covered with blood; D – Table set and covered with blood; E – Chair in which Mrs. Kemlo sat; F – Sink in which the knife was found; G – Pool of blood."

Bloody doings had never been splashed so gruesomely across the pages of any major New York paper the way they had been since Joseph Pulitzer's takeover that spring of the moribund *World.* When a dozen people were trampled to death on the pedestrian causeway of the just opened Brooklyn Bridge a few weeks after he took charge of the paper, Pulitzer headlined the tragedy "BAPTIZED IN BLOOD." His headlines were particularly effective at celebrating the ghastly; among other early gems were "A FIEND IN HUMAN FORM" to describe the arraignment of a man charged with sexually molesting a young girl, "A MOTHER'S AWFUL CRIME" to cover a case of infanticide, "SCREAMING FOR MERCY" to depict how one resisting prisoner went to the gallows, and:

> BUNGLED BY THE HANGMAN
> ALEXANDER JEFFERSON, THE NEGRO,
> SLOWLY TORTURED TO DEATH
>
> He Struggled While His Body Swings, Tears the
> Black Cap from His Face, and Stretched Out
> His Arms Pleadingly to the People—Sheriff
> Stegman Faints in the Prison.

Such vulgar but compelling exploitation of humanity at its vilest was a wide departure from the original fare of the *World,* established in 1860 as the most moralistic of the city dailies. Funded by ardent churchgoers, it omitted news of scandal, lewd crime, the theater (and theatrical advertising), and other degenerate subjects. Prosperity, alas, did not follow, even after merger with the once imposing *Courier and Enquirer.* Only when it fell into the hands of Democratic politicians and financiers and under the editorship of the scholarly, adroit former Boston newspaperman Manton Marble did the *World* rise to fifth place in sales. Very well edited, it made money but suffered from the swift surge of the *Sun* under Dana, and when Marble was implicated in the shady plot to reclaim Tilden's stolen presidency, he got out of journalism. The *World* passed for three years to a railroad tycoon and three more in the grip of the egregious Jay Gould, who used it shamelessly to promote his exercises in corporate piracy. By 1883, the *World* was back in the red, and Gould unloaded it with pleasure to the odd-looking Mr. Pulitzer, a Hungarian-born Jew who paid $346,000 for a paper whose circulation had fallen to 11,000. Not a promising prospect, particularly in light of the competitive situation.

But Joseph Pulitzer had come equipped with more ambition than newlywed Reid of the *Tribune,* more flair than Jones of the bland *Times,* more financial acumen than Dana of the *Sun,* and far more constructive leadership than the absentee owner of the front-running *Herald.* Pulitzer had been a study in directed energy since he got off the boat in Boston in time to serve as a teenage enlistee in the Union cavalry for the last year of the war. In St. Louis, with its large German-speaking community, he worked as a common laborer while learning English, then turned to journalism with the city's ranking German-language paper, which in time he bought. An ardent supporter of Greeley in the 1872 election, he was so distressed by the collapse of the Liberal Republican cause that he switched to the Democratic banner, became a lawyer, served as a reformist member of the lower house in the Missouri legislature, and in 1878 put together two foundering St. Louis papers and quickly built them into the leading entry in the evening field. The *Post-Dispatch* made its mark by flaying grafters, tax-evaders, and a whole bestiary of other civic vermin. But Pulitzer was not so swept up in his work in the nation's heartland that he failed to note the immigrant masses that had begun to pour into America through the portal of New York. In them he saw an opportunity unpursued by the existing papers.

But unlike a latter-day Horace Greeley, who believed the downtrodden might all rise to prosperity and fulfillment if only they would bestir themselves, Joseph Pulitzer saw that in an increasingly crowded and combative industrial society, class conflict was a stark fact of life; Greeley's wishful evasions, a feckless dream. Pulitzer chose his side, and it was with the poor immigrant, the sorely used workingman, the brutally crowded tenement dweller. The plight of the poor was news, and the *World* alone told what life among them was like. It may not have made for pretty reading, but it was gripping when written up in simple, even slangy, highly graphic language so that the marginally literate had no problem absorbing it. In crusading against the conditions of degradation—typical pieces bore headings like "Poverty's Christmas" and "Lines of Little Hearses"—Pulitzer believed injustice would shrivel only under the burning light of publicity. His newspaper did not by any means ignore activities of the well-off, but they were amply covered elsewhere, particularly by the *Herald*; in placing its stress on the lower end of the economic scale, the *World* served to dramatize the common humanity of the city's disparate elements who had few other meeting grounds. In seeking to inspire and uplift the dispossessed through his highminded editorial page, he took after the rich as no one had before him. Luxuries, inheritances, and incomes above $10,000 should be taxed, he argued; large corporations ought to be stripped of their oppressive privileges, and the tariff was justifiable only as a revenue measure and not as a cloak for exploitive practices by native industrialists. The very charities the *World* sponsored underscored its social purpose: coal for the needy in winter, ice in the summer—and a pedestal for the great green goddess of freedom sent over by France and raised in the harbor largely on the mountain of pennies Pulitzer gathered by appeal to the least affluent of the city's liberty-lovers: his readers.

To lure a readership of the scale he had envisioned, Pulitzer enlisted reporters with skills specifically tailored to his market. He wanted both terseness and strong descriptive powers, humor where appropriate and originality that was not obscure, and the most assiduously pursued level of accuracy in the gathering of facts. Above all, he sought a quality of compassion in his writers that contrasted sharply with the sardonic or downright cynical styles that had become the hallmark of the *Sun* and *Herald* sophisticates; the *World* wanted men who had not lost the capacity to be shocked and saddened by life's unending travail. If, as a result, their copy often bordered on, or even swam in, sentiment, Pulitzer did not object. His aim was to move the masses. He introduced bigger headlines, larger body type, and lavish use of drawings, diagrams, and cartoons to put his message across. And he paid well for talent, better than his rivals.

Beyond shock and pathos, Pulitzer supplied the common man—and especially the common woman—with the basic data needed for getting along, and ahead, in the urban jungle. Most evident was the sort of material that twentieth-century newspaper people have come to call service copy; on the *World*'s women's page, the reader received abundant advice about beauty and hygiene, cooking and nutrition, style and taste, health care and etiquette. Sports coverage was institutionalized by the *World,* which paid particular attention to boxing and baseball, with their mass followings. The Sunday paper was filled with light, heavily illustrated material implicitly instructive in urban mores. In short, the *World* was performing at two cents a copy a critical acculturating function for an overflowing polyglot population that had turned New York into the most dynamic, diverse, and socially complex metropolis on earth.

Within a year and a half of his purchase, Pulitzer had driven the circulation of the *World* past the *Herald*'s. Before a decade was out, the combined readership of the morning edition and the *Evening World,* which Pulitzer inaugurated in 1887, was nearly 350,000, the largest in the United States. Its competitors cut their selling price, to little avail. And the advertising came flooding in to Pulitzer, who offered a mass marketplace at low rates to the new department stores and brand-name producers reaching across the old class lines for the consumer dollar. Bennett fulminated as Pulitzer seized the *Herald*'s long-dominant lead in classified advertising, and when the newcomer charged the large shopping emporiums no more for the inclusion of illustrative material in their display ads, Bennett perversely stuck to his antiquated rules against such eye-appealing, customer-aiding advances; only type could be used in *Herald* ads, and column rules were not to be dispensed with, on the ground that such gross and lavish huckstering would overwhelm the presentation of the news and be unfair to smaller, old-line merchants. Whatever merit the *Herald* policy contained ignored the incontestable fact that advertising itself now brought highly useful news to readers anxious to stretch their hard-earned dollars.

In 1890, a mere seven years after his arrival in New York, Pulitzer erected a sixteen-story, 310-foot, bronze-domed home for the *World,* topping the *Tribune*'s tall tower and every other building in town. Reid may have preferred to put out a newspaper by brainy writers for likeminded readers, but Pulitzer, reaching for their hearts and souls—and, along the way, their pocketbooks— had left the *Tribune* and every other paper in New York trailing in the dust.

IV

Tempting as it was to his enemies, to attribute the *Tribune*'s steadily rightward political drift during the final decades of the nineteenth century to Whitelaw Reid's marriage into great wealth and, with it, access to the highest rungs of society would be to understate the ample evidence of his original fidelity to the propertied classes. Making money interested him far more than it had Greeley; Reid's preference for rugged individualism left him relatively little compassion for those locked into society's lower levels.

On casual inspection, the brand of conservatism Reid's *Tribune* began to espouse was unexceptionable. Large combinations of either capital or labor were equally inimical to the commonweal, the paper avowed. The worker should be free to bargain for his services as he saw fit. The creditor must not be robbed of his due by proponents of an inflationary greenback monetary policy; hard money was the only good money. But with the industrial revolution already almost a century old, such views came to be increasingly and unmistakably understood as repressive toward those of limited skills, means, and incentive. Industrial cartels had a power to fix prices immeasurably more antisocial than unions had to fix wages. The solitary worker could not meet on equal footing with his employer in a steadily expanding labor market. Without an adequately growing money supply, aspiring entrepreneurs could not obtain credit to challenge established firms. The impact of Reid's value system was fully revealed by his paper's response to the protests surrounding the rate and wage policies of the nation's railroad giants. When workers struck massively in 1877, the *Tribune* was among those who most loudly asserted that the strikers should be put down by governmental force. And when Western farmers united in the Grange movement to avoid extortionate freight rates, the *Tribune* denounced the effort as punitive to the railroads' profits, which it said were needed to pay their workers a decent wage.

Reid's antipathy toward labor was almost certainly hardened by his own problems with the *Tribune*'s printers. After he had slashed wages and replaced the union crew in 1877, an uneasy peace prevailed in the shop until late in 1883, when the typographers, despite their pledge not to strike, grew disgusted by reports of the paper's much-improved profit picture and their own depressed wage scale. On top of that there was rankling displeasure over the tyrannizing practices of the shop foreman, W. P. Thompson, accused of arbitrarily imposing penalties, loan-sharking, and generally making the printers' lives miserable. The paper was again struck. Scabs were harder to round up this time, and under competitive pressure Thompson conceded that a union shop could be reinstalled at union scale provided he otherwise had free rein over the shop, typesetting machines could be installed without interference, and the one-year agreement could be severed by either side with thirty days' notice. Reid, out of town at the time, apparently balked at the imposition of the union shop, but Thompson persuaded him not to upset the pact. The peace was short-lived. Thompson claimed the union sent him inferior workers and sabotaged his shop; the union claimed Thompson was waiting to abrogate the contract only until he had assembled a new scab work force. At any rate, the police were called and the *Tribune* printers were given the choice of accepting a cut in wages or leaving on the spot—a plain enough violation of the thirty-day notice requirement. Fifty-nine of the sixty-four printers left, and the full fury of the union fell upon Reid.

The boycott of the *Tribune,* thoroughly organized and earnestly pressed home, lasted eight years. The union targeted the paper as "the most pronounced opponent of the workingmen of America" and called upon subscribers, newsdealers, and advertisers to have nothing further to do with it. In January 1884, the first issue of a union weekly called *The Boycotter* was published; it continued for years, carrying news of printers' activities but primarily attacking Reid in far from polite terms. It reprinted articles from the *Sun* that had vilified Reid as Greeley's murderer for his role in the "Crumbs of Comfort" episode and in effect stealing the *Tribune* from its founder. He became "Whitelaw 'Rat' Reid," "Son-in-Law Reid . . . champion editorial dude," "the cold-blooded, pulseless, heartless Snivelling Sneak of the Tower." By the end of May 1884, *The Boycotter* was calling him "the acknowledged tool of . . . Jay Gould and other Wall Street sharks who have successively purchased him" and claiming that he had converted the *Tribune* from champion of the rights of the weak and oppressed into "a canting organ of what he is pleased to style 'the better classes.' "

Though a goodly measure of such vitriol may be discounted as a propaganda weapon, the fact of the *Tribune*'s growing callousness toward the plight of the poor was documented repeatedly on its own editorial pages. That first February of the boycott, for example, the paper was blaming the squalor of the neighborhoods in the lower reaches of Manhattan upon the moral degeneracy of its residents. Such squalor, moreover, was said to be the normal condition of these ignorant and brutalized classes. And landlords in the slums were entirely justified in charging high rents to the tenants for the privilege of turning the buildings into pigsties. This, at a moment when the *World* had come upon the scene and was regularly exposing economic travail as a rebuke to any claim that New York was a civilized community.

The *Tribune*'s labor troubles were no parochial affair. A persuasive case can be mounted, in fact, as the printers themselves did, that Reid's intransigence cost his good friend James G. Blaine the presidency in 1884. When the Republicans nominated the elitist Senator from Maine, with his close ties to major industrial interests, the union called upon the party to be true to the faith of its founders and denounce the party house organ (i.e., the *New York Tribune*) for dealing unscrupulously with laborers. When Blaine stuck by Reid, *The Boycotter* put out a sustained drumbeat, urging the more than 3,000 union printers and an estimated quarter of a million members of the Knights of Labor in New York state to vote Democratic that November. New York's electoral votes, as it turned out, provided the margin of victory; Grover Cleveland carried the state by just 2,000 votes.

Reid was by no means without recourse in his effort to combat the union printers. His principal weapon was a machine that he hoped would make them obsolete. With Mills money at his disposal, he helped its inventor fund the endless experimenting needed to refine it. And when its prototype was finally ready for commercial use, it was installed in the *Tribune* shop, and Reid himself, upon watching its first successful operation, gave the large, clanking, ingenious thing its name: the Linotype.

Machine-set type was the missing link in the chain of technological advances that turned printing into one of the earliest mass-production industries. Stereotyping, introduced at the beginning of the Civil War and providing curved plates for high-speed presses, was soon followed by the development of newsprint made from wood pulp instead of costly rag paper, the web-fed perfecting press printing from a continuous roll of paper, fast-drying inks, and automatic folding machines. The gathering and recording of news itself had been much speeded up by the arrival of the telegraph, the telephone, and the typewriter. But a device that could economically mechanize the costly handsetting of type proved maddeningly elusive. To work, such a machine would have to be able to assemble characters, justify them in even lines, cast them in metal, and redistribute them automatically—and require no more than a single operator. Hundreds of moving parts intricately coordinated and swiftly functioning were needed; human ingenuity had not yet progressed to that point. But it was not for a lack of effort. Between 1870 and 1900, patents were issued for some 127 typesetting machines. Only three of these inventions proved practicable. The first and the best of them was built by a young machinist whose workshop Reid had sent his foreman, the labor-baiting Thompson, to inspect. Here was the potential solution to the printers' nagging demand for a living wage: each machine could replace any number of compositors, who would then be in oversupply and unable to make unreasonable demands. Reid eagerly awaited the day when the invention was ready so that relatively low-skilled machine operators could be substituted for the high-priced handsetters.

The beneficiary of Reid's patronage was a German immigrant named Ottmar Mergenthaler, who had come to America at seventeen and made a living in Washington building models for patent seekers. Aware of the prize that awaited the man who could perfect a typesetting machine, Mergenthaler opened his own shop in 1883 when he was twenty-eight and devoted himself fanatically to the challenge. Previous inventors had pursued one of three paths: to compose founder's type mechanically, to type a lithographic transfer, or to type a mold from which stereos could be cast. None succeeded. Mergenthaler at first worked with a movable metal matrix bar which could be summoned like a typewriter key to mold a line character by character. The difficulties of the method nearly drove him to abandon the effort; then he hit upon the idea of creating small matrices, one for every character to be set, that would fly down a channel to their proper places in the line at the touch of a key. These small brass slabs, though, had to fulfill high demands, for as they moved through the machine, they were continually being gripped and carried, lifted and pushed, pressed together and spaced out, and therefore had to be highly durable and made with utmost precision; bent, they would cause the whole device to malfunction.

Mergenthaler was understandably receptive, then, to Reid's offer to finance his efforts. The inventor was given a thousand shares in the company Reid organized for the purpose; numbered among its stockholders were out-of-town newspaper publishers, non-President Blaine, and Reid's father-in-law and brother-in-law. With 7,000 shares, the Reid interest dominated. It was only natural that when Mergenthaler's miraculous machine was ready to debut, the *Tribune* should have been the site. The date was July 3, 1886. Soon a dozen of the Mergenthalers were installed.

The following year, fearful that Reid's anti-labor plans would succeed, *The Boycotter* infiltrated the *Tribune*'s composing room for a firsthand report on the progress of the Linotype. Not surprisingly, the union paper called the invention a disaster. "REID'S RATTLE BOX!" the article was headlined, with the subheadings "Scheming to Push his Type-setting Machine into Union Offices . . . How the 'Tribune' Office has been Converted into a Machine Shop . . . Whitelaw Reid Spending His Friends' Money in a Vain Attempt to Destroy Typographical Unions." The article claimed to see little threat in the machine to the jobs of the 60,000 compositors it said Reid hoped to throw out onto the street. The machine-cast type was often broken and uneven due to wear and tear on the matrices, the machines and their operators required constant attending, great expense was necessary to power the machines and keep their casting lead molten, and the slightest miscalculation sent burning metal squirting in all directions. "Of course it is not perfect," the union sheet quoted Thompson as conceding, "but it beats anything yet invented. I am educating a number of young men to operate the machines, and once they are in an office, that settles the union."

Within five years of the introduction of its prototype at the *Tribune,* a thousand of the machines had been installed nationwide. Reid prospered accordingly. By lowering the labor cost of printed materials, the Linotype in time created many more, not fewer, jobs for the printers. Their war with the *Tribune* did not end until 1892 when Reid was forced to accept a union shop in order to win the vice-presidential nomination on the ticket headed by Benjamin Harrison; to have held out longer would have jeopardized Republican chances that fall. The anti-labor label, though, did not come unstuck so easily. The Harrison-

Reid ticket was defeated by Grover Cleveland and Adlai E. Stevenson, whose grandson and namesake would twice fail to gain the presidency.

V

No matter the vagaries of party politics or convulsions of New York newspaperdom, the *Tribune* under Whitelaw Reid's stewardship, as before it, continued to attract to its staff men of surpassing talent and character. The best of them moved on before too many years, often to other fields, but not until they had forwarded its standing as the embodiment of the Newspaper as Literature. Perhaps by definition, the very idea is self-contradictory: A newspaper is designed to have the lifespan of a housefly, so for its prose to aspire to longevity would seem an exercise in futility with results almost predictably pretentious. Literature is writing that by its style and insight endures (or deserves to); it is rarely produced under a deadline.

One man able to bridge the gap was John Hay, among the most agreeable people ever to serve on the *Tribune*. By the time he joined its staff in 1870 at the age of thirty-two he had already been exposed firsthand to enough history, politics, and culture to serve a lifetime. The son of an Indiana doctor, he had been sent east to Brown University, where his gifts as a good-humored colleague who spoke, wrote, and thought well were abundantly evidenced. He once woke a classmate to witness the aurora borealis, then published a poem, among the first of many fine ones he would produce, to celebrate the event. After college, he studied for the law in his uncle's office in Springfield, Illinois; next door, Abraham Lincoln practiced. At twenty-two, Hay went to the White House with him as a private secretary and served him affectionately if not reverentially throughout the most protracted crisis in the life of the republic; he and fellow secretary John Nicolay long afterward paid monumental homage to Lincoln in a joint ten-volume biography. For six years after the war, Hay held appointments on the American legation staffs in Paris, Vienna, and Madrid, preliminary to a later diplomatic career that would culminate with his distinguished seven-year term as Secretary of State.

But first he joined the *Tribune* as one of the bright young men Horace Greeley enlisted in his last years. Having felt the sting of Greeley's carping over the Union's conduct of the war during his years at Lincoln's side, Hay considered him an editor prone to snap judgments and loose reasoning—one who too often "dipped his pen of infallibility into his ink of omniscience." But he also recognized Greeley's earnestness and was fond of referring to his paper, only half facetiously, as "the G.M.O."—the Great Moral Organ. He stayed for five years, writing editorials, night-editing, occasionally corresponding, and grew closer than anyone else on the staff to Whitelaw Reid, who valued his witty companionship during that stressful time when he came into control of the paper.

When Chicago nearly burned to the ground in 1871, Reid sent Hay to report on the devastation. His initialed articles were gems of literary reportage. The last of them, appearing in the October 17 issue under the heading "The Cradle and the Grave of the Fire," revealed a virtuoso journalist's ability not only to see but also to understand, to know both which details to select and how to phrase them most affectingly, and—Hay's special knack—to make connections that supply dimension and meaning where others never plumb below the surface of brittle fact.

His article opened: "Man is the only animal who wastes his time in efforts to find out how things began for the mere pleasure of knowing." He made his way to "a mean little street . . . with dirty dooryards and unpainted fences falling to decay," where slatternly women lounged at the gates and "a dozen absurd geese wandered with rustic familiarity." Down a fire-gutted alleyway, by then quite flat and cool, he encountered "small gutter-boys marching through the lots, some kicking with bare feet in the light ashes for suspected and sporadic coals, and others prudently mounted on stilts, which sunk from time to time in the spongy soil and caused the young acrobats to descend ignominiously and pull them out." Finally he came upon a "warped and weather-beaten shanty of two rooms," the only structure left standing on its unpaved street, out of which the previous Sunday night had come a woman bearing a lamp to the barn behind it "to milk the cow with the crumpled temper, that kicked the lamp, that spilled the kerosene, that fired the straw, that burned Chicago. And there to this hour stands that craven little house, holding on tightly to its miserable existence." Around to the rear, he found the Man of the House sitting with a pair of friends. "His wife, Our Lady of the Lamp—freighted with heavier disaster than that which Psyche carried to the bed-side of Eros—sat at the window, knitting." Hay asked the man what he knew about the origin of the fire; the answer, civilly given, was very little; the alarm had awakened him in time to fight the blaze and save his hovel. At every sentence he indicated his friends and added, "I can prove it by them." Hay here inserted:

> He seemed fearful that all of Chicago was coming down upon him for prompt and integral payment of that $200,000,000 his cow had kicked over. His neighbors say this story is an invention dating from the second day of the fire. There was something unalterably grotesque in this ultimate atom feeling a sense of responsibility for a catastrophe so stupendous. . . .

Hay then set out to trace the path of the horrific blaze and came at last to the German cemetery at the gate of Lincoln Park, "by the shining beach of the Lake," where "hundreds of the hunted fugitives of the North Division, hotly chased by the fire, came to pass that first miserable night of hunger and cold." Having painfully lugged with them what household possessions they could rescue, the survivors were forced, as the night chilled, to fight fire with fire of their own, breaking up their cherished remnants for kindling. A group of German singers "from a low cabaret saloon, who flew out into the night with nothing but their tawdry evening dresses," sat huddled and shivering in the lee of a tombstone, "their bare arms and shoulders blue and pinched, and the tinseled flowers in their hair, shining with frost." At times "they cheated their misery with songs," soothing "that sorrow-stricken place [with] the soft impurities of the Vienna muse, and the ringing and joyous jodel of the Tyrol. Nearby the fragments of a Methodist congregation had improvised a prayer meeting, and the sound of psalms and supplication went up mingled with that worldly music to the deep and tolerant heavens." In juxtaposing the sacred and profane, Hay found redemptive shards; here was blasted humanity celebrating what life remained to it instead of bemoaning the oblivion it had narrowly eluded but that yet lay in certain wait. Every word was picked with poetic sensibility, every sentence was structured for maximum flow.

In a letter to Reid accompanying his article, Hay explained how it had been impossible to find a telegrapher to wire back his piece, so he had had to resort to the mails. "I have done as well as I could. I have a clean conscience. Your condemnation will not gall my withers. I have given the Great Moral Organ 16 hours a day ever since I arrived."

Three years later, Hay married the daughter of a wealthy Cleveland railroad builder and industrialist and retired from journalism to the shore of Lake Erie and a temporary career as assistant magnate. When Reid himself married in 1881, it was Hay to whom he turned to take charge of the *Tribune* during his seven-month wedding trip. Hay obliged—even as his grandson would oblige Reid's grandson seventy-seven years later when the paper faced imminent extinction.

A different sort of literary contribution—this one to the early annals of urban anthropology—was made by a busy little *Tribune* police reporter in a wing collar. Arriving in America from Denmark at twenty-one in 1870, Jacob August Riis found only odd jobs for his carpentering skills, went hungry a lot, trained as a telegrapher, and finally drifted into journalism as a reporter for a New York news service that provided supplemental coverage to the city papers. Later he wrote for and edited a political sheet in Brooklyn, where his neighbors included one W. F. G. Shanks, the city editor of the *Tribune*. Riis, with his fussy spectacles and droopy mustache, hardly seemed the spirited reporting type, but Shanks took him on at space rates; through the fierce winter of 1877, Riis would have to show his mettle.

One awful night word came that a tidal wave had ripped away part of the Coney Island shore, carrying houses and people with it. In pursuit of the story, Riis went by streetcar as far as he could, then continued on foot through knee-deep slush as the storm raged about him until he reached Sheepshead Bay, only to find that the ice and the tide had shut off all approach to Coney Island. Unable to gather firsthand evidence, Riis polled the hotelkeepers of the bay, who were forthcoming with vivid accounts of the wreckage, replete with a kitchen stove floating by, a live cat perched forlornly on top. Notes pocketed, he rented a sleigh, drove back frozen stiff to the paper, and wrote up his story, the only extensive account of the disaster to appear in a New York paper the next morning. When he reported for duty that day, Riis was confronted by editor Shanks regarding him sternly over the edge of the paper. "So you went to the island last night, Mr. Riis?" Riis confessed he had not got across, that no one could have done so. "Eh?" asked Shanks, lowering the paper an inch. "But this very circumstantial account—" Riis explained his sources and his confidence in same, vowing he would have braved the bay had a single boat been available. "Right," said Shanks, softening now and eyeing the bill for Riis's return sleigh ride that was already on his desk for approval. "We'll allow the sleigh—we'll allow even the stove," said Shanks of the floating apparition, "to a man who owns he didn't see it, though it is pretty steep." With a dismissing wave, he added, "Next time, make them swear to the stove. There is no accounting for cats."

It was a struggle to eke out a living; Riis frantically pursued every line of type he could get into the paper so there would be bread on the table for his family. Another howler of a night, he raced around the corner on his way back to the *Tribune* building and plowed directly into editor Shanks, who slowly extricated himself from a snowbank and asked Riis what the confounded hurry was all about. The sheepish reply was a meeting he had attended, of no great importance, that Riis was running to get into the first edition.

"And do you always run like that when you are out on an assignment?"

"When it is late like this, yes. How else would I get my copy in?"

Riis awaited dismissal in the morning. But his bowled-over supervisor thought the *Tribune* needed nothing better than such a fireball to man police headquarters on Mulberry Street. Riis was promoted to staff membership at twenty-five a week, but his pace did not relent. His fellow police reporters, not the most industrious lot in New York journalism, were prone to pool their material, taking turns going out for stories so their office card game could continue essentially uninterrupted. Riis went after everything, logging brutally long hours but learning the byways of crime and squalor, especially in the surrounding Lower East Side, better than any of them. The enormity of the problem was quickly apparent to him: one-third of New York was forced to beg, borrow, or steal to survive in those "dens of death," as he called the tenement rookeries where so much physical and moral contagion resided. He did not agree with Whitelaw Reid and the *Tribune* editorialists that those woebegone denizens were degenerates by nature; in his reports he dealt with their victimization as sympathetically as he could and paid the price of constant negotiation with his editors, who complained that his style was "altogether editorial and presuming, and not to be borne."

To prevail in his daily combat, Riis was sustained by a spiritual pride in the way he reported "the tumult of passions . . . and not rarely a human heroism that redeems all the rest." It was his task, he felt, to go beyond the facts and portray what he witnessed so that "we can all see its meaning, or at all events catch the human drift of it, not merely the foulness and the reek of blood." If he succeeded, his murder story might "easily come to speak more eloquently to the minds of thousands than the sermon preached to a hundred in the church on Sunday." Yet he saw no sacrilege in that aim. Indeed, he felt that his work was consistent with the Lord's, and beseeched the aid "of Him who is the source of all right and all justice" whenever he had a big story, "whether a fire, a murder, a robbery, or whatever might come in the way of duty." Some may have found ludicrous or irreverent "the notion of a police reporter praying that he may write a good murder story," but that was only because, as he wrote in his autobiography, "they fail to make out in it the human element which dignifies anything and rescues it from reproach."

One spring morning in 1888, having crossed New York harbor by ferry from his Staten Island home with an armful of flowers that his children had picked for him to distribute to "the poors," Riis began to walk toward his office but within minutes had had his arms stripped clean by wide-eyed youngsters eagerly touching the blossoms to make sure that they were real. The episode inspired Riis to insert a notice in his police-news column asking other commuters to bring to his office a few blossoms from their gardens to gladden the day for a feverish child or a shut-in mother. Health Department doctors on their tene-ment rounds had agreed to help distribute the flowers. Such a profusion of blooms appeared the next day, express wagons of them, that youngsters jammed the streets clamoring, policemen came out of headquarters to gape at the glori-ous spectacle, and even surly rival reporters helped hand out the precious gifts. The flowers continued to arrive daily; several boxes came from a women's group that invited Riis to speak before a large meeting at the Broadway Tabernacle, the city's leading lecture hall. As a result, a committee was formed to help improve the conditions of the poor, and Riis was launched on a second career. One of his early listeners at a church lecture was an editor on *Scribner's* magazine who asked him to contribute a piece on tenement life, accompanied by photographs Riis had taken. The article appeared in the December number of 1889 under a title Riis had copyrighted some time before—"How the Other Half Lives." An invitation to expand the piece into a book followed.

Drawing on his newspaper experience of a dozen years, using his reporter's notebooks and scrapbooks of his articles, nagging Health Department officials for hard data to supplement his own compassionate convictions, Riis composed one of the great books of American journalism. A by-product of his *Tribune* work, *How the Other Half Lives* was published in 1890 with the subtitle *Studies among the Tenements of New York.* Here were hauntingly portrayed Italian immigrants living beside garbage dumps under the evil protection of *padrones* exploiting their dumbly trusting countrymen. Here were Jews packed twelve into a little room, their sewing machines whirring from dawn till they dropped, yet still ready to fight for their rights as if they "had not been robbed of them for eighteen hundred years." Here were the blacks, "loyal to the backbone, proud of being an American," withstanding "poverty, abuse, and injustice alike . . . with imperturbable cheerfulness." Though marred by excessive stereotyping of ethnic-group traits, the book was an intensely observed indictment of intolerable social conditions and a prescriptive plea, toward the fulfillment of which Riis devoted most of the remainder of his life, for basic human urban rights: a decent job, adequate schooling, a bearable place to live, safety from fire, crime, and epidemic. He switched to the *Sun* for a while, then went full-time into social reform, opposed by landlords and most politicians. An exception among the latter was Theodore Roosevelt, who as police commissioner of New York, and later governor and President, allied himself with the aims of the former police reporter and helped usher some of them into law. Roosevelt, while preaching for good citizenship in 1903, pointed to Riis as "the ideal American," one who had acted squarely, worked hard and cheerfully, and fought for high ideals.

Riis, like most reporters of his day, labored anonymously so far as the reading public was concerned, and Hay's editorials, like nearly all after Greeley's time, were unsigned. But one *Tribune* staff writer whose initials appeared regularly at the end of his articles was Lemuel Ely Quigg, its star correspondent for most of the nine years starting in 1885, when he was twenty-two, that he worked on the paper. His writing, encountered nearly a century later, retains much of the energy and fluency that won him prominence at an early age. Most striking was his seemingly total command of the material he wrote about, so microscopically observed and confidently selected, then presented in long, seamless paragraphs that overwhelm the reader with the intelligence and sensibility that shaped them.

A masterful example of Quigg's work was presented to the *Tribune*'s readers in June 1893 when he was sent to cover the trial of Lizzie Borden. His pieces, beginning in the right-hand lead column on page one and spilling over onto the second page, ran to four or five thousand words each for two weeks straight. Among the whole body of works dealing with the case—two dozen books, countless articles, stage, screen, song, and ballet have all celebrated it and promoted Lizzie to the pantheon of American folklore—none has surpassed Quigg's brilliant dispatches, written under nightly deadline pressure. An imposing figure of a man inclined to drive home his speech with a stabbing forefinger, Quigg wrote the same way; in his Borden trial articles, though, he dwelled not on the unfolding testimony but the psychological framework of the case and its tantalizingly paradoxical circumstances. Consider the surprise opening of his first piece, devoid of factual or narrative statement and instead almost wholly interpretive, relying for impact upon an elaborate metaphor:

> New-Bedford, Mass., June 7 — It is plain that the State does not expect to prove that Lizzie Borden killed her father and stepmother. The most it hopes to prove is that nobody else can be reasonably suspected of the crime; that she may be suspected, and, therefore, that she must be guilty. Judged by its effect in carrying this conviction, the evidence thus far submitted is undeniably strong. It has been presented in much

the same way that scraps of a torn paper might, when all collected, be put together. Gradually the writing is shown in something like the original form, with most of the letters in place, the torn edges fitting. . . .

Quigg made little effort from the first to hide his growing skepticism of the prosecution's case, but to charge him with lack of objectivity would be to reduce the true reporter's function to dumb stenography. The daily testimony was amply rendered in the lower sections of his articles, but Quigg interposed a judgmental overlay on the collateral facts as they emerged by stressing the direction to which they pointed. Noting, for example, that Lizzie's mother had died thirty-one years before the murders and her father had married Lizzie's stepmother three years later, Quigg added, ". . . so that if, as the prosecution asserts, she was the object of Lizzie's profound and bitter hatred, it follows that the prisoner had put up with her for a long while." Such asides may be considered evaluative rather than subjective; their intent to alert rather than persuade.

Every witness was meticulously scrutinized and assayed with regard to outward appearance, apparent inner character, and likely veracity; none was spared his wit. Of one of Lizzie's neighbors who offered damaging testimony, Quigg wrote, "Miss Russell wears an expression of countenance suggestive of an acid diet. She is not young, and does not create the impression that she ever has been." But it was for Lizzie herself that Quigg reserved his severest attention, fascinated by the unlikelihood of her guilt, sympathetic with her plight, yet ultimately uneasy about overtly taking her side. There is a charged quality to every careful sentence as he presented her, for example, in the swift-flowing second paragraph of his story on the trial's fourth day:

> This woman, thirty-three years old, unmarried and without a lover, is accused of having hacked her infirm old father and the stepmother with whom she had lived from her infancy to their deaths, and of having done it with a hatchet which, the handle having been broken off near the blade, she must have grasped by the iron head. Her very fingers must have sunk into the wounds they made. She is not an adventuress; she has lived her life without making any other history than that which comes to the ordinary New-England girl who lives in the home of her parents and busies herself from morning to night in adding to its comforts. . . .

Throughout the trial, Quigg's acute eye caught the emotive detail with which he fashioned the variable moods of the setting and manner of the players:

> It has been a damp, cold day. The heavy grass on the court-house lawn and the leafy archway of elms that gives a stately covering to its approaches have worn a sombre hue, as if whispers of the tragic tale that was being told beyond the Grecian portico that fronted them had come out through the open windows. Within there was a deeply interested audience. Sometimes, moved by [defense counsel] Governor Robinson's almost savage satire, they ventured to smile, and once or twice they had the hardihood to let what may have been a titter escape them. Then the portly person of the High Sheriff of Bristol County would visibly enlarge. His swallow-tailed coat of Websterian blue would elevate itself at the back and stand out at the tails as if

electric with indignation, and the uncountable brass buttons that adorn and beautify him, catching the gleam of his eyes, would flash and sparkle with reflected ire.

At the end, with the testimony all in but the verdict pending, Quigg's only reservations applied to the doubters among the assembled. "The belief in the prisoner's guilt is now confirmed," he wrote, "to that class of people who are naturally suspicious, who have at least a tendency to hard-heartedness, and who are also so narrow and prejudiced in their views that, having once obtained an impression, they can never allow themselves to part with it."

By contrast with Quigg's essays, the *Herald* carried a clear, brisk narrative, in choppy paragraphs, with little of the intensity or color of the *Tribune* presentation, and it was detectably down on Lizzie. The *Times* account, bland and straightforward, relying much on direct testimony and daring little by way of interpretation, read like wire-service copy. Other papers sensationalized without challenging the reader's morbid curiosity. But L.E.Q., as the *Tribune* identified him at the close of each piece, produced both literature and history that fortnight. The following year, he began a five-year career in Congress and drifted off afterward into industrial promotion, never again to write with the authority and élan he brought to his coverage of Lizzie Borden's ordeal. Acquitted, she herself survived on the inheritance from her slain father until 1927. The murders have never been solved, though the literature on the case keeps growing.

VI

As the nineteenth century drew to a close, decay implanted by complacency was overtaking the New York newspapers that had sprung to brawling life a half century earlier. The *Tribune*'s case was the most advanced, except in its owner's eyes.

The daughter of a multimillionaire whose riches she loved to spend, Elisabeth Mills Reid drew her husband farther and farther from newspapering, where he saw no new worlds to conquer and recognized no talent or property superior to his own. Never in awe of the powerful since familiarizing himself with their world in Civil War days, Whitelaw Reid frankly enjoyed immersion in their ranks. Money added to suavity, intelligence, and undeniable competence crowned his social ambition; he was now an authentic American aristocrat, by marriage and disposition, and one of the nation's most influential citizens, by trade and access. And he lived like a lord. The Mills millions bought the couple two magnificent homes, a rococo mansion at 451 Madison Avenue in the city and an estate called Ophir Farm, a veritable castle of gray stone set in more than seven hundred superb acres in suburban Westchester, not to mention a rustic

complex hidden away upstate in the Adirondacks among other luxurious re-
treats of the well-heeled.* His newspaper grew more conservative and patently
Republican as his own comforts multiplied; in the middle of Grover Cleveland's
first term, for example, the *Tribune* devoted almost an entire issue to an analysis
of the Democratic President's performance to date; it was more a demolition
job than journalism. Yearning for recognition when the Republicans reclaimed
national power in 1888, Reid was rewarded with the post of American minister
to France; from that moment until his death twenty-four years later, he became,
practically speaking, an absentee newspaper owner.

Unlike Greeley, who left vigorous subordinates in charge when he was away
from the *Tribune,* Reid designated civil-servant types who risked little and let
the paper glide along on inertia. A "class" publication whose conservative,
educated, relatively wealthy, but shrinking clientele was still numerous enough
to attract advertisers, the paper was earning an annual profit in the vicinity of
a quarter of a million dollars at the beginning of the 'Nineties. Reid, meanwhile,
relished his diplomatic work, more ornamental than functional, in Paris; the
import status of American pork was about the weightiest issue with which he
was concerned during his three-year tenure. When his attention wandered from
the glitter of international society to home thoughts, it was not the *Tribune* that
concerned him but Ophir Hall, upon the improvement of which he and Elisabeth were lavishing the finest treasures and architectural talent money could
buy. Frederick Law Olmsted, the nation's premier landscape architect, and
Stanford White, its most masterly interior designer, were engaged for the task
with the encouragement of D. O. Mills, who footed most of the bills. Reid sent
back a steady stream of detailed instructions and comments on the proposed
embellishments and, by way of participating more directly, purchased two
complete Louis XIV rooms from a château near Paris and had them shipped
to Ophir, at a cost of $14,000, to be installed as the drawing room and adjoining
parlor. From Donald Nicholson, his longtime former secretary, whom Reid had
left in charge of the paper, the American minister to France wanted to hear as
few troubles as possible. And if they did reach him, Reid was inclined to dispose
of them in a fashion that suggested that party loyalty had thoroughly routed
journalistic integrity as his secular god. When the *Tribune*'s veteran Washington bureau chief, Max Seckendorff, wrote severely of the Pension Bureau,
President Harrison complained and asked for the source of the data upon which
the offending article was based. Seckendorff declined to supply it, citing the
newsman's imperative to shield his informants. Nicholson, a full-bearded, inoffensive Welshman, declined to intervene. But when the President's son wrote
directly to Reid to pursue the matter, the owner recommended that his man in

---

* The Reids' other principal piece of property, of course, was the *Tribune.* Within two years after
their marriage, the couple and D. O. Mills among them owned nearly three-quarters of the newspaper's stock. Reid continued to buy up shares—anonymously, through intermediaries—as they were
offered for sale; given its modest profits, few others were attracted to the paper as an investment.
In due course, the *Tribune* was wholly owned by the Reids and Millses.

Washington go to the White House, fully explain the nature of the confidentiality practice, and then reveal the name of his informant.

When the *Tribune* marked its fiftieth birthday with a celebration at the Metropolitan Opera House, Minister Reid was not on hand. Close observers of the 3,000 loyal subscribers who attended the occasion noted that most were well on in years. This tendency did not concern Reid, who was pleased with the reports he received about the high dignity with which the affair was conducted. Other papers may have been well ahead in gross numbers, but the *Tribune* was still the circulation leader at Newport and Saratoga in season and the special favorite of the clergy all year round. His was a sound paper for the soundest element among the citizenry. Neutral commentators, however, credited it with sustained editorial excellence only in its critical departments. No New York paper boasted a more knowledgeable threesome than William Winter, the drama editor, Henry Krehbiel, the music critic, and Royal Cortissoz, the art critic. Winter and Cortissoz, though, were antiquarian in their outlook—Ibsen, for example, the *Tribune*'s drama expert found a Norwegian crank and Shaw did not rate much higher with him—while Krehbiel's pro-Germanic bias bordered on obsession. But the three, who each served for more than forty years, were as entrenched and apparently unshakable as the institution that employed them.

If there was a more prominent American in Paris than Whitelaw Reid during his ministerial tenure, it was James Gordon Bennett the Younger; certainly he was more conspicuous. But the Commodore was less the cutup now; he saw himself as the voice of America in Europe, thanks to his having established a Paris edition of the *Herald* in October 1887. Bearing only an incidental resemblance to its New York parent, "Le New York," as it was known at Paris kiosks, was a somewhat eccentric sheet that reflected Bennett's impulses— restaurants that did not serve him like royalty, for instance, were excoriated in print—and crotchets. Its letters column one day carried an inquiry signed "Old Philadelphia Lady," asking how to convert centrigrade temperature into Fahrenheit and vice versa; Bennett's exceedingly misshapen funnybone was so struck by this that he ordered the letter to appear every day thereafter, without answer or comment—and it did for more than thirty years, until a few days after his death. The Paris paper appealed mainly to three groups of readers: tourists, expatriates, and members of the international set from among the royal courts of the Continent, their titled outcasts, and pretenders who found in Bennett himself an easy mark for their dubious charms. The Paris *Herald* ran $100,000 in the red every year but at least had the beneficial effect of distracting its owner from mercilessly torturing his employees in the home office via cable.

That office, though, was never long out of mind, and when Joseph Pulitzer put up his golden-domed quarters, Bennett decided to answer back with a new home of his own but of a very different sort and in a location far from the *Herald*'s Park Row rivals. Aware that the nexus of the city's commercial activity was moving uptown, he selected the triangular block, then known as Dodge

Place, bounded by Thirty-fifth Street, Broadway, and Sixth Avenue. Upon it, Stanford White designed a long, graceful two-story anomaly with an arcade supported by slender white columns on three sides. Modeled after a Veronese palazzo, the new *Herald* building was a rebuke to the granite-and-steel shafts that were poking high into the sky throughout downtown New York. Bennett was nothing if not extravagant and independent, and his office building had to be likewise. The area south of it, renamed Herald Square, soon became one of the city's commercial hubs, but the site and the building itself proved impractical.

In addition to squandering *Herald* profits on his dissolute style of life, his Paris paper, and his new New York headquarters, Bennett indulged in a battle with Jay Gould for control of the transatlantic telegraph cable, of which the Commodore may have been the largest single user. The money could have been better spent improving and promoting the *Herald,* which soon fell below 100,000 in circulation and continued to lose ground to the *World.* A soundly edited, reserved-looking paper like the *Herald* simply could not match the dynamism that Pulitzer had brought to his bright, déclassé sheet. Though he grudgingly admired Pulitzer's success, Bennett would take no step to imitate it.

He was actively repelled, though, by the appearance in New York in 1895 of a young California man with a partial Harvard education, seven and a half million dollars recently inherited from his father, and the determination to out-Pulitzer Pulitzer in appealing to the masses. William Randolph Hearst had done well building the family-owned *Examiner* in his hometown of San Francisco; he came to the nation's communications capital at thirty-two, hungry for attention and impatient for power. He picked up the bedraggled *Evening Journal,* a distant also-ran known in the trade as "the chambermaid's delight," and began pouring out his money like Napa wine in pursuit of the *World.* His formula was a yet more lurid display of sex, crime, and scandal news, confected scoops and crusades, and an editorial page favoring such avowedly populist causes as the eight-hour workday, public ownership of utilities, and the cheap-money monetary policies of William Jennings Bryan. Truth and taste were tiresome encumbrances to Hearst's noisy, splashy brand of sensationalism, which had little of Pulitzer's redeeming idealism. What the two publishers shared was a recognition that a new class of reader now lived in the thronged city who looked to his daily newspaper as his principal source of entertainment —for he could afford no other—as well as information. Facts were still useful, to be sure, but how the sensationalized sheets dressed them up into "a story" provided the spice in the day's recipe for circulation success. In redefining news, Pulitzer had tipped the balance toward whatever *interested*—whether it amused, titillated, thrilled, or horrified did not matter—and away from historically approved standards of what was *important* in the affairs of men and states. Hearst sent the balancing apparatus right off the table.

Within a year, the *Journal*'s penny-apiece circulation vaulted past the *Herald*'s to 150,000 but the paper was still losing $100,000 a month. Hearst intensified the war by hiring away almost all of Pulitzer's Sunday staff to build up his own flashy Sabbath edition, brimming with lushly illustrated articles of shameless superficiality. In countering the *Journal,* the *World* degraded itself.

A year after Hearst, another newcomer to the city bought up a moribund daily and began to revitalize it in utterly the opposite manner to Hearst's and in pursuit of the very readership that the older establishmentarian papers—the *Tribune, Herald,* and *Sun*—felt was comfortably theirs. Adolph Simon Ochs brought no fat patrimony with him to New York, only the conviction that *The New York Times,* $300,000 in debt and its circulation shriveled to 9,000, could be resuscitated if placed in his hands. A small, blue-eyed mass of energy, Ochs had employed hard work and as much credit as he could get to take hold and make a success of a paper in his adopted city of Chattanooga, Tennessee. Not himself a journalist, he prized straightforward news content in abundance rather than showy style as the chief commodity he had to sell. Without vanity except as embodied in the prosperity and dignity of his paper, he viewed the editorial page as a necessary evil and went to great pains to avoid stirring controversy in his. It was as a kindly commander of men's loyalty, though, and not as a showman or disciplinarian that Ochs excelled. He worked harder than any employee and lived no better than most; profits went to enhance his paper rather than to inflate or display his ego.

To the aging stockholders and anxious creditors of *The New York Times,* Chattanooga was a far cry from Gotham, and Adolph Ochs was a greenhorn Southerner without big-city experience; he was also a Jew seeking a toehold in an intensely competitive marketplace that his co-religionist, Joseph Pulitzer, had emerged out of similar obscurity to dominate. To make his play for control of the *Times* yet more problematical, Ochs had neither much capital to invest in it—only $75,000—nor any strikingly innovative program for its revitalization. But in his appealingly exuberant way, he radiated confidence that sound business management and vigorous renewal of the paper's traditional stock-in-trade—dignified, trustworthy, nonpartisan news coverage in abundance—would do the trick if he was correctly appraising the New York newspaper market. Ochs saw a *Tribune* whose steadily more reactionary Republicanism had driven its circulation down,* a *Herald* that had become a society sheet out

---

* There is no reliable basis for assertions about the circulation figures for American newspapers before the 1920s and the coming of the Audit Bureau of Circulation (ABC). All numbers cited herein are based on publisher claims or unaudited guesses by outsiders, including postal authorities. Often the available data are in conflict. Meyer Berger, for example, in his *Times*-sponsored centennial history of that newspaper, stated that the *Tribune*'s daily circulation at the time Ochs bought the *Times* was about 16,000, ahead of only the *Times* among the city's major papers. But he cites no source for the figure. Harry Baehr, in his post–Civil War history of the *Tribune,* states its circulation at the time of Ochs's arrival to have been about 76,000 and cites *Ayer's Newspaper Annual.* It should be noted, however, that members of the Ayer family had been *Tribune* stockholders prior to that time. Michael Schudson, a highly competent young sociologist at the University of Chicago, elected to use Berger's much lower figure in his useful book, *Discovering the News: A Social History of American Newspapers* (Basic Books, 1978), and cited Berger's book as the source—but a sourceless

of touch with the broader issues of the day, a *Sun* that was well written in its featurish way but deficient in hard reporting and scope, and in the blatant journals of Messrs. Pulitzer and Hearst, newspapers that were unfit to enter any refined home. The *Times* would purvey solid quality to readers eager for it.

To demonstrate his self-assurance, Ochs premised his bid for a controlling interest in the *Times* on his ability to put it in the black and keep in there for three consecutive years. While the financiers contemplated this outlandish proposition, its author cheerfully pursued his quarry for months; when time permitted, he would dreamily bicycle through the great city to familiarize himself better with its character. Since there was no more attractive offer, the greenhorn's was finally accepted.

He did nothing radical to the paper or its editorial staff. But he brought intensive supervision to bear on the other departments, quickly slicing away $2,000 a week in unwarranted expenses. Then he made his main conceptual contribution to the renaissance of the *Times*: henceforth it would become the bible of the city's powerful financial and mercantile class, whose interests it would serve only incidentally on the editorial page but massively by expanded coverage of business and industrial news. Mondays the *Times* carried an authoritative summary of the national economic scene, long lists of arriving out-of-town buyers were added as a useful service feature for the city's wholesalers and manufacturers, and heavier tabular and statistical matter helped it as well to vault past every other paper in New York in its completeness of attention to the metropolis's most vital running story: money. Ochs also reached out for the city's intelligentsia by introducing a Saturday literary supplement and fattened the starveling Sunday edition with a new illustrated supplement. The forbidding gray typography was lightened somewhat, a telephone solicitation campaign was undertaken with emphasis on the respectability of the *Times*—it did not figuratively soil the breakfast table as the *World* and *Journal* did with their exhaustive accounts of sordid incidents—and a contest to furnish the revitalized paper with a suitable motto came up with none better than Ochs's own coinage: "All the News That's Fit to Print." Within a year the *Times* had swept past the slumbering *Tribune*'s circulation but still was far behind the *Herald* and not even on the same racetrack with the *World* and *Journal*. But when the latter two helped concoct a nice little war between America and Spain to stimulate their sales, Ochs most shrewdly demonstrated his business acumen.

Hearst had agitated openly for the United States to free Cuba from Spanish oppression and then reward the liberated island with annexation. The *World,* in its most ignominious hour, joined in, berating President McKinley for diplomatic pussyfooting instead of boldly acting. Both papers greeted the blowing up

---

source is no source at all. In view of the *Tribune*'s rank partisanship, sedate news presentation, becalmed management, and three-cent price, the correct figure near the end of the century was probably closer to Berger's than that of *Ayer*'s—at any rate, close to the rear of the pack among the city's papers.

of the battleship *Maine* with fist-high headlines, turning an act of uncertain espionage into an irresistible provocation to a war America could not lose. The *Tribune* lashed out at "the hot gospellers of sensational jingoism," but its voice was feeble against so much thunder. For the ten weeks the conflict lasted in the spring of 1898, the Hearst and Pulitzer forces collided in fiercer combat than was seen on the battlefield. As many as five hundred American writers, photographers, and artists were on the scene, including Hearst, who exposed himself to enemy fire. The *Journal* spent $3,000 a day on coverage reported in red-headlined extras whenever the bloody news offered the slightest excuse for it; the *World* was not far behind. Both their circulations soared over the million mark as readers feasted on the lopsided encounter in the Caribbean, marking America's hemispheric dominion and the expulsion of decadent Old World power. Aroused in his far-off exile by all these sanguinary doings, James Gordon Bennett ordered the *Herald* to regain its faded glory by spending freely to cover the war; his troops responded with the soundest, fairest coverage provided by any American newspaper, and its circulation vaulted to 500,000 for the duration. The *Tribune,* opposed to the trumped-up barbarism of the war, used wire-service copy and some stringers to cover it, and at its most excited, reported American victories under a discreetly proud two-column headline.

Adolph Ochs, struggling to attain competitive respectability, knew he could not afford to cover the hostilities against the mass-circulation papers and did not waste his money trying. Fearful, though, that the renewal process he was carefully nurturing would be overwhelmed by the war hoopla and the clamorous descent into yellow journalism by the mass-market dailies, Ochs took a bold gamble that, in retrospect, purchased his newspaper's destiny: he cut its price from three cents to a penny, underselling the *World* and *Journal,* both at two cents and spending so much in their competitive war that they could not afford to meet his price. The *Times,* at any rate, was not serious competition. Some of Ochs's own staff members feared the penny price presaged an imminent descent into cheap journalism; who ever heard of a quality newspaper selling so low? Precisely, replied Ochs. Within a year, as the war hysteria passed and the *Times*'s virtues as a serious chronicler of news uncolored by political or commercial considerations began to manifest themselves, its circulation tripled, and by the turn of the century, it stood at 82,000, on the threshold of major competitive status.

For Whitelaw Reid, the Spanish-American War proved a personal triumph even if it did little to arouse his languishing journalistic aptitude. In the six years between his return from Paris to run for Vice President and the onset of war in Cuba, Reid had been in virtual retirement. Rarely seen at the *Tribune,* he traveled widely, ranging from his father-in-law's estate in California and stays in Arizona to treat a lingering asthmatic condition to tours of Egypt and other far-off foreign places. The Cuban crisis concerned him sufficiently to order a nonmilitaristic stance on the *Tribune*'s editorial page, but when the outcome of the war became apparent, Reid disclosed a strong new imperialistic streak. The

United States was no longer an enfeebled infant, asserted the paper (and Reid himself, in articles and speeches); it was time for America to take its place on the world stage as a major power. He favored and forcefully espoused a grand U.S. position in the Pacific: annexation of nearly the entire Philippine archipelago and the Hawaiian Islands, heavy reparations from Spain, and construction of an inter-oceanic canal via Panama. Such expanded dominion, he believed, would serve not only American grandeur but the interests of the primitive peoples incapable of self-government who would fall under Uncle Sam's beneficent rule. Indeed Whitelaw Reid had begun to make no secret of his low opinion of the non-Aryan peoples of the earth. He was expressing alarm over the "extraordinary change in character" of the immigrants flooding into the United States, noting that they were diluting the Anglo-Saxon character of the nation and turning it into "the common sewer of Christendom." God and nature, he proclaimed in the *Tribune,* meant for Great Britain, Germany, and the United States to be at eternal peace with one another as the bulwark of civilization.

Named to the five-man peace commission that met in Paris to work out terms with vanquished Spain, Reid operated with assertive confidence. His easy command of French, the language of diplomacy, the ready availability of his landau to taxi his co-commissioners to and fro, and his intermediate position between the isolationists and the extreme expansionists in the American delegation made him its most influential member. The final terms were essentially his terms. *The Times* of London called them even harsher than those Germany had imposed upon France in stripping her of Alsace and Lorraine, among other indignities, in 1872.

After his diplomatic feat, Reid retired once more to private life, still hungering for laurels but indifferent to the health of his newspaper. Year by year throughout the 'Nineties, its profits ebbed. By 1901 they had evaporated entirely. Instead of diverting his and the Millses' resources into its rehabilitation, so that it might compete at least with its traditional rivals, Ochs's resurgent *Times* and Bennett's again prospering *Herald,* Reid elected to cut costs and reduce the once proud *Tribune* to the status of pensioner. But to sell it would have been unthinkable: it was his duty as a Republican Christian gentleman of impeccable Nordic stock to sustain the old dowager. Yet in a dynamic metropolis served by twenty-five daily newspapers, most of them locked in furious combat for readers, to view the *New York Tribune* as a private charity case, as its lofty proprietor did at the dawn of the twentieth century, was almost certainly to doom it to extinction.

PART TWO

1900-1941

*This new journalism is . . . bound, I think, to become less
Napoleonic at the top and less bohemian at the bottom, and to take
on the character of a liberal profession. . . . It has never yet been
a profession. It has been at times a dignified calling, at others a
romantic adventure, and then again a servile trade. But a profession
it could not begin to be until modern objective journalism was
successfully created, and with it the need of men who would
consider themselves devoted, as all the professions ideally are, to
the service of truth alone.*

—WALTER LIPPMANN, *writing in* The Yale Review, 1931

6

The Girl with the Goods

The small young woman, who had about her the expensive fragility of a fine china miniature, looked smaller still measured against the wrought-iron gates guarding the courtyard of the brownstone mansion. Executed in the Italianate manner that American *nouveaux riches* embraced as the epitome of Old World elegance, the grand residence occupied the entire eastern blockfront of Madison Avenue between Forty-ninth and Fiftieth streets. It had been constructed originally for Henry Villard, who quit reporting after his Civil War adventures on the *Herald* and *Tribune* and made his fortune building railroads in the Northwest. Its present mistress, to whom tiny Helen Rogers was about to apply for the position of private secretary on this early June morning in 1903, was that formidable hostess and stout pillar of the international social set—Elisabeth Mills Reid. At Barnard College, from which she just graduated, Miss Rogers had gathered that Mrs. Reid was a woman of majestic whims and artless candor with a notably low threshold for tolerating stupidity among her servants. Not quite as uneasy as Cinderella among the swells but anxious at the prospect of intimacy with the fabulously rich, Helen Rogers drew herself up to her full height of five feet and the better part of one inch and marched crisply to meet her fate.

There had been no doubt she would be a working girl. "I'm sick of this dependence and I can't stand the feeling of draining mother," Helen had written to her sister Florence at the beginning of her senior year at Barnard. The youngest of eleven children, she had been left fatherless at the age of three, and everyone in the Rogers family of Appleton, Wisconsin, had to pitch in to make ends meet. At an early age Helen had become a passable seamstress, refashioning her older sisters' dresses to fit her smaller self, and at boarding school she was by no means too proud to help work off her tuition and upkeep. Blessed with a clear, orderly mind and a spirited, unfrivolous nature, Helen seemed to justify the sacrifices the family had to make to stake her to a first-rate higher education. She did her best to reduce the burden; between and after classes at Barnard, she tutored, supervised a dormitory, and ran a typewriter in the bursar's office, yet still found time to sing in the student choral society, stage-manage for the drama club, and as a senior, turn the yearbook into a paying proposition. A fine manager, she had grit to her that her delicacy of appearance belied. Her round face had a moonlike geometry Helen did not much care for, and there was an angularity to her features—the firm, square jawline, the thin wide mouth, the strong cheekbones—that, when taken with the fine soft hair curled close to her head, gave her a kind of incisive look not usually perceived as sweet. Most striking were her eyes, large and pale in a hue somewhere between a grayed green and faint blue, that seemed to probe with an almost metallic glint whatever object they focused upon; if the object was human, the effect, chilling or cauterizing as their owner's mood dictated, could be decidedly unsettling. The steely character those eyes conveyed was captured by Barnard's Class of 1903 poet, who wrote of her: "We love little Helen, / Her heart is so warm, / And if you don't cross her, / She'll do you no harm. / So don't contradict, / Or else if you do, / Get under the table / And wait till she's through." Bright if not clever, a demon for detail, a go-getter out to escape the genteel poverty she had known all her life, Helen Rogers had one other quality that her overseers in Barnard could commend to Mrs. Whitelaw Reid—persistence. What nature or fate had not kindly bestowed upon her she would strive to win by industry.

"I wish you could have seen her look me over—I nearly died," she wrote to Florence when the ordeal was over. But she survived the scrutiny and was engaged to conduct Madame's correspondence, keep track of her social engagements, and balance her ample checkbook; the pay was two hundred a month, generous for the times.

If she was awed by the splendors of the Reids' Madison Avenue mansion, with its dining room large enough to accommodate fifty guests easily, Helen was all but overwhelmed by their estate in Purchase, a few miles east of White Plains, that Mr. Reid had renamed Ophir Hall; Ophir Farm had come to seem too consciously understated for the grandeur that now filled it. The coach that met her at the railroad station required a ten-minute drive *after* passing the Reids' gatehouse to wind through the grounds and reach the castle at the summit. The view from there, commanding a full sweep of lush countryside and the distant sparkle of Long Island Sound, was nature's modest prelude to the jeweled setting within: rose marble floors, Tudor timbered ceilings, Vandykes and other old Dutch and Flemish masters on the walls, furniture in Venetian velvets, Coromandel screens, fine rugs and tapestries in profusion, the most heavenly red leather chairs and divans in the library, and the great soaring halls softened by abundant arrangements of lavender orchids and other tropical blooms. Each time she came, a different coach and driver in the Reids' livery would fetch her at the station; after five she stopped counting them.

The work proved far more interesting than Helen had expected, and her employer, far less forbidding. *She is a woman of great good sense and a better heart,* Helen wrote Florence in a revealing correspondence that constitutes a running eight-year chronicle of her career among the Reids, *and best of all she is very democratic.* One day that autumn when the rest of the family was away, Mrs. Reid had Helen join her in the massive dining room for *a little paltry five-course luncheon. . . . We had a butler apiece and unless I had added a little muscle of late in polishing floors, I never could have lifted the silver.* Though careful not to overstep her bounds, Helen surprised herself by doing most of the talking. Emboldened by her study of classics, in which she had nearly majored before abandoning plans to be a teacher, she was articulate and well-spoken; Elisabeth Reid, for all her family's wealth, lacked Helen Rogers's schooling. But in terms of protocol, Helen had far more to learn than to teach. For a series of house parties that kept Ophir Hall busy much of that autumn, she tried her best to master the complexities of seating the guests by drawing up table diagrams based upon such small knowledge as she had gleaned of them; invariably, after inspecting Helen's seating assignments, Mrs. Reid would shuffle them. *You see, two people can't sit next to each other two meals in succession and there are about twenty here all the time.* And there were occasional telltale signs that Helen's attire was not quite presentable, such as Mrs. Reid's urging her to buy "some sort of little handbags for coming up here with. You just get whatever you like." That meant (1) Helen's old belt bag was just too shabby to be seen at Ophir and (2) her employer would pay for its replacements; the sting was balmed with kindness. Her benefactor was *not a woman given to praise so a little is much appreciated. It makes me so anxious to prove myself of real value to her.* That she was doing so Mrs. Reid plainly signaled on Christmas with "a little remembrance of the day," a gold pin with three big heart-shaped amethysts and ten natural pearls. Helen was charmed, flattered, buoyed, and drawn deeper into the web.

She was not, of course, without a life of her own. Her mother had come east to chaperone, sharing her apartment but hardly dampening her social life. Helen attended an occasional suffragist meeting and related her budding feminist sentiment to her mother, who had at first disapproved but then came to see in her daughter's pluckiness a validation of the rights at issue: Helen Rogers was worth as much as any man, and a damned sight more than most. Her openmindedness drew her out one thoroughly enjoyable evening with a group of socialists for dinner and a performance of *The Master Builder* by Ibsen. *You know Socialists are very interesting people and not of necessity queer at all. I have always felt toward them about as I do toward anarchists—but they really can be most conventionally nice and good looking.* And she began to see and correspond with a Princeton man named Francis Nash, who also came from Wisconsin of a family with relatively slender means. He had her down to the Yale-Princeton football game and took her to the theater and wrote the most amusing letters, if one discounted—as she readily did—a certain quantity of drivel among the *bons mots.*

Distinctly on the periphery of Helen Rogers's world were the Reids' children, Jean, two years her junior, *who is not pretty but very animated,* and Ogden, six months older than Helen, who was *very good looking and has a beautiful smile.* But inevitably, the longer and more closely she worked with Elisabeth Reid, the more familiar she became with her children and the anxieties they induced in their parents: an unswanlike daughter of decidedly marriageable age and a son with looks but a feckless character to go with his invincibly sunny disposition.

Broad-shouldered, dark-haired Ogden Mills Reid, then in the last year of his undergraduate career at Yale, was his father's pride and despair. Forty-five years old when his son was born, Whitelaw Reid had taught the boy to ride and swim and shoot and took pleasure in his aptitude for each; indeed, he soon excelled his father in them. But he showed little of his father's intensity or powers of concentration. Ogden was an indifferent pupil at the Browning School, not slow so much as uninterested. A year off for tutoring preceded his admission to Yale's Class of 1904 but did little to improve his academic performance. At the first opportunity, he dropped Greek and Latin, to his father's displeasure, and still just barely managed to pass. There were other traits that distressed the senior Reids: the boy was reckless, driving too fast and drinking too much and partying too late; and careless, forgetting one semester to send in his tuition payment until the bursar called the unpleasant matter to his father's attention; and thoughtless, almost never writing home—and when he did, he had the most annoying way of forgetting to date his letters, as if life to him was an endlessly burbling stream of easily navigable rapids. He was, after all, well liked by his colleagues and renowned in New Haven as the star of the swimming and water polo teams, both of which he captained. He could not justifiably be termed a wastrel, so it was hard to object when he took his polo ponies with him to Yale for his senior year. They were evidently as much a distraction as a comfort to him, for within two months of his projected class commencement, the dean of students wrote the Reids that Ogden was not attaining satisfactory grades in organic evolution and elementary statistics and was thus in grave peril of not receiving his degree. Alerted, the indulged prince of Purchase cheerfully dismounted and did what he had to do, graduating on schedule if not with distinction. Now, perhaps, he would get on with life's more solemn business, or why else were his father's pride and his mother's money sustaining the *New York Tribune*? Yes, Ogden would take over its direction at the earliest possible moment, but maturity was needed first, and so on he would go to Yale Law School to improve his reasoning powers and discover his better self.

The lessons Ogden Reid did not soak up from his parents' world Helen Rogers did. *I wish I could talk politics with you for a while. I am getting so fearfully wise about things, and it's such fun. . . . I don't suppose there's another house in New York where one would find such an interesting mingling of the social and political atmospheres.* Her usefulness to Mrs. Reid increased with her worldliness, and the little gifts betokening approval came regularly now: a silver drinking cup in a leather case, a looking glass with a mother-of-pearl handle, *a stunning old rose brocaded silk work bag. It's big and beautiful and I keep it hung over the bed post to feast my eyes upon.* By her second Christmas, she was the recipient of a fur-lined coat from Elisabeth Reid. *"Isn't she a star?"* There was a still more exciting gift: At sixty-six Whitelaw Reid's social and political careers were capped by his appointment as American ambassador to the Court of St. James's—and Helen was invited to join the official family in London, continuing as Mrs. Reid's secretary, at a no doubt more frenetic pace, and filling in on Mr. Reid's staff when and if the need arose. During the spring of 1905, she studied stenography and brushed up her typing; *Burke's Peerage* became her bedside reading. "Keep your nerve, little girl," her Princeton friend Francis Nash wrote her as embarkation neared, "you've got the goods and it will be all right before long."

His newspaper was now losing money at the rate of $2,000 a week, but Whitelaw Reid felt his protracted absence would in no way diminish its true role in his, and the nation's, life. "I have long looked upon my ownership of the *Tribune* as a sort of trust," he wrote to President Roosevelt by way of assuring him that, once installed in public office in London, he would not be involved with it in any way that might prove embarrassing to the administration. The paper stood for "good morals, good citizenship, and the public policies with which the public has learned to identify it . . . [and] I should be sure its general course would not depart from these established lines during my absence." Reid divested himself of the title of editor-in-chief that he had worn for one-third of a century and handed it to a thoroughly dependable watchman, Hart Lyman, a Yale man, a clubman (the University), a Republican, and a staunch conservative, who had spent twenty-nine of his fifty-six years on the *Tribune,* mostly in the comfortable seclusion of the editorial page and lately serving as assistant to Reid's previous inoffensive surrogate, Donald Nicholson. Reid's departing instructions held no surprises; Lyman was to keep the paper on course as the most "trustworthy and the best family newspaper in New York—the one which a gentleman (at least one of Republican leanings) is better satisfied to read every morning himself and to have read in his family." Dignity was all, and Mr. Lyman did his gentlemanly best.

During his seven and one half years as U.S. ambassador to Great Britain, the Whitelaw Reids crossed the Atlantic sixteen times, always in the highest of style, taking a three-room suite for themselves on the great ocean liners and accommodations for the maids, valets, and secretaries who constituted their entourage. Helen Rogers was among the latter, but a notch above. Mrs. Reid's maid dressed her every morning on shipboard. *I hardly know what I should have done without her. Oh, it's fun to have a maid button your shoes and do your hair.* The Reids' London residence, Dorchester House, was a fairy-tale setting, every room a museum piece, with a staff of thirty-five; Wrest Park, the country estate the ambassador also rented, was only slightly less opulent. And the Reids themselves gloried in the life of the court, she in her exquisite Parisian gowns festooned with lace and encrusted with pearls, he in his silk knickerbockers and long stockings at the reception for the King of Spain or whatever other ceremony summoned them in that twilight of extravagance before cataclysm routed the ruling classes of Europe. *I wish you could see her in all her jewels. . . . The big frontispiece heavy collar with the . . . three wonderful ruby pendants and the tiara.* [*Mr. Reid*] *looked every inch a King in his sable lined coat with its beautiful collar and cuffs—he really is a handsome man you know.*

The line between the Reids' world and hers continued to blur. Mrs. Reid insisted that Helen take cabs everywhere in London, that a maid pick up after her and tend to her wardrobe, that Helen have ten pairs of her long white suede gloves when only lace would serve for her now. *Do you know what the feeling of having ten pairs of long gloves is like? I sort of want to tell it to everyone I meet.* Yet she confessed to *feeling rather glum with my belongings* [*and wanting*] *to have more suitable clothes for Dorchester House and the people whom I meet there. . . .* Sometimes she would breakfast in Jean Reid's room and chatter away with her in sisterly fashion. Sometimes she would dine merrily and innocently with Ogden when he summered with the family, and he would take her to the theater, but usually he escorted girls from the proper social set and, at any rate, would soon be off to another term at law school. She was with them, more and more, but not of them.

That she was ambitious to cross this line began to occur to others perhaps even before Helen herself was aware of it—certainly before she could admit it and the torment that followed from it, given her innate decency and family values. Tongues wagged that brainy, efficient, pert little Miss Rogers would make just the sort of wife that affable but lackluster Ogden Reid required to put his life in order and on the road to responsibility. He was known to like the girl, to have squired her around a bit, and if it was just social slumming on his part, why hadn't Elisabeth Reid stifled the relationship in the bud? Because she cherished Miss Rogers, and Jean was also well disposed to her. And who could blame Miss Rogers for not discouraging the boy's attentions? It was just that she was so—well, that her background was so—so common. By London's ironclad social rules, the ineligible Miss Rogers looked rather like a gold-digger; democratic friendship with the help really ought not to be encouraged.

Elisabeth Reid was pained by such whisperings, partly no doubt because she recognized their validity; Whitelaw Reid was even more pained because he had worked so hard to win his way into the Brahmin ranks and did not relish the prospect of his son marrying well beneath him. In the nicest possible way, therefore, Mrs. Reid had a painful and probably not entirely candid talk with Helen at the end of the Christmas holidays during Ogden's last year at law school. The whole family was so fond of her, of course, Ogden included, as was so plainly evident by the attention he had just paid her, taking her to the automobile show and so forth over the holidays, but people did talk and he was, after all, a somewhat immature and impressionable boy still who might misunderstand her kindness to him, and if she might somehow manage to be, well, perhaps a bit more standoffish with Ogden . . . The conversation stunned Helen; the innocence suddenly drained out of her friendship with Ogden, casual and intermittent though it had been. *I at least know where I stand and the game I must play though the good Lord knows how I'm going to play it. . . . Mr. Reid is the real trouble plus the talk of a few accursed people. His changed manner started my unhappiness . . . and try as I might to believe it was my own imaginings I knew very well that there could be only one thing the matter.* She boiled with resentment, felt her pride trampled on, and if she did not harbor such deep affection for Ogden's mother *and it weren't too hard to live on nothing I'd fling my dependence on her to the wind.*

Instead, she paid more attention to the lovesick importunings of Francis Nash, who was struggling to get ahead with his business career, first doing some sort of managerial thing at a lumber company in Arkansas and then something a little more respectable in Kansas City. She saw him on one of the Reids' trips home, finding him handsomer than she remembered, though rather haggard from a bout with malaria, and still able to stir her. Back in the lap of luxury in London, she was glad for the renewal of creature comforts, yet she was not proud of herself for this materialistic tendency, bemoaning *the almighty struggle for adjusting and manipulating everything for myself—which I seem to have done for so long—against the very peaceful and naturally feminine state of having every possible care and comfort done for one.* But she steeled herself against such lures. Ogden, who was clerking for a law firm while waiting to take his bar examination, joined the family for the Thanksgiving holidays, and Helen found him *a nice boy and I rather enjoy him, a beautiful, likeable disposition but without a ray of cleverness. What in thunder he's going to do with the Tribune I give up but mayhap he'll unexpectedly make good.* She would not deceive herself about the rich boy who could make her life a waking dream or the poor boy out West pining to make her his. The socialites Ogden went out with she was able to view with almost clinical detachment, preferring a certain little Southern girl to one whose whole family she judged, no doubt partly on the strength of Jean's reports, to be lying in wait for him. But her correspondence with Florence during the first half of 1908 revealed an increasingly troubled state of mind, oscillating between love and contempt for Ogden. She wrote that she wished she could *lay the whole awful complication before you. . . . I'm sure he's pure gold really and yet I have a dreadful feeling every little while I'm idealizing him beyond all reason.* She would reconcile herself to his marrying one of the girls in his set, then try to feign pleasure over her own ineligibility because *the difficulties would be simply intolerable and I have to let myself dwell on them every once in a while for the sake of antidoting my caring.* But the caring would not go away. When word arrived in March that Ogden had failed the bar examination, her frustration turned into fury against him. *I've no doubt that the stupid, lazy, irresponsible boy will flunk them again and make a failure of life before he has even started it.* He passed on his second try, and the family celebrated; Helen bristled at his lackadaisical attitude toward it all and his sweet obtuseness to her hours of lecturing him how he ought really to knuckle down and make something of the advantages life had dealt him. By late spring she was certain that it would be best for both of them for their affection to ripen no further. For all its graces, she recognized the snobbery of his world—indeed, of his family—and how her elevation into it would strike her own friends as a betrayal of her independent character. *We are totally incongenial in much, we could never have any intellectual pleasure in common, he is 49 years younger than me in his experience of responsibility and in his feeling of life as a whole. . . .*

The rightness of that judgment was reinforced by Jean's marriage that year to an Englishman twice her age but with all the best social credentials this side of a peerage. John Ward, the younger brother of the Earl of Dudley, had posted a splendid military record and served as equerry to King Edward VII. His modest fortune was augmented by a gift of $100,000 each from Jean's parents and grandfather Mills. After the wedding, which the King and Queen attended, the couple settled down on a 2,500-acre estate. Something of the sort was what they had in mind for Ogden.

What Ogden had on his mind just then was the *Tribune.* That summer he began a nearly four-year apprenticeship that would end with his appointment as managing editor by his thirtieth birthday. That he would concentrate on the editorial side had been a foregone conclusion; he was poor with numbers, and business details bored him, even as the minutiae of life in general did not much concern him. What, after all, did a young fellow on a $2,500-a-month allowance have to worry about?

He might have swaggered into the place and thrown his weight around, but that was not Ogden Reid's makeup. By being a good-natured novice eager to learn from the professional retainers surrounding him, he won the affectionate loyalty of the staff instead of what might easily have been profound resentment. Swagger, moreover, would have been ludicrously misplaced at the *New York Tribune* in 1908. The Tall Tower his father had erected as its proud home thirty-three years earlier was now a hard-used monument to shabby gentility; its staff and their product seemed souvenirs of a bygone eminence. Revenues that year came to $839,000, well under what the paper was taking in during the latter part of Greeley's reign, and losses had reached nearly $3,000 a week. Expenses kept being cut accordingly, which merely accentuated the downward slide, although staff members were almost never summarily dismissed—they were simply not replaced when they fell from that withering vine. The editors were kind, the work pace casual, and the resulting newspaper reflected a total absence of dynamism. In an article appraising New York's daily press, *The Atlantic Monthly* that year ranked the *Tribune* as close to the worst in the city; its financial pages were found execrable, its news columns readable but utterly commonplace, and its rubber-stamping of Republican policies made it the last sheet in town operated as a servant of party machinery. Whitelaw Reid, who thought his paper the truest keeper of the pure party flame, ordered up an editorial in response that characterized the *Atlantic* as a formerly distinguished literary periodical that had outlived its usefulness.

Ogden began work as a reporter and journeyed nicely around the office with stints on the copy desk, city desk, rewrite desk, and night desk. By all accounts, he was no worse than marginally competent; by some, he displayed talent and judgment. A most welcome early report reaching Dorchester House came from Lord Northcliffe, publisher of *The Times* of London, who wrote from New York to the ambassador about a reporter whom the *Tribune* had sent to interview him: "At my first encounter with him neither my secretary nor I had any notion that he was your own son and we were much pleased with the very conscientious way he set about interviewing me." Afterwards, Northcliffe observed Ogden "at public meetings and other places which I went. I must say that I think you have in young Mr. Reid the material for a very good journalist and a conscientious one." Similar but more suspect commendatory letters arrived in London from the *Tribune*'s editors, and Helen Rogers was obliged by her employer to listen to them recited *ad nauseam* and offer her opinion in response, as if it mattered to her that *every office boy adores him. They probably do—I never knew a servant yet who wouldn't lick his boot if he looked out of the corner of his eye at them. . . . [B]ut I wish to goodness they wouldn't talk to me about him. The book is closed and I don't like having to read over back chapters.*

The less likely Helen's entanglement with Ogden appeared, the less disagreeable toward her Ambassador Reid became. The cessation of hostilities between them seemed confirmed by the spring of 1909 when he brought flowers to her bedside while she was in the hospital for an appendectomy, though Helen was certain Mrs. Reid had put him up to it. Nevertheless, they drew closer together, even sharing meals in Elisabeth's absence. *Solemnly we lunch together and solemnly dine with a flunkey standing in each corner of the room. . . . Without exception I believe he's the strangest combination of human particles extant. Such a mixture of greatness and weakness, of simplicity and snobbery, of kindness and hardness, of wisdom and blindness, and I never decide which tips the balance except in moments when I hate him.* In a burst of anguish that evidenced the fierce hold the Reids had upon her, she declared to her sister: *Oh, Flossie, won't I ever be able to tear this out of me! It seems as if I should never be able to get away from it as long as I live in the midst of these people. . . .*

But remain among them she did, abandoning Ogden to a Louisville flame who was reportedly warming his heart while she responded with intensified interest to the ever more ardent pursuit by Francis Nash. For the first time now, she began seriously to contemplate exchanging the life of luxury and glamour that her service to the Reids had won her for a struggling existence in some Midwestern nowhere by the side of an adoring husband. It was a bargain, she tried to tell herself, that she would readily make if her character was worth five cents. But she was unsure whether Francis's companionship, however "perfect," compensated for the troubling realization that he loved her more than she did him. Nor, she confessed to her sister, did she want to be poor, and Francis's ambition struck her as deficient. How she wished she had money of her own, she confided in a deepening orgy of indecision.

By the end of 1909, Helen declared finally that she wanted "with all my heart" to marry Francis, who now began to speak of pursuing a career at law. Their engagement was announced the following spring in the Appleton newspaper, the pain of impending separation from her beloved benefactor was confronted—and Ogden Reid took the news less airily than all had supposed likely. She explained it to him in New York in March, and they each shed tears, and it was all rather unpleasant, but as she sailed back to England with his parents, convinced her relationship with Ogden was dead, she professed satisfaction, or at least relief. *I should love dearly all the material comfort and intellectual interest that his life touches but so far as real sympathy and understanding are concerned a life with him would have been hell. Also I know perfectly well that I'm a darned sight cleverer than he is and that isn't a very happy kind of a basis.*

But then Francis began pressing her hard to set an early wedding date despite his still far from bright financial prospects, and when she saw him again in the fall, it was over. *He's the ideal absent lover if there ever was one.* He trailed her back to New York to try to rewin her but would not come aboard the boat to argue his case, preferring to gaze on her from the dockside crowd in broken-hearted anguish. Ogden was in London to console her but did not press his own suit; she found him calm and strong and comforting throughout her ordeal of guilt over having finally flung over the poor boy she had for so long kept on a string. Francis wrote after she had asked him not to, his mother wrote asking what Helen had done to her son, and she was tortured by fond memories of his devotion to her, but she would not yield. Spinsterhood suddenly looked attractive to her as her twenty-eighth birthday passed. *And yet all the time Ogden thinks he is going to marry me and just calmly goes on assuming it without any reason for so doing.* At times she found him a dear and at others rather horrid; there were fights and tears, and she was unhappy because she knew he did not love her the way Francis did, was incapable of that sort of suffering passion, and she did not want to offer herself up in the end to be taken as a prized possession of the Reid dynasty. They already possessed quite enough.

But she did not. Her pride and independence were perhaps less negotiable than most other young women's of her station in life, yet she was no longer a dreaming schoolgirl insistent on a grand passion at the core of her life. And Elisabeth Reid badly wanted her for a daughter-in-law now. She would bring order and responsibility to Ogden's life, she had acquired the necessary social graces through more than seven dutiful years with the Reids, and the bestowal upon her of a generous monthly allowance would purchase for her a sense of freedom and an assurance of well-being not dependent on Ogden's moods or wayward attentions. And so the bargain was sealed.

The wedding took place in March 1911 in Appleton, Wisconsin. Whitelaw and Elisabeth Reid were the only guests to arrive in their own railroad car. *Ogden is a pretty wonderfully sweet person and so much finer than even I suspected that I feel almost ashamed of myself. . . .*

The *New York Tribune,* without anyone on its atrophying staff suspecting it, had acquired a new life force that in ways both subtle and exceedingly obvious would dominate its course for nearly half a century.

II

Upon his designation as managing editor of the *Tribune* early in 1912, Ogden Reid continued to exasperate his father by small, irresponsible acts of omission. He forgot, for example, to ship to London as instructed copies of the paper on a regular basis so the elder Reid could assess his progress and make suggestions. And there was the London correspondent whose pleas for a directive from Ogden went unheeded for so long that they were finally sent to the ambassador, who was not amused by his son's delinquency. But there were unmistakable signs that Ogden, or somebody, was on the job in the New York office.

His first test had come late on the evening of April 14 when distress signals from the leviathan luxury liner *Titanic,* on its maiden voyage, reached the city. The *Tribune* kept its forms open until 4:30 the next morning to publish the latest fragmentary news; no paper, despite claims to the contrary by historians of *The New York Times,* brought its readers fresher word of the disaster in its April 15 edition. And for the next several days, while the liner *Carpathia* steamed incommunicado toward New York with the survivors, the *Tribune* held its own against the massive coverage of the city's prosperous papers despite its far smaller staff, circulation, and news hole. An excellent sailor himself, Ogden Reid directed the paper's coverage with evident relish. The critical test came when the *Carpathia* docked and newsmen fell upon the survivors and over one another in a mad scramble to reconstruct that night of horror at sea. Ogden had hired a couple of tugboats to try to board the rescue ship before it docked—they were repulsed in New York harbor—and installed a battery of four telephone lines at dockside to relay news back to the office; a corps of sixteen reporters, nearly the entire city staff, was shuttled to and fro by a small fleet of vehicles, and the resulting news presentation in the *Tribune,* the city's smallest major paper, was every bit as informative, colorful, and moving as that in the big sheets. The *Times*'s play was somewhat more compendious but, aside from an

exclusive though overblown interview with the *Titanic*'s radio operator, no
more thorough—and less orderly and readable; the *Herald*'s spirited coverage,
directed by the aging Commodore himself, who happened to be in New York
at the time, was stronger than any paper's in nautical knowledge but choppier
than the *Tribune*'s and less solid than that of the *Times,* which had by then
succeeded it as the city's most industrious news-gatherer.

One week's bravura performance, however, did not change the fact that the
Tribune, even with the owners' son now titular head of the editorial staff, was
a distant straggler in its field. Ogden may have been well provided for materially,
but his paper continued on a near-starvation diet. Still, there were signs that his
parents were inclined to deal somewhat more generously toward the *Tribune*
now that Ogden was actively on board. In the five years preceding his arrival,
the Reids had subsidized its losses by a total of approximately $425,000; over
the next five years, in the face of declining revenues, the red ink accumulated
in the amount of $1,135,000. Sustaining the operation at the moribund level to
which Whitelaw Reid had let it fall was hardly strong enough medicine to stop
the hemorrhaging. Not until the ambassador died in London that December at
the age of seventy-five was his paper released from bondage to an orthodoxy that
had nearly buried it with him.

Reid's estimated $1.4 million estate consisted largely of his stock in the
Tribune, which he willed to his wife. Added to her own holdings, the bequest
made Elisabeth Reid practically the sole owner of the paper. Two years earlier
she had inherited a great deal, the probable equivalent of something between
twenty and twenty-five million, from her father. During the remainder of her
life, she elected to make the *Tribune* principal beneficiary of her generosity. The
process began in March 1913 with her appointment of Ogden as editor-in-chief
and her granting him a free hand to change the paper as he saw fit. By 1920 he
and his appointees had substantially remade the *Tribune* and consumed nearly
$4.4 million of his mother's fortune doing so. Even then it was still not paying
its way, but it was undeniably alive and kicking.

The paper he took command of had a circulation of under 50,000—it was
probably closer to 25,000; there are no reliable figures. The number was almost
certainly no higher than it had been when Whitelaw Reid obtained control forty
years earlier; in the interim, the city's population had more than quadrupled and
the competition had bolted far ahead in laying claim to its readers, mostly
among the lower economic tiers. The *Sun,* oldest of the *Tribune*'s main rivals,
was the closest to it in circulation as Ogden surveyed the volatile newspaper
market; fifteen years after Dana's death, its sales were down to about 75,000,
and while it remained a well-written sheet, it had the same aging, threadbare
look about it as the Reids' property.

The *Herald,* its second-oldest rival, came next with about 90,000; the decline
in its sales from the city's leadership a generation earlier had been steady except
for a bulge during and just after the Spanish-American War. Bennett's eccentric

and tyrannical absentee ownership and his milking of the paper's profits to sustain his exorbitant standard of living would have been sufficient in themselves to assure the *Herald*'s steady slippage, but his own infuriated displeasure over the rising fortunes of the egregious William Randolph Hearst had exacerbated the problem. Bennett would not forgive the upstart for the *Journal*'s having covered the war against Spain as if it were one big tawdry sex murder; its simplistic, inflammatory editorials and distorted, jingoist news presentation were a disgrace to the profession, in the Commodore's view. When Hearst had the effrontery to cable Bennett asking if his paper was for sale and, if so, at what price, the reply read: "PRICE OF HERALD THREE CENTS. FIVE CENTS SUNDAY. BENNETT." And when Hearst's blatant political ambitions, which made Greeley's look decorous in retrospect, drove him into an expedient alliance with Tammany Hall for a Democratic nomination to Congress in 1902, the *Herald* led the choral scoffing at the transplanted Californian's claim to be a champion of the common man. Hearst, victorious, threw himself and the city a giant fireworks celebration in Madison Square, and when some of the materials awaiting use exploded, killing seventeen and injuring another hundred, his *Journal* buried the story on an inside page. When Hearst bid for the presidency in 1904, the *Herald* led those who charged he was trying to buy his way into the White House. And when Hearst obtained the Democratic nomination for governor of New York and threw his money and the massed weight of his organization into the campaign, Bennett ordered his troops to unsheathe their long knives. Their attack was incessant, raking over Hearst's whole dubious past, from his dismissal from Harvard for a smart-aleck prank (a gift-wrapped chamber pot delivered to each of his instructors with its recipient's name prominently embossed) to his alleged complicity in the assasination of President McKinley by running several editorial-page suggestions that that unworthy, who had failed to make war on Spain as fast as Hearst had wanted, was as ripe for removal from office by violent means as any other bad regime or ruler.

Blaming his narrow loss of the governorship—and with it the smashup of all his political dreams—on Bennett's mad-dog pursuit of him, Hearst sought revenge and soon found it. A prime source of the *Herald*'s popularity for decades had been its "Personals," which filled the first several pages of the paper long after its rivals had given theirs over to presentation of the news. With their thumbnail tales of need and privation, hope and despair, opportunity and assignation, they made for reading every bit as fascinating as the news columns. They also functioned as a buyers' guide to the demimonde, featuring such unmistakable come-ons as:

Refined young woman desires immediate loan.

Woman finds paddling her own canoe dreary task, seeks manly pilot.

LADY: loyal, loving, lovable, with famished heart craves devotion of but one man financially worth while.

Attention! Is there a man of honor and sterling worth who can appreciate the cruelty that impels a gentlewoman, superior mental and physical attractions, age 34, to adopt this means of release from hated bondage? No Shylocks or triflers.

Dollar-a-line announcements by "chic Parisian ladies with cozy suites" and "masseuses with highly magnetic manners" gave a decidedly risqué tone, especially in its Sunday edition, the city's biggest seller, to the otherwise society-minded *Herald*. Bennett had long been warned by his editors of the paper's vulnerability on this score, but no stranger himself to the courtesan's trade, he defended the ads as a public service; besides, they were keeping him in champagne and châteaux. Hearst put one of his ablest investigative bloodhounds on the trail and, after a year documenting the nature of the *Herald*'s profitable flesh-peddling, spread the findings all over the *Journal* at the same time they were being presented to a federal grand jury on the charge of sending obscene material through the mails. Bennett, found guilty, appeared in person and disdainfully peeled off thirty-one thousand-dollar bills to pay the fine and marched right back up the gangplank of the ship that had brought him from Europe.

The damage, though, could not be so tidily repaired. The disappearance of the suggestive "Personals" and the residual taint left by their elaborate defrocking sent the *Herald*'s circulation into a slide from which it never really recovered. Remembering the Stanley-finds-Livingstone glories of his youth, Bennett tried to recover the lost ground by staking an explorer to a $25,000 expense account for the story of his impending trek to the North Pole; the *Times* paid Robert E. Peary $4,000 for the same story, and the race was on. The *Herald*'s man claimed victory in 1909, but his report lacked convincing documentation and was soon acknowledged a fraud. The *Times*'s victory solidified its stature as the new leader for accuracy and enterprise in the collection of the news— a role long prized by the *Herald*.

Third oldest of the *Tribune*'s rivals, the *Times* under Adolph Ochs had rewon the ground it had lost in the forty years since the Tweed Ring revelations and showed no signs of slowing its growth. Like Whitelaw Reid, Ochs professed that ownership of his newspaper was more like serving as temporary custodian of a public trust than running a business primarily for profit. The difference in their custodianships was that Reid saw his trust as a museum piece requiring only an occasional dusting and airing while Ochs saw his as an organic, growing entity that needed constant tending and nourishment. In the thirty years of their marriage, the Reids might have invaded the Mills fortune to build the *Tribune* into the dominant national institution that Pulitzer, Hearst, and now Ochs were trying to establish; instead, the Mills money went for a life of luxury while the *Tribune* turned into a trinket betokening their social and political eminence. Ochs had no fortune to build with, so he kept reinvesting the *Times*'s modest earnings until they began to compound themselves. He was at the paper every day, all the time, learning the mechanism inside out, viewing himself not as the keeper of the flame of any political faith or social creed but as a builder of a never-ending monument to public enlightenment—and in that end saw a viable business enterprise. All the leading newspaper figures before him had been journalists, ambitious for literary distinction; Ochs was not so infected. He was a public-spirited businessman selling a commodity—information—in abundance, with high-quality ingredients, untainted by partisanship, free of self-aggrandizing additives, all plainly wrapped and delivered at a low price. He was confident the public would recognize excellent value when offered it.

To implement the marketing program that he pursued with such single-mindedness, Ochs turned over the news side of the operation to a sixteen-year veteran of the *Sun* whom he enlisted in 1904 and who over the next twenty-five years served as the shaping hand of the *Times*'s journalistic destiny. Managing editor Carr Van Anda had a consuming intellectual curiosity that was as keenly focused on scientific and technological developments as on battlefields and legislative chambers. He had a mind capable of spotting an error in one of Albert Einstein's calculations and detecting a forgery in a freshly unearthed 4,000-year-old panel of hieroglyphics. His formidable intelligence was yoked to an omnivorous appetite for news from every corner of the earth—news that with the development of the automobile, airplane, and wireless was more readily accessible than ever before. He wanted it fast and accurate and complete, and Adolph Ochs provided him with the money to get it reported and the white space to get it printed. And he did not want it stylistically garnished; the *Times* was not a showcase for aspiring poets, novelists, or philosophers—and if some criticized it as elephantine, they were invited to seek diversion elsewhere. The *Times* was for people of intelligence, of propriety, of vested interest in the orderly working of society, and reading it, with its almost unrelieved seriousness of purpose, became a badge of rectitude. By 1912, Ochs and Van Anda had driven its circulation past 200,000, and the *Times,* while still well behind the *World* in copies sold, was closing fast and about to challenge it as the most important and influential newspaper in America.

In mounting this effort, it is instructive to note, the *Times* studiously resisted the spectacular forms of news presentation used by Pulitzer and Hearst in favor of a format grounded in an entirely different set of values and judgments. Its conservatism in appearance and layout—until well into the twentieth century its front page was unillustrated except when major news broke, and its basic, classic headline was and continues to be set in slender all-capital letters resembling a neat picket fence one column wide—bespoke a philosophical and not merely esthetic preference. The *Times*'s apparently encyclopedic rigidity declared, by its very modesty and balance, that life on earth was essentially orderly, comprehensible, measurable, encompassable, and the *Times* was there to tell you what had happened yesterday within a historical framework. While its placement of stories conveyed an editorial judgment of their relative importance within the twenty-four-hour period just ended, its editors steadfastly declined to pretend by inflated typographic display that the news, weighed by the absolute standard of historic moment, was more important than it really was. This absence of excitability calmed and reassured, so that when extraordinary events did occur, the *Times*'s habitual reader had not been numbed to them by false daily declarations of catastrophe or revelations of evil. Joseph Pulitzer's *World,* on the other hand, and a growing number of papers in its mode, viewed the world each morning as if it had been minted fresh the day before, its happenings deserving to be writ large, displayed lavishly, narrated breathlessly. Its currency was not analysis but emotion; its subjects were far less likely to be the official ones that filled the *Times* than the elemental commonplaces of everyday existence: love, death, violence, vice, wealth, and poverty. Thus, the *World*'s and its progeny's editorial judgment of the news was exercised against the narrowest frame of reference: whatever, relatively speaking, could be most arrestingly rendered became the sensation of the day and was so displayed typographically. This process was not carried out, in the *World*'s case, in a vacuum of social responsibility; indeed, the sincerely held principles of its editorial page—equal justice for all classes and civic incorruptibility—overlay the *World*'s selection and play of the news. But its prevailing characteristic was an excitability which, though toned down somewhat in the wake of Pulitzer's death in 1910, was still sufficiently appealing in 1913 to attract nearly twice as many readers as the *Times.*

And Hearst's *Journal,* with its morning edition renamed the *American* to fend off charges of treason linked to its vilification of the slain McKinley, was recording even greater commercial success by still more grossly distorting the *World*'s techniques. The news was habitually overblown for ease of digestibility until hyperbole became an end in itself; editorials, simplistic and inflammatory, were also set in large type now, and the bizarre, the erotic, and the half-truth raucously colored its news columns. On the strength of this approach, the youngest of the *Tribune*'s rivals was able to sell a million copies of its combined morning and evening editions—more than twenty times the sales of the frail bark of which Ogden Mills Reid was now handed the captaincy.

III

So moribund was the *Tribune* that no infusion of cash from Elisabeth Mills Reid or appointment of a strong editor like Van Anda could have resuscitated it until the windows were opened and the suffocating solemnity of the place was aired out. And Ogden Reid did that—or, more accurately, he permitted it to be done.

Perhaps in reaction to the very formality and orthodoxy that governed his parents and came to characterize the family's newspaper, young Reid was partial to the light, bright touches that were introduced under him and served as counterpoint to the *Tribune*'s essential seriousness throughout the thirty-three years he was in charge of it. The writing grew livelier; bylines were introduced, encouraging reportorial and stylistic enterprise. Headlines grew larger and friskier. Many more pictures, maps, and charts were used, and by 1920 the typography had been so entirely redesigned that the *Tribune*'s graphic elegance and readability made it the national pacesetter. Its sports pages, carrying the witty Heywood Broun, romantic Grantland Rice, and caustic William McGeehan, became a fan's delight. Its editorial page offered shorter, brisker commentary and a popular new feature column, "The Conning Tower," a curious mélange of verse, epigrams, *pensées,* parody, parable, and scattershot irreverence edited and partly written by Franklin Pierce Adams, known to two generations of newspaper readers simply by his initials. A pictorial section in rotogravure, humor pieces by Robert Benchley, and an expanded drama and cultural section leavened the Sunday package. Weekday cultural coverage was improved with the launching of a daily book column, pioneer reports of the movies and radio, and a far more biting and contemporary tone to the theater reviews. And—the ultimate lightening and brightening—the comics got bigger and better, and three cartoonists of distinction were integrated into the mainstream of the paper: Clare Briggs, creator of "When a Feller Needs a Friend" and other nostalgic evocations of domestic comedy of a uniquely American smalltown brand; H. T. Webster, whose best-known single-panel satirical creation, "The Timid Soul," added the appealingly put-upon character of Caspar Milquetoast to American folklore; and Jay Norwood Darling, better identified as "Ding," the name he signed at the bottom of his drawings, whose editorial-page caricatures gently lampooned the wicked and the blunderers.

But nothing better conveyed the fresh spirit at the *Tribune* under its new head than a zest for combat that landed it in court on three occasions between 1914 and 1918, each time over a matter of principle. The last of them said little for the paper's historic highmindedness, but the merits of its position in each instance mattered less than the fact that it was aroused and swinging.

The first case stemmed from a pair of scoops scored by the paper's veteran shipping-news reporter, William E. Curtin, known among his colleagues as an accomplished raconteur, whose special gift was mimicking the colorful waterfront characters he encountered on the job, and as a less than accomplished writer. Typically he would phone in his stories to a rewriteman. He had attained the rank of *Tribune* legend by returning to the office one day with a hot story in plenty of time to write it himself. But the thing kept eluding him, lead after discarded lead landed in the wastebasket, and the city editor, a polite, almost shy gentleman named George Burdick, grew impatient for the piece as the deadline neared—and that, of course, tightened Curtin's fingers and brain all the more. Sympathetic to the reporter's predicament, the city editor approached him and gently spoke into his ear the patented Burdick relaxant for writer's block: "Mr. Curtin, just one word after another."

No such problem plagued Curtin in December 1913 when one of his sources around the U.S. Custom House tipped him off to a pair of investigations being conducted by Treasury Department officials involving conspiracy to defraud the government by smuggling jewelry into the country. Since those charged with the crimes were of some social standing, the stories, garnered two weeks apart, each made front-page exclusives. Divulging such activities, however, was a violation of Treasury Department regulations, so Curtin and his mentor, Burdick, were both summoned before a federal grand jury and asked the source of the leaked information. Even as Whitelaw Reid, during his term as Greeley adjutant, had stoutly defended the right of confidentiality between newsmen and their sources when the Senate put a pair of *Tribune* reporters on the grill, so Ogden Reid, in the early days of his command, backed his staff members. In promising freedom of the press, however, the First Amendment said nothing of such a privilege—the press was free to publish what it wished but not with total immunity to the consequences. Journalists had long argued that to serve the public interest, they should be accorded the same unaccountability in their dealings with confidants as was extended to doctors in their confidential relationship to their patients, clergymen in relation to their parishioners, and spouses who were not obliged to testify against each other in court. But since this privilege had yet to attain any legal standing, Curtin and Burdick based their refusal to comply with the federal prosecutor's demand on the Fifth Amendment ground exempting self-incriminating testimony; the *Tribune* men could conceivably have been prosecuted for conspiracy to violate a governmental regulation. The newsmen were assailed for having undermined the judicial process—although the alleged culprits in Curtin's stories had been duly tried and convicted—and having caused suspicion to be cast upon many customs officials as the likely tipsters, but the *Tribune* men held fast. Even when they were resummoned and presented with pardons signed by Woodrow Wilson excusing them from any penalties that might arise from their testimony, Curtin and Burdick refused to accept them. The government then took them to United States District Court, where the eminent jurist Learned Hand ruled against the pair. Of Burdick, he wrote: "If he obstinately refuses to accept [the pardon], it would be preposterous to let him keep on suppressing the truth, on the theory that it might injure him."

Ogden Reid, the formerly feckless, irresponsible boy, stiffened his back and ordered the *Tribune*'s lawyers to carry the case to the Supreme Court. Their brief was a scalding indictment of the government's tactics. The purpose of the President's pardoning power, it noted, was to temper justice with mercy, not to coerce information from witnesses. Nor had any legitimate reason been given to interrogate the newsmen or to grant them a pardon, for it was no violation of the law for the information in question to have been given out—only a departmental regulation had been breached—and it was a crime neither to have received such information innocently nor to publish it. The real perversion of the judicial process was the government's because the court to which it had appealed was powerless to inquire whether the grand jury had, at the federal prosecutor's instigation, been acting in good faith investigating a crime "or was being used as an instrument of inquisition at the insistence of a member of the President's Cabinet" in order to locate the source of "uncomfortable news . . . so that the person furnishing [it] might be summarily punished not by criminal proceedings but by dismissal from office." If the government won its case against the *Tribune,* its lawyers contended, every federal department would thereby "be supplied with a most potent, indeed terrorizing, instrument for preventing any of the acts or omissions of its officials from being made known to the public and subjected to wholesome criticism." In short, the government's executive officers were seeking the inquisitorial and punitive powers of a criminal court for enforcing their own regulations.

The entire American press saluted the *Tribune*'s stand. In January 1915, the Supreme Court overruled Learned Hand—but not on the basis of the eloquent *Tribune* brief. Acceptance as well as delivery of an executive pardon was essential to its validity, the Justices ruled, since the granting of it carried an imputation of guilt and its acceptance a confession of it; no court could therefore force the acceptance of a pardon nor did its refusal forfeit a witness's right to claim Fifth Amendment protection against self-incrimination. Nothing was added by way of sustaining the claimed journalistic privilege to keep reporters' news sources confidential, but the ruling in *Burdick v. U.S.,* as the *Tribune* case was styled, "had the effect of settling that point," according to the editorial page of *The New York Times.* That estimate would not be disturbed until the second half of the century; for the time being, the long-slumbering *New York Tribune* was the toast of its profession.

Two years later, the paper was entangled in another major legal battle, and again it presented itself as the champion of the people, *all* the people, not merely the propertied sector as had been its wont. Its opponent this time was one of New York's largest retailers, which was also one of the *Tribune*'s biggest advertisers (of which there were not an excessive number); Gimbel Brothers sued the paper for a million dollars for besmirching its reputation. And so it had —well-deservedly, too, the *Tribune* contended. The episode cast the paper's management in a light that allowed it to appear thoroughly principled while following a policy that was calculatedly expedient. Indeed, the *Tribune* had done nothing so enterprising on the business side since Whitelaw Reid decided to fund the Linotype machine.

To spur its drowsy revenues, the *Tribune* in September 1914 hired as general manager Richard G. Waldo, who had for nine years been business manager of *Good Housekeeping* and helped create its immensely successful money-back guarantee to readers who were not satisfied with any of the products advertised in the magazine. Within a few months, the *Tribune* launched a similar campaign, casting itself as the Caesar's wife of New York dailies and proclaiming as its new motto: "First to Last, the Truth: News, Editorials, Advertisements." Any reader dissatisfied with a product or service advertised in the paper would be fully reimbursed, either by the vendor or by the newspaper; meanwhile, the *Tribune* was establishing its own Bureau of Investigations to check up on any complaints from the public with a promise to publicize its findings on continual offenders.

It was a cheeky maneuver. At the time the paper's claimed circulation of 50,000 made it a dubious candidate to serve as watchdog of the city's advertising morals. But its very slenderness meant it had little to lose. The money-back gambit had the effect of saying to readers, "We may not have a lot of advertisers but the ones we do deal in quality," and to advertisers, "We may not have a lot of readers but the ones we do have money—and they trust our advertisers." And since advertisers who did not make good on the *Tribune*'s guarantee faced the prospect of being exposed in print, few were likely to argue with complainants.

To put teeth into the effort, the *Tribune* brought in Samuel Hopkins Adams, a lively writer who had won a name for himself with a series of ten muckraking articles in *Collier's*, starting in 1905, that exposed the proliferation of quack medicines, phony physicians, and fraudulent "health institutes." His work was a major contribution to the public outcry that resulted in a series of federal and state legislative reforms of which the Roosevelt-sponsored Pure Food and Drug Act of 1906 was the most prominent. By 1915 New York state had passed a law against fraudulent or misleading advertising. To help publicize the law—and its own purity, and therefore desirability as both a marketing vehicle and a buyers' guide—the *Tribune* assigned Adams to write a series on the subject and then take command of a regular column called "The Ad-Visor," empowered to report on readers' complaints about dubious advertising practices not only in the *Tribune* but anywhere else as well. It was a groundbreaking exercise in pro-consumer journalism that would not be surpassed until the establishment of Consumers Union in 1936. Written with candor and gusto, Adams's column attracted attention out of all proportion to the *Tribune*'s circulation. That it was also flagrantly serving the *Tribune*'s own interests, there could be no doubt. When, for instance, a reader called to his attention a Wilkes-Barre paper that had canceled a mail-order company's fraudulently offering a borax powder, Adams commended the action and added, "The manner of the Bennett-Hearst-Pulitzer type of newspaper to exposure of the dishonesty of an advertisement is to continue to publish that advertisement and to profit from the fraud."

Among advertisers attracted to the *Tribune* by its new feisty spirit was Gimbel Brothers department store, a huge emporium opened on Herald Square in 1910 following successful outlets in Philadelphia and Milwaukee. Gimbels took a 100,000-line contract, the equivalent of more than ten full-page ads, at the bargain rate of five cents a line—a loss leader for the paper but an important incursion among the city's mass merchandisers of lower-priced wares. Soon, though, the *Tribune*'s lofty principles were put to the test. Reports began filtering in that Gimbels bargains were not what their advertising proclaimed. Always there were plausible excuses, and always the complaining customers were recompensed. But the dubious practices did not cease, and Adams insisted on exposing the store in print. Waldo urged caution, telling Adams to build his dossier until the case against Gimbels was irrefutable; meanwhile, the paper's investigating bureau would keep trying to get the store to reform. Adams agreed, going so far as to defend Gimbels in his column when a reader denounced the store for gross misrepresentation of consumer habits in war-torn France with an ad in the *Times* that read: "Every woman in Paris is wearing two pearl pins. The whim of the moment . . ." A huckster's romantic hyperbole, Adams suggested. But his, and the *Tribune*'s, patience was exhausted when Gimbels threw itself a sixth-birthday extravaganza, advertising all sorts of alleged bargains that investigation disclosed to be overpriced frauds. On October 22, 1916, Adams attacked; the headline read: "GIMBELS ADVERTISING CLAIMS PROVE FALSE," and below was an exhaustive, caustic indictment with passages like this:

> With singular appropriateness, the hopeful birthday shopper was greeted, on entering the sale on the Thirty-second Street side, by a display of "Iceland Fox." There they lay, white, graceful and shining, under a "birthday" placard specifying attractive prices for scarfs. Have you ever seen an Iceland fox? It is a curious animal with strange and disconcerting habits. It has an artificial face, a hand-made tail, and hooks instead of claws, wherewith it tears open the pockets of the guileless and draws forth their money. . . . That is to say, the Iceland Fox (Gimbel) is Mary's little lamb under an alias. In other words, it's a howling, bleating, baa-ing fake!

And the paper promoted the exposé to the hilt, issuing it as a separate pamphlet titled "The Gimbel Story" and rooting on its author in print with the line, "Go to it, Adams—the sky's the limit!"

Gimbels sued for a million, naming the Tribune Association, Ogden Reid, Richard Waldo, G. Vernor Rogers (one of Helen Rogers Reid's brothers, a vice president on the paper from 1913 to 1923), and Adams as respondents. The store denied wrongdoing and countercharged that the whole thing was a plot by the *Tribune,* which "had gradually lost its great prestige" and become a paper of "but little power and influence," to restore itself to glory by bludgeoning advertisers into its columns. Having signed up Gimbels at an advertising rate it soon regretted, the paper concocted the attack, the store claimed, merely as a way of getting out of its contract.

But by then the *Tribune*'s circulation and confidence were decidedly on the upswing. It answered with a massive, masterful brief that spelled out the Gimbel Brothers' alleged history of tawdry dealings, including the sale of impure canned goods and failure to correct fire hazards at its Philadelphia store and bribery of public officials and white-slavery practices involving its low-paid salesgirls at the Milwaukee store. The net effect of the suit was to defame Gimbels all the more and enhance the *Tribune*'s standing as champion of the consuming public; the litigation was eventually dropped. Whitelaw Reid would have said *caveat emptor*; his son saw the profit in siding against capitalist purveyors of bad goods.

The *Tribune*'s third court fight of the period grew out of a combative righteousness reminiscent of nothing so much as Greeley's extremism in promoting the cause of free-soil Kansas against the onslaught of the slavocracy.

In this case, the locus of evil was Kaiser Wilhelm II's Germany, and the *Tribune* more than any other American paper called for its defeat.

German atrocities in Belgium the month the Great War began were given boldface, double-column coverage by the *Tribune*'s special correspondent, the dashing Richard Harding Davis, whose mother had written editorials for the paper in the 1870s. Davis filed from London:

> ... For two hours on Thursday night I was in what for six hundred years had been the City of Louvain. The Germans were burning it, and to hide their work kept us locked in the railroad carriages. But the story was written against the sky, was told to us by German soldiers incoherent with excesses; and we could read it in the faces of women and children being led to concentration camps and of citizens on their way to be shot.
>
> The Germans sentenced Louvain on Wednesday to become a wilderness, and with the German system and love of thoroughness they left Louvain an empty, blackened shell. . . .

Extension of the German blockade of Allied shipping to include U-boat warfare in the Atlantic against American and other neutral vessels was widely denounced but nowhere more fiercely than in the *Tribune,* which called it a violation of international law and an outrage against mankind. German warnings in no way excused or mitigated the sinking of the *Lusitania* in May 1915, and six months later, fed up with what it considered President Wilson's unmanly response to the Germans' lack of contrition over the taking of innocent American lives, the *Tribune* was lamenting that the vast majority of its countrymen "have no appreciation of the meaning of the present conflict in human history. . . . We are permeated with pacifist flapdoodle." The nation was turning its back on honor and duty, choosing instead "the road of safety and prosperity" while the very structure and conception of democracy as a global force were endangered by the Germans' outlaw conduct. The *Tribune* called for a weakling America to rouse itself by conscription and rearmament against the inevitable day the nation would have to join the Allied cause. The crescendo reached a climactic note in an editorial titled "The Anniversary," published a year after the *Lusitania* sinking. Written by Frank A. Simonds, a political reporter turned staff military specialist, it cried out more in sorrow than in anger because

> we have insisted upon applying to the German mind our own standards and upon believing that the German thought as we thought, believed as we believed, but were [sic] temporarily and terribly betrayed by a military spirit and by dynastic madness.
>
> . . . These things which we name crimes are neither accidents nor excuses; they are not regretted or condemned by a majority or even a minority of the German people. They are accepted by Kaiser and peasant. . . .
>
> We did not see. We have not yet as a nation, or as a people, perceived that the German phenomenon is an attack upon civilization by barbarism, a barbarism which combines the science of the laboratory with the savagery of the jungle. . . .

The piece concluded with the assertion that "the battle of Great Britain, of France, of Russia, is our battle. If it is lost we are lost." To many in a nation whose President was running for re-election on the slogan "He kept us out of war," such words were undiluted warmongering; to others, they were the height of patriotism—and so perceived by the trustees of Columbia University, who, under the terms of Joseph Pulitzer's will establishing a school of journalism and endowing a set of annual awards for excellence in the field, named the *Tribune* recipient of the first Pulitzer Prize to be given for editorial writing on the strength of Simonds's piece.

The paper's kettledrumming grew more thunderous as the presidential campaign progressed. The Republican nominee was celebrated as the far more likely candidate to endorse "a complete and aggressive nationalism" than the pusillanimous Democratic incumbent, and the *Tribune*'s news columns sprouted large, boxed, urgent articles on the country's military deficiencies ("The most powerful battleships possess very large guns capable of being elevated thirty degrees . . . and are able to make from twenty-five to twenty-eight knots per hour [sic]. *We have not one battleship combining their qualities*"). And when war finally came for America, the paper turned to shrill insistence on "an absolutely united front" against the foe. There could be no doubters, no dawdlers; all pacifists were denounced as radical subversives whose utterances were to be suppressed. And if the First Amendment presented certain obstacles to this crushing of dissent, the *Tribune* suggested other ways to achieve it. *The Masses,* the pacifist Marxist magazine, for example, could be squelched by courts-martial now that the nation was at war. And all domestic manifestations of pride in German culture and heritage—the German-language press, German societies, German as a course in schools—the *Tribune* wanted wiped away. And it cooperated *sub rosa* with top officials of the Post Office, who, eager to mobilize public opinion so that convictions might more easily be obtained against the dissemination of seditious writings, leaked to the paper its files on suspected traitors; the result was a witch-hunting *Tribune* series entitled "Enemies Within" that tossed progressives and radicals indiscriminately in with opponents of the war and branded the lot of them as un-American. In the fall of 1917 the paper followed up by unleashing its most lethal cannon, Samuel Hopkins Adams, demolisher of the Brothers Gimbel, in a series of articles with the blunt title "Who's Who Against America." Its prime target was William Randolph Hearst.

It was as if the *Tribune* had seized Hearst's discarded suit of jingoist armor. Hearst's papers had indeed cried out against American involvement in the European conflict, but its motives, despite *Tribune* contentions to the contrary, were not so much pro-German as anti-British. His early bellowing against British war censorship and heavy-handed suppression of Irish home-rule agitation at a time Britain was supposedly holding high the torch of democracy against bloody autocracy had caused Hearst's operatives to be banished from the Allied camp. The *Tribune,* frustrated by the slowness and apparent ineptness of Wilson's War Department in sending adequately trained and armed Yanks into the fray, lashed out at Hearst for complicity in this delay. *Tribune* editorials implored the administration to adopt a War Cabinet as an emergency measure so that knowledgeable businessmen (i.e., efficient Republicans) could help shape the faltering American effort to save Europe. By the spring of 1918, U.S. doughboys had joined the fight, but the war still looked endless, and the *Tribune* shifted its fire from Wilson back to Hearst. In doing so, it adopted his most tendentious style of crusading. A daily column headlined "Coiled in the Flag—Hear-s-s-s-t" contained such simplistic charges as this:

> Since the United States entered the war the Hearst papers have printed: 74 attacks on our allies, 17 instances of defense or praise of Germany, 63 pieces of anti-war propaganda, 1 deletion of a Presidential proclamation—total 155—or an average of nearly three a week, while America has been engaged in the life and death struggle with civilization's enemy.

The *Tribune* issued pamphlets and circulars shrilling for the shutdown of the Hearst chain, and one community in the heart of the *Tribune*'s strongest readership area—the large Westchester suburb of Mount Vernon—obliged by passing an ordinance forbidding the sale of Hearst papers within its boundaries. When several metropolitan area newsdealers tried to drop Hearst papers from their stands, what had been a gnatlike whine by the little *Tribune* against the huge Hearst enterprise became a free-for-all involving the entire New York press. The publishers' association ordered the American News Company, in its role as principal wholesaler and distributor of the city's dailies, to withhold delivery of all other papers to any dealer boycotting Hearst—a step taken less out of sympathy for "The Chief," as the grand wizard of far-off San Simeon styled himself, than out of fear that any break within their ranks would open them to price-cutting by dealers already resentful at being made to swallow a new and higher price structure. The *Tribune* broke ranks and promised to deliver its own papers to any dealer who was boycotting Hearst and, as a result, got boycotted by the other city papers. The other papers then ordered American News not to deliver the *Tribune* to any dealer not selling Hearst papers. The *Tribune* tried to set up its own distribution network, tempers and expenses rose, Congress began investigating Hearst, lawsuits flew—by Hearst against the *Tribune* for conspiracy, by the *Tribune* against all its city rivals for restraint of trade —and confusion reigned. All of it seemed to help the *Tribune*'s circulation, which passed the 100,000 mark. The old paper had not stirred such a fuss since Dana's "Forward to Richmond" incitements.

So gripped had the *Tribune* become by war psychosis that at the first sign of German interest in a negotiated peace on the basis of Wilson's Fourteen Points, the paper reversed its support of the President's position, citing its fear that Germany would get off too lightly, and editorialized, "with no diplomacy, that we hate the Hun, that we mean to crush him utterly, that his hand is a stinking abomination" never to be shaken. From there it was a short hop to rejection of the League of Nations as a toothless wonder—the victorious Allies, with Japan and Italy as junior partners, would maintain the peace as they saw fit—and a muddled call for "order and staunch nationalism to stand against Bolshevism, pacifism and all that brood of anarchy and confusion." It even endorsed as justified, though illegal, New York mayor John F. Hylan's call to ban the red flag of communism from city street demonstrations. Two years ahead of time, the *Tribune* named its choice for President in 1920—Theodore Roosevelt—saluting his platform of militant nationalism, universal military training, and "anti-hyphenation," which meant "the complete Americanization of all alien groups and elements." The paper's voice had grown xenophobic, isolationist, delusionary, and not far from hysterical. Certainly it was beneath the dignity of a Whitelaw Reid. But he was gone, and his good-natured, easygoing son was riding high in the stirrups. Peace returned, Congress found Hearst free of treason, and he and the *Tribune* forgot their legal differences. Each had found a new obsession in the Red scare now troubling domestic tranquillity.

IV

The desolemnization of the *Tribune* in the early years of Ogden Reid's stewardship was best exhibited in its snappy feature writing, and no one performed that function with more verve than a bulky, heroically sloppy young man who joined the staff in 1912, two years after he had completed his studies at Harvard (except for neglecting to pass French). Degreeless, he took his revenge by going to work for the least cerebral paper in New York—the *Morning Telegraph,* a sporting sheet with particular expertise in the activities of racehorses. When in due course he requested a pay increase from twenty-five to thirty dollars a week and found himself out of a job for his temerity, he presented himself, again as if perversely, at the most reactionary newspaper shop in town.

No one quite like Heywood Broun had appeared among the fussbudgety gentlemen of the *Tribune* since Greeley died. His necktie was askew, his suit rumpled as the proverbial unmade bed, his tousled hair hopelessly out of control, but his good nature was irrepressible; he had all the grace and appeal, as his future biographer put it, of a baby elephant. And while he exuded indolence and a certain forlorn air, he in fact proved to be a good worker, starting as a copyreader on the overnight lobster trick. But big as he was, he felt overlooked while working the wee hours and laboring over other men's writing, and so he petitioned city editor Burdick for liberation. Though lacking in dispassion, the ideal of the reporter's trade, he did his job well enough to win a spot on the rewrite desk, where one of his colleagues—they were not exactly boon companions—was Ogden Reid. Broun's lively writing style, when shoved directly beneath the nose of the sports editor, caught his eye, and Heywood was assigned to cover the 1913 campaign of John J. McGraw's New York Giants. Sportswriting has not been the same since.

In the press box at the Polo Grounds, the Giants' ballpark, he found his natural habitat, littered as it was with cigar stubs, tobacco quids, and half-empty beer bottles, and in his assignment a wide-open playing field for his verbal energy. His usual chic supplemented by a black slouch hat that accented his new sportiness, Heywood dwelled there among such notable writers as Damon Runyon of the *Journal* and Grantland Rice, then on the *Mail* but soon to join the *Tribune* as both writer and columnist. Broun's slightly overheated prose, full of fun, odd allusions, and occasional Homeric epithets when his beloved Giants performed deservedly, won him a regular byline, which had the effect of further stimulating his talents.

His forte was in celebrating the commonplace, in having a good time with the thoroughly routine, as in this lead of his on an early July game:

> An eye for an eye and a tooth for a tooth may have been a good policy in Mosaic days, but it represents only an average of .500 when applied to baseball. Just now it is the doctrine which the Giants seem bent on upholding. . . .

His specialty was the critical put-down, preferably aimed at the Giants' opposition, the Philadelphia Phillies in this instance. A trade announced in the course of the game would soon have the therapeutic effect of replacing the current Phillie shortstop, of whom Broun remarked, "He does not look like a shortstop; he does not act like a shortstop; and only by grossly circumstantial evidence will he ever be convicted of shortstopping. Now he may drop his disguise and go back to the outfield." The following paragraph read:

> Oeschger was in the box for Philadelphia, but his delivery is not nearly as difficult as his name. He was hit so hard that [Philadelphia manager] Charlie Dooin was driven at last to send in another pitcher of such obscurity that he was not even indicated on the scorecard. Matteson was the newcomer. He lacks more than a few letters of being a Mathewson. . . .

For a time Broun doubled as a sports editor, but the details of the job he found tiresome, and the orders that he issued were more by way of an apology than a command. Nor was he ever comfortable on management's side in labor relations, as he would amply illustrate two decades later as the organizer and founding president of the American Newspaper Guild. When, as *Tribune* sports chief, he was authorized to hire a new columnist at a salary of fifty dollars but up to fifty-five if absolutely necessary, Broun lured over the splendid stylist William O. McGeehan, recently arrived at Hearst's *Journal* from San Francisco and writing under the pseudonym "Right Cross." After discussing with him the preferability of writing under his rightful name, Broun clinched the deal by advising, "Mr. McGeehan, I am authorized to offer you a salary of fifty dollars or fifty-five—which would you prefer?" After that they named Broun the *Tribune* drama critic.

His qualifications for the job were that he had studied drama writing at Harvard, wrote with wit, and got his copy in on time. And he loved the theater—but not so much that he was blinded by what he saw on the stage. When he commented that the performance of a certain actor was the "worst to be seen in the contemporary theater," the malefactor sued Broun for damaging his reputation; while the case was still pending, the plaintiff appeared in another play, and his performance prompted Broun to report, "He is not up to his usual standard." Of a play titled *Just Outside the Door,* he wrote that "whenever the long arm of coincidence intrudes, the author seizes it and shakes hands." But Broun's own performance went well beyond a facility with snide one-liners. He was generous to playwrights seeking to break new ground in the drama, particularly those cultivating realism where sentimentality had long been the mainstay of the commercial Broadway house. Of one taboo-breaking play he remarked, "It is our experience—bitter, too—that the rewards of virtue are by no means certain. Life, we find, does not deal in exact judgments," and it was fine with him to come upon characters who were not all one thing or another.

When the controversial content of his reviews made the paper's managers too uncomfortable, Broun was replaced by George S. Kaufman, the no less caustic future playwright, and given charge of the drama section—a titular promotion that he accepted like a trooper but did not relish. His gifts, though, were not fully utilized in that inside job, and when war came, someone got the idea that Broun was just the fellow to report on the preparations and shipment to Europe of the American Expeditionary Force. Never was a journalist so superbly miscast for an assignment. An instinctive pacifist who hated bloodshed, a free spirit who hated regimentation, a natural slob who hated military spit and polish, Broun brought with him to the job a monumental irreverence and the conviction that no true glory was ever won on a battlefield. Grim, chisel-chinned John J. Pershing, the American commander, felt otherwise; the two were on a collision course from the first.

Upon the arrival of the first sizable contingent of American troops in France, Pershing issued a statement thankful that "not a man or an animal was lost or injured" in the transatlantic transfer and noting that the U.S. soldiers, "all fine, husky young fellows, with the glow of energy, good health and physical vigor," were being "exceptionally well camped and cared for." Broun, hands tied by Pershing's strict censorship, could not report how the troop transport he came over on had narrowly escaped being torpedoed. But he did file a report on the troop landing, carried at the top of page one by the *Tribune,* that offered a portrait of the arriving doughboys slightly less wholesome than their commander's:

> In a few moments gangplanks were down and the first American force began to click heels on French soil. Since little things are important at moments when history is being made, it may be recorded that the first remark of the first soldier to land was: "Do they allow enlisted men in the saloons in this town?"

His own defeat by the French at Harvard no doubt in mind, Broun went on to report, "A query which was repeated again and again during the course of the day was, 'Don't any of these people talk American?' " The article concluded with a note on a ritual performed by a small circle of the Americans that attracted special attention from their hosts: "The French stood six rows deep around this group and watched with breathless interest. They realized that history was being made. For the first time 'craps' was being played on French soil."

Besides refusing to write about the Yanks as if they were tin-helmeted gods, Broun presented himself as a parody of the conquering military hero. Forced by Pershing's orders to wear a uniform, he sported one that made him resemble a pajamaed Bedouin; his odd little salutes were the scandal of the American encampment, and when he stood for review in front of Pershing, his state of disarray prompted the general to ask, "Did you just fall down?"

What Broun saw during most of his six-month stay with the AEF were wretched training conditions and troops ill prepared for battle. But he was forced to restrict his reports to developments on the lighter side, such as his efforts to return a British officer's salute that he described as resembling "three nip-ups and a swan dive." Finally he decided to circumvent military censorship of the Atlantic cable by sending letters to the paper detailing the poor training conditions; soon he was the *persona* most *non grata* among the U.S. press corps and got summoned back to New York, where he vented his pacifist soul by announcing, "Of all cleaning fluids, blood is the least effective." The *Tribune,* critical of Wilson's military policies for alleged laxity since the war began, ran Broun's anecdotal revelations of U.S. military bungling in France until one day he lambasted the army for sending thirteen major generals to Europe on the same troop carrier; he had failed to check the story (which was not true) and lost his standing as a military correspondent.

During his final three years on the paper, Broun returned to the cultural beat, producing lively literary reviews in a column called "Books and Things." As with the stage, he favored the real and the ironic over the ethereal, fanciful, and cosmetic. A sensibility that rained high praise upon Lewis's *Main Street* did not appreciate the youthful romanticism of Fitzgerald's *This Side of Paradise.* Beyond that, he would not refrain from denouncing the work of such *Tribune* sacred cows as Nicholas Murray Butler, president of Columbia University. And when no promising book presented itself for discussion, Broun did not hesitate to take off in any direction that suited him, whether mocking a fundamentalist church reformer or denouncing Warren Harding's Attorney General for the massive and arbitrary deportation of foreign-born alleged radicals—heresies that did not delight his employers. His gracious letter of resignation to Ogden Reid thanked him for the many opportunities, however abbreviated each had proven, that he had been given by the *Tribune,* which he confessed "is very fairly and frankly in a political camp opposite to my own convictions." At the *World* and later the *Telegram* and *World-Telegram,* he became the most celebrated liberal columnist of his time. At his death late in 1939, President Roosevelt, a man much to his liking despite owning a Harvard diploma, said of Heywood Broun, "He wore no man's collar." Other political and cultural liberals prospered on the *Tribune* after him but none more defiantly.

V

No solitary genius blueprinted the rebuilding of the *New York Tribune* during the second decade of the twentieth century as the paper neared the climactic stage of its existence. Many hands did the job, and Ogden Reid had the grace to know his own limitations, select able people to function under him, and let them operate with an exceedingly light rein. Four people, though, who joined the staff in the early years of his rule were of special importance in energizing the paper and readying it for its rebirth of greatness.

The one who stayed most briefly had the most immediate impact.

When he came over from the *Times* in 1916 at the age of thirty-eight, Garet Garrett told Adolph Ochs he had grown too comfortable there and that the *Tribune* was a paper in the making and therefore a greater challenge to him. A small, almost impish man whose tailored tweed suits and gilded-age walking stick lent him an air of elegance, Garrett had overcome a lack of higher education to rise from a Chicago printer's apprentice to a spot on the editorial board of the *Times.* His specialty had been financial journalism, which he practiced on a number of New York papers, and it was to revamp the business coverage of the *Tribune* that Ogden Reid hired him. But his abounding energy and intellect commended him for more sweeping authority, and in 1917 he was named managing editor. As temperamental and decisive a man as Reid was not, Garrett had the courage of his strong pro-business convictions; it was he who led the *Tribune*'s crusading against Wilson's management of the war effort, calling for a bipartisan Cabinet staffed by the best business brains in the nation to stop the bumbling. And it was Garrett who called loudest within the *Tribune* councils for the suppression of pacifism and the campaign against Hearst as a dangerous subversive.

But his most important contribution to the paper was not as the incendiary crusader whose lamentable excesses would be all too visible once the passions of war had begun to cool; it was, rather, upon the appearance of the *Tribune* that he made a lasting mark. So simple yet so effective was the facelift he imposed that for the next half century, the paper would be regarded as the standard-setter for typographic excellence in the U.S. press.

Like most American papers, the *Tribune* was then dressed in a jumble of headlines in various typefaces of mostly nineteenth-century origin; the main heads were in all capitals that did not allow much room to tell the story, and the heavy blackness of the infelicitously contrasting type styles produced a muddy effect. The flow of spectacular war news required adroit display treatment that was beyond the skill of most makeup editors, who were neither by instinct nor by training estheticians. The resulting layouts were often chaotic at a time when readers most needed clarity and cohesion. Garrett, who had apprenticed at the typecase, worked hard on the problem. His principal solution was to limit the *Tribune* headlines to a single family of type, varying its use by size, column width, and a decorous sprinkling of fussier italic heads—usually for feature stories—amid the basic roman style, and set the main heads as well as the subsidiary ones in capitals and small letters (called upper-and-lowercase in the printing trade) for ease of readability. No paper had done that before. After much experimentation, Garrett settled on a typeface that had been designed in Parma, Italy, by Giambattista Bodoni in the late eighteenth century yet retained a classic, timeless, and distinctly readable look:

ABCDEFGHIJKLMNOPQRSTUVWXYZ
abcdefghijklmnopqrstuvwxyz
1234567890

ABCDEFGHIJKLMNOPQRSTUVWXYZ
abcdefghijklmnopqrstuvwxyz
1234567890

The tall uprights and long descenders of lowercase Bodoni type, requiring more than normal space between lines, lightened the solidity of the style, and the exaggerated contrast between the thick and hairline-thin parts, especially of the capital letters H, M, N, O, U, and W and in the loops of the small a, b, d, and g, lent it a decided elegance. And yet, for all its fine-art origins, Bodoni type did not break apart when submitted to the heavy use of the stereotype machine and high-speed modern presses; on the newspaper page, it almost seemed to sparkle. It could also be used in fonts large enough to declare the importance of a story without bludgeoning the reader to attention.

Almost at once its new Bodoni dress distinguished the *Tribune* from every other paper in the city; soon the typeface was being widely used by high-style magazines, in which it appeared to particular advantage on slick paper. Two-thirds of a century later it is still the staple of *The Washington Post, Boston Globe, Miami Herald,* and many other prominent, prospering dailies. Its fused formality and simplicity somehow achieve a geometrical tension that adds importance to the words it forms and quality to the personality of the publication that uses it artfully.

His finest handiwork done, Garrett left the newspaper business in 1919 to become a free-lance writer, mostly of short stories for popular magazines, and the *Tribune* would not find another commanding figure to serve as managing editor for a dozen years. The year Garrett departed, however, the business side of the paper was much strengthened by the arrival from Hearst's morning *American* of the stubby form of Howard Davis. Bald at forty-three, somewhat crotchety, addicted to cigars, he was not a magisterial figure. But he would rapidly prove to be the best business manager in the paper's history. Without any more formal learning than Garrett, Davis had steeped himself in the news-paper business in his hometown of Scranton, Pennsylvania, where he had worked on the advertising side of two papers. He joined the Hearst organization in 1904 and for nine years starting in 1910 was the business manager of "The Chief's" New York morning sheet. Bluff and occasionally gruff, he set about bringing the same order to the chaos of the circulation, production, and book-keeping departments of the paper that Garrett had imposed upon the appear-ance of the product. His plainspokenness and arch-Republicanism made him a quick favorite of Ogden Reid, who vested almost total trust in him to oversee the parts of the enterprise in which he had the least interest.

A third reshaper of the *Tribune* was another stout-figured man whom Reid had hired from the *Sun* in 1913, but unlike the other two, he was very well edu-cated indeed, with bachelor and law degrees from Columbia, and had the kind of lineage that sat well with the Reids. Geoffrey Parsons's great-grandfather had been the chief justice of Massachusetts and a framer of the Bill of Rights; his grandfather served as dean of Harvard Law School. A man of wit and *joie de vivre,* Parsons himself had practiced law for three years before joining the *Sun* as a reporter, later writing for its editorial page and then directing it. His civility and broad learning added both style and substance to the *Tribune* editorial page for eleven years before he was named in 1924 as its chief editorial writer. That year he published his first book, a well-reviewed history of the world. More than anyone else, he steered the paper away from the shoals of extremism in its advocacy of free enterprise and patriotism; his was a progressive brand of Republicanism, and if Ogden Reid did not always care for its latitudinarian divergences from orthodoxy, he was genuinely fond of its shrewd formulator; the two drank companionably as fellow members of the Century Association. His closeness, too, with Helen Rogers Reid, whom Parsons had been acquainted with during their overlapping college years on Morningside Heights, added to his power on the paper; both Reids would in time defer to him in matters affecting the cultural department of the paper, to its vast benefit.

A still more fateful role than those played in remaking the paper by Garrett, Davis, and Parsons was taken up by the owner's daughter-in-law and former private secretary. Helen Rogers Reid had been superbly trained for her duties as society wife and matron, and during the first seven years of her marriage, while Ogden busied himself trying to repair the damage his father's indifference had done to the *Tribune,* she organized the rest of their busy life like a small, relentless dynamo. There were two children to attend to—Whitelaw the second, born in 1913 and known, as his grandfather never was, as "Whitie," and Elisabeth, who arrived two years later—and two sizable households, a city place at 35 West Fifty-third Street, just off Fifth Avenue, and Ophir Cottage, a misnomer for a thirty-room residence in Purchase just across the road from the Ophir Hall estate. When World War I erupted and American involvement called forth gestures of patriotism, it fell to Helen to direct the conversion of her mother-in-law's showy spread into a model working farm that produced dairy products of a richness befitting its lush greensward. The family was often on the go, shuttling between city and country homes and summering at Camp Wild Air in the Adirondacks, and she and Ogden and Elisabeth were heavy entertainers, in keeping with their social and business standing. It was Helen who kept the whole entourage functioning smoothly, whether bustling the unpunctual Ogden off to the office on time or arranging a dinner party for two dozen or a lawn party for two hundred or making sure that Whitie's ice skates fit him. With characteristic perseverance, moreover, she trained herself to become a suitable companion to Ogden the sportsman. Not athletic by nature, she learned to share her husband's love of the water; with an unsqueamish but not very artful dive, she would swim in her methodical way, and with her full share of the burden in overland carries between lakes and ponds, she would canoe the Adirondack waterways, and with charts and maps and binoculars, she would sail as Ogden's first mate while he would do it all by instinct, winning trophies racing Long Island Sound or mountain lakes. She learned to golf and shoot as well, but nothing so characterized her approach to the game of life as her technique at tennis. Hardly overpowering, she worked hard to develop steady ground strokes and a little flat serve that was pingingly effective; she did not charge the net. In all things, she was still very much a working woman. Fittingly, she gave what time she could to the suffragist drive, helping New York women raise a quarter of a million dollars in their struggle for the vote. Not by coincidence or mere timely mellowing did the *Tribune* editorial page patronizingly note the suffragist activities when they picked up steam in 1912 and then wholeheartedly endorse the female franchise when the campaign reached its critical stage in 1918.

The domestic nature of her manifold duties did not, however, fulfill Helen Reid. She wanted to make a more useful contribution to the family fortunes, which were intimately tied to the *Tribune.* The paper was doing better now but still relied heavily on Elisabeth Reid's purse. A keen admirer of Helen's abilities, Elisabeth encouraged her daughter-in-law's active participation in the paper; Ogden, though certainly exceeding his mother's expectations, still needed all the help he could get. The trick was to find a role for Helen that would not impinge upon Ogden's dominion. The happy solution was to enlist her efforts in the department of the paper that needed shoring up the most and that interested

Ogden little—its advertising. That Helen had had no experience whatever in the area hardly mattered; with due diligence, she could master anything. And so in the fall of 1918, after arranging for her no longer married sister Florence, called Sally by the family, to move in and help care for the children and the household, Helen Reid went to work for the *Tribune.* She stayed thirty-seven years and, for better or worse, became its driving spirit.

For a few months, she served in the ten-person advertising sales department, and then, with scarcely a wink at the protocol of corporate democracy, assumed direction of the department. Since women were responsible for 80 percent of American consumer buying, she would counsel skeptics, what could be more natural than a female advertising director of a newspaper? Her performance on the job was a more convincing argument. She organized, she planned, she set targets, she motivated by praise and fear; no problem was too big or small for her attention, whether helping a salesman storm the steepest barricade or suggesting improvements in a block of copy for a wavering account. Every Monday at 9 a.m. sharp, she assembled her staff and pep-talked them for the week's battles. Progress reports were demanded, problems were openly confronted, failures lamented but not belabored, and triumphs celebrated: there was a cardboard cutout of a tree, standing for the *Tribune,* and each time a targeted new account was acquired, a cardboard apple went up on the tree. A speaker from the editorial or circulation department would come to apprise the salesmen of latest developments on the paper, the better to arm them for their customer calls, and sometimes they would sing songs proclaiming the glories of the *Tribune* and their devotion to it.

But mostly Helen Reid led by example. Whatever her title, she was Mrs. Ogden Reid, Mrs. *New York Tribune,* and she did not hesitate to march through the doors which only that fact opened to her. Once inside the executive suites of the city's principal retailers, she was no wilting violet. As petite and feminine as she appeared, she sought no special courtesies because of her sex, and the objects of her pursuit quickly learned that there was nothing fragile about little Helen Reid. The prime ingredient in her sales approach was an uncontainable enthusiasm for both what she was selling and what the customer was. What the readers of the *Tribune* lacked in numbers they compensated for by their wealth, position, and power, she would argue, though not quite so directly, and then concentrate on the needs and problems of the merchants whose wares she wanted advertised. She would listen to them carefully, ask a lot of questions, and next time bring along suggestions for a new copy approach or proposals for a new campaign or send them by letter and follow up by telephone or at a luncheon. She was dauntless, and early successes with the New York department-store owners, most prominently Macy's Jesse Straus and Rodman Wanamaker, two of the city's largest-volume retailers, made her more so. An increase in space by the big stores and finer specialty shops was especially critical to the struggling *Tribune*'s aspirations toward real competitive status among the city's dailies. Although local retailers benefited from a low advertising rate on the theory that what they showcased in the papers was news and therefore a form of public service, the marginal profitability of such business was more than compensated for by the attention that heavy local advertising won from national advertisers, who paid top dollar. Then Helen Reid went on to Detroit and Chicago and anywhere else she could land big national accounts. In those places, she was less known, the door harder to open, the sale more difficult to consummate, but she tried all the more vigorously and kept going back, and when she failed, the defeat was never final.

Typical of her approach and follow-up was a letter she sent in December 1922 to Philip D. Armour, head of the giant Chicago meat-packing firm, with whom she had met in his Union Stockyards office and discussed the problem of the high cost of advertising national products in local papers:

> Dear Mr. Armour:
> You were very good to send me the advertising proofs of your sausage campaign in [Decatur and Quincy,] Illinois, and I enjoyed enormously going over them.
> It seems to me a most interesting as well as effective piece of work, and I do not wonder that the campaign met with gratifying results.
> Why don't you experiment with the same schedule in New York? It would give you much valuable data about the market here, and you could dominate the field at a comparatively reasonable cost. My recommendation would be to use the World and the Tribune in the morning field, and the Sun and Globe in the evening. The total cost of the schedule would be $13,888.80. . . .
> Why wouldn't it be sound business to take a market like New York and feature either two or three of your products each year? The effect from even one would, I should think, be a definite help to the business generally.
> I enjoyed talking with you so much when I was in Chicago, and I am looking forward to seeing you some time when you are in New York.

Cordial, flattering, aggressively but constructively soliciting, direct, specific—with the hint that her prey would not be safe from her until he capitulated. In her first full year on the job, the *Tribune*'s gross revenues rose from $1.7 million to $2.7 million; by 1920, her second full year, they were up to $4.3 million, with circulation responsible for probably no more than 10 percent of the increase. Helen Reid was a go-getter. "She'd surround things," said her son, Whitelaw, remembering long afterward the mornings in Purchase when she would have the household under control and herself coolly presentable before hurrying off for the 7:53 train from White Plains to be at her desk by nine.

Her influence on the *Tribune*'s course was not limited to the advertising side, but she was careful to tread with a light step into her husband's editorial territory. Even before she joined the working staff, she urged Ogden to bear in mind women readers in the improvements he was implementing. Accordingly, the paper devoted more space, especially on Sundays, to the club and social activities of women, concentrating on Westchester, northern Essex County in New Jersey, and Garden City and the north shore of Long Island. Its fashion coverage and illustrations improved, gardening news and instruction grew, and in 1915, as part of the paper's clean-advertising campaign, the *Tribune* established what it called a "home institute," a kind of kitchen-laboratory to test recipes and household products instead of writing them up uncritically as most other papers did. The home institute long outlasted Samuel Hopkins Adams's "Ad-Visor" column and, supplemented with market reports on food prices and seasonal availability, established the *Tribune* as a national leader in domestic-service copy. Helen Reid had a hand in all that. She was less influential swaying the editorial-page positions of the paper, aside from assuring its wholehearted if belated backing of the Nineteenth Amendment enfranchising women. She had favored Prohibition, but the *Tribune* wavered on the issue, finally preferring to leave the matter up to the discretion of the individual—which is to say it was all wet; she also favored U.S. participation in the League of Nations, but the paper did not. Her influence, moreover, did not extend to the department of hard news. Perhaps because this was Ogden's special preserve but just as likely due to lack of instinct and aptitude, she never really functioned as a journalist. Her priorities in judging editorial personnel may be inferred from a letter she wrote her mother-in-law in March 1922, when the *Tribune* hired as managing editor Chicago newsman Julian S. Mason, a graduate of the elite Phillips Academy of Andover, Massachusetts, and Yale (six years ahead of Ogden) and grandson of the mayor of Chicago at the time of the great fire. "He has all the things we want," Helen wrote Elisabeth, "background, cultivation, love of his work, admiration for the Tribune, a gift for managing and winning people, and an extra amount of sound common sense." Except for "background," she might have been speaking of herself. Notably absent from her list was editorial talent, which, after all, was what the man had been hired for.

New features, new appearance, new people, a new spirit, rising circulation and advertising revenues—it was not surprising that the *Tribune* found itself outgrowing the old tower at 154 Nassau Street. In 1921 work was begun on a new home for the paper on West Fortieth Street midway between Seventh and Eighth avenues, almost exactly three blocks from the *Times*'s new offices. The Reids had pumped in six million dollars to keep the *Tribune* alive since the turn of the century, and now that there were clear signs the investment might eventually pay, they did not stint on a major capital improvement that was essential if the paper was to become truly competitive. With the help of a $1.25 million mortgage on the old *Tribune* building provided by the Metropolitan Life Insurance Company, the new seven-story structure was to be devoted entirely to the newspaper's operations. Without pretense of architectural distinction, the paper's new home was planned by general manager Howard Davis for maximum efficiency. Davis, as much a newspaperman as he was a businessman (and as Helen Reid was not the former and Ogden Reid not the latter), arranged the departments to follow the flow of gravity: business and advertising on the top two floors, editorial on the fifth, composing room on the fourth (instead of above the newsrooms as at most papers), presses on the third and second, and distribution and circulation on the ground floor. The arrangement won wide praise within the newspaper business.

The new building opened in April 1923 and was inspected in detail that June by former Ohio newspaper publisher Warren G. Harding, whose residence in the White House was to end prematurely just two months later. The visit by the President was testimony to the ascendant status of the *Tribune.* Its new headquarters, built to accommodate twenty years of happily anticipated growth, would prove inadequate within two.

7

Bigger than
a Cat Trap

A t the age of seventy-three, American expatriate James Gordon Bennett, Jr., began to redeem himself from a life of dissipation and dishonor. With the outbreak of the European war in August 1914, the French government and most French newspapers abandoned Paris for Bordeaux, and the capital turned into a garrison city. But Bennett, considering himself the leading citizen of neutralist America and loathing the Kaiser for fancied social slights in the past, vowed to remain. His Paris *Herald*, by then in its twenty-seventh year of nonprofitable operation, had nevertheless won a creditable reputation on the strength of its competent if condensed international reports, extensive continental weather forecasts, and comics, and Bennett did not intend to pack it in despite the approaching rumble of German guns.

To demonstrate his solidarity with the French cause, he promised to pay full salary to the wife of every *Herald* staff member who went into military service; soon he was down to a skeleton crew, and his own horses, carriages, and automobiles were commandeered to fight the Boche. There was only one thing to do: walk to the office and put out the paper himself. And so for the first time in his career as a hereditary prince of American journalism, he became a working newspaperman, editing copy, sweating over headlines, and writing editorials that urged French heroism at the ramparts and called on his country-men back home to rally to the Allied cause; he even covered a few stories himself, including one about the abandoned canine population of Paris. And when the paper was put together at night—it had been reduced to a two-page flyer, the back of it in French to serve the natives in the absence of French journals—Bennett was there, hanging over the printers' composing stone and directing. Some nights there would be large blank spaces in the paper where the French censors had intervened; other nights, having argued long and loud with government ministers and waved his finger under the noses of generals, Bennett would defy the censors. They would reprove him sharply the next day and threaten to close him down, but his value to the war effort was too high for that —and besides, the Americans were sooner or later coming to the rescue of France. When they did, finally, an astonishing thing happened to the Paris *Herald*: it began to turn a profit. The decidedly monolingual AEF wanted something to read, and Bennett's sheet helped provide it.

Back in New York, however, the *Herald* suffered just the opposite fate. Its shriveled staff was run by a bunch of unhappily yoked yes-men. Circulation could not keep pace with rising costs, and the paper plunged into the red in 1917. Its decline had been evident for a decade, but its aging absentee owner, dealt a severe blow by the vengeful Hearst, lacked the energy and resources to undertake a major recovery drive. For a time, his *Evening Telegram* sustained the joint operation, but it, too, began to slip. By the last year of the war, the *Herald* was selling not many more copies than the rising *Tribune* and only one-third of the *World* and *Times* daily totals and one-seventh of Hearst's *Evening Journal,* by then pushing out more than 800,000 copies a day. For the first time, the financially strapped Bennett was living more or less modestly— and no longer as a rake; late in life, he had married the widow of one of the members of the Reuter family, which had founded the British news agency of that name, and at last could claim to have been domesticated. When he died in the spring of 1918 at the age of seventy-seven, he had drawn an estimated thirty million dollars out of the profits of the newspaper his father founded and, after living a life of extravagance unmatched by any of his countrymen, left the goose that had laid the golden egg a nearly dead duck. Bennett's will commanded that the *Herald* should be published in perpetuity and that his widow and others of his designation should receive annuities totaling nearly $150,000. Both instruc- tions could not be followed; there was simply not enough money in his estate. In 1920, the *New York Herald,* its Paris edition, and the *Evening Telegram* therefore passed into the welcoming hands of a man whom Bennett had disdain- fully called "that grocer." The price was four million, but the discovery of a million in cash in the Paris paper's bank account from swollen postwar sales effectively reduced that by one-fourth.

Frank Munsey, a bachelor who lived in New York's Ritz-Carlton with one hundred Brooks Brothers suits to hang on his wiry frame, had a long bony face that he thought made him resemble Bennett, whom he had much admired. Upon assuming control of the *Herald,* Munsey began to brush his hair and trim his mustache in the late Commodore's fashion in order to stress the similarity and suggest a continuity. But where there had been fire and wicked intelligence in Bennett's eyes, Munsey's close-set, vacant pair betrayed a dim and preening ego.

A former boy telegrapher who once managed the Western Union office in Augusta, Maine, Munsey had come to New York with forty dollars in his pocket and dreams of making his fortune as a magazine publisher. He started with a children's magazine, *The Golden Argosy,* added an adult version without the gilding, then began a weekly named after himself and converted it to a monthly of no special literary or journalistic distinction. But he cut its price and vigorously promoted it and by the early years of the twentieth century he was making a million a year. He branched into real estate and the grocery-chain business and made even more before being fatally bitten by the ambition to own a string of daily newspapers, to which he would apply the same managerial know-how that had succeeded for him in the grocery business. In short order, therefore, he bought or founded newspapers in New York, Philadelphia, Washington, Boston, and Baltimore; by 1917 he had sold or suspended all of them. The key, Munsey now decided, was consolidation; there were just too many newspapers around—at least 60 percent more than the reading public needed, he calculated. And the most overcrowded place of all, he saw, was New York, where the greatest rewards—profits, fame, power—were to be gathered by a daring impresario, i.e., Frank Munsey.

First on his list was the *Press,* a Republican morning paper founded in 1887 with strong sports coverage and a somewhat sensational personality, which Munsey bought in 1912 for a million dollars. It did not immediately prosper. So in 1916 he bought both the morning and evening editions of the *Sun* for two and a half million, merged the larger and far older morning edition with the *Press* (which effectively disappeared in the process), and spent an additional two million over the next four years to establish the fattened *Sun* as a major factor in the morning field. But it remained in eclipse. That was when he decided to buy the *Herald,* merging the two pioneers of the penny press, now both citadels of conservatism. The new company, called the Sun-Herald, dropped the *Sun*'s name from the morning paper while hoping the *Herald* would retain its readership and changed the name of the *Evening Sun* to the plain *Sun*—that is, the only *Sun* that was left.

Seated proudly at the late Commodore's small, rarely used French desk in the elegant *Herald* building, Munsey resolved to inject renewed life into the starved scarecrow he had purchased from Bennett's executors. The tenth paper he had bought, it was the first to possess even a residue of greatness. But his reputation had preceded him—Munsey's eccentricities, while not in Bennett's league, were legion; he was known, for example, to disapprove of fat men and soon separated them from his employment. And his distaste for smoking caused it to be outlawed from the premises of his properties, though the ban was rarely enforced among his heavily puffing employees except when he was on the scene. Quirks aside, newspapermen considered Munsey to have a bookkeeper's mentality, to be a man who manipulated his papers like toys with an eye fixed firmly on the balance sheet. The *Herald,* with the *Sun* morning circulation added, improved somewhat editorially through infusions of Munsey's cash, but it did little better than hold its own in sales. Its circulation at the beginning of 1924 was 166,000, less than half the morning *World* and *Times* daily figures and only 35,000 ahead of the slowly but steadily climbing *Tribune,* which had not benefited as the *Herald* had from absorbing two competitors (the *Press* and the morning *Sun*). Munsey was doing better in the afternoon field. In 1923, he paid two million for the *Globe.* Founded in 1904, it had absorbed the *Commercial Advertiser,* a relic from the six-penny era, and become a surprisingly fresh, liberal, and independent voice in New York newspaperdom. Its accomplishments notwithstanding, the *Globe* was promptly merged into Munsey's evening *Sun* with positive results; by 1924, the *Sun*'s circulation was up by one-half and its advertising by one-third, and it was earning a million and a half a year. Munsey's far flashier *Telegram,* which had come in the purchase package with the *Herald,* was also doing nicely in the evening field. But he continued to be frustrated by the inability of his morning entry to attain fiscal health, and the competitive situation looked darker than ever.

New York had seventeen English-language daily newspapers in general circulation in 1923, and among them they ran 160 million lines of advertising; Philadelphia had six papers dividing 85 million lines, and Chicago, six with 80 million lines. Too many mouths in Gotham, and not enough food. Compounding the problem was the jump in costs: newsprint was now selling for twice what it had ten years earlier at the beginning of the Great War, and wages in the mechanical departments had risen nearly as much. Something, plainly, had to give, and Munsey thought he knew where the next act of attrition should occur.

The three morning Democratic papers were running neck and neck in the circulation race. The *World* in early 1924 was selling 355,000 copies of its morning edition, the *Times* was at 341,000, and Hearst's *American,* 320,000. There was little doubt, though, that the *Times* was ascendant. Its advertising linage was 40 percent ahead of the second place *World*'s and its stature continued to grow, though the *World,* under flamboyant executive editor Herbert Bayard Swope and editorial-page editor Walter Lippmann, retained a strong following among liberals and intellectuals. But under Ochs and Van Anda, the *Times* attained supremacy in the completeness and accuracy of its newsgathering, particularly on the strength of its coverage of the war. No other American newspaper came close to it. Ochs placed no budgetary limit on Van Anda, and the managing editor instructed his correspondents to file at "double urgent" rates from the war zone so the *Times* could carry next-day reports on the latest fighting. Cable costs soared to $750,000 for the last year of the war, but by then circulation had grown nearly 50 percent since the fighting had begun four years earlier; clearly, the superior editorial product was being rewarded by results at the newsstand. By comparison, the up-and-coming *Tribune*'s overseas reports looked pitiable; its war coverage depended on a man in London and a single correspondent in the field—Wilbur Forrest, former chief of United Press correspondents in Europe, who had taken over for Heywood Broun—supplemented by wire-service reports and an occasional piece by a syndicated reporter of some celebrity, as Richard Harding Davis had provided in the early stages of the fighting. Determined to maintain the *Times*'s lead in international reporting at war's end, Adolph Ochs asked his young ace war correspondent Edwin L. James what it would cost for the paper to carry the best, most comprehensive global coverage in the world; James answered half a million a year in peacetime. Ochs decreed it. In the twenty-four years he had owned the *Times* by 1920, it had recorded total profits of some $100 million—all but four million of it put back into the paper to nourish its solid, continuous growth. It was no secret why Ochs was outstripping all rivals. Bennett had milked his paper; Whitelaw Reid had nearly starved his; Pulitzer's heirs had none of his fight or genius and failed to reinvest earnings; Hearst spent lavishly for vast circulation but his newsprint bill was correspondingly huge and the gaudiness of his products did not attract quality advertisers who could pay the high rates needed to cover costs. And Munsey, scavenging, thought he could succeed by splicing together the stragglers.

New competition as well clouded the scene as 1924 dawned. The morning paper with the largest circulation by then had been operating for only five years. Joseph Medill Patterson's *Illustrated Daily News,* as it was first called, was based on a tabloid format that had met with success in England; in nearly every way, it was the mirror opposite of the *Times.* Its news stories, devoted almost entirely to love, violent death, and crime—all the news unfit to print in Ochs's very proper paper—were short and ended on the page where they began. It had very little serious world or national news but many pictures, with an announced preference for pretty girls among the subjects, and entertainment features. Arriving in the wake of the cataclysmic bloodbath in Europe and just at the outset of Prohibition and the spree of lawlessness it set off, the *Daily News* was perfect morning reading for anyone who did not want to ponder the world's troubles. Its vaguely populist editorial stand, "aggressively for America and the people of New York," echoed Pulitzer's stance as champion of the masses. The *News,* though, had very little substance and evidenced slight concern for social justice. All it did was sell. By 1924, it was up to 633,000 copies a day, just about even with Hearst's evening mainstay for the city leadership in circulation. Before the year was up, Hearst would join the tabloid sweepstakes by launching the *Mirror,* and pulp-magazine publisher and health faddist Bernarr Macfadden would weigh in with the yet sleazier *Graphic.* Competing as well now for public attention and advertising dollars were the infant radio industry and a new generation of periodicals like *Time,* the weekly newsmagazine, and the *Reader's Digest* with their massive readership potential.

In view of such a brawling competitive marketplace, Frank Munsey decided the only step that made sense for him was to buy the *Herald*'s remaining morning rival for conservative Republican readership—the *Tribune.* What could be more natural? The bitterly feuding founders of the two papers had now been in their graves more than half a century, and ownership of each had passed to unrelated hands. Whatever their philosophical or journalistic differences had been long ago, now they were both eminently respectable senior citizens of the New York newspaper scene, appealing to essentially the same conservative constituency. The *Herald,* once the saucier and more irreverent of the pair, had become the more somber; its appearance was so lackluster that it made the Bodoni-dressed *Tribune* look like a young gadabout. Separately, the two papers would struggle to survive, probably lasting only as long as their owners' fortunes; together, they could prosper as the rejuvenated elder statesman among the city papers, the venerable leader of the political opposition in Democratic New York. Munsey put his proposition to Elisabeth Mills Reid, who owned 144 shares of the *Tribune,* and her son Ogden, who held six: Would they sell?

For her, the temptation must have been sizable. The *Tribune* corporate minute books suggest the scale of the financial transfusions the paper had been receiving from the family: by 1921, it owed her more than $5 million of principal and some $1.25 million in interest; it owed Ogden more than a million. And still it was losing, though the gap had narrowed considerably. After apparently having decided to forgive the paper most of its debt to her and the accrued 3 percent annual interest charge in 1920, Mrs. Reid changed her mind the following year; perhaps her attorney had misunderstood her view that the loans were uncollectible and therefore ought to be written off. At any rate, the debt was restored to the *Tribune* books and continued to grow, now at 5 percent and then, the next year, at a 6 percent rate. When would it ever end? Suddenly, there was a buyer at hand.

But Frank Munsey was not at all Elisabeth Reid's kind of person. There was little refinement, no social grace. He was a grabber, an executioner of other people's newspapers; what a shame it would be to sell this man Whitelaw's fine old paper, especially now that Ogden and Helen were working so hard to make a go of it. Why not, Mrs. Reid asked Mr. Munsey at her Madison Avenue mansion soon after New Year's Day of 1924, sell us your *Herald* instead? Yes, the Reids had put a pretty penny into saving the *Tribune*—she even told him how much, by way of emphasizing how deeply the family felt about it—and probably Munsey was right: it was foolhardy for the two old Republican papers to continue competing with each other when there was so much other competition massed out there. The only question was under whose auspices the amalgamated paper would operate. No, she said, she would not sell; she would only buy.

Munsey viewed her answer as just an opening parry. By now he considered himself the spiritual successor to the Bennetts and Dana, with Greeley, too, in imminent prospect if only the Reids would behave rationally. It was of vital importance, furthermore, for him to have a platform to argue his political and social positions—against the veterans' bonus, against U.S. involvement with the corrupt Old World, against any wavering in the government's fiscal conservatism; the combined paper would speak to those issues with a voice more than twice as loud as the sum of the two. And who were the Reids, anyway, to respond so arrogantly to his proposition? He had spent many more millions than they on sick newspapers, and what did he have to show for it? A *Sun* that was profitable but without major influence. He would wait for the Reids to come around.

By early February, New York newspaper circles were full of rumors that the *Herald* was about to buy the *Tribune*. So heavy were the reports among advertising agencies and newsdealers that the *Tribune* ran a wry editorial of denial. Its effect was to stir Munsey's acquisitive juices; a new appointment was scheduled to discuss merger. Helen Reid apprised her mother-in-law, vacationing in France, of every development. That Munsey's overtures had evoked profound reflections in Whitelaw Reid's widow is suggested by Helen's February 2 letter, assuring Elisabeth that "you are not the only person who worries about the financial relationship between you and the Tribune. It has been a nightmare for years and I have longed more than you can ever know for a solution that would relieve you of the Tribune responsibility." But *Tribune* general manager Howard Davis's meeting with Munsey did not go well, Helen reported two days later; Munsey saw himself as indispensable to the shaping of public opinion: "He has a megalomania about his own wisdom and experience and he frankly says the situation has changed materially since the first part of January. . . . He refuses to be convinced that you are interested in going on. He reiterates his sympathy for your heavy losses and how he wants to help you out of your difficulties. He was astonished to learn how much money you have lost on the Tribune." That Elisabeth wanted to get something back besides cash for her heavy investment, he could not fathom.

Two weeks later, the parties met again. Now Munsey seemed to waver, or perhaps it was just a new gambit. "Our newspaper friend refuses point-blank to sell," Helen wrote Elisabeth, "unless we are willing to substitute his newspaper's name at the end of one year. He is half crazy I believe." It seemed absurd to kill either name when each had its own loyal following, and, at any rate, if one were to go, it should surely not be the buyer's. "Perhaps when you get back you can have some effect on him. . . . [H]is personal vanity seems to be intertwined with the success of his morning paper and he is determined to force us to sell if he possibly can." But Helen refused to give up hope, speculating that "if we can proceed to make a better paper during the coming months we may succeed in getting the Herald by fall."

Still another round of fencing followed. Munsey said he wanted to reduce his New York newspaper holdings to a single paper and tried to get Ogden Reid to swap the *Tribune* for the moneymaking *Sun,* whose owner asserted it would surely earn $30 million over the next decade—an alluring prospect, he supposed, to the Reids, longtime sailors on a sea of red. Ogden stressed what he took to be a sacred duty of the Reids to sustain the *Tribune*; Munsey could claim no such heritage. Helen wrote her mother-in-law that only she could persuade Munsey that the Reids would never sell to him.

And so she did. He yielded to that assurance and the handsome price offered for his paper: five million, one-tenth of it for the Paris edition, payable in ten $500,000 notes beginning six years hence, all personally endorsed by Elisabeth Reid. Munsey had in effect paid three million for Bennett's properties, the *Herald* and *Telegram*; the Reids' offer, even taking into account what he had invested to build up the *Herald,* would leave him ahead—and of course he would still retain the profitable if undistinguished *Telegram.* The businessman in him won out over the newspaper collector.

On Monday evening, March 17, 1924, Ogden Reid summoned his staff and did his best to look the picture of dejection. "I have a big news story to break to you," he began. "I have just come from an important business discussion with Mr. Frank Munsey." Groans filled the room; the grim executioner of journalism had struck again. But Ogden could not long continue the pretense. "I have purchased the *Herald,* " he declared, taking filial liberty with the truth, and joy reigned. In the tumult, no one heard Greeley and old Bennett revolving in the ground.

Over at the *Herald,* there was no meeting, only a brief notice on the bulletin board. Reading it, a *Herald* veteran remarked to Leland Stowe, a young reporter, "Jonah just swallowed the whale."

The buoyant *Tribune* ran a half-page-wide boxed announcement of the merger at the top of page one the next morning: "This will unite two of the historic names in American journalism. It will establish one of the great publishing enterprises of the country."

"I sold," Munsey told the *Times,* which played the story in the off-lead position in column one of page one with its customary detail, "because I could not buy."

"I will make the best newspaper I know how," Ogden Reid was quoted as saying by *Editor & Publisher,* the trade weekly. "I have a son, Whitelaw, 10 years old, and a daughter, Elisabeth, 8, who will be looking for jobs some day." The magazine went on to report that contrary to Munsey's theory that circulation could not be bought and that in taking over papers he purchased only their character, New York newspaper circles thought the *Tribune* would hold a large part of the *Herald*'s readership, given its political stance and the lack of duplication between them. Ogden Reid said that the *Tribune* would do what it could to make room for *Herald* staff members, but in fact his paper took only twenty-five on the news side; the *Sun* took forty. Six hundred from all departments lost their jobs. Among the transferees to the *Tribune* were the *Herald*'s popular sports columnist, W. O. McGeehan, who had moved there from the *Tribune* only two years earlier after an abortive run as managing editor; young reporter Leland Stowe, who five years later would win the first Pulitzer Prize awarded to the *New York Herald Tribune,* and three young editors who would shortly play an important part in the merged paper's challenge to the *Times* for national pre-eminence.

The merged paper was, with very few changes, the *Tribune* intact. Added to it were the *Herald*'s popular Sunday radio magazine, some of its comics, its extensive weather information, a few society-page features, and McGeehan's column, "Down the Line," which had run in the *Tribune* from 1915 to 1920. The *Tribune*'s handsome Bodoni headdress was retained along with its odd trademark, the baroque dingbat in the center of the nameplate at the top of page one. Greeley's paper had absorbed Bennett's.

Of all the congratulatory messages Ogden Reid received that week, none better captured the spirit of exhilaration on West Fortieth Street than the note penned by Elisabeth Reid's current private secretary, Eleanor Goss, who at the time also happened to be the second-ranking women's tennis player in the nation. Miss Goss would summer with the Reids at Camp Wild Air, their thirty-acre compound of large "cottages" (with tennis courts) in the Adirondacks, where departing guests were given a distinctive little cheer as they pulled away from the camp dock in a motorboat, usually after dinner and under starry skies, for the train station at Lake Clear. The Reids' Wild Air cheer, in the nonsensically collegiate style of the day, echoed over the lake and turned what might have been a melancholy moment into a gay send-off. Miss Goss's note to Ogden borrowed liberally from it:

> A beebo, and a-bybo, and a-beebo bybo bum!
> Bum! get a rat trap bigger than a cat trap!
> Bum! get a rat trap bigger than a cat trap!
> Bum! bum! Cannibal!
> Rah hoorah, siss-boom-ah!
> Ipsoo razoo, Billy blow you bazoo!
> Ipsidee aye-kye, hit 'em in the right eye!
> We'll show Uncle Mun how to run a newspaper!
> Tribune! Tribune! Tribune!

A year after the merger, the *Herald Tribune*'s circulation was 275,000, or about 90 percent of the two papers' total daily sales the year before. It was now in the running with the big boys in town. That same year, Frank Munsey died, leaving a fortune of twenty million and his two afternoon newspapers, the *Sun* and the *Telegram*, to the Metropolitan Museum of Art—and nary a pang in the soul of any journalist who had worked for him.

II

In the middle of August, a slow news season, that first year of the *Herald Tribune*'s existence, Dwight Perrin, the able city editor, sent out one of his most industrious and reputable young reporters to check up on rumors that a floating nightclub was operating in defiance of Prohibition off the shore of Fire Island some sixty miles east of the city.

Sanford Jarrell, twenty-six, had been on the *Tribune* two years when he got the assignment. The city desk allotted him a small bundle of cash to hire a motorboat for pursuit of the allegedly seaborne liquor dispensary and told him to keep in touch. For two days, he searched, calling in from Bay Shore, Long Island, to report only limited progress. Nobody was rushing him and, after all, the limpid sea air was far more pleasant than the muggy city that time of year.

On the third day, Jarrell phoned in to report success. He had found the boozy *Flying Dutchman,* and it was no myth. He would supply all the details. The city desk geared up for a big exclusive. Back in the office, Jarrell told of his great adventure: the trouble he had had in convincing his motorboatman that he was not a federal agent, how they had hit a submerged log and drifted helplessly ten miles out to sea while the propeller was being repaired; the dimensions of the mystery ship and all its posh appointments, what everything on it cost, and the nature of the clientele. It was some whale of a tale, and the paper so played it: a copyrighted lead story with a four-column, three-line headline, plus a three-column map showing the ship's location and a box beneath it itemizing the pleasure charges ("Boat fare, round trip . . . $70, First admission charge . . . $5, Four sloe gin bucks . . . $8, Promenade deck stateroom . . . $15"). Jarrell's bylined story began:

> Fifteen miles off Fire Island, beyond the pale of the law, is anchored a floating bar and cabaret that is the playground of the rich and "fast." It is a large ship, more than 17,000 tons. On board are silverware and other fittings, marked with the name of the Friedrich der Grosse, a former North German Lloyd liner.
>
> A negro jazz orchestra furnishes the music to which millionaires, flappers and chorus girls out of work, whirl on a waxed floor with the tang of the salt air in their lungs. A heavily manned bar serves both men and women. An excellent cuisine lends tone. Drinks of every conceivable character may be obtained at prices that melt the fat wallets of the customers. Revels de luxe are in vogue. . . .

Midway down the page, the story broke into a first-person narrative of the reporter's derring-do, all the more convincing as detail piled on detail: how he had been rescued from his stranded motorboat by another bringing customers to the luxury ship from Atlantic Highlands on the Jersey coast; speculations about the provenance of the ship, its British crew and Union Jack ensign; the champagne that flowed after midnight when the jazz musicians hit many a clinker but the fox-trotters and one-steppers were too pie-eyed to notice. There was an occasional touch of ersatz Fitzgerald to Jarrell's prose: "On deck here and there were comfortable canvas chairs, where one could sip drinks in tall thin glasses, listen to the clink of the ice and the swishing of the waves, gaze on the rays of the moon playing on the water and make love marvelously." And like a refrain through the narrative were references to a certain bobbed redhead named Irene "with the laughing eyes," who danced by the *Tribune*'s faithful correspondent and called with vixenish delight, "This is an epic lark!"

The story caused the sensation the editors had played it for. The Coast Guard ordered a massive search for the rogue vessel. The Treasury Department directed pointed inquiries to the British government. Dozens of reporters from rival papers scrambled to recover on the *Tribune*'s delicious scoop. Jarrell himself had a follow-up story in the off-lead in the next day's issue on the latest intriguing developments; meanwhile he dwelled in the bower of reportorial ecstasy—he had set the town on its ear.

But the more elusive the oceanic saloon proved, the more uneasy Jarrell's editors grew. They had backed him when envious competing sheets scoffed at the story. But now they noticed that the details of his follow-up pieces were getting hazier, and when they asked for corroborative evidence, Jarrell could supply only unessentials. Still, he swore the story was true. The *Tribune* commissioned an independent investigation, and Jarrell's veracity was found wanting. Well, he conceded, he may have embellished a little here and there, but his story was true in its essence. He left the office, vowing to obtain proof of his handiwork to satisfy his increasingly skeptical superiors; he never came back. Instead there was a note confessing that the story was "wholly without foundation" and containing, along with his resignation, assurances of his "sincerest regret."

With a painful front-page clearing of its throat under a single-column headline, the August 23 issue of the *Herald Tribune* acknowledged a week after breaking its big floating nightclub exclusive that it had been suckered by a previously trustworthy employee. Resignation, though, was too good for the villain. The final paragraph of the piece conceding the hoax stated, "Sanford Jarrell has been posted on the bulletin board of The Herald Tribune editorial room as dishonorably dismissed."

No one ever knew what made Jarrell do it. He had in fact gone out to Bay Shore and hired a motorboat to prowl the ocean off Fire Island for a fee of $110, but the boat ran into the difficulties Jarrell wrote about and he paid the skipper half the promised fee. But instead of proceeding to the mythical ocean liner, the rescue launch took him and a certain redhead he had been squiring on their "epic lark" back to shore and a high old time of it. During the post-midnight hours he had supposedly spent cavorting on the liquor ship, Jarrell was actually sleeping at a little hotel in Bay Shore, his subconscious perhaps concocting the extravagant hoax. If he had been drunk when dreaming it up, he had surely sobered by the time he executed it in convincing detail. Perhaps he did it to win a bet, perhaps to impress the redhead. Whatever the reason, it was a sin that newspapermen do not forgive.

And yet, when Jarrell died thirty-seven years later after having drifted west and worked obscurely on several dozen papers, the last of them in Long Beach,

California, the *Herald Tribune* ran a substantial obituary recalling the "Hoax Story Reporter" who had betrayed it. Whether the obit was an act of grace or final vengeance remains no clearer than the explanation for the infamous prank itself. In 1924, at any rate, the stunt did little to enhance the stature of a newspaper aspiring to greatness.

III

Of the legitimate talent that had begun to mass by the 'Twenties in the news-room of the *Tribune*—most people in the business still called it that and never "the *Herald*"—none was more valued by the editors than Robert B. Peck, the quietest man there.

Peck came to the *Tribune* in 1912, the same year Ogden Reid took charge of it; he remained forty-three years, his work in such favor that he was long the best-paid writer in the city room among the regular staff. As a reporter, he had been no great shakes, but he soon proved a wizard at rewriting other men's overlong or underenergized stories or taking telephoned reports from legmen and turning them swiftly into tight, seamless copy that hardly ever needed a comma altered.

Bob Peck looked like a slightly pudgy, slightly grizzled cherub with his perpetual little shy smile. He came to work at five in the afternoon, claimed his place at one of the four desks that composed the rewrite bank right beside the city editor, shed his jacket, unbuttoned his vest but never removed it, rolled up his sleeves but never lowered his tie, had a drag or two on a cigarette, and turned to his typewriter. He worked the machine methodically, clackety-clacking along without apparent effort in his flat-fingered way, turning out between five and fifteen stories a night—about four or five thousand words on average. He could radically compress the copy of a conscientious reporter who had written at twice or three times the length the editors had allotted so that the piece gained speed and grace with brevity. But he could also write in a more leisurely, often witty style reminiscent of the old *Sun,* where he had spent five years, not hesitating to drop in a pleasing allusion to Dickens, Shakespeare, or classical mythology. His best work was done on breaking local stories phoned in by reporters cover-ing the police or the courts. He would listen intently for details that he could seize upon to make something special out of; then, hanging up, he would characteristically run his pencil along the slats of the back of the city editor's chair, signaling that the story was routine or remarking, "I may have a little something here," which meant he would run with it in his special fashion. No editor had to tell him how long or short to write it, and, the least temperamental of men, he grew testy only when instructed to write funny. Instinct told him when and how to play it light. But Peck was also capable of writing with pathos all the more affecting for its understatement, as in the piece he turned out in April 1934 when the *Tribune*'s Jersey City legman called in the court case of a forty-nine-year-old tailor who had been given a thirty-day jail sentence and hundred-dollar fine because he had charged thirty-five cents for pressing a suit of clothes when the minimum charge permitted by the cleaners' and dyers' code of New Jersey was forty cents. Out of that nickel difference, Peck shaped a thirteen-paragraph parable of bureaucratic imbecility and its bewildering effect on a simple man struggling to earn an honest living. It read in part:

> He has no helper. He starts work early in the morning and, if there are jobs to be done, he works late in the evening. He doesn't get around much. Changing social orders don't interest him so much as changes in the price of thread.
>
> His observation has led him to believe that the only reason one man gets more business than another is that he gives more value for the money. Application of that principle has permitted Mr. Maged to survive in a world which seems to him unnecessarily full of tailors. It is a theory of business which seems to Mr. Maged incontrovertible. . . .

Peck's sole drawback as a journalist was an elfin strain that sometimes got the better of him. Once, piqued over man's inhumanity to beast, he wrote a story about a car crash caused by an incautious deer and reported that while the animal was so badly injured it had to be destroyed, the driver "was deemed worth saving and taken to the hospital." The driver's family was not amused. Nor was the managing editor when Peck one day decided to mock what he took to be aviator Charles Lindbergh's studied ingenuousness in using "we" to share credit with his aircraft for his exploits aloft. Peck embellished a wire-service short about Lindbergh's arrival by train in Cleveland after poor flying weather had kept "we" on the ground; he quoted the celebrated pilot as walking up to the locomotive after the trip, patting its steamy flanks, and declaring, "Well, we made it." So did the story, until it got yanked from the city edition. Likewise spiked was his account of the fellow with a long Polish name who died, according to the rewriteman, from "contraction of the vowels." And then there was the suicide who had fired a shotgun up his own anus —a feat Peck memorialized with a proposed lead noting that the deceased "had supple legs." Assigned the kind of routine weather story he loathed, Peck one time submitted a piece that ran, in its entirety, "It snowed yesterday with the usual results."

The paper tried for years to get him to work as an editor, just as *The New Yorker* magazine kept soliciting him for contributions, but all Bob Peck wanted was to be a rewriteman. No one was better at it. When he retired to the Catskills, admiring colleagues asked if now, finally, he would write books or articles of his own choice. "I have written," Peck said and, having composed perhaps forty million words for the *Tribune,* wrote no more.

IV

If Bob Peck was the best inside man on the *Herald Tribune* writing staff in the years of its ascent to greatness, the best all-around reporter—adept at gathering facts under often arduous conditions and returning to the office to fashion them speedily into a brisk run of evocative prose—was a small, sturdy Scotswoman of large dignity.

When Ishbel Ross arrived at the *Tribune* in 1919 at the age of twenty-three with a couple of years on a Toronto paper behind her, she had been preceded in the newsroom by only one female reporter. Two women of high competence had served as literary editors in the nineteenth century—the intellectually formidable Margaret Fuller and Ellen Mackay Hutchinson, who gave up the job to art critic Royal Cortissoz upon marrying him. Others had worked on the women's and society pages, but regular reporting, with its long, late hours, often difficult travel, and frequent contact with disreputable characters, was considered man's work. The *Herald* made an exception of spirited Frances Buss Merrill, who before editing its women's page had been a gifted feature writer, riding atop an elephant at the head of the parade when the circus came to town, exposing the cruel work conditions of women at a dye plant in Staten Island, relating the pain and shame of an unwed teenage mother whose baby had just died at Bellevue Hospital. Mrs. Merrill was not less concerned with the exclusionary conditions confronting would-be newswomen in the late nineteenth century, such as the absence of toilet facilities, and took the lead in organizing a feminist Rainy Day Club, devoted to, among other practical goals, the sanction of shorter skirts so that working women required to be mobile in even the most inclement weather could more easily manage on muddy streets.

Emma Bugbee, who graduated from Barnard six years after Helen Rogers Reid, became the first woman reporter on the *Tribune* in 1911 and remained on its staff fifty-five years, to the last day it was published. She was neither swift nor clever as a writer, but greatly devoted to the paper and her pioneering role on it, and she served responsibly and never less than competently. Her subjects were invariably women and their activities, and she endured her share of hardships to cover them. She tramped through snow for a week in the winter of 1914 accompanying a band of suffragists on a pilgrimage from the city up the west bank of the Hudson to Albany, where they appealed their cause at the statehouse; every night Bugbee managed to find a phone, still an uncommon instrument in rural areas, and call in the day's developments. Her first byline was earned in a comparable ordeal, braving winter's blast in remote northwestern Connecticut to interview a woman just released from a forty-year jail term for a crime she continued to deny having committed. Miles from the nearest hotel or inn, she stayed the night in her subject's unheated cabin under piles of blankets and survived to breakfast on mince pie and coffee. In time the eminence of her hostesses and the accommodations they provided would greatly improve; in the 'Thirties, she became a close friend of Mrs. Franklin D. Roosevelt, whose activities she regularly covered, and several times stayed the night at the White House.

Ishbel Ross, coming to the *Tribune* eight years after Miss Bugbee, was not limited in her assignments to stories about or of special interest to women. She wrote too well for that. There was a finished, swiftly paced smoothness to her copy, a literary sensibility quick with insights and nuances yet not at all precious —you'd never know a woman wrote her stuff, the men in the city room were forced to concede.

Women were not exactly beloved objects on American newspapers as they crashed sexist barriers in the 'Twenties and 'Thirties. Diehard anti-feminist editors claimed that a disturbingly high proportion of them were incompetent vixens, adepts at office politics and exploiting their male colleagues while subject to going to pieces in a crisis; worst of all, they sat on your desk all the time. Petite Ishbel Ross was not like that. She had dark brown wavy hair that never seemed untidy, bright blue-gray eyes, a pleasingly modulated voice with a trace of her native Highlands still detectable, and looked to many a tobacco-stained, liquor-loving, dirty-collared male reporter-around-town as if she had just stepped out of a couturier's front window. She had reputedly been the first Canadian female journalist to fly in a plane, accompanying a stunt pilot for a story and recalling the daring feats of Nellie Bly on the *World* a generation earlier. But Ishbel Ross displayed little personal flamboyance; only her writing scintillated. Perhaps it was her eagerness to dispel the bias against the female of the reportorial species as coy, catty, and at heart a puddle of emotion, but more likely it was simply her natural reserve that held her back from mingling with the men in the city room. She covered everything from dance marathons and the Easter Parade on Fifth Avenue to the hottest crime stories of the era, and did it in such clear, compact prose that her editors in time forgot all about her sex in choosing her assignments. In the field, she could be as aggressive as necessary but was rarely more so. In the office, she was always a lady as well as a woman, always "Miss Ross" and never "Ishbel" to them, though they were not averse to casting a sideways glance at her ankles whenever she sat cross-legged in one of the little phone booths scattered around the city room and neglected to close the door. When she got married, it was not to an office love but to a rival reporter on the *Times.* Together but separately, they covered the biggest murder trial of the 'Twenties, involving an adulterous minister and his married lover, slain on a rural lane in the midlands of New Jersey. The climactic moment in the 1926 trial came with the testimony of a bizarre witness who claimed to have seen the revenge murders; Ross's story, in a style expertly blending color and economy, began:

SOMERVILLE, N.J., Nov. 18 — Jane Gibson, the Amazon "pig woman," who rode Jenny the Mule in her sturdier days and guarded her farm with a shotgun, was borne into court on a stretcher to-day—a helpless, mummified figure, wrapped in blankets and close to death.

For four blistering hours she dominated the Hall-Mills trial from the pillows of a hospital cot—an eerie figure waving waxen fingers at the four persons she now links with the murder scene on the Phillips farm in September, 1922. . . .

When her story was finished and her self-control at an end, she pulled herself up and screamed in a mad crescendo: "I have told the truth, so help me God. And you know it—you know it!"

Her wild eyes blazed from their sunken sockets at Mrs. Hall. Her skinny arm was levelled at the still figure in black. A faint smile of pitying scorn touched the lips of the rector's widow. . . .

When the biggest crime story of the *next* decade broke six years later some twenty miles due west of the site of the Hall-Mills murders, it was too close to deadline for the *Tribune* to send a reporter to the obscure Sourland Mountains of west-central Jersey; wire-service copy and stringer reports had to suffice. But the kidnapping of Charles Lindbergh's son was such big news that, although the final edition had closed, assistant night city editor L. L. Engelking wanted the paper's best reporter on the scene, even in the bitter-cold pre-dawn hours of March 2, 1932, for the following day's paper. Engel (as he preferred to be called), big as he was, was slightly intimidated by the cool, correct, and superbly reliable Miss Ross, little as she was, but he knew she was the one to call. The time was 4:45 in the morning. Richard G. West, a young Harvard man then on rewrite, never forgot the office end of the conversation: "H'lo, Miss Ross? . . . This is Engel at the office. I'm sorry to bother you [shuffling his feet and chewing hard on his habitual dead cigar], but we've got a big story here and we wonder if you'd like to come up and cover it. . . . Well, pretty soon. We've ordered a Carey Cadillac here at five-thirty. . . . Sorry to get you out of bed. . . . Well, that's fine." Engel hung up and mopped his brow. "What a woman! She's coming up."

In forty minutes she appeared, every wave in place, as if she had just come from the beauty parlor. Engel started to apologize again for rousing her so early. "Oh, that's all right," Miss Ross said, "I hadn't been to bed yet."

Not long after she had departed, several men on the night city desk crew, their duties over, decided they wanted to share in the excitement and piled into night editor Henley Hill's car for the drive to the Lindbergh place near Hopewell. Maron J. Simon, a rewriteman at the time, recalled the scene: "It was a damned cold winter dawn, and the place was crawling with cops and officials and reporters—it looked as if an army had bivouacked there, the place was so filled with mud—and there in the middle of all that muck and mire was little Ishbel, wearing her red cloth coat with the fur collar and her high-heeled shoes —no boots or galoshes. She'd worked all the previous day and hadn't slept." After getting their fill of the spectacle, Miss Ross's admiring colleagues went to the nearby Princeton Inn for some sleep; she labored on, reporting back to the paper at 7 p.m., dripping wet, and wrote the eight-column lead story, juggling her own copy, new leads from the wire services, inserts, kills, and sub-graphs until they let her go home at two the next morning.

Having proven she was both as durable and as capable as any man in the business, Ishbel Ross quit newspapering the next year when her first novel scored a commercial success and wrote books for the rest of her seventy-nine years. None, though, was as good as her reporting had been.

V

On slow news days, it was customary to test the mettle of cub reporters by sending them on impossible missions. In that spirit one afternoon shortly after the close of World War I, Maurice Jay Racusin, a twenty-six-year-old cub up from Philadelphia, was told to go down to Wall Street and interview John Pierpont Morgan the younger. What nobody told Racusin was that Morgan did not give interviews and his lair was all but impenetrable.

Racusin took along a *Tribune* calling card to present and, upon reaching Morgan's office, wrote on the back that Mr. and Mrs. Ogden Reid had sent him to see the great financier. In a matter of minutes, he was ushered to the deskside of one of the most powerful figures in the world. What was it the Reids had sent him about, the young reporter was asked. "Well, sir," said Racusin, "you've just toured abroad, and the American people would be very interested if you'd be willing to share your assessment of the world economic prospect with them."

A reasonable enough premise, politely put, and Morgan began to talk—and talk. Racusin began to take notes, many notes, and when the agreeable meeting was concluded, Racusin had the foresight to ask Morgan to initial his notes so there could be no doubt of the authenticity of the story he would write. Morgan obliged. Racusin returned to the office, composed his piece, and handed it in as if it were a perfectly routine piece of work. Around the city desk there were murmurs; plainly the story was a phony. Called to account for it, Racusin produced his Morgan-endorsed notes and swore that he had not been drinking. Still, the editors were uneasy about the piece and played it in a substantially cut version well inside the paper. But the *Tribune*'s syndicate sent all of it out across the nation, and many leading papers front-paged it.

It was the first of many times during the course of his forty-three-year career on the *Tribune* that Jay Racusin demonstrated he was nothing if not resourceful. He had attended the University of Pennsylvania's law school and comported himself with a barrister's air of self-confidence. Designated the paper's prime investigative reporter, he soon uncovered racketeering practices in the housing industry, inequities in the administration of veterans' benefits, and fresh evidence around Washington in the Teapot Dome scandal. For one undercover assignment he grew a beard, swapped his normal well-tailored suit for rags, and posed as a pushcart peddler for two weeks on the Lower East Side, where he found graft rampant among city licensing officials.

So skillful did Racusin prove as a ferret that the *Tribune* management would borrow him from time to time as a sort of house detective, investigating anyone who brought libel actions against the paper. Over the years, he saved it a lot of money. There was, for example, the gentleman testifying before a Long Island grand jury whom a *Tribune* stringer identified on the phone to a rewriteman as a convicted bookmaker. The outraged fellow sued for $50,000, and "Rac," as he was known for short in the city room, swung into action. The case was child's play for him; a little digging disclosed that the complainant had been convicted as a bootlegger, not a bookmaker—the two trades sounded similar on the phone, the paper's lawyers suggested to the plaintiff, offering to explain the mix-up in print and go into all the particulars of the bootlegging conviction while they were at it. The offer was declined, and the case was dropped. From it and others like it, Rac evolved the twin maxims of his special craft and passed them on to the next generation of *Tribune* muckrakers: (1) Everyone has something in his past to hide and (2) it is impossible to destroy a reputation that never existed.

At times Jay Racusin violated the textbook ethics of his trade but claimed higher ground to justify himself. His most spectacular success in underhandedness came in 1940 after Ansel Talbert, the *Tribune*'s aeronautical and military specialist, had broken the story of the unheralded arrival in New York of Gerhardt Westrick, one of Germany's most skillful lawyers, sent by Hitler to secure relations with American companies supplying the Third Reich's war machine. Talbert had to leave town on another assignment, and Racusin was told to keep tabs on the German agent. The disclosure of his activities, Rac learned, had caused Westrick to move from the Plaza Hotel to the quieter Carlyle on upper Madison Avenue. To find out whom Westrick was seeing and dealing with, Rac handed a twenty-dollar bill to the hotel's telephone operator to get the numbers called by the Nazi operative; then he used his undercover contacts at the telephone company to trace the locations of the numbers. The one most often called turned out to be a residence in fashionable Scarsdale that had become Westrick's true base of operation. Rac and other *Tribune* reporters kept a close vigil on the place for weeks, noting the license plates of the German's clandestine corporate visitors. Among those he dealt with most frequently was Torkil Rieber, the Norwegian-born chairman of the Texas Oil Company, one of the world's largest oil refiners, which had also been kind enough to supply Westrick with a company car for his convenience. Rac prowled around Rieber's affairs, too, and while the Texaco chief denied any sympathy with fascist governments, he conceded that his company had not hesitated to supply Franco's side in the Spanish Civil War and was in business, after all, to turn a profit. So damaging was the publicity that followed Rac's disclosures that Rieber was forced to resign within days. The potential effectiveness of Westrick's mission was at an end—a blow mainly inflicted on the virulently anti-Semitic Nazi regime by one of the few Jews then on the *Herald Tribune*'s editorial staff.

VI

Its improved appearance had helped a lot, but it was the writing throughout the paper that had most reinvigorated the *Tribune* and put it into contention with the *Times* and *World* for leadership in all-around quality among the dailies of New York and the nation. Its two most luminous stylists in the post–World War I era worked without supervision by the city desk or any master, really, other than the pleasure of the managing editor and Ogden Reid. By wide assent within the profession, the pair of them performed their tasks—as sports columnist and drama critic, respectively—in wittier, more engaging, more knowledgeable fashion than any other practitioners then serving on an American newspaper. Each came to the paper from the West at a relatively advanced age for the news game, each proved to be expert at a light sarcasm in fields where journalistic booster- ism had been more the custom, and each served sixteen years on the *Tribune* staff and died while in its employ, due largely to abusing their bodies even while they were ennobling their profession.

Like so many before him, William O'Connell McGeehan learned upon arriving in New York that, although he had a distinguished career record elsewhere (in San Francisco, where he had risen to managing editor of the *Bulletin*), no one in the big city knew who he was. There was just so much talent in town, so many papers, such fierce competition; New York was the sternest test of his calling, and so he was glad to catch on with Hearst's big evening paper even though they made him write his column under a pseudonym. When Heywood Broun brought him over to the *Tribune,* Bill McGeehan was thirty-six and the only man in the place who still rolled his own cigarettes out of brown paper and Bull Durham.

His column, "Down the Line," was immediately popular because it showed no reverence for its subject. Sports to him were above contempt but beneath apotheosizing. Writing about the subject had been the lowest-paid and least- regarded branch of journalism for the twenty-five or so years since the sports page became a regular feature on most papers. Sportswriters, not surprisingly, were therefore easy prey for promoters and team owners eager to have their heroes spoken of glowingly in print and thereby improve receipts at the gate. Their persuasion took a variety of forms, ranging from salary supplements in the form of cash payments—bribes would be perhaps one degree too strong a term, but close—to liberal applications of free food and liquor, complimentary tickets, and travel accommodations on the house. Until after World War II, many newspapers accepted this last practice as a way for major-league baseball clubs to assure ample coverage of their road games. It was no wonder that many sportswriters turned out copy not far removed from pure press-agentry.

W. O. McGeehan, as he signed his column, saw sport as part games, part business, and wrote about it without stars in his eyes. Like his contemporary Ring Lardner, he recognized that most athletes, especially the professional variety, were not very bright, personable, or well-mannered, but they were his meal ticket, so he did not go out of his way to mock them. His scorn was directed largely at the promoters and hustlers who often exploited the competitors. McGeehan was especially deadly when writing about boxing, the most ardently followed of all sports in that era; he called it "The Manly Art of Modified Murder." This iconoclastic approach, styled by Stanley Walker in his 1934 book, *City Editor,* as the Aw-Nuts school of sportswriting, was a welcome antidote to the Gee-Whiz school, whose chief proponent, McGeehan's colleague and later rival, Grantland Rice, wrote as if the Trojan War were being rerun every other autumn Saturday on the gridiron of South Bend.

McGeehan was so sophisticated a journalist that Ogden Reid, himself an earnest sportsman and fan, appointed him managing editor of the *Tribune* in 1920. It was a mistake. McGeehan had a problem with the bottle, not a fatal handicap to a columnist free to roam, pick his subjects, and set his own hours, but as office routine it was another matter. McGeehan went off on occasional binges to avoid the pressure and responsibility, and in 1922 got fired. The *Herald* was glad to take him on as sports columnist, as which he had no peer, and when the Reids bought out Frank Munsey, they welcomed McGeehan back to the fold as sports editor and columnist.

McGeehan had the look of a friendly priest, but his deadly pen skewered impartially and ecumenically. His stylistic virtuosity made his column unpredictable; in it he was capable of anything from musings on the bastardy of thoroughbreds to satires on *Macbeth*—his was called "Macbroth, or the Fatal Sausage," featuring in the title role Harry M. Stevens, the hot-dog impresario of sports arenas—and *Julius Caesar,* retitled "Hylanus Geezer," spoofing New York's mayor, John Hylan. Now and then, the *Tribune* directed his fine acidic spray at appropriate subjects beyond the sports page, such as the Scopes trial, which he helped cover in 1925. He was never better. Of the young state attorney general who prosecuted the case with fanatical dedication, McGeehan wrote:

> He made this trial with its preacher-judge and its boyish defendant the Verdun of Fundamentalism, and he shouted that the forces of knowledge should not pass. These foreign lawyers were invading holy ground. It was the South against the North. He waved no bloody shirt, but he certainly waved an ensanguined skull cap. He sounded the call to arms to the hill people of the Cumberlands to stand in their galluses with staves of hackberry in their hands to repel the invasion of the brutal and bespectacled professors from Yale, Harvard and Johns Hopkins, who were coming to invade the green hills of Tennessee and to shackle the free-born Tennesseans with thought.

He lasted to 1933. Toward the end his drinking made his output so unreliable that the paper paid him only on delivery of his columns—$100 apiece—a fact unknown at the time to colleagues who frequently covered for him with their best imitation of the inimitable Bill McGeehan.

In the midst of his unhappy tenure as managing editor, McGeehan scored one triumph that had eluded others on the staff: traveling to Chicago, he succeeded in dislodging the veteran drama critic, Percy Hammond, from Robert McCormick's *Tribune.* It may not have been, as it proclaimed on its logotype, "The World's Greatest Newspaper," but in Hammond the *Chicago Tribune* had the nation's best writer on the theater. Such distinction, McGeehan argued to Hammond, was wasted on Chicago.

At forty-seven years of age, however, Percy Hammond was uneasy as to whether his transplantation to the Great White Way would take. Why risk his unchallenged stature as cultural arbiter of the heartland stage? He knew the answer. New York was the undisputed capital of the arts in America, and no art or entertainment form was more dependent on the press for its success or failure than the Broadway stage, which mounted a dozen productions for every one seen in Chicago. The *New York Tribune* may have been small potatoes in circulation when compared with its Chicago namesake, but in cultural matters it had the advantage of long tradition and a front-row seat. So he came to New York in 1921 and brandished his stiletto gingerly at first, then began slashing away with a kind of verbal energy and learned playfulness previously unencountered by New York theatergoers; the pontifical school of play-reviewing, of which the *Tribune*'s longtime aisle-sitter, William Winter, had been a patron saint, was dead.

Percy Hammond was quite a sight returning to the office after an opening-night performance. He would come panting into the city room, maneuvering his huge bulk ponderously to his desk in a far corner, cast aside his walking stick, doff his broad-brimmed black hat and evening jacket, and settle down to an hour-long duel with the English language. His weapons were a pencil—he never was comfortable typing his reviews—a mug of Prohibition gin (at which he sipped intermittently until doctor's orders dictated its replacement by a pot of coffee), and a dictionary and thesaurus. He had a passion for the tactical deployment of odd or unexpected words, preferably polysyllabic, and phrases of unlikely wedded components that could be amusingly esoteric; they were not only clever, they were precise and usually devastatingly dismissive. But he was no pedant and knew the difference between art and entertainment and between entertainment and trash. When he reported on "last night's disturbance on Broadway," it was likely to be more with sorrow than relish. "How is my time? How is my time?" he would keep asking the copy desk urgently as his deadline neared and the sweat poured off him.

Hammond was capable of turning out memorably succinct put-downs like "Mr. Ziegfeld should remember that the human knee is a joint, not an evening's entertainment" and "The farce had many names before 'Gertie's Garter' was finally selected. What it seems to need, however, is not a name, but an epithet." Of a soft-voiced duo, he might write, "The little one sings a battle song in the manner of a germ going to war," or about acrobats "performing easy feats with great difficulty." But he could also be generous to players caught in a disaster, as he was in his first season on Broadway to the young Helen Hayes: "Honest, tricky, brilliant, taking many risks and making few errors, Miss Hayes is one of those artists, apparently, who can dare extravagance and by her charm and her deft obviousness blur the line between acting and exhibition. She will be a big thing in the theater before long, I predict."

He was never merely glib, though, and the reader looking to catch his drift when a serious work had engaged his attention could not scan it for a single telling snatch; Hammond packed too much thought and sensibility into every paragraph. His best reviews were dense but never long. His 1931 review of Eugene O'Neill's *Mourning Becomes Electra,* vintage Hammond, showed both his disinclination to be overwhelmed by large reputations and his toleration of well-executed commerce even if it did not transport him. Once more, he reported, O'Neill was examining "an agonized New England household . . . using the tools of Greek tragedy considerably modernized but none the less vivisective." The playwright led his characters "through a morbidly fascinating series of experiences, including murder and suicide . . . tinged with deft, Theatre Guild suggestions of lust, romance and incest." The sin-drenched female lead, whom Hammond had not hesitated to criticize in past performances for hyperemoting, he now commended with an edge of mockery: "Nazimova glides to and fro with now and then a graceful dart of her cobra head, more mesmerically reptilian than ever. . . . I shall not forget what [she] did to my emotions last night, when she walked up the steps of the Greek temple that was disguised as a New England mansion, defeated, mysterious, desperate and planning to blow out her brains." Having remained neutral for most of his essentially descriptive report, Hammond then closed in. O'Neill's "eminence as the First Playwright," he wrote, allowed him to disregard the rules governing dramatists "of lesser vogue" by employing as much time and space as self-indulgence invited. Lest he be misunderstood, the critic concluded:

> Were I not fretful that I should be hissed as a blasphemist, I should suggest that Mr. O'Neill is a blend of the sincere artist and the shrewd mountebank. Even when, as some contemporary satirist has said, he is "Thinking, Thinking," he has his mind upon the gadgets of the Drama, the little talking points of salesmanship. The Greek "chorus" device in "Mourning Becomes Electra" is, I suspect, but the saleable nostrum of a cunning vendor of theatrical produce. This, no doubt, is legitimate practice in the most charlatan of the arts; and it is to be praised for the dignity and skill with which it achieves results.
>
> Accordingly, it is possible to remain calm while attending [the play]. . . . Its ugly people and their gloomy perversions may be observed with tranquility by cooler playgoers, who will have almost as good a time as the fanatics.

He was, moreover, capable of dealing objectively with his own as well as others' work. In a review of a collection of his own pieces, he remarked: "He [Hammond] can say nothing in more words than any musical comedy librettist. . . . *But—Is it Art?* is only a printed museum of piffling affectation and . . . adds nothing of value to the literature of show business." Perhaps, but its author added much to the literature of journalism, puffing all the way.

VII

The euphoria born in the spring of 1924 for Helen Reid, with her mother-in-law's purchase of the *Herald* and early signs that the merger would at last bring financial stability to the *Tribune,* dissipated that December with the death from typhoid fever of her second child, Elisabeth, halfway through her tenth year. Caught up as she had been with her work at the paper, Helen blamed herself for having neglected the child and fell into deep grief. For a while she kept a death mask of Betty, as the family had called the child, by her bedside—evidence of how painful the parting was proving. "Almost every night Betty comes back in some form in my dreams," Helen wrote her mother-in-law in March 1925, "as if I could change it all if I only knew the way." Three months later, at the age of forty-two, she gave birth to a second son, Ogden Rogers Reid; the boy, like the sister he never saw, resembled his father.

The baby was hovered over from the first by a singularly devoted nursemaid, who assured him from the start and throughout his childhood that he would grow up to become President of the United States. To differentiate his name from his father's—and no doubt because it made a nice chromatic contrast with his older brother Whitie's—the family called him Brownie for his tendency to tan so readily at the beach.

Assured that the unplanned, perhaps providentially sent child was healthy and under capable supervision, Helen Reid plunged back with fresh vigor into the building of the *Herald Tribune.* "She believed in the paper the way a religious person believes in God," recalled Monroe Green, who worked closely with her for half a year before falling from her grace and transferring to the *Times,* where he swiftly became the colossus of newspaper advertising directors and Helen Reid's archrival. Her work on the *Tribune* was so vital and met with such success that it now became an extension of her family life; there were two sons to build it for, and she would not stint in her efforts. Behind the wonderfully soft voice lurked a tigress, pale greenish eyes flashing when opposed; inside the velvet glove, an iron hand.

In 1926, for example, she went after Bankers Trust Company, which had been giving its financial advertising to the *Times* in the morning and the *Sun* at night. Contending—cordially at first—that *Tribune* readers "include a large proportion of the bond holders whom it is important to reach with this advertising," she grew more pointed in remarking to the bank's president on reports her salesmen had received from his underlings that the *Times* had been favored because it was a big depositor. While advertising should no doubt be placed "on a strictly merit basis," Helen Reid argued, that apparently was not how the game was being played, in which case the bank ought to bear in mind that "the owner of [our] paper, Mrs. Whitelaw Reid, has for many years carried a large account with Bankers Trust Co. and has transacted through the bank a great deal of business for the Herald Tribune as well as for herself." Beyond that, using a morning and an evening paper guaranteed duplication of readership, and the *Tribune* not only had a circulation of 30,000 higher than the *Sun* but "I believe there is no question but that it has a larger following among the readers of financial pages than the *Sun,*" witness the two million more lines in related advertising that it carried the previous year. Nor was she above appealing to the Republican sympathies of financiers, as she did the following year in berating the Union Trust Bank of Pittsburgh for advertising a $25 million bond issue for Koppers Coke exclusively in the Democratic *Times.*

She could be even more direct when thwarted. After pitching the Institute of American Meat Packers for a full advertising schedule in mid-1927 and obtaining a good deal less, she wrote to the executive vice president, who had sent her a floral bouquet for her train ride home from Chicago, "If you thought you were sending that lovely basket of flowers to my funeral, you will be disappointed. . . . When I saw the flowers the next morning [after her meeting with him], I thought they were in celebration of a closed episode rather than a consolation prize." She promised to renew her efforts to persuade the meat packers that the *Tribune* was "the outstanding food paper in New York City," as testified to by its home institute's receipt of 20,000 letters the previous year regarding problems about food and other household questions. Her recipient thanked her for "your shrewd, interesting, ungracious letter."

But she could be very gracious indeed, particularly when fending off reader complaints about advertisements in the *Tribune.* To a man registering disgust over an ad for Kotex sanitary napkins and wondering whether others would follow, proclaiming the joys of toilet paper, she answered that the product was "an extremely good one," the copy was "simple and dignified," and if the health of many was aided by advertising its benefits, what was the harm? Where she served the paper poorly, however, was in those instances when her fierce competitiveness caused her to view the *Tribune* primarily as a merchandising vehicle instead of an editorial product. During the Paris fashion shows in the spring of 1927, for example, she was annoyed by the decision of one of the big houses to advertise only in the *Times* in New York on the theory that its ads in the Paris edition of the *Herald Tribune* addressed the portion of that paper's readership most likely to include its potential customers. "Perhaps you can pass along a good word some time at Deuillet's," she wrote to Fanny Fern Fitzwater, the paper's fashion writer and illustrator, "from the standpoint that they need to pave the way with Americans before they go to Paris and familiarize them with the names of the best houses." To assign a sales function to a feature writer was to jeopardize the editorial integrity of the paper. Such a tendency and her related vulnerability to pressure by advertisers seeking friendly news coverage were part of the reason Ogden Reid kept his wife, for all her zeal, from intruding into the news side of the operation.

Helen Reid's diligence did not go unrewarded. For the progress the paper was making, for the care she was taking of Ogden, for the next generation of Reids she was rearing, her mother-in-law expressed gratitude in various material ways, of which a sizable cash gift on each wedding anniversary was but one. Thanking her in March 1927 for what an insensitive outsider might have termed her annual retainer, Helen wrote: "I don't believe that any girl ever had a mother in law who could be mentioned in the same sentence with you and if I loved you less I could probably tell you much more easily how I feel on the subject. . . . When you started out sixteen years ago to give me an income of my own you did something that I don't believe a mother in law ever did before —and it has just made a world of difference to so many people." Helen noted that while she did not dispose of Elisabeth's largesse in ways that would have provided maximum satisfaction to her benefactor, "I know you sympathize with the responsibility I feel for various members of my family." Thus, Helen not only shared the Reid wealth with the Rogers clan but made no secret of the fact. "My appreciation and gratefulness for all your goodness is much more than I can ever put into words," she concluded, "but at least you know that I love you and my one ambition is to live to see you enjoy the Tribune debt free, standing firmly on its own resources. You smile credulously [sic] and I don't blame you —but some day you *may* smile differently." While there is no evidence whatever for questioning Helen's sincerity in these annual letters of thanks, they appear as if she were under increasing stylistic strain to persuade Elisabeth of the fact. "I am convinced that no queen or Empress ever lived who could touch you for greatness," Helen offered in her 1929 response to her anniversary gift.

Helen Reid's arrangement with her mother-in-law had yielded all the trappings of luxury that Mrs. Whitelaw Reid's former secretary had agonizingly bargained for twenty years earlier. She, Ogden, and the boys now moved into a large, five-story townhouse at 15 East Eighty-fourth Street, a few steps from the Metropolitan Museum of Art. But their truer home continued to be constantly enlarged and improved Ophir Cottage in Purchase, from which the family commuted to the city during the pleasant spring and autumn weather. Through August and till mid-September, the family joined Elisabeth and a small regiment of friends at Wild Air, their wonderfully cool Adirondack retreat 310 miles from Purchase by rail, motor, and launch. Rustic it may have been—all those huge cedar logs hewn to perfection on instructions from Messrs. McKim, Mead, and White—but how little of rough-camp austerity it imposed may be surmised from its inclusion of a main "cabin" with twenty-three bedrooms and baths, a separate cabin for the billiards table, and two cabins just for the help.

Over the Christmas holidays, the family traveled by rail and ferry to Norfolk, Virginia, then by car over a muddy back road to Flyway, their 400-acre private wildlife preserve and duck-shooting range—Ogden was always a bit ambivalent about the preservation issue—on a little inlet of the Atlantic Ocean just above the North Carolina border. Less grand than Wild Air, it had a main house, huge barns, and a boathouse, employed by the family only briefly during the year. In March, the Reids went to Palm Beach, renting a place for the month for five or six thousand dollars while Helen and Ogden stayed in regular touch with the office by phone and wire. At Purchase they kept eight automobiles; at Flyway, four. They employed a couple of dozen in help, including the caretakers at Wild Air and Flyway. And Helen herself owned at least several hundred thousand dollars' worth of jewelry and furs, bought her petite dresses at Bendel's (vivid colors preferred, shades of regal purple most of all), and popped into John Frederick's stylish millinery salon five or six times a year for a fetching variation on her standard *chapeau,* a beret ornamented with something fussy—sequins, say, or flower petals or a diamond clasp. All that, thanks to Elisabeth Mills Reid —and the paper, too. A little girl from smalltown Wisconsin was entitled to overflow with thanks.

How deservedly she retained her mother-in-law's favor may be at least partially inferred from the financial progress of the *Herald Tribune.* By 1928, just four years after the merger, it turned a profit—if one did not count what the family was owed on its loans (and since the family owned the paper outright, the cash infusions might properly have been considered capital investment)— of more than a million dollars. Circulation reached 289,000, more than 60,000 ahead of the *American,* just 13,000 behind the slumping *World,* and 77 percent of the pacesetting *Times*'s total. That year the city-editorship passed to perhaps the most celebrated holder of that position in the annals of American journalism —Stanley Walker; the *Tribune*'s golden age of cityside coverage was about to begin.

For all her pluck, enthusiasm, efficiency, and the conveniences and grandeur they had brought her, Helen Reid was not constructed of steel. She could not continually add to her family, professional, and social responsibilities. At a dinner party on Long Island in the fall of 1928, she collapsed at the table and was carried upstairs with a faint pulse. Nervous exhaustion, the doctors said; she would have to abstain from the office while she regained her strength.

In her absence, the paper continued in good health. In 1929 its circulation crossed the 300,000 milestone, and profits climbed to nearly a million and a half. Construction began on a new home for the Paris edition of the paper and a twenty-story addition to the six-year-old *Tribune* building, joining it at the rear and fronting on Forty-first Street, where the main entrance was now located; the upper stories unneeded by the paper would provide rental income.

The crash on Wall Street that October had almost immediate effects on the *Tribune*'s—and its rivals'—profit picture, although circulation held firm. Consumer purchases of larger items fell off fast, thereby reducing advertising linage, but few were so hard pressed as not to be able to spare a couple of pennies for the morning paper. The Reids were at Palm Beach as usual in March 1930, but could not escape the gathering threat to the reversal of their recent good fortunes. General manager Howard Davis, in his weekly report to Helen, wrote that operations had run $1,000 in the red compared with a $38,000 profit for the same week a year earlier and that it was proving increasingly difficult to rent out space in the new addition to the *Tribune* building—"a fair reflection of the present changed business condition as affecting our newspaper. To me it is most serious."

"The Reids never reef" was a family motto applied literally to their hearty seamanship on the often gusty waterways of the Adirondacks. But in a figurative sense as well it spoke of fixity of purpose and security anchored in wealth and social position. That June, the family took a six-week trip to Europe, courtesy of Elisabeth Reid's checkbook, and inspected the newly rising headquarters of the Paris edition of the *Herald Tribune* just off the Champs-Elysées. It had been too long a wait for prosperity to attend their proudest possession for the Reids to go into mourning at the first sign that the 'Twenties party was over.

VIII

Among the Pulitzer Prize winners announced while the Reids were in Europe in the spring of 1930 was their Paris bureau chief, thirty-one-year-old Leland Stowe. He was commended for his coverage the year before of the intensive, multibillion-dollar horse trading at the reparations conference in the French capital among World War I belligerents. It was the paper's first Pulitzer for reporting, and the Reids celebrated by taking young Stowe out to a Parisian feast. That they did not order his salary increased or even award him a bonus struck Stowe as ungenerous, but there was, after all, a world financial crisis going on and, anyway, he had a dream of a job and splendid professional prospects.

A short, peppery fellow from a small town near Waterbury, Connecticut, Stowe had graduated from Wesleyan and undergone a spirited reportorial apprenticeship on the *Telegram* in Worcester, Massachusetts. What appealed to him about newspaper work was how it taught you much more about the community and human nature and life in general—and much faster—than any other profession. He rode the fire trucks and the police ambulance, covered city hall and interviewed leading citizens all the time, roamed the countryside in a Model T as county correspondent, felt pity stir in him at the sight of the purple face of an electrocuted steelworker; death was always good for a story. He jumped from Worcester to the *Herald* in New York, one of the last reporters ever hired by it, came over to the *Tribune* after the merger, and partly on the strength of his coverage of a visit by the crown prince of Sweden, won assignment to the paper's Paris bureau in 1926. But he did not hit it off with bureau chief Wilbur Forrest, the former United Press man who had performed serviceably but no better in covering U.S. forces for the *Tribune* during the war. Forrest found the newcomer too pushy and not properly deferential. Stowe found little in his superior to defer to; Forrest seemed to possess all the intellectual curiosity of a burned-out police reporter with an aggravated case of cultural antipathy to the French: he never went to the theater or museums, still spoke the language abysmally after nine years in Paris, insisted on eating in the cheapest restaurants when for a few francs more one could dine better than anywhere else on earth. And when Stowe did share a meal with him, the conversation was vacuous and repetitive; all Wilbur Forrest seemed to care about was his golf game.

When the biggest story to hit Paris since the Armistice came along, it was not surprising, therefore, that Stowe was left back at the office on rewrite while Forrest headed the field coverage of Charles Lindbergh's thrilling landing at Le Bourget airport on the evening of May 21, 1927, after his historic solo flight over the Atlantic. Forrest's version of his reportorial activities that night, as recounted in his 1934 book of memoirs, *Behind the Front Page,* paints a self-portrait of a supremely enterprising journalist who singlehandedly scooped the world not once but twice on the Lindbergh story, first in reporting his landing and then in obtaining an interview with him. At the distance of half a century, this claim appears to have been a gross distortion of the journalistic exploits of the men involved that frenzied evening.

According to Forrest, he had anticipated the mob scene that would greet the flier at Le Bourget and jam the five-mile road between the airfield and the city, and so had arranged with a cable company to post a man in a second-floor storeroom in an auxiliary building that looked out over the field. Once the plane was down, Forrest would supply only the official time of landing to the cable man, who would relay the word by private phone line to his office, where a pre-written bulletin would be flashed almost instantaneously to New York.

The plan worked perfectly. Forrest, in a sea of 30,000 Parisians, decided he could do a better job from the second-floor lookout with the cable-company man. As Lindbergh's frail silver moth circled the floodlit field and glided in for the landing, the crowd broke down the iron restraining barriers and swept out to greet the hero even before the plane's engine had stopped. It was 10:21 Paris time. Forrest's message flashed to America before any other. Now the trick would be to get hold of Lindbergh for an interview before he was spirited away by staffers of *The New York Times,* which had purchased exclusive rights to his story. Once they closeted him, all other papers would have to copy. But reporters down on the field, *Times* men included, lost track of Lindbergh in the melee as French military aviators rescued him and his plane, brought the flier to a hangar on the far side of the field, and chauffeured him by back roads to the American embassy. Officials there steadfastly denied his presence to reporters so that the presumably exhausted aviator could recover in peace from his ordeal.

In his published memoirs, Forrest wrote that it took him hours to get back to his office after he had sent the landing bulletin and a few other details that were messengered over to the *Tribune* bureau. Then he took over the writing job. "I did not see Lindbergh at close range at the airfield that night at all," he would recount. "The first I saw of him was when he sat on the side of a bed in the American embassy a few hours later and told the story of his flight"— and over the next several pages of his book, he described the hunt for Lindbergh as if he had been part of it and included the interview with Lindbergh at the embassy as if he had written it for his second big journalistic coup of the night.

A different version emerges from the memories of three other newsmen who were in Paris that night—Stowe, writing the Lindbergh story out of the *Tribune* bureau; Al Laney, a deskman next door on the Paris edition, of which he published a history in 1945; and William L. Shirer, the journalist-historian, who was at Le Bourget for the landing as a foreign correspondent for the *Chicago Tribune*.

Two weeks before the Lindbergh crossing, a pair of French aviators, Charles Nungesser and François Coli, attempted the flight in the opposite direction, leaving from Le Bourget in the middle of the night under trying weather conditions. Their effort had been postponed several times, and when the takeoff was finally certain, Forrest was off and Stowe was manning the *Tribune* bureau. Forrest instructed Stowe to remain at the bureau, relying on legmen from the Paris edition to call in reports on the Nungesser-Coli takeoff. But Stowe, feeling uneasy with that arrangement, especially in view of the unreliable French phone system, defied his orders and went to the field—it was the only way to get the story right, to his way of thinking. The Commercial Cable Company, he recalled, kept an agent at Le Bourget with a direct line to the main Paris office; Stowe knew the fellow and, given the approaching deadline of the New York paper and the long distances that had to be covered on foot at the airfield, left him a message to be transmitted urgently to America the moment the French fliers' craft left the ground—the very arrangement Forrest was to claim as his own invention for reporting the Lindbergh landing, only he embellished it by suggesting that the presence of the cable-company man at the field had been his idea. The Frenchmen's plane was never seen after leaving French territory, but Stowe's plan worked; he sent a short follow-up description of the takeoff that caught the New York paper's run and was strongly commended by the editors back home. Although Stowe's story carried Forrest's byline, since he was the bureau chief, the episode did not sit well with Forrest, who had been upstaged by his disobedient assistant and, according to the latter, never forgave him.

Thus, Stowe found himself deskbound when the Lindbergh story unfolded. He ground out some 4,000 words for transmission to New York as information on the landing trickled in from all over Paris, including Forrest's flash and a few supplementary details sent over to him from the Commercial Cable office. When Forrest finally made it back, he put a fresh lead on the story and added firsthand details; as usual, only his own byline ran. Meanwhile, the hunt for

Lindbergh went on all over town; the *Times* men, with a proprietary interest in his story, were in as much of a quandary over his whereabouts as everyone else.

Sometime around three in the morning, when the Paris edition of the *Tribune* had all but completed its run, a twenty-eight-year-old deskman and occasional reporter named Ralph W. Barnes took it into his head that Lindbergh had to be at the American embassy. A big, lumbering, painfully earnest Oregonian with a graduate degree from Harvard, Barnes was an anomaly on the Paris *Herald* (as the paper continued to be referred to, even after the merger, out of deference to its origins). Among an editorial crew of has-beens, drunks, young expatriate transients on a lark, and a nucleus of able technicians, most of them Britons with French wives, the inexperienced Barnes was intent on mastering his craft—no small task since he had more or less fast-talked his way onto the staff after a short, shaky start back in New York on the desks of the *Brooklyn Eagle* and the *Evening World.* He was always loaded down with books and papers and magazines, always arguing idealistically in the after-hours talkathons at Harry's New York Bar or Le Dôme. His wickedest outburst was "Golly Moses!" and his worst sin was a tendency to knock things off people's desks as he brushed by them in a coat and jacket loaded to the lapels with heavy-duty reading matter. He had covered the cross-Channel swim by Gertrude Ederle the year before, enduring seasickness, an offshore drenching, and a desperate hunt in the dark for a farmhouse with a telephone to call in the story. But Barnes was still perceived as a novice on the *Herald* staff. Until some four and a half hours after Lindbergh had landed, he played no role in the paper's coverage of the event.

But now, filled with certainty, he returned to the paper from a bar where he had been speculating on Lindbergh's whereabouts with a bunch of other American newsmen and demanded taxi fare for one final assault on the embassy. The night editor, detecting the light of revelation in Barnes's eyes, complied and ordered a skeleton crew to stand by in the composing and press rooms. A wedge of competitors, similarly persuaded, trailed Barnes to the embassy, where they made their presence thunderously known to the ambassador, who finally conceded that Lindbergh was upstairs asleep and would meet the press first thing in the morning. "But golly Moses, Mr. Ambassador—" Barnes began, fiercely determined to get at the hottest news source on earth. The next instant word reached the embassy foyer that the flier, perhaps awakened by the rumpus below, would meet briefly with the gentlemen of the press. Barnes led the charge upstairs, where Lindbergh sat on a bed in pajamas and asked if anyone was there from the *Times.* A dozen rival pencil points poised like daggers to do him in if he demanded exclusivity, the *Times* man allowed that Lindbergh, his agreement with Mr. Van Anda notwithstanding, might offer a few highlights of his historic flight to the waiting world.

Incoherent with excitement, Barnes came bursting back through the office door. "Write!" they ordered him and alerted New York to stand by; there was still a little time to catch the tail end of the Sunday run. The story was so immense, the intensity of the moment so extreme, that the fear of failure all but consumed Barnes. "Golly Moses, I've got to check my notes—" No notes, they told him; just write it. They shoved the paper into the typewriter for him and poised his fingers over the keys. Nothing. Even as they were about to order him to move over and let somebody else write it while he talked it out, Barnes cleared his brain and began to peck it out. Very slowly. They snatched the copy from his typewriter a paragraph at a time; it was set almost simultaneously in the Paris and New York composing rooms. When Barnes paused and reached for his notes, they grabbed them away from him: "Just write!"

His 600-word piece was composed almost solely of quotations; the world, after all, was hanging on the airman's words, not some reporter's.

Yet not only did Barnes fail to get a byline for his feat that night, any more than Stowe had been credited for his part in it or the Nungesser-Coli story, but Forrest claimed both their accomplishments for his own, without mention of either of them, when he published his memoirs seven years later.

In 1929, the two young *Tribune* men teamed up to cover the war reparations conference in Paris that culminated, after months of blustery talks, in a plan put forth by Owen D. Young, head of the American delegation, to create an international clearinghouse for the involved governments' central banks. It was a difficult assignment because none of the bankers, economists, or finance ministry officials on the seven participating delegations wanted to be quoted for fear of aggravating the already sensitive negotiations, in which the Germans proved especially ruthless and artful. Pooling their material but writing separate pieces, Stowe filing to New York, Barnes for the Paris edition, the two *Tribune* reporters worked longer hours than their competitors, stayed with the story constantly while the other news organizations rotated the men covering, and did a better job of mining sources, especially within the Japanese delegation, whose members were flattered by the *Tribune*'s attention while the other newsmen largely ignored them. As a result, the *Tribune* coverage consistently scooped the opposition; Stowe counted twenty-three exclusives. Their last was the best. A quiet, amiable member of the Japanese team handed Stowe and Barnes the still secret text of the Young Plan, which in effect established an international bank to handle the reparations payments; the text had to be returned that same evening without fail and its source kept strictly confidential, of course. The photocopier had not yet been invented, so the *Tribune* men typed feverishly all day and into the night, proofreading with care as they copied. The whole thing ran exclusively the next day in both the Paris and New York editions. Barnes, though, was again denied a share in the glory because his accounts of the conference appeared in the Paris edition; it was Stowe's for the home paper that were given the Pulitzer.

Their careers on the paper went in directions opposite from what might have been expected. Stowe was recalled to the New York office, where he was a fifth wheel on Stanley Walker's gifted city staff. Wilbur Forrest, who did not like him—"Stowe was definitely on Wilbur's shit list," recalled Richard W. Van Horne, a *Tribune* reporter and deskman in the late 'Thirties—and who by then had been chosen to serve as Ogden Reid's executive assistant, saw to it that he was kept shackled. When war broke out again in Europe, Stowe was denied his request to go overseas by Forrest on the alleged ground that he was, at thirty-nine, too old for the job. He switched to the *Chicago Daily News* and turned in his share of crack war reporting.

Barnes, meanwhile, moved among the *Tribune*'s European bureaus—Rome, Moscow, Berlin, and London—as war flared, and won a reputation among his colleagues for boundless energy and scrupulous integrity. The latter did not sit well with the Nazi regime, especially dispatches like his March 13, 1938, piece from Berlin that began:

> With Reich German bayonets controlling Austria this morning, the German government has bluntly rejected the strongly-worded French and British protests against invasion as if they were two equally worthless scraps of paper.
>   . . . When German soldiers wearing a uniform similar to that in which their fathers left the trenches in 1918, set foot on Austrian soil at 5:30 yesterday morning, the official time announced by Dr. Josef Goebbels, the mask was torn from the new version of Prussian militarism. . . .

Barnes was permitted to continue filing from the German side as late as the battle of Dunkirk, but after reporting the likelihood that Hitler would in time violate his 1939 peace pact with Stalin, he was sent packing. He filed for a time after that from the Balkans and Greece; the British bomber on which he was flying in November 1940 was shot down over Yugoslavia. Barnes was the first American newsman to die in a war his nation would not join for a year. Many newspapers, including the *Times,* saluted his gallantry. The *Tribune* had not known his like since Smalley at Antietam.

8

The Sawed-Off Texan
and Other High Spirits

To challenge the institutional gravity of *The New York Times* and the readability of the *World,* the *Herald Tribune* needed more than talent, brighter features and graphics, dynastic determination, and the pluck of little Helen Reid. It also had to have better editors. When the marginally competent Julian Mason was invited after four years to look elsewhere (and wound up editing the *Evening Post*), he was replaced as managing editor in 1926 by a white-haired Southern gentleman out of New Orleans who looked like a statesman, drank too much, and knew too little of his craft. Armistead Richardson Holcombe made one appointment, however, that in itself justified his five-year term as head of the news side. To run the city desk he picked a sly, sawed-off Texan who had precisely the right temperament, taste, and aptitude to provide inspired coverage of that Age of Wonderful Nonsense.

In its postwar binge of self-indulgence, the nation had turned away from the dull Presidents and other vapid Throttlebottoms who officially led it and toward those who could provide distraction from the stultifying regime of home, office, and factory. It celebrated athletes, aviators, tycoons, evangelists, flagpole sitters, celluloid lovers, frenetically capering youth, and anyone out to flout the hypocrisy of Prohibition. Nowhere, of course, was there a larger supply of human folly eager to be ballyhooed than in shameless New York. The very size and vigor of the place seemed to insulate it from sensitivity to exposure in the way that smaller cities and towns were quick to take self-conscious offense at printed reports sullying their reputations. Such a climate was paradise for journalists confronted with gray men in high office and the countinghouse. And none of them appreciated it more than those who came to it from farthest away, like Harold Ross of Aspen, Colorado, who in 1925 resuscitated the name of Greeley's old magazine, *The New Yorker,* and turned it into the nation's most successful literary periodical, and Stanley Walker of Lampasas, Texas, who at the end of 1927, when he was just thirty, was named city editor of the *Herald Tribune.* Perhaps the only city editor ever to become better (if more briefly) known to the public was the terrible-tempered Charles E. Chapin of the *Evening World,* who ate reporters for breakfast and was put away in Sing Sing for murdering his wife; he died there in 1930. Walker had a less spectacular approach to life.

The city room has always been the nerve center of American newspapers, which, in contrast to the leading journals in many European countries, have primarily been local institutions most heavily devoted to the chronicling of local lives and events—a function that has somewhat declined since the arrival of the atomic age and television, which jointly redrew the horizon line of every American community. In that less grim day before global responsibility began to press heavily on the public mind, the city room served as part seminary, part abattoir, presided over in legend—and now and then in fact—by short-fused curmudgeons who seemed to their terrorized recruits to possess occult powers and misanthropic souls; city editors knew everything and everybody in town, their very function was in fact to define the community, and when they cracked a smile, which was rarely, it was usually at the expense of something the rest of humanity held sacred. Stanley Walker, although he did not hold a high opinion of human nature, earned the admiration of his colleagues by attending life's circus as a wry roustabout and coaxing his reporters to join in.

He was small, five foot seven or eight, and wiry, probably never weighing more than 125 after the biggest meal in his life, and had wavy black hair with auburn tints, a thin, aquiline nose, and assertive hazel eyes. He smiled mostly with his eyes because he was sensitive about his ugly, discolored teeth. There was hardly a hint of Texas in his quiet speech, which had a rapid, staccato beat, but he had little small talk and did not speak when he had nothing to say. When he did, his talk, like his writing, had a zinging, pithy quality to it, acerbic but not acidic, blasphemous but not boisterous. To idle inquirers about the specific whereabouts of his hometown, which seemed to them as remote from Broadway as the far side of the moon, he would characteristically respond that, on the contrary, Lampasas, Texas, was located "at the exact geographical center of the area immediately surrounding it." He rarely raised his voice. When angered, he barked briefly or just looked disgusted. He dressed in conservative navy blue, liked a good cigar, was something of a gourmet and a serious drinker—mostly of scotch, of which he was said to be able, in his prime, to consume a dozen to twenty shots a day and hold it.

He grew up on his family's ranch about sixty miles northwest of Austin, where he attended the University of Texas for three years and worked on the *Austin American* as a reporter before taking a deskman's job on the *Dallas Morning News.* On a cold December morning in 1919, he arrived in New York wearing an overcoat that was too thin and bearing a letter of introduction from a Texas newsman to an old Spanish-American War buddy who was an editor on the *Herald,* then on its last legs and about to fall into the eager grasp of Frank Munsey. Hired as a reporter on a shriveled staff, he got around town smartly, exploited every assignment for the contacts it could yield, and came to know the pols and the cops, the clerics and the vaudevillians, the promoters, gangsters, and financiers. As a writer and then a deskman, he was fast, accurate, and reliable, if not brilliant. When the *Tribune* bought out the *Herald,* Stanley Walker was one of only two dozen editorial hands invited uptown to join the new operation. His versatility earned him swift advancement. The nervous energy with which he worked and the quiet, economical, but diverting way he spoke were in sharp contrast to the habits of the incumbent city editor, who screamed a lot at his reporters when he was not slumped at his workplace, sound asleep. Soon the job was Walker's, along with a mandate to clean out the rumpots, slackers, and incompetent progeny of aristocratic old families who weighed down the city staff.

First, the screaming stopped. Reporters were called "Mister" again when summoned to the city desk to receive an assignment, and respect was repaid with respect. Second, the energy level in the city room rose as the decibel level sank. Walker showed the way, logging fourteen-hour days that began at 10 a.m., three hours before his reporters arrived. The parade of visitors to his desk, the likes of which had assailed no *Tribune* editor since Greeley had been besieged in his heyday, featured press agents, tipsters, job-seekers, columnists, mobsters, police inspectors (three at a time once), politicians, actors, writers not seeking jobs, and preachers—how he used to love to roll out the name of the Reverend Christian Fichthorne Reisner! And the endless phone callers, whom he dealt with himself when he was not on another call, were divided about equally between the bizarre and the celebrated; Governor Al Smith might be croaking away at the other end or dapper Jimmy Walker, no relation, from City Hall or wherever his fancy took him, or Police Commissioner Edward P. Mulrooney or the Right Reverend William T. Manning, Protestant Episcopal Bishop of New York—or some old crony from Texas advising him, exclusively, that Wyatt Earp had just died. Amid the hubbub he was a rock of efficiency and imperturbability. He knew how to pace himself throughout the long day and evening, executing with sudden bursts of energy and then retreating into becalmed, often cryptic inscrutability. The scotch fueled him. After dispatching his troops about the city between one and one-thirty, he would depart for lunch and refreshment at Jack Bleeck's speakeasy directly next to the Fortieth Street façade of the *Tribune* building; by the time he reappeared, there was a detectable softening in his manner until the troops returned and results had to be assessed, story lengths decided upon, copy blessed or fixed or gutted, night assignments made, the front page laid out in conference with the other editors. And all the time he would not raise his voice.

There were times, though, when he was sorely tempted. Early in his tenure, he was accosted at his desk by a *Tribune* advertising salesman seeking a plug in the news columns for a client he was soliciting; Walker politely declined the favor. The exchange was overheard by Howard Davis, the tough little cigar-chomping general manager, who commended the city editor and added, "Next time you needn't be polite—throw the bastards out the window if they try to bother you." With profits accumulating for the first time on the paper's twentieth-century balance sheet, its editorial soul was for sale less than ever, and that stiffened Walker's back. So did his admiration for Ogden Reid's politics, gentlemanliness, journalistic values, and fondness for alcoholic spirits; these mattered more than his insistence on possession of the editor's title even though he could not write worth a damn and did precious little editing. Disdain for such drudgery befit Ogden's aristocratic heritage, which invited, as Walker calculated, five basic assumptions that governed the owner's dominion over his paper: (1) the Republican Party was usually best for the country, (2) the national defense must be kept strong, (3) censorship was dangerous, (4) a first-rate newspaperman was the most admirable of God's works, and (5) there was no need to be ashamed of laughing. Ogden Reid was Stanley Walker's kind of benign boss.

The paper's sudden prosperity provided the city editor plenty of white space to fill every day. Politics and economics bored him, by and large, and he preferred to devote the space, as he claimed, to "women, wampum, and wrong-doing"; in fact, he gave over much of it to a new kind of social journalism that aimed at capturing the temper and feel of the city, its moods and fancies, changes or premonitions of change in its manners, customs, taste, and thought —daily helpings of what amounted to urban anthropology. To replace the deadwood on staff, he recruited a few solid veterans from outside, like Pulitzer Prize winner Alva Johnston, who was being poorly utilized by the *Times,* Edward Angly from the Associated Press, and Joe Driscoll from the *St. Louis Post-Dispatch,* but for the most part, Walker grew his own talent—beginners with brains and educational background—and inspired their devotion and hard work by convincing them it was an honor to practice such a magical profession on a newspaper of such high character and literacy.

"Most of the music in journalism is played by ear," Walker would write. Indispensable to its artful practice were strong legs, unlimited energy, inquisitiveness, accuracy in recording perceived events, and verbal facility. Those you either had or did not; the rest could all be learned, within three months in most cases, six at the outside. Reporting, moreover, was no business for a married man with family responsibilities. The hours were long and irregular, the pay low, the work often physically and emotionally debilitating. And younger men were more malleable in work habits and outlook, less jaded with or broken by life, still susceptible to being moved by the tragicomedy of the human race. Reporters did their best work, Walker felt, between twenty-five and thirty, when the calling was still an adventure for them; after that, it was likely to become a grind of thrice-told tales and settling for the first serviceable quote to dress up a story instead of pursuing sources day and night all over town for the ones that lent conviction.

So he enlisted what he would later call "eager, intelligent, unterrified young-sters" who gave the *Herald Tribune* its distinctive flavor and *The New York Times* a run for its money. He taught them not by imposing stylistic orthodoxy but by letting them evolve their own style. He was patient and he was tolerant, and his genius lay in matching the reporter to precisely the right assignment. When all the elements of Walker's approach meshed, the results made for extraordinary journalism, as in a 1933 piece produced by St. Clair McKelway, then twenty-eight, who was given a short report from the City News Association about the slaying of a minor hoodlum and turned it into a graphic study of low life in the underworld; in so doing, it broke many of the prevailing rules of the craft. McKelway began:

> Joseph Leahey, better known as "Spot," a West Side gangster and desperado whose long career of racketeering has been characterized by assaults and killings of studied cruelty, was stabbed in the throat just after dawn yesterday as he climbed to a second floor speakeasy at Broadway and 105th Street. He was left to die in an untidy heap at the bottom of the stairs. Since his right arm was shattered by an adversary's bullet four years ago Spot had tried to teach himself to shoot with his left hand, but had given it up as too awkward and had adopted a short, sharp knife as his favorite weapon. It may have been this, his own knife, police say, that his murderers used to slit his jugular vein. . . .
>
> Leahy was recognized as a master of terrorism, an artist in mayhem with a knife or a broken beer bottle, and for years a valued gorilla on the outside staff of one of the bigger beer barons. . . . His tendencies were too sadistic and his methods generally too boisterous for him ever to reach the upper fringe of racketeering, where the big money lay. But throughout his career he appears to have been treated with a certain deference by the courts and in the Upper Broadway district, where he finally met his death, he occupied a position of dominance.

Walker's journalistic values were transmitted partly by osmosis to those in his vicinity but in larger measure by his own writing, which reached a far wider professional readership. He wrote for the smart magazines of the day—the *American Mercury, Vanity Fair, Harper's,* and *The New Yorker*—and turned out three books during the seven years of his city-editorship: *The Night Club Era,* a rogues' gallery of Manhattan's Prohibition profiteers and patrons; *Mrs. Astor's Horse,* a miscellany on the spectacular lunacies of the post–World War I era; and *City Editor,* spirited shoptalk about his craft. All were rich in judg-mental irony. He also oversaw the 1934 publication of the *Herald Tribune Style Book,* a 125-page compendium on language usage that was almost certainly the most instructive such work yet produced by an American newspaper solely for the guidance of its own staff. From these works, supplemented by his later writings and by the collective memories of those who worked and drank with him, the essence of Walker's professional precepts, which helped educate a generation of journalists, may be distilled.

First and foremost, *don't ever betray a confidence or knife a comrade.* (2) *Always get the other side of the story.* That's why you have legs and a voice. (3) *The higher you go for a source, the more likely you are to get comment*—but don't call after midnight. (4) *Great reporters can cover any story.* Yours is not a divinely inspired art form. Greatness at it requires good wind to go with the legs, a touch of imagination to lead the brain, sleepless curiosity, and ability to write the blunt Saxon tongue. (5) *Monotony is your chief occupational hazard.* There is no shortcut to waiting for something to turn up—or someone to die. Or searching out the little details that turn your piece into gospel. When you're out at tedious charity luncheons, testimonial dinners, or organizational meetings that yield drab copy, use the occasion to connect with sources—and eat well. (6) *A servile reporter is sickening; just be polite.* (7) *Never ask your editor how to get to Canarsie* or what to do next on your story. Editors are not wet nurses. If you are not resourceful enough to figure it out for yourself, beat it. (8) *Don't drink on the job.* Your writing will only suffer. (9) *Most of what you need to know about libel:* Every story that imputes unchastity to a woman or crime to anyone is actionable; better be sure you've got it straight. Even then, no story is worth ruining a woman's life for. (10) *Don't let the paper down.*

He was equally direct in his strictures on style. His minimum requirement for satisfactory copy was that it be clear, vigorous, informative, and accurate; charm and vividness were prized but not essential. Dullness was his cardinal sin. Risk fresh phrases and dancing verbs and don't be cowed by journalism-school discouragement of lively language. Do not, however, get carried away on a tide of swollen ego when given a major assignment and turn out "Taj Mahals of verbal flubdub." Fancy writing is the sign of an insecure craftsman. Reach only when appropriate—and almost never for whimsy. Pick adjectives as you would a diamond or a mistress; too many are dangerous and produce diminishing returns. Let verbs tell the story; "said" happens to be a perfectly good one—your sources need not "state," "declare," or "aver" to make their point. Avoid slang, coarseness, and contractions. Be specific; don't say the accident occurred at the corner of Park Avenue and Fifty-seventh Street when all the world knows that intersection has four corners. Look up the correct usage of words you are not certain about: e.g., "different than" may be common in the spoken language but is an abomination in print. Culprits are "indicted for" and "convicted of" their crimes; don't write ". . . following his conviction for larceny." The "active passive" voice, as in, "Johnny was given a horse for his birthday," is an illiteracy; it wasn't Johnny who was given—it was the horse. Thus, "Johnny received a horse," "the soldier was presented *with* a medal." And use titles correctly: write "the Rev. Francis P. Smith" and "the Rev. Mr. Smith," not the provincial form, "Rev. Smith." Don't call him Congressman Jones—Congress has two houses; he is either Senator Jones or Representative Jones. And that august fellow in the robes is the Chief Justice of the United States, not merely of the Supreme Court.

II

Advised that it was pointless for him to try to match the local coverage of *The New York Times* because its enormous staff had a man to watch every rathole in the city, Stanley Walker characteristically responded that the *Herald Tribune* would succeed by assigning a rat to watch every manhole. His recruits were, if anything, more royal than rodent; almost all were college-educated, many at the best universities in the nation. A typical case was James T. Flexner, Harvard '29, who arrived with his freshly won Phi Beta Kappa key plainly visible, no journalistic experience, and a preference for a job in publishing or publicity. Instead, Ivy Lee, one of the leading public relations counselors of his day, had directed young Flexner to the *Tribune* as "the only paper to work on." That Flexner was the son of the director of the Rockefeller Institute of Medical Research did not hurt his application. His first outside assignment was to cover a picnic given by a Hibernian society; in his copy the novice described the event as "fascinating"—an adjective, Walker's least favorite part of speech, and a poor one at that. "Don't proclaim it," the city editor said upon summoning the fledgling and indicating the offending word, "show it." "It was as fine a piece of advice as I've ever had," recalled Flexner, the future Pulitzer Prize biographer of George Washington.

Other lessons came fast. His shyness, for instance, in telephoning the bereaved to get material for obituaries was misplaced, Flexner discovered. The grieving, approached politely, welcomed the human contact and distraction from sorrow. A more complex lesson, on what constituted printable news, followed Flexner's attendance at a Tammany Hall testimonial dinner at which a bottle of illegal hootch was on every table, cops and crooks rubbed elbows, priests joined wardheelers at the gaming tables, and presumably nonpartisan journalists solicited contributions to the party. Brimming with these orgiastic tales, he reported in to the city desk and asked how much space he might have; one paragraph, he was told—"you were their guest." Complicity, evidently, was preferable to exposure of official immorality, even if practiced by the party to which your paper was editorially opposed. "Actually, I rather admired the bravado of the whole thing," Flexner remembered. "We were really without much social consciousness." Next to dullness, piety was the least welcome visitor to Stanley Walker's city room.

Of the dozen or so bylines Flexner won during his two years on the *Tribune*, none was more resourcefully obtained than an interview he had been assigned with Theodore Dreiser, known not to be receptive to such intrusions. Flexner went to Dreiser's apartment house on West Fifty-seventh Street and rang him on the house phone, asking to come up. "You've just destroyed the novel I've been working on," came the reply, "but since the damage has already been done, come ahead." Dreiser prefaced his remarks by saying he thought all such interviews were fatuous and betting Flexner ten dollars that he could not get the substance of Dreiser's gloomily anti-capitalist views printed in the *Tribune*. Flexner took the wager and proceeded to include the fact of it in the lead of his story. It did not appear the next day. But on the day following it did, with Flexner's byline and a rejoinder, on the editorial page, chiding the acclaimed writer for berating the social system that had allowed him to own a duplex apartment opposite Carnegie Hall and a country estate in Mount Kisco. "What pathetic nonsense!" the paper wrote. "We are not sure what it all goes to show, unless it be that novelists should never be interviewed, or . . . that a man may be a great novelist and still be something of a fool." Dreiser promptly sent Flexner a ten-dollar check and a note that read: "Fair enough. . . . Incidentally this makes me slightly less pessimistic."

Mingling with the famous and powerful became routine for Flexner and emboldened him not a little. When the notoriously unpunctual James J. Walker arrived late for an interview with the *Tribune*'s young man, Flexner told him, "The prettiest girl in Greenwich Village is getting angrier and angrier at me." The mayor asked why and was told his lateness would cause the reporter to forgo their planned social evening so that he could get his story in. Grieved, Jimmy Walker put his limousine and driver at Flexner's disposal for the rest of the night. "And believe me," he remembered fondly, "the young lady was very impressed when we ran the red lights."

III

Easily the most ornate and preposterous of Stanley Walker's reportorial acquisitions was the tall, foppish figure who presented himself for inspection one midsummer day in 1929—a flagrant boulevardier, right down to the yellow gloves holding the jaunty walking stick. The city editor, in a playful mood himself that day, wearing what the job applicant would later describe as Walker's ratcatcher outfit—a Sherlock Holmes checked suit, a deerstalker's cap with the earflaps tied overhead, curved pipe, magnifying glass in hand—studied the yet more outlandish spectacle before him. Lucius Beebe's credentials, like his manners, were impeccable. At twenty-seven, he had a degree from Harvard, where he had done a year's graduate work in literature—no mention was made just then of his having been thrown out of Yale for a drunken jape—and a fistful of clippings from a couple of creditable Boston papers. And he called Walker "sir" with booming deference. There was no reason not to take him on, except for the costume. On reflection, Walker decided that that was all right, too: might improve the sartorial state of the staff.

At Bleeck's saloon a few nights after Walker had hired him, Ogden Reid caught his first glimpse of the *Tribune*'s newest employee. He was wearing his usual nocturnal gear when out on the town: white tie and tails, top hat, red-velvet-lined opera cloak, heavy gold chain adorning his midsection, silver-tipped black stick; he was smoking a cigar less than a foot long but not by much.

"Quite a sight," Reid said to Walker after their introduction and Beebe had exited to light up the night. "Is he good for anything?"

The city editor nodded. "I hired him as a sort of sandwich man for the More Abundant Life."

Reid's appreciative bellow echoed all over Hell's Kitchen.

Beebe was indeed partial to life's velvet comforts. "All I want," he once said, "is the best of everything—and there's very little of that." His grand manner and Wildean ways were attributable, some said, not to an aristocratic upbringing but to a bourgeois one he hoped to extirpate. His father had been in the leather business and later ran the local gas company in Brockton, Massachusetts, serving, too, as a bank director. Beebe would refer to him as a banker. Whatever the neurotic nature of his family bond, his parents were known to send him three hundred dollars a month, nearly three times the salary paid to young reporters on the paper, and he comported himself accordingly. The extravagance of his wardrobe was mirrored in the tangled wildwood of his prose: he avoided the vulgar tongue whenever he could get away with it. Such a style was not much suited to reporting on small fires—which he did on at least one occasion while wearing a morning coat—or covering routine speeches at dinners where he himself was likely to be an object of as much curiosity as the guest of honor. Once, when he had been assigned to cover a dinner address by the president of the New York Central Railroad to his assembled engineers, Beebe instead showed up at a gathering of the Caledonian Society being held in the same hotel. Why the railroad chief should unaccountably have decided to address his men on aspects of Scottish culture, the reporter was uncertain, but he wrote it all up dutifully and was puzzled by the ensuing uproar; one damned dinner, after all, was very like the next.

They transferred him to the drama section, where his talents were better utilized in second-string reviewing and expansive interviews (whose subjects, however, all tended to speak in the upholstered vocabulary of their interviewer). In 1933, the director of the Herald Tribune Syndicate proposed that Beebe write a column on New York nightlife—not the most promising of subjects at a moment much of the nation was wallowing in economic misery. Yet it worked. No doubt it would have reinforced the *Tribune*'s not altogether desirable reputation as the paper of the plutocrats if it had been written in a flat style, but Beebe's "This New York," devoted to what he called "the nervous hilarity of the damned," was social reportage that proved its author to be a penetrating satirist. Subject and style meshed perfectly. He would write of "calamitous potations," "vaguely anonymous spaniels," and "the purlieus of magnificence"; food and drink, for him, were always "comestibles." He became, over the next two decades, the historian of the upper stratum of New York's café society and its showy habits. If you wanted to know anything about vintage champagnes or the best buy in Alfred Dunhill's humidor or how to outsnob your maître d' or why the insignia of the Plaza Hotel consisted of spine-to-spine P's in a wreath,* Lucius Beebe was your man. He stalked the town by night on his long legs— all night—often showing up in the office at dawn, still in white tie, to bang out his copy. He would catch a few hours' sleep, then reappear in late morning, less formally outfitted, for some office chitchat and attending to callers; by midday, he would turn to anyone handy and say, "Hey, keed, let's you and me go downstairs for a gag," short for a "rye gag," a calamitous potation of his own devising. A besotting lunch was followed by a nap and a Turkish bath and then careful wardrobing for his round of public appearances that evening. He was said to be the only staff regular whose work allowed him to get drunk twice each day. When Stanley Walker felt called upon once to deny that his staff of superior young men were in fact a bunch of playboys, he added, "Excepting, always, Lucius Beebe."

The rest of the city room learned to take him in stride. One post-midnight weary, Henley Hill, the brusque night editor, stopped by the city desk on his way home and demanded, "Where's my hat?" He had a hat in his hand. "This isn't my hat," he said. "Where's my hat?" When someone noted that Hill hung his hat in the drama department, it was suggested that Beebe might have taken it in error. Hill telephoned and found him home. Witnesses reported the office end of the conversation running thus: "Beebe? Hill, at the office. You got my hat? . . . What? . . . Well, go look. [Hand over mouthpiece.] Son of a bitch, he's going to look. [Back again on the phone.] Yeah? Well, get down here with it right away. . . . That's right. I want it." Over his shoulder, walking away: "Son of a bitch had it."

Beebe weaved in through the Forty-first Street door half an hour later, hat on head, none in hand. Hill accosted him: "Where's my hat?"

"Well, Mr. Hill," mumbled Lucius, "I'm sorry. I took your hat by mistake and later in the cab something funny happened to it. I didn't feel very well, you know, my stomach . . ." Hill was speechless. "I'll buy you another."

Hill stalked off and the remorseful Beebe hung his rear over the edge of a tall wastebasket of the sort favored in newspaper offices and carried on a disjointed conversation with the late crew. His seat slipped, and he sank slowly into the basket, jackknife fashion, receding like a ship over the horizon. He was extricated with great difficulty. A few days later, Hill reported to the city desk that Beebe had indeed bought him a new hat. "Better than I had."

* The P's stood for Park Plaza, the hotel's original name, Beebe noted for the uninitiated, who made up the preponderance of his readership.

His admirable character went beyond haberdashery. Beebe was an avowed enemy of the American Newspaper Guild, which tried to organize the city room for nearly ten years before succeeding. He hated all unions with Bourbon contempt, arguing that they were "for the benefit of the worthless, incompetent and discontented to harass their betters and to prevent ambitious, hard-working people from getting ahead." But when the day came to vote on turning the *Tribune* into a Guild shop, the poorly paid copyboy in Beebe's department—a staunch advocate of the union—was home ill, and gentlemen did not take advantage of others' misfortune; Beebe abstained—for one of the few times in his career.

IV

Sometimes the way Stanley Walker fired a man said as much about the character of the city editor as how he picked him in the first place.

He took an early liking to an excessively shy fellow named Joseph Mitchell, fresh out of the University of North Carolina and eager to crash bigtime journalism with a small stake from his father, a cotton and tobacco dealer. Walker saw in him the same Southern agrarian background as his own and a pleasingly understated personality; brashness in the young, even (or especially) young reporters, displeased him. But Joe Mitchell was a certified rube, and Walker suggested that he familiarize himself with the city, live in different parts of it—the Upper West Side, the Village, Brooklyn—get any work he could find, as a soda jerk, even, that would let him savor the variety of metropolitan life, and then come back and talk about a job.

Mitchell latched on to a copyboy job at the fading *World* and got promoted to slipboy at police headquarters, making him a sort of apprentice reporter. That sped up his indoctrination in the wicked ways of Sodom-on-Hudson. Walker agreed to take him on then on a trial basis, and Joe Mitchell soon showed his mettle. He worked the police shacks around town and was good at dockside interviews with arriving and departing celebrities. His specialty was gangster funerals and their picturesque floral arrangements, such as a twelve-foot-high tower of roses with a silk cummerbund reading "Good-by, Old Timer"; many a florist, he soon discovered, fronted for the numbers racket. He could not have been happier in his work. To be able to phone someone on a story and identify himself as "Mitchell of the *Tribune*" validated his presence on the planet—"the paper had a tony ring to its name—it was like invoking the British Empire," he recalled. "The *Times* was just a dull newspaper as far as we were concerned. We didn't even think we were in competition with it."

All that euphoria faded for him one February day in 1931 when Mitchell turned in his best piece of police reporting. He had been at the Fifty-first Street police reporters' shack the morning after a well-paid prostitute with an unsporting habit of blackmailing her prominent clientele had been found murdered in Van Cortlandt Park. Overhearing several detectives arrange to inspect the victim's apartment on East Thirty-seventh Street, Mitchell tagged along and witnessed the discovery of her highly illuminating diary and a letter she was in the process of composing to the Seabury Commission, a state panel about to begin a probe of the police vice squad. "My God," whispered one of the detectives. Soon his superior appeared on the scene, grasped the situation, and taking one look at the frantically scribbling Mitchell, screamed, "Get that guy out of here!" Mitchell phoned Stanley Walker, who urged him to hang around as long as he could, collecting as much as possible on the prostitute, her clients, contacts, property—anything. When he got back to his desk, he was told to write for all he was worth. But as night came on, managing editor Holcombe decided the story was too hot to be entrusted to one of Walker's cubs and ordered him to turn over all his material to Wilbur Forrest, back from Europe and being groomed for the executive office next to Ogden Reid's. Deprived of his scoop, back pounding the pavements of the Bronx on routine police stories, Mitchell burned. He did not know exactly who was responsible for what had happened, but his anger focused on Ogden Reid, the editor-in-chief and Forrest's prime patron.

One afternoon the following fall, calling in from an assignment that had fizzled, Mitchell was asked by Walker to stop at the hotel room of a recent staff addition and help him out; the newcomer, it seemed, was a very heavy drinker wrapping up an important story for the paper and, not trusting himself to avoid the temptations of booze, had locked himself in his room and thrown his shoes out the window to guarantee that he would stay there until the piece was done. Now that it was, he was marooned, shoeless and sober. Perhaps Mitchell could scare up Lucius Beebe; his feet were thought to be about the same size as the new man's—and, at any rate, he had plenty of shoes to spare.

Beebe showed up with a selection of shoes and a bottle of Medford rum to celebrate the occasion—"it didn't take much of one for Beebe to celebrate," Mitchell recounted—and before long, their spirits soared. After Beebe had gone off to his Turkish bath, Mitchell and his newly shod companion went roaring over to the paper to deliver the latter's copy. Mitchell, still bitter about being made to give up his big story the previous February, decided to deliver something of his own—he would tell Ogden Reid exactly what he thought of him. The sloshed pair scuffled a bit with the *Tribune* guards but managed to make their way upstairs, where the new man, seeking the lavatory but turning the wrong way, relieved himself in a corner of the coatroom while Mitchell marched on Reid's office to tell him off. The boss was away, as he was more often than not, but his secretary said she would try to find him. Mitchell used the interlude to invade Ogden's paneled office, grab the fancy inkwell from his desk, and hurl it full force at the wall behind. "I still remember the beautiful crescent pattern the ink made."

The security guards came and carted the pair of them away. Walker called Mitchell at home the next day and said that Ogden wasn't bothered much but Holcombe insisted that the cutups be made examples of. His firing could not have come at a worse time for Mitchell; he was about to get married, and jobs were scarce. Oddly enough, the newly amalgamated *World-Telegram* took him in while many a veteran from the lately deceased Pulitzer sheet went jobless. Walker, of course, had got him the job, which Mitchell parlayed into a career as one of the best-respected reporters in the business, especially on *The New Yorker.* When he tried to thank his benefactor, Walker told him, "I don't know what you're talking about." He had also arranged employment, on the *Boston Evening Transcript,* for Mitchell's drunken colleague—"and Stanley didn't even like him."

If Joe Mitchell had survived on the *Tribune* a few weeks longer, he would have had the satisfaction of seeing the man who had really taken away his big scoop—Armistead Holcombe—stripped of the managing-editorship, in part because of his drinking, and replaced by his assistant, the first truly competent journalist to direct the news operation of the paper since Whitelaw Reid in his prime half a century earlier.

Grafton Stiles Wilcox moved across the city room with the gravity of a battleship. It was not his size so much as his bearing that commanded respect. Of medium height, he held his broad shoulders and large head very straight, and if, at the age of fifty-two, there was a certain jowliness to the face and a bay window that his double-breasted suits could not quite conceal, there was also a courtly presence about him. His large eyes, high brow, and firm but gentle speech strengthened the aura he projected that here was a good, wise, solid man. Nobody called him Grafton.

Like his two immediate predecessors as managing editor, he had a presentability that was the *sine qua non* for the social-minded Reids, yet at a time when more and more college men were coming into the field, they chose a man who had not gone beyond high school as their chief news executive. The son of a Congregationalist minister, Wilcox had grown up in west-central Illinois and served his newspaper apprenticeship in Waukegan and Chicago, specializing in political coverage. He reached Washington in 1910 and served sixteen years as a leading correspondent for the Associated Press, *Chicago Tribune,* and *New York Tribune.* A sociability that complemented the solidity of his performance won him the presidency of the National Press Club and membership in the Gridiron, the capital's journalistic elite. The Reids brought him to New York in 1926 as assistant managing editor under the provincial Holcombe, who lacked Wilcox's familiarity with national politics and world affairs. In command now and in concert with Walker, a city editor who knew much of New York and Texas and little in between, he gave the paper confident direction. He was not strong in cultural affairs, but others were. He showed keen judgment in evaluating breaking news, worked conscientiously, remaining at the office until the city edition came up for scrutiny and whatever revamping was required, and was considered scrupulously fair in his dealings with the news staff. "Wilky," they called him, but never to his face.

In the ten years he held the managing editor's position, Grafton Wilcox never succumbed to delusions of grandeur. He steered clear of the foursome who wielded the intramural executive power that Ogden Reid increasingly delegated —Howard Davis, Helen Reid, Wilbur Forrest, and chief editorial writer Geoffrey Parsons—and remained always a working journalist, no mere company man. When the *Tribune* cut back from a six- to a five-day workweek in 1934 under pressure on the newspaper industry by the New Deal's National Recovery Administration, its prissy sports editor, George Daley, denounced the move to Wilcox as a lot of damned nonsense and said any good newspaper executive would agree. Wilky studied Daley for a moment, then with the slightly ironic tone he used to register disdain said, "Well, George, if you want to work six days a week, I don't think the Reids will object, but as for me, I'm damned well going to take my two days off and enjoy them."

V

Most of Stanley Walker's intrepid young men of brains and breeding served with zeal and sooner or later moved on. But one stayed, the better part of thirty years, to become one of the nation's most powerful political commentators and critics. None of Walker's recruits, Lucius Beebe included, had looked more unpromising at first.

Joseph Wright Alsop, Jr., Harvard '32, carried nearly 250 pounds on his short frame and found the simple act of crossing his legs about as easy as a penguin would have. To get that fat, he wrote several years later, "you give yourself up to orgies of doing nothing." Besides being an unsightly blob, he spoke in the manner of the English upper class, whose lovingly elongated vowels and clipped consonants sounded intimidatingly superior around egalitarian American newsrooms. And he could not type. Or drive a car. And he had done no extracurricular writing at Harvard. His only credential for a reporting job on the *Herald Tribune* was that his grandmother had been a friend of the Whitelaw Reids, and since his parents, deciding he had had enough of academic life at Cambridge, did not know what else to do with him, they extracted a promise from Helen Reid that Joseph would be given a tryout in the city room. "There," said Stanley Walker to an aide after interviewing the unthinkable prospect, "goes a perfect example of Republican inbreeding."

Joe Alsop was not a favorite of the copyboys. None of them was well-off or had had the advantages that instantly got him a writing job most of them panted for and had to wait years to win. Chief copyboy Homer Bigart, five years in menial servitude at that point, was told to find a piece of wire-service copy believed lodged somewhere in Alsop's desk and found in the course of his search a bunch of uncashed *Tribune* paychecks, apparently too meager for Alsop to bother to take to the bank. Nor was he gracious to the commoners who typed his copy for him. "Boy!" he snapped from one of the city-room telephone booths to copyboy Barrett McGurn, a mere Fordham graduate with solid experience as campus stringer for the *Times* and *Tribune* and editor of the undergraduate weekly *Ram,* "get me a pencil." He wore gabardine suits and colored shirts with white collars and French cuffs and his shoes were handmade and he was always reaching for the handkerchief prominently displayed in his breast pocket to mop his copiously sweating brow. His domestic needs were tended to by a Japanese named Buto and his wife, a cook, who lodged with him in a spacious apartment on East Eighty-fourth Street, not far from the Reids' place. When on occasion the city desk called on the phone to summon Alsop for an assignment he preferred not to accept, he would give his best nasal approximation of Buto's accent and say the young master was not at home at present.

Testy and snobbish, he was also a natural as a journalist. He was smart and enormously well-read and not only spoke the King's English but wrote it with easy mastery. And he had undeniable skills as an interrogator not easily cowed by reluctant sources. Walker stuck with him, and in six months Joe Alsop was turning in excellent feature copy, often on recondite topics that would have baffled others. Between assignments, he would sit at his desk reading. Once it was a volume in English of Proust's *A la recherche du temps perdu,* which he was comparing with the original for a review he was writing for the paper's Sunday book section. To the better-bred young men among the reportorial staff whom he found suitable social companions, like Phil Boyer, Sandy Vanderbilt, Ring Lardner's son, John, and his cousin, Richard Lardner Tobin, Joe Alsop could be exceedingly cordial and generous. He would sometimes pick up their checks at Bleeck's and have them to his apartment for dinners prepared by his cook, after which there would be poker games, free-flowing Cutty Sark, initiation of the host into the thrill of shooting craps, and other pastimes not included in his refined upbringing.

Early in 1935, Joe Alsop got his big break. He was assigned to the *Tribune* team covering the trial of the accused kidnap-murderer of the Lindbergh baby. Some three hundred reporters overran the little Hunterdon County Courthouse in rural Flemington, New Jersey, and Alsop, asked to provide color stories to supplement the lead running account, was forced to perch atop a radiator in the jammed courtroom to observe the proceedings. The most heavily covered murder trial in history, it proved a ghoulish spectacle at which souvenir salesmen peddled miniature likenesses of the stepladder the accused had allegedly fashioned to reach his child victim's bedroom. Tickets to the courtroom were sold to spectators for as much as fifteen dollars a day. The scene provided a field day for feature writers, and Alsop's pieces won him a daily front-page byline.

The day the defendant appeared to testify in his own behalf, Alsop began his piece:

> FLEMINGTON, N.J., Jan. 24 — Bruno Richard Hauptmann, so long publicized as the dark "mystery man" of his own trial, stepped down from the witness stand today still something of an enigma, but one of a new sort. Instead of a creature of inhuman malevolence, he seemed no more than a simple Bronx carpenter of German extraction, fond of music and the outdoors and given to saving money in a penny-pinching way. The enigmatic thing was the great pall of suspicion hanging over such an ordinary-appearing man.
>
> After all the talk of the strangeness of his eyes and the sinister composure of his demeanor, his testimony had exactly the effect that would be produced if the actor cast for Hamlet's tragic attitudinizings suddenly began playing Polonius.

It was not the sort of copy that Damon Runyon was filing for the Hearst papers. After a day's cooking atop his courtroom radiator, Alsop would say, "I have to change my linens," and then, freshly attired, would join a group of colleagues to find a suitable country inn instead of dining at "this terrible old drummers' hotel," as he called it, across the street from the courthouse. His reward was transfer to the *Tribune*'s bureau in Washington, where his social connections among the Ivy League New Dealers reached as high as his distant relative in the White House.

Stanley Walker soon followed Joe Alsop out of the city room he had revolutionized and turned into the habitat of New York's best local reporting staff, according to the contemporary judgment of *Time* magazine and many others in the news game. For a while, Walker had lent an occasional zany touch to the paper's atmospherics, like the time he sent a pageful of commas to a suburban stringer whose copy was habitually devoid of them; or mocked the pompous style of the second-string music critic by assigning one of his feature writers to assess in like fashion the performance of the first organ-grinder and monkey of the spring season; or joined a giddy cab ride all around the town to determine whether there were more snow-white horses or redheaded women extant on the streets of Manhattan—a lark that yielded a column and a half of weightless copy. But as the breadlines lengthened and the economic news became increasingly oppressive, such antics waned, along with the large news hole that had once been at the city editor's disposal. News from Washington and Berlin and Rome and Shanghai, most of it unremittingly grim and all of it indisputably more important than the airy stuff Walker's cubs were so good at, had sapped Walker's zest, and he lacked the depth and flexibility to adjust to the new day.

There were other factors as well. He complained that the *Tribune* refused to pay his reporters enough, and they were always leaving him. And the paper had not been excessively generous with him, either. So when Arthur Brisbane of the *Daily Mirror* trotted him off to Dinty Moore's to try to lure him over as managing editor to turn the gossip sheet with its half-million circulation into a quality tabloid, Walker was receptive. The salary was double the $10,000 the Reids were paying him, and the fresh challenge was irresistible. Besides, being city editor too long burned a man out. His departure was not universally lamented at the *Tribune.* Some said that he played favorites with his reporters, that he exploited them in writing his books and articles, that he took too much money from them in bets on the Match Game at Bleeck's, and that he generally displayed an embittered cast of mind as the mood of the 'Twenties steadily dissipated. Perhaps he had begun to believe his own legend; what other city editor was featured in full-page advertisements in *The Saturday Evening Post* endorsing Gruen watches?

But things did not go well for him at the *Mirror.* The talk around town was that Hearst had hired him, not to overtake the *Daily News,* a million copies ahead of the *Mirror* in daily sales, but to unman him, in vengeance for the uncomplimentary things Walker had written about "The Chief" and his papers in *City Editor.* Whatever the reason, he was soon sidetracked and left the *Mirror* after a year. He joined a magazine called *New York Woman,* but it went under. An editor's job on *The New Yorker* did not suit him; he needed the rhythms and excitement of a daily paper. The *Public Ledger* in Philadelphia, in a survival struggle, took him on as its top editor, but the owner would not invest adequately in the staff, preferring to give expensive parties, at which Walker stood around dazed and unhappy, talking nervously and pining for New York. The only good thing he claimed to have found in Philadelphia was an all-night delicatessen. He and other high-priced talent were let go, and the *Ledger*'s demise soon followed. They took him back on the *Tribune* for a time as an editorial writer and then he contributed pieces at space rates, hanging about on the fringes of the paper, drinking too much at Bleeck's, and remembering the glory days.

Prizefighting taught two lessons that applied to life in New York, he would later write: "(1) Each man must protect himself at all times, and (2) only a sap keeps on fighting after the bell has rung." In 1946, Stanley Walker heard the bell and went home to his ranch in Texas. But he always kept in touch with his friends on the *Tribune.* He had a ram on his ranch that he called Ogden because the silly creature kept getting its head caught in its feed bucket, not unlike the way he remembered the *Tribune* proprietor's head falling into his bowl of soup at Bleeck's when an alcoholic haze lulled him to blissful sleep. In 1962, suffering from cancer of the throat, he sent a characteristic note to Belle Rosenbaum, the assistant literary editor, whom he had known since they had worked together on the *Herald*:

> . . . For some time now I have had a red hot fish hook in my throat. Tomorrow I go down to Houston and there, under the best of auspices, the boys with the short knives will do their stuff. The gimmick is on the wall near the voice box, and it is too big. We shall see. Don't worry, and there isn't anything to do that isn't already being done. I just thought you ought to know.

It was signed "All love, S. Walker, The Sweet Singer of Hummingbird Mesa." But he never went to Houston. Instead he stuck a shotgun in his mouth and put his stamp on the front page, for the last time, of the *Herald Tribune*.

VI

The rapid decline of the New York *World* from its rank as the most vibrant and readable, if no longer the best or most influential, newspaper in America was a major contributing factor to the corresponding rise in reputation and economic health of the *Herald Tribune*. A severe case of split personality leading to heart failure brought death to the *World* in February 1931, but not until a heroic effort had been made to revive the patient.

The *Times* had caught the *World* in circulation and surpassed it in advertising and reputation by 1920, the year Joseph Pulitzer's sons handed command of the paper to Herbert Bayard Swope, the tall, florid, jaunty former star reporter and correspondent. His strategy was to give the stumbling enterprise both more substance and more glitter, offering thoughtful readers enriched fare and at the same time reclaiming the masses which Pulitzer had originally staked out as his and who were now being heavily drained off by the *Daily News*. The paper would become more exciting, more entertaining, more argumentative— qualities the voluble Swope himself embodied. And to a significant extent, he achieved his goal. The news columns were enlivened and returned to splashy crusading against corruption, the Ku Klux Klan, and other manifestations of civic and social pathology. "Pick out the best story of the day and hammer the hell out of it!" Swope ordered, reviving the sensationalist style of news play that had characterized the *World* in its heyday. At the same time, in an innovative step the whole industry would later follow, he set aside the page opposite the editorial page as a showcase for an array of gifted, controversial columnists, of whom *Tribune* transfers Heywood Broun and F.P.A. and his "Conning Tower" were among the leading attractions. The cultural department was also greatly strengthened with the addition of such sophisticates as Alexander Woollcott as the drama critic, Deems Taylor as music critic, and book reviews by Laurence Stallings, author of the hit anti-war drama *What Price Glory?* And to run the *World*'s editorial page, Swope in 1922 enlisted a thirty-three-year-old philosopher-journalist who consorted with leading intellectual and political figures of the day and was widely admired as a writer and thinker.

A boy socialist at Harvard, Walter Lippmann plunged into the waters of progressive politics and the reform movement as both observer and participant. He worked as a Boston reporter, a legman for Lincoln Steffens, and an editor for the liberal *New Republic*. His political involvement ranged from the municipal improvement of Schenectady, New York, to the formulation of President

Wilson's Fourteen Points through close association with the Chief Executive's intimate adviser, Colonel Edward M. House. He wrote for many magazines and in 1913, at twenty-four, published his first book, *A Preface to Politics,* which at once established him as a leader of a new generation that was rejecting the outworn ideologies, assumptions, and morality of the past; he wanted a political system that was both just and workable.

The year he joined the *World,* Lippmann brought out the book that more than any other of the twenty-two he would write in his long career was to help establish his position as probably the foremost American political thinker of the twentieth century. In *Public Opinion,* he argued, with the clear-sightedness that made it so increasingly difficult to assign him to a partisan niche, that democracy in modern mass societies could no longer be conceived of in the ideal terms that applied to its ancient Greek city-state model. Issues to be decided had grown so much more complex, variable societal factors so much more numerous, contending interests under universal suffrage so much more intense and insistent, that it was blindness to believe the collective citizenry could be relied upon in its wisdom and dignity to elect able governments and create just laws. At a time when social psychology was in its infancy, Lippmann wrote that the public expressed its will not coolly and rationally but in ways refracted through the prisms of emotion, habit, prejudice, and self-interest. The most the press could do was to function "like the beam of a searchlight that moves restlessly about, bringing one episode and then another out of the darkness."

With such a weighty and provocative mind writing its editorials—he produced some 2,000 of them during his nine years on the *World*—and Swope energizing the city room, the paper was freshly embraced by liberals and intellectuals. But there were not enough of them in a decade in which the country spurned reformers and refused to be serious about many things other than moneymaking. Its flashier news play satisfied neither the masses who preferred the elemental and gory tabloids nor solider citizens who found the *World* too full of features and too thin in coverage of world and national events; serious readers turned more and more to the moderate *Times* and the conservative *Herald Tribune.* Trying to be all things to all men, the *World* seemed an unstable emulsion; the parts no longer complemented one another as they had in Joseph Pulitzer's day, and the competition was now far fiercer.

The *World*'s business management, moreover, was almost willfully shortsighted. Pulitzer's three sons milked the operation of its profits and declined to make the sort of investment in staff and white space that Swope needed to achieve the solidity of its quality competitors; flair alone would not work. A decision to raise the sales price from two cents to three in the mistaken belief that the *Times* and *Tribune* would follow proved fatal; circulation fell off 20 percent, seriously damaging ad revenues. By the time the lower price was restored several years later, it was too late. By 1929, the *World* was losing money; by the next year, as Depression struck, most newspapers were doing the same, but the Pulitzers lacked the nerve to resist the economic tide. Swope was two years gone, Broun had transferred to the *Telegram,* other defections had dampened its spirit, and the Pulitzers decided it was all hopeless. They sold out for five million to the Scripps-Howard chain, which killed the flagship morning edition and merged the *Evening World* into the *Telegram,* which it had purchased in 1926 from Frank Munsey's beneficiary, the Metropolitan Museum of Art.

"There was deep gloom in the editorial rooms where the news events of half a century have been fearlessly recorded day by day," Ishbel Ross wrote in the *Tribune*'s lead story on the *World*'s demise. Adjacent ran the text of its last editorial, which was unsigned but credited to Walter Lippmann, who had concluded with a quotation from Mr. Valiant-for-Truth in *The Pilgrim's Progress*: "My sword I give to him that shall succeed me in my pilgrimage, and my courage and skill to him that can get it." Lippmann was the last survivor, the personification of the *World*'s former greatness, and there was no one who wanted to get his sword, courage, and skill more than Helen Reid.

It was a daring ambition, one that seemed alien to the partisan heritage of the *Herald Tribune.* But it was also an extremely shrewd risk, for if the paper was to continue to grow and challenge the *Times* for supremacy as New York's quality paper and therefore probably the nation's most influential, it would have to reach out to a wider readership. Its conservative roots were sound and deep, but it must no longer be parochially pro-business and socially retrogressive, or be perceived as such, especially at a time when the nation's economic fabric was unraveling and the very foundations of the republic were trembling. Fresh thinking and a variety of views were needed, not the pitiable bromides of Calvin Coolidge, whose latest thoughts, admirably brief as befit the intellect that framed them, were then being run each day at the top of the *Herald Tribune*'s front page. In Lippmann, thought Helen Reid, who in her youth had found that socialists were not necessarily all that queer, the *Tribune* might find its way to real political independence. Lippmann was the way to lure over the Wilsonian Democrats and intellectually minded independents who had formed the core of the *World*'s readership and now had nowhere to turn. She broached the idea to Ogden and Geoffrey Parsons, thinking Lippmann might be persuaded to come over if offered the chance to write signed editorials—a sort of loyal opposition to the *Tribune*'s prevailing view—as well as other articles of his choosing. Ogden, to his credit, agreed. Helen phoned Lippmann and arranged a meeting between the two men at the Century Club, to which they both belonged; the fellow may have been rather too left for the *Tribune*'s comfort and a Jew at that, but by all accounts he was a gentleman.

Not only the *Tribune* wanted him. Harvard offered him a professorship in government; the University of North Carolina, its presidency. The newly merged *World-Telegram* asked him to run its editorial page; Hearst, to write a syndicated column; the *Times,* to direct its Washington bureau. In his talks with Ogden Reid, Lippmann made clear that he was less interested in a job with administrative duties than in a platform to present his views—a column without inhibitions imposed by any management that might hire him. The *Tribune*'s only comparable feature was a Washington column by conservative Mark Sullivan, far more partisan and "inside" than the analytical overview that Lippmann would likely take. That was all right with Ogden, but others in the *Tribune*'s upper reaches were not so certain, fearing defections among the paper's conservative constituency.

To bolster the *Tribune*'s pursuit of Lippmann, Helen Reid sought to enlist the backing of the paper's owner, her mother-in-law, then in Paris. "Ogden has thought up a wonderful plan for getting Walter Lippman [sic]," she wrote at the end of February. "I hope he will decide to come. I know you will feel he is a great addition to the writing strength of the paper. . . ." A few weeks later, she was still sounding the same note. "Please pray that we may find the way to get him for I believe it would mean such a lot for the paper. We need a fine writer and a man of character and he is both. Do send a word of encouragement to Ogden if you can for he is not getting much at the office." To ease any ideological reservations Elisabeth may have harbored, Helen went on to argue that Lippmann is "not really a democrat [sic]—he is actually a [Theodore] Roosevelt man and he has made a remarkable position for himself. Incidentally he is a delightful human being and we could always be proud of his representing the paper. . . . We are being very quiet about it because I know how much Mr. Ochs wants the man."

During the monthlong romancing of Walter Lippmann, he was featured on the cover of *Time* magazine and tendered a testimonial dinner at the Astor at which his remarks made him seem an even more suitable acquisition for the *Tribune*. It was wrong of the public, he argued, to vilify business in the worsening economic crisis; capital was the creator of national wealth, not its enemy, and the sooner all elements in society could agree on that, the earlier the nation could get on with the repair job that had to be done. Horace Greeley himself would have concurred. The Reids pursued Lippmann all the harder. They saw him in Florida during their annual Palm Beach stay, and he seemed cordial and encouraging but said he could make no final decision until the end of the month after meeting with a certain party in New York. Without asking, the Reids knew who that was.

But that obstacle quickly vanished. Adolph Ochs wanted Lippmann for his Washington chief, not as a columnist. He did not believe much in the idea of giving writers, however eminent, a signed column in which to express their opinion; the *Times* had an editorial page for that. So it was agreed between Lippmann and the Reids that the column would appear four times a week— soon cut back to three—and be like no other then carried in an American newspaper. His observations of men in power and their dealings would furnish the materials for his higher purpose of seeking to shape a public philosophy and clarify the values of his society. If the best of ordinary journalists were historians on the run, Walter Lippmann would slow his pace to a stroll, bringing a broader perspective to his analyses. His salary was set at $33,000 a year plus a secretary, travel expenses, three months off for research and reflection, and half the revenues from the syndication of his column after the *Tribune* took the first $15,000. It is unlikely that a newspaper writer up to that time had ever received anything even approaching this. Within a year, his column, "Today and Tomorrow," was running in a hundred papers with a combined circulation of ten million; eventually he would appear in twice that number of papers. No serious-minded American writer had ever before regularly addressed so large a readership.

There were times, especially in the beginning, when Ogden Reid must have regretted the whole thing. In April 1932, for example, Lippmann implicitly forecast the expanded power of the central government in a column decrying the foolhardy history of Prohibition: "[N]ot only do the American people insist that the written law be uncompromising with unrighteousness; they insist at the same time that the government which exercises these laws shall be weak. . . . It is fair to say, I think, that we have the strongest laws and the weakest government of any highly civilized people. . . ." A month later, in a column titled "The False Gods," Lippmann was denouncing "the moral apathy of those in high places" during the previous decade that had resulted now in "profound spiritual bewilderment" of the people; throughout the whole period, marked by "stupendous lawlessness and corruption" feeding off Prohibition, "no candid word, no straightforward utterance, no honest inquiry" had come from the nation's leaders—he did not specify them by name or party or economic position, and did not have to—only talk of the people's destiny to have "two-car garages and eight-tube radio sets . . . to become acquisitive, to seek feverishly to become richer and richer. . . . It is not only against the material consequences of this decade of drift and hallucination, but against the essence of its spirit that the best and bravest among us are today in revolt. They are looking for new leaders, for men who are truthful and resolute and eloquent. . . ." It was, therefore, small surprise to the Reids when their new fourteen-carat trophy called for the election of Democrat Franklin Roosevelt later that year. But when he sharply put down Herbert Hoover, whom they greatly admired, with the charge of trying to use the economic relief programs he had tardily set in motion for blatant political advantage, the *Tribune*'s proprietors began fully to grasp the painful bargain they had made. Two years later, delivering the Godkin lectures at Harvard, Lippmann seemed to be proclaiming the death of laissez-faire by suggesting that the state was ultimately responsible for the complex economies of modern societies—a towering heresy by the *Tribune*'s lights.

Still, just when the paper must have been ready to write him off as a committed New Dealer and Keynesian whose nascent socialist impulses had never died, Lippmann showed that he could not be categorized so simplistically. He quickly soured on New Deal efforts at massive, long-range planning; men could not prudently plan their future, "for they are unable to imagine it." He opposed the pro-union Wagner Act, favored a federal sales tax that liberals branded as regressive, and, fearing rampant Caesarism in the White House, parted company with Roosevelt in the 1936 election. He was like that throughout his career; he had no political allegiances that were not readily overridden by weightier considerations.

At times his Olympian prose had a leaden quality that could repel a reader trying to digest it over the breakfast table. At times the sweep and assurance of his judgments smacked of intellectual arrogance. One could never say whether he was a hardheaded liberal or a warmhearted conservative; tomorrow's column might subvert a premise that yesterday's, if insufficiently considered, appeared to bolster. And he could sound as persuasive when he was wrong —as in opposing efforts to expand American armed forces three months before Pearl Harbor and in favoring the confinement of Japanese-Americans in detention camps not long afterward—as when he was right. But for two generations, he instructed readers on a quest for meaning in a volatile world filled with totalitarian dogma and ceaseless strife, foreign and domestic, and he did this largely on the payroll of the *Herald Tribune,* under whose aegis he was awarded two Pulitzer Prizes. He brought new stature to the paper, broadened its readership, helped expand the permissible educative function of all newspapers—and if those who followed him were sometimes demeaned for committing acts of "punditry," Walter Lippmann was at fault mostly for having established so formidable a standard of comparison.

VII

A month after Helen and Ogden Reid shared the triumph of snatching Lippmann out of the grasp of the *Times,* their own and their newspaper's financial security seemed suddenly as imperiled as that of the rest of the nation: Elisabeth Mills Reid died at seventy-three in the south of France while visiting at her daughter's villa.

The obituaries spoke of her as "a brilliant leader of international society" and praised her charitable works in behalf of the Red Cross, hospitals in California, and the Episcopal Church. A transitional and uniquely American social figure, she had bridged the world of her upbringing in a California setting scarcely removed from raw frontier days and the salon world of New York's *arriviste* mercantile society and London's hermetically tight aristocratic set. Kind, direct, forthright in speech and decisive in action, she had more of the pioneer about her than the cosmopolite, for all the grandeur with which she happily surrounded herself. But it was the survival of the *Tribune* more than anything else she did with her life and the money she had been bequeathed that exalted her above the rank of self-indulgent dowager. The paper editorialized:

> . . . Especially in the last decades of her life this newspaper was her central concern and interest. Her relationship to it was typical of her unselfish and courageous nature.

How greatly its success was built on her indomitable will, her understanding, her loyal trust, those who worked with her can best testify. If a newspaper lives first of all by its character, the fairness, the courage, the sound judgment of Elisabeth Mills Reid are part of this newspaper's priceless heritage. May it not forget them!

Far more than her husband, for whom she no doubt regarded it as a living memorial, she financed the improvement of the paper and permitted it to grow when merely to have sustained it, as he had done, would have only prolonged its death agony.

She had lived long enough to see it within reach of economic self-sufficiency, although at the end of her life it had slipped back into the deficit column amid the hard times afflicting the national economy. The year she died the *Tribune* would lose nearly $650,000. But it was now a strong enough institution under sufficiently committed management to ride out the storm, as the *World* had not been. By 1933, it had climbed back into the black by some $300,000, and it would remain there for nearly twenty years. The profits, though, except for several years during World War II when rationing of newsprint benefited the *Tribune* at the expense of the *Times,* were rarely more than a few hundred thousand, insufficient to nourish growth, yet apparently enough to satisfy the Reids. For fifteen years after her death, the newspaper Elisabeth Reid had saved by the generosity of her purse would prove able to keep approximate pace with its principal rival, albeit several lengths to the rear. By 1937, for example, the *Tribune*'s daily circulation had moved up to 350,000—Walter Lippmann's presence had helped, but made no spectacular claim on the allegiance of former *World* readers, who seemed to have dispersed in all directions—and the Sunday paper crossed the half-million mark. These figures were just under 70 percent of the *Times*'s totals—a ratio that would hold, give or take a few points, for another decade.

The dimension of Elisabeth Mills Reid's benefactions to the paper did not become fully evident until her will was probated; the estate she left was rather smaller than might have been expected twenty-one years after she had become co-heiress of the D. O. Mills fortune. She left her control of the paper to Ogden; three million each in trust funds to him and his sister, by then known as Lady Jean Ward; $200,000 each to Helen and to Jean's spouse, Sir John Hubert Ward; $100,000 to each of her four grandsons; and some three million to charities and in assorted smaller gifts. Most estimates of her financial assistance to the *Herald Tribune* placed the total at about $15 million. The only difficulty over her generosity in this regard was that the bulk of the funding was in the form of loans, not capital investment to protect her own equity interest in the property. Those notes, which Elisabeth Reid willed in equal amounts to her two children, were calculated the year after her death to have a value payable on demand to the holders of more than $7.4 million; Ogden held another $4.2 million in notes, funds that had also derived from his mother. "Grandmother had always intended to tear up those notes," her grandson Whitelaw recalled half a century after her death, "but she just never got around to it."

Neither would any of the other Reids, with results that were catastrophic. The potential severity of the problem was foreseen in 1933 when the *Tribune*'s treasurer, Robert Cresswell, proposed a recapitalization of the paper in view of the fact that the enterprise was technically insolvent, and "were it not for the fact that about $12,500,000 of the liabilities are owed to creditors who have a financial and sentimental interest in the corporation's operations, the situation would be impossible to retrieve." The Reids, in effect, held a mortgage on their own property. Such an arrangement, Cresswell pointed out, "effectively prevents any financing of the corporation either on a short term or a long term basis. Bank loans are out of the question with such a discrepancy [more than $6 million] between assets and liabilities, and so is public financing. . . ." As long as working capital could be replenished or new cash investments made by the principal stockholders when operations required it, the treasurer added, the condition of the balance sheet was "of academic interest only," but in view of the hard times the paper and the nation were experiencing, the problem could grow acute. The obvious solution was for the debt-holders to convert all or a major portion of the notes into equity. But Ogden, already holding virtually all the *Tribune* stock, could see nothing to be gained by such a bookkeeping transaction, and his sister, by all reports, was not eager to surrender her financial claims against the paper for a relatively small ownership share of a business that her financial advisers did not think ever likely to prove very profitable. By the end of 1933, at any rate, things were looking up, the paper was at least marginally profitable again, and the owners saw no need to heed Cresswell's advice. When they finally did make the move twenty-two years after, it would be too late.

VIII

A free-floating poetical fragment from the unannotated lore of New York's print media history declared: "Drink is the ruin of the *Herald Tribune* / And sex is the curse of the *Times.*" On the alleged latter affliction, this volume stands mute beyond the comment that, if true, it appears to be out of character. Of the *Tribune*'s enslavement to alcohol, nothing statistical may be ventured to distinguish it in fact as boozier than other newspapers, but there was a widespread perception during its lifetime, and it persists in the memory of living men, that the *Herald Tribune*'s staff was indeed a hard-drinking crew. John F. Ryan, head of the New York chapter of the American Newspaper Guild from 1937 to 1947 and something of a clearinghouse for such intelligence reports, was unequivocating in his estimate: "There was more drinking on the *Trib* staff than anywhere else in town." The impression was extravagantly reinforced by the roughhouse deportment and barfly's-eye-view of the world of the staff *enfant terrible* in the paper's final years, Jimmy Breslin.

That newspapermen in general, especially reporters, and most especially young reporters, should relish their reputation as heavy drinkers is plainly linked to the romance of the trade. For its more accomplished practitioners, mingling with the famous and powerful was a form of daily self-validation; extracting information from them, spreading their fame or exposing them to ridicule, sharing in their exalted lives and fortunes—all that raised the reporter's psychic metabolism and promoted the illusion of self-importance. When the workday was done, the overcharged reporter was often unable to return comfortably from the uplands of celebrity or the lists of controversy; some suffered the opposite reaction, landing too harshly, emotionally spent, without other resources or satisfactions to comfort them. Either way, liquor was quicker.

A more detailed analysis of the phenomenon at the *Tribune* would be unlikely to turn up much that is not already known from dozens of novels, movies, and plays. But it is certainly true that the perquisites and logistics of the reporter's job encouraged drinking. People threw booze at you—promoters, politicians, sports moguls, corporate public relations types—at luncheons, dinners, parties, receptions, or any old time, all in the interest of prominent and favorable treatment in print. Freeloading came with the franchise, and some found it hard to resist. Christmas cheer in pinch bottles overflowed the city room and was hidden away in many a bottom desk drawer. Sometimes there was nothing hidden about it. A bottle of scotch and a stack of paper cups were fixtures on the copy desk as deadline neared in the financial-news department.

For serious drinking, however, the *Herald Tribune* was blessed with its own quasi-official clubhouse just off the premises. The place, at 213 West Fortieth Street, was formally called the Artist and Writers Restaurant. The name, in Old English letters on the swinging sign out front, looked like a typographical error —why "Artist," singular, and "Writers," plural?—but its original proprietor, a saturnine import from St. Louis named John Bleeck (pronounced "Blake") insisted otherwise: the singular artist was one Langston McCormick, a stage designer, who gave the establishment its mellow English chophouse ambiance when it opened as a respectable speakeasy for males only in 1926. There was nothing light about the place, including the food, which was vaguely German and generally digestible. The decor featured ersatz Tudor timbering overhead, wrought-iron chandeliers, wainscoting and stuccoed walls in glazed oxblood, high-backed paneled booths, polished oak-top tables without cloths, and odd props mounted here and there—a tennis racket said to have been abandoned by Bill Tilden, a stuffed striped bass said to have been landed by the elder J. P. Morgan, the original of a cartoon by customer James Thurber, a suit of armor rescued from the scenery discards of the Metropolitan Opera House around the corner, a nonfunctioning fireplace to suggest coziness amid all the clatter and clamor. The centerpiece of the establishment was the forty-two-foot-long bar in the front room, where the clientele piled up two and three deep at lunch and dinnertime. Most of the regulars were from newspapers and magazines; the balance were in press-agentry, advertising, and show business. The majority called it Bleeck's after the owner; at the *Tribune* they just called it "downstairs."

They were its privileged customers. Jack Bleeck, a stern disciplinarian rather than a genial host, liked the lively engagement of the *Tribune* people and the politics of the management. Its employees were given preference in seating and service and credit when they needed it, so long as they made good on payday. The bartenders knew what the *Tribune* customers drank—and which ones could not drink, like its diminutive women's features editor, Eugenia Sheppard, and photographer Morris Warman, a small man, who were served, without having to ask for it, tea or other nonpotent beverages disguised as highballs. Besides its function as a decompression chamber from the day's or night's labors upstairs, Bleeck's served a number of other uses for the paper. Officers and enlisted men met there without the restraints of the workplace between them. The formidable L. L. Engelking, for nearly twenty years the terror of the city desk, might make a man rewrite his lead a dozen times and, encountering him afterward at Bleeck's, say, "This one's on me." There was a family feeling about the *Tribune* nurtured more at Bleeck's than on the paper's premises. "It was our club, our male redoubt—you went there for conversation and companionship," remembered John Crosby, who joined the staff in 1936 and after the war would become the nation's best critic of radio and television programming. "It was a rallying place, a comradely place," recalled sports columnist Walter W. (Red) Smith. Bleeck's was a home for many; they fought there, received mail there, planned their assignations there. Lonesome new staffers from out of town made their first New York friends there. And it was convenient. The city desk, far from worrying about Bleeck's debilitating effect on staffers, was comforted by the knowledge that if a story broke late and reinforcements were needed, a bunch could almost certainly be rounded up in a hurry downstairs.

Bleeck's prices were not cheap, especially in view of the pay scale prevailing among his chief clientele, and less social-minded *Tribune* people did their drinking across the street at the déclassé London Grill, which featured a horse parlor in the rear in that era when off-track betting was as illegal as the sale of alcoholic beverages. But Bleeck filled his drinks to the brim and provided a suitably clubby, discreetly rollicking retreat.

No women were permitted in Bleeck's until the repeal of Prohibition, and even then the owner did his irritable best to discourage female customers. One prominent exception was Tallulah Bankhead, who one night after a performance allegedly stood on her head on a table while singing "God Bless America." Such rowdy conduct was relatively rare and brief: singers, shouters, and solicitors were discouraged. Also blacks. The king of Siam, who was not exactly black but looked that way to Bleeck, was a house guest of the Reids in 1931 when he came to America for an eye operation; Ogden Reid and his new executive assistant, Wilbur Forrest, brought the king downstairs to enjoy a little local color and a libation. "Mr. Bleeck," said Forrest, "I'd like you to meet the king of Siam." Bleeck, often the butt of practical jokes, replied, "Mr. Forrest, get that nigger out of here." Everyone in the office had heard the story before the evening was over. Bleeck and his bartenders were equally ferocious about *Tribune* charge customers who did not keep their account clean. Roy Wilder, Jr., who joined the paper as a reporter not long before World War II, was away in service for four years; on his return, he was presented with a prewar bar bill totaling under five dollars. Jack Bleeck neither forgot nor forgave.

He did permit a certain amount of gaiety, of course, or the *Tribune* crowd would not have materialized. Some of it, of a largely irreverent nature, grew out of shoptalk, such as the 1939 papal pool, in which bets were made on who would emerge as the new Pontiff, or the "ghoul pool" in which lots were drawn for which one of a selected list of aging statesmen, celebrities, or other eminences would be the first to die. Wagers on claimed aptitude for memorizing the pointless, like the names of all the monarchs of Great Britain in sequence, were common. Minor athletic contests were held, like a standing broad jump with the aid of a rolled *Tribune* as a prod. Once Stanley Woodward, the best sports editor in the *Tribune*'s, or probably any paper's, history, won a bet by moving the massive oak bar an inch or two; he was very strong, and stronger still when under the influence, which he frequently was. Sometimes they refused to serve him. "One night," recalled Seymour Freidin, a reporter and editor, "they said, 'Stanley, go home,' and the old woodpecker got so sore he reached over the bar and lifted the spigots right up out of their slots and got his drink."

By far the most celebrated of *Tribune* pastimes at Bleeck's was the Match Game. Any number could play. Each player put his hands under the table or behind his back, placed one, two, three, or no matches in the fist of his choice, and presented it firmly sealed for inspection. Each participant then guessed how many matches were sealed collectively in the lot. Whoever guessed right was eliminated, and the next round began. The last one in lost and bought everyone else drinks. Side wagers on individual rounds were common. Lucius Beebe played with gold matches that had little diamonds in their heads. The game was nothing more than a means of structuring conviviality, a way to fill in the drinking sessions and to prevent the conversation from turning too heavy. It was more of a psychological encounter than a contest of skill, accompanied by much staring deeply into opponents' eyes to study their likely behavior under competitive stress.

Compounding the influence of Bleeck's on the drinking habits of *Tribune* people was the example set for them by one of its most prominent and loyal customers. On nights when he was not obliged to go to the opera or show up at home for one of Helen's elegant soirees, the president of the *Tribune* was wont to appear at Bleeck's around nine or nine-thirty and stay late. He was often accompanied by Wilbur Forrest, who reminded him of the names of staffers, for whom he might buy a drink, and made sure he did not fall down on departing. Then the boss would go back to his office and sleep it off.

Nobody knew why Ogden Reid drank so much, but there were several theories. The most benign was that the better the staff Ogden surrounded himself with, the less there was for him to do, even if he had known how, so he drank and lent moral support to his troops—and they provided him with physical support when he needed it. The most unpleasant explanation was that he drank in response to his wife's highly motivated and disciplined personality. It was a fact, at any rate, that the more involved Helen became in the *Tribune* management, the less so Ogden became. Whether her growing activity was cause or effect of his gradual withdrawal was no easier to determine than whether he appreciated or resented her expanded role. Still a third theory, at least as plausible as the other two, was that the world of the 'Thirties was no longer a very appealing place to Ogden Reid. He turned fifty the year Franklin Roosevelt became President, and the social programs of the New Deal, however imperative, violated the values and standards Ogden had absorbed as his birthright. Office legend held that upon hearing reports the New Deal was contemplating a confiscatory tax on all incomes in excess of $25,000, Ogden remarked to a fellow member of the Union League Club, "Why, a man can't even keep clean on twenty-five thousand a year!" Money was not something real to him; great sums of it had always been at his disposal, and he had trouble grasping what the lack of it did to other men. One night, en route to Bleeck's, he encountered a cluster of editors and deskmen and asked what the matter was. An indigent old copyreader had died, he was told, and the hat was being passed around the city room to cover the burial expenses. Before contributing, Ogden asked, with apparently genuine puzzlement, why the funeral cost could not just be deducted from the fellow's estate. In a similar vein, Ogden got to chatting one night in 1940 with veteran deskman Jules Frantz about the likely outcome of that fall's presidential election. When Frantz voiced the opinion that Roosevelt was likely to be re-elected, Ogden looked glum and asked him to name one truly commendable act of the New Deal. Perfectly aware of his employer's archconservatism, Frantz sought an unexceptionable answer. Finally he suggested that the creation of the Federal Deposit Insurance Corporation had served the public's interest and bolstered confidence in the banking system. "What good's that?" Ogden protested. "It only insures a depositor's first ten thousand dollars."

And so the farther out of touch with reality he drew—reality now consisting of this Hitler fellow and the tinhorn Caesar in Rome and the bloody awful business tearing Spain apart and a dozen other unpleasant developments overseas as well as at home—the more he seemed to drink. And the more overt his drinking, the more pitiable and endearing a figure he became to his employees. For all his social obtuseness, they could not hate him. True, he and his family lived like royalty while paying his staff (with certain prominent exceptions) like peons, but he cared about the paper, took obvious pride in it, knew what good journalism was—and there he was, drinking with them democratically at Bleeck's as if he were one of the gang.

One Friday night in 1939, Ogden noticed an unusual amount of roistering among a group of *Tribune* men in the back room at Bleeck's and wandered over to their booth. Ted Laymon, a rewriteman, was getting married the next day and being tendered an impromptu bachelor party. "Sounds like an occasion," Ogden said and, joining in, proceeded to pay for everyone's drinks for the rest of the night, which turned out to be very long. When Bleeck's closed at three, the group tottered across the street to the London Grill, which had the decency to stay open till four, at which point the merry band hailed a taxi and set out for the Kit Kat Klub, a dozen unnavigable blocks away. It, alas, had closed, so they wound up at a distinctly sleazy second-floor joint on Eighth Avenue around the corner from the office. Ogden, "feeling no pain," as Laymon recalled the occasion, led the way upstairs and made no strenuous objection when a gap-toothed female slipped onto his lap, blew up an exotic variety of condom in his face as if it were a balloon, and asked, "Say, don't I know you from somewhere?"

"Probably the Racquet and Tennis Club," said co-reveler Milton Lewis, a *Tribune* reporter specializing in crime news.

Laymon went home by dawn's early light, and the others hauled Ogden around the corner and carefully lowered him into his office Morris chair. He was such a gentleman, even in his cups, that he reached up, shook Lewis's hand just before expiring, and said, "Congratulations." It was the proper sentiment to cap the occasion, even if he had blessed the wrong bridegroom.

9

Writers of the
World, Unite

Although the owners and managers of most American newspapers have been overwhelmingly conservative in their social sentiments since daily journalism became big business about two-thirds of the way through the nineteenth century, the net effect of the messages they have been collectively printing defies easy location on the political spectrum. This is due less to the enlightenment of press proprietors or the decreasing influence of their editorial pages, which have by and large dutifully reflected their staunch pro-capitalism and Chamber of Commerce mentality, than to the countervailing professional and personal values of their staffs. It is they, of course, who in the daily routine actually decide what material shall be printed or omitted, how prominently it shall be displayed, and how sympathetically, critically, or neutrally it shall be written. Thus, even a paper like the *Herald Tribune,* which until 1940 was viewed as a spokesman for and guardian of mainstream Republicanism, could reasonably be said to reflect in its daily presentation of the news something close to a national political consensus. The massed weight of management was pitted against the essentially creative and socially sensitive labors of unpropertied hired hands. But it had never been an even battle—the ruling interests in any community, press lords prominent among them, rarely favor departures from the status quo—and has usually been characterized by guerrilla warfare in the city room.

A representative combatant in the *Tribune*'s rebel ranks, John M. Price joined the staff as a mail clerk in 1926 and went on to perform editorial services of a high order for the next thirty-nine years. A tall, spare man with a square face and high cheekbones who parted his hair in the middle, he was one of those anonymous city-room figures in a green eyeshade, worn to absorb the glare of the ceiling lights, whose job was to examine and improve the copy written by other men. Quiet almost to the point of reticence, he was viewed by those who worked with him as calm, deep, erudite, and sensitive to the prose he edited. "He helped give the paper its quality," said Don Cook, a veteran *Tribune* correspondent, summarizing the staff estimate of John Price's work. What made him remarkable was a capacity uncommon among newspapermen to get angry at what was going on in the world. His anger took the form of sympathy with leftist ideology, and while there is no evidence that he ever formally joined the Communist Party, he openly expressed his belief that America had something to learn from Soviet Communism in the quest for social justice. He did not walk around the city room trying to proselytize his co-workers, but he fought against the *Tribune*'s anti-Soviet instincts in the play of the news—an effort he was uniquely situated to make during nearly twenty years' service as the cable editor. All overseas dispatches passed through his hands. And when economic conditions within the office invited him to put his philosophical convictions into action, he did not hesitate to do so. In the end, still loyal to the paper but heartsick over what it had become, he was made to pay for his heresies.

In 1932, as an anti-Depression measure, the *Tribune* cut by 10 percent the salary of everyone earning more than thirty dollars a week. John Price voted the Communist Party ticket in that year's presidential election. The next spring, while Ogden and Helen Reid were spending $10,000 for the rental of financier Otto Kahn's "Pink House" in Palm Beach (plus $358 for the garage and $300 for the telephone), their managers at the *Tribune* were imposing another 10 percent pay reduction, this one affecting all staff members, regardless of salary size. The loudest lament in the city room came from those at the bottom. "There is a responsibility every employer must consider," declared an editorial in the *Copyboys' Call,* an intramural little four-page sheet generally given over to broad jesting, "and that is his obligation to pay his help a living wage. Even copyboys have a standard of living," and most of them were having trouble getting by on the fifteen a week the *Tribune* paid them; 10 percent less, as now mandated, "is an imposition, a social injustice, a direct attack on a fundamental necessity, food. . . . [A] mild hunger is no incentive to increased efficiency nor to fond regard for our employers." The protest was unsigned, but the head copyboy at the time was an energetic stutterer named Homer Bigart, earning $17.50 after five years on the paper. John Price, his salary on the cable desk down now to $52.65, noted the copyboys' protest with approval.

Price was further aroused by the role taken by the *Tribune*'s general manager, Howard Davis, in frustrating efforts by the new Roosevelt administration to bring the newspaper industry within the precincts of the National Recovery Act, aimed at spreading employment under minimally humane working conditions. The American Newspaper Publishers Association, of which Davis was president from 1931 to 1935 and a figure of high standing thereafter, insisted that the press ought to be exempted from such a program. The power to license an industry conferred the power to control it, the ANPA argued while reaching for the First Amendment to shield itself from any federal threat to its freedom. NRA efforts to outlaw child labor both as uncivilized and as a depressant on the demand for adult workers also drew the publishers' fire because of the direct threat such a reform posed to the newsboy delivery system. John Price watched Howard Davis, spokesman for the masters of the American press, as he crossed the *Tribune* city room and saw "an evil-looking, puffy-faced go-getter" determined to resist any inconveniences the national economic emergency might impose on the newspaper owners. And when the *Tribune* voluntarily complied with the NRA call for a forty-hour week, aimed at encouraging employers to add workers to their payroll and thereby cut joblessness, Price noted that the paper failed to add anyone new to the staff; the effect, therefore, was merely to have the same staff perform the same work at the same pay but within a shorter workday—in other words, a speedup, clearly against the spirit of the NRA goal. Elsewhere, the situation was far worse. Newsroom staffs were cruelly slashed, and reporters in many cities were forced down to as little as twelve to fifteen dollars a week. News hands seemed to be the most readily dispensable part of any newspaper operation, their advancement opportunities were drastically curtailed as the Depression deepened, and an alarming rise in alcoholism reflected their plight. Few could avoid noting their helplessness in comparison with the protections enjoyed by the unionized men in the newspapers' mechanical departments, where the printers had won the eight-hour day as early as 1910 and the forty-hour week in 1930 and nobody was fired without cause. Editorial people had long explained away the higher pay and greater security won by shop men as their reward for performing what the white-collar worker saw as mostly dirty, brainless, repetitive labor. Now the situation had changed.

When Heywood Broun's August 8, 1933, column in the *World-Telegram,* titled "A Union of Reporters," called for newsmen to unite to protect their interests, the nationwide reaction was far more positive than could have been forecast from the traditional posture of journalists as rugged individualists outside the main social stream. And when the first group of *Tribune* newsmen met quietly to organize themselves a few months later at the Hotel Pennsylvania, John Price was on hand. When comparable groups from all papers in New York gathered soon after to form a citywide organization, *Tribune* reporter Allen Raymond, a political conservative, was named their first chairman. And when groups from many cities convened to organize nationally, it was another *Tribune* reporter, Edward Angly, who proposed the name adopted for the new organization—the American Newspaper Guild. They were craftsmen, men of high skill and honor, not peons to be exploited at their employers' whim, Angly argued in urging the name, and he saw no degradation in the idea of journalists allying themselves as trade unionists with the American Federation of Labor.

But 90 percent of the early Guild members opposed open alliance with the labor union movement. Most favored a professional association, something akin to the American Society of Newspaper Editors, that would speak up for the nonsupervisory personnel in the newsrooms of the nation. Collective bargaining and rowdy strikes they viewed, at first, as beneath their dignity. And many editorial people bristled at the very thought of a lockstep salary structure that would not reward excellence in individual performance. Newspapering's unwritten tradition had long held that the journalist would willingly sacrifice money, comfort, sleep, love, food, and hope of eternal salvation to the spirit of his craft; his compensation was to be on the inside of things, to know the dynamics of his society, to confer celebrity or promote social justice and to feel he was as good as any man through his access to the printed word. But his license expired the moment he was put off the payroll, and many newsmen, fearful of management reprisal, kept away from the Guild. Broun countered that far from reducing journalists to the status of regimented drones, unionization would earn them enhanced professional standing, free of the chronic threat of arbitrary dismissal and adequately rewarded to spurn proffered bribes that had long tempted underpaid newsmen to run or kill stories. The Guild, in short, would make the individual journalist more independent, not less. But Broun, who became founding president and spokesman for the Guild while leaving most of the organizing work to others, was dismissed by many as unsound, as a joker, as a radical, and his efforts as self-seeking; at the *Tribune,* he was remembered as antic, unsightly, and unmanageable, not the sort that gentlemen dealt with if they could help it.

In November 1933, charter Guild member John Price was promoted to cable editor of the *Herald Tribune,* responsible to managing editor Wilcox for all foreign news flowing into the paper, and given a 30 percent salary increase. Earlier in the year, he had been helping out at the *Daily Worker* in his spare time and had joined the Pen and Hammer, a society of Soviet-line writers. "We were really going broke," he wrote to his brother in reporting his promotion. But now John Price was a supervisor at the *Tribune,* that venerable champion of embattled capitalism, and he might well have turned his back on the infant Guild movement. Instead, he became chairman of the Guild's *Tribune* chapter the following June and arranged the first meeting with the paper's executives to discuss improved working conditions. President Reid, general manager Davis, and managing editor Wilcox were asked to rescind the two 10 percent wage cuts management had made, to formalize the forty-hour workweek and apply it throughout the newsroom from copyboys to editors, and to extend severance notices; other key Guild requests, such as a $35 minimum weekly salary after one year on the paper and paid vacations, were held in abeyance. The *Tribune* managers listened and said nothing. When a month passed without response, John Price directed the paper's Guild chapter to begin issuing a weekly bulletin, called the *New Lead.* The first number, dated July 31, 1934, carried the heading "Bargain, Mr. Reid?" and politely took the ownership to task for failing to react to the Guild's initiatives. But the overseers of the *Tribune* had no intention of dealing with the upstart effort of underlings to tell them how to run their news operation; they reacted instead with what the Guild's longtime head New York organizer, Jack Ryan, called "polite scorn."

City editor Stanley Walker, closest of the *Tribune* brass to the Guild incursions, was certainly scornful toward the whole notion. No one, except the Reids, was going to tell him whom he could hire and fire—a prerogative that a closed union shop would remove from him. More than that, he strongly objected to reporters who chose sides; they were to be above the battle. As it was, Walker felt, reporters tended too readily to side with the underdog; how could they deal objectively with stories relating to labor if they were all enrolled in a union? He did not, however, raise a similar objection to the daily reality of sanctioning a man who regularly voted Republican to cover a Democratic mayor, or a Presbyterian to interview a Roman Catholic prelate. For all his partiality to youth, Walker was displeased with the prospect of reformist impulses like the Guild that placed too much power in the hands of "boiling youngsters."

Walker's superiors on the news side, Wilcox and Ogden Reid's alter ego, Wilbur Forrest, were still more conservative in their social views. Forrest, writing in March 1934 to Laurence Hills, general manager of the paper's Paris edition, registered the prevailing management view by noting that the decision to place reporters and copyreaders on a five-day week was "in response to the demands of the Guild, aided and abetted by our dear President [Roosevelt], who will be just about as popular with newspaper owners as a skunk at a lawn party unless he ceases to make it more and more difficult to do business. What he is doing actually is to play the workers against the owners who pay their wages."

Beneath the intransigence of management, another factor was at work that made the city room of the *Herald Tribune* uniquely difficult for the Guild to organize. "You'd go out on assignment in those days," Jack Ryan recalled, "and the *Tribune* guy who showed up was almost always young and bright and well dressed, and his suit was pressed." The extraordinary flow of college-educated talent that was Stanley Walker's prime contribution to the paper was earning the *Tribune* widening renown as "the newspaperman's newspaper," better written and better edited than any other. The *Times,* by contrast, read as if it had been "edited with a shovel," Guild organizer Ryan added. And nowhere else in town were reporters and deskmen treated so cordially as on the *Tribune,* nowhere was the atmosphere more casual and clublike, nowhere was the talent given more freedom to express itself and gain self-respect. "We all felt we were working on the best newspaper in America," remembered Carl Levin, who joined as a copyboy and left twenty years later as a Washington correspondent for a lucrative career in public relations. "It was just a wonderful place to work," said Nat Fein, who was a *Tribune* staff photographer for more than thirty years, "the kind of place where you'd come in a half hour early just to see what was going on." Thomas R. Waring, more nearly typical of the well-bred young men who remained on staff only a few years, called his *Tribune* stint "the best learning experience in my fifty years in journalism," a career in which he was long the ranking editorial figure on newspapers in Charleston, South Carolina. Robert Shaplen, who reported for the paper starting in the late 'Thirties and later became a distinguished correspondent for *The New Yorker,* found the *Tribune* an ideal training ground for a young writer because its small, companionable staff allowed him to be given attractive assignments almost from the first and front-page bylines could be earned within a year; by comparison, he found the *Times* city room "a morgue" when he went over there often after work to pick up his father, who reported for it on labor affairs. Emma Bugbee, who reported for it for longer than anyone else, caught the prevailing tone with the memory that "we just thought we were cleverer than the other papers." And they were clever. On a slow night in the city room, a bunch of high-spirited *Tribune* writers and deskmen, instead of sharing dirty jokes or scanning the racing charts for the next day's entries as was customary in other city rooms, were apt to kill time by organizing an elaborate parody of their own craft. The Second Coming was a favorite topic. Starting with a simulated AP flash from Jerusalem ("MESSIAH ARRIVES"), they would concoct the entire running account of the Next to Greatest Story Ever Written, complete with day leads, night leads, sixth and seventh leads, kills, inserts, and corrections, each piece coded and timed as the story moved westward with the sun and developments unfolded. In a city room full of such high morale and playful irreverence, class struggles were not easily ignited.

John Price, however, did not view his efforts to organize the Guild as subversive to the integrity of the *Herald Tribune,* which he held in as high esteem as any man there. Camaraderie did not preclude economic security. Stanley Walker's merry young men came and went, largely indifferent to the concerns of careerists, but others could not afford to be so blithe. "We were nervous about our jobs," recalled Frank Waters, then working under Price on the cable desk. "We wanted protection."

Slowly, meeting before and after office hours in small groups at the London Grill and other places where they did not play the Match Game, Price and his colleagues made headway. Deskmen and other insiders were easier to sign up than sporty reporters. They scoured the news department and won Guild recruits in all areas, from copyboys and library clerks to Walter Lippmann. Within several months of accepting its leadership, Price had the *Tribune* chapter's roster up to 155 members out of 275 eligibles. But the numbers were misleading. Of the total, only about fifteen were active, working members, perhaps forty or fifty others were actively interested, "and the rest," he wrote his brother, "we drag $1 a month dues out of and are trying to stir up. . . . What we need is the check-off."

As Price plugged steadily away, the *Tribune* management stiffened its resistance to a union among its editorial employees. And it sought spiritual alliance with the ownership of its larger, more powerful rival, *The New York Times,* which took particular objection to the idea of its news people all belonging to a single outside organization, as a closed Guild shop would have required, thereby "polluting the well-spring of editorial objectivity," as the *Times*'s new president, Arthur Hays Sulzberger, would later characterize such a threat in testimony before the National Labor Relations Board. In June 1935, discussing the status of the New York newspaper publishers' troubled talks with the printers over a new contract, the *Tribune*'s Howard Davis wrote to his opposite number on the *Times,* Julius Ochs Adler:

> . . . I hope we are able to sit tight and take a strike if necessary, rather than concede anything to the [International Typographers] Union. I think they now have more than they are entitled to and if we surrender anything further, it will affect not only our contracts with other Unions but will have a serious effect on our Guild situation and non-Union departments as well.
>
> The Guild is still driving us hard. I met their Committee yesterday and told them flat that we would make no agreements or contracts with them.

Given its employees' pride in their product and its highly agreeable working environment, the *Tribune* had the luxury of thus resisting the Guild drive for recognition and bargaining parity with management. Elsewhere, though, less paternalistic ownerships inspired greater militancy, which in turn drew reprisals in the form of firings and demotions to punish Guild activists. Before long, editorial hands were bearing placards on the picket line in uncoordinated and most ungentlemanly strike actions, including a rowdy series in the New York metropolitan area at the *Long Island Press, Newark Star-Ledger,* and *Brooklyn Eagle.* Dedicated Guild members on New York papers, Heywood Broun among them, marched with the strikers through long winter months, and the pickets discovered that the police who befriended them in the normal course of their journalistic duties forgot to be mannerly when dealing with newspapermen as mere laborers seeking a fair shake from the boss. W. R. Hearst, still paying some of his reporters below twenty a week, complained that the Guild was taking the romance out of newspapering and engaged in combat with its enlistees in Seattle and Madison, Wisconsin. The striking Hearst newsmen survived partly on the generosity of Guildsmen elsewhere, and a growing sense of brotherhood surged through the organizing campaign as it became clear to journalists everywhere that it was no game the Guild had embarked upon. Sentiment grew to ally the Guild with the trade union movement through membership in the American Federation of Labor (AFL), and even those who were repelled by the prospect of journalists' adopting what they called "the bricklayer's mentality" were coming to think of newsroom occupants as exploited underdogs. The more firmly that newspaper managements opposed bargaining with the Guild, the farther left they drove it.

At the *Tribune*, the Guild suffered a setback when John Price was felled by tuberculosis, which kept him off the job for most of 1936. But other, younger hands picked up the slack. The new college men who stayed on the paper and a number of city-room veterans parted company politically with management. "The New Deal was contagious," recalled Richard Tobin, who came to the paper in 1932 from the University of Michigan and a small-town Republican background. "It wasn't a matter of whether you were left or right in your politics—the New Deal had opened up new possibilities for what government could achieve in bringing social justice closer." And it produced almost constantly exciting news, endearing it to journalists no matter what their previous political allegiances. *Tribune* management continued to view the New Deal as a diabolical influence upon the free-enterprise system, but its field hands had seen the casualties of that system's massive malfunction and understood, in growing numbers, that their own interests and those of the American Newspaper Guild coincided. Dick Tobin and others like him succeeded John Price as chairmen of the *Tribune* chapter.

By the time Price came back to work late in 1936, his energy level reduced by disease, the Guild had won its first contracts with New York papers. The *Post,* now under liberal ownership, agreed to modest pay minimums and decent severance terms, and the *Daily News,* more prosperous through the hard times than the city's other papers, became the first major daily to yield to the pressing social imperative to treat its editorial personnel no less equitably than its blue-collar people. These breakthroughs spurred intensified Guild efforts at other papers, and pervasive interest in the Spanish Civil War and its galvanizing effect on the social conscience of the New York intelligentsia added to the ferment. Communists and Communist sympathizers, gaining respectability from the so-called Popular Front linking otherwise widely divergent leftist and reform movements, became a more active and effective element in the Guild's organizing drive; few doubted their motives or had their patience to sit through endless meetings or conduct the thankless petitioning and dues-gathering.

Hardly unaware of the trend, the *Tribune* management sought to undermine the Guild with tactical daubs of honey. Small raises, of two to five dollars, were awarded to discourage new enlistments and imply that a union was unnecessary to deal with so benevolent an ownership. A number of the Guild's ablest younger leaders, far from being punished, were promoted to posts not coincidentally intended to make them less combative; Tobin, for example, was advanced to the city desk, and reporter Joseph F. Barnes, a proud left-wing intellectual out of Harvard, was sent off to become Moscow correspondent. And John Price, who might have been uncharitably dealt with during his nine-month bout with TB, instead was paid his full salary; his martyrdom would only have kindled the Guild bonfire.

Nationally, that fire blazed in 1937 as more radical elements assumed dominance in the Guild. Affiliation with the AFL, approved by the national Guild convention the year before, was proving a disappointment; the trade union movement was toadying to management, in the view of Guild militants, and only membership in the new Congress of Industrial Organizations (CIO) and opening the Guild ranks to white-collar workers outside the news department were likely to provide it with enough muscle to force more publishers to the bargaining table.

Spirited contests within local Guild units were waged for control of delegations to the June 1937 national convention. When the more militant faction won, speedily voting the Guild into alliance with the CIO, the alarm of the newspaper publishers was manifest. "I believe in a Guild," said Howard Davis, "but not this kind of a Guild." By "this kind" he evidently meant one with teeth. Davis and other press executives summoned the ANPA to an emergency closed-door session in Chicago that turned into a workshop on how to combat the Guild. Its entry into the leftist CIO was cited as *prima facie* evidence of Red domination, its call for a closed shop in the nation's city rooms was denounced as a blatant danger to press freedom, and manuals were issued to newspaper managements detailing sixteen ways they could fire troublemakers without running afoul of the new Wagner Act, designed by the New Deal to facilitate union organization in resistant industries.

The *Tribune* fully supported the ANPA's diehard resistance. Wilbur Forrest, a member of the three-man committee that management was now forced to field to negotiate with the Guild, wrote in early June to Laurence Hills that the Guild's alliance with the CIO made it "an out and out radical labor union" in the eyes of the paper's managers. "Our shop is organized," he went on, "but the bulk of Guild membership here are the little people[,] among them office boys, library employees and others of the nether brackets. All the Jews in our employ are active in the movement with one or two exceptions. . . . We are called upon to meet with a little Jew named Kaufman, secretary of the New York Guild, a man named Hathway of the *Daily News* and a man named Kieran of the *Times.*" Forrest hinted at management's increasing anxiety by going on to note that New York's Mayor La Guardia, "a red," was in open sympathy with the Guild, so that in the event of a strike and picketing, "we would have no guarantee of police protection for loyal workers." By the end of June, Forrest was advising Hills that the *Tribune* "may have to make some sort of an agreement with the Guild if they are willing to accept our version of economic possibilities," which excluded a closed shop, the checkoff, "and interference with hiring or firing."

But Howard Davis, who headed the *Tribune* negotiators, demonstrated his considerable adroitness in seven or eight sessions with Guild officials. "He felt he was negotiating for the future of the paper," in the opinion of George A. Cornish, then newly installed as Sunday editor. Davis's hand was strengthened by the closing down earlier that year of Hearst's morning *American,* throwing hundreds onto the already crowded New York job market, and the Guild's defeat at the *World-Telegram,* Broun's home paper, in an election to establish it as authorized bargaining agent. Instead of pushing for such a make-or-break vote at the *Tribune,* both sides preferred discussing a contract that might incorporate a number of Guild requirements. Some, like the five-day, forty-hour week, were readily yielded; others, like the closed shop, Davis flatly rejected, and when the Guild prudently withdrew this demand as long as enough other provisions were acceptable to management, Davis insisted that the Guild's international executive committee approve in writing elimination of the closed shop from the proposed *Tribune* contract—a concession sure to be gravely debated at the highest Guild levels. By the end of August, the Guild was accusing Davis of bad-faith negotiating; the *Tribune* general manager, pleading illness, recessed the bargaining sessions to an unspecified date. They did not resume in earnest for five years. "There is no doubt that he used Fabian tactics," recalled one of Davis's admiring assistants, John Bogart, grandson of the *Sun* city editor who coined the man-bites-dog definition of news. "He handled the Guild like a chess player."

The setback badly strained cable editor John Price's devotion to the Reid management. In July 1938, claiming he had heard a rumor that Henry R. Luce was discussing the purchase of the *Tribune* with Ogden Reid, Price wrote directly to the head of Time Inc. to ask if it were so. He added:

> It seems unlikely. But if it isn't true, why shouldn't it become true? We at the Tribune . . . would welcome it. Mr. Reid is a very kindly and likeable man but an intelligent and enterprising owner could work wonders.
>
> This suggestion does not ask a reply, of course. Yet I should be glad to help in any way possible.

The brash note was rewarded with a reply two months later. Luce called Price's the most complimentary letter he had ever received, somewhat cryptically denied the rumor, but invited the *Tribune* man to lunch. During their rendezvous at the Rainbow Room atop Rockefeller Center a few weeks later, Luce was noncommittal about the idea of buying the paper but speculated openly about what might be done with it. In a memoir of the occasion in which Price described himself at the time as " a left-wing independent, generally sympathetic to the Communists," he wrote, "I remember arguing that the American press was scandalously unrepresentative of popular sentiment, with which he [Luce] disagreed." Even so, Price was enough encouraged by the meeting to divulge its substance to the *Tribune*'s gnomish night editor, Everett Kallgren, a brilliant journalistic technician and something of an odd duck. Pleading confidentiality, Price wrote him at his Essex House bachelor's apartment: ". . . all I have in mind at present is that it would be a hell of a lot more fun working for a smart owner than it is working for a dumb one; and that we might get somewhere if we presented to Luce a comprehensive and eye-catching scheme for making the paper a knockout."

Kallgren discouraged the mutiny, but Price apparently achieved his purpose. Luce in fact called Ogden Reid and asked to meet with him. Reid obliged, asking Wilbur Forrest to sit in on the session, which proved brief. After a few preliminaries, Luce said, "Ogden, I would like to buy the *Herald Tribune.*"

"Harry," replied Reid, "the *Tribune* is not for sale."

Transfer of ownership to Luce's empire would no doubt have provided the paper with the working capital for which it hungered throughout the rest of its life. Whether the editorial product would have been inventively enriched or fatally manipulated to suit the new helmsman is arguable. Time Inc.'s political position, though, would likely have proven no more satisfactory than the Reids' to John Price, whose admiration for the great Soviet socialist experiment had not been dimmed by the Moscow purge trials of 1937 and 1938—Frank T. Waters, who served as a *Tribune* deskman for thirty-five years, remembered Price remarking that anyone Stalin purged had probably deserved it—or the 1939 pact between Stalin and Hitler. But a substantial number of *Tribune* Guildsmen, along with many liberals everywhere who had admired the Soviet effort to reclaim Russia from the dark ages, were appalled by these acts, and some, like Homer Bigart, quit the Guild because Red-line members seemed to him to predominate.

The Nazi conquest of Europe made Price's cable desk one of the busiest spots on the paper. Overworked and stricken now with pleurisy, he did not object when the new position of foreign news editor was created above his and given to returned European correspondent Joseph Barnes, who shared Price's fascination with the Soviet Union, although what he had seen there firsthand, and Stalin's handshake with Hitler, had badly undercut his enthusiasm. Still, the fact was that the *Herald Tribune*'s foreign news coverage was largely in the hands of a pair of editors whose political sympathies diverged sharply from those of the management.

Barnes lent his stature to a revived Guild effort in 1940, and when the *Times* news department voted that September by a margin of more than two to one to accept the Guild as its bargaining agent, the *Tribune* unit's hopes were bolstered. Under the leadership now of thirty-year-old deskman Fritz Silber, an educational campaign was waged to convince the city room that being a leftist did not make you a Communist or a Stalin-lover. Silber's supervisor, copy desk chief Allan Holcomb, made his disapproval of the Guild as clear as Stanley Walker had in the early days of the organizing effort. "It was a fairly bitter time," Silber remembered, "with much literature being circulated by both sides and sharp words being exchanged in the lulls between editions." The German invasion of Russia and then the American entry into the war quieted the quarreling, and it was not until June 1942 that the issue at last came to a vote at the *Tribune*. Preceded by a rally run by the Guild's New York office at which Washington chapter member Eleanor Roosevelt, author of the popular syndicated column "My Day," appeared and strongly urged a pro-union vote, the victory went to Silber's side, 178–79.

Even then, though, the *Tribune* ownership did not surrender gracefully. With the onset of the Guild enlistment drive, management had again begun passing out merit raises, more substantial than in the past and more widespread, to discourage union participation, but this had not been enough to head off the Guild. Forced finally to negotiate at a time when it was posting record profits but still paying a minimum scale below those at the Associated Press and the *Bronx Home News,* the *Tribune* fought provisions of the Guild contract so determinedly that the union had to take its case to the National War Labor

Board in Washington. There, at a full-dress hearing, the Guild accused the paper of excessive hostility, citing "despotic treatment of questions of job tenure, protracted negotiations and aspersions cast by management on the Guild's right to represent the employees" even though it had been certified as bargaining agent by the National Labor Relations Board. The government ordered a compromise.

For nearly ten years, the gentlemen running the *Herald Tribune* had kept out the Guild. Only the archconservative *Sun* and *Wall Street Journal* would resist longer among New York papers. Unionizing that clubby newsroom somehow seemed unsporting, but in the clinches management acted anew on the premise Whitelaw Reid had heartily expounded—that labor, white collar no less than blue, was a commodity, infinitely replaceable and no more important than newsprint simply by virtue of being flesh and blood.

II

When John Price, writing to Henry Luce, called Ogden Reid kindly and likable if deficient in intelligence and enterprise, he was not patronizing his patron. That was the city-room consensus. Milton Lewis, who began on the *Tribune* as a copyboy and would serve it nearly thirty years as a superior, if testy, reporter styled in the tough-guy image of actor Edward G. Robinson, spoke for many on the paper in describing its owner as "a dolt who let the professionals run it for him. He was regarded as kind of a joke—but not without compassion."

Somehow this large, craggy, balding gentleman with his four homes and annual income of between $300,000 and $400,000 escaped blame for the tight-fisted wage scale and antiquarian social outlook of the men who managed his prized possession. He was good old genial "Oggie" Reid—though nobody called him that to his face—who would drink with the least of them at Bleeck's and was all newspaperman at heart. Few of them took his boozy geniality for the tragedy of dysfunction it had long since become.

The family had been alerted to the clinical severity of his alcoholic addiction as early as 1925, when he underwent a minor operation on his nose. Following it, he hemorrhaged badly; the doctors could not control the flow, and for days his life was in peril. "I can still see him lying on his bed with a big clamp on his nose," his son Whitelaw recalled. "His blood, which didn't get checked in advance, had so deteriorated under the impact of alcohol that he was in no way fit for an operation."

He was placed under the close, comradely scrutiny of Arthur Draper, the able former political correspondent who bore the title of assistant editor and whose principal task was to curb the owner's self-destructive tendencies. Ogden was still capable of occasional journalistic contributions, like the one he made the day after the ocean liner *Vestris* went down off Virginia with 324 aboard in November 1928. The ship took ten hours to sink, and Ogden, himself no mean sailing man, told Stanley Walker he thought it would make a fine story to try to figure out what had gone on in the captain's mind during those desperate hours of the losing struggle. Other city editors might have balked at the challenge of reconstructing the mental processes of a man who was at the moment ten fathoms deep in the Atlantic, but the resourceful Walker put his troops on the trail of psychologists, experts on navigation, and other plausible authorities and came up with a unique front-page piece.

But an occasional brainstorm did not compensate for a general state of pickled lassitude. Ogden came and went by whim, and if he kept explorer Richard Byrd waiting at his office for two hours while he reduced himself to stupefaction over lunch at one of his many clubs, the discourtesy was purely unintentional. Watchman Draper himself was judged to be too fond of the grape and was replaced, at the urging of Elisabeth and Helen Reid, by the more sober and gentlemanly Wilbur Forrest, then back in the city room after serving with social, if not journalistic, distinction in the *Tribune* Washington bureau. Ogden would continue to bestir himself on occasion, as in his active role in winning Walter Lippmann to the paper or as on the evening late in 1935 when he attended the annual stag bash of the New York Illustrators Society that got broken up by police who carted off five young models for indecent exposure. Far from distancing himself from the latter event, Ogden tore into the city room, reportorial heart beating fast, told the city desk all about the revealing festivities held before an audience of highly respectable New Yorkers, and handed over to rewriteman Maron Simon notes that he had had the presence of mind to take. " 'Sulzberger was there, too, but I didn't see him taking any notes,' " Simon remembers Reid boasting. "He seemed so pleased to be useful." Ogden waited eagerly at Bleeck's till the first edition came up and noted with pleasure the story's overplay at the top of columns two and three on the front page.

Arthur Sulzberger may have lacked Ogden Reid's reporting reflex, but the handsome, courtly sophisticate with the slightly self-deprecating manner who had taken command of the *Times* that year had more important gifts for mastering the institution he had married into. Adolph Ochs had turned the paper over to him only after Sulzberger had undergone an eighteen-year apprenticeship to familiarize himself with every technical aspect of the *Times,* starting with its newsprint supply. Despite its absence of creative spark, the *Times* was methodically adding to its reputation as an indispensable tool for serious students of public affairs. Thoroughness had made it a standard reference. Such unspectacular but unmatched services as its annual index to the news and the new Sunday section summarizing and analyzing the past week's events suggest why the *Times* kept ahead of the *Tribune* and all other American papers in sales on out-of-town newsstands, in the classroom, and to mail subscribers. And Arthur Sulzberger, building cautiously on his father-in-law's achievement, was a skillful coordinator of other men and very much on the job. Ogden Reid, in marked contrast, reigned but did not rule. Not quite so docile as a figurehead, he sat more like a constitutional monarch, deferring to ministers of his choice and occasionally exercising a veto so that everyone would remember he was not altogether inert.

The operating direction was tacitly vested in a consortium of four, whose power was delicately balanced and played off against one another's. Of them, Wilbur Forrest held the least sway in his own right—his authority was entirely derived from the fact of the owner's disability—but it was he who was professionally and fraternally closest to Ogden Reid. He got up early each morning at his home in Manhasset and read all the papers to know what the opposition was up to. And he wrote the letters and memos that bore Ogden's signature, sat in for him at all the meetings the owner had neither the patience nor stamina to attend, and tried to settle policy and personnel problems that would only have bored Ogden, while keeping him company and trying to monitor his drinking with an attentiveness that went beyond duty. Theirs was an old-shoe relationship that worked precisely because the retainer rarely forgot he was in fact a servant.

Bill Forrest was what used to be called a man's man, a bear of a fellow with a gruff voice, a warm smile, an Oriental cast to his eyes, and a fondness for the outdoors. Golf and hunting were his favorite pastimes, which endeared him to Ogden almost as much as his indifference to things intellectual and esthetic. He was amiable in a low-key, almost stuffy way that wore well on his master. Insolence was not in his makeup; besides, he was genuinely fond of his charge. "Dad really loved him and felt he was worth taking care of," recalled Forrest's daughter Yvonne, "exasperated as he sometimes became with him. The loyalty went beyond feeling sorry for Ogden because he was wounded."

A native of Pekin, Illinois, near Peoria, where he briefly attended Bradley University, Forrest was a heartland Republican and meat-and-potatoes journalist whose pre-*Tribune* career had been with the United Press wire service. At twenty-five, he was running its Milwaukee office, the youngest bureau chief in the organization, and after stints in Cleveland and Washington, went off to Europe to cover the Great War. An early beat interviewing survivors of the *Lusitania* on the Irish coast earned him plaudits; he reported the mad butchery at Verdun, where a correspondent next to him stood up to see the action and lost an eye to a bullet. Bill Forrest was not a man who tempted fate. No lover of combat, he found covering the war to be mostly "the glorified dissemination of government propaganda." His work for the *Tribune,* whether on the Lindbergh landing or an interview with Mussolini upon his conquest of Rome or on politics out of the Washington bureau or on the Seabury investigation disclosures when he was back in the city room, was generally reliable and almost never much better or worse than competent. His chief accomplishment aside from the Lindbergh flash was getting elected president of the Gridiron Club, a social distinction that recommended him to the Reids as a suitable companion for Ogden. A greater talent or bolder spirit would not likely have taken the job.

He proved the perfect company man. Rarely would he oppose the Reids on policy matters. When they cut down the size of the paper by two pages in 1933 as an economy move to offset a decline in revenues, he did not argue that such a step would hurt the *Tribune*'s momentum in its drive to establish itself as an equal to the *Times,* which was willing to absorb the losses and not cut back on its news volume. "Our slogan is brevity consistent with the news, good writing and careful editing," he reported to Laurence Hills of the Paris edition. "The *Times* adheres to the scoop and shovel policy. . . ." Of Hills's own efforts at belt-tightening the next year, Forrest wrote, "We were all thrilled with your economy program." That such programs on both sides of the Atlantic might be penny-wise and pound-foolish, he could not conceive. What pleased him was the *Times*'s red ink.

Forrest's combativeness was reserved for Geoffrey Parsons, in charge of the paper's editorial page and the second member of the reigning directorate. Forrest felt the *Tribune* ought to stand as a beacon against any leftward turn in national or international politics and questioned Parsons's soundness on the issue. The contrast between the pair could hardly have been sharper. A subtle charmer, Parsons was the paper's cultural chief, a man who viewed the political landscape from a historical and social perspective that the xenophobic, literal-minded Bill Forrest did not pretend to. The chief editorial writer, while a certified Republican, was independent enough to admit the failures of the fallen order and, whether assessing the policies of the New Deal or a Labor government in Britain or a Socialist one in France, not to judge by reflex. A trained lawyer from a family with a tradition in jurisprudence, Parsons was also a steadfast civil libertarian and tried to hold the paper on that course. And he was neither pompous nor dogmatic in pushing his views. His highly sociable nature and breadth of interests—he and his wife vacationed in Europe every summer and were fond of giving musicales at their Stanford White–designed home, where Parsons himself performed on the piano—made him a favorite with both the Reids. While he was closer to Helen in his political and cultural leanings, he drank companionably and more than moderately with Ogden in the male-only sanctuary of the Century. Not surprisingly, then, Bill Forrest was wary of such an accomplished associate with whom he could not hope to match intellect or *bons mots.* "There were terrible conflicts with Geoffrey," Forrest's daughter said in recalling how her father was "capable of great anger" whenever he felt Parsons was trying to exercise undue influence on Ogden and extend his hegemony from the editorial page to the entire paper. "They worked closely together but they were never really friendly."

Howard Davis, the third wielder of power within the inner circle, held a social and political outlook still more conservative than Forrest's, and his antipathy to the New Deal and the kind of trouble it stirred up for honest Republican businessmen was evidenced in the vigor of his dealings with the Guild. While an ardent believer in the separation of the entrepreneurial and newsgathering functions of the paper, the plump little general manager let his bias take over one day in 1936 when he suggested to Grafton Wilcox that the *Tribune* might perform a true service for the electorate in that presidential election year by assigning one of its best reporters to investigate the extent of Communist infiltration into the New Deal. The managing editor was agreeable and put Pulitzer Prize winner Leland Stowe on the job. Stowe, advised of the origin of the idea, was skeptical; he viewed Davis as a doctrinaire conservative, "a Rotarian type . . . who oozed self-satisfaction and superficial amiability whenever he strode through the city room." Sensing that he was being ordered to do a partisan hatchet job, Stowe said he would discover everything he could but distort nothing to suit Davis, Wilcox, or the Lord Himself. Two months of investigation in Washington yielded a ten-part series in which the New Deal was found to be free of Red personnel and influence, except for a handful of participants in the WPA's Writers' Project. Such a judgment was unwelcome at a time when the paper was plumping hard editorially and in its play of the news* for the election of Republican presidential nominee Alfred Landon, and Stowe's series was quietly spiked.

Howard Davis's power, in short, was real but circumscribed. "Mr. Reid trusted him greatly," the owner's longtime private secretary, Eve Peterson, said of Davis, who had so competently handled negotiations with Frank Munsey on the *Herald* purchase, the construction and efficient layout of the new *Tribune* building, and lately the annoying agitation of the Guild. He knew every phase of the newspaper business and, in rough times, how and where to cut costs and, in good times, how to try to make them still better. But he did not have the power of the purse. In a pair of "Dear Ogden" memos in 1936, for example, he strongly urged the owner to capitalize on the upsurge in the *Tribune*'s volume by making plant improvements, the continued absence of which would "hamper further development of this newspaper, in both circulation and advertising, due to mechanical limitations." What was the point in spending money for attractive new editorial material and circulation promotion if the paper lacked the machinery to accommodate its sales success? "Therefore it seems to me we must do one of two things," Davis warned, "and do it quickly":

> Cut down the expenditures for general promotion, news and editorial developments for the time being, sufficiently to take care of the cost of necessary plant maintenance

---

* The *Tribune*'s political bias was by then much less evident in its news columns except in presidential election years, when, as in 1936, the Republican candidate was more likely on any given day to be given the edge in story placement if not quantity of coverage. Thus, if Roosevelt and Landon both gave major speeches before sizable audiences, the latter was likely to be featured in the lead. The *Times*, by contrast, was scrupulously fair. It would typically, in the example cited above, carry a single three-column headline, devoting the top line to one candidate and slotting his story in lead column eight and covering the other candidate in the second and third lines of the head and dropping the story on him off column five, with a photograph occupying the top of columns six and seven. Other, less subtle manifestations of *Tribune* favoritism in that campaign were the continuing prominence it gave to the notorious *Literary Digest* poll—which reported, in contrast to other polls, that Landon was ahead—and a regular column it carried by an identified Landon campaign organizer.

and development, the amount of such reduction to be definitely decided upon and set up as a monthly reserve for that purpose,
or
raise new capital for these mechanical necessities.

Otherwise it will be impossible to meet the public demand for the newspaper and its services created by promotional and editorial efforts and of course a newspaper either goes forward or backwards—it never remains stationary.

But neither course was followed, any more than was the urgent suggestion three years earlier by treasurer Robert Cresswell, calling on the Reids to review the paper's capital structure, which was so badly burdened by notes against loans to it by the family that it was technically bankrupt and ineligible for outside financing. Without his mother to turn to now for cash infusions, Ogden Reid seemed incapable of risking his own resources or reducing his claims against his own paper in order to raise outside funds to try to turn it into a truly profitable enterprise. Profits were not why the Reids ran a newspaper. Howard Davis, for all his acknowledged expertise, was essentially a caretaker baying at the wind.

The fourth member of the regency that operated the *Tribune*—Helen Reid —was its most powerful one, but her influence, too, was cabined. As queen, she was closest to the monarch, but she was not sovereign and took pains not to pretend otherwise. When *Time* magazine featured her on its cover in 1934, implying that she and not "bald, likable, easy-going" Ogden wore the pants in the family, she let it be known around the paper that she was greatly displeased with such acclaim, particularly the article's finale. She had called Ogden "the most independent-minded man I ever met," to which *Time* added that "it is Mrs. Reid who often helps that independent mind make itself up."

In truth, she did not put herself forward in his stead until it became plain that her husband was physically and mentally incapable of leading the paper. His drinking had shamed her, but she did her best to tend to him without being overly obvious, phoning the office at night to ask clerks to see if he was all right or to call the stationmaster at Grand Central to hold the last train to White Plains until they could bundle him onto it. His titular command of the *Tribune* was a charade she played at in order not to unman him more than he did himself; she made constant excuses for his inattentiveness, saying he was tied up on the phone or at a meeting when he failed to show up for an important occasion. Her celebrity came at an increasingly painful price.

While Helen Reid was never a working newspaperwoman in the sense of having professional knowledge of journalistic techniques, her imprint on the tone and reputation of the *Herald Tribune* as an advocate of humane progressivism was unmistakable. From the moment she came on the paper, she was a moderating influence on its excessively partisan and occasionally extremist editorial rhetoric. It was she who urged Ogden to serialize the first major biography of Woodrow Wilson and the memoirs of his chief aide, Colonel House, as it was she who recognized the value in securing Walter Lippmann upon the death of the *World*. And she forcefully defended such departures from a limiting orthodoxy; to one typical complainant among the paper's militantly right-wing readers, she wrote in 1932: "We believe that Mr. Lippmann is today the most distinguished writer from an independent or Democratic viewpoint and as such we have found that our readers are interested in knowing what he has to say. Many people disagree with him who still enjoy reading him. . . ." Besides, reading Lippmann had the virtue of stirring Republicans "to work harder for Mr. Hoover's re-election."

It was not politics, though, but Helen Reid's lifelong feminism that provided the main conduit for her liberating and liberalizing influence on the *Tribune*. Starting with her own employment as a highly visible representative of the paper in New York's business community, she sponsored the placement of more women in positions of responsibility on the *Tribune* than were on any other major U.S. newspaper. A strong advocate, for example, of the Sunday book-review supplement launched by the paper in 1924, she befriended Irita Van Doren, who took charge of the literary section in 1926 following the sudden death by drowning of Stuart Sherman, the founding editor, a conservative professor from the University of Illinois. A curly-haired Floridian married to Columbia historian Carl Van Doren, the new literary editor traveled in liberal intellectual circles and moved easily between academia and the more bohemian life of Greenwich Village. The book review rapidly became a repository for writers and thinkers of a decidedly more liberal bent than *Tribune* readers were accustomed to encountering in its columns; books chosen for most attention similarly reflected the enlightened taste and curiosity of Irita Van Doren's world, and her friend Lewis Gannett, a polite but passionate social egalitarian, became the *Tribune*'s daily book reviewer. Similarly, when the paper started up a new magazine for the Sunday edition in 1926, Helen Reid enlisted little Marie Mattingly Meloney, called Missy, a former newspaperwoman then editing *The Delineator,* a magazine appealing mainly to women. It was in tandem with Missy Meloney that Helen Reid dreamed up and ran the inspired promotional idea of the *Tribune*'s annual Conference on Current Problems, begun in 1930 and drawing its audience at first from metropolitan area clubwomen. Helen used all her formidable skills as a saleswoman to attract a blue-ribbon roster of speakers, and soon, rechristened the Herald Tribune Forum, the three-day affair was playing to standing-room-only crowds at the Waldorf-Astoria and being broadcast across the country as a nonpartisan current event of the first magnitude. By running it, the *Tribune* began changing its image as a blindly conservative foe of social change; by 1934, Mrs. Roosevelt was delivering the keynote address and the President offered closing remarks.

Her power at the paper steadily growing, Helen lobbied successfully in the mid-'Thirties for the hiring of two women feature writers of remarkable competence who quickly established their appeal to readers. The first was the daughter of a prosperous Kansas farmer and carried on a lifelong love affair with the fruits of the earth. Before she came along, the *Tribune,* like most papers, used to drop in a few menus and recipes and other filler copy to accompany the heavy food and marketing advertisements that traditionally ran in the Thursday edition. Food was food, and there did not seem to be a lot to say about it. Clementine Paddleford changed all that.

No amateur dabbler in the culinary arts, she did not address herself much to restaurant fare, which by and large repelled her. Her subject, rather, was the metropolitan homemaker's market basket and the delights it could place upon the dining table. Trained as a journalist in Kansas and New York, Clem Paddleford edited a Chicago-based magazine called *Farm & Fireside* before arriving at the *Tribune* with her almost poetic power to evoke the sensory qualities of food. "Pick a tomato fresh from the vine," she wrote. "It lies warm in the hand, a vermillion globe subtly charged with properties of life-giving sun . . . plump and round at its juice-heaviest. . . . Slice it for supper in thick meaty pieces to rest in curly edged lettuce, no dressing, just salt and freshly ground pepper." Or at apple harvest: "The teeth crack into the brittle flesh, a winy flavor floods the mouth—the soul of the apple blossom distilled." Her copy also dealt straightforwardly with practical detail:

> When you buy apples, treat them right. To retain the full flavor, to keep the fruit crisp, store it in the refrigerator. . . . Buy Rome Beauties that are firm and of proper color—which is a yellow or greenish skin mottled with bright red and striped with carmine. An apple that is the right color for its variety will have well-developed flavor. . . . The old story still holds: a bad apple can spoil a barrelful—so store only the sound ones.

Her workday began as early as 5 a.m. as she tramped through the markets of the city, looking for values to pass on to readers and, en route, drinking in the aromas, of which the heavy, sultry, slightly charred smell of coffee roasted daily on Water Street was her favorite. Home again, she would consult her encyclopedic files and write her daily article by hand; each week she turned out six regular pieces and one for *This Week,* the slick syndicated supplement with which the *Tribune* replaced its own Sunday magazine in 1935—enough prose to have filled a couple of newspaper pages. No one surpassed her output. This devotional outpouring of effort, which would in time draw as many as 100,000 letters a year from readers, was managed despite the effects of cancer that in 1932 had claimed a part of her larynx and vocal cords, requiring her to breathe through a tube in her throat, its aperture concealed by a black ornamental ribbon, and leaving her with a somewhat sepulchral voice that she could summon only by placing a finger to the breathing tube. Undaunted and uncynical, Clementine Paddleford, during her thirty-one years at the *Tribune,* elevated writing about food from pulpy service copy to a legitimate place in consumer journalism.

A more controversial addition to the paper was Helen Reid's acquisition in 1936 of Dorothy Thompson, who would quickly become the most influential woman journalist in the nation. Presented to Ogden as a sort of distaff counterpoint to Walter Lippmann, she was recognized at the age of forty-two as an

unremitting foe of European fascism, then mobilizing on the civil war battlefields in Spain. There were those on the American political right who preferred fascism and its promise of orderly economic development to the perceived
anarchy of bolshevism, and Ogden Reid acceded to his wife only when Thompson promised that whatever she wrote about would not diverge markedly from
the editorial position of the paper; one Lippmann was enough.

She was a formidable figure. Large, prettily even-featured, rosy-skinned,
prematurely gray-haired, and possessed of a commanding voice to fit her stature,
Dorothy Thompson wrote in a gutsy, vigorous style of absolute certitude. If her
treatment of an issue tended to the simplistic, at least the reader was in no doubt
about where she stood. The daughter of an impoverished Methodist minister
from upstate New York, she graduated from Syracuse University on a scholar-
ship, delivered stump speeches in behalf of the suffragist movement, wrote
advertising copy in New York, and after World War I embarked for Europe
with aspirations as a free-lance journalist. On the boat over, she fell in with a
group of Zionists headed to a conference in London and wrote her first inside
exclusive. Confident and nervy as a writer for the *Philadelphia Ledger* and the
New York Post and later free-lancing, she was at her best obtaining interviews
with subjects at the edge of the news—the hunger-striking mayor of Cork just
before his death in the cause of Irish freedom; the secluded claimant to the
Austrian throne, whom she reached by disguising herself as a Red Cross nurse;
a rising German politician named Adolf Hitler, to whom she took a towering
dislike and did not hide it. When he came to power, Thompson was given a
one-way ticket out of the Reich and began to call attention to the imminent
threat of fascist domination of Europe. She was soon writing on world affairs
for the *Tribune* in a style that nicely contrasted with Lippmann's. Thompson
emerged from the printed page as a very wise, warm, and caring earth mother,
mourning the world's frailties, bolstering its sagging confidence, and appealing
to its conscience at a time of rampant political wickedness.

Others spoke out against the new tyrants and pleaded for their victims, but
no one did it more persistently or courageously than Dorothy Thompson. When
Lindbergh appealed by radio to the American people in 1938 to look kindly on
Herr Hitler's efficient regime as the wave of the future, she cried madness and
got splattered with hate mail. The next year she drew worldwide attention by
so loudly heckling a German-American Bund rally at Madison Square Garden
that the police had to escort her to safety before any harm befell her. Her stormy
marriage to Sinclair Lewis, the leading American novelist of the day, added to
her fame. Within a year of her debut as a *Tribune* columnist, she was being
syndicated to seventy other papers, soon to another hundred, which sold eight
million copies a day among them. Add to that three million monthly readers
of the *Ladies' Home Journal,* for which she wrote a column, and the estimated
five million who listened to her weekly radio broadcast, and it is possible to grasp
the scale of Thompson's standing as the prime female social commentator of the
pre–World War II period. And Helen Reid was her sponsoring angel. Perhaps

the truest tribute to Helen's instincts as an impresario of editorial feature talent was the follow-the-leader behavior of the *Times,* which gave Arthur Krock a column for political commentary two years after Lippmann began in the *Tribune* and Anne O'Hare McCormick a column on world affairs the year after Miss Thompson began in the *Tribune* and, seeing the success and usefulness of Clementine Paddleford's work, several years later expanded its own coverage of food as news.

The city room remained beyond her reach, but Helen Reid advanced women to executive posts on the business side of the *Tribune,* among them the promotion director, the first director of industrial relations, and the assistant advertising manager. Disciplined and dead earnest, her carefully bobbed and waved hair gray now and her thin straight lips slightly tinted, Helen herself remained the driving sales force. She still presided over the weekly meeting of the advertising salesmen in the paper's ninth-floor auditorium and hosted luncheons for a dozen in the executive dining room—"Helen's chophouse," the staff called it—at which leading merchants were surrounded by public figures and *Tribune* editors and none too subtly sold on the pulling power of the paper. Assured of her position as the most eminent woman executive in her business, she grew yet more determined in her dealings with balky advertisers. Surfeited with flattery by the head of Russek's Fifth Avenue department store over her trailblazing role for women the country over, Helen replied with gratitude for her correspondent's approval of the *Tribune*'s progress but pointedly added, "I would feel happier in knowing of your conviction that it is essential to the growth of Russek's." When Bloomingdale's threatened to cancel its advertising after the paper raised its rates in 1937 to counter a profit squeeze, she would not be bluffed or bullied. "I want you to know that no action on your part can effect [sic] either the Tribune's thinking or action," she wrote, softening the reply by noting that the paper's rates were still below the 1931 level and that the store had established a considerable following among *Tribune* readers, "which it will be unfortunate for you to lose." She brought the political sell to a new level of artless candor in her February 1935 pitch to Andrew W. Mellon for a share of the Alcoa advertising schedule, then divided in New York between the *Times* and the *World-Telegram,* nominally Democratic but not ardently New Dealing in their editorial orientation:

> . . . I do not mean to suggest that advertising should necessarily be placed along political lines, but when a paper is the outstanding Republican one in the country and one of the two great papers of New York City, it seems strange that it should not be used by the Aluminum Company. . . . In the last analysis it seems to me that the New York Herald Tribune is working to accomplish through public opinion the objectives for which the Aluminum Company of America stands—namely, the right handling of both capital and labor—more than any other paper. . . .

Rarely did she miss a selling opportunity. Returning from New Haven after a Yale football game in 1936, the Reids discovered the delights of a new, low-priced restaurant chain called Howard Johnson's. Off went a letter to the ownership, praising the friendly service and delicious food and suggesting that they call their fine establishments to the attention of the many *Tribune* readers who might be as unfamiliar with them as Helen Reid had been; her promotion department stood by to help if desired. On occasion, though, her selling zeal led her astray. Faced with a national economic slump in 1937 that nearly plunged the paper into the red, she approved the sale to the Cuban government of a promotional advertising section that looked suspiciously like journalism. It bore the designation "Section XII" of the November 21 Sunday edition, carried on its cover the heading "Cuba Today: Land of Peace and Progress," and featured a main article headlined "Colonel Batista's Life Dedicated to Relieving Cubans from Oppression." Even *Editor & Publisher,* the industry's lapdog, shook its head.

Had the Cuban section been presented to Ogden Reid for his approval, he might have vetoed it, but by late 1937 the president of the *Herald Tribune* was suffering so acutely from alcoholism that his need to be hospitalized was apparent. Meanwhile, the paper's profit margin, down to a sliver despite nicely climbing circulation, was all the more alarming in view of the annual half-million-dollar installment it was still paying off out of operating revenues to Frank Munsey's beneficiary, the Metropolitan Museum of Art, for the purchase of the *Herald.* The precarious finances demanded attention at precisely the moment the paper's owner was clinically incompetent. Where would fresh operating cash come from? The four who ran the paper for Ogden were powerless to solve the urgent problem.

Ogden's sister, Lady Jean Ward, was summoned from England to help meet the emergency. More British by now than the British, she was remote from the paper except for the more than three million dollars in notes against it that she had been willed by her mother—a debt she had, like her brother, declined to call, for it would have meant the *Tribune*'s bankruptcy. Bad enough to realize nothing on the notes, but to be asked now to provide the paper with fresh resources struck her and her advisers as impertinent in the extreme. Compounding the problem was a growing estrangement between Jean and her sister-in-law. Although Helen did everything for her when she would visit in America—put her up, gather her old friends for a dinner party, and in general look after her —Jean could never overcome the memory that Helen had been her mother's secretary and on occasion still called her Rogers. Of his aunt at this sensitive moment, Whitie Reid would say, "She couldn't, I think, take in the fact that H.R. [as he referred to his mother] had become a substantial figure and a more active newspaper executive than her brother." Nor was she eager to accept how badly Ogden had slipped and how essential his hospitalization was. "She thought it was kind of a plot cooked up by me and H.R."

But a deal was struck. The *Tribune* obtained a loan of $800,000 from Irving Trust after Jean and Ogden agreed to subordinate their claims on the paper, so that the bank now became its first creditor. As the critical condition of the deal, an oversight committee composed of Howard Davis, Wilbur Forrest, and Robert Cresswell, the paper's treasurer, was empowered to direct *Tribune* operations until Ogden, admitted to the Silver Hill clinic in Connecticut, was judged fit to resume command. Helen, due probably to a combination of her sister-in-law's jealousy, her own lack of financial acumen, and the male chauvinism of the other top figures on the paper, was placed at arm's length from its treasury.

Since two of the three members of the so-called economy committee were from the business side and the third, Bill Forrest, favored a leaner paper that was easier and quicker reading than the *Times,* the news budget was not surprisingly a prime candidate for sacrifice. Among the first to feel the knife was the *Tribune*'s news-gathering operations in Europe. At precisely the moment that events were hurrying the continent toward the bloodiest war in history, the only American newspaper with a European edition, the one paper that might have been expected to do the best job of all in covering the epochal news out of the Old World, decided to reduce its foreign file. And it placed its overseas personnel under the unified control of a man held in contempt by almost every American journalist in Europe.

III

Upon discovering the bonanza that had fallen into his hands in the form of the Paris edition of the *Herald* in 1920, Frank Munsey gave only one instruction to the man he placed in charge of the operation: keep costs down. And Laurence Hills, regarding the command as if transmitted from Sinai, made it his life's work thereafter.

Washington bureau chief of Munsey's *Sun,* Hills had gone to Paris to cover the Versailles peace conference after a successful career on the paper as an investigative reporter and national political correspondent. He stayed on as the Paris man for the *Sun,* which was suddenly merged into the *Herald,* and found himself installed as well as manager of the Paris edition. He did not relish the prospect, and nothing in his background or character recommended him for the task. Owlish in his horn-rimmed glasses, he suffered from a somewhat irascible nature that made it difficult to tell from his expression whether he was smiling or his teeth pained him. The pleasures of postwar life in Gay Paree, however, compensated for his new armchair assignment, and Hills, a man with a decided inferiority complex who did not take kindly to even bantering criticism, soon found himself a figure of importance in the American colony with its own club, church, and hospital. Restaurants, theaters, and nightclubs were pleased to receive him as their guest, and the freeloading lifestyle became second nature with him.

After the *Herald*'s bloated circulation figures vanished with the Yank troops, good journalism, of which Hills was not ignorant, was jettisoned for economy of operation. No real effort was made to cover Paris. Staffed only by deskmen and a few feature writers and stringers, catering to American expatriates and tourists, the thin sheet consisted chiefly of rewritten cable copy from New York and the European services, publicity handouts, and inoffensive gossip from the fashionable spas of the continent. Any story that suggested prosperity was not permanent had difficulty reaching print, and nothing excited Hills's tenor-pitched wrath like a piece that had somehow slipped through the net and drawn protest from French officials or the business community. Haphazardly put together by a poorly paid staff and messily printed on deteriorating presses, the Paris *Herald* was often outperformed journalistically by the other two English-language papers in the French capital, the European edition of the *Chicago Tribune* and the continental version of the London *Daily Mail.* But its reputation as the established English-language paper, more aggressive distribution in resort areas, and hold on advertising by shipping lines and the travel industry kept the *Herald* profitable. And its esthetic shortcomings were minimized by comparison with the Parisian press, distinguished only by its corruptibility. The news columns of nearly all the hundred French papers that appeared daily were said to be for sale, and Havas, the national news agency, exerted its own influence by doubling as the principal vehicle for the placement of advertising.

The Reids retained Larry Hills as general manager and editor of the Paris edition upon their purchase of the *Herald* and extended him nearly carte blanche in its direction so long as it remained out of the red. He did better than that with the arrival of boom times, and as revenues rose, the paper brightened. It was manned by a crew of curiosities, starting with managing editor Eric Hawkins, a diminutive British ex-pugilist with a perfect disposition to absorb Hills's harassing tantrums from above and the resentments of his ill-paid editorial staff and French-speaking shop. Among the mainstays of the news staff were cosmopolite Vincent Bugeja, a multilingual Cambridge honors graduate who had been head of the leftist labor party in his native Malta; William H. Robertson, known as Sparrow, an endearing little man well into his sixties, who wrote a syntactically riotous diary of his night-crawling among the favorite American dives and haunts in Montmartre and referred to everyone, including the Prince of Wales, as "my old pal"; and Al Laney, a young, soft-spoken, and expert pencil-wielder who always wore his hat in the office to conceal a surgical dent in his head and who, in his spare time, read to and wrote letters for the nearly sightless James Joyce. There was also an editor whose Russian wolfhound came to work with him every night and curled up under the city desk till his shift was up.

"Laurence Hills is entitled to great credit," Ogden Reid wrote to his mother in 1927, reporting on the salutary condition of the Paris edition. By 1929, its circulation stood at a solid 35,000, it was carrying three-quarters of the total advertising linage appearing in the three English-language papers published in

Paris, and its staff, now numbering thirty editorial hands, had outgrown the dirty little office at Les Halles with its abundance of nearby bistros and zinc-top bars that made working for the *Herald,* even at paltry wages, so alluring. Instead of investing in personnel, the Reids characteristically put their profits into real estate; a splendid H-shaped office building to house the paper and its new presses rose on the rue de Berri, a block off the Champs-Elysées.

The construction was completed just as the first fearsome effects of the Depression hit Paris. Larry Hills, chronically cranky now as he feared for the paper and the comfortable way of life it had afforded him, undertook retrenchment with zeal; he had lost his journalist's heart. Survival was all. "Our whole effort recently has been to keep the losses down," he wrote to Wilbur Forrest, at Ogden Reid's right hand, late in 1933, "and by compression of expenses we have not been doing any worse than last year, although the volume of advertising is 15 percent under 1932." In his fear of economic collapse and encroaching anarchy, Hills sought new political gods and thought he found their embodiment in the strongmen seizing or contending for power in Italy, Germany, Poland, Portugal, and Rumania. He wrote an editorial in the May 22, 1932, issue of the Paris edition titled "Fascism for America" that hailed the new movement and said in part: "Whatever its special characteristic or name, it has always consisted essentially of a mobilization of moral force. . . . The hour has struck for a Fascist party to be born in the United States. . . . It may [take the form of] the clean youth and imagination of a Charles Lindbergh calling upon men of good will to join him in a party of law and order." Shocking as such a proposal appears at the distance of half a century, it was no more so at the time than comparable suggestions from the other side of the political spectrum to remake the unraveling capitalistic democracies along selfless socialist lines. Fascism had not yet revealed the full force of its brutal hand, and the Paris edition of the *Herald Tribune* did not hesitate to run considerable copy friendly to the emerging Nazi regime, Mussolini's already entrenched *fascisti,* and other authoritarian movements across Europe.

Hills was rewarded with continued advertising by the German and Italian shipping lines and other government-controlled businesses and agencies after Hitler took official charge of the Reich. Alone among American papers, its ad columns sprouted swastikas and *fasces.* Hills was pleased to lease office space in his new building to the *Berliner Tageblatt,* the once renowned liberal paper whose Jewish owner had been forced to relinquish his control a year earlier; "it will help us in many ways," Hills wrote Forrest in June 1934. The next month he commented with pride on the paper's recent exclusive interview with Hitler. The extent of Hills's sensitivity to the fascist threat was reflected in the concern he expressed to his superiors in New York that war talk was bad for tourism and thus the Paris paper's revenues.*

---

* Hills's indifference to the most rabid manifestation of the Nazi pathology—its virulent anti-Semitism—may perhaps be inferred from remarks in an April 1935 letter to Forrest in which he

The ambitions and inhumanity of the fascist dictators went on unmistakable display in Spain as the civil war there erupted in 1936. After that, those who favored strongmen as the best hope for social stability in Europe were declaring their yearning for authoritarianism over liberty and serving as accessories to tyranny. Laurence Hills was one of these. To him the choice in Iberia was between Communist anarchy and the order of the right. And he did his best to impose his view on the paper he ran. When a *Tribune* correspondent referred to "Loyalist" troops, Hills had it changed to "reds." Pro-Loyalist letters to the editor were suppressed as offensive to the fascist governments to which he saw the Paris paper's economic fate inextricably tied.* In a letter to Forrest in September 1936, Hills noted that he had urged his copy desk to refer to the Republican side and Franco's rebels as "reds" and "whites," presumably in the interest of chromatic clarity, and, while denying any bias in the instruction, conceded, ". . . personally my sympathies cannot help but run on the rebel side in this Spanish business." He not only escaped censure but was tacitly encouraged in his attitude by Forrest, who replied that there was not much patience in the New York office with the anarchists, Communists, and syndicalists "who seem to be in thick" with the Spanish government, and that several articles Leland Stowe had written for the home paper suggesting that the Republican government was good for the people had been badly received.

Nothing better illustrated the *Tribune*'s preference for anti-Communism in the guise of neutrality over honest reportage than the short shrift given in both the New York and Paris editions to the findings of John T. Whitaker, who had infiltrated Franco's forces and obtained damning evidence of their murderous mentality. Whitaker was one of the bright young men Stanley Walker had hired in 1929. After an able performance in the city room, he had been made a foreign correspondent and done well in the Berlin bureau and even better in Rome, where, despite his loathing of fascism, he had ingratiated himself with Mussolini and still more with Il Duce's daughter. In 1935, Whitaker was the first American correspondent on the scene when Italian troops tried to bully their way to an African empire in Ethiopia, where the temperature during the fighting reached 140 and you had to put your hands under your armpits to cool them. Still, he was unprepared for the horrors he encountered in Spain, "where men talk

---

alludes to the recent death of *Times* publisher Adolph Ochs, who had dropped into the *Tribune*'s Paris office from time to time and through intermediaries, according to Hills, tried to hire him. "All the time I felt that while a Jew publisher, he was a great figure in our business." Forrest's attitude on the same subject was suggested earlier in his letters to Hills regarding the Guild and in a December 1938 letter to Hills in which he reported that the home office in New York had received complaints about the anti-Semitic content of letters to the editor that had run the previous month in the Paris edition. "These are letters which we would shy away from here in Semetic [sic] New York," Forrest wrote, "but which are undoubtedly more innocuous in Paris." *Tribune* management, he added without chastising, would of course deny any anti-Semitic sympathy in its Paris office.
* Hills's position was strengthened when the *Herald Tribune* bought out the *Chicago Tribune*'s European edition, in some ways a superior effort, for $50,000 in 1934.

constantly and knowingly and lovingly of Death as if it were a woman," he would write of the experience six years afterward, "and where the smell of rotting corpses was with us so steadfastly that once I put brandy in my nostrils." It was the slaying of innocents that pained him most, and the cruelty was to him by no means equally apportioned between the foes. "We've got to kill and kill and kill, you understand," one of Franco's press officers told him, in order to reduce the proletariat to manageable numbers and stamp out social unrest; the real problem, other fascists explained, was modern plumbing because before its arrival plague and pestilence had served to thin out the complaining masses. This was not just talk. Whitaker passed several days every week at Franco's base camp in Talavera and awakened there each dawn to the volleys of the firing squad in the courtyard: "I watched the men and women they took into the Cartel each day to provide their quota for the next dawn. They were simple peasants and workers, most of them Spanish editions of Caspar Milquetoast. It was sufficient to have carried a trade union card, to have been a Free Mason or to have voted for the Republic." Each victim was given a two-minute hearing and then capital punishment was pronounced. He watched a cluster of 600 Republican prisoners tremble in one convulsion as Franco's soldiers machine-gunned them down, heard their commander explain that he could hardly have dragged the victims along as his troops advanced, and later listened to official denials that such atrocities had ever occurred.

And almost none of this appeared in print in the *Herald Tribune* on either side of the Atlantic. Larry Hills had put his sympathies into effect.

Yet it was Hills to whom the cost-cutting committee that had been handed financial control of the *Tribune* turned late in 1937. "We are in for a very rigid regime of economy here due to a sag in projected revenues," Forrest wrote him on October 26, advising of the creation of an oversight committee "with rather broad powers." Citing a need for "synchronized cooperation," Forrest said that the paper's foreign service would surely be involved "and in that connection the committee may ask your cooperation in holding down expenditures abroad." Hills could hardly wait to wield the ax. He replied that he had been planning to write New York questioning outlays for foreign correspondence because "frankly, from what I have observed, I think a great deal of money is being spent unnecessarily, if the results were to be appraised."

He was speaking not of the Paris edition, of which he was in total charge, but of the *Tribune*'s independently operating bureaus in London, Paris, Rome, Berlin, and Moscow. Though autonomous, each was in regular touch with the chief of the Paris bureau, John Elliott, a somewhat remote Princeton man whose bespectacled features and flying hair gave him the air of the proverbial absent-minded professor. As the senior correspondent, Elliott acted as go-between with the others and coordinator of coverage and travel plans with the home office. That ended abruptly after Hills was summoned to New York and a cable over managing editor Wilcox's signature was sent to Elliott on December 1:

EFFECTIVE DECEMBER 1 LAURENCE HILLS APPOINTED DIRECTOR OF EUROPEAN
SERVICE NEW YORK HERALD TRIBUNE WITH FULL EDITORIAL AND FINANCIAL
AUTHORITY UNDER MANAGING EDITOR NEW YORK STOP DECISION BASED ECO-
NOMIC REASONS SOLELY WITH VIEW TAKING ADVANTAGE FACILITIES PARIS
HERALD TRIBUNE STOP CONTINUE IN YOUR PRESENT CAPACITY UNTIL MR HILLS
RETURNS WHEN YOU WILL REMAIN AS PARIS CORRESPONDENT. . . . REORGANIZA-
TION PLAN . . . CONTEMPLATES EVENTUAL MERGING CENTRAL FOREIGN BUREAU
WITH PARIS HERALD TRIBUNE. . . . HOLD DOWN COVERAGE TO HIGH SPOTS LEAV-
ING ROUTINE TO AP AND UP BOTH READY TO COOPERATE INFORMING YOU THEIR
DAILY COVERAGE

"The cable was a bombshell," recounted Walter B. Kerr, who had arrived
in Paris as Elliott's assistant a few months earlier, "to Elliott and the rest of us
overseas—and not because John was no longer 'European manager.' It was
because everyone understood it to mean that the *Herald Tribune* was dropping
out of the fight with the *Times,* that we were no longer to compete with the
Times, at a crucial time in the history of the world. And this mattered to us.
We were not working for money; we were working for the paper. . . . We felt
we could adjust to almost any financial requirements of the paper, that if they
were stringent we could think of a way to minimize their effect. But no one
asked."

Back in Paris, Hills sped out a directive to the bureaus confirming their worst
fears. "It is no longer the desire even to attempt to run parallel with the New
York Times in special dispatches from Europe," the memo instructed. "Relying
more than ever on the agencies [Associated Press and United Press] for routine
what the paper wants from our service are dispatches that in a sense seem
exclusive in news, as well as presentation. This means short stories, as well as
long. Crisp cables of human interest or humorous type cables are greatly appreciated. Big beats in Europe in these days are not very likely." Hills added,
by way of making clear his new power as czar of the paper's European coverage,
that the New York and Paris editions "are to be considered one organization
and that the men abroad are employees of both."

Elliott described the situation to John Whitaker, who by then had transferred from the *Tribune* to the *Chicago Daily News* foreign service. His reply
of December 20 suggests the prevailing estimate of Hills among the correspondents:

> He represents everything which is bad in American journalism. He boasted
> during the Versailles Conference era that he got his publisher [Frank Munsey] to
> come out against the League because it would make the paper different from the rest
> and build circulation. He has accepted humiliating terms for advertising from certain
> governments. He proudly claims that his chief accomplishment is in chiseling down
> salaries and cheating reporters into writing for by-lines and promises. He has the
> integrity of a cockroach.
>   . . . No one has ever told the Reids about this man. Wilbur [Forrest] is a

bootlicker too but he and Lee Stowe . . . know about Hills and they would support the whole foreign corps if you wrote and asked their help. . . . Good luck if you fight —to hell with you all if you take it lying down.

IV

The opportunity for journalistic distinction that its superior personnel presented and that its headless management squandered by misguided retrenchment was nowhere more marked than in Moscow, where the *Herald Tribune* had posted early in 1937 a superbly qualified correspondent of twenty-nine. He knew the Russian language, the land, the people, the history, and the bureaucracy as no other American correspondent did and had arrived to represent the paper just as the terrorist nature of the Soviet regime was being bared to world scrutiny.

Joseph F. Barnes, a broad-shouldered six-footer with a long, strong face and great personal charm to match his good looks, had grown up not quite a child prodigy in a highly unorthodox household. His father, a social progressive, was an itinerant scholar and Chautauqua lecturer who had not learned to read until he was twenty-five, traveled in academic circles throughout the nation and abroad, and would take young Joe with him sometimes on the speaking circuit. Joe's childhood was passed "in masses of rooms full of masses of books and masses of guests," among them Harold J. Laski, the British political scientist, whose socialist views Joe was exposed to and favorably taken with during the year Laski lived with the Barnes family in Philadelphia. Admitted to Harvard at fourteen, Joe was sent off instead to stay for a year and a half with friends who lived a dozen miles outside Oxford, to which the boy biked daily to study Latin and absorb what he could of British civility. Then, at Harvard, he became president of the *Crimson,* the undergraduate daily newspaper, and numbered among his friends a free-spending, hard-drinking princeling named Frederick Vanderbilt Field, a great-great-grandson of Cornelius Vanderbilt and a boy even then burdened with an uneasy conscience over the indulgences of the rich. Field and Barnes went off together after graduation in the Class of 1927 to the London School of Economics, where Laski and other thinkers of the left were teaching. Fred Field fell under Laski's influence and, upon his return to the United States, joined the Socialist Party; Joe Barnes, with his more supple, questioning intellect, was unexcited by economic ideology. His choice was to study the Soviet Union itself, where great if not wholly admirable things were happening.

Switching to the School of Slavonic Studies, Barnes spent three months in a crash course in Russian, one of the first ever offered. For the rest of the year he absorbed as much as he could from books about Russian life and history and then, in the expectation of writing a doctoral treatise on peasant communal land ownership, went to the Soviet Union. He was there for seven months, all on his own at the age of twenty and nearly broke most of the time. Moscow in revolutionary ferment was one of the most exciting places on earth to be just then. Barnes lived in hostels, haunted the central municipal library of Moscow, perfected his use of the Russian language, and persuaded the commissariat of agriculture to let him visit a government farm in the south of Russia and share the peasants' hardships. He read some Marx, too, finding much of it impenetrable but grasping its appeal to victims of oppression.

If he had been captivated by Communist thought, he picked a peculiar way to implement it on his return to America. He worked for several years in the very bourgeois banking business, starting in the commercial credit department of a branch on Madison Avenue. He even made some money on investments, got married, and was able to ride out the early ravages of the Depression. But banking was not the career for his restless mind, and in 1931, with the help of press credentials obtained through his brother Howard, who for twenty-five years would serve as a film and theater critic on the *Tribune,* Barnes went back to the Soviet Union accompanied by his wife to reinforce his mastery of the language and study the progress of the Red regime. He also helped the idealistic correspondent Ralph Barnes (no relation) open up a *Tribune* bureau in Moscow —an enlightened step at a time when few American papers were willing to bear the expense or the domestic political risks of representation in the Soviet capital —and wrote some pieces for the paper on Russian life. He had extensive dealings with the Soviet bureaucracy for the first time when he was hired as an interpreter and guide for a group of scholars from the Institute of Pacific Relations (IPR), a New York–based research foundation devoted to Asian affairs, who were crossing Russia from west to east for an international conference in Shanghai. The experience excited Barnes enough for him to take a staff position with IPR back in New York, where he edited its fortnightly bulletin and renewed acquaintance with his Harvard friend Fred Field, now a politically active leftist on the IPR staff, and his wife, Elizabeth. The institute, fueled largely by Rockefeller, Carnegie, and corporate funding, was a curious mesh of establishment patronage, missionary zeal, and Marxist-socialist sympathies among many of the staff intellectuals. In time, China-lover Henry Luce hired Joe away from IPR and set him to work for seven months on the dummy of a projected magazine that was to be a sort of *Reader's Digest* of foreign articles. When the idea died on the drawing board, Joe was hired by Stanley Walker as a *Tribune* cub.

From the day he entered the city room, he was special. Handsome, reflective, courteous, he also evinced a youthful enthusiasm for people and ideas that he would never lose. Some found him too subtle; others took his self-possession for arrogance. Said one city-room contemporary, "He was one of the few men I've ever seen who could strut sitting down."

But he worked hard. He put in his time as a district man on the police beat, did hundreds of obituaries on rewrite, and hit the streets as a cityside reporter specializing in stories about science and education. Yet his fondness for journalism was tempered, he related in a remarkable memoir recorded in 1951 for the

Columbia University Oral History Project. Joe Barnes was attracted to newspapering because it made him feel a part of his tumultuous times. Many young intellectuals had turned to Marxist doctrine as something solid to pin their hopes to. Joe had seen the Soviet prototype and harbored hopes but few illusions. And now he was out there witnessing his own troubled society up close, and the paper gave him his ticket as legitimate observer of its infinitely varied forms. "Every day is done when the paper goes to press," he mused, "and next morning the world starts as if it had been created afresh for you." But there were days when he was convinced that the prime qualification for excellence in reporting was "a limitless capacity to be bored." The fascinating personalities with whom legend said he was to be in steady contact were far outnumbered, he found, by tiresome ones—by dumb cops and timeserving politicians whose ineptness and insensitivity he could not openly challenge. He did his work well, though, and joined the newly formed *Tribune* unit of the American Newspaper Guild because he did not think twenty-five dollars a week was an excessive reward for the demands of his trade. And in a complex and painful romance involving the breakup of both their previous marriages, he wed Fred Field's former wife, Elizabeth, known as Betty, a Bryn Mawr graduate with a serious and independent mind, who considered herself radical but in no way politically doctrinaire. No city-room agitator, Joe was nevertheless known to be leftist, so managing editor Wilcox put him to the test of covering the national convention of the Communist Party in 1936 to name its presidential ticket. His handling of the weeklong assignment in thoroughly objective fashion convinced his bosses that he could be trusted not to let politics distort his reportage. Named as Moscow correspondent, he sailed in February 1937 with his wife, Betty, and her five-year-old daughter, Lila. En route, he stopped in Paris and met Laurence Hills, who was much taken with him; Hills wrote to Forrest that Barnes "strikes me as one of the best young men I have seen picked for foreign service in a long time." Forrest concurred. Neither of them alluded to his private politics.

Covering Russia, at a time when the savagery of the Soviet secret police system was turning the purge, detention, and liquidation of political deviance into daily acts of state, was probably the most difficult journalistic assignment in the world for a correspondent from a capitalist nation. The Soviets offered no help. There were no press conferences, no access to the commissars, no interviews with official spokesmen. Every extracted fact was treated by the regime as a piece of potential military intelligence. An American correspondent's main news sources were the Soviet press, what he could see on the sidewalk with his own eyes, and, if he knew the language without need of an interpreter (as only Barnes did among the American correspondents then in Moscow), casual contacts with the people on the street, in shops, or at the theater. All cables were censored, all phone calls and mail monitored.

Under such circumstances, the Barneses elected to live not within the safe confines of the foreign colony but across the Moscow River in a neighborhood of ordinary Russians. They rented a split-log house with three good-sized rooms and a veranda overlooking a little garden. Contact with Russians was uneasy; foreigners were viewed as possible political contaminants. The Barneses' main link with their neighbors proved to be little Lila, who played with their children and attended a Russian kindergarten. The Barneses were at pains not to draw suspicion to their neighbors, but they themselves did not feel constrained to live in privation. Indeed, on Joe's $75-a-week salary, augmented by an expense account, a car (it was an old Dodge) and chauffeur, and a highly favorable exchange rate on the black market used almost universally by foreigners with hard currency, the Barneses were able to live in comfort, entertain often, and enjoy frequent visits to the ballet, symphony, and theater.

The oppressive political climate affecting Soviet citizens, moreover, did not restrict Barnes from traveling widely as long as he could fend for himself and make do with rough accommodations. He cruised down the Volga and over other inland waterways, mingling freely with the people, and was allowed to roam from the Ukrainian breadbasket to the new trans-Ural industrial heartland at the edge of Siberia. On such treks especially, the line between work and recreation disappeared for him and he relished the chance, as he would write in the chapter on foreign correspondence he contributed to *Late City Edition,* "of finding the sort of all-absorbing immersion in a new experience which some men would pay for." He learned the correspondent's priorities of survival—a bed, a cable or wireless office, a way of getting out of town, food and drink, local currency, and "some natives who are not too dishonest"—and suffered from what he called "the corrosive psychological effect of knowing" that wherever stationed or whatever his pay, the American reporter abroad was an aristocrat compared to the people he was writing about.

The hardest part of the job for him was its professional loneliness. There were never any instructions from New York or Paris about what to cover, never a rebuke when the *Times*'s veteran Moscow correspondent Walter Duranty scooped him, and only an occasional note of commendation from Wilcox or Sunday editor George Cornish. "I got almost nothing," he would write of his employers, "but freedom and silence." And from the Soviets, cold scrutiny and nightly struggles on the telephone with the censor. Once he put through a call to the *Tribune* bureau in Berlin and, thanks to careless monitoring, was able to get out a list of 1,200 Soviet officials of every rank who had been victims of the purges. The feat nearly got him deported. But he did not back down or disclose fear. "Joe was a very cocky guy, full of himself and ambition, and not fraught with anxiety or uncertainty," his wife recalled. Such grit earned him the suspicion not so much of the Soviets as of those in the self-ghettoized American colony who did not speak the language as Joe did and did not choose to live across the river with the people and socialize regularly with those of other nationalities. "No doubt we were disliked for not being humble about our differences," Betty Barnes surmised.

How Barnes was viewed within the American colony is suggested by the recollection of George F. Kennan, long a leading U.S. authority on the Soviet

Union, who was then attached to the embassy in Moscow. "Joe, as I remember him, was, at least up to 1939, much more pro-Soviet than the rest of us—naïvely so, it seemed to me," Kennan recounted. "I saw him as a warm, generous, if naïve, idealist, captivated, as so many had been in that early post-revolutionary period, by the excitement and the ostensibly progressive aims of the Soviet regime of that day."

A different contemporary view was offered by Henry Shapiro, who was a Moscow correspondent for forty years, starting as a *Herald Tribune* stringer in 1933, then becoming Reuters bureau chief, and switching to head the United Press bureau late in 1937. Shapiro found Barnes not more pro-Soviet than other American and Western correspondents, as Kennan judged him, "but less anti-Soviet." Most of the American press corps, in Shapiro's estimate, had a cultural and political bias against the Soviet regime. "The very fact that Joe knew the language was enough to cast him under suspicion," Shapiro said. "Joe's problem was that he didn't suffer fools gladly—he was head and shoulders over the rest of the correspondents, and he'd let you know about it. He'd been used to dealing with academics and others with a background in the area. . . . He was very critical of the Soviet Union when dealing with people with whom he thought he might have an intelligent conversation."

Word came from New York at the beginning of December of his first year in Moscow that he was to hold down his filing as part of the *Tribune*'s economy drive. It had a chilling effect on Barnes. To be put, in reality, under the supervision of Larry Hills made matters even worse. Instead of protesting to the ownership as John Whitaker had urged them, the paper's European correspondents got together and signed an aide-mémoire among themselves, pledging cooperation to help meet their mutual problem and agreeing to take collective action only as a last resort. In January 1938, Hills praised Barnes by writing, "I think you have been holding your stuff down beautifully." So discouraging was this perverse cheerleading that Barnes felt constrained at the end of that month to write Hills and explain like a schoolboy why he wished to take a two-week trip to the Urals and beyond to see, as no American correspondent had in eight years, the huge new Soviet industrial developments. It represented, Barnes carefully explained, "probably the biggest single shift in economic and military geography since the opening of the American West or the industrialization of Japan." Hills cabled back: "TRIP PERMISSION GRANTED ON CONDITION NO EXPENSE TO PAPER. . . ." On the successful completion of his voluntary assignment, Barnes was greeted by word that he would not be reimbursed for his rail fare to and from Paris in December for a visit during which he had held extensive discussions with Hills.

The *Tribune*'s self-defeating policy of fielding a corps of highly competent foreign correspondents and then drastically curtailing their output was illustrated in all its folly by the highly compact but unduly pinched accounts that Barnes filed on the great set piece of terrorist politics in the Stalin era—the purge trials for treason against twenty-one formerly prominent Soviet officials in

March 1938. Years later, some would accuse Barnes of having slanted his copy toward the regime, but a close reading of his stories as published (after having been edited by the avowed Soviet sympathizer John Price) discloses no such bias. There were instead such skeptical phrases as "this plot for a Hollywood scenario" and "one of the strangest prisoner's speeches in the history of political crimes" that amply conveyed the correspondent's belief that he was witnessing a carefully staged drama. The trouble was not with what Barnes wrote but what he was not allowed to write. For the opening day of the trial, when the *Times* carried the entire text of the indictment of the alleged traitors and separate articles of commentary by anti-Stalinist exiles Kerensky and Trotsky in addition to the long main story—a full page of type in total—Barnes filed only 560 words, which when expanded from "cablese" came to a sixteen-paragraph story of about twice that length, skimpy in the extreme compared to its rival's coverage. And things got worse as the trial progressed despite Barnes's best efforts to compress his accounts. On most days he cabled fewer than 400 words, and even his longest piece, only twice that length, showed both the art and the strain of colorful compression; it began:

> MOSCOW, March 8 — The thin ice of theoretical quibbles collapsed today in the sixth day of the Soviet Union's most spectacular treason trial, dropping the entire proceedings into the political underworld. From Henry G. Yagoda, former head of the secret political police, and a trio of famous doctors who had worked on his instructions, the court martial heard a strange tale of the deliberate medical murder of four well known men as a last resort of the desperate conspirators struggling for power.

Barnes continued to cooperate without protesting the myopia of the paper's cutback of its foreign correspondence. In April he again wrote Hills, politely asking if he might go to the Ukraine, where "this year's harvest is likely to have overwhelming importance for the whole Soviet situation. As with my Magnitogorsk trip, it is understood that . . . I will pay all the expenses personally." The correspondent, in short, was subsidizing his employer. But by May, Barnes's patience was becoming exhausted. He politely but firmly wrote to Hills objecting to the paper's decision to run an AP story on the May Day parade instead of his own interpretation of the event. Not only was the wire-service piece wrong on the facts, such as stating that U.S. Ambassador Joseph E. Davies was present when he was actually in bed with indigestion, but it missed completely the point "clear to nearly everyone except the A.P." that the parade was less military than in former years and more a display of proletarianism. By July, his unhappiness was turning to disgust. After the *Times* correspondent had filed a piece of 750 words on a subject about which Barnes felt free to send off only 300, he wrote to Walter Kerr in the Paris bureau that "anyone comparing our stories will think I was lazy, inept, or both" and added:

> But this is a general problem, applicable to every story every day, especially since [*Times* correspondent] Walter [Duranty] has come back with ants in his pants, and

is sending a think-piece every day. The Moscow bureau is increasingly becoming a luxury for the Trib., and one that doesn't even carry prestige so long as I don't file anything.

"I never had the feeling," Barnes would say of his Moscow tenure, "that the *Herald Tribune* was more than remotely interested in my being there"; his was more of a promotional than an editorial presence, he concluded.

The rest of the *Tribune* foreign corps was reaching the same conclusion. In May, John Elliott wrote Barnes that Hills had urged him to send New York part of a piece that the Paris edition had run under the headline "Avenue de l'Opéra to Be Lavishly Decorated / With Roses for Visit of British King and Queen"; Hills went on, "I would appreciate it greatly if you and Mr. Kerr would keep your eyes open for anything that could be cabled in the way of a short to incite interest and bring Americans to Paris. As you know this helps the European edition and that means Mr. Reid. I am afraid we are threatened with a rather poor American tourist year." This, two months after Nazi Germany had seized Austria—without a *Tribune* correspondent on the scene—and four months before the Munich Pact that would sentence Europe to war. Elliott also passed on word of the demoralizing effects of the economy drive in the New York office from Leland Stowe, who had written him: "As for foreign news, it has no champion in the upper hierarchy here—and may never have. To know what is happening abroad you simply have to read the Times and that will be the case ad infinitum, I fear. We have thrown away countless opportunities to become really a competitor and now are in retreat. . . ."

The pusillanimous policy that led the *Tribune* to curtail its European coverage when it should have been expanding it and its European manager to appease fascist regimes—all because its owners were unwilling to deprive themselves of personal luxury or seek adequate outside financing so the paper would not have to live hand to mouth—was laid bare late in July 1938 when the Paris edition suppressed a column by Walter Lippmann. Hubert Roemer, assistant general manager of the Paris edition, acting in place of Hills, who had been hospitalized with intestinal cancer, wrote the New York office explaining the decision, which had angered Lippmann: ". . . it would be very foolhardy to prejudice what he [Hills] has built up by publishing some of Mr. Lippmann's pieces. If there is no war in Europe this summer and we had published this particular article, we would have scared a lot of tourists needlessly." He sent the New York management a copy of the letter of explanation he had written Lippmann, in which he stated that he knew the columnist appreciated "the rather unique position of the Herald Tribune's edition over here. . . . [W]e cannot take the definite risk of antagonizing other nations or in frightening tourists by presuming to tell the former the faults of their regime or the latter by explaining to them, through our columns, the dangers of an immediate armed conflict over here." After adding the gratuitous intelligence that in some countries the *Tribune*'s distinction between signed columns and official editorial policy was not recognized,

Roemer concluded by insisting he was not assessing the situation "from a purely commercial point of view." But no other was cited; it was simply dishonorable journalism. Wilbur Forrest cabled Roemer back: "REID AND I AGREE HILLS POLICY MUST PREVAIL PUBLICATION LIPPMANN ARTICLES. YOUR LETTER OUTLINING POLICY EXCELLENT."

It was the same sort of dollars-first abandonment of principle that had permitted the paper to publish the shameful supplement touting the joys of totalitarian Cuba the previous autumn. Hills's power, strongly backed by Forrest in the name of the owner, was not curbed until the end of 1938 when Dorothy Thompson wrote to Helen Reid that while she hesitated to interfere in matters

> which you may think are none of my business . . . I feel that I ought to tell you that when Larry Hills was put in charge of the foreign service, practically every American journalist in Paris was appalled.
>
> I have many old friends there and they write me candid letters, and they tell me that the Paris Herald Tribune is playing the fascist game from start to finish. Inasmuch as this is certainly not the policy of the Herald Tribune, I feel that you ought to do something about it.

The *Tribune* did. Hills, by then a terminally ill man, was summoned home and told there would be no more pulled punches in covering European fascism. He was stripped of the power to write editorials except of a purely local and nonpolitical sort, but direction of the paper was not removed from him; he had been, after all, a creature of the Reids and done their bidding all too well.

The measurable effects, meanwhile, of the economy drive on the health of the *Tribune* as the news heated up on the eve of World War II lent substance to Bill Forrest's contention, as expressed to Hills early in 1938, "that a well edited and closely written paper—in normal times—is a better newspaper and that volume has to stop somewhere due to the sheer inability of the reader to absorb it. . . . I think the Times has a policy of long windedness which may prove an increasing embarrassment." By the end of 1938, a year that was hardly "normal times," and despite the reduced filing from foreign bureaus, the half-million-dollar slash by the economy committee in operating expenses, and the fact that the *Tribune* was running six fewer pages in its daily edition than the *Times,* it was the latter that suffered a larger circulation drop—of more than 20,000 in the daily edition compared with the *Tribune*'s loss of 1,500—after both papers raised their price from two cents to three in May. "It is my personal belief —not entirely subscribed to by some others here—that we should never go back to loosely edited papers," Forrest wrote Hills with the end-of-September ABC circulation figures in hand. The *Tribune,* he argued, "should surrender completely to the Times its unenviable obligation to publish full texts and other volume for the rag paper edition and library trade and publish a paper for people who have only part of the day to devote to it. In other words we should maintain our newly gained journalistic individuality."

Whether this was an artful attempt to make a virtue out of a shortcoming or an earnestly held conviction among higher management, the cutbacks eased the financial squeeze without apparent damage to the *Tribune*'s competitive position. And the coming of war, with its imposed restrictions on newsprint availability and limitations in overseas filing due to crowded military traffic on cable lines, would freeze the relative positions of New York's two great dailies for nearly a decade and lull the runner-up into a false complacency.

10

The Soul of a Newspaper

The jury in the murder trial of the century had been out since 11:21 that morning, and now, at 10 p.m., February 13, 1935, in the city room of the *Herald Tribune*—an hour before the first edition was due to hit the street—the tension was peaking around the desk of the night city editor, Lessing Lanham (Engel) Engelking. There were three possible verdicts: Bruno Richard Hauptmann would be found guilty and sentenced to die for the kidnap-killing of the Lindbergh baby; guilty with a jury recommendation for mercy and thus a mandatory sentence of life imprisonment; or not guilty. All three outcomes were already set in type, along with a lot of "B" (for background) copy, so that once word was flashed from Flemington, Engelking had only to instruct the composing room which version to slap on the press. They waited, Engel puffing harder and harder on his huge Corona as the clock edged ahead.

At the courthouse, security was very high; the sheriff was determined that no word of the verdict would leak out prematurely. The courtroom shades were drawn upon the jury's return, so that no hand signals could be transmitted to confederates on the street or hanging off nearby rooftops. But the Associated Press man on the spot was equally determined to beat the world with the news. His briefcase, which never left his hand during the daylong vigil, contained a tiny shortwave radio device to signal the AP dispatcher planted in the court-house attic.

At about half past ten, four minutes before the jury returned and fourteen minutes before it rendered the verdict, the AP reporter sent his secret signal; it worked like a charm. In the *Tribune* wire room, the bell jangled in a frenzy, the teletype chattered, and the waiting copyboy hurried the flash to Engel. "Guilty-life!" he boomed at Walter Hamshar, Sr., head copy clerk on the night desk. Printers scurried.

No documentation has surfaced to explain the AP's error, but there were many rumors. One was that in addition to the three possible verdicts, the AP man had arranged a fourth signal to indicate the return of the jury and that the dispatcher in the attic confused that signal with the one for guilty-life. A more plausible explanation, the one that *Tribune* people heard the following day, was that the AP had a payoff in with a court attendant who was eavesdropping outside the jury room and the spy got things wrong. In any case, the wrong verdict was dispatched to the world. At the *Times,* the presses were already rolling.

But at the *Tribune,* Engel was puzzled; he had expected the death sentence. Better to wait for corroboration from the United Press, even though it was traditionally the less solid and reliable service. No word came, though, for puzzling minutes. The pressmen stood by. Finally, more bells and the UP flash in purplish ink on yellow paper: Hauptmann was sentenced to die in the electric chair. "Hold everything!" Engel boomed a second time and, large as he was, disappeared into an impenetrable cloud of smoke. *Times* delivery trucks were already reported on the street. Attempts were made to query both wire services, but in the confusion nothing was clear. Engel puffed on in excruciating silence. Joe Driscoll, the *Tribune* man on the scene, telephoned in routinely a few minutes later. "Guess you heard the news?" Driscoll said.

"What news?" Engel demanded.

"He's going to fry."

Engel rose through his self-generated pillar of smoke and roared, "Guilty-death—goddammit!" A new front page was swiftly snapped on the press, and the *Tribune* rolled with the correct story. In the office, they heard with delight that the *Times* trucks were in hot pursuit of the mistaken copies already being hawked by newsdealers at the top of their lungs.

The sentence was not carried out for nearly fourteen months. Pleas to the governor of New Jersey for a stay of execution pending a new trial and, that failing, commutation of the sentence to life imprisonment were finally exhausted on the evening of April 3, 1936. On hand at the state penitentiary in Trenton to report the scene for the *Tribune* was twenty-five-year-old Richard Tobin, by ten years the youngest reporter in the death chamber. His byline had led the paper almost daily since the beginning of the year over coverage of the Hauptmann lawyers' efforts to spare the condemned man's life. Now he sat in the third row among the fifty-seven witnesses, ten feet from Hauptmann. Only the doomed man's nose and chin were visible after they strapped him in. He confessed nothing, blamed no one, was silent to the end. The electricity surged through him, and his head shot back. The lights did not dim. There was no crackle of energy or any sound in the twenty-two-by-eighteen room. "But you could smell his burning flesh—it was very acrid—his insides were burning up," Tobin recalled long afterward. "I have never forgotten the smell." After three minutes, they shut the power off, Hauptmann's head slumped forward, and he was pronounced dead.

Over the next forty-five minutes, Tobin filed 2,000 words to the *Tribune*. Engelking was on the other end of the wire, encouraging, questioning, reminding. Exactly how many witnesses had there been, did he have the executioner's age and middle initial correct, why did his account and the wire services' differ on the exact moment that death was pronounced? The death chamber clock turned out to be half a minute faster than the one in the warden's office. The *Tribune* chose the latter; Tobin's story put the moment of death at 8:47 1/2 p.m. "That was Engel for you," said Tobin.

There was not a word in the printed story, however, about the odor of incinerated human innards that pervaded the death chamber in ghastly testimony to the barbarity of capital punishment, although Tobin had included it in his story. The detail presumably would have offended the sensibilities of *Tribune* readers. That, too, was Engel.

Emotionally spent, Tobin retired to the bar of the Hotel Stacy-Trent and drank well into the night—a sure way to fend off haunting dreams. Hung over the next day, he gamely made what he envisioned as his triumphal return to the paper by dropping in at Bleeck's "for a little hair of the dog." Among the first people he ran into at the bar was Ogden Reid, who looked up from the scotches lined up in front of him and asked genially, "Where you been, Tobe? Haven't seen you around." Here his byline had been on prominent display over a Trenton dateline for thirteen weeks on the biggest story in the country, and the owner of his paper did not connect him with it. Perhaps the owner was kidding? "No, he meant it," Tobin recalled. "He had no sense of humor—none of the Reids did."

The incident persuaded Dick Tobin that eminence and power at the *Tribune* were not to be won by the reportorial route, and a week later he asked for and was granted transfer to the city desk. For the fact was that the *Tribune* was primarily an editors' newspaper, not simply in the usual sense that the editors selected the writers, made the assignments, and dictated the angle of the stories and their ultimate placement, but because the paper was so strapped for money, manpower, and news space that it had to use its wits and talent to the hilt to remain in the game against the leviathan *Times*. No other American paper faced such a competitor. Every paragraph in the *Tribune* had to be well utilized, and only alert editors could hope to achieve that ideal. Of them, none was more able than Engelking, a dominating presence, vocally demanding and challenging— the real force behind Stanley Walker, some said. Yet when Walker's successor as city editor was chosen in the period between Hauptmann's sentencing and execution, Engel was passed over for still another Texan.

Charlie McLendon, a big, beefy man with large black eyes swimming in his fleshy face, had been neither a reporter nor a copyreader but a makeup man on the nightside, an able technician who had served his time and looked as if, by sheer physical force, he could assert authority over the city room that Stanley Walker had once exercised with a few words and a quick brain. McLendon, though, had no brilliance in him. And he was crude. He sat there in dubious command, chomping on wooden pencils and scratching away none too furtively at his private parts. The copyboys called him King Kong. "If this were a b-b-bank," remarked Homer Bigart, the stuttering, long-suffering copyboy recently advanced to reporter, noting the announcement of McLendon's appointment as city editor on the office bulletin board, "there'd be a r-r-run on it."

The consternation among the city staff over management's failure to elevate Engelking was explained away by McLendon's seniority and Engel's relative youth—he was thirty-three at the time—and his high value on the nightside, where the action was heaviest. McLendon proved a jovial and easygoing commander despite occasional displays of irritability and an office reputation as "something of a tosspot." His shortcomings were compensated for by the strength of his assistants. One of them, Lewis B. Sebring, Jr., the methodically neat assistant night city editor, held McLendon in thinly disguised contempt. A born snob and ardent whip-cracker who thought reporters ought to put in twelve-hour days, Sebring brought superior editorial tools and an authoritarian frame of mind to his job; he was known to have hung a Nazi flag on the wall of his home as a souvenir of a vacation trip to Germany and to be equally admiring of the British royal family. Given his rightward political bias, he was impossible to persuade of the newsworthiness of a report one night that the police were headed over to Rockefeller Center to cover the huge mural there by Marxist painter Diego Rivera; only when the *Times* city edition played up the outrage prominently did Sebring relent. He was similarly unresponsive, due to a wholesome hatred of press-agentry, when public panic greeted the exceedingly realistic adaptation of H. G. Wells's *The War of the Worlds* by Orson Welles's radio troupe on Sunday evening, October 30, 1938; the whole thing, Sebring insisted, was a publicity trick, unworthy of prominent attention in a dignified newspaper. The copyboys accused him of premature senility.

McLendon's inability to control Sebring and his own tendency to go off on a bender at inopportune moments underscored his unsuitability for the key leadership post in the city room, and in the fall of 1939, Grafton Wilcox summoned L. L. Engelking to his office and told him the city staff was his to command. And command it he did, more demonstratively than any predecessor or successor, during a tenure that was slightly longer than Walker's and no less memorable to his charges or important to the product they crafted.

Like Walker and McLendon before him, he had come up out of Texas, a long, lean, sandy-haired lad of twenty-two, rough as a cob and eyes filled with wonder at the city's thrilling waterfront and elevated trains and soaring new towers and newspapermen who wore hats and carried canes. His family, German pioneer stock, had settled in Texas in the 1830s; his father, by choice an itinerant schoolteacher with a passion for Shakespeare and by necessity a railway mail clerk, was killed accidentally in the Houston yards when his son was fifteen. His mother died the next year, and from then on the boy was something of a loner. He worked his way through the University of Texas in five years and served, as Stanley Walker had, on the *Austin American,* where he learned never to whistle in the city room or steal the pastepot off someone else's desk. He also discovered that he preferred editing to reporting despite the anonymity and his lack of fluency at writing headlines, an essential skill for a deskman on a small daily. "It's a gift," he would later remark—one so elusive for him that when laying out the *American* front page, he would give preference to stories for which headlines came readily to his mind.

In New York, he wrote his way onto the *Tribune.* First he put in a year as a reporter on the *Bronx Home News,* a sort of farm club for the major-league papers in town. It was a loosely edited sheet carrying as much news about people and events north of 110th Street as its constantly changing cast of reporters could grind out on the busy morning shift. Afternoons, they were free to pursue feature stories downtown and jobs on the big papers. Engel landed on the *Telegram*—"one of the worst papers in the world at the time," he would say of it—as a rewriteman. Required, with two or three colleagues, to turn out the bulk of the copy for the paper's endless edition changes, he learned speed and finesse and the fine art of cosmetic journalism; he covered the Hall-Mills murder trial by rewriting the wire-service accounts all afternoon. Meanwhile, he stalked Stanley Walker for a job on the rising *Tribune* and in 1927 was taken on, the tallest man in the city room at a slightly hunched and awkward six-foot-four, with arms and legs so gangly he did not quite know how to arrange them. He would put in a dozen years, the last five of them in charge of the city desk at night, before winning the city-editorship, which he considered the best job on the paper.

He worked at it with rare devotion to the ideal paper he wanted the *Tribune* to become. Like Walker, he was primarily an energizer of talent, but he was a more exciting, hectoring taskmaster and more openly competitive with the *Times,* which he knew the *Tribune* would never outman but could damned well outwrite and outedit. His moods pervaded the city room. "Engel was so dedicated to the product," recalled Robert J. Donovan, who joined the staff as a city reporter two years before Engelking's promotion, "that he affected everybody's life on the paper."

He would come in every morning, looking all cloudy and frozen, with an unlit cigar jammed in his mouth and the front brim of his big slouch hat folded back Texas style to add to his immensity, and he would put one foot up on his desk, on which that morning's paper would be spread, and start turning through it slowly, looking for gaffes, circling questionable items, making a note of what stories to follow up on, and occasionally bellowing a phrase or two of admiration. His booming praise, though, could be as embarrassing as his wrath. And his wrath could be terrible indeed. The telephone was a particular target of his

NEW YORK

Herald Tribune

THE "DINGBAT," *the complex allegorical device depicting antiquity on the left and the progressive American spirit on the right, first appeared as part of the front-page logotype on April 10, 1866, the twenty-fifth anniversary of the* Tribune's *founding, and remained there for the succeeding 100 years of the paper's life. The significance of the time shown on the clock remains a mystery.*

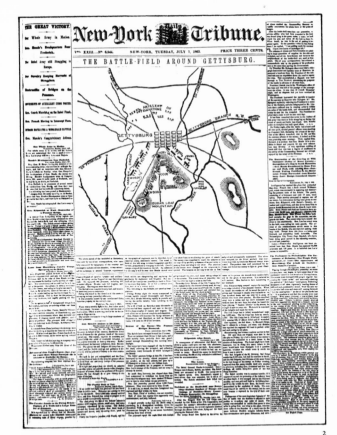

4

5

FDR'S FIRST RE-ELECTION,

issue of November 4, 1936

HORACE GREELEY, *founder and editor*
of the New York Tribune, *ca. 1865*

THE
NOMINATION

LAMPOONED *candidate Greeley rejoices* (right),
*at the news of his nomination for President by the
Chicago Democratic convention in 1872.*

GREELEY'S FARM *in Chappaqua, N.Y.* (below),
from a Currier & Ives drawing of 1872

JAMES GORDON BENNETT (above left), *founder and
editor of the* New York Herald, *drawing from a photograph
by Mathew Brady, and his son and successor as* Herald *publisher,
James Jr.* (right), *from an engraving by A. H. Ritchie*

CONFEDERATE SYMPATHIZER *Bennett is attacked
in 1860 cartoon (below).*

"Good, my lord; what is the cause of your distemper?". . . . .
"Sir, I lack advancement.   **SHAKESPEARE**

TALL TOWER, as the ... building on Park Row ...own, rose 260 feet and was ... only to the Trinity Church ... Wall Street as the highest ...re in New York when it was ...ted in 1875—a striking ... of self-confidence by the ... new owner and editor, ...aw Reid (inset), pictured ... his days as a Civil War ...ondent.

17

16

ABSENTEE OWNER *Reid was in his prime as a diplomat and political figure when this photograph* (right) *was taken in 1897; his wife, Elisabeth Mills Reid* (below), *whose family's fortune sustained the* Tribune *for seventy-six years, is shown in a portrait by Laszlo de Lombos, ca. 1920.*

EER WOMAN *Helen Rogers, ca. 1905 as*
ary to Elisabeth Reid and later (ca. 1920)
g transatlantic voyage with her husband, Ogden
Reid, Tribune *president from 1912 to 1946*

21

20

POLITICAL FOES *of the paper, Eleanor Roosevelt and New Y*
Mayor Fiorello La Guardia, were nevertheless pleased to particip
in the Tribune's *annual forum, directed by Helen Reid (center).*

23

THE DOMINANT FORCE *on the business side of the paper,*
Mrs. Reid (above) concentrated her efforts on advertising sales.
After her husband's death, she deferred increasingly to William
E. Robinson (left), *who served as advertising and business*
manager and then publisher of the Tribune.

25

GREAT CITY EDITORS *of the* Tribune: *Stanley Walker* (left), *who served in that capacity from 192 to 1935; his fellow Texan, Lessing Lanham Engelking* (below left), *1939–1946; and Joseph C. Herzberg* (below), *1946–1952*

26

GENTLE SATIRIST *H. T. Webster,*
Tribune mainstay, created Caspar
Milquetoast, "The Timid Soul."

NO
LOITERING

MR. MILQUETOAST SHIFTS
FROM FIRST TO HIGH

© 1936 N.Y. TRIBUNE INC.

29

28

THAT COMPASS
DOESN'T POINT THE WAY
I WANT TO GO.
CHANGE IT.
NOW!

F.D.R.

SUPREME
CONGRESS

FAVORITE TARGET *of political*
cartoonist Jay Norwood Darling, who signed
his work "Ding," was President Roosevelt,
here needled for his 1937 plan to pack the
Supreme Court.

GENTLEMANLY *George A. Cornish, here shown in the* Tribune
city room, was the paper's top-ranking editor from 1940 to 1959.

31   32

INTELLECTUAL *leadership and progressive political influence
on the* Tribune *were exercised from the mid-'Twenties to the
late 'Forties by (from left to right) chief editorial writer Geoffrey
Parsons, literary editor Irita Van Doren, and foreign correspondent
and editor Joseph F. Barnes.*

34

"THE BABE BOWS OUT," *the Pulitzer Prize–winning photograph*
by Nat Fein, poignantly captured Babe Ruth's final appearance at Yankee
Stadium in June 1948 without showing the subject's face.

35   36

SPORTSWRITING *was lifted to new levels of literacy and elegant*
craftsmanship by sports editor Stanley (The Coach) Woodward
(left) *and Walter W. (Red) Smith* (right), Tribune *columnist for*
more than twenty years.

37

DARING AND DEVOTION *marked the comb correspondence of Homer Bigart* (left), *two-time Pulitzer winner, as he covered the Pacific theater in World War II, and Marguerite Higgins* (belo *pioneer woman war correspondent, shown in September 1950 during the Korean conflict.*

WASHINGTON BUREAU *chiefs Robert J. Donovan* (left), *regarded as the ideal* Tribune *reporter—fast, accurate and lucid—and Bert Andrews* (below), *who played an active role in the Hiss-Chambers affair.*

39

41

40

POLITICAL PHILOSOPHER *Walter Lippmann, shown not long before he joined the* Tribune *in 1931.*

42

CULTURE CRITICS *John Crosby* (above left),
who wrote on radio and television, and Walter Kerr
(above right), *on the theater, set high standards for
critical writing in daily journalism.*
POLITICAL-SOCIAL SATIRIST *Art Buchwald*
(right), *soon after he began working on the paper's
Paris edition in 1948*

SITES IN *temperament*
ersonality, the brothers Reid
he third and final generation
r family to head the
ne. Whitelaw (Whitie),
, served as president from
o 1955; Ogden (Brown),
from 1955 to 1958.

LAST PRESIDENT *of the* Tribune, *lawyer-financier Walter N. Thayer* (left), *hired in turn Robert M. White II* (below), *an affable small-town Missouri publisher, and John L. Denson* (below left), *the intense former editor of* Newsw[eek] *to energize the paper editorially.*

47

49

LAST EDITOR *James G. Bellows* (at left, top), *in the* Tribune *composing room with John Hay (Jock) Whitney, who owned the paper from 1958 until its death in August 1966. Feature writers Tom Wolfe* (left) *and Jimmy Breslin* (above) *broke fresh ground in daily newswriting during the paper's last three years.*

EDITORIAL HIGH COMMAND *during the* Tribune's *innovative but doomed effort to survive included (from left to right) editor Bellows, editorial page chief Raymond K. Price, Jr., managing editor Murray M. (Buddy) Weiss,* New York *magazine editor Clay S. Felker, associate editor Richard C. Wald, and editor-in-chief/publisher Whitney.*

fury; angry, he would slam it down loud and hard, or, angrier still, chop off its cord with scissors and hurl the receiver into the trash basket, or, at his angriest, just rip out the whole damned contraption. At least once he threw a chair surprisingly far across the city room. Staffers he could paralyze with a single hard look, and when in a less punitive mood, he was adept at needling his prey, like the time reporter Leonard Ingalls spelled a man's name three different ways in the same story and Engel sniped, "Thanks for giving us a choice." Or he could be clumsily playful, like the day when Otis Guernsey, Jr., a fledgling reporter and the only one tall enough to look Engel straight in the eye, showed up in a spanking new seersucker suit and the city editor announced to the room, "Well, I do believe Mis-ter Guernsey has come to work today in his pajamas." His sallies and outbursts were never meant to be personal; he hollered at everyone democratically, including on occasion his superiors, and without malice. But his abusiveness got out of hand now and then, and staffers learned to keep their distance when he was in an explosive mood. After it passed, he was likely to be apologetic in private to those he had flogged in public. Some would not take the bullying and talked back, like rewriteman Maron Simon, a sturdily constructed Vanderbilt University graduate, who one evening while Engel was still night editor handed in a story that set him off on a tirade. "What the fuck does this thing mean?" the Texan growled. "Why don't you write the god-damned thing right?" and on and on. Simon said nothing and remedied his copy, but on his way down to dinner, Engel followed him out to the elevator and made sounds meant to placate. Simon did not respond, and Engel soothed on, but Simon remained tight-lipped. Finally Engel asked, almost plaintively, "You aren't mad at me, are you, buddy?" to which Simon said quietly, "Don't ever talk to me that way again or I'll knock the shit out of you, big as you are." Engel would later make him day city editor.

Behind the bluster lurked affection he worked to mask until the growls became habitual and, to those who knew what prompted them, almost appealing. "He was my terrifying, godlike teacher—he scared me to death but I loved him deeply," Margaret Parton wrote of him. Fendall Yerxa, a strapping veteran of four years in the Marines and future top *Tribune* editor, was no less frightened upon encountering Engel in his last and most irritable year in the job when "he tilted his huge frame back on the rear legs of his battered wooden chair, hurled his cigar butt across the room, and shouted your name as if it were an obscenity. I never realized until after he left the city desk what a shy, gentle person he could be." Otis Guernsey perhaps best explained the esteem with which the city editor was regarded by his abused legion: "He taught all the young men on the staff that this was an honorable profession, not one for hacks, and that they should think well of themselves for performing it." Walker, in his very different way, had tried to teach them the same lesson, but fewer of his pupils stuck with newspapering.

Engel's differences from Walker were more important than their similarities. Their polar-opposite temperaments were the most obvious contrast, but if Engel could be faulted for his volatility and a certain sullenness, he surpassed his predecessor in the depth and complexity of his concern for the news; he grasped issues that bored Walker and approached their coverage more analytically. He became an expert on municipal affairs, and his love for New York far outlasted Walker's. The latter went home to Texas to stay; Engel, after 1938, never went back.

As a mentor, he preached absolute honesty and accuracy in rendering the news—he was obsessive about small errors of fact that suggested sloppy habits of work and thought by a reporter—for it was in details that the truth about an event or a man's character might be revealed if you were trained to spot them. In a 1933 book review for the paper, he cited with admiration a reporter's acuity in noting that the gangster Al Capone appeared in a Chicago court without garters to prevent his socks from drooping; too few newsmen, Engel wrote, understand that sometimes "the little thing is the big thing."

When a major story broke, he was incomparable at scanning his reporters' copy for both the big and the little things, as he did in objecting to the lead on the *Tribune*'s account of the Hartford circus disaster in early July 1944. Working with wire-service copy but relying more heavily on the phone reports of the paper's three legmen on the scene, rewriteman M. C. Blackman had begun this way:

> HARTFORD, Conn., July 6 — At least 139 persons, most of them children, lost their lives here this afternoon and 224 more persons were injured in a fire that raced in less than ten minutes through the nineteen tons of canvas in the main tent of the Ringling Brothers and Barnum & Bailey Circus.

With his stickler's eye, Engel noted that Blackman had the circus name correct: the first "and" spelled out, the second an ampersand. But something struck him wrong as he kept fussing with the sentence. "Just a damned minute," he said. "What's this 'less than ten minutes' business? Nobody's going to believe a fire swept all the way through and destroyed the big tent of the circus, with that many victims, in that short a period."

"It happened," Blackman said. The wire services had hedged on the time element, but the *Tribune* reporters had checked it with survivors, plenty of them, and "I believe our guys."

It was Engel's business to be less credulous. "How could it happen?" he asked. "Was the canvas coated with gunpowder?"

"Almost," said Blackman, called Inky by everyone on the paper. The tent had been waterproofed with a solution of paraffin melted in gasoline, he explained, and was highly inflammable.

Engel's eyes widened. "Can't we say something of the sort in the lead to make the ten minutes sound reasonable?"

"I don't want to play it up," Inky explained. The only source for the paraffin-gasoline mixture was the mayor of Hartford, from whom *Tribune* reporter Ted Laymon had extracted the exclusive report, and since five circus officials were already under arrest on a manslaughter charge and their approval of inflammable waterproofing was likely to make the circus vulnerable to yet more millions in liability claims, the paper was better off to tread lightly, Blackman thought. Engel concurred but changed the "in less than ten minutes" to "with incredible speed" and told the rewriteman to elaborate a few paragraphs below and attribute the information to the mayor. No other paper had anything on the waterproofing angle until the second-day stories appeared and picked up the *Tribune* report, which proved to be correct. The circus paid heavy damages and its officials went to jail.

Attribution of material vital to a story was a cardinal element in the Engelking canon of journalistic ethics. Nothing riled him more than sources who declined to be identified but let reporters give the substance of their remarks or quote nameless "officials." Reader confidence, he felt, required names and titles; anything less constituted slipshod journalism. "No more quotes from anonymous fence posts," read the notice he once posted. He taught integrity not by proclamations but by affirming acts. Saks Fifth Avenue, a prominent *Tribune* advertiser that catered to the same carriage-trade clientele as the paper, once tried to block the report of a shooting in the department store by a berserk customer who claimed he could not find a satisfactory necktie. Someone had phoned in a tip to the paper about the incident, but crime reporter Walter Arm was confronted with denials by store and police officials until a precinct sergeant whom he had befriended in his district days slipped him a note saying that the fix was in. "I know," said Engel when Arm told him back at the office. "They tried to put one here, too, through the advertising department." Then he gave the reporter his grimmest look and ordered, "I want you to start the story with the store's name. I don't mean in the first sentence—I mean the first words."

Much less of a writer than the facile Walker had been, Engel would stew and fret over copy that he thought needed to be crisper and more vivid. Once he pondered a laborious Board of Estimate story on city finances and boiled its lead down to the simple statement that the body had met ". . . and nibbled at the 1937 budget." If he had ever composed a manual on newswriting, its first precept would have been: "The right verb is the shortest path to maximum impact." He was open to the colloquial but cautious about its use. When a reporter turned in a story using the word "boondoggle," then a new entry in the political lexicon, Engel chased all over town after him to learn its precise meaning. He kept learning as well as teaching. And if he sacrificed income to follow his calling, as every teacher did, it was worth it to him.

Early in 1940, Wilbur Forrest wrote to Laurence Hills that Engelking had reorganized the city staff "and is plastering the Times daily. Our coverage is far superior" and was recording ten to fifteen exclusives a day under Engel. That was the same Wilbur Forrest who not long before had wanted to take the *Tribune* out of competition with the *Times* "and maintain our newly gained journalistic individuality." But there was, and would remain, only one real basis for comparison of the *Herald Tribune*'s performance as a news disseminator and selling medium—and that was the trouble.

II

While the managing editor was ultimately answerable for everything in the paper and the city editor controlled the bulk of its staff-produced contents, the operational responsibility for getting the *Tribune* out on time and in pleasing condition belonged to the night editor. He was the glue that held the whole works together; after the managing editor went home, it was his paper. He could do anything he wanted with it—alter the makeup, change headlines, rewrite stories, whatever news developments dictated, in his judgment. From 1935 to 1961, the night editor of the *Herald Tribune* was a mysterious little one-eyed man whom half the staff hated but who everyone agreed was a mechanical wizard.

His name was Everett Kallgren, but everyone called him the Count—or, in direct address, just "Count."* A less lordly fellow would have been hard to invent. Slightly built, pallid, and baldish, he looked like a dwarf jeweler with his small, even features and rimless glasses as he hovered over piles of page proofs, humming "Jesus Loves Me" or some other spiritual when he was not making snide cracks about the incompetence of the help, his own night desk crew excepted. He had lost one of his eyes climbing a tree in childhood, but nobody in the office was sure which was the glass one. Because he was known to harbor in his locked desk a collection of pornographic magazines and obscene, or at least suggestive, pictures taken by *Tribune* photographers, the story circulated that the Count was something of a voyeur in his off-hours, and if you could ever catch him after a protracted session of telescopic peeping out of his Essex House apartment, you would know at once from its telltale bloodshot condition which was his good eye. Every night he ate alone at Longchamps— none of Bleeck's conviviality for him—and every night, it was said, his meal consisted of steak and potatoes, because of some dietary deficiency. A bachelor till late in life, he was anything but a fashion plate, favoring cheap brown suits —at least they looked that way on him—and yet he could afford to live in one of the city's most fashionable residences and in 1940 bought the gold-painted Lincoln Zephyr that had been a showpiece of the Ford Motor Company exhibit at the just concluded New York World's Fair.

Count Kallgren's job was to impose quality control on the complex mosaic

* None of the more than two hundred former *Tribune* staff members interviewed for this book could even hazard an authoritative guess about the origin of Kallgren's nickname. The most often cited theory was that he had a drop or two of noble blood somewhere back in his Swedish ancestry.

that coalesced each night after the managing editor's late-afternoon conference laying out the front page. Aside from the sports, financial, women's, cultural, and editorial pages, which were self-governing, all news copy flowed to the night desk from its originating city, cable (for foreign news), or telegraph (for national news) desks. The Count and his assistants checked stories and heads for accuracy, clarity, duplication, and logical placement in the paper by related subject. His news judgment was rated high and corroborated nightly by the *Times*'s play of the day's stories when its first edition reached the *Tribune* city room. Often, though, Kallgren would concede a misplay and alter the *Tribune* layout to conform with the *Times*'s, only to discover when the late city edition arrived that the *Times* had done likewise; respectfully following each other's judgment, in other words, the two papers would reverse their play of the same story. A more important task for the night desk was to make sure the *Tribune* "recovered" swiftly on stories in the *Times* it had missed altogether and that Kallgren judged essential for inclusion.

The Count was at his best, though, not when he was worrying about the *Times* but when coping with major late-breaking news that required him to pull the paper apart and remake it under severe time pressure, as he did the night of August 31–September 1, 1939, when Hitler's troops swept into Poland and launched World War II. Deftly manipulating a string necklace that he used instead of a ruler to measure the length of typeset stories, he would relish making a series of split-second decisions that might have slowed a more reflective man. Without any higher education (though his brother was dean of Colgate University), political preference (so far as anyone in the city room knew), or apparent intellectual curiosity beyond the best bets at the racetrack the next day, he came as close as any man in the profession to its ideal of clinical objectivity in evaluating a news story. He was a marvel at condensing; he could take a soggy seven-take piece on a real estate scandal that he had to bump for a breaking story and reduce its essence to a long caption under the accompanying photograph. The Count's first maxim of editing-under-the-gun was "There's no story that can't be cut." His other two were "There's no problem that can't be solved" and "Our only rule is the rule of common sense," and he would recite them with what veteran *Tribune* copy deskman Lorimer Heywood characterized as the Count's "old-maidish schoolmarmism."

His technical virtuosity, when in high gear, was astonishing. One-eyed or not, he could spot faster than anyone else an extra one point of leading—1/72 of an inch of white space—that a printer had inserted where it did not belong. His greatest gift was as a headline writer. The surest measure of the seriousness and thoroughness with which a newspaper was edited in the pre-television age was its headlines. They set its tone, its standards for precision, its formality of language. Did they accurately encapsulate their stories so that the reader knew which were important for him to pursue and which he could skip, confident that he had absorbed their gist? Or did they forfeit all nuance for shopworn phraseology that happened to fit the allotted space? Did they use slang and contractions and abbreviations, out of either laziness or a wish to be instantly comprehensible even at the price of stooping to vulgarity? A *Herald Tribune* headline was required to fit tightly into lines of equal length, but its elegant Bodoni typeface consumed more space and its individual characters were more irregular than the less attractive types in the *Times* and were thus harder to compose. The Count was a zealous guardian of their fitness, often bouncing headlines back to their authors on the copy desk with a snide criticism scrawled alongside in red. Did they convey the point of the story or had the writer reached down to the third paragraph for the idea that his headline stressed? Or was the head right in its emphasis and ought the story to be changed around to conform? When a head came up in proof from the shop and was too long or too short, he would caution the deskman who wrote it to "Watch your count!"—so constant an admonition that some came to believe it was the origin of Kallgren's nickname. For all his insistence on meticulous fit and meaning, he also wanted the heads to be alive and inviting. Forced to grind them out by the dozen, copy editors were occupationally prone to settle for the routine. Kallgren's night desk tried to add spark without cheapening the product. Thus, an obituary headed "Heroic Navy Chaplain Dies at 58" when it crossed under the Count's eye would be pegged instead to a quotation in the story and wind up reading: " 'The Bravest Man I Ever Knew,' " while a dull statistical piece comparing the dangers of smoking to those of inhaling New York's polluted air would be topped: "You Can Quit Cigarettes / But You Can't Quit Breathing."

The Count's mastery of his craft made him impatient with the underskilled, and the press of the clock often precluded his explaining what was wrong with heads he chose to change with apparent arbitrariness. His conduct at times ranged from waspish and insensitive to rude and autocratic, and his shattering comments and unexplained alterations had a particularly demoralizing effect on the copy desk and its chief, Allan Holcomb, who was as dedicated to his work as the Count and personally attached to the men arrayed around him on the big horseshoe desk. Kallgren's sadistic nature struck even at copyboys, whom he would typically instruct to bring him three-eighths of an inch of copy paper and then browbeat if the stack proved fractionally off. "He was mean to those powerless to fight back," thought Stefan Kanfer, a *Tribune* copyboy who rose to become a top editor on *Time* magazine. Others, like copy deskman Alden Whitman, who switched to the *Times* after nine years on the *Tribune,* felt Kallgren judged a man by his work and justly harangued those found wanting.

Off the paper, almost nobody knew who he was. But his handiwork was amply recognized. The Ayer Cup, awarded annually for typographic excellence among American newspapers, was presented to the *Herald Tribune* eight times and the paper was one of three honorably mentioned in twelve other years during Kallgren's twenty-six-year tenure as overseer of the paper's appearance. Only the *Times* came close to that record.

III

Without explanation Joseph Barnes was ordered to close up the *Tribune* bureau in Moscow at the end of 1938 and move forthwith to Berlin to cover the Nazi regime. One of the unhappiest years of his life followed. Hitler's totalitarianism was far more hateful to him than the Soviet brand, and Germany's territorial demands were threatening world war. The Berlin censors, moreover, were more painstaking than those in Moscow, although, oddly, in neither authoritarian state did he find that news of any real importance was suppressed.

On the night when word came that Stalin had signed his cynical peace pact with Hitler, Barnes was in a Berlin tavern with fellow correspondent William L. Shirer, then connected with the Columbia Broadcasting System. The two would remain close friends for thirty years, and Barnes would eventually edit two of Shirer's books, including *The Rise and Fall of the Third Reich.* No moment of their relationship was more indelibly marked in Shirer's memory than their post-midnight exchange in the Café Taverna in early August of 1939. "Joe was absolutely stunned," he recalled. "Everything he'd believed in about Russia went up in smoke. Till then he had been very sympathetic to the Soviets and their aspirations"—a sympathy Shirer thought went beyond a dreamy socialist utopianism. "It took a long time for him to become disenchanted," and in Shirer's opinion, Barnes continued to believe, even as John Price did on the *Tribune* foreign desk, that World War II had been ignited by capitalist interests.

The outbreak of war and the torrent of news from abroad convinced *Tribune* management that the paper had to have an experienced student of global affairs as foreign news editor serving over the no longer robust Price, who, while a highly competent technician, was untraveled, unsophisticated, and by the Reids' measure, politically unsound. Joe Barnes was the obvious choice. Polished, informed, intellectually and physically attractive, he was soon taken up by Helen Reid and Geoffrey Parsons as their special newsroom favorite. Price, anything but resentful, noted in his diary that Barnes had the knack of making anyone with him feel he was Joe's best friend. Barnes was a hearty partaker at Bleeck's, drinking well into the night with, among others, Ogden Reid, back from his drying-out interlude but far from cured. After a session together, Joe would pass Ogden in the office hallway the next day and get hardly a nod of recognition. Even so, some envious detractors thought him too haughty by half and too busy buttering up management.

The more closely Barnes was in regular contact with the owners and other editors, the surer became his perception of the newspaper as an institution beyond the operating control of its proprietors. "The only distinctive feature of the mass media in an historical sense isn't the technology that makes them possible," he would suggest in his oral memoirs, "but the fact that they are collaborative, collective enterprises." He came to believe that "the soul of a newspaper" was rarely shaped or created by the owner; indeed, owners were "illiterate in terms of craftsmanship. The number of big American newspaper owners today who could perform any operation on the paper except sweeping the floor . . . could, I think, be numbered on the fingers of both hands." The reading public he found to be "equally incompetent, untrained, uninterested." Newspapers were shaped, rather, by a handful of editors who over time, over drinks, in stand-up deskside huddles, on the fly down a corridor, at postmortem dinners and a thousand other close encounters, developed a kind of shared set of values and outlook toward life that had little to do with politics, economics, or philosophy and almost everything to do with craftsmanship. The day's hurtling events were sifted, collegially, and life's jumble was given structure, pattern, and priorities for posterity's future inspection. That posterity would care, they never seemed to doubt.

Reflectiveness was not unique to Barnes on the *Tribune* foreign desk. John Price, who still did the rewriting and copyediting of the overseas file, was also a thoughtful man worried about the fallibility of his craft. In a 1939 talk before an editorial workshop run by the New York chapter of the Newspaper Guild, Price confessed his belief that "all newspaper stories more than five lines long —and most of those shorter than five lines—are ludicrously full of errors." There were multiple causes, but mainly he faulted the shortage of competent practitioners and of time to check information carefully within the daily production cycle. Even if these shortcomings were remedied, the fact remained that "the chief sources of news are governments and politicians. . . . [A]s I see it, every good editor and every good reporter is engaged in an unending struggle to sift out, as well as he can, the news from the propaganda. I am afraid most of us do it badly." The challenge was compounded with regard to foreign news, he said, because the main conduit of overseas developments—the Associated Press—had tie-ups with semi-official foreign news services and thus appeared too ready to accept government versions of events and interpretations of policy. Price viewed the AP as unduly conservative in its entire approach, an outgrowth of its cooperative ownership by the biggest and richest American papers. The United Press, while more independent, was also far less reliable than its chief rival, he had found, and prone to sensationalism and fakery.

Having isolated what he regarded as the prime task for journalistic vigilance, Price raised a related issue that would eventually affect his own professional fate —how to handle news *about* propaganda. Suppose, he posited, a major Nazi newspaper ran an editorial attacking President Roosevelt and his Cabinet as "Jewish Communists" in the most unrestrained language. Is that news? Should a report on it be printed in American papers? "My own inclination has always been to do so," Price said, "but I am sometimes overruled, and I can see good reason for it. One must remember how many people accept whatever is printed as gospel truth."

The expanded implications of the question have grown far more troublesome with the growth of mass media, especially television. Is it not the responsibility of the press, when conveying charges by public officials—or anyone else, for that matter—to make an accompanying effort to assess them for accuracy or to obtain a rebuttal? Even minimal standards of fairness would seem to dictate such an obligation, but in the hurry of the news day, with the shortage of personnel to check out the facts involved, such niceties have more often than not been disregarded, and the ruling "fact" of the story becomes the charge itself. The line between authentic news dissemination and propagandizing by governments, self-seeking individuals, and special-interest groups has been badly blurred by the intervening half century of refinements in public-relations techniques and TV newscasts on which ninety seconds constitutes major play. What can happen when irresponsible charges are given currency in the press without being adequately challenged would be grotesquely apparent eleven years later with the emergence of Senator Joseph McCarthy. Among his ambivalent accomplices would be the *Herald Tribune*; among his victims, John Price.

IV

In his youth, Rufus Stanley Woodward narrowly escaped blindness. Surgery spared him his central vision, but his peripheral sight was never again very good, and he wore thick glasses the rest of his life, except when playing guard on the football team at Amherst; to succeed at the sport, he groped a lot. It helped that he was very large—six foot three and 225 pounds. Even so, his football career left him a physical wreck requiring five bone operations in later years to keep him ambulatory. His Amherst line play also helped turn him into the most knowledgeable student of the game in American journalism and probably the profession's best sports editor. These distinctions never seemed like much to Stanley Woodward, but during the twenty years he graced them, the *Herald Tribune*'s sports pages achieved an unmatched level of pungent literacy.

Graduating from college in 1917, he served in the merchant marine and at the end of the war joined the news staff of the *Gazette* in his hometown of Worcester, Massachusetts. Three years later he was city editor. When he moved to the *Boston Herald* as a writer in the 'Twenties, Woodward turned back to his love of sports, which was generating keen reader interest in that age of spectacle and flimflam. Writing about football, his specialty, had become a kind of verbal spasm featuring florid phraseology and wallowing in jargon. For a time Woodward pumped his own football stories full of hyperbole, as his editors expected, until shame and experience toughened him and he decided the best way to report was to become "an expert of such thundering complexity," as he later wrote, "that no one would have any idea what I was talking about. . . . I saw things in games that nobody else saw. Leaving symbolism and nature completely out of my work, I became unique as a football writer. Like the others, I didn't know what I was talking about, but I showed it in an entirely different way."

Having learned the game in the trenches, he knew the importance, for example, of the direction and velocity of the wind on the playing field; such things sometimes mattered a lot in a fair evaluation of the play. Most of all, he knew it was a game that, for all its fierce combativeness, was supposed to be fun and, with its complex formations and colorful personalities, offered more variations for lively coverage than any other sport. On the *Tribune,* beginning in 1930, he wrote about it with wit, carefully avoiding chauvinism or excessive reverence. He once called the Holy Cross–Boston College game "the annual Jesuit hair-pulling"; a strong Princeton squad became, for him, "Old Nassau's Implausible Brats"; and the University of Miami eleven he tagged "Old Sun Tan." Even after twenty years, he brought verve to an account of the most ordinary game, such as the October 19, 1947, meeting between Holy Cross and an injury-wracked Harvard team, which prevailed, 7–0:

> . . . Once the Harvards got ahead, they returned to their role of self-defense in their own territory. They confounded the enemy with the weirdest, most inconstant and upsetting defensive patterns ever devised by the existentialistic [Coach] Harlow. They played eight-man lines, nine-man lines, five-man lines. They blew their back-ersup, charged in parabolas and S's and generally loused up the honest, straightforward and powerful Holy Cross attack.
>
> The Crusaders of Worcester were in Harvard territory frequently, but in the horrid dream world of last-ditch Harlow defense they bogged down and couldn't move.
>
> It was a dull game. . . .

He always brought a pint of something alcoholic with him when covering cold-weather sports and approved of taking a few nips to remove the tension and fine edge of self-consciousness before writing—he did not speak of staying warm; too much booze, though, and "you dull your sensibilities and erase your self-criticism."

In 1938, to the joy of most of his colleagues, Woodward succeeded the fatuous George Daley as sports editor. Almost as tall as Engelking and nearly as cantankerous when displeased, he was a massive man of bull-like strength, with short hair, a strong jaw, and clipped New England speech that criticized tartly and praised generously. When intoxicated or on the way, he could become a cussed, stumbling giant. His staff was not eager to displease him. What he demanded of it was the same crisp, clear prose he himself wrote, avoidance of the hackneyed, and exceedingly spare use of superlatives. One autumn Sunday about noon, *Tribune* sportswriter Harold Rosenthal was alone in the sports department when Woodward phoned in from Lenox Hill Hospital, where he was recuperating from surgery. Rosenthal naturally asked him how he was feeling, and Woodward said, "Terrible—I've just been reading your story of yesterday's game." Rosenthal had included a sentence that began: "The second half saw the tide of the game turn . . ." A period of time cannot "see" anything, Woodward remonstrated, adding, "Do it again, and I'll jump out the window."

He waged a constant battle against abuse of the stylistic freedom that the sports page offered writers. Heightening this tendency to overembellish, Woodward suspected, was evidence that sports were "of extreme interest to the immature," who swelled the ranks of job applicants to the point where he had eight candidates for every staff opening. Because those without experience in other aspects of reporting proved to be the most prolix and idolatrous sportswriters, he prescribed two or three years' training on cityside first, so that his people were newspapermen before they were sports enthusiasts. Even then, the freedom to create their own style so overwhelmed newcomers to the sports page that they tended either to gush Niagaras of purple prose or to lapse into a coma; usually it took them six months, he calculated, to get used to "the hooray and hubbub" of the sports world. And if they were good, they were likely to be a different sort of newsman—"more volatile, less profound, less socially conscious, more nimble-witted, less thoughtful, quicker in the fingers, lighter of touch, better dressed, better known, better paid, more indispensable and less valuable than the city staff man."

The most expert and treasured contributor to the sports page, in his view, was the baseball writer. The circulation people had told him that 25 percent of the paper's sales were attributable to the sports pages, which was why they were allotted as much as 15 percent of the total daily news hole, and the biggest reader attractions were the coverage of, in order, baseball, football, and boxing; thus, a good baseball writer was "worth more to a paper perhaps than anyone else." Since baseball had the longest season of any organized sport, its writers came to know even the most subtle aspects of the game. Woodward expected his baseball writers, indeed all his writers, to indulge only in "exact adjectives that reproduce the scene." Action verbs were better for telling the story economically and well. The superior writer should say, for example, whether the run-scoring single had been "lined" or "blooped" into left field. Hanging around the clubhouse or traveling with teams on the road for the 154-game season and its spring-training prelude, baseball writers inevitably got to know more about the professional and private lives of their subjects than they could begin to write about. Woodward worked to see that his people were not excessively kind in print to the players and their owners and stressed that even if the club management picked up their travel expenses, the deal was between the paper and the ball club—the writer was in no sense a guest of the team and therefore its captive.

The same went for other sports. Rosenthal, a *Tribune* sportswriter for more than thirty years, never forgot the time he was being exceedingly careful and polite on the phone with Madison Square Garden officials while trying to dig out the status of a pending middleweight title fight between Sugar Ray Robinson and Rocky Graziano that was imperiled by the latter's having allegedly slugged a military policeman. Woodward had been hovering nearby during the exchange, and when Rosenthal hung up, the sports editor said, "Don't be so fucking obsequious next time you talk to them." Rosenthal was struck more by the style than the substance of his upbraiding. "It was the first time I ever heard those two words together like that. He was tremendously overqualified for his job—he should have been running the newspaper."

Indeed, some of those closest to Stanley Woodward attributed a latent bitterness in him and his occasional terrible outbursts of temper, generally aimed at those he loved best, to a self-contempt for devoting his career to the chronicling of games. He rarely directed the contempt at those he supervised. "He was a leader who commanded loyalties almost as fierce as the loyalty he gave," Red Smith said of him. Woodward shrugged off such praise. The most he would say of his own efforts was "Over the years I tried to write English and see that others did, too"—as noble an epitaph as any newspaperman could ask.

V

Not since Whitelaw Reid's efforts in behalf of his friend James Garfield in 1880 did the *Tribune* play as prominent a hand at kingmaking as in the presidential campaign of 1940. Indeed, no newspaper people may ever have exercised more decisive influence upon the nomination of a major party candidate than *Tribune* staff members did the year that Franklin Roosevelt outraged the Reids and all orthodox Republicans by daring to seek a third term in the White House. There was nothing surprising in the paper's fierce opposition to what it viewed, along with millions of others, as the incumbent's monarchical designs on presidential power, but its choice for a champion to dethrone Roosevelt was unlikely in the extreme: the man had never run for an elective office and, until two years before, had been a registered Democrat. Perhaps as interesting was the fact that the dashing Republican candidate the *Tribune* did so much to promote was engaged before, during, and after the campaign in an adulterous love affair with the literary editor of the paper. Everyone on the *Tribune,* from the Reids down, knew of the relationship, as did Franklin Roosevelt, but a generation would pass before any word would reach print even hinting at the true bond between Irita Bradford Van Doren and Wendell Lewis Willkie.

Willkie's political career was meteoric. The capitalist system has probably offered up no more qualified, articulate, or enlightened spokesman before or since in presidential campaign history. He had a large frame and large gestures, and his massive head seemed still larger for its thick shock of dark, often tousled hair. His voice was wonderfully sonorous, his smile captivating, his intellect as formidable as it was insatiable; he was a vital, incandescent figure at a time when the Republican Party lacked leaders of much wattage. Former President Hoover was discredited and cranky. The party's last nominee, Alfred Landon, had been overwhelmed in 1936 in the nation's biggest electoral landslide. The way was open to a fresh Lochinvar.

Willkie had been a highly successful trial lawyer in Akron for ten years and a director of an electric utility company in northern Ohio before being summoned to a Wall Street firm and named general counsel to Commonwealth and Southern, a utility giant with holdings spread from Georgia to Michigan. The public outcry against electric companies for allegedly extortionate rates grew with the Depression. Willkie, conceding some abuses and the need for a degree of governmental regulation of the industry, was handed the presidency of Commonwealth in 1933 at the age of forty-one and set out to revitalize it. He did so, pushing up the company's volume by 300 percent in a four-year span—a remarkable performance in a still recuperating economy. But the company's newly won prosperity was imperiled by the New Deal's huge Tennessee Valley Authority project, one of whose aims was to furnish cheap hydroelectric power throughout the same area served by a Commonwealth subsidiary, the Tennessee Electric Power Company. Willkie cried foul, and casting himself as the earnest David of free enterprise locked in combat with the Goliath of an oppressive government, he used every opening and platform presented to him through speeches, magazine articles, radio debates with federal officials, and extensive coverage in the press, with whose representatives he enjoyed an easy, bantering relationship. Willkie made good copy, and as he became a defiant voice against what he styled as the growing government peril to capitalism, his national fame spread. In 1938, Helen Reid had him speak at the *Herald Tribune*'s annual forum at the Waldorf, where he gave a beguiling performance. As a guest at the Reids' dining table, he met Helen's friend and confidante, Irita Van Doren, two years divorced from Columbia historian Carl Van Doren and by then a figure in her own right in the New York literary world. Willkie had never before encountered socially a woman who was his intellectual peer and at least his match for charm.

Born in Birmingham, Alabama, the eldest of four children, she was the daughter of a merchant and mill owner who moved his family to Tallahassee, Florida, where he was murdered by a fired mill hand when Irita was nine. She was brought up thereafter in reduced but comfortable circumstances by a mother who gave music lessons and sold preserves to make ends meet. By seventeen, Irita had completed Florida State College for Women and had her eyes opened to the wider world on a trip to New York with her mother and a sister. After obtaining a master's degree back in Florida, she returned to New York to pursue a doctorate in literature at Columbia, and she stayed the rest of her life.

Her aptitudes, it developed, were more social than scholarly; her dissertation topic, uncompleted by the time she married fellow Columbia graduate student Carl Van Doren in 1912, was "How Shakespeare Got the Dead Bodies Off the Stage." Equally merry and serious, she was an animated woman with sparkling dark eyes, a low, gentle Southern voice, a mass of soft pretty curls, and a slender figure even after bearing three daughters. Besides brains, warmth, comeliness, and gaiety, however, there was a vein of iron in her. She wanted to do more with her life than raise a family and serve as charming hostess to a widening circle of friends at their Greenwich Village apartment and the farmhouse she and Carl bought at West Cornwall in northwestern Connecticut. In 1920, she joined the advertising staff of *The Nation,* the liberal weekly on which Carl served as the literary editor, and three years later succeeded him in that position. Well read without ambition to become a writer herself, well connected with the rising generation of academics, she brought taste and an alertness to topicality to the editor's chair. Among the critical essays she edited for the magazine were those by Stuart Sherman, on the University of Illinois English faculty and an old friend of Carl Van Doren. When Sherman was chosen to edit the new literary supplement of the freshly merged *Herald Tribune,* he asked Irita to assist him. She remained on the paper thirty-nine years, all but the first two as literary editor following Sherman's death in 1926.

The job did not require the sort of pencil-editing skill by which a city-room deskman made his living. Most of the reviews in the Sunday book section were by professional writers not on the *Tribune* staff; Irita Van Doren's great gift was in enticing capable authorities, and often eminent ones, to undertake the largely thankless and ill-paid task of book-reviewing by making it as pleasant as possible. Only a few newspapers were sufficiently devoted to cultural developments to produce a literary supplement rather than a weekly book page or column covering a mere handful of titles, and only the *Times* and *Herald Tribune,* serving the nation's largest book market, attempted comprehensive coverage of serious new books. To be asked to review for the *Tribune,* therefore, bore a certain cachet, and Mrs. Van Doren brought grace to the wheedler's art. "I don't know whether it's your natural Southern sweetness," Lewis Mumford wrote back to her in accepting an assignment in July 1930, "or my professional respect for your skill as an editor, but I find you very hard to resist, and have almost given up trying to. . . ." She had a sixth sense about which titles would interest which reviewers, who harbored jealousy or a grudge against whom, and what tone and level of critical writing suited the readership needs of a metropolitan newspaper. She was receptive to bright new intellects eager to break into print, provided they could write accessibly; among her discoveries were Henry Steele Commager, a young instructor at New York University when he began reviewing for her in 1928, and Alfred Kazin, a raw City College graduate without academic credentials when he did his first *Tribune* piece in 1935. Above all, she avoided reviewers out to make their reputations by carving up those of others. If there was a weakness to her book section, it was in its civility and reluctance to pass a negative judgment. A certain lack of critical rigor resulted. But such a humane and genteel attitude made Irita Van Doren an immensely popular and sought-after figure on the New York publishing scene, then very much a gentleman's game. In 1936, she went on the board of *The American Scholar,* the journal of the Phi Beta Kappa society, and two years later began to preside as mistress of ceremonies over the popular monthly book-and-author luncheons sponsored by the paper at the Waldorf and featuring informal addresses by leading writers of the day. Her marriage had ended by then, but her career, wide circle of acquaintances, and resources of character assured her emotional stability. Quick to laughter, quick to tears, constant in devotion, she was someone people confided in, and none did so more than Helen Reid.

The two had much in common, particularly their escape from provincialism and respectable poverty, ambition decisively enhanced by their marriages, and a softness of manner that veiled a powerful will beneath. Helen, with all the trappings and some of the substance of power, was locked into a difficult marriage that provided decreasing companionship with the passage of years and increased responsibilities requiring high discretion. There were few to whom she could turn in trusting confidence. Irita Van Doren, her own professional position established, was one. The friendship won Irita considerable personal power and wide latitude for her social views, political preference, and literary taste. "She could be very influential when she wanted to," said Joe Barnes's wife, Elizabeth, of Irita. "She had a first-class mind, the necessary background to form a point of view, and the charm and articulation to promote it without getting anyone's back up. She understood the uses of power."

The mutually magnetic and instantaneous attraction Wendell Willkie and Irita Van Doren felt for each other was not surprising. She found him "terribly attractive," remembered her daughters Barbara Klaw and Margaret Bevans, in their early twenties at the time. A student of history, he had "an exaggerated respect for writers," so that the public perception of their relationship was that she initiated him into her world rather than the other way around. He provided her with hints, though, of the world of wealth and power in which he normally dwelled, like the time he visited Irita's country place in West Cornwall and proudly exhibited a freshly received trophy of his five-year battle with the federal government—a check for $8 million, the first part of the $79 million settlement he had won for the sale of Commonwealth and Southern's Tennessee subsidiary. He was a virile, larger-than-life emanation from a social stratum utterly different from hers, where nobody had any money to speak of.

He was also married, at least nominally. Willkie had outgrown his devoted spouse, Edith, whom he had married when they were very young, but would not cruelly discard her. She lived with him in a fashionable Fifth Avenue apartment when Willkie was in New York, but he was on the road perhaps half the year and even when in the city often traveled without her. His rumpled good looks and driving personality won him what female companionship he needed, and while Mrs. Willkie knew of his dalliances, she recognized that she was not in a strong position to prevent them and had no desire to ruin his career so long as the outward forms of their marriage were preserved. That had been no problem while Willkie's affairs were not serious; his attachment to Irita Van Doren, however, proved to be different.

She stimulated his intellect no less than his heart, becoming his literary adviser, helping edit his speeches and articles—a role that nicely explained the increased time they passed together. "Irita directed Wendell's immense energy and broadened him," said William Shirer, one of a number of leading foreign correspondents, including John Gunther, Vincent Sheean, and Joe Barnes, with whom the lovers were on close terms. By 1939, Willkie was staying weekends at her Connecticut farmhouse and accompanying her frequently to the Reids' for dinner. That summer, they spent a week together at Dorothy Thompson's Vermont farm. Irita encouraged him to think more about his future in political terms and challenged him to work out his views on major issues so that he might express them more forcefully and confidently in his writings and speeches. His devotion to her grew; on the road, he called or wired her every day.

Believing his private life nobody else's business, Willkie took minimal precautions to cloak his feelings for her. He would take a taxi from the city or reserve a roomette on the train when he visited her in the country, but there was nothing furtive about his visits to her apartment on West Seventy-seventh across Central Park from his own. "They were not terribly circumspect," said Barbara Klaw. "He was in and out of that house a great deal." Those closest to and fondest of the pair took it for the deep love affair it was and no little fling. At the Reids', "it was not a topic up for discussion," recalled Whitie Reid, by then a reporter on the *Tribune* but still living with his parents. At the paper, where Willkie was often seen, the relationship was an open secret, although Van Doren almost never mentioned it to her associates. Nor did she push Willkie to divorce his wife and marry her. She knew that as his presidential bandwagon began to roll, divorce and remarriage would doom his ambitions, which she had done so much to stimulate.

He was a dark horse for the Republican nomination, but despite his lack of political experience, Wendell Willkie looked like an increasingly attractive prospect. He had stood up to the New Deal in the name of free enterprise and took an internationalist view of American responsibilities abroad in light of fascism's conquests, favoring Roosevelt's call for a draft to prepare U.S. armed forces and the so-called Lease-Lend arrangement with the British to provide them weapons and supplies to stave off Hitler's gathering horde. Such a political creed won Willkie the fervent backing of Helen Reid, the two highly influential syndicated columnists she had enlisted for the paper—Walter Lippmann and Dorothy Thompson—European-oriented chief editorialist Geoffrey Parsons, and Ogden Reid himself, who took a back seat to no one in his antipathy for the newly rampaging Hun; for Ogden, it was as if World War I had never ended. Other key anti-isolationist Republican opinion-molders soon joined the Willkie camp, most notably Henry Luce and his Time Inc. properties and the Harvard-educated Cowles brothers, John and Gardner, whose big pictorial magazine, *Look,* and dominant newspapers in Iowa and Minnesota gave Willkie a cheering section in the heartland. In the spring of 1940, with his wife, Edith, dutifully at his side, Willkie barnstormed for delegates. But his thoughts were never far from Irita. "ON THIS EXHILARATING OHIO SPRING MORNING AN INDIANA BUCCA-

NEER GREETS A FLORIDA SCHOLAR AND SAYS THE HELL WITH ILLINOIS," he wired from Columbus. From Santa Barbara, he wired Irita that he had stopped by Osborne's bookstore, where the clerk handed him a copy of the *Tribune*'s literary supplement and "WE HAD HEATED DISCUSSION SHE INSISTING THAT IT WAS THE BEST BOOK REVIEW PUBLISHED IN AMERICA. I OF COURSE DID NOT AGREE. I AM LEAVING TONIGHT FOR SAN FRANCISCO AND WILL SEE YOU FIRST OF NEXT WEEK. MUCH LOVE." His campaign aides were privy to these messages and their unmistakable implication and feared their damaging exposure, but the press corps, especially the New York chapter that was familiar with the Van Doren affair, never wrote about it.

Whatever chance Willkie's two chief rivals for the nomination, conservative Senator Robert A. Taft of Ohio, and the young racket-busting New York district attorney Thomas E. Dewey, may have had soon faded. Taft's diehard isolationism was totally out of keeping with the national mood on the brink of war. And Dewey seemed lacking in the kind of experience necessary to deal with the world crisis.

On June 27, 1940, the day balloting for the party nominee began in Philadelphia's Convention Hall, a copy of that morning's *Herald Tribune* was placed on every delegate's chair by the same managers who arranged to pack the visitors' galleries with crowds chanting in practiced cadence, "We want Willkie!" The *Tribune* declared in an editorial at the top of page one headlined "Wendell Willkie for President" that the big man from Indiana with the wayward forelock had the extraordinary abilities that the times demanded and had demonstrated his capacity to unite the country during his pre-convention campaign that "has been the despair of the experts." It ended:

> ... A man of the people, a Middle Westerner who knows all of America, a Democrat for many years, a Republican by choice, he seems to us heaven's gift to the nation in its time of crisis.

From a remote balcony seat, Irita Van Doren watched as the convention designated Willkie its nominee on the sixth ballot. She had known that the campaign would shove her into the background of his life, but she had urged it on him, had helped vitally in shaping and polishing his public character, and now she thought as she left the auditorium and its last echoing cheers that she had lost him forever.

If his campaign had gone better, she might have. Late in August, word reached Franklin Roosevelt that Republican operatives had obtained copies of letters that his running mate, Henry A. Wallace, had once written to a White Russian mystic. "Dear Guru," they began, and their purloiners were reportedly showing them to friendly newspaper publishers. In tape-recorded remarks that surfaced forty-two years later, Roosevelt speculated to an aide on the possible need to fling mud back at the Republicans by pointing to his opponent's romantic involvement: "Awful nice gal, writer for the magazine and so forth and so on, a book reviewer. But nevertheless, there is the *fact.*" One "very good way of bringing it out," Roosevelt mused, would be to point out what he perceived as the similarity between Willkie's convenient display of his wife for public consumption during the campaign and a $10,000 payment Jimmy Walker had made to his estranged wife to accompany him to Albany during the trial that would strip him of his New York mayoralty. *"Now, now* Mrs. Willkie may not have been *hired,* but in effect she's been hired to return to Wendell and smile and make his campaign with him. Now, whether there was a money price behind it, *I don't know,* but it's the same idea."

Roosevelt's own, far more closely guarded relationship with Lucy Rutherford Mercer no doubt made him reluctant to attempt blighting his opponent with scandal. Willkie's campaign, moreover, was not going well. He was widely seen as a "me, too" candidate who shared the President's main goals of social and economic justice and differed only in the particulars to achieve them. And in the rough going, he yielded to the imploring isolationist wing of his party and painted Roosevelt as a warmonger, declaring that "we shall not undertake to fight anyone else's war. Our boys shall stay out of Europe." The flame of idealism had been quenched by expediency. Two of Willkie's most ardent and powerful *Herald Tribune* supporters defected from his cause. Walter Lippmann, who had been an informal adviser to the Willkie camp, dropped out and remained neutral in his columns on the choice that faced the voting public. Dorothy Thompson went further. Distressed by the turnabout in Willkie's handling of the war issue and the global peril of fascism on which she had written so stirringly for years, she went to see Roosevelt and came away reassured that, as she told her readers, although Willkie was "a very good human being," the President "has assets on his side that nobody can match."

Willkie was philosophical about the blow, telling Van Doren that Thompson's true motivation had been "to ride with a winner." At the *Tribune,* Thompson's painful reversal was viewed as treachery. Its editorial page assured readers that the paper disagreed with her. A column following up her Roosevelt endorsement with reports she claimed to have from Europe that the Axis powers favored Roosevelt's defeat was suppressed by the paper, and no effort was made to curb attacks on her by the paper's old-line conservative columnist, Mark Sullivan. After the ballots were counted—Willkie won 6.5 million more votes against Roosevelt than Hoover had in 1932 and 5.5 million more than Landon had in 1936 but still lost the popular vote by ten percentage points and was crushed in the electoral vote—Helen Reid urged Dorothy Thompson to write on nonpolitical subjects; she did not add "or else," but that was the implication, since the columnist's contract was coming up for renewal the following March. Unapologetic about her switch from Willkie, denying that she had ever promised Ogden Reid that she would be blindly obedient to the *Tribune*'s editorial stands or keep silence if she disagreed, Thompson rejected Helen's pointed suggestion and said that unless she remained free to say as precisely as she could "what I think upon any issue I am afraid I won't be able to write at all." Then she compounded her sin by arguing that Roosevelt had in fact been the true conservative candidate because he had recognized the need for "far going social and economic readjustments at a time when the alternative might have been chaos and revolution." There was no softening on the Reids' part. Late in January, Thompson wrote Helen Reid, "I think we shall be happier divorced. . . . I feel an unbridgeable hostility in the Tribune. . . ." Her forced resignation from the paper and its syndicate sent her career into a tailspin; her most important work, as watchwoman in the night of Europe's dissolving liberty and American indifference to it, was behind her.

Willkie's close relationship to Van Doren and the *Tribune* family resumed during the four remaining years of his life. When reporters needed to reach him for a comment at night, they sometimes apologetically telephoned her apartment. It was there that after his 1942 global trip accompanied by Joe Barnes, who served as his interpreter in his meeting with Stalin, he wrote *One World*, his *cri de coeur* for international justice, the end of colonialism, and strengthened democracy's coexistence with Communism; winning the war was not enough. Irita pencil-edited the manuscript, her daughter Margaret, who lived across the hall, typed it, and Simon and Schuster, where Margaret's husband, Tom, worked, published it. One of the most influential books issued in wartime America, it sold two million copies and greatly enhanced Willkie's reputation as a visionary statesman. His party, however, found him too outspoken, too independent, too internationalist, and turned elsewhere for leadership.

Among the consoling notes Irita Van Doren received after Willkie's death in October 1944 was one from Dorothy Thompson, who called him "our vital conscience" and added: "You did so much to create Wendell—or rather to help him create himself—and all that is part of you and of America, forever."

VI

While the New York–dictated economy drive was keeping other *Tribune* correspondents in Europe anchored to their bureau desks, a twenty-six-year-old Yale dropout was frantically shuttling around the hottest spots of a continent on the brink of conflagration. Bright, tightly wired, socially proper Walter Boardman Kerr had prepared for college at Andover and been forced by the Depression to quit New Haven after one year in the Yale Class of 1934. Now, having worked a couple of years as a reporter on the *Post-Standard* in his native Syracuse and three more in the *Tribune* city room, he was covering the *Anschluss* in Vienna and appeasement in Munich and meantime dashing back to Paris to act as the second man in the bureau while awaiting yet another crisis assignment. "I'd worry all the time about just getting the story," he recalled. "I was young—I didn't know the language in most places—I didn't know my way around these

cities—and I couldn't afford to be beaten. I had to get up early and stay up late."
And all the while he felt shadowed by what was coming. "You had the feeling
that there was an avalanche rumbling above you and you couldn't do anything
about it."

Kerr was answerable to Laurence Hills, who found him "a first-rate chap
whose ideas on news . . . are excellent and he works well under my guidance."
The admiration was not mutual; Kerr saw Hills for what he was—a sour
pinchpenny who turned the heat down when he left the still busy office at 6 p.m.
on winter evenings and a political blind man who was still writing to New York
in the spring of 1939 that "things may right themselves when a real stabilization
of Central Europe's affairs occurs. . . ." The outbreak of war and the improved
economic outlook at home eased the pinch on *Tribune* foreign news, and when
Stalin launched a bullying war in the winter of 1939 to push back the Finnish
border, too close for comfort to Leningrad, the unenviable assignment of covering it fell to the paper's youngest European correspondent.

The real story was not who would win the Russo-Finnish War but how good
was the Red Army, said to be poorly equipped and disciplined. To cover the
conflict, waged in a dead-white winter, Kerr had two prime assets besides his
wits. The first was a greatcoat and fur hat, purchased in Stockholm en route to
the front and inhabited almost continuously for the four months the war lasted.
They did nothing, though, for his feet and hands, which he protected by keeping
constantly on the move during weather that varied from ten to forty degrees
below zero. Kerr's second blessing was the *Tribune*'s newly installed foreign
editor in New York—Joe Barnes, who understood the difficulties of coverage
and filing in far-off, hostile places and doggedly tracked him down in obscure
towns and villages from which he had arranged for his war correspondent to
report by means of telephone recordings.

Kerr returned to France later that spring in time to witness, with only a
handful of other American correspondents, the fall of Paris and with it the
suspension of the *Herald Tribune*'s fifty-three-year-old European edition. The
belief had persisted in Paris that the Germans would beat themselves into a froth
against the Maginot Line, which had not been extended to the sea in the
confidence that the Belgians would put up the same fierce resistance they had
in the first war. But the Germans confounded those expectations by charging
through the tangled Ardennes, and the rout was on. French censorship prevented the story from being fully told either in the Paris papers or by the wire
services, and the European edition of the *Tribune* appeared now with large
blanks where sensitive material had been excised. As the war news worsened,
Kerr found Hills wandering befuddled around the office—a man broken in
health and spirit, his once robust form shrunk, eyes blinking continuously
behind his thick-rimmed glasses. Early in May, after the Germans plunged into
the Low Countries, the same Hills who had toadied up to tyranny for nearly
a decade wrote a front-page editorial bearing his initials and titled "Hitler's
Latest Victims." "It is useless to blind one's self," it began, "to the deadly

dramatic import of yesterday's developments. . . . Nothing can possibly justify Germany's latest invasion. The excuse offered is more hollow than even in the case of Norway. . . ." He ended by stressing the contempt that Germany held for genuine neutrality and, in a plea to his native land similar to the one that James Gordon Bennett, Jr., had made twenty-five years earlier under almost identical circumstances, urged America to put aside useless diplomatic protests and act quickly to stem the Huns' advance.

As his world collapsed around him and he acknowledged the fact, Hills's tragedy was played out for the whole *Tribune* office to see. Even those who had held him in lowest esteem viewed him now more with pity than censure. "Was he that much different from many men who think of themselves before all else?" asked Kerr. "Some of us get away with it. Some of us die before we realize how wrong we have been—the lucky ones. Larry Hills knew before he died that he had betrayed every honorable instinct he started out with."

His cancer incurable, Hills resolved to stay in Paris and try to strike a deal with an occupying German government which he thought might treat the paper as if it were in the same category as the American embassy. His assistant, Hubert Roemer, wrote New York disapproving of such a plan. "I do not believe that we would be permitted to issue anything except a handbill for the official German news agency," he said. Hills had told him, he added, that he knew of no better way to end his career than to be put before a German firing squad, but the real point was that any effort by the *Tribune* now to keep functioning in Paris, "instead of leaving with the rest of the papers and keeping its independence on untaken French soil," would surely imperil its future after the end of the occupation. Ogden Reid settled the issue. As the Germans swept forward, he cabled Hills on June 7, 1940: "DO NOT BELIEVE HUNS WILL REACH PARIS THIS CENTURY BUT IF THEY SHOULD YOU AND MRS. HILLS SHOULD BE ELSE-WHERE. WE WILL NOT PRINT PROPAGANDA AND UNDER INVASION COULD NOT PRINT NEWSPAPER."

Reluctantly, the Paris *Herald Tribune* staff departed, most of it waiting until the Germans were nearing the gates of the city. The last issue, a two-page flyer with the back side blank except for some small ads and the masthead, appeared June 12. The only byline in it belonged to Walter B. Kerr, who wrote of the flight of the Parisians and the movement through the city of many from surrounding areas:

> . . . They came in long straggling parades, farmers from the country, taking away their families and things on those old-fashioned French hayricks, drawn by three horses in single file. These ricks went along in groups of ten, twenty, and thirty. The parades entered the city from every road on the right bank of the river and crossed the bridges toward the south.
>
> . . . Where they are going and what they expect to find when they get there are unanswered questions. Th[ere] cannot possibly be enough food for them all, even for a few months. . . .
>
> These people are taking things with them that they could never use and the stuff

is weighing them down. I have seen old men and women carrying baggage that would tire a strong man after a while.

The number of push carts is as astonishing as it is tragic, but you cannot push a cart all the way to Bordeaux or wherever it is they are going. . . .

It was from Bordeaux that the holdout Americans on the paper got the last boat home. Managing editor Hawkins, a Briton and therefore an enemy national, made it out just in time; Bugeja, the Maltese deskman, and others hid out with the Maquis in the French underground. The only American newsmen on hand to watch the Nazis goosestep down the Champs Elysées were representatives of the AP, UP, and *Chicago Tribune,* and Larry Hills, little old Sparrow Robertson, the Paris *Herald Tribune*'s ungrammatical gossipist, and Walter Kerr. Hoping to send out an account of life in the dimmed City of Light under the Nazi heel, Kerr remained for a dispiriting month, but the Germans had brought American correspondents with them from Berlin, including the *Tribune*'s Ralph Barnes, shepherded their every move, and censored every dispatch. There was no point in staying on. Kerr was in the defunct *Tribune* office clearing out his things when the Sparrow, as everyone called the tiny octogenarian, came by close to dawn to say goodbye to his sole remaining "old pal." Kerr was grateful and at the end urged Robertson to take a taxi home to avoid getting picked up for breaking the German curfew. "Get away from me with that *stuff,*" the Sparrow replied. "These swine don't worry me. I go anywhere, anytime." And for a while, he kept defying the Germans, making the rounds of the few night spots still open, writing up his copy as always in his little office cubicle, and dropping it on the empty city desk for transmission to the silent presses below. Finally he stopped and just sat alone in the dark, cold, empty office. He and Hills died the next year.

When Kerr reached neutral Lisbon from Paris, he sent home two long, graphic dispatches that censors on both sides had prevented him from filing before. Each got prominent play on the *Tribune* front page. The first told of life in occupied France, "an economically twisted country, with its millions of people broken in spirit and doped with propaganda," and of its gray-clad conquerors, their equipment, personnel, and insignia everywhere as they worked "night and day for the coming attack on England." The Germans, he wrote, occupied all the hotels in Paris, their officers operated out of all the public buildings, and their aircraft dove on the Arc de Triomphe for practice and skimmed the rooftops for fun.

And yet there is an undercurrent of resistance. Some weeks ago posters were displayed urging the people to have confidence in their German friends, that they had been betrayed by their leaders and now were being fed by German soldiers. The penalty for defacing one of these signs was death, but I do not know of one of them in Paris that has not been ripped and torn.

The second dispatch, which French censorship would have killed, was yet more affecting. It began: "It now seems quite clear that there never was a battle of France, a battle for Paris, or whatever it was called in the days before the country's collapse." From the breakthrough at Sedan near the Belgian border, French morale was shattered and its army was done for as a competent fighting force. "That is the unpleasant truth that Frenchmen are beginning to understand." Carefully citing first-person observations and talks with refugees from the front, Kerr demythified the belief that the French troops "were simply driven back by a highly mechanized army that rolled forward on a wave of flame and steel." There were no battlefields, he reported sadly—only flight and humiliation.

> It is not easy to explain why all this happened. Many factors are involved: eight months of idleness after September [when the war had begun in Poland]; German propaganda that England was the real enemy, not France; a censored press that was not allowed to hint that anything was wrong; the unwillingness to defend a city and thereby cause its destruction; no training to withstand air and tank warfare; not enough radio equipment and so easily severed communications; not enough planes; too little mobile artillery; an ineffective 25-mm. anti-tank gun; the average French soldier's belief that he was to fight in the Maginot line and not away from it; the rude awakening.
>
> And the result was a feeling among the men that they had been betrayed. They still think so.

VII

As Walter Kerr headed west out of Lisbon for home, he crossed paths with another young *Tribune* man passing through the Portuguese capital on his way to the hellfire threatening to engulf all of Western Europe. With German shore batteries and planes pounding English Channel ports, it would take Whitelaw Reid, twenty-seven-year-old first son of Ogden and Helen Reid, eleven days by freighter out of Lisbon to reach Britain. When the ship finally put in at Bristol, he was stirred by the sight of "this brilliant green grass on either side of us as we moved up the estuary." He was moved, too, by the immense resolve of the people to resist the invasion they feared to be imminent that he immediately encountered at the dock, where the customs inspector who passed him into the country said he had told his daughter that she was to stick a broom handle into the neck of the nearest beer bottle, break off its end, and "make sure any Nazi who came through the door got it in the face."

More poet and printer than journalist, Whitie Reid had a keener eye for natural imagery and the character traits of the individual than for affairs of state and conditions afflicting society as a whole. His instincts and responses were those of the esthete, not the analyst; there was a dreamy, almost remote quality about the graceful young man with the whippet-lean body that took the form of a self-effacing shyness. It was as if he knew he had been born to rule, and while he would not shirk the responsibility, the prospect did not fit well. His was not a forceful personality, for while the features of his long, narrow head more closely resembled his mother's—the fair complexion, light brown hair, strong cheekbones, and especially the startling pale blue eyes—he was more his father's son in temperament and aptitude. Kind, gentle, decent, he was no stuck-up brat, and though quite serious about life amid the setting of wealth and the surround of important people he had been born into, there was nothing bookish about him. His considerable athletic skills, unlike those of his more powerfully constructed father, depended more on fluency of movement and coordination than strength. He was, even as a lad, a superior sailor, horseman, and tennis player, and while a strong swimmer, he lacked his father's endurance in the water.

Early on, even as he loved the man, Whitie Reid recognized his father's shortcomings, manifested for the boy especially in his parent's inability ever to do things on time. "After waiting an hour and a half—or two hours and a half —to go riding with him, I wasn't in a very good mood and it made me at best snippy with him," he recalled. "This kind of waiting occurred, too, in the case of shooting—when you wanted to get out early for the first flight of duck—or fishing or anything else. As a result, the fun of doing things with him became increasingly marginal, and I wound up doing more with H.R., even in the area of sports." For much of his life, on the paper as well as in outdoor sports, his mother would substitute for his father as director and companion if not guide and model.

From the first day he slid down the pole in the *Tribune* pressroom to the reel room below at the old Nassau Street building, "it was a foregone conclusion that I would go on the paper," said Whitie. He did not have a vote in the matter, really, any more than in the decision that he leave the progressive Lincoln School in New York and with it a future as a promising figure skater for a more traditional, rigorous, and socially suitable education at St. Paul's preparatory school, where hockey was what you did on skates. It would be like that much of his life: artistic gifts and sensibilities were dismissed as sweet but irrelevant to the true manly business that needed conducting.

At Yale he majored in sociology rather than history on the premise that "it was a better way perhaps of learning about the elements I'd have to deal with" on the *Tribune*. But he was in no hurry to begin the strictly vocational aspects of his training. He joined the freshman glee club instead of heeling for the *Yale Daily News*, and while he later worked diligently on the college paper and became its assistant business manager in his senior year, journalism by no means consumed all of his extracurricular enthusiasm. He lettered on the swimming team and played for the 150-pound football squad, performed for the drama society in several minor roles, participated in the political union and student government activities, and joined the Delta Kappa Epsilon fraternity—in short, he was an all-around good fellow and highly active solid citizen, though not really a big man, on the New Haven campus. Summers he would play and travel rather than work on the *Tribune*. Even after graduating in the Class of 1936, he exhibited no impatience to begin at the paper. Instead, he and six classmates went to Norway to pick up a forty-nine-foot schooner, which they sailed home on a circuitous and sometimes perilous seven-month voyage. More months passed while he carefully organized photo albums and movies of the great adventure and tutored his little brother Brownie; the *Tribune* could wait for the second Whitelaw Reid.

The grooming began slowly and at the bottom. Perhaps because he seemed to lack his father's interest in the news and his mother's brass at salesmanship and promotion—or because they truly wanted him to master the intricacies of how the paper operated—his initial training was in the mechanical departments, where his esthetic bent was evidenced in concern with graphics. He was sent off to the Rochester Athenaeum and Mechanics Institute to learn how to set type and pull apart and reassemble a Linotype machine: manual rather than mental training. His father's hospitalization for alcoholism and the surrounding financial crisis at the paper in the fall of 1937 drew Whitie back to New York, and after further technical instruction at the Mergenthaler Company in Brooklyn —the same company his grandfather had played so pivotal a role in establishing —he finally went on the *Tribune* payroll in the wait-order room, where all advertising matter was processed. His job was to trail the ads from type specification down to the final stereotyping stage, where he had to make sure the text and illustrative portions of each plate were properly shaved clean of surrounding metal so that no unsightly ink patches would appear on the printed page. He marveled at the finicky persistence of Lord & Taylor, a blue-ribbon advertiser, which ran the most chic and stylized ads of any department store, insisted its instructions be followed to the minutest detail, and required the paper to provide it proof after proof until perfection befitting a slick fashion monthly had been obtained; they got their money's worth. Whitie moved on to the production manager's office to learn the overall work flow through the plant and be indoctrinated into the properties of newsprint, the single costliest item in the budget. Mingling freely among white- and blue-collar personnel, he was struck by the high dedication of the *Tribune*'s work force. It was not unlikely, of course, that those workers functioned with still more dedication than normal upon detecting in their vicinity the unmistakable upper-class intonations of the boss's son.

When they finally put him in the newsroom, Whitie Reid proved to be a better than competent writer with a decided flair for the descriptive. He did features mostly—pieces on the Chinese New Year, skiing in Central Park, the development of sulfa drugs—and Engelking, his wrath discreetly muzzled for a change, warmly encouraged him. He might have gone on to become a solid cityside reporter but "I was convinced the impending Nazi invasion of England would be the biggest story since the coming of Christ," and, exercising the prerogatives of proprietorship, he won overseas assignment without the prior local newsgathering experience required of others.

Bottom member of the five-man London bureau, he was overwhelmed by the human drama on all sides of him. "They were totally unrealistic about their strength," he recalled of a people whose army had been narrowly rescued from oblivion at Dunkirk a few months earlier, whose tattered air arm had been removed to the Midlands beyond easy range of the Luftwaffe that had pounded its coastal fields into inoperability, and whose civilian population had been so ignorant of the fury of modern warfare that one woman Whitie interviewed in London told him she intended to tie a mattress to the roof of her car to deflect any falling bombs. Like everyone else on the staff, he donned a tin helmet left over from World War I whenever he went outside to cover the Blitz, which began that September. He shuttled between London and the Channel coast, gathering color stories on British morale through the ordeal. At Dover, Whitie took a room at the Grand Hotel to be near the expected invasion site and walked out on Shakespeare Cliff. The sky was filled with great barrage balloons that were often hit by lightning, and he could see the flash of guns on the Calais side and would hear the incoming whistle of the shells as they pounded the town. Undeterred by the destruction of a wing of his hotel, Whitie flew out on a 700-mile air reconnaissance mission along the German-held North Sea coast and another night rode in a Channel patrol boat with the full expectation of being blown skyward any moment by a mine. Part of his dispatch to the paper on that mission read:

> Flares over the French ports, appearing through field glasses as fiery spider webs, first indicated that the Royal Air Force was warming up to the attack. The flares lingered two minutes or more, pencilling trails of light across the water to the side of the trawlers. The whole stretch of water might have been a small Adirondack lake set glimmering in the lights of boat houses on the far shore.
>
> Searchlights shot skyward in a forest of beams. Anti-aircraft fire spat in their midst, and the diffused light of bomb explosions flashed with the intensity of sheet lightning. Now and then so-called flaming onions, seen exploding as twisting streamers of red balls, added to the color of the panorama.

"I was living on the edge of life," he recounted; the intensity of the experience surpassed that of even his own military service as a naval patrol pilot over the less perilous stretches of the Pacific a few years later. When he went home at the end of the year, by which time the choppy winter seas had all but ruled out a cross-Channel invasion of Britain at its most vulnerable, Whitie felt "a little as if I were deserting"—so much so that once back in America, he did not return to the *Tribune* but gave himself to lecturing, always a painful business for him, on the bravery of the British and the need of American preparedness. James Reston of *The New York Times,* who made several trips through the south of England with Whitie during the German raids, said of him, "I always found him a very shy but quite courageous young man."

That holiday season, while the British manned the last bastion of genuine democracy in Europe and the Germans intensified their firebombing of London, the *Tribune* ran an editorial titled "Dover Beach" after the Matthew Arnold poem. It was written by Walter Millis, who had joined the paper's editorial-page staff when Geoffrey Parsons took charge in 1924 and, over the thirty years he would serve the paper, demonstrated a skill unsurpassed among American newspaper editorialists to compose literate commentary of high emotional impact when the occasion demanded it. The last week of 1940 was such an occasion. Millis's first and last paragraphs follow:

> Christmas brought no respite, truce in the air brought no relief, to the armed men who watch on Dover's cliffs. Each moment of calm upon the Narrow Seas, each hint of mist, drifting across the waters that are England's slender moat, redouble the menace banking in the East.
>
> . . .
>
> But Dover Beach is not a military problem primarily. It is a problem in what men believe in, in how much they will stand, in whether they are overcome by the essential blankness of the external world or whether they are resolved to overcome it, to impress upon its pain and horror their own conviction, to wield their Bren guns not as the instruments of a shrinking defense but as the weapons with which they will shape their world to what they believe to be worth while. Such matters unavoidably escape the military expert. They are the larger part of what wins wars.

VIII

The resignation in the spring of 1941 of Grafton Wilcox, for ten years the stabilizing rudder of the *Tribune* news department, left the paper in an interlude of uncertainty at a moment of heightening global conflict. Wilcox's downfall was intestinal rather than alcoholic or professional in nature; there had been several bouts with amoebic dysentery and related gastrointestinal complications, aggravated by a belly bloated from too much beer, ice cream, and candy. And there was an emotional toll taken by tending to his wife, judged by those few on the staff who knew her to be eccentric if not certifiably unbalanced. Under Wilcox, the *Tribune* had accumulated a young, vigorous staff of editors and writers who made it one of the ranking newspapers of the world; it was imperative that his successor maintain that standard.

At such pivotal moments, Ogden Reid exerted the prerogatives of ownership. The choice of managing editor was his alone to make. He solicited the views of the four regents who operated the paper, but they were divided in their preference among the candidates, and so their counsel was effectively neutralized. His strong inclination was to promote from within the organization; internal morale would be hurt if he went elsewhere and thereby declared a shortage of homegrown talent.

The leading contender was Wilcox's senior assistant, the brusque but adept

Henley Hill, universally regarded in the city room as "a helluva newspaper-man," who had performed expertly as night editor before the job was turned over to Everett Kallgren. A nice-looking, two-fisted, sandy-haired fellow who dressed carefully and commanded decisively, Henley Hill lacked only one credential for the top news position on the *Herald Tribune*: he was not a gentleman. A womanizer and unsubtle about it, he showed up at sporty restaurants and leading nightclubs, where he performed suavely on the dance floor with women who were not precisely from the *Social Register*. "He didn't have Wilky's class," said Richard Tobin, summing up the staff consensus—and Helen Reid knew it.

A candidate who possessed Wilcox's stately bearing, and a far more dazzling intellect besides, was thirty-three-year-old Joseph Barnes, off to a strong start in the post of foreign news editor. He had, moreover, powerful sponsors in the *Tribune*'s highest echelon. Helen Reid, Geoffrey Parsons, and Irita Van Doren found young Joe Barnes a delightful companion. According to the testimony of Whitie Reid, Eve Peterson, who was Ogden Reid's personal secretary at the time, and others close to the family, Mrs. Reid and Parsons strongly urged the appointment of Joe Barnes as managing editor. He had youth, brains, talent, courage, and polish. But the managing editor's job was a far larger responsibility than foreign editor, and Barnes lacked seasoning. What he had instead and in spades was the same breadth of cultivation and savoir-faire that Parsons did—and that Forrest did not; plainly, Forrest's own influence would have been degraded by the elevation of an aggressively glib intellectual to the top news job. Forrest's opposition to Barnes's candidacy also reflected uncertainty about the foreign editor's ability to lead a newsroom that harbored some suspicions—along with envy—of his easy social access to the Reids and their circle. Beyond that, there was the matter of Barnes's politics. Disenchanted by the Stalin regime, he was still unapologetic about his fondness for the Russian people and their aspirations, and that made him a fellow traveler in the eyes of conservative staff members. He had lent his name, too, to the Newspaper Guild's continuing effort to organize the *Tribune*; his photograph and words of endorsement appeared at the head of a list of New York newsmen supporting the more militant slate of Guild candidates at the 1941 annual national convention. Such activism almost surely doomed Barnes's cause with the most conservative of Ogden Reid's close advisers, Howard Davis, who, according to his assistant, John Bogart, opposed the appointment of Barnes. Perhaps the fatal flaw in Barnes's candidacy was, ironically, the very factor that gave it greatest strength: Helen Reid's support. It was the kiss of death. Out of necessity stemming from the weakness of his character, Ogden had ceded to his wife working leadership of the paper, but he steadfastly drew the line of her decisive influence at the newsroom door. If Helen was for Joe Barnes, Ogden was against him, however attractive the fellow was.

Why not Engelking, then? The big Texan had breathed fire into the city staff even if he did it raucously and inspired dread at times. He would be a strong leader and exercise good news judgment, and his recent marriage to the daughter of veteran *Tribune* editorial-page writer William Houghton, Ogden's Yale classmate, had made him more socially acceptable. His emotional volatility caused concern, though, and it seemed imprudent to risk converting a highly effective city editor with a limited news range to the high command; Engel was a superb line officer, not a chief of staff. Stanley Walker, too, was available, but a string of setbacks, while probably all beyond his control, had tarnished his reputation; his day had passed at the *Tribune,* and the overseas orientation of the news would only have emphasized his limitations if he had been elevated to the managing editor's office. Everett Kallgren was also gifted enough to hold the job, but the quirky little night editor, for all his talent, did not fit the Reids' requirements; the Count bordered on the asocial and physically repulsive.

Ogden Reid turned his attention from this roster to one of the less voluble men in the city room. George Anthony Cornish, a courtly Alabaman of subdued charm, had been on the staff nearly eighteen of his forty years when he was called to the owner's office in January 1941 and told he had been selected over Henley Hill, the other assistant managing editor, to direct the news staff of the *Herald Tribune.*

He had never seen a copy of the *Tribune* before arriving in New York with two years of reporting experience on the *Birmingham Age-Herald,* a diploma from the University of Alabama, and the soft, smooth Southern speech that refined Northerners take as testimony of genteel ancestry. George Cornish's father, a farmer with a law degree, made his living as publisher of the weekly *Times* in the west-central Alabama town of Demopolis. Like many lads, George loved to hang about his father's place of work; he wrote small social items for the paper and, later on, editorials while attending the local high school. At the university at Tuscaloosa, he began with the ambition of becoming a lawyer, but the tug of the family profession proved too great; he worked on various student publications and discovered that editing suited him better than writing—"I was one of those countless people who want not to write so much as *to have written,*" he said. On graduating, he headed for Birmingham, Alabama's metropolis, and the *Age-Herald* with its staff of barely a dozen, editors included. Working seven days a week, noon to midnight on most of them, he covered every sort of local story, from service-club luncheons to murder trials to President Harding's visit to the city. After his first year, he also became night AP correspondent and got two whole paragraphs of his printed unchanged in the New York *World*; his destination in life was fixed.

When he reached New York in 1923, he landed a spot on the copy desk of the *Tribune,* anathema to Southerners ever since Greeley's antislavery crusades. But he worked his way up steadily, unspectacularly, from copy desk to cable desk, eventually to Sunday editor, then assistant *to* the managing editor, then assistant managing editor—safe, sound, solid George Cornish. He was pleasant and polite to all but rather on the impersonal side; some said he would have been perfect on the *Times.* If Henley Hill had lacked the social grace for the managing editor's job, Cornish was vulnerable to the charge of having too narrow a news background compared to Wilcox's; he had been an inside man his whole *Tribune* career and knew little firsthand about national or global affairs. But Ogden Reid, Bill Forrest, and Howard Davis thought he was just the ticket: urbane in an understated way, exquisitely diplomatic—he had never been heard to utter an unkind word about anyone—and a loyal organization man who had not solicited advancement. "Mr. Reid thought he had strong staying qualities," Eve Peterson recalled. Others sensed hidden depths to him, and if he lacked Wilcox's breadth of news experience, Cornish was far more au courant in the world of the arts, thanks in part to his wife, Constance, a former actress.

In designating him chief steward of the soul of his newspaper, Ogden Reid told George Cornish there were only three things he could not do on his own: add a continuing feature, like Lippmann or that Thompson woman; change the type style; or appoint a major editor or foreign correspondent. There were no further instructions.

The Cornish appointment shattered the career of Henley Hill, who lingered futilely for nearly a decade on the fringe of the newsroom, but it gave the *Herald Tribune* its ranking editor for the next twenty years. Essentially a stabilizing force and a master mollifier, Cornish would see the paper through its best days and darkest time. Six months after his appointment, Helen Reid let Bill Forrest know she thought the choice had been the right one.

PART THREE

1941-1958

Freedom of the press is guaranteed only to those who own one.

—A. J. LIEBLING, 1960

11

On Higher Ground

A century after its founding, the *Tribune* was hardly less embattled than it had been in the beginning. In its central precept—that liberty was the paramount democratic virtue and that equality of opportunity, not of attainment, was the highest ideal of social justice—the Reids' paper differed remarkably little from Greeley's. What had changed drastically was the role of newspapers as moral preceptors. Greeley had been pre-eminently a teacher, a reformer, and used the paper as a vehicle for civic betterment; its distinction resided in the rhetorical fervor and relentlessly argued positions of its editorial page. By 1941, technology and social upheaval had dimmed the thunder of the *Tribune*'s editorial page, and most others. Its power to persuade had been overwhelmed by the rush and magnitude of events; public opinion was shaped far more now by the writers and editors who created the front page, imposing their judgment on the undifferentiated mass of information that flowed into the office almost instantaneously from all over the world. Radio and motion pictures exercised their more elemental tug at the mind and heart strings. Within the paper itself, columnists like Lippmann and Thompson, with their own individual voices, had reduced the relative importance of the editorial page.

Still, what the *Herald Tribune* editorials said mattered. Not only had its institutional continuity been strengthened since the merger by the improved quality of its staff and its broadened, far less partisan treatment of the news, but the imperial presidency of Franklin Roosevelt cast the paper in the role of spokesman for the loyal, responsible opposition. It stood on recognizable ground. It did not indulge in the mad-dog fulminations of its party's extremists, represented by the *Chicago Tribune,* the other journalistic claimant to be keeper of the true Republican conscience. Shrill fundamentalism would no longer serve to purvey truth and wisdom in a society struggling to reconstruct itself without resort to revolution or abandonment of its founding values. To orchestrate its institutional voice under such circumstances, the *Herald Tribune* had the ideal man.

Geoffrey Parsons was cordial, learned, balanced, highminded, and seasoned with a dash or two of earthiness. He was also a master office politician, foxy enough to regulate the key, tempo, volume, and length of vibrato of the paper's six or seven daily editorials without degrading their anonymous authors. Quite the opposite. By writing few of the pieces himself, he preserved the power of supervisor over the output of his half a dozen junior colleagues. The chief editorial writer was not *primus inter pares*—he was the president of a most exclusive club of essentially like-minded gentlemen, and he set the rules and procedures. At the *Times,* the editorial writers sat around the table and talked things out, striving for consensus and tending toward homogeneity in the final product. At the *Tribune,* with very rare exceptions, there were no meetings. Instead, Geoffrey Parsons appeared around eleven each morning in the large single room the editorialists shared and moved discreetly about the clubhouse for a little chat at each desk. Head cocked, he was an intent listener on his rounds and decided who would write about what for the next morning's paper after he got the drift of each man's thinking. No one, of course, was required to write anything he did not believe. But if a writer's views were at too sharp a variance from Parsons's or failed to embody the paper's historic or current position on any subject, he would not be asked to write on it. More typically, the writer was invited to address dissenting arguments or mitigating considerations in his treatment of the topic so that even if his finished editorial did not precisely or even predominantly reflect his own sentiments, they were prominently represented in it. The editorial was not, after all, a form of personal expression. The writer's ego and uniqueness were subsumed in the institutional nature of his craft. He labored under the likelihood that neither fame nor riches would be his lot in life; rather than aspiring to a declaration of individuality as the reporter or columnist or author of books did, the editorial writer derived fulfillment as an exalted ventriloquist: his was the voice of the *Herald Tribune,* exponentially larger than any he could cast on his own. Every day, moreover, he was writing on important subjects, often touching on the fate of millions if not mankind itself; what bylined writer could say as much? Nor was the microcosm ignored; *Tribune* editorial writers were encouraged to seize on minute or apparently trivial topics if they inspired useful thoughts. "Nothing human is alien to an editorial page," Parsons taught; sometimes the not quite human would do as well, as in the handsome editorial tributes the paper paid to the racehorse Man o' War and the original Elsie the Borden Cow on their deaths.

Writing anonymously for Parsons's edit page had its liberating aspects as well as its compromises with the paper's institutional imperatives. He did not want the pieces all to sound alike and encouraged stylistic distinctions in the belief that such diversity gave the page character and prevented it from sinking into a formulaic singsong that was the greatest peril to its readability. At the end of each deskside mini-conference, Parsons was comfortably able to say to the assignee, "Well, anyhow, write it as you feel it." There was no noise, no acrimony, no jealousy in his club. Everyone went off to luncheon and ate heartily and spent the afternoon peacefully researching and writing, and when they were done, their offerings were placed, triple-spaced on yellow paper neatly folded in half with the reading matter showing, behind the inkwell on Parsons's desk for his calm inspection. It was all very civilized. And if a man's work did not suit, his offering was not slashed to ribbons or passed to other hands to recraft; Parsons kindly indicated the problems to the writer, who was invited to correct them himself. Parsons never berated one of his people for stylistic infelicity, believing that every writer "is himself and writes as God made him" and in deriding him the editor of editorials would "be destroying the only thing that can make [his] page come alive."

Parsons strove to make his page its liveliest on Monday mornings, when reader attention, he felt, was likely to be refreshed after a weekend free of toil. His other operating precepts were few but pointed. He favored catchy though not tricky headings and bright, grabbing leads for his editorials. There was no room in the well-composed miniature essay for a break in continuity, for digressions or charming irrelevancies, and its conclusion ought to leave the reader "completely conquered." Style and vocabulary might vary widely, but the reader must not be written down to. Fancy writing, though, availed little, and it was "fatal to pursue a metaphor for too long." Finally, time ruled art on a daily newspaper; the editorial writer was no freer than the police reporter to polish a gem that missed the deadline. Eloquence and profundity were too dear a luxury for historians on the run.

At its best, however, the *Herald Tribune* editorial page was unsurpassed in its contribution to the literature of journalism. Its best tended to come forth at moments of crisis, as in the subdued and therefore all the more powerful lead editorial on the morning of December 8, 1941, which began:

> In this solemn hour the first thought of every American will be of his country. "The drumming guns that have no doubts" have spoken. That union in face of peril, which was grievously lacking, is at hand. How to co-operate, what one can do to aid the flag that protects us all, becomes the instinctive thought of every citizen.

With the same nonpartisan allegiance to the President's stated policies against international tyranny that Parsons's page had commended throughout the long prelude to war, the editorial went on to note: "It had been the hope of all Americans that the liberal elements among the Japanese people might be able to restrain these reckless aggressors. Mr. Roosevelt and Mr. Hull deserve all

praise for their patient efforts to support these elements and preserve the peace."
Such generosity to the administration weighed heavily in the award of the
Pulitzer Prize to Geoffrey Parsons for the 1941 performance of the *Herald
Tribune* editorial page—"an outstanding instance," the citation remarked,
"where political affiliation was subordinated to the national welfare, and a
newspaper firmly led its party to higher ground."

II

In recognition of his credentials as the most broadly cultivated man on the
paper, Geoffrey Parsons served as the *Tribune*'s unofficial commandant of the
arts. In selecting critics, the Reids relied heavily upon his judgment—no small
matter in view of the *Tribune*'s historic leadership in journalistic coverage of
the American muse. With the demise of the *World,* no paper in the country
matched the *Tribune* for stringency of critical standards, quality of critical
writing, or range of critical assessment.

Few papers were even in the running for the distinction. Only New York,
the unchallenged cultural capital of the nation, provided enough activity in the
arts to justify a newspaper's employing a corps of fulltime critics. And only the
relatively well-to-do and educated readership of the *Times* and *Tribune* cared
enough about the arts to justify devoting substantial space to the papers' critical
departments on a daily basis. Of the two, the *Tribune* did it with more enthusiasm. The *Times* thrived on hard news; under Ochs and for several decades
afterward, it was squeamish about being judgmental. "Criticism was always
more of a chore than anything else for us," conceded Turner Catledge, a *Times*
managing editor for fifteen years, who faulted the *Tribune* for an elitist approach
to its arts coverage. The identical charge might, of course, have been levied
against the *Times*'s approach to its news coverage.

Of all the art forms, none is more difficult to comment on critically and
engagingly than music. Describing a new musical composition or a concert
performance that once given is gone forever—disembodied sensory phenomena
—is an elusive skill, a complex exercise in transforming sound into a vocabulary
intelligible to the amateur listener. For forty-three years beginning in 1880, the
Tribune employed the acknowledged dean of American music critics, Henry
Edward Krehbiel, a tall, ruddy-bearded arbiter renowned for the catholicity of
his taste—he wrote admiringly, for instance, of the Negro spiritual at a time
when few others were willing to grant it artistic status—and for the integrity
of his judgment. Scorning promoters, he cared only for the merit of the performance; serving on many an international jury, he won respectability abroad for
American cultural life. Krehbiel's successor, Lawrence Gilman, produced less
magisterial but thoroughly knowledgeable music criticism for the *Tribune* for

seventeen years. To replace him in 1940, Geoffrey Parsons enlisted a major and unique figure in twentieth-century American music.

At forty-four, Virgil Thomson had long since surmounted his provincial origins in Kansas City to become a cosmopolite, more at home in Paris, the Old World's art capital, than in New York, which was beginning to challenge it for cultural supremacy. He knew everyone in the modernist movement and wrote brilliantly on music in leading magazines; his 1930 book, *The State of Music*, was a major work of explication. As a composer he blended a folk-flavored American idiom with Parisian sophistication in works notable for melodic mastery and clarity of texture. Nine years into his reign as *Tribune* music critic, he was awarded the Pulitzer Prize for his musical score for the motion picture *Louisiana Story.*

Why would such a man apply himself to the daily grind of journalism? For one thing, Thomson saw himself as "a species of knight errant . . . rescuing musical virtue in distress"; his commission was not to aid careers or promote Music Appreciation among the masses. His weapon was musical polemics, with which he pledged to dislodge the nimbuses of worshipfully regarded composers, conductors, and performers. He was not in awe of the genius as "a special kind of man," he later wrote. "I respected only sensitivity and workmanship." His second and not entirely incidental motive was the hope that the celebrity and power that would flow to him as music critic on one of the two most influential papers in the country in cultural coverage might encourage the performing of his own works.

Thomson's reviewing on the *Tribune* was remarkable first of all for its brilliance of descriptive analysis; it was explicit, clear, and comprehensible. By way of an example is his March 14, 1942, review of a competent but quite ordinary performance of Strauss's *Der Rosenkavalier* at the Metropolitan Opera. He explained at the outset that the work was not a favorite of his:

> . . . I can take a catnap here and there without seeming to miss anything, because when I wake up the music is always doing what it was when I dropped off. It is full of waltzes that all sound alike and that have nothing to do with the play. . . . It is full of broken-up vocal lines that have no musical necessity, because the orchestra always has the tune anyway, and that always have to be sung loud because the orchestra is thick and pushing, due to Strauss's constant overwriting for the horns. . . .

After assessing the individual performers, he concluded his piece, which typically ran to only four chunky paragraphs:

> Erich Leinsdorf conducted all right, too, though an ideal rendition would have been rhythmically more flexible. . . . With so many quite good elements involved . . . it seemed a shame that I couldn't get up anything like the enthusiasm about [the performance] that the audience did.

Thomson's second distinction as a critic was that he did not restrict himself to evaluating repertory works at famed concert halls. Indeed, he railed against the shopworn programs dictated by establishment tastes, sought to deflate musical reputations he thought undeserved—that of Sibelius, for example, and many of the Germans, especially Wagner—and called for the performance of more American music, which too many managers, impresarios, and well-heeled but tasteless patrons judged beneath their dignity to recognize. Thomson was always on the prowl for the new and sought pleasurable, stimulating sound in forms and places other critics disdained—a Bach oratorio by amateurs at a neighborhood church, Holy Thursday services at St. Patrick's Cathedral, performances of suburban and regional orchestras, the sound track of Disney's film *Fantasia,* and even a group of recent Juilliard graduates performing *The Marriage of Figaro* without sets or costumes to only piano accompaniment.

It was his writing, immensely informed and fun to read, that more than anything else distinguished Virgil Thomson's criticism. But when his very first effort, a review of the opener of the New York Philharmonic's ninety-ninth season, turned out to be a pan of brutal overstatement, which Thomson titled "Age Without Honor" and which included the first person singular seventeen times, his uneasy *Tribune* patron, Parsons, decided he had better intervene. What ensued over the first years of Thomson's stay on the paper was a series of memos which the critic conceded "corrected me kindly, clearly and with reasons," even as Parsons "admired me, forgave me, and adopted me into his family." Parsons's cautionary notes survive as a primer for the defense of artistically stringent standards waged with civility and compassion, qualities in which Thomson was at times self-defeatingly deficient. After his initial butchering of the Philharmonic and the audience's unaccountably warm response to its performance, Thomson was offered two cardinal rules of reviewing by his guru: (1) Never criticize the audience and (2) don't appear to be superior; his job, rather, was to make clear to the Philharmonic subscriber,

> who can read words of more than one syllable, that so far from being a Young Pedant in a Hurry, with a Paris condescension, you are a fair, patient judge, anxious to help. It is a great tragedy for the city that the Philharmonic should have relapsed into such stodginess. . . .

When Thomson undertook a guerrilla war against conductor Arturo Toscanini, snipping at his "wow-technique" on the podium, a "couldn't-care-less" attitude toward modern music, an apparent preference for second-rate singers, and the overbearing nature of his publicity, Parsons urged discretion and damning by faint praise: "He is the town's local hero but I know you can do the trick and get away with it." When he hammered uncharitably at a suburban Connecticut orchestra and made no concession to wartime personnel shortages and other problems in mounting a small-town ensemble, Parsons lamented that the critic served no one in casting "a large wet blanket" over the effort. The rebuke prompted Thomson to note in his memoirs, "Discouraging suburbia about anything, I understood, was imprudent. For suburbs, like churches, accept only praise."

Even after two years, Parsons had to rein him in from time to time. "Anyone who sits in judgment as you do," he wrote Thomson after a fresh demolition job of the Philharmonic in November 1942, "should be damned modest and generous, remembering the personal equations involved. . . . The thing that readers most want from a critic is a reliance on his judgment. When you use slang, or become petty and personal in your criticisms, you compromise yourself with all your readers. For Christ sake, what's the matter with you?" A year later, after Thomson noted of a Met performance that "Lily Pons, the official star of the evening, sang prettily enough in her pale and bird-like fashion" and that the other singers "all dragged and mostly flatted," Parsons again lost patience but began to sound himself like an advocate of boosterism as he chided, "You will defeat your own ends and destroy your influence if you sound like a carping school teacher rapping his pupils over their knuckles."

Despite enraged protests from smug music-lovers who did not enjoy seeing their predispositions shredded in print, the paper stood behind him. Threats were made by concert managers to cancel advertising, and unhappiness was registered by eminences in the cultural community, like A. Conger Goodyear, who had served for ten years as president of the Museum of Modern Art when he wrote Helen Reid in November 1941 that Thomson's latest assault on the Philharmonic had reached "a new level of stupidity and ignorance." Mrs. Reid conceded that her music critic had annoyed a number of people but among the experts she had consulted, Thomson's comments were considered "well justified." The consensus soon swung heavily to Thomson's side. For a decade, before his attention began to wander, Virgil Thomson's reviews in the *Tribune* made him "a force in American cultural life," in the estimate of Robert Craft, among the leading musicologists the nation has produced. Thomson's work was succeeded by a reign of mandarin commentary—critics writing primarily for one another; his reviews, essentially reports about events in the marketplace, have survived the test of time that most journalism fails and belong, according to Craft, "to the small library of permanent music criticism."

III

By the time of World War II, little pretense remained that Ogden Reid ran the *Herald Tribune.*

Inside the paper, on days when he was up to it, Ogden might still go through some of the motions of proprietorship, like reading proofs of the next morning's editorials or checking with the city desk to see what was dummied for the front page, but so far as the outside world was concerned, Helen was in charge. When, for example, Norman Thomas, the Socialist leader, had a complaint in February 1941 about how he and his party had been dealt with in a column by Dorothy

Thompson, he registered it with Helen "as the person most responsible for the Herald Tribune." People in power all over the country knew who she was. Missy Meloney, back from a West Coast trip in March 1941, reported to her that Louis B. Mayer "admires you tremendously" because when she had bearded the head lion in his den at Metro-Goldwyn-Mayer for an advertising commitment to the *Tribune,* Helen would not leave until she had clinched the deal with his signature on the dotted line. "It was not just your charm," Meloney noted, "but that you had the intelligence to make him see the importance of the Herald Tribune."

As she neared her sixtieth birthday, Helen identified herself even more closely with the Reids. When the page proofs of the special centennial edition of the *Tribune* were presented to her for approval in April 1941, she changed the word "patriarch" that led off the caption under the front-page picture of Horace Greeley to read "statesman," as if it were too painful to her to concede to history that the paper had not always belonged to the Reids. Her pride also stiffened her resistance now to advertisers who tried to second-guess the way the paper was run; more and more, she stood by her editorial people, even at the risk of jeopardizing ad revenue or the allegiance of potent allies. As she did in backing Virgil Thomson, so she stood fast when Philip Le Boutillier, president of Best & Co., one of the city's top carriage-trade retailers, protested to her in December 1941 that the publicity given in the *Tribune*'s fashion section to a coat being featured by decidedly unexclusive Ohrbach's department store was "entirely out of character for the Herald Tribune and totally ridiculous to me." Helen fired off a "Dear Philip" salvo that declared, ". . . in my judgment you are the person who is wrong. The Herald Tribune does not cover the news of Fifth Avenue and Park Avenue alone. Happenings on Second Avenue and Fourteenth Street are of equal concern."

Nothing so became Helen Reid as her handling of a pair of complaints lodged in the summer of 1942 by the previous and the current tenant of the White House, each protesting the attack on him by a *Tribune* staff member of the opposing political persuasion. Both cases corroborated the perception in high places that she was indeed the paper's chief executive and demonstrated her loyalty to the staff even if it meant offending the mighty.

Herbert Hoover had co-authored a new book titled *The Problems of Lasting Peace,* which the *Tribune*'s daily book critic of thirteen years' standing, Lewis Gannett, gently dismissed as naïve in a one-paragraph review tacked on to the end of his "Books and Things" column, the bulk of which was devoted to a pair of unweighty novels. From his suite at the Waldorf-Astoria, Hoover wrote to Helen Reid on June 24, expressing deep concern "that a journal of such importance to America as the Tribune should maintain a Communist book reviewer engaged in the destruction of books dedicated to the American System and in the eulogy of all books of Communist flavor." Despite such subversion, the book was selling very well, especially in the Midwest, the ex-President advised.

It was not the first time Lewis Gannett had been called a Communist. Son of a Unitarian minister and a mother highly active in the causes of women's suffrage and racial equality, he grew up in a world devoted to social reform. A Quaker by choice and a pacifist by nature, he graduated from Harvard, where, like his near-contemporary Walter Lippmann, he was gripped by socialist visions of economic justice. After working as a reporter for the *World,* he went to the Great War with the Quaker ambulance corps and returned to serve as a writer and traveling correspondent for the left-liberal weekly *The Nation,* which exactly suited his ideological frame of mind. With Irita Van Doren's help, Gannett came to the *Tribune* in 1928 at the age of thirty-six and began writing a daily book column that was informal, unpedantic, and readable. His style, or absence of one, was not the test of his value to the paper. An unfailingly cheerful, quietly humorous man, he had an enormous range of interests, from world history to wildflowers, and he read very fast. It took him just three hours to read a book, and he often covered several in a single column; over twenty-seven years on the *Tribune,* he reviewed some 8,000 titles. He never fancied himself a critic, preferring the role of a reporter whose beat happened to be books; books were news, and his job was to winnow it from the hundreds of pages he consumed each day. His reviews were, in the words of John K. Hutchens, his junior colleague in later years and himself a grainier and more compelling writer, "like a conversation with an enlightened, sometimes indignant, incessantly curious observer of life."

Throughout his career, he had lent his name and what money he could afford to liberal, pro-labor, pacifist, and occasionally pro-Soviet causes, of which the famine relief effort in Russia in the early 'Twenties was the most sinister. In working to heal the warring factions of the labor movement, Gannett had believed for a time, along with many liberals, that Communists were simply the most radical elements of the left and capable of cooperating in a united front rather than inevitably subverting organizing drives to their own ends. His most ardent support was reserved for the Newspaper Guild, of which he was a charter member, and the National Association for the Advancement of Colored People. This disgraceful record earned him a Red label and had prompted Helen Reid to ask him directly early in 1941 if he was a Communist. He said no and in an elaborating memo sent on Washington's Birthday explained the extent of his fellow traveling:

> . . . I was excited about Soviet Russia's experiments, and it still seems to me that it will stand in the perspective of history somewhat like the French Revolution—very mixed but with much that was creative and fermenting in it. I worked for Russian recognition. I believe, intensely, in trade-unions as an American pattern of evolving democracy. . . .

"Dear Herbert," Helen wrote Hoover. "In spite of the inadequate handling of your book by Lewis Gannett and my complete disagreement with his judgment of its importance, I want to place on record the fact that Lewis Gannett is not a communist. . . . In fact, he is, by creed and all his tendencies, a Quaker. You would actually have much in common." She added that the paper never considered an individual's politics in its hiring practices "with the exception of those who write editorials" and, in an insouciant postscript characteristically dismissive of the wound her retainer had opened in Hoover's hide, suggested that the seven-column advertisement for his book that had run in the *Times* the previous day "should also reach Herald Tribune readers[.] I'm afraid you have wished to punish me."

Two months after Hoover's complaint about Gannett, it was Roosevelt's turn. In a letter headed "Personal, Confidential, and 'Off the Record,' " the President wrote to Helen that although "I have, during a long course of years, acquired, of necessity, the skin of a rhinoceros," there was a limit to his imperviousness. Because "the good old Herald Tribune has on the whole a decent respect for veracity, I think a cartoon which is based on the opposite of veracity is something that you and Ogden and Mr. Parsons ought, for your own sakes, to take up." The offending drawing, which had run on the August 19, 1942, *Tribune* editorial page and been distributed to papers across the country by the Tribune Syndicate, showed a golfer who resembled Roosevelt and wore a beanie labeled "Administration" lining up a short putt to a hole labeled "Politics"; nearby, holding the pin flag labeled "Nov. 4," which was election day that year, his squat partner, labeled "Congress," was hushing the third main figure in the cartoon—a frantically leaping fellow labeled "Public" with a water bucket under his arm who was screaming "HEY!" and pointing to thick black clouds labeled "The War" on the horizon, where a remote likeness of Uncle Sam, shirtsleeves and trousers rolled up for the supreme effort, was madly bailing to put out the fire. The cartoon was captioned, in words the artist was plainly putting in the "Congress" figure's mouth, "Sh-h! Can't You See We're Busy?"

The perpetrator of this item was the *Tribune*'s Pulitzer Prize–winning Jay Norwood Darling, a Midwestern conservative, who had been turning out a daily cartoon for it and its syndicate since 1916 except for a year and a half when he defected to the New Deal as a bureaucrat in the Interior Department's conservation program. The President's letter declared to Helen Reid that "the amount of time taken by me from war work hours in relation to the . . . political situation was exactly zero," and he itemized a few phone calls and brief meetings with Democratic chieftains—a total in time that was "not much longer than the very nice visit I had with you the other day. . . . Don't for a minute imagine I am sore about this, but I have always thought that the Herald Tribune was big enough to know when it had printed something when it was not true."

A week before the cartoon in question appeared in print, its creator had written to a friend:

> . . . There is nothing that so completely spoils Roosevelt's day as an intimation that he and his New Deal associates do not, within themselves, contain all the factors necessary to do any and all jobs better than anyone else. I had a ringside seat at his show for two years and witnessed this supreme satisfaction with his own wisdom. . . . Roosevelt hates the New York Herald Tribune only a little less intensively than he hates me. . . .

The animosity was clearly mutual. Indeed, Darling felt that the reason he had been offered the job running the Interior Department's Biological Survey was not his lifelong concern with conservation issues but Roosevelt's desire to halt his cartoons. He may have been right, for the President had few more pesty or effective detractors. Darling, who got into the habit of signing his drawings "Ding" for student publications at Beloit College, had made his newspapering mark in Iowa, where his cartoons were eventually featured on the front page each day of the *Des Moines Register.* But he wanted a national showcase for his work and joined the *Tribune*'s syndicate at the age of forty while remaining essentially an Iowan unsullied, except on regular visits to New York, by metropolitan attitudes. His drawing style, trading in gentle but unmistakably barbed ridicule, was exceedingly simple as befit his conception of his craft as "a spotlight service" and "an emotional medium" that was in essence "a primitive and very abbreviated form of thought and expression." He was a strong patriot and believer in the promise of rags-to-riches opportunity for every American. His Pulitzer-winning cartoon of 1923, titled "In Good Old U.S.A.," depicted the humble origins of three Americans who had risen to power and prominence. With the coming of the New Deal he continually chided the Roosevelt administration for alleged shackling of big business, subservience to organized labor, handouts to the idle and undeserving, and usurpation of libertarian values.

Helen Reid answered Roosevelt's protest evasively by suggesting that there was a general belief afoot in the land that "Congress was under the influence of the Fall elections" and went on to lecture the nation's chief executive: ". . . I have believed that you would best gain your end and strengthen your control as our war president if you kept both your time and your endurance free from politics. It has seemed to me that this procedure would increase the wholehearted support from the country and would decrease what I know are an incredible number of demands on yourself." At the end she added, in self-expiation, "It might surprise you to know how often this paper is berated for its support of you. . . . Some times I wonder if you ever see the bits of genuine applause that appear on the editorial page. Perhaps they count for more than . . . if there were continuous agreement." Perhaps, too, Helen Reid had not forgotten that a few months earlier Eleanor Roosevelt addressed a rally of the New York Newspaper Guild that urged *Tribune* staff members to designate the union as their official bargaining agent at the office election a week hence. Helen's letter could scarcely have mollified Roosevelt any more than the appearance, a few days after its receipt, of another Darling cartoon, showing Washington buried under a blizzard of pointless bureaucratic paperwork. Titled "What a Place for a Waste Paper Salvage Campaign," it was awarded the Pulitzer Prize, Darling's second, for the best political cartoon of 1942.

Helen Reid's growing stature kept pace with her level of self-possession, which was creeping suspiciously close now to arrogance. In May 1944, *The Saturday Evening Post,* then in its heyday, ran a two-part series on her titled "Queen Helen"; the subheading read: "Hostess to the famous, mistress of an old fortune, a high-powered sales executive with sandpaper persistence, Mrs. Ogden Reid is one of America's remarkable women." Buoyed by such acclaim, she was deterred by little in seeking to advance the *Tribune*'s ends and her own will. That November, as the Allied armies drove the Germans back toward the borders of the Fatherland, Helen wired the supreme commander of the liberation forces—General Dwight Eisenhower—to approve the reopening of the *Tribune*'s European edition: "Ours was the last and only American newspaper published in Paris before occupation following 53 years uninterrupted appearance. Believe soonest possible resumption will benefit your efforts. Will appreciate answer care of New York Herald Tribune. . . ."

Eisenhower said yes. The man she sent to meet with him in Versailles to work out the details would play a significant role in the general's ascent to the presidency; in the interim, he would become the most powerful figure on the *Tribune* by his conquest of Queen Helen.

IV

By the time she hired him to succeed her in August 1936 as advertising director of the *Herald Tribune,* William Edward Robinson had earned the reputation as the best newspaper space salesman in New York. A driving, hard-fisted, amiable extrovert, he was not precisely the Reids' idea of a gentleman either through family, schooling, or professional affiliations. Somewhat florid in manner and appearance, he had a substantial frame with a fleshy face, heavy brows, cleft chin, and assertive, often mesmerizing voice. Bill Robinson, they said, could sell suspenders to a scarecrow, but what he was best at selling was Bill Robinson.

After a Catholic boyhood in a Rhode Island milltown, he attended a private parochial school in Providence and then headed at his first opportunity for New York, where he held what he called "every conceivable job short of stealing" while putting himself through New York University's School of Commerce. During the 'Twenties boom, he wrote promotional brochures and letters for a firm selling mortgage bonds and in five years became its sales manager; he would later refer to this as his period "on Wall Street."

Through a mutual friend, Robinson was summoned to the office of magazine publisher Bernarr Macfadden, who asked the young securities salesman to help him decide whether to accept an offer from Hearst to buy out his flamboyant tabloid, the *Graphic,* then losing $850,000 a year. Hearst's plan was to merge the *Graphic,* best known for its Broadway columnist Walter Winchell, sports columnist and later television personality Ed Sullivan, and trick photographs, with the *Mirror* and make a real run at the *Daily News* for dominance of the tabloid market. Robinson analyzed the situation, concluded that the *Graphic* was "the lowest form of newspaper life," with a circulation that gyrated wastefully according to the degree of sensation of its featured distortion that day, and counseled Macfadden to sell. And what could be done to rescue the paper if he chose to hang on? Robinson prescribed patience, money, a less blatantly fabricated editorial product, an honest advertising rate card instead of peddling space in the sheet for any price its salesmen could get, and Macfadden's complete backing of a new boss. In 1928, at the age of twenty-eight, without a day's experience in the newspaper business, Bill Robinson found himself president of the nation's most notorious daily.

He imposed a modicum of integrity on the news columns, ended the rate bargaining with advertisers, stopped the extortionate practice of stacking newsstands with copies of the *Graphic* that dealers could not sell but had to pay for if they wanted an ample supply of *True Story* and the rest of Macfadden's hot-selling magazines, and cut the paper's loss in half in his first year at the helm. But the key to profitability, he recognized, was attracting advertising from the big department stores. Macy's was the bellwether account, and Robinson himself went after its advertising manager. Three times the fellow broke appointments with him, and Robinson indignantly wrote to Macy's president, Jesse Straus, arguing that it was his ad manager's duty to see the representative of a newspaper that sold 300,000 copies a day and reached a lot of potential Macy's customers. That got him inside the door for fifteen minutes, during which the ad manager said that persistence alone would not earn Robinson a sale; instead he issued a challenge: volume Macy's had plenty of, but if Robinson could figure out within ten days how his *Graphic* could help the store raise its average sales check—and thus its lagging profitability—an advertising contract would be forthcoming.

Robinson did nothing else for ten days but study Macy's ads in other papers and ponder the problem. At the end of his allotted time, he returned to the store with the solution: since the *Times, Tribune,* and *Sun* had readers who could afford to buy higher-priced merchandise, that was what the store ought to feature in those papers, transferring its lower-priced items to advertisements in the *Graphic,* whose readers could afford them and would be responsive. It was so clean and simple that Robinson was whisked upstairs to Straus's suite for commendation and, after a bit of haggling during which it was established that the *Graphic* rate card was the same for Macy's as for everyone else, he was presented with a 200,000-line contract—a major breakthrough. But before he could apprise Macfadden of his triumph, Robinson was told that the impatient owner had rehired one of the key business executives who had been let go under Robinson's rehabilitation program—a violation of his understanding with Macfadden, who had promised him a free hand. Instead of placing the Macy's contract in front of him as testament to the better prospects just ahead, Robinson urged Macfadden to reconsider his broken pledge; when the owner said he could not, Robinson resigned and returned the contract to Macy's with the statement that he could not vouch for the integrity of the *Graphic* under someone else's direction.

After two years as local advertising manager of the *World-Telegram* and three as overall ad manager with its principal rival, Hearst's *Journal,* Robinson moved to the *Herald Tribune* and relieved Helen Reid of the day-to-day burden of supervising the sales force. Though lacking in pedigree, he was a big, strong, forceful fellow who had worked at smoothing away his rough edges. He told a funny story well, held his liquor, golfed in the low eighties, played an expert rubber of bridge, danced a spirited rumba, and was at ease in a steambath with Bernard Gimbel. In newspaper circles, Bill Robinson would get to be known as a heartier and less pompous operative than his opposite number on the *Times* —Monroe Green—and, by consensus, one tough cookie.

He knew he had to sell the paper by its quality, not quantity, and he did it with the certitude of an evangelist. In a 1940 speech to an association of dry-goods merchants, he typically cited a number of unique service features the *Tribune* offered its readers, who knew, for example, that the food described in Clementine Paddleford's columns had been cooked and tested in the paper's own model kitchen. The *Tribune* carried more food and fashion news, he contended, than any of its competitors and was considered the official newspaper by practically all women's clubs in the metropolitan area. More than that, it was considered a friend by its readers and,

> like a good friend, has performed a great many services for hundreds of thousands of our readers. The Herald Tribune is a guide to the philosophy with which they conduct their lives. It is a reliable and sure guide for the little homely things they must do every day to make their living and the conduct of their homes more pleasant, more gracious, more efficient. . . . The market for you is pre-tested, pre-sold, predisposed before your advertisement is written. Accordingly, when it appears [in the *Tribune*], it functions with greater efficiency which results from greater reader interest and the confidence we have built for you.

In less formal settings, he would reduce his quality-over-quantity pitch to the one-liner "Why buy the whole cow when we'll sell you just the steak?"

With the expansiveness of a super-Rotarian, he made himself into a persuasive booster of his city at a time New York was losing influence and power to Washington and manufacturing jobs to the South and West. In May 1943, he wrote a series of three editorials for the *Tribune* arguing that whatever losses the city had suffered had been more than made up for by its burgeoning new industry, business management, with its workshops in great office buildings instead of lofts and factories, as corporate America centralized direction of its far-flung operations and depended increasingly on New York's unsurpassed and growing supply of liquid capital. Mayor La Guardia was so pleased that he ordered 50,000 reprints, and the *Tribune*'s—and Robinson's— stock rose in the business community. So strong had the paper's competitive position become that year, in fact, that it was challenging the *Times*'s lead in retail advertising linage and, partly due to a brief boycott of the *Times* by the leading department stores over a rate increase, the *Tribune* actually carried more ad volume from Macy's, Bloomingdale's, and Altman's in 1943 than its chief rival.

The *Tribune*'s enhanced position, according to media historians and *Times* personnel, was due only to temporary constraints imposed on both papers by wartime rationing of newsprint and ink, and its opportunistic short-range gains were achieved at the expense of its long-term health. In *The Kingdom and the Power*, a popular 1969 study of the *Times*, Gay Talese noted that newspaper publishers around the nation had to decide whether they would cram their pages with advertising, readily available due to the war-induced economic boom, or resist the easy revenue and maintain the news hole; he went on:

> . . . Sulzberger chose the latter alternative with a resoluteness that the *Tribune*'s owners did not try to match, and as a result *The Times* conceded millions during the war years, but produced a superior newspaper. . . . the additional space that *The Times* was able to devote to war coverage instead of advertising was, in the long run, a very profitable decision: *The Times* lured many readers from the *Tribune*, and these readers stayed with *The Times* after the war into the Nineteen-fifties and Sixties.

A slight variation on this generally held theory was that in accordance with *Times* publisher Sulzberger's order that the news hole was not to be reduced to accommodate the abundance of advertising dollars available, the *Times* stringently rationed its ad space in keeping with prewar use by advertisers so that smaller space buyers would not be crowded out of the paper; national accounts were limited to a maximum of one-third of a page for any insertion, and classified ads were limited to two or three lines, depending on the category. These voluntarily adopted rules gave the *Tribune* a chance to fatten up on the *Times* overflow—"and it did just that," said Monroe Green, the *Times* ad manager. Bill Robinson did not ration his space to keep small advertisers happy the way the *Times* did; instead, he took all the linage he could get from the big department stores. "Helen Reid thought that her day had come," recalled Ivan Veit, a veteran of more than half a century on the *Times* business side and eventually its executive vice president. "Our advertising department was in great anguish as we saw the *Tribune* creeping up on us." But as soon as the war ended, according to this version of the two papers' postwar fate, rationing was lifted, the *Times* opened its pages to all the advertising it could get, and the big stores severely cut back on their linage in the *Tribune*, inducing malnutrition and eventually death.

Neither of these theories, both dependent on alleged greed by the *Tribune*, appears to be supported by the facts. Both papers, as the accompanying table shows, actually increased their ratio of advertising to news during the war years —the *Times* from 42.58 percent for 1941 to 49.68 percent for 1945, the *Tribune* from 37.58 percent for 1941 to 49.32 percent for 1945—and at no time did the

Comparison of *Tribune* and *Times* During World War II

	TOTAL PAGES	ADVERTISING % & annual change	WEEKDAY CIRCULATION [Sept. figs.]	SUNDAY CIRCULATION
1941	NYT 23,468	(42.58%)	455,825	788,546
	Trib 19,756	(37.58%)	330,138 [72.4% of NYT]	538,005 [68.2% of NYT]
1942	NYT 22,458	(44.98%) +2.4%	440,086	790,334
	Trib 18,429	(39.88%) +2.3%	310,447 [70.5% of NYT]	534,363 [67.6% of NYT]
1943	NYT 22,238	(50.02%) +5.0%	419,447	805,907
	Trib 18,570	(45.60%) +5.7%	296,197 [70.6% of NYT]	548,250 [68.0% of NYT]
1944	NYT 19,598	(50.14%) +0.1%	449,409	817,960
	Trib 16,394	(48.37%) +2.8%	306,372 [68.2% of NYT]	565,965 [69.2% of NYT]
1945	NYT 18,824	(49.68%) −0.5%	531,458	851,982
	Trib 16,236	(49.32%) +1.0%	336,393 [63.3% of NYT]	598,915 [70.3% of NYT]
1946	NYT 24,654	(55.64%) +6.0%	538,914	1,002,765
	Trib 20,682	(51.49%) +2.2%	348,626 [64.7% of NYT]	708,754 [70.7% of NYT]
1947*	NYT 27,000	(58.13%) +2.5%	543,583	1,092,054
	Trib 21,240	(50.22%) −1.3%	319,867 [58.8% of NYT]	680,981 [62.4% of NYT]

Source: *Tribune* treasurer and author's computations.
Tribune raised price to five cents at end of 1946.

Tribune carry a higher proportion of advertising matter than the *Times*. But because the *Tribune* published a paper that was between 15 and 20 percent smaller in total pages printed than the *Times* and because it began the war carrying a 5 percent lower ratio of ads than the *Times,* the *proportionate* increase in the *Tribune* seemed greater than it was in absolute terms. The evidence that this disproportionate increase in the *Tribune*'s advertising content left its readers feeling deprived of war news coverage and sent them in droves to the *Times* is, at best, highly ambiguous. The *Tribune*'s weekday circulation as a percentage of the *Times*'s slipped slightly from 72.4 percent in 1941 to 70.5 percent in 1942, rose to 70.6 percent in 1943, fell off to 68.2 percent in 1944 but rose in absolute numbers by 10,000, fell off more sharply to 63.3 percent in 1945 but rose in absolute numbers by 30,000, and in 1946, with rationing off, rallied to 64.7 percent. For the Sunday edition, which represented nearly half the total number of pages both papers published each week, the *Tribune*'s circulation actually increased during the war, both in absolute terms (by 60,000 copies) and as a proportion of the *Times*'s (from 68.2 percent in 1941 to 70.3 percent in 1945), and in 1946 reached its all-time high of 708,000. Far from profiteering from its increased ad linage, the *Tribune*'s net income during the war years was less than half the *Times*'s in dollars and substantially less than that when measured as a percentage of gross revenues, never rising as high as 4 percent. The major change in the relative circulations of the two papers did not occur until 1947 and can almost certainly be attributed to a factor unrelated to wartime advertising policies or supposed reader perception of a diminished editorial product: in the last days of 1946 the *Tribune* raised its newsstand price from three cents to five; the *Times,* offering a heftier paper, held fast at three cents for another three years. The immediate result was a loss of nearly 30,000 daily *Tribune* sales in 1947; the *Times* gained only 5,000, indicating not wholesale defection to it but a probable much greater drop for the now costlier *Tribune* among people who had been taking both papers.

The most, then, that can be safely ventured about the effects of their wartime advertising policies is that the *Times* published smaller papers and sold fewer of them than it would have and the *Tribune* as a result published more advertising—though not grossly more—than it would have; at the end of the war, they reverted to their antebellum positions until the *Tribune,* with Bill Robinson by then in charge of its business operations, raised its price in what was to prove a major blunder.

Robinson may have been emboldened in the price rise decision by the success he had scored earlier with the reopening of the *Tribune*'s Paris edition. Its presses there were already being used to print the European theater edition of *Stars & Stripes,* the American armed forces' paper, when Robinson arrived to meet with Eisenhower on December 19, 1944, to gain approval for needed allocations of fuel and newsprint, then under military control. But the Battle of the Bulge had begun three days earlier, jeopardizing the whole Allied western front, and Robinson fully expected his meeting to be canceled. No such word arrived, though, so Robinson showed up at Eisenhower's Versailles office. The general, alone in a large, bare room unadorned even by big battle maps, sat drinking coffee and smoking a cigarette. Robinson was apologetic about bothering him with a nonmilitary matter and spoke fast. Eisenhower put him at ease, saying that this was the only time the *Tribune* man would get to him and it was best to go over the arrangements carefully. "Bill was so undone, so completely snowed by the calm of the general in the midst of such a panicked atmosphere, dealing with a relatively minor matter while shifting whole armies around the face of Europe," said Sylvan J. Barnet, who would later direct the business side of the Paris edition, "that he came away from the meeting convinced he had met a truly great man."

Even with stars in his eyes, Robinson was hardheaded. He ordered Eric Hawkins, back in harness as the managing editor of the Paris edition, and Everett Walker, assistant managing editor of the parent paper, on hand to see that the reopened offspring measured up more closely to New York standards, to start up the presses a day earlier than planned lest Eisenhower change his mind. He also overruled Parisian advisers who had urged him to retain the prewar sales price of one franc and instead raised the figure to five francs, the equivalent of ten cents at the official exchange rate of fifty francs to the dollar. His decision was based on exploitation of the black-market exchange rate that lured 300 to 400 francs for the hard American dollar, which most of the Paris

Tribune's potential readers would have access to; the paper, meanwhile, would pay its French workers and newsprint suppliers at the officially pegged rate and fatten up on the differential.

His wartime performance left little doubt that Bill Robinson would be named business manager to succeed Howard Davis, who retired almost the moment the guns stopped. Robinson appeared to be a more dynamic figure than the aging Davis, but some on the *Tribune* felt he did not know much about the business beyond the advertising side and it was far from clear that he knew how to manage it. But Helen Reid liked his style and confidence—he was the sort of two-fisted fellow she felt the paper needed to lead it into the promising postwar era.

When 1946 proved to be the best financial year in *Tribune* history, with revenue up by one-third and profits of over a million, the paper decided to make some badly needed improvements in the pressroom—a decade after Howard Davis had urged the step. The outlay left management in a cash-tight squeeze once more, and so Robinson calculated that in the rising tide of revenues and profits, the moment was at hand for the *Tribune* to increase its newsstand price to a nickel. Even if circulation slipped by, say, 10 percent, the paper would come out well ahead in total revenues. And the *Times,* also needing the cash to fund its postwar expansion plans, would surely follow the *Tribune*'s lead in short order. Richard Pinkham, who was about to succeed to the post of circulation manager, which he would hold from 1947 to 1951, said of Robinson's decision, "I told Bill I thought it was a mistake to raise the newsstand price without our knowing if the *Times* would come along. He said, 'We need the money,' and that was that."

At the *Times,* where memories were still fresh of the *Tribune*'s wartime performance, the decision was made to leave their prime competitor out on a limb. "We didn't want to give them any quarter," recalled Nathan W. Goldstein, *Times* circulation manager from 1948 to 1974. "Our numbers were on the rise, and we didn't want to do anything to jeopardize them. 'No free rides for the competition' was the way we looked at it. The idea was to keep the pressure on them." Ivan Veit concurred: "While it might have been good to pick up the added revenue, it was better to keep the pressure on them." He recalled a favorite Arthur Hays Sulzberger homily that stated, approximately, "If the car is taking you uphill, don't stop it and look under the hood to see if you can make it go better."

During the three years before the *Times* raised its price to five cents, its circulation advanced only marginally, but the *Tribune* was unable to recover more than a small part of the loss it suffered in the first year of the higher price. The momentum with which it had come out of the war was blunted by its own pricing policy. And after raising its advertising rates to meet postwar inflationary pressures on income, the *Tribune* was charging advertisers nearly three-quarters as much for the same space as the *Times* did but had only 57 percent of the latter's circulation by 1950. It was a premium that fewer and fewer advertisers would be willing to meet, no matter how glowingly Bill Robinson talked of selling them choice sirloin.

V

The unexamined premise of Gay Talese's book on the *Times* was that in its twentieth-century version it was incomparably the best newspaper in America and, weighting its comprehensiveness more heavily than any shortcomings in editorial acuity, probably the world. The contention here is that, all things considered, especially readability in terms of both prose and typographic presentation, and judged over its entire life span, the *Tribune* was not inferior to the *Times*—only less successful. Talese's presumption is exemplified by a passage dealing with the approximate time period under discussion here:

> . . . *The Times* was unquestionably the best newspaper in sight, even though the *Tribune* in those days was a serious and interesting newspaper, and was no doubt a more congenial place for reporters wanting literary freedom. For straight reporting, however, and depth of coverage, *The Times* was incomparable. It was especially clear during World War II, when *The Times'* staff so outnumbered and outdistanced the *Tribune*'s, despite the remarkable efforts of some *Tribune* reporters who were as good as *The Times'* best, that the *Tribune* could never again gain on *The Times* in circulation or advertising.
>
> The decision to increase *The Times'* staff and spare no expense in covering the war was Arthur Hays Sulzberger's. . . .

No evidence of this alleged wartime editorial superiority is provided; it is simply asserted. Surviving data from the *Times* archives disclose that its news and editorial department expenses, rather than leaping ahead to pay for coverage of the global conflict as Talese implied, were actually below the prewar level in four of the five war years:

YEAR	*Times* EDITORIAL EXPENSES
1940	$3,826,000
1941	3,759,000
1942	3,752,000
1943	3,484,000
1944	3,746,000
1945	4,219,000

The *Tribune* never had fewer than a dozen correspondents covering the war, and if the *Times* contingent outmanned them, just as it had done steadily on all fronts since the turn of the century and Ochs's ascendancy, it did not necessarily outreport them by any measure but total number of words—and it did not outwrite them by any measure of the language. A good deal of war news was embargoed or limited by military censorship, and much of the basic coverage took the form of expanded official communiqués from military headquarters, relayed indiscriminately by the wire services. The war was, in effect, one large, continuous story, and the *Tribune*, with enough gifted hands in the field to supplement wire reports, its superior typographic display, and a battery of first-rate editors coordinating production in the newsroom, at least held its own against the *Times*'s legions.

Its first lead paragraph of the war seemed to forecast that the *Tribune*'s martial prose might revert to the overheated level of chauvinism that characterized much of its World War I coverage. Recently installed Washington bureau chief Bert Andrews began his double-column lead story on the effect of the Pearl Harbor attack this way:

> WASHINGTON, Dec. 8 (Monday) — Japan has forced the United States into war in the Pacific, and today all the might of America's Army and Navy is being marshaled for a fight to the finish—Japan's finish.

More typical of the subdued yet stylish writing that followed the initial round of flag-waving was Roy Wilder, Jr.'s lead on a military training story as the nation geared up quickly for combat: "Mud is what Fort Dix has the most of."

Probably the most productive *Tribune* correspondent in the field, in terms of amount of combat copy filed, was John J. (Tex) O'Reilly, a former copyboy whom Stanley Walker elevated to reporter in 1928 after he had reputedly won $167 in a city-room poker game late one night. The happy-go-lucky O'Reilly prospered as a feature writer specializing in animal and nature stories under Engelking, whom he called "Massa" for the verbal whippings he administered to his staff. O'Reilly's closest brush with mortal combat before he went overseas had been a confrontation with an uncaged leopard during a circus rehearsal at Madison Square Garden in April 1940. The beast had climbed up the side of its topless cage while its keeper was otherwise occupied and bounded off in the direction of fleeing spectators; O'Reilly was in its direct path of flight. Not looking back until well down a dead-end hallway, he spotted the oncoming leopard about the same time as his hand brushed against an abandoned piece of canvas and, as he reported:

> Picking up the canvas, I held it between myself and the leopard, like a bullfighter using a tent for a cape. The cat would at least have to hit the canvas before he hit me. Somehow, I couldn't turn my back and run. Leopards can run faster than men. The time I held that canvas between me and the leopard seemed as long as a political campaign. It was less than a minute. But I'd seen men get killed in less than a minute, and I once saw a man get married in four minutes.
>
> Finally several animal trainers came running up the steps to our corner. The first one, probably thinking I was putting some plan into effect, shouted, "Hold him. Hold him there."

O'Reilly's understated comic gift was epitomized in that "our corner." He had few opportunities for mirth in his war correspondence, which began in the

African campaign and went right through to the German surrender at Rheims. He became a city-room legend, though, while covering the Free French forces on their march up from Lake Chad to a rendezvous at Tripoli with British troops for a joint westward push into Tunisia. Unable to find time to keep fastidious track of his expenses, O'Reilly made his account balance by listing "One camel—$350." Perplexed *Tribune* auditors decided the dromedary was a capital expense and wired O'Reilly: "WHERE IS CAMEL?" He wired back: "ATE IT."

If O'Reilly's solid wartime performance had been predictable, the same could scarcely be said of the staffer who turned in by far the most daring and accomplished job of any *Tribune* combat correspondent. Indeed, few less promising candidates for renown had ever entered the paper's city room than skinny, stuttering Homer Bigart, taken on as a nightside copyboy in 1927, about the time of his twentieth birthday, for twelve dollars a week. He came down from Hawley, a mill town in northeastern Pennsylvania, where his father ran a little factory that made woolen sweaters. A frail six-footer with very blue eyes and a solemn mien that masked a withering wit, he looked scholarly enough in his wire-frame glasses and at New York University chose to study English literature and journalism. A friend from home helped him find night work at the *Tribune,* and for two years he carried the double load. But when the great economic crash began in 1929, his father's business, like that of so many other marginal manufacturers, approached the edge of bankruptcy. Homer decided not to strain the family resources any longer; besides, he did not think much of the offerings in journalism at NYU. He took a room in the Park Slope section of Brooklyn for three dollars a week, lived frugally, and managed to send a bit from his meager *Tribune* earnings to his hard-pressed folks.

Progress came slowly at the paper. A copyboy's work was menial, and there were few chances to practice the craft he had diffidently chosen. The chances went to the young, vastly more sophisticated graduates of Yale and Harvard and the University of Michigan and the better Southern colleges whom city editor Stanley Walker enlisted. Homer Bigart, meanwhile, could only sharpen pencils and haul copy paper, fetch coffee and cigarettes, and wait to be noticed.

Now and then they let him write an obituary. Phoning up the bereaved for biographical information on the deceased and sounding consoling in the process was not easy when you stuttered, but working the telephone was an occupational necessity for a newspaperman, so he persevered. Once, he even managed to scoop the *Times* by scanning its long agate columns of paid death notices and spotting one announcing the demise of a college president. Sundays he would cover the sermon at one of the leading churches in the city and earn an extra three dollars. But mostly he labored obscurely—a painfully self-conscious, self-effacing young man who was no good at office politics. Homer Bigart was not a natural communicator.

By the time he made head copyboy, he was twenty-six, old for the honor, maybe older than any copyboy the paper had ever had. But he served with a mustached distinction that would have been almost laughable in one more prepossessing. He wore a dark suit and vest all the time, even in summer heat that approached the unbearable in the *Tribune* city room, and resembled nothing so much as a mortician-in-training. He would stand in the middle of the city room directing the other copyboys like a traffic cop. On errands himself, he moved with a swift, stiff-legged gait thought to be military in manner and therefore highly efficient. On the job, his charges saw him as something of a tyrant; off it, they thought him almost a recluse. He often donned a crooked smile that was sometimes taken by its beholder as a sneer or sign of disapproval —a trait that did not measurably speed his advancement. Life at the paper looked so unpromising to him, in fact, that he began to wonder whether he ought not to head for some other, less fiercely competitive part of the country. It was then that they made him a reporter, at twenty-five a week.

Normally he might have started out working the police beat, probably in the shacks in the outer boroughs, calling in routine stories to the rewrite bank and gathering background when something big broke. But Homer Bigart did not like cops—uniformed authority figures who paraded their power would be anathema to him his whole working life—and resisted the assignment. Anyway, turning him into a legman, a reporter who used the telephone instead of the typewriter as his principal tool, would have been torture to him. Nor did he want a beat like politics: too confining. And he did not think or write fast enough, he himself recognized, to handle big breaking stories or a heavy diet of spot news. His copy was full of cross-outs and there was not much of it per page, so that you could almost see his painful thought process unfolding as he composed.

They put him on routine general assignment—fires, speeches, sailings, harmless features—and hoped for the best. He was no ball of fire. Assigned to Pennsylvania Station to cover the inauguration of coach service to Florida on one of the two rail lines that ran between there and New York, he went to the wrong track and wrote up the non-event ballyhooing the wrong rail line. There followed a command appearance in the office of Helen Reid, who informed him in her frostiest manner that he had made "a terrible mistake," one that had cost the paper a plump advertisement. Bigart awaited the blade. But the *Tribune* did not execute its loyal retainers for misdemeanors; barring acts of repeated irresponsibility or towering incompetence, they were kept on, and on, at low pay and lower status. The day after his flub, Bigart felt a gentle hand on his shoulder and a voice fifty degrees warmer than the one that had lacerated him the day before. "It's all right, Mr. Bigart," said Mrs. Reid, "we got the ad back."

Being tolerated, though, was not exactly the pathway to the stars. A mentor in the city room or someone in power kindly disposed to him might have helped. To those staffers Stanley Walker preferred, the wispy, hard-shelled city editor, a celebrity in his own right, was communicative enough, occasionally dispensing a stylistic tip and even drinking with them downstairs at Bleeck's. But Homer Bigart could not afford to go drinking with his boss, even if he had been invited. Walker, at least, did not bawl out those he did not favor—and would just look disgusted when they failed him. His successor as city editor, Charlie McLendon, showed Bigart even less preference; he ragged him for his stutter. Engelking, too, induced dread in him, but Engel had a great love of the language and a compassionate side that invited loyalty in the form of extraordinary effort by his reporters. Under him, Bigart began to get a few breaks. His assignments improved, and his writing, still slow but steadier now in its flow, started to sparkle, particularly in occasional feature spreads. His brisk front-page piece on the 1940 St. Patrick's Day parade held in a snowstorm displayed his growing gift for sardonic observation. "The snow lay an inch deep in the folds of the Mayor's large black felt hat," he wrote, "by the time the County Kerry boys went by singing, 'The hat me dear old father wore' . . ." Now his stories were enriched, too, by specificity in small brushstrokes that produced a marked graphic quality in almost everything he wrote. Where other papers, for example, reported a fire gutting a Greenwich Village candy company, Bigart's lead identified it as "a gumdrop factory."

Apparent now, too, in his work was the product of what his competitors would come to call "Homer's All-American dummy act." The license to ask questions that no one else in society is sanctioned to put freely is perhaps the truest form of power the American journalist wields. Homer Bigart's style of interrogation was unique. He made a strength of his handicap. He would appear on the scene of a story as a stuttering, bumbling incompetent, helpless and harmless, and approach his quarry, disarming him by the pitiable spectacle he presented. A. M. Rosenthal, who as a rival and eventually one of Bigart's editors on the *Times* would come to know and admire the technique, parodied it thus: "Hello, I'm Homer Bigart, can you tell me about it? . . . I don't understand . . . I'm stupid . . . Explain it to me . . . Is this a coffee cup? . . . What's a coffee cup? . . . Why is it a coffee cup? . . . Explain it to me again." And of course he would wind up with twice as much information from the sympathetic source as any other reporter.

By 1942 he was handling major out-of-town assignments with high competence. His day-after account late in November of the Cocoanut Grove fire in Boston in which 491 people were burned, suffocated, or trampled to death was a model of succinct narrative, dwelling on the testimony of a few survivors and rescue workers to render the horrifying consequences of the unleashed herd mentality. It was also the last big piece he would write as a city reporter for the *Tribune*. A healthy bachelor in his thirty-fifth year, he was faced with the choice of being drafted into military service or working as a war correspondent. Red badges of courage did not appeal to him, and, at any rate, he had done his share of soldiering on the streets. His salary before he left to join the paper's three-man London bureau was, after fifteen years on staff, eighty-five dollars a week.

The war served as a release for him. Mostly, he wrote what he chose to, although at first the variety of subjects was slim. The worst of the Blitz was long past and the nearest land combat was in North Africa; in Britain, the only real story was the air war.

He would wait for word by phone at the bureau—"Big poker game tonight" and the like—and take the train in the direction indicated by the cryptic message to a country depot from where he would be jeeped to an airbase to await the return of that evening's mission. Sometimes he made it to the planes to talk to the crews before they came in for debriefing, but security and morale considerations prevented his reporting candidly on the terrible casualties—25 percent at times or even higher—the Luftwaffe inflicted at first. Everything he wrote had to clear the censors. When the chance came for him to go on one of the missions, he did not hesitate.

Trained for a week at one of the air bases, the reporters chosen underwent physical examinations and received instruction in aircraft identification, first aid, how to handle oxygen masks in temperatures that would drop to 50 below zero 27,000 feet above the earth, how to fire 50-millimeter machine guns (in violation of the Geneva Convention, which outlawed the arming of noncombatants), how to operate a parachute and, no less important, to inflate a rubber raft, without which they would not survive thirty minutes in the North Sea in midwinter. His press colleagues on the raid, men several years younger than Bigart, included Walter Cronkite, then with the United Press; one representative each from the Associated Press and Hearst's International News Service; Andy Rooney of the American military's *Stars & Stripes;* and Robert P. Post of *The New York Times,* by far the best known and most highly regarded of their number.

The correspondents were each to fly in a different plane for the mission; the target—the U-boat pens at Wilhemshaven—was one of the most heavily defended bases in Germany. Post, who insisted on going despite the base commander's urgings, got a place on a bomber in the middle of one of the four formations —it was a better vantage point, he was told, but in fact the position was regarded as relatively the safest, befitting a representative of *The New York Times.* Uncelebrated Homer Bigart of the *New York Herald Tribune* was assigned to the lead plane of his squadron. The date was February 26, 1943.

After they crossed the Channel, there was no fighter escort. Their safety depended upon flying so high that the effect of antiaircraft fire was reduced and upon keeping a tight formation that put out a deadly field of fire against enemy fighters harassing them. What struck Bigart most about the mission was not its peril or his fear—the drama was so intense and theatrical there was almost no time to be scared—but his sense of loneliness and isolation. And the cold, which nearly did him in before the real show began. At minus-20 degrees, ice formed when he drooled into the breathing apparatus on his oxygen mask. The curtailed air supply made him woozy, and he knocked into another crew member, who saw his trouble and quickly stuck an emergency pipe into Bigart's mouth.

As they reached the Dutch coast, the Luftwaffe fighters rose up to meet them. "You see them far ahead, mere specks in the sky," he would write afterward, "and they are on you in a minute. He's doing about 400 an hour and you are not exactly standing still, so you have only a few seconds to put the bead on him and press the trigger." Bigart himself never did manage to aim, but he did keep the bullets flying.

The flak thickened as they neared their target—nasty black puffs of it that left curious smoke trails in an hourglass shape. The nearest burst two hundred yards from them, but it was heavy around the squadron ahead of them to their left. And then he saw one of the planes up there go down and only two chutes open; it was his worst moment of the raid.

As soon as their own bombs were dropped, the pilot "had us shifting like the Notre Dame varsity, changing course just often enough so that the Focke-Wulfs sitting there against the horizon never had a chance to set us up for a frontal attack" on the big glass noses of the B-17s. The Focke-Wulfs were replaced by twin-engined Messerschmitts that dogged them halfway to England. When they were finally in the clear, the pilot, a twenty-six-year-old captain from Pine Bluff, Arkansas, flying his thirteenth mission, passed judgment over the intercom with a bravado the RAF had patented in its heroic defense of Fortress Britannia: "A piece of cake."

On their ride back to London from the air base, Bigart asked Cronkite what he thought of the experience. "I've got my lead all set," answered the future television newscaster. " 'I've just returned from an assignment through hell— a hell of . . .' " and then he rattled off the rest of a long, melodramatic opening.

"You-you-you wouldn't!" said Bigart, whose own taste favored understatement. Cronkite argued that the UP's clients would expect a sensationalized treatment. The debate ended when they reached their offices and learned that the bomber *Times*man Robert Post had been flying in was shot down and he was not among the survivors. Piece of cake.

Bigart remained in London under six months, but they were enough for him to leave his mark. Soon after arriving to take charge of the UP's London bureau, Harrison E. Salisbury went one day to the Ministry of Information for an air communiqué. The ministry was housed then in a huge auditorium which was empty at the moment "except for this solitary figure—a skinny, very serious young man hunched over his typewriter and very slowly, very carefully typing his story." Salisbury watched him for a while, fascinated by the fellow's obliviousness to being observed. "I'd heard about him—that he was a beautiful writer and said to be meticulous, to spend more time on a story than anyone else, which of course made him a pain in the ass to his competitors. I never knew a more tenacious reporter," Salisbury recalled after exposure to Bigart in action. "I think he was a legend within weeks of his arrival in London."

Bigart's metamorphosis from city-room frog to a prince among war correspondents was quickened by his transfer to the Mediterranean theater in the summer of 1943. Land combat taught new lessons that he could learn only in the field. It was a hot, loud, dirty, bloody field where, more than ever, he was on his own.

Modern mechanized warfare does not lend itself readily to being rendered by journalists who do not, as Homer Bigart did not, like to take its perpetrators' word for what was happening on the battle line. World War II was fought with more masses of men and concentrations of weaponry over vaster distances than any conflict before or since. No man could hope for even a bird's-eye view of more than a small sector of battleground. For most reports, correspondents were reduced to transmitting official news only: what military commanders chose to issue for home consumption. Censorship was a condition of access to the war zones.

To act as a mere conduit, though, powerless to observe events full-scale and form independent judgment of their meaning, was a waste of his presence, Bigart soon calculated. The wire services would provide the *Tribune* with whatever portion of the big story American military headquarters decided to put out. Instead of grand strategies, Bigart would devote himself to small tactical operations that, if carefully reported, would bring a dimension of reality and understanding to readers back home. So long as he did so, confining himself to limited actions already concluded and making no mention of pending troop movements, the brass and its censors were happy to let him pursue the war at the cannon's mouth. No one else did this so often, so persistently, so evocatively, and lived.

The first big land mission he chose to go on was nearly his last. He accompanied a weary battalion, only recently back from a rugged action, on an amphibious probe behind the German lines in Sicily. The enemy reacted swiftly to the landing, and Bigart found himself with a unit pinned down behind a hilltop, a sitting target for shelling if the Germans had not been facing heavy pressure on their front. Sweating out the wait for relief, Bigart blamed the stupid, vainglorious venture on the man who had ordered it—George Patton—because the general had been frustrated in his lust for laurels by stiff German resistance.

The next time, deeper into the Sicilian campaign, that he courted extinction he had only himself to blame. Out near the shifting front trying to locate a unit, he reached a spot where there wasn't anybody—but well within range of enemy gunfire. He dove for a foxhole and prayed for invisibility. Guns chattered sporadically around him. The wait was eternal. The Sicilian sun baked him, and the dust intensified his raging thirst, and the incoming shells seemed ticketed for him personally, and he was alone. Finally he began to make notes he hoped to live long enough to use. During a lull in the shooting, he scrambled desperately away, took almost as large a risk by dipping his canteen into the nearest muddy stream to cool his burning throat, and managed to flag down a jeep that returned him to the American lines.

On the job, he wore fatigues and a helmet and chain-smoked two packs of cigarettes a day—indistinguishable on the exterior from the GIs he covered, except that he was older and went unarmed. After the air attack on Wilhelmshaven, he did not carry or fire a gun for the rest of the war. His most valuable possession was his bedroll. In the field, under enemy fire, it got damned cold, and that far from the press facilities in the rear there was nobody to look after him. He had to be mobile and resourceful. His typewriter he would lug to a point beyond which it would be a burden to his survival. When they gave him a place to write, it was often elbow to elbow with other correspondents. Sometimes he had to write without notes—there was often little opportunity to take them amid the cross fire and perilous logistics—but he discovered how remarkably retentive the human memory can prove under the dire circumstances of battle.

Even after the campaign crossed over to Italy, he would hardly ever see a copy of the *Tribune,* know what they were doing to his copy or where they played it. His editors back in New York might as well have been on Neptune. They never cabled him a story suggestion and only rarely sent a letter expressing general approval of his work. He wondered if he was really performing a useful service—his copy was, after all, largely supplementary, inflated sidebars that could hardly have made much difference in the paper's daily summation of the global war. But the longer he kept at it, the more he came to view the absence of feedback as a blessed form of freedom. His competitors on the *Times* were in ceaseless communication with the home office and often grew depressed as a result: assignments from a distance of 4,000 miles that made little sense at the scene, arguments with censors, copy butchered by a surfeit of deskmen, worry over filing deadlines. Bigart covered what he saw fit, labored over it, handed his stuff to the censor, and moved on.

At Anzio he was on the beachhead the first day and remained there throughout three murderous German assaults to push the U.S. forces back into the sea. He watched an American general go to pieces in the face of threatening disaster and felt for the first time what it was like to be fired on directly by a tank: loud, nasty, and imperative. The lines were so close he could see the German troop movements—here was no distant, disembodied menace but flesh-and-blood ranks and mighty armor wheeling for a kill, all visible to the unaided eye. Tension was high within the American lines, fights arose over little things, and Bigart had to restrain his revulsion over a fellow correspondent who never changed his underwear. One day Bigart accompanied an artillery spotter atop a stone tower, a vital observation post and prime target for the long German guns. It was not a pleasurable experience, and when he had endured enough to gather a sense of it, he left the spotter to his fate—and in the process came to understand truly the difference between the correspondent's life, even that of an intrepid one who insisted on up-front exposure, and the soldier's: The reporter could beat it when he chose and go back to sleep on a cot in a tent; the soldier had to face the possibility of momentary annihilation as the central fact of his being. It was one reason Bigart never regarded himself a hero.

A month after the Anzio landing, when U.S. forces had broken through the ring of German steel, Bigart treated himself to a rare day off and went out rowing in a rubber boat. Suddenly a German fighter plane swooped down from nowhere and used him for target practice. The bullets missed. Not long after, a 20-millimeter shell ripped through the wall in the villa where Bigart was billeted and wound up in his bathtub. Bigart was away at the time. During the long struggle that followed for the abbey at Monte Cassino and its commanding heights, Bigart was crossing a just liberated field one day on the killing plain below the monastery, began climbing a fence, and happened to notice beside him a large, flat, pancakelike object clinging to it—a live mine that a retreating German hadn't had time to plant. A few weeks later, as Allied troops raced to liberate Rome, Bigart hurried in a jeep ahead of the main body—freedom's outrider, eager to record the sense of elation among the Italian people as they flung open their shutters to the conquerors of fascism. Around a bend in the road he was confronted, at no more than two hundred yards, by a German tank, its crew calmly eating lunch. Bigart's jeep flew into reverse even faster than it had advanced as the Germans bolted for their guns; ever after he would remember the hair on the back of his neck standing on end till his jeep was out of range. For all this, he refused in the lulls between action to think about getting killed; it was something that happened to other people.

Bigart's daring, however foolhardy other correspondents rated it, awed them. Turner Catledge, who would become the ranking editor of the *Times* in the postwar era, was with him once at a field headquarters in Italy. "We had to get under a fence in a hurry while the area was being shelled. Homer would stop and check a few facts even while we were under fire." Yet what Catledge recalled most about the experience was Bigart's modesty.

For Catledge's bearded *Times* colleague Milton Bracker, competing head-on with Bigart on a day-to-day basis inspired more exasperation than awe. He could not let the *Herald Tribune*'s man outdo him during the long Cassino siege, with its pelting rains and deadly raking fire from the German-held heights, so he stuck doggedly to Bigart's trail. One night well after supper the two of them and an AP man got back famished to the American lines and prevailed upon an army cook to put up some eggs. The AP man left his typewriter and fell on the steaming platter. Bracker eyed Bigart, glued undistracted to his typewriter, and asked if he would be breaking for a bite. "Not hungry" was the reply. Afraid that if he ate, Bigart would file first and if he did not, the wrath of the kindly cook would descend upon him, the starving Bracker settled for bringing his plate to the typewriter and picking at it between paragraphs. At midnight, after his story was in, Bigart devoured a crust of bread, all that was left. The day Cassino fell, Bracker was off on a story in another part of the sector, and when he got back to camp weary at nightfall, discovered Bigart had been up at the monastery when the Americans finally seized it. To match Bigart's dateline, Bracker had to make his way up to the abbey through the dark, over still heavily mined fields; traversing the same fields by daylight the next morning, two British correspondents were killed by mines.

Bigart's growing reputation was garnished by now with stories of his wit as well as his prowess. Most of them had one element in common—their subject reportedly stuttered at just the artful spot in delivering the punch line. When, for example, the post-liberation Italian Cabinet met for the first time, an aide emerged in the antechamber and told a cluster of correspondents that it would be just half an hour more before the officials, as one of their first acts, finished drafting a law to abolish fascism. "All they have to do now," Bigart was said to have cracked, "is put in the l-l-loopholes."

By the time he returned to New York in October 1944 for a month's vacation before reassignment to the war in the Pacific, Bigart had attained national stature. His stories, at once simple and detailed, were almost always on the *Tribune* front page and won prominent display by other papers subscribing to the Herald Tribune Syndicate. *Newsweek* ran a piece on his exploits, calling him "the hardest kind of worker and the fairest kind of competitor." Back in the city room, with a little time on his hands, the prodigy, his mustache long gone and looking stockier now, still declined to read his clips. If he was prospering in a fool's paradise, why undo the delusion?

In the island campaigns of the Pacific, Homer Bigart produced his best work of the war.

He preferred the tropical climate to the frigid campaigns in Europe—"I'd rather be terrified in a warm place," he said—and the smaller battle arenas that he could more easily reconnoiter, but he did not prefer the more fanatical enemy. With the Germans, there had been at least an occasional display of humanity, such as Kesselring's command to stop firing at American ambulances bearing the wounded away under Nazi gunsights at Cassino, a gesture that the correspondents were forbidden to mention in their dispatches. With the Japanese, there was no sense that they valued human life, their enemies' or their own. "You definitely got the idea we were going to have to walk over piles of their corpses to get to Tokyo," Bigart remembered. "This was a more awful war."

Nowhere was the diehard Japanese resistance fiercer than on Iwo Jima, ten square miles of grimly contested territory only 750 miles from Tokyo and thus a strategically important prize for the stationing of U.S. planes. Just reaching it was an ordeal for Bigart. There was no harbor and the sea was very rough under the landing craft to which he had to descend from his ship by crawling down a rope ladder carefully lest he get smacked by the bobbing LST. What he found ashore inspired an explanatory dispatch in prose that was evolving into a sinewy, evocative style recognizably his own:

> For this desolate heap of volcanic cinders the marines have paid in blood, and more casualties will be counted before the island is secured. But the toll was certainly not exorbitant. Anyone visiting this macabre piece of real estate, as treeless and bleak as slagpiles in Pennsylvania coal fields, may well wonder how the marines were able to land at all.

He detailed how the Japanese buried pillboxes in the crests of hills, covered them with timbers and sheets of concrete, then heaped on stone and dirt and planted grass on top, so thoroughly camouflaging the emplacements that the marines could not detect them until they were directly in front of the enemy's gun slits. The subterranean defenses, under construction since World War I, were impervious to the big U.S. naval guns offshore and aerial bombardment. Heavily supplied and manned by 20,000 troops, a great many for so small a place, with guns trained on every beach, the Japanese positions left no room for maneuver —there could be no end run to ground left undefended. He concluded his dispatch with a terse judgment that was as close as he would ever come to chauvinism: "We had to have Iwo, and we will have to pay for it."

He almost paid for it himself. In the tangled jungle terrain of the Pacific island wars, it was often hard to know where the lines were, and they had an unpleasant way of shifting without signs being posted. In his perpetual quest for a unit whose pain and valor he could document, Bigart holed up one night in a hut with a pair of exhausted GIs and left in the morning before they awoke. Soon after, he learned that the hut had been destroyed and its sleeping occupants with it.

Even such close calls did not inhibit him. He seemed, rather, to thrive on danger. One of his most memorable articles told of an air-sea rescue raid in which he accompanied an amphibious landing party, reinforced by paratroopers, who wiped out a Japanese garrison of 243, many by knifepoint, and freed 2,100 civilian internees from a prison camp twenty-five miles behind enemy lines in the Philippines. In 1,600 succinct words of rousing but not overwrought narrative, he compacted a story that could easily have filled a novel or served as the scenario for a full-length motion picture. It transported the reader to the scene of mingled joy and horror nearly half a world away, and enmeshed him in it:

> . . . Immediate evacuation was essential, but in their moment of liberation the internees were too hysterically happy to appreciate the peril of delay. They began picking up rags, rusty pans and blankets accumulated during three years' imprisonment. . . . Aged internees hated to leave their beds and beach chairs behind. There were frantic, last-minute hunts for cats and dogs that had somehow escaped being eaten during the last weeks of acute hunger.

He wrote of the sadistic Japanese commandant who reduced food rations to 200 grains of rice and corn a day, though there were heavy growths of coconut trees right beside the camp; of one heroic doctor among the internees who performed 300 major operations with the most primitive of equipment; of how wood for coffins had to be scavenged from old buildings lest the exposed dead spread tropical contagion; of the birth and survival—amid such ghastly travail—of two babies just a few days before the rescue. The names and numbers and chronology and quoted reactions by the rescued were all there, and the feelings of outrage and elation, without redundancy or moralizing. His subject, as he had recognized from the first, was so inherently dramatic that it did not require ornament from him.

He became a master now of economical scene-setting, a most useful virtue in view of the rationed wordage allotted to him on wires that had to serve hundreds of clamoring correspondents throughout the Pacific theater. This is how he sketched the backdrop of a first-person report on a Japanese air attack on American ships unloading supplies at Okinawa:

Our duck was jolting across the coral shallows when black smudges of ack-ack bursts appeared on the seaward horizon. Through the murk overhead we heard the faint hum of airplane motors. On the long flat deck of an LST tied up on our right we saw the gun crews standing ready. All eyes stared upward at the cloud curtain.

It was lanced through so quickly that the machine-gunners barely had time to let loose a burst. In one instance a Zeke seemed to slow down as though the pilot was undecided which of the wealth of targets he should choose. . . .

In New York, his editors inserted the bracketed intelligence that a "duck" was an amphibious truck and a "Zeke" a Zero fighter. But mostly they added nothing—and found little that was superfluous.

These word pictures of his, in the pre-television age when newsreel photography could capture only flashes of combat conditions but little of the detail and none of the sweep of battle, made Bigart's work of special value. At home, Elmer Davis, running the Office of War Information, singled him out for praise at a dinner of the Overseas Press Club. So highly regarded had Bigart's knowing dispatches become that when he dared to question the wisdom of the U.S. frontal-assault strategy on Okinawa, a far larger island than Iwo Jima and one where an attack on the enemy's rear might have shortened his resistance, syndicated columnist David Lawrence seized on the suggestion and labeled the American operation a fiasco. In a statement rare in American military annals, Fleet Admiral Chester W. Nimitz was forced to defend the course followed by the commander at Okinawa but pointedly declined to criticize Bigart's reporting. His care, accuracy, and courage were, in fact, so well thought of by the military that the *Tribune*'s management received a letter from the War Department expressing alarm at Bigart's habit of voluntary exposure to danger. Helen Reid, who a decade earlier had scolded the city-room also-ran for costing the paper an advertisement, now wrote to him:

> . . . It was good of [General Chase] to bother to write but I can assure you that we have all been considerably disturbed over your determined habit of being almost ahead of the front lines. We will enjoy knowing that you do not take perilous chances all the time. . . . We are praying that the collection of your articles for the Pulitzer Committee will receive the award it deserves. . . .

He was flying back from a raid on Kumagaya, a rail hub on the Japanese mainland, when World War II officially ended. He felt more relief and exhaustion than euphoria. When the armistice papers were signed on the deck of the battleship *Missouri* a few days later in Tokyo Bay, Bigart was aboard. But the scene was so thronged and so many correspondents were on hand that he could not file to the paper; only pool reports were sent.

For him the war did not truly end until he witnessed the devastation of Hiroshima. As he had been with the first party of reporters to view the bombing of Germany, so at the end he was with the first group of newsmen to observe close up the cataclysmic force of atomic energy. While he felt the decision to drop the bomb had saved no fewer than 200,000 American lives that would have been spent in an invasion of Japan, he was overwhelmed by the spectacle that greeted him in early September, a month after the explosion: ". . . only flat appalling desolation, the starkness accentuated by bare, blackened tree trunks and the occasional shell of a reinforced concrete building." The cloying stench of death clung to the streets, and residents were still dying at the rate of a hundred a day. He was surprised to discover no crater at ground zero, testament to the primarily lateral force of the blast, and contrary to reports he had heard of the obliteration of matter on the site, he discovered the usual rubble of war at his feet, only the particles were smaller.

Asked a generation afterward whether any journalistic techniques or principles had consciously guided his war reporting, he replied, "I just tried to get the goddamned story written."

For those "goddamned" stories of his in 1945, Homer William Bigart was awarded the Pulitzer Prize.

VI

Shortly after the capture of Berlin by the Red army in April 1945, Carl Levin, a small, peppery man who had succeeded Homer Bigart as the *Tribune*'s head copyboy and worked his way up to the Washington bureau before going overseas for the paper, began poking through the rubble of Hitler's bunker beneath the ruins of the Reich Chancellery. A Russian bayonet was pressed against his belly, sheathed smartly in an Abercrombie & Fitch uniform, until Levin identified himself and gained admission along with his driver. Face down amid the wreckage of the building was a bronze sculpture, about twice life size, of Hitler's head. The Russians had pumped five dumdum bullets into it, toppling the work from its pedestal and causing considerable damage to its rear.

With some difficulty Levin and his driver lifted the sculpture, wrapped it in the latter's overcoat, and bustled the thing past Soviet guards. When the crate containing it arrived some weeks later in the office of *Tribune* managing editor George Cornish, it was shoved unopened under the conference table around which he and the other editors met late each afternoon to plan the next morning's issue, and stayed there for some time. When at last a janitor was summoned to pry open the formidable container, it was found to bear a note from Levin suggesting that the bullet-raked head might be a fitting monument to the noble service rendered by the paper's war correspondents. Cornish agreed, and the bronze stood on the windowsill for his remaining fifteen years in that office.

Levin's most dangerous moment of overseas service occurred not under German gunfire or the scrutiny of Russian guards but several months after the surrender when he was covering the American army of occupation. The civilian government established in Bavaria under the U.S. Third Army commanded by

General George S. Patton, Jr., included a number of prominent Nazis. Levin noted the fact in articles that were played prominently in the Paris edition of the *Tribune* and *Stars & Stripes*; the disclosure did not endear him to Patton's staff. Soon after, Eisenhower lifted a ban he had imposed on his generals against holding press conferences, and Patton agreed to meet with correspondents at Third Army headquarters at Bad Tolz. He strode in, placed his pearl-handled revolvers on the table, and, as Levin recalled, "began to critique us on how he won the war." At the end, Patton greeted the newsmen informally, and Levin used the opportunity to ask him why he seemed to be dragging his feet on the denazification program in force elsewhere in the fallen Third Reich. Patton's answer made a hot story: " 'This Nazi thing,' he explained, 'is just like a Democratic-Republican election fight.' For this reason, he added, he has never seen the reason for a denazification program." Patton went on to say that more than half the German people had been Nazis and therefore, "We've got to compromise with the devil a little bit to get things going before trying to get a simon-pure system."

In the celebrated movie *Patton,* as in the biography by Ladislas Farago on which it was partly based, the Levin-like reporter was portrayed as putting the words into Patton's mouth that Nazis were really no different from members of the two main American political parties. Levin insisted the words were the general's. Whoever uttered them first, they drew Eisenhower's stiff rebuke and an order to apologize publicly. Patton complied, in his fashion, but Eisenhower soon stripped him of his command and assigned him to direct a paper army. Patton, fuming, went off on a hunting trip, during which he was killed. When Levin climbed aboard the funeral train bearing Patton's body to Allied head-quarters in Luxembourg, the general's staff members accused the *Tribune* correspondent of causing their commander's death and, according to Levin's vivid memory, tried to edge him off the train that was hurtling a hundred miles an hour across the terrain Patton had helped liberate. "After the funeral, I said to Eisenhower that I was sorry if my stories had forced his hand, and he said, 'On the contrary, Mr. Levin—you made it possible for us to do what had to be done.' "

VII

Not all the best *Tribune* men were sent abroad to cover the great war. Among those who stayed behind was reporter John G. Rogers, who had come over in 1937 from the *American,* where he had been a legman pining to write, and turned into one of the city room's finest performers for nearly thirty years. Several times considered for city editor or foreign correspondent, Rogers never wanted to do anything but local reporting, just as Bob Peck could not be enticed from the rewrite bank. Rogers did not mix much with his colleagues at Bleeck's—he did his work and went home—but he thought a lot about his craft and was proud of it.

The modern newspaper reporter, Rogers once wrote, was the most prolific and widely read writer who ever lived, but that was hardly cause for excessive egotism while cranking out his short-lived wares, because his readers sought information from him, not inspiration or beauty. Yet to John Rogers there was a definite kind of beauty in good newspaper writing, which he defined as "an expert job of simplification"—crisp, clear intelligence stated in the fewest and shortest appropriate words. His piece on President Roosevelt's funeral, more of a color story than a straight news account, Rogers felt was the best thing he ever wrote for the paper. It read in part:

> HYDE PARK, N.Y., April 15 — The hedge-girdled rose garden on the Roosevelt estate was bright with sunlight but ruffled by a sharp wind at 9 o'clock this morning when preparation began for the service that buried the wartime Commander in Chief in the home soil that he loved. . . .
>
> Through that long gauntlet of sailors, military police and much-decorated marine veterans of Pacific fighting, Franklin Delano Roosevelt was to pass as he came home for the last time to the meadows and hills that were his boyhood playground.
>
> The pall of gravity, the stern sense of finality that pervaded Hyde Park today extended completely to these several thousand young service men whom chance had selected to participate in this closing chapter of an era. Even when they stood at ease during their long waiting, they smoked little and talked little.

A few weeks later, Adolf Hitler died ignominiously by his own hand. The stylistic contrast between the *Tribune* and the *Times* may be at once perceived by examining the obituaries that the two papers ran on May 2, each a biographical essay consuming approximately a full page of text. The unsigned *Tribune* obit was by John Durston, a somewhat melancholic rewriteman. The articles began:

TRIBUNE VERSION

Adolf Hitler sought to enslave the world and almost succeeded in destroying the civilization which it had taken Europe 2,000 years to achieve.

History can hardly deny him a place beside Genghis Khan, Attila the Hun, and the other great conquerors and scourges of human freedom, but in all the annals of mankind a stranger or more unsavory figure was never enthroned in their questionable Valhalla.

He combined the appearance of a low comedian of the music halls with the savagery of a South Sea Island head hunter. Womanish hysteria was as much a part of

TIMES VERSION

Adolf Hitler, one-time Austrian vagabond who rose to be the dictator of Germany, "augmenter of the Reich" and scourge of Europe, was, like Lenin and Mussolini, a product of the First World War. The same general circumstances, born of the titanic conflict, that carried Lenin, a bookish professional revolutionist, to the pinnacle of power in the Empire of the Czars and cleared the road to mastery for Mussolini in the Rome of the Caesars, also paved the way for Hitler's domination in the former mighty Germany of the Hohenzollerns. . . .

Before the climax of a career unparal-

his character as the ferocity which drove him to start the worst war in history. He could simper over the prettiness of a flaxen-haired child in one breath and in the next gloat over the bombing of a hundred British children of equally Aryan blondness.

His was a character of tortuous complexities and astonishing contradictions. The sufferings of his victims left him unmoved, except by childish glee, but Wagner's music made him weep . . .

Hitler restored tyranny to history. He hung chains on a civilization that thought it was finished with slavery. . . .

leled in history, he had subdued nine nations, defied successfully and humiliated the greatest powers of Europe, and created a social and economic system founded upon the complete subjection of scores of millions to his will in all basic features of social, political, economic and cultural life.

Sixty-five million Germans yielded to the blandishments and magnetism of this slender man of medium height, with little black mustache and shock of dark hair, whose fervor and demagogy swept everything before him with outstretched arms as the savior and regenerator of the Fatherland. . . .

VIII

Whatever its virtues, *The New York Times* was not "unquestionably the best newspaper in sight," as Gay Talese called it; inarguably, it was the most complete. On any given day or story, the *Herald Tribune* was capable of matching or outperforming it. A case in point was its coverage of the July 28, 1945, crash of a B-26 twin-engine Army bomber, lost in a morning fog over Manhattan on a flight from Boston to Newark, into the seventy-ninth floor of the Empire State Building. Spewing high-octane flames in every direction, the plane incinerated its three crewmen and ten office workers. If it had not been a summer Saturday when the department stores and most offices were closed, if rain had not just begun to fall and discouraged sightseers who normally thronged what was then the world's highest structure, the toll would have been catastrophic.

At the moment of the plane's impact, a subway train from Queens was a couple of minutes from delivering Peter Kihss to the Empire State Building. A tall, lean man who sometimes stooped as if self-conscious of his height, he had a narrow face with soft, kind eyes behind glasses that gave him a bookish look. Despite his efforts to join the navy, weak eyesight had kept him from military service. Now a few weeks shy of his thirty-third birthday, Kihss had spent the war as a newspaper reporter, first with the evening *World-Telegram,* where he had started in 1936, and for the past two years with the *Herald Tribune.* He liked that better. There was a friendly, almost family feeling about the city room, where he would spend the nine happiest years of his career.

Others wrote better and won more prizes than Peter Kihss, but it was widely agreed among the city's working press that, during a career spanning nearly half a century, no more dedicated or thorough reporter worked the town. He was not smooth or tricky or swashbuckling. His distinction resided in the tense resolve and barely contained excitement with which he approached his assignments and mined them for all they were worth—and sometimes more. His approach to the story that brought him to work that last Saturday morning of July in 1945 was typical: A leading official at the regional quarters of the Office of Price Administration (OPA), located in the Empire State Building, was to be dismissed at a press conference scheduled for noon. Conscientious nearly to the point of obsession, Kihss had decided to arrive at the scene early and nose around. You never knew what might turn up.

The subway deposited him at the south side of the Empire State Building that midsummer morning. As he emerged onto the sidewalk, a brick landed near him on Thirty-third Street. Kihss looked up, but the upper reaches of the building were shrouded in fog and smoke. Instinct and deduction drove him around the block to Thirty-fourth Street, the side of the building that the plane had hit moments before. The first sirens wailed now through the wet morning. Bystanders told him of the terrible concussion and the burst of flame far above.

He raced for a phone booth on the street and called the *Tribune* city desk, ten blocks away. They had not heard the news. Even while he was on the line, another deskman was telephoning word to city editor Lessing Engelking, who at the moment was in the bathtub at his home in Forest Hills. Engel roared instructions to Kihss to stick with it. As he got back to the building's entrance, Mayor Fiorello La Guardia and his fire commissioner were just arriving. Kihss fell into step with the pair, who knew him well, and beelined for the elevators. He did not ask them if he could go along. You never asked La Guardia for anything because the answer would always be no—especially to Kihss. The two had had a blustery relationship ever since the *World-Telegram* had taken to sending Kihss to City Hall anytime a politically explosive question had to be put to the combustible mayor; that way the paper's City Hall beat man could be spared La Guardia's enmity. But the mayor had more on his mind just then than past irritation with the press, so Kihss rode the elevator up with him in tense silence. Behind them on the ground floor, the police barricade went up.

When he got out on the sixty-seventh floor, which was as high as the elevators were working, Kihss found no other reporter on the scene. For the next hour or so, the story—and the inferno that greeted him after an additional twelve-story climb on foot—was his exclusively. As a rule the press was kept out of most disaster scenes until the gore had been cleaned up by rescue workers and the bodies removed or humanely covered by sheets. In this instance, the sole representative of the press was ahead of almost everyone.

The heat assaulted him first and then the smoke and the smells of burned oil and metal and flesh—rank fumes of the battlefield that Peter Kihss had been spared until that moment. The seventy-ninth floor had been shredded into a blackened tangle of stone, glass, metal still cracking and crumbling from the heat, charred wood, and papers turned to ash. Iron railings and steel doorframes had been twisted like bailing wire, and the buckled floor was becoming a dark, debris-strewn swamp as firemen worked their hoses, snaked from miraculously still-functioning standpipes on the floors below. Others searched for trapped survivors. Directly in the path of the plane had lain the war relief office of the National Catholic Welfare Conference. There the devastation was almost total. Metal partitions had been flattened, and some lifted in molten fusion with shards of windowpane to form ghastly stalactites on the ceiling. They would stab at Kihss's memory for the rest of his life.

As the fierce heat cooled, the grimmest work began. Charred body fragments were lifted with shovels and placed gingerly on surviving desk tops. What looked like a wad of water-sogged paper proved to be a torso. Two sets of shoulders, bloody and crushed, were dredged up near each other, along with scorched tatters of an airman's uniform bearing European campaign ribbons. Here was part of an arm, upturned at the elbow, as if frozen in convulsive reflex to ward off oblivion; there, the shriveled head of a stenographer, its singed blond hair somehow still in place.

With pencil and pad, Kihss wrote it down as fast as he knew how, diagramming as he went, snatching words on the fly, mapping the path of the disintegrated bomber by the wake of its destruction. His mind outraced his hand and his legs. He was thinking every instant, knowing amid the bedlam that this was one of the great and terrible stories of the year, of the age, of his career, and he did not want to miss a thing. The dead were gone, he told himself, beyond help and further pain, part now of the inanimate rubble; only the whiff of their souls remained, and he had to put them out of his mind. The cries of survivors would have been a different matter, but here there were no cries of the pinioned; death had come in a second. There were injured, twenty-six, some badly, but they were being tended to. So he did his job.

He took down everything because there was no telling what would finally make a story for the *Tribune,* partial as it was to color as well as substance in its reporting. On the eightieth floor, where the fire had leaped up the elevator shaft and burst out into the hallway and then into the suite of the Caterpillar Tractor Company's New York office, he found a tantalizing lead. In the back wall of the rear room of the suite, an oval hole two and a half feet high had been gouged with what must have been desperate haste as a means of escape from the fiery blast. Behind it, an empty room under renovation in an unoccupied suite led to safety. Kihss rummaged over the desk in the Caterpillar office and found the name and phone number of its occupant, the assistant manager. Astonishingly, the telephone was working. He tried the man's home number in Middle Village, Queens. His wife answered. Her husband, she said, had called a short while ago and was on his way home but had not said why; Kihss chose not to alarm her. Instead, he called his city desk and alerted Engel to a potentially heroic tale. Within minutes, Margaret Parton, among the most gifted of the women who had found places on the city staff during the wartime manpower shortage, was on her way to interview the Caterpillar man.

A dozen other *Tribune* reinforcements were working the story now, too, and reporters from the other papers were trudging up the stairs to survey the sorry spectacle. But before quitting the scene, Kihss felt he had to learn for certain what had become of the airplane's engines. One of them had wound up in an elevator shaft, driving an empty car down to the subcellar beneath its weight. The other was nowhere to be found. After a moment's reflection, he followed the plane's path the length of the building and hypothesized the hurtling engine out through the punctured south wall, from which debris had fallen near him as he left the subway. The engine might well have shot entirely across Thirty-third Street. He hurried down to the twelve-story building directly across from the Empire State. There, in a sculptor's penthouse studio, he found a cleanup crew tending to the disfigured remains of the missing engine. It had come to rest at the foot of a statue of an angel; on the floor just below, seventy-five toolmakers were doing war contract work. No other reporter had yet been there.

It was midafternoon by the time he reached the *Tribune* building on West Forty-first Street. Deadline for the big Sunday edition was 6 p.m. Engelking might reasonably have assigned the lead story on the crash to Bob Peck or one of the other rewritemen adept at weaving together the disparate elements of such a drama, and asked Kihss to type up his notes for inclusion as the writer chose. He had, after all, put in a nonstop burst of legwork under draining conditions —hardly ideal preparation for turning out a long, demanding story under the tyranny of the clock. But Engel wanted him to write the story himself; he had been there before anyone else, knew it better than anyone else, could write it better than anyone else.

On his desk Kihss found a mountain of material: all the wire-service copy on the crash, duplicates of side stories by others on the *Tribune,* memos on information gathered for him by phone, including volunteered eyewitness accounts, and clips from the library on plane crashes, famous fires, and the Empire State Building—all of it to be digested and blended with his own hurried notes, mostly scrawled in dark corridors or rooms and hard to decipher. The nightmare he had to render now in words would be the centerpiece of a great metropolitan paper that would sell 600,000 copies of its ten-section Sunday edition the next morning. It was a task made no less daunting by the tumult around him: jangling telephones, a miniature anvil chorus of typewriter keys, murmured conversations, queries from the city desk, copyboys adding to the pile of material walling him in—and, worst of all, there was Engel, lumbering about the place, eyeing him anxiously from afar, chewing up his big unlighted cigars with tension born of pride in his paper and his writers' ability to outperform that great gray eminence, *The New York Times,* two blocks to the north.

It was not a moment for the fragile flower of creativity to wilt. Indeed, the muses were not invited to participate. It was not art at all that Kihss was required to practice now under extreme duress—it was craft, and it had to be produced fast and without temperament, and it had to be as right in all its small parts as in its large lineaments, and as dramatic and affecting as his gifts could summon on the instant. He could not await the arrival of inspiration. This was history on the run.

His slice of it that day came to 4,000 words in print, with his byline at the head. He never had the chance to read it all the way through until it was over; his story had moved to the city desk in takes, then to the copy desk, then the night desk. In transit, the story had been little altered. The rule at the *Tribune* was: good editors don't fix writing that doesn't need fixing. The only fix Engel insisted on was that Kihss drop the word "blond" in describing the shriveled head of one of the victims he had seen; it was too shockingly graphic and would only add to the pain of the dead girl's family.

That mysterious two-and-a-half-foot hole in the wall in the Caterpillar Tractor suite would provide the *Tribune* with an exclusive follow-up, thanks to Kihss. A woman elevator operator, it seemed, had parked her car on the eightieth floor a moment before the plane hit. The impact blasted her into the Caterpillar office, where she sought help from the assistant manager and one of his salesmen in the back office. But the flames followed her, trapping the three. "I opened the door a crack and saw that it was a furnace out there," the assistant manager told the *Tribune*'s reporter. "Then I looked at the windows and the flame was sweeping up them. The room was filling with black gas smoke, and we all began to cough. The floor was beginning to get hot, too." At the last moment, he remembered a claw hammer kept in the supply closet, grabbed it, and began pounding away at the rear wall. The plaster was four inches thick. But when his desperate flailing opened a hole big enough to reach his fist through, he found the wall was made of hollow brick. A spasm of superhuman effort forged an opening for the praying, sobbing girl to squeeze through, and the two men followed. On the other side was a room carpenters and masons had been using to store their equipment while renovating the next-door suite. From there they fled down the stairs to the fifty-sixth floor and took an elevator to safety. Kihss included a portion of the intensely dramatic account high in the lead story while the full version ran on an inside page. The *Times* stumbled along behind, inserting a shorter version of the horror tale in its late city edition, largely a rewrite from the *Tribune*.

A generation later, near the end of his newspaper career, Peter Kihss would say it was "luck" that had placed him at the scene moments after a bomber had crashed into the Empire State Building that misty morning a few weeks before World War II ended. But it was not luck that had prompted him to take the subway in from Queens two hours before his scheduled assignment. Or luck that he knew not to ask the mayor if he might join him on the elevator to the scene of the disaster long before any other newsman could follow. Or luck that wrote, at top speed, in clear, graphic prose, his indelible account of the appalling event. It was his life, and his newspaper thrived on it.

12

Cooking Cabbage

The firing of Lessing Lanham Engelking, the best city editor the *Tribune* had ever had, did not come as a surprise.

By his own later admission, he had been "in a low state of mind" since the end of the war and had become increasingly difficult to work under. In his unconsciously cruel perfectionism, he would berate subordinates with little or no justification. On the day Roosevelt died, Engel came back from supper and found a pile of as yet unattended copy in the wire basket beside his night city editor, Joseph G. Herzberg, a speedy craftsman who had been laboring heroically in the city editor's absence to keep up with the torrent of news. When Engel lashed out at him for having fallen behind, Herzberg, whose back and shoulders had been disfigured by infantile paralysis, rose up to his full stooped height, seized the basket of unedited copy, dumped it on his tormentor's lap, told him to edit the stuff himself, and stalked out. Engel had turned into a moody martinet, consumed by the job; on his summer vacation, he would come into the office and work up the election tables for the following fall. His tirades served no purpose now and only demoralized the city room.

In the spring of 1946, the big Texan rallied his resources and extended his lease on the city desk—extended the desk itself, in fact—by annexing the newly established United Nations as part of his territory. It was a shrewd move, for the news from abroad and Washington had continued to dominate the paper even after the war's end; the opening of the UN in New York seemed to promise a reversal of the trend by establishing the city as the capital of the postwar world. The Reids, moreover, were surrounded now by such internationally minded counselors as Lippmann, Parsons, and Barnes, who, in contrast to the circle directing the paper after World War I that had swayed Ogden from supporting the League of Nations, were strong believers in the need to create an arena for the peaceful settlement of global disputes. During the discussions held in San Francisco the previous spring to thrash out the UN charter, the Reids had rented a large home in the Bay City and remained for some six weeks, hosting a sizable delegation of *Tribune* people on hand to cover the event and manifesting their wholehearted backing for the UN.

Engel struck quickly to create a beachhead; he assigned about ten of his city staff of sixty, including Peter Kihss, John Rogers, recently returned foreign correspondent Walter Kerr, and Robert S. Bird, a smooth-writing transferee from the *Times,* to a special UN bureau and went up himself to the Bronx campus of Hunter College, the temporary site of the Security Council, to ride herd on the branch operation. All went well until Washington bureau chief Andrews and foreign news editor Barnes found their space allotment being unmercifully squeezed by Engelking, who fought for every story his troops brought in. Inevitably Cornish cut down on the UN overplay, and Engel started boiling. The day Cornish moved up the deadline for local copy—a change that was apparently not relayed with sufficient clarity to the city editor—was the day Soviet delegate Andrei Gromyko, in response to an assault on the Soviet Union's provocative activities in Iran, staged the first of his several walkouts from the UN. Engel came back to the office brimming with hot copy but found room left in the paper for only a fraction of it. When the next day's *Times* thoroughly outplayed the *Tribune* on the story, Engel was enraged. "He was so shocked and humiliated," Robert Donovan recalled, "that he absolutely stopped functioning. He was really sick that day—why hadn't he been told—why wasn't the change fully explained to him?" Until then, the city room had been his shop; no one meddled in his direction of the city staff. But now his ambition had put him on a collision course with other gifted and ambitious editors, and Cornish, without an adequate echelon of assistants directly under him to plan and coordinate the increasingly complex news-gathering process, had to arbitrate, sometimes summarily, as never before. Engelking was not a gracious loser. "I've never been renowned for diplomacy or for not stating my opinions," he said years later of his slipping hold on the city room. He stayed at his desk after the Gromyko episode to fight more effectively for his UN people, but he was growing snappish, then almost paranoiac as he began to suspect that his underlings were out to unhorse him. In the end, he did himself in when Helen Reid came down to the city room one day—something she did more and more frequently as Ogden's health failed—with an item she wanted run and, according to Whitie Reid, Engel "exploded in a most intemperate manner, saying something like 'I don't want to run this kind of horseshit.' " In his proprietary passion for his work, he had forgotten who owned the paper. "Helen Reid wanted me kicked out—she didn't care for me anymore," Engel reminisced long after, but the truth more nearly was that the job was a man-eater, it had devoured the man who had held it longer than anyone on the paper, and it was time to go.

A quick survey around town disclosed that he would not find adequate employment elsewhere, so Engel asked Cornish if there was some other job on the paper he might be given. Geoffrey Parsons offered to take him onto the editorial page as a specialist in municipal affairs, and so after nearly twenty years of abstinence, Engel became a writer again and stayed—a large, brooding figure smoking his oversized cigars and loyally haunting the corridors as a living legend for twenty more years. Beneath the tree in his Forest Hills home that glum Christmas of 1946, he found a thirteen-volume set of the Oxford English Dictionary with a nameplate that read: "To L. L. Engelking, with esteem and affection—The City Staff, New York Herald Tribune."

His successor had served a twenty-one-year apprenticeship on the paper, during which he had overcome physical adversity and demonstrated beyond doubt that he was qualified to rule the city room. Disease had not only humped his back but left his hand with a sometimes violent palsy. Yet the shake did not slow his pencil as it flew over every piece of copy he attended with an almost miraculously beautiful script, nor was his aim diverted at the billiard table in the pool halls he frequented around Times Square in his off-hours. For Joe Herzberg was a man of the streets—he did not hide his misshapen form from them or his beloved city's theaters, saloons, and ballparks. Here was no outlander from Texas or Alabama but a native of the Bronx who had graduated from the Townsend Harris high school for bright students and gone to work in 1925 at the age of eighteen as a *Herald Tribune* copyboy to help his parents make ends meet. A self-made intellectual with an encyclopedic mind, he became an omnivorous reader, always carrying a book with him to work as he advanced to reporter, then crack rewriteman, then to the city desk, eventually directing its nighttime operation. He could discourse with equal authority on the works of Cézanne or the liturgies of Roman Catholicism and was probably the only man in the city room who could recite every major-leaguer's batting average at the moment or give the location and spelling of such remote city oases as McCoombs Dam Park.

More than an accomplished dilettante and useful trivialist, Joe Herzberg was treasured in the *Tribune* city room as a "copy doctor." He had mastered the paper's preferred style of crisp, vivid writing and knew how, with a minimum of fuss, to add a stroke or two to brighten, or cut a word or phrase to tighten, the copy that poured across the city desk. His memory was almost as useful as his stylistic sense. Upon receipt of a story from Don Irwin about a Park Avenue robbery that had been broken up by a dog with a rather grand name, Herzberg advised, habitual cigarette dangling from his lips, "If you check the clips, I think you'll find that that pooch won a blue ribbon at the Westminster dog show last year."

He was not the cheeriest soul in the city room, but neither did infirmity turn him antisocial—he was an avid after-hours card player, excelling at hearts—or curdle his dry wit. When Henley Hill one night brusquely overruled his handling of a story, Herzberg hollered after him, "When bigger heels are made, they'll walk these floors"; even Hill warmed to the parting crack. Joe Herzberg could be nastily supercilious at times or just withdrawn into his craft, but he could also be a generous teacher, going over a novice reporter's flawed copy with him word for word instead of just sliding it over to Bob Peck for a swift re-write.

For all his qualifications, what most distinguished Herzberg's appointment late in 1946 to succeed Engelking at the paper's nerve center was that he was the first Jew to serve as a top-ranking editor of the *Herald Tribune*.

While hardly exclusionary toward Jews—there were perhaps a dozen to fifteen of them working in the news department before World War II and a good number in the classified advertising and circulation departments—the *Tribune* did not encourage their presence or facilitate their advancement to the managerial level. For a newspaper ostensibly serving a readership area with the largest concentration of Jews in the world and dependent for prosperity on a retail trade dominated by Jewish ownership, such an attitude would appear, in retrospect, to have been both insensitive and imprudent. The same might be said for its insistent identification with the Republican Party when it was published in a community that was overwhelmingly Democratic. But in staking its claim for customers, the *Tribune* had never tried to appeal to the masses. Its primary constituency ever since the highminded but slightly disreputable Greeley's death and Whitelaw Reid's takeover was gentlemen of property, propriety, and breeding, not devoid of social conscience yet persuaded that the fittest ought to rule society. And to the greatest extent possible, Reid had decreed, his staff ought to consist of gentlemen of the same stripe. By the prevailing standards of the age, Jews were not gentlemen; they tended, with rare exceptions, to be too new, too crude, too radical, too demonstratively ambitious. The *Tribune* was not actively hostile to them as readers or employees; they were simply not the clientele it sought to reach, and so why invite them into the clubby confines of an identifiably Christian, conservative organization?

While it did not practice anti-Semitism of the virulent kind, it is nevertheless the case that until the last two decades of its life, the *Herald Tribune* engaged in the more genteel variety common to the social class of its proprietors. Its attitude was almost certainly exacerbated by the fact that the paper's two principal twentieth-century competitors, the *Times* and the *World,* were owned by Jews.

Writing to her mother-in-law in February 1923, for example, Helen Reid reported, "The Times has taken away a man who has been assistant Managing Editor but he is a Jew and although clever I believe Mr. Mason is going to build better without him." The editor referred to was Lester Markel, an imperious man who went on to build the Sunday *Times* into an overwhelming editorial package; Julian Mason built nothing. Four years later, Helen wrote to Elisabeth Reid about "most disturbing news" concerning the possible sale of property adjacent to their place in Purchase for division into small lots to be offered to members of a certain country club; she wished she could buy up the land in question because "I hate the thought of Whitelaw and Brownie growing up with nothing but Jewish neighbors around." Some Jews, like Walter Lippmann, were socially acceptable to her, as Helen made clear four years later in letters to Elisabeth, stressing his gentlemanliness—no mention was made of cleverness. But Walter Lippmann was a most recessive Jew indeed, who favored the imposition of a Jewish quota for admissions to Harvard, his alma mater, who shied from writing about Hitler's genocidal rantings and policies toward Lippmann's co-religionists, and who in general sought to distance himself from the faith. According to Joseph Alsop, whose social background put him on a "Dear Helen" basis with her despite the generation between them, "The *Trib* was the voice of the WASPs at that time when Dick Whitney was made head of the stock exchange to keep a Jew from being appointed. Anti-Semitism was taken for granted in this social sphere. Helen Reid used to be quite overt about it—except when peddling the department stores." Before Lippmann's, there had been no recognizable Jewish byline on the *Tribune* until sportswriter Jesse Abramson emerged in the late 'Twenties, and, according to his widow, Dorothy, he was urged by sports editor McGeehan to alter his name for byline purposes to "A. Bramson." When Carl Levin was about to get his first byline in 1931, managing editor Holcombe suggested that a different name might fit better into the *Tribune*; Levin told him, "If you don't like my name, don't use it." Milton Levine, on the other hand, thought his advance would be faster if he changed his name to Milton Lewis—a common enough kind of alteration by Jews eager to assimilate. None of the pioneering Jewish staff members ever complained that their careers on the paper were affected by their religious affiliation, but management's prevailing attitude toward them may be inferred from Wilbur Forrest's complaint, noted earlier, that the Jews were disproportionately active in efforts by the Newspaper Guild to organize the editorial staff. Jews were tolerable, that is, so long as they did nothing disagreeable or deviant.

On the business side, however, Jews were limited to clerical and other low-level positions. In Helen Reid's advertising department the discriminatory policy took several forms. In 1932, the paper had issued a booklet on standards of acceptability for advertising and, in noting the *Tribune*'s pioneer role in monitoring truth in newspaper ads, cited its current taboos, which it said excluded from its columns personal attacks, use of the flag for sales purposes, obviously speculative financial ventures, matrimonial bureaus, massage parlors, fortune-telling and astrological ads, and "advertisements whose wording discriminates against any class, religion, or race." But when in January 1934 an unemployed Jewish bookkeeper-secretary called the paper's attention to its blatant failure to honor this last standard, Helen Reid was unmoved. Stella Choyke, a resident of West Fourth Street in Manhattan who described herself as a college graduate, refined and personable with a fine occupational record, had been looking in the *Tribune* help-wanted section and found that

> in one advertisement after the other the word "Christian" or "Protestant" appeared as one of the required qualifications, and I happen to be a member of the Jewish race. Of the 125 office positions listed, 70 of them call for Christians. Actually, there are more than that number from which Jewish applicants are barred because certain employment agencies, while not specifying religion in their ads., do so when the applicant calls at their offices. . . .
>
> While there is so much indignation among Jew and Gentile in America against the hardship the Jew is suffering in Germany at the present time . . . it seems strange that manifestations of it exist in America unnoticed. . . .

An examination of the *Tribune* and *Times* classifieds of this period reveals that the former ran vastly more discriminatory help-wanted insertions. The only condition the *Tribune* attached, by way of a reform measure Helen Reid had imposed in 1930, was that discriminatory insertions had to be written in an affirmative way; the words "only" or "exclusively" (as in "Christians only") could not be used. Mrs. Reid cited this policy in replying to Miss Choyke, noted that it was an unfortunate fact of life that some employers had strong feelings in the matter, and went on:

> The Herald Tribune itself has no reservations about its own employees—we are only interested in the ability of individual applicants—but we do believe it is fairer for an advertiser not to interest people in applying for jobs if, because of some religious point of view, there is no possibility of employing them. On this point I think you will agree.

Miss Choyke did not. Her point was that the *Tribune* was making itself a vehicle for religious intolerance. She answered in part, "You inform me that [the *Tribune* does] not allow a negative form of advertisement excluding persons of any religious group. Doesn't the affirmative form make the same exclusion in quite as emphatic a fashion?"

The following year, Helen Reid hired a 1927 graduate of the University of Pennsylvania's Wharton School named Monroe Green as an advertising space salesman. Green, who was Jewish, had risen to the position of advertising manager of Macy's after five years with the department store. At the *Tribune,* he was naturally assigned to selling the major stores, which with the exception of Lord & Taylor and Wanamaker's were owned by Jews. Before Green, few if any Jews had served as field representatives soliciting advertising for the *Tribune* under the Reids—and after him there would be fewer still. For Monroe Green soon discovered that he was so good at what he was hired to do, especially selling hitherto problem accounts, and on such good terms with management in the person of Helen Reid, whom he regarded as "a very fine woman— attractive, charming, bright . . . regal," that he thought he ought to be paid more nearly what he was worth. Besides, his wife had recently given birth and living costs in New York were higher than elsewhere. He was told to wait a bit. Two months later, Green tried again. "Oh, Mr. Green, you're just too impatient," said Helen Reid, who nevertheless made plain her admiration for his work and every other week or so would drop him off on her way home in her limousine after a nice informal chat en route. After his second rebuff, Green promised her that he would not ask again but would merely notify her after he had made other arrangements if economic need caused him to leave the paper. "Oh, you won't leave," Helen Reid said cheerily, stressing his unlimited future on the *Tribune*. When he did leave after six months on the paper—an unreasonably short span, Green acknowledged in retrospect—to join the *American* as retail advertising manager, Mrs. Reid told him he was making a big mistake and even tried to enlist his friends in an effort to dissuade him. But Green had already signed a contract with the Hearst organization, where he would remain six years and rise to advertising director of the *Journal-American* before joining the *Times*. Whenever Green ran into Helen Reid after that, "I sensed her personal animosity toward me. I would hear from people whose credibility I could not doubt that she said, 'I will not hire another Jew as long as I live.'"

At the *Times*, Green excelled. It was he who hit on the idea of making its Sunday magazine section a showcase for manufacturers in the garment trade, New York's largest industry and much of it Jewish-owned. After becoming *Times* ad director in 1946, Green was a leader in the development of so-called vendor-paid advertising, a cooperative arrangement that began with apparel manufacturers' bearing all or most of the cost of display advertising that featured their merchandise and was placed by department stores which could buy space at the low retail rate. Green's aggressive salesmanship left *Tribune* ad salesmen trailing in the dust.

The *Times* bedeviled Helen Reid's ambitions throughout her *Tribune* career. In 1940 she tried to strike back by hiring Turner Catledge, her rival's star Washington reporter and a highly personable native Mississippian, to run the *Tribune* bureau in the capital. During their conversation, she asked him why he wanted to keep working for "those Jews on Forty-third Street" when the *Tribune* would allow him to travel "in a different social circle" and, with Willkie in the White House, provide him unique access to Washington's most powerful figures. "I think it was a slip of the tongue on her part," Catledge recounted. "She asked if she might talk with Mrs. Catledge about the social part of it and stressed the influential role I would have in the Washington press corps." Catledge declined the honor; he would serve as the *Times* managing editor from 1953 to 1968.

Whether from animus or obtuseness or both, Helen Reid persisted in refusing to hire Jews even in those departments where they might have been most helpful to the paper. When her nephew Kenelm Winslow, the *Tribune* circulation manager whom contemporaries described as "a little bit of a thing in a Brooks Brothers suit," was getting ready to retire in 1945, Mrs. Reid hired as his heir apparent a Yale classmate of her son Whitie named Richard Pinkham. His social background was highly suitable, his navy war record was outstanding, and his prewar career—as advertising manager of McCreery's department store and then an ad agency copywriter—would prove useful in the newspaper field; what he did not know about the circulation business, he could be taught. The first thing Pinkham learned was that he was as miscast for the circulation job as Winslow had been. "He did his level best to talk me out of the area," Pinkham said of his predecessor, who was "a very precise, very uptight, very decent man who had been very earnest about his job but hated it—and the people he was dealing with—the newspaper wholesalers who he felt had him at their mercy. They were mostly first-generation Jews, some of them just one level above being thugs, and they'd come into his office in a group and surround him and give him a hard time, and afterwards he'd have to go out and walk around the block a couple of times to cool off." Not until ten years later would the *Tribune* hire a Jewish circulation manager, but in no other business department except classified advertising—an inside operation—was a Jew assigned to a position of prominence.

Joseph Herzberg's appointment as city editor, therefore, was a *Tribune* milestone. If his religion "was never mentioned" at the time, as Whitie Reid, then serving as an assistant to his father, remembered the occasion, it was because Herzberg's qualifications for the job were undeniable by every measure but the paper's social standard. Herzberg expressed his gratitude two years later by dedicating his book *Late City Edition,* a useful collection of essays by *Tribune* editors and writers on their craft, "To Ogden Reid (1882–1947)."

II

For years after Ogden Reid was gone, they would tell the story of how one evening in his declining years he came by the night desk and asked Everett Kallgren, as he often did, to see the proof for the next morning's front page. The Count obliged. The owner sat at a nearby desk and diligently studied the page for a time. Returning it, he remarked, "Not much news tonight, eh, gentlemen?" It was only after the boss had retired to his paneled inner sanctum that the Count noticed he had given him a proof from the previous day's paper.

For all his apparent obliviousness, though, Ogden Reid was not to be ignored, even in his last ailing years. There was the July night in 1944, for example, when Franklin Roosevelt was nominated for his fourth term as President and Adolf Hitler had been slightly wounded in an assassination plot. The *Tribune* city edition was already rolling with the Roosevelt story in the lead and the Hitler story in the off-lead when Reid came by, studied the front-page layout, and ordered the Count to reverse the play of the two stories. The Count, unused to such direct countermanding orders from above, nodded and said, "We'll catch it on the first lift," meaning when the city run halted momentarily for any late development. Ogden Reid said simply, "Now." He was, still, at moments of his choosing, demonstrably the owner.

On the night the paper was preparing to run a story, about which it had been tipped by a Republican Party publicity man, to the effect that the New York state Democratic organization owed the telephone company a rather hefty sum from the previous election campaign, a deskman dutifully telephoned its substance to the owner, who was at home that evening. "And do we know whether the Republicans owe anything?" he asked. A longish silence ensued, followed by an embarrassed confession that this obvious angle had been overlooked. "Find out," the owner said, and hung up. The Republicans turned out to be almost equally in arrears to the phone company; the story did not see print. Ogden Reid may have been a staunch political partisan, but he was a journalist first.

And he had taste till the end. Soon after the war, William Robinson, the new *Tribune* business manager, proudly presented to the owner for his signature a contract he had negotiated for the paper to carry and syndicate a column by financier-showman Billy Rose. It would be "a swell brightener" and surely boost circulation, Robinson contended with his usual hearty salesmanship. "Not while I'm alive," said Ogden Reid, returning the contract unsigned.

They did not have to wait long to put Billy Rose in the *Tribune*. After his 30,000-mile trip to the Orient with Wilbur Forrest in the autumn of 1945, Reid's health declined; he lived through 1946, the best financial year in the paper's history—and as a newspaper the *Tribune* never had been better. A recurring throat cancer hospitalized him late in the year, and Helen had to nurse him through his dwindling days and run the paper, too, as she had done for so long. The estrangement between them had grown steadily as he came to work later and later and sometimes even stayed the night, but she never acknowledged it or gave vent to her sorrow and frustration. Everett Walker, who held a number of ranking editorships during his forty-two years on the paper, remembered once seeing Ogden drop a full cocktail shaker on a glass table at the Reids' home in Purchase and watching Helen, without grimace or fuss, march over and clean up the resulting mess. He may have been an awful lush, but Ogden Reid was not a failure. Of the seven morning newspapers operating in New York when he took over the managing-editorship of the *Tribune* in 1912, only two were still publishing the day he died nearly thirty-five years later—his and the *Times*. It may be debatable which of the pair was better, all things considered, but it would be hard to deny that the newspaper Ogden Reid left behind, which had been more important for its past than its present when he received it from his father, was no worse than the second-best daily in the United States and one of the ten best in the world.

Helen, their two sons, and his sister Jean were with him when the cancer, complicated by pneumonia, took his life on the evening of January 3, 1947. City editor Herzberg had alerted all desks that there might be a front-page obituary before the night was over. When word came by phone from Harkness Pavilion, it was 10:35 p.m.—too late to catch more than the tail end of the city edition. The prepared obituary needed only to be topped by a few paragraphs giving the particulars of the death, but the Reids wanted to be sure the wording was perfect. By the time Whitie got to the office and finished going over the text with his mother by telephone, the late city edition run had begun. The presses had to be stopped for a lift; the *Times*'s late city edition beat the *Tribune* to the streets with the news of its own owner's death. It was an ill omen.

If his lawyers had not advised him to create a charitable foundation in 1942, the notes totaling some six million dollars that Ogden Reid held against his newspaper would have been taxable at their face value at his death and the family forced to sell the paper or obtain major outside financing. Instead, the financial albatross was bequeathed to the Reid Foundation, which eventually provided a modest number of stipends for worthy journalists traveling abroad but was primarily and transparently a device to keep the tax collector from the *Tribune* door. The rest of Reid's estate was valued at slightly more than three million dollars after taxes, about half in liquid assets—a figure suggesting that he had long been invading principal to maintain the family's extravagant living style. His stock in the *Tribune* he willed to his wife with the proviso that it would pass in its entirety to their sons upon her death.

At the moment of its peak performance the *New York Herald Tribune* became legally and officially what it had long been in fact—a matriarchy.

III

The day in 1946 after Mayor William O'Dwyer announced that New York's police force had driven the bookmakers from the city, *Herald Tribune* crime reporter Walter Arm went into midtown Manhattan and inside a couple of hours found six thriving bookies. It did not take masterful detective work. He walked into a cafeteria and sat near a group of bettors studying the form charts. After they had conferred, their choices would be recorded on a scrap of paper, and one of them would head off as a courier to the nearest horse parlor. Arm followed, at a distance. One courier wound up in the back of a barber shop. Another led the reporter to a rear room at a municipal court on the West Side, where press, police, and bail bondsmen mingled freely. He wrote it all up for the paper, omitting only the specific addresses. When a pair of plainclothesmen invaded the city room the next day seeking the particulars, Arm declined to supply them; if he could uncover the illicit activity that easily, he said, no doubt they could, too. *Exeunt* cops, cursing.

Walter Arm had not made his reputation as one of the best police reporters in town by mocking New York's finest, but he was no press agent for the force, either. He was, rather, part of the new breed of professional crime reporter, dogged, accurate, speedy, objective, serving a newspaper that considered crime news a necessary evil and did not deign to sensationalize it. It could not be ignored, however, and learning how to cover it was considered part of most *Tribune* reporters' basic training. The police beat was more colorful and exciting than most; Walter Arm once handled two front-page stories within an hour— one about a bad water-main break that flooded a subway station, the other about a lone brunette foiled in the act of holding up a Chinese restaurant in Times Square. But police coverage could also be boring, sordid, and decidedly grue-some; manifestations of despair, misery, and madness were never-ending in the city, and those witnessing them night after night had to resist mightily not to succumb to a diminished regard for human life. Cynicism was the minimum price usually paid by the crime reporter, but as Arm wrote in *Late City Edition,* "... if he wishes to remain an asset to his newspaper and a human being as well, he retains some feeling and compassion as a balance."

Most reporters fled the police beat at the earliest opportunity. Walter Arm made crime news his specialty for most of his twenty-five years on the paper and, along with his sidekick and eventual successor, Milton Lewis, gave the *Tribune* superior personnel even in the trenches of the trade. Arm came on the paper in 1930 as a twenty-one-year-old copyboy with a diploma from Brooklyn night school. A poor, unpolished city boy, he advanced slowly, working as the night swingman among the roach-infested "shacks" close by the borough police head-quarters or command precincts around town. The oldtimers among his fellow reporters were, for the most part, poorly educated and spoke the language of the streets, having apprenticed as cop camp-followers, fetching coffee and run-ning other errands for the officers and operating as tipsters to the papers. Some thought like cops and carried guns. They were prone to drink hard on and off the job, no doubt partly to insulate themselves from the grubby, grisly nature of their work and environs. They were adept both at cards and at labor-saving devices like pool coverage of their beat—why should eight men cover a routine story when one could do it for all of them while the other seven went on playing cards in the shack? Few considered themselves writers; the telephone was how they communicated. And fewer of them were eager to hold down a city-room desk. "They were looking only for the story, damn the victims, and nothing was sacred or worth considering beyond that," Arm recalled. On the *Tribune,* at least, crime reporters were not expected to steal photographs from the homes of the subjects of their stories—a common requirement of those working for the tabloids or the sensationalist papers.

Walter Arm was a bad cardplayer and a worse drinker, so he spent his spare time in the shacks studying law by mail and cultivating the cops—hundreds of them over the four years he worked the districts. Unless they knew who he was, their standard response to his round of inquiries was "Nothin' doin'." There was nothing better than personal contact, reinforced night after night. The key to covering crime, Arm learned, was understanding the policeman's mentality and not scorning it. A reporter might conceive of himself as a guardian of the public morals and welfare, but to the policeman he was an agent of a highly competitive, profit-seeking enterprise. The cop's job was to subdue violence, apprehend evildoers, gather evidence, and complete his shift without a reprimand or a bullet in his hide. All else, the press included, was secondary. Police had been trained to have as little to do with reporters as possible, Arm discovered: "A reporter means questions; questions mean answers; answers may be embarrassing, and embarrassment is something a policeman can do without."

Nor was it his job to determine what made a good newspaper story, any more than the reporter was responsible for solving the crimes he covered. One dull night while monitoring the police teletype and sifting through report slips in quest of a story, Arm came upon an item about a woman who had died in her bed on East Third Street; the report ended: "Contagious. Nothing suspicious." Wondering what the fatal disease might be, he hopped a taxi to the scene and checked with the sergeant standing guard at the deceased's apartment. "Aw, there's nothing to it," said the officer. "There's nothing contagious." The cop on the beat had been told not to touch the body until the medical examiner arrived, so he mistakenly thought the woman had had a contagious disease. Arm shrugged his thanks and turned to leave when the sergeant added that if there had been any contagion, the woman's children would have been sent to the hospital instead of a shelter home. What children, Arm asked. The sergeant explained that the woman had been dead for three days and her three-year-old daughter and one-year-old boy were living on scraps while waiting for their mother to wake up; if the neighbors hadn't complained about the smell, the children would have still been waiting. "You don't think that's a story, do you?" the cop wound up. It made page one.

Besides his *modus vivendi* with the police, a first-rate crime reporter needed a sure sense of what his paper considered newsworthy. The more famous or infamous the criminal or his victim, the classier the neighborhood that was the scene of the crime, the more unusual, flamboyant, or ghastly the act, the better the chance the *Tribune* would give it space. Undisguised racism dictated minimal attention to all-black crime news until the civil rights movement of the 'Sixties. Unless the crime was so heinous, such as a multiple killing, or a white was involved as a victim or perpetrator, it rarely rated reporting in the *Tribune*; the other New York papers were not notably less biased. "There was so much of that cheap stuff up there," Milton Lewis explained in defense of this omission of crime news emanating from Harlem, "and if it happens all the time, it's not news." Even more important than racial priorities for the police reporter was a constant awareness of the clock. Nothing was more inevitable or perishable than crime news, and the reporter who missed an edition deadline in an effort to turn his story into an epic was soon relieved of the beat.

The best police reporter was also a master telephone inquisitor. It was essential to supplement whatever information he obtained from the police at the scene with material gathered in person from victims, friends, relatives, and witnesses. But often these were unavailable or inaccessible at the moment; the accomplished professional returned to the office and kept working the phone, risking the thin line between polite inquiry and invasion of privacy with his drumbeat of questions, probing until the last possible moment for what Lewis called "that extra bit of information that can make a story fascinating."

Knowing what to do with "that extra bit of information," of course, remained essential. Walter Arm once hit the front page with the story of an unemployed middle-aged actress found murdered in her West Fifty-seventh Street apartment, a tale poignant enough in itself. But what gave the piece an extra touch of pathos and made it clear how brief fame is, and what a very tough profession in a very tough town the woman had pursued, was its concluding sentence: "Even before the victim's body had been taken to the morgue for autopsy, the building superintendent was besieged by a dozen people seeking to rent her blood-stained flat."

He never operated on the theory, beloved by hard-boiled cops in their dealings with the press, that one hand washes the other. But his social perception, integrity, and respect for police work at its best eventually earned Walter Arm appointment as deputy commissioner in charge of community relations of the New York Police Department, a position he held with model efficiency and candor for ten years. The job paid a lot better than crime reporter and came with a car and chauffeur; on the *Tribune* only Mrs. Reid had traveled as grandly.

IV

Although its composing room, the mechanical heart of the newspaper, was never really modernized after the move uptown to West Fortieth Street in 1923, the *Tribune*'s shop was manned by "the most productive work force in the city," according to Bertram A. Powers, who emerged after World War II as the most powerful figure in the printers' New York local. This relatively high per-man output of the *Tribune* "chapel," as the typographers' union called its unit at each paper, was achieved with the same pay scale as on all the other New York dailies and despite an editorial philosophy notable for its historically pro-capital, anti-labor tilt. Such efficiency is worth noting in view of a widely held notion that its labor force, especially Powers's International Typographical Union Local No. 6, was primarily responsible for the financial decline and death of the *Herald Tribune.*

The mechanics of the printer's craft underwent a major revolution in the *Tribune*'s final years and in the decade immediately following its demise, as the costly, bulky technique of molding lead—"hot type"—was replaced by far more efficient photocomposition. But no major newspaper and none of the *Tribune*'s New York competitors was yet being produced, in the two decades after World War II, with the new materials of film, paper, and paste. And the

Tribune shop, while aging, was kept in good working order. Its seventy-three Linotypes were constantly attended by four full-time machinists who cleaned the space bands twice daily and responded quickly when the red light went on over any malfunctioning machine. Old but well-cared-for Linotypes yielded the same output as new ones—six lines a minute—and since the state of the printing arts had not changed much between the last decade of the nineteenth century and the middle of the twentieth, an era that was otherwise marked by the most extraordinary technological advancement in history, its horse-and-buggy printshop could not really be said to have put the *Tribune* at a competitive disadvantage.

Its shop, moreover, was honest. The same could not be said of some of its rivals. Seniority rules and rated work minimums were honored; there was no favoritism. By comparison, the *Journal-American,* the largest afternoon paper, was "corrupt," according to Bert Powers. "There were buyouts and side deals" involving how much work was really expected and where the men could slide and fudge, no matter what the contract or union regulations specified. At the *Daily News* in the postwar era, Powers added, "there were bookies and drinking all over the place. The *Tribune* was much stricter and more tightly run. There's something about the character of a newspaper that goes through the whole building."

The *Tribune*'s shop routine also encouraged greater flexibility in the use of the typographers' multiple skills than at the *Times.* ITU regulations provided that when a printer first came in to work and specified his preferred job classification (machine operator, ad compositor, page makeup man, or proofreader), he could not be made to spend more than three hours at another job; the *Tribune,* though, was inclined to use its printers interchangeably as much as possible. It was not unusual for a man who worked "the hand side" composing department-store advertisements in the morning to be assigned after his lunch break to assembling the news pages or to spend an hour or two in the proofreading room. And every journeyman typographer was trained to operate a Linotype, one of the most complex and temperamental machines man ever invented. While this shifting of men around was not universally relished in the *Tribune* chapel, it did keep their various skills honed and challenged.

"There was a closeness in that shop I never saw anywhere else," said Anthony Sessa, who served for a time as chairman of the *Tribune* chapel and later became one of Powers's assistants in the printers' hierarchy. In place of a certain sourness that prevailed in several other New York newspaper shops, *Tribune* printers got along well with one another and their white-collar supervisors, and few curses were sounded against the paper's ownership. This was partly due, no doubt, to the pride that management took in the appearance of its paper—all those Ayer Cups for typographic excellence bespoke a caring about craftsmanship all the way up and down the line. Editors like Henley Hill and Everett Kallgren knew and respected the printer's trade, and provided enlightened supervision along with demanding standards. And in the paper's

later years, acrimony between the unions and an increasingly frustrated management was minimized by the skills of the paper's bluff, salty director of industrial
relations, John Bogart, son of a Massachusetts publisher who had lost his
newspaper during the Depression. A prewar transferee from the editorial department, Bogart was schooled in the mechanical and business aspects of *Tribune* operations by Howard Davis but brought a firm yet more compassionate
attitude to his dealings with labor than the old general manager. "He was so
damned good," Sessa said of Bogart, whom he credited with knowing the paper
"from top to bottom."

More than any other single factor affecting productivity at the *Tribune* was
the quality of supervision. "Management had very good control of the work
force," in Powers's judgment—a condition less attributable to the talents of its
mechanical superintendents than to the dedication of the shop foremen, union
members who believed they owed it to their craft to provide the paper a fair
day's work for pay received. Among the most valuable of these union supervisors was Frank Spinelli, known at the paper more affectionately than not as
"Little Caesar," after the motion-picture role made famous by Edward G.
Robinson, whom he resembled in shortness of stature and facial features. A
Brooklyn boy with two years' school training in the printing trades, Spinelli
went to work in 1918 as a seventeen-year-old apprentice in the old *Tribune* shop
on Nassau Street. He put in five years at tasks like pushing the locked-up page
forms from the composing stone to the stereotyping room on rolling, steel-top
tables called "turtles" and breaking down the forms and collecting the type for
reuse after the edition had closed. As a journeyman, he could do every job in
the shop and do it well. After World War II, they made him foreman of the day
shift—a post he hesitated to accept because of the divided loyalty it entailed.
He held it for twenty years; when the *Tribune* died, he had been on its payroll
forty-eight years.

He was given the foreman's job, Spinelli explained in retirement, "because
I had the loudest voice in the place and wasn't afraid to use it." But he never
directed it abusively at his men. "You cucumber, you!" was his fiercest form of
expletive. He commanded obedience, rather, by the example he set. "He worked
from the minute he came in the door," Tony Sessa remembered, "and if you
didn't do your job right, he'd do it for you." He shamed the malingerers into
productivity. "I had to set a pace for certain people" was how Spinelli put it.
He knew every man's talents, and if a printer given a fresh assignment was
legitimately experiencing trouble in handling it, Spinelli was there to lend a hand
or made sure someone else was sent to ease the pressure. His men were the
princes of the printing trade to Frank Spinelli, and he expected them to behave
accordingly. But if a man gave him backtalk or stirred up trouble by fussing
about whether a window was open too wide in winter or kept showing up at
the last second before the starting bell rang, he would feel Spinelli's wrath.
This usually took the form of assignment to the most onerous job the foreman
could find—generally, setting "bogus," the make-work duplication of adver-

tisements that had been delivered by the advertiser in a form ready for use.

While he liked to refer to himself as "a 60/40 man" in terms of his allegiances, he never revealed whether management or the union owned the larger portion of his heart. But he was indisputably a union loyalist. When his hegemony was challenged by management—like the time the august Geoffrey Parsons sent down an editorial and requested a particular Linotype operator to set it posthaste—Spinelli rebelled; neither Parsons nor anyone else in the place could tell him how to run his shop. And he made a point of never testifying against a union man at a grievance hearing, even if management's charge was justified—as it was, for example, against a chronically disruptive compositor who had returned drunk from lunch one day, causing Spinelli to order him off the composing-room floor as a menace to himself and his colleagues.

If a spirit of comradeship keener than that in the shop existed anywhere at the *Tribune,* it was in the pressroom. Here were the men who actually printed the paper, but tradition dictated that only the men in the composing room be called "printers"; the huge, two-story presses were operated by "pressmen," whose intricately folded newsprint hats were the emblem of their craft.

Theirs was heavy, dirty, physical work, requiring real muscle power and athletic limberness rather than the manual dexterity and basic literacy essential for typographers. Each lead page plate that had to be lifted onto the presses and locked into place weighed more than fifty pounds; they were usually lugged across the pressroom one on each hip. A lot of climbing was involved in threading the rolls of newsprint through the presses and rewebbing the paper whenever it broke during a run. There was constant danger from the gears and cutters and rollers and formers all moving at lightning speed, and it was not unknown for the presses to hurl a loose plate across the room like a piece of jagged shrapnel. And the noise could deafen; some pressmen wore earplugs. And a mist of ink, spun off the rollers by the high velocity of the presses, filled the room, matted the hair, coated any exposed skin, penetrated orifices. The walls and floors had to be mopped thoroughly every day, and the men showered at the end of their shift.

Only the strong could endure the grind, and a proud fellowship naturally grew up among them. They labored together, bet on the ponies and the numbers together in their own intramural gambling parlor, drank beer and played poker together in the foreman's little room suspended from the ceiling over the presses so he could monitor the run, laughed and heckled together in the showers after work, and had a nightcap together at the London Grill. Until the later 'Forties, admission to the pressmen's union tended to be restricted to close relatives of present or past members, and a man who did his job poorly dishonored his family name in that tight, inky, thunderous world.

Pressmen did not grant the typographers' claim that newspaper craftsmanship ended at the composing-room door. A pressman like Nick Thalasinos, a wiry six-footer who worked in the *Tribune* pressroom forty-one years, considered himself as responsible as any man in the building for the typographic excellence of the paper. One of thirteen children who grew up on a tiny farm on the Aegean island of Cos, Thalasinos came to America in 1907 at the age of fifteen and performed whatever unskilled labor he could find to survive until he figured out that he had to acquire a trade before he could earn dignity. After apprenticing on a Greek paper in Brooklyn, he entered the *Tribune* pressroom in 1916 and eventually rose to floorman and shift foreman. "He had the best eye in the place for the color of the printing," recalled his son Gus, who worked with him for thirteen years. "Color" in black-and-white printing meant the evenness of the gray tone; too much or too little ink was unsatisfactory. Nick Thalasinos had the perfect touch in adjusting the keys that controlled the flow of ink, one key per column of the page, to achieve uniformity of print. He knew if the rollers had been set precisely, just barely kissing to provide the right pull; too little tension and the ink would be pale, and too much would smear and blot the printed page. During the paper's run Thalasinos would roam the aisles between the press units, feeling the impression that the press plates were leaving on the paper as they contacted the cushioning blanket cylinder beneath—excessive pressure would cause the paper to emerge looking as if it had been printed in braille—and fine-tune the whirring presses with his wrench as he went.

Editorial hands were not the only kind that labored with pride of craft at the *Herald Tribune*, by wide assent the most graphically attractive American newspaper of its day.

V

At war's end Stanley Woodward set out immediately to make the *Tribune* sports pages the best in the business.

The nucleus of talent was already in place—men who disdained the bizarre patois of the craft and wrote with exactness and erudition. Among the mainstays was Jesse Abramson, a fanatically accurate reporter whose knowledge of track and field was so extensive that competitors had dubbed him "The Book." A joyously argumentative man who often talked at a shout, dark brows undulating above a myopic squint, Abramson was as tough as Woodward and ideally equipped to cover the grubby world of prizefighting. "I have no heroes in boxing," he once said. "I try to write what I see." A meat-and-potatoes kind of writer, he probably turned out more bylined prose in his forty-two years on the paper, spanning the entire lifetime of the merged *Herald* and *Tribune,* than any other member of the staff.

Equally expert in his fields of specialty, tennis and golf, was Al Laney, a slight man with an omnipresent, Confederate-gray, snap-brim fedora, who spoke so softly that Woodward once threatened to have him wired for sound.

After ten years as a deskman and night editor of the Paris edition, Laney had joined the New York sports staff in 1935 and began writing in exceedingly long, graceful sentences shaped with an almost conversationally casual vocabulary. "A couple of felicitous phrases go a long way in a sports story," he said with characteristic self-effacement. He liked to cover golf because it was the only competitive sport not played on a regulation field and reporting it took him to attractive places; it, like tennis, was not considered a rigorous game but as a recreation for the country-club set, and both were relegated to the status of minor subjects on the sports page until professionalism took hold of both in the postwar era.

At the opposite extreme was football, of which Woodward himself had no peer as a reporter, and his staff had to meet his standards. For horse racing, Woodward enlisted Joe Palmer, a former college English instructor and the star columnist of a Kentucky-based weekly devoted to horse breeding called *The Blood Horse.* A burly, slow-talking native of bluegrass country, Palmer lived for only five years after joining the *Tribune* in 1946, but during them, when he was not railing against the potential evil of off-track betting as a menace to the survival of the sport of kings, he wrote with color, wit, and knowledge-ability that turned racing journalism from a tout game into something close to literature.

To help cover baseball, Woodward elevated Harold Rosenthal, who had hung on at the paper by his fingernails for nearly ten prewar years, writing at space rates on schoolboy sports, Parks Department tennis tourneys, Coney Island road races, and anything else they would let him do. He was no stylist, but he was dependable and he knew his stuff, and Woodward gave him staff status and sent him off to cover the Brooklyn Dodgers in their heyday, with impressive results. He caught the intimacy of Ebbets Field, the Brooklyn ball-park; the oratorical style of the team's innovative president, Branch Rickey, who brought the first black players into the major leagues during this time; and the exasperated affection of its raffish, street-hardened fans. "There were times you felt you were missing something by devoting yourself to so trivial a subject—you knew life would go on without sports," Rosenthal recalled. "But all writing is tough—it's a lonesome business—you have to shed people." It had its forms of recompense, though, like wide recognition within his specialized realm—and the color television set the Dodger management delivered by truck to his front door one Christmas. After five years covering Brooklyn, he was assigned to the Yankees, methodical victors in that era and therefore less fun to write about. Among Rosenthal's successors on the Dodger beat for the *Tribune* was a young reporter named Roger Kahn; out of his experiences on the paper and with the ball club, he would write his notable book, *The Boys of Summer.*

The only real weak spot on the *Tribune*'s sports pages was its columnist. No first-rater had emerged to fill the role since McGeehan's death. Woodward and Laney were taking turns at the job but without the special zest or stylistic flair it required; both were essentially crack reporters. To fill the position, Woodward had his heart set on Ring Lardner's son John, a deadpan humorist who had put in three years as a *Tribune* reporter under Stanley Walker and since 1939 had been writing a column devoted mainly to sports in *Newsweek* magazine. Laney had another candidate in mind.

Early in the morning of the mid-May Saturday that the Preakness was being run at Baltimore's Pimlico racetrack in 1945, Laney spotted him high in the press box, alone, hunched over his typewriter before most of the sports world had awakened. Walter Wellesley Smith had been slaving away for nearly ten years as a sports columnist for the Philadelphia *Record,* the third-, or possibly the fourth-, best paper in town—he had worked for also-rans as well in Milwaukee and St. Louis—and for his seven columns a week was paid ninety dollars. A Notre Dame graduate, he had been struggling for twenty years to make a living in journalism. He was married, with an eleven-year-old daughter and seven-year-old son by then, and trying to cover family expenses left him perpetually broke. That early morning at Pimlico, when Al Laney of the big-time *Herald Tribune* came upon him, Red Smith was writing *Terry and Bunky Play Football,* a children's book, to pick up some badly needed cash. "He was a lovely little guy with reddish blond hair then and very shy in his way," Laney remembered. He had a thin face and wore rimless glasses that might have given him a severe look except for the mischievous twinkle that animated his features, his speech, and his prose. Fellow sportswriters knew him for his light touch and easy company, but nearing his fortieth birthday, he seemed destined to pass his career obscurely on second-rate papers, pounding away about what he called "these games little boys play."

Yet Red Smith never thought sportswriting was beneath him or his talents. Sports were for him an authentic aspect of American culture, and he recognized the elemental nature of their attraction. "It doesn't take a monumental brain to figure that three strikes are out," he would remark in later years, "and a six-year-old could referee a boxing match." His approach was that of a professional spectator; most people attended athletic contests for the fun of it, and reading about them ought also therefore to be fun. "The natural habitat of the tongue is the left cheek," he once said, and delegated reports of gritty scrimmage-line collisions and breathless locker-room banalities to others in the trade.

Having fun watching and writing about sports in Philadelphia took applied effort during Red Smith's decade there. Its two baseball teams were chronic losers, its professional football team was not much better, and basketball and hockey had not yet arrived as pro sports. Smith learned to write above and beyond the event, to understand what made losing teams lose—the double play that went unexecuted, the extra base not taken—and how a great but unspectacular player like Joe DiMaggio beat you with his apparently effortless grace in the field and sudden acceleration on the base paths as well as with his bat. He found that much about life if not about winning baseball could be derived from a pre-game chat with the Philadelphia Athletics' ancient owner-manager, Connie Mack. Anyone could look good writing about conquering heroes; real writers understood that all of life was a game of sorts, with far more losers than winners, and that joy had to be extracted from other elements in the contest besides the outcome. To Red Smith, the score was never the point.

By his own account, he grew up "small and weak and yellow and had no reflexes" and no special interest in sports during his boyhood in Green Bay, Wisconsin. But he loved to wander the woods and fish, and he would remain a celebrator of the outdoors his whole life and find in nature more than in organized sports the truest repository of his pleasure. Some of his best columns were about fish. He worked his way through Notre Dame, cheering for Knute Rockne's powerful football teams and reading Grantland Rice, who turned them into legend; what undergraduate writing he did was for the yearbook and not the sports page. On the *Sentinel* in Milwaukee, he was a mediocre reporter —"I couldn't cover a three-alarm fire in hell," he said, claiming that he thought of all the best questions only when he was back in the city room—but became a workmanlike copy editor, though he did not much like the job. In that capacity he moved to the *Star* in St. Louis, became a proficient rewriteman, and was rescued from tedium on the desk by a managing editor needing sportswriters. Asked if he knew much about sports, Smith said he knew how the games worked. The editor then asked him if he was honest, and Smith nodded. Finally the editor asked if he would take twenty dollars from a fight manager to push his pug, and Smith said, "That's a lot of money." Sports, then, was mainly his ticket back to writing—"I was pretty high on myself and the romance of journalism and tired of writing lousy heads on the desk"—and St. Louis was a good sports town. Smith was especially fond of covering wrestling "because they let me write whatever I wanted." The night the floodlights were first turned on at the Washington University football field, Smith wrote about it from the perspective of a glow-worm and his mate, burrowing up to the surface and feeling pretty rotten about being so hugely outshone. After that, they knew he was something special.

Such charming antics earned him a spot on the *Record* in Philadelphia, much nearer his goal of New York. "It was like wanting to play the Palace, it was the communications capital of the country, and to me a New York sportswriter was about the most godlike character who'd ever been created." Within six months he was doing a Sunday column using the "Red Smith" byline for the first time. But writing a once-a-week column was hard for him; he would get an idea and play with it all week and by the time he had to write, it was cold. The more he wrote, the better he got. "My antennae were standing up all the time, and I fell into a kind of gait. It's harder to break into a run from a standing start." Even some of his admirers felt that seven columns a week was a punishing grind and inevitably weakened his performance, but Smith preferred it that way, arguing that if he produced a poor effort one day, he could recoup the next. There were not many bad performances. He extracted the best from a variety of influences—Ring Lardner's rhythmic sentences but not his comic grammar, Damon Runyon's blend of the ridiculous and the sublime, Frank

Graham's keen ear for the way sports people really spoke, Grantland Rice's poetic vision though not his sentiment, and most of all, the flowing clarity of E. B. White, not even a sportswriter. And then he imposed upon the blend his own special hallmarks: the unexpectedly comical turn of phrase, the easy shift from the erudite to the vernacular, the sudden but never venomous skewer. Before him subtlety had not been the mark of the sportswriter; Red Smith left a lot of things unbelabored. Overwriting was to him the worst of sins; of a colleague pushing too far he would say, "That guy tried to leave writing dead on the floor."

Stanley Woodward admired Red Smith's work on the *Record,* although he felt he was writing too much, and could not figure out at first why no other New York newspaper had brought him up from Philadelphia. It was not that they were unaware of him; Runyon and Bob Considine of the *Journal-American* had paid him the compliment of founding a mythical "Keep Smith Out of New York Fan Club" lest he make the rest of the local sportswriting fraternity look bad. Woodward finally decided that because most of the other sports editors were also or even primarily writers or columnists themselves, they did not want to hire anyone who could outperform them. "I took the opposite view on this question," the *Tribune* sports editor explained in his memoirs. Abandoning his quest for John Lardner and responding to Laney's lobbying, he hired Red Smith at $125 a week. But he did not make him a columnist, at least not right away. Smith went back to regular reporting, in his special style, until Laney took a sabbatical from the column, which he considered a chore, and went off to write a book about the Paris *Herald.* Smith filled in for him and never relinquished the job.

At a staff meeting to plan coverage of the World Series early in Smith's tenure, Woodward handed out all the usual assignments, and when he got to the columnist, he told him, "Get me the smell of the cabbage cooking in the halls." Smith understood instinctively the nature of his charge. "If you've got a good soft brain to begin with," he quipped in explanation of the knack, "you can go to any game and take a nice impression . . . like soft wax, and you'll come up with a column idea." It was not what he wrote about that mattered so much as how. "He was so resourceful in expression," Woodward noted of Smith at his peak, "so gifted in stating an ordinary case." Among his unique skills was the apparent ability to interview someone without taking notes and render in print the substance of the subject's remarks with high precision. The trick was in eliciting the words in the first place. "I felt I could conduct a looser, less self-conscious interview if no pencil or paper was in view—if I just stood or sat there and chatted," he explained. He had a good memory and fixed in mind the essence of the exchange, especially how things were put—"everyone has his own individual means of expression"—and then at the first opportunity, preferably a few minutes afterward, he would go to his typewriter in the press box or take out his note pad in the car and set down the most memorable and useful words;

he did not dredge them out of thin air four or five hours later at deadline. But the legend grew that he had supernatural powers of retention.

He composed with great deliberation. Writing for him, he often said, was "like opening a vein and letting the words come out drop by drop." The results were artistry, achieved six times a week for fifteen years, then reduced to four during the last five years of the *Tribune*'s life—a total of something over 5,000 columns. To keep his pieces fresh, he never wrote ahead, preferring to turn each column in like clockwork by 6 p.m. the day before it appeared. This schedule, while keeping his copy alive, had the disadvantage of requiring other newspapers subscribing to his column to pay telegraph charges usually running to more than the cost of the column itself. And since most papers preferred to feature a homegrown columnist on their sports page, syndication of Smith's column grew slowly at first. By 1949 he was carried in only eighteen other papers. Three years later, he was up to eighty papers and earning five times the salary he had started at on the *Tribune*. Eventually the total would reach three hundred; the reason, as *Time* put it in 1961, was simply that Red Smith wrote "the most polished, literate, and readable sports column in the country."

Almost any paragraph plucked at random from any of his columns reveals his deft touch and faintly comic tone. This is how, in the middle of a 1950 column, he described a scene of carefully outfitted anglers on stylish Martha's Vineyard:

> At Menemsha Bight the bass-slayers got into hip boots and rubberized overalls and waterproofed parkas and lugged their tackle down to the beach. The tide was rampaging out through a narrow cut and there were perhaps half a dozen fishermen casting into the current from the rock jetty, with a dozen or so more strung out along the beach flinging their feathered jigs into the surf. The jigs, or plugs, or tin squids, are cigar-sized gobbets of lead with feather tails which, it is optimistically hoped, will look edible to large stupid fish.

He drew his subjects from almost anywhere in the world of nature—once he climbed a ponderosa tree to interview a baby eagle—or of competitive sports, excepting only hockey and basketball, which he disdained as "those back-and-forth games." His bread-and-butter subject, though, was baseball.

There was something almost miraculous for him about the uniquely American game, starting with the very geometry of the playing field. "Ninety feet between the bases," he liked to say, "is the closest approach to perfection man has ever achieved." The dimensions were essential to baseball's delicate balance between offense and defense, he noted: "The fastest runner alive, hitting a sharp ground ball to a shortstop who fields it cleanly, cannot beat out the throw—but it's awfully close." The tempo of the game, deemed slow by detractors, was to Smith another of its virtues if the spectator was properly attuned. "You don't pace a Greek tragedy the way you do a George Abbott musical—each is right for its own style," he said. Baseball constantly absorbed Smith, with the balletic movements of its players and its power to build suspense so that ideally the outcome awaited the last pitch to the last batter in the bottom half of the last inning with the score tied, the bases loaded, the count full, and everybody on base running on the pitcher's delivery. "No playwright ever wrote a better climactic moment than that."

With Red Smith in place, Woodward achieved his ambition of assembling the finest sports department in the American press. His people were contemptuous of the *Times*'s department, tagging it "Chowderhead Kelly's Mill." "They had pages and pages to fill," Smith remembered, "and didn't know how. . . . It was laughable." Smith did not laugh, though, when his opposite number on the *Times*—Arthur Daley—was awarded the Pulitzer in 1956 for his column, "Sports of the Times." Many in the New York sportswriting fraternity knew that Daley often filled his columns with blatantly fabricated quotations attributed to athletes who could not string two coherent clauses together and felt that Smith was by far the more deserving of the honor. But having waited so long to get to New York, Red Smith was not embittered; he was, after all, the most widely read and respected sportswriter in the land by then.

He was always grateful to Woodward for having given him the chance to make it big. He expressed the feeling, however, in subtle gestures. One night the two of them were out drinking with Jock Sutherland, the University of Pittsburgh's behemoth of a football coach. Woodward, about as big, got well oiled and challenged Sutherland to a wrestling match on the spot. "A quarter-ton of beef smashed to the floor," Smith recounted. "The house trembled. Stanley was pinned. He lay gasping. 'Smith,' he said weakly, 'help me up.' I handed him a scotch and soda where he lay. He knew I went into newspapering because I disliked lifting things."

VI

It was baseball that provided the subject for the single most celebrated picture ever taken by a *Herald Tribune* photographer.

Newspaper photography, like the rest of daily journalism, rarely aims at or achieves high art. News photos have generally served to break up the monotony of gray columns of type rather than to add true graphic dimension to a story. Many are static shots of staged ceremonies or are taken at too great a distance to reveal nuances of facial features or other details. Because photoengraving was based on a screen process that broke the picture down into a fine mesh of dots, only crude gradations of tone were possible in the era before more sensitive photo-offset composition and printing were adopted by most American papers. Simple subjects rendered in sharply contrasting shades reproduced best—a daunting limitation for subtle cameramen. A second occupational hazard was the high tension of the trade born out of the photographer's perpetual anxiety that he had botched the assignment by leaving the lens cap on, moving the camera, using the wrong speed or opening, shooting from the wrong angle, or any of a dozen other mistakes that could not be repaired; reporters could always try to compensate for their omissions with words. Thus, the photographer's habitual cry of "Just one more shot!" at gatherings of the celebrated.

Nathaniel Fein suffered no handicap, then, over the lack of subtlety in his work. He began as a *Tribune* copyboy in 1932 and three years later invested ninety-five dollars in a Speed Graphic because it seemed the fastest route to advancement, quickly turning himself into a competent press photographer with a flair for staging shots. He made it a habit to carry handy props in the trunk of his car, like a shovel for ground-breaking ceremonies or a lucky horseshoe for candidates to pose with on leaving the voting booth on election day. A streak of daredeviltry not uncommon to the trade sent him routinely to high, dangerous places for unusual shots, like the ones he took atop the wind-whipped towers of the Verrazano Bridge while they were under construction. There were more artistic photographers on the paper, such as Morris Warman, who was perhaps the best portraitist in U.S. daily journalism, but Nat Fein had enough of the esthete in him to frame a poignant picture for the *Tribune* of a drifter walking through Central Park after a heavy snowfall and beneath the mellow light of a street lamp that softened all the usual hard edges of the New York cityscape. Fein's specialty, though, was the funny animal picture, a little heavy on the anthropomorphism, like one he arranged of a kangaroo emerging from a subway entrance.

Fein was assigned to Yankee Stadium on the day in mid-May 1948 when fifty-three-year-old George Herman Ruth, a cancer of the throat sapping his life away, climbed for the last time into his pin-striped uniform with the large 3 on the back and stood at home plate to say goodbye to the fans of the sport he had once dominated. The field was swarming with photographers. Fein snapped away continuously, starting with a shot of the Babe coming out of the Yankee dugout, and circled entirely around the scene. One of his shots was a rear-angle composition that so effectively caught the former hulk of the athlete with his spindly legs and wasted body now bent with pain that his identity was unmistakable even without the sight of his face; to the side, ranged along the first-base line, Yankee players stood in homage. A press-service photographer snapped Ruth from almost the same unlikely angle, using a flash, while Fein went with natural light on the overcast day.

Tribune photographers had one advantage over most of their competitors, although they viewed it as a mixed blessing: they developed, printed, and cropped their own pictures. This money-saving practice had the added benefit of allowing the photographers to get the most out of their fieldwork by artful use of the darkroom. Fein, for example, was fond of shooting action shots too fast and then compensating by overdeveloping. He handed the photography editor four prints of the Ruth farewell ceremony; the editor immediately selected the striking rear-angle shot for the first sports page. After the city edition, it was moved to the front page and captioned "Babe Ruth Bows Out." The wire-service photographer's similar shot was widely used by out-of-town papers, but his flash washed out the rest of the scene that was essential to Fein's softer composition. It was Fein's version that was awarded the Pulitzer for the best news photograph that year. After that, he would ask himself with every shot he framed whether it was worthy of a Pulitzer winner: "You wanted each one to measure up. I felt on the spot all the time, an extra tension—not the best thing for a photographer to live with."

VII

In twentieth-century America, there were really only three comprehensive national newspapers. Many excelled at local news coverage and sports, a few at international reporting, but only the *Times, World,* and *Tribune* ranged as well over the mass of daily developments in finance and culture, centered in New York, and political news emanating from Washington, the locus of vastly enlarged federal power. To qualify as a national paper, a New York daily required most of all aggressive and resourceful representation in the capital.

From 1941 to 1953 the *Tribune*'s Washington bureau, composed of between a dozen and fifteen men, the second largest—after the *Times*—of any daily, was headed by Bert Andrews, a mediocre writer but a highly skilled reporter of the old school. He was not deep, but he was fast, wrote clean, had an almost preternatural instinct for where news lay hidden, and loved his work with a passion that blocked out most other pleasures from his life except Chesterfield cigarettes, which he smoked continuously, and good bourbon, of which he drank too much. A. J. Liebling, press critic of *The New Yorker,* once noted with approval that Andrews indulged in metaphor "as sparingly as a Montclair housewife employs garlic"; his style called the reader's attention to the story rather than its author. Already strong on stylish writers, the *Tribune* especially needed a hard-news man to spearhead its Washington coverage—a gritty go-getter who could stand up to men wielding vast power over the nation's public life, a writer who thrived on deadline pressure, a reporter who loved nothing better than to scoop the opposition. "He was a shark—he tasted blood in the water," recalled James Reston, a prominent member of the *Times* bureau during Andrews's years in Washington. "He used to give us a lot of trouble. He liked to say, 'We can make you guys look silly on any given story.'"

Brought up in San Diego, Bert Andrews dropped out of Stanford despite doing well academically and became a vagabond newspaperman during his twenties until he reached New York and settled down on Hearst's morning sheet as a solid reporter and lightning rewriteman. At the *Tribune* he confirmed his skills, was advanced to Albany correspondent during sessions of the New York legislature, and was tapped for the Washington job in mid-1941. A believer in the natural adversarial relationship between journalists and politicians, he was an ideal choice as the top man in the capital for a paper that cast itself as Franklin Roosevelt's enlightened opposition. Although he had voted for Roosevelt in 1932 and 1936, Andrews was a political conservative by nature who rarely allowed partisan considerations to deflect him from pursuit of a good story. And he found Washington a journalist's paradise. Big-time politicians were more accessible and talkative than the local hack variety, and he liked to get out of the office and use his legs instead of the telephone to track down sources. Neither a glib storyteller nor a card-playing crony, Andrews was regarded by official Washington as a straight shooter who kept confidences and worked the cocktail circuit with discretion in his endless prowl for leads.

But he was a lone wolf with a dark side, too. His marriage disintegrated during his Washington years and the job consumed more and more of him. The administrative aspects of his work, where he might have found consolation and companionship, left him cold. He was not a gentle disciplinarian or an avid instructor, and the young reporters surrounding him viewed Andrews with mingled awe, admiration, and resentment for being what one of them termed "a story hog." That lack of generosity to his subordinates was no small shortcoming in a crowded bureau that was packed into Room 1285 of the National Press Building, a space perhaps twenty-by-twenty-five feet, where desks, papers, and private lives overlapped and a perpetual frenzy of jangling phones and clattering typewriters did not promote serenity.

Personality aside, Andrews suffered professionally from only one serious drawback, but it was an important one in light of his strategic position in postwar Washington. He was much better at handling big, breaking hard-news stories about concrete events than the more abstract policy stories that were becoming increasingly important—the kind of story that Reston did so well for the *Times.* Two of the biggest stories that Andrews was credited with in the postwar period illustrated both his virtues and his limitations as a Washington journalist. Both dealt with an aspect of the major, basic, ongoing issue of the age—anti-Communism—and both were handled in the tradition of hot-off-the-griddle scoop journalism.

In the early fall of 1947, Carl Levin, by then back from Europe and reinstalled in the *Tribune* Washington bureau, where he had a reputation as "the house liberal," was approached with a promising story by Paul Porter of the New Deal–connected law firm of Arnold, Fortas and Porter. The State Department earlier in the year had dismissed ten employees as security risks but declined to detail the charges, disclose who had made them, let the accused confront their accusers, or otherwise honor the tenets of due process or the department's own administrative regulations. Token hearings proved to be star-chamber proceedings at which the summary judgments were upheld. The dismissed officials engaged Porter's liberal firm to represent them and appeal to

Secretary of State George Marshall, on civil-libertarian grounds, to reopen their cases or, at the very least, wipe their records clean of the unproven charge of disloyalty to their government and country. When no word was forthcoming from State, Porter tried to stir up interest in the case in the press. Levin went to Andrews with Porter's story "and tried like hell to get permission to write it up." But Andrews, wary of liberal causes and causists and anything that smacked of softness toward Communism, was unsympathetic.

Later that fall, Porter's eminent partner, Thurman Arnold, found himself seated next to Helen Reid, by then the president of the *Tribune,* at its annual forum at the Waldorf in New York and told her about the State Department's summary dismissals. For all the compromises with idealism she had had to make during her long ascent to power, the liberal and reformist instincts of her youth had never entirely deserted Helen Reid. Appalled by Arnold's story, she instructed Bert Andrews to pay attention to it. Levin was advised that it would be best if the story was not written by a known liberal—the outrage should not be confused by partisanship—and Andrews did it himself. To dramatize the story, he focused on the case of Bernard Nortman, one of the ten fired men, whom he identified in the paper only as "Mr. Blank" and whose firing after five years of government work had been preceded by eight months of FBI investigation prompted by charges from unnamed accusers that he and his wife had been active Communist Party members in the mid-'Thirties. Nortman had learned that much about his phantom foes when FBI agents came to his home to inquire about the charges, which he flatly denied; it made no difference in the State Department's decision. Milton Freeman, an associate of the Arnold and Porter law firm at the time, recalled working with Bert Andrews while he was preparing the article: "It was not a political question to him. It was a nice, simple, civil liberties case to him—and, after all, the owner of his newspaper had been offended by it."

Andrews's 4,600-word story, chastely headed "A State Department Security Case," sprawled over the Sunday, November 2, issue of the *Tribune* and read like a political nightmare out of Kafka. A new Red scare was subverting essential American values. The impact of Andrews's story and his follow-up pieces caused the State Department to remove the disloyalty charge from the records of the fired officials and to pledge that it would not, as Arnold put it in his letter of thanks to Helen Reid, "repeat this disgraceful performance."

The following August, a few months after he had received the Pulitzer Prize for his "Mr. Blank" story, Bert Andrews received a call from a young member of the House Committee on Un-American Activities (HUAC)—Republican Representative Richard M. Nixon of California. The committee had taken closed-door testimony from an alleged former Communist Party member named Whittaker Chambers, then an editor on *Time* magazine, who claimed to have had dealings of a subversive nature in the 'Thirties with a number of U.S. government officials including Alger Hiss of the State Department. Hiss had denied the accusation. Corroboration of Chambers's story was largely lacking, but Nixon had a hunch he was telling the truth; if, on the other hand, Chambers was perpetrating a fraud, it would be, as Nixon later wrote to Andrews, not only "a great wrong to Hiss and the others named . . . but it would be a death blow to effective and necessary investigation of the Communist conspiracy in the United States." Nixon therefore wanted Andrews to read Chambers's testimony for his opinion of its veracity. In his book *Six Crises*, Nixon explained that he thought the *Tribune* bureau chief would be "predisposed to believe Hiss rather than Chambers" because of his Pulitzer-winning articles exposing the State Department's loyalty purges, but he also believed that Andrews would be objective. The unspoken consideration for letting him in on a potentially very hot story was that Andrews was a powerful journalist representing a powerful paper, the beacon of the Eastern liberal wing of the Republican Party, and Richard Nixon was an ambitious man.

Andrews came to Nixon's office, read Chambers's testimony, agreed with Nixon's judgment, and accepted his invitation to drive with him to Chambers's farm in Maryland to meet the informer firsthand and appraise his character. Nixon would write to Andrews four years later that "the whole course of the investigation was determined by that visit." The private, off-the-record meeting lasted three hours, during which Andrews grilled Chambers with the relentless skill of a veteran newsman; afterward, he told Nixon he was sure Chambers had known Hiss and urged that a confrontation of the two men be arranged before HUAC members—a step that was soon taken. During the long, sensational investigation that ensued, Andrews became, along with chief HUAC investigator Robert Stripling and Chambers himself, Nixon's close adviser in the pursuit of Hiss. Nixon once spoke to him on the phone at night for three hours from his room at the Commodore Hotel in New York to seek advice as the case unfolded. At one point, when the probe was in danger of being dropped because HUAC investigators had not uncovered sufficient proof of Chambers's story, Andrews scoffed at the cursory nature of their effort, especially in checking on the existence of an old Ford that Chambers claimed Hiss had given him. "How hard have you worked?" Andrews asked Nixon. "I'll bet that somewhere in the District of Columbia some records about that car survive. Why don't you put the whole staff of investigators to work on it? Maybe just one investigator just politely inquired in one place and accepted a plea of no information. But there must be a dozen places to check. Did someone own it before? What is Hiss's story of what became of it? Did Hiss trade it in when he got a new car? Most people do. Or did he sell it? At any rate, who got it? And why can't you trace the subsequent owner?" Bert Andrews, in short, steeled Richard Nixon's resolve at critical moments in the investigation. And when Hiss sued Chambers for libel and HUAC was told by both principals that they could not cooperate further without risking a contempt charge by the court hearing the libel case, Andrews made his most fateful contribution. "You were too nice to Chambers," he told Nixon after the Congressman and Stripling had returned from a fact-seeking trip to the informer's Maryland farm. "Did you just ask him for anything he had? Or did you slap a subpoena on him?" The subpoena followed the next day, and that evening Chambers produced from a hollowed pumpkin behind his farmhouse microfilmed copies of confidential State Department documents he said Hiss had transmitted to him. Although no proof of this charge was ever produced, evidence that the papers had been copied on a typewriter once belonging to Hiss was vital to his being convicted for perjury in claiming that he did not know Chambers. There was substantial reason, then, for Nixon to write, in a March 1, 1950, note to Helen Reid, that "had it not been for Bert Andrew's [sic] work, the Hiss case might never have been broken at all."

Throughout the Hiss-Chambers affair, Andrews and the *Tribune* had the inside track on its coverage. As a result, the paper played the story in a far larger and splashier way than the *Times,* and Andrews, while never disclosing his behind-the-scenes role as Nixon's counselor, did not hesitate to promote in print the California Congressman's Red-hunting activities. In the pumpkin-papers story, which the *Tribune* led the paper with under a four-column headline (and the *Times* gave a one-column head in the off-lead), Andrews wrote:

> . . . Mr. Nixon, all reporters in Washington know, has been more responsible than any other member of the committee for bringing Hiss-Chambers facts into the open. It was Mr. Nixon, in fact, who ordered a subpoena served on Mr. Chambers—and who got a pumpkin and its contents.

The *Times,* James Reston contended a generation afterward in appraising Andrews's part in the Hiss-Chambers affair, would "not have stood for any such debasement of news coverage." Was Andrews guilty of abandoning his objectivity? Or had he, like any good reporter, merely jumped at the chance to get on the inside of a juicy story and exploited his prime source even as he himself was being exploited in return? That his participatory role in the Hiss-Chambers case may have gone to his head is suggested by the remark he once passed to Robert Donovan, that he intended to make Dick Nixon President someday. By the time Nixon was residing in the White House, Bert Andrews had been dead fifteen years—a burned-out case at the age of fifty-two. He lived long enough to see Nixon elected Vice President, largely on his reputation as a vigorous anti-Communist.

VIII

When Don Irwin, an earnest young *Tribune* reporter who specialized in municipal and state politics, was asked to write a piece on the minor candidates in the 1948 presidential election, he made a small, understandable mistake. He mixed up the candidates put forth by the Socialist Workers Party and the Socialist Labor Party. When the unfortunate error was pointed out, the paper promptly published a correction. But that did not satisfy Edward Teichert, the Socialist Labor candidate, who argued that because Farrell Dobbs, the Socialist Workers candidate, had served in jail under a Smith Act conviction for sedition for trying to create dissension in the armed forces in 1941, the mislabeling would materially damage his candidacy; he sued the *Tribune* for $100,000.

In the ensuing negotiations between the parties, a settlement figure of $3,000 was put forth by the aggrieved Socialists. Reporter Irwin, being a well-mannered Princeton graduate and usually very conscientious about his job, was so guilt-stricken that his blunder should cost the financially pressed *Tribune* such a sum that he wrote a note to managing editor Cornish offering to repay the paper out of his salary. Cornish wrote back, declining the offer with thanks and saying that if the paper did not think Irwin was worth more than that, it would not be keeping him on. All nicely honorable and gentlemanly.

But that was not the end of the matter. For the *Herald Tribune* did not like to settle libel actions brought against it. Its special counsel for such matters— E. Douglas Hamilton—was strongly persuaded that such settlements in the long run would likely prove more costly to the paper than combating them, because giving in would only invite more suits. By resisting, Hamilton believed, and convinced *Tribune* management, "our potential adversaries knew they'd be in for a very tedious case of it." A little research into the activities of the litigious Mr. Teichert's party disclosed that it published a weekly newspaper called *The Guardian,* which, upon inspection, appeared to Douglas Hamilton to consist in significant part of material cribbed from other publications, including the *Herald Tribune.* Further inspection revealed that no one actually owned *The Guardian.* "They all did," Hamilton recalled. "They were true believers." So he filed suit against them all, Teichert included, for copyright infringement, and when the Socialists failed to drop their libel action against New York's staunchest press defender of capitalism, the *Tribune* countersued again, and then again, citing a lengthening list of alleged infractions. In time, the Socialists gathered that they had far more to lose than to gain by pursuing the case and dropped it.

In his twenty-nine years of defending the *Tribune* against libel charges, Hamilton lost only one contested case—a 1939 judgment of $2,500 that he got reduced to $1,000; and that one was lost, Hamilton always insisted, because the judge charged the jury incorrectly. Such a record was remarkable not merely because of the almost infinite number of instances of publication of unavoidably defamatory material in a newspaper of the *Tribune*'s scope but also because of the nature of libel law itself. Under it, the usual legal procedures seemed to be stood on their head: all that the complainant then had to do was prove that the offending story was published and claim that it was untrue and had damaged him; the defending newspaper then had to demonstrate its innocence—not presumed until proven otherwise, as is the general standard of Anglo-American justice—by showing the truth of the libel. However heavy a burden this might have placed on the press, it was not a jurisprudentially unsound one, for as

Hamilton himself noted in *Libel: Rights, Risks, Responsibilities,* co-authored with Robert H. Phelps, "the publisher of a libel is standing in the shoes of a prosecutor since he is accusing someone of bad conduct, while the person named in the publication is—as he should be—presumed innocent of the accusation."

A direct, good-humored man who wore a homegrown miniature rose as a boutonniere and had a touch of the carnival barker about his almost offhandedly witty speech, Hamilton was one of the nation's leading authorities on libel law and a powerful asset to the *Tribune* editorial department. Where most lawyers make their living by cautioning clients against taking unnecessary risks, Hamilton was so thoroughly comfortable with both his own mastery of libel problems and the *Tribune*'s willingness to resist intimidating restraints on its freedom to publish that his characteristic counsel was one of boldness. Charles Portis, who spent several years as a *Tribune* reporter and deskman before going off to write *True Grit* and other works of fiction, remembered Hamilton's typical response to city desk inquiries about a story suspected of indefensible libel: "Well, they'll sue—but we can beat it, so go ahead." A graduate of Harvard College and Law School, Hamilton in 1927 joined the New York law firm that had been handling *Tribune* legal matters since at least 1885, when Whitelaw Reid asked its principal member, Henry Woodward Sackett, to prepare a pamphlet for the staff summarizing the most important things for them to know about the law of libel. One of Sackett's successors in the firm, Harold L. Cross, revised and updated the pamphlet, which proved so useful in its clarity and brevity that he began using it as a text when Columbia University's new School of Journalism asked him to become its first lecturer on the subject in 1915—a role he relinquished after thirty-five years to his junior colleague, Douglas Hamilton, who held the job twenty-seven more years. Titled "What You Should Know About the Law of Libel," the pamphlet was also made available to many newspapers around the country. With such expertise readily available, the *Tribune* could afford to be courageous. "The feeling I got impregnated with early," Hamilton recalled of his handling of libel questions for the paper, "was that if it's possible to publish it, let's publish it—what if we do get into a few libel cases? No paper worth its salt can escape from the problem."

He would make himself available to the city desk all hours of the day and night, and when out for an evening would leave a telephone number where he could be reached, as doctors did. His principal lesson to reporters was to make every effort to get the other side of a libeling story, out of both fairness and the need under evolving case law to demonstrate absence of malice by the paper. If the defamed party offered comment, he was thereby giving tacit consent, in Hamilton's opinion, to publication of the damaging contents unless he explicitly warned the paper against printing them. Aside from stories about people under investigation by grand juries, no problem was a more frequent source of libel action than that of mistaken identification, even if innocently made. Hamilton taught the wisdom of adding the home or office address of any individual, company, or organization cited in an unfavorable context to avoid the possibility of confusion with an innocent person of the same name. Another of his prime lessons dealt with a newspaperman's professional privilege, in covering legislative proceedings, to report defamatory and even false remarks, although, under other circumstances, repetition of a libel by a speaker or another publication was in itself a libel. In criticizing artistic performances, *Tribune* hands were warned never to comment on the motivation of the artists—a lesson painfully learned by Horace Greeley and Thurlow Weed in demeaning James Fenimore Cooper a century earlier.

Prevention, then, was the surest defense against libel. But when that failed and a potential litigant indicated that mere correction would not do, Hamilton's first instinct was to ask the writer involved what else he had of a defamatory nature on the offended party. When the Philadelphia police force threatened suit over a report in Red Smith's column that one of their number, unnamed, had let spectators without tickets into an Eagles-Giants football game for a cash consideration, Hamilton recommended publication of the offender's badge number, which Smith had obtained before writing about it from the Eagles' owner, a witness to the event. If the writer had no such additional ammunition, Hamilton would put reporter Jay Racusin on the case to dig up dirt on the litigious party's past; the mere hint of its publication was usually enough to end the action. In fact, Hamilton went to trial in no more than a handful of cases in all his years representing the *Tribune*. "He was one of the people who made the paper great," said Judith Crist, for twenty years a *Tribune* reporter, editor, and film critic. In its last days, Jimmy Breslin, the paper's most freewheeling and potentially libel-provoking writer, would listen in to telephone conversations between his editors and Hamilton reviewing the dangers of his copy. When Hamilton gave his customary go-ahead, he would hear a whispered "God bless you, Doug" from the temperamental Breslin.

IX

Even those who were fond of Joe Alsop conceded that he was a mite imperious; others found him downright arrogant. No doubt he could be rude and overbearing and cruelly dismissive of people who bored him—as more did than not— but some who admired his undeniable intellect and journalistic talent detected a studied quality to Joe Alsop's offensiveness, even as they did in his high Oxonian speech. It was as if these mannerisms were designed to distract those encountering him from his unsightly girth, to insult before being insulted, to terrorize lest it be disclosed that he was the one who was terrified. Whatever the truth behind his peculiar personality, it did not precisely endear him at Harvard or in the *Tribune* city room, where Stanley Walker had taken him on at Helen Reid's behest, and where he proved, within six months, to be a highly capable performer. Advanced to the Washington bureau, he found the perfect habitat for his hauteur and his banker's suits.

Prewar Washington numbered few among its press corps with young Joe Alsop's educational and social background, his tribal links to the Roosevelts and old school ties to the Ivy Leaguers and patrician types manning the New Deal. Within weeks he was making all the right parties and connections and learning the necessity of cordial relations with those one neither liked nor trusted. Soon his *Tribune* correspondence was earning him assignments from *The Saturday Evening Post,* and when the North American Newspaper Alliance offered him a syndicated column while he was still in his mid-twenties, the lure was irresistible.

Alsop had the shrewdness to team up with a slightly older reporter well versed in the ways of Congress and the bureaucracy—Robert Kintner, who would one day preside over the National Broadcasting Company. "The Capital Scene," they called their column, a chatty inside report informed by plenty of legwork and leads Alsop began to pick up at soirees he assembled about his round dining table, where his often bitchy and outrageous talk helped loosen guests' tongues. No longer "a chubbo," as he referred to himself, after melting off weight under the supervision of Johns Hopkins doctors, he now had both self-confidence and a syndicated showcase. In 1940, the *Tribune* welcomed him back as a syndicated columnist until the war interfered.

His wartime experience, most of it in the Orient connected with General Claire Chennault's "Flying Tigers" after a brief internment by the Japanese when they captured Hong Kong, shifted Joe Alsop's journalistic horizons. Global affairs and American national security replaced domestic politicking as the prime subject of his new column, called "Matter of Fact," launched at the beginning of 1946 with a new partner, his brother Stewart. Three years younger than Joe, taller, handsomer, more personable, and without Joe's Britishisms, Yale man Stew Alsop had been a junior editor at a publishing house before the war, from which he emerged as a genuine combat hero. Their complementary natures meshed professionally. The result was a provocative column that blended erudite background, calculated opinion, and yeasty gossip.

Much of the Alsops' early reporting was given over to the Soviets' use of tyrannical terror in bringing Eastern Europe under their domination in the immediate wake of the war. The more they saw and heard, the more strident became their cold-warriorism and their insistence on America's need for vigilance in a perilous world—to the point that Washington insiders nicknamed the brothers "Doom and Gloom." An early example of their woe-mongering came at the end of their first month in partnership when they uncovered the gist of "the first authoritative study of the strategic meaning of the atomic bomb and other new weapons" made by the War Department's operations and plans division. Its general conclusions, "as reported on high authority, should be the subject of anxious, sleepless consideration by every thinking American," they wrote. The War Department thinkers reportedly warned that in the atomic age, the nation that struck first in war would almost surely be victorious, but that the United States, given its bothersome democratic traditions and clumsy governmental structure, was unlikely to take such an initiative, however provoked; the Alsops interpreted:

> ... in other words, if we permit the world again to reach the condition in which war is likely, we may expect to be destroyed as the result of our own easy negligence and complacency.
>
> That makes bitter reading . . . in conjunction with our postwar relapse into national weakness and complete demilitarization, which has already vastly reduced our power to influence the course of world events. . . .

By hammering on this theme, they ran the risk of being most boring when they were most right, Joe Alsop later noted, but their warnings were amply vindicated at the onset of the Korean War when the depleted strength of the U.S. military arm was grimly evidenced. To their considerable credit, the Alsops never linked the external peril of militaristic Communism to an alleged domestic conspiracy to turn the country over to the Soviets—a handy phantom seized upon by demagogues across the American political landscape to quash dissent. The real threats to American strength and unity, in the Alsops' view, were witch-hunting politicians who fed on the myth of an insidious Red menace at home and, by creating divisiveness, helped the Kremlin's cause.

The Alsop column succeeded because it was rooted in hard reporting. Joe Alsop, claiming a quota of no fewer than four in-person interviews a day, had discovered that officials in Washington and other national seats of power were glad to talk with a reporter who had done his homework, spoke their language, and approached them with the assurance that all America anxiously awaited their views. At its best, "Matter of Fact" served the function, not unlike that of the chorus in classical Greek tragedy, of describing those parts of the drama that did not take place on the open stage. Within a year and a half, the Alsops were syndicated in more than a hundred papers; at their peak, the number would be 137, including a majority of the nation's most influential papers. When the brother act broke up amicably after a dozen fruitful years and the older partner carried on alone, *Time* magazine commented, ". . . the eloquent voice of Joe Alsop, amplified by syndication, has dedicated itself to the cause of scaring tranquil humanity into its wits."

X

In his freshman year as a member of Yale's Class of 1935, John Campbell Crosby had the misfortune of being caught in his dormitory room with a young woman at an impermissible hour and was thrown out of the university. The event, reported on the front page of the *Herald Tribune,* inspired a novelette in *The Saturday Evening Post,* adapted into a Broadway play by Howard Lindsay, which in turn became a movie titled *She Loves Me Not,* starring Bing Crosby, no relation. None of this directly benefited John Crosby, but fate compensated him the following year when, readmitted to Yale as a member of the Class of 1936, he made the acquaintance of Whitie Reid, a fellow member of the freshman swimming team.

Economic hard times forced Crosby's withdrawal from Yale at the end of that school year and later, after a promising start in a journalistic career, his layoff from the staff of the *Milwaukee Sentinel.* Out of work and luck, Crosby wrote of his plight to Whitie Reid, who invited his former classmate to spend the Christmas holidays with the family in New York. That led to a tryout on the *Tribune* city staff, to which he was officially added in June 1936, the same month Whitie graduated. For five years, Crosby worked as a quiet cityside reporter, covering the police, routine local news, and the entertainment business and doing his best work in the form of interviews and an occasional minor review for the drama section. On his own time he tried his hand at playwriting and actually came close to having one of his efforts staged on Broadway. An eye condition kept him from combat during the war, in which he served as a press officer in San Francisco, and when he reappeared in the *Tribune* city room after the war was over, George Cornish was not sure what to do with him. He had hardly been a fireball in his prewar career on the paper.

For some time, Cornish and Helen Reid had wanted the *Tribune* to launch a regular column evaluating radio programming as an art form, but wartime pressures on the news hole had made it impossible. Newspapers had been wary till that point in their treatment of radio, a competitor for advertising dollars. The public listened to it, in great numbers, but few took it seriously—certainly not as an art form. Papers ran daily program logs on their back pages, occasional press releases, and gossipy, uncritical personality pieces on its performers, but no real criticism. After interviewing a few dozen candidates for the job, Cornish remembered John Crosby's bright touch with theatrical subjects and invited him to become the nation's first newspaper radio critic. The astonished Crosby, who did not even own a radio and rarely listened, accepted the challenge. The column, called "Radio in Review," began in May 1946, five months after the Alsop brothers made their debut and as Red Smith was beginning to make his mark as the new sports columnist.

Crosby's approach was that of a listener writing for other listeners, just as Smith cast himself as a sports spectator rather than an inside-dopester. In his first column, he took off after the morning talk-show vapidities of Ed and Pegeen Fitzgerald, who had the grace to appreciate the humor in Crosby's barbs and the inspiration to reprint his remarks in *Variety,* helping at once to establish the *Tribune*'s new ear as a receptor to be reckoned with. He poked fun at the pontifications of popular news commentators Fulton Lewis, Jr., Gabriel Heatter, and H. V. Kaltenborn ("the last of the free-wheeling larynxes"), roasted the crime drama series "Mr. District Attorney" for remoteness from reality, and praised what few islands of taste and sophistication, like the dry wit of nasal comedian Fred Allen, he could find while roaming the dial out at his cottage in Ocean Beach, Fire Island. As an assignment, it was a lot more pleasant than the police beat. As cultural criticism, by turns subtle and robust, "Radio in Review" was a trailblazer. It scored the prosperous broadcasting industry for pandering to the lowest common denominator while practically ignoring any obligation under its licensed control of the public airwaves to cultivate the American intellect.

His very application of an esthetic standard honored the medium he scorned and therefore made Crosby a scold, but a highly respected one, even by those he lacerated. Fan mail rolled in. His salary was raised four times in his first year as radio critic. Press agents for the broadcasters clamored for his attention, but Crosby declined to deal with them. Their publicity handouts piled mountainously on his desk, along with endless invitations to lunch, but he was unmoved. Besieged by phone calls whenever he came to the office, he sprinkled some fan mail atop the heap of press releases and appealed to Cornish for a secretary all his own to help answer his readers; approved and installed, she served mainly to insulate the critic from the industry that wanted to drown him in martinis.

By the end of 1949, Crosby's column was running in twenty-nine papers with four million readers. The next year he began to shift his attention largely to television, by then in some eight million American homes (compared to forty-five million with radios), and entered his most fruitful period as a critic of popular culture. He pleaded with the new industry not to make the same mistakes in its programming that radio had, especially in the presentation of the news. The comics may have been the most popular section of many a newspaper, he wrote, "but no editor would dream of filling the whole paper with them." If it heard, the electronic Cyclops never blinked.

XI

Newly independent India was being torn apart by religious strife and bloody rioting of a mass brutality that appalled the *Tribune*'s recently arrived correspondent, Margaret Parton. The subcontinent's saintly leader was just recovering that September of 1947 from a fast, his only weapon to protest and combat the violent behavior of his countrymen, when Parton received a letter to convey to him from Helen Reid. Would Gandhi come to New York, it asked, to address the *Herald Tribune*'s annual forum on current problems? Barring that, might he at least send a message to the forum and, through it, to the peoples of the world eager for his inspiring thoughts?

Parton duly delivered the request to Gandhi's headquarters in New Delhi and, upon hearing nothing in response, set about seeing if it had been considered. After two weeks of trying, she was granted an interview with the nationalist leader for 2:30 one afternoon. At 3:45, his secretary led her in, whispering that the Mahatma had just had his inhalator treatment and would not be able to speak more than a few sentences. When Parton entered, the great man was lying flat on his back, receiving a hot mudpack treatment on his chest from two young Indian girls. She knelt on the floor, in the vicinity of his left foot, a posture appropriate for venerating the near-skeletal figure she had come to regard as the greatest mortal in the world. Invited to begin, she asked if he had seen Mrs. Reid's letter. He had not. She produced a carbon copy. He held it six inches above his head and read it through twice, very slowly. Then he tossed it back to the American correspondent, indicating he did not care to answer it personally. "Whether God intends me to go to America someday I do not know," he said. "Certainly today it is out of the question." Silence.

Parton conceded the impossibility but persisted in asking whether he might transmit a message to the *Tribune* forum, perhaps a restatement of his pacifist faith, which most people accepted but were somehow unable to honor. Being a Quaker, she made her little speech with some conviction. "My only preoccupation is with India," he answered her. "I am not interested in world affairs." Silence again as the girls finished the mud slapping and pinned a white swaddling cloth around Gandhi's chest.

Parton understood how, since his message of peace had failed to pacify his own country, he was not disposed to offer it to a world unlikely to be more hospitable. Desperately, she put a few questions to him about the Indian situation, hoping to pluck a message of some sort from his answers. "I have nothing to say about India," he said. "I do not care to discuss anything." He closed his eyes then and apparently went to sleep. The interview had lasted seven minutes.

What mattered about Parton's mission was not its absurdity—had Gandhi not refused, what would he have *worn* to the Waldorf?—or fruitlessness or that under the circumstances she should have been after a news story, not come on a social call, but that it signaled Helen Reid's return to business as usual. The forum was a consuming project that she felt called the world's attention to the paper and well worth her efforts in trying to enlist notable speakers for it. Some on the *Tribune* thought it distracted her from far more pressing business, for the forum did not, after all, broaden the paper's circulation base or enhance its advertising revenue; what it promoted mostly, they said among themselves, was Helen Reid's ego, serving her need to mingle with the mighty and to use the paper as a vehicle for extending her personal sway. Whatever its purpose or efficacy, she was throwing herself back into the effort after a protracted spell of grieving over her husband's death. He had left her the paper to do with what she liked, but without him it was not the same.

At first she could devote herself only to his memory; she handwrote nearly five hundred responses to condolence notes she had received with the methodical, compulsive attention to detail that had most distinguished her work habits.

And there were estate matters to attend to, financial headaches, and bittersweet memories that were especially poignant when she vacationed at Wild Air that summer. She wrote Irita Van Doren:

> . . . I wish you were here today. The trees and water are breathtakingly beautiful. I dreaded seeing it again without Ogden, but I am thankful now to be here and perhaps the outdoor world helps one to get in better balance. I have felt like half a person and without roots of my own. . . . Meanwhile, there is plenty of work to be done and whatever I have is in the warp and woof of the paper going forward. . . .

She would soldier on, alone and brave—as in many ways she had been doing even while Ogden was alive. Now, though, she was truly Queen Helen, regal and chic, looking every inch the part. She had always known how to dress her tiny self smartly but in a way that made her seem larger: never an outfit that cut her in half, nothing with a short skirt, shoes with two-inch heels, hair puffed up and out, hats of a vertical rather than horizontal design. Her manner became more and more that of her late mother-in-law: grand, elegant, certain of her dominion. Britishisms began to creep into her speech; the word "issue" she would pronounce "iss-you" and "schedule" lost its "c." Her presence in a room would dominate it, and among her employees she inspired respect bordering on awe, but not a great deal of affection. Those eyes could still freeze or cauterize or look through what they elected not to behold. To rule the paper, however, did not necessarily require the love of the staff. What she needed most were resolve and vision forged of wisdom, experience, and imagination. But at sixty-five, the age of retirement for most of her contemporaries, was it reasonable for Helen Reid to assume such a burden? For her, the question was rhetorical; she would not abdicate her responsibility so long as health permitted. Behind that stubborn devotion was a pride that had grown with the years faster than the wisdom that should have governed it, and as a result, what Helen Reid demonstrated when installed as president of the *New York Herald Tribune* were not her virtues, which were numerous, but her limitations, which, if unchecked, could prove ruinous.

Iphigene Sulzberger, Adolph Ochs's daughter and wife of his successor as publisher of the *Times,* served on the Barnard College board of trustees with Helen Reid, and while respecting her intelligence and accomplishments, never forgot the time Mrs. Reid insisted that the board drive a hard bargain with the Rockefeller interests over a real estate matter involving the college's property. In Mrs. Sulzberger's eyes, Helen Reid had failed to see that the college's larger interests lay in dealing generously with the Rockefellers, given their power and possible future benefactions.

So it was with the *Tribune.* She was a master of minutiae but missed the main point, the larger problems confronting the paper and their underlying causes. She let her energy be siphoned off by attentiveness to details, believing with invincible hope and confidence that her cause was just and would prevail in the end. Her talent as a letter writer, for example, was formidable, but even the most routine letter to her got a personal response. If a publicity person sent her a copy of a handout already dispatched to the city desk or one of the departmental editors, her reply would include good wishes for the event it sought to publicize, and the press agent receiving it assumed the way was open for him to the front page. More important letters were often carefully revised. "They were almost always in the end good letters," George Cornish recalled, "but it troubled most of her executives that she and her secretary spent such incredibly long hours working on them." Her involvement with the forum was similarly taxing.

Chief executive officers cannot be mired in petty matters and remain effective. Nor can their thinking be governed by personal considerations, of the sort that rates loyalty to the company above ability and efficiency. What infuriated Helen Reid most were employees who ungratefully chose to leave for nothing more admirable than additional pay. The *Tribune* staff, she liked to believe, were members of her extended family, but she came to view them in fact as family retainers, to whom she attended, more or less, in their hour of need and from whom she expected fealty the rest of the time. She preferred that this benign autocracy remain undisturbed by reality. Outsiders were not invited to appraise her rule; the *Tribune* board of directors was a rubber stamp composed of family members and executives on the paper, and hard numbers were not presented for its inspection. Her manner was rarely tyrannical, but her hold on power within the organization was complete. Modern management disperses power and shares responsibility and encourages collective judgments and rule by consensus; Helen Reid was not a modern manager.

Nor was she linked by professional competence or personal feeling to the *Tribune*'s primary community. New York City to the Reids was a place for doing business, a source of news and revenue, the site of cultural exhibitions. Its people, though, were not her people—they were too loud, numerous, unruly, and, well, common. Her sort lived in the rectangle bounded by Park Avenue on the east, Fifth Avenue on the west, Eighty-sixth Street on the north, and Fifty-ninth on the south, and in the leafy suburbs beyond the outer boroughs. She cared more for the backyards of Bronxville and the gardens of Greenwich than the preservation of Central Park, to which Iphigene Sulzberger devoted considerable effort. The major global and national iss-yous concerned her and she dearly loved to lure powerful figures from the larger world to her dining table and her forums to discuss them, collecting these eminences like charms on a bracelet. But she evidenced social consciousness and visceral concern for the city in which her paper published no more than her husband had. The Fresh Air Fund, the *Tribune*'s own philanthropy, which had provided summer vacations in the country for poor city children since 1877, was to her way of thinking at least as much a shrewd form of promotion as a manifestation of noblesse oblige. "Her interest in the Fresh Air Fund was wholly monetary," in the estimate of Frederick H. (Bud) Lewis, who directed the fund's activities for twenty-five years. "She never inquired about our program philosophy, our educational aspirations, our long-range goals." But every New Year's Day, she would call Lewis at his home in Scarsdale at 8 a.m. to inquire if the annual fund drive, vigorously promoted in the paper and ending the midnight before, had surpassed the previous year's total. And if she was indifferent to the city's humble, she was not connected to its true movers. She knew many of its leading merchants on Fifth Avenue, but it had been years since she dealt with them on a regular basis and, at any rate, advertising was placed now by the lower echelons, not by orders from on high; numbers, not personal acquaintance or peevish letters, were what sold newspaper space in postwar New York. The Seventh Avenue garment industry was *terra incognita* to her, as were Madison Avenue's advertising agencies and the Wall Street financial community and City Hall with its alien Democrats. Her connections were social, where they existed at all, but barriers of rank, religion, party, and sex closed her off from genuine working relations with those who ran her city and held the fate of her paper in their hands.

The real trouble was that Helen Reid began to be blinded by dynastic pride. The manifest excellence of her paper and the caliber of its readership would see it through, even as the Reids would continue to direct it, whatever their short-comings. Instead of reaching outside the family or the paper for a strong hand to shape it editorially, she chose her older son, Whitelaw, to become editor, succeeding his father. Still shy and modest at thirty-four, he was not prepared for the job. His postwar experience had been limited to work on the Fresh Air Fund, the forum, and whatever odd jobs came his way in the office adjacent to his father's. "I hadn't projected the idea," said Whitie of his accession to the editorship, but neither would he shirk the job once his mother concluded it was what her husband would have wished. That the *Tribune* required something more, and urgently, did not occur to Helen Reid. What Whitie did not know, he could learn. The point was that he was the next Reid in line to edit the paper, and edit it he would. "The Reids began to conceive of themselves as infallible —as a kind of untouchable upper crust," said Richard Tobin, who worked for the *Tribune* twenty-five years in an editorial and promotional capacity and was on easy social terms with the owners. Tobin, like many on the staff, came to see them as the Romanoffs just before the Revolution, concluding in their insular arrogance, "No need to summon the Duma this year."

Nor would Helen Reid heed a friend of the *Tribune* like Walter Hoving, prewar president of Lord & Taylor and postwar head of Bonwit Teller and Tiffany & Company, all three carriage-trade emporiums, who urged a more realistic advertising approach upon her. "Helen Reid was quite a stubborn woman," Hoving contended. "I said to her many times, 'Why don't you promote your paper the way the *Times* does?' " He had in mind Monroe Green's program of sending thousands of free copies of the Sunday paper to merchandise managers around the country, the wholesalers and buyers who read it to see what was going on in the retail trade, of which the clothing manufacturers were the heart; with the manufacturers putting up the money under Green's vendor-paid approach, *Times* salesmen were able to offer their retail accounts space in the paper at greatly reduced cost. "But she couldn't see it at all," Hoving said of Helen Reid's preference to hold out for top dollar on the elitist premise that she was selling to the cream of the consumer market, "she couldn't see the fundamental point. She thought her do-gooding with the annual forum was the way to promote the paper. What she failed to understand was that her paper had to get the advertising bulk first to be able to afford that kind of high-class institutional approach."

The only person she seemed to listen to now was William Robinson, her business manager. She liked his confidence, his strength, his size—a big man like Ogden, but self-made, driving, outgoing, a born salesman. Her eyes seemed to light up when he was around, those in and close to the *Tribune* executive offices remembered, and Bill Robinson played to her admiration, like a platonic gigolo, using power instead of sexual favor. He had all the connections around town that she did not—he knew the retailers, the bankers, the brokers, the operators, the politicians, the showmen—and if he did not travel in the Reids' social set, if there was a certain excess to his hail-fellow-well-met manner, if he drank rather too much and had a tangled domestic life, no matter; he had broad shoulders and plenty of polish to smooth the rough spots. "He burnished himself," said circulation manager Richard Pinkham, not one of Robinson's admirers, and others felt that Robinson played Sir Walter Raleigh to Helen Reid's Elizabeth and emerged the ranking minister of her court. No one else rivaled him. Wilbur Forrest drifted off into retirement after Ogden's death; he could have served no other master. Geoffrey Parsons was nearing seventy and had no familiarity with the business side of the newspaper. George Cornish was an accomplished technician, not a policymaker or a power-grabber or a catalyst of change; he was there to maintain the *Tribune*'s editorial standards if permitted to. And Whitie Reid was a novice, nominally presiding over the 11 a.m. meeting in his office of the editorial-page writers and being taken out to a weekly breakfast by the top editors, whom Helen Reid charged with the task of speeding his on-the-job training. There was no strong figure on the editorial side of the paper to challenge Bill Robinson's hold on Helen's heart—and with it, direction of the paper.

Robinson was no bull in a china shop. He moved gingerly for a big man, but he moved. As early as August 1947 he felt free to send a memo to Mrs. Reid expressing concern about an anti-business bias he thought he detected in the editorial staff and a liberal tilt to the editorial page, symbolized by the cartoons of Bill Mauldin, whose work ran for several months as a counterpoint to the steadily more conservative drawings by Jay Darling. A typical Mauldin cartoon showed a repressive Franco with the blood of the Spanish people on his hands and a figure representing that country's Catholic clergy looking on approvingly. Robinson, a Catholic, contended that Mauldin had veered "pretty close to the Communist line," and that was not where the paper's readers wanted to be taken. Precisely at a moment when the *Tribune,* with its three most conservative executives—Ogden Reid, Wilbur Forrest, and Howard Davis—lately retired or in the grave, began to reach toward a more liberal readership, Bill Robinson emerged to exert a cautionary pull back toward the paper's orthodox constituency.

He enhanced his standing in Helen Reid's eyes that fall by enlisting the pen and lasting friendship for the paper of perhaps the most attractive public figure in the nation—Dwight Eisenhower, then completing his term as Army Chief of Staff. Greatly impressed by the general while dealing with him over the reopening of the Paris edition, Robinson visited Eisenhower in his Pentagon office in October 1947 and urged him to write a book about his wartime experiences; no American since Benjamin Franklin had succeeded so well at getting on with the nation's European allies when to do so was a matter of historical necessity. The *Tribune* would gladly help fund the project in return for the right to syndicate a condensed version, Robinson said, and he himself would gladly serve as Ike's agent in finding a publisher. Eisenhower was reluctant; writing a self-serving book did not appeal to him. But he conceded distress at some of the distorted accounts of the war that had begun to appear. Moreover, he had no money in the bank, and he had hopes of retiring someday to a nice home in a small town somewhere. Selling, always selling, Robinson told Eisenhower he would make no less than a million dollars on his book. In a follow-up letter, he added, ". . . [I]t is an imperative necessity for the American people as well as the historians of the world, now and in the future, to have your story." On reflection, Eisenhower yielded. Robinson obtained a contract for him with Doubleday & Company, which put up two-fifths of the price; the *Tribune* supplied the rest, along with the services of its foreign editor, Joe Barnes, who had worked with Willkie on his book and knew the grand strategies and lesser battles of the war as well as any newsman in America. Eisenhower, who had taught English at West Point and served as a speechwriter for then Commandant Douglas MacArthur, dictated the text over a fourteen-week period in the spring of 1948 before assuming the presidency of Columbia University. Syndicated that November and appearing in book form soon thereafter, *Crusade in Europe* sold 300,000 copies in its U.S. hardcover edition alone and was issued in twenty-two nations abroad. It brought Eisenhower the financial security Robinson had promised and enhanced his stature as a warrior-statesman. The two men became fast friends, and Robinson's nearly professional skills as a golfer—he was a long driver and an excellent putter—and bridge player made him a favorite Eisenhower recreational partner. Impressed, Helen Reid put the *Tribune*'s private two-engine plane at Robinson's disposal to fly Eisenhower down to the Augusta National golf course on occasional weekends.

Robinson and Mrs. Reid together faced their sternest test as co-commanders of the paper in the three-year span following Ogden Reid's death. It was the *Tribune*'s last chance to remain competitive with the *Times.* Although the *Tribune* had raised its price to a nickel at the beginning of the period and lost

10 percent of its daily circulation by the fall of 1949, the *Times* was unable to make any weekday circulation gains of its own. On the other hand, the lowered circulation of the *Tribune* and higher per-unit advertising rates caused its ad volume to remain static in the 1947–49 period, though its overall revenues rose 20 percent on the strength of its higher selling price. The *Times,* meanwhile, posted a 26 percent gain in advertising linage and a nearly 40 percent jump in overall revenues despite holding the line on its three-cent daily price. The *Tribune*'s profits averaged only $300,000 in those three years, and the *Times,* with its much larger overhead, was only fractionally more profitable. But there was a critical difference in the performance of the two papers' managements, with consequences that would become evident soon after the century reached its midpoint.

The *Times*'s profits were low, indeed almost invisible, in the early postwar years because it was reinvesting heavily in its plant, staff expansion, and amenities that lifted employee morale. It spent nearly $2 million in 1948 just on air-conditioning its newly modernized and expanded offices on Forty-third Street and added an employee lounge, a game room, and a circulating library; its composing room grew by 40,000 square feet, almost an acre. At the *Tribune,* in marked contrast, a total of only $3.2 million went into capital expenditures: a long-overdue expansion of press capacity, improvement in the *Tribune*-owned building next door to the paper's offices, and liquidation of $1 million of the paper's long-term debt to the Reids ($400,000 was paid to Jean Ward, Ogden Reid's sister, and the rest to Ogden's estate). Nothing was invested in the rapidly deteriorating *Tribune* offices, beastly hot in the summer, when a fine layer of grit sifted through the wide-open windows and covered every flat surface in the city room. The year-round grime was so offensive to one veteran copy editor, Constantine Nicholas (Mike) Messolonghites, that upon reporting to work each day, he would go to the men's room and return with a cardboard tray bearing a mess of wadded, moistened paper towels, which he used to scrub off his chair, his telephone, and the portion of the copy desk allotted as his work space; "Mike and His Portable Swamp," observers labeled the daily performance.

Instead of proposing an investment of capital, creativity, and energy to make inroads into the *Times*'s daily circulation, stalled at about 535,000 during this period, Robinson chose to rationalize away the 160,000-copy lead it held over the *Tribune*. In a revealing memo dated July 20, 1948, he argued that "not less than 75,000 transient readers every day" bought the *Times* solely for its classified ads, adding, "If it has what they want, they tear out that page and throw the rest of the paper away. . . . They never read anything else in the paper." Another group, which he estimated to be of the same size, "buy the Times primarily for [its] business service in the apparel trades." A third group, which he said numbered about 50,000, were Jews who faithfully read the *Times* obituary columns "to be sure that they will know of the passing of relatives and friends" since the Jewish religion prescribed burial within twenty-four hours.

This adds up to something like 200,000 copies of the paper sold every day to people who are impelled to buy it for a reason other than the news and editorial excellence of the Times. It is my firm belief, therefore, that more people in the New York area (city and suburbs) buy the Herald Tribune because they prefer it as a news and editorial product than the New York Times.

The numbers were confected out of thin air and the contentions behind them were wishful thinking. Even if they had been right, what made 75,000 garment-industry readers of the *Times* a less significant total than a comparable number of *Tribune* readers who preferred it for its coverage of Wall Street? What made 50,000 Jewish readers of the *Times* obituaries inferior statistically to 50,000 Presbyterians who might have bought the *Tribune* solely to read its sports page? The *Tribune* business manager then compounded this masterpiece of self-delusion by proposing to combat the *Times,* not by strategic expenditures to improve or reconceptualize his product or distribute it more effectively, but by a massive act of belt-tightening. The bind Robinson found himself in was difficult, without a doubt. The cost of publishing a newspaper had doubled in the ten years since the *Tribune*'s last big economy drive, in 1937, and while many other papers were feeling the same cost squeeze, the *Tribune*'s situation was unique. Its newsstand price had already been raised two cents above that of its heftier rival, and its advertising rates were so high in proportion to its circulation that the paper was becoming a deluxe option for space buyers. Other hard-pressed papers around the country were not required, as the *Tribune* was due to the nature of its competition and its conception of reader service, to devote half its contents to editorial matter; most ran 40 percent or under. To Robinson, there was only one answer to the *Tribune*'s dilemma:

> . . . [W]e must for these next two years follow an austere and frugal policy under which we will constantly improve the caliber and quality of our news, feature and editorial content. Every dollar we can store up by careful, prudent operation will be a blow stored away for the day when we can take advantage of our lesson, and switch readers from the Times to the Herald Tribune in wholesale quantities.
>
> With a year of two of constant gains against them, they [the *Times*] will be panicked into all kinds of expedient measures, while we pursue our firm purpose to develop this newspaper as the best NEWSpaper in the world. . . .

This sloganeering mentality, based as the 1937 economy drive was on the preposterous contention that a better newspaper could be produced with fewer resources if everyone just worked at it, prevailed, and Helen Reid handed Bill Robinson an ax. A million dollars was to be slashed from the operating budgets for the next two years. Personnel reductions were made in all departments. The *Tribune* page size was reduced slightly to save on newsprint. Prices in the paper's cafeteria were raised to put it on a paying basis. And about twenty-five men were dismissed from the news department—in an effort, Mrs. Reid would explain to a *Time* magazine interviewer, to bring the staff back to its prewar level; the paper simply could not afford to retain both returning veterans and their wartime replacements. The biggest cut came in the number of men cover-ing the police districts around the city, reduced from ten to three on the defensible premise that after the horrors of war news, the general run of local fires, muggings, and stabbings no longer seemed worthy of exhaustive daily documentation. But younger foreign correspondents were also recalled from their expensive overseas postings, out-of-town assignments were curtailed and the telephone substituted, the daily news hole was reduced by four columns, and a perceptible thinning of the news product was underway. What remained was still of high quality, and the new postwar features, such as the columns by Red Smith, John Crosby, and the Alsops, made the *Tribune* more readable than ever. The cutbacks, though, were a severe blow to morale, a confession of weakness, or unwillingness or inability to raise fresh capital to combat the *Times.* Nobody in the upper reaches of the *Tribune* was happy about the economy drive. Never before had the paper engaged in mass firings. "It became a case of having to shorten sail in a big blow," Whitie Reid recalled, dipping into the nautical metaphors favored by his family. If the situation had been no more complex than that, then the strategy would have made sense. But the simple truth, perfectly visible at the time, was that the *Tribune* ownership would not invest in the paper—was in fact siphoning off badly needed working capital to pay itself back long-standing loans that should have been written off or converted into equity decades earlier—at precisely the time its powerful competitor was arming itself massively for the years ahead.

XII

At the time of Robinson's cutbacks, sports editor Stanley Woodward was asked to submit the names of two members of his department for sacrifice on the altar of economy. Woodward listed himself and Red Smith.

He was like that. His excellent if short-lived turf writer, Joe Palmer, said of Woodward that he was "often contemptuous of superiors, barely tolerant of equals, and unfailingly kind and considerate to subordinates." His contempt for his immediate superior, George Cornish, was heightened when the Alabama-reared managing editor declined to place on the *Tribune* front page an exclusive report of a threatened strike by the St. Louis Cardinals over the appearance in their ballpark by the Brooklyn Dodgers' Jackie Robinson, the first black to compete in the major leagues. Woodward thought Cornish a spineless company man, tight with the owners' money, and so cautious and safety-minded an operator that he dubbed him "Double Rubber George," a prophylactic sobriquet that clung to the courtly Cornish during the rest of his long tenure as the *Tribune*'s ranking editor. Woodward had still lower regard for Cornish's new titular superior, Whitie Reid. Whitie's father he had admired as honest and fearless, and never forgot the time when Larry MacPhail, owner of the New York Yankees, had sent a letter of complaint over something derogatory Woodward had written about him and urged Ogden to fire his sports editor. Wilbur Forrest, answering for Ogden, who he said had gone out of town, wrote back: "Before leaving he suggested that I tell you that he will call on you in case he decides he needs aid in running his business." When, by contrast, Woodward wrote a column panning Madison Square Garden boxing promoter Mike Jacobs for scheduling a heavyweight match too close to the *Tribune*-sponsored Fresh Air Fund charity football game between the reigning professional champions of the previous season and a team of college all-stars, Whitie Reid wrote to Jacobs apologizing for Woodward's printed attack and told the sports editor about it after the fact. "I considered the column undignified," Whitie explained. Woodward shot back that nobody in authority on the paper had ever before gone behind his back on a matter of office business and that if what Whitie prized in a sports editor was dignity, he had better hire someone else.

Woodward's fiercely independent soul finally ran afoul of Helen Reid. He had become aware of her growing power during Ogden's declining days when, as he wrote in his memoir, *Paper Tiger,* an advertising man appeared in his office one afternoon "and gave me detailed instructions on how to run the Sports Department. . . . The Editorial Department was no longer verboten to the commercial minions of Mrs. Reid." In the spring of 1948, the intrusion became unbearable for him. Noting that the *Times* on a slow sports day had run an eight-column headline over a roundup story on women's golf matches at Westchester courses, Helen Reid sent Stanley Woodward a note asking that the *Tribune* follow suit. Woodward replied in a sardonic note to Cornish, arguing that he did not have the space for such marginal news, of likely interest only to the participants and possibly their husbands, and that it would be demeaning to assign one of his regular writers to such a story, which, if absolutely necessary, could be done on the phone by a copyboy. Whitie Reid remembered that Woodward, as an act of protest, then cut some of the charts giving the horse-racing results in order allegedly to make room for the first Westchester women's club golf results. "It seemed an act of deliberate sabotage," Whitie Reid recalled. "He was thumbing his nose at us." So the *Tribune* fired the best sports editor in the United States. "I have never been able to communicate with you, even though I sat across the desk from you," Woodward wrote in his parting note to Mrs. Reid. The real problem, as he himself would later put it, was that he had addressed management "in terms of insufficient servility." Grainy types were not Helen Reid's dish.

A still more troubling loss in 1948 was the departure of foreign editor Joe Barnes to take editorial charge of the mortally ill left-wing tabloid *PM.* Although the *Tribune* wished him the best in a farewell editorial, Barnes's leaving was almost certainly greeted with furtive sighs of relief by its top management, which had all but forced his exit by giving him too little to do.

Barnes had demonstrated resourcefulness in jockeying his small staff of correspondents around the globe to compete—or at least to give the illusion of competing—with the *Times*'s foreign coverage. They had, by 1947, fifty-nine overseas reporters working out of twenty-seven bureaus; Barnes had eight bureaus, several manned by part-timers, and hardly that many correspondents. To compensate, he developed a kind of roving coverage, spotting his people where stories occurred, and began to assign correspondents not by geographical areas as had been the universal practice of the trade but by their specialized knowledge, such as diplomacy, economics, military affairs, and cultural developments, letting them float from country to country to report on their specialty. He also pioneered in team coverage. A group of four *Tribune* correspondents spent three months in Eastern Europe gathering material for a twelve-part syndicated series titled "Behind the Iron Curtain," which left readers in little doubt about the repressive tactics of Soviet-dominated Communist governments. But by 1948, the foreign news hole, which had run as high as forty columns during the height of the war, was down to nine or ten columns a day, and Barnes was left with a handful of correspondents.

Starting in February 1948, the misanthropic Westbrook Pegler, then a syndicated columnist for the Hearst papers, launched a series of assaults on the *Tribune*, which he said had veered sharply leftward since Ogden Reid's death and "reflects the editorial and political policies of Joseph Barnes," whom he styled as a radical. Pegler's prime evidence for so characterizing Barnes's political posture was a passing reference to him in *Mission to Moscow*, a memoir by Joseph E. Davies, American Ambassador to the Soviet Union during part of Barnes's tenure as the *Tribune*'s Moscow correspondent. Davies himself cited no examples of Barnes's alleged radicalism and alluded to him not as a sinister fellow but as one highly knowledgeable about Russian life. Facts, though, were small impediments to Pegler when he was on a tear. "Almost any way you turn," he wrote, "you find politically queer people, un-Republican people, sounding off their ideology in the Herald Tribune"—as undocumented a claim and gross a distortion as the charge that Barnes had become the dominant editorial influence on the paper.

The Reids remained publicly undisturbed by Barnes's politics. Helen Reid's confidence in his clearheadedness and patriotism was evidenced in her answer to a 1945 letter from the virulently anti-Communist William Loeb, then the publisher of the Burlington, Vermont, *Daily News*, who had accused Barnes of fellow-traveling and possibly Communist Party membership; she wrote him:

> It has been my experience that there are always people who rush into designating as a communist or fellow traveler any one who believes in being informed on Russia or who considers that the future security of the world is dependent on the United States and the Soviet Union being friends. I hold this latter conviction myself as does Joseph Barnes, our Foreign Editor. He is not, however, either a communist or a fellow traveler. . . .

Yet the family in effect invited him to leave by stripping him of staff and space in the paper instead of advancing him to a position of higher responsibility, such as successor to aging Geoffrey Parsons as editor of the editorial page, a job for which he was ideally suited. Plainly they considered him too politically risky for that sensitive post. That summer, Whitie Reid's younger brother, Ogden, whom everyone called Brownie, worked during his vacation from Yale as a researcher for a House of Representatives subcommittee studying national security. "Brownie reported the FBI had damning evidence against Joe Barnes," his brother recalled, and Brownie himself long afterward acknowledged, "There was some information about him given to me by the government . . . that raised some questions," but he declined to reveal what sort of questions; the "information," he conceded, was "not necessarily conclusive." But it was enough to dishearten his brother and cause him to warn his editorial writers to be wary of Barnes when they brought up his name at one of their daily meetings in his office. "I didn't know how far over he'd been" on the political left, Whitie explained. When *PM,* rechristened the *Star* by Barnes and his group, ran out of money early in 1949 despite the genuine progress it had made as a responsible news product under his guidance, the *Tribune* made no effort to lure him back.

"Joe deserved a kinder fate from the Reids," William Shirer said of Barnes. "He was never given authority in keeping with his gifts."

A reading of the minutes for the 1947–49 period of the *Tribune* planning board, a monthly convocation of the paper's top people initiated by Mrs. Reid in mid-1947, discloses how little the organization could afford the loss of Woodward and Barnes, two of its most gifted and imaginative editors. Precious few ideas were introduced to deal with the *Tribune*'s basic dilemma, which was becoming increasingly apparent—journalistically it may have been the best newspaper in New York, but was there a market for it as conceived? For all its editorial sprightliness, would it languish forever in the shadow of the *Times*? How long could it go on functioning with precariously thin profits?

The problem was not that the people who ran the *Herald Tribune* were blind, but that they loved it too well to want to change it very much. A little tinkering here and there was all they could countenance; Bill Robinson's cheerleading would lead them out of the wilderness into economic stability. There was no talk about the need to refinance the operation, only a continuing call for economy and efficiency by Robinson and A. V. Miller, the cold, tight-lipped treasurer. They would leapfrog in their planning discussions, remarking on the need for more pictures or more local news or more human-interest copy or better comics or even a slogan that would more vividly capsulize the virtues of their product than the dreary incumbent, "You're Missing Plenty if You Don't Read the Herald Tribune." But nothing was sustained, no major innovations broached. Although the circulation of the Sunday *Tribune,* which produced half the paper's advertising revenues, was hemorrhaging before their eyes—it lost nearly 100,000 sales over the three years while the *Times* was adding almost that many Sunday customers—they seemed baffled by the trend and powerless to counter it. *This Week,* its airy Sunday supplement, Cornish claimed to be as worthy an entry as the *Times Magazine,* a heavyweight in more ways than one; his main suggestion to improve the Sunday package was to produce its weekly news review section as a tabloid—it would bulk up better that way. Parsons thought the section ought to be improved first, "but not at this time—perhaps when we are in a position to do something about it." No one insisted that the improvement had to occur then and there, that time was not on their side, that the Sunday *Times* was a leviathan that could not be harpooned with toothpicks. Only Whitie Reid proposed an interesting new idea for the Sunday edition—a "home" magazine, gathering together material on design, decoration, family finances, gardening, living styles—but he did not push it with his elders. Whitie Reid was not a pusher.

Only one man in their midst was. Richard Pinkham, the young circulation manager, seemed to grasp the severity of the problem while there was still time to do something about it, and he spoke out. "Here we sit with the world's best newspaper and only some 300,000-odd readers," he declared. Bold innovations were required. Pinkham pushed hard to win readers for the *Tribune* among the world's largest Jewish community, which shunned it for the *Times,* and began to make incursions. The *Tribune* embraced Zionism, as the *Times* had not until the state of Israel was an all but accomplished fact, covered the Palestine war extensively with Homer Bigart and one of its best young correspondents,* ran the condensed memoirs of Chaim Weizmann, a prime mover in the establishment of Israel and its first president, and launched other features, like "Pitching Horseshoes," Billy Rose's column, and a list of arriving out-of-town buyers like the one in the *Times,* all thought to appeal primarily to Jewish readers. But the gains were limited, possibly driving away as many Christian readers as the Jewish ones they attracted. Pinkham pushed, too, for more vigorous promotion of circulation. In 1948, he got money to sample some 30,000 homes and achieved an extraordinary 12 percent success rate. But in Robinson's austerity drive launched that year, such expenditures were judged a luxury and curtailed. Still, Pinkham persisted. In the spring of 1949, he argued that no matter how well his circulators performed, they could not succeed with the current product. "So tremendous is the reputation of *The New York Times* for authenticity, for objectivity and for completeness and so inconspicuous to the average reader's eye are the ways in which the *Herald Tribune* is a better paper," he asserted,

---

* Kenneth Bilby, the young *Tribune* reporter involved, covered the conflict mostly from the Israeli side and, while sympathetic to the Zionist cause because of Hitler's slaughter of European Jewry and admiring the Jewish army in Palestine as "an infinitely superior fighting force," did his best to report the war objectively. But he felt the *Tribune,* newly eager to win Jewish readers, was selective in how it played his reports and sacrificed integrity in failing to run one he filed on the misery and bitterness he encountered in the Arab refugee camps. Pinkham told the planning board about one New York rabbi who had lately become a *Tribune* reader because of "our fair treatment of the Palestine story"—a switch in the lifelong reading habit of the rabbi, who confided that "every single morning when I bought [the *Times*] at the newsstand I would have a thrill of pride to think that our people could produce such a great newspaper."

no dramatic progress was foreseeable unless the *Tribune* revamped itself. "This is really the main chance," Pinkham told them, and specified what ought to be done. Without abandoning a hard core of news and informed opinion, the *Tribune* had to provide more color and entertainment for readers, had to bridge the gap between mass and class, had to have "Li'l Abner" and other top comic strips and a gossip columnist as good and refined as Leonard Lyons of the *Post* and an informed society columnist like Charles Ventura of the *World-Telegram* and whatever else was required to make it irresistible reading. "I'd like to see [the *Tribune*] shake loose from its current reputation as a second *New York Times* and establish itself as the happy-medium newspaper in the vast middle ground between tabloids and tedium. All it takes is faith, guts and money. We all have the faith. I know Bill Robinson has the guts. All we need is the money."

It was heresy, of course. Most of them would rather have seen the paper perish than prostitute itself. But they missed the main thrust of Pinkham's proposal: to live, the *Tribune* had to take itself out of direct competition with the *Times* and somehow create a new identity. At the December 1949 planning board session, Pinkham was urging the adoption of "Never Dull" as the *Tribune*'s slogan and placing it on millions of light bulbs as a promotion stunt. They all liked Dick Pinkham, but after that they rated his thinking as rather too bizarre to be taken seriously.

13

'Fifties
Follies

T he *Sun* set on the fourth day of 1950.

A museum piece by then, without any of the sparkle or bite that had distinguished it at its height under Dana, the afternoon paper was down to sixteen reporters and rewritemen at the end and served a circulation that had dwindled to about 275,000, smallest in the city following the postwar merger of the *Post* with the *Bronx Home News.* The *Sun*'s archaic political and social policies—it was the only New York paper other than *The Wall Street Journal* to keep the Newspaper Guild from organizing its news and commercial departments—still claimed the loyalty of a wealthy clientele that for years attracted almost as much weekday advertising as the *Herald Tribune,* but that patronage had begun to fall off sharply in 1949. There were simply not enough dogmatic conservatives in metropolitan New York to sustain the *Sun,* any more than there had been enough doctrinaire leftists to provide an adequate readership nucleus for *PM,* which had been as sprightly in its reporting on labor, racial injustice, consumer affairs, and the glories of psychotherapy as the *Sun* had been fusty in its devoted coverage of the financial markets, antiques, cat care, and motorboating.

The death of the *Sun* left seven dailies in New York. The *News,* selling 2.3 million copies a day, was by far the largest—a snappily written, cleverly edited digest emphasizing the seamy side of the local scene. The *Mirror,* its pallid imitator, sold about half as many copies, enough for second place in city circulation, but drew little advertising. Hearst's other New York entry, the splashy, almost unsightly *Journal-American,* paced the evening field with 700,000. The *Times,* fourth in sales with 537,000, led all papers in advertising on the strength of its readers' high average income and prominence in the city's commercial and cultural life. Then came the *World-Telegram* with 366,000 customers (about to grow substantially, if temporarily, through its absorption of the *Sun*), the *Post* with 355,000, and last, the *Tribune* with 323,000. And other threats to the *Tribune*'s solvency, its editorial distinctions notwithstanding, were beginning to manifest themselves. *The Wall Street Journal,* serving a readership of similar social outlook, was up to 142,000 copies a day—a 100 percent increase in only four years—and *Newsday,* the quality tabloid serving suburban Long Island, a *Tribune* stronghold, had grown as rapidly and crossed the 100,000 mark.

Despite its rank at the rear of New York papers in size, the *Tribune* remained economically viable because of its advertising revenues, third highest in the city. But unless its circulation improved, especially in relation to the *Times*'s, its prospects for financial health were gloomy despite Helen Reid's pluckiness and Bill Robinson's cheerleading. A few weeks after the death of the *Sun,* the *Tribune* got a break that gave it some breathing room. The *Times,* having held its newsstand price at three cents for more than three years while the slimmer *Tribune* was going for a nickel, was finally forced to follow suit. The *Times*'s net profit had slipped from a 1946 high of nearly 8 percent to under 1 percent in 1949 as it continued to pump resources into the product. The two cents added to its selling price were to cost the *Times* some 30,000 sales a day and bring its circulation down to just slightly above half a million copies, a plateau on which it would be stalled for four years.

Occurring almost simultaneously, the demise of the *Sun* and the price rise by the *Times* presented the *Tribune* with both the necessity and the opportunity to widen its claim on the readership market. The *Sun*'s failure triggered a round of rumors that the *Tribune* was likely soon to follow it to oblivion or at least go on the auction block. Richard Pinkham had heard the whispers while vacationing out at fashionable Fishers Island the previous summer, Bert Andrews told Helen Reid that similar reports were circulating in the National Press Building in the capital, and Walter Winchell was feeding the rumor mill even while printing the *Tribune*'s denial that it was about to be bought by the Cowles family, which had offered $8 million. There was reason now, though, for increased anxiety about the reports of the *Tribune*'s troubles because they appeared to be increasing in number and not accidentally. "Advertising salesmen from the Times are circulating around town with a confidential report which is so confidential they can only let agency men and other advertising executives get a glimpse of it," William D. Patterson, head of the Fred Smith & Company agency, wrote to Whitie Reid. "They won't leave it with anyone." The gist of the *Times* men's report, Patterson alleged, was that the *Tribune* was losing a lot of advertising "and isn't it terrible . . ." The strategy behind the effort, Patterson concluded, was to discourage advertisers from patronizing a sinking ship, "and the Sun is always mentioned by the Times in discussing the Trib." The *Tribune*'s revenues had in fact slipped 4 percent in 1949, but the *Times*'s had grown by only 4 percent that year, and if *Times* ad salesmen were undercutting the *Tribune,* their purpose may have been as much defensive, over an anticipated drop in circulation due to the new five-cent price, as malicious to their chief rival. Yet other *Times* men were heard around town bad-mouthing the *Tribune.*

"They didn't play like gentlemen," said George H. Allen, promotion manager of the *Tribune* in the immediate postwar years, summing up its view of the *Times*'s tactics. That the *Times* kept heavy pressure on its main rival by holding down its price and ad rates while settling for what George Cornish characterized as "ridiculously low profits" infuriated *Tribune* executives. For its part, the *Times* was merely practicing aggressive free enterprise and viewed *Tribune* protests about poor sportsmanship as so many sour grapes. "The Ochses and the Sulzbergers poured their money back into the paper and lived relatively modestly," commented Harrison Salisbury, a veteran *Times* correspondent, editor, and latter-day historian, "while the Reids didn't do either of those things."

Helen Reid, sufficiently aroused in the spring of 1950 by the damaging rumors to sniff a conspiracy against her newspaper, went to the state's friendly Republican administration to seek help. New York's attorney general responded by announcing an investigation and declaring, "Erroneous reports alleging that this important and world-known newspaper either is about to be sold or is seeking buyers have cropped up repeatedly despite vigorous denial by the management. . . . Pressure by false rumor can become a serious threat not only to the New York Herald Tribune but to any member of the free press." The statement also included Helen Reid's forceful insistence that her paper was operating at a profit. She did not say how narrow it really was.

But the *Sun,* too, had made such disavowals of impending doom in the months before it went under, so more convincing evidence of the *Tribune*'s strength was required. It was forthcoming with the appearance that spring of the Early Bird, a new edition of the *Tribune* dreamed up by Bill Robinson, aimed at reaching Manhattan newsstands by 8 p.m., a full three hours earlier than the *Times*'s and its own city editions and about the same hour that the tabloid *News* and *Mirror* hit the streets. Robinson had three ends in mind: to catch the tail end of the homebound commuter crowd, heavy buyers of the *World-Telegram & Sun;* to compete directly against the tabloids with a *Tribune* edition tailored for the job; and to steal a march on the *Times.* Some 1.3 million papers were sold in the city between 8 p.m. and 1 a.m. every night, and Robinson believed that the new, brighter Early Bird edition could increase the *Tribune*'s piece of that market by from 50,000 to 100,000 copies.

To achieve that goal, an earlier edition of the regular *Tribune* would not do. After the cares of the day, readers wanted lighter, easier material in the newspaper they read at night, so the Early Bird featured an eight-column streamer headline and two columns of the day's sports results on page one, larger head-lines and more pictures throughout the paper, and the addition of show-business news and personality features. But it also had to include the recognizable nucleus of the traditional *Tribune* and the complete closing Wall Street prices and other service data expected of a great newspaper of record—in short, the *Tribune* contracted a case of self-induced schizophrenia in order to create an edition midway between the mass and class markets. Circulation manager Pink-ham, while eager for a brighter, more entertaining paper to sell, was doubtful that the Early Bird was the way to go about it. He thought the additional investment it would require in composing-room, distribution, and promotional outlays might better be spent on improving the basic product with more local news and first-rate feature material; cosmetics and a new delivery schedule would not materially improve the *Tribune*'s position, he argued. But Dick Pinkham's was not a powerful voice in the *Tribune* councils. Helen Reid was all for the Early Bird, even thought up its name, and sent a memo strongly urging all department heads to cooperate with the new venture that she hoped would provide the key to the paper's prospects for growth. At the *Times,* with their own circulation falling, they watched the takeoff of the Early Bird anx-iously. "It was an irritant," said circulation manager Nathan Goldstein, "and a cause for concern."

The new venture suffered a setback at the outset when columnist Billy Rose, whose light essays tuned to the big town's street-smart ethos were precisely the fare on which the Early Bird hoped to thrive, quit and moved to the *News* after the *Tribune* declined to run one of his pieces. Its libel lawyer, Douglas Hamil-ton, beloved in the city room for his latitudinarian view of what could be printed and successfully defended, objected to Rose's attribution of gross anti-Semitism to opera singer Kirsten Flagstad, who was about to be hired by the Metropolitan Opera. But other papers ran Rose's syndicated column. The incident did not improve the *Tribune*'s standing with Jewish readers, whom the Early Bird sought especially to attract. A replacement of sorts, fortunately, was waiting in the wings.

So badly did Hy Gardner want to write a show-business column for the *Tribune* that he had been lobbying for a year and a half. For a month he wrote such a column to show how it could be done with dignity befitting the paper, had it set in type at his own expense, and sent proofs of it to the *Tribune*'s top executives and editors. George Cornish, whose principal mission was not to dream up new ideas but to guard the integrity of the editorial product, had been sufficiently impressed by Gardner's sample work to approve it for the Sunday drama section; the paper could not afford more space than that for celebrity chitchat. But once a week would not attract the following Hy Gardner wanted. As a high school boy in New York, he had been a legman for Walter Winchell and Mark Hellinger, the two most prominent show-business columnists of the day, and later apprenticed in Hollywood for Hedda Hopper. His other journalis-tic training was limited to a prewar stint on the *Brooklyn Eagle*; essentially he was a publicist with stars in his eyes and a few among his clients, of whom band leader Tommy Dorsey was the most famous. When Billy Rose left the *Tribune*, the paper decided to give Gardner his chance—but only in the Early Bird. Lively, decent, and honest, Gardner's column lacked Rose's style and polish but made a mildly diverting potpourri of anecdotal name-dropping and the vagaries of show-business high life on both coasts. Gardner's main claim to journalistic distinction was the accuracy of his material, no small achievement in covering a field where hype and hoopla reigned. "New York is a double-talk town," he said of his beat, "but in Hollywood nobody told the truth." He invented a format he called "Tip-Off and Check-Up" that gave him the chance to report on intriguing rumors by allowing their subjects to confirm or deny them. The column proved sufficiently appealing after three months to graduate from the Early Bird to all editions. Hy Gardner considered himself a bona fide newspaperman thereafter, but many in the *Tribune* city room, where he was sardonically called "Mr. Broadway," thought him a bit of a slippery operator and his pieces too trivial to warrant regular inclusion in a great newspaper.

Gardner's gossip complemented another personality-centered feature Whitie Reid had enlisted from the world of celebrity the year before in keeping with his own and Pinkham's conviction that the *Tribune* needed more diversion in its columns. "New York Closeup" took the form of a question-and-answer interview ostensibly conducted by the husband-and-wife team of Tex and Jinx McCrary, who already presided over radio and television talk shows, both prominently cited at the end of each column. McCrary, a slender, solemn-faced live-wire whose monotone voice belied his restless energy, had graduated from Yale a few years before Whitie and crashed New York's media world by serving as assistant to the *Mirror*'s chief editor, Arthur Brisbane, and marrying his daughter. The marriage did not hold, but McCrary kept parlaying his social and professional connections and turned himself into a celebrity by a postwar marriage to former model Jinx Falkenburg. The couple resided in a small house on the estate of sportsman-investor-philanthropist John Hay Whitney, whom Tex had come to know during service in the wartime Army Air Force. McCrary's Whitney connection would have bearing on the fate of the *Tribune* at a critical juncture in its history, but in the beginning his contribution to the paper took the form of superintending "New York Closeup" by determining its subjects and suggesting the main lines of the interview; the actual fieldwork and writing were done by several young members of McCrary's staff, most prominently an unpolished, indefatigable twenty-year-old named William Safire, who would become one of the few newspapermen ever to reach the heights of the profession *after* a successful career in public relations.

The disdain that most *Tribune* newsroom veterans felt for the glossy, often self-promoting copy turned in by Gardner and McCrary was symptomatic of a far deeper distress over the whole Early Bird concept and how it was damaging the quality of the *Tribune*. The paper's hallmark had always been good writing and good editing, but both suffered in the production of Bill Robinson's brainchild. In effect, the same staff had to turn out two different newspapers within hours of each other. To make the Early Bird deadline, reporters were required to curtail their research, crank out hasty and often incomplete stories, and try to repair the damage in time for the later editions. "It wrecked us," recalled Peter Kihss, an exhaustive news-gatherer. The problem was worse for the Washington bureau, whose sources were often unavailable to the press until they got home in the early evening. Filing for the Early Bird under such circumstances entailed "a serious loosening of standards," according to Robert Donovan, then based in Washington. Sportswriters, directed to compose play-by-play accounts of afternoon baseball games for the Early Bird as well as their regular stories, paid as much attention to the clock as to the action on the field. "It destroyed my writing," said Harold Rosenthal. Editorial-page writers lost the opportunity "to write as close to the news as possible," as August Heckscher put it. And carelessness crept in all along the production line. On the copy desk, overwhelmed with work to clear enough material to fill up the Early Bird, stories got "railroaded"—there was time only to check them cursorily against obscenities and obvious libels. "You wrote the first plausible headline that came to mind," deskman Alden Whitman remembered. "The place became a sweatshop." In the composing room, where the work shifts were staggered to accommodate the crush, many stories had to be set twice—once for the Early Bird, its revision for the regular runs—and most pages made over. Typographers were practically colliding with one another; overtime soared. The city desk flirted with pandemonium trying to keep everything straight. "It was a horror," said day city editor Richard West.

What the creation of the Early Bird signified was the takeover of the *Tribune* by its business-side mentality. Editorial integrity was sacrificed to boost circulation; improvement of the product in the form of expanded staff or deepened coverage to achieve the same goal was not seriously entertained by management. But even as an economic expedient, the Early Bird was badly conceived. In the first place, no one had really assessed the impossibility of the queen of newspapers dressing herself up gaudily as a lady of the evening and parading the city streets like a tabloid tart. Then there was the unpleasant fact that you could sell the paper only once a day to its readers, and many who picked up the Early Bird were already regular *Tribune* customers who simply switched their reading of it from the morning to the evening—and of them, a number started to take the *Times* the next morning and thereby defeated one of the prime aims of the venture. Finally, the timing of the idea was wrong in many ways. The Early Bird reached the streets too late to catch any sizable contingent of commuters, and by the time the theater and evening movie crowds broke, the first edition of the *Times* was also available. In a larger sense, the Early Bird was exquisitely mistimed because it failed to take into account the tidal wave of television, which by 1950 was already radically altering the nation's nighttime habits; fewer and fewer people were on the streets now in the evening. The *Daily News* lost 100,000 in circulation on Tuesday nights when New York television sets were massively tuned to the new medium's most popular show, the Milton Berle comedy hour. "Something had to be done," said Everett Walker, assistant managing editor, in recognition of the *Tribune*'s need to improve its circulation. But it was the wrong idea put forth at the wrong time and undertaken in the wrong place. For as the 'Fifties unfolded, the real battlefield for circulation among New York newspapers was not within the five boroughs of the city itself, where buying habits were fixed, but in the suburbs, where the *Tribune* was strong—and the *Times* was girding to challenge its supremacy.

In its first year, the Early Bird raised the *Tribune*'s circulation by about 25,000, less than half of Bill Robinson's minimum expectations for it. Within two years, the paper's circulation was back where it had been before the Early Bird was launched. After four years of wobbly, misdirected flight, the creature was put to rest, unlamented.

II

Susceptibility to a disabling emotionalism was the charge that newspapermen long levied against women of the press and used, along with alleged physical limitations and vulnerabilities, to keep them in largely subordinate roles. Wartime necessity forced L. L. Engelking to put aside such cant. Of the unprecedentedly high number of women reporters he brought onto the *Tribune* city staff in the first half of the 'Forties, three excelled by any standard of the profession.

Warm, matronly Margaret Parton was the least menacing to male suppositions. Though an acute observer and strong writer, she had a certain fragility about her, a sensitivity that was almost poetic and caught her up in her assignments in a way some felt skewed her objectivity. A journalist too enmeshed in his or her story errs as much as one coldly detached.

Judith Klein was made of sterner stuff. Smart and assertive with the help of a remarkably expressive face, she served her *Tribune* apprenticeship under Dorothy Dunbar Bromley, a liberal activist whom Helen Reid nevertheless hired to move beyond society and club notes in infusing the postwar Sunday women's page with socially significant substance. But Klein did not want to be pigeonholed as a woman writing about women. She asked Sunday editor Robert Moora for assignments in the main sheet. One of the first dealt with the higher cost of candy, and she labored over it until satisfied, only to have Moora change her lead to: "The kid with a penny is a pauper today. There is no penny candy." He had taken her adequate opening and, with an easy stroke, personalized and individualized it to win reader intimacy. A quick study, Judy Klein soon showed grace and energy in her writing style and versatility in her reportorial range.

Her marriage to public-relations man William Crist in an age when even career women were wont to use their husbands' names professionally induced a certain self-consciousness in her, beginning with Mrs. Bromley's expression of regret because, as she put it to Judy, "I so liked having a Jewish byline on the page." Judith Crist replied that you could hardly do better than her new name for genuine Jewish origin. Still, she took the precaution of asking the composing room to have a batch of her bylines always available in type so no unfortunate misspelling could occur under deadline pressures. A certain anxiety persisted, though, and surfaced now and then, especially in stories involving the Catholic church. She encountered, for example, considerable community animosity for a series she wrote documenting how the relatively wealthy city of Yonkers, New York, was starving its public schools due to the indifference of a largely Catholic officialdom and a parochial school enrollment that accounted for one-third of the city's student population. "Dear Judas Christ," some of the hate mail began. Nothing tested her edginess on the subject as much, though, as the Story of the Weeping Madonna.

The wire services had reported how a little girl in an upstate city had found a plaster statuette of the Virgin Mary and set it on a shelf in her impoverished home, whereupon the object began to shed tears and kept on doing so until neighbors were thronging the tenement to observe the phenomenon and pronouncing it an authentic miracle. Under Bill Robinson's austerity program greatly curtailing out-of-town assignments, Crist had to deal with the story by telephone. She started with the wire-service stringer—a co-religionist of hers, as it happened—who told her, "I'm Joosh, but I seen it with my own eyes, lady." So she devoted most of her reportorial efforts to rationalizing the phenomenon, calling up psychologists who spoke learnedly on the idiosyncrasies of human perception, scientists who speculated on the properties of plaster to absorb and emit water, and diocesan officials whose lips were sealed on the miraculous nature of the happening. Mightily she labored on the piece and got it in just before deadline to assistant city editor Ted Laymon, who thanked her and, after a glance, handed it over to Bob Peck for rewrite. Judy went downstairs to Bleeck's for dinner with her husband and dissolved in tears, real ones, convinced that her efforts had gone unappreciated. When the city edition came up, there was her story with a double-column head and a deceitful "Special to the Herald Tribune" slug instead of a byline on top. Through red-rimmed eyes Judy read her story transformed into a thing of beauty—the reader was there alongside the crowds, pushing upstairs to see the weeping Madonna, and the long lines of people outside, singing and chanting adoration in their hunger for a miracle. The possible explanations were there, too, but in their place. "The real story wasn't whether a plaster statue could weep real tears," she recalled, "but about the phenomenon of credibility—only I had been so afraid that those people might really believe that I wound up trying to prove my own skepticism. I had missed the whole point of the story." She missed little else in a career on the *Tribune* that spanned twenty-one years.

Marguerite Higgins was the third of the *Tribune*'s star female recruits from World War II and, throughout a staff career as long as Crist's, became an object of love, hate, admiration, envy, and intense resentment. No other member of the editorial staff ever stirred such emotions. For Maggie Higgins was a driven and at times ferociously determined woman who did not play by the rules to get what she wanted.

Her problem stemmed in large measure from her beauty. A five-foot-eight windblown blonde, possessed of a round, babyish face and a high-pitched voice that gave her the look and sound of a teenager well into her twenties, Higgins also had a voluptuously curved, unmistakably adult body that, by all accounts, proved useful in the advancement of her career. She did not flaunt its attributes but neither was she coy about her sexual appetite. "She had a sort of movie-star prettiness, almost like a cross between Betty Grable's and Marilyn Monroe's," Judith Crist remembered, "with a super figure and those absolutely blue eyes. She looked taller than she was because she was so slender."

Born in Hong Kong, where her volatile Irish-American father worked as a freight agent for a shipping line, Marguerite grew up speaking English, Cantonese, and French, her mother's native language. The family moved to Oakland, where she was educated at a private girls' school and then at Berkeley, where even then, working on *The Daily Californian,* she got a reputation for overaggressiveness. At Columbia's School of Journalism, she attracted attention as the *Tribune*'s campus correspondent by following a nurse into the off-limits room of Madame Chiang Kai-shek, a patient at Columbia-Presbyterian Hospital at the time, and obtaining an interview, forbidden to other reporters. Nothing easily stymied Maggie Higgins when she was in pursuit of information she felt she and her newspaper were entitled to have.

Admitted to the city staff at twenty-two, she was a pretty but messy sight, fingernails dirty and forehead smudged from handling carbon paper and typewriter ribbons, hair and copy paper flying in all directions as she artlessly pounded out her stories and then followed them around the newsroom to see how the editors changed them. And they made a good many changes; writing was not Higgins's strength. But her stories were worth the effort it took to repair them, for she was a human vacuum cleaner at sucking up intelligence about any subject she was assigned to, and Engelking nurtured her resourcefulness by preaching the need to figure things out for herself. She had cyclonic energy and an uncontainable need to prove her worth anew every day, not a major handicap in a journalist. Her only limitation was literacy. "She had to learn how to write —and we all broke her in, some in more ways than one," remarked an accomplished reporter who said he had been on sexually intimate terms with her for a year before he left to become a foreign correspondent for *The New Yorker.* There was another reported long-running affair with an older, gifted but alcoholic rewriteman, claims of one-night stands with her by others, and along the way a short-lived marriage to a young college philosophy instructor who went off to war and out of her life. Office-watchers were divided over whether she was intimate with more than one man at a time or took them up and discarded them *seriatim.* It all would have been nobody's business except for one thing: a substantial body of evidence suggests that throughout her working life Maggie Higgins selected most if not all of her bedmates for intensely practical reasons, to add to her power or promote her career. Few men could wield their sexuality so strategically. Was it feminism, then, to use her beauty in such a fashion— or a travesty on the goal of emancipation for her sex? It was unlikely that the question ever framed itself that way in her mind; rather, she was simply incapable of separating her private and professional lives. All else seemed secondary to her advancement. Her aggressiveness became an office legend, replete with charges that she stepped on those who got in her way, snatched off desirable assignments, arranged to phone in the legwork of others as if it were her own when out on a team assignment, and otherwise comported herself with a competitiveness bordering on the pathological.

These charges gathered momentum during the five years she spent in Europe as a *Tribune* correspondent—an assignment she won by appealing over Cornish's head to Helen Reid. But she made a good case of it: she spoke more languages than anyone else on the staff, having grown up with three, studied Spanish and Russian besides, and picked up some German along the way; she was a nervy and relentless reporter; she was young and energetic and, anyway, why shouldn't the *Tribune* have a woman as a war correspondent? The fighting was still going on when she arrived, but they would not let her get near it. There was plenty of news for her to cover behind the lines, though, and enough of the war's horrors fell her way to write about, like the liberation of the Nazi death camps for the Jews, to teach her that she had to compartmentalize her emotions if she was to master her trade. Her manipulativeness did not abate; when fellow *Tribune* correspondent Carl Levin succeeded in obtaining an interview with the interim French president, Higgins purred at him the night before, "Carl, your French isn't very good—wouldn't you like me to come along?" She had a way of grabbing the main story on shared assignments and leaving her colleagues with a sidebar. "Men didn't do that to other men," said Levin.

Still, she did well enough to be named Berlin bureau chief at the age of twenty-six. The former German capital was no longer a seat of power at the time of her appointment, but it soon became the focus of East-West tensions, and Higgins was sitting on top of the hottest running story in the world for eleven months as the Russians blockaded the city and the Allies relieved it from the air. She thrived under such conditions and became practiced at dealing with the military mentality, which she found oafish in its responses to the press. Her notoriety grew with her continued practice of taking useful lovers, among them a leading member of a competing Berlin bureau and an ample selection of ranking American Army officers—preferably the kind with stars on their shoulders—in liaisons behind sturdy castle gates. One general she befriended, with a wife and four children back in the United States, did his best not to be compromised by her allures, given the vital military intelligence function he was charged to perform in that incendiary climate, and failed: William Hall fell in love with Maggie Higgins, and she, uncharacteristically, with him. By the time they married in 1952, she had become the most famous newspaperwoman in the world.

In 1950, however, the prospect appeared unlikely. The paper ordered her out of Europe. "She was a dangerous, venomous bitch," said Stephen White, a *Tribune* European correspondent at the time, offering the consensual assessment of Higgins then, "and a bad reporter." She was aggressive and worked hard, White conceded, but ignorant, and she tried to compensate in ways that antagonized sources, associates, and rivals, all of whom were essential to a correspondent covering the postwar complexity of Europe. Her particular sin was the transparency with which she sought to extract information from other journalists while declining to share her own. "Maggie treated all reporters as enemies," White recalled, "even the one or two she slept with to my knowledge. They were competitors." Nor was she innocent of overdramatizing her copy, White added. "Maggie used to get annoyed because I would never hype a story. 'I'd have had that one on the first page,' she'd tell me. I said to her once that I was human enough to enjoy seeing my name on the day's lead story, but I was sensible enough to realize that it was the story that led the paper, not me. She didn't disagree—she simply did not understand what I was saying." But she was not unaware of the enmity she invited. In her 1955 autobiographical book, *News Is a Singular Thing,* Higgins recognized that she suffered from "a one-track preoccupied personality [that] can be very wearing and in many ways unattractive." By the time she was sent to Tokyo in mid-1950, a novel titled *Shriek with Pleasure* by Toni Howard had appeared dealing with a man-eating female correspondent stationed in Berlin who had an Irish name and a knack for combining business and bed. Before she was thirty, Marguerite Higgins was part of the lore of her trade.

For the first months there, she found Tokyo unbearably dull after the cold-war confrontations of a divided Europe. She shared an office with *Chicago Daily News* correspondent Keyes Beech, a thirty-seven-year-old Tennesseean who had been through the thick of World War II combat in the Pacific as an official correspondent with the marines and was, in his reserved, flinty, and witheringly honest way, able to withstand her wiles. Her reputation had preceded her, and she was up to it, picking the brains of every correspondent in sight even while deriding the Tokyo scene, under the iron rule of its five-star American semi-deity, as no more exciting than a duck pond. "But it was the only story we had," Beech recalled, and the Tokyo press contingent was ungrateful to her for scorning it. Beech, especially unhappy when she took to tagging along with him on assignments, was in the process of looking for a separate office when word was flashed from Korea that war had begun. Once more, Maggie Higgins was on the spot when the biggest story in the world unfolded.

She and Beech made the last American plane into Seoul ahead of the invading North Koreans and then barely got out alive. The South Koreans began blowing up the bridges over the Han River, killing and maiming hundreds of their own people while trying to slow the advance of the Communist invaders. Beech grabbed a jeep abandoned by the American military advisory mission and tried to race out of the South Korean capital over one of the remaining spans; Higgins rode in another jeep with an Army colonel:

> A bright red sheet of flame was seen by this correspondent as I was about to cross the bridge. The structure was ripped by the explosion, and two other correspondents who were closer to the dynamiting were injured. . . .

The injured men were Beech's passengers. He was resourceful enough to get his jeep across the river on a makeshift ferry under Red artillery fire while Higgins, separated from him, made it over on a boat the U.S. military personnel commandeered at gunpoint. Without transportation, wearing a navy-blue skirt and flowered blouse and lugging her typewriter amid the civilian throngs, she had to flee on foot for fourteen miles before being rescued by Beech. The *Tribune* ran her copyrighted account of the escape on the front page, accompanied by a column-and-a-half-wide file picture of Higgins looking pretty, pensive, and fragile.

For the first week of the war she covered for the paper by herself, traveling in Beech's jeep and pooling all her information with him in return for the mobility he provided. Without it, she could never have kept up with the pace of events; as Beech put it: "An army on the run—which ours was in Korea—is not very good about offering you transportation. With it, you could beat the hell out of the others who had to hitchhike around the front and to file their stories in the rear. I would have killed to keep that jeep." Higgins, needing him, was on her best behavior. Beech, while doubting her intentions, nevertheless felt in his Southern cavalier bones that he ought to look after her. It soon became apparent that, dressed now in incongruously becoming army fatigues and tennis sneakers, she was quite able to take care of herself. "I early developed a quick eye for protective terrain," she wrote in *War in Korea,* a 1951 account of her combat coverage, "and can probably hit a ditch as fast as any man." She also had not forgotten how to catch the eye of the military brass. Supreme Pacific commander Douglas MacArthur, on a hurried visit to survey the desperate situation of the thin American garrison backpedaling down the Korean peninsula, gave Higgins a hitch back to Tokyo and en route an exclusive interview, disclosing that he was about to request fresh ground troops from home.

She was not back in Korea long when Homer Bigart, the *Tribune*'s best reporter and its expert on warfare, arrived and told her to go back to Tokyo and run the bureau, as she was supposed to; he would cover the fighting. He had covered a lot of fighting since the end of World War II, shuttling from one danger zone to another and adding to his reputation as an intrepid troubleshooter and a special favorite of providence. Now nearing forty-three, he was heavier and more grizzled, more than ever the loner, a ceaseless witness to the world's woes and their incomparable chronicler. Maggie Higgins was twenty-nine, obviously unsuited to battlefield conditions, untested under gunfire, and a known troublemaker. He did not need her.

But she would not leave. Korea was part of the Tokyo beat, and Korea was where the news was. She had been doing well and saw no reason to be exiled to the rear; there was enough war for both of them to cover. Bigart, though, was insistent and cabled his editors in New York that he wanted Higgins out of his hair. Higgins cabled no less insistently that her removal was unjustified. New York ruled that Bigart was the prime correspondent but, given the developing gravity of the war, Higgins could stay and file whatever color or sidebar pieces she could find. Bigart protested no more; he just turned his back on Higgins and pretended she was not there. But she was, and he knew it, and she had Beech's jeep at her disposal, and he had no jeep, so he covered the U.S. Army as he had in World War II, at the cannon's mouth or as near as he could get or just standing out there in the middle of some road, seeming dumb and helpless with his jack-o'-lantern grin and disarming stutter as younger reporters who admired him fed him their stuff.

Their work appeared side by side on page one for the first time on July 6. Bigart had the lead with a dispatch in his familiar lean and powerful style on the rout of green American troops in their first engagement with Communist regular forces, spearheaded by Russian tanks. Pulling no punches, his sixth paragraph asserted, "There is no denying that the first action was a rude shock to the Americans. It became apparent that the Korean campaign may be a lot tougher and rougher than was expected a few days ago." Higgins's piece was a closeup—"As this correspondent watched from a near by hill"—of the first U.S. infantryman to die in Korea. Her writing lacked the power of Bigart's; the verbs were not as hard-edged, the adjectives as tersely evocative, the vision as wide-angled or penetrating, but it was serviceable, well reported as far as it went, and eager to proclaim gallantry. Her feature, datelined "AN ADVANCE COMMAND OUTPOST IN SOUTH KOREA," closed:

> The medics brought the dead soldier's body in here, tenderly lifting him from a jeep. The lifeless form was shrouded in a blanket which kept the pelting rain off the blond young face. As medics brought the body in, one young private said bitterly, "What a place to die!"

He would be followed to the grave by 33,628 American soldiers in Korea. The second line of the two-column head on Higgins's story read: "Woman Reporter Sees the Battle," an unvarnished disclosure of her value to the paper as a novelty and stimulus to readership.

A few days later, Bigart filed his longest and most memorable piece of the war. Headed "From a Foxhole in Korea," it stands with Smalley's account of Antietam and Whitelaw Reid's of Shiloh as a classic of American military journalism, but its approach was typically microcosmic, the only way mechanized warfare can be rendered effectively, rather than sweeping like theirs, and it was transmitted within hours, not days, of the event. The 4,000-word story dealt with one of a series of desperate holding actions by U.S. troops trying to retreat in good order to what would soon shrivel to a small quadrangle with an iron perimeter in the southeastern corner of the Korean peninsula, there to await reinforcements for the counterattack. The account of the combat, in which a heavily outnumbered company of poorly equipped and badly supported soldiers in an exposed hillside position narrowly escaped annihilation, was worth detailing, Bigart wrote, "only as an example of what happens when men are thrown into action without adequate preparation." He set the scene for the six-hour engagement:

> The fatal element in our defeat was a ground fog that rose quickly at dawn. It billowed upward from the plain, and under its protective screen the North Koreans moved swiftly and decisively. Not until 8 o'clock was the curtain lifted, and by that time the enemy was in position to deal the death blow.
>
> I found a foxhole within hearing distance of the colonel's, and made this log of the attack:
>
> 5:55 a.m. — We hear the enemy jabbering over on the left, but can't see fifty feet through the fog. The show starts any minute now. . . .

In prose narrating events so inherently dramatic that it needed no embellishment, Bigart recounted how the young colonel urged his men not to fire blindly into the fog, thus revealing their positions; how he steeled his hard-pressed left flank to hang on till reinforcements could reach them; how their remnants tried vainly to regroup when they were overrun; how air support kept not arriving to attack the enemy tanks and when two jets finally made a feeble run at their shrouded targets they missed; how their own artillery shells, aimed under the misconception the Americans were already in retreat, began to fall dangerously close to them and pinned them in place as the enemy closed in. All along he registered the dread, without stating it, that the massed, jabbering enemy would emerge at any moment and destroy them all. They got out just after noon:

> On signal from the Old Man, we leaped from our holes and ran, crouching and dodging, across open ground to an orchard sloping down to rice paddies.
>
> Crossing these paddies when you are very scared and in a hurry is like walking a tight rope for the first time. The little earthen levees holding back the water are not very wide at the top, and you keep slipping knee-deep into the mud.
>
> At this precise moment, two jet planes, looking for enemy infantry, came over [and] started what looked like a strafing run at us. We had no casualties, but some of the boys acquired a life-long aversion to rice.

Aside from their own heavy losses, they found afterward that seven soldiers, trying to bring in ammunition, were captured and, their hands tied behind them, shot in the face. Bigart also learned then that the other two correspondents covering the action died in it—the first newsmen to fall in Korea. Commenting editorially on their deaths, *The New York Times* called attention to Bigart's "remarkable story" in the *Tribune* and how it showed "what the correspondent as well as the soldier must face in Korea. We are proud of our soldiers and we should be just as proud of our newspaper men."

Higgins renewed her own claim on fame a week later by again being ordered out of Korea, this time by General Walton Walker, who stated that this was "not the type of war where women ought to be running around the front lines," where conditions of dress, language, and sanitation were primitive and, presumably, no member of the fair sex should be allowed to risk her pretty little neck. Incensed, Higgins wired Helen Reid, who promptly sent off an urgent plea to MacArthur in Tokyo, arguing that her correspondent had demonstrated "personal strength and courage both in Korea and in Europe" and that Walker's ban "will be a blow to profession which has rated newspaper women on equal terms with men. Also it will be severe blow to this newspaper and to others which have been giving her dispatches first page prominence. Would appreciate your help in reconsidering decision. Greatly hope it can be changed." Higgins had hardly touched down in Tokyo when she saw a copy of MacArthur's reply:

ZEBRA ONE ONE EIGHT ZERO BAN ON WOMEN CORRESPONDENTS IN KOREA HAS BEEN LIFTED. MARGUERITE HIGGINS IS HELD IN HIGHEST PROFESSIONAL ESTEEM BY EVERYONE. SIGNED MACARTHUR

The *Tribune* front-paged her restoration and included her MacArthur-like resolve to redeem defeat: "I walked out of Seoul and I wanted to walk back in."

Together, then, but separately, Bigart and Higgins provided their paper with remarkable coverage of one of the saddest chapters in American military history —the frantic, often chaotic retreat of troops with weapons inadequate to pierce enemy armor and a tendency to run before they should have. Hanson Baldwin of the far larger *Times* contingent on the scene asked Keyes Beech, "Why are Homer and Maggie beating our asses off out there?" Beech answered, "That's easy—they hate each other. The competition is a lot fiercer between them than between them and you." Higgins matched Bigart for valor. At the end of July a surprise enemy attack reached within seventy-five yards of a regimental command headquarters where she was having breakfast and, after hugging the floor to avoid bullets tearing through the building, she helped medical corpsmen administer plasma to the wounded who were brought in while the attack was being driven back. Her report on the incident did not mention her own role, but the officer in charge, Colonel John Michaelis, wrote to Helen Reid that his unit "considers Miss Higgins' actions on that day as heroic, but even more important is the gratitude felt by members of this command towards the selfless devotion of Miss Higgins in saving the lives of many grievously wounded men." When the brakes gave out one day soon after on Beech's jeep, she sustained a concussion in the crash and, though bleeding from the nose and mouth, refused to lie down on the stretcher brought for her; she rode beside the ambulance driver instead and quickly fled from the hospital lest the uninjured Beech should abandon her while she recovered. She could not, would not, miss any of the action so long as she could stand. The high point of her heroism was her coverage of the Inchon landing in mid-September, which she and Beech managed to accompany on the fifth landing wave while the usually resourceful Bigart was left back on a big transport ship to file an overview of the vastest amphibious action since the Normandy landings six years earlier. Though the four previous landing waves got through with little trouble, Higgins's wave came under heavy fire and was pinned down for hours behind a seawall. She emerged soaked but unscathed.

By then she and Beech were close friends, sharing her sleeping bag as well as his jeep, though neither mistook the convenient sexual relationship for love. She still had a way of walking over people, of dismissing those who could or did not help her. "Obviously this man doesn't know what the hell he's talking about," she would say of a sentry trying to be helpful but lacking hard information, "so let's get out of here." And she would quarrel with Beech, who had an earlier deadline than hers since he wrote for an afternoon paper, about when they ought to head for the rear to file. But he could not help liking her. She was brave, at times almost foolish in the risks she drove them to, and durable, and would never accept the more comfortable accommodations she was occasionally offered because she was a woman. And, most important to Beech, she would not play her stories in a way they both suspected her editors in New York might have most wanted—from the woman's angle. "She never stooped to that," he said.

His fondness for her was sorely tried one night after Inchon as U.S. forces were preparing to recapture Seoul. "Just as we were getting ready to cross the Han River, Maggie got the curse." Beech emitted a rousing "Aw, for crissakes!" by way of registering his opinion that she should have been prepared for that contingency, then turned his jeep around and drove twenty miles "through a whole army of trigger-happy marines" in pitch darkness under a military blackout to Inchon, so Higgins could obtain a sanitary napkin from the hospital ship. "I was particularly ungracious that night," Beech recalled, but he mellowed and they killed a bottle of scotch before the sun came up and talked over a lot of things they never got to while on the run all day, like how they prayed to God to get them out of whatever jam they were in and would promise never to get themselves back into that tight a hole again and why the next day they would be right back in it. He heard all the rumors about how she played dirty tricks to get her stories cabled out fast by putting them on top of the pile and how she nuzzled her breasts under pilots' noses so they would let her hitch flights around the front and how she got wounded men bumped off a plane to make room for her, but Keyes Beech never saw her do such things. He wrote that "she had more guts, more staying power, and more resourcefulness than 90 percent of her detractors. She was a good newspaperman."

By October all America knew about Maggie Higgins. *Life* magazine ran a major feature spread on her with many pictures of Maggie winsome in GI fatigues. Movie and book offers were tendered for her story, and Helen Reid brought her home to speak at the *Tribune*'s annual forum. Then she went back to the cold of that punishing Korean winter and did some of her best work of the war, covering the pullback of marines who had to fight their way to safety through waves of Red Chinese:

> The men were ragged, their faces swollen from the cold and bleeding from the raw bite of the icy wind, their ears blue. Their mittens were torn and raveled. Some were without their fur hats. A few walked barefoot. They had to—they could not get their frost-bitten feet into their frozen shoe-pacs.

A few weeks after writing that, she cabled Whitie Reid asking if the paper planned to submit her work for a Pulitzer.

Bigart, who had one and had validated his claim to it dozens of times over, did not bother to ask. He just kept turning out first-rate stories and surviving. Philip Potter of the Baltimore *Sun,* who watched him perform in Korea, recalled, "He worked over his copy more than any of the rest of us correspondents who were anxious after a hard day in the field to get our copy written and filed so we could get a drink. Homer would still be at his portable, crossing off one word because he had thought of a better one. . . . [H]e was always the last one to get his copy to the censor. . . . He observed things that we had missed." When he ended his coverage in January 1951, *Newsweek* wrote: "By the almost unanimous agreement of colleagues there—and of many State-side readers—Bigart left the Korean battlefront as the best war correspondent of an embattled generation."

But he had also won for Marguerite Higgins a sympathy from her colleagues that she decidedly lacked when he came to Korea, ordered her out, and kept ignoring and resenting her presence long after she had demonstrated her qualifications for being there. Other newsmen gave coins to Korean waifs to jeer "Homer loves Maggie!" outside press billets where he stayed, and they wrote chiding lyrics to the tune of "Lilli Marlene" that went: "Marguerite Higgins / Telephones the news, / She gets exclusive / Front-line interviews / While Homer crawls / Through rice fields wet / To scrounge some stuff / That she can't get. . . ." He thought her stories dealt too much with her own exploits, that she hero-worshipped MacArthur and was too reverential of the military command in general, and he bore his grudge long afterward: on being told Marguerite was pregnant, he asked, "Who's the m-m-mother?" His bitterness was almost certainly the result of the conviction, which he confided to Stephen White among others, that Higgins nearly got him killed in Korea for making him take chances he would not otherwise have had to—surely more of a confession of his own character than hers. "No way can I make my behavior toward her appear in a favorable light," he conceded more than thirty years later. His dispute with her, he said, was territorial, not personal. "I wanted her out of there in the worst way but couldn't get her transferred. . . . The desk in New York loved it."

The Pulitzer Prize in the international-reporting category was given in the spring of 1951 to six correspondents for their Korean coverage. The first three in alphabetical order were Keyes Beech, Homer Bigart, and Marguerite Higgins.

III

One noon hour not long after William Robinson had been named executive vice president of the *Herald Tribune,* he came into the paper's private dining room and began describing to a dozen or so of its top people the promotion campaign that he had just helped a major department store plan for a new product, the portable dishwasher. Robinson detailed the virtues of the machine, how easy it was to roll around and hook up to the kitchen faucet, what a splendid job it did —all with great enthusiasm.

Just as he was finishing, Helen Reid came in with a new summer purse she had picked up at an East Side boutique. Made of white plastic, the purse came with interchangeable button-on fabric covers to match or complement the wearer's outfit of the day. She had two of these covers with her, showed how easy they were to change and how fine the purse was without any cover, and said what a bargain it was. Her secretary was going back to the store that afternoon, she added, and would pick up more of the purses for any of those at the table who wanted them. Several of her listeners took up the suggestion.

After the president and executive vice president had left the room, Geoffrey Parsons, the *Tribune*'s genial senior statesman, took a final sip of his coffee and said, "Gentlemen, you have just seen two of the world's greatest salesmen at work."

The otherwise trivial incident serves to illustrate how, beneath their very different exteriors, Helen Reid and Bill Robinson were kindred spirits and to explain why he was invested with so much authority. He functioned, some even felt, as her surrogate husband, although she was old enough to be his mother. His strength and confidence sustained her waning powers, and if she was overly suggestible to his seductive salesmanship and unshakable faith in the *Tribune,* no one was willing to step forward and say burly Bill Robinson was whispering sweet nothings into Helen Reid's ear. In 1949 she gave him a fifteen-year contract at an annual salary of $50,000 and a $5,000 expense account, making him one of the best-paid newspaper executives in the country. But as the century slipped past its midpoint, the price the *Tribune* paid for her misplaced notion that supersalesmen made superior business managers became increasingly evident to others around them, if not to Helen Reid.

When Richard Pinkham came on the paper as a bright young recruit who would soon take over the circulation department, she introduced Robinson to him as "someone you're going to admire a great deal." She was wrong. Pinkham concluded before long that Robinson was a shallow and very limited man, for all his surface charm and vigor. His character, too, Pinkham learned, left something to be desired. As the *Tribune*'s Sunday circulation plunged at the end of the 'Forties, Robinson summoned Pinkham one day, explained that in order to sustain the circulation level guaranteed under the paper's advertising rate card in the ABC's forthcoming semiannual tally, it would be necessary to show 10,000 more sales in the next several weeks, and instructed his circulation manager to have the suburban distributors swallow that many extra copies for a while. That meant padding the paper's sales figures by any of a number of expedients, the simplest of which was not to credit the distributors for their full number of returns and forcing them to pay up the difference or chisel it out of their dealers by charging them more or requiring them to share the burden. Pinkham objected. Despite the *Tribune*'s strength in the suburbs, it did not have the muscle to exact that sort of homage, he said. Besides, he added, it was crooked.

"Do it or you're through," said Robinson.

Having no other immediate job prospects, Pinkham did what he was told. The distributors, unaccustomed to underhanded dealings by the principal pillar of Republican rectitude, grumbled—loud enough for the *Times*'s hustling new circulation director, Nat Goldstein, to detect—and soon Bill Robinson was called to a special panel of inquiry maintained by the Audit Bureau of Circulation to inspect fishy figures. Robinson told Pinkham he was to come along to the hearing. Pinkham protested that he had been against the scheme, as Robinson knew, and could not defend it. "I don't give a good goddamn about that," said Robinson. "You're coming with me."

Before the ABC interrogators, who included a number of leading executives in the advertising business, Bill Robinson denied the charges. Told that there was documentary evidence against the paper, he said he knew nothing of any such subterfuge and if it were so, the skulduggery must have been the work of his circulation people—and indicated his junior colleague. Pinkham was left twisting gently in the breeze, his reputation damaged. The *Tribune,* in view of its previously sterling record, got off with a stiff reprimand. "I hadn't trusted him before that happened," recalled the fall guy, "and I certainly didn't trust him afterward."

But Dick Pinkham soldiered on, trying to be constructive. When Robinson hatched his Early Bird, Pinkham registered his reservations. When they were ignored, he fell in line and urged that the new edition ought to be promoted more extensively. Robinson was unresponsive. The gap between them widened still farther in their assessment of the Sunday situation. As the *Tribune*'s sales on its big edition of the week fell 100,000 below the figure three years before, Pinkham drafted a memo in March 1951 saying that small improvements in the Sunday drama and financial sections were not nearly enough to reverse the downtrend and challenge the ever-fattening Sunday *Times.* The latter's success, as he analyzed it, was due first of all to the prestige of its magazine, even though "to many of us, each issue is exactly like the previous one"; it always contained at least one article of real substance and "a lot of handsome advertising," whereas the *Tribune*'s counterpart, *This Week,* was pretty frail by comparison and syndicated at that. The great bulk of the *Times,* moreover, while superfluous, made it an irresistible package on the one day of the week when many people had the time to invest in it and therefore represented a far better buy for the price than the *Tribune.* Finally, its classified, real estate, and financial advertising columns were so loaded as to make its attractiveness overwhelming in a toe-to-toe comparison with the *Tribune.* The only way to counter this disadvantage, Pinkham asserted, was for the *Tribune* to offer Sunday attractions that the *Times* did not and likely would not possess. He proposed three: tabloid supplements devoted to news and local advertising of the major suburban regions, where the *Tribune* outsold the *Times*; more and better comics, a feature the *Times* considered beneath its dignity; and a separate magazine or supplement devoted entirely to television, which he said was about to undergo explosive growth as "America's top pastime. . . . It will dwarf and may absorb the movies. It will reduce books still further in our U.S. pattern of self-entertainment. It will become the absorbing interest of most of our lives, dominating the leisure hours from 7 p.m. to midnight every night of the week."

Robinson's response to these proposals was a smug memo to Mrs. Reid a few months later, minimizing the Sunday problem by noting that other city papers were suffering a similar slump in sales due to price rises that had caused many New York area families to curtail their habit of buying more than one Sunday paper. And "a simple analysis of Sunday papers and reader requirements would indicate," he airily added, "that there is very little possibility of our making a dramatic improvement in news content or news presentation which would lend itself to any dramatization or promotion of improved value." His only suggestions, which Helen Reid promptly approved, were a gradual improvement of the comic section and an outlay of $600,000 to bolster *This Week* by adding six pages per issue tailored specifically to the interests of New York area readers and grandly promoting the addition.

Pinkham left the *Tribune* in frustration soon after to join his friend Sylvester (Pat) Weaver at the National Broadcasting Company and help in the development of the "Today" and "Tonight" shows for television. "I cared a helluva lot about that newspaper," he said thirty years later.

Pinkham's innovative bent was shared by two other figures of prominence on the business side—Alfred B. Stanford, the tall, lean, Lincolnesque advertising director, a contemporary of Robinson who had joined the paper after a distinguished career in the wartime navy, and James Parton, the promotion director, a creative spirit twelve years their junior and the grandson and namesake of Greeley's best contemporary biographer. "I was never any kind of advertising salesman," Stanford recalled, but he brought to his post two important credentials. He knew how the advertising business worked, having been a co-founder of the successful Compton agency before the war and later the executive director of the Bureau of Newspaper Advertising, a trade organization aimed primarily at preventing national accounts from heavily patronizing the magazine industry. "At some point, all business is local," he would preach on his lobbying rounds, by which he meant that all products and services were ultimately purveyed by local dealers and that only newspapers allowed manufacturers and other national companies to tailor their sales pitch to markets where it would do the most good. Al Stanford also knew something that Bill Robinson did not: in postwar America, newspaper advertising was bought, not sold. Media departments had been established at all major agencies and were now mapping out most campaigns by the numbers. That usually meant that they bought the largest paper with the wealthiest readers in any given newspaper market—and in New York that meant the *Times*. Department stores, too, were increasingly buying newspaper space on a scientific basis, and department heads were being given the decisive voice in how their ad dollars were allocated; top executives and store ad managers, the people that Bill Robinson used to romance, deferred more and more to their buyers, who were held accountable for how well their goods moved. The change meant that Robinson's personal sell and the efforts of those like the *Tribune*'s star national ad salesman, Bill Butler, who pursued his accounts with what Stanford described as "breathe-down-your-neck-let's-go-to-lunch persistence," grew more ineffectual with each year as the *Tribune*'s numbers, based on stagnant circulation and rising ad rates, looked less and less attractive to media buyers. Robinson continued to rely on his pitch that the *Tribune* was, in effect, a special case, catering to the most influential segment of the most influential market in the country and therefore worth the premium it charged because so little of its relatively small readership was wasted. But the claim ran into increasing skepticism, and Stanford strongly urged the paper to invest in market research, a new concept at the time, to document its self-proclaimed value as a selling vehicle. The problem was nicely put by Percival White of the Market Research Company of America, in response to an approach for help by the *Tribune:*

> . . . [Y]ou postulate the ring leaders, the bell wethers, the stormy petrels of our community [as the bulk of your readership]. . . . All right, can you prove it? . . . Your problem is not merely the positive one of proving that the Herald Tribune constituency is all wool and a yard wide. You must also demonstrate that your esteemed contemporary [i.e., the *Times*] is weeviled with Job-Seekers, is moth-eaten with Fair Dealers, and is riddled with Needle Workers. . . .

White proposed a random sampling of 2,200 *Tribune* readers to test its contentions. Stanford also brought in Alfred Politz, a leading pioneer in market research. But Robinson and Mrs. Reid "were not persuaded," said Stanford, whom they found ineffective at what they continued to perceive as primarily a job for good old-fashioned salesmanship. Finding the situation "hopeless," Stanford, like Pinkham, also quit in 1951.

At the *Tribune* forum that October, little Helen Reid climbed up on a platform to reach the microphone after the last speaker was done at the final session around 10:30 p.m. and in an occasionally quavery voice read the text of the editorial that would appear on the paper's front page the next morning. Titled "The Time and the Man" and echoing the phrases with which it had endorsed Wendell Willkie for the Republican presidential nomination eleven years earlier, it announced its support—before any other paper in the nation—for Bill Robinson's friend Dwight Eisenhower: "By deed and by word General Eisenhower has shown himself a keeper of the great liberties to which Republicanism is dedicated." He possessed, it said, "the vision of the statesman, the skill of the diplomat, the supreme organizing talents of the administrator, and the humane sympathies of the representative of the people," and the *Tribune* would work for his election.

In the ensuing months, Bill Robinson began to insert warm words about Eisenhower's virtues as part of his regular sales talks around the country on the importance of advertising in the *Tribune*. Increasingly he was becoming the partisan voice of the paper and urging Mrs. Reid to return it to conservative orthodoxy. In a memo to Whitie Reid that June, the essence of which he shared with her, Robinson asserted that the prime reason the *Tribune* was losing ground against the *Times* was "a disappointment or a disagreement with our editorial policy on the part of our basic Republican readership. . . . [W]e must be *proponents* of the Republican Party if we are to hold this important segment of our readership. . . . [W]e must contrive to strike blow after blow for the Republican Party. Very often this could take the form of a violent attack on the Democratic side." Then he added, approaching self-parody, "I would hope that you could consider the adoption of a more militant Republican editorial policy which could be pursued with honesty and integrity and with no dilution of our claim as an independent newspaper."

It was for such civic and social ends and the personal fulfillment they yielded that Robinson and Mrs. Reid ran their paper, not for making money. Their priorities were not those of businessmen. Their actions and decisions were those of a holding operation that generated prestige and preserved family pride. Meanwhile, the *Herald Tribune* sank into the red in 1951, and further into the red in 1952, and still further in 1953.

In those same years, while stuck on a circulation plateau, the *Times* continued to make steady revenue gains and position itself, through an improved product and more aggressive merchandising methods, to achieve such decisive numerical dominance as the 'Fifties lengthened that the *Tribune*'s proprietors, old and new, would abandon hope of ever overtaking it and worry only about survival. In good years and slow ones, Arthur Hays Sulzberger maintained his father-in-law's basic managerial policy of strengthening the institution of which his family was the proud custodian instead of aspiring to a personal fortune. Indeed, in the twenty years of the paper's coexistence with the *Tribune* after World War II, *The New York Times*'s net profits averaged but 1.6 percent annually despite an average annual increase in revenues from newspaper operations of 10 percent. In the first half of the 'Fifties, the *Times* continued to improve its plant and, "sensing the movement of history," as James Reston put it, to pour additional resources into its coverage of national and world events as New York kept on losing ground as the prime generator of the news. Its contents grew more sophisticated and its writing more felicitous under a new top editorial team of managing editor Turner Catledge, his style-conscious assistants, Theodore Bernstein and Robert Garst, and Washington bureau chief Reston. Production schedules were revamped to make sure all of its editions were available to customers before or no later than the *Tribune*'s except for the Early Bird, which soon proved by its ever-narrowing gyre to be no bird of prey.

The *Times*'s principal strategic move in this period was its decision to outflank the *Tribune* in its stronghold, suburbia. In 1940, the weekday *Tribune* outsold the *Times* in the New York suburbs of Westchester and Long Island by a total of 15,000 copies, in New Jersey by the same figure, and in Connecticut by not quite 5,000. Ten years later, as the postwar exodus from the city got underway in earnest and new Jewish suburbanites in particular took their old *Times* reading habit with them, the *Tribune*'s lead was on the wane, down to 3,000 in Westchester, while in Nassau County the *Times* had actually edged in front; in Jersey, the *Tribune* remained in front by 10,000 and in Connecticut's Fairfield County, the suburban territory most resistant to a Jewish influx, by 4,000. "Their suburban dominance was our first project," said Nat Goldstein, who in 1948 replaced a *Times* circulation manager deemed unsatisfactory. Goldstein soon pressed the editors, with whom he grew close, to add features that would be especially appealing to suburban rail commuters but had been considered too frivolous to include in the weekday *Times,* although the *Tribune* had had them for years; thus, the arrival of a daily crossword puzzle and bridge column, sufficiently cerebral entertainments to be deemed permissible.

Goldstein's main effort to overtake the *Tribune* in suburbia was based on muscle, money, and a recognition of the nature of the terrain. The last was the key. In New York's vast suburbs, population density in the 'Fifties was not heavy enough and the distances between neighborhoods and tracts under development was too great to permit deep enough penetration by any one morning city paper to justify delivery by newsboys. Most other cities and their suburbs were more compact: fewer papers competed for readership; there were not many local suburban papers to contend with, and newsboy carriers worked well and economically there. In New York's suburbia, Goldstein saw, he would have to use adults in cars to establish home-delivery routes for the *Times*—a more costly expedient—and local dealers supervising these deliverers would have to be subsidized in the early stages of this vital missionary work. Out of the additional two cents grossed in the *Times*'s 1950 price rise, Goldstein earmarked a half cent for this purpose and to gain preferential display position and handling on suburban newsstands. By offering a deliverer a premium "until he could maintain the economies of the route," Goldstein calculated that the *Times* would eventually add to its profitability because every home-delivery sale reduced waste in the press run by limiting the number of returns; the more home sales, the less guesswork in setting the nightly print order. By the same token, Goldstein undertook a steadily heavier sampling campaign in the suburbs, of the sort Pinkham had launched at the *Tribune* but had not received the money to sustain. When the *Tribune,* under Robinson's cost-cutting policies, decided to end its participation in a Welcome Wagon program which offered the paper free for a time to new suburban residents, the *Times* quickly took its place; in some areas as many as one out of three recipients became paying customers after the period of free delivery expired. Goldstein had not only a bigger bankroll behind him but a basically different attitude from the *Tribune*'s toward the distributors. Newspaper delivery, especially of morning papers in outlying areas, was a hard, cumbersome business requiring unpleasant hours, travel over long distances, physical exertion, and reliable performance in often appalling weather; and in New York, the competition was so intense that no paper could afford its own fleet of suburban deliverers. With these realities in mind, the *Times* was willing to give up a larger piece of its circulation income than the *Tribune,* where even the forward-looking Dick Pinkham was unsympathetic to his distributors' problems in doing business. With the smallest paper in the field, Pinkham felt himself at the mercy of wholesalers who, he said, "made unconscionable profits of one cent a sale and all drove around in Cadillacs."

Nothing better illustrated the difference in the two papers' attitudes toward distribution and their determination to master the prized suburban territory with its well-heeled readership than their response to demands by Henry Garfinkle's American News Company for tribute money. Because American News controlled newsstands at train stations and other key distribution points throughout the metropolitan area, it was powerful enough to insist upon what were euphemistically called "retail display allowances"—kickbacks, in common parlance—from the newspapers. Those that complied, like the *Times,* enjoyed prominent display; those that did not, like the *Tribune,* got buried or placed in harder-to-reach positions on the counter. In conceding this knuckling under to Garfinkle, Goldstein said that even more hateful to the *Times* than such extortionate payoffs was anything that caused "a disturbance in our numbers. . . . It was cheaper to buy our way out of trouble—like our labor relations people did in yielding to the unions rather than taking a strike." This soft-on-labor policy stemmed from the *Times*'s long-standing belief in its institutional indispensability as *the* newspaper of record; any unpleasantness, like a strike, that might interrupt its publication would deprive posterity of something vital—almost as if events that went unreported in the *Times* had never really occurred. This self-invested importance, validated with the passing years by the public's recognition of the *Times* as a primary research tool in schools, libraries, and other repositories of civilization, was reflected in the counsel given by its general manager, Julius Ochs Adler, when sending his labor-relations department to the bargaining table to negotiate a new contract with the unions. "Don't give them anything," he would say, according to veteran *Times* executive Ivan Veit, "but I don't want a strike." And so generally the *Times* gave ground, especially on manning issues. Such softness, though, was mitigated by the certainty that the *Tribune* would have to go along with the costly concessions and would be hurt worse by them. A similar attitude governed the setting of advertising rates at the *Times,* always undertaken, Monroe Green acknowledged, "with the *Tribune* very much in mind." By holding its rates down, the *Times* aggravated the *Tribune*'s desperate need for cash; by 1953, it cost advertisers 44 percent more per reader reached to buy space in the *Tribune* than in the *Times.* At the *Tribune,* they found such policies ungentlemanly—indeed, downright unscrupulous. But Jack I. Straus, who at the time was running Macy's, the biggest advertiser in New York, did not see it that way. He knew and admired Helen Reid and Bill Robinson "and his social outgo." But he also knew Arthur Sulzberger and Julius Adler, "and they were smarter—more able" and picked stronger managers to run their paper; Helen Reid, he thought, "didn't pick the people."

As vital as the harvest of new readers to be reaped on the suburban battlefield of the 'Fifties was the *Tribune*'s ability to retain its strong hold on national advertising, especially in the key automotive and travel categories, in which it ranked second among New York papers and among the leading papers in the country, largely on the strength of its leadership in the affluent suburbs. As the *Times* intensified its efforts there, the *Tribune* would have been well advised not to dissipate its resources on the Early Bird in a forlorn quest for in-city readers but instead to solidify and expand its position in suburbia. In James Parton, the last imaginative executive to serve on the business side of the *Tribune* under the Reids' ownership, the paper had a vocal advocate of such a strategy.

Harvard graduate Parton, a short, assertive man approaching forty, had left a promising career with Time Inc. in the editorial and promotion departments to buy a chain of giveaway shopping papers and convert them into a newspaper serving suburban Los Angeles communities by means of zoned editions. He ran out of money before the venture could take hold, but the *Los Angeles Times* at once picked up the idea of zoned editions that helped build it into a colossus with the largest advertising linage in the nation. It was not surprising, therefore, that Parton joined Pinkham in pushing the *Tribune* to greater efforts in the suburbs when he came on the paper to run its promotion department in 1950. He urged Robinson to tell the *Tribune*'s suburban story in a separate promotion booklet instead of joining other New York papers in a joint project. Robinson rejected the idea, as he would every innovation Parton proposed. The promotion man pushed hard for suburban supplements that might run in either the Thursday or the Sunday edition, contended that Robinson was wrong in his belief that the paper had lost nothing in dropping its Jersey Sunday supplement before the war, and asserted early in 1951, "I come back to my conviction that nothing would help us so much as the split run with the localization of news which it would make possible" and the opportunity for the *Tribune* to attract substantial local advertising. "I was told there was no money for it," Parton recalled, "and it couldn't be done." It was then that he understood the largest single obstacle in the way of the *Tribune*'s path to prosperity: the shortage of working capital and Helen Reid's unwillingness to obtain it at the cost of yielding any of her control.

Early in 1952, Parton sent Mrs. Reid a remarkably candid memo about what ailed the *Tribune* and directed a copy to Robinson, whose management policies it sharply criticized. The paper's budgetary controls, he said, were a bad joke, "full of skeletons in the closet," done in a last-minute rush, haphazardly monitored, and needful of being broken down by months or quarters instead of unwieldy semiannual periods. Management, though it had "superb inspirational leadership from the top and a number of extremely capable managers at the operating level," had nobody in between and was thus "a very loose operation. We are a car that needs tightening in every joint. We are a collection of individuals, not a team." What was required was a thoroughgoing staff reorganization with a real executive committee. Worst of all was the paper's lack of a long-range program. It was all right to follow a policy of weathering the storm, Parton asserted, if you expected it to pass eventually, but "I, for one, don't expect it to abate." The *Tribune* required objectives beyond simply "trying to best last year's figures and keep abreast of our competition." But Helen Reid had her mind heavily on the election of Dwight Eisenhower that year and the gain in influence that would accrue to the *Tribune,* his principal newspaper sponsor, if he led the Republicans back to the White House after an absence of twenty years. And that fall, when Robinson produced his friend the President-elect at the surprise seventieth birthday party for Helen Reid in Purchase, his power at the *Tribune* was greater than ever.

Parton, elevated to assistant to the president in addition to his other duties, continued to vent his frustration. At the end of April 1953, he wrote Mrs. Reid, this time without a copy indicated for Robinson, that the reason the paper was not as successful as "we all know it ought to be," despite "your inspirational leadership and the shining integrity of Whitie's editorial team," was that "the third wheel—business management—is woefully weak and wobbly." He lamented the "present acute bottleneck of authority and decision at the top" and went on to propose a radically different, "modern" Sunday edition based not on bulk but on offering to "perceptive people of better means" a series of sections devoted largely to their leisure pursuits and pleasures. With real prescience, he added a plea for investigating advances in printing technology looking toward a streamlined plant "controlled by teletypesetter from clean, compact editorial and sales offices in, say, Rockefeller Center" and perhaps shared with the *World-Telegram,* which he hoped the *Tribune* might be in a position to take over in the near future. Helen Reid's response to Parton's daring and risky words was shortly to name Robinson publisher of the *Tribune*—a title never before bestowed in the paper's history. "Bill did not ask for it or in fact for anything," she explained to Geoffrey Parsons. "I am merely a strong believer in getting all the values for the paper that we can following his important work in the [Eisenhower] political campaign. I know you will understand."

Parton had one last project to propose. He advised Mrs. Reid of reports that the venerable *Brooklyn Eagle,* a Democratic paper with a circulation of 125,000 among largely Catholic and Jewish buyers—an ideal complement to the *Tribune*'s demographics—was failing fast and could be bought at a bargain price. If even half the *Eagle* readers could be retained by a new zoned edition, the *Tribune* circulation would jump to 80 percent of the *Times*'s, and with this Brooklyn base secured, the paper might strike out forcefully after new readers on Long Island, where many Brooklynites were emigrating. "But Robinson peed on that idea, too," Parton recalled, and Mrs. Reid said there was no money for such an ambitious risk. Parton then produced his friend Robert Straus, of the Macy's Strauses but not connected with the store operations, who visited Mrs. Reid's office and offered to put up half a million dollars toward a joint purchase of the *Eagle* by the *Tribune* and him. The offer was declined, and Parton assumed that was the end of it.

That summer, over lunch with another wealthy friend, John Hay (Jock) Whitney, who had made a modest investment in his ill-fated Los Angeles newspaper, Parton confided his unhappiness with the *Tribune*'s prospects and his intentions to look for employment elsewhere. Whitney, a sophisticated multimillionaire, confided in return that Helen Reid had approached him through Robinson about the possibility of his investing in the paper; Whitney's social and ethnic background apparently made him a more attractive investor than Straus in her eyes. When Whitney said he had not yet decided on the matter, Parton urged him to wade in and, bending the dictates of discretion, discussed the paper's troubled finances, how it was living hand to mouth, and its vital need for a big enough bankroll to fight back successfully against the *Times.* Parton then went off to vacation in Vermont but was soon abruptly summoned back to New York by Robinson, who by then could have harbored little love for him, for an emergency meeting with Mrs. Reid. "Bill tells me that when he was playing golf with Jock Whitney the other day," she began as Robinson hovered in the background, "Jock said you had struck him for a job." She went on to charge Parton with telling Whitney that the *Tribune* was for sale and making financial disclosures he had no right to make. Parton said Whitney must have misunderstood him regarding his own situation, denied saying the paper was on the market, and admitted discussing some numbers with Whitney but only because Parton had been told Robinson had made overtures to him about investing in it. Whether Whitney had misunderstood or Robinson embroidered, the *Tribune*'s new publisher clearly was using the opportunity to pull the rug from under his severest and perhaps only open critic on the staff. Parton was done.

Even while Parton was cleaning out his desk, Robinson was signing an option agreement for the *Tribune* to buy the *Eagle* for $805,000. No records have been found or memories uncovered to indicate whether the funds for the purchase and ensuing higher operating costs were to be provided by Whitney, some other outsider, or bank loans. What is known is that *Tribune* staff members spent six weeks studying the proposed deal from every aspect—how many of the ninety-four editorial staff members would the *Tribune* retain, would they have to be paid at the *Tribune*'s higher scale, would fifty news columns a day be enough to retain the bulk of the *Eagle*'s readership, how would the loose and flashy style of the *Eagle*'s afternoon-paper typography be integrated with the *Tribune*'s more formal look? In its first issue of October, *Editor & Publisher* reported the deal as pending. But two weeks later it was reported dead. The *Eagle* management blamed the intransigency of unions, but the causes of the collapse were more complex. *Tribune* accountants found concealed expenses, meshing the two editorial products looked like a far stickier problem than anticipated, and the outlay needed to sustain the enlarged undertaking jumped with each run-through of the calculators. Helen Reid wrote to son Brownie, then working on the Paris edition, that if the *Eagle* owner "had kept quiet, we might have had the chance to secure some agreements" with the unions. "It was a bitter disappointment to give up the plan, but in the end we were greatly relieved. Meanwhile, the news that the purchase was a possibility proved a tonic in our organization and was of considerable value on the outside."

Helen Reid's power of self-deception was as sizable as Bill Robinson's capacity to pass himself off to her as what he was not—and to convince her that her newspaper was capable of surviving without a major infusion of capital and talent. Perhaps buying the *Eagle* would have changed nothing basic, but it would have been a far more promising step than the Early Bird, Robinson's biggest blunder. By the end of the year, probably sensing that the situation was beyond his control as he watched the paper's annual loss reach $700,000, the worst ever, and despairing of ever obtaining any equity in it, Robinson resigned with passionate expressions of gratitude to take charge of a large Manhattan public relations firm—precisely the right slot for his aptitudes. Now there was no one left from the prewar days for Helen Reid to lean on. And at seventy-two, she was not prepared to bring in a stranger to take over the operation. Instead, she made a deteriorating situation worse by turning to her two sons.

14

Whitie, Brown, and the Reds

Upon his father's death and his succession to the editorship of the *Herald Tribune,* the second Whitelaw Reid had not undergone a radical transformation of character. At thirty-three, retaining the same ascetically slender, boyish look of his prep school days, he was likely to arrive at the office wearing a tiny, brilliant green bow tie, a battered gray fedora, and pants several inches too short for him, because, as one waggish subordinate suggested, "he could afford to." In an interview with him shortly after he became editor, a reporter for *The New Yorker*'s "Talk of the Town" section found "an air of modest determination" about Whitie Reid, who put in thirteen-hour days and often still ate in the employees' lunchroom.

His modesty was justified. Since the war Whitie's main contribution to the paper had been to assist his mother with the annual forum and to take over as president of the Fresh Air Fund, helping teach 10,000 city slum children each summer that there is beauty in life as well as pain. An accomplished horseman, skier, swimmer, tennis player, and woodsman, he found the wholesome outdoor aspects of this charity work perfectly suited to his aptitudes; the fund-raising part of it he liked less well, for as Fresh Air Fund supporter and board member Laurence Rockefeller told him, he would never extract the money needed from wealthy donors unless he asked them for it forcefully. But forceful was not Whitie Reid's manner. To the editorial side of the paper, Whitie's prime postwar contribution had been to persuade management of the logistical and promotional value of buying a two-engine passenger plane, prominently stenciling the *Tribune* logotype on its side, and using it for the swift dispatch of reporters to the sites of breaking news. "The Flying News Room," it was proudly dubbed until ignominiously grounded on landing in the mud after a flight to cover a massive fire in Texas City, Texas, following which it was referred to by the staff as "The Flying Men's Room" and relegated to largely recreational use.

After a seemly interval, Whitie took his father's large, paneled office but, even as the new editor of one of the world's great newspapers, was so rarely seen in the city room that the impression grew that, for all his acknowledged physical courage, he was scared to mingle with his troops. And when he confronted them, neither a smile nor a greeting formed easily on his lips. The solemnity with which he cloaked an almost pathological shyness could have been explained far less by fear than by the highly sensitive nature of a man freshly elevated to power he had not earned and self-conscious, as his father before him had not been, that his rank and command were due entirely to the accident of birth. Ambition to validate his lot in life did not suddenly overtake him now. Instead, he chose to interpret the title of "editor" in its narrowest context, limiting his responsibilities primarily to the editorial page and its policies, still tended by the safely avuncular Geoffrey Parsons. The equally courtly George Cornish had the news operation well in hand, and Whitie would not have dreamed of wresting it from him. Those few who dealt with him advised the rest that behind the skittish personality, the nervous giggle, and the eyes like pale blue marbles that seemed to deflect all effort at contact and register no human emotion, Whitie Reid was a kind, decent, fair man desperately eager to do the right thing. As a prewar cub reporter, he would ask the city desk, like every other staffer on assignment, for permission to make any phone call that would cost the economy-minded paper more than a nickel; as editor, he was no more inclined to pull rank. Such grace was widely mistaken for dumbness.

It was not a substitute, however, for what the *Tribune* needed most at that juncture—leadership. His inadequacies in this area were foreshadowed toward the end of his first year as editor when he hosted a program at the Yale Club of New York featuring several of the correspondents who had collaborated in the *Tribune*'s "Behind the Iron Curtain" series. After a few of the Old Blues attending offered remarks critical of the series for not being sufficiently disapproving of the Communist regimes of Eastern Europe, Whitie began to hem and haw instead of boldly defending his people. "I asked myself what kind of gutless management I was working for," recalled Paris-based correspondent William Attwood. "After all, I didn't have to show up there like a performing seal for the boss." This incapacity to give effective expression to a position and argue it persuasively was characteristic of Whitie's public diffidence. Addressing audiences of any real size was painful for him and added to the impression that he was a terribly nice fellow but hopelessly impotent when it came to seizing the reins and driving the team. His very niceness, his disinclination to inflict pain, served him ill, for distinguished editors, whatever their other traits, must be as able at flaying creative talent gone astray as at recognizing and encouraging its skillful performance. Gentle Whitie Reid knew good writing, but he could neither inspire nor scold. Nor was he a skilled communicator up close; he had no small talk and none of the common touch called for in an editor of a large newspaper in a great metropolis. An intensely private man, he was rarely known to have a sustained conversation about anything with anybody outside his immediate family, and while a serious fellow, he was no intellectual, rarely reading books or attending theater or concerts. There was a dreamy, almost wistful sense about him, as if he might have preferred being in another time and another place, and his dreams were less likely to be of social utopias than of white-water canoeing in the Adirondacks or the perfection of the coconut cakes Mrs. Roach used to bake for the family on its annual winter sojourn to Palm Beach.

The problem, of course, was his mother. So long as she remained on the premises, it was Helen Reid's paper, not Whitie's, and much of what was taken for indecisiveness on his part stemmed from filial devotion to the woman he thought of as "one of the big people of her time." When fashion editor Eugenia Sheppard asked him about the paper's paying for her first trip to Paris to write up the new collections, he told her, "I'll have to check with Mother." When the Alsops wrote a series of columns critical of Pan American Airways and its head, Juan Trippe, a friend of Helen Reid, it was scuttled in the *Tribune* after the first installment—and the editor felt powerless to intervene. He was perceived, therefore, as something of an overgrown mama's boy, a ditherer and a procrastinator, an executive who would sit down to attack a pile of correspondence and after disposing of half a dozen letters would be victimized by a short attention span and get sidetracked into something else, rarely central to the paper's business. As an editing editor, he was more a fiddler than a fixer; instead of instructing the writer of an editorial that did not satisfy him to redo the troubling passages, as Geoffrey Parsons was wont, or rewriting it himself, as he was capable of doing, he would hover and dwell over the copy, picking at it, daubing at it, worrying it endlessly, and settling finally on changes that seldom affected it overall.

What Whitie Reid badly needed, his mother decided, was a managing woman behind him, just as his equally decent but less conscientious father had had, and she did her best to promote an acceptable romance for her socially recessive older son. She placed at least two comely candidates for marriage before him—her assistant in running the forum, Helen Hiett, who possessed a Phi Beta Kappa key from the University of Chicago, a steel-trap memory, and a fondness for the outdoors akin to the Reids', and tall, pretty Mary Louise Stewart, the top scholar in Barnard's Class of 1946 and head of the student government, whom Helen Reid, as chairman of the Barnard board of trustees, invited home for dinner with the family. Helen Hiett would have married Whitie Reid, she confided to longtime *Tribune* man Richard Tobin, "if he'd only proposed"; instead, she married someone else and died tragically young while mountain climbing in the Alps. Nor did Whitie spark to the equally formidable Mary Louise Stewart, but his brother did and married her the year after Whitie, nearly thirty-five, took a bride just slightly more than half his age.

Joan Brandon was a leggy, lively teenager when she caught Whitie's eye, hanging around the *Tribune,* as she had so many other city rooms, waiting for her mother, Dorothy, a well-traveled, divorced newspaperwoman, to finish work. Whitie had hired Dorothy Brandon from the *Pittsburgh Post-Gazette,* where she had written a column on bringing up teenagers. For the *Tribune,* she did a column called "Today's Moderns," dealing with activities of the young-at-heart—part of Whitie's program to leaven the paper with "human interest" features. In the package came Joan, a "news brat" as she called herself, who trooped the country with her mother and had attended seventeen schools by the time she completed twelfth grade and was dating Whitie Reid. Both mothers encouraged the bachelor-bobbysoxer relationship, Dorothy for the financial security and social advancement it would bring her daughter and her, Helen for the companionship badly needed by a dear son who seemed to confide in no one and had such difficulty employing the first-person singular. The Reid line, moreover, needed propagating. On their first date, Whitie told Joan what he was worth and the subject of money did not arise between them again. She and her mother were invited to Ophir Cottage as house guests and survived the ordeal of being waited on by servants, one of whom eventually presented the nubile youngster, in Whitie's behalf, with a grapefruit containing an engagement ring —not exactly the wooing technique of a Don Juan. But the ring fit.

At a party in Purchase not long afterward, Helen Reid bestowed a pearl necklace that had once been her mother-in-law's upon her daughter-in-law-to-be despite the young woman's deficiencies of background and refinement; nearby was an ecstatic Dorothy Brandon, considered by some in the *Tribune* city room a vulgar old news hen who had flaunted her daughter before Whitie. Not everyone viewing the rite of passage at Ophir that day was rapturous over the obvious social unsuitability of the newcomer to the family and what her arrival said of the perils of primogeniture. The wife of one of Helen Reid's nephews attending the occasion was close by Whitie's brother when the family heirloom was passed to Joan. "You just had to see the look on Brownie's face," the relative later told reporter Judith Crist, "and you knew the whole future course of the *Herald Tribune* was written on it."

The poolside marriage at Ophir Cottage was held right after the Republican convention in the summer of 1948. Whitie built his wife a splendid modern house about a mile from his mother's and poured much of his own esthetic nature into the details while working with the architect. Just running the new household and learning how to become a Reid was enough curriculum for Joan Brandon Reid, who dropped out of Barnard early in her sophomore year and rebuffed her mother-in-law's efforts to get her to work at the *Tribune* and involve herself more with Whitie's struggles there. A bolder person than her husband, she knew her strengths and limitations—she could never be another Helen Reid—and directed herself accordingly; Whitie, honor-bound by his own way of thinking to persist in the role his mother had thrust upon him, never made the same sort of self-assessment. He lacked his mother's ambition and will but was at least her match in stiff-necked pride.

In his five years as editor, Whitie Reid was not without influence on the artistic contents of the *Tribune*. He was a persistent advocate of bright, terse copy in both the news and feature departments—he particularly admired daily book reviewer John Hutchens for his "beautifully clean and simple prose"—and had his say in the hiring of new art critic Emily Genauer and drama critic Walter Kerr (not to be confused with the *Tribune* foreign correspondent of the same name), who shortly emerged at the top of their professions, and show-business gossipist Hy Gardner. He saw nothing amiss with the introduction in 1950 of the Early Bird edition. He was, at any rate, not about to do battle with the Early Bird's chief proponent, Bill Robinson, whom he regarded as "a most likable human being" and an essential presence on the business side of the operation. By neither instinct nor training was Whitie Reid suited to the rough-and-tumble of business. His idea of economy was, when driving from home to office and back, to avoid the toll on the Triborough Bridge by going many blocks out of his way and taking one of the free spans over the Harlem River. And so he deferred to the forceful, outgoing Robinson, in almost every way Whitie's opposite, and never pushed hard for innovations the executive vice president rejected, like Whitie's suggested "home" magazine for the ailing Sunday edition or the section devoted entirely to television that Richard Pinkham had espoused. When Robinson and his mother ruled the ideas too costly a gamble, "I didn't argue with them," Whitie recalled.

As Helen Reid turned seventy in 1952, she passed the presidency of the *Tribune* to Whitie and took the title of chairman for herself, but did not retire. During his two-and-a-half-year incumbency as president, Whitie paid little more attention to the business side than he had as editor but was better able to put his imprint on the editorial product. His abiding interest in typography now resulted in a cleaner, modern look to the paper, achieved largely by eliminating most of the subheadlines that had crowded its pages and consumed too much space; besides, television news was usurping the former function of newspaper headlines as a digest service and doing it in some instances half a day before the morning papers were in readers' hands. Whitie's other chief contribution was a new editorial team more to his liking—amiable fellows all, but less than scintillating or innovative. He had begun the process in 1948 with the selection of his Yale classmate Bob Cooke to replace the deposed Stanley Woodward as sports editor. Smooth and cordial, Cooke was a decent enough writer but not half as good as he thought himself and altogether lacking in Woodward's grainy quality as mentor and administrator. Whitie's somewhat better choice as city editor in 1952 was Fendall Yerxa, a strapping, jut-jawed ex-marine who had put in six years as a cityside reporter and speedy rewriteman but had never served on the desk and was not particularly knowledgeable about New York. The handsome Yerxa was liked by the staff as a square shooter but faulted for a certain subdued quality unbecoming in a city editor. Joe Herzberg, moved from city editor to Sunday editor, was not given the budget or personnel to revamp the badly lagging Sunday paper and began to wither on the vine. George Cornish was moved up to the new title of executive editor—a cosmetic change, really —and his loyal lieutenant, Everett Walker, somewhat closer to Helen and Whitie Reid than Cornish, was named managing editor. The appointment most emblematic of Whitie's values and standards, though, was the man he named to succeed Geoffrey Parsons, who retired following the 1952 Republican convention after twenty-eight years as chief editorial writer and the unseen shaping hand behind the *Tribune*'s re-emergence as a major national political and cultural force.

By rights the job should have gone to Walter Millis, then a seasoned fifty-three, author of several respected books on military history and, on the strength of his rare gift for compact prose with bite or lyric power as the occasion called for, widely regarded as an editorial writer second to none. Millis looked rather like a character out of a Marquand novel, with his twinkly blue eyes, all that white hair, his fondness for sailing, and a projected sense that he was going to put his arm around your shoulder at any moment and talk banking. But his domestic politics were at least one shade too liberal for the Reids, and he was undiplomatic in his dealings with Whitie, whose wits he regarded as deficient and who in turn found Millis "very independent and abrasive," like Woodward and Engelking. Instead of Parsons's job, he was tossed a large bone in the form of a column on global armaments. Placed in charge of the editorial page was another of Whitie's Yale classmates, a voluble, somewhat airy fellow of suitable credentials but not in Millis's league as a writer or thinker.

August V. Heckscher was as articulate as Whitie Reid was not. A tireless, and at times tiresome, conversationalist and facile writer, he also had much in common with Helen Reid's older son—great family wealth stemming from nineteenth-century financial and real estate operations, an education at St. Paul's and Yale, a humane and progressive social outlook despite patrician upbringing, and a fondness for bow ties (with polka dots in Augie's case). But at Yale, Heckscher had been a star: captain of the debating team, a co-founder of the political union, a columnist for the *Yale Daily News*, and Phi Beta Kappa. He went on to graduate studies in politics at Harvard, taught for a time at Yale, wrote a book about politics, and was serving as editor of the *Auburn Citizen-Advertiser*, a small daily in upstate New York with a readership about as conservative as the *Herald Tribune*'s, when Whitie lured him to the editorial-page staff in 1948 with a clear shot at Parsons's job if he did well. The only thing peculiar about his being brought to the *Tribune* was that Augie Heckscher was an authentic New Deal liberal. But he was pragmatic enough to recognize his opportunity under Whitie's patronage and swallow a few of his principles to serve, as he put it, "as the interpreter of a great journalistic tradition." He was capable of turning out intelligent and persuasive editorials; he was also capable, when his pen outran his head, of ponderous and pedestrian work. On his advancement to the chief editorial writer's job, his work came increasingly under Whitie's exasperating scrutiny. "He thought he had to make his personality felt," Heckscher recounted. Where others found a conversation with Whitie Reid "like talking to a zephyr," Heckscher, who dealt with him probably more than anyone else on the paper did, found him "ambiguous and complex—as if there were a veil of steel over him. He had an inflexibility about him that was not the same thing as simple stubbornness. You could see the muscles in his jaw working sometimes when he was listening to you. I had the sense that he was always under heavy pressure, as if he had been told he ought to stand up to Heckscher."

And, in effect, he had been—by Bill Robinson, who made no secret of his conviction that the *Tribune*'s editorials under Parsons's and then Heckscher's supervision were too liberal for the paper's good. It was precisely that liberalism, however, that was Whitie Reid's principal contribution to the *Tribune*'s history; no one else among the three generations of Reids that owned it approached him in the possession of social conscience. Whatever his other failings, however ruffled the relationship with Heckscher occasionally grew, Whitie saw to it in his soft yet fixed way that neither his aging mother nor the opportunistic Bill Robinson nor anyone else steered the *Herald Tribune* away from the progressive Republicanism that quirky old Horace Greeley had bequeathed it. Thus, the postwar *Tribune* sought to blend libertarian and egalitarian principles, recognizing the social needs of the growing American and global populations while hoping they could be served without inordinate reliance on centralized government, with its tendency toward tyranny. Civil rights and civil liberties were insisted upon in *Tribune* editorials, and capital punishment was denounced as a vile vestige of barbarism. The right wing of the Grand Old Party, a sanctuary for the privileged, was encouraged tactfully to concern itself with the overall quality of life on the planet. Taftites and others in the party xenophobically wary of the United Nations were chastened, and the Democratic administration of Harry Truman was occasionally approved of even if the circumstances offended Republican fire-eaters. The *Tribune* supported the President's decision to relieve Douglas MacArthur of his Korean command for insubordination, and it understood Secretary of State Acheson's decision not to turn his back on former State Department official Alger Hiss. While unflagging in their anti-Communism, *Tribune* editorials recognized that totalitarianism by the political right was no more commendable than that of the left. Imperialism by any nation could no longer be countenanced, starting with America's own, and the paper was unequivocating in its call for the independence of the Philippines, a U.S. colony for half a century due to the efforts of Whitie Reid's grandfather and namesake as much as any man's. And whatever Helen Reid's lingering distaste for aggressive Jews, particularly her Forty-third Street rivals, her older son seemed uninfected and his editorial page viewed Zionism with compassion; Palestine, at any rate, was at a safe remove from Purchase. All in all, it was not a creed that endeared the *Tribune* to the diehard isolationists and mossbacks. But it was a noble creed, and for the most part Whitie Reid tried to sustain and spread it.

As president of the *Tribune,* however, he was a failure because he had no feel for power—how to use what he was handed of it, how to delegate it, how to guard it from those who thought him unworthy to wield it. When Helen Reid in 1953 named Bill Robinson publisher of the paper, in effect reducing Whitie's presidency to a figurehead status, he did not object; his mother, he would maintain long afterward, had just been "trying to make Bill happy with his lot on the paper." He was a pliant son. And when Robinson resigned before the year was out, opening the way for Whitie to dominate the operation and save it from sinking, he demonstrated what by then should have become painfully obvious: he did not know how—and his mother should never have asked him, out of misconceived reverence for the family honor, to go against his nature. His brother saw that, along with the unseemly bestowal of Elisabeth Reid's pearls.

II

Having accepted the responsibility for the death at nine of her daughter Elisabeth, Helen Reid entrusted the second son who was born soon afterward to the ceaseless care of a large, forbidding nurse. Because his parents had had him in their forties, when his father's health was already failing, his mother preoccupied with other responsibilities, and his only sibling a dozen years older and beyond easy companionship, little Ogden grew up a somewhat lonely and pampered child. Called Brownie by everyone in the Reid clan, he was given a toy red electric car at an age when most children got a tricycle, followed by expensive radio and camera equipment and membership in the Knickerbocker Greys, a pint-sized platoon of the sons of New York's social elite who received uniformed military drill twice a week at an East Side armory. Nurse Davidson, inculcating the belief that the sun rose and set upon him, turned Brownie into a small terror around the various Reid households, overbearing toward the help and behaving in general, as his brother remembered without pleasure, "like a little tin god."

To absorb a bit of discipline and toughen him in wholesome surroundings, Brownie was sent off to a boarding school in the Colorado mountains, which were very far away indeed to a lonesome boy. Whitie visited there to buck him up and later at Deerfield, when they brought him East to prep for college, and spent part of a summer tutoring his little brother, who hero-worshipped him and would try all his life—and fail—to emulate his athletic prowess and feats of physical grace and coordination. Small for his age, darkly handsome like his father, Brownie was teased for his whiny, nasal voice—"Oggie the Froggie," they called him—and more than once asked his family to fetch him home. But no Reid, of whatever age, was allowed to reef in a storm, and so he stayed and began to blossom at Deerfield, becoming a competent photographer and member of the swimming team. And when he was home, there was frequent exposure to the famous and powerful; he dined with Wendell Willkie and Amelia Earhart, walked around the Central Park reservoir with Anthony Eden, and trekked in boots through the marshlands of Queens as Robert Moses showed him the future boundaries of New York's great international airport, Idlewild, later renamed JFK. Not much awed the teenaged Brownie Reid. At the 1940 Republican convention, he climbed up on a piano to snap a picture of Kate Smith singing the national anthem; the photograph made the *Tribune.* He took others for the paper at sports events that an unknowing editor once had the temerity to decline until told the identity of the photographer. He was an indulged boy.

The war interrupted his years at Yale. At eighteen he volunteered for the paratroopers, which seemed to him a dashing outfit, and was trained for intelligence work as well but never saw combat. Stationed with U.S. occupying forces in Japan, full of swagger and high spirits, he led a jeepload of colleagues on an unauthorized sortie into Tokyo to probe the mysteries of the Black Dragon and other native secret societies. When he reported their findings to his superiors, his initiative as an off-limits investigator was rewarded with quarters arrest. Brownie hurriedly telephoned *Tribune* correspondent Frank Kelley in Tokyo and dictated a cable to his mother, asking that the Secretary of War dig out his file, showing that he had been trained for intelligence work, so that he could answer the charges causing his barracks detention. Two days later Helen Reid cabled back: "I WILL DO NO SUCH THING. TELL YOUNG MAN TO STAND ON HIS OWN TWO FEET." Kelley's acquaintance with General Robert Eichelberger, a good Ohio Republican and *Tribune* admirer, spared Brownie more than a reprimand. His service record was further notable for his leading a group of newsmen on an unauthorized reconnaissance flight over the Russian-occupied Kurile Islands to check reports of military activity; it sounded to Brownie Reid like a good news story. But his general performance as a public information officer was good enough to make up for such boyish derring-do, and he returned to Yale in 1946 with an adequate service record.

He was a casual college student, more enthusiastic about motorcycling and flying than studying. Through a family connection he worked summers as a junior researcher in Washington for a federal commission, chaired by former President Hoover, investigating the capabilities of the national security apparatus, including the military services' state of preparedness and the skills of the intelligence-gathering agencies. This job gave Brownie Reid a precocious education in the operations of big government and its misuses of power. Power interested him a great deal, and he became convinced that his country did not have enough of it. He cultivated contacts in the capital, chief among them FBI director J. Edgar Hoover, and was watched over by *Tribune* bureau chief Bert Andrews, whose conservative political preferences he absorbed. Andrews brought his friend Richard Nixon to the party marking Brownie's engagement to Mary Louise Stewart. During his senior year, he essentially commuted between Purchase and New Haven, sometimes arriving home in the middle of the night and, as his then sister-in-law recalled, "asking the cook to make him the most impossible things." A spoiled boy-man, often thoughtless of others, he sometimes even issued orders to Joan Reid, who did not take kindly to them. "He didn't mean anything by it," she said. "It was just his way." His way, in nearly all things, was not his older brother's.

Brownie and Miss Stewart, who was then working for the CIA, were married in the summer of 1949. (Their romance had been temporarily interrupted by his attention to the pretty Olympic figure-skating champion Barbara Ann Scott.) Soon afterward he went to work on the *Tribune* as a reporter, letting it be known that he wished to be called Brown instead of Brownie; the diminutive was beneath his dignity. So Brown it was, but behind his back they called him the Dark Prince. His unfortunately nasal voice, more of a honk than a whine now, sounded snobbish to his fellow reporters, and his behavior did not help matters. On his first day in the city room, he leaned over to the neighboring desk and told science writer Earl Ubell "the worst anti-Semitic joke I'd ever heard." Ubell, who happened to be Jewish, had never heard an anti-Semitic word on the paper before then. "I'm sure he did it without malice," Ubell said. "Given his talent," he added, "Brown rose through the editorial ranks much more rapidly than I did."

The vehicle he rode in that rapid ascent was anti-Communism. After putting in some time on routine feature stories—which proved him to be a less than remarkable writer—he needed another outlet through which to show the paper what he was made of. Whether by calculated choice—which he later denied— or spontaneous attraction, he seized upon the most scarifying issue of the times and exploited it.

III

When the Mexican painter José Orozco died early in September 1949, Whitie Reid had instinctively reached for the phone and called the *Tribune*'s newly designated art critic, Emily Genauer, to ask her to write an editorial tribute. For Genauer, it was a sensitive task. Her move to the *Tribune* had been triggered by an argument with *World-Telegram* president Roy Howard, who thought she was paying too much attention to the modernist movement, and by implication to "Communists and left-wingers," of whom Pablo Picasso was the pre-eminent example. Genauer had told Roy Howard she did not give a damn about an artist's politics, and if that was how he felt, she would take up the standing offer from the *Tribune* to practice her craft there. Now, on the phone, she told Whitie Reid that Orozco was a very great painter indeed, better in her view than his countryman Diego Rivera, but did Reid know that he was definitely a Communist? "Miss Genauer," Whitie told her, "I really don't care about his politics." She knew then she had come to the right place.

But the quiet confidence of values embodied in that brief exchange began to evaporate rapidly as the national mood approached hysteria over the menace of Communism. The 1948 attacks on the *Tribune* by Pegler that were instrumental in tarring it as "the Uptown Daily Worker" had left Helen Reid fearful that the paper was in danger of losing major segments of its conservative readership —an anxiety that Bill Robinson fed. As the *Sun* died at the beginning of 1950 and rumors spread, reportedly fanned in part by the *Times,* that the *Tribune* would shortly follow it to oblivion, Pegler renewed his onslaught, joined now by fellow Hearst columnist George Sokolsky. The air was full of loose, angry talk of un-Americanism born of frustration over the spectacle of the Soviets' new domination of Eastern Europe, their behavior in Berlin, their development of a nuclear arsenal, the 1949 takeover of China by Mao, the trial that same year of leaders of the American Communist Party, and the espionage charges made against Alger Hiss, an establishment State Department figure, and the prominent scientist Klaus Fuchs in Britain. The Reds seemed to be on the march. Suggestions that the *Herald Tribune* was soft on Communism were taken by its management as an appeal to defection of its right-wing constituency and a genuine peril to the paper's already endangered financial stability.

Following the death of its old-codger columnist, Mark Sullivan, the *Tribune* installed in January 1950 a yet more militant conservative, David Lawrence, in his place, ran him daily and more prominently than it had Sullivan, and took charge of his large syndication that had made him the most widely read commentator on the American political right. A dry, persistent critic of the New Deal and its heirs and a thoroughgoing anti-Communist, Lawrence served to still charges of the *Tribune*'s fellow-traveling. When he received mail attacking his alliance with the *Tribune,* Whitie Reid wrote to assure him that the paper's anti-Communist soul was pure: ". . . Hiss might well have never been convicted if it had not been for the perseverance and hard work of Bert Andrews, Chief of our Washington Bureau. . . . The idea that the paper is leftist has been studiously spread by some venomous people and also in part by our competition which has propagated the idea that the paper would have to be sold." Helen Reid gave an interview a week or so later that was prominently played in *Editor & Publisher,* plugging the birth of the Early Bird but aimed no less at disarming the charges of leftism. "No paper in this country is a stronger Free Enterprise paper than the Herald Tribune," she declared, and cited as examples of its firmness the "Behind the Iron Curtain" series dreamed up by Joe Barnes, a similar series on Red infiltration of Asia, and the anti-regime reporting of *Tribune* Moscow correspondent Joseph Newman, who was refused readmission to the Soviet Union after he left it to be married.

Barely a week before Mrs. Reid's remarks were published, Senator Joseph McCarthy of Wisconsin had begun his sensational crusade charging that the

State Department was honeycombed with Communists and their sympathizers. The allegations—largely fabricated, mostly unsupported, and when documented found so faulty as to provide no legitimate basis for dismissal or prosecution—were soon directed against other parts of the government. Fully familiar with the mechanics of the press, McCarthy dispensed his charges and innuendos in a way that milked maximum coverage from almost every paper in the country. He was, after all, a U.S. Senator, and what he said was news almost by definition. That much of it was also false or at best based on the unsupportable ground of guilt by association was not then perceived as a serious concern of the American press. If there was time to check with a McCarthy target for his reply, reporters might make the attempt, but often deadline pressures intervened—the Senator's timing was usually exquisite in that regard—and few papers honored the niceties of fairness in their rush into print. The press services vied feverishly to get the latest McCarthy charge on the wire fast. Headline writers rarely had the space to bother about nuances in McCarthy's language. And when his victims proclaimed their innocence, their words hardly ever caught up with or gained the prominence of the original smear. Early coverage of his recklessness was particularly prominent and complicitous, even by some of the papers that disapproved his excesses. *The New York Times* ran 333 column inches on McCarthy's charges in the first month of his onslaught; the *Herald Tribune,* 230 inches. But the *Tribune,* so eager now to display its attentiveness to anti-Communism, placed on the front page five of the dozen McCarthy stories it carried that month; the *Times,* only one. And neither paper would follow the example of the *Denver Post,* which in time adopted the policy of treating McCarthy's words as if they were not protected by senatorial privilege; his attacks would not be run unless accompanied by his subjects' responses. The widespread toleration, if not active endorsement, of McCarthy's conduct by the press, in its blurring of the distinction between fact (i.e., the uttered charge) and truth (i.e., the validity of the charge), was due in no small part to the political alignment of the principal players—McCarthy was a Republican, most of his targets were Democrats; the Republicans had been out of power in Washington for nearly two decades; and a heavy majority of U.S. papers were owned by Republicans.

The onset of the Korean War that summer turned the Red scare into a forest fire. American blood was being spilled in a far-off land against Godless Communism, and anti-Communists could do no wrong. Under such circumstances, Brown Reid, at twenty-five, moved to put his stamp on his family's great but wobbly newspaper.

Commandeering star reporter Robert Bird to do the writing, Brown utilized many of the contacts he made during his Hoover Commission internship to prepare a ten-part series titled "How Strong is America?" that ran in the *Tribune* during August 1950. As a piece of investigative reportage, it would have been laughable except for the gravity of its subject. Sweeping judgments were offered with little to base them on, and when data were supplied or evaluated, there were almost no named sources. After faulting U.S. intelligence operatives for failing to predict Tito's defection from Moscow and Mao's triumph in China, for badly overestimating Arab military strength in the Palestine war, and for underestimating the number of Soviet-made tanks given to the North Koreans by 233 percent, the Reid-Bird series advised readers that the Soviets were spending half their national income on the military and that the Red army numbered 175 fully activated divisions—how did the authors know that if not from the same intelligence sources who were so badly misinformed in the other instances cited?—compared with one battle-ready U.S. division and nine others partially activated. Similar unverifiable comparisons abounded. Whatever hard facts there were, moreover, were overshadowed by contentions that the Truman administration itself was soft on and neglectful of "Communism's stealthy advance." All was cryptic, murky, and frightening. The series concluded with assurances that "the plans and suggestions outlined in this report are considered by responsible leaders as minimums for safety." Which leaders? How much would it all cost and what were the priorities? Correctives were badly needed, as the near-disaster in Korea was demonstrating, but the Reid-Bird series read as if it were running in a house organ for the military-industrial complex.

But this was nothing compared to the series that Brown got Fendall Yerxa to work on with him a few months later. Essentially a lengthy recitation of several documents of dubious origin supplied to Brown by the FBI, which was not acknowledged as the supplier, "The Threat of Red Sabotage" premised an active network of Communist agents diabolically masterminded by Moscow and bent on destroying American society. No overt evidence of success by this Red network was cited—only the peril. The series began on the *Tribune* front page at the end of November with the statement: "A merchant seaman's hunger aroused by an innocent looking sardine can recently brought to light the most insidious Communist weapons of subversion, violence and revolution ever to penetrate the borders of the United States," and was accompanied by a four-column picture of a sardine can not detectably different from any other. But this can, it seemed, was part of a spoiled cargo on a freight ship (unnamed, as were its ownership and origin) being tossed away (date unspecified) in Philadelphia. When the can was opened—the seaman, presumably, was partial to rotten sardines—it was found to contain thirty-three tiny pamphlets carrying instructions for saboteurs-in-training on how to set fires without being detected, murder by stealth, batter turbines useless, cripple machinery with emery dust, and the like. "Never before in this country's bitter internal struggle against international communism have printed orders been found, outlining in such minute detail a direct course of action," the article reported. What "bitter internal struggle," the article did not elaborate upon. And not until the fourth paragraph did it disclose that the tiny pamphlets were made even stealthier by being printed in Spanish, "a convenient disguise in an English-speaking land." The rest of the series was only slightly less ludicrous. Reporter Yerxa, Brown's collaborator in this epic of phantom malevolence, had been ordered by his superiors to work on the series, like it or not, and had trouble pinning his partner down on some of his sources—"Brown would just brush me off," he recalled. His uncertainty should have ended when FBI chief Hoover issued a statement commending the series for removing "any remaining doubts Americans may have as to the true objectives of the Communists and their willingness to resort to any tactics . . . to fulfill their objectives of undermining, weakening, and eventually destroying our American democracy." Brown Reid, in short, was Hoover's cat's-paw, with the consent of his mother and brother.

It was about then that, as many staff members remembered, Brown took to wearing a pistol around the *Tribune* office. Earl Ubell looked up one day and saw a foot planted firmly on the corner of his desk. "I followed that foot right on up along the leg till I got to the hip," he recalled, "and saw a large gun, and I said, 'Brownie, what are you doing with that gun?' and he said, 'These Communists are really getting upset about my series—you can't be too careful.' "

Brown's gun-toting was short-lived but his Red-baiting was not. The following spring it was institutionalized in a weekly column, "The Red Underground," bearing his byline and appearing in the Sunday news review section. A grab-bag of short items about the allegedly secret doings of Communist Party operatives, their fronts, and collaborators, the column raised more questions than it answered. The August 26, 1951, column was typical; it began:

> A new national order that trickled down through the Communist underground by word-of-mouth courier last week warned members that the party would consider "any meeting of more than three" as "a serious breach of security regulations."

Who gave the order? From where? How did the reporter find out? Why were the quoted words in quotations? What was the significance of the order? The only elaboration offered in the rest of the four-paragraph item was that the alleged order was in response to an FBI crackdown, details of which were not offered.

Nor were the other items more credible or better substantiated. For example:

> A new Communist front or mass organization, "The Stockton Peace Council," was formed last week in Stockton, Calif. More than 100 persons attended the first meeting. The majority of the council's officers are underground party members.

How did the reporter know that the event took place, how many attended, and how many of the officers were party members? The final item read:

> FRUIT, GRAIN, TOOL SHED: Recently a few important underground Communists were given the secret code meaning of these words as used in the sentence: "The load of fruit and grain has been placed in the tool shed." Fruit: ammunition, grenades, small arms, guerrilla type weapons. Grain: gunpowder. Tool shed: secret cache or ammunition dump where fruit and grain are to be kept hidden until needed.

Which "important underground Communists"? Were the code meanings transmitted in sardine cans?

It was almost all like that, full of revelations that the reader had to take almost totally on faith. Open meetings by leftist groups were smeared as subversive by the simple act of including them in a column with such a name. No distinction was drawn between legitimate social protest and subversion or sabotage. Those who defended the rights of even acknowledged Communists to protection under the Constitution they would destroy were vilified. And when it paraphrased or summarized the publicly stated positions of outspoken figures on the left, the column was often careless or maliciously misleading, as in its report that I. F. Stone had asserted there was more freedom in Russia than America—to which Stone replied in the *New York Compass,* a short-lived leftist successor of *PM* and the *Star,* "I consider a statement of that kind wholly untrue and politically idiotic. The very fact that I can speak and write as I do rebuts the statement attributed to me."

The problem with "The Red Underground" was not that what it reported on was untrue but that there was no way for a reader to determine the accuracy or significance of its contents or the true scale of the conspiratorial peril it proclaimed week after week. Brown's prime sources were, in fact, the FBI, with whose chief he was on close terms, and an FBI-approved counterspy named Herbert A. Philbrick, who had emerged from nine years of undercover party membership to testify at the 1949 federal trial of Communist leaders for conspiracy to overthrow the government. Preceded by a letter of introduction from Hoover, Brown went to see Philbrick in Boston, decided that his story was authentic, and persuaded him to write a book about his experiences with the full cooperation of the *Tribune,* which would help him with the writing and editing and find a publisher in return for syndication rights, even as it had done with Dwight Eisenhower. Meanwhile, Philbrick provided Brown with material for his column—"I fed him a lot of the stuff—maybe 60 to 70 percent of the column," he said. And Brown gained attention within the profession as a fearless crusader; "Ogden R. Reid Hits Reds in Herald Trib," Ray Erwin reported in a full-page panegyric in *Editor & Publisher.*

Brown Reid was, in short, now playing Joe McCarthy's own reckless game. The *Tribune* ran the column and tried hard to syndicate it, though with few takers. It was "frankly an effort to counteract the damage" done to the paper by Pegler and extremists on the right, as Whitie Reid conceded a generation later. "One went along—but always reluctantly."

IV

Among the early victims of McCarthyism and the complicity in it of the American press was Joseph Barnes, one of the most gifted and poorly rewarded staff members of the *Herald Tribune.*

Three years off the paper and by then working as an editor at Simon and Schuster, Barnes was summoned to a two-hour closed-door inquisition before the Senate Internal Security Subcommittee, whose only attending member during that July 5, 1951, session was James O. Eastland, a Mississippi reactionary. Barnes appeared without a lawyer—his friends later chastised him as foolhardy for so doing—and gave what, on re-reading a generation later, would appear to have been the full, frank, and fearless answers of a man remarkably free of paranoia to a long list of questions apparently based on reports that during his years on the *Tribune* he was excessively sympathetic, if not in clandestine league, with the Soviet regime and its American collaborators. He had never been a Communist, he said, and his contacts with the Soviets had been almost entirely professional; his knowledge of Russia and the Russian language— undoubtedly a major cause of the suspicion and resentment toward him— bespoke nothing sinister but the crying need for more Americans to learn about their Russian adversaries, who were master semanticists fond of distorting language "to confuse us."

In spite of the effectiveness of Barnes's responses, the same subcommittee, in open session a month later, put questions about him to witnesses who, in a two-week period, four times described him as a Communist or Soviet agent. These witnesses ranged from the head of the Russian-language desk at the Voice of America, a Soviet defector, to Louis F. Budenz, a former managing editor of the *Daily Worker,* who made a career for himself as a paid FBI informer and professional anti-Communist and was later largely discredited. All the charges were reported in the papers, along with Barnes's vehement denials and his demand to be called by the subcommittee in open session in order to clear his name. He never was.

Barnes's widow felt that the charges against him "left a large wound. . . . His verve was drained off, and he lost heart for combat." Peter Schwed, long the publisher at Simon and Schuster, recalled that after the charges had been made, Barnes stayed out of office politics and played a role beneath his capabilities for the rest of the nearly two decades he worked there. And the *Herald Tribune,* which ten years earlier had seriously considered Joe Barnes for its top editor, stopped asking him to review books for it in the wake of the attacks on him. "A less Communist-oriented man would have been hard to find," said Betty Barnes.

V

It was only a matter of time before Brown Reid caught up with the authentic Communists and their close sympathizers on the *Tribune.*

According to one of their number who asked that the disclosure not be attributed to him, there were about ten Communist Party members on the *Tribune* staff at the outset of the McCarthy campaign. One of them was Alden Whitman, who had joined the party in 1934 and the *Tribune* in 1942 as a copy editor. "The Communist Club at the Trib was not conspicuous," Whitman recounted. "All its members were doing what good Communists were expected to do—to be active in building the union where they worked. . . . Our group met periodically, often in my apartment, to discuss the state of the union, collect dues, compare notes on *Trib* union problems and personalities. We were low-key and probably not very effective in union politics," although Whitman helped negotiate the Guild's first contract with the *Tribune* and served for a time as chairman of its grievance committee. Management never bothered him about his politics, he supposed, because he did his work competently, had the protection of the Guild behind him, and was no apparent threat to the internal security of the nation or the editorial integrity of the paper. But if he had stayed past the middle of 1951, when he moved to the *Times,* he would likely have paid for his political sympathies as John Price did that year.

In his eighteenth year as cable editor of the *Tribune,* Price was not a member of the paper's Communist cell, according to his own assertions and those of his closest colleagues, his family, and at least one member of the Communist group. But he was an avowed Soviet sympathizer, almost certainly the highest-ranking member of the staff in that category. For some time he had been growing disheartened with the direction the *Tribune* appeared to him to be taking after Ogden Reid's death: too featurish, too little hard news, especially foreign, too much dominance by the business side as manifested by the creation of the degrading Early Bird edition—and, most of all, an escalating anti-Communist slant in the selection and play of the news. It riled him that the term Iron Curtain was almost never placed within quotation marks, an omission that meant to him, as he wrote in his diary, that

> reporters and editors alike assume that the Communist world wants to shut itself off from the non-Communist. "Satellite" is complacently and matter-of-factly applied to Russia's smaller friends; our small friends are "allies." News stories consistently refer to allegations of Western "imperialism" (with quotes) and to Russian imperialism (without quotes)—a perversion of truth that would be hard to beat.

When Soviet premier Stalin made his first public statement in two years in the form of an interview with *Pravda* in mid-February 1951, Price was appalled at the *Tribune*'s handling of the story. "We should have led the paper with it, as all other papers did," he wrote to himself, "and printed the full text, as the Times did. . . . I was ordered to hold the Stalin story within a column, and it had a minor place on page one, with a snide head. It was not only a disgraceful bit of biased editing but a stupid one."

The appearance of Brown's "Red Underground" column soon thereafter deepened Price's sense of the propagandistic direction he felt the paper was taking. And then its own internal purge began. Price recorded in his diary that three not very prominent staff members "who were or were believed to be Communists" were let go—"smoothly, without any scandal or fight with the Guild." Another man was demoted for working after hours on the *Compass,* and several others who had been promised they would be rehired were not because, Price believed, *Tribune* management now considered them too radical. And then Alden Whitman left, entirely of his own volition, for a more economically secure workplace on the *Times,* but his politics had plainly endangered him. Now reports reached Price, as the charges against Joe Barnes hit the headlines, that Brown Reid was searching through the desks of suspected Reds and sympathizers in the *Tribune* city room for hard evidence against them. According to his prime collaborator on "The Red Underground"—Herbert Philbrick—Brown did indeed search through Price's desk and found stashed in the drawers whole dispatches and scissored pieces of others unfavorable to the Soviet Union. "Price was plainly censoring the news," Philbrick said.

That Halloween, George Cornish summoned Price to his office and, in his usual quiet way, said that in line with a number of changes being made in the organization, "we feel that no one should remain too long in one job, and of course you have been in the cable editor's job for Lord knows how many years." He was to transfer the following week to a spot on the copy desk—the word "demotion" was not uttered—with no reduction in salary, "and later on we may be able to find another spot for you."

In his diary that night, Price estimated that there was no more than a 30 percent chance Cornish had been candid with him. Dissatisfaction with his work he thought was a 10 percent possibility; the likelihood that "the reason for my demotion was my well known opposition to the paper's political views" he placed at 60 percent. He was aware, of course, of the *Tribune* management's sensitivity to attacks upon it from the right, "and since I had never made a secret of my pro-Communist views—although I have not pressed them on anyone, either, it is possible that they feared Pegler might some day 'get into' me and attack them for letting me edit their foreign news." Precisely, as Cornish would acknowledge long afterward in retirement. But the order to render him harmless originated, according to Philbrick, with Brown Reid, whom Price characterized in his diary the night the ax fell on him as "a very loud-mouthed, arm-swinging, swaggering young stinker. . . . He does a lot of conferring with Cornish, who defers to him, and with the front office people. . . . No doubt Brownie will become more influential and powerful as time passes—indeed, because he is so much more vigorous and aggressive than Whitie, he may very well oust him from control eventually."

Four years later, as Senator Eastland was preparing to bring his Internal Security Subcommittee to New York to investigate alleged Reds on the city's newspapers—Alden Whitman was among those called—John Price was given that other spot Cornish had said they would try to find for him: on the sports desk. Price knew next to nothing and cared less about sports. But he learned, and did not quit, and they did not fire him, so he stayed ten more years, disgruntled but always the professional. He found solace in reading, studying mathematical theory, playing chess, and birdwatching in Rockland County, where he had built a home and was active in church work.

VI

Brown Reid's pet project, turning the exploits of domestic anti-Communist spy Herbert Philbrick into a book under the *Tribune*'s sponsorship, proved highly successful. It was both a commercially and patriotically appealing saga: how a mild-mannered, curly-headed, unsophisticated, decent Christian young man of twenty-four from a small town in New Hampshire applied his modest talents to a copywriting job for a mail-order company in the Boston area and, in his after-work avocation as a Baptist churchman, joined the Cambridge Youth Council, which he soon discovered to be a Communist front. So rather than just quitting, he went to the FBI and was told he would be performing a great service to his country if he remained an active member and filed surreptitious reports on the front's subversive activities.

It became the consuming mission of Herb Philbrick's otherwise quite ordinary life. For nine nerve-wracking years, he held down a regular job by day but by night skulked about at interminable secret meetings, rising in time to be what he called "a member of the highest intellectual level of the Communist apparatus in the U.S." He was hard at work trying to colonize the John Hancock insurance company for the party when the FBI brought him out from under cover to tell all in public and help put the party leaders behind bars.

To tell his story, the *Tribune* advanced Philbrick $4,000, got him a $20,000 advance from McGraw-Hill for book rights, and assigned Fendall Yerxa to work with him in a little office at 10 Tremont Avenue in Boston. The FBI, which did not employ Philbrick but paid some of his expenses, assigned its public-relations expert, Cartha (Deke) DeLoach, to the premises to check over his revelations so that its agents and interests were not compromised; in short, the government censored the text. Yerxa was more skeptical of Philbrick's story than Brown Reid had been, but the detailed nature of Philbrick's account and his patent sincerity finally left him satisfied with its essential authenticity—a judgment reinforced by the fact that "we always had Hoover's guy hanging over us." It was a true *Tribune* team effort: Yerxa rewrote Philbrick's earnest but awkward prose, Frank Kelley broke it down in New York into installments handy for serialization, Helen Reid thought up the title—changing the bland original, *Nine Years,* to the more intriguing *I Led Three Lives*—and Brown would call at all hours to check on progress and spur them on during the writing stage.

Hailing Philbrick for his "genuine contribution to public enlightenment," the *Tribune* ran his story in seventeen installments at the top of page one early in 1952 and syndicated it across the nation; in book form, it became a bestseller. The *Times* called it "a dour tale," but in the *Tribune*'s book review section, Erwin Canham, editor of *The Christian Science Monitor,* found "the immense utility" of the book to be in its revelations of Communist techniques to seduce the innocent and distort and undermine the American political process. "Philbrick is no fanatic," Canham wrote, echoing the widespread praise for the author as a patriot and no mere turncoat. "The job he did was very tough."

There were few polemics or lurid passages in *I Led Three Lives,* certainly, but it was not innocent of hysteria-spreading passages like: "Anyone can be a Communist. . . . No one is safe. No one can be trusted. There is no way to distinguish a Communist from a non-Communist." It was one thing, moreover, to spy for a time on those perceived as lethal to your nation's security, but nine years was making a career of it. What had begun as a public service soon showed signs of turning into a private crusade, for the book brought celebrity with it, wide adulation against the sound of Joe McCarthy's tumbrels, a television series, a ready audience, and a power to command attention not easy for any man to renounce. But to protract the adventure, the peril had to be presented as genuine and continuing, whatever the facts, and if fanaticism was not in Herbert Philbrick's nature, he had embraced an obsession he could not let go of—and the *Tribune,* success in hand, would not let go of Herb Philbrick.

They put him on the payroll as an advertising salesman at first, but his accounts were more interested in talking to him about Reds, the FBI, and himself than about the paper. Brown and Bill Robinson worked out a better scheme: he would take over "The Red Underground" from Brown—he was already its prime source, and city reporter Newton Fulbright, as rabid an anti-Communist as there was on the staff, would team with him for several months—dividing his time between that and personal appearances in behalf of the *Tribune,* thereby aligning it beyond doubt with the forces battling the Red peril. Philbrick's reception in the city room, however, was on the chilly side— "there were icicles hanging out all over the place," he recalled. His mail was tampered with, his desk rifled, he claimed, and the files he and Brown were using in the library at night would be messed, with allegedly sensitive contents removed, by the following evening. So Philbrick was given an office all his own on the eleventh floor behind unmarked steel doors, especially installed to discourage break-ins, and outfitted with a sizable library of Marxiana and anti-Communist literature donated by a financier foe of the Red peril. The place became a rendezvous for old Mensheviks, FBI agents, informers, grudge-bearers, and anyone else on the warpath against the Commies.

"A weekly column of shocking importance to every American!" the *Tribune* promotion department trumpeted the Philbrick version of "The Red Underground" to papers it tried to enlist for syndication. Now a traveling celebrity, Philbrick had the help of an *ad hoc* network of tipsters, but his column no more qualified as authentic journalism than it had under Brown Reid's byline. George

Cornish tried to legitimize it—"he provided extremely good advice, suggesting things that I'd follow up on," Philbrick said—but what ran in the papers was mostly a potpourri of allusions to an undemonstrated menace, of a vagueness and insubstantiality that would have been tolerated nowhere else in the *Herald Tribune* and was in fact carried in no other paper of solid journalistic reputation.

Herbert Philbrick's speeches, furthermore, delivered around the nation under the aegis of the *Tribune,* whose sponsorship he rarely failed to mention, would have warmed Westbrook Pegler's heart. Four years after *I Led Three Lives* was serialized in the *Tribune,* Philbrick was still telling groups like the Northeastern Retail Lumbermen's Association that the underground Reds were "the greatest problem that the United States of America has ever faced in its existence." His sincerity was not the issue; it was the *Tribune*'s duty, though, to separate his self-interest from its own, and in continuing to sponsor obsessive, propagandistic copy and oratory to placate its phobic detractors, it smeared itself and its claim to greatness.

What August Heckscher termed "Brown's enormously malign influence" on the *Tribune* during McCarthy's heyday caused chagrin and fear throughout the city room. Night editor Everett Kallgren—the Count—privately called the Reid-Philbrick column "a lot of shit" but was no more willing to object out loud to it than managing editor Cornish or Sunday editor Herzberg, who also knew what it was. And if the best editors in the newsroom were afraid of crossing Brown, his effect on the lower ranks was yet more chilling. Second-string film critic Joe Pihodna was cornered one day by Brown, who wanted details on a Russian film at an Eighth Avenue theater he had reviewed a few weeks earlier. Pihodna checked his clips and said it dealt with Russian attempts at sabotage during the German invasion. Smelling a rat or possibly a sardine can, Brown said he thought it might be an attempt by the Russians to teach esoteric sabotage methods to their agents in the United States. Pihodna noted that the film had cleared customs without difficulty, was regarded by most critics as just another propaganda film showing how bravely the Russians had resisted the Nazis, and its sabotage methods could be figured out by any intelligent high school student, but if Brown wanted to see it, the critic would arrange a screening. Brown seemed irritated at Pihodna's response and declined the offer, but the critic was soon ordered to submit his reviews to new city editor Yerxa for clearance. Earl Ubell was similarly confronted by Brown after writing up a paper on the state of Russian psychiatry, delivered to the American Psychiatric Association by a prominent New York professor who was reputed to be a left-winger. "Why did you write about that Commie?" Brown demanded. Ubell explained that his beat required him to report on developments of scientific significance. "He's one of those subversive bastards!" Ubell recalled being told in reply. "Now when the son of the owner of the paper says something like that to you," Ubell reflected, "that's intimidation." When city reporter Robert Poteete did a gently mocking article on a new First Army pamphlet circulating on Governors Island telling enlistees how to spot a Communist, he was sharply reprimanded by the desk.

Brown Reid began talking about the possibility of imposing a loyalty oath on the whole staff; Roscoe Drummond, a new *Tribune* columnist at the time, writing from a moderate Republican viewpoint, recalled Brown's urging him to write columns favorable to McCarthy. And Philbrick was emboldened to send memos to Cornish, complaining about what he regarded as a leftist slant to some stories. "We embraced McCarthyism," contended Poteete, a thorough City Hall reporter, later an able assistant city and Sunday editor. An embrace it was not, but at least a frequent hearty handshake.

Brown's anti-Communism opened a rift with his older brother that never fully healed. "There was considerable friction between us," Whitie said. "He was always seeing Communists around the paper. He was much more in line with Bill Robinson's thinking." When Brown took it on himself to pass the word that the *Tribune* would throw its support to Taft if Eisenhower was not nominated by the Republicans in 1952, Whitie's annoyance rose. But he took no overt step to swat his kid brother down. "He was probably awfully conscious of being twelve years younger and that I seemed to have had a long headstart on him," Whitie speculated.

Brown himself retrospectively conceded that his anti-Communist efforts might have been on the flamboyant side but denied they were ever "a conscious effort to project myself." Through security clearances that so young a man was rarely granted, "I had seen the disarray of our defenses," he said, and thus alerted, got caught up in the temper of the times that invited him to vent his own nature: "I've always gone full tilt at everything I've ever been involved in." His wife, who did not fully share his concern over the peril of domestic Communism, justified Brown's behavior as "an effort to counterbalance what seemed an excessive leftist influence on the paper."

When he went off to Europe in the middle of 1953 to take charge of the ailing Paris edition, few in the city room were sorry to see him go. At that distance, his influence was sure to wane, they supposed. But when he returned a year later, he was stronger than before.

VII

In its postwar reincarnation the Paris edition of the *Tribune* had done very well at first. It earned $200,000 in 1945 and was a much better newspaper than its prewar version, closely integrated now with the home edition in appearance and policy.

But as the American troops went home and few tourists replaced them until Europe had had a chance to mend from the trauma of war, readers were harder to come by. Worse, the paper was under the command of a pair of cheerful souls, editor-publisher Geoffrey Parsons, Jr., a Harvard dropout with eight years as a *Tribune* correspondent in Chicago and London, and general manager William Wise, a charming mediocrity, whose fondness for francophile gaiety resulted in a wonderfully relaxed, unbusinesslike atmosphere about the rue de Berri operation. Staffers came and went on irregular yet remarkably productive schedules and the phones jangled incessantly with inquiries from traveling Americans who wanted to know where to eat, how their dollars could be most profitably converted on the black market, or the latest baseball scores. Parsons comported himself as if he were the vice-ambassador to France, at least as attentive to the latest NATO reception and Parisian high life as to overseeing the paper; Wise, manipulatable and eager for Parsons's approval, declined to rein in their expense-account living style. Meanwhile bills got shoved into drawers and taxes owed the French government on the paper's 200-man payroll went unpaid. The product itself became a scrawny six-pager with too little news and too much filler, surviving on its stock exchange quotations, the comics that appeared in its military edition, and a subsidy in the form of bulk sales to the State Department, which gave it away to foreign officials. When the fiscal omissions and oversights were finally detected and corrected, the joy was gone; profits turned to red ink, growing from $100,000 in 1947 to $300,000 in 1949. Parsons and Wise were finished.

To replace them, from New York came the manager of the Herald Tribune Syndicate, Buel Weare, a Princeton man with a Harvard master's in business administration, a socialite fond of riding to hounds, and a cost-cutter in the misanthropic mold of Laurence Hills. Weare cleaned up the financial mess and office clutter in short order and got the operation back into the black, but his martinet manner demoralized the place. And he overstepped his charge, claiming editorial control of the paper that was nominally being shared by the technically able managing editor, Eric Hawkins, and the more sophisticated Walter Kerr, who had succeeded Joe Barnes as foreign editor and then was put in charge of all European correspondents for both the New York and the Paris editions. Internal tensions were matched by external pressures as competition grew in the form of the *Rome Daily American,* a ludicrously emaciated edition of *The New York Times* printed in Amsterdam and carrying two-day-old news, and a new generation of military papers. Collecting revenues in several dozen currencies amid constantly shifting exchange rates also caused a chronic massive headache.

At this point a new *Tribune* star arose, one quite as unpromising in appearance and manner as anybody since Joseph Alsop. But Alsop had a Harvard education and breeding; Art Buchwald was a mutt.

He was twenty-three when he showed up at Hawkins's desk in 1948—a tubby little fellow in a loud checkered jacket and tortoiseshell glasses that gave him what the Paris managing editor later recalled as an "owl in the moon" look. In a voice unmistakably acquired on the pavements of New York's least stylish neighborhoods and unmodulated in transit, Buchwald asked for a job reporting Parisian nightlife—a severe lacuna in the *Tribune*'s coverage, he pointed out.

As Hawkins was quick to discover, the applicant was supremely unqualified for such a plum assignment. Lately arrived in Paris, where he learned that GI Bill benefits would allow him to study, he did not know the French language, cuisine, or culture and had no connections, and his writing credentials were limited to work on undergraduate publications during three years at the University of Southern California and as an eight-dollar-a-week Paris stringer for *Variety*. But Art Buchwald had what he called "a slightly curved way of looking at life." Kicked around during a homeless childhood, he turned to comedy for solace, protection, and revenge. His stint in the marines in the Pacific during the war while he was still a teenager was more pleasant than the rest of his youth had been, he would always say. When Eric Hawkins told him the *Tribune* had no interest in a reporter to cover nocturnal Paris, and if it had, he would surely not have been the choice, Buchwald went away and waited till Hawkins took a vacation. Then he approached easygoing publisher Parsons and said, with his patented deadpan honesty, "Mr. Hawkins and I have been talking about my doing a column—"

At first he had a single piece a week on night spots and got twenty-five dollars. His prose was as unpolished as everything else about him, but he learned fast from the copy desk fixes. When Guild regulations required that he be paid the fifty-dollar minimum and Parsons balked at paying him that much for what he was doing, Buchwald talked his way into a second weekly piece, this one reviewing French films. Unhampered by familiarity with the language, his criticism tended to the generous side; he was forever trying to drag colleagues to the cinema with him to translate. One con job led to another. Soon he had a third weekly column, on restaurants. "His idea of gourmet dining was to begin his meal with *crème caramel,*" recalled Robert Yoakum, a reporter and city editor of the Paris edition of that era. Skillful rewriting of French menus lent an authoritative tone to Buchwald's copy, and soon American tourists were consulting his "Paris After Dark" columns as culinary gospel. There was a fourth column, too, about personalities, which he wrote with Yoakum for a time before the latter left the paper, so that inside of two years he had invented a dream job for himself against all odds. "While the rest of us were going out and drinking too much, talking politics, sex, and religion, and trying desperately to get laid," said Yoakum, "Art was sucking up everything available in the writing end like a vacuum cleaner."

His success invited envy, admiration, disbelief, and resentment in about that order. The whole office would hush to listen when he got on the phone with an obviously French speaker on the other end and began conversing in English garnished with an increasingly French accent that was supposed to make him understood. It was that earnest whimsy of his—the persona of a Chaplinesque innocent abroad, baffled by long wine lists, intimidated by haughty waiters, exasperated by a thousand and one native customs lurking to entrap the foreigner—that served him so well. He was deft, too, at tweaking the French—an unthinkable practice on the prewar paper—even while kidding the gaucheries of his countrymen. With mock seriousness, he reported on his own scientific poll revealing that 99 percent of all Citroën drivers were sadists, he crusaded fearlessly against the custom of permitting French diners to bring their dogs into restaurants with them, he needled the delicacy of haute cuisine by tracking down the reigning garlic expert of France in his quarters on a barge in the Seine, and he satirized art connoisseurs by ardently admiring the collection of counterfeit masterpieces in the possession of the Paris prefecture of police.

Upon the discovery that visiting American celebrities were so worried about going unrecognized in Paris that they would gladly give him an audience if he just rang them up, Buchwald would make the rounds of the big hotels, search through the guest registers that publicity-hungry management was only too happy to make available to him, and soon be seated at the George V bar or on the terrace at Fouquet's opposite the famous and powerful. The relaxing mood of Paris and Buchwald's own unthreatening manner invariably put his subjects off guard, and they would say more than they should have. And soon he was famous himself, welcomed at every first-class restaurant in town like a visiting potentate, then moving out around the continent, crashing the coronation of Elizabeth II of Great Britain or a posh Venetian costume ball, visiting Yugoslavia to sample the slivovitz or Vienna to report on the state of the *schlag*. His humor derived from the situation rather than his style, which seemed to be no style at all in contrast to that of inspired newspaper humorists of the past, like Finley Peter Dunne and Petroleum Vesuvius Nasby, who depended heavily on dialect, or Will Rogers with his homespun irreverence. Here, for example, is a passage from the column on his caper in Venice:

> At seven-thirty sharp, dressed in the full costume and wig of Louis XIV, I climbed into a motorboat and set sail from the Lido for the Bestegui Labia Palace. I won't deny my knee britches were twitching. I had a lot to worry about. If I got thrown out of the palace by the Venetian aristocrats who thought me a commoner, I would probably get stoned to death by the populace who mistook me for an aristocrat.
>
> As we motored up the Grand Canal, I waved to the watching people and screamed, *"Vive la République,"* and as we turned into the Canale di Cannaregio, where the palace was, I yelled, *"Vive le Roi."* But when we touched the dock, I found to my dismay that I was two hours too early. . . .

At a time when it badly needed brightening, Art Buchwald was helping sell the Paris paper. By 1952, he talked Helen Reid and George Cornish into trying him in the parent paper. Under the title "Europe's Lighter Side," he appeared twice a week, alternating on the bottom of the showcase split page with John Crosby, then at the top of his form, and was taken for syndication by *The Washington Post* and several other leading papers. His sudden celebrity won him immunity from rebuke as the office zany. He would stand up in the middle of the Paris city room and read his copy aloud. He would hand in the most preposterous expense accounts, like the one for a 4,000-franc lunch with his guest, the Aga Khan, which left Hawkins unamused. "He ate a lot," Buchwald explained. "All I had was a piece of bread and a glass of *vin ordinaire.*" But they all laughed when he brought a giant poster of Stalin back from East Germany, pasted a Coke bottle in his hand, and slapped the collage up on the city-room wall. Then word arrived that Brown Reid was coming. Stalin, Hawkins had heard, was no laughing matter to the owner's younger son. The poster came down.

Brown's detractors, who heavily outnumbered his admirers on the paper—and he knew it—said that his mother had sent him to take charge of the Paris paper to get him out of everyone's hair in New York. The more plausible reason was that she wanted him to learn the business side of newspaper publishing, and since the Paris operation appeared to be stagnating, perhaps Brown could infuse it with his abundant energy.

To give the threadbare sheet more substance, he ordered it to carry the full text of important speeches by Eisenhower and Dulles, nowhere else available on the continent, and editorials from other U.S. papers besides the *Tribune* so that European readers might have access to a wider spectrum of American opinion. These additions only made the paper more ponderous, not better, in the estimate of Sylvan J. Barnet, who had been the New York advertising representative of the Paris edition and joined Brown as his assistant in Paris. "Brown simply did not know how to make a newspaper," Barnet said. "There wasn't room for all his politicized attitudes. It was an inadequate paper that needed to be made more informative and interesting." Barnet, by his account, called for more financial and sports news, complete stock listings every Monday of the previous week's activities, more stories on page one, more comics, and a society columnist, among other improvements, "and Brown bought it."

On the business side, Brown obtained a loan from the Chase bank in Paris to give the paper more working capital and pledged only his word as collateral. He got the bookkeepers to eliminate accounting irregularities and make sure cash receipts and reported sales actually balanced. He cut down on expense accounts, merged the military and civilian editions, intensified the circulation effort by enlisting more vendors at hotels and military bases, and utilized the printing plant more fully by pushing harder for job printing.

It was on the social side that Brown undoubtedly did best. An attractive couple, he and Mary Louise rented a grand house in Versailles and entertained grandly, showing the *Tribune* flag to a wide assortment of political, diplomatic, military, and business leaders. Brown made what he would recall as "my usual number of gaffes," like the time Jean Monnet, architect of the European Economic Community, offered him a brandy that he declined with thanks and got offered again and again and declined again and again until Mary Louise kicked him under the table and he remembered at last that M. Monnet had a proprietary interest in brandy-making. But Brown was, after all, only twenty-eight.

Perhaps his most important tactical success was what those who did not like him referred to as the courtship of his aunt Jean Ward. She held notes against the *Tribune* totaling nearly $3 million, and while she had refrained from collecting any of it since the paper had fallen into the red, it was apparent that unless she and the Reids were willing either to forgive the combined sum of more than eleven million they were theoretically owed by their own property or to subordinate their claim to any new funding that might be arranged, the *Tribune* would starve from lack of working capital. But Lady Jean had never shared her parents' or brother's feeling for the paper. And her sister-in-law, having eclipsed Ogden as the dominant figure in the *Tribune* operations, was not her favorite person in the world. It was not only that Jean was social and titled and Helen, when you got down to it, was a careerist and a commoner, but that the Wards, whether by geography, temperament, or social attitude, were perceived by the Reids as remote and no one meticulously advised them of developments at the paper. Brown, though, had never found Lady Jean overly formidable. For all her British eccentricities, like regularly turning the lights out throughout her manorial home and declining to lay fires in the grate till the whole place was freezing, she seemed to him a sporting old gal who still liked to ride hard and had not lost her zest for life. He would visit in the evening beside her bed, where she liked to curl up with a good mystery, and fill her in on what he was doing and everyone he had met and tease her perhaps about her inexpert fishing technique. She appreciated the attention and enjoyed her nephew's brashness, so different from the stiffness of her own two sons, and she saw in Brown's wife a bright and composed lady. He left with her assurances of cooperation in whatever steps were required to save the *Tribune*—and, not incidentally, with an invaluable ally for the struggle ahead.

That it would be a struggle was plain from the dismaying news that kept arriving from New York.

Bill Robinson had quit and left no one strong to take his place; he had seen to that. The paper had recorded its heaviest loss ever in fiscal 1953, and with labor and newsprint costs continuing to rise, revenues stagnating, and Sunday circulation plunging toward the 500,000 level—below which major advertisers could be expected to reduce their *Tribune* schedule sharply—bold measures would have to be taken almost immediately. The most obvious steps were to try to enlist a sizable investment from outsiders who would not demand control of the paper and its policies in return, or a merger that would open new markets for readership and revenue. His mother and brother, though, had been exploring these avenues while he was away, with no results, and Bill Robinson's approach to Jock Whitney had fared no better. Whitie had had talks with Republican multimillionaires Paul Mellon and Nelson Rockefeller and *Wall Street Journal* president Bernard Kilgore and got nowhere. He and Helen had even gone to Texas to talk with Sid Richardson and other oil barons about an investment. And merger explorations with the non-union Macy chain in Westchester, the *Brooklyn Eagle,* and *The Journal of Commerce,* which had been overwhelmed by the rise of *The Wall Street Journal,* had either never really got off the ground or had broken down over the costs and dubious gains that would accrue to the *Tribune.*

And then there was the slackening in the anti-Communist cause at the office in his absence. Joe McCarthy was being reined in, and the press was growing bolder now in its attacks, especially Joe Alsop, stalwart against him from the first, who had written a column discussing reports rampant in Washington about allegedly immoral relationships between McCarthy and his two most prominent aides. "This unfortunate affair has been handled with the greatest relish by the Red faction in our office," Brown's city-room spy, Newton Fulbright, wrote him in March 1954. Complaining that he himself had not been able to get any anti-Communist pieces on the editorial page and that the Sunday paper under Herzberg was also closed to him, Fulbright added, "I can't wait till you get back here and see what's going on." With so much else to absorb him, Brown nevertheless retained much of his anti-Communist zeal while in Paris. When Buchwald came back from Ireland with a pointed piece narrating his efforts to check into the genealogy of the McCarthy clan—it traced through alleged multiple rapings and pillagings by the black McCarthy branch of the family and concluded, "No one knows where they are now"—Brown killed it, according to Buchwald, who sold it to *The New Republic.* Now, in the spring of 1954 as McCarthy neared his Waterloo, Brown ordered the Paris city desk not to run Albert Einstein's picture on the front page on the occasion of his seventy-fifth birthday because, as staff members remembered Brown's sentiment, the physicist was a fellow-traveling "peace nut." And when Herbert Philbrick wrote him expressing anxieties similar to Fulbright's and wondering what was in store for him and the paper, Brown wrote back reassuringly that he would return to New York for good in early May and renew his association with Philbrick. He added: "I have no intention of allowing anything serious to happen to the Herald Tribune and you can be sure that my point of view will be made quite plain before much longer."

VIII

Talent kept flowing into the *Tribune* even as its troubles mounted and defections grew. In 1951, the year master reporter Peter Kihss left for the *Times,* a new drama critic arrived who turned out to be the best in the *Tribune*'s history and, after the retirement of the *Times*'s Brooks Atkinson in 1960, reigned for nearly twenty-five more years as the unchallenged dean of U.S. newspaper drama critics.

Quiet, with a dry wit to his speech and writing, Walter F. Kerr* was serious but never dull about his lifelong affair with the theater. He wrote about it with

---

* Born in 1913, he was a year younger than Walter B. Kerr, the *Tribune* foreign correspondent and later foreign editor and Washington bureau chief.

a grace, passion, and authority that grew out of deep immersion in his subject and a practical knowledge of the working stage that began when he was a student at Northwestern. Starting in 1938, he taught and directed drama at Catholic University in Washington for eleven intensive years. As early as 1941 he was collaborating on material for Broadway productions and by 1944 had his first solid credit in the big time with the Theatre Guild production of his play *Sing Out, Sweet Land,* which ran for 103 performances. Material that he and his wife, Jean, had developed with Kerr's students at Catholic turned into the 1949 musical revue *Touch and Go,* which ran for six months both on Broadway and in London's West End. On the strength of this success, the Kerrs moved to a modest home in suburban New Rochelle to be near the heart of the theatrical world.

To his dismay, Kerr found scant interest in his creative gifts. But a rather professorial piece he wrote for the *Times* drama section attracted a large reader response, and Kerr began to grasp that his true talent was not as a creator for but as an analyst of the theater. For a year the Kerrs lived off their royalties from *Touch and Go* while Walter served, at thirty dollars a week, as drama critic for *Commonweal,* an intellectual Catholic journal. When he heard that the *Tribune* was looking for someone to replace Howard Barnes, Joe's alcoholic brother, as its theater critic, Kerr applied by letter to Whitie Reid. "It seemed like the least likely thing in the world," he recalled, but high-powered press agent Richard Maney, who was a regular at Bleeck's and had done the publicity for *Touch and Go,* and others in the theater world who knew of Kerr's rich background and amiable disposition lobbied hard for him. He was offered a one-month tryout but insisted on three; reviewing under *Commonweal*'s leisurely weekly deadline for a small, select readership was very different from grinding out a pithy piece under the excruciating one-hour deadline for New York's second most influential paper, with its substantial effect on the commercial fate of each production.

He wrote too much in the beginning—*Variety* called his first review longer than the play—and had to learn not to ramble and how to keep in the background all the historical and philosophical inventory he had gathered during the long courtship of his muse. "No one wants to read about catharsis in a first-night notice," Kerr noted; his heavyweight insights ran Sundays in the drama section. Well before the tryout period was up, they gave him the job. He reviewed 101 productions that first season, at the end of which he was widely rated as the strictest but brainiest newspaper critic in town.

His reputation as a serious critic would be built mainly on his careful, instructive, and lively Sunday articles and the books that largely grew out of them, but it was his first-night reviews—almost literally criticism on the run—that made him a household name in New York. Evenings when he had a play to review were always an ordeal for him because he knew the price in human effort and hope that went into each production yet had to distance himself from them to perform his vital function rigorously. For him there was no other way.

At first he and Jean used to take the train into the city on review nights, but worrying about schedules being met only added to his anxiety, so they would drive and leave time for dinner, usually at Bleeck's or Sardi's, joining Brooks Atkinson of the *Times* and his wife once a month or so. Kerr's first rule of reviewing was only one drink before the curtain—a relaxer. Then a short walk to the theater, where he sat on the aisle of the fourth or fifth row center, at the end opposite Atkinson's. He would have preferred the last row because, when he himself had mounted productions, he had begun on stage, in close with the actors, then retreated to the front rows of the orchestra to see how the show played, then finally went to the back of the house for maximum perspective and to hear how the lines carried. Sitting close also made him pivot his head a lot to follow the action. But the prestige of his paper demanded the up-front seating. And the aisle, of course, allowed him to make the necessary fast getaway at the final curtain. Note-taking, which he found vital to prevent his reviews from rambling and to brace his memory, was also much easier while aisle-sitting than being hemmed in on both sides. Soon he had the note-taking down to a science: he would take two pieces of yellow typing paper, fold them in half, making a nice little eight-page booklet, and assign each page a different critical use, the first for possible leads or tag lines for his review, the second for remarks on the lead performers, the third for other performers of note, the middle two pages for color—scenic design, costumes, flashy effects, anything that might make his copy come alive and be more graphic in rendering the spirit of the play—and a page for direction and music and choreography when needed. He became adept at thumbing through the pages in the dark and jotting without taking his eyes from the stage.

Walter Kerr always took his seat hopefully, for good plays were easier to review and gladdened him while bad ones consumed his energy in the hunt for redeeming qualities. "There's no worse feeling than when you've written three or four negative notices in a row and you want this one to be good," Kerr recalled, "and it isn't. It's a sinking feeling because you don't want a reputation as a chronic naysayer." Acute awareness of the weight his opening-night judgment bore often painfully restrained him from what would otherwise have been a spontaneous reaction, especially to comedy, of which he was a keen student and fan. Once, though, he nearly fell into the aisle laughing over the one-man performance of Victor Borge—and earned a reproachful stare from the starched Atkinson at the other end of the aisle.

Twenty minutes into most performances, he knew if anything of value was happening on the stage. He found it essential, though, to be cautious and never to make up his mind by the intermission for fear the second act would not hold up. And while not eager to go galloping off as the lone dissenter among the New York reviewing corps, he made it a fast rule during intermission never to discuss the show with his peers—or anyone else, even Jean, whose reaction he could generally guess. Instead, there would be a pleasant chat about anything else with Richard Watts of the *Post* or Louis Kronenberger of *Time*; Atkinson stayed in his seat. By the curtain he knew his mind and was already framing possible leads as he and Jean dashed for a taxi to make the *Tribune*'s 11:55 deadline.

At the office there was no door to hide behind, no privacy or quiet. He was out there in the goldfish bowl of a city room with the clock running and his wits whirling and all of Broadway awaiting his verdict. "I used to trick myself to help concentrate—to get the right mental set—to know I had to move quickly and precisely," he remembered. "I used to adopt the prim, in-charge mentality that my mother would have had if she were addressing the problem, as in 'Now you're going to *sit* down at this typewriter and you're *going* to do this, and you're going to do it *right.*' Not that my mother ever wrote." Drama editor Otis Guernsey had told him on taking the job that he would bleed to death every opening night, "and he was right. You really do sweat it out—and tear your hair if you think it's going badly. You're really in the oven—it's such a delicate thing —and it's got to be done, and you want it to be at least defensible—and sometimes you know you've got a bum review on your hands and five minutes to go and you just can't do a thing about it." As a literary form, he found the opening-night review an abomination because it got fed into the machinery in pieces, with only his wife to screen it for him against frantic incoherence; by the end of his *Tribune* career, he still had not accustomed himself to the routine and had to take medicine for high blood pressure. But he had the satisfaction of knowing that what he did was good, and in his day no one was better at rendering a thoughtful verdict as quickly as the marketplace demanded.

IX

Even while his brother in Paris was reasserting his anti-Communist impulses, Whitie Reid was indirectly revealing the gulf that had opened between him and Brown. The brothers, in effect, symbolized the two wings of the Republican Party, just as their parents had. In addressing the annual banquet of the *Yale Daily News,* on which he had served as an undergraduate, Whitie hinted broadly at the difficulty the *Tribune* had had in maintaining its editorial integrity a few years earlier when the whole climate of political debate bordered on hysteria. If one had so much as suggested that the federal government should "do something to safeguard health—so it need not be a prerogative of only the well-to-do—straightway one was accused of being Socialist or Marxist. . . . Those were the days when it was hard for a Republican to speak out for what was decent and a little bit forward-looking without getting a barrage of mail." Now, in 1954, with the arrival of the moderating Eisenhower administration, he assured his young Yale listeners that the schism was being healed.

Whitie Reid dwelled in a paradise of self-deception that year, as if unaware that growing financial perils would soon dwarf all his good intentions and make them, and him, appear to be impediments to the *Tribune*'s survival. That spring he rejoiced over the paper's receipt of the Ayer Cup for typographic excellence among all U.S. dailies—the highest recognition of the streamlined makeup he had had a large hand in fashioning the previous year. It was the eighth time in the twenty-four years of the Ayer competition that the *Tribune* had been named the handsomest American newspaper (plus twelve honorable mentions); the *Times* had won six times, and only one other paper, a small Illinois daily, had won even twice. But good looks were not boosting sales or advertising any more than good intentions had.

Toward the end of that summer Whitie tried to rally the editorial staff to improve the product. But it was a wan, tentative, and badly belated message. "Our aim is to make reading the Herald Tribune as compelling as possible," he wrote in a two-page open memo, adding:

> It no longer seems good enough to come out with a well-balanced digest of news that could serve as a course in government. We want the paper out of the ivory tower and an accurate reflection of life itself in this somewhat difficult and turbulent time. . . .
>
> To win the newspaper niche in New York that the Herald Tribune deserves, it has got to be so obviously more interesting than other papers that its supremacy is unmistakable. . . .

But how to gain that recognition? The memo spoke of more "news features," more attention to the suburbs, shorter page-one stories whenever possible, and writing with "good taste and simple, direct language." He was the dutiful Dutch boy inserting a finger in the dike about to burst upon him.

The very week Whitie's memo was circulating, his mother was fending off reports that a sale of the paper was being negotiated with the Cowles publishing company. She had, in fact, had two meetings with Gardner Cowles aimed not at selling the *Tribune* but at attracting an investment in it. Cowles now responded to her plea to clear the air on the matter by advising her he had told inquirers that he understood the *Tribune* was definitely not for sale—"a completely honest answer because I have never felt you would want to relinquish control." And that, of course, was a principal reason the paper could not attract funding from outsiders; why sustain the Reids' control when they had not demonstrated competence to make the paper a money-earner? Their appeal left no rationale for investment in the *Tribune* except civic conscience—i.e., the belief that, as edited, the paper was an invaluable national and party resource and had to be perpetuated. However admiring, no one so far approached was willing to pay for this privilege.

Whitie, meanwhile, continued his largely ceremonial role, presiding that fall over the twenty-fourth annual Herald Tribune Forum in place of his mother and fussing endlessly over notes on his three-by-five index cards in order to get his introductory remarks before each speaker just right. His real role at the paper had become, in the eyes of many, that of protector against the ambitions of his brother. When Brown was elevated in February 1954 to vice president of the *Tribune* and president of its French subsidiary, far-leftist deskman John Price confided in his diary that he might leave the paper after twenty-eight years because of his feeling that "Brownie, whom I consider Fascist-minded, is likely to shove aside his weak older brother and gain control after their mother dies. I think he would turn the HT into a Hearst-type rag, which would be very unpleasant to work for even if I did not get fired out of hand. . . . But I feel fairly safe as long as Mrs. Reid is alive and Whitie is editor." Many others shared his apprehension.

It was not misplaced. Brown Reid's intention of taking charge of the paper and leading it vigorously was transparent from the moment he returned from Paris early in May 1954. From his viewpoint, that intention was above any petty plotting for personal power. The 1954 losses were accumulating more heavily than those of the previous year, the worst ever. "The money was running out," he recalled, "and it was very clear that something had to be done to save the paper as a family enterprise, a national institution, and one of the great newspapers of the world." And with Bill Robinson gone and no dominating personality on the payroll to replace him, Brown saw himself as the chosen instrument—by his brother's default—to achieve that salvation. His aim, he said, was "to reach for new initiatives within the *Herald Tribune* tradition." And his mother encouraged him by effectively handing him supervision of the business side of the paper. Whitie remained, at least in theory, in charge of the editorial side, while as president his unexercised authority extended to both realms.

As he dug into the financial operations, working closely with treasurer A. V. Miller, Brown was shocked by how badly the situation had been allowed to deteriorate. But recriminations now were pointless. His mother was old and giving him his head; his brother was no businessman and made no pretense of being one, and Robinson, who had held the real power to manage and used it poorly, was gone. The only energetic executive Brown found on the business side was the dapper, lewd-humored circulation manager, Barney Cameron, who had been well trained on Scripps and Hearst papers on the West Coast and in Pittsburgh. In a long, explicit memo he drew up within weeks of Brown's return, Cameron spelled out a number of proposals that were soon to become a basic part of the paper's survival strategy. A survey of *Tribune* circulation had recently revealed that one-third of its readers were over fifty-five, 58 percent were over forty-five, and 82.5 percent were over thirty-five. Plainly, something had to be done to attract younger readers, he wrote, and while greater outlays for promotion and home delivery would undoubtedly help, "it is my sincere feeling that we have gone about as far as we can go in circulation with our present product"—about the same conclusion that Richard Pinkham had reached. And like the brainy Pinkham, the earthy Cameron called for an increase in light and entertaining features, which he thought could still rescue the Early Bird edition, along with an expanded sports section run on colored newsprint, service features like the "Worry Clinic," a daily horoscope ("of which there are many on the market"), a full page of pictures, and an expanded weather map in view of television's emphasis on that topic. This same sensibility applied to the grave Sunday problem led Cameron to conclude, "As I view Sunday circulation in the New York field, it takes a gimmick to sell the paper." The *Journal-American*'s gimmick in achieving a vast Sunday sale was comics; the *Times*'s was bulk. Suburban sections and "a Home section featuring many do-it-yourself features" would help the *Tribune* on Sunday but not a fraction as much as a pocket-sized television and radio magazine modeled after the enormously successful *TV Guide*—all ideas that the departed Pinkham, Parton, and Stanford and the still present Whitie Reid had unsuccessfully pressed on Helen Reid and Bill Robinson. But now a different Reid was listening. He heard, too, Cameron's most un-*Tribune*-like suggestion that in order to test the long-standing belief among them that circulation would rise considerably "if only the public had a real opportunity to sample our product," the paper ought to run a contest called "Tangle Towns," an eight-week-long series of puzzles each containing a batch of scrambled letters that when properly rearranged spelled the name of a municipality in the paper's region. Such an educational contest would "get results in New York *without hurting our prestige*" as it had succeeded for "fine newspapers from Boston to Seattle"; Cameron urged the *Tribune* to launch its version of Tangle Towns shortly after Labor Day.

Advertisers and others Brown spoke to told him the editorial product was inadequate: too thin, too formal. George Cornish was rated by his callow boss as a fine technician when it came to conventional handling of the news but "short on imagination," and imagination was what the paper needed. Brown became a regular fixture around the city room, where his brother had rarely been seen. The very prospect of his return had prompted renewed vigilance on the anti-Communist front and was almost certainly a factor in the decision to kill a long piece by Homer Bigart, then assigned to the Washington bureau, preceding the Army-McCarthy hearings and pointing out that for all his fulminations, McCarthy had not been responsible for rooting out a single authenticated Communist. Bigart's copy in covering the hearings, moreover, was carefully screened for anti-McCarthy sentiments and frequently toned down. Upon his return, so intense did Brown's interest prove in the ongoing hearings, which were to speed McCarthy's downfall, that while sitting in on the front-page makeup conference of May 17, he overruled George Cornish and directed that the lead story the next day should be about a week-long postponement in the hearings instead of the Supreme Court's monumental decision that morning unanimously outlawing segregation in the nation's public schools. When the *Times* first edition came up that night bannering the desegregation story, Richard Tobin, then promotion director of the *Tribune,* urged Cornish to follow suit, but the executive editor declined to confront Brown Reid, and the *Herald Tribune* was perhaps the only newspaper in the country to run an eight-column head on a routine political development in preference to a landmark in American social history. Whitie Reid recognized the blunder in a letter the next day to Eric Hawkins, commending him for the general attractiveness of the Paris edition and the major play it gave the Supreme Court story. But Whitie had failed to exert his own authority at home by mandating similar coverage.

Further evidence of the weight Brown was now throwing around came the following month with the dismissal of liberal Walter Millis, allegedly on the ground that his column, "Arms and Men," was not being well received by the *Tribune*'s syndicate customers (but then neither was Philbrick's "Red Underground"). The unacknowledged reason was almost certainly a pair of columns Millis had written strenuously objecting to the Atomic Energy Commission's decision to deny Robert Oppenheimer, supervisor of the development of the atomic bomb, further security clearance because of his acquaintance with known Communists and failure to report an approach made to him by a Red agent. Whitie, already disenchanted with the insufficiently servile Millis, did not object. But he by no means wilted entirely before his brother's incursions. "He'd push awfully hard for what he wanted," Whitie recalled. "Things got fairly abrasive when he had the nerve to take an editorial out of the paper, and I had to overrule him."

By September, with cash low after the usual summer slump in revenues and Sunday circulation at 528,000, down another 20,000 for the year, Brown made his first two major moves. Aided by family friend David Rockefeller, head of the Chase Bank, he persuaded the Massachusetts Mutual Life Insurance Company that the *Tribune* was more than just another cash-short business, that it had strong political pull in the White House, where it was the President's favorite paper, was a vital force in the necessary reshaping of the Republican Party to face the modern world, and in any other city but fiercely competitive New York would have been a rousing success. The insurance company granted the *Tribune* a $2,250,000 mortgage, enough to retire an existing mortgage with Mutual Benefit and leave the paper with some badly needed working capital. As a proviso, the operations of the paper were placed under the constant scrutiny of a committee of three quasi-trustees: Robert Whitfield, a recently retired Chase vice president recommended by Rockefeller; Roy Gasser, the pedantic New York attorney who represented Lady Jean Ward; and Brown Reid, who had no trouble persuading his aunt to join the rest of the family in agreeing to subordinate their notes against the paper to the mortgage. And since the Massachusetts Mutual money would be a stopgap at best, Brown paved the way for the family finally to convert its claim of more than eleven million dollars against the paper into preferred stock—an expedient reluctantly accepted within eighteen months, thereby opening the way at last to additional outside funding. These time-buying financial maneuvers served to vault Brown over his brother in their mother's eyes as her prime hope of keeping the *Tribune* in the family.

Brown now also threw his weight behind Barney Cameron's Tangle Towns proposal, and the promotional effort ran in the paper most of that fall with the accompanying hoopla—$25,000 in prizes, 1,000 spot commercial announcements on television and radio, thousands of subway and bus cards, billboards

in the suburbs, kits for school teachers. "It was distasteful," Whitie Reid recalled, "but things were grim, and we thought we'd give it a try." Along
Madison Avenue's advertising row, where the gimmick was seen as a sign of the
Tribune's weakness, the paper's salesmen argued to the contrary, describing it
as a device to get the public to sample their superior product. At the *Times,* the
Tangle Towns contest was viewed as a desperate measure. "You do that when
you run out of ideas," Ivan Veit summed up the *Times* consensus. In the view
of *Times* circulation manager Nat Goldstein, newspaper contests were "like
opium"—with only briefly pleasing effects and a cure for nothing.

To persuade new readers attracted by the contest that the *Tribune* was a
lively sheet and not a daily textbook, crime and entertainment news was given
more prominent play; photographs of sexy women, known on racier papers as
"cheesecake," now appeared in their more demure variation, and an anecdotal
book about celebrities called *Champagne Before Breakfast* by the *Tribune*'s
show-business columnist, Hy Gardner, by then on close terms with Brown Reid,
was serialized on the front page. The idea seemed to be working. Everyone was
talking about Tangle Towns, though not entirely favorably, librarians were
being besieged for research help by contest entrants, and *Tribune* circulation
rocketed to 400,000—a gain of some 60,000 sales a day, enough to cover the
costs of the promotion. What remained to be seen was what portion of the gain
the paper would hold.

While the results were being awaited, Whitie Reid took an initiative of his
own to ease the paper's financial crisis. He flew out to Fishers Island off eastern
Connecticut to meet with multimillionaire investor and philanthropist John
Hay Whitney, a strong Eisenhower backer and prominent supporter of and
contributor to the liberal Republican wing. Whitney's financial participation in
the paper would have had additional justification because of the close friendship
between the first Whitelaw Reid and Whitney's maternal grandfather, John
Hay, who had worked on the *Tribune* and had even run it for Reid during his
wedding trip. And Whitney, nine years Whitie's senior, was also a Yale man.
So there were social, political, family, and old-school ties between the Reids and
Jock Whitney that suggested the plausibility of his coming to the aid of the paper
if approached directly by the family rather than through an intermediary like
Bill Robinson, who had done so the year before.

On December 3, 1954, Whitney returned the financial and other data Whitie
had presented for his review and said that upon consultation with the managing
partner of his venture capital firm, J. H. Whitney & Company, he had decided
an investment in the *Tribune* of the scale required would be "inadvisable" in
light of his existing commitments. But Whitney concluded, in words foreshad-
owing his opposite decision three years later:

> I want you all [the Reids] to know, also, that I understand the emotional
> involvement which you have with the paper, and I realize fully that this is not just
> any business venture to be analyzed. Generations have woven these roots deep into

your hearts in an almost passionate attachment. I can share that feeling, but, after all, it is not my business or my child, and I must put my own affairs first. I know you understand this, but I wanted you surely to know that I am profoundly sympathetic to your problem.

Whitney's gracious but firm turndown spelled the end of Whitie Reid's tenuous hold on the *Tribune,* although his brother and mother would not deliver the coup de grace for several months. There was no clue to his awareness or resentment of his pending doom in Whitie's fond, cheery holiday note to Brown: "Your Flyway greens filled the house and gave all our rooms an especially Christmasy look. Nothing could have been more appreciated. . . . I can only say that you made Santa Claus seem very real. The best from us all and much gratefulness for all you did in honor of the 25th." But Whitie should have remained in no doubt that the season of goodwill was over when a few weeks into the new year *Editor & Publisher* ran an article headlined "Brownie Reid Guides Herald Trib Forward," called the Tangle Towns promotion "a spectacular success," and dwelled on the virtues of "young, war-hardened, serious-minded Ogden R. Reid, who charts the course and calls the signals for the business side of the Trib these days."

Tangle Towns was a bust; the entire circulation gain would be lost by September 1955. A quick fix was not the answer. The oversight committee, of which Brown and his aunt's nominee were in control, concluded that the *Tribune* could not survive under Whitie's ineffectual and indecisive leadership—and Helen Reid was forced by the facts to concur. "There was never any doubt that Whitie was the senior son and closer to H.R., especially in personal matters," Brown's wife, Mary Louise, said. "But Brown could deal with business people and bankers whereas Whitie did not relate well to these kinds of people." The solution of removing Whitie from the presidency was "a terribly, terribly painful one," Brown said, because "you couldn't have a better or finer brother. But Whitie's cast of mind was limited to the editorial side." His brother's ouster was "the hardest family moment" of Brown's life, "but there was no graceful way it could have been handled. No matter what I did it would have been hard on him."

It would not have been quite so hard, however, if Helen Reid had not compounded her mistake of installing one unqualified son in the presidency of the paper by replacing him with her other unqualified son, who was not yet thirty. An outsider of stature could have been recruited to take charge of the *Herald Tribune,* for all its financial problems; Whitie could have remained as editor with ceremonial duties and his authority limited primarily to the oversight of the editorial page, and Brown could have served as executive vice president while he gained seasoning and perhaps modesty to go with his energy. But Helen Reid did not want an outsider running her paper, any more than she wanted outsiders' money if it meant yielding control to them. No, it would have to be Brown or nobody; he had her spunk and ambition, and perhaps his youth was precisely what the paper needed. Whitie would succeed her as chairman, she would clear out of Brown's way and let him run the operation without her looking over his shoulder all the time, and on Barney Cameron's suggestion, fifty-four-year-old newspaper executive Frank W. Taylor, who had taken over Hearst's ailing *Milwaukee Sentinel* in 1942 and made it profitable over the next ten years before resigning in a policy dispute, would become executive vice president of the *Tribune* and provide Brown with solid daily counsel.

Whitie understood his mother's decision that he ought to be replaced; the replacement selected was another matter. "She was really rooting for me, but I guess I hadn't got things together enough," he said, "and she was in a corner." But the prospect of yielding his place to his younger brother was a heavy and humiliating blow. "I was really appalled that the editorial fortunes of the paper were being put into Brown's hands." His mother used all her considerable selling talents "to tell me I'd be bigger than ever as chairman," but he knew Brown would have the final word in all matters and that was unacceptable to him.

The night before the announcement was to be made of Brown's ascension, Whitie summoned those closest to him in the office—among them managing editor Everett Walker, city editor Fendall Yerxa, Sunday editor Joseph Herzberg, editorial-page editor August Heckscher, deputy edit-page editor Harry Baehr, and his own executive assistant, Jack Mearns—to a midnight meeting at his apartment in the Dorset Hotel on Fifty-fourth Street west of Fifth Avenue to talk over whether anything might be done to prevent the White Prince's surrender to the Dark Prince. The only member of the editorial high command not on hand was executive editor George Cornish, who was seen by the rest of them, as Yerxa put it, "as a straddler—always smooth but notoriously cautious." Whitie felt Cornish had been "sliding along with the times, letting Brownie infiltrate more and more into the newsroom"—as if Whitie himself did not bear the main responsibility for his younger brother's usurpations. His absence from Whitie's meeting would always bother Cornish for what it said about how he was viewed by the other editors. His highest duty, though, he felt in his own heart, was not to take sides between Helen Reid's warring sons but to serve only the paper. To the others, the time for such evenhandedness was past, for it was precisely their own sense of duty to the paper's imperiled integrity that drew them to the meeting. "It was a terrible spectacle to watch the family tearing itself apart in that fratricidal struggle," Heckscher said.

The gathering of editors turned out to be little more than a handwringing session, at the end of which they designated managing editor Walker to speak with Helen Reid the following day. "But Whitie called me early the next morning and said not to bother seeing his mother as everything had been set and it would do no good," Walker remembered; Whitie vacillated to the last. That morning, having heard about the midnight meeting at Whitie's, Helen called Walker to her office anyway and explained why she thought the change would be best for the paper. She added that "the bank had insisted" on the change—apparently a reference to the position of Robert Whitfield, the Chase Bank nominee on the oversight committee that Brown had been instrumental in establishing—and that Brown would do a good job and prove easy to work with. "She also asked me to do everything I could to help him." Within a year, all those who had attended Whitie's hotel meeting were gone from the *Tribune* except Harry Baehr, whom Brown placed in charge of the editorial page and then replaced, and Everett Walker, whom Brown effectively stripped of power and left in limbo.

To preserve the appearance of family unity, Whitie made no public statement of protest, appearing to accept the title of chairman in place of his formally retiring mother, who nevertheless retained ultimate authority by virtue of her controlling stock ownership. But Whitie's pride would not permit him to remain under his brother's shadow. "She begged me to use my feminine wiles on him not to leave the paper," Joan Reid recalled of her mother-in-law's efforts to reconcile Whitie to his demotion, "but I told her it was not my place to interfere and that if she hadn't been able to convince him to stay, it wasn't my place to try to. Whitie behaved with great filial propriety and would never have hurt her willingly." Nevertheless, he left. "I couldn't give her any comfort," Whitie said. He decided the best way he could help the paper was to go off and try to make some money, so he went to California to look into the helicopter business, but nothing came of it and he flew down to Venezuela for a time and went exploring in the jungle. Eventually he got into the food-vending business in a modest way, divorced Joan and remarried, and devoted himself to his new family, tennis, horses, skiing, and the Fresh Air Fund, for which he helped to develop a permanent camping site. But he never again worked for the *Tribune* or for any other paper; if you were a Reid, there was only one.

Later in the day that Whitie's fate was announced, his chosen chief editorial writer, Augie Heckscher, came upon Helen Reid in her office, holding her head in her hands and looking disconsolate. "This is the most difficult moment I've known," she confided to him, "since my little daughter died."

Two months shy of his thirtieth birthday, Brown had the paper. The very aspects of his character that stirred such trepidation among the staff were also, oddly, a cause for hope. Even his fiercest ideological foes on the paper shared in it. John Price wrote in his diary of the change he had foreseen: "Brownie is very much an aggressive personality. I think the coasting era has ended or will end pretty soon, there will be a lot of drastic innovations, and the paper will become a profitable property or collapse."

15

Enter the
Perfect Patron

The last of the Reids to preside over the *Herald Tribune,* the surviving confluence of two of the four great newspapers founded in nineteenth-century New York, was not tentative about assuming control.

Ogden Rogers Reid was the mirror opposite of his brother in the forcefulness of personality that he displayed, the hopefulness he radiated to the staff, and the high opinion he held of himself. Brown was as much a leader by nature as Whitie was not, but now there was little time to refine the techniques of leadership or to acquire a vision of what the paper should become in order to achieve prosperity in the ever more deadly competition in New York's communications industry. Brown Reid's sins were therefore ones of commission; his older brother's had been ones of omission. If Whitie had had Brown's energy and decisiveness, if Brown had had Whitie's taste and reflectiveness, the *Tribune* might have remained the Reids'.

Brown's first task was to transform himself into a judicious executive and statesman of his profession. His gun-toting, motorcycling, Red-baiting days he put behind him now as he donned blue serge suits and silver ties and went forth to reclaim the *Tribune*'s rightful place as a national and global force. Within weeks of his taking power, he was presenting to the annual convention at the Waldorf of Sigma Delta Chi, the honorary national society of journalists, his credo for a free press:

Today, we are the first estate and not the fourth, for without the free press, there can be neither freedom nor free government.

We must help make history—not just write it. A passive press that only records, will write itself and freedom into oblivion.

The story, with the "creed" set in boldface, was generously displayed on page five of the next morning's *Tribune,* accompanied by a photograph of the paper's new leader. "In touching on the Communist peril in today's world," the paper went on to report, "Mr. Reid said: 'The tensions of the cold war, fed by Soviet subversion and propaganda, place a premium on accurate, dispassionate reporting.' " Anti-Communism remained his war cry, but the domestic danger receded in his recital of social evils; indeed, he urged chief editorial writer Heckscher to be on the lookout for civil liberties causes that the paper could support, by way of ridding himself of the McCarthyite label. Co-existence with the Soviets on terms of parity, however, was unthinkable. During his interview for a job on the editorial page early in Brown's presidency, Nicholas King offered the conviction that the United States must match the Soviet initiative anywhere on earth, to which Brown replied, "Match—and surpass."

While ideology and ceremony aroused his enthusiasm, Brown was no dilettante about his duties. From the first, he was all over the place, displaying his intention to lead and motivate. He was a demanding boss but worked long hours and had his hand in all aspects of the operation. He had a fetish for the telephone, wielding it like a field marshal summoning his officers to receive their latest advisories and issue them instructions. "Let's stir the pot," he would instruct his executive secretary, Dee Kellett, on arrival in the morning. "There was the constant illusion of his being fantastically busy," she recalled. At editorial-page conferences, his familiarity with world and national issues made him more intrusive than Whitie had been, although Brown was hardly an original or profound thinker. But he had to make his presence and outlook known, even if in redundant ways. He would scan an editorial already in type declaring, "The State Department must be told in no uncertain terms that . . ." and insert "forthright and" after the "in" for emphasis. Told that the change would require the entire paragraph to be reset, he said, "Yes, I know—but it's important." His enthusiasm could take a similarly unprofessional form when he conferred with his newsroom editors. City editor Fendall Yerxa remembered Brown's setting a meeting at a perversely early morning hour, then showing up late, "rubbing his hands in glee over some presumed journalistic coup for which he took personal credit and adding, 'Well, I guess we wiped the *Times*'s eye with that one.' It was embarrassing and humiliating."

Yet his zest for combat was a welcome change in the city room, where Brown appeared in the early days of his reign and spoke to the gathered staff about the *Tribune*'s bright future. Platitudes, uttered in his nasal, grating voice, did not readily inspire his listeners. What did register was his caring, and the commitment behind it. "He was serious and ponderous and young," recalled

William Safire, then a publicist with Tex McCrary's firm, which had the *Tribune* as a client during Brown's presidency, "and when you are all those things, you invite a lot of resentment. But Brown was no softie as his brother had been, he had a sense of history—and he wanted that paper to live."

To save it, he put his own people into key spots. Chief among them was to be the new executive vice president, Frank Taylor, who was found, he told the staff upon introducing him at the city-room pep rally, after a nationwide search for the best possible man. Taylor's old West Coast friend, Barney Cameron, now elevated to business manager of the *Tribune,* had boosted him as "a delightful and knowledgeable guy" with "tremendous ability on both the editorial and business side." Those virtues were not immediately apparent to the staff. Taylor told the city-room assemblage of big but unspecified plans afoot, of the winning team that would be fielded, of their competitors' future resentment "when we put our thumb in their eye"—and of how "I always feel I should have two paychecks, one to put in the bank and the other to wrap around my heart." But he was a bona fide newspaperman who had come up through the reportorial ranks before shifting to the business side and had reputedly enjoyed considerable independence in the Hearst organization, where he was said to have stood up to the old man. Besides, typography was his hobby—he had a small printing press in his basement—so maybe that heart he wanted to wrap his paycheck around had genuine printer's ink pumping through it.

More important than Taylor in the day-to-day operation was the new city editor Brown installed to succeed the conscientious but lackluster Yerxa, who happily moved to Wilmington, Delaware, to become executive editor of the morning-evening monopoly paper there. Luke P. Carroll swiftly and loudly dominated the *Tribune* city room as only Engelking had in his prime, and his fealty to Brown was unquestioned. By background, he was an unlikely choice. A "dead-end kid" brought up on the far west side of midtown Manhattan, Carroll had had only a parochial school education when he went to work as a district police reporter for the old City News agency in the Depression. Joining the *Tribune* in the same capacity, he demonstrated extremely modest skills as a writer, but he was a resourceful, reliable fact-gatherer who knew his way around the troubled streets of the big town, and when he was assigned to Chicago to become the paper's Midwest reporter, he did well there, too. Whitie Reid, who found him "a rough-and-ready sort," brought Carroll in as his assistant, and his native intelligence and ambition soon asserted themselves. Promoted to the newly coined job of news editor, working as a liaison officer between Cornish and the city, national, and foreign desks, Carroll watched Brown Reid advance on his brother's terrain and cast his lot with him; Brown, without many friends on the news staff, reciprocated.

A throwback to the boomer tradition of city editors, Carroll made his presence felt by a no-nonsense, unintellectualized approach to hard breaking news. If his limitations as a story formulator and pencil editor were apparent, so were his efficiency and doggedness. He refused to coddle talent but managed, unlike Yerxa, to extract raises for some of the deserving city-room denizens. Even those who said he dressed like a bookie and called him "Old Yellowshoes" for the footwear he sported to match his camel's-hair coat, agreed he was fair in parceling out assignments. Crime news was his favorite. The murder of a police captain's daughter he insisted be given a three-column headline on the front page, and he remained enough of a votary at the shrine of scoop journalism to allocate a couple of hundred dollars to enlist the exclusive services of a tipster who promised to finger the murderers of mobster Frank Costello. His class difference from most of the rest of the city room also made Carroll more tolerant than they of Hy Gardner, who in his capacity as *Tribune* show-business columnist had inducted Brown Reid into the world of celebrity and now became his informal court jester, always ready with a joke to brighten the day of his incessantly serious boss. Gardner occasionally came by the city desk with celebrities in tow, introduced them to Carroll, got him show tickets, and otherwise solidified his alliance with the starstruck city editor, who was ordinarily a cold-lipped disciplinarian. Not surprisingly, entertainment personalities began to command more attention in the *Tribune*'s news columns, and Gardner's appointment to the job of public relations director for the paper aggravated the fear of staff purists that its seriousness as a news disseminator was gravely jeopardized. Accentuating this concern was Brown's demotion of managing editor Everett Walker to work with Joe Herzberg on the troubled Sunday edition without providing the pair, both highly accomplished news technicians but viewed as allies of the dethroned Whitie Reid, with the money or manpower to attack the problem. Only George Cornish was left in place as executive editor —his reward, apparently, for having been receptive to, or at least polite toward, Brown's newsroom incursions before the transfer of power. Cornish still presided over the daily news conference that supervised the layout of the paper, and while this function allowed the continued exercise of his highly regarded news judgment, his chronic disinclination to back that gift with the force of personality made him more than ever a conciliating rather than a commanding or creative presence in the newsroom. Luke Carroll, while nominally outranked by Cornish, became the driving figure on the news staff, and it was he to whom Brown Reid turned to do his bidding.

The editorial page he kept for his own domain, as Whitie had, but where his brother had had Geoffrey Parsons and then Augie Heckscher as shapers of the *Tribune*'s official opinion, Brown selected a more sedate figure. When Heckscher, like Yerxa, chose not to remain on the *Tribune* under Brown—he became director of the Twentieth Century Fund, a research foundation—the editorial-page job went to his deputy, Harry Baehr, who had been writing lucid, if not precisely arresting, editorials for the paper for fifteen years. A donnish, prematurely bald man who always looked wise beyond his years, Baehr had graduated from Dartmouth and gone on to earn his doctorate in history at Columbia under Allan Nevins; his dissertation, a history of the *Tribune* from the Civil War on, was published in 1936—a largely admiring but nonetheless creditable study. He joined the paper the following year, writing mainly for the Sunday edition. Under Parsons, he showed a rare gift for taking other men's opinions and turning them into judicious, persuasive little essays of grace and conviction. It was not that he had no convictions of his own but rather that he knew the paper's historical and institutional point of view, largely concurred in it, especially as it had evolved under Parsons and Millis, and found fulfillment in expounding it well. Like Cornish, he had exceptional judgment and a temperament that did not clamor for attention; the pair of them might have served with distinction as State Department career officers. "He had the most perfect dignity of any man I ever saw," his younger colleague Nicholas King said of Baehr. His presence was unquestionably a moderating force on Brown, who had the good sense to rely on him. Harry Baehr's loyalty went not to Brown or any of the Reids but, like Cornish's, to the paper itself.

With his team in place, Brown Reid was ready to act boldly. A year and a half earlier, two of the Reids' wisest counselors, newly installed Washington bureau chief Roscoe Drummond and retired edit-page chief Parsons, had drafted separate memos proposing that the *Tribune* consider a major departure in news coverage by stressing interpretive reporting. Drummond, a self-effacing little man who styled himself "a liberal conservative," had won wide respect as an editor and columnist for *The Christian Science Monitor,* which was in effect a daily newsmagazine; he urged a similar approach on the *Tribune* by noting: "Spot news has become a declining—and I believe sharply declining—salable commodity for a morning newspaper" because the conventional approach was based on news already a dozen hours old and familiar to most readers through radio and television. To keep itself a mandatory morning habit, the *Tribune* ought selectively to cover the biggest news with "three-dimensional reporting" that brought events into immediate perspective by melding background on their causes, analysis of their meaning, and a carefully drawn assessment of their likely consequences. There was no point in pretending any longer, Drummond added, that the *Tribune* was or should be a paper of "exhaustive record," but there might be frequent occasions "when we could cover one thing with such imagination and detail that we will begin to create the impression of indispensability among our readers." Parsons recommended essentially the same tack:

> . . . [T]he older conception of objective reporting is no longer adequate without interpretive material to supplement it. In a sense our leadership in creating and printing columnists was a pioneer job in just this function. . . .
>
> What I am suggesting here . . . might be termed background articles. Perhaps "objective interpretation" suggests the precise goal. That is to say, they should give neither the opinions of the writer, nor his predictions, nor his guesses, but the news of leaders, popular reactions, journalistic opinions, stories about people, happenings which are not exactly news, and in general all the factual material that serves to set the bare facts of an event or a situation against its background, past, present and future. . . .

To free staff members to produce such material, which might include articles of a kind not ordinarily carried in the *Tribune* such as "[a] résumé of a strange murder trial, a portrait sketch of a prominent figure in any walk of life, social and economic changes in the life of a city or a country," the paper would rely on wire-service reports of routine news, provide time to plan and develop these new kinds of stories, and display them "in such fashion that our readers will quickly realize what they are getting." Both men were saying, in short, that the *Tribune* ought not to be locked in any longer by conventional notions of "news" as the very latest events, which might instead serve as no more than a point of departure for a more profound set of disclosures that were timely in a general sense but became "news" by the very prominence accorded them, their freshness of subject, richness of revelation, and the clearer understanding they brought to the attentive reader.

Such a reconceptualization of the *Herald Tribune* had been beyond the imaginings of Helen and Whitie Reid, but given the critical financial health of the paper whose control he had been handed, Brown Reid might have entertained a basic recasting of its news presentation. He was not blessed, however, with a venturesome mind—only an energetic disposition. His ideas were prosaic in the extreme, which is not to say that he was unintelligent. But he could not see, any more than the rest of his family, that the larger risk for the paper was not in change but in failing to change. The men he enlisted or elevated to key positions—Frank Taylor, Barney Cameron, Luke Carroll, and Hy Gardner— were all experienced professionals who saw the *Tribune*'s salvation only in greater appeal to the masses by simpler presentation of the news, leavened by entertaining features that distracted rather than instructed readers. Theirs was a plausible enough strategy, but it betrayed the history and nature of the *Herald Tribune* and did not address its embattled position in the New York market, where the tabloids and the Hearst and Scripps-Howard evening entries were amply providing readers with all the airy distraction they could want. The *Tribune* would have been better advised to heed Drummond and Parsons by emphasizing a qualitative difference in its traditional serious engagement with news and culture. Brown Reid, perhaps because he was himself so unseasoned, took only those steps that seemed to promise immediate improvement in the paper's balance sheet; grand designs would have to await prosperity. Meanwhile, he would try to emphasize the paper's importance as a political force, a special case in American journalism by virtue of its links to the Eisenhower administration; the President, after all, read the *Herald Tribune* every morning, and his partiality to it was no secret.

Brown's most immediate problem was the Sunday edition, the paper's chief moneymaker, which dipped to sales of 519,000 in May; if it continued downward, triggering mass defection by advertisers, the whole enterprise would be lost. To halt the slide, Brown promptly implemented Cameron's ardent call for inclusion in the Sunday package of a pocket-sized magazine devoted to television and radio listings for the coming week and related articles. Such an addition, handy and useful throughout the week as the highly successful *TV Guide* had proven, would in itself be worth the cost of the paper and allow a badly needed increase in the price from twenty cents to a quarter. Every effort was made to adopt a format typographically resembling *TV Guide* as closely as possible without inviting legal reprisal. Launched in May under the editorship of Hy Gardner, the miniature TV magazine was an immediate success. Not only did it neutralize the higher newsstand price, which would otherwise certainly have driven sales still farther down, but in fact it sent the Sunday circulation surging by 50,000, so that when the September ABC figures were released, they showed the long-troubled edition with average sales for the prior six-month period 7,000 copies ahead of the year-earlier figure. The slide had been stopped and reversed.

Brown ordered several other editorial improvements that were announced with fanfare, including the addition of between ten and twenty news columns per day, the bulk of them to fatten the financial section, and four new foreign correspondents. Soon after Labor Day 1955, with still louder fanfare, the *Tribune* appeared in a new three-section package, of which the most notable departure was a sports section printed on mint-green newsprint. Other papers, especially of a sporty or sensationalist tone, had used colored newsprint as an eye-catcher. Why not the *Tribune,* argued Frank Taylor, who had worked with it during his years in the Hearst chain. Since the color was restricted to the sports section with the daily radio and television listings in the back—all basically recreational subjects—the essential dignity of the paper would not be affected. Accessory units called balloon formers were installed high above the massive presses to weave the green paper into the regular run, and an additional cost of several hundred dollars a night for the tinted paper and the added handling it required was budgeted for the purely decorative change. The green may have evoked playing fields or money or mouthwash, but it altered nothing essential. It was in keeping, however, with the tactics that Brown Reid and his managers were adopting to "brighten" their product—more short articles, fewer long ones, bigger pictures, greater attention to show-business celebrities and the bosoms thereof, and the regular inclusion of contests of the Tangle Towns variety of word game, among them one featuring biblical names—even if all that meant cheapening the paper. Numbers were the unabashed object now instead of more Ayer Cups or prizes for literary content, none of which had gained the *Tribune* financial success. Absent from this line of reasoning was any recognition of the countervailing argument that what had denied the paper prosperity was not an excess of editorial quality but a shortage of working capital and enlightened ownership willing to spend money in order to make it.

One innovation of the new three-section *Tribune* did have an editorially substantive purpose. The front page of the second section, which inside was devoted to women's features and financial news, was given over entirely to city and suburban news. Here was a way to distinguish the paper from the *Times,* with its top-heavy national and international flavor; the *Tribune* would henceforth prominently display local area news, and while the suburban material consisted in large part of mere snippets from outlying communities lumped indiscriminately under a catch-all department heading, it was at least a start toward organized coverage of the most dynamic growth sector of the metropolitan population.

Two weeks after the greening of the *Tribune,* the Early Bird edition was unobtrusively dropped, along with the supplemental pages produced for the *Tribune* edition of *This Week.* These two economies, laying to rest Bill Robinson's principal contribution to the editorial side of the paper, saved some $700,000 at scant sacrifice of content. The savings, added to a half-million-dollar increase in circulation revenue from the higher-priced Sunday edition and a 4 percent rise in advertising linage, allowed the paper to close out 1955 with a profit of $45,000 after four years of deepening deficits. Brown had succeeded, furthermore, in enhancing the political stature of the paper. At the Geneva summit conference that summer, he led a large party of *Tribune* people on hand to cover and support President Eisenhower's efforts. A big batch of the Paris edition was trucked in each day to service the American delegation and international press corps; no other English-language paper was logistically capable of such a showing. When the President suffered a heart attack later in the year, Brown ordered the Paris paper to issue an extra on a Sunday. The feat required much dashing about and bending of French laws but once again boosted the *Tribune*'s standing in Europe. Domestic ties to the White House were also strengthened through capital bureau chief Drummond, who during his work on the Marshall Plan staff in Europe had come to know Eisenhower, then heading up the North Atlantic Treaty Organization, and helped draft the statement announcing his run for the presidency. Brown's own cordial relationship with Vice President Nixon—Bert Andrews's principal legacy to the paper—continued to grow. And midway through the year, *Tribune* White House correspondent Robert Donovan was selected to write a book, based on materials put exclusively at his disposal by administration officials, that would purportedly reveal the inside story of Eisenhower's first term in office.

All these favorable developments prompted *Business Week* to put a picture of Brown Reid on the cover of its first issue of 1956 and portray him inside the magazine as a striving young publisher in pitched battle against fierce competition—all true, as far as it went. What was not true was Brown's assertion that the *Tribune* had ended 1955 "comfortably in the black." And the article kindly omitted the dispiriting fact that for all the progress Brown's activity had apparently generated, his paper was still losing ground to the *Times.* The latter had gained five times as much advertising linage for the year as the *Tribune,* whose ad volume thereby dropped from 49 percent to 45 percent of the *Times*'s total. Worse still, the *Times* had at last broken out of its circulation plateau around the 500,000 level on its daily edition and by year's end was outselling the *Tribune* in its suburban strongholds of Westchester and Bergen counties and even in some Connecticut towns like Westport. Brown Reid, though, had stirred the pot.

II

In 1956 the *Tribune* took longer strides toward apparent economic well-being. Its Sunday edition added 40,000 sales, reaching to just below 575,000, and its weekday circulation climbed 20,000; in both categories, it kept pace with the growth of the *Times*. Revenues grew by more than 7 percent, and the paper's profit amounted to $110,000, which, while still far from being "comfortably in the black," represented movement in the right direction. But the inadequacies of the paper and its managers became more apparent through the year.

The pocket-sized Sunday television magazine, for example, was in fact a shabby little item. Run on a shoestring, graphically uninviting, it was edited with one hand by Hy Gardner, who, according to Marie Torre, the paper's television news columnist and a subordinate editor of the magazine, "was always coming up with harebrained ideas for articles. He had a very narrow perspective of news—he was not a real newspaperman." But he was quite good at publicity and adept at obtaining, for little or no money, articles by leading television personalities whose artistic stature would thereby be enhanced while the *Tribune* benefited from the glamour of their bylines. A typical issue offered comedian Red Skelton writing on "Mirth Needs Warmth," high-collared singer Dorothy Collins on her own inspirational wellsprings, children's entertainer "Captain Kangaroo" on the good taste of tots, a psychiatrist on the popularity among older women of androgynously mannered pianist Liberace, and the president of one of New York's independently owned television stations on why viewers should tune to his channel. It was almost all contrived, self-serving, and obviously ghost-written. The only honest materials in the package were the critical columns by John Crosby, whose standing as a cultural arbiter and social conscience had sprouted during television's phenomenal infancy, and the news and gossip pieces on the industry assembled by the *Tribune*'s new Hollywood reporter, Joe Hyams, and Miss Torre in New York. The fluff content was easily rationalized: the articles were only window dressing for the program listings. But such insubstantiality was not the hallmark of the *Herald Tribune*, which prided itself on the expert knowledge of its staff writers on even the most specialized subjects, from Walter Terry on dance to Ernest Kehr on stamps to Florence Osborn on bridge to Walter Hamshar covering the waterfront.

This junking tendency was further revealed with the debut in September 1956 of the *Tribune*'s new Sunday magazine. Called *Today's Living*, it was aimed at bulking up the Sunday package and, with cute covers of painted suburban motifs, winning away from the *Times*'s plump Sunday magazine a portion of the Seventh Avenue apparel manufacturers' advertising. Here was a chance to display flair, wit, and usefulness to the paper's prime suburban constituency; instead it was handed a dog. Featured were antic exercises in popular psychology and self-help, like "What Your Boss *Really* Means," skimpy civics lessons and social insights ("You *Can* Fight City Hall" by the mayor of Mamaroneck), chuckly outdoors pieces on bird-watching, fox-hunting, and other pursuits of the gentry, and some soft fiction and lightly satirical cartoons. It was trivial and unoriginal in conception and clumsy in execution; its writing tended to ramble and talk down to its readers. The only first-rate entries in *Today's Living* were the informative, ungushing fashion articles by the *Tribune* women's feature editor, Eugenia Sheppard.

The incompetence of the new magazine signaled not only the continuing failure to create a distinctive Sunday paper to replace the skinny imitator of the overstuffed *Times* but also the lack of resolve to exploit the political, social, and religious affinities of suburbanites—so like the *Tribune*'s own—whose activities it declined to cover in a serious, organized way. Even the few solid stories and the roundup of tidbits it had begun to carry on the first page of the second section as part of the September 1955 repackaging were eroded whenever material deemed more promotable, like Hyams's multi-part series on Clark Gable, presented itself. Covering the suburbs in a way that might have attracted substantial numbers of readers would undoubtedly have been a costly, space-consuming operation. But the money the paper was spending on game contests would have bought the services of a number of outlying correspondents and stringers, and the money spent on green newsprint for the sports pages would have bought additional white paper that could have been devoted to daily suburban coverage, and the money spent on *Today's Living* would have bought grittier Sunday regional supplements dealing with genuine suburban concerns and offering seriously researched reportage. Only lip service was ever paid to the suburbs, and perhaps no more than that could have been expected from the *Tribune* editor in charge of metropolitan coverage—Luke Carroll, a city boy who wore yellow shoes and did not much mingle with the commuter set.

Carroll's other limitations were still more damaging to the performance and morale of the paper because it was he who effectively controlled the city staff and, through it, the heart of the *Tribune*'s news-gathering machinery. Carroll knew the city well, had a good memory, and was properly skeptical toward all suitors for the space he rationed. But he never learned the difference between coddling the talented—an unmanly practice, by his lights—and respecting them, a vital distinction for an effective city editor. He was no inspirer of effort or loyalty, as Stanley Walker and L. L. Engelking had been, or instructor in style as Joseph Herzberg could be when he chose. Indeed, Carroll was often a brutal, bullying ruler, favoring nasty confrontations. He was also an unsubtle office politician, storing debts owed him by reporters and printers for any kindness he dispensed and calling them in as needed. Personality aside, Luke Carroll's news judgment fell far short of the *Tribune*'s traditional standard. He retained a police reporter's mentality, which had its uses, but in an age when the news was growing increasingly complex, something more was required to direct the daily operations of a sophisticated metropolitan newspaper. Symptomatic of Carroll's values was his ruling, bulled through in reversal of the decision reached at the daily conference of editors under Cornish's direction, to play the obituary of popular singer Mario Lanza on the front page and assigning the one on art historian Bernard Berenson, who died the same day, to the inside obituary page. Berenson's life work was for the ages, as the *Times* recognized in placing the story of his passing on its first page while relegating Lanza, stout of frame and large of lung, to the rear. Popular journalism to Luke Carroll too often meant being guided by sensation; history to him was for libraries, not newspapers.

Carroll may have been flawed, but the man Brown took for his titular second-in-command—Frank Taylor—was a washout almost from the moment he arrived. Whatever professional competence he once possessed had been consumed by alcohol; he was detected drinking vodka out of a water glass during *Tribune* working hours. His personality made Luke Carroll seem the soul of charm. Taylor was grossly deficient in education, manners, and culture and the editorial people rated him a blowhard who tried occasionally to throw his weight around and then retreated glumly into the shadows of dysfunction. He ordered the removal of a story on cancer treatment from an inside page because, on the basis of his experience as a former director of the American Cancer Society, he felt such reports belonged on page one if legitimate or nowhere in view of the false hope they fanned. Another time he ordered the national desk to begin regularly checking out the accuracy of sources quoted in wire stories—until the exorbitant telephone charges for this pointless task became apparent. The day he summoned *Tribune* veteran editor Everett Walker to his office to tell him the front page of his Sunday edition looked "like horseshit," Walker told Taylor right back that people on the *Herald Tribune* did not talk to one another that way. "He was a son of a bitch who drank too much," Walker said. "He was a bad joke, a blunderbuss, a con man," recalled one longtime deskman, expressing the consensus, "and Brown fell for it." But it served Brown's purpose to be yoked to a powderless blunderbuss. Enjoying a good salary and not anxious to part with it, Taylor gave his boss little trouble and less counsel; the green sports section was his sole contribution to Brown's efforts. He survived by not interfering and depending on three subordinates to run the business side—Cameron, who knew the mechanical operation; advertising manager Jack Thees; and new circulation manager Lester Zwick, the first Jewish executive on the paper outside of the news department. But neither Cameron nor Zwick had ever worked for a quality newspaper, and their ideas about what would sell the *Tribune* were no more inventive or exalted than Carroll's or Taylor's.

With such a team in charge, lapses of taste and judgment became common as the editors gyrated in response to Brown's latest hot idea. If Lord Beaverbrook advised him that the *Tribune* ought to have no fewer than twenty stories on its first page, as his prosperous *Express* did in Britain, then the *Tribune*'s beautiful front page turned to scrambled eggs for a while: little one- and two-paragraph stories with ungainly large heads were all over the place. If someone else told him the paper ought to try massive coverage of the next big news break, then half the front page and eighteen inside stories were devoted to the announcement by Dr. Jonas Salk that he had developed an anti-polio vaccine. The paper wore a ragged look throughout. Prepositions began to appear at the ends of lines of multiple-line headlines—a sloppy practice for the once punctilious *Tribune* night desk to allow—and inside heads too large by past standards for the stories they topped added to the appearance of decadence. Political coverage of the presidential campaign, while not blatantly partisan, gave a decided edge in story placement to Eisenhower's efforts. A box on the front page quoted the latest odds on the outcome of the election—Eisenhower was heavily favored—although where they came from, what they were based on, and why they were there went unexplained; whatever the answers, no serious newspaper could run such an item without creating the impression it had suddenly become a tout sheet. Indeed, there were days when the paper seemed to be desperately groping for promotable material. Perhaps a nadir was reached with the celebrity-based copy of former movie fan magazine writer May Mann, which driveled on and on—and got printed. A typical Mann confection, this one from her series titled "How to Make a Good Husband," began:

> No one Hollywood couple has more to tell of the growth and development of a happy marriage than Mr. and Mrs. Alan Ladd.
> A projectionist at Mr. Ladd's studio once whispered to me: "They still hold hands and sneak kisses in the dark when I'm running a picture."
> A strong athletic type, Alan was not ashamed to visit a lingerie store to buy his wife a fancy nightie with matching negligee. Or to have her name "Sue" monogrammed and entwined with little red hearts, or add satin mules sprinkled with rhinestones to match.

Even Luke Carroll threw up his hands when she submitted a long series on Marilyn Monroe devoid of a single fresh revelation. Frank Taylor got the job of sacking the poor woman.

A few weeks shy of the thirtieth anniversary of his employment on the paper, copy editor John Price decided to attend the Twenty-five Year Club party held in the ninth-floor auditorium of the *Tribune* building. He went because he thought his show of allegiance might somehow improve his endangered status as a Marxist employee. A bourbon and soda in hand, he stood around talking with book reviewer Lewis Gannett, another veteran of the left, who had joined the *Tribune* two years after Price and, like him, survived at Brown Reid's sufferance. "We agreed that the paper had changed for the worse," he entered in his diary afterward, "and that we could see the effects in ourselves—no more will to fight for anything." He added:

Everyone was seated, and Hy Gardner, the Hollywood gossip columnist who is now a power in the management, announced that there would be entertainment. Joey Adams, the night-club comedian, took over and began telling off-color stories which were very funny. Then an acrobatic tap dancer performed.

Brownie Reid delivered his standard inspirational speech in his cracked, grating voice—the free press, free world and Herald Tribune team—every word of it false. . . . The vulgarity and slickness of the "party" seemed to me perfectly symbolic of what the paper is becoming under its new bosses.

That May, after thirty-one years on the paper, Joseph Herzberg resigned and moved to *The New York Times,* where Homer Bigart had gone the previous September after twenty-eight years on the *Tribune.* The pair of them embodied the dedication and craftsmanship that had lifted the paper to the pinnacle of American journalism. At his death twenty years later, Herzberg was lauded in a *Times* obituary editorial titled "Lover of the City" for his "formidable record as city editor of the New York Herald Tribune in the years of its greatness." Those years were clearly over when Herzberg left, bitter with a *Tribune* management lacking, as he said, in "talent, experience, and wisdom." He felt ill used by the paper, cast aside for Brown Reid's flunkies, like Luke Carroll, whom he rated incompetent. Indeed, the whole city staff was being ill used, Herzberg thought, and neglected in the paper's obsession with shoddy feature material— Hy Gardner and May Mann "violate everything a true reporter is trained to write"—and national and international copy aimed at boosting Brown's prestige. Meanwhile, legitimate city news, like the big real estate boom of the mid-'Fifties, was going uncovered except with puff copy in the soft Sunday real estate section. And through all this defiling of taste and dismantling of integrity, executive editor Cornish was, thought Herzberg, "afraid to move in any direction whatsoever."

Many on the paper concurred in that view of George Cornish, reduced to a departmental figurehead under Brown and apparently a survivor at any cost. But others offered a more charitable appraisal. William Zinsser, a postwar arrival who, as a writer for the Sunday news review section and then drama section editor, film reviewer, and editorial writer, was on staff during most of Cornish's tenure as the *Tribune*'s ranking editor, found him "a witty, urbane, charming man, and rather like Hamlet—a study in courtly introspection who rationalized much and never really did anything but survive as the embodiment of the paper at its best. So long as he was there, you had the sense that things were not as bad as they could get. At a certain point, though, you had to ask yourself, 'Where is his pride?' Stanley Woodward wouldn't put up with that crap—he drove them crazy with that pride of his." But Cornish was not Woodward; his role was to keep the crew from mutiny and the ship on course. "He was one of the deftest diplomats I ever met," Zinsser said. "The garden editor could go in there with a gripe and leave with the impression Cornish thought there was nothing more important in the world than begonias." But it was always a retreating action for Cornish, a tragic hero to Zinsser, who suspected that "putting up with all that garbage must have killed him." Among the garbage George Cornish tolerated was Brown Reid's 1958 order to him to remove William Zinsser as the *Tribune* film critic because his caustic comments on some of Hollywood's more flatulent extravaganzas were believed to be costing the paper advertising revenue.

III

Brown Reid was a study in perpetual motion during his three-year reign over the *Tribune.* He thrived on conferring by phone with New York state Republican chairman Judson Morhouse or Secretary of Defense Neil McElroy or showing up for a Rotary luncheon or a function at one of the twenty-seven other clubs and societies to which he belonged (among them the Sons of the American Revolution) or making a speech on the Soviet peril at an affair for the Jewish Theological Seminary and being presented with its annual Eternal Light award —apparently in gratitude for the *Tribune*'s enduring support of Israel. Philo-Semitism had come at last to the Reids.

But superhuman character would have been required of a man as young, untrained, and innocent of life's hard knocks as Brown Reid was to provide the *Herald Tribune* with the leadership it needed. And he did not have such a character. He had a superficial mind, a short attention span, and an inclination to heed the advice of the last persuasive person to get hold of his ear. His dedication to the task before him was unquestionable, but it produced an obsessive self-centeredness. He thought nothing of asking his private secretary to stay up all night on a train to Chicago to type the speech he was to deliver there the next day. At a time when the *Tribune* was struggling for survival and sacrifices were being asked of its loyal retainers, no secret was made of his purchase of a sixty-five-foot, $85,000 yawl.

Of all Brown's limitations of character, it was his judgment of people and policies that served him least well. He did not surround himself with strong, able, farsighted people. Oddly enough, one of the most capable men whom he reached toward for help and who served him very well—Tex McCrary—was someone whom professional propriety should have told him to avoid.

The shrewd, melancholy, aggressively well-connected McCrary, while still running radio and television interview shows, had launched a public relations firm early in 1956, representing among others building tycoons William Zeckendorf and William Levitt (of Levittown fame); the Roosevelt Field shopping mall on Long Island, then the largest such installation of its kind in the nation; and the troubled New Haven Railroad. To this list he happily added the *Herald Tribune,* selling his services on the strength of his ability to enhance its young boss's stature and to rout continuing rumors of its financial weakness; his backdoor access to the Eisenhower administration would be a further help.* Brown bought the proposition, and Tex pursued it, talking up the paper all over town and on his shows, arranging speaking dates for Brown before audiences that would do the paper most good, pushing for articles in *Time* and other top magazines on Brown's vigorous efforts to rebuild the paper, and urging influential business people of his acquaintance to look kindly on the *Tribune*. He wrote department-store mogul Bernard Gimbel, for example, that he ought to get to know Brown Reid, who "will run for President, and be elected some day," McCrary told him. "And I think you can have a hand in guiding his career, at the very time that he needs to be *respected* by his elders." McCrary added:

> Incidentally, getting down to business:
> I got some figures on The Trib's retail lineage; I remember what you told me about The Trib, but I would like to try to change your mind. I think The Trib today can do a lot better job for your Big Store, because The Trib is a *new* newspaper under Brown Reid. It has muscle again.

McCrary arranged clever promotions for the paper, like the election-night program on New York's local Channel 5 that originated from the *Tribune* newsroom and featured many of its writers, editors, and columnists. On New Year's Day 1957, a long list of influential New York residents got a photostated copy of the *Tribune* front page for the day they were born and accompanying greetings from the management that began: "This is where you came in . . ." McCrary reportedly played a key role in Brown's election to the board of directors of Loews, Inc., a theater chain. And it was no accident that the *Tribune* editorial page of December 24, 1956, carried a flattering send-off to McCrary's Long Island landlord, Jock Whitney, as he embarked for London as Eisenhower's second-term ambassadorial appointee to the Court of St. James's. "Betsey [Mrs. Whitney] and I were completely overwhelmed by your editorial this morning," the ambassador wrote Brown. It would soon prove a timely piece of flattery.

However gifted McCrary was at his trade as publicist, Brown Reid exposed the paper to serious questions of professional conflict by employing McCrary's firm. For one thing, McCrary still functioned as a broadcaster and therefore as a quasi-journalist; establishment of a public-relations firm left him, as the *New*

---

* A combative sort who had flown fifty air force missions and made sixteen parachute drops during World War II even though he was a public relations officer and not required thus to risk his neck, McCrary found in politics an outlet for his aggression but let it get out of hand and went unrewarded for his efforts. He had orchestrated a giant rally at Madison Square Garden for Eisenhower early in 1952 that was so enthusiastic it reputedly helped the general decide to seek the White House. But in the ensuing campaign for the nomination, McCrary's partisanship got him into trouble for his on-the-air criticism of Eisenhower's chief foe, Robert Taft, who claimed he was being called a liar. And there were charges that McCrary was involved with planting Eisenhower hecklers in Taft's audiences during the New Hampshire primary. At any rate, he was not invited to join the Eisenhower administration and resented it, but he retained entrée to its key members.

York Post wrote in an unflattering 1957 series on McCrary and his wife, "blithely working both sides of the street." There was the further implicit conflict of representing the *Tribune* while at the same time trying to obtain access to its news columns for his other clients. And in the course of his efforts to obtain write-ups on the *Tribune*'s progress, McCrary worked hard to enlist the cooperation of Luke Carroll, who had the professional aversion of most lifelong newsmen toward press agents or, as they became known yet more disdainfully to the next generation of journalists, "flacks." How hard city editor Carroll resisted may be inferred from the closing paragraph of an October 4, 1956, note from McCrary to Brown:

> If we can just get Luke thinking in terms of promotion, half the battles won't have to be fought to plant The Trib Story all over town. Luke is your best performer, once he learns to enjoy it.

McCrary apparently meant that Carroll was convincing as a hard-boiled spokesman for the paper, but should he have been implicated in the *Tribune*'s promotional schemes? Would Carroll, knowing the alliance between the paper and its publicist, be more or less receptive to the next press release bearing the "Tex McCrary, Inc." letterhead or that of any of his clients? McCrary and others at his firm were, of course, aware of the potential conflict—or coincidence—of interest, but it did not much faze them, for according to William Safire, who had done most of the writing on McCrary's "New York Closeup" column for the *Tribune* during 1949–51 and was now a full-fledged associate in his office: "We had to work harder to get something into the *Trib* than into other papers." Then why represent the *Tribune*? Surely not for the money, which amounted to an annual fee in the $20,000–$25,000 range and in consideration for which McCrary devoted nearly half his time to the *Tribune* account, according to Safire. If he was not doing it for the money or for the advantage it gave his other clients in terms of access to the paper's columns, the only other reason McCrary could have had was the personal influence and resulting power it brought him —not a dishonorable motive, certainly, but one that induced caution and suspicion among most *Tribune* people other than Brown Reid. "I used to get a lot of stuff from Tex's office for the edit page," Harry Baehr recalled, "and put it in the wastebasket. When I told Brown about it, he just looked solemn." But Brown enjoyed the celebrity McCrary was winning for him and was untroubled by the accompanying compromise of journalistic principle; if he had understood it, he could not in clear conscience have accepted a position on the board of Loews, then involved in a fight for control of Metro-Goldwyn-Mayer, a major film studio, because of the shadow his outside role cast over the *Tribune*'s objective coverage of Loew's dealings and M-G-M movies.

In policies that affected foreign coverage and the Washington bureau, Brown exercised a capricious intrusiveness that, like his hiring of McCrary, strained the best traditions and highest values of newscraft. If he had known more, he would have butted in less. But it was all his fiefdom to romp in, and like a high-spirited colt, he relished using his muscles. There was the case, for example, of the care and feeding of Marguerite Higgins.

Glamour had clung to her after Korea as she divided her time between roving diplomatic correspondence from abroad and whatever she could dig up as a somewhat glorified member of the *Tribune* Washington bureau. Her celebrity preceded her wherever she wandered overseas, readily obtaining interviews with heads of state and their leading ministers. So well known had she become that her articles generally bore her name not merely as a byline but in the headline. A typical dispatch of hers out of Hong Kong carried a "kicker" or smaller, underscored italic line reading "Marguerite Higgins Reports" followed by the main, larger head, "Russia Sending Peking Long-Range Bombers"; often her name was part of the main head. Her tone grew increasingly anti-Communist with the years—not surprising for someone who had experienced the Berlin airlift and the Korean War firsthand and was married to a general—but not to the point of undermining her value as a reporter. She did some of her best work when her ideology was most apparent, as in her late 1954 series on the Soviet Union, where her militancy was no secret; her interview with Soviet premier Khrushchev caught his star qualities as a personality but rendered no less vividly his hardness as a foe and brutishness as a man. Back in Washington, she and General Hall lived in an attractive townhouse off Massachusetts Avenue near embassy row, whose residents she was adept at luring to her home for weekday expense-account luncheons that often propelled her into the *Tribune* office by midafternoon with an exclusive story; as always, work and pleasure were inextricably combined for Maggie Higgins. Her reputation had crystallized in the capital as a hard worker, an intelligent reporter, a sloppy writer, and a bad dresser. And her aggressiveness had not much abated. Roscoe Drummond, who directed the *Tribune* bureau from 1953 to 1955, recalled that his industrious crew, working in cramped quarters, "kept out of each other's way, except for Miss Higgins. . . . She was always trying to take away someone else's story." And she did not hesitate to go over Drummond's head to the editors in New York, "but they always backed me up."

When Drummond found the double burden of managing the bureau and writing a daily syndicated column to be too heavy, former foreign editor and correspondent Walter Kerr was placed in charge of the paper's Washington operation. But no one told him that at the beginning of 1956 Higgins had extracted a two-year contract from Brown Reid that made her a privileged character among her peers and, from the practical standpoint of running a daily paper, unmanageable except by her own consent. The key clause in her contract defined her duties as "a Correspondent attached to the Washington Bureau . . . on White House assignments, or on top-flight assignments as mutually determined from time to time by the Editor of the Herald Tribune [i.e., Brown Reid] and the Author, and to write news stories, Special Articles or Columns as assigned by the Head of the Washington Bureau or the Editor. . . ." Her strong anti-Communism and celebrity value to the paper made her an attractive property to Brown and worthy of kid-glove handling.

The ascetic, somewhat withdrawn Kerr had no real problems with Higgins until he moved to fill the job of White House correspondent, temporarily vacated by Robert Donovan, who was on leave to write a book on the Eisenhower administration (with the *Tribune* benefiting through syndication rights). Kerr's choice was thirty-seven-year-old Earl Mazo, who had been a reporter for papers in South Carolina and editor of the Camden, New Jersey, *Courier-Post* editorial page before joining the *Tribune* in 1950 as a political reporter in New York and New Jersey. Kerr obtained Brown's approval of his choice—Mazo was deemed to be politically safe (and would in future years draw close to Richard Nixon)—but had trouble convincing Mazo to relocate in the capital. When he finally succeeded and Mazo's choice new assignment was made known to the Washington bureau, Higgins's talons were unsheathed; she wanted the White House job for herself and asked Kerr for permission to go up to New York and argue her case to Brown. Aware she would do so with or without his blessing, Kerr consented. Suggesting that the language of her contract gave her first call on the White House assignment and her credentials were infinitely superior to Mazo's, she won Brown over. Humiliated by the reversal, Kerr went to see Brown and protested. "If I made a mistake," Brown said, according to Kerr, "it's your job to protect me." Soon thereafter, Brown jumped at the chance to replace Kerr with Pulitzer laureate Don Whitehead, a highly regarded former Associated Press correspondent then completing a book on the FBI with the cooperation of its chief, who was Brown's favorite bureaucrat. He asked George Cornish to recall Kerr to New York to resume the post of foreign editor, which he had filled after Joe Barnes left. "But I didn't think I'd be happy there," said Kerr, "with Brown running the paper." Kerr went on to run *The New York Times*'s new international edition out of Amsterdam, wanderlust gave Higgins second thoughts about the confining White House beat, and Donovan finished his book in time to be reinstalled at 1600 Pennsylvania Avenue.

Donovan's book and the paper's hearty endorsement of it fit nicely into Brown's strategy to achieve financial health for the *Tribune* by gaining it broad recognition as a political force. The problem with this strategy was the partisanship involved. At least in theory, great newspapers prized their objectivity. And Brown Reid premised his efforts on the claim that his was a great paper. In belying that claim, its excessive partiality to the Eisenhower administration had the added invidious effect of skewing the vision of one of its finest and most principled reporters—Bob Donovan.

It was said of him that he had the exuberance and decency of a beloved high school basketball coach. Denied a college education by the Depression, Donovan spent four years as a reporter in his hometown of Buffalo and after repeated applications to the *Tribune* finally wore down city editor Charlie McLendon. In 1937, at the age of twenty-five, Donovan began a career that, by the time he left the paper at fifty, had won him acclaim as the epitome of a *Herald Tribune* newsman. They put him on the street as a cityside reporter for a couple of years and then advanced him to cover City Hall under the flamboyant rule of Fiorello La Guardia. Though the paper was no fonder of the mayor than it was of President Roosevelt, Donovan was scrupulously evenhanded in his coverage. He was also a resourceful threader through the bureaucratic maze, finding a white-haired oldtimer buried away in the financial department who could translate the byzantine numerology of the latest municipal budget for him or the omniscient subcommissioner who would volunteer nothing but if deferentially consulted off the record could explain the hidden trade-offs behind the latest construction project. He was good at spotting a local story that was in fact of much wider interest—a school to be closed, beloved buildings to be razed for a new parkway or housing development. He was even better at writing with exemplary clarity about complex subjects.

And he was conscientious. One bitter-cold night in January 1942 during the annual budgetary tug-of-war over city aid between Albany and New York, the *Tribune* desk had a tip that La Guardia was to meet with key state legislators that evening in strictest confidence at the Engineers Club on East Fortieth Street across town from the paper. Donovan hurried over to the club, spotted out front the police car that the egalitarian mayor used in place of a limousine, but was firmly barred from entering the building. There was no lobby or even a vestibule to take shelter in, and he could not wander off to a nearby bar or other spotter's post for fear he would miss La Guardia's getaway and a possible scoop, so he had to stay outside and wait and wait—"and it was one damned cold night," Donovan remembered ever after. Finally the mayor and his entourage emerged, the political deal almost certainly struck but not to be revealed until the niceties of statecraft were honored back in Albany. "Oh, the look he gave me when he came out of there," said Donovan. "And he had this marvelous way of dancing away from you when he didn't want to talk—a sort of sideways twisting and turning that kept his head away from you." La Guardia had reached his car by the time Donovan got to him, and when the reporter leaned down to question the mayor, the edge of the closing door caught Donovan's cheek and opened a gash in it. La Guardia stopped the car, ordered it to back up to the wounded newsman, and in a voice suddenly solicitous asked, "Did I hurt you?" "You almost killed me, you son of a bitch," said the copiously bleeding Donovan. Grieving, the mayor explained he could not help him on the budget story, but while Donovan tried to stanch the flow, La Guardia gave him another, and better, exclusive by way of expiation: the city had decided to tear down the Tombs, its antiquated municipal prison, and donate the steel bars to the war effort. A bloody apparition on his return to the office, Donovan was bandaged up and, writing from clips on the Tombs while the presses were already rolling, whipped out a front-page beat for the late city edition.

After the war, Donovan was promoted to the Washington office under Bert Andrews, but neither the conservative bureau chief nor anyone else on the

Tribune ever told Bob Donovan to slant a political story; his journalistic integrity remained unimpeachable. He liked Harry Truman's grit (and would later write a biography of him) and admired Adlai Stevenson's intellect, but his stories on his favorite Democrats revealed no more bias than the ones he wrote on Eisenhower, although he knew the home office would be receptive to almost anything he put on the wire about Ike. His emotions thus grew tangled upon learning over luncheon with White House aide Kevin McCann one midsummer day in 1955 that the President had read and admired a book Donovan had written about the assassination of historical figures and, in view of his obvious journalistic qualifications, favored him to be the author of a book about the first Eisenhower term. Virtually unlimited cooperation was promised.

"I smelled a campaign book," Donovan recalled. And the fact that Roscoe Drummond had already declined the same offer on the ground that it would compromise his independence as a columnist reinforced Donovan's concern. But McCann persisted. At a second lunch, Donovan fended off the White House man by pointing out there were vast areas of the administration he had not covered and knew nothing about and was therefore plainly not qualified to undertake the project even if he were so inclined. McCann countered that the President's staff was prepared to supply whatever material Donovan might need to fill in the gaps; among the information to be made exclusively available to him, moreover, would be the notes taken by a Lafayette College historian at Cabinet meetings and other executive sessions as well as further data that McCann said he was sure would be of keen interest to the *Tribune* and its readers. "By this point I was bug-eyed," recounted Donovan, who sensed a scoop as big as the Capitol dome. A visit followed with Sherman Adams, the President's chief of staff, who assured Donovan that there was no objection to the truth being told "warts and all"; behind this broad license, Adams said, was a feeling among the Eisenhower people that "we haven't gotten our story across very well to the public"—a revelation that astounded Donovan in view of the President's popularity. In the end he took the deal, which had two main provisions: (1) no one in the administration could see the book until it was in print, except for portions dealing with national security, which Donovan would submit for clearance, and (2) he would get it done in time for publication by June 1956 and the ensuing re-election campaign. This trade-off—no censorship in exchange for delivery in time for campaign use—looked fair enough, but it could have left only an exceedingly obtuse author in doubt that a kindly disposed work was anticipated.

Before the arrangement was sealed, Donovan had to ask Brown Reid for a leave of absence and whether the paper had any objection in principle to his doing the book. Calling the proposition "an extraordinary offer" that presented him and the *Tribune* with "a great opportunity" to turn out "a fascinating narrative with an inside-the-White-House flavor," Donovan added:

Naturally, my own feelings toward the President, as they undoubtedly know, would lead me to a sympathetic approach toward the subject, but I would consider it my function neither to praise nor to blame, but to let the facts speak for themselves.

Whether there was any real likelihood that the "facts" would, under the circumstances, say anything other than the expected, Donovan soon found himself submerged in vast quantities of raw material, literally wheelbarrows full of it, as he worked away in a secluded White House office. "The whole thing was an agony," said Donovan. There was too much to plow through and too little time; he did what all journalists do in composing history on the run—the best they can. He had to confine his narrative and analysis to what he had in front of him and could produce in 260 days of nonstop work. There was no opportunity, let alone inclination, to get the other side of the story and do outside checking, but since by definition he was rendering "the inside story," that did not seem to matter. In the preface to the finished book, Donovan said he had done his best to write "a reporter's book, straightforward and objective." How, though, could an objective reporter's book be confined to one side of the story—even the "inside" account of it? "Inside" accounts especially needed testing and verification to qualify as reportage. Donovan did not even meet with Eisenhower himself in preparing the book. "I didn't want to," he explained. "I felt that if I talked to Ike . . . on a special basis, I would be obliged to use a lot of things he gave me, and I didn't want that. . . . I wanted to take the material and make my own story out of it." It was a disingenuous disclaimer.

What emerged at the beginning of July 1956 was a 423-page volume, *Eisenhower: The Inside Story,* which raced up the bestseller lists and sold some 50,000 copies that summer. Donovan did not glorify Eisenhower in the book, and there was some material that, he was told, had, when printed, embarrassed the President, such as his musing about the possibility of starting a third party because of the Republican right wing's coolness to some of his attitudes and programs. Donovan offered useful insights into the pragmatic idealism of his subject, like his insistence on referring to foreign aid as "mutual security" grants by way of stressing that his administration was not just tossing money away overseas but applying it for America's own good. Some reviewers praised the authentic and intimate qualities of the narrative, while others noted its true nature. "This book, frankly a campaign document, is the best case yet made for the Eisenhower administration," said Gerald W. Johnson in *The New Republic,* while the *Tribune*'s own Sunday reviewer called it "much more than a campaign document." The purpose of the book, nevertheless, was not primarily to serve posterity but to help the President get re-elected and the author pay off the mortgage while pleasing his employer. None of those was an ignoble motive, but they did not add luster to Robert Donovan's previously unblemished integrity. Reporters on great American newspapers, as Brown Reid seemed not to know or care, were not supposed to serve partisan interests, even when on leave. For when their leaves were up and they returned to action, how vigorously might their readers expect them to pursue negative or damaging stories about the figures whose causes they had supported in campaign season?

During the Eisenhower years, recalled Benjamin Bradlee, then Washington bureau chief of *Newsweek* and later executive editor of *The Washington Post,* the *Herald Tribune* had a reputation in the capital as "the company paper"— precisely the status that Brown Reid had set out to achieve for it and that Donovan's book abetted. Later that summer of 1956, Brown had a letter of thanks from Richard Nixon for his help on the Vice President's acceptance speech for his renomination. It was "reassuring to know that you were offering suggestions and standing by," Nixon wrote.

IV

The sharp fall-off in circulation after the end of each new promotional contest the *Tribune* ran—to levels only marginally higher than what they had been before the contests—suggested that the various changes in format and content introduced under Brown Reid had not materially improved the paper's position except to avert disaster for the Sunday edition. Reid and his publicist, Tex McCrary, could claim progress of a sort, but the numbers still provided no margin of comfort; most of the promotional shouting was bravado.

The early 1957 figures were discouraging. Costs were up, due in part to a late 1956 wage settlement of 9 percent over the next two years that *Tribune* officials said was 50 percent higher than it should have been because *Times* negotiators had once again caved in rather than risk a showdown and strike; revenues, meanwhile, were slowing. Reid appointed an editorial committee to figure out what the paper needed beyond cosmetics and contests to get its momentum going again, but he failed to turn to outsiders for fresh ideas. The committee, composed of Cornish, Carroll, Walker—career *Tribune* men all—and Roscoe Drummond, came to the inarguable conclusion that the paper should be made more engrossing in both substance and presentation but not at the cost of being trivialized. Nor was further typographical razzle-dazzle in order; "meat and muscle" were needed. The committee called for no additional spot news or emphasis on foreign coverage—where the *Times* was strongest—but for more "behind the scenes" copy and quality features. Included among the two dozen editorial columns of recommended new material were regular features on house-hold finance, emotional problems, and child care on the women's pages; added coverage of mutual funds, Wall Street personnel, and the garment industry in the business and financial section; a horse-racing handicapper, an outdoors column, and local golf results on the sports page; an inside-Washington column, patterned after the Kiplinger Letter, and a "hard-hitting" column on local politics; a regular real estate column; serialization of books dealing with problems of everyday living; and—as if an afterthought—"more suburban news." Especially needed, though the committee did not say so, were more and better editors to plan and supervise. The top staff was already stretched imprudently thin; Luke Carroll was serving in effect as foreign and national editor as well as city editor—a burden many in the city room felt contributed to his irascibility.

To make any or all of these solid improvements and get away from the quick-fix measures that had attracted attention but not much admiration for the paper required money. But as 1957 lengthened, profits disappeared; by the end of June, operations were $70,000 in the red, and the circulation figures were alarming. Weekday sales for June averaged 37,000 a day below the year before and were off 14,000 from the 1955 figures—a retrogression in the two years since Brown had taken control. And Sunday sales were off 56,000 from the 1956 mark for June and 9,000 from the 1955 figure, suggesting that the TV magazine had made no lasting impact. When circulation manager Zwick tried, for some reason, to boost *Tribune* sales in the Democratic stronghold of Hudson County, New Jersey, forty-five newsboy canvassers could enlist only three new subscribers. And signs of a serious downturn in the national economy during the second half of the year portended an even grimmer economic picture by the end of 1957. There were only two plausible prospects for covering the anticipated deficit and obtaining enough working capital to improve the property. The first, raising the daily price from a nickel to a dime, ran the risk of killing the paper if the *Times* did not go along almost at once. The afternoon papers were already selling for ten cents, and if the *Times,* which could improve its narrow profits with the added revenues, acted in concert with the *Tribune,* their resulting mutual circulation losses would probably neutralize each other without causing much change in their relative advertising linage. But a decade earlier, the *Times*'s strategy had been to wait three years before matching the *Tribune* price increase; now, with its smaller rival hurting financially and groping editorially, it was not likely to be any more cooperative—and less likely still to take the lead in a price doubling that would give the *Tribune* breathing space. "We were in a box," said Brown Reid. His only real alternative was to find a partner.

In the interim since his mother and brother had tried without luck to interest outside investors, the capital structure of the paper had been revamped, unburdening it of the more than eleven million dollars in notes the Reids had reluctantly converted into stock. This intramural transaction made the *Tribune* at least a credible investment vehicle. Brown, moreover, whatever his limitations, was a dynamic young man who was plainly trying hard to turn the paper into a moneymaker. But Brown and his principal financial adviser, retired Chase banker Robert Whitfield, saw that in order to raise enough capital and end the hand-to-mouth existence the *Tribune* had survived in the twenty-five years since Elisabeth Mills Reid died, the Reid family had to be prepared to give up voting control. That realization pointed toward a partner not already in the newspaper business—one who would allow Brown to remain as editor and president, directing it along lines long favored by the Reids.

Helen Reid made the first approach, to her friend and longtime *Tribune* reader David Sarnoff, founding chairman of the Radio Corporation of America. Sarnoff, intrigued, summoned Kenneth Bilby, the executive vice president of RCA's prime subsidiary, the National Broadcasting Company, told him the *Tribune* was available for "not too much," and asked Bilby how he would like to run the newspaper on which he had spent six years as a city reporter and foreign correspondent. Disparaging his own credentials for the job, Bilby told Sarnoff he thought there was still room in New York for the *Tribune* and trying to save it might be fun but RCA would have to bring in outstanding people to direct the operation since the main problem with it, in his view, was "the boys." Sarnoff went as far as referring the question to RCA's corporate lawyers, who soon returned with the doleful opinion that the antitrust division at the Justice Department might look with disfavor on an NBC-*Tribune* combination, thereby jeopardizing the network's station licenses. Since Sarnoff had spent a considerable portion of his career in disputes with the government over its patent licensing practices, "he had no stomach for another protracted battle," Bilby recalled.

It was at this precarious moment that Tex McCrary, in his capacity as goodwill ambassador for the paper, reintroduced the name of John Hay Whitney as the perfect partner for the Reids. True, two earlier attempts to interest Whitney—one through Bill Robinson in 1953 and the second by Whitie the following year—had failed, but Whitney, now in his first year as U.S. ambassador to Great Britain, enjoyed being cast as a statesman and might well prove receptive now, thought McCrary, who knew the multimillionaire well and rented a small house known as the Mouse Hole at Greentree, the Whitneys' 600-acre estate on Long Island. The appeal to Whitney this time had to be civic, not financial, McCrary knew. He was no longer surrounded by his numbers people at J. H. Whitney & Co. in Rockefeller Center; now he was a world figure, trying to repair Anglo-American relations strained by the Suez crisis of the previous fall and graciously attending the Queen of England, as his grandfather Hay and Brown's grandfather Reid had done before him. During Whitney's diplomatic leave that summer, McCrary brought up the subject of the *Tribune,* and the ambassador was sufficiently interested—especially if, as McCrary assured him, eventual control of the paper and not simply a junior partnership was the prize—to meet with Brown.

"There was a certain remote quality about him," Brown recalled. "He was very shy and hard to read." McCrary, though, could break through that barrier and speak to Whitney in a way that for others would have been impertinent. "I think the decisive point was my suggesting to him that if he owned the *Tribune,* he would no longer have to explain himself," McCrary said—justify himself, he meant, to people who were always coming to Whitney and urging him to run for office or take over some institution or invest in some worthy, or perhaps not so worthy, cause or venture and thereby define just who and what he was. For most men that question was generally answered well before their fifty-third birthday, which Whitney marked that August, in terms of the careers they had staked out and achievements recorded along the way. Jock Whitney, though, was no careerist; he was a protean figure, wrapped in aristocratic privacy, whose widest celebrity had come from his appearance on the cover of *Time* magazine years before for being a stellar polo player. Still, there was little mystery about the factors that made him seem the perfect patron and savior of the *Herald Tribune*.

Necessarily first was his money. He was probably worth somewhere between $150 million and $200 million in 1957; *Fortune* magazine estimated his wealth to be $250 million in 1964. By any standard he was fabulously rich. And attractive. An athletically solid six-foot-one, he had a strong, impassive face with ruddy good looks, abundant brown hair, and beautifully lashed hazel-gray eyes behind the clear-framed glasses that he had switched to from light shell frames when embarking on his ambassadorial assignment. He had a princely bearing about him, accentuated by immaculate wardrobing and grooming, but there was no hint of flamboyance to his mannerisms, no demonstrative claim for attention. He had intelligence, taste, impeccable social standing—unaffected by his decision to take his name out of the *Social Register* at the end of World War II on the ground that such compilations were a travesty on democracy— and large influence in the Republican Party. He was a friend, though not a courtier-crony like Bill Robinson, of Dwight Eisenhower, whom he played bridge and golf with and invited to his thirty-two-square-mile plantation in southern Georgia for quail hunting. During his life he had been called, successively, a society playboy, a socialite sportsman, a patron of the arts, a philanthropist, a venture capitalist (but nothing so crass as a mere investor or banal as a businessman), and lately a diplomat. None of those addressed the most notable quality of John Hay Whitney: his character. What was remarkable about him was that, having been handed so much so young, he turned out to be such a decent and civilized human being with so strong an emotional need to make himself and his money useful. This is not to say he abjured indulging himself grandly—indeed, he lived like a sultan, surrounded on all sides by luxury and alternating his whereabouts with the seasons of the year among his eight splendid residences run by a permanent staff of more than a hundred. But he knew how fortunate he was and was moved by a desire to repay society for the hand fate had kindly dealt him. Jock Whitney's principal virtue was "his utter, complete sincerity—his always wanting to do the thing that was right," according to Walter N. Thayer, who was the managing partner of the Whitney investment firm in that summer of 1957. How easily Whitney, the very personification of noblesse oblige, might have turned out like his father, Payne, who never did a serious day's work.

His parents' wedding was attended by President Theodore Roosevelt and members of the Cabinet, Congress, the Supreme Court, and the military and diplomatic corps. John Hay, the father of the bride, was the Secretary of State after a career that began as Lincoln's White House secretary and continued as journalist, diplomat, poet, biographer, and son-in-law of one of the richest men in Cleveland. William Whitney, the father of the groom, was hardly less accomplished and considerably richer. Lawyer, politician, and freewheeling investor, he was allied with Democrat Samuel Tilden in the reform of New York's Tammany Hall, then used his political connections to help build a fortune by financing railroads and public utilities and dealing in the city's booming real estate. As Secretary of the Navy under Grover Cleveland, he took the lead in modernizing the U.S. fleet and was so highly regarded that Henry Adams spoke openly of him as Cleveland's likely successor in the White House. William Whitney's brother-in-law was Oliver Payne, treasurer of Rockefeller's Standard Oil, who gave Payne Whitney and the former Helen Hay $150,000, jewelry, and a townhouse on Fifth Avenue at Seventy-ninth Street as wedding presents. On Oliver Payne's death fifteen years later, almost all of his $50 million fortune and Greenwood, his plantation in Thomasville, Georgia, went to his favorite nephew, Payne Whitney, whose own estate, when he died just ten years later, was appraised at nearly $179 million.

John Hay Whitney was his parents' second and last child, born in 1904, a year after his sister, Joan. They grew up at Greentree, the Manhasset, Long Island, estate Payne had bought the year Jock was born. Befitting Payne's sporting interests—he had been stroke of the Yale crew in '98 and a devilishly good polo player—the grounds included stables, kennels, three grass tennis courts, one of the country's handful of enclosed court-tennis courts, and its own nine-hole golf course, with a caddy always at the ready, not to mention four Rolls-Royces stored in a garage that could accommodate twenty-eight vehicles.

A pudgy boy with protruding ears, poor eyesight, and a stammer that would remain with him all his life, young Jock was not the princeliest of children. Naturally wary of strangers and carefully protected by a phalanx of servants, his life arranged for him in minutest detail, he was nevertheless not pampered into brathood or sissiness. He was taught young how to defend himself with his fists, and he shared both his parents' love for horses. From his father, who gambled and drank to excess, he learned never to turn down an advantage and how to play hard at games and partake of life's earthier pleasures. From his mother, who had her father's literary bent and became a poet of some renown as well as one of the nation's leading horsewomen (two of her thoroughbreds won the Kentucky Derby), he learned decorum, dignity, and life's more refined pleasures. But no one taught him about money.

At Groton, he went from mediocre to senior prefect, the school's top honor. At Yale, sprung at last from the scrutiny of his parents and their servants, he had a high time of it; amid the privileged youth who partied scampishly in the 'Twenties, Jock Whitney was right up there near the band, doing the Charleston rather too slowly, testing his capacity for gin and bourbon, developing a trencherman's appetite, and, his boyish ungainliness behind him, discovering women.

He flunked freshman mathematics but otherwise got by academically, poloed and crewed (and missed out on the crew captaincy because of an attack of rheumatic fever), and despite his stammer took minor roles in several under-graduate stage productions. Upon graduation in 1926, he went to Oxford for more studying and partying. The following year, his father died during a tennis match at Greentree, and Jock sailed home to an immediate inheritance of $30 million, with a good deal more to come through his mother's estate, and a life that suddenly became more serious. Just learning how to preserve that much money was an occupation in itself, though not one that could fulfill a spirited fellow like Jock Whitney; without parental guidance and unmoved by the ac-quisitive drives and social ambitions normal to most educated young men in their formative years, he set out to define a life for himself that would not leave him a jaded, aging playboy.

First he went to work as a $65-a-week apprentice at the old-line brokerage firm of Lee, Higginson to learn the vocabulary and mechanics of Wall Street and train himself to overcome an antipathy to things mathematical. He also became adept at distinguishing wise counsel from the exploitive and self-promotional sort—a rich man's first line of defense. Before long he was making calculated investments on his own and doing well with some speculative companies like Freeport Sulphur and what was to become Pan American Airways. But he was more attracted to the creative and artistic worlds, to humanist more than materialistic values—it was no accident that since early manhood he had worn his grandfather Hay's signet ring—and began investing his money and efforts accordingly, with happy results. Over twenty years, he backed some forty Broadway plays, including *The Gay Divorcee* with Fred Astaire, the long-running *Charley's Aunt,* and the still more successful *Life with Father,* which returned him $300,000 over five years. He was a pioneer of Technicolor and joined with his close friend David Selznick to fund such notable film productions as *A Star Is Born, Rebecca, The Prisoner of Zenda,* and, most spectacularly, *Gone With the Wind,* which Whitney bought for the screen for $50,000 before it was published and ceaselessly nurtured through its prenatal period amid much skepticism about the cost of the venture. Always, though, he remained behind the scene, conscientiously overseeing the advertising, booking, and foreign dis-tribution aspects of the movie operation with Selznick. He took small pieces, too, of interesting publishing ventures like *Newsweek, Scientific American,* and *PM,* the adless new daily launched by former Luce editor Ralph Ingersoll, in which Whitney put $50,000 before its idealistic impulses swerved sharply leftward.

In all these undertakings, except for his inspired reach for Margaret Mitch-ell's novel, he was never the instigator, never the leader, never the organizer. "I was always just a participant in things," he once lamented. His friend Nelson Rockefeller said of him that one of Whitney's few problems was that he never had time to concentrate sufficiently on any one thing that interested him. If so, it was because Whitney chose to spread himself, to hedge his bets by diversifying them, for he had no need to invest himself or his money unduly in any one venture; besides, it was more enjoyable to have his hand in lots of things. Nor was there any reason for him to rush decisions; he could afford to be contemplative and developed a ruminating nature that was written in the seriousness of expression he generally wore. He became an art collector (favoring Post-Impressionists) and patron *extraordinaire* who knew his priorities; his money was for being well invested, doing good with, and living off well. The do-gooding took many forms, most prominently gifts to New York Hospital and the Museum of Modern Art, both of which he served as a board director for many years. And he made plenty of time for play, especially polo on the twice national champion team with ten-goalers Tommy Hitchcock and Pete Bostwick. The fun was partially by way of compensating for an unhappy marriage in 1930; his private life filled up instead with other friends, theatrical and literary people as well as the smart social and café society set. No snob, he crossed class and professional lines easily. Probably because his speech impediment made him measure his words, he was direct in his remarks, searchingly curious about the news others brought him of realms vastly different from his own, thoroughly appreciative of a good joke or yarn, bright, involved, and, once committed to a companion or a cause, unshakable in his loyalty. His friend Robert Benchley said of him in 1940 that Jock Whitney "has the general approach, body displacement, and personal menace of a Newfoundland dog who might once have rowed on the Yale crew. Has a loud laugh, followed by 'that's marvelous' or 'I don't believe it,' followed by a loud laugh. . . ." He was a gentle man without being soft— except when it came to firing people, which he did poorly and sought to avoid altogether.

In 1942 he married again, this time to the former Betsey Cushing, daughter of an eminent Boston brain surgeon, and adopted her two daughters by her first marriage to James Roosevelt, a son of the President. After placing his mammoth investment portfolio in the capable hands of Samuel C. Park, Jr., who had graduated from Yale a year ahead of him and gone on to Harvard Business School and a career with the investment banking house of J. P. Morgan, Whitney volunteered for military service at an age when he need not have; his life, a lesser man in his position might have felt, was worth vastly more than that of most GIs, but he did not look at the world that way. He did what they let him for Air Force intelligence, made captain, and angled to get a crack at a combat mission. Late in the summer of 1944, he was sent to southern France to investigate field operations of the Office of Strategic Services and fell into German hands. Held prisoner for eighteen days, he was finally packed into a boxcar with twenty-eight fellow American captives, who he was shocked to learn had appallingly little awareness of Nazi barbarism or other reasons their country was fighting the war. During a midnight air raid on their slowly moving prison train, he managed to escape and make his way back to American lines, winning a medal for his efforts.

Returned to civilian life, he was a more purposeful and considerably richer man, thanks to Sam Park's adroit handling of Whitney's investments, especially in such technologically innovative companies as IBM and 3M. More serious about his philanthropic impulse, Whitney set up a foundation of his own that gave away a million a year, mainly to improve educational and economic opportunities for the underprivileged. Then, seeking a more constructive approach than mere enhancement of his capital, he established J. H. Whitney & Co., devoted to supplying seed money to promising new enterprises, particularly those pursuing new products, processes, or markets. Never a nine-to-five chair-warmer or much good at managing the details of a complex business, he surrounded himself with a small crew of well-educated, socially compatible professionals, mostly lawyers and Wall Streeters, who hitched their ambitions to Whitney's outsized wagon and made their fortunes while enhancing his. Men of ability, character, and judgment, they worked within the general guidelines Whitney put down, screening thousands of proposals to find the most attractive investments. They put the firm into a wide array of enterprises, ranging from Spencer Chemical, which hit it big in the fertilizer business, to Minute Maid orange juice, one of the first commercial applications of the frozen-food process developed during the war, to Australian mineral properties, to American television stations. Always a team player comfortable behind the scenes, Whitney made sure his elite recruits had things running well, touched base regularly with the operation, headquartered at 630 Fifth Avenue in Rockefeller Center, and mostly let it function without his intruding. The $10 million with which he funded the firm was said to have multiplied between ten- and fifteenfold within two decades.

He next began to give his time and resources to the Republicans, once the party had handed its leadership to Eisenhower, whom Whitney rated a humane and moderate figure sure to stand firm against the retrogressive and isolationist right wing. As 1952 financial chairman of Citizens for Eisenhower-Nixon, a nonpartisan fund-raising drive, he had no qualms about putting the bite on rich friends in both parties; two years later, he headed the New York state Republican funding drive and in 1956 chaired the regular national Republican drive for contributions to re-elect Eisenhower. He was rewarded with the ambassadorship to Britain, a non-policymaking post but one rich in prestige that also needed delicate handling after America had denounced the Anglo-French fiasco at Suez. To prepare for the job, he took lessons that helped him overcome his aversion to public speaking. After the rousing editorial farewell paid him in the *Tribune* on instructions from Brown Reid, Jock and Betsey Whitney took command of the ambassador's residence in Grosvenor Square; the annual salary was $27,500, about what their weekly maintenance bill came to back home. Under his direction were seven hundred employees of America's permanent mission to her mother country—the first time in his life that Whitney had sole charge of a sizable organization.

Why, then, in the first euphoric flush of his new public role, was he now open to the Reids' overtures? First, because his post in London, while largely ceremonial, validated him as his money alone never could, and he enjoyed being constantly in the midst of large events and important, interesting people. Similarly, the *Tribune* situation would stimulate him, long after his ambassadorial days were over, in a way that J. H. Whitney & Co. no longer could. Second, he did not want the *Tribune* to die, and saving it would be both a public service and a personal fulfillment. "He wanted his voice to be heard," said his close political ally and friend Jacob K. Javits, "and he believed in the liveliness and style of the paper." To Whitney's daughter Kate, the *Tribune* appeared worthy of consuming him for the rest of his life because of "the constant source of excitement, the challenge of rescuing it, all the new people, his love of literature. . . . It was always important to him how you wrote and spoke." His brother-in-law, William S. Paley, founder and chairman of the Columbia Broadcasting System, put it more bluntly: "Jock was a bright man who didn't have anything to do after London. Running the paper would give him status and let him have fun."

Brown Reid and a small group of his *Tribune* confidants including banker Whitfield and columnist Drummond were thus welcomed at the Whitney offices in Rockefeller Center to pitch the strong points of the paper and the plans to improve it editorially to its potential ideal benefactor. Whitney meanwhile asked his own people to begin investigating the situation. Robert F. Bryan, financial specialist among the Whitney partners and a Yale Ph.D. economist with Wall Street, government, and industrial experience, had an intensive visit with *Tribune* treasurer A. V. Miller and came away pessimistic. In an eighteen-page report to Whitney, Bryan noted the paper's static position over the past decade, which was traceable in no small part, in Miller's view, to the managerial shortcomings of Helen and Whitie Reid and Bill Robinson. Brown Reid was at least bringing energy to the paper, but money was badly needed to improve the product, which, as Bryan pointed out, had been comparatively malnourished during the previous ten years; editorial expenses over that span had increased a total of only 31 percent, far less than other costs. In view of the gathering national recession, Miller predicted that the paper's losses for 1957 would reach $650,000 and be close to double that for the following year, but thereafter he projected a marked improvement with profits of over a million by 1960—a prayerful prospect, in Bryan's opinion, and one based not on increased circulation and advertising sales but on a rise in the selling price and ad rates. Among the attendant encumbrances that came with the *Tribune,* Bryan added, was a debt of $3.5 million in retirement and severance benefits that Whitney would be contractually and morally obliged to pay if the paper went out of business under his ownership. He went on:

> The failure of the Tribune to build circulation and advertising volume during the past ten years, especially the dramatic decline in its share of Sunday circulation and advertising lineage, the change in character of the New York City population resulting from the trend to the suburbs, the competition from the tabloid morning papers, the keen competition in the news and entertainment area from radio and television,

the number of failures and forced mergers of newspapers in other cities in recent years, the strength and aggressiveness of the labor unions in the newspaper field (the Tribune's employees are divided among twelve different unions), the age of much of the Tribune's plant, the great prestige of the Times and the momentum it has gained since the War, as well as its alleged willingness to forego large profits in order better to carry out its public service responsibilities, the loss of circulation felt by the World Telegram after its increase to 10 cents—all these things would seem to warrant a gloomy appraisal of the odds against the Tribune.

It could "not go on indefinitely without drastic changes," Bryan concluded, and rescuing it would require a commitment from Whitney of no fewer than ten years and five million dollars.

In the more knowing opinion of Samuel I. Newhouse, whose network of papers would surpass the Hearst and Scripps-Howard chains and included dailies surrounding Manhattan in Newark, Jersey City, Bayonne, Staten Island, and Queens, Whitney was already too late to save the *Tribune.* "He was convinced it couldn't be done," recalled Walter Thayer of the Whitney firm, who consulted with Newhouse at the time, "because the paper had been badly run for too long. But he thought Jock ought to try—and would never regret it."

This almost recreational aspect of the undertaking—Whitney, after all, as owner of Greentree Stables, was used to sporting challenges that he could afford to lose—became the prime rationalization among Whitney's friends and advisers in assessing the *Tribune* situation for him. Among his intimates only Sam Park did not approve of indulging the boss in such a fashion, but in the view of Frank Streeter, Park's assistant and successor as overseer of Whitney's personal finances, Park failed to credit sufficiently the expansiveness of spirit that the *Tribune* would provide Whitney and the attractiveness to him of the team play involved in trying to rescue it. Park was not the only one to miscalculate; Streeter commented, "I doubt that Jock ever fully understood the financial implications of the *Tribune* picture."

But the rest of the J. H. Whitney & Co. office understood it all too well. "The *Herald Tribune* made no sense as a venture capital investment, and it was doubtful that it made sense as any kind of investment," thought the Whitney firm's senior partner, Benno C. Schmidt, "except as a public service." Managing partner Thayer recalled, "We never considered it as a financial investment—it was a matter of 'Let's set it up so that he can do it if this is what he wants.' "

The partners urged a strictly limited commitment on Whitney's part in the beginning, and the Reids accordingly offered him a 10 percent interest in the paper's stock for a modest $100,000 with a two-year option to obtain majority control for another $400,000 plus $2 million in a low-interest, long-term loan. With Whitney's name and status—and the potential of his fortune—behind him, Brown was inclined to risk raising the *Tribune*'s daily selling price to a dime regardless of whether the *Times* went along. But Bill Paley, who was perhaps Whitney's closest friend and a titan of the communications industry, thought raising the paper's price, with its depressing effect on circulation, would make the job of salvaging it that much tougher; furthermore, he feared any premature equity position that Whitney might take would raise expectations of his eventual heavy involvement and entrap him psychologically. So Paley, Park, and the firm partners counterproposed that Whitney simply make a loan to the paper of $1.2 million, enough to cover the deficit Brown said he expected through the end of 1958; with the loan would come the option to obtain 51 percent of the common stock by lending the paper another $1.3 million. Either form of the deal was attractive to the Reids because Whitney's money would allow them to improve the paper and give value to their then all but worthless stock in it without, they hoped, forcing the family to relinquish operating control.

While Whitney was pondering the commitment and showing signs of hesitation, Brown and Tex McCrary flew to London in mid-September to try to clinch the deal. McCrary confided that his friend Edwin W. Pauley, a wealthy California oilman and a force in the Democratic Party, was waiting in the wings to step in if Whitney did not want the paper—an offer that, if true, had never been transmitted to the Reids, who, according to Brown, would at any rate have been hesitant to accept it. Whitney accused McCrary of bluffing, but the very suggestion served its purpose; so, apparently, did McCrary's remark, as they passed the plaque in the embassy lobby bearing the names of Jock's and Brown's grandfathers as former ambassadors, that fate had tapped Whitney to own the *Tribune.*

The announcement was made in a modest article on the page opposite the editorial page in the October 1, 1957, issue. Whitney's statement read:

> I am happy to make this investment in the future of the New York Herald Tribune and in this manner participate not only in its ambitious program for increased service to its readers but also in the future of the newspaper medium as a vital instrument of public information. . . .
>
> Until such time as I may become a stockholder of the paper, I will have no connection with its management or its editorial policies. The paper will continue under the leadership of Ogden R. Reid, its president and editor.

In its lead editorial, titled "Renewing a Valued Association," the paper made a point of the historic ties between the Reids and the Hays lest anyone miss the strengthened position in which the Whitney loan placed Brown. But *Time,* despite Tex McCrary's and William Safire's best efforts to extract kudos on the occasion from its "Press" section, expressed a skepticism that would rapidly be shared by Whitney and his people:

> The new *Herald Tribune*'s unknown quantity, to many staffers, is still Publisher Reid, a portentously high-minded young man who sincerely believes that "the *Trib* is one of the world's most important papers"—and yet must take the blame for much in the recent past that has made it merely trivial. Even last week, as *Trib* men spoke earnestly of their plans for a better paper, radio commercials and full-page ads for a new circulation-boosting Tangle Towns contest struck a dissonant note. . . .

V

When the Soviet Union announced that it had hurled its first Sputnik satellite into orbit on October 4, 1957, and ushered in the space age of mankind, *Tribune* science editor Earl Ubell was fortunately attending a reception at the Soviet embassy in Washington in honor of global scientific amity during that designated International Geophysical Year. Ubell scurried about, collecting what scraps of detail he could from attending Soviet scientists and reaction to and speculation about the epochal development from other experts on hand. Then he dashed to the *Tribune* bureau and without clips or other supporting data at his fingertips wrote up one of the big stories of the century mostly out of his head.

Two things were remarkable about Ubell's story that night. The first was that the *Tribune* placed it below the fold—on the bottom half of page one—for the city edition with a one-column headline. Night city editor Murray Weiss, known for his sure news judgment, and news development editor Arthur Hadley, a staff newcomer who had covered the Pentagon for *Newsweek* and knew a lot about air technology, fruitlessly urged executive editor Cornish to play the event big, but whether out of untypical miscalculation of the story's importance or intimidation after years of being subjected to Brown Reid's reflexive disparagement of all things Communist, he would not. Only when the *Times* first edition came up with an eight-column banner and half its front page devoted to the Russian breakthrough did Cornish relent. And then there was Ubell's remarkable story itself, beginning "Our planet has a new moon tonight," and written with a panache that made the *Time*'s conventional factuality look positively arid.

A good-looking boy of sixteen with prominent cheekbones, a slight Tartar cast to his bright eyes, and his mop of hair well lubricated with Vaseline tonic, Earl Ubell had showed up at the *Tribune* in the middle of World War II wearing his black suit and asking for any sort of work they might have. They started him as messenger, but he could type and learned shorthand and had zeal, and soon he was night secretary to managing editor Cornish, reorganizing the files and learning how to be courteous and in between chores doing his homework on the 6–11 p.m. shift. He stayed five years in this clerical status, helping defray his own and his family's upkeep while finishing high school and City College of New York, where he earned an A average as a physics major. After service in the navy, he was made a city reporter. His studies qualified him as a natural candidate for covering science and medicine, a beat then badly neglected by most newspaper editors with their liberal arts backgrounds and impatience with stories that were technical and abstract. But Ubell had a knack for turning scientific complexities into everyday prose. Soon he was on science full-time.

More than any other qualities, the job required hard, steady work and dogged curiosity. He read sixty scientific and technical journals a month, sifted through 250 press releases a week and forty or fifty letters pertinent to his beat, and made ten phone calls a day to try to obtain more detailed understanding of developments he could translate into stories digestible by laymen. Researchers would be questioned in depth on their printed claims, likely consequences would be hypothesized, skeptics would be consulted for opposing evaluations. His contacts were usually glad to talk about their work. "Scientists don't begrudge you their time," said Ubell. And he made it his urgent business to attend the annual conventions of the ten biggest national scientific associations, where he was regularly informed and educated by the most brilliant men in their fields, giants like Rabi, Bohr, Oppenheimer, Pauling, and Salk; he mingled with ambitious younger scientists sometimes all too eager to share their findings and traded tips and insights with others in the small but growing science-writing fraternity.

But to acquire depth as well as range of knowledge, Ubell took to heart advice he received while doing a series on the Institute for Advanced Study in Princeton. He had asked former diplomat George Kennan why he had holed himself up in that lofty retreat to study some of the more arcane aspects of Russian history; Kennan told him that if you know one subject in depth, it allows you to know a lot of other things in depth. Not long afterward, a ranking figure in the then avant-garde field of X-ray crystallography invited Ubell to take a free two-week evening course on the subject at Brooklyn Polytechnic Institute; it was the key that opened his understanding of atomic and molecular structure —the central arena of so much basic research. He followed up by using his accrued vacation time, which was considerable because of the long and irregular hours his beat dictated, to work without pay at leading university laboratories. In Linus Pauling's lab at the California Institute of Technology, he and a colleague spent a summer shining hair-thin X-ray beams at a crystal of moleic anhydride and measuring the angle and intensity at which they were deflected in order to make a grid model that enabled them to determine the microscopic structure of the crystal down to the atom. It was the first genuine scientific work he had ever done and allowed him "to experience the fascination of doing something nobody else had ever done before. It was an invaluable way of understanding what drives these guys."

One of his reports in the less abstruse behavioral sciences opened *Tribune* readers' eyes while *Times* readers searched in vain for comparable intelligence. Late in the summer of 1953, Ubell spent a week on the campus of Indiana University, reading the galleys of the forthcoming book by Alfred Kinsey on female sexual behavior—the result of fifteen years of research. When he returned to New York, he told Cornish that if the story was to be done right, the usual taboos about what could appear in a dignified family newspaper would have to be repealed temporarily; Kinsey was science. Cornish concurred, and Ubell produced an extraordinarily frank analysis of Kinsey's findings that filled some five columns of the paper and did not shrink from clinical terminology. Thus, "orgasm" made the front page of the *Tribune,* probably for the first time, accompanied by a report that the average American married couple said they had sexual relations 2.8 times a week; "oral-genital contact" was reserved for the continuation on page eight. The *Times* limited itself to a chaste Associated Press summary; the *Times,* after all, only promised all the news fit to print.

Ubell saw that for much of his work to be effective, conventional reportage had to be abandoned, especially in the longer Sunday pieces he turned out. "I began to realize that the inverted-pyramid style [i.e., aspects of the story presented in descending order of importance] was a killer of readers," Ubell recalled. "It says, 'The more you read me, the less interesting I get.' No other literary form uses that approach." Starting in 1955, after attending the Atoms for Peace Conference in Geneva and observing how British science writers for even the most popular papers were able to write seriously on their subject in a bright, accessible way, Ubell turned to a more open, essaylike form of reporting and related developments wherever possible within a human frame of reference. These techniques, which he refined during his thirteen-year tenure as science editor and continued after the *Tribune*'s death as a leading television science reporter, required some educating of his editors on the part of the lively and argumentative Ubell. After reading a piece of his about developments in the fight against leukemia, which Ubell dealt with dramatically by narrating the efforts to save the life of one small boy and not disclosing until the final paragraph that the child had died anyway, city editor Luke Carroll complained that the only trouble with the story was that it made him read it through to the end to find out what happened.

VI

In mid-October 1957, for the third time in three years, a "new" *Tribune* was unveiled. It was to be Brown Reid's last effort to save the paper that his family had owned for eighty-five years, and with an infusion of $1.2 million of Jock Whitney's money behind him, he managed a perceptible improvement: a product more varied yet coherent, deeper yet livelier.

Gone now was the nonsensical green newsprint in the sports section, which under a rearrangement of the three-section paper was combined with the financial pages to form a unit primarily appealing to male readers. The local-area news page, which had previously fronted the second section but was often conceptually destroyed by the intrusion of unrelated feature material, was transferred to the middle of the first section and its integrity maintained as a metropolitan news dispensary. The second section led off instead with redesigned and expanded women's features, three snappy pages of them, dressed in a slender, modern headline type and anchored by Eugenia Sheppard's "Inside Fashion" column, a new way of writing about clothing styles by linking them to the people who designed and wore them; business editor Donald Rogers writing on family finances; Charles Ventura, hired away from the *World-Telegram* to do his long, name-filled column on the pursuits of the terribly rich ("Doris Duke Reported Ready / To Take Be-Bop to Newport"), and the durable Clementine Paddleford on the infinite delights of gastronomy.

The first section, too, was busy with new life. Major front-page stories carried a lead-all or "focus" paragraph set in larger, bolder type and aimed at providing instant perspective for what followed; although more cluttering than illuminating, it was an interesting attempt to lend immediate significance to the bare headlines. New inside features included "World Insight," a gathering of notable but secondary developments abroad condensed into a single paragraph each; "Across America," a similar collection of items on the domestic scene but lighter in tone; "Radar Screen," four or five unsourced "inside" items set double-column in typewriter type that dealt with expected developments or speculated on the meaning of recent events—the sort of thing the *Times* would never countenance; "Man to Watch," a sketch on an important figure in the news rather than a mere celebrity; and a regular departmentalized home for news of science and medicine, for which Earl Ubell was given an assistant, and of education, recognized now as a subject of ongoing newsworthiness. In addition, the paper began to carry with far more frequency in-depth series that dealt with serious social issues but were not necessarily pegged to recent news, such as Robert Bird's pieces on the condition of New York's black population, for too long *terra incognita* on the *Tribune*'s pages. The paper's editorial page, too, came to life with sharp comments on the lassitude of the Eisenhower administration's response to the challenge posed to the United States by the Soviets' launching of Sputnik.

George Cornish, interviewed by *Editor & Publisher* on the occasion of the revamped paper, said his staff's handiwork had resulted in a *Tribune* that was "complete, convenient, lively." The latter two, at any rate, were supported by the evidence. Business manager Cameron commented that the paper was just at "the beginning of a long campaign of improvement."

Major contributors to this reformation were a pair of authentically gifted but equally volatile new editors enlisted by Brown Reid. The more visible of the two was Arthur T. Hadley, a Yale '49 classmate of Brown and an exuberant soul full of bright ideas and journalistically worthy instincts. Grandson of a Yale president, son of a partner in the Wall Street law firm of Milbank, Tweed, himself a Phi Beta Kappa man with strong social connections, a heroic war record, and six years on *Newsweek* covering the Defense Department and the White House and editing its "Periscope" department, Hadley was given the amorphous title of director of news development and a four-desk brainstorming outpost in the *Tribune* city room. In anticipation of his arrival, office wags placed a folder on each of the desks under his command and in large red penciling labeled them in turn "IDEAS," "MORE IDEAS," "STRAY THOUGHTS," and "SECOND GUESSES & POSTMORTEMS." Once the eager Hadley materialized, spraying suggestions in all directions followed by his uninhibited laughter booming over the city room, the ribbing of the news development editor only increased. Veterans would stop by his desk and ask in mock seriousness, "What's developing, Art?" Others would wait until they saw him heading for the door, then dial his telephone extension, just to watch him bound zealously back to his desk, and hang up before he could answer. In fact, an alert, energetic editor who was thinking about stories beyond the day's breaking news and planning in anticipation of events instead of in reaction to them was precisely what the paper needed. Some of the series and features he dreamed up moved the paper in directions it had not gone before, like Bird's pieces on black New York and a series on Puerto Rican families, followed in detail from their origins on the island to their struggle for survival and acculturation in the city. The latter, written by Peter Braestrup, whom Hadley had known at Yale and brought to the paper from *Time*'s national affairs desk to work with him on feature material of social substance, drew city-room skepticism from those who felt *Tribune* readers learned all they wanted to about New York's downtrodden by glancing at Harlem out of their commuter train windows on the ride in from Chappaqua and Darien each morning. "Art's position was that we had to show them how the other half lives," Braestrup recalled with admiration. His Puerto Rican stories led to follow-up series on corruption in the garment center, where many of the newcomers worked at menial jobs, and then to a wider-angled investigation into the activities of organized crime as well as so-called lifestyle reports such as how New Yorkers of varying income levels and in different job categories spent their money. It was serious, unsensational, yet promotable investigatory journalism of a sort only the liberal *Post* practiced with any regularity among New York dailies of that era.

Hadley also functioned as Brown Reid's professional conscience, sending him frequent memos of a candor no one else on the staff dared to express. Encountering "many masters—and none" in the city room, he urged Brown to reorganize the news department: "This new paper will not work unless a managing editor is in control doing—not just suggesting or planning—what must be done." He also pleaded against continuing Tangle Towns and the other puzzle contests, which he thought demeaned the paper; anatomized the failings of *Today's Living,* the limp Sunday magazine; urged the paper to appeal to suburban readers by assigning good reporters to cover civic and social trends in the bedroom communities and upgrading the allocation of suburban news space to parity with news of the city; and proposed that Luke Carroll, whom Hadley regarded as unsympathetic in the extreme toward his efforts, be transferred to running the Sunday paper and replaced by Engelking, mothballed on the editorial page for the past eleven years but "emotionally stable" enough now, Hadley believed, to resume the city-editorship and reinspire the staff.

Almost as brainy and irrepressible as Hadley but of a totally opposite background was William J. Miller, whom Brown brought over from *Life* and installed over the loyal Harry Baehr to breathe freshness into the editorial page. Recommended to Brown by the staid, sensible Roscoe Drummond, Miller told the *Tribune*'s young leader that he thought most newspaper editorial pages were bland and predictable, and he wanted to bring a diversity of ideas and ways of expressing them to the *Tribune*'s page. Among the eighteen innovations he proposed were written debates on a given issue, supplementing the paper's own view; first-person-singular pieces by people whose opinions rarely appeared in print, like the feelings of one of the black schoolchildren who were then integrating Little Rock's Central High School under the protection of federal troops or of a New York dock-walloper explaining why he felt victimized by his job; editorial excerpts from other publications; and the reintroduction of the essay, preferably with a satiric bent, as a gracious and useful art form. And why not? Brown waved him on board.

VII

In the days immediately following the introduction of the new, improved *Tribune* in mid-October, Brown found himself caught up in a legal squabble that tested his resolve over a principle upon which he was prepared to lecture—and did—at every opportunity: freedom of the press.

Earlier in 1957, his paper's new, hardworking, and thoroughly competent television and radio news columnist, Marie Torre, had written about the difficulties CBS network officials were having in getting singer Judy Garland to settle on the format and date for the first of several television shows she had contracted to do. In her article, Torre attributed to an unnamed CBS "spokesman" the remark that Garland did not want to work "because something is bothering her." Asked to elaborate, the company official "nodded vaguely and said, 'I don't know, but I wouldn't be surprised if it's because she thinks she's terribly fat.' " A response by Garland's agent, which Torre solicited, disputed the CBS allegation that the problem was the entertainer's fault, and was duly printed in the *Tribune* the next day. A few months later, Garland sued CBS for $1.4 million for libel and breach of contract. When Torre was summoned before the contending lawyers for a pre-trial deposition, she was asked to supply the name of the company "spokesman" who made the crack about Garland's avoirdupois. She declined to comply, citing her profession's sacred insistence upon the confidentiality of its news sources. But how could Garland ever win her case unless she could prove that someone at CBS had made the remarks Torre attributed to him? The First Amendment may have guaranteed the freedom of the press to print what it liked, but not totally without regard to the consequences—or else there would have been no law of libel—and not without its responsibility to comply with the fair and orderly operation of the judicial process as mandated under the Sixth Amendment. Garland's lawyer brought Torre before U.S. District Judge Sylvester Ryan, who gave her a week to reveal her source or go to jail for contempt of court.

Anxious now and fearful that she would have to give in—as she understood many other newspapers required their reporters to do rather than get them entangled in costly litigation—or be fired, Torre was called to Brown Reid's office, where the paper's lawyers were trying to talk him out of defending her. No precedent under federal law then existed on the exact point at issue— whether a reporter could withhold information pertinent to, indeed at the heart of, a civil case to which he or she was not a party. If the paper were to fight on the issue, the lawyers argued to Brown, it ought to do so in a case of far more importance to the public; this one, they said, was too trivial. They pressed Torre to explain why she could not cooperate. Her source, she said, "had done me a favor, given me information I was after, and now I couldn't repay his kindness and helpfulness by revealing information that would probably get him fired— I just wasn't going to do that." The lawyers were unmoved by Torre's gallantry and pressed Reid to stay out of the case—to let his reporter go to jail if it came to that. "You don't understand, gentlemen—I *want* to fight this," said Brown. "I wanted to kiss him," Torre recalled. When she returned to court the following week to face the judge, the *Tribune*'s lawyers were at her side, loudly proclaiming First Amendment protection for their client's employee.

It was the judge's turn to be unmoved. "I know of no rule of law or no decision that extends the privilege that Miss Torre asserts as to personal functions in her capacity as a journalist," said Ryan, who nevertheless agreed to frame his ruling against her in a way to facilitate an appeal "without inflicting too much hardship upon the lady who willingly steps forward as the Joan of Arc of her profession." In a public statement, Brown vowed to carry her case to the Supreme Court if necessary and instructed his editorial writers to issue a ringing proclamation of faith in the next day's *Tribune*. The case itself might be "a relatively trivial one," the paper editorialized, but the enshrined principle it challenged was decidedly not. Torre's right to protect her source was more important than Garland's acknowledged right to obtain the facts relevant to an injustice allegedly done her, the *Tribune* contended, "not because any newspaper should be above the law or defy the law . . . but because the basic freedom of the press is the ultimate guaranty of all individual liberties, including those of Miss Garland to redressal of her injuries, if any."

The unquestionable sincerity with which Brown Reid held this view hardly blinded him to the flattering light in which it cast the *Tribune* as a valiant leader of the national press and drew to it the support and commendation of many other papers during the ensuing year as the Torre case climbed the judicial ladder. And it could not hurt his own standing and the attractiveness of the paper in the eyes of its backer and potential savior in London. But in the first few months following the Whitney loan, even as the paper improved under

Brown's hand, the inadequacies of his leadership were displayed. To the option holders of the *Tribune*'s fate, Brown appeared to be, however earnest, a haughty boy sent to do a man's very difficult job.

Brown's handling of the two most talented people he had hired on the editorial side—Arthur Hadley and William Miller—was indicative of his erratic direction. Hadley no doubt made matters difficult for himself by a certain quirkiness of behavior that reduced confidence in his judgments, which were usually perceptive and often brilliant. From time to time, for example, he was seen performing what were taken to be yoga exercises under or in the vicinity of his desk—a form of therapy, he explained long after, to ease the pain of war wounds induced by the constant stress of his job. In a rare moment of manic satisfaction, he was heard to declare across the snickering city room, "This news business is fun-fun-fun!" More often it was frustration. Hadley was never given the money or manpower needed to develop news features—only Braestrup worked under his supervision—and wound up in frequent shouting matches with Luke Carroll, who eyed him as a rival for power and spared him few reporters to carry out his ideas. "I never had a clear mandate," Hadley said. Nor did anyone bother to educate him to the differences in resources, capability, and timing between weekly journalism, the world from which he had brought fresh thinking and techniques, and daily journalism, with all its priorities of urgency. For the new "Radar Screen" column—a variant of the "Periscope" page he had directed at *Newsweek*—Hadley cabled all *Tribune* correspondents to be on constant lookout for contributions, "intelligent guesses" on future trends in their regions, and offered as an inducement for every two of such valuable insights the munificent reward of five dollars. "I was too young to know how to play office politics," he conceded. Veteran reporters who saw him as a naïf began ignoring his directives with impunity, and Arthur Hadley ended up perceived as being as unseasoned and unworthy of power as his boss.

William Miller, too, thought he had Brown's clearance to produce the "virile, hard-hitting" editorial page that the *Tribune*'s promotional ads were trumpeting: "a point of view with guts." But he soon learned otherwise. Convinced that the economies of Treasury Secretary George Humphrey and the habitual delegation of authority by the President had caused the United States to lag behind the Soviets in arms and to suffer a powerful blow to its prestige as the world leader in technology—a view in which Brown largely concurred —Miller wrote: "This nation has been asleep. The urgency of the crisis argues for the summoning of a special session of Congress to launch a scientific and research program in keeping with the supreme challenge of this apocalyptic age." There was a good deal more of this on the *Tribune*'s editorial page, and it did not escape the attention of either the President or his embarrassed ambassador in London. On a visit to New York, Whitney offered some discreet words of caution to Brown regarding the awkwardness of his position as part of an administration being strafed by the presumably loyal newspaper in which he had invested. Discussions with Miller ensued, the sting was excised from his more extreme statements on national security, and by December, Brown was able to advise Whitney of a definite modification in the *Tribune*'s editorial policy. The paper, he wrote,

> must assert powerful and enlightened leadership. We must do so in a calm and determined fashion. To date we have raised various alarms, some may have felt we over-did the case. Be that as it may, our job *now* is to help build public confidence, Executive action, and Congressional support. We must do this, I repeat, calmly and resolutely. This, in a word, is the time for a steadying hand and for support of the Administration.

For all his declaiming on the independence of the press, Brown bowed to expediency, though it left him with a deflated chief editorial writer. Miller also began to demonstrate a certain lack of discipline in his habits of work and thought. He was sometimes less than meticulous in his research and use of supporting data and indulged himself by writing long and crowding out the work of other editorial writers. After he had left the office, Cornish would check over the next day's edit-page lineup and countermand Miller's orders when necessary. And Harry Baehr was recruited to tone down the extravagances or unacceptable policy statements of the man who had been hired to replace him as chief editorial writer. Eventually Miller stopped showing up when he was supposed to and after about eighteen months on staff just drifted away without saying goodbye to people who had misused him.

Like a solitary sailor trying desperately to hang on to the tiller of his storm-tossed craft on a sea too vast for it, Brown Reid tried to dominate the *Herald Tribune* in order to save it. But will was no substitute for an understanding of the techniques and teamwork required. At the daily editorial meetings, he always had some useful thoughts to offer, like urging his editors not to overlook the current troubles of teeming Indonesia in the news play or suggesting that the women's page offer more guidance on the preparation of frozen and prepackaged foods or that the drama-page layouts needed to be pepped up. But most of his suggestions and complaints were trivial or misguided. He reacted almost petulantly when the *Times*'s London bureau scooped the vastly outmanned *Tribune* office there. He liked the light stories featured on page three so much that he wanted them preplanned and always available, ignoring the need for such material to be a spontaneous outgrowth of the day's news. He picked over graphics details, like the size of the type in standing departmental headings, asked for special treatment of the film *Windjammer* because he himself sailed, and incessantly dwelled on Republican activities at the local, state, and national level, all but ignoring Democratic developments despite the high density of Democrats in the *Tribune* readership area. Nor did he stop trying to dream up ideas that he hoped would add to the paper's luster but too often bordered on the crackpot, like the decision to begin one of the paper's regular columns on the front page each day—and each day a different one—simply to show that the *Tribune* had the best collection of columnists in America.

"Once you pointed out his excesses to Brown, by and large he backed off," Arthur Hadley recalled, citing a series on near-collision flights involving Pan American Airways. Long friendly with the Reid family, Pan Am pressured Brown to soften the negative stories until his editors impressed upon him the gravity of the subject. "He was limited," Hadley added. "If he'd had more time to develop, he might have made a real contribution."

His limitations were less forgivable because of his egotism. Raymond K. Price, Jr., whom William Miller had brought over from *Life* as his assistant on the *Tribune* editorial page, worked closely with Brown and respected him for his "shrewd eye for nuance in dealing with public issues" and a strong sense of the paper's responsibility to where the public interest lay in any given policy question. But Price felt Brown was incapable of educating his subordinates to do things his way and instead ordered them to be done as he instructed, imperiously, brandishing the authority he had been handed by his mother but never earned.

This insensitivity in personal dealings carried over, ruinously, to Brown's handling of Howard Brundage, the junior partner from the Whitney firm who had been sent down to the paper to familiarize himself with the operation, to be of any help he could, and to funnel intelligence back to Walter Thayer and Jock Whitney. Brown appeared to view Brundage only as an intruder on his domain and little better than an errand boy. "He looked over and under me," recalled Brundage, a Dartmouth graduate well trained in finance at the Wall Street house of Morgan Stanley and the Hanover Bank before joining the Whitney firm. "I thought Brown was a very self-satisfied, snobbish guy, who was supremely confident that this was just a temporary problem and saying to us, in effect, 'Just give us the money, and we'll lick it.'" If Brown executed an executive leadership, Howard Brundage did not see it. As Roscoe Drummond put it in melancholy recollection of that unhappy era of the *Tribune* under Helen Reid's sons, "Whitie Reid didn't know how to make any decisions—and his brother didn't know how to make any right ones."

As early as December 1957, Walter Thayer and William Paley, Whitney's closest counselors on the *Tribune* situation, were advising the ambassador that their earlier suspicion about Brown Reid had become "a deep conviction," as Thayer put it in a letter to London—namely, that the paper required "a new and strong personality in command" and that its problems could not be properly dealt with by Brown "in view of his background, experience and emotional ties." They had, moreover, conveyed that view to Brown, who, Thayer wrote, "professed to be in agreement. I cannot say with certainty that he understood the full scope of authority we feel should be given to the person brought in. . . . I anticipate difficulty in nailing Brown down."

Thayer's instinct was soon borne out when he paid an exploratory visit to Lee Hills, the executive editor of the *Detroit Free Press,* recommended by Brown himself, McCrary, Drummond, and a number of others as the ideal candidate to take charge of the *Tribune.* Upon learning of the meeting, Brown objected strongly that he had been left out of it and said that while he would be willing to give new management "full authority" in the event the Whitney option to assume control of the paper was exercised, he wanted to remain as chief executive officer. That Alice in Wonderland attitude prompted Thayer to write Whitney again later in the month that he did not believe Brown was willing to face the circumstances required to bring in "a Lee Hills or a reasonable facsimile thereof."

But the year-end figures on the paper's 1957 financial performance left Brown without bargaining room. The *Tribune* had lost nearly $1.3 million, the most ever and nearly twice what treasurer Miller had projected as late as August. It was the only newspaper in New York carrying less advertising than it had been ten years earlier, its share of the market in terms of ad linage had dropped from 15 to 12.4 percent while the *Times*'s had risen from 23.4 to 30.6 percent over the decade, and the *Tribune*'s plight, in view of the deepening recession, was expected to darken still further in 1958 despite all Brown Reid's efforts.

By the time Jock Whitney came home over the New Year's holidays, his advisers were planning how he might assume control of the paper in a fashion that would best insulate his personal fortune yet provide the *Herald Tribune* with the wherewithal and leadership it had badly lacked for the preceding twenty years.

PART FOUR

1958-1966

*The American stake in literacy as a technology or uniformity
applied to every level of education, government, industry, and social
life is totally threatened by the electric technology. The threat of
Stalin or Hitler was external. The electric technology is within the
gates, and we are numb, deaf, blind, and mute about its encounter
with the Gutenberg technology, on and through which the American
way of life was formed. It is, however, no time to suggest strategies
when the threat has not even been acknowledged to exist. . . . Our
conventional response to all media, namely that it is how they are
used that counts, is the numb stance of the technological idiot. . . .*

—MARSHALL McLUHAN, Understanding Media (1964)

16

Sick Chicken

When Walter Nelson Thayer III graduated from the public high school in the small mid-Catskills town of Ellenville, New York, in 1926 at sixteen, his parents thought him too young to go away to college, so he worked for a year as a junior reporter on the weekly Ellenville *Press* at twelve dollars a week. News in Rip Van Winkle country was on the drowsy side, but Walter enjoyed the work and later, in tandem with his brother, would for a time even own the Ellenville paper. But although he was drawn toward a career in civil and social service—his physician father ran one of the state's two reformatories for "defective delinquents" and would serve as New York commissioner of corrections under Governor Franklin Roosevelt—young Thayer did not find his fulfillment in newspapering. He turned instead to the law, at which he succeeded in both public and private practice. Yet thirty years after his teenage journalistic fling, he would find himself cast involuntarily in the central role of trying to preserve one of America's great newspapers. For the last nine years of its life, the *Herald Tribune* was associated in the collective mind of the news profession with the fortune and benevolent spirit of John Hay Whitney. In the practical, operating sense, however, the paper's fate was placed in the hands of his principal business adviser. But Walter Thayer was never in doubt about his priorities: his loyalty to Whitney's well-being came first, then his own ambitions, then the *Herald Tribune.* So long as he saw a mutuality of interest among all three, he remained the keystone to the paper's survival.

Thayer's early career revealed the warring impulses—public service and personal advantage—at work within him. A Colgate graduate, he first held a civil service appointment as a state parole officer, then opted for Yale Law School and, with a little help from his father's former employer, then presiding in the White House, a two-year stint as an assistant U.S. attorney in New York's Southern District, where he won a reputation as a careful, principled prosecutor. After private practice with a medium-sized Wall Street firm for several years, he went to Washington during World War II and served with distinction as a government lawyer with the War Shipping Administration and the Foreign Economic Administration.

At war's end, he returned to private life and for nine years had his own small firm, representing clients as diverse as Rolls-Royce and the Philadelphia Eagles. Smart, clear-thinking, hardheaded, as personable as any man when he chose to be, Thayer also came to be perceived as cold, guarded, very private, and almost ruthlessly dismissive of those he found unworthy or unuseful. Responsible in part for this was a certain wintry look as he reached his late forties. His hair, already a striking white, nicely set off his strong, mineral-blue eyes and neat, even features; his low, pleasing voice resonated with confidence and command. He bore a resemblance, one veteran editorial writer at the *Tribune* would later say, to Calvin Coolidge sucking a lemon; others said he looked more like Barry Goldwater. He was probably as smart as Coolidge and Goldwater combined, yet there was something flinty and chilling about Walter Thayer.

He had remained public-spirited over the years, and in 1952 he served as legal troubleshooter for the fund-raising efforts of Citizens for Eisenhower, the non-partisan campaign in which Jock Whitney was prominently involved. The two men quickly formed a bond. Whitney liked the clear way Thayer spoke and got to the nub of a problem, how he told a story and played golf and sociably drank his bourbon. He invited the lawyer to join J. H. Whitney & Co., but Thayer declined at first. He was doing well on his own and not much interested in becoming an organization man; also he was more of an analyst, a calculator, a negotiator, and a dealmaker than a businessman or administrator. Yet Whitney sensed that Thayer's acute but tough intellect was ideal for appraising the opportunities that kept being presented to the Whitney firm. Offered the managing-partnership in 1954, Thayer accepted—without even discussing the financial arrangements. Mutual trust was the glue to the two men's thirty-year friendship. Thayer became a lawyer with only one client, Jock Whitney. It was an almost ideally complementary relationship: the attorney as compatible counselor, coolly rational, analytically Apollonian, and his fabulously wealthy but emotionally vulnerable employer, with his esthetic, humanistic, Dionysian nature. Thayer's candor and loyalty won him power with Whitney that he exercised with discretion, gentlemanliness, and good cheer, all of which served to vault him into the role of Whitney's prime professional adviser. (Whitney's brother-in-law, Bill Paley, remained his closest male confidant on the strictly personal side.) Thayer succeeded most of all by keeping his not inconsiderable vanity under tight self-control and operating carefully within the territory Whitney granted him.

Accordingly, he did not regard it as his duty to try to argue Whitney out of involvement in the *Tribune.* His task, once Whitney had resolved to get into it, was to protect his client's interest. Early in 1958, as all the rapidly accumulating evidence persuaded him that only massive overhaul of the paper's management could rescue it, Thayer adopted an all-or-nothing policy toward the *Tribune* as Whitney turned to him increasingly for counsel in the matter. The stopgap $1.2 million loan already extended, Thayer believed, should be the extent of the Whitney bailout effort in view of the reports reaching him from Howard Brundage, the firm's representative on the *Tribune*'s premises. Brundage felt any money put into the Reid-owned enterprise was to be written off just as surely as if Jock had given it away to Yale. Nothing basic could be done unless the Reids stepped aside, and to meet Whitney's standard of acceptably graceful conduct, they would have to go willingly, not under compulsion. If Brown Reid believed that the rescue mission would be further funded by Whitney monies while leaving him in control, Thayer's first task was to disabuse him. And even with the Reids out of the picture, a Whitney takeover made sense to Thayer only if two conditions were met—a mechanism to limit the financial drain and a first-rate newspaper executive to take charge.

Even before Ambassador Whitney returned to London in the first weeks of 1958, his financial advisers were urging him to take maximum advantage of the tax laws to fund the *Tribune* if he elected to exercise his option. The way to do this most prudently, they suggested, was to build a hen house around the sick chicken—that is, to surround the paper with one or more properties in the same or a related field that would throw off enough profits to cover the *Tribune*'s losses for a sustained rebuilding period; at least five years would be required, everyone agreed. Whitney's fortune would provide the collateral for loans with which the hen house could be constructed; the interest on them was of course tax-deductible, and whatever profits the newly acquired properties earned would serve to neutralize the *Tribune*'s losses. A package of properties with a collective price tag in the $10–$15 million range and netting about 10 percent of the purchase price was thought adequate to accomplish the job, and so in the first months of 1958 Walter Thayer went shopping. At the top of his list were radio station WINS in New York, a collection of three newspapers and a radio and television station under single ownership in Huntington, West Virginia, and *Family Weekly,* a syndicated Sunday newspaper supplement.

Since no one in the Whitney organization knew anything about the newspaper business, finding the right man to guide them was as important a precondition of taking over the *Tribune* as acquiring the hen house to shelter it. Thayer's initial approach to Lee Hills, the fifty-one-year-old executive editor of John Knight's *Detroit Free Press,* had been based on seeking his help simply as a consultant, but it soon became apparent to him and Whitney why Hills was so highly regarded within the profession and being recommended from all quarters as the likeliest newsman in the nation to straighten out the *Tribune*. Understated and detached in an almost scholarly fashion, Hills had little of the newspaper romantic about him on the surface, but beneath the formality was a dynamic, devoted craftsman who had mastered every editorial aspect of his trade and demonstrated to his employers that quality could produce profits. Thayer liked the clinical way Hills diagnosed what he termed the *Tribune*'s "staggering" problems: reversing a long-stagnant newspaper operation might be achieved, but "not easily and not quickly." Yet Hills saw hope in the relatively thin coverage of metropolitan New York's five million families by any of the city's dailies, including the *Times,* especially in the growing, balkanized suburbs, where Jock Whitney's bankroll might still allow an improved *Tribune* to make headway.

That Hills seemed to speak Thayer's language may have been partially attributable to the law degree he had earned studying at night while covering crime news for a paper in Oklahoma City. Precocious at his trade—he had edited a small daily in Utah by the time he was twenty—Hills moved steadily eastward, to Memphis and Indianapolis and Cleveland, and upward, reaching the managing-editorship of the *Miami Herald,* which along with Jack Knight's *Free Press* in Detroit, *Daily News* in Chicago, and *Beacon Journal* in Akron constituted the best newspaper chain in America. All were lively yet dignified, using the Bodoni headline type that the *Herald Tribune* had introduced into U.S. journalism but in a bolder, more imaginative fashion and set off with enough white space to avoid a cluttered look. Knight's papers, conceived and edited with care and utilizing scientific sampling to determine reader needs and preferences, were easy to read, informative without pretending to be definitive, and journalistically enterprising as well as graphically appealing. Under Hills, the *Miami Herald* won a Pulitzer in 1951 for a series exposing the activities of mobsters who wintered in Miami. Convicted for contempt for criticizing the rulings and opinions of judges in certain mob-related criminal cases, the paper appealed to the U.S. Supreme Court and won a reversal. Transferred to the top editorial job on the *Free Press,* which was waging a running three-way dogfight for circulation supremacy with the *Detroit News* and *Times,* Hills added to his reputation by winning the 1956 Pulitzer for "aggressive, resourceful, and comprehensive reporting" of the automakers' complex negotiations with their unions over the guaranteed annual wage. Who better to assume command of the *New York Herald Tribune* and create for it a distinctive personality beyond the shadow of the *Times?*

But Hills was not looking to move. He did not have the sort of outgoing nature ideally suited to make a splash in the big-city pond, and the Knight management prized him; his salary of nearly $60,000 made him one of the best-paid editors in the country, while a 5 percent ownership of stock in the Knights' Miami TV station was testimony to his standing in the company. Although he met with Thayer on a number of occasions in New York, joined now and then by Whitney, Paley, Tex McCrary, and Brown Reid, Hills never set foot in the *Tribune* building throughout the seven months they tried to land him. He was cautious not only out of loyalty to the Knights and to protect his position with them but also out of concern about the strength of Whitney's resolve to save the *Tribune*. He was not sure that Whitney understood what he was getting into, and stressed that he ought not to bother unless he was prepared to make the paper the most important part of his professional life, unless he understood that the struggle to save the paper would "obsess and frustrate him, nag and drain and worry him," unless he was capable of backing up his staff even when it made mistakes and alienated his friends. But if Whitney really wanted it more than anything else, Hills advised, and if he was willing to organize it against failure—i.e., with the hen-house approach—well, then it would prove "the most exciting, challenging and personally satisfying thing he's ever done and add stature to him . . . and luster to his family name." By mid-February, Hills was drafting a more programmatic memo, cautioning against the outdated concept of the *Tribune* as a party organ, insisting that the paper had to develop "a different voice . . . not just a conservative one." The *Tribune* would work for Whitney "only if his motivation is really how best to use his money to help mankind," in which case nothing could be better and the paper "could be the climax, the crowning achievement of his life—or it could cost him a fortune."

"He measures well," Thayer reported to Whitney in passing on Hills's caveats, and while the Detroit editor continued to express doubt that he could be lured to New York, Thayer felt he was purchasable and stayed on his trail as the effort to buy the hen-house properties moved forward. More troubling was Brown Reid's blithe attitude despite Thayer's assurance to him in February that Whitney "has no present intention to increase his commitment" to the paper. But Reid, advised of the hen-house scheme and aware of the romancing of Lee Hills, seemed to think that both could work to his family's advantage. If, as originally presented, the hen house took the form of profitable *Tribune* subsidiaries, the Reids' minority interest under the Whitney takeover plan would at once make their holdings potentially valuable. And if Reid had to turn over editorial direction of the paper to Hills, he could step up to chairman and retain power and dignity in that fashion. And so Brown stayed in steady touch with Whitney by letter, assuring him that the paper was doing its best to cut costs and that once the business recession eased, the red ink would evaporate. By 1959 they could raise the price to a dime, and profits would soon follow. Meanwhile, he kept Whitney informed of political developments, as if the pair of them were already in league, advising, for example, of his recent private lunch with White House chief of staff Sherman Adams at which were discussed "specifics of what the Herald Tribune would do to help the Administration and the Republican Party." Regarding Thayer's dire warnings, Brown added, with studied casualness, "It is still my hope and belief that something can be worked out that will make sense on a business basis."

But by March, Thayer had moved well beyond hinting that a Whitney-Reid team was not in the cards. Lee Hills was the key to the plan, he advised, and while Brown might remain as chairman until Whitney's retirement from the ambassadorship, real operating direction of the *Tribune* and its hen house would have to reside with Hills—if they ultimately got him. Hills, meanwhile, had asked that discussions between them be suspended until one or more hen-house acquisitions were imminent.

Although Brown remained reluctant to accept Thayer's message, he was helped along toward reality by a pair of letters from his own financial mentor, Robert Whitfield, the retired Chase banker, writing from his home in Greenville, Mississippi, with an avuncular kindness. Brown would shortly have to decide, Whitfield said, between saving the *Tribune* by surrendering his command or going down with the ship. Nobody in Brown's position and with the limited resources at his disposal could have done much better, but if Whitney was to pay for the rescue operation, he was entitled to pick his own management and reap the lion's share of any profits that might accrue. Far better now for Brown to step aside and work with a distinguished organizer and administrator (like Hills) so that "adding age and experience to your brilliant mind and outstanding abilities along certain lines you might well succeed to the No. 1 spot again and become a really great, all-around newspaperman." In a follow-up letter, Whitfield wrote that even if Brown had to swallow Thayer's terms,

> you will be in a position of having taken over an impossible situation, having saved the paper from bankruptcy, having saved the family's prestige, having saved the historical traditions and policies of the paper, having assured the continuance of the paper in proper hands, having saved for the Reid family, Lady Ward and the [Reid] Foundation the only possibility of ever realizing anything from their investment, and having thereby won for yourself an enviable position in the public eye. . . . [Y]ou simply must not let anybody jockey you into the position of doing anything that might possibly jeopardize the consummation of a deal with Jock. . . .

Brown's apparent acceptance of this bracing line of thought was reflected in an April 8 letter Whitney sent to his immediate superior, Secretary of State Dulles, telling him of the efforts to take over the *Tribune* and "to return it to its former prominence in national conservative leadership." The patient, sadly, was "a good deal sicker than when we began," Whitney noted, and "the only ray of hope" was that the paper's financial situation had become "so desperate that Brown now agrees to step down in favor of a really top newspaperman."

Walter Thayer's idea of a deal, though, grew increasingly one-sided as the *Tribune*'s plight deepened. By the end of the first quarter of 1958, its losses were running 50 percent over expectations, and the breathing room provided by the Whitney loan, supposedly to tide the paper over through the end of 1958, would be gone before the year was half over. Although the picture could be expected to brighten as the national economy improved, at the current rate *Tribune* losses would hit $3 million for 1958, and Thayer was not inclined to pay a premium for the privilege of taking over what was now, commercially speaking, a large white elephant. The more its losses grew, the more Whitney would have to pay for the hen house to shelter it. The required investment was scaled up to the $15–$20 million range, and Thayer began to dicker for profitable *Parade* magazine, a close runner-up to *This Week* in the Sunday supplement field, as the first sturdy wall of the hen house; Marshall Field had it on the market, but had turned down a $9 million bid for it, although he was eager for cash to buy out Knight's *Daily News* in Chicago and pair it with his *Sun-Times* against the McCormicks' *Tribune* and *American* morning-afternoon combination. The greater the projected Whitney stake grew, the more the Reids stood to gain through the hen-house door, so at the end of April, Thayer restructured the deal. Instead of becoming *Tribune* subsidiaries, whatever new properties Whitney bought would, along with the paper itself, all be subsidiaries of a Whitney-controlled holding company; the stock in the paper would be held 51 percent by Whitney, 39 percent by the Reids, and 10 percent by Hills. The hen house, that is, would be all Whitney's, and the Reids would be left with 39 percent of their sick old hen. But since the whole point of the effort, at least in its inception, was to restore that old hen to health and thereby add luster to the Whitney and Reid family names, there was a certain fairness in the proposal.

Confident that the Reids would recognize this, Thayer intensified his efforts to land Hills, whom he offered a thirteen-year contract, personally guaranteed by Whitney, which called for a $100,000 annual salary, ample expenses and benefits, and an option on 10 percent of the *Tribune* stock at an inside price—and he would run the hen house, *Tribune* and all. That Hills was ready to accept the offer was plain from his April 29 memo to Thayer, stressing the care with which the *Tribune* takeover announcement ought to be made. The whole arrangement "could backfire if people got the idea JW had *bought* LH, that ORR [Brown] was still his major partner, that LH is simply a hired manager out for a fast buck; the rich man's whim thing, etc.," Hills wrote. The basic ideas to get across to the public were that the *Tribune* was here to stay, that Whitney would build on past traditions but move in fresh directions, that while he viewed the paper as a public trust it was not to be sustained as a charitable institution —"We believe strongly that the best newspapers are solvent ones, and intend to operate the *Tribune* with that in mind"—and that though nobody "should expect any overnight miracles," the new ownership ought to move promptly to dispel "the reported widespread beliefs that [the] Tribune has no editorial direction, is changing and indecisive, ruled by columnists, stoops to cheap promotions, compromises its integrity for advertisers, etc." With such a proprietary attitude reflected in his communications with Thayer, Hills looked to be all but in the bag.

But the Reids now balked at Thayer's hard bargaining. Their lawyer counterproposed, early in May, that if the *Tribune* was to recede to a subsidiary status, Whitney ought to recognize the huge investment the Reid family had made in it over the years—$20 million was cited as the total, in the form of net capital advances, interest accrued on those advances, profits left in the business, and salaries not taken, over the 1924–57 period—and that the nearly $6 million the Reids retained in the form of preferred stock ought to be paid to them through promissory notes over a fifteen- or twenty-year period, or they would in effect be giving the *Tribune* away for nothing. The Reids ought also to receive "X percent" of the *Tribune* stock, meaning that the offered 39 percent was not enough in view of the paper's downgraded standing in the projected Whitney holding company setup, and in addition, "Ogden Reid would undertake to continue as the executive head of the paper," meaning, presumably, under Lee Hills's charge.

Thayer interpreted this as a lawyer's bargaining position and steeled Whitney to hold firm. From the embassy in London, Whitney replied with great cordiality, emphasizing to Brown that he did not want there to be any misunderstanding between him and the Reids but just as plainly stressing that they were now discussing "a different basic relationship" from his original involvement as a participant on a "look-see" basis. The paper's "greatest hope of success," Whitney wrote, was to invest Lee Hills with its command. "I could not take on the required responsibility without a person of Lee's experience, stature and ability in this post." Hills would have Whitney's "unlimited proxy," and Brown would have to join him in announcing the fact of Hills's primacy and then perhaps "take on an assignment abroad to give Lee a clear road in becoming known and regarded as the executive head of the paper." With regard to the financial arrangements, Whitney added that "in the judgment of those who are advising and helping me," he ought not to take on the burden of "current and prospective losses, the heavy present liabilities for severance pay and other debts, and add to those the burden of $5.7 million of preferred stock of the present corporation." The whole object of his takeover would be to get the paper on a self-sustaining basis as soon as possible; profits were not likely to materialize "for a considerable period of time." He would try to save the *Tribune* because he shared the Reids' conviction about its importance to New York and to the nation, but he would not do so "under circumstances which you may now or later believe to be inequitable to you or to members of your family." That amounted to an exquisitely worded take-it-or-leave-it.

Brown's reply a week later, while equally gracious, was a masterpiece of ambiguity. It said on the one hand that Whitney's points had been "completely clear to the Reids for some time" and that furthermore Brown was "much moved by the spirit of equity that has characterized your thinking." On the other hand but in that same spirit, his family had reviewed its position and "should a firm proposition be made to the Reids and should that specific proposal meet with the acceptance of the several parties, I would do everything possible to help in the transition." To Thayer, that sounded like face-saving legalese for capitulation, and a meeting was set for the first Saturday in June among Whitney, Brown, and Hills to wrap up an agreement. If the Reids proved unexpectedly difficult, Thayer counseled Whitney, it was not too late for him to walk away from the whole situation, possibly adding $500,000 to his previous loan to give Brown time to find a new buyer—or taker—for the paper.

Just before Whitney was to meet at the St. Regis Hotel with Brown and Hills, he received a note from Helen Reid, who still held the decisive hand for her family in settling the *Tribune*'s fate. And she was unhappy. Her note expressed the hope that "your plan may be in some degree improved. I care so much about its going through, but there are other worth-while investors who believe that there is a better alternative for the paper. They are people who value more the Reid identity and investment—in work as well as dollars—than perhaps you or your business advisors do. . . . What I care about above everything is the right preservation of the paper. And with some changes in your current thinking I believe that your magic can bring about a powerful Herald Tribune that will result in a rewarding experience for you."

At the age of seventy-five, Helen Reid was indulging in self-delusion about her newspaper for the final time. To think that Whitney and his people would believe, at that late date, that other investors were waiting in the wings with a sweeter proposition for the ailing paper was preposterous. But Helen and Brown Reid were battlers—to the end. When Brown showed up at the Saturday meeting at the St. Regis, instead of shaking hands on the existing Whitney proposition he put a fresh proposal on the table that contained his mother's notion of a plan "in some degree improved": the Reids would yield the paper in return for 39 percent of the new parent company Whitney was assembling around the *Tribune*—and Brown's role at the paper was still left up in the air.

Hills said at once that he could no longer be included in their arrangements. On the phone with Brown the next day, Whitney offered to go ahead as earlier outlined even without Hills's commitment—they felt Hills would still come along once the deal was clinched and the anticipated purchase of *Parade* concluded—but Brown continued to hold out for better terms. By Thursday, Whitney had had enough. "I am sorry that our plans have not worked out as I knew we both had hoped," he wrote, and while there were no doubt people other than Lee Hills who could take on the *Tribune* job, the time and effort required for the recruiting "make this impossible for me. Therefore, Brown, I reluctantly and sadly conclude that I cannot provide further financing for the Herald Tribune beyond my present commitment. . . . I hope the alternative source of financing to which reference had been made will prove successful."

But there were no alternative sources; Helen Reid's bluff had been transparent. Brown, stating that "the future of the Herald Tribune is our only and principal concern" and that the family had merely taken literally Whitney's invitation to express to him openly any reservations it had about his terms, caved in at once. His note concluded:

1. I will step out of the Tribune today or next month if you so desire.

2. The Reids will yield on the improved deal if it is your view that we should, for legal, or other reasons.

The decision is yours.

As always, our best regards,

"We were going to the back benches for the foreseeable future," Brown recalled. "The shock was deepest and greatest for Mother. I had read Walter somewhat earlier. But there was really no viable alternative."

"The 'alternative,' " Thayer wrote to Hills, referring to Helen's bluff, "has evaporated faster than dry ice on a New York sidewalk in August. . . . [F]rom here on there won't nobody be kiddin' nobody." But even in the face of Brown's unconditional surrender, Hills was not persuaded. The Reids' last-minute tactics, he wrote Thayer, put the onus "squarely on Jock and, by inference, on me. . . . It made him look like a Shylock driving a hard bargain with people who were desperate. . . . It just isn't the congenial kind of thing with the Reids I had thought from the first it would and must be." Brown, he supposed, probably still did not believe that Hills was "very happy where I am; that I haven't been after his job; that I became interested because you and Jock outlined a program which seemed to give the Tribune a real chance for success. . . ." In view of "the whole basic disharmony" of his relationship with Brown, Hills was bowing out for good, he advised. Even then, Thayer and Whitney did not give up on him.

With that much raw emotion having been expended in the showdown with the Reids and without the man they badly wanted to run the paper and its potential hen-house relatives, Whitney might have backed off the undertaking if he had not received a remarkable letter dated June 13 from the White House. Helen Reid had just been in to see him, the President wrote. "My morning was a high pressure one and I really had no time for a conversation, but she was so insistent that I agreed to the meeting." Mrs. Reid had two points she wanted Eisenhower to convey to Whitney. The first was that Brown would get out whenever Jock wanted; the second was that Ike believed that the *Tribune* "has a great and valuable function to perform for the future of America." The President assured her that he and Whitney had spoken often about his proposed takeover of the paper, which he looked upon as "a civic service of the highest order." Still, to please her and to repay the paper for its long support of him, he wrote to Whitney,

> I told Helen, once more, that I did attach the most tremendous importance to the project and that I, of course, would be most happy to see it go through. . . . She obviously attaches such tremendous importan[ce] to your taking over the Herald Tribune and is so confident of the complete readiness of the Reid family (especially Brown) to comply with the conditions you have laid down that she wanted me to reassure you on these points as well as of my own abiding interest.

It was, in all likelihood, the one instance in American history in which the transfer of ownership of a major newspaper was decisively affected by the timely intervention of a sitting President.

Whitney's new possession, Walter Thayer predicted to the ambassador's wife, Betsey, "will tap Jock's wide range of talents and interests better than anything else could."

II

Copy desk veteran and onetime cable editor John Price, arriving for work around 4 p.m. on Thursday, August 28, 1958, entered the *Tribune* elevator and encountered Whitie Reid, rarely seen on the premises in the three years since his removal from power. The two men smiled at each other and said hello. The deskman thought he saw Whitie glance nervously at him to see if his hand would be proffered for shaking. Instead Price asked pleasantly, "Is today the big day?"

"Every day," said Whitie, giving nothing away, "is a big day."

After eighty-six years, the Reids surrendered control of the *Tribune* to a man who was not there for the occasion, probably out of respect for the emotional delicacy of the moment. The purchase of *Parade* for approximately $11 million had been consummated a month earlier in the name of Plymouth Rock Publications, as the hen house was formally named—a lofty evocation of Pilgrims' pride but in fact a veiled reference to the breed of fowl. Attached to *Parade* by a new long-term contract came its president, Arthur H. (Red) Motley, a vigorous salesman who had increased the magazine's revenues more than tenfold since taking command eleven years earlier. With that first solid wall in place, the only reason to have held up announcement of the *Tribune* takeover was the hope that Lee Hills, assured of the availability to the paper of *Parade*'s nourishing profits and the imminent departure of Brown Reid, would now accept Whitney's ultimate challenge to his abilities as a journalist.

Thayer kept advising Whitney that in the end they would get their man, but in mid-August the canny Hills gave his final no to Whitney's generous offer. It was, he wrote the ambassador, "the most difficult decision of my life." Tex McCrary, who had pushed his candidacy from the first, remarked in a letter to a friend after the final turndown, "Hills had no guts." Bill Paley, who had been a party to the effort to land him, felt afterward that "Hills strung us along" and in the process won a better deal for himself where he was. But Whitney's junior partner Howard Brundage, following Thayer's long tracking of his prey, had a more generous assessment of Hills: "If it took him six months finally to say no, it was because we didn't give up on him—we felt we really wanted him." In fact, Jack Knight did increase the rewards to his prize news hand and held out to him the imminent prospect, which was duly fulfilled, of *de facto* editorial supervision of the Knight newspapers, leading in time to command of what would become the Knight-Ridder chain. There was, too, the mitigating circumstance at the time of Hills's wife's ill health; she had recently suffered a heart attack. But in the complex human equation that confronts some men with the opportunity for greatness in their field if they will only risk it, Hills chose to stick with the success and comfort he was enjoying in Detroit and places smaller than

to gamble against failure and frustration in the nation's main media arena. Not everyone has his price.

The hope had been to announce Hills's appointment simultaneously with Whitney's takeover by way of demonstrating the size and quality of the new broom about to sweep through Horace Greeley's old *Tribune*. Whom they would find in place of Hills was too important a question for them to rush the answer, but the anxiety swirling through the city room—would Whitney take over and save the paper or walk away and let it die?—had to be stilled; a caretaker regime, with Brown remaining for a short transitional period, would stay in place while Thayer now intensified the search.

And so at 4:30 that late August afternoon—too late for the evening papers to carry the story—the Reids appeared in the *Tribune*'s ninth-floor auditorium, little Helen in blue brocade, light bonnet, and white gloves, Brown in his all-business navy, Whitie in summer-weight gray with an aggressively patterned tie, to announce that they had turned over control of the paper to Ambassador Whitney. And to smile when they said it. Half sitting on the corner of a desk, Brown read the mimeographed announcement. The Reids would retain "a substantial interest" in the paper, but Whitney would hold "clear, working control." The ambassador believed "in its continuing future as a great newspaper," his statement said. "I propose to preserve its character and to build upon its great tradition as an independent Republican newspaper"—the Greeley hallmark of political alliance free of slavish partisanship. Helen, who had stood behind her sons for most of the announcement meeting, came forward at the end to answer questions as Brown slipped a supporting arm around her waist. It was a fine step for newspapers in general, she said gamely, to have a man like Mr. Whitney enter the field. Over the years, there had been many offers to buy into the paper "but nothing that management or ownership cared to consider" —a trooper right up to the curtain. "We never contemplated selling the paper. We are not selling it now."

And when would Whitney appear on the scene and begin to work his restorative magic? He could not take part in the paper's daily publication "at this time," his statement read, "but I will follow its progress closely and consult from time to time on long-range policy and plans for its expansion. At a later date I will devote my major attention to the New York Herald Tribune."

"If I had just bought a newspaper of that importance," retrospectively remarked a woman who long ran one of the nation's most influential dailies, "I'd have come home from London. Jock had to make up his mind—the paper or the ambassadorship. . . . He didn't understand the newspaper business. Papers can't be run *in absentia*."

But Jock Whitney had never really run anything in his life. For him now suddenly to have taken command of the bleeding *Tribune* and begun issuing rousing orders to undermanned and inadequately directed troops would only have perpetuated the Reids' folly of pride; he had not bought the paper to turn it into a rich man's plaything. It was a job for professionals of the highest acquirable skills, and Walter Thayer would find the right man to put in charge as he had found and bought *Parade,* for the paper was to be run as a business, not as a charity or a tightly clutched family heirloom. And if enough time, money, and talent were expended in the effort, the odds were at least even— in Thayer's judgment—that it would succeed and, as Thayer, Paley, and McCrary were in accord, provide Whitney with the most fulfilling patronage of his career.

There was the further consideration of Whitney's own loyalty to the President and sense of patriotic duty serving, even if only ceremonially, in London. Jock and Betsey Whitney were a great hit in Britain, functioning, in her words, as "a joint venture. I was more a part of Jock's life then than at any other time." Pleasurable aspects of the ambassadorship aside, "he never would have thought about deserting the ship," Betsey Whitney added. The *Tribune* could go on without him—so long as he was footing the bill.

It would also go on now without the further affiliation of the man who may have done more than any other to bring the Reids and Whitney together. Tex McCrary, having served the *Tribune* and his own new public-relations firm well by promoting Brown as the boy wonder of U.S. newspapering, had persuaded the Reids that their best bet for saving it was Whitney. He also persuaded Whitney, in the face of the massed disapproval of his financial advisers, that the paper would secure his standing as a useful and influential citizen. And when Jock hesitated at the brink, McCrary kept pushing. He was at least party to the discussions that helped create the hen-house concept—afterward he would claim the idea had been his—and he had strongly championed Lee Hills to run the enterprise. And when *Time* kept trying prematurely to break the story of Hills and the hen house, McCrary managed to keep getting it killed. When progress had been slowed in the spring, he told *The Wall Street Journal* that Whitney's full-scale involvement was imminent (and, not incidentally, that he had been instrumental in enlisting Whitney). Given this involvement, Thayer had asked, through Brown, whether the publicist expected a finder's fee if the deal went through; McCrary waived so material a measure of his value to the paper. Whether as an officer or director, possibly with a small piece of the stock, or at the very least as its well-paid publicist, McCrary anticipated an ongoing relationship with the *Tribune* under Whitney's ownership; it was the least they could do for him. But then, and not for the first time, his own combativeness and zeal shortcircuited his ambitions.

When the President's lord high chamberlain, Sherman Adams, who was the very model of the stern, frugal, hardworking New Englander, was suddenly disclosed in the spring of 1958 to be an old friend of a flamboyant, corner-cutting Boston industrialist, Bernard Goldfine, and a recipient of his gifts, McCrary engineered a scenario designed to take the heat off the White House. While it was true that Adams had been in contact with government agencies about Goldfine's dealings, his intention was said to have been merely to gather information, not obtain favors for his friend, whom McCrary was meanwhile busy portraying as a rags-to-riches entrepreneur up from an immigrant youth and now being victimized by oppressive congressional investigators and Democratic politicians out to embarrass the President. McCrary beat Adams's foes to the headlines by working closely with Goldfine's attorney and staging a media campaign in downtown Washington just before the industrialist was summoned to a grilling on Capitol Hill. McCrary and his staff people succeeded in uncovering efforts by House investigators to plant an electronic recording device in Goldfine's hotel rooms and then used the bugging attempt to authenticate their claims of harassment in a steady counterattack before radio microphones, television cameras, and eagerly attending print reporters. McCrary had little trouble prevailing upon Brown Reid, who was eager to please both Eisenhower and Whitney, to place the *Tribune* in the vanguard of those indiscriminately defending the White House, although some in the paper's Washington bureau warned against the step. The *Tribune*'s first editorial on the subject went windmilling off to the rescue:

> Whoever knows Sherman Adams knows that he is honest as the day is long. . . . Those who are using the matter of Boston hotel bills as an attack upon his character will find such tactics only boomeranging upon themselves.

But flaunting his manipulative skills too vigorously to remain submerged, McCrary was himself questioned at one of the press conferences he had stage-managed about his role in the Goldfine camp. He and his people had come to Washington, he said, without fee and because of his friendship with Goldfine's counsel. Pressed further to explain this generous outlay of his firm's services, McCrary said, "My concern, if any, is with the *New York Herald Tribune*. I am trying to help the *Herald Tribune*," which was his client. What connection the paper had with Goldfine or Adams, he did not explain; it is hard to make yourself understood with your foot in your mouth.

In the end, Adams was found guilty of impropriety, his usefulness to the President was at an end, and he resigned; Goldfine went to jail for tax evasion, and the *Tribune*, associated with a public-relations ploy in Adams's behalf and too eager to dismiss the whole affair as a teapot tempest, was revealed as nakedly partisan. McCrary, furthermore, was both visible and vocal that spring and summer in espousing the Republican candidacy of Nelson Rockefeller for governor of New York—a position eagerly embraced by the *Tribune* as well. But McCrary's elevation within the organization and blatant use of its power as a political instrument were not precisely what Jock Whitney had in mind. With the takeover announcement imminent, Thayer advised Whitney that it was imperative for the paper to distance itself from McCrary. He was too hot, too indecorous and indiscreet, and his services, Thayer later told McCrary as decently as he could, would no longer be required or helpful.

In an outraged letter sent a week before the takeover, McCrary stormed at Whitney for his ingratitude. "You never would have known how much you wanted the Trib as a way of life if I had not stubbornly pushed you back to the decision each time you pulled away from it," he railed. Whether or not he knew it, Whitney needed him now, but if he was to be discarded, he demanded public acknowledgment of his role in the deal and a finder's fee that he had waived in expectation of other, more satisfying forms of thanks. Whitney never answered his letter; their friendship was never the same afterward. William Safire, McCrary's admiring younger associate, who had been highly active on the *Tribune* account and in the Goldfine embroilment, would remain unforgiving. "I think there's no doubt that Tex got a screwing," Safire said long afterward, "and that Jock acted dishonorably toward him. The facts of Tex's role are indisputable."

Bill Paley thought McCrary had exaggerated his part in the *Tribune*'s change of hands but favored his being paid off in some fashion. Thayer thought that might be done but only at a later date, when McCrary could be dealt with rationally. Brown Reid recalled that, from where he sat, McCrary's further participation in the paper "was neither understood nor discussed."

Brown's own future participation would not extend beyond the end of the year, and the only real hope of his ever again becoming master of the paper lay in a "recapture" clause his lawyer had won as a concession from Thayer whereby the Reids were granted the first right to negotiate for any *Tribune* stock remaining in Whitney's estate at the time of his death; no terms or negotiating formula was specified. Still, Brown seemed to take his required departure in good grace; he was just thirty-three, with his life in front of him. Whitney, through the President, and McCrary, through his friendship with Nixon, were trying to arrange an appropriate—i.e., not major—ambassadorship for him. A few days after the takeover was announced, Brown wrote a long farewell report to Whitney, prescribing what he thought were the paper's most pressing needs, prominent among them a new set of editors. He signed off, in the fashion of the nautical Reids, "The ship is yours. The very best of luck."

Deskman John Price, who had been on the *Tribune* almost as long as Brown Reid had been alive, used the rite of passage to forgive the former ownership for the mess they had made of the paper and the crimp they had put in his career. He addressed his sentiments, not to Brown, whom he held in low regard, but to Brown's mother. Speaking for himself but reflecting the prevailing view among *Tribune* editorial people, Price wrote to commend "your hard decision which was announced yesterday" and added:

> For my part, I have owed a debt of gratitude to Mr. Reid and you for some thirty years of secure employment, which I have ever sought to repay with good work. It will be sad not to have your wisdom and integrity still guiding the paper, but the best parting gift you could make was to assure its continuity as an institution, which you have done.

She thanked him and wished him well.

III

Although the Whitney era of hope had begun, 1958 ended on a series of low notes at the *Herald Tribune*. The new owner and the new leadership he was expected to bring were nowhere to be seen—only his surrogate, "acting president" Howard Brundage, slightly older, more corpulent, and a good deal more financially astute than Brown Reid but even less knowledgeable about how to operate a successful newspaper. The national economy picked up, but for eighteen days in December, including the period when the heaviest pre-Christmas advertising would normally have run, all the New York papers had been shut down by a strike of the deliverers' union. It was the most intractable and mischievous part of the labor force and possessed an inordinate power to toss a monkey wrench into the machinery because of where its members' unskilled services were rendered in the manufacturing process—at the very end. The work stoppage was the first and least damaging of a series that would finally convince Walter Thayer that newspapers were not like other businesses. The lost revenues the strike inflicted left the *Tribune* with a record loss of nearly $2 million for 1958.

The day after the deliverers' strike ended, which was the next-to-last day of the year, Brown Reid came into the newsroom around five in the afternoon, summoned whoever was there to the vicinity of the city desk, and delivered what even the unadmiring John Price conceded was "a pretty good little farewell speech and received a polite round of applause, although"—he added in his diary—"everyone, so far as I know, is glad to see him go."

Not quite everyone.

Even as Brown was clearing out his desk, television news columnist Marie Torre was entering jail for a ten-day stay to defend the principle that Brown had chosen to espouse more ardently than any other: democracy depended upon freedom of the press. Torre not only shared this conviction but was grateful to Brown for giving her the opportunity through personal ordeal to be the instrument for dramatizing it to the world.

Torre always believed that ultimately she would be spared the degradation of going to jail for declining to disclose the name of the CBS executive who had told her the network believed singer Judy Garland was not living up to her commitments because of unhappiness over her weight. The worst that would happen, her friends assured her, was that Judge Ryan would give her a suspended sentence. Indeed, Ryan could well have ruled in Torre's favor, holding that in the absence of any clear precedent to the contrary in nearly 170 years of federal adjudications, members of the press were entitled to the same privilege of confidentiality in their relationship with news sources as the courts extended to lawyers' dealings with their clients, doctors' with their patients, and clergymen's with their parishioners. But Sylvester Ryan was a practical jurist, able but intellectually limited, and not eager to write federal law. He might have withheld judgment of Torre's claimed privilege by awaiting the outcome of Garland's case against CBS to determine the materiality of Torre's information. For, ironically, even if Torre had revealed her informant's name, thereby confirming the libel, many legal observers felt Garland could not have won her case because the network would have cited truth as a defense—i.e., the entertainer's weight problem and its resulting miseries (or was it the other way around?) were common knowledge, and the CBS official had merely dared to utter to a reporter what was already well known in private to be true. But without Torre's cooperation, Garland could probably not have had her day in court, regardless of the result, and thus the singer's constitutionally mandated right to a fair trial would have been abridged.

At Brown Reid's insistence, the *Tribune*'s lawyers went before the Second Circuit of the U.S. Court of Appeals and argued that the freedom of journalists to gather their information unencumbered by court-ordered disclosure of their sources was as integral to First Amendment protection as the freedom to publish that information. Brown Reid's sincerity in this belief "was almost palpable," recalled Sheldon Oliensis, part of the team of *Tribune* lawyers defending Torre. " 'My reporters are not going to disclose their sources,' he said. It didn't matter to him whether the case was about a missing dog or a fat entertainer. Defending the principle involved was more important to him than winning." Brown himself, having been apprised that the paper's case would have been more promising and heroic if it had involved, say, corruption in high places or a comparable instance in which the public's need to know could have been invoked, recalled: "I took the position that you can't always choose the ground on which to fight."

At the end of September, a year after Torre had refused before U.S. District Judge Ryan to yield up the name of her CBS source, Potter Stewart, writing for the Second Circuit appeals tribunal just before his elevation to the U.S. Supreme Court, ruled against her. Compulsory disclosure of a journalist's confidential sources "may entail an abridgment of press freedom by imposing some limitation on the availability of news," Stewart held, but "the duty of a witness to testify in a court of law has roots as deep as the guarantee of a free press," thereby justifying "some impairment" of First Amendment guarantees. Press freedom, "precious and vital though it is to a free society," was not absolute. "[B]asic too are courts of justice armed with the power to discover truth," for there was "a paramount public interest in the fair administration of justice."

Appealing to the Supreme Court, the *Tribune* lawyers contended that the Second Circuit opinion, unless reversed, would have an immediate chilling effect "on the willingness of news sources to transmit news in confidence to reporters and news media. It will lend aid to any forces seeking to choke off the flow of news. . . . The First Amendment mandates against restraints at any stage of the flow of news to the public," so the Stewart opinion "strips from newsgathering the essential protection of the amendment." The Supreme Court, with dispatch and only civil-libertarian absolutist William Douglas in dissent, declined to take the case, thus upholding the decision below.

When Marie Torre, her legal remedies now exhausted, reappeared before Judge Ryan and still refused to disclose her source, he blew up at her. "Make this girl talk," he yelled at the *Tribune* attorneys. "I don't want to send her to jail." But she would not. Ryan, angered and insisting that a journalist, of all citizens, ought to set an example by cooperating with the courts, was ready to pack Torre off to jail on the spot until her lawyers noted that she had a husband and two infant children at home and it would be humane of the court to give her a few days to make domestic arrangements before incarceration.

Even then Torre's friends tried to keep her from serving time in jail. Boston barrister Joseph Welch, who had become something of a television celebrity after his 1954 on-the-air tongue-lashing of Joe McCarthy for the Senator's shameless tactics in ruining the careers of innocents, telephoned Torre, told her she had done more than her share to defend the honor of her profession and should now ask her CBS informant to stand up like a man, and if he refused, she ought to reveal the cad's identity. But Torre would not. She did take Welch's advice to call a leading Wall Street lawyer for reassurance that she would not be indefinitely subjected to the same demand for disclosure and continuing punishment by the court even after she had served the jail sentence. She was told that Ryan, unlikely to risk public censure for appearing to persecute her, would probably let the matter drop after her release. Before going to jail, she did tell one person the name of her source just in case anything happened to her—city editor Luke Carroll, who promptly called the source and asked him to spare Torre by coming forward. He declined but phoned her to express his admiration for her principled behavior. "I didn't know Luke was going to do that," Torre recalled. "I didn't urge him to, and if I had known he was going to, I wouldn't have told him."

She was up at 5:30 that very cold late December morning to prepare. There were the pre-court interviews to be given at her apartment, the children to be calmed and reassured about her return, the things to take with her to jail— cigarettes, candy, two dresses, a copy of *Dr. Zhivago*. At 10 a.m. sharp she rose upon Judge Ryan's arrival in court and came forward to face him for the last time. The final confrontation lasted hardly a minute, and when she refused again to name her informant, the judge ordered her taken away by two marshals, through the silent courtroom packed with many of her newspaper friends to lend her moral support, past her father, who she was afraid would have a heart attack on the way back to his office after having seen her hauled away, and the photographers who kept popping away at her down the endless corridor while she struggled to smile pluckily. "I had a feeling of such loneliness—because my country was doing this to me—sending me to jail when I knew I was not a bad person and had not done a bad thing." In the marshals' office, her pent-up emotions gave way, and she cried for a time before they took her across the river to the federal lockup in Hudson County, New Jersey.

The episode was not a lark. Marie Torre got fingerprinted and photographed like a common criminal and had to wear a uniform. Early in the mornings she was presented with a bucket and mop and ordered to clean up. Her closest companion among the inmates was a husband killer, and her greatest peril a woman given to violent spasms, threats, and profanity who had to be tied down from time to time. When the novelty wore off after the first couple of days, there remained long, lonely hours to pass—there were no recreational facilities, no yard, no therapeutic activities. The reality of being caged was "mostly a wretched, empty world with nothing in it but despair."

Near the end of her ten-day term, she wrote to Brown Reid, regretting that he had left the *Tribune* and saying, "You gave me 20-20 vision into the dangers of a shackled press, plus more legal and moral support than any reporter has ever received from an editor. The praises that have been showered upon me since my incarceration really belong to you. . . . Thanks for giving me the biggest opportunity of my career."*

The issue at stake that was first brought to public prominence in *Garland v. Torre* has yet to be settled. Many more states now have laws shielding the press from obligatory disclosure of their sources, but many still do not. A growing and complex body of legal opinion surrounds the question, which has received more attention as public concern has grown over the power of the press and its potential for abuse. It is posited that the privileged anonymity of sources might be used to cloak careless reporting or to spread malicious charges concocted by grudge-bearers. The courts now go through a delicate balancing act, trying to weigh sensitively the colliding constitutional rights and applying pragmatic tests as to how vital the reporter's withheld information really is and what stake society has in its forced disclosure. In serious criminal cases, like the one involving *New York Times* reporter M. A. Farber's information about a New Jersey doctor charged with committing multiple murders, journalists have been required to testify or—as Farber did some twenty years after Torre—go to jail. The legal consensus appears to hold that journalists, who are privileged characters in many ways and deserve to be in light of their quasi-public function, are not constitutionally sanctioned to interfere with the orderly enforcement of the law, any more than are Presidents of the United States, as Richard Nixon discovered.

IV

A whole year would pass between Jock Whitney's taking title to the *Tribune* and the installation of a new president of the paper, but Walter Thayer, who was in charge of recruitment, at least did not make matters worse by fol-

---

* Asked by the author nearly twenty-five years later to identify her informant—in the interest, he said, of history—Torre would not.

lowing a suggestion indirectly made by the President of the United States.

A few weeks after his earlier letter written on Helen Reid's behalf, Dwight Eisenhower again wrote to Whitney about the *Tribune,* which, he felt, "operated under your political philosophy," would prove helpful "to preserve sound and moderate government." He had been having long talks on the subject, he went on, with Bill Robinson, by then the president of the Coca-Cola Company. "My respect for his opinions and for his dedication to the country is high indeed," Eisenhower stated. To succeed, the self-promoting Robinson had told the President, every newspaper needs a partnership between two key men, one on the editorial side and one on the business side; in Lee Hills, who had not yet taken himself out of the running irrevocably, Whitney had the editorial star he needed, by Robinson's estimate. And who better to team with Hills, Ike intimated, than Robinson himself? "His devotion to the paper and friendship for you would guarantee his cheerful assistance in any way that might seem fitting to you." But why would Robinson give up the pay and perquisites of heading one of the nation's stellar marketing organizations to return to the newspaper that he had done as much as anyone to run into the ground? Thayer, well connected with the Georgia industrial aristocracy through his membership in the Augusta National Golf Club, soon discovered that Robinson had made the mistake of confronting and contradicting Robert Woodruff, the chairman and dominant force of Atlanta-based Coca-Cola, before a meeting of company officials. On top of that, Coke was being outperformed lately by its chief competitors. Robinson, on his way down and out of the company, had turned to his friend in the White House to try to win his way back onto the Whitney-funded *Tribune.* Thayer, though, knew enough about the man and his record to flatly oppose his return. Whitney, all grace, thanked Eisenhower but said his new Plymouth Rock publishing venture had the ideal complement to Hills in Red Motley, the hard-selling head of *Parade,* which he was about to buy.

Within days of Hills's withdrawal, Thayer was meeting with the man Hills unequivocally endorsed as the best in the country to take on the *Tribune* challenge—Bernard Kilgore, the forty-nine-year-old president of the Dow Jones Company and architect of the extraordinary rise of *The Wall Street Journal.* Its circulation had grown from 32,000 in 1940 to 480,000 in 1958 on the strength of its comprehensive business coverage, jargon-free reporting, shrewd front-page format (tightly written world and financial news digests, a pair of "leaders" on widely varying and unpredictable but business-related subjects, and a rotating column on trends in taxes, labor relations, merchandising, and the securities markets), and a literate if conservatively doctrinaire editorial page. To a new generation of businessmen and growing numbers of investors eager to share in the postwar boom, *The Wall Street Journal* was becoming a bible, their indispensable second morning paper, which, through pioneering use of teletypesetting and other techniques in automation, was printed at several plants across the nation and delivered to every subscriber's desk with the mail. No American newspaper had won such swift and phenomenal success since Joseph Patterson's *Daily News* hit New York after World War I.

For a time, both Thayer and Bill Paley, who was filling in for his brother-in-law, thought that Barney Kilgore, well fixed though he was at Dow Jones, with a handsome slice of the profits, was intrigued by the challenge of remaking the *Tribune* and tempted to take it on. Thayer pressed his case and extracted a number of sensible thoughts from Kilgore on what direction the *Tribune* should take—namely, toward a more compact, conservatively presented paper for readers who did not have the time to deal with the bulk of the *Times*, with stress on metropolitan rather than global and national coverage as had been its glorious but financially unrequited tradition. Kilgore soon decided against shifting to the *Tribune*; instead, he became Thayer's close adviser and sounding board and served as a director of the burgeoning Whitney communications enterprise.

While the search went on, the *Tribune* was glutted by rumors of possible successors to Brown Reid, among them Tex McCrary, an inappropriate contender in the combined Thayer-Whitney judgment; Harry Ashmore, editor of *The Arkansas Gazette*, whom Hills characterized to Thayer as being uncomfortably far to the left; and Ralph McGill, editor of the *Atlanta Constitution*. In fact, Thayer had an open mind on the subject; he wanted a man with energy, courage, and competence on both the editorial and the business side of newspapering. He would have preferred someone who knew the complex New York market, but neither of the pair whom Hills suggested—Francis M. (Jack) Flynn, who ran the *Daily News*, and Seymour Berkson, publisher of the *Journal-American*—seemed right. A *News* man was not the ideal sort of gent for a Whitney-owned *Tribune*—it would send the wrong signal to the trade—and Berkson, though well regarded, was running a money-losing operation for Hearst. A more logical move would have been to raid the *Times* for one of its stars, like James Reston, to whom Brown Reid had sent Sylvan Barnet to try to enlist as a well-paid syndicated columnist for the *Tribune* in 1956, or business manager Amory Bradford, the polished Yale man who had left a top Wall Street law firm and risen swiftly at the *Times*. But even if either of them or other *Times* people had been interested, it would not have been seemly to steal someone from the competition, for Whitney people played the game by Marquis of Queensberry rules and traveled first-class. And, at least as relevant, to have turned to the *Times* for a new leader would have been a confession of the *Tribune*'s badly reduced standing in the head-on competition for New York's quality newspaper readership. For a time, Thayer pursued a pair of New Yorkers hardly among the leading lights of journalism but recommended to him as highly knowledgeable—J. Montgomery Curtis, the politically conservative director of the American Press Institute, a kind of advanced vocational training center linked to Columbia's School of Journalism, whose chief operational credential in the field was five prewar years as a Buffalo city editor, and Weston Pullen, Jr., a Time Inc. vice president and clubby Princeton man. Neither made sense, given the size of the task, and Thayer started asking around the country for other suggestions.

As the search began to look more difficult than he had imagined—the problem was that those qualified to take the *Tribune* job knew how difficult it would be and shunned it, while those likely to be most eager were probably not up to it—a division of opinion arose between Whitney's two closest advisers. Sam Park, installed as titular head of Plymouth Rock but continuing as Whitney's personal financial overseer, thought it made most sense to keep Brown Reid as the editor, though fastened to a short leash, bring in a strong advertising and promotion man to match Barney Cameron's strengths as a circulation and production manager, and fill in with a few other needed personnel until Whitney returned from London for good and stepped in with both feet. Howard Brundage would remain at the paper, meanwhile, to represent the Whitney interest and install financial controls. Thayer, who considered Brown to have been a disastrous chief executive, sharply disagreed, arguing it was essential to install a strong figure at the top as soon as possible and a mistake to staff at the lower levels first; the new chief ought to be free to make his own selections. He wrote to Whitney that "we are beginning to go off in different directions" and asked him "to call the signals." A few weeks later, while Whitney was deciding whom to side with, Thayer registered a more urgent plea, noting that his own view on the paper's management problems "differs materially from Sam's" and Brundage's and conceding that "they may be absolutely right." But he contended that the paper was living on borrowed time, "three years at the most," unless its situation improved dramatically, and that could happen only if it promptly enlisted "aggressive, imaginative, resourceful and confident management." He added, by way of galvanizing Whitney, "This thing is dynamite," losing $5,479.45 every day of the year at its current rate. "I have lived with it almost day and night. It scares the hell out of me. I think it's the toughest assignment you have ever taken on."

When the management consulting firm of McKinsey & Company, Inc., hired to analyze what ailed the *Tribune* and blueprint a future course, handed in its first report a month later, saying it thought the paper could be salvaged but had "an urgent need" for managerial direction, Whitney sided with Thayer. Brown was invited to leave four weeks hence, at year's end, and Brundage was put in as temporary chief executive with instructions to get the repair job underway while George Cornish, restored to full power as the egregious Luke Carroll was demoted to his assistant, held the fort on the editorial side. Thayer intensified his hunt for the right man.

Although no new figure appeared until late in the summer, two personnel changes occurred early in 1959 that cheered *Tribune* veterans and brought back hope for the restoration of faded greatness. Sports editor Bob Cooke and chief editorial writer Bill Miller, both poor administrators, left the paper. With the departure of Cooke, Red Smith wrote to Whitney, imploring him to bring back Stanley Woodward, whose firing "for fighting too loudly for a better newspaper" had been "a ruinous mistake." Woodward, then in his sixty-fourth year, had been producing strong sports sections for papers in Miami and Newark and doing magazine work. Drink and failing health had drained his powers, but so quick and accurate a judge of men was he and so "full of fierce integrity" that inspired unquestioning loyalty, Smith assured the new *Tribune* owner, that long before age could be a factor Woodward would have the run-down sports staff back in great shape. Thayer, seeking fresh talent, opposed the idea, but Whitney overruled him, and "the Coach," as Woodward was by then universally known in the sportswriting community for his broad knowledge of the world of athletics, came back to the paper in mid-February—"my dream for years," said Red Smith of the man who had brought him to the big time and was then himself unceremoniously bounced from same. And named as acting chief of the editorial-page writers was Lessing Engelking. For a good part of that year, then, the *Tribune* was returned to the aging hands of three men who had shaped it during its heyday two decades earlier.

Thayer, however, did not bank heavily on nostalgia and by mid-February was telling Kilgore that the Brundage-Cornish team lacked the spark, energy, "and even the enthusiasm for the job that has to be done." In response, Kilgore offered a new name with an interestingly varied background for the *Tribune* job —fifty-one-year-old Eugene S. Duffield, who had been "a brilliant writer" when Kilgore hired him to report for *The Wall Street Journal*'s Washington bureau in the mid-'Thirties and a fine handler of men when elevated to bureau chief. "I cannot think of a better bet," said Kilgore.

On inspection, Duffield looked like the genuine article. A graduate of the University of Wisconsin, where he later taught history and served in the deanery, he had written for David Lawrence's *U.S. Daily* and the *Chicago Tribune* in Washington before his stint with Kilgore's *Journal,* then served in government as an assistant to the Secretary of the Treasury and more closely with James M. Forrestal in the Navy Department. After the war, he had been an executive and director at the McGraw-Hill publishing company, assistant publisher of the *Enquirer* in Cincinnati, and vice president of Federated Department Stores, a retailing giant, where he had a reputation as a tough-minded administrator. The man had range but had never run anything; now seemed the right moment. But Thayer was a little late. An old-line firm that published the successful monthlies *Popular Science* and *Outdoor Life* had offered Duffield its top job, a safe and well-paid slot. And Duffield stressed to Thayer that he wanted to be his own boss at last rather than work with or for someone, even as passive a proprietor as Whitney was likely to be. Thayer urged Whitney to reassure Duffield, and the ambassador cabled:

MY POLICY AS IN OTHER ENTERPRISES WILL BE TO GIVE YOU THE ENTIRE RESPONSIBILITY WHICH TOP JOB REQUIRES. . . . I HOPE SEE TRIBUNE BECOME GREAT NEWSPAPER AGAIN AND BELIEVE IT CAN BECOME SO ONLY IN HANDS OF DEDICATED AND PROFESSIONAL MANAGEMENT WITH OWNERSHIP WHICH UNDERSTANDS AND APPRECIATES THAT FACT.

But Duffield chose *Popular Science* instead. Thayer's irked reaction was to contemplate buying the company Duffield was joining, adding it to Plymouth Rock, of which Duffield would serve as president, and thereby obtaining his services for the *Tribune* by putting him over whomever Thayer finally got to run the paper. "This is a difficult, frustrating, depressing experience," Thayer wrote to Whitney after Duffield's rejection. "I can't ever remember being involved in any endeavor which took quite so much patience and effort."

He did not wallow in discouragement for long, for the McKinsey consulting firm shortly presented him, as part of its ongoing assessment of the paper, with a report that he characterized to Whitney as "a severe indictment" of current management. Thayer concurred. Only that reinstalled curmudgeon, Stanley Woodward, whom Thayer was man enough to recall he had opposed bringing back, was doing well, having "substantially improved the sports section." And no one was more disappointing than Howard Brundage, J. H. Whitney & Co.'s own man at the paper, who Thayer felt had offered no original ideas, demonstrated no independent judgment, added nothing to the development of an organization, and "struck out without even a foul tip." Perhaps this assessment was harsh, Thayer noted, since Brundage had never been projected as the permanent chief executive of the paper, "but he could have carved out an important spot for himself" if he had shown reasonable ability. Brundage, in his own defense, recalled that he was working with a crew of leftovers who could hardly have been expected to generate a revitalizing effort. His assistant, Charles Rees, a junior finance man also sent over to the paper from the Whitney office, thought that Brundage had been given "a limited mandate" that was plainly understood to be a holding action. To Thayer's way of thinking, however, Brundage, who had done well for the firm in looking out for its investments in the orange-juice and frozen-food business, ought to have been adaptable enough to become quickly useful in the newspaper business. It would take Thayer several years to concede that, as managerial assignments, newspapers and oranges could not be compared.

From holdover Barney Cameron's perspective, the Whitney era at the *Tribune* was off to a fine start "until Walter Thayer moved his McKinsey whiz kids in. They knew nothing about newspapers and went to see every bellyacher in the place. We could have got along very well without Thayer and his efficiency boys."

But it was Thayer's judgment that prevailed, and with his anxiety increasing by the week, he was perhaps wishfully receptive when Barney Kilgore telephoned during a break in a meeting of Associated Press members being held in the city in early April 1959 and said he had somebody with him who he thought should be considered to run the *Tribune*. A more unlikely candidate would have been hard to imagine. Robert Mitchell White II was running the little daily that his father and grandfather had passed down to him in Mexico, Missouri, a county seat in the east-central part of the state about two hours' driving time west of downtown St. Louis. The *Mexico Ledger* was a quite ordinary smalltown sheet, with a circulation of under 9,000, though its attention to world and national news made it less provincial than most papers its size. Bob White was proud of his town and his newspaper, but his own reputation within the American journalistic fraternity was out of proportion to the charms of Mexico, Missouri, or the virtues of the *Ledger.* His name had appeared on one of the lists Lee Hills had given Thayer of those worth considering for a top editorial job. "Very attractive, good speaker and good editor," Hills had noted, "in his 30's." In fact, White was then forty-three but had a craggy, ageless face, cropped haircut, and ramrod military posture that made him look younger. He also smiled a great deal—a wide, boyish, ingratiating smile that was highly photogenic—and shook hands with a firmness that declared here was somebody fine and forthright. He was a Democrat, a Mason, a Methodist, a Rotarian, a wholesome product of heartland America, and within a short time of being introduced to him, Walter Thayer was hearing from some of the biggest newspaper people in the Midwest—Jack Knight and Mike Cowles and Marshall Field, Jr.—that this Bob White, this unlikely specimen from a burg nobody at the *Herald Tribune* had ever heard of, was a special human being.

Newspapering was in his blood. When his grandfather, Robert Morgan White, bought the *Ledger* in 1876, one of his first editorial campaigns was against wearing six-guns around town. His younger brother, Albert, went into a saloon one night, and a couple of fellows started raising hell with him about the damn fool things his brother was writing in the newspaper. "One thing led to another, and a fight started," as Bob White often and pridefully retold the story. "Albert knocked one of the men down and turned on the other when the man he had dropped drew and shot Albert in the back, killing him." According to the code of the country, grandfather White had to kill his brother's killer or leave town. "But instead of strapping on his guns, he did another editorial, denouncing the cowardly murder of Albert White, saying only a man with a yellow streak a yard wide down his back would do such a thing and, at that, it would take the kind of coward who could only exert his manhood by carrying a six-gun. Happily, that fellow left town. And I'm here."

White's father had continued that principled tradition by heartily opposing the locally prominent Ku Klux Klan, and an idealistic young Bob was sent east to West Point for his college education. He flunked out after one term, was admitted to more genteel and less rigorous Washington and Lee, where he played football and was graduated in 1938, went to see Europe before it was engulfed by war, came home, and set to work for the *Ledger,* reporting, serving as sports editor, and learning his way around the advertising and circulation ends of the business. For a little while he worked in the United Press bureau in Kansas City. During the war he was in the South Pacific for three years, part of the time on General MacArthur's staff, before being transferred to the War Department's public-relations office in Washington. At war's end, he wrote editorials for a few months at the *St. Louis Post-Dispatch,* then came home for good to take charge of the *Ledger* while his father moved to the background.

Papers like the *Mexico Ledger* were the cement that held together the mosaic of American communal life in non-urban places, supplying them with identity and cohesiveness in a broad countryside where man and nature abided in uneasy alliance. "Covering the news like the dew covers Little Dixie," ran the *Ledger*'s motto, referring to the band of ardently Democratic counties it had carved out for its readership zone. The paper was full of local names and pictures of local fires and car crashes and a lot of wire-service copy and canned columns and other material from the syndicates, and although it could demonstrate enterprise when a big story broke, it was shaped more by complacency and boosterism than journalistic doggedness or craft. Its articles were in diagrammable English and its sans-serif headlines were serviceable, but its writing style and layout lacked grace, and its editorials, most of which Bob White wrote himself, were notable for the primerlike quality of their prose and heavy dependency on platitude for their thought.

Bob White's real skills were social, not editorial. Crops might fail, storekeepers prosper or struggle, office-holders come and go, but smalltown newspapers, like banks, were the bedrock of their communities, and Bob White was an immensely secure man in his surroundings, a leader of the local aristocracy. Yet he was also eager to shine in a wider orbit. He thus became active in the Missouri Press Association and the American Society of Newspaper Editors and the National Conference of Editorial Writers and the Inland Daily Press Association, of which he was serving as chairman when Kilgore commended him to Walter Thayer, and Sigma Delta Chi, the national fraternity of journalists, of which he had been treasurer in 1958. Bob White not only joined and dutifully attended the gatherings of these professional organizations, to which most working newsmen could devote only occasional and usually indifferent attention; he *starred* at them, winning friends in high places with his hearty handshake, all-American smile and good looks, gift for ingratiating gab, and absolute sincerity. Jack Knight offered him a place in his chain, but White declined cordially, saying he preferred to stay top frog in his small but familiar pond. But when Marshall Field, heir to the Chicago department-store fortune and owner of the *Sun-Times,* set about expanding his newspaper operations, he invited White to become his executive assistant and consultant. White accepted on a part-time basis and for two years starting in 1956 commuted between Missouri and Chicago. His work with Field, his only extended experience in urban journalism, became the principal credential on his dossier other than his inherited editorship of the *Ledger* as Walter Thayer began weighing his qualifications to run the *New York Herald Tribune,* one of the most sophisticated—and troubled—newspapers in the nation.

According to Emmett Dedmon, then the assistant managing editor of the *Sun-Times* and soon to become its top editor, Marshall Field, who was not the most emotionally stable of men, met White at an editors' convention, was much taken with him, and, in a manic mood, brought him back to Chicago and gave him an office next to his. "But White had no metropolitan experience and didn't know what was going on," Dedmon recounted. "The paper was very much in a building process then, and the last thing we needed were amateurs from the provinces. He was kept out of the newsroom, as remote as possible from the daily operation, and made no impact on the *Sun-Times* during his time there." Marshall Field's wife, Katherine, who after being widowed and remarrying became a successful newspaper executive in her own right, recalled White's role more charitably. He and Field did indeed become "very good friends. It would be difficult for me to point to specific effects of Bob's consulting, but I do know he was extremely important to Marshall during a period of major decision-making."

When Barney Kilgore, who had met White over a cup of coffee at a Sigma Delta Chi convention eleven years earlier and found him pleasing, brought him up to Rockefeller Center to meet Walter Thayer, Jock Whitney's deputy was also smitten. Thayer sent Whitney a picture of White and wrote that he "appears to have the kind of editorial imagination, spark and talent we want . . . [to be] a unique and rare young man . . . [who has] won every award in the book for his newspaper. . . . He is self-assured without being cocky, and he has courage. If we take him, he has to have help on the business side." Kilgore proposed teaming White with Duffield, presumably still obtainable by the purchase of *Popular Science*; he called them "the two best newspaper minds I know in America." Thayer liked the concept and flew White to England, where he met, charmed, and lost at golf to Whitney. They discussed life and values and their different party labels, discovering that not much separated White's moderate Democratic views from Whitney's progressive Republicanism. The *Tribune* would have to be rebuilt brick by brick, White suggested, but neither Thayer nor Whitney pushed him to say what shape the completed edifice might assume. That was just as well because White could not have told them. "It would have been a showboat answer if I'd listed a lot of specifics," he recalled. The revamped paper would have to evolve.

Why did as shrewd and hardheaded a man as Walter Thayer, who never even asked to see a copy of the *Mexico Ledger,* fail to probe more deeply into White's background and skills? Primarily because he felt unqualified to appraise the editorial worth of White's paper. Instead, he was relying on the judgment of certified experts, and the chief among his advisers was rated an authentic genius of twentieth-century American journalism. "If White had come in and asked me for a job to run the *Herald Tribune,* I would have laughed," Thayer recounted. "But Kilgore was absolutely convinced he could do the job. Bob talked a good game—he looked and sounded good—he was pleasant and attractive, he exuded self-confidence, he was available and wanted the job—and here was Barney Kilgore telling me, 'This is your man.' What more could I ask?"

But White was as troubled as Duffield had been by his answerability to Whitney and sought reassurances in this regard. Pushed once again to waive effective control of the newspaper he was rescuing, Whitney wrote to Thayer late in May of his sudden misgivings over the entire venture. He had thought that "my life's experience . . . gave me a reason and a challenge for personal activity on the paper, which would be exciting, useful and proper. This may have been a half-baked, really an unbaked reason for what *otherwise* would have been an idiotic, Quixotic contribution to the survival of a tradition," but it had seemed valid to him, "[a] bit, perhaps, because Ike believe[s] in its importance —as everyone does who doesn't have to pay more than a nickel for it!" Now, however, he was faced with a challenge "to my romantic notion that I can perform a working function in this revival." He understood that saving the *Tribune* was essentially a job for professionals, but he was shaken by the advice of friends in journalism who were telling him "you can't be a chairman of a newspaper as you can of a company" because of the instantaneous nature of the decision-making process of the daily press. He was "not at the moment convinced that if Mr. Duffield and the Sage of Mexico [i.e., White] will do this that I will give it to them, on their terms." He believed that "unless the new Tribune is associated with the Whitneys, as it once was with the Reids, there's no sense, no sense at all, in my giving it a reputation and a fortune, in both of which I have a proud stake, and which they can exploit. I can cut it now, and I think you should know I am prepared to."

If Walter Thayer had been as calculating and indifferent toward the *Tribune* as some on the paper would come to think in the years that immediately followed, he could have used that moment in 1959 to cultivate Whitney's distress and spare him a financial bloodletting. Persuasive evidence suggests, however, that Thayer's loyalty went beyond the bottom line, beyond gratitude for the generous way of life his association with Whitney allowed him, to the man himself, for he understood Jock Whitney's complex psychological needs and uncertainties. "You have a tremendous talent to bring to the venture," he wrote back to Whitney, adding:

> I am sure there is no endeavor you can pursue which would *tap* or *use* to such full extent the great assets you have to offer. . . . [N]ot for a single moment have I contemplated a management solution that would bar active participation for you. . . . [I]t makes no sense to me for you to put your wealth and reputation at risk in a business from which you are excluded.

Thayer was convinced, he continued in a telltale comment, "after these two years of pretty close scrutiny that there is nothing unique about the business of running or editing a newspaper," and he challenged the wisdom of Whitney's friends in the field who doubted he could serve usefully as a working chairman. It was the ownership that was responsible for the ultimate success or failure of the enterprise "by the picking, backing, driving, and giving general direction to the efforts" of the hired professionals. "This is the *tough* job. It's a lot easier to be on the firing line than in the firing seat." The people they had been seeking to hire were understandably suspicious of Whitney's motives, Thayer suggested, "because so many amateurs have used newspapers to satisfy their personal desires for public recognition and power." Thayer objected, furthermore, to

Whitney's aspiring to a role comparable to the Reids', for they had not been smart enough, he said, after Ogden's death, to quit meddling "every day and every way." The men Thayer was trying to enlist to operate the paper knew Whitney would not behave that unseemly way; they also would not expect him to surrender his rightful role as the ultimate arbiter of their performance. Yes, Whitney could get out of the whole thing then and there, perhaps even at a profit, and Thayer would not mind being relieved of the unfamiliar burden he had been handed. But it would "also be a disappointment that all this didn't work out as you, and I, had hoped. Maybe, however, this is the nature of the beast—and as it's your beast with your name you ought to have a good look at it while it still can be farmed out."

His resolve stiffened, Whitney waved Thayer on. Bob White rejected the idea of being yoked to Duffield but accepted the *Tribune* presidency on the condition that he would report directly to Whitney, who would grant him full authority to run the paper until his ambassadorial days were over, at which point the two of them would figure out their future working relationship or, if Whitney preferred, White would pack up and go home. He was so confident that he could preside over the *Tribune*—the only difference between running it and the *Ledger*, he would later recall believing at the time, "was the number of zeroes" —that he did not ask for a contract.

The announcement was made in mid-July, to the amazement of the New York newspaper trade. "I think we have found a man with the dynamic ideas and sound newspaper background we were looking for," Whitney's statement said. But there was no direct evidence that Robert M. White II had either of those qualifications as he stepped into the most challenging job in American journalism.

V

By the time Bob White arrived at the *Tribune* in early August 1959, a substantial collection of ideas about what to do with the paper had accumulated.

The clearest and most concise advisory had come from Barney Kilgore in a memo he headed simply "(No strings attached to this)." "Generally speaking, advertisers will not 'support' a newspaper," he wrote to Walter Thayer. "They regard it only as a sales tool." The paper had to set its course and demonstrate for a time that it knew what it was doing before it could hope to improve its advertising volume substantially. His main conceptual strategy was for the *Tribune* to take advantage of the formidable size of the news package that the *Times* produced each day by issuing a paper of comparable quality in what it contained but leaner, more compacted, and far more local in its coverage emphasis. Its national and foreign reports ought to be interpretive rather than try to deal authoritatively with breaking news, which the wire services could cover. City and suburban news should be handled in a livelier, even spicier fashion but within a more typographically conservative format. Such a paper, perhaps issued in a single section (as *The Wall Street Journal* then was), would win over some *Times* readers who until then saw no intelligent alternative to plowing through all the news fit to print; more important, it would be an upgraded alternative to the tabloids, whose function as a graphics-oriented news summarizer was being usurped by television. "A new formula designed along these lines may not result in a 'great' newspaper," Kilgore advised Thayer, and it would not sell as far away from New York as the *Times* did. "But it would stand a chance to survive."

The same day that Kilgore offered his suggestions, the *Tribune*'s London bureau chief, Don Cook, by then a fifteen-year veteran of the paper, wrote to Whitney at the U.S. embassy there and urged a precisely opposite course. As the only American newspaper with a true foreign edition and an established presence in Paris, the *Tribune* ought to have the finest overseas correspondence of any U.S. daily, Cook argued. Instead, the paper's small foreign corps was "a frustrated lot," underutilized and badly in need of guidance and reinforcement. The Paris edition, more a scissors-and-paste job than a real newspaper, needed direction and coordination with the parent edition. His thinking was echoed the following week with the arrival of Brown Reid's prescriptive list of suggestions in his farewell memo to Whitney. Brown, always global and a bit megalomaniacal in his view of the *Tribune*'s mission, called on its new owner to make it "the most important newspaper in the world"; his formula: more news in a complete, easy-to-read package. It was such insights that prompted Thayer to want him separated from the place at the first opportune moment.

From the first, these conflicting aims—greatness versus survivability—seemed to present irreconcilable solutions. Whitney had undertaken to save the *Tribune* because of its national and international standing and literate, sophisticated style; to save it, he was now being told with increasing frequency, he would have to turn it into something less important and more common, if not vulgar. Spyros Skouras, head of Twentieth-Century-Fox films and an old friend of the paper, proposed a more middle-class approach stressing local issues and crusades, somewhat in the manner of the *World-Telegram*. Robert Beith, executive editor of the Gannett chain's morning-evening combination in Portland, Maine, recommended an even more parochial tone by converting the *Tribune* into "a hometown paper in a big city," loaded with the names and activities of ordinary people, as no New York paper was, and shorn of its "hard coating of sophistication." Even a sophisticate like Robert Manning, then London bureau chief for Time-Life, pressed Whitney to focus his paper more on metropolitan news. Manning had other sobering thoughts for the new owner of the *Tribune*: the common view of his paper in journalistic circles was that its political objectives and well-known partisan affiliation had infected its news interests and judgment. Manning also thought the paper suffered from "an abrasive inferiority complex" toward the *Times,* ought to become a leaner and more disciplined sheet, rather as Kilgore had proposed, and perhaps might best serve its own ends by getting out of the Sunday field entirely rather than remaining a bedraggled also-ran. Above all, said Manning, whom Whitney would hire as his Sunday editor two years later, the *Tribune* needed an editor with "new ideas and techniques." Added Osborn Elliott, a senior editor at *Newsweek* who would shortly rise to its top editorial post, "The last thing the Tribune needs is a back-slapping, speech-making dilletante [sic] type."

From within the *Tribune* itself, the only creative ideas about how to reshape the paper came from the derided Arthur Hadley, the news development editor. In fact, Hadley was ahead of his time. In a series of memos offered to the new ownership, he argued that the old core-city concept had been replaced by the social patterning of "interurbia" that was radically altering how people in the *Tribune* readership area lived—where they worked and shopped and took their recreation (namely, more and more outside the city limits), what they valued, how they thought. By continuing dependency on breaking news to shape each day's paper, New York editors were ignoring this sweeping trend in the urban style of life and the accompanying problems, challenges, and subjects to write about. Psychology and sociology did not have to be the exclusive province of academia, Hadley preached, but, by preplanning and use of outside writers and experts to supplement regular staffers, could be probed and dramatized in a steady flow of articles that would broaden and deepen the accepted capabilities of the daily newspaper. As part of the *Tribune*'s new "youthful, vigorous personality," business news ought to be presented more in terms of people than of cold numbers, suburban coverage ought to be massed for impact, and the Sunday paper ought to be totally reconceived as "a complete entity" in the form of a single standard-size front section containing the latest news and sports results and encasing a collection of tabloid-size magazines, among them "Program" on arts and entertainment, "Money" on all aspects of finance, and one on "People-Opinion-Events." Hadley's suggestions went unheeded.

To help guide them, the Whitney people enlisted professional researchers and analysts, including Elmo Roper & Associates, who in May 1959 interviewed some 3,000 metropolitan area residents and concluded that the *Tribune* readership was "too old, too Republican, too upper class, too suburban, too highly college educated, too Protestant and too heavily male" to be commercially successful in the New York market. This was not a revelation, but such corroborative findings served to move the paper toward a formal course of action. A bundle of useful insights was drawn from the Roper and other data by a marketing consultant named Victor Ratner, former advertising manager at Macy's and "the fellow Bill Paley told me a long time ago was the most brilliant man they ever had at CBS," Thayer explained to Whitney in putting him on the *Tribune* payroll for six months. Ratner traced the paper's slide to having bet too long and heavily in the prewar era on too small a segment of the public —the rich and refined. After the war the *Tribune* had failed to broaden its appeal, Ratner contended, while advertisers went after the newly prosperous masses. *Tribune* managers badly underestimated the appeal of the *Times,* which they scoffed at as dull and dependent upon quantity instead of quality in its news presentation. And when they tried to counter the *Times*'s growing lead, they sacrificed dignity for gimmickry and superficial additives that, except for the little magazine with TV and radio listings in the Sunday edition, provided no real added news service. As a result, Whitney was now in possession of a newspaper in imminent peril of collapse as an advertising medium; the *Tribune* was surviving "thanks to yesterday's advertising habits," Ratner said, and cited persuasive evidence of a short life expectancy. Recently, for example, the Benton & Bowles agency had omitted only the *Tribune* among city papers from its schedule kicking off a big campaign for Maxwell House coffee. The *Times* had definitely surpassed it in most suburbs, and even the *Journal-American* was proving a better medium for selling cars. In the city itself, with its increasingly nonwhite demographics, things were worse; the pivotal residential newsstand at the northwest corner of Broadway and Eighty-sixth Street in Manhattan was now selling 1,000 copies of the *Times* each morning, 525 of the *News,* 300 of *The Wall Street Journal,* 250 of the *Herald Tribune,* and 200 of Spanish-language papers. The pulling power of the *Tribune,* moreover, as measured by the responsiveness of its readers to advertising, was abysmally low relative to cost and the effectiveness of the *Times* and *News,* due largely to the fact that the *Tribune*'s older, wealthier readers "much more often buy what they want *when* and *where* they want it because they *do* have more money"—that was the mortal danger in the Roper data. The *Tribune* and the Republican Party with which it was aligned faced the same basic problem: how to attract and hold younger, more active people. An all-out effort in that direction was imperative: "anything less is unthinkable at the present time. . . ." And how to achieve that end? Not by presenting "more news in less time," as television was providing, and not merely by identifying itself as New York's hometown paper, though that was a good idea, but by moving away from its "very conventional" handling of the news toward "a fundamentally changed approach." But Ratner did not suggest what that approach might be.

Less intuitive and prescriptive but nevertheless useful was the series of studies by McKinsey & Co., which had recently consulted extensively for the prosperous *Los Angeles Times.* At the root of the *Tribune*'s problems, the McKinsey people counseled early on, was its ambition; with only 58 percent of the *Times*'s circulation and 30 percent of its advertising revenue, the *Tribune* was carrying a ruinously disproportionate 85 percent as much editorial content as its main rival. Yet there was little fat on the *Tribune* payroll, McKinsey found, since the paper's problems had for some time been attacked "by a consistent program of expense reduction." A smaller news hole was the chief and obvious economy to be introduced. Yet such a proposal seemed to fly in the face of the circulation increases that the consulting firm targeted for the paper to reach the break-even stage within five years: an annual growth of 30,000 sales for the daily paper and 70,000 for the Sunday edition—hardly a realistic goal, considering that the *Times* had averaged a gain of only 9,000 a year over the preceding decade. But the longer the new ownership delayed in installing a vigorous management team, said the consultants, the costlier the reclamation project would prove.

Among the most important of the McKinsey suggestions in the spring of 1959 was the desirability of shaving costs by sharing production facilities with one of the afternoon city papers or a suburban paper with an underused plant. More than that, the idea of shifting the entire *Tribune* operation to the afternoon field seemed to have enough "potential advantages to warrant thorough exploration." Such a shift would have the immediate and enormous benefit of taking the *Tribune* out of direct, disastrous competition with the *Times* and *News,* the best papers of their kind in the country, not to mention *The Wall Street Journal* with its strong appeal to executives of the sort who were the backbone of the *Tribune* readership. In the afternoon field, the *Tribune* would be the class entry, and if it came into the market at its current five-cent price, it might make swift inroads against the *Journal-American,* with its field-leading circulation of 564,000, the *World-Telegram & Sun* (with 454,000), and the *Post* (343,000), all of which charged a dime. A more expensive but ultimately sounder way of making the move might be to buy one of the afternoon papers and merge it into the *Tribune.* Home-delivered, an evening *Tribune* would have far greater appeal to advertisers than the current morning version, McKinsey advised after canvassing New York area merchants.

This radical move was at once presented as a possibility to the holdover *Tribune* management by acting president Brundage, who thought it preferable to continuing an unwinnable fight against the *Times.* His executives were dubious. An afternoon *Tribune* would need a lot more of what they called "gee whiz" to be competitive, and its current editorial team, used to producing the journalistic equivalent of holy scripture, was felt to lack both the know-how and the inclination to put out a flashy enough paper. What they overlooked was that the *Tribune*'s most distinctive features—its wide array of columnists, its cultural coverage, and the quality of its writing—were strengths that would likely have translated readily into the evening field, and a news approach that retained the *Tribune*'s essential dignity while adapting somewhat to the time pressures of afternoon publication might be precisely what would have made it attractive to better-educated readers who found the existing evening papers frivolous.

Circulation manager Zwick felt that transfer to the evening would cost the *Tribune* 100,000 daily sales in the school, mail-subscription, and "country" markets. And he did not think it would sell more than 50,000 in the suburbs, less than a third of current suburban sales.

The only way afternoon publication made sense to Zwick, Frank Taylor, Barney Cameron, and advertising manager Jack Thees was for Jock Whitney to buy out the *Journal-American* and, after cannibalizing the best of its columnists and comic strips, kill it, thereby presumably ending future competition of

the sensationalist sort. But the logic behind such a purchase, which they estimated would require $10 million if Hearst management was willing to part
with its New York flagship, was elusive. Unless the *Journal*-ingested evening *Tribune* retained sufficient *eau d'Hearst*—unless it became a celebrity-
mongering sheet written at the fan-magazine level with a decided Catholic
orientation in its news play—ex-*Journal* readers would likely desert it by the
tens of thousands. A more plausible course might have been to buy out the more
moderate and journalistically worthy *World-Telegram,* amalgamate its best features, which would have suited the *Tribune* better than the *Journal-American*'s,
and establish the newly combined paper as the clear preference of the bourgeoi-
sie and suburban markets that were of greatest interest to advertisers.

Boldness and imagination were scarce among them, however, and Brundage,
who had the advantage, at least, of fresh perspective, saw himself as no more
than a caretaker. And Jock Whitney was in London. And Walter Thayer, who
was a prudent man, gave no sign, then or afterward, of favoring a massive outlay
of capital that would probably have been required to reposition the *Tribune*
competitively. Whitney had obtained the paper at virtually no cost, and if he
could nurse it back to health by surrounding it with profitable properties, that
would be fine; to raise the ante exponentially would have been madness.

VI

When Robert M. White II sat down to his desk as the new president and editor
of the *Tribune,* he was greeted by an advisory letter from his mentor and
sponsor, Bernard Kilgore, who himself had come out of the Midwest—Indiana
was where he had been raised and educated—and scored a professional conquest
of New York. "Don't assume the city is much different from the small town,"
Kilgore counseled. "People are people wherever you find them."

How much to heart White took that arguable advice was reflected in a signed
editorial he wrote for the August 3, 1959, paper, proclaiming his arrival on the
scene and the immense goodwill he had brought with him—as if New York
cared. "Our belief is that newspapers are important because you—the reader—
are important," it began. "The most basic cause a newspaper can serve is telling
you—the reader—the facts, the truth, the news," it went on. "That shall continue to be our basic effort. . . ." There was another traditional cause the paper
would serve, "that grand, old American right, American privilege, and, we
believe, American duty of standing up to be counted." This the *Tribune* would
do, but it could not promise that its studied convictions would always be right.
"What we can promise is that they will be dead-level straight, from the shoulder,
sincere, our best." In conclusion, "we ask for time. . . . We must build well

because newspapers are important. . . . And will be important just as long as our way of life is of, for and by you—the reader."

These stirring reassurances were followed the next month by a second editorial by White, this one unsigned but appearing on the front page in both English and Russian and addressed to Soviet premier Khrushchev upon his arrival for an extended visit to the United States. "One thing we believe you can learn to understand here," the editorial lectured the Red leader, "is wealth— wealth in terms of more people living better than anywhere else on earth." It continued:

> Ask why so many workers can live so well in the U.S.A.
>
> Ask why our masses, our "peasants," are educated, are proud, are a vital source of power to this nation.
>
> Ask why, Mr. Khrushchev.
>
> For when you answer that question, then you will understand our country, our way of life.
>
> Then you will understand why you will not "bury" us; you will understand why our grandchildren will not live under your brand of "socialism."
>
> For our greatest wealth, Mr. Khrushchev, is of the spirit. It lies in our people —a free people. A people who are volunteers, not conscripts, in citizenship, in labor, in their way of living.
>
> Know them, Mr. Khrushchev, and you will know our country. . . . and a strength far greater than that of mere wealth.
>
> Know them, Mr. Khrushchev, and go in peace.

That truth and freedom are good was not an unworthy utterance, however corny it might have seemed to busy New York, which needed reminding now and then of the fundamentals of American life. But such pure, basic values were generally the starting point, not the sum and substance, of discussion in a newspaper like the *Tribune,* which sought to stimulate the public to reflect on issues, not merely to congratulate it for its sterling virtues. New York's tempo, anxieties, and interests were not White's, and whether out of smugness, insecurity, or wariness, he made scant effort to involve himself in them. He bought a two-hundred-year-old house in suburban Rye, far from the heart of his constituency. He preferred Western movies to the Broadway theater. When he moved into his office at the paper and saw yards of empty bookcases, he instructed outgoing president Brundage's assistant, Charles Rees, to stock them. Rees, thinking a man in White's position would be partial to works of history and current affairs, asked him what sorts of titles he would prefer. "I don't care," White said pleasantly, "just fill 'em." He kept regular commuter's hours, took his time meeting the staff, stayed out of the city-room operations, felt rather than pushed his way into the job, and limited his displays of leadership to uncharismatic pronouncements, like his appeal to the Washington bureau to produce "straight, honest news." In the early weeks of White's tenure, Whitney quipped in a letter to Thayer that he had heard via the journalistic grapevine that "Bob is a wholly dedicated joiner, whose ambition in life is to make the Board of the A.P. His taking our job is primarily to achieve that high purpose." Whitney, though uneasy about his young Lochinvar's undertaking "indiscriminate memberships" and unhappy that "his writing verges on appalling," was nevertheless optimistic. "The more I know of him," he said of White, "the more I respect his professional preparedness in the administrative . . . side. He will not be stampeded—he will form good judgments."

Bob White's first judgment was that he had taken over a badly demoralized operation. The staff had been buffeted by so much uncertainty, so many commands and demands and changes, that it had become "almost numb," he recalled. "Nobody had patted them on the back in a very long time." And the doleful effects of underfunding were noticeable to the newcomer at every turn. The building struck him as dirty and the walls badly in need of paint. Salaries had been held at minimal levels too long for too many, and the absence of a pension system had caused superannuated personnel to clog the payroll. Yet everywhere White detected an abiding loyalty to the paper and memories of its tattered glory still intact.

His first mission was to soothe the staff with assurances that no massive purge was impending. "I was surprised that he didn't start riding herd on us when he came," business manager Cameron remembered. Instead, backs got patted, lofty standards of professionalism reinvoked, and the physical plant spruced up. The balance of 1959 Bob White devoted to meeting New York's leading merchants over lunch—eighty of them during his first four months on the job—and assembling a new management.

George Cornish, after thirty-six years on the *Tribune,* and secretary-treasurer A. V. Miller, after twenty-six, resigned voluntarily. Frank Taylor, who White rapidly concluded was paid a lot for doing nothing, was shown the door. Next went Luke Carroll, whose dealings with the staff, like his judgment of the news, was rated "heavy-handed" by White. And to complete the removal of Brown Reid's leading appointees, White dismissed the one truly creative editor on the staff whose unorthodox ideas and acute insights the paper badly needed —Arthur Hadley. White thought him short on common sense and of scant use in the daily grind. "Art's value from deadline to deadline was as limited as his experience," said White, missing the whole point of Hadley's conceptual approach to the evolving definition of "news" and the forms it was assuming. "He told me that my trouble was that I didn't have any good old-fashioned, police-reporting news sense," Hadley remembered.

White's highminded but almost slavishly traditional approach to his trade was evidenced by the caliber of his staffing. To replace Taylor as number-two man he advanced Barney Cameron, a proven but pedestrian professional, who had touted Taylor and Tangle Towns and the miniature television magazine as cures to what ailed the *Tribune*; none had proved to be. To succeed Cornish as director of the news operation, he brought back Fendall Yerxa, who had served four years as executive editor of the Du Pont–owned Wilmington papers. As the new financial man he hired Richard Steele, an accountant by training and the cost-conscious associate publisher of the Worcester, Massachusetts, *Telegram and Gazette,* a decidedly profitable operation, on which he had worked his way up for seventeen years. To take over the editorial page he enlisted Dwight Sargent, a moderate Republican who had held the same post for eleven years on the Gannett combination in Portland, Maine; like White, the convivial Sargent was devoted to the fraternal aspects of the profession. All three new men came from monopoly papers in small cities; all were able, likable, and uninnovative.

As White moved at a relaxed pace through his first months of orientation, confident that Whitney wanted him to build well and with due deliberation after the years of rashness and misdirection the paper had endured, the *Tribune* balance sheet kept getting worse; the cost of standing still mounted month by month. Losses for 1959 were approaching $3 million. The Plymouth Rock hen house could not accommodate its venerable invalid at such a cost. That October, Whitney and Thayer took the decisive step of converting what had essentially been a corporate shell into a powerhouse in the communications industry by adding to it the Corinthian Broadcasting Corporation, a network of five television stations, two with radio affiliates—WISH in Indianapolis, WANE in Fort Wayne, KHOU in Houston, KOTV in Tulsa, and KXTV in Sacramento—that J. H. Whitney & Co. had built with a minimum of cash into a $37-million property in just five years. Whitney had been a bit reluctant to get into television, partly out of fear that old cronies from his prewar days in the movie industry and other would-be impresarios might besiege him to fund new enterprises in show business, which was too raffish a field for his tastes now. But he was encouraged to jump in by Charles Wrede Petersmeyer, a young partner at the Whitney firm, who argued that television was as much a communications industry as an entertainment medium and one in which the news content would become increasingly important. A Harvard Business School graduate with a short tenure at the McKinsey management consulting firm, Petersmeyer proved an extremely able manager in the infant TV industry, parlaying success upon success, to the point that General Electric made a substantial offer to Whitney for the entire Corinthian chain. Acquiring properties in new industries obtained through mostly borrowed funds, building them through tight and aggressive management, and selling out at a hefty profit was just the pattern that J. H. Whitney & Co. liked to follow, but in view of the *Tribune*'s escalating needs, Whitney let the GE offer go, paid his partners the appraised value of Corinthian, and transferred the TV properties to Plymouth Rock, which was renamed Whitney Communications Corporation (WCC). Whitney owned 86 percent of the stock; the balance was held by executives in the constituent companies, of whom Petersmeyer, with 4 percent, had the largest stake. In addition to the *Tribune, Parade,* and Corinthian, Whitney fattened WCC with two smaller ventures, *Interior Design,* a profitable decorating monthly, and the VIP Network, a string of four suburban New York radio stations—in Mineola, New

Rochelle, Mount Kisco, and Kingston—in which he shared ownership with Martin Stone, a Yale-trained lawyer and wartime colleague of Walter Thayer in Washington.*

The hen-house era was over. In its place had been erected a grand château, on the grounds of which the *Herald Tribune* was relegated to the financial doghouse. It refused to be ignored, however, which was not pleasing to a dynamic young executive like Wrede Petersmeyer, who knew that the profits from the television stations he was so ably overseeing would go not to improve broadcast facilities or buy new properties but to keep the *Tribune* afloat. But he could hardly carp at this decision since it was Whitney's wealth that had fueled Corinthian's creation. "It was not an economic question, it was an emotional one," Petersmeyer recognized. The paper had never been treated as a business venture by the Whitney firm's partners. "It was Jock's personal thing, a love of his—something he wanted more than anything else in the world. It was his right to buy it, and since he had given me a great opportunity with Corinthian," Petersmeyer moved over to WCC as requested, hopeful that with sufficient infusion of money and professional management, the *Tribune* turnaround could be achieved soon.

Nor was anyone else at WCC in the early years of the operation inclined to tell Whitney he was letting his heart rule his head in granting the *Tribune* a preferred position among the constituent properties. "They all knew how much the paper meant to him," recalled Martin Stone, who once rode with Whitney in his limousine and heard him confide that he had bought the paper because he did not want to be thought of as just a rich man but as someone important in his own right. "He was impressed that the *Tribune* was read in the Kremlin as well as the White House," and was helping shape the opinions of important people around the world. "You accepted Jock's interest," added Stone, a smart marketing and promotion man who had developed "The Author Meets the Critics" and the "Howdy Doody" children's program in the early days of television, "and felt you had to make sacrifices or concessions to help keep such an institution alive."

To orchestrate the now vastly expanded communications enterprise, Whitney detached Thayer from the managing partner's post at his investment firm office on Fifth Avenue and installed him as president in WCC's headquarters one long crosstown block away in the new Time-Life Building. The more passive Sam Park was moved aside to chairman of the WCC finance committee, and J. H. Whitney & Co.'s top financial analyst, Robert Bryan, joined Thayer on the new management team, on which the *Tribune*'s White, *Parade*'s Motley, the

* During Whitney's joint ownership of WFYI, the Mineola station's small radio transmitter was upgraded to 50,000 watts when it was transferred to a fifteen-acre parcel at the edge of Greentree, his estate in nearby Manhasset. Unfortunately, it was discovered upon completion of the new transmitter that the red lights atop its tower to warn off aircraft flashed directly into Whitney's bedroom. He was tactfully told that it would be easier for him to adjust his sleeping arrangements than to move the tower—and he acceded.

VIP Network's Stone, and Bernard Kilgore sat as directors. Just how radically the new setup altered the *Tribune*'s prospects was foreshadowed by a letter Thayer sent Whitney shortly after taking command of the greatly enlarged operation:

> I think WCC has two *basic* functions to perform: They are (1) capital management and (2) the creation of a community of interest (through cross-fertilization and otherwise) in this group of companies and enterprises. The "capital management" function is a clear-cut necessity, readily recognizable by all concerned. It involves the control of cash flow so that ends meet in all enterprises, cash is available when and where needed, investments (Parade plant, color printing equipment [at the *Tribune*], radio stations, TV stations, etc., etc.) are made in order of priority *so far as the health and welfare of the entire project is concerned.* In order to make these decisions, WCC will have to have a current and continuing flow of financial information and projections from all WCC companies . . . [Italics added.]

The *Tribune* may have been the *raison d'être* for the creation of WCC and the apple of Jock Whitney's eye, but it was surrounded now by successful entities run by able and ambitious men who, however respectful of their patron, were not likely to put up with the floundering of his pet project indefinitely.

Barely two months on the job, Bob White got his first inkling that the balance of power had shifted and that his cherished independence of action as master of the *Tribune* was compromised. As their commuter train pulled into Grand Central Station one morning, his traveling companion, Walter Thayer, guided White into the station bookstore for a little confidential chat. As White recalled the occasion, the president of WCC told the president of the *Herald Tribune* that he would like to have monthly reports on the paper's financial standing, including a breakdown on advertising sales—and, by the way, when was he going to start improving the still dragging Sunday edition? Surprised at being subjected to such surveillance, which he had not bargained for, White agreed to cooperate by supplying the financial data but said he did not want to tamper with the product itself until he had assembled his new management team —a process he was industriously pursuing; the rebuilding of the paper, he reminded Thayer of his pledge to Whitney, was to proceed at a careful brick-by-brick pace.

Within the next month, Thayer's new, steady scrutiny became apparent. When the Herald Tribune Syndicate sent out a promotional mailing piece on John Crosby's column, featuring his stinging commentary on the dubious artistic and ethical standards of the TV industry, Thayer objected on the ground that the effort might redound to the harm of WCC's Corinthian properties. And when TV officials were brought before congressional investigators probing scandals involving payola and rigged quiz shows, an anti-industry editorial in the *Tribune* drove Thayer to complain not to White but directly to the new editorial-page chief, Dwight Sargent. Under Thayer's "community of interest" policy, WCC's siblings ought to be looking out for their mutual welfare, not sniping at one another.

White was riled. In mid-November, he went to Thayer's office and demanded to know who was running the *Tribune*. He had taken the job on the understanding that he would be answerable to Whitney and no one else; if Whitney did not approve of the job he was doing, he had only to ask for his resignation—White, after all, had no contract. But so long as he was in charge, White wanted no meddling with the paper's independence. The basic difference in perspective between them, at any rate, was now clear to him. "I thought of WCC as a corporation to which Jock had assigned enough of his holdings to give him a strong, useful, rewarding *Tribune,*" White recounted, "while Walter clearly thought of WCC as the dog wagging the paper as its tail."

Such a metaphor somewhat overstated the case. In recognizing the paper's privileged status, Thayer did not want it indulged to the point that it would imperil the rest of his financially robust operation. And Bob White, he decided soon after the Missourian's arrival, was "not budget-minded . . . not a tight operator." Thayer, who from the first had pushed him to bring in a top financial man quickly, rejoiced over the impending arrival of Richard Steele in January 1960. "We will all be better off when we are less dependent on Bob," Thayer wrote Whitney near the end of 1959. WCC "must run scared until we *know* what the Trib picture is going to be. . . . Bob is going to try end-runs around me and you have got to send him right back or we will be in a mess."

At long last, the *Herald Tribune* was under the direction of—or, as sentimentalists might have put it, at the mercy of—modern management.

17

Who Says
a Good Newspaper
Has to Be Dull?

I
t was ironic that the last proprietors of the *Herald Tribune* should have turned to television, with its elemental appeal to a mass viewership, to provide the financial means for rescuing the troubled old newspaper, which had always considered the culturally sophisticated and socially refined as its natural clientele. In those cases—and there were a good many—where newspapers lived in happy symbiosis with radio and television stations under single ownership, the electronic media were almost always an outgrowth of the paper, usually a civic and financial power in the community. The stations were primarily purveyors of entertainment with a license to coin profits that added to the institutional solidity of the ownership. At the *Tribune,* it was different. Few people on the paper knew or cared that its financial survival was dependent, with the establishment of Whitney Communications, on five television stations west of the Alleghenies or that VIP, the suburban chain of radio stations, was proclaiming itself on the air as "the Herald Tribune Network." From Helen Reid on, *Tribune* people rated radio and TV as inferior competitors for advertising revenue and reader attention; their disdain for the new media as cultural Saharas and journalistic pretenders was nicely expressed by John Crosby's steady sniper fire. But no sooner was the paper married to the Corinthian TV

network under joint WCC ownership than Walter Thayer was cautioning its writers against, in effect, biting the hand that was feeding them.

Just how greatly dependent the *Tribune* had become under the newly carpentered WCC roof was stressed to its recently installed president and editor, Robert M. White II, at a gathering of the company's executives at Greenwood, Jock Whitney's white-columned manse near Thomasville, Georgia, during the second week of January 1960. After the shooting and golfing and goodfellowship, there were the numbers to reckon with: profits for the year were projected at $7.9 million, mostly from Corinthian, but interest on the aggregate WCC debt of more than $25 million would take $1.2 million and another $3.4 million would go to paying off the principal; what was left, or as much of it as necessary, would go to subsidize the *Tribune*. The fragile debt structure, built to drain off as little as possible of Whitney's fabulous collateral by leveraging—i.e., borrowing against it in the expectation of earning far more than the cost of the loans—was "entirely manageable," in Thayer's judgment, provided that careful financial oversight was maintained by all concerned. But as corporate secretary Charles Rees noted, there was "little elbow room" in the arrangement. Heavy debt service was an acceptable risk for young and rapidly growing enterprises, but WCC was saddled with—indeed, had been created to salvage—a newspaper that was neither. In his remarks at Greenwood, Thayer contended that WCC's finances had been arranged in a way that would allow the *Tribune* adequate resources with which to become a self-sustaining partner. But by confining those resources to the cash throw from its profitable partners, Thayer effectively put a lid on the funds that the paper could expect from the rest of the operation. Walter Thayer was a practical man, a lawyer ably serving his client by protecting him from his costly, if noble, impulses.

While at Thomasville, Thayer spoke with Bob White about the cordial relationship, born of their mutual interests, that he thought should prevail among members of the WCC family. *Tribune* carping against the TV industry would not help to secure that linkage and, in view of the paper's dependency, was not seemly. But Robert White was a proud man, a newspaperman, and viewed WCC purely as a means of restoring the *Tribune* to its former greatness. Thus when John C. Doerfer, chairman of the Federal Communications Commission, proposed that the shortcomings of the TV industry might be counteracted by requiring the networks, on a rotating basis, to set aside a half hour of prime time each evening for public-service programming, the *Tribune* responded with a negative editorial. Such conscience time was hardly adequate to meet the problem, the paper contended, and Doerfer, who had been criticized by congressional probers for fraternizing with leaders of the industry his commission was supposed to monitor, was denounced for his failure to bring greater moral suasion and regulatory scrutiny to bear against the corrupt and culturally degrading practices of television.

Thayer's response was swift and sharp. In a letter to White, he was resentful of the editorial writer's implication that all TV fare was bad; plainly the fellow had not heard—as White had—Wrede Petersmeyer's outline of Corinthian's programming plans. He did not wish to interfere with the paper's freedom of expression, but

> ... When an editorial writer gets on a subject ... which directly affects the interests and welfare of the [WCC] "family," my interest is in seeing that the facts within the family knowledge, and the views and opinions of the various members of the family, are known to him. *He may disregard those views and facts* but at least he will have been exposed to them [italics Thayer's].
>
> Pressure is not involved. Nor is the integrity of the editorial page. No one is going to tell anyone what he can or can't write. But I do ask that the editorial staff acquaint themselves with the thinking of their associates in this venture on subjects affecting those associates. . . .

Corinthian favored Doerfer's proposal and would so testify to the government, Thayer added, and since Whitney owned Corinthian, he could not dissociate himself from the policies and views of the publicly regulated TV stations as he could from the editorial positions of his unregulated newspaper. It was all very embarrassing and potentially damaging to WCC.

That Thayer was not overstepping his charge as Whitney's surrogate was emphasized a few weeks later when, following two other editorials along much the same line as those that had provoked Thayer's memorandum, Whitney wrote White from London in annoyance over "these two pieces of fatuous piety." Even if he had had no financial stake in TV, Whitney asserted, he would have been upset: "God knows there's plenty wrong with television, but there's plenty wrong with newspapers, too," and no one was suggesting that government regulators ought to step in and cure what ailed the press. "I don't think we can afford to be holier-than-thou, and to *my* personal taste I think it is cheap."

Under such pressure from above, White was faced with a crisis of conscience when, a few weeks later, just before Doerfer was due to testify before a House committee investigating unethical business practices, David Wise of the *Tribune* Washington bureau uncovered evidence that during the previous month the FCC chairman had spent nearly a week aboard the yacht of George Storer, president of Storer Broadcasting Company, a leading independent radio-TV chain somewhat larger than Corinthian. Fearful that the *Tribune*'s disclosures would poison Doerfer against WCC, whose stations would soon be up for licensing renewal by the FCC, Thayer was not coy about trying to discourage the paper's investigative initiative. According to White, Thayer said he understood that the *Tribune* reporter involved tended to be irresponsible and drink too much.* In fact, he was one of the best journalists the paper ever produced.

A cool, confident, well-spoken six-footer, the son of a Manhattan attorney, David Wise had started on the paper right out of Columbia in 1951. His aggressive techniques and lack of awe toward authority did not win him city-room

---

* Thayer denied to the author that he exercised any dampening influence on the Doerfer revelations in the *Tribune*.

popularity contests, but his performance, especially in the political arena, gained him swift advancement. In Albany, he more than held his own, turning out three or four stories a day against a team of *Times* reporters when the legislature was in session. At City Hall, his investigative aptitude was both whetted and frustrated. He and his colleagues, he felt, did not begin to touch the levels of corruption that were poisoning the body politic, especially in the collusive dealings of office-holders with organized crime. "You couldn't get at it," Wise recalled, "but you knew it was there."

In Washington, he did better at exposing betrayers of the governed. Together with several other reporters, none on New York papers, he blasted open the Adams-Goldfine story. To the credit of Robert Donovan, by then the *Tribune*'s Washington bureau chief, Wise was in no way inhibited from pursuing the story at length and keeping it alive, despite Donovan's earlier involvement with the White House over his "inside" book on Eisenhower's first term. Yet for all the play his Adams stories were getting, Wise had the feeling that the *Tribune*'s editors in New York were handling his copy with tongs. Then executive editor Cornish showed up on one of his infrequent trips to the bureau. "I had always thought him the most stiff-assed of all the *Trib* people—a very formal, perfectly pleasant, but remote man," said Wise. "He stood behind me for a time while I was typing up the latest Sherman Adams hotcake and then he said *sotto voce* with that nasal quality of his, 'Wonderful stories, David—keep it up.' He was a newspaperman."

Wise was soon recognized as one of the best diggers among the capital press corps. He cultivated sources artfully. The best of them, he found, were middle- to lower-level bureaucrats usually unfulfilled in their ambition and eager to share embarrassing inside information, not because of grudges they bore to their superiors or policy differences with them, but for the thrill of influencing history by seeing their disclosures show up in the papers—"even if nobody else knows they did it," as Wise put it. While the cultivation of such people was of course exploitive, he acknowledged, "you have to be genuinely interested in people to develop them as sources—you can't fake it." One "funny little man I had befriended," a fellow whose domestic tribulations he had dutifully heard out, rewarded him with the information that in February 1960 FCC chairman Doerfer had again accepted the extravagant hospitality of broadcaster Storer. Wise checked out the tip by carefully establishing Doerfer's movements during the week in question and determining that his time was not otherwise accounted for by legitimate public business, but still he lacked the "smoking gun" with which to pin the fatal indiscretion on the powerful Eisenhower appointee. He decided on a gambit. Obtaining the name of Storer's yacht (*Lazy Girl*), which he learned was berthed at Indian Creek Island near Miami Beach, he telephoned the marina there and asked to be put through to the boat. It turned out to be in dock and plugged in electrically to the marina's line. One of the deckhands answered. As if he were a friend just trying to get in touch, Wise asked to speak to Doerfer, although he knew the FCC chief was back in the capital. "Oh, he go back to Washington," the man said in a pleasing Scandinavian lilt and went on, as Wise gently pumped him, to spill the whole itinerary at sea during Doerfer's stay aboard *Lazy Girl.* He then phoned Storer, who said the report Wise had received of Doerfer's week-long stay on his yacht was "an exaggeration," but when asked to explain just how, Storer clicked off. Doerfer was unavailable for comment.

When Wise filed his fresh hotcake to New York, managing editor Yerxa apprised Bob White of the sensitive story. White told Yerxa only to be sure that Wise was solid on his facts. Wise was, and the exclusive story ran in the off-lead on the top of page one. For good measure, Donovan weighed in with a background piece that could have left nobody in Washington in doubt that he was not in the White House's pocket.

Doerfer, due to testify before the House ethics oversight subcommittee the very day Wise's story ran but spared his appearance for twenty-four hours by a snowstorm, denied the charge and said in a public statement that he had been on board Storer's yacht only for a two-hour cruise. David Wise's career was on the line; the feeling around Washington was that either he or Doerfer would soon be out of a job. The next day, under oath before House investigators, Doerfer not only changed his tune, confessing to the six-night visit on Storer's yacht, but did so defiantly, insisting that he had done no wrong, that he was not a second-class citizen and could pick what social acquaintances he wished, and that Storer had had no matters before the FCC at the time. He conceded, though, that Storer's stations would be up for license renewal within two years and that he had not known Storer prior to his 1953 appointment to the FCC. Wise, greatly relieved, asked Doerfer afterward if he intended to resign and drew in response a terrible glare and defiant no.

Bob White and the *Herald Tribune,* its lifeline to the TV industry notwithstanding, would not let it go at that. White, chastened by Walter Thayer's earlier upbraiding, telephoned him to say the paper was preparing an editorial calling upon Doerfer to resign. Thayer, while not defending Doerfer, "strenuously disagreed" with such a step by the paper, according to White, and urged the editor to call Whitney in London before proceeding. "If Bob calls you about his proposed Doerfer editorial," Thayer wired Whitney at once, "please call me. The implications of what he is considering could be serious." But White did not call Whitney. Instead, the *Tribune* ran an unequivocating editorial titled "Mr. Doerfer Should Resign," saying that "he is lacking in the moral perception required by his office." White sent off a copy of the editorial and a seven-page letter to Whitney, explaining that he had thought the matter over carefully and was taking full responsibility for the decision, and tactfully asking Whitney not to create any sacred cows for his paper's editorial writers. Thayer's anxieties about the effects of the paper's actions in the Doerfer matter were misconceived, White added, because "among the people in Washington who count, keen attention will be given to FCC treatment of WCC. And because this is true, FCC will, of course, lean over backwards to be completely objective in handling WCC."

The day after the *Tribune* editorial ran, David Wise got a call from House ethics subcommittee member John Moss, who told him, "You've got a scalp on your belt, David—the President has just accepted Doerfer's resignation." "I was shocked that he would look at it in personal terms," Wise recounted, "and would express it that way. I had never met Doerfer until the day he testified— I even felt a little sorry for him. My only emotional reaction was of relief and vindication—I was really out on a limb—and of being on a newspaper that would give me room to do this."

At the annual Gridiron Club dinner, the social centerpiece of the Washington press establishment, White's ears were filled with praise for the paper's handling of the Doerfer case. These admirers, he duly reported to Whitney, "know this paper could not have had David Wise do the objective reporting he did, without your approval." The episode served to inculcate "the deep conviction that Jock Whitney wants a great paper and one dedicated to high ideals." Whitney, asking in response only that *Tribune* editorial writers henceforth refrain from swatting at straw men, was disarmed.

II

Among the chief managers of the properties composing Whitney Communications Corporation, Robert White of the *Tribune* was the only one to report directly and regularly to Ambassador Whitney in London. This was perhaps only fitting since the paper was Whitney's first love and the reason for the establishment of WCC.

From the start, White was convinced that the *Tribune*'s best and perhaps only chance for survival was to sustain Whitney's interest in it for the rest of his stay in London so that he would eagerly plunge into its management with whatever resources were necessary upon his return. Toward that end, he sent the ambassador a constant flow of long, chatty, upbeat letters that managed to be both self-promoting and fawning. His January 25, 1960, letter was typical, advising that a lot of talented people were now applying for work on the paper and that "each of these applications is a tribute to the Herald Tribune. And also a tribute to the ownership. . . . These men know you mean it when you talk about making a great newspaper out of the Herald Tribune. And what they mean by applying is that that greatness is: Publishing the truth."

But by early February, half a year into White's term as president, this Panglossian tone began to ring hollow, and Thayer called him on it by advising Whitney that the cheery reports from the paper were deceptive. January revenues had sunk 10 percent, reflecting a citywide slump in the newspaper business, but if the *Tribune* was truly making progress, it should have been able to buck the trend. "The critical problem we face today is the accelerated rate of loss," Thayer told White. "Time is now a critical factor." All financial matters ought to be placed at once in the hands of financial vice president Dick Steele while White concentrated on whatever changes he had in mind for the editorial product. "We are forced to a point where we may have to make them quickly or not at all. . . . Now is the time to make decisions." No one was expecting White to put out a great paper—the *Tribune* had been suffering from a complex of "pseudo-greatness" for fifteen years, Thayer remarked—but White ought to recognize that his newspaper was "fighting for its life" and get on with improving it.

White, confident of Whitney's commission to rebuild the paper "brick by brick," did not concede the urgency Thayer had invoked. White's choice to run the daily editorial operation—Fendall Yerxa—had just reported to work; it would take him time to adjust and to decide with White what needed to be done. The week after receiving Thayer's goading memo, White wrote to Whitney, as if in rebuttal, that it would be "the rankest kind of folly to radically alter our news formula in a desperate effort to find a short-cut to success." Instead, earnestness and professionalism would win the battle. White described how Yerxa had addressed the city room on his arrival, calling upon the staff's talents and ideals and the potential right there within themselves to lift the paper, which happily was no longer being run on the basis of perpetual crisis. "And in the depth of his sincerity," White wrote, maybe the note cards Yerxa was speaking from "were shaking a little. But his voice was firm and sure," and at the end there was "that quick, sudden, enthusiastic, solid kind of applause" that meant the speaker had hit the mark.

Yerxa was no more inclined than White to make wholesale changes in the paper. "My approach was conservative," he acknowledged in retrospect. "I wanted the old *Trib* back again, the paper that was recognized even beyond the profession as the newspaperman's newspaper" with its stress on individuality of style among its writers. Yerxa, trained in the city room under Engelking and Herzberg, had "total faith" that a *Tribune* restored to such a standard of excellence could prosper—"and that was the basis on which I tried to operate." Within months, he came to understand that this approach was not satisfactory to top management—i.e., Walter Thayer. "However, I don't recall that it was ever made explicitly clear to me just what they did want."

What Thayer wanted was progress, measurable on the monthly balance sheet. When White, snatching at straws by the end of February, reported almost gleefully to Whitney that circulation for the previous week was up a few thousand over the year-earlier figure and that the Sunday drop was only 5,000 compared to the 36,000 falloff for that period in 1959, Thayer lamented over the "unfortunate Alice-in-Wonderland air" about White's sanguine attitude and noted with foreboding that if the current rate of loss was sustained throughout the year, the *Tribune* would be afloat in an ocean of red ink—a deficit of $4.6 million, or 50 percent higher than WCC operations could meet. By early March, Thayer was growing more insistent that Steele supplant Barney Cameron, the last holdover of the Reid regime, as the ranking financial officer and controlling force in the budget being drawn for the *Tribune*'s new fiscal year. "The financial picture and success of Whitney Communications Corporation depends on what happens at the Tribune and whether this apparently unmanageable financial drain can be gotten in hand," Thayer instructed White, who continued to view the paper as the rightful beneficiary of WCC's prosperity rather than an impediment to it. "I expect to stay close to these financial and business problems until we see our way out of this dilemma or until we raise the white flag."

Just how closely Thayer intended to oversee the situation became distressingly clear to White at the beginning of April when the paper suffered further reversals on the advertising side. Grey Advertising excluded the *Tribune* alone among the city papers from the new programming promotion for its client, NBC; the *Tribune*'s low-saturation coverage of city dwellers made it twice as costly as the *Times* and five times as expensive as the *Daily News* to reach New York residents through its pages, according to Grey's media buyers. The still worsening Sunday circulation, again dipping close to the 500,000 level, prompted a jolting warning from Walter Hoving, then the president of Tiffany & Co., long a steady *Tribune* advertiser, that unless the paper's Sunday picture brightened considerably within the next six months or it cut its ad rates to a realistic level, he would have to slash the big jewelry store's *Tribune* advertising allotment in half. Its share of the New York newspaper ad pie, meanwhile, had slipped from 11.95 percent in 1959 to 11.68 in the early months of 1960. Alarmed at these signs of falling revenue without a corresponding drop in expenditures, Thayer unilaterally created an executive finance committee consisting of himself, White, and Steele and declared it sovereign over the paper's business operations. The move sent an unhappy Bob White off to London to ask Jock Whitney who was running his paper and to offer his resignation if he no longer held Whitney's confidence.

After several days of talks, Whitney felt obliged to reduce their renewed understanding to paper because of a peculiarity he had now become aware of in White's manner: "You don't react person-to-person. In fact, as you described it to me, you don't react at all if you do not agree or if you don't think the point being made is worth your consideration. . . . This means in all the hours that we have talked I may have not received any sure impression of the order of importance to you of the things we discussed." Thayer's role regarding the *Tribune,* Whitney emphasized, was the same as it was for the other parts of WCC—making all the ends meet. "His interest in this respect is my interest and no other." Thayer's financial talents were welcomed by the other WCC members. "Nowhere else is it thought to be an intrusion." Yes, White was in charge of and totally responsible for the *Tribune,* but his power was derivative and not autonomous. The newly imposed finance committee was a device to help him, not undercut him. Having digested all this, much of it withering and cautionary, on his way to the airport, White phoned Whitney at the embassy to express his pleasure and gratitude for what he interpreted as a vote of confidence. "He is too deep for me—or something," Whitney wrote in informing Thayer of what had transpired.

Back in New York, White was quick to advise his subordinates that his mandate had been confirmed. Thayer was displaying "an entirely new attitude," White sensed—casual, almost—and noted in a private memorandum that the WCC president had disclosed upon inquiry that if the *Tribune* could be brought to a break-even position, his net worth, based on his ownership of, or option on, 5 percent of the company's stock and the current earnings of the other subsidiaries, would be enhanced by $250,000 a year—and that White, with a 1.5 percent share of the stock, would be enriched by $60,000 annually. What Thayer sought to impress upon White as their mutual vested interest in straightening out the paper White took to be an essentially mercenary approach by Thayer without due regard for the historic and civic values involved. For a week or so, Thayer held back, hoping that White would demonstrate more resolute leadership. But it was clear that the *Tribune* management was locked in an irreconcilable power struggle. When at a mid-April budget-planning session, Steele, who had come to the paper assuming he would supersede Cameron as the second-in-command, tried to move the discussion from narrow budgetary considerations to the larger issues of the stagnant circulation and absence of general planning to attract substantial new revenues, Cameron charged, in effect, that Steele was overstepping his authority. Steele, a man without artifice, thought such bickering absurdly obstructionist. In his view, Cameron was a deft office politician who had been tossing his weight around the paper for years without ever having had to answer for his misjudgments and managerial limitations. He had curried favor with White and been repaid in kind, and now the pair of them appeared to be using each other to fend off the threat Steele represented to their sway.

For him to function properly, Steele felt there could be no more dawdling and cover-up of bungling, and he went over White's head to write Thayer that "if exploration of present or past financial matters results in an embarrassment of any individual or group of individuals this cannot be helped. The Herald Tribune is an institution of far more importance than any individual." Steele, whose job took him to WCC headquarters each month to pick up the check to cover the *Tribune*'s deficit, inevitably was drawn into Thayer's camp. Steele was hardly fond of what he regarded as Thayer's authoritarian manner—"Old Cold Eyes" was how he thought of him—and recognized that Thayer was using him to inform on White. But he also felt that Thayer's growing disrespect for White was justified and that White's incompetence all but invited divided loyalty.

By the end of April, Steele's disenchantment overflowed in a grim report on the financial status and trend at the paper. First-quarter losses topped a million dollars, prospects appeared to be deteriorating rather than improving, and he feared that "the beginning of the end is at hand" unless "unlimited resources are available to keep the pump primed." He called out plaintively for a blueprint of what the paper ought to be, concluding that "the Herald Tribune needs action —the sooner the better." White and Cameron tried to convince Steele that his gloom was unwarranted and that his projected deficit figure for the year was based on preliminary departmental budget requests and other raw or uncorrected data, but to no avail. Even before Steele filed his cauterizing report,

Whitney was registering impatience with White. He was distressed by accounts of "unduly protracted inactivity on the news side." Ten days later, with Steele's grim report in hand and Thayer at his side in London, Whitney in effect revoked the hedged vote of confidence he had given White just a month earlier. He had not looked for overnight miracles, Whitney explained in a letter to White, but he had expected "a clearer assessment of our situation and a more definite indication of a program than I heard from you during our many hours of conversation when you were here in early April, and from [what] Walter is now able to bring me." Thayer was therefore being instructed to take a more active role at the paper—"the role I would attempt to fill if I were in New York at this time." Thayer was given, "without limitation, the authority he may require," and that included "the full right to make changes in the present organizational structure" of the paper.

Two months after his principled stand in the Doerfer matter, Robert White's independence in running the *Tribune* was fatally circumscribed; only prompt action, starting with his immediately putting Steele in over Cameron, could have rewon it for him. But whether out of stubbornness or continued obliviousness to his imperiled position, he did not act. When Thayer pushed him on the Steele matter, arguing that it was essential for the paper to use his financial acumen to the hilt, White "responded as he always responds, with platitudes and generalities," Thayer told Whitney. Thayer was still more downhearted after attending an "incredible" meeting in White's office at which it became apparent that chief editor Yerxa "did not know that there was pressure of this kind to complete the program for product change and he did not know that Jack Thees was relying in part on product change to bolster his advertising sales. I can't imagine what kind of conversations Bob and Yerxa have had." He found no evidence that White had contributed any ideas to Yerxa for improving the paper; rather, White seemed to have led Cameron and Yerxa "to believe that time and money are unlimited so far as you [Whitney] are concerned." Thayer was left after that numbing session "where I have been for the last 60 days— that we cannot do this job with White at the helm."

White was down but not out. He bestirred himself to ask all *Tribune* department heads (or their ranking subordinate in cases where he had picked the head) to summarize progress in their areas since he had taken charge. He then sent off the batch of reports to London, telling Whitney they were important not only for the specifics but also "for the feeling it will give you of staff interest, morale, dedication and activity here." *Tribune* treasurer Charles Hupp spoke of tightened financial controls. Circulation manager Lester Zwick noted that the latest semiannual ABC report showed a 1,500 gain for the daily edition compared with a 26,000 loss for the year-earlier period; the downtrend, at least, had been halted. Advertising director Jack Thees reported "a marked improvement in the sales atmosphere," even if there were not yet numbers to validate his claim. Harry Baehr said that he could not remember a time when the editorial-page staff worked under more favorable conditions, even in Ogden Reid's heyday. Everett

Walker, returned to power as Yerxa's principal deputy, asserted that the paper had been improved in content, quality, and appearance, that there were no more sacred cows grazing intrusively in the city room, that the valueless features introduced during Brown Reid's frenetic manipulations of the editorial content were blessedly gone, and that there was far less nagging emphasis on competition with the *Times*. Summarized personnel director John Bogart, who had begun his *Tribune* career as a cub under Stanley Walker and was temperamentally disinclined to paint a rosy picture at White's bidding: "There has been a great lift in morale. The fears and anxieties of recent years have disappeared. The paper is squared away on a new course."

Unquestionably, White had improved the situation in his calm, personable, and passive way by ending the turmoil that had afflicted the staff under the Reids and by improving the paper through the simple expedient of delegating its operation to Yerxa and Sargent, rather as Ogden Reid had set standards but not insisted on placing his personal imprint on the daily edition. Even Thayer conceded that the paper under White was better than it had been before he came. And few doubted that White was well-meaning and capable of kind gestures, like learning enough of sign language so that at the annual Twenty-five Year Club party he was able to greet and congratulate qualifying mute typographers in a way that had special meaning to them.

But his shortcomings were equally undeniable. He lacked dynamism and creativity when both were desperately needed, and Yerxa was no stronger in either department. Nowhere in the budgets White was supposed to shape and approve was there an item for changes or improvements in the paper. Nowhere was there a sign of a fresh idea. He voiced only noble sentiments and worthy ideals that nobody contested. Restoring the paper's hallowed past was demonstrably an insufficient strategy for staving off disaster, especially since even at its editorial peak—except for a few freakish years during World War II—it was a financially marginal operation run on largesse and family pride. Yet nothing Thayer or Steele or Whitney said served to shake White's maddening vagueness or to ground his rhetorical arabesques. He seemed all smile and precious little substance. "We got nothing but marshmallows and cream puffs from him," said a member of the Washington bureau. In London, the resident *Tribune* correspondents who saw Whitney frequently during this period recalled his frustration over White's torpor. London bureau chief Don Cook said Whitney felt he had given White license to remake the paper yet nothing new was forthcoming from him. "Jock was terribly disappointed that White couldn't figure out how to put his money to constructive use," said Cook's junior colleague, Richard Wald. "Those early years were pissed away while management tried to get itself together."

In fairness to him, White felt undercut by Thayer, who he said "increasingly and consistently accentuated the negative" in his assessments of the paper's progress. And submerging the paper within the WCC complex had the self-defeating effect, White believed, of keeping it alive without curing its sickness;

the $3.5 million ceiling Thayer imposed on its 1960 operational deficit "clearly limited investment of funds that could have been used to rebuild the paper." But White never forced the issue, never presented Thayer and Whitney with concrete proposals. A week after he sent Whitney the reports from department heads citing improvements at the paper under him, White dispatched his "Overall Program for [the] Herald Tribune," calling it "the most important document I have sent to you." It was little more than a packet of windy generalities and unexceptionable banalities. The section titled "Product Improvement" began: "It is always well to remember: The only reason for the existence of a newspaper is the product you put in a reader's hands. You can be totally expert in all other areas, but if you fail in the one area of product—editing—your newspaper fails."

White's professional limitations, hardly surprising in view of his provincial experience, also began to surface in misplaced enthusiasms and naïve indiscretions. He warmly praised rewriteman Sanche de Gramont for a stock piece of sentimentality about a child lost at Coney Island on the Fourth of July; de Gramont, winner of the *Tribune*'s last Pulitzer for a 1960 obituary written under extreme deadline pressure on a Metropolitan Opera star who died in mid-performance, rated the editor "not a quality person." At the 1960 Democratic convention in Los Angeles, White expressed amazement at the swift, ceaseless flow of copy from the typewriter of Robert Donovan; later at the Republican convention in Chicago, watching over Donovan's shoulder, White turned to deskman Charles Kiley, part of the *Tribune* coverage team, to ask of the Washington bureau chief's copy, "Do you think he's caught the flavor of this thing?" For some months, White commuted to work by limousine, in theory to free him from the dictates of the train schedule and allow him to work privately while in transit. But White never worked long hours and did not require this convenience, and newsmen, always a defiantly democratic lot, were not pleased by such lordly affectations, which particularly rankled while the paper's pay scale remained low—many in the Washington bureau were then receiving the Guild minimum—and its employees lacked a lounge, its cafeteria was substandard, and its toilets unsightly. White gave up the limousine but remained remote from the staff; the door to his office was not open in the informal fashion favored on many papers where the constant, daily pressure of big and little problems implicates the editor and president, who in this case were the same man. White avoided such involvement, did not attend Yerxa's daily editorial conference to plan the next day's paper, almost never waited around for the city edition to come up. "I didn't want Fen to become dependent on me," he explained long afterward. Instead, he preoccupied himself with soft-soaping Jock Whitney and trying forlornly to evade the deputized iron hand of Walter Thayer.

By June, Thayer was certain that White was less an asset than an obstacle to rescuing the *Tribune,* which he told Whitney could still be turned around if no more time was wasted. "You were a hero to him if your outfit was doing well," Corinthian Broadcasting president Wrede Petersmeyer said of Thayer, who was unstinting in his praise of WCC's head of television operations. "He was tougher on people than on policy," Petersmeyer added, meaning that Thayer's scrutiny was directed less at operational detail than results obtained. Thayer himself stated his managerial philosophy as: "Get the best men you possibly can and turn them loose. If they work out, fine; if not, get someone else."

White sealed his fate early in July by deciding to follow the *Times* in raising the price of the Sunday edition from thirty to thirty-five cents without bothering to consult Thayer first. Infuriated by such unilateral action in a matter affecting WCC's overall cash flow, Thayer revived the idea of buying *Popular Science* and bringing in Eugene Duffield over White; the less humane solution was simply to send White packing back to Missouri. Whitney, though, urged caution. "Like it or not, we brought Bob into this picture, and impossible as he has been, he is still our vaunted boy," Whitney said in a handwritten note that sympathized with Thayer's responsibilities but discouraged any tricky moves like the Duffield stratagem. He added that "you, and only you can know how hopeless it is with Bob. But at the same time you must know what an explosion will arise when we launch him and how right we must *appear* to be—and *be!*" In a follow-up, Whitney noted that White had "summoned some very useful disciples" and for WCC to push him off the mountaintop to which they had hoisted him "would break many more bones than his." Thayer did not soften his conviction; he replied to Whitney on July 13, a year after White had been appointed:

> . . . Everything has been running in our favor this year—the economy, sensational news, the election year, etc. We are not holding our position in advertising . . . and our whole Sunday picture is deplorable and still deteriorating. I do not have confidence in the "new" product. . . . Bob is a washout as far as this is concerned as he has nothing to contribute to it. . . . He can be a valuable asset, if his pride and vanity will permit, but he misses by a wide mark what is required in the form of ability and leadership to do the job.
>
> This is my best judgment. . . .

Thayer was pacified somewhat by White's finally installing Steele over Cameron to control the paper's business operations. What patience Whitney retained toward White, however, was badly strained during the Republican convention that August when the paper ran an editorial critical of the keynote address by Representative Walter Judd, the Minnesota missionary-politician, for being too partisan. Whitney found it "a proper loin-girder for the faithful—which, 'fore God, is what a keynoter is or it is nothing." The speech seemed to him wise, decent, and honorable, he told White, "a Republican appeal which our Republican paper should have had better taste than to dismiss in the manner and style of the editorial in question." He did not want to give the impression that "we are on-the-fence Republicans" or that "we might endorse Kennedy if he plays his cards right." Perhaps the offending editorial had been written because someone at the office "thinks we should make Republicans earn their praise from the

Herald Tribune. O.K. But not during the battle. During the battle, Bob, we fight."

The futility of hoping for a sudden blossoming of White's executive skills was demonstrated at a mid-September meeting of the paper's executives when White confessed puzzlement over the lagging advertising support for what he termed the paper's stronger Sunday product. Dick Steele, having seen only minor rejiggering of the Sunday format, in which the most exciting change had been placement of the editorial page at the front instead of inside the weekly news review section, exploded. How was the Sunday paper better, he demanded to know. White's answer amounted to a claim that the *Tribune*'s improved morale was producing inspired journalism. Steele complained to Thayer that he had heard White and Yerxa "talking in circles" about the Sunday paper since he had come to the *Tribune* at the beginning of the year, but all that had been forthcoming were excuses about lack of time to formulate changes and claims that the Sunday drop-off was decelerating—hardly a basis for attracting advertising. No plan yet existed to improve the situation, yet "each Sunday now is critical in fighting to maintain some semblance of a 500,000 circulation. . . . The present posture of the newspaper is such that it will not respond to theory and semantics." When White and Yerxa finally got around to more substantive Sunday changes in the latter part of November, the only eye-catching one was a new "Lively Arts" section, combining the former drama section and the book review in a tabloid format on newsprint that had a muddy, jumbled look. They said they would get around to revamping the limp *Today's Living* magazine sometime "later."

But by then it was too late. The ABC report for the period ended September 30 put the daily circulation at 336,000, a gain of 10,000 during White's year at the helm but no higher than it had been two years before when the paper passed to Whitney; it was on a treadmill growing more costly to operate all the time. And the Sunday circulation was at a disastrous 488,000, the lowest since 1936. Right up to the end of October, White was still trying to convince Whitney that there had been notable progress, particularly if one considered that an entirely new management team had been assembled. An extensive circulation drive was now underway, a major advertising sales effort was being formulated, a new concept and technique for the coverage of major stories had been unveiled—just what these were, White did not explain—and the *Tribune*'s editorials "may be the most widely republished in the U.S." The decision, though, was in; Whitney would return from London at the expiration of Eisenhower's term of office in January and assume the title of president and publisher. To save face, White would be allowed to retain the title of editor if he chose to stay on.

White was not advised of his options until after election day. The paper's coverage of the campaign had been trying for Whitney, starting with the critical editorial on the Republican keynote address and continuing with the endorsement of John Kennedy, their fellow Harvard alumnus, by columnists Walter Lippmann and Joseph Alsop and detectably heavier news play of Kennedy's campaign that led Nixon to complain. "Kennedy was the better story," Robert Donovan recalled by way of explanation. The final blow was the *Tribune*'s premature conclusion in print that Kennedy had won the election. As Nixon whittled down the margin in the post-midnight vote count, the *Times,* by contrast, slowed its press run, ceasing altogether at 5:30 a.m., when it still had 200,000 copies to print, and not resuming until seven when it named Kennedy the apparent victor but reported that the contested vote in Illinois might yet alter the outcome. "We ran an hour ahead of the Times in declaring Kennedy the winner," White reported proudly to Whitney. A few days later, he was summoned to London and told that Whitney would take his place as head of the *Herald Tribune.*

Properly commendatory statements were issued in praise of White's service during a difficult transitional period—Whitney told a skeptical *Newsweek* that White's appointment had been for a trial period, and no ignominy attached to his replacement—and the staff read with interest Whitney's assertion that "I want to jump in . . . head first, because I feel I must get *immediately* into an active, responsible working relationship" with the paper's top people. "I know I am taking on an immense job," he wrote to White, "but I have come to the conclusion that only the owner can *be* the paper and to do that he must really command." Well regarded in Britain for his work there as ambassador, Jock Whitney was coming home in an expansive, determined mood. But nearly two and a half years had passed since he took control of the *Tribune,* and there was still no light visible at the end of the tunnel. He had succeeded only in lengthening the tunnel.

In January 1961, Bob White went home to Mexico, Missouri, a victim of his own imperturbable nature and a blissful ignorance of metropolitan urgencies. It was not that he had done a bad job. Editorially he had restored the *Tribune*'s dignity, and according to an annual poll of editors around the country conducted by Edward Bernays's public relations firm, it was rated by its peers in 1960 as the sixth-best daily in the United States, up from tenth the year before. A similar poll by *Saturday Review* of journalism school faculty members taken right after White's departure placed the *Tribune* seventh. But there were no bold initiatives, no prospects of ending the financial tailspin. "It was a great idea, but it didn't work," Walter Thayer would later say of his selection of White. But it was not a great idea, even if the genius behind *The Wall Street Journal* had proffered it. "If White had been a well-rounded, broadly experienced newsman with courage and administrative talent," reflected Richard Steele, the results might have been different. Steele himself, convinced the paper's problems were too massive to be overcome and fearful that Thayer would inevitably dominate the operation, elected to go home to Worcester and accept an offer to become publisher of the paper there that he knew so well. Whitney received Steele's resignation on his first day as boss of the *Tribune.* That left him without an editor or a business manager to face the most formidable challenge in American journalism.

III

The *Times* welcomed him home with a commendatory editorial, and its newly retired publisher, Arthur Sulzberger, sent him a framed print of Horace Greeley's farm in Chappaqua with a note reading: "We hope that it will cheer your office and bring you luck." But the one gesture from his dominant rival that would have cheered Jock Whitney's return—raising its newsstand price from a nickel to a dime so the *Tribune* could do likewise and reap some badly needed revenues—was nowhere in sight. Gentlemanly words aside, the extinction of Whitney's paper would have suited the *Times* far better than its revival.

His resolve to save the *Tribune* was tested at once by Whitney's associates at WCC, who at Walter Thayer's direction gathered all the pertinent data and thinking and presented to the head of the company what treasurer Robert Bryan described as "a very stark picture." The partners from J. H. Whitney & Co. who had joined him in the creation of WCC had understood from the start that the enterprise would be encumbered by Whitney's indulgence in the *Tribune* but expected this obstacle to their ambitions to be hurdled or set aside before it could threaten the solidity of the new company. "We weren't ordered to do this," said Bryan of the move to WCC, "but we were all indebted to Jock—and doing things for Jock paid off for people." There were clear signs now, though, after two and a half years of Whitney ownership and subsidized losses totaling $7,125,000, that the situation was getting out of hand.

Annual losses in the range of one to two million—within hailing distance of break-even—might have been tolerable for a protracted period; twice that amount, with still heavier losses as the immediate prospect, was a different story. It was painfully evident, Thayer said in early January to a gathering of his executives in anticipation of Whitney's momentary return, that "we have some important decisions to make . . . [regarding] whether the progress we are making justifies the losses we are incurring and the serious continued drain on the other companies." No longer was there a question, as Thayer framed the matter in businesslike fashion, of WCC's priorities; the only question was John Hay Whitney's priorities. Thayer knew that whatever else the *Tribune* represented for Whitney, his starting premise was that the paper had to be operated as a business and not on indefinite subsidy. Anyone with great wealth could buy and sustain a newspaper as a rich man's toy—the challenge for Whitney was not merely in having the *Tribune* and commanding its voice but in getting it to stand on its feet. Could that be done, however, within the framework of WCC, which saved Whitney from invading his capital to underwrite the paper but sharply delimited the resources available for the herculean task? For Thayer, it was the only rational way for Whitney to attempt it; "[you] should know the financial limitations within which this venture must be operated," Thayer told his WCC colleagues, thereby defining what he regarded as the prudent extent of the risk that Jock Whitney would describe to Nelson Rockefeller three months later as "the most important undertaking of my life."

Reinforcing Thayer's position was the built-in grievance of the *Tribune*'s sister properties under the WCC umbrella—the companies whose growth programs were being indefinitely postponed because, as Thayer pointedly put it, "all of their cash is being siphoned off for the Tribune." Wrede Petersmeyer of Corinthian Broadcasting, WCC's main provider, was troubled not only by the drain of his profits but also by what he perceived as the *Tribune*'s hostility to the television business. Thayer focused Whitney's attention on these "feelings of frustration, if not despair" at Corinthian.

But Whitney was far from ready to toss in the towel. He recognized that Thayer, for all the sincerity of his efforts, had failed to find him a vigorous, talented man to run the *Tribune*; no wonder it was worse off than when he took title to it. But neither was he ready to make a bold move, like taking the paper into the afternoon field, where it would be the star, perhaps merging it with the *World-Telegram* or *Journal-American* or even both, as Thayer's WCC council briefly considered, or linking it with a suburban paper or group of papers for joint advertising sales and production facilities. Before any of that, the paper had to be redefined, and no one was yet on hand who could do that for him. Perhaps he himself could do it, now that he was taking personal charge? Over dinner with the Whitneys before their return to the United States, London correspondent Don Cook's wife, Cherry, remarked to Betsey Whitney how essential it was now for Jock to impose his taste and sensibility on the paper. Mrs. Whitney replied, according to Cook, "Jock will never impose himself on anything—that's not the way he is." He was a patron, an encourager, and though anxious to jump in with both feet, as he had written Bob White, he had one great advantage over the Reids besides his fortune: he knew what he did not know.

The most accomplished among the *Tribune*'s outside advisers—Bernard Kilgore—came forward in his role as a WCC director and urged Whitney to remember that his first goal for the paper had to be its survival, which could not be accomplished by what Whitney himself referred to in private as the "shower of gold" effect, the assumption that with his millions behind it, the *Tribune* staff no longer had to worry about money. Kilgore called for a tight ship, for running a one-man Washington bureau if that was all the paper could afford, and using the wire services for foreign and national coverage if that was what the balance sheet dictated. An indefinitely subsidized paper lacked integrity, he argued; many useful papers were put out on budgets far smaller than the *Tribune*'s. Why not turn it into "the compact model paper"? Better to have "a good regiment than a weak division," Kilgore said. Piecemeal retrenchments were a retreat from reality. "My father used to say it is a mistake to cut off the cat's tail an inch at a time. Doesn't help the cat."

A similarly prescriptive recommendation for a less ambitious kind of *Herald Tribune* came from the paper's director of research and promotion, Richard

Sheldon, who reminded Whitney that the central cause of its financial woe was its disproportionately high editorial content. In 1960, the paper ranked seventh nationally in total columns of news matter published—just behind *The Washington Post* and just ahead of the *Chicago Tribune,* both vastly stronger operations; in total advertising linage, it ranked No. 113 nationally, between the Syracuse, New York, *Herald-Journal* and the Portland, Oregon, *Journal,* much smaller papers in much smaller markets without ambitions for national influence. Sheldon urged the *Tribune* to scale itself down accordingly, retaining editorial distinction by extensive use of outside contributors and experts on call when the news dictated instead of maintaining expensive Washington and overseas bureaus and a news hole befitting a prosperous giant in the field.

Fully apprised now of the costs, Whitney was caught between his lingering dream of restoring the *Tribune* to its status as a great institution and pressures for running it as Thayer counseled and conventional business wisdom dictated —on a budget-conscious basis. This ambivalence was reflected in an interview he gave to *Editor & Publisher* soon after his return to New York. "Herald Tribune Must Pay—or Else, Whitney Says," the article was headlined. But in making clear he had no intention to subsidize the paper forever, he also declared, "I think our paper should have much more national influence than it does today." It had been slack in seeking national readership, "and I intend to push this."

In fact, Whitney did not push anything; he enlisted people to do the pushing for him. Confronted with the enormity of the *Tribune*'s problems, he made his first and only truly fateful decision as proprietor of the paper in selecting the man to preside over its financial well-being—he asked Walter Thayer to leave WCC's offices at the top of the Time-Life Building to join him in the grubbier surroundings on West Forty-first Street. Thayer would retain the presidency of WCC, but the rest of its operations were in highly capable hands and prospering; the *Tribune,* with its seemingly intractable troubles, was where he was needed to apply direct, continuing attention. At least as relevant was Whitney's personal diffidence. "Jock had an unreasonable lack of confidence," said his brother-in-law, William Paley. "He was scared to death to go down to the paper and try to run it alone." He trusted Thayer thoroughly and needed his clarity of vision and toughness of mind. "He leaned on Walter tremendously," Paley noted. For Thayer, the command invitation had the unenviable effect of making him directly responsible for the paper's performance, and his background hardly suited him to the assignment. But those inside the Whitney enterprise surmised that Jock had made an irresistible offer to his prime counselor in which he said, in effect: Let's go down there together and have some fun trying to save this thing—and I can assure you that you'll never be the loser financially. "Walter's loyalty to Jock made any other choice impossible," said WCC director Martin Stone.

Taking the interim title of chairman of the *Tribune* executive committee and still shuttling between the paper and the WCC offices a dozen blocks away,

Thayer promptly put the McKinsey & Co. management consultants back on the job to lay out an action plan that would make up for the time lost under Bob White's easygoing reign. The McKinsey people responded in two useful ways. First was to supply a target, premised on a series of connected conditions that, if met, would put the paper in the black within five years or sooner. If circulation increased at 5 percent a year, McKinsey reasoned, and if the editorial content —the news hole—was reduced by 10 percent, and if the staff was cut by between 12 and 15 percent, break-even could be achieved by 1966 without any major increase in advertising. There was nothing inherently absurd or contradictory about projecting higher sales of a leaner paper put out by a smaller staff, provided that the paper itself could be made more attractive. Just how that could be done, McKinsey could not, nor was it expected to, say. What it did develop, though, was a highly specific set of management controls designed to provide the direct unit costs of each activity and component of the operation. Knowledge of such items as the distribution cost for every thousand copies sold on suburban newsstands or the net per-line contribution of every advertising category was essential if modern management techniques were to be applied to reduction of the paper's deficit.

Thayer then made two personnel moves to implement these programs. The first was to hire a general manager to replace Dick Steele as the paper's top operating financial officer. His choice of Thomas L. Robinson, who had recently been bought out as owner of the Charlotte, North Carolina, *News* by the Knight chain's rival *Observer,* would soon prove as unfortunate a selection as Robert White had been. But Thayer's other appointment, with Whitney's concurrence, was a man who brought to the *Tribune* the only authentic touch of editing genius it had witnessed since Greeley's death. And he did it fast.

IV

Based on its clean, classic look as restored by managing editor Fendall Yerxa and night editor Everett (the Count) Kallgren, the March 15, 1961, issue of the *Herald Tribune* was awarded the F. W. Ayer Cup, emblematic of typographical excellence, for the tenth time, re-establishing the paper's reputation as the handsomest in America. The day before the prize-winning issue was prepared, the *Tribune*'s new editor, John Lee Denson, arrived from *Newsweek,* where he had been the ranking editor for eight years. Within a fortnight of his arrival, Yerxa was out, the Count was in permanent eclipse, and the *Tribune*'s glorious front page, with all its formal elegance, was gone forever.

A critical mass of intensity and irascibility relieved by interludes of amiability, John Denson was a throwback to Greeley in the three characteristics that made them both remarkable journalists: a ceaseless curiosity about the world, an excitability that activated energies when other professional observers grew jaded, and a sense of showmanship that did not need to traffic in the tawdry. Neither had much formal education and, partially as a result, both tended to black-and-white judgments of contemporary personalities and social issues. But where Greeley was essentially a man of ideas, a teacher and preacher, Denson was primarily an inspired technician, preoccupied with the forms and flourishes of news presentation.

He was a native of the Louisiana hill country, where relatives ran the parish weekly. By sixteen, he had quit military school in Maryland, where his family had moved, and gone to work as a copyboy on the Washington *Herald.* There followed the impulsive wanderings of the prototypical American journalist of the early part of the twentieth century. He worked on close to twenty papers throughout the eastern half of the nation, ranging from Miami to Chicago, doing whatever they asked him to, always learning, always producing, always moving on. There was a two-year stint in the late 'Twenties in the *Herald Tribune* Washington bureau, followed by several years in New York on the *World* and *World-Telegram* before more responsible editing jobs on the *Post* in Washington and under flamboyant editor Louis Rupple, a resourceful generator of story ideas, in Chicago. From daily journalism, he turned to periodicals—a shift that allowed him to master new professional techniques and form a somewhat broader perspective on events and definition of what was news. He wrote for *Fortune,* served as second-in-command of *Time*'s busy Washington bureau during World War II, became the first managing editor of *The Kiplinger Magazine* (later called *Changing Times*) and one of the last managing editors of terminally ill *Collier's.* He came to *Newsweek* in 1952 at the age of forty-eight, a long-traveled journeyman with a conquered case of alcoholism in his past and a record with creative flashes but no major triumphs.

Rising swiftly to managing editor and then the top of the masthead, John Denson brought *Newsweek* out of the shadows of *Time* during the ensuing decade and, with his wits, typographic flair, and an alertness for the sociological and technological frontiers of the news, turned his magazine into what Madison Avenue media buyers referred to as "a hot book." Where writing style was *Time*'s trademark, graphics was Denson's forte. He broke up texts with arrows, bullets, dingbats, circled sections of photographically enlarged documents, boxes that highlighted or detailed complex elements of a story, and an array of other devices all aimed at improving reader comprehension. He used pictures with an artfulness rare in word-oriented editors, specializing in facial close-ups cropped in a way that emphasized a subject's characteristic features and lopped off ears and other uninteresting parts. He put the magazine heavily into coverage of space and the atom, new styles of living and leisure, and the emerging crisis over racism in the United States. His chief journalistic god was clarity—"I'm a simple man," he would say, exhorting his staff to reduce big issues and complicated events to the man-in-the-street sensibility that Denson himself epitomized; he was never an urban sophisticate. Thus, it was said that *Time*'s typical reader was a Westchester or Winnetka suburbanite while the classic consumer of Denson's *Newsweek* was a druggist in Greenville, South Carolina. His affinity for Main Street once led him to put the president of Rotary International on the cover—an unthrilling selection based on the reasonable premise that for that one week, at least, a lot of businessmen who were the core of their communities would definitely have *Newsweek* on their minds.

Not a deep thinker, he saw the news in terms of heroes and villains—he loved George C. Marshall, Douglas MacArthur, and other military stalwarts, hated Harry Truman and John Kennedy among politicians, whom he viewed generally as frauds and rogues—and personalized issues and events through a mind shaped by cracker biases accumulated in youth and never shaken. He was xenophobic, anti-Catholic (or at least anti-Papist), and anti-Negro. There was nothing in the world cuter than a black baby, he would say; "they only get ugly when they grow up." He was often fascinated by silly things that caught his attention, like the introduction of a new football kicking tee, which he ordered prominently displayed in *Newsweek*'s sports section, or the development of the square tomato, a sorrowful example of which he put on the cover, where it sat, inert and inscrutable—a dud as measured by newsstand sales; not all John Denson's inspirations clicked. Short on intellectual resources of his own, he was a scavenger of other people's ideas and knew, usually better than they, how to package them.

On the job, he was a study in concentration. "It wasn't just that he worked hard—he never stopped," said one associate. Of medium height, slender except for a little potbelly, he had a small man's compact face with very pink skin, an emphatic jaw, slightly bulging eyes that looked weepy behind his thick, tinted glasses, and breath minty from pills he was forever gobbling for what colleagues supposed was an arrested case of ulcers that he fed with a diet of scrambled eggs, ice cream, and black coffee. His grooming was fastidious and his wardrobe right off the Ivy League rack—perfectly pressed dark suits, blue oxford-cloth button-downs, rep ties from De Pinna. Though he labored at a demonic pace in the center of the production process, amid mounds of copy over which he ran a restless editing pencil, photographs that he loved to crop experimentally with the nearest straightedge, and headlines that he compulsively rewrote no matter how inspired the original, he never worked in his shirtsleeves. It was almost as if to shed his finery would have been to risk his rank and authority. Even at the end of one of his fourteen-hour days, he looked as neat and pink and crisp as when he began, without a wrinkle in his garments or a hair on his head out of place. The only physical evidence of the pressure he was under was his heavy smoking and the eerie clicking and grinding of his dentures when tension mounted. His crankiness was an office legend. Peter Wyden, then a special-projects writer working out of the Washington bureau, remembered the sound of Denson's "gnashing, snarling voice on the phone, asking you to go out and round up the Atlantic Ocean for him by Friday. If he decided you were a fuck-up, you could bring him the Second Coming of Christ as an exclusive and it would do you no good, but if he decided you were a pro, you'd have to rape the President's wife for him to find fault with you."

Though he surrounded himself with a small circle of sycophantic aides, he broke with the old *Newsweek* habit of promoting by social pedigree, and for all his grumpiness was warmly loyal and tactfully generous to old cronies who were forever showing up at his office door. To the mass of subordinates who were neither yes-men nor aging pals, John Denson was a chameleon in his personal relations. "He could turn on you in a moment," recalled one. He harbored a deep sense of his own indispensability and operated as a one-man band to promote the illusion. After a long day's work, his idea of recreation was to drop by the out-of-town newspaper stand in Times Square, buy up a three-foot-high stack of papers, and spend the rest of the night at his apartment scouring them for story ideas. The next day he would fire off a batch of memos to his editors, advising them of developments in a dozen far-off places, suggesting whom their reporters might contact, and not bothering to attach the news clipping on which the suggestion was based—that would have destroyed his well-nursed image of omniscience. He would work without let-up for weeks at a time until nervous exhaustion overcame him and then head with his wife, Kitty, to their 125-acre farm near Brattleboro, Vermont, where, according to house guests, he would do little but stand in the window watching the snow fall and saying over and over, "Boy, it's really comin' down." For diversion he would go into the back room to watch very old movies through very poor reception and holler in periodically, "Kitty, are there any more Es-kee-mo Pies?" Away from the office, he almost never talked politics or national issues, preferring to reminisce about his newspapering days. When Kitty threw an occasional cocktail party at their Tudor City midtown apartment, he would lounge around uncomfortably on the fringes. Those who knew him best thought John Denson was a lonely man; the same was said of Horace Greeley.

By 1961, he had done what he could at *Newsweek*. Circulation had risen nearly 50 percent during his years as its editor and stood at 55 percent of *Time*'s—a small but important improvement in its relative standing. He left behind a distinctively different news weekly from the one he had taken over and a younger generation of journalists, among them Ben Bradlee, his Paris and then Washington bureau chief, who said of Denson, "He taught me the sizzle is important, not just the steak."

Denson's name had shown up on Walter Thayer's list of candidates to run the *Tribune* after Lee Hills had rejected the offer, but somehow he was never seriously considered. Reports of his volatile personality persisted in the news business, but none of them had reached Thayer's ears. His credentials for the job were as overwhelming as Bob White's had been deficient, and when asked, he jumped at the challenge: if he could put *Newsweek* on the road to competing seriously with *Time*, surely he could outfit the *Tribune* with an attractive new personality that would end its forlorn yearning for equality with *The New York Times*. One *Times*, he believed, was enough.

Throughout his magazine career, newspapers had remained his first love, and becoming editor of the *Tribune,* on which he had worked in Washington a generation earlier, was "like coming home," John Denson said. But he was hardly thrilled by what he found. "I've never seen so much no-talent in one place," he remarked over dinner one night with circulation manager Zwick. Thayer presented Denson with all the reports, analyses, and recommendations that had accumulated during the mark-time Whitney ownership, said that neither he nor Whitney expected overnight miracles—even as they had told Bob White—but did not repeat the mistake of inviting an open-ended timetable for the metamorphosis. The redesigned *Tribune* needed to be ready for a big post–Labor Day unveiling, Thayer said—that gave Denson six months to tinker. Beyond indicating that everyone agreed the revamped paper ought to be "compact," Thayer prescribed nothing specific. The Sunday edition, he added, required priority attention.

Denson proceeded to pay as little attention as possible to the Sunday problem. He had his own sense of priorities. The first was to rekindle the excitement and excellence the paper had displayed in its heyday while finding a serviceable format that did not stray so radically from the old mold as to make it unrecognizable. No longer could its columnists, features, and political allegiance carry the paper, he recognized. To broaden its readership, the treatment of the news itself would have to become the selling point. But he had no more bodies at his disposal to do the newsgathering, for while Whitney did not order the editorial staff pruned in heeding his efficiency experts' call for a reduced payroll, neither did he expand Denson's budget—a shower of gold would be the kiss of death, Barney Kilgore had counseled. Denson did have several critical factors in his favor, though. He had the freedom to wing it, to break the mold and bring to his assignment a forty-year working lifetime of accumulated ideas. And the era in which he was to remake the *Tribune* could hardly have been better suited to produce the news. It was the early months of the Kennedy presidency, and almost everything the new young leader said and did made splendid copy.

Rather than issuing detailed instructions on what he wanted done, Denson installed himself in the Count's place on the night desk, the nerve center of the city room after dark, and did much of the work himself. Swift superimposition of his methods was easier than trying to restaff the place in his image. And since he would concentrate his efforts on the front page, the showcase of the paper, the remodeling process was not beyond the powers of one man so long as he worked, as was John Denson's habit, with an almost pathological intensity. The resulting front page had something of the flashiness of afternoon papers but was far more disciplined and careful in every detail. Retaining the *Tribune*'s elegant Bodoni headline typeface and declining to spice its columns with smut, gore, or the trivial pursuits of entertainers, the Densonized front page was much more informal, declarative, grabbing, and—to many of the paper's inveterate readers —repellent than its prize-winning predecessor. Liveliness had supplanted dignity as the dominant trait of the *Herald Tribune* personality. Whatever else it was, John Denson's handiwork was not dull.

V

Denson's touch made itself evident in the March 19, 1961, issue, only a few days after he got to the paper. The entire top left quarter of the front page was devoted to the first part of a weeklong series on Cuba under Castro as reported by the *Tribune*'s UN correspondent, Joseph Newman, who had spent nearly a month watching the island in the process of transforming itself from a bourgeois revolutionary state to a Marxist-Leninist regime with undeniable authoritarian tendencies.

Too lacking in detail to pass for first-class investigative journalism, the series was nevertheless readable and prescient, and John Denson gave it maximum impact with typographical sleight of hand. Instead of a conventional headline, he put on it a provocative label: "CUBA-S.S.R?" It was set all in capitals, as *Tribune* heads had not been in more than forty years, and italics for added vibrancy, and floated in ample white space to attract maximum attention. By use of the question mark, a Denson trademark, the heading served to pose the issue in the fewest possible words—a shorthand instantly comprehensible to all but the dimmest readers. The clinching, overdrawn subheadline, "Communist Gun at the Head of Latin America," was substantiated only by a silhouetted picture of a Castro-like figure in military fatigues holding a pistol in an extended arm and aiming it at Newman's story. A boldface box in the white space beside the picture explained what the series was about, and tucked into a corner of the wide-column text was a sidebar on Newman's background with a half-column picture of him incised. Typographically intricate, unmistakably sensationalist in the tone and implications of its framing, discordant with the rest of the front page, the apparatus of its presentation commanded the reader's eye and lured him in.

Denson soon thereafter introduced the interpretive news technique practiced at *Newsweek* by supplementing a report on President Kennedy's officially positive reaction to the outcome of a Southeast Asia Treaty Organization conference in Bangkok, summoned to consider collective action in the Laotian crisis. A large box next to the story carried two side-by-side columns, one headed "SEATO: What We Wanted," the other "What We Got." By tersely comparing and contrasting, the box disclosed how American aims were compromised; it was a useful corrective to the White House claim of satisfaction. And the "We" in the boxed heads pierced the traditional veil of editorial objectivity by acknowledging that the reader, the members of his government, and the creators of his newspaper were all countrymen who presumably shared a national interest. The following day, the *Tribune*'s story on the new municipal budget for New York featured a large chart labeled "How the Budget Grows," a graphic civics lesson instantly absorbed.

At a more rapid pace thereafter, Denson swept away the old front-page architecture, essentially vertical in structure, with its heaviest thrust to the reader's upper right and the rest a stylized patchwork of mostly one- and two-column headlines that snugly filled the space between column rules and marched predictably down the page. In the old format, everything seemed to be slotted, only slightly less so than on the front page of the *Times,* which appeared to vary little day after day in its good, gray, understated fashion. Denson's papers rarely looked the same two days running. His modular approach, using chunks of type and artwork as building blocks of infinitely various sizes and shapes, pulled apart the staid verticality of the page and started each day with a fresh canvas. The format ought to accommodate the news, not the other way around. Stories now slashed across the page horizontally, they were boxed or indented or set wide-measure, they were matched as twin or triple "readouts" conveying different aspects of the same major story and run as dependencies of a catchall main head. Headlines, in unorthodox lengths and shapes, were set flush left and right in the old *Tribune* fashion, or centered and surrounded by white space for readability and starkness, or indented less radically but enough to achieve a cleaner look, or underlined or boxed and enclosed by rules on the top and sides in a "hood," or staggered flush left on the top line and flush right on the bottom. Italic type, with its graceful cursives, was used more generously and blended for enhanced contrast and variety. And the headlined words themselves were no longer conceived as a mere repetition of the opening paragraph or two of the story but as cryptic enticement or flavorful toppings, like "The Windy City?—It's N.Y. / During the Easter Parade," which in nearly every element was a departure from past practice. There was Denson's favorite interrogatory opener, followed by the abrupt dash dictating a reflective pause, then the conversational contraction "It's" and the informal abbreviation of "New York"; even the "the" in front of "Easter Parade" went against conventional headlinese, which usually dropped all articles to gain a kind of telegraphic urgency. When the Russians sent their first cosmonaut into space—a feat almost every *Tribune* reader knew about before he received the April 13 issue—Denson picked up where the television coverage left off. "How a Man Got Out of / This World . . . and Where / Do We Go from Here?" his headline read in part; it said nothing at all, really, but conveyed a celebratory sense of the epochal achievement; in this case, his "We" meant not America but all mankind—his way of personalizing the outsized event for the reader to share in it better.

In the week of April 17, only a month after Denson began, his jarring techniques were put to full use as the Bay of Pigs fiasco unfolded, producing news sensations day after day. On Monday, the top one-third of the front page was devoted to the first of three articles on an extensive interview with Soviet

premier Khrushchev by Walter Lippmann, accompanied by candid photographs of the two men paired at opposite sides of the page, as if putting the
journalist-philosopher on a par with the Russian leader as world statesman. The
top of the *Tribune*'s front page was no longer necessarily reserved for the most
important news of the day by the conventional definition of the word. It was
now an element of a conscious composition. Denson's boxed headline, "Khrushchev to Lippmann—Face to Face. No. 1," did not even pretend that hot news
had emerged from their exchange, but here was something new and thought-
provoking and unavailable on TV screens the night before. The main hard-news
story below the Lippmann piece was a miniature eight-column banner set in
capitals, "CASTRO—'KENNEDY IS LIKE A CAT . . . ,' " which even with its
two-column subheadline did not make clear that the Cuban leader's comment
was in response to an air attack on his military airfields by anti-Communist
rebels under U.S. protection. The reader learned that by reading the story; the
headline was there to draw him into it. To the left, the third leading element
on the page was headlined "Here's the Story / Eichmann Will Tell," with an
overline or "kicker" that proclaimed with Hearstian immodesty, "Exclusive
Interview!" The interview by Robert Bird was in fact with the Nazi war criminal's lawyer on the eve of his trial in Jerusalem; again the headline said nothing
of substance and by the very omission challenged the reader to delve into the
text. The stories themselves were hardly a departure from *Tribune* style, but
now they were invitingly gift-wrapped. It was typographical showmanship.

The top of the next day's paper was devoted to a horizontal band of five
paragraphs of equal depth, each tightly summarizing the Bay of Pigs misadven-
ture from a different perspective—"On the Invasion Front," "In New York,"
"In Washington," "In Latin America," and "In Moscow"—and together providing the reader with a sense of the magnitude of the drama as his eye swept
across the page and gobbled up the wide-measure, extra-leaded, easy-to-read
capsulizations. The banner below did not waste itself repeating what readers
had already learned from TV and radio but sought instead to relay the sense
of crisis in a conversationally elliptical manner: "CIVIL WAR IN CUBA . . . '5,000
ASHORE' . . . / THE FIRST 24 HOURS MAY DECIDE IT."

The next day's main headline took an openly jingoist tone: "Kennedy Tells
Off Khrushchev / . . . We'll Meet Force With Force." And the flanking subhead-
ings on the two prime related stories showed Denson's headlining at its most
provocatively direct—"Bluster, Not Bomb, / That's What U.S. / Expects From
Reds"—and tauntingly speculative—"Does Khrushchev / Seek to Paralyze /
U.S. With Fear?" All across the top ran an inch-high box with the overline "A
MESSAGE FROM THE ANTI-CASTRO UNDERGROUND IN CUBA TO AMERICANS,"
and beneath it the text: "If Cuba is not liberated now, there will not be another
Latin American nation with the guts to shake off the Communists." Beneath,
in Denson's mosaic of East-West confrontation, ran a horizontal gallery of
pictures of five involved world leaders, wearing suitably somber expressions,
with captions that disclosed latest developments; Khrushchev's read: "Moscow

expresses joy at the Cuban people's victory." The main stories were yoked by a headline that projected an almost wistful quality: "WHERE'S CASTRO—WAR VICTIM? / KENNEDY—A PROMISE TO CUBA." A lot of sizzle, not much steak, and the merest hint of a verb.

By the weekend, it was time for reflection and evaluation as the din of the aborted invasion faded. "THE STRANGE AND TANGLED STORY OF CUBA—FROM ALL SIDES," said the overline above the five text blocks at the top of the page; each bore a small italic headline that compactly gave a different angle as elaborated in stories below: the invaders' assessment ("It's No 'Defeat' "), Castro's ("It Was Crushing"), the responsible people in Washington ("Who Said 'Go' "), the reasons the attack failed ("What Upset It"), and the likely consequences ("The Next Round"). The précis under "What Upset It" read in its entirety:

> What went wrong? A number of miscalculations, Washington sources now say. For one, there was an underestimation of how much Fidel Castro's strength had been beefed up by Communist aid—jet fighters, tanks, artillery—and by Red technicians. Rebel sources said—after landing—they were surprised at the amount of hardware thrown against them by Castro forces and the speed with which it was used. Another surprise was the professionalism displayed by the Castro troops in using the Communist-supplied weapons. The biggest overestimation was in the number of Cubans who would defect to the rebels when the invasion was triggered. The Premier apparently has a tighter hold on the Cuban people than had been estimated.

It was the merest gloss on a complex of factors, as was each of the other four pieces of exactly the same length, but such editorial compression required care and skill; for many readers, the bare-bones treatment was all they had the time or interest to absorb.

The week ended with another outbreak of civil war. Denson led off the Sunday paper with a big boxed overline, "Two Great Crises Rock the Free World," and below it the main linking head, "Algeria: Revolt Gains, De Gaulle Acts; / Cuba: Ike Confers, Mr. K. Threatens." Wherever he could, Denson tried to tie together stories related in subject or, as here, in scale. Previously, "Ike" had been an impermissible indignity in *Tribune* headlines, although "Eisenhower" took up a great deal of space; "Mr. K.," which Denson would soon shorten to just "K," would have been an unthinkable abomination to designate a head of state. But people called him Ike—it was an affectionate nickname, after all. And the Soviet leader's name was equally space-consuming in headlines and even harder to spell, so why not shrink him to a single letter—he wasn't our icon.

In his diary, *Tribune* copy editor John Price expressed great ambivalence toward Denson's revolutionary methods. They were more packaging than journalism, he wrote, and were based on too few facts and too much innuendo and guesswork; it was essential now to read the *Times,* Price felt, to know what was really happening in the world. But John Price was a professional student of global affairs, with an ideologue's interest in the struggles of socialism; how many readers wanted as much detailed reporting from their morning paper? How many had the time? And as Price acknowledged of the Densonized *Tribune*: "This is a thoroughly professional job . . . silly but expert silliness."

Without question, Denson's new packaging was capturing attention in the nation's media capital. *The New Yorker*—in a deft satirical putdown by Roger Angell titled "Syndrome? What Syndrome?"—described the emotional collapse of a fictional *Tribune* reader overdosed by Denson's questioning headlines. Whitney was amused; Denson was not, perhaps because his existence went unnoted in the piece. What left the paper's business managers unamused was the disruption of the production process that Denson's custom-tailoring of the front page was causing. Standard typesetting specifications did not apply to page-one story candidates because there was no longer such a thing as a standard page one; copy was set in various widths as Denson's eye and taste dictated. As a result, many stories were held back from the composing room till the last minute, causing bottlenecks. And when the page proofs came up and Denson was displeased, considerable resetting and recomposition were required. The paper was running late. And the more refinements Denson devised, the later the paper ran. Near the end of April, general manager Tom Robinson sent Denson a memo from the production department head, who demanded to know, "Have we any deadlines or are we on a when, as and if basis . . . [?]" One night, after a 9:02 p.m. press start—two minutes late—Denson had stopped the press four minutes later to change the lead headline, remove a border from around a picture, and transpose a cutoff rule. "How many papers did that sell?" the foreman wondered. A few days later, business manager Barney Cameron, who was responsible for the production department, warned of disaster "if we are to continue with complete disregard for copy deadlines, copy flow and edition closing times. . . . As I have been saying . . . for the past two weeks [which included the Bay of Pigs crisis], something simply must be done to change the situation."

But Denson's paper was selling. Circulation for April was up 40,000 over April 1960—a figure somewhat buoyed by the extraordinary news events yet surely traceable in some measure to the eye-catching new format. In May, a less spectacular news month, circulation was up more than 20,000 from the year before. By June, Denson's news-compacting methods were coming into their own. When the Supreme Court issued a flurry of complicated rulings on the same day, Denson gathered them under an omnibus headline, "SUPREME COURT—GOD, BIRTH CONTROL, EVIDENCE, UNION MONEY IN POLITICS," summarized each in a tight package, and referred interested readers to detailed accounts on the inside. His conception of reader service was further amplified a few mornings later following Kennedy's TV report to the nation on his Vienna meeting with Khrushchev and talks with other European leaders. The *Times* ran the full text of the President's remarks, but the *Tribune* broke out carefully selected excerpts and labeled each by subject in an inviting sampler across the top of the page. The main headline read: "What Kennedy Meant: We're in

Trouble; / K Sure of Conquest Without Great War," and before White House correspondent David Wise's interpretive lead article, an intervening double-column "precede" set in italics began: "As the President made his candidly serious report to the nation on his conversations abroad, this was the crisis news elsewhere. . . ." and a series of four terse short-paragraph summaries, each set off by a decorative printer's mark, followed. John Denson was more interested in sweep than depth. But he could also turn expansive. When Pope John XXIII issued his 25,000-word encyclical *Pacem in Terris,* on the duty of prosperous nations toward needy and backward people, Denson played it as part of a historic trilogy and presented it across a whole page in digest form with Pope Leo XIII's 1891 encyclical on conditions of the working class and Pius XI's 1931 treatise on justice in labor-management relations as a means of preventing class warfare. Denson may not have cared for Pontiffs past or present, but he knew good copy when he saw it.

His early work revitalizing the *Tribune* won mixed grades from the profession. In mid-July, *Time* noted that the paper was trying hard to find a level of its own amid such uncertainty about where it should be and that its old front page, which used to win beauty contests, had taken on the look of "a parquet floor—all overblown pictures, klaxon headlines . . . and framed summaries of the major news." Indeed, the *Tribune* under Denson seemed "more summary than news" to *Time.* But an extensive and far more favorable commentary on Denson's efforts appeared about the same time in *Saturday Review,* which said the *Herald Tribune* was being talked about over the past few months as it had not been for years. Written by Robert Shaplen, a former *Tribune* city reporter and by then a fixture on *The New Yorker,* the piece reported that the Densonized paper was enjoying the largest circulation gains of any daily in the city and spelled out the editorial philosophy of "its lively new editor." Denson told Shaplen he wanted his paper read, not just printed, and hoped to make it useful to busy people in a busy town and to establish "a warm relationship between the writer and the reader" by means of a format that tried to humanize the news. He was working to turn the *Tribune*'s lack of bulk into a virtue through "brightness, clarity, explanation, and significance. . . . We want to talk to our readers as if we were chatting with them in the living room [and saying,] 'Hey, pals, this is the way it is, this is the score.' " The *Times* had succeeded by being formal and aloof; the *Tribune* would regenerate itself by becoming informal and engaged. "I want," said Denson, "to make the *Herald Tribune* a heart paper again." At times his stints in the Hearst organization showed through.

Over at the *Times,* John Denson's innovations were watched with uneasy contempt for their debasement of classic *Tribune* craftsmanship but also with grudging admiration for their catchiness and shrewdness. Harrison Salisbury, then attached to the *Times* city staff, remembered how managing editor Turner Catledge began returning to the city room after supper, as he had not done for a long time, to be on hand when Denson's city edition came up. For fifteen years, the *Times* had been outdistancing the *Tribune* to such an extent that they were hardly in the same race any longer, but suddenly, Salisbury said, there was a fear that Denson's jazzed-up version "just might catch on." Catledge would invade the sacrosanct confines of assistant managing editor Theodore Bernstein's "bullpen," the equivalent of the *Tribune*'s night desk, and sit down to study what typographic flimflammery Denson had wrought that night. Sometimes, as a result, he ordered changes in emphasis or news play in his paper, but mostly he just watched Denson's experimenting with rapt attention. "After a few months he decided it wouldn't work," said Salisbury.

By the end of August—the date Walter Thayer had asked him to have whatever changes he planned ready for introduction to the public—Denson was becoming a celebrity as he never had been while on *Newsweek*. Appearing on "WCBS-TV Views the Press," he explained that the *Tribune*'s purpose was not only to clarify the news but to "cleanse" it as well: "We must be on guard against the words of statesmen who say things they do not mean. We should be on the alert for politicians who often say the opposite of what they really believe. We must escape somehow from the propagandists and the publicists who fill news columns that lazy newsmen have been handing over to them."

Inside the *Tribune* office, he was not a beloved figure. Oscillating between crusty gregariousness and studied aloofness, he took no man's counsel. With a fearsome visage, eyes bulging, face flushing, teeth clicking as he worked, trimming text blocks he had ordered to fit a precise hole and dreaming up headlines of a kind no one else seemed able to get just right, he looked like a mad genius, wrapped in cigarette smoke, redoubtable and combustible and half the time on the verge of apoplexy over the exigencies of the clock and the ineptness of subordinates. They called him the Lone Ranger.

From *Newsweek* he brought two devoted young aides with him—*Trib* men referred to them as his Tontos—to protect him and see that his strange ideas were carried out. Tall, dapper Freeman Fulbright, with Clark Kent good looks and a toothpaste-ad smile, was the more forceful of the pair, though his primary duty, in the view of city-room veterans, was "to hold John's coat for him." More emotionally supportive was Robert Albert, affable, self-effacing, and highly literate, who Denson-watchers said "held John together." Among older *Tribune* hands, Denson latched on to the genial and unthreatening Frank Kelley, who had been serving as foreign editor, and brought him into his tiny inner circle of assistants. Titles hardly mattered anymore; being a Denson assistant was about as high as a man could hope to rise now.

Only one editor seemed to operate as a free, happily functioning spirit in Denson's city room—Murray Michael Weiss, called Buddy, who had defected to the *Times* and was brought back after six months to be Denson's city editor. An NYU English major who at twenty-one began working on the *Tribune* as a clerk in 1945 after military service, Weiss swung over to the night desk and received an intensified trade education under Everett Kallgren while during the day pursuing a master's degree at Teachers College. Bright, quick, and feisty, he was made assistant day city editor in 1959 and put his teaching career aside.

Shifting to the *Times* as assistant makeup editor for more money and security, he found work there unfulfilling; there were so many people "and not enough honest work for everyone to do." Back at the *Tribune,* radiating energy and warmth, Weiss had all the tools Denson needed in the man to run the city room: he knew type, layout, production, good writing, and how New York worked. And he had keen judgment of news and of people, instinctively grasping what was eating them and how to lighten spirits with a wisecrack. High-domed, short-haired, and wide-eyed, Weiss was the best-liked man on the news side in the last years of the *Herald Tribune.*

But while John Denson was there, it was his show and no one else's, not even Jock Whitney's. Very thoughtfully, very carefully, he was downgrading the paper to make it more readable and accessible to masses who had never considered taking it. And it was beginning to catch on. "He understood what readers were interested in," said Buddy Weiss. His methods and high-handedness caused wide resentment among the older deskmen, who felt their skills rendered useless. Most, though, like John Price, understood what he was up to and went along because, as assistant night editor William Taylor put it, "the alternative seemed to be the death of the paper."

VI

For Jock Whitney, making the rounds of merchandising tycoons to help push advertising, traveling to West Virginia to address a national gathering of advertising agency executives, planting the flag of the *Herald Tribune,* which he served gamely, if not delightedly, as roving ambassador-at-large, here, there, and everywhere, there was finally something new and exciting to sell. Whitney liked the look John Denson was bringing to the paper and the excitement created by his emphasis on "sweep" and instant interpretation. But he also exercised a cautionary role, to ensure that his editor did not exceed the tolerable limits of journalistic showmanship, and asked of him that the paper "encourage the serious reader as it satisfies the short-order one."

At the office, he underwent on-the-job training, sitting in on as many meetings a week as he could manage, from the promotion-planning session to the daily front-page conference. Mostly he listened and asked questions, often shrewd ones that probed and stimulated. Even at the editorial-page conferences, where he would have been entirely within his rights to set policy guidelines, he was extremely deferential. Edit-page chief Dwight Sargent, knowing of Whitney's role as a longtime director and benefactor of New York Hospital, once dropped by to get his approval for an editorial on an aspect of health-care services. "If you had to come to me every time an editorial touches something I'm interested in," Whitney told him, "there'd be no time to write them." His tall, broad, exquisitely tailored form became a common sight around the city room and at Bleeck's, where he mingled with the makers of the paper to which he had committed his name, his fortune, and now his presence. His initial effect on it, given his professional limitations and managerial diffidence, was slight at best. Like Ogden Reid's, his presidency was largely titular, as he himself soon realized, and he traded in the title of president for that of editor-in-chief—a measure of the romantic attitude he harbored toward his would-be role and a confession that the business and administrative side of the enterprise bored him. He retained the title of publisher, and with it the responsibility for whatever ran in the paper, but to oversee its operations as a profit-seeking entity, he made Walter Thayer president of the *Tribune* as well as of WCC in June 1961.

From then on, Thayer made the paper his main base of operation. "I went down there against every instinct in my body," he recalled. "It was not a situation where we could afford on-the-job training. . . . I would have been much happier sitting up at WCC and watching it. It was very difficult work in a field in which I didn't feel I had any particular competence."

But Thayer pitched in manfully. In Denson he had found a reason for hope and lost no time proclaiming his optimism. "I am very much encouraged by the progress we are making," he told *Editor & Publisher* upon his ascension to president and, revealing the rudiments of the McKinsey & Co. five-year plan for the restoration of black ink, spoke of his confidence that "what we have planned will take us out of the red well ahead of the projected five years." It was part bravado, part war cry to let the *Times* know that the *Tribune* was not going to fold, so the titans of Forty-third Street might as well raise their newsstand price to a dime. His self-assurance, grace of bearing and utterance, and calm but forceful analytical aptitude brought to the paper a figure of the sort who dominated American corporate boardrooms. Yet as superintendent of an organism as emotion-laden and often unresponsive to the dictates of reason as a troubled newspaper, Thayer stood on alien ground. The impression he gave of unapproachability, reinforced by his wintry looks, made him a shadowy figure to those on the creative side of the paper who collectively sensed that he was present against his will and better judgment in order to monitor Jock Whitney's investment—and end it at the earliest seemly moment. The impression was supported by the disclosure of the McKinsey five-year plan, which struck many on the staff as imposing a deadline rather than offering breathing space. In the city room, they called Walter Thayer "the North Wind."

In fact, with his name now appearing on the masthead in each morning's edition, Thayer worked faithfully—within the limitations he had set—to save the *Tribune*. He preached the gospel of resurrection where he performed best, in small gatherings like the board of directors of Bankers Trust, to which he artfully explained the new compact-model *Tribune,* and the paper's own advertising staff, who had not been pep-talked so ardently since the days of Bill Robinson. In John Denson, he told them, the paper at last had a man who could produce the kind of newspaper that would "meet the strong competitive test of this market."

Cheerleading on the business side helped some, but Thayer's larger contribution after having enlisted Denson was to install a modern management team to control costs and exploit sales of the brighter editorial product. Barney Cameron did not measure up to Thayer's standards and was soon on his way back to the *Post-Gazette* in Pittsburgh, where he worked until retirement. Impatient for action, Thayer also quickly decided that his choice of Tom Robinson as the top man on the business side had been a blunder—the fellow seemed incapable of coping with a balance sheet and actually managing daily operations—and stripped him of power and masthead listing. In their place came younger, broader-gauged, and better-trained professional operatives who knew little about the newspaper business but were amply qualified as modern managers. Ralph Schwarz, a Lehigh-educated engineer with graduate study in law and comparative religion, came to the paper from Bethlehem Steel to serve as Thayer's executive assistant. Winslow Maxwell, who had been manager of budgets and forecasts at giant General Dynamics after an apprenticeship at the top New York accounting firm of Arthur Andersen & Company, was appointed controller of the paper, a new post. And, in his most important move, Thayer turned to Robert Taylor MacDonald, a thirty-one-year-old account executive with McKinsey & Co., who had been involved from the first in the firm's consulting work with the paper, to take administrative charge of operations. A Yale graduate with a master's in business administration from the University of Pennsylvania's Wharton School, MacDonald had begun his working career selling space for a Mount Kisco, New York, weekly and later been business manager of a small shipping monthly called *The Mariner*. These were hardly overwhelming credentials for a man chosen to serve as Thayer's surrogate as whip-cracker at the *Herald Tribune*. But the cool, ambitious MacDonald, who bore a resemblance to actor James Stewart, knew the *Tribune*'s problems inside out, having been paid to study them in depth and recommend steps toward their solution. Without a stronger product to sell, he recognized, no amount of cost accounting, deadwood pruning, or master strategizing could turn the *Tribune* around. Now Denson had charged up the place, and young Bob MacDonald, his fortune in front of him, accepted the challenge of converting efficiency-expert theory into everyday practice. "You know what has to be done around here," Thayer told him. "Do it." In no time, he was all over the building—a self-programmed badgerer, full of politic suggestions and gentlemanly reprimands, sometimes overzealous in his scrutiny but always emitting high hope that it was all going to work. Thayer's selections of Denson and MacDonald were rapidly turning out to be as wise as those of White and Robinson had not been.

The September 30, 1961, ABC report showed that Denson's paper was holding its early gains; average sales for the half-year period, including the summer doldrums, were up about 20,000 from the year before—well above the targeted rate of gain of 5 percent annually. At the end of October, one-quarter of the front page—the entire first two columns—was given over daily to a systematic rendering of Denson's technique of compression and interpretation. More of a guide to than a summary of the highlights of that day's edition, this new double-column feature, under the standing boxed head "IN THE NEWS THIS MORNING" —or "Quick, Denson, the News," as Whitney paraphrased it—was artfully tricked out in a blend of roman and italic body types, divided into "Topic A" (since Denson's inventive layouts sometimes left the reader in doubt about what was the top story of the day) and then global, national, metropolitan, and other news categories for easy digestibility. "The world has never been so well reported, nor, at the same time, seemed so confusing," explained a front-page message from publisher Whitney on the debut of the innovation. The daily news review was "one more of the ways in which we have tried—and will continue to try—to clarify at least what can be clarified, to respond to the need to know and to brighten so far as possible the newspaper-reading minutes of busy people." A typical paragraph entry, from the November 24, 1961, issue went:

IN THE WORLD—
   Sharing the burden of Western Defense. The U.S. is getting set to begin (and soon) active negotiations with other NATO countries for greater contributions to the $3 billion yearly cost of maintaining U.S. forces overseas. West Germany has agreed to pay $700 million, but the Kennedy administration wants all fourteen other NATO countries to match or better (proportionately) Germany's figure. Purpose is to reduce the U.S. balance of payments deficit ($3.9 billion last year, an estimated $2.25 billion this year). *Washington's efforts to spread the burden mean long, painful negotiations with our allies, some with troubles of their own. But prosperity in many NATO countries will give us a strong argument.*

It read like nothing so much as the text of a superior TV newscast, but the eye could absorb it all far more quickly than listening to it would have taken.

As Denson's concepts were refined and the new paper better defined, management began to spend money to promote it. Seven circulation branch offices were opened in the suburbs—four in New Jersey, one each in Westchester, Nassau, and Fairfield counties—to push home delivery. And a young, irreverent advertising agency, Papert, Koenig & Lois (PKL), whose principals were all in their thirties, was hired to ballyhoo the improvement. George Lois, one of the agency partners, recalled, "Denson had taken this dull-ass paper and turned it around." Dealing from strength, the agency came up with the simple but inspired idea of putting on a one-minute commercial at the beginning of the local CBS late-evening news show four nights a week, featuring a close-up of the next morning's *Tribune* front page and explaining what was different about it. "Now there's a new way to edit a serious morning newspaper," the voice-over asserted, and elaborated on Denson's reasons, given to an agency copywriter after the front-page conference at the *Tribune* office scarcely five hours earlier, for playing the news as he had. "We loved him," Lois said of PKL's dealings with Denson. "He was so crotchety—everything you wanted an editor to look like and be like—it was *Front Page,* baby. He took one look at us and decided we were these Madison Avenue faggot fuck-ups . . . and he'd come out with some right-wing ape-shit stuff, and we'd say, 'Fuck you, you fascist Hitler.' . . . I never met such a cynical man—I mean politically cynical—the black humor—but he did it with love—he came with a passion for his work—and he wasn't a young man."

From this unlikely alliance of sensibilities sprang a highly effective campaign of commercials, created with a speed that defied the practices of the advertising industry, which told viewers, in effect, that the news they were about to see was junk compared to what they could find in the next morning's *Tribune*. For a while, Lois remembered, "Whitney's people in their three-piece suits" would show up at the studio, hang over the shoulders of the frantically busy agency talent, ask to check over scripts, and second-guess them the next day. But soon all that stopped, and the agency people were putting their creations on the air without client approval—or even the approval of their client's lawyers. "We could have gone to jail," said Lois. Instead, they won acclaim for themselves and the product. "It was being part of a living thing—it was pumping blood— it was ball-busting—but it was a thrilling account to work on. There's nothing like the newspaper business." Out of this fecund creative environment, Lois's partner Julian Koenig dreamed up the slogan that became the *Tribune*'s banner of defiance in its long territorial war with the *Times:* "Who says a good newspaper has to be dull?"

The swift acceptance of and growing attention to his handiwork did not perceptibly mellow John Denson. It just seemed to make his wicked sense of humor grow more misanthropic and manic. Buddy Weiss came to the office one morning that November and found Denson doing a mad little Hitlerian caper around his desk. Wire reports that Nelson Rockefeller was flying back home in grief over the loss of his son Michael, who had drowned off New Guinea, had inspired the *Tribune*'s editor. "All you need is one great idea in life," he announced, then explained that his was to charter a plane, fly to meet Rockefeller as soon as he touched down on American soil, and offer himself up for adoption to the multimillionaire governor.

Denson was riding high as 1961 closed. He would hold forth at Bleeck's when the city edition came up and, wielding a big grease pencil, flip through the pages, scrawl changes on them with a flourish, and feed them off to the veteran Everett Walker, whom he had reduced to a flunky. Men whose skills had long been serviceable to the paper but whom Denson now found wanting and useless— like Walker and the Count—he brushed aside with ill grace. Christmas week he pulled Walker off the daily and assigned him to make a complete survey of all editorial personnel—there were more than three hundred—indicating their job and salary history, current duties and hours, and then do a similar study on all the paper's stringers. It was a glorified clerical job for a man who not long before had been one of its ranking editors. "You have been at the daily news grind for a long time," Denson wrote him in a peremptory memo, "and this should be a challenging change."

He knew how to break a man, especially one who was not patently loyal or had the temerity to push his own ideas, as Robert Manning did—briefly. While in London, Whitney was impressed by the lively Manning, who had covered the State Department, White House, and UN for United Press before joining *Time* and rising to bureau chief for all Time-Life publications in the British capital. Thoughtful and articulate, Manning had urged Whitney to consider taking his Sunday edition out of direct competition with the weighty *Times* by adopting a slimmed-down format stressing analysis and top-flight writing along the lines of London's Sunday *Observer*. Consumed by his efforts to redesign the daily, Denson had paid almost no attention to the Sunday paper beyond redesigning the logotypes for each section and canceling the sole innovation of the White-Yerxa era, a tabloid section combining the arts and entertainment departments and the book review. Sunday circulation was plunging toward the 450,000 level, and something had to be done. Whitney suggested that Denson take on Manning, back in the United States to try his luck at free-lancing.

Over luncheon at Voisin to celebrate his hiring, a principal topic of discussion among Manning, Whitney, and Thayer—as Denson listened impassively—was whether the publisher had enough pull to get his new Sunday editor's son admitted to the exclusive St. Bernard's grammar school in time for the fall term. Denson, who had no children and little sympathy with the elitist circles into which the new man was being ushered pell-mell, decided on the spot that he did not much like having Manning or anyone else foisted on him, whatever his talents. Manning himself soon got the picture. Without a real budget, staff, or mandate to reshape the Sunday edition, he was reduced to trying to cajole feature pieces from top *Tribune* byliners like Robert Donovan in Washington, who received no extra pay for their articles. Denson was inaccessible to him, and Manning had to deal with his aides, whom he considered stooges. When he managed to obtain an interesting piece on the travails of *Life* magazine written by Clay Felker, one of *Esquire*'s bright editors, Denson killed the article at the last minute without explanation. However inspired a technician, Denson was to Manning "a mixture of impatience and sourness, with an anemic sense of what the world was all about."

In early November, Manning drew up a detailed proposal for major improvements in the Sunday edition, which he wanted to aim at younger, more intelligent and worldly readers, with stress on New York area life and how to cope with it—a sharply different emphasis from that of the globally minded *Times*. Manning asked to scrap parts of the Sunday package he considered an embarrassment—the TV magazine and *Today's Living* ("a failure since inception")—and upgrade the travel section, which he rated as little better than a collection of publicity handouts, and the real estate section, in which he said the trade-off of editorial space for advertising was "blatant." Among his proposed innovations were national syndication of the moribund book section, to be taken from the aging hands of Irita Van Doren and brightened with articles on all aspects of the literary life; a new magazine with something of the bite and flair of England's *Queen,* "sophisticated but not haughty"; and special major articles and series by top non-staff contributors, to be commissioned by the *Tribune* in collaboration with out-of-town papers. To accomplish this or any major part thereof, Manning asked for money and manpower as soon as possible in view of the continuing erosion of the Sunday circulation.

Denson's sole response was to order the Sunday comics, until then printed in color as a separate section, changed to black and white and incorporated into one of the other sections. Newsdealers, Denson argued, could not be dissuaded from wrapping the comics around the rest of the Sunday paper, thereby obscuring the changes in tone and format he had wrought.

With his principal sponsor, Jock Whitney, recuperating in New York Hospital for six weeks from a relatively mild heart attack complicated by influenza, Manning had nowhere to turn. Tormented into a bundle of frustrations, he explained in his December 19 letter of resignation that he had thought he was going to have "sufficient scope in judgment and initiative to make a creative contribution." Whitney, while regretful, solidly backed Denson, whom he wanted to be "the architect of the Sunday paper as well as the daily paper" and in whom he retained full confidence "to build the organization and employ methods which will make the paper as successful on Sunday as I believe it is becoming on weekdays." With a boost from Whitney, Manning went to work for a short time in the State Department and later became editor of *The Atlantic Monthly.* His replacement as Sunday editor was Denson acolyte Bob Albert.

By year's end, everything had gone Denson's way. Even *Time,* which had sneered at his efforts the previous summer, now wrote that under him the *Tribune* was "steering a bold matutinal course" and "emphatically succeeding in its effort to avoid looking, sounding or acting like . . . the *Times.*" During the preparation of the *Time* article, Whitney told a researcher that he regarded Denson as "an artist" who had fired up the whole paper with enthusiasm. Denson, in turn, called Whitney "a great humanitarian." There was truth as well as hyperbole in that mutual admiration. John Denson could plausibly be rated an artist because he refused to wait upon events and concede his impotence before destiny by issuing a quiet sheet the morning after a slow news day. That was fine for the *Times,* which prided itself on not overstating the case; proportion was all. For Denson, every day had to be exciting—with all those billions churning around the face of the earth, enough interesting things *must* have transpired in the preceding twenty-four hours for him to shape into a mentally stimulating and visually compelling composition of type and ink and newsprint. He was imposing his will on fate, his vision on history, and if the facts got a little nicked or watered in the creative act, so be it; liveliness was all.

18

Studies in Stubbornness

lthough the *Times* was outselling it by nearly twice as many copies daily and nearly three times as many on Sundays and carried well over three times as much advertising a year, hope for survival and regeneration lingered at the *Herald Tribune.* It was sustained by more than John Denson's creative hand. No one at the paper realistically expected to attract many new advertisers until truly substantial circulation gains were registered. But the *Tribune* continued to sell ad linage out of all proportion to its readership in precisely those categories that were most lucrative. In 1961 it ranked second in the nation in financial advertising, third in airline advertising, and fourth in total national advertising, trailing only *The New York Times,* the *Los Angeles Times,* and the *Chicago Tribune* in this last category. In New York, it carried the most tobacco linage and was second in travel, new cars, and media ads, ahead of all the afternoon papers. And the *Tribune* still attracted a disproportionately high volume of advertising from certain quality retail stores, showing linage nearly equal to the the *Times*'s for Abercrombie & Fitch, Lord & Taylor, and Brooks Brothers and more than half the *Times*'s linage for almost all the others.

The *Tribune*'s enduring strength with purveyors to the carriage trade was in part attributable to the financial condition of its readership; among all New York newspapers, it had the highest percentage of customer families with an annual income of more than $10,000. But there was another important factor behind this durability as an advertising vehicle despite weak circulation. The paper possessed a pair of columnists so consummately knowledgeable on their subject and skilled at presenting it that they were required reading among a small but critically influential sector of the metropolitan market. A number of *Tribune* columnists and specialists were good enough to attract and hold their own constituencies—among them Walter Lippmann, Red Smith, John Crosby, Walter Kerr, and Clementine Paddleford—regardless of whatever shortcomings were perceived elsewhere in the paper. None of its writers, though, was more important to the *Tribune*'s economic survival than Joseph Kaselow or Eugenia Sheppard.

Kaselow, a New York native who joined the paper as a copyboy in 1937, was a foot soldier covering business news until told by George Cornish one Thursday in 1953 that, beginning the following Monday, he was to write a weekly column on the advertising industry. Before that day was over, the frequency of the column was raised to daily except Saturday. Madison Avenue, which he had covered sporadically, rewriting over-the-transom items into an inconsequential collation, became his beat, and nobody told him how to organize its coverage or presentation—a freedom typical of the *Tribune* and traceable in large part to the thinness of its editorial supervisory ranks. Uninstructed and unhectored —"I never had anybody say to me that I should be nice to this advertiser or agency," he recalled—Kaselow kept his finger on Madison Avenue's volatile pulse for the remainder of the *Tribune*'s life and grossed for it countless millions with his light touch and evenhandedness.

If Joe Kaselow made himself an indispensable habit on Madison Avenue, Eugenia Sheppard became an international power in her realm, beyond the massed institutional strength of her competitors on the *Times* or the influence of any other individual fashion writer. *Vogue, Bazaar,* and the *Times* Sunday magazine may have been the prime showcases for U.S. fashion advertising, and the Fairchild trade journals were the authoritative monitor of commercial developments in the world of apparel, but it was Sheppard, at her peak in the 1956–66 decade, who defined who and what was chic in New York.

A tiny, strong-willed, compulsively energetic, and remarkably nervy woman, she was a great deal like Helen Reid, except two inches shorter. But there was a crucial difference between them: Eugenia Sheppard was a professional newspaperwoman with a talent for her craft; Helen Reid was essentially a vendor. But Mrs. Reid had the wit to recognize Miss Sheppard's gifts and the paper's need to utilize them fully.

After graduating from Bryn Mawr in 1921, she had returned to her native Ohio, passed through two unsuccessful marriages, and gone to work on the women's pages of the *Columbus Dispatch.* She arrived in New York in 1939— with ringleted blond hair, cornflower-blue eyes, and looks that are called cute rather than pretty on small women—and after eighteen months as a fashion reporter on *Women's Wear Daily* was hired by the *Tribune*'s fashion editor, Kay Vincent. War news and material shortages reduced the attention that could decently be paid to women's styles, and the fashion section atrophied. Vincent was taken by alcohol and other distractions, and in 1947 Sheppard replaced her. Two years later, her title was upgraded to women's feature editor, supervising the ninth-floor department devoted to news of fashion, food, furnishings, beauty, and other subjects thought to be of primary interest to female readers. And supervise she did, with a competence and independence bordering on the autocratic; grown men in the city room feared her iron manner as they marveled at her efficiency and ogled the pretty young women from her department who passed through.

On taking command, she asked for and received sufficient staff of her own, including a managing editor and a layout artist, who achieved a look of elegance by the use of very large fashion photographs and a slender variant of Bodoni headline type. Sheppard also insisted upon enough space to make her offerings inviting on a daily basis, not just occasionally, and throughout two decades of convulsive policy and management shifts and self-defeating economy drives she fought successfully to defend her territory. In its coverage of fashion, the *Tribune* outstripped the *Times* in volume as well as quality; no New York paper ran more fashion copy. And of herself and her staff, Eugenia Sheppard demanded a standard of journalistic detachment rarely found on women's pages in U.S. newspapers, historically a repository for soft, puffy copy. Sheppard's stress was on accurate, fair, straightforward presentation, indifferent if not oblivious to the influence of large advertisers. Now and then there would be efforts at egalitarianism in story selection, so that a budget-conscious reader might learn, for example, how to furnish her apartment by haunting flea markets, junk shops, and auctions or be advised what such middle-class emporiums as Macy's, Gimbels, and Saks 34th Street were showing in the way of fashions. But Sheppard, try as she might to keep an open mind, found fashions for the masses to be generally "ghastly," and the emphasis and taste standards on her pages were unashamedly elitist. More than anything else, her section was distinguished by good, clear writing, as exemplified by her own terse, breezy style of short sentences charged with the strong verb, picturesque adjective, or arresting image—but rarely all three together. There was little reaching for effect. The former Ann Pringle, who wrote for Sheppard's pages in the early postwar years, recalled: "What Eugenia was getting across was that the story was not simply a report on something else—it was a thing in itself. The responsibility of the writer was to make the story interesting—a primary rather than a secondary experience for the reader."

Sheppard's influence grew as the war economy lifted and Paris reclaimed its position as world capital of high fashion. Her reports from there were especially influential among U.S. manufacturers and wealthy buyers because they ran the next day in the Paris edition of the *Tribune*; no other American fashion reporter had such swift exposure. Using an almost defiantly American frame of reference, she could be pleasantly analytical ("The new Paris fashions are positively wholesome . . . [and] look like a slightly jazzed up version of Harriet Beecher Stowe") or pointedly carping as in her 1957 summary of the Parisian designers' fascination for buttons and bows: "It's all terribly cute, but like giving a girl candy when she craves steak." Her critical jabs were deft and economical when she was confronted with a dress that had, say, too much front ("Believe me, you could be having twins") or too little shape ("Just a gunny sack, with diamonds"), but rarely did she bludgeon. Once she denounced the new collection of couturier Yves Saint Laurent as "hideous" and got herself banned from his showroom and others in Paris, but she managed to file accurate reports anyway, and her growing influence and following became too great to deny. Leading houses in Paris and New York would not begin their shows until Eugenia Sheppard was in her front-row seat.

With the introduction in 1956 of her thrice-weekly column, "Inside Fashion," Sheppard revolutionized the journalism of style by adjusting its focus from inanimate fabric to the people who designed and wore it. In her first column, she dwelled on film actress Grace Kelly's preparations for marriage to Prince Rainier of Monaco, including the intimate details of her trousseau; the big news was that her lingerie was yellow—a scoop Sheppard mined from her sources in the trade. "Nobody considered this sort of thing news before then," Sheppard recalled. "There was just no room for it in the paper." Fashion journalism had been obsessed with colors, fabrics, hemlines, necklines, and a whole encyclopedic recitation of sartorial grace notes. "Readers had been drowning in ruffles and tucks and seams," Sheppard said. "I tried to simplify." More than that, she vivified. To her, the clothes were less interesting than those who created and bought them, and she began to write about the relationship between the two groups. "Eugenia made the clothes come to life —she brought intimacy to fashion," said Bill Blass, one of the designers whose career she advanced by publicizing his work; until then, manufacturers had received more attention in the press than designers, who were treated as faceless.

She also made the startling discovery that the fashion-conscious rich no longer craved privacy, and loved nothing better than to have their taste validated by attention in the public prints. They were, after all, women who worshipped clothes, unapologetically spent much of their time and a good deal of money shopping for them, and found Sheppard's appeal to their narcissism irresistible. By deciding whom and what to write about she could create a whole new pattern of social commentary. It was those who were featured on the crisply written, attractively presented women's pages of the *Tribune,* more than in any other paper, who qualified as members of the subculture that came in the 'Sixties to be called the Beautiful People. Epitomizing them was the young, slender, strikingly attractive brunette who entered the White House at John Kennedy's side—the first non-dowdy First Lady within the memory of fashion-watchers. Jacqueline Kennedy was not squeamish about buying elegant, if generally understated, clothes and displaying them at every opportunity. Eugenia Sheppard's column, fully recording the chain reaction in fashions she set off, acquired wider readership and influence than ever.

II

Soon after assuming the editorship of the *Tribune,* John Denson went down to Washington and told the members of the paper's bureau there, "You guys are all I've got." Like much else about Denson, the remark was characterized by hyperbole. But it served to point up that the bureau, since 1957 under the direction of the affable Robert Donovan, had been rescued from turmoil and rebuilt into an alert, efficient newsgathering machine, better than at any other time in *Tribune* history.

There were few better reporters in Washington than Donovan himself, and none wrote with more assurance, clarity, or speed. A mostly easygoing coordinator of individual talents that needed stroking and blending, Donovan became something of a father figure to the bureau and his suburban Virginia home a kind of clubhouse, the site of parties like the one given for Jock Whitney on his return from London, featuring an alcohol-fueled game of touch football in which Joe Alsop dished off a well-aimed lateral pass to his host, who promptly cracked a rib on a downfield banister.

On the strength of his investigative skills, David Wise won the bureau's choice assignment, covering the Kennedy White House. At the Pentagon, Donovan had stationed the resourceful Warren Rogers, Jr., practiced after a dozen years of wire-service reporting at turning out slick copy moments before deadline. On Capitol Hill, he had the ambitious and well-connected socialite from the Philadelphia Main Line, Rowland Evans, Jr., whose nasal voice, selective story eye, and fondness for breakfasting with sources at the exclusive Metropolitan Club, to which he belonged, made him the haughtiest bureau member since Joe Alsop. Covering the State Department was Marguerite Higgins, by then the mother of two, less peripatetic than before but still manipulating colleagues and deadly to rivals, and caught up in a sustained affair with Peter Lisagor of the *Chicago Daily News*—the least secret illicit romance in the capital. To the little luncheons at her home for diplomats whom she tried to mine for stories, Higgins sometimes invited Warren Rogers "because I knew what questions to ask—she was not a detail person. Her idea was that she was the star and I was there to help her." She would also turn for help to the good-natured Don Irwin, who was known on occasion to carry her typewriter for her, and to national political correspondent Earl Mazo, with his pipeline to the upper reaches of the Republican hierarchy. Out of reach in the corner was Joseph Slevin, covering the economics beat and often on the phone gathering intelligence for the bond newsletter he turned out on the side.

Donovan kept the place happy and productive by outflanking Higgins. He made clear to her that, as bureau chief, he would handle the biggest stories, and then, by assigning Wise to the White House and Rogers to the Pentagon, he took the two hottest beats in town out of her grasp. Higgins did not give up without a fight. Wangling magazine assignments, she showed up at national conventions and summit conferences to which she had not been assigned and managed to file sidebars for the paper. But Donovan avoided confrontations with her because he understood the value of her byline to the paper.

The *Tribune* was still viewed widely in Washington as what Ben Bradlee called "the company paper" in spite of its handling of the Sherman Adams and Doerfer scandals, so at the beginning of the Kennedy administration, Donovan moved shrewdly to position it as politically neutral. In David Wise, the paper had an acknowledged Kennedy admirer. Wise had attended the 1956 Democratic convention in Chicago and been assigned to interview Senator Kennedy, then an underdog contender for the vice-presidential nomination, at his hotel suite. During their discussion, Wise admitted he did not know exactly what farm parity was, and Kennedy took the trouble to explain it; Wise came away certain he had just been talking with a future President. Like many of the new breed of well-educated Washington reporters, Wise found Kennedy a highly attractive figure, with remarkable poise and far less artificiality to him than most political stars—the sort of man the younger members of the capital press corps, by their schooling and background, would have liked to number among their friends. "But I had no trouble dissociating my personal regard for him," Wise said. "I always knew what I had to do."

Donovan himself moved closer to the Oval Office by accepting a commission from McGraw-Hill, soon after Kennedy took office, to write a book about the President's wartime exploits as commander of an ill-fated PT boat in the South Pacific. "I believed that it would be a good way to develop valuable entrée to the Kennedy White House," Donovan said. The resulting book, *PT-109*, became an even bigger success than Donovan's 1956 book on the Eisenhower White House, sold over a million copies in paperback, was made into a movie, and added to the iconography of John F. Kennedy. Not incidentally, it succeeded in its purpose of putting its author in high standing at the White House. And, just as he had insisted with his volume on Eisenhower, Donovan said, "I never had any feeling of being compromised by the book. It was written almost as a documentary."

The paper itself got off to a friendly start with Kennedy by yielding to his request, in the national interest, to swallow a scoop it was about to break four days after his inauguration. Donovan had learned that the White House planned to make a major announcement on an undisclosed subject at two o'clock in the morning—too late for most of the *Tribune* run—so the presses in New York were halted while the bureau, in a feat of fast post-midnight teamwork, tracked the story down. David Wise telephoned White House press secretary Pierre Salinger, who began to sputter, as Wise later wrote, "like a Roman candle in a light rain." But he neither denied nor elaborated on the report, saying only that it had to remain secret and he could make no comment. Warren Rogers then called one of his sources and bluffed confirmation of what the *Tribune* team had surmised—that as a gesture of conciliation to the new President, Soviet premier Khrushchev had agreed to the release of two U.S. fliers who had been shot down in an RB-47 reconnaissance bomber, or spy plane, six months earlier and held prisoner since. When Wise called Salinger back for confirmation, acknowledging that the *Tribune* press run had been interrupted so the news could be included in the maximum number of copies of the last edition, the press secretary said that the deal with Moscow depended upon simultaneous announcement by both governments. Wise urged Donovan to accede to the White House's wishes. Donovan, concurring, phoned New York and the *Tribune* presses resumed rolling without the big story. For its restraint, Kennedy commended the *Tribune* in a telegram to Jock Whitney the next day.

Thus, on the arrival of John Denson, the paper's Washington bureau stood high in the eyes of the Kennedy people and its peers in the Washington press corps. So solid a performance had it been turning in under Donovan's leadership that the home office, with all the shifts in owners and editors to contend with, was glad to let it function as an almost independent entity. But Denson, after commending the bureau on his early visit to it, moved rapidly to make it answerable to him and his needs for the sort of newspaper he proposed to fashion. The trick was not to trim it back but to get the most mileage from it.

At *Newsweek,* Denson had become accustomed to shaping the news to meet his own preconceptions rather than relying on his bureaus and subeditors to exercise their own judgment. This self-reinforcing, highly egocentric syndrome often resulted in arbitrary and sometimes frivolous play of the news—a depressing new reality that Donovan and his people now had to contend with. What bureau deskman Fred Farris recalled as "a blizzard of messages" began to descend on them from New York, directing not only what stories were to be covered but also how they were to be angled. Denson was on the phone constantly, Farris said, "ordering up stories. He wouldn't say, 'We'd like a story that looks into such-and-such'—he'd say, 'We need a story that says . . .' and he'd tell us what he wanted."

Sometimes Denson concocted a headline that he hoped a story could be found to bear out. One evening in 1962 at a time of growing U.S. anxiety over unstable conditions in Laos, the phone on Warren Rogers's desk rang as he was hurrying to file a big, technical piece on weapons research that he had been developing exclusively. It was Denson calling. "Hey, kid," Rogers remembered him saying, "how does this sound for a headline—'U.S. Pulling Out of Southeast Asia?' ?" Rogers said he supposed the head was fine if the word count fit, but it did not exactly jibe with the facts as he understood them. Over lunch a few days earlier, Rogers said, he had heard that the prospect was for more, not fewer, U.S. troops in Indochina. Denson snapped up that straw in the wind and ordered Rogers to build a haystack around it. The reporter dropped his weapons story and got on the phone right away with State and Defense Department sources, who spoke to him on "deep background" (i.e., off the record and in no way traceable to its sources but still a knowledgeable rendering of inside policy information). Even before Rogers could get to Denson with his findings, the editor was back on the phone to him. "I've been thinking about that headline, kid," he said. "How's this sound—'U.S. Beefing Up Southeast Asia Force?'?" He had done a 180-degree turn in minutes. "To him a story was a story," said Rogers, whose serious, carefully researched, nuts-and-bolts piece on weapons development Denson later ran inside the paper while the troops story, hastily woven from filaments of fact and a lot of extrapolation, he played on the front page. The root of Denson's peculiar genius, in Rogers's estimate, was that "he didn't know a goddamn thing—he never read anything—but he sure had an instinct for knowing what other people were interested in reading about. I loved to work for him." Others in the bureau were far less appreciative even while recognizing Denson's flair. David Wise summed up for the doubters: "His approach was too simplistic—it all looked a little like an Army clap film to us."

The *Tribune,* its acknowledged Republicanism notwithstanding, shared in the honeymoon Kennedy enjoyed with the press for most of his and Denson's first year in their respective offices. So gladly were the media wrapping the attractive First Couple in the robes of royalty that when David Wise was gauche enough to write that a reception the Kennedys had given at Mount Vernon for Pakistani president Ayub Khan fetched up images of sumptuousness like nothing since the grandeur of the French court at Versailles, Jacqueline Kennedy was displeased and let Wise know it through staff aides. "With the Kennedys you were either for them or against them," Wise recalled. "They had great trouble accepting that I wrote my stories as I saw them." Mostly, though, the *Tribune* rode the tide of adoration. Denson carried Donovan's syndicated *PT-109,* and even the paper's editorials were so muted in their criticism that the President commended them to Donovan for the responsibility he felt they displayed.

But in the spring of 1962, Denson's latent animus toward Kennedy surfaced. When the President applied the full might of his office against U.S. Steel for allegedly violating its pledge to him to hold the price line in the nation's bellwether industry in order to contain the threat of explosive inflation, the *Tribune* painted him as a tyrant. Denson saw the episode as an epic athletic contest, a sort of David and Goliath mismatch, in which it suited his purpose to cast the federal administration as the outsized ogre and the steel industry as the underdog hero of the free-enterprise system. "The Steel Story: Kennedy's Fury," Denson's opening headline read; it was supported by a photograph of the President's emphatically accusatory finger and Robert Donovan's more evenhanded lead, which told of a chief executive "striking with the scorn, contempt and defiance of a man who felt himself duped." The next day's *Tribune* pressed its characterization of White House strong-arm methods by boxing at the top of page one a story on how an FBI agent had awakened an AP reporter in the middle of the night to obtain his notes on a Bethlehem Steel stockholders' meeting; the *Times* account of that day's developments reported the FBI intrusion in the tenth paragraph. When the industrialists backed down the following day, Denson headlined the event: "Big Steel's Retreat on Prices; How Kennedy Cracked the Whip," and beneath ran a gallery of photographs of White House aides who had played major roles in the crisis—"The Administration's Muscle Men," they were labeled. In follow-up stories, Republican denunciations were given prominent and continuing play, and Joseph Slevin wrote in an interpretive piece, which Denson handled like hard news, that the nation was headed for "an era of bigger and more powerful government." Serious journalists call such strongly angled and unnuanced overdramatization "hype." When he had something hot in his hands, John Denson hyped. It sold papers.

He kept after the Kennedy crowd with the hard and steady play all that spring of the Billy Sol Estes scandal. In March, when the FBI arrested Estes, a financial manipulator from Pecos, Texas, and charged him with using government subsidies to get rich quickly in schemes involving cotton acreage allotments and elusive grain and fertilizer storage tanks, Denson put Earl Mazo on the story. And before long the *Tribune* blossomed with extensive accounts of Estes's operations, abetted by the influence if not outright connivance of Democratic legislators and Kennedy administration officials. When the story showed signs of slowing down, Denson sent twenty-six-year-old cityside reporter Laurence Barrett, who had never covered a big national story or set foot in the Lone Star State, to the little rural county seat of Franklin in east-central Texas to look into the alleged suicide of an Agriculture Department official said to have helped uncover Estes's schemes. Told by the sheriff's deputy that bad things were known to happen in those parts to nosy strangers, Barrett persisted for a month and found out that the dead official had been discovered in a pasture on his farm, slain by five shots from his own bolt-action .22-caliber rifle—surely an extraordinary feat of self-destruction—and that there had been no suicide note, no known motive for suicide, no fingerprint test made on the rifle, no autopsy or other official examination of the body, and that the inquest by the coroner, who was not a medical doctor, was conducted without any sworn statements and very little questioning. Other big-city reporters came flocking, and eventually a grand jury looked into the travesty—all splendid grist for Denson's mill.

The paper's anti-Kennedy vendetta peaked in the May 19, 1962, issue. Pierre Salinger had just returned from Moscow, where he had met with Khrushchev, and hurried to report to Kennedy, who was staying at the Hotel Carlyle in New York. The *Tribune*'s front-page story on his return was accompanied by a large cartoon by staff artist John Fischetti, which depicted the President and his press secretary emerging from a columned building as Salinger reported in the caption: "Mr. Khrushchev said he liked your style in the steel crisis." Adjacent was a double-readout blast on latest developments in the Estes scandal, topped by a linking two-column-wide quotation of Secretary of Agriculture Orville Freeman's remark earlier in the month that the scandal was "getting ballooned out of proportion" and Denson's needling headline: "The 'Ballooning' Estes Scandal— / Mystery Meeting, Shooting Probe." Salinger phoned David Wise early in the morning and said he thought the *Tribune*'s White House man might like to know the President's reaction to that morning's edition of his newspaper— which was, Salinger quoted, "The fucking *Herald Tribune* is at it again." The press secretary urged Wise to pass those very words on to his publisher. "Kennedy knew very well that Denson was out to get him," Bob Donovan recounted, "and suspected that our Estes coverage was part of the crusade."

The question was no longer in doubt after the May 30 *Tribune* arrived in the White House. In January, the President had disclosed that federal stockpiling of strategic materials was discovered to be in excess of established emergency requirements by some 75 percent—due, according to congressional investigations proceeding casually that spring, to contracts entered into late in the Eisenhower administration and producing windfall profits for a number of corporations, among them the M. A. Hanna Company, of which Ike's Secretary of the Treasury, George Humphrey, had been an officer. "Kennedy regarded it as a rich man's scandal," Donovan remembered, but the slow-paced Senate subcommittee inquiry into the alleged stockpiling irregularities seemed like dry, tame stuff and, given the steady stream of exciting news out of Washington and the paper's limited bureau manpower, was generally left for the wire services to cover. At the end of May, witnesses were due to offer testimony expected to be damaging to the old Eisenhower crowd, but nobody in New York asked Donovan for staff coverage and the wire-service report on the May 29 hearing made only the late city edition of the *Tribune*; it was the city edition that circulated in Washington. When the President read the next morning's *Tribune,* he found nothing in it on the Republican embarrassment—but he did find two fresh stories unfriendly to his administration on top of page one, the first headlined "New Scandal," with a picture of Secretary Freeman and dealing with further instances of alleged corruption in the Agriculture Department, and the second just below, headed "Old Scandal," on Estes. Kennedy ordered the twenty-two copies of the *Tribune* delivered to the White House each morning to be replaced by a like number of the *St. Louis Post-Dispatch.*

Denson seemed almost gleeful. "WE GET A CANCELLATION FROM WASHINGTON," crowed the headline over the *Tribune*'s front-page editorial the next day. Signed by "The Editors," it piously expressed the hope that the action had not been taken "because of hard reporting by our greatly respected staff" or the occasionally critical nature of the editorial page and trusted that the President did not display the same attitude to all "who may find reason at times to criticize his program." Jock Whitney, unhumbled by the White House rebuke, sent Denson a note praising him for "a superb piece of writing under pressure" and adding, "I go west today with even greater admiration and affection for you and your leadership."

Although Kennedy's cancellation of the *Tribune* was widely criticized as thin-skinned pique and rated a blunder that served to enhance rather than diminish the standing of the paper, many in the bureau were embarrassed by the presidential slap and acknowledged privately that their editor had over-played a partisan hand.

The extent to which Denson's partisanship could be exercised in the artful angling of a major story was demonstrated to the chagrin of the Washington bureau a few weeks after the cancellation episode. Robert Toth, a new man on the staff, filed a carefully objective lead and balanced report on the U.S. Supreme Court's June 25, 1962, ruling against the permissibility of prayers in public schools. Denson's disapproval of the decision dictated a less clinical approach in the next morning's *Tribune*. "School Prayer 'Unconstitutional,'" declared the banner head, supported by a boxed smaller headline reading: "A 6–1 SU-PREME COURT DECISION—SPELLMAN SHOCKED." Before the double-readout coverage—Toth's story from Washington was "twinned" with a piece on the reaction of clergymen—the text of the proscribed prayer appeared in large, wide-measure italic type set off with exaggerated indentation and interlinear leading so that the reader could be in no doubt of the offending words. The eighth column, where tradition placed the lead story, was given to the church-men's reaction, and Toth's story, beside it in column seven, was rewritten to begin: "The highest court in the land ruled yesterday that a 22-word New York school prayer asking God's blessings is a Constitutional peril to the nation." Taken together, this typographic presentation—placement of quotation marks around "Unconstitutional" in the main head as if to question the legitimacy of the ruling, the spotlighted text of the prayer as if to argue for its utter harmless-ness, the equal play given the clergy's response, and the loaded language of the rewritten dispatch from Washington—made Denson's bias appallingly obvious. The only saving factor for Toth in the handling of the school-prayer story was that his byline did not appear on it—only the line "From the Herald Tribune Bureau." Two months earlier, Toth had been sent to cover the splashdown and recovery of astronaut John Glenn's spacecraft after the first U.S. manned orbital flight. Because only a handful of pool reporters were allowed aboard the aircraft carrier to which Glenn would be returned for debriefing, Toth filed his account from nearby Grand Turk Island in the Bahamas. But Denson changed Toth's dateline to "ABOARD THE CARRIER RANDOLPH AT SEA," had Toth's piece rewritten to include more of the material coming from the wire-service reporters on the ship without crediting it to them, and left Toth's byline on it. Toth had protested in a letter to Denson, and now Denson remembered to leave Toth's name off the school-prayer story. But Toth had had enough and switched to the *Times* bureau. "He ruined the integrity of the paper. . . . Whatever was unique in it had become suspect."

III

John Denson's compulsion to try to shape the news was perhaps most apparent in the *Tribune*'s handling of foreign affairs. His news-weekly approach cast overseas correspondents not as the glamorous, independent operatives of the past but as fact-gatherers whose dispatches rated no higher than wire-service copy. Denson's chosen instrument to concentrate on the foreign file was *Tribune* alumnus Seymour Freidin, a large, lumbering man as sociable as Denson was not, who was given to expressing rapid and sweeping opinions based, in roughly equal portions, on a substantial body of firsthand knowledge, devout anti-Communism, and amiable bluster.

Freidin, who had worked his way up from copyboy to World War II foreign correspondent, was best remembered on the paper for his feat of having met up with elements of the Soviet army in the closing days of the war in Europe and, after much hearty consumption of bacon fat and vodka with the conquering Red heroes, contriving to drive his jeep in their midst on their sweep into Berlin. The only American correspondent on hand to witness the Red occupation of the Nazi capital, he managed to smuggle a melodramatic dispatch past Soviet censors via a German courier.

Denson brought Freidin back to the paper at the beginning of 1962 as one of four approximately equal executive editors he named to bring at least a semblance of organizational structure to the news department. Until then, the staff chart consisted of Denson at the top and everyone else as an appendage —an arrangement suited to promoting Denson's indispensability and general anarchy all around him. Buddy Weiss became executive editor (metropolitan), a grandiose version of city editor; Freeman Fulbright, executive editor (national), which meant he served primarily as Denson's messenger boy to the Washington bureau; Freidin, executive editor (foreign); and a newcomer, James G. Bellows, a quiet man of innate authority, executive editor (news operations), which in effect made him managing editor, the position he had held at the *Miami News* before joining the *Tribune*. For Freidin, there was vindication in the appointment.

His rightward ideological bent and inclination to overwrite had put him out of favor with foreign editors Barnes and Kerr after the war. Pro-Soviet cable editor John Price, who had to wrestle with Freidin's prolix and purplish dispatches, thought him the worst of the paper's correspondents. Summoned home during the staff cutbacks of 1948, Freidin found himself a fifth wheel around the city room and, embittered after a dozen years on the paper, went back to Europe as a free lance working out of Vienna. Although he knew the languages, players, and politics of the Soviet satellite world, his friends in Vienna and Paris detected a large element of pretense to Si Freidin's trenchcoated swagger. It was not surprising that in the period between his leaving and rejoining the *Tribune*—but not while he was on the paper, according to Freidin —he was affiliated with the Central Intelligence Agency.

He was never paid by the CIA beyond having his bar bill picked up, Freidin insisted after his involvement in the spy business was disclosed in the late 'Seventies. Given his ready professional access to people and places either off-limits or awkward to reach for CIA station or U.S. embassy personnel, Freidin's main function with the agency was as a go-between with the Soviet KGB apparatus. His *modus operandi* was "the double-check and cut-out game," in which he would serve as the third man in discussions between the two sides until the subject got too delicate for him to remain. Denson might conceivably have hired Freidin back even if he had known of the CIA link, but former *Tribune* men learning of it long afterward viewed it as a betrayal of their profession. Freidin himself viewed the matter quite differently. In his book *The Forgotten People,* completed just before he rejoined the *Tribune,* he wrote with conviction of the "death watch" he had stood during the subjugation of Eastern European peoples by Communist terrorism: "I have seen too many die, even if they continued to live. I do not believe in what is still sometimes described as 'objective reporting.' To me this is an all too simple solution of trying to reflect man's fate by accepting none of the responsibility for it." Those more cynical about Si Freidin's character would in later years paint his CIA involvement as the dark secret he hid from the profession in order to achieve success and make himself useful to his country, even if nobody else could know of it. Those more charitable saw him not so much as an ideologue and cold warrior as a tough-minded and unsentimental patriot at a time when primitive anti-Communism was not fashionable in America.

At any rate, he served Denson's purposes. He knew how to weave together colorful, interpretive stories from diverse sources and did not cavil at a bit of imprecision of language or stretching of the facts to achieve what he and Denson defined as maximum readability. Compare the openings of the same lead story that ran in the April 16, 1962, issues of the *Tribune* and *Times*:

By Seymour Freidin *Executive Editor, Foreign News*	By MAX FRANKEL Special to the New York Times
Under the toughest, tensest circumstances since World War II, the United States will try today in Washington to talk a Berlin solution to the Soviet Union. This time the divisive pressure is Western-made, menacing the future relationship of the main allies in NATO. It all popped, like a raging boil just lanced, over American proposals that will be broached to the Russians on the future of Berlin and Germany.	WASHINGTON, April 15—Secretary of State Dean Rusk will resume exploratory talks on Berlin with the Soviet Union tomorrow on behalf of a bickering Western alliance. The Secretary of State is scheduled to meet with Anatoly F. Dobrynin, the new Soviet Ambassador, at 2:30 p.m. Much of their first meeting is likely to deal with arrangements for the continuing Berlin dialogue, but Mr. Rusk is willing to dis-

The propositions, dismaying the West Germans, were leaked in the Federal Republic's capital on the misty banks of the Rhine in Bonn. Publication deeply discomfited the administration in Washington. The State Department chewed out the West German ambassador.

It was a lecture that only sent temperatures rising. The two principal protagonists, President Kennedy, for the U.S., and Chancellor Konrad Adenauer, for West Germany, are reliably reported downright furious—at each other.

cuss the substance of the issues if the Ambassador is ready.

French objections to this search for a settlement and West German reservations about a number of proposals the United States and Britain would like to offer make it necessary to keep the talks informal and at what is being called the "subnegotiation" level.

The Secretary of State will advance a number of ideas for a possible Berlin settlement to gauge the Soviet reaction. Although the Russians have relaxed pressures against Allied positions in Berlin in recent weeks, they have shown no greater interest than before in a compromise agreement.

Unquestionably, Freidin's copy, with its generally urgent, overdrawn, and often awkward language, made for more gripping reading than the calm, careful, often plodding prose of the *Times,* but it did not inspire the same confidence. The *Tribune*'s veteran European correspondent Don Cook found his dispatches being regularly rewritten in New York for maximum dramatic effect, with or without his byline attached. "Freidin fancied himself an all-American rewrite-man," Cook said.

By the time most *Tribune* correspondents, who were usually on the run between assignments, caught up with the paper and saw what Denson and Freidin had done to their copy, it was weeks too late to protest. But one of their number who was better connected and more articulate than the rest—Richard Wald—fought back. During the Berlin crisis, reports circulated around the world that Russian warplanes were buzzing U.S. aircraft in the air corridor linking the isolated former German capital to the Western-occupied zones. Wald accompanied Lucius Clay, the U.S. High Commissioner for Germany, aloft to check the reports and found little to justify the rumors. Some routine Soviet military exercises in adjacent airspace had been understandably mistaken in that hair-trigger setting for unduly provocative conduct. Wald wrote as much, but the AP continued to send out scare stories that, in Wald's estimate after firsthand inspection, were "patently false." Denson, operating on what Wald and others believed to be the theory that the better story should run regardless of strict veracity, ran with the wire-service account and put Wald's byline on it.

This flagrant disregard for the integrity of his correspondents' work stirred Wald to phone New York and protest. It got him nowhere. But when Denson came to Paris that summer of 1962, Wald's resentment boiled over. During a dinner given by the Whitneys at the Ritz for their editor and his overseas reporters, Denson defended his diminution of the traditional role of the paper's correspondents by insisting that he and his editors were closer to the interests of their readers and so reserved the right to alter foreign dispatches as they thought best, even if that occasionally meant accepting a wire-service version of events. Then, citing Wald's low-key Berlin reports as a negative example, Denson turned to him and said, as Wald recalled it, "You don't know how to report." Wald, whose harried face was often brightened by a puckish grin, answered darkly, "You don't know how to edit." Don Cook reminded the thirty-two-year-old junior correspondent that he was addressing his boss. But Betsey Whitney intervened and urged Wald to have his say. In a long lament that sounded to foreign correspondent Sanche de Gramont as if it had been rehearsed, Wald revealed his feelings about the Denson hype and did not restrict his remarks to foreign coverage; Denson's anti-Kennedy play of the steel price-rise crisis that spring, he said, had been "reprehensible." When Wald finally fell silent, Jock Whitney broke the pall by turning to him and saying, "I think you ought to have another drink."

Perhaps because he had delivered badly needed criticism of the sort that the diffident Whitney did not himself care to administer, or more probably because the owner had become fond during his ambassadorship of the self-possessed young man who had served as a London correspondent, Richard Wald was not sacked on the spot. Within months, he would become the third most powerful editor of the *Herald Tribune* and its principal articulator of modified Densonism. "I started out hating his innovations—partly it was the makeup," Wald recalled. "I had loved the old look, and I didn't like the flashiness of the new one . . . and the dishonesty of it—the way they hid the wire copy, for example, and tried to make believe it was something else. But then I began to see that we weren't competing anymore with the *Times* and it was good that we were beginning to work out our own destiny."

IV

A year into the Denson revolution, the *Tribune* city room was no more serene than when it began. Among staff veterans, grousing was all but universal. In winning wide attention for the paper, the new editor had succeeded mainly in making it notorious, they felt. His techniques were said to have tortured accuracy, trashed the paper's dignity, and cast a blind eye upon its special pride, good writing. And it was a mighty thin package Denson was so meticulously wrapping—the front page *was* the paper, many contended; the rest of it was being ignored. Rewriteman Inky Blackman was appalled at being handed a headline along with notes and clips for a story and told to write accordingly; that was turning journalism on its head. On John Denson's *Herald Tribune,* there was only one creative force, from whom all inspiration had to flow. On the copy desk, the consensus was that at best Denson possessed "a screwy talent for doing odd and striking things," in the words of John Price. His colleague Lorimer Heywood thought the editor "a smart, superficial bastard." Editorial-page writer Nicholas King considered him "a brutal and obsessed man," and many felt the sting of his acerbic tongue. Those who did not yield to his arbitrary rule paid for it, like the stubborn assistant editor Charles Kiley, who declined to cancel his long-planned family vacation at the last minute as Denson had requested and found himself demoted to the copy desk. Night editor Kallgren thought he detected "the eyes of a madman glinting behind those goggles." In the composing room, resentment was widespread over the new editor's extraordinary demands for unorthodox composition; every night it was something different, and every hairline rule had to be perfectly in place. Those whose skills he scorned—and that included many of the most experienced people in the place—found themselves obsolescent overnight and privately vented their unhappiness.

Among the oldtimers who granted that the expediencies of survival justified Denson's experimentation and its inevitable excesses, a few with longer perspective admired the creativity being brought to the rescue mission. Editorial writer and *Tribune* historian Harry Baehr thought Denson the only editor the paper had had in the twentieth century who was touched with genius. At his best, as he was early in 1962 when the nation celebrated the first manned space flight by an American, Denson exhibited a flair unique among newspaper editors of the day. To chronicle the spectacle that the world had witnessed on television the previous day, the February 21 *Tribune*'s front page was dominated by a six-column close-up picture of the astronaut smilingly recumbent on a medical examiner's table; above the photograph ran the exultant italic overline "We're Thrilled, We're Proud, John Glenn." The main head said "A 'Fireball' Space Ride; / Astronaut —I'm Excellent," and from it depended quadruple readouts—four equally played stories subheaded "The Flight," "The Man," "The Future," "The World." And as he had caught the human quality of that moment in a manner alien to the *Times,* the newspaper of record, so Denson captured the terrible irony the following week when New York began to give a tumultuous greeting to the nation's greatest hero since Lindbergh at almost the precise moment a jet passenger liner was carrying ninety-five people to their death in nearby Jamaica Bay. Denson cleared the March 2 front page of all other stories, and the two supremely contrasting events were played in identical horizontal blocks, the one above headlined "TRIUMPH—The New York Way," and the one below, "TRAGEDY—End of Flight 1," and over both of them he ordered up a short editorial, written by Herbert Kupferberg, which began: "Man reaches for the stars, but he stands upon the earth." The *Times,* locked into a format that made no allowance for emotional truths more powerful than any sanitized recitation of events can render, clinically separated the stories on opposite sides of the page and between them ran a one-column piece about a Fifth Avenue bus strike.

Among the *Tribune*'s younger generation of reporters, Denson's efforts were generally admired. They attracted a newcomer like thirty-year-old Notre Dame graduate Maurice Carroll, who after an apprenticeship on Newhouse papers in Jersey City and Newark and the *Journal-American* came eagerly to what he felt was "the most exciting newspaper in the business." Laurence Barrett, five years out of Columbia's School of Journalism and then serving as the paper's City Hall reporter, saw in Denson an inspiring intensity—someone was finally in charge who cared greatly and knew what he was doing and did it without resorting to the tawdry or smutty or inane but within the bounds of serious news subjects. "Yes, he would goose up a story now and then," Barrett conceded, "but basically it had to be there in the first place. His charter was to save the paper, and to do that he had to get attention." Denson worked with his reporters, sometimes overdirecting or worrying a story to death in a way they found constricting, but they knew the boss was paying attention and they exerted themselves accordingly. "He was an exercise in problem-solving for me," recalled Stuart Loory, "but he respected what I did, and he let me do it."

Loory was a twenty-eight-year-old Cornell graduate with three years on the *Newark News* and three more on the *Tribune,* mostly covering science under Earl Ubell, when Denson sent him into the thick of the nation's racial strife in May 1961. Loory went without hesitation, although his wife was about to give birth to their first child. The *Times,* in a court challenge with the state of Alabama, which was trying to obstruct its coverage of the civil rights war there, had no reporter on the scene as Loory drove all night in a car with other reporters from Birmingham to Montgomery behind a busload of "freedom riders" and stepped out into a scene of unpoliced bedlam. A white mob at the Greyhound bus terminal began to beat the emerging riders with a vehemence that stunned Loory, and as the attackers turned their rage upon the accompanying newsmen, smashing the conspicuous equipment of photographers and TV cameramen, he fled in momentary panic with a carload of reporters. But before he got around the corner, Loory realized he was running away from the story—"and I couldn't do that." Back he hurried into the melee, alone in a strange and hostile city and afraid of being hurt, but steeled to his professional duty. There was no way he could shrink into the shadows of the horrific scene—in his jacket and tie he stood out as an intrusive irritant to the mob—so he got out his note pad and pencil and started "walking around and listening and smelling and tasting. . . . You couldn't believe this was happening—it just couldn't be."

When Loory began filing his eyewitness story, Denson sent word to him to write it in the first person, but Loory said he was not trained at that and the office could do it for him if it wanted. The piece ran at the top of page one, and Loory was instructed to remain in Montgomery for follow-ups. Watched wherever he went, invited to leave the city room of the *Montgomery Advertiser,* denied use of his car because the agency that had rented it to him feared it would be damaged, Loory appealed directly to Denson to be careful how he handled and played his copy if the editor valued his future services. Denson assured his correspondent that he was not in any trouble and all he had to do was invoke the magic name of the *Herald Tribune.* "He was certain that a big ol' New York paper was invulnerable down there, especially if I just explained it all to those crackers." Denson had obviously lost touch with his native Dixie.

But in the eyes of Robert Poteete, elevated to day city editor after a decade on the paper, Denson had a good grip on what mattered in New York. A good-hearted country boy who had come to New York from the *Arkansas Gazette* with something of a moralizing tendency—"he was full of 'should,'" said a city-room colleague—Poteete cared passionately about the *Tribune* and his work on it in what one of his superiors called "an undemonstrative, shit-kicking, Arkansas way," and was willing to devote twelve- and thirteen-hour days to proving it. His conscientiousness in covering City Hall was rewarded in 1958 with a prize-winning exposé of a larcenously high overpayment by municipal officials for marshland in farthest Queens. Promoted to the city desk, Poteete was offended by what he considered Denson's "virulent prejudices. John was a racist and a woman-hater. He'd say that [*Times* publisher] Arthur Hays Sulzberger's dream in life was to go to sleep and wake up an Episcopalian. He'd mock Mayor Wagner's wife, Susan, as a drunk, never granting that maybe she was drinking to dull the pain of a cancer that was killing her. But I loved him." Poteete approved of the kind of anecdotal approach and seamless prose Denson prescribed, and he did his best to rewrite stories, captions, and "precedes" to suit his demanding master. Poteete and his immediate boss, Buddy Weiss, succeeded in pushing Denson into more extensive city coverage. Larry Barrett was given a weekly City Hall column, Bob Bird produced a multi-part series on life in Brooklyn—the sort of popular urban sociology that the departed Arthur Hadley had forlornly urged the paper to run—and most attention-catching of all, the front page for a time featured a pothole-of-the-day campaign in an effort to rid the city streets of battlefield conditions. This is how the drive was described in one of the Papert-Koenig-Lois television commercials that ran before the CBS local late-evening news show:

> The New York Herald Tribune versus Manhattan Borough President Edward Dudley.
> April 16. Last Monday the Tribune says there are too many holes in New York. Here's one on Wall Street. Mr. Dudley fills it right up.
> April 17. Tuesday the Tribune finds another one. This time on 51st Street. Mr. Dudley fills that one.
> April 18. Wednesday the Tribune seeks out this ditch on Sixth Avenue. Mr. Dudley, not even breathing hard, has filled it even before we go to print.
> April 19. Thursday, intrepid Tribune reporters, warming to the hunt, come up with a doozy on Chrystie Street. Within three hours Dudley fills it, recapturing the lead.

April 20. Tribune advance scouts discover a new one on 82nd Street. But Dudley's repair crew, showing discouraging speed, is already on its way. Demoralized Tribune reporters turn to editor John Denson. Says Denson, "This means war. The Tribune will continue to find new potholes if you reporters have to dig them yourselves."

Citizens of New York, follow this gripping battle in the New York Herald Tribune!

Who says a good newspaper has to be dull?

Probably nobody in the city room more admired Denson's skills or learned more from them than the man who would succeed him as the last editor of the *Tribune*—James Bellows, a gifted craftsman of few words, high tensile strength, and quick arms and feet, who burned up a lot of calories as *de facto* managing editor in trying to get the paper to press without antagonizing his perfectionist superior. Never one of Denson's yes-men, always cautious and watchful lest the volatile editor resent his competence and cast him as a would-be usurper, Bellows led the charge of editors following the belated breakup of the nightly front-page conference, moved copy and layouts so the bottlenecked production began to flow, hovered with a grease pencil to get the crop marks just right on the artwork Denson had selected, and pushed him ever so gently as deadline approached with a "Hey, we're way late, John—you've got to decide." What he respected most was Denson's power of concentration as the editor sat there, false teeth grinding, thick lenses glittering, face buried in page proofs, brain weighing the impact of every headline, pondering the precise fit and wording of every caption, fretting over how much white space to leave around a picture he wanted enclosed with rules. "It all had to come together for him," Bellows remembered. "He was developing a total esthetic out of the front page." The Denson hype he partially excused as an unavoidable concomitant of the end in view, which Bellows described as "trying to get the team back into Yankee Stadium."

Denson's most important fan was, of course, Whitney. Although the owner had no special fondness for his editor as a human being, he considered him brilliant in his use of type and handling of the news. The front page of the April 20, 1962, issue of *What's Going On,* the paper's house organ, bore a signed greeting from Whitney on the completion of Denson's first year at the *Tribune*: "John Denson has played the major role in shaping the paper to fit the job we believe must be done in today's world. . . . Happy anniversary, John Denson! We know that another exciting year lies ahead."

By the fall, as Denson began to extend the front-page innovations to the inside of the paper, circulation was the highest it had ever been without the aid of contests. For the first week in October, sales of the daily were averaging above 400,000, well ahead of the *Post,* and, according to fresh research data, the paper was attracting new customers where it had been most badly lagging—in the city, especially among Jewish readers. And then, as quickly as he had arrived unheralded, John Denson was gone.

V

One mid-autumn day in 1961 while Jock Whitney was recuperating from his heart attack, his wife, Betsey, was excused from his room at New York Hospital during a visit by the president and the editor of her husband's newspaper. Mrs. Whitney left with good grace but from the hallway soon heard loud voices raised across the patient's bed. The noise grew into "such screaming and shouting for ten or fifteen minutes," she recalled, that she became infuriated, followed the two visitors to the elevator after they had left the room, and gave Walter Thayer and John Denson a piece of her mind for their inconsiderate behavior.

That unpretty hospital scene foreshadowed a year of smoldering strife carefully hidden from the outside world while the newspaper to which the three men were devoting their efforts had apparently been reconceptualized with success and was progressing nicely toward solvency. The clash between its two principal employees, however, worked like a slow poison on the *Tribune*'s frail health and left its owner trapped between a pair of personalities more forceful than his own.

Their ostensible flashpoint was Denson's continuing failure to stick rigidly to production schedules. Thayer, who was a rational man, thought he could have both Denson's inspired creativity and an orderly operation—or, to be more precise, that the one without the other would not save the paper. Denson felt that his efforts ought not to be arbitrarily governed by unimportant deadlines. He believed that the *Tribune*'s fate would be settled within the New York metropolitan region; it therefore mattered little to him if the early edition was not punctually aboard trains that supplied its small out-of-town readership. But circulation managers live by the clock and value every sale, and the *Tribune*'s dutiful Lester Zwick was distraught over the habitual lateness of Denson's paper, complaining vigorously to Thayer the next day after each fresh violation of the schedule. To Zwick, much of Denson's fine-tuning was willful self-indulgence, not in the paper's overall interest, and one night toward the end of November 1961, soon after the heated exchange between Thayer and Denson over Whitney's hospital bed, Zwick ordered the presses not to stop for what he regarded as a minor alteration in a front-page headline Denson wanted made late in the run. The editor exploded, saying it was up to him and not the circulation department to determine the contents of the paper and that unless such humiliations were guaranteed not to recur, he was through. In view of the success his innovations were achieving, Denson's sovereignty over the product was reconfirmed—a decision Thayer would later regret as an act of appeasement that served only to embolden the editor, leave the operation dependent on his whims, and make it impossible ever to rein him in. But Thayer succeeded in extracting from Denson his agreement to distribute a portion of his work by naming a slate of executive editors, including Bellows, who was brought in specifically to facilitate production.

Some improvement followed, but press times remained erratic, overtime continued in the composing room in defiance of McKinsey & Co. efficiency methods that the new administrative vice president Robert MacDonald was monitoring, and out-of-town sales, important to Whitney's ambition to bolster the *Tribune*'s standing as a national paper, suffered. As chronic tension built, Whitney's admiration for his editor grew strained. In a memo to Thayer after one exasperating night, Whitney wrote: "This is a really horrifying bear we have by the tail. I feel so much like shaking him till his poor old teeth fall out that I can hardly resist going out to the bullpen [the night desk, where Denson stationed himself] and shouting at him. But then I sit here in my office knowing that if I really let fly he'd have to go and then so would we. That disastrous indispensability—how long will we have it?"

Compounding that dependency was growing evidence that John Denson was not a stable man. To those closest to him, he often seemed out of control, unaware of or unwilling to acknowledge his own physical and emotional limitations. On magazines, he had become accustomed to weekly or longer deadlines and a rhythmic production cycle of ups and down; on the *Tribune,* he was confronted with the unvarying pressure of that night's press time. He did not know how to pace himself. He would work constantly at a nerve-shredding rate for three weeks running and then collapse, retreating for days to his Vermont farm to recharge his drained energies and grumble about what his subordinates were doing to his beautiful paper. And then the agonizing cycle would resume. At *Newsweek,* he had had the time and talent to shape the editorial creation satisfactorily in his image, but at the paper, as Bellows put it, "you might not be able to get it right—just exactly right—that night, and that was very frustrating to him."

That frustration, which lowered the never high threshold of Denson's irascibility, did not elicit much sympathy from Walter Thayer. His executive assistant at the time, Ralph Schwarz, said of Thayer, "He was approaching the *Tribune* as a regular business and did not understand the emotional content of the newspaper or of newspapermen." Thayer's chief administrator, Bob MacDonald, had a broader view of the problem. As the prime installer of the new financial controls system that provided overnight reports of plant productivity for the previous day's paper, MacDonald knew better than anyone else what Denson's stubbornness was costing in lost sales and overtime, but he also recognized the larger rewards at stake. Denson would be snide and sarcastic toward him when MacDonald inquired about the lateness problem. "He was a guy with a lot of rough edges. But he was a great editor, and people like him are cut from a different cloth." When MacDonald probed to learn just why it was that Denson was having so much trouble meeting deadlines, the editor told him, "I've got to get it right—and I don't want to get it out of here till it is." MacDonald understood even if he did not approve. "He was really putting his heart and soul into it and driving himself to perfection, and when you're in a death struggle, that's the kind of editor you want—not a Bob White. I urged Walter not to force the issue."

And Thayer did hold back as Denson's success reinforced his self-importance. His inability to share his power or brook any challenge to it was dramatized in April 1962, when he began censoring columns by sports editor Stanley Woodward. At issue allegedly were questions of taste; Woodward had needled readers of the Sunday *Times* for buying it by the pound and had said a few kind things about the Kennedys. But Denson's kills of the offending passages almost certainly reflected both his private political biases and his sensitivity over his failures to turn around his own paper's Sunday circulation. When he failed to grant Woodward's claim that he had the same right to express himself freely in the paper as Walter Lippmann, the sports editor gave a year's notice of his retirement. Denson replied that if Woodward felt that way, he ought to leave at his earliest convenience. So for the second time, Woodward left the paper he loved in disappointment and rage. In his book *Paper Tiger,* Woodward put his finger on the source of Denson's chief shortcoming of character: "Denson once said to me, 'Everybody on this damn sheet thinks he has a proprietary interest in it.' His attitude was that people employed by the *Herald Tribune* should work there for the money he paid them, do what they were told, and shut up." But it was precisely that proprietary interest that was the true strength of the paper, Woodward argued, and in refusing to cultivate it, in riding roughshod over it to impose his will, Denson defeated himself. No modern, complex newspaper, especially one with the *Tribune*'s range of coverage, could operate as a one-man band. At Denson's editorial conferences and out on the city-room floor where he supervised the paper's nightly assemblage, there was really no give-and-take among the editors, Jim Bellows recalled. "You would try to pass along a little idea to him that he'd hear and chew over, but it wasn't a matter of a thing being taken or rejected—it would all sort of go into the mix. It was *his* front page, his paper, and you had that sense of his feeling, 'I'm the one doing this.' He wasn't really ever asking you for an opinion so much as confirmation of his instincts."

Pressurized by too little time to work his nightly miracle and too few hands judged worthy to assist, Denson seized increasingly on Thayer as his tormentor when in fact his own character was a far greater menace to his creative freedom. He refused to pay deference to Thayer as he did to Whitney and would often come late or not at all to management meetings called by the president. And he inflated Thayer into a demonic figure, Jock's Mr. Moneybags and the implacable foe of the editorial department. When a vice president for production was hired and a tough taskmaster brought in to oversee the composing room and overall copy flow, Denson griped louder about the incompetence of the shop and inadequacies of the machinery at his disposal; the real problems were mechanical, not Denson-made, he snarled. But his ceaseless tinkering and revising could not be blamed away, and as his commands slowed the composing room and forced corrections for the rest of the paper to be backed up while the latest version of the front page was rejiggered, reporters complained about all the typos in their stories that got into print, sub-editors fretted impotently, circulation manager Zwick went back to his old job on the Boston *Record-American,* the new production boss quit, and the city room ran an almost nightly fever from the tension. "We were desperate," Thayer recounted. Denson's conduct was "hurting morale, losing us circulation, and costing us a lot of money."

But Thayer's principal subordinates on the business side of the paper did not agree with that appraisal of Denson's net value. Besides MacDonald and Schwarz, who felt the editor was worth all the aggravation, the new circulation manager, Roy Newborn, and the controller, Win Maxwell, disputed Thayer's charge. Newborn, who had spent seventeen years as a *Tribune* circulator and four years at the *New York Post* as circulation director, estimated the circulation loss traceable to Denson's delays at no more than 3,000 nightly, most of it in out-of-town sales. In the New York area, meanwhile, Denson was selling a lot of papers. "He really had a touch," said the admiring Newborn. "He put out a marketable product that sold wherever it went. Our school circulation doubled during Denson's time." Controller Maxwell added, "I'm a numbers man—and we were hitting our expense numbers under the McKinsey plan, even with Denson's overtime," which did not exceed $100,000 a year. While advertising volume had not yet rallied in proportion to the daily circulation gain and Denson continued to be "strangely silent" in addressing the Sunday problem, "the plan was working," in Maxwell's view. "I was surprised when they let him go." To Ralph Schwarz, Denson's departure was "a tragedy." A similar consensus among the top editors, who suffered directly from Denson's chronic irritability, was expressed by the indefatigible cable editor, Harry Rosenfeld: "Sure, they tinkered and they shoved and they squeezed and they broke everyone's balls with the delays, but they got the paper over 400,000—the man was a presence. They were getting a lot more out of him than he was costing them. Who was out there buying all those papers if Denson was getting it out too late? For your savior you put up with idiosyncrasies. . . . They should have tickled him behind the ears more."

But Thayer was not an ear-tickler, and his efforts to reason with Denson, who had become increasingly irrational toward the business side, were a failure. "He was impossible to talk to—and I tried and tried and tried," Thayer recalled. "Everything would have been fine if only he had met his deadlines, but he was constitutionally incapable of it."

Those close to the feuding pair saw the problem in terms of an irreconcilable clash of two lone-wolf personalities, each used to having his own way. "Walter finally just got fed up with John, who was challenging his authority, and he wasn't going to let him get away with it," MacDonald suggested. Maxwell put it more bluntly: "Denson was too much of an oddball to pay proper deference to Thayer." Just how far short Denson had fallen of being even civil to Thayer may be inferred from the latter's memory of his efforts "to be helpful by hanging around the office at night. It got so bad he'd throw things at me—he'd snarl at me to get out of his office. I was the butt. He was just a mad artist."

John Denson was also someone Jock Whitney believed in. Acquainted with the volatility of the artistic temperament from his prewar experience in the movie business and investments in Broadway shows, Whitney tried in his fashion to broker peace between the two feuding men. "I think it became a political situation," said MacDonald, "in which Walter may have become jealous of Jock's relationship with John." Schwarz thought it was rather more a matter of Thayer's fear that Whitney was being led astray: "Walter was afraid of John's power and influence over Jock," who was entranced by the editor's inventiveness and therefore willing to sit down and try to reason out the production problem with him. "It was precisely when he got through to John and vice versa that Walter would be hurt and apprehensive," Schwarz added. "Jock and Walter were not talking there much for a while [because of Denson]." In the end, Whitney had to choose between them. "Walter pushed him into getting rid of John," Betsey Whitney believed. Thayer argued that while Denson was undoubtedly talented, others could carry on his work without the uproar; that much of Denson's circulation gain was due to the heavy advertising and promotion drive that had been thrown behind the redesigned paper; and that since losses were still running at more than three million a year, the place had to be put on a businesslike basis, genius or no genius. Whitney was persuaded.

Thayer accomplished the execution in a more polished fashion than the way he dispatched ex-general manager Tom Robinson, whose resignation he asked for while passing him in the hall one morning. After checking around in the industry on how the Denson dilemma might be solved without a fatality, Thayer hit upon the entirely reasonable idea of taking the nightly lockup of the paper out of the editor's hands and giving it to Bellows. On almost every paper, the closing was delegated to a subordinate and not held on to fiercely by the presiding editor. Before revealing the plan to its target, Thayer asked his valued metropolitan editor, Buddy Weiss, where he would stand if Denson quit as a result. "With the paper," said Weiss. Bellows, too, recognized that Denson had placed his ego above the general welfare of the *Tribune*. Informed of the imposed change, Denson hollered that the plan was just a scheme to box him in and, for the first time, went charging through the interconnecting door between his office and Whitney's and demanded to know who was running the paper. Whitney told him. Denson's resignation on October 11, 1962, was marked by a revealing note he fixed to the fifth-floor bulletin board:

> I am stepping out as Editor of the Herald Tribune. I am sure that you all know that the independence of the editorial department has always been one of my principal concerns.
>
> In parting, I am happy to say that the September weekday circulation figures— all but five issues were under my command—will have a cheerful ring; that results from the first issues of October—also under my command—appear even brighter.

I am deeply grateful to all of you who gave me an earnest and honorable helping hand during my stay on the paper. All the luck in the world.

Whitney ruled that no outsider would be brought in to succeed Denson. Instead, Bellows's title was changed to managing editor. His first act was to replace national editor Freeman Fulbright, Denson's prime satellite and the only one of the four executive editors to fall devotedly on his sword. In his place went foreign correspondent Richard Wald. Denson became an operating and then consulting editor with the Hearst organization and left behind him at the *Tribune* the mold for a new approach to daily journalism. Even his harshest critics in the city room agreed that things were duller after he had gone.

VI

"Long Range Planning / For Herald Tribune," asserted the headline in always obliging *Editor & Publisher* the week after Denson left as the paper moved promptly to assure the industry that his departure would not hamstring its recovery drive. And indeed fears of the editor's indispensability were quickly dissipated after the new, young editorial team pulled together to put out a strong run of papers during the Cuban missile crisis. The essentials of Denson's typography were retained and refined; the headlines were perhaps less snappy and the layout less idiosyncratic, but the look and style were a faithful imitation of the master's touch—and the paper got out on time.

Commending managing editor Bellows on his good start, Jock Whitney noted with approval early in November that the front page was less self-conscious than it had been under Denson and that "occasionally a verb appears in a headline." Although the departed editor had created excitement and some extraordinary papers, Whitney told his successor in an assessment that revealed why the owner had not fought harder to hold Denson, his overall performance lacked consistency: "Instead, the face [of the paper]—the new face—sometimes became a mask which covered a lack of quality." Insufficient effort had been expended on improving the writing and layout throughout the run of the paper; only the front page had been the beneficiary of Denson's magic. And "we have not given our readers more insight, more depth and, really, not much more 'ease of understanding.'"

If Whitney was pressing his editors for a better product, a memo from Thayer to Bellows two weeks later made clear that the *Tribune*'s president was operating on a different set of priorities. Distressed that the proposed editorial department budget for the November 1, 1962–April 30, 1963, period called for a 3 percent increase of $64,000 rather than the 8 percent cut of $200,000 he had hoped for, Thayer wrote, "It is essential that we find the ways and means to reduce personnel in those areas where employees are not carrying their share of the load." Undoubtedly the president was determined not to let yet another editor defy him and was making it clear from the start who was boss, but the diverging guidelines put down by publisher Whitney, who wanted a stronger paper, and president Thayer, who wanted an economically sane one, told Jim Bellows he was out on a high wire. To ask for a tighter editorial budget just at the time the redesigned paper was proving attractive to readers—especially since Denson's new techniques had not added much to his department's costs —was as self-defeating an economy proposal as the cutbacks William Robinson had mandated in 1948 just as the *Times* was deciding on the opposite strategy of reinvesting heavily in the quality of the paper. If there was fat in the *Tribune* budget late in 1962, it was in the promotion and advertising allocations, lavish by the paper's traditional standards. But they, too, were proving effective. For the month of November, the *Tribune* was selling 412,000 copies a day—a record level—and without Denson. Was that the moment to propose cutting back?

The question became academic within days. For on December 8, in the very midst of the Christmas shopping season, with retail advertising at its annual peak and the *Herald Tribune* riding a tide of hope, it was closed down for 114 days along with the other New York City dailies as a result of the most disruptive and costly newspaper strike in American history.

Within four years of the end of the strike, four of the seven citywide daily papers would be dead, and the intransigence and shortsightedness of the unions —especially of New York Local No. 6 of the International Typographical Union, which called the great 1962–63 walkout—would be widely blamed as the single most prominent cause of the fatalities. In its zeal to compensate for what it regarded as a decade of meager gains at the bargaining table and to reclaim for the blue-collar craft unions the initiative they had yielded to the white-collar American Newspaper Guild, the aggressive new leadership of the New York printers' local miscalculated the ability of the city's newspapers to meet its price and overplayed its bargaining hand, thereby protracting the ruinous strike. But the real tragedy was not that the settlement finally extracted, a two-year package of wage and benefit increases totaling $12.63 per worker per week, was so exorbitant—the publishers had been ready to pay $10.20 on the eve of the strike nearly four months earlier—but that largely because of their own disunity, shortsightedness, and lack of resolve, the newspaper publishers failed to win in return the slightest gain in productivity from their work force.

Local No. 6 of the printers' union (ITU), known in the printing trades as Big Six, controlled the work force at 600 commercial printshops and twenty-eight publications in New York, making it the largest and most powerful local of what most labor historians believe is the oldest continuous labor union in the United States. The ITU, by its continuity, conscientiousness, reliability, and pride over the decades, had won greater control of its working conditions and rate of productivity than probably any other labor union in the world. Symbolic of its power and often cited by its critics as evidence of labor's worst abuses was the practice of bogus, imposed upon management since the end of the nineteenth century, requiring the duplication of any work done outside a newspaper's composing room—usually advertising matter in the form of papier-mâché mats —for inclusion in the paper. Bogus, carefully composed only to be destroyed, was classic make-work, repugnant to almost all printers but fiercely defended as a weapon against union-busting, since heavy importation of outside work could obviously reduce any given paper's manpower needs in the shop. But such waste as bogus and other featherbedding and overmanning practices were substantially balanced in the case of the printers by a number of benefits that newspaper publishers had come to take for granted. Big Six functioned as a twenty-four-hour employment agency for the New York papers, providing them with a ready supply of generally qualified printers to get out whatever work was required. Weekends were considered part of the regular work week, and printers working on those days did not receive premium pay. The union allowed management to expand or contract its work force as needed on forty-eight-hour notice, thereby permitting far more flexibility than management enjoyed in most other industries. The printers' own fraternal code, furthermore, prohibited overtime work, which often cost employers a higher wage than regular time; instead, the printers, in order to spread the work among their colleagues and keep more of them employed, provided a convenient supply of substitutes if there was more work than the assigned crew could handle. Big Six was also a union free of corruption, run along genuinely democratic lines and composed of workers who were among the most skilled and versatile in the American labor movement; all its members were supposed to be capable of operating the highly complex Linotype machine, meticulous assemblage of thousands of pieces of precisely fit metal for the composition of newspaper pages, and proofreading and general knowledge of the English language—a rare combination of mechanical aptitude, dexterity, strength, and brains that required six years of apprenticeship. For such laborers, take-home pay of $118 a week in 1962 was not a princely sum.

The real problem, then, was not that New York newspaper owners were being gouged by their labor force but that they were wedded to antiquated technology that had changed little in three-quarters of a century. The *Times* and *News* and even the *World-Telegram* to an extent had been experimenting with automation and photocomposition, but the *Tribune,* which had been the first American paper to achieve high-speed printing by the introduction of curved press plates in 1861 and the first to encourage high-speed composition by the introduction of the Linotype twenty-five years later, had shown no inclination to pioneer new technologies in the twentieth century. This failure bespoke irresolute management, especially in the early 'Sixties, when the paper was in a struggle for survival, when it was owned by a multimillionaire whose previous business was a venture capital firm devoted to encouraging new products and industrial processes, and when it had hired a management consulting firm that ought to have stressed the possible economies the paper might realize in production costs from new technology. Indeed, the *Tribune*'s principal outside adviser,

Bernard Kilgore, headed a newspaper that for ten years had already been making extensive use of teletypesetting (TTS), a technique of automation involving perforated tape created at a typewriter keyboard with ordinary clerical skills and then fed into a device that actuated the keyboard of an unmanned Linotype. As early as 1954, *Tribune* officials were aware that the stock market quotations requiring seventeen of its Linotypes two hours to set each night were composed by TTS at *The Wall Street Journal* on only six machines and in half an hour less, but no move to introduce the technique was made by the cash-short Reids after obtaining Big Six approval.

Union intransigence rather than management hesitancy was generally cited as the main obstacle to the introduction by New York papers of TTS and photocomposition, which used far less bulky and far less expensive film in place of lead, yet the issue had never really been joined up to the eve of the 1962 printers' strike. The ITU had won jurisdiction over TTS and photocomposition techniques in the mid-'Fifties, establishing the right of its men to operate the new machinery; what the union also wanted was (1) the right to control the rate at which these time- and labor-saving techniques would be introduced and how they would be manned, (2) the assurance that a single wage scale would apply to their operators—even for the TTS tape-punchers, who required far less skill than journeymen printers—and that no men would lose their jobs as a result, and (3) cash payments to the union treasury for cost savings realized by the publishers from the new machinery. Publishers were willing to promise that no printers would be laid off due to the new technology, settling instead for payroll savings through attrition, but balked at tribute payments to the ITU. The union contended that such savings ought to be diverted, at least in part, to the maintenance of the printers' pension fund, which would be threatened by the shrinking roster of active members once the labor-saving machinery had been installed. An even more troubling issue was the owners' desire to use TTS tapes transmitted from outside sources, like the wire services and syndicates, which would allow quicker, cheaper typesetting of such material as financial tables, baseball box scores and racing charts, the texts of important speeches and documents, and syndicated columns. Here was a cost-cutting process applicable to editorial matter that was precisely analogous to the economies that newspapers had tried to realize from the use of mats produced outside their shops for the composition of advertisements but that had long been blocked by the union's requirement of bogus. The use of outside tapes was perceived by the union as no less a direct threat to printers' jobs in the 1960s.

And yet the ITU was not merely poking its head in the ground and denying the arrival of a new technology; in fact, it had already built a large training center at its national headquarters in Colorado, where union members could learn without cost to use the latest equipment. What the union wanted was to obtain for itself as large a share of the productivity savings as it could pry from management. But that battle had not been joined in New York as the profit-making *Times* and *News* experimented with the new processes, and when Big

Six elected Bertram A. Powers as its new president in mid-1961, he recognized the union's vulnerability: the papers were legally entitled to install whatever new equipment they wanted, provided only that ITU members operated it; there were no other restrictions in the union's contract. "The danger was clear to me," Powers recalled. In the coming 1962 negotiations, he knew he would have to "duck and bob and weave," as he put it, to stave off any concerted effort by the publishers to force the automation issue at the bargaining table.

The publishers, although negotiating as a unit to prevent their being picked off by the unions one at a time, were a discordant bunch. The *Times*'s vulnerability was its institutional imperative to keep publishing at almost any cost—it owed no less to history and civilization—and its reluctance to face down unions and risk a strike was well known. The *News,* less motivated by its responsibility to mankind, was far more willing to challenge the unions, but it could not do so alone, especially while it remained in competition with the *Mirror,* its pale imitator but still the second-largest-selling paper in the United States. The *News* continued to exert economic pressure on the *Mirror* by holding its selling price to a nickel, just as the *Times* was doing against the *Tribune,* when all four papers would have been in far better health if the profitable two had relented. In the afternoon field, the two chain-owned papers, the *Journal-American* and *World-Telegram & Sun,* were in the red and came to the biannual union negotiations with one end in view—the cheapest possible settlement; fancy new equipment was not about to be lavished on them by their corporate managers, so fighting for the right to unlimited use of the new technology would have been a largely pointless exercise for them. The independent *Post,* with its pro-labor editorial policy, came to the contract sessions with one arm tied behind its back. It had survived on grit and the personal bankroll of its publisher, Dorothy Schiff, whose wealth was a fraction of Jock Whitney's and who had no elaborate corporate superstructure to insulate her from the losses in lean years. The *Post,* therefore, could not afford to worry much about the potential blessings of automation or photocomposition, which would have required heavy capital investment. The *Tribune,* however, could have afforded such an investment if its owner's financial commitment to it had not been so carefully hedged. All the New York papers—perhaps the *Tribune* more than any of them—could have gained by determination to challenge Big Six through a sweeping proposal that would have fairly rewarded labor for allowing management to realize significant gains in per-worker productivity. Perhaps the printers would have been flexible in manning requirements, the use of outside tapes, and the elimination of bogus if the papers had been willing to offer guaranteed employment, shorter hours, substantial contributions to the union's pension fund, and a wage scale pegged to a proportion of genuine gains in productivity. But no one at the *Tribune* was thinking in such sweeping terms at the time; capital investment in new technology would have to await improvement in the balance sheet. If Whitney could have been persuaded that his paper's best chance to regain health lay in boldly embracing the new production technology, matching the boldness of the new editorial product John Denson had begun to create, the *Tribune* might have tried to lead the industry to a new deal with its unions or, failing that, might have struck its own bargain geared to the long view, creating a model for other papers willing to make the investment. Its top management, however, was composed of novices in the field of industrial relations, and Walter Thayer, hardly eager to raise the stakes of the game, saw the 1962 contract negotiations as a costly inconvenience, not an opportunity for a revolutionary relationship with the unions, who were certain to resist the idea.

Instead, the bargaining and ensuing strike were dominated by Big Six's Bert Powers, a forty-one-year-old former printer, who understood the publishers' weaknesses and was fixed in his own goals. A tall, lean, handsome man with whitish-blond hair and soft, clipped speech that retained traces of his working-class Boston area upbringing, Powers conducted himself with a stubborn resolve, physically manifested in erect bearing that seemed a denial of his indigent youth and a defiance of an auto accident in his early teens that had shattered a hip and left him with a stiff-legged gait and in permanent pain. An apprentice printer at sixteen and self-educated thereafter, he took pride in his craft and worked well at it on papers in Boston and New Haven before arriving in New York to work on the *Star*. When it folded, he went to a commercial shop on South Street, invariably earning a fifteen-dollar weekly bonus for his output, and became active in Big Six. A clever man who chose his words with care, he was on the union's executive committee by the age of twenty-seven and became its chairman two years later, gaining precocious insight into the bargaining process. He watched as the photoengravers struck the city's newspapers in 1953 for nineteen days and the deliverers walked out for two weeks in 1958—and saw that in neither case did the strikers succeed in obtaining a better settlement than the publisher's pre-strike offer. Powers was particularly unhappy with the pattern bargaining by which the publishers first reached agreement with the white-collar Guild, whose 6,800 members made it the largest of the ten unions comprising the 19,000-man work force on the city's papers, and then imposed the settlement terms on the blue-collar craft unions, whose two-year contract regularly expired early in December, five weeks after the Guild's. In Powers's view, the Guild was inclined to be too easy in its bargaining, partly because, as the only vertical union in the newspaper trade, its leaders deftly split up the newly won wage-and-benefit package so that its more skilled workers, on a higher scale than the others, received a proportionately larger piece of the pie and were not locked into across-the-board increases. Powers's 3,800 newspaper printers, operating on a single scale, unwilling to accept overtime pay that the lower-scale pressmen benefited from regularly, too honest to engage in side deals and payoffs of the sort the deliverers routinely inveigled, were falling further behind their fellow unionists in relative take-home pay each year.

The new Big Six leader was determined to change the situation as he approached the 1962 negotiations. His goals were a single expiration date for all the union contracts, thereby ending the Guild's dominant position; an hour-anda-quarter reduction in the work week to thirty-five hours, already enjoyed by the Guild; a healthy gain in hourly wages, which had increased by a total of about 33 percent over the previous decade; and establishment of the principle that the printers were entitled to a major share of any savings the publishers achieved through new technology—and until he had won these goals, Powers was prepared to keep his men out for a long, long time.

Since Big Six had not struck in seventy-nine years—the last time was over Whitelaw Reid's union-busting tactics at the *Tribune*—the publishers saw little reason to deviate from the pattern bargaining of the past. But Powers gave them fair warning of his militancy, starting in April 1962 with the establishment of a unity council that called for honest bargaining by the publishers with all the unions instead of relying on settlement with the relatively docile Guild as the inflexible pattern for the rest. Despite the early start-up of contract talks, no real numbers were put on the table until the Guild negotiations began. By then, Powers had exhibited some muscle-flexing with letters to his shop stewards and rank and file, telling them to be prepared for a long strike since anything less, judging by the ineffectual walkouts by the engravers in 1953 and deliverers in 1958, could be absorbed by the publishers without much pain. There was no bluffing in his position. "If you're really ready to go out, you might not have to," Powers recounted. Nor did he have much doubt that the papers could afford to pay his price. The *Times* and *News* were financially solid. The *Post* was at least marginally in the black and tightly run and had a rich owner. The *Mirror, Journal-American,* and *World-Telegram* were owned by big chains that could afford to subsidize their New York outlets. And Jock Whitney, he knew, was writing off the *Tribune*'s losses against other profit-making properties—and if he got tired of doing that, Powers believed, some other wealthy figure would almost certainly come forward to take over the paper and sustain the voice of Eastern Republicanism. "It was a comforting self-delusion," the printers' president recalled. And if by any chance one of the papers did succumb during a marathon strike, there was plenty of work for his printers at the city's busy job shops. To underscore his determination, Powers organized a unity rally in October, shortly before the Guild contract was due to expire, and attracted 4,000 workers from all ten newspaper unions—an unmistakable show of strength.

After an eight-day strike against the *News,* the Guild settled for a two-year, citywide package of $8.50 a week, which was better than the seven-dollar increases of 1958 and 1960 but far from satisfying Powers's ambitions. The unity council, which had agreed that no union should accept a contract that a majority of the others felt was too low, voted six to four against the Guild pact, but the Guild membership nevertheless ratified it. Thus rebuffed, Powers asked Big Six to take a strike vote and won authorization for a walkout by a vote of 2,003–47. Early in the evening of December 7, when the craft unions' contracts were within hours of expiration, the publishers finally made Powers an offer of $9.20 and were prepared, if he made a reasonable response, to go a dollar higher;

beyond that, the papers were ready to take a strike. Powers bided his time until after midnight and then gave his counterproposal: he wanted a wage-and-benefit package of $38 and would give no ground on the continuance of bogus or use of outside TTS tapes.

"I want to assure you that the future of the Herald Tribune—our future—is a most hopeful one," Whitney wrote to all his staffers four days into the strike, and went on to say that the paper's upward momentum would resume as soon as the strike was over. But the year ended without progress while Powers waited for the publishers to improve their offer and the publishers were shielded by their strike insurance, totaling $2.25 million and covering the first twenty-nine days of forced stoppage of publication. Strikers are rarely popular with an inconvenienced public, and Powers was prepared for the vilification that soon descended upon him as a headstrong obstructionist out to make his mark in the labor movement without regard for the impact of his actions upon the community or the publishers' ability to pay. He would not submit his case to the court of public opinion by accepting arbitration of the dispute; the publishers would have to stand and negotiate with him, he said—not dictate terms as they had become accustomed to doing. And when the mayor, governor, and Secretary of Labor joined in January to name a board of public accountability, composed of three judges, to weigh the merits of each side's case, Powers declined to appear before the unofficial tribunal. "It was a stacked deck," he believed, in the sense that the judges were closely linked to the political and social establishment and therefore inclined to side with the publishers. In its findings, the judges blamed the publishers for waiting far too long to start serious negotiations, but the panel came down far more heavily on Powers and the printers by charging that the strike was "not a move of last resort to which they were driven after a full exploration [of the publishers' position]. . . . It was a deliberate design formed by the printers' representatives as the opening gambit in negotiations."

As Powers seemed to harden into a statue of calm, cool intransigence, Walter Thayer came forward in a series of radio and television appearances that projected him as an attractive, utterly reasonable spokesman for the victimized publishers, forced to deal with a willful foe who wanted everything and would give nothing in return. Shredding Powers's disingenuous claim that the union was willing to negotiate separately with the papers on the basis of their ability to pay, Thayer asked whether the union had a discount division of printers for hire at discount wages and asserted that any paper unable to meet the higher scale could not hope to attract enough qualified manpower to stay in business. In answer to the charge that the publishers were stalling in the post-Christmas season when advertising normally ebbed, Thayer argued, "We're out of touch with our readers—five and a half million of them," who were "finding other things to do, other things to read, other ways to spend their time," and with their advertisers who were finding other ways to spend their money. "We don't want them to get into the habit of doing this." In courteously but firmly rebuking Powers, he conceded that the union leader was "trying to overcome some history" but called him unrealistic for trying to accomplish too much overnight. Regarding Powers's claim that the future viability of his union was at stake in the strike, Thayer counterpunched: "The principal issue is money—and it's just that simple," and went on to charge that the union had made no concessions that would reduce the publishers' costs. But that, of course, was to gloss over the unspoken central issue of higher productivity for higher wages. The publishers were demonstrating no initiative in coming forward with a plan that would offer the union real incentives for granting management freedom to modernize their plants.

After a telecast in which they were interviewed from separate rooms in the CBS studios, Thayer and Powers met privately and talked settlement. The Big Six chief stated that he would settle for $16.42, but that was still 60 percent higher than the publishers had been willing to go on the eve of the·strike—too large a gap for them to begin yielding ground. The pair met again for a private lunch on Fourteenth Street, hoping for a breakthrough on a man-to-man basis. Thayer found Powers, a well-tailored Long Island suburbanite married to a Ph.D. who taught high school history, to be several cuts above the usual run of labor leader—"an all-right guy but impossibly stubborn." Powers, a guarded sort with the resolve of a man who has had to fight all the way for his respectability, found Thayer a savvy antagonist and easy to talk to but granted him little trust: "He'd cut your throat out." Still, the *Tribune* president got through to him during one of their talks when, after Powers had argued that the WCC write-offs of the paper's losses and the federal corporate tax rate meant Jock Whitney was really paying only twenty-five cents on every dollar of red ink, Thayer replied, "Yes, but when there are millions of them, it hurts."

After the eighth week of the strike, the printers began to receive unemployment insurance, and in a national referendum the ITU membership voted to contribute 3 percent of its wages to the New York local's strike benefits. Between these funds and their own strike kitty, Big Six members were taking home as much money as when they were working—hardly an incentive to surrender. Other unions were suffering more, but they recognized that Powers was negotiating for all of them and so remained solid behind him. Late in February, President Kennedy stated at a press conference that the New York newspaper strike had gone beyond public endurance and placed the burden of the blame on Powers by name. This denunciation from on high embittered Powers, who had campaigned door to door for his fellow Irish Bostonian in 1960, but reconfirmed him in his role as underdog pitted against the massed might of the politicians and plutocrats. By month's end, though, his price had come down to below fourteen dollars.

After weeks of continuous negotiating at City Hall had worn down the publishers and left them anxious to start up the presses in time to catch the spring and Easter advertising, Mayor Wagner and mediator Theodore Kheel, trusted more by Powers than the publishers, offered both sides a settlement package. Under it, all ten union contracts would expire simultaneously; the printers' workweek would be reduced to thirty-five hours by the simple expedient of eliminating their daily fifteen-minute allowance for wash-up and toilet use; the publishers granted the union the right to share in the savings achieved by use of TTS and other new technology—the papers were free to use outside tape to set the stock market tables but nothing else—with the extent of their sharing to be determined by future negotiation, deadline unspecified; the wage-and-benefit price was $12.63. Even after the negotiators had accepted the deal, which represented a massive triumph for Powers, three weeks were consumed by political infighting among the unions before the settlement was ratified. The papers reappeared on Monday, April 1, 1963, the *Tribune* proclaiming with Densonized exuberance, "Read All About It / Oh, What a Beautiful Morning!"

But there would be scant cause for celebration at the *Tribune* counting table when the fiscal 1963 year closed at the end of April. Losses had reached $4.2 million. Jock Whitney's total investment in the *Tribune* now stood at $16.6 million, and he had just been saddled with an expensive new set of labor contracts that in no way enhanced his paper's prospects.

19

The Trail of
the Blue Darter

or Walter Thayer, the great New York newspaper strike of 1962–63 had
only two positive results. It finally allowed—indeed, it forced—the *Tribune* to raise its price from a nickel to a dime; where else, other than the
deep pockets of Jock Whitney, would the money come from to pay the higher
wages won the strikers? Even before the strike was settled, the *Times,* too, had
decided on the higher price. If it had been as wicked in its rivalry as *Tribune*
people preferred to believe it was, the *Times* might instead have followed the
same course as the *Daily News,* which, aware of the mounting losses of the rival
Mirror, kept up the economic pressure by holding the price line and denying
its faltering competitor badly needed circulation income. The other benefit of
the strike for Thayer was that during its agonizing course he had become a close
friend of Orvil Dryfoos, the gentlemanly publisher of the *Times.* Through their
friendship, Thayer believed he had found the salvation of the *Tribune.*

Dryfoos, a solid, modest, friendly figure, had been handed the reins at the
Times early in 1961 after a twenty-year apprenticeship to his predecessor and
father-in-law, Arthur H. Sulzberger, to whom he bore a close resemblance in
many ways. Both were handsome men of taste, intelligence, quiet dignity, and
dependable nature, raised in German-Jewish mercantile families in New York,
Ivy-educated, and devoted to sustaining the grandeur of the great institution
that Sulzberger's father-in-law, Adolph Ochs, had built. Eager to put his own
stamp on the *Times,* Dryfoos had launched a West Coast edition of the paper

in the fall of 1962, expecting it shortly to attain a circulation of 100,000. How-ever, without a supplementary editorial staff or contents tailored to the regional interests of Western readers, and with the paper's appealing bulkiness reduced by the absence of classified advertising and display ads by New York retailers, the expensive Los Angeles–based branch operation was running into trouble. And the long strike in New York had further frustrated Dryfoos, whose con-ciliatory disposition was not matched by the aloofness of the *Times*'s general manager, Amory Bradford, an able executive who let himself be baited and taunted by Bertram Powers of the printers' union and was replaced in the public eye by Walter Thayer as the prime spokesman for the newspaper publishers. Out of the candid companionship that grew from their united front against the union, Thayer and Dryfoos discussed the possibility of ending the 112-year rivalry between their two papers.

As the strike lengthened, collapsing the momentum the *Tribune* had been building in the fall of 1962, Thayer concluded by the spring of 1963 that if the paper had a future, it was probably in the afternoon field. "It looked like a natural," he recalled. The brighter Denson format would stand up well against the flashy afternoon entries, yet the paper would still clearly be the class of the field. Its staff and resources would also stretch farther in the afternoon, where it would no longer have to offer the comprehensive coverage that its illusory competition with the *Times* demanded. And in James Bellows, Thayer had as his chief editor a man who before joining the *Tribune* had played a key role in building the *Miami News* into one of the best afternoon papers in the country. Most important of all, as Thayer weighed the risks of switching, the *Tribune* could realize major operational economies by selling off its antiquated plant and sharing the production facilities and business staff of the *Times* in return for vacating the morning field and thus allowing its erstwhile rival a lucrative monopoly of the quality market. Just what share of their pooled revenues would be allotted to the Whitney interests would require careful negotiation, but the mutual advantage to the two papers seemed clear to Thayer, who pushed the idea with Dryfoos. The *Times* publisher was receptive.

As the strike wound down, Thayer had his *Tribune* administrator, Robert MacDonald, and his chief financial man at WCC, Robert Bryan, work up projections of a joint venture with the *Times.* MacDonald was especially san-guine. He estimated that the sharing of facilities and personnel other than editorial would save the combined operation between ten and fifteen million a year. The *Times* circulation, fattened by inheriting almost all of the *Tribune*'s former morning readers, would rise to the 900,000 level while the *Tribune*'s afternoon sales were calculated at about 300,000 —figures that would yield some seven million above their combined revenues if the *Tribune* stayed in the morn-ing field. The *Times-Tribune* morning-afternoon combination would become an exceedingly attractive package to advertisers, MacDonald predicted, but even if the linage totals did not rise, the higher circulation would allow for a rate increase producing an additional ten to twelve million. All in all, the *Tribune*'s switchover would mean a gain for the two papers in the $30 to $35 million range, MacDonald asserted—more than half of it stemming from the *Tribune*'s abandonment of the morning field—and "each newspaper would achieve financial strength far greater than either could hope to achieve alone." Bryan, habitually cautious, thought such estimates hard to make with much hope of accuracy and expected that as an "inevitable" part of such a deal with the *Times,* the *Tribune* would have to drop its Sunday edition—a step MacDonald did not contemplate. Thayer, thinking that the *Tribune*'s chances in the afternoon field would be improved by purchase of or amalgamation with one of the current entries, began exploratory talks with Dorothy Schiff, whose *Post,* while marginally in the black, would have been most vulnerable to the *Tribune*'s challenge and made more sense as a takeover candidate than the money-losing chain entries. "I think Walter was after our Jewish readership," said Mrs. Schiff, who was surprised by the *Tribune*'s overtures.

Thayer further strengthened his case with the *Times* by hiring a pair of powerful New York lawyers to attend to potentially troublesome aspects of the projected consolidation. Milton Handler, who was struck by Thayer's eagerness for the deal as the logical way to stem the *Tribune*'s financial hemorrhaging, was confident that the Justice Department of the Kennedy administration, to which he was well connected politically, would raise no objections to the deal on antitrust grounds even though it would represent a lessening of competition by marrying the first and third papers in the city in terms of total advertising revenues. So long as the troubled *Tribune* had vacated the morning field in the interest of its own survival, any charge of a monopolistic tendency could be readily repelled. Theodore Kheel, architect of the 1963 strike settlement, was summoned by Thayer to assure the *Times* management that the unions were not likely to oppose the consolidated operation since it would save jobs that the demise of the *Tribune* would cost.

Before the terms could be thrashed out, the idea had to be presented to the *Times* management for careful assessment. "Dryfoos was for it," Thayer said. And so was his father-in-law. Infirm but still lucid at seventy-two, ex-publisher Sulzberger was almost sentimental in his attitude toward the idea. "He hated more than anything to see a good newspaper die—it tore him up," recalled Sulzberger's son, Arthur. Arthur's sister Marian, who was married to Dryfoos, thought her husband's enthusiasm for absorbing the *Tribune* was a blend of sentiment—the rescuing of a gallant foe—and high practicality; it had the additional virtue of immediately clearing the morning field of a weakened but still feisty competitor, bankrolled by one of America's largest private fortunes. Monroe Green, the advertising director of the *Times,* saw in Dryfoos's support of the *Tribune* venture a vehicle for the publisher's ambition to prove his mettle —here was a relatively low-risk way to add to the *Times*'s grandeur, and at a time when its West Coast edition was showing signs of foundering.

Wearied by the strike, Dryfoos had gone on vacation to Puerto Rico. Stricken by a heart attack, he was flown home to Columbia-Presbyterian Hospital. Thayer went to visit him there and came away reassured of Dryfoos's continuing support of the merger. Ivan Veit, the *Times* business manager, saw Dryfoos shortly after Thayer and corroborated his publisher's backing of the *Tribune* consolidation. Speaking to Veit through an oxygen mask, Dryfoos said, "Do all you can to help this thing." Dryfoos did not leave his hospital bed alive. He died on May 25, 1963, at the age of fifty.

Just four days later, the top brass of the two papers gathered in secret at the Carlton House on Madison Avenue to explore the transaction that would have been a fitting memorial to Orvil Dryfoos. Thayer took the initiative and spoke favorably of a prospective "joining of forces," tactfully avoiding the word "merger." Probably the entire net benefit of the joint venture would be reflected in the *Times* results, Thayer stressed by way of apportioning the likely financial rewards; Jock Whitney's chief ambition in entering into the discussions was the enhanced chance for survival of the *Tribune* by partnership with the *Times,* upon which it ought not to prove a burden in view of the readily realizable economies.

How vital Dryfoos had been to the chances for the deal became apparent at once when Amory Bradford, a possible choice as his successor, answered Thayer for the *Times* by indicating that his people anticipated far smaller savings from the pooled staff and printing arrangement than the *Tribune* was projecting; that the *Times* had in mind a much less binding deal between the two ownerships; and that perhaps the wisest course all around would be for the two staffs to remain entirely independent and for the *Times* to offer the *Tribune* a printing contract at attractive terms. That, of course, would scarcely have rewarded the *Tribune* for vacating the morning field and in no way allowed it the benefit of the *Times*'s broad shoulders to share the burden of its precarious finances. Monroe Green, who a generation earlier had briefly been the *Tribune*'s star advertising salesman, struck a more positive note from the *Times*'s side of the table. From the advertisers' perspective, Green thought, seven New York newspapers made no sense; four were enough—one morning and afternoon paper each to serve the class market and the mass market. The *Times* and the *Tribune,* if switched to the evening field, would be the class papers; the *News,* absorbing the *Mirror* in the morning field, and the merged *Journal-American* and *World-Telegram* (with the *Post* readers scattered between it and the *Tribune*) would be the mass entries. An afternoon *Tribune* could prove "very successful," Green argued, because the New York department stores "feel acutely the need for a quality evening paper," and, furthermore, with home delivery available, the *Tribune*'s circulation could blossom. All that served to make the switchover more inviting to the *Tribune*; none of it addressed the benefits that the *Times* would realize. These Green and the other *Times* executives minimized. He estimated that total advertising gains of a *Times-Tribune* package would probably not exceed five million dollars because of heavy duplicated readership. And the projected higher circulation revenue was a chimera since, even at the new ten-cent price, the *Times* lost three cents on every copy it sold due to heavy labor and material costs. Finally, any real chance of mutual benefits from the deal required the *Tribune* to quit the Sunday field. Advised that the *Tribune* was formulating plans for a radically different kind of Sunday paper that would hardly affect *Times* sales, Green remarked he was doubtful about the prospects of such "experiments."

Despite the sizable gap between the two positions, discussions involving the managements and their lawyers continued throughout 1963. Any real chance for an agreement ended, however, on June 20, when Arthur Ochs Sulzberger, Adolph Ochs's only grandson and then assistant secretary of the *Times*, was named its publisher at the age of thirty-seven. "Punch" Sulzberger had been widely viewed at the paper as an amiable lightweight with little apparent ambition to fulfill his dynastic role. His sunny disposition and wandering attention had not made a student of him; at seventeen, he joined the marines and saw action in the Pacific during World War II. The experience toughened and focused him; he did well at Columbia, passably on the family paper as a reporter, and endured a broken first marriage, recall to military service during the Korean War, and training stints at the *Milwaukee Journal* and in the Paris bureau of the *Times*. When he came home, he assisted his father but was not jumped up the ranks or to the top as Helen Reid had imposed her sons on the *Tribune*. "You don't inherit the ability to run any business—you've got go learn it from the ground up," remarked Punch Sulzberger's mother, Iphigene, in contrasting his grooming for the *Times* throne with that of the Reid boys. Whitie "lacked confidence"; Brown Reid "had pep, but they pushed him too fast. We sent Punch to Milwaukee—you can learn a lot working where you're not the boss's son." And when Punch worked in Paris, he went as the low man in the five-man *Times* bureau, Mrs. Sulzberger noted; Brown, only a year older than Punch, went to the Paris *Tribune* as its boss. A far more modest young man than the *Tribune*'s dark prince, Punch Sulzberger recognized his own limitations and, upon inheriting the crown from his brother-in-law without having been adequately trained for the responsibility, listened carefully to the professionals surrounding him before reaching judgments.

Among his first decisions was one scuttling any deal with the *Tribune*. His family may have been sentimental about the idea; Punch Sulzberger was not. "I was the hardnosed one," he recalled of the proposal, which he felt "did not make any long-term sense to me. For the good of *The New York Times* I thought we'd be better off letting nature take its course." But out of deference to his father and late brother-in-law, Sulzberger let the talks drag on. The *Times* lawyers, headed by former U.S. Attorney General Herbert Brownell, kept raising objections in what the *Tribune*'s attorney, Milton Handler, remembered as "a very pleasant, very courteous way," until he concluded they were simply stalling and so advised Walter Thayer. If Dryfoos had lived, Thayer estimated the chances were at least even that the deal would have gone through; Veit of the *Times*, who strongly opposed it, thought Dryfoos would surely have brought the proposal to his board of directors, where "it might well have carried." Punch was "very young and very, very inexperienced," a wistful Thayer recounted. He was also to prove as tough-minded and unsentimental as Thayer. The bottom line began to matter now at the *Times* as it had not since Adolph Ochs's early days at the helm. In January 1964, Punch shut down his brother-in-law's ill-considered Western edition. Unlike Walter Thayer, however, as the ensuing decades would demonstrate, Arthur O. Sulzberger turned himself into a newspaperman.

II

The fallout from the strike was worse than feared. Circulation losses, expected because of the doubled newsstand price, were heavy at both the *Times* and the *Tribune* but proportionately far worse at the latter, with its far smaller reader-ship base. Advertising suffered accordingly.

Yet Jock Whitney had not lost heart. In a mid-July memo to Walter Thayer, James Bellows, and Robert MacDonald, his principal subordinates, he wrote that "the Trib is the only really *interesting* newspaper I know," and that "lots of people" were telling him, "I'm crazy about your paper."

Thayer, depressed by the numbers and stymied by the *Times*'s stalling on his proposal for a joint operation, was less than enthusiastic in response. He conceded that the post-strike *Tribune* was proving to be "an improved, interest-ing and exciting newspaper" and that he, too, heard good words about it. But he found "a very special danger" in their being lulled by "what our mass of readers and our bigger mass of non-readers think" as a guide to the paper's chances of successfully competing in the killing New York market. He added his "serious doubts" that the *Tribune* was succeeding in its avowed aim of expertly compacting the news for busy readers while interpreting it authorita-tively for more attentive ones.

Whitney's ardor was unquenchable. Even when the paper launched a major muckraking series titled "Our Sideline Legislators: A Double Standard of Eth-ics" by reporters Richard Madden and Martin Steadman early in August, Whit-ney seemed not to mind that among its prime targets were leading figures in the New York Republican Party, of which he was a major financial supporter. In an expansive August 13 memo he wrote of his aspirations to own a newspaper that was "at once humane and practical" and might save New York "from the fright-ening prospect of dependence on the Times." Because television, with its inevita-ble oversimplification, "puts a premium on glibness, on photogenics, on all the qualities we normally associate with show business rather than public policy . . . [w]e have to catch and hold readers by making the facts themselves more interest-ing." In helping to meet that challenge, he regretted acutely his lack of newspaper background, which "makes me hesitant to exercise a firm, direct operational control" on the paper; instead, he had to settle for trying to give it "style and direction," thus granting Jim Bellows—whose title had by then been upgraded from managing editor to editor—maximum freedom to do his best, "which I think we're discovering is very good indeed." But because Thayer, to whom the memo was directed, bore "the principal and legal responsibility for the paper's fortunes and performance" in his capacity as president and chief operating officer, and because Thayer knew "how deeply I respect your judgment and your ideas," Whitney wanted his thinking to be heard in the editorial councils of the *Tribune* and to find its way frequently into the paper itself.

Thayer's pointed response ten days later revealed the widening divergence between him and Whitney in their evaluation of the *Tribune*'s virtues. Thayer did not share Whitney's admiration for Bellows's editorial touch, citing especially a tendency he detected toward too many "cryptic and uninviting" headlines and the horizontal makeup of inside pages with overblown four-, five-, and six-column heads that served to expand rather than compact the news presentation. Most of all, Thayer lamented "the lack of a definite personality or image that reflects our purpose and intent. . . . One ought to know what to expect when he picks up the paper"—next to which Whitney wrote "NO" in the margin and underscored it three times. This alleged lack of personality was particularly apparent on the editorial page, Thayer felt, and was evidenced in unpredictability, which he rated as much a character defect in a newspaper as in a man: "I think if a newspaper is not predictable it suggests that it hasn't a mind of its own"—a judgment which drew from Whitney the marginal scrawl "Disagree."

As to his own participation, Thayer made it plain that he was a conscript and not a volunteer in his role as operational head of the paper and that it was Whitney, not he, who was "responsible for the paper's fortune and performance and this is a responsibility that you cannot delegate to someone else." The best business organization in the world "cannot make a success out of a poor editorial product," he said, then noted that "the aftermath of the strike is beyond the worst apprehensions of any of us"—the fact that all the papers in the city had been badly hurt was irrelevant—and that it would take "a long, long time and very substantial additional losses" for the *Tribune* to get back to where it had been before the strike. "Now you can afford this. The available cash throw from WCC is ample to meet projected losses. The decision, therefore, as to the value of the paper to you—and, as you see it, to New York and the country—can only be assessed by you." Thayer's own position from the start, he said, had been that WCC ought not to contribute to the *Tribune* "beyond the point where it became clear that it could not stand on its own feet," and until then he had felt it could achieve self-sufficiency even though "some of our associates have taken the position this was wishful thinking on our part." Now, however, Walter Thayer had joined them: "I cannot . . . any longer honestly say I believe this goal to be attainable within the bounds of any reasonable outlay. I find myself, therefore, in a very difficult position with our associates. . . . [I]f the decision is to continue indefinitely you must make it clear that this is *your* plan and intention." Indefinite subsidy of the paper by WCC would stifle the initiatives of the parent company's "better people," Thayer concluded, striking the same chord he had struck when Whitney returned home from London two and a half years earlier—but it had a far more funereal resonance to it now.

The realities with which Thayer was confronting Whitney were manifest in the circulation figures tabulated at the end of September. For the six months following the strike, the *Tribune*'s weekday sales averaged 282,000—a decline of more than 50,000 midway through the five-year recovery plan set up at the end of Whitney's ambassadorship, a drop of 77,000 from the year-earlier figure (the *Times* was off by 78,000), and nearly 130,000 below the paper's pre-strike peak. In mid-October, two weeks after these appalling numbers were tallied, the Hearst Corporation announced that the New York *Daily Mirror,* with the second-highest circulation of any newspaper in the United States, was going out of business. The city was down to six papers.

As circumstances conspired ever more perilously against the *Tribune,* John Hay Whitney seemed to grow in stubborn gallantry. He would neither heed the judgment of his most trusted adviser nor reach into his personal fortune, beyond the arbitrarily limited corporate machinery assembled for the rescue mission, and move boldly by acquisition, merger, or technological innovation to confound the fates. Instead, he invested his hopes for remission of the *Tribune*'s apparently terminal illness in the editorial and human skills of forty-one-year-old James Gilbert Bellows, an elusive figure who coursed through the paper with the speed and trajectory of an arrow on an urgent, endless mission.

A native of Detroit, raised mostly in Ohio, educated at a small Connecticut prep school and Kenyon, one of the best small liberal-arts colleges in the country, Bellows unaccountably had about him the aura of a Southwesterner, the lean, rugged, resolute look of a man of brief words and decisive action. He might have stepped out of a Gary Cooper horse opera or a Marlboro cigarette advertisement as the hero-cowboy, to judge by the haunted earnestness in that low, soft twang of his or the intentness behind those strong dark eyes and firm brow. He was nobody to have against you.

Bellows had shown no interest in journalism until he was twenty-four—indeed, his mother had nourished hopes he might enter the ministry—when he completed his college work after a distinguished record as a wartime navy flier and joined the *Columbus Ledger* in southwestern Georgia as a cub reporter. On the job about a year, he caught wind of plans for a mass mountaintop gathering of the Ku Klux Klan and, joined by a photographer and another reporter, managed to witness the fiery proceedings before being detected, forced to drink himself into an alcoholic stupor, and placed unconscious in a compromising position with one of his colleagues in the back of a car that was left conveniently accessible to the police. Bellows's story was all over the front page. He had more courage, though, than writing talent; his real journalistic strength was working on the desk, appraising what was news, deploying staff, and all the time feeding his hunger to learn his craft—the uses of type, the power of print to come alive with the pulse of the community. Deskmen were generally sedentary sorts; Jim Bellows prowled the offices he worked with a chain-smoking restlessness that hinted of an inner turmoil. But all that sublimated energy produced on-the-job results. After serving as city and state editor of the *Ledger,* he moved to the *Atlanta Journal,* which had probably the most talented city room in the South at the time, and rose over five years to news editor, starting to demonstrate now the quiet authority that would become his trademark. "He was bright and bold and a horse for work," recalled Eugene Patterson, then editor of the *Journal.* But there was the bleakness of the loner about him, too. "Nobody ever really gets to know him," Patterson said of Bellows. "He reminds me of a man standing alone in a dark room, looking out into the bright sunlight and worrying about something."

His skills were further refined by the demanding standards of Lee Hills during a two-year stay at the *Detroit Free Press,* where Bellows worked on the copy and city desks and with the arts and magazine departments. Then Patterson boosted him for his first major position, managing editor of the *Miami News,* under the same ownership as the Atlanta papers and a distant also-ran to the Knight-owned *Miami Herald.* Bellows immediately brought fresh life to the paper, helping it capture the beat and mood of the new oceanfront metropolis. "He was a very enterprising, innovative competitor," said Lee Hills, who by then was supervising both the Detroit and Miami outlets of the Knight chain. Bellows's witty superior, editor William Baggs, nicknamed his cheerless-looking managing editor "Sunny Jim" and, alternately, "the Blue Darter" for his perpetual motion. Three years in Miami earned him a reputation as one of the best news mechanics in the business—precisely what Walter Thayer convinced John Denson he needed to get the *Herald Tribune* out on schedule. Fascinated by Denson's typographic and conceptual innovations, the quick-learning Bellows had to walk on eggshells not to antagonize his crotchety new boss yet retain his own professional dignity. But in less than a year Denson was out, and when Jock Whitney decided to promote from within, the quiet, efficient, somber Blue Darter was put in charge.

Like Denson, Bellows had an agglutinative kind of mind—or, as one *Tribune* city-room wag put it, "He stole well." With his highly pragmatic intelligence, he borrowed or adapted whatever ideas he thought would work to turn out a brighter, hipper, yet sounder paper than the one he had inherited. Compactly packaging the news and distilling its essence in instantaneous interpretations were useful borrowings from news-weekly journalism, but Bellows recognized that, when carried over to a daily paper with its merciless time and space demands, they inevitably invited superficiality of treatment, hyped headlines, and purple prose. Denson's genius had been the intricate format he devised; through excitement of presentation, it provided as much stimulus to readership as Bellows thought legitimate. To claim more for a story than the facts, backed by judicious judgment, warranted was to degrade the integrity of the news hole, and he would not do that.

He differed sharply from Denson in two personal traits as well. Secure in his own gifts and limitations, Bellows was unthreatened by the talents of others, readily encouraged them, and knew how to delegate to those whose skills and character he trusted. Also unlike Denson, he hated confrontations yet managed to leave no one around him in doubt about who was in charge. His style of leadership was an amalgam of authentic shyness, projected humility, and studied inarticulation. His low, country-boy speech trailed off like whiffs of smoke in baffling ambiguity—"You couldn't ever really hear him," recalled Judith Crist—and his hands would fill in the interstices with busy milling motions or describe airy geometric shapes or tie a fancy bow, as if to finish off his cryptic instruction with a flourish, and then off he would dart. His elusiveness had a seductive quality to it—"You sort of wanted to help him out," Earl Ubell recalled. And if you had done your work well, he would let you know, and then the next time he came by with his gesturing hands and half-heard mumblings, you knew what he meant, more or less. What was unmistakable in his manner was that beneath those vaporous words, behind that steel-edge look, a very private, very self-contained man of mystery cared deeply about his mission and was waging war with a combative tension coiled just below the surface. If you did not share his purpose, his body English made plain, you had no business being there. He inspired, then, not by dread, as Denson had, but by letting the staff know it was needed; wiser than Denson in his personnel dealings, he never fancied himself a one-man band.

And he knew how to use his subordinates. The commonsensical Buddy Weiss, as open and wisecracking as Bellows was clenched and serious, ran the city staff like a lovable morale officer. Large, big-hearted, blustering Seymour Freidin was understood to be a cold warrior, and his prose and judgments in the handling of foreign news were now monitored accordingly. Freidin's principal value to Bellows was as a bulky protector against Walter Thayer, whom the editor deeply distrusted and did his best to avoid. Bellows's marital status figured importantly in the rift between them. Married to a Georgia woman while working at his first newspaper job and the father of two children, Bellows became romantically involved in 1962 with Maggie Savoy, the women's editor of *The Arizona Republic,* whom he met during an Associated Press convention in New York; like him, she was married and had children. Their affair persisted across the continent, largely by phone and mail, until Maggie's husband died in a car accident, and she drove her white Lincoln Continental to New York —an earthy, easygoing, vibrant woman, casual about her looks and dress, with a great wide beautiful smile that thoroughly demolished the editor of the *Herald Tribune.* His wife, seven months pregnant, declined to give him a divorce. The day he brought her home from the hospital with their third child, he moved out of their suburban home and into an apartment with Maggie. "It was a terrible thing to do," Bellows conceded, "but it was something I could not keep myself from doing. Call it star-crossed—whatever." His wife called it something else as she sailed into the *Tribune* office one day and drew blood from him with a well-aimed candy dish that belonged to Bellows's secretary. Thayer sympathetically recommended the services of a lawyer friend to Bellows to help him out of his unhappy situation, but in time Bellows heard reports that Thayer was characterizing him as emotionally unstable, hardly the kind of man to pilot the paper at so critical a moment, and Bellows never forgave him.

Although Si Freidin was useful to Bellows as an intimidating presence against Thayer, Bellows found his foreign news chief increasingly unreliable in his professional capacity and persuaded him to transfer his base of operations to London at the end of 1963 and to delegate the line work to Harry Rosenfeld, the effervescent young cable editor who was as skilled and controlled a rewriteman as Freidin was not. Freidin's dispatches, filed several times weekly, got sanitized in New York, an arrangement that left him increasingly embittered, but the civilities between him and the home office continued to be observed. Rosenfeld meanwhile learned just how careful Bellows expected his editors to be. One day Bellows had blamed him for letting something get by in a dispatch from Sanche de Gramont, so the next day Rosenfeld went over de Gramont's follow-up piece with special care, only to earn another Bellows rebuke, this time for messing unnecessarily with the correspondent's copy. "You mean I'm damned if I do and damned if I don't?" he asked. "That's right," Bellows replied; each story was a separate test of an editor's judgment, and he was as accountable for his actions as the reporter. "I was being defensive about my ego," Rosenfeld remembered, "and the point he was making was that you don't invest your ego in the decisions you make—you invest it in what appears in the paper finally. You're making decisions all day long, and what may look like a five-inch story at 11 a.m. may wind up a twenty-three-inch story in the first edition. A good newspaperman has to roll with the punch, constantly reevaluating the story."

With Freidin gone, Bellows relied increasingly on Weiss and even more on his thirty-three-year-old national news editor, Richard C. Wald, who had a cold streak in him that occasionally suggested arrogance. If he was not beloved throughout the city room for his glib intellect—no one like him had risen so high on the paper since the departure of Joseph Barnes fourteen years earlier—his keen knack for analyzing the components of a big story and knowing how to attack them made Dick Wald a valuable adjutant. He also had one special friend on the paper who gave him unique power, and Bellows knew it.

Supposing the American ambassador to be a man of great dignity and rather forbidding nature, Wald got his first look at Jock Whitney in his large overcoat and hat, entirely filling the doorway of the private dining room at London's deluxe Connaught Hotel, and feared his anxiety had been warranted. But as Whitney, peeling off his coat, moved toward Wald and Don Cook, his London correspondents, with whom he was to dine, he burbled, "I'm a couple of drinks behind, from the looks of you two," and gave every sign of being decidedly human. After a gingerly start to their conversation, they all warmed up, and Wald began to tell himself that the multimillionaire diplomat was just like everyone else. He laughed heartily, spoke well and not without charm, asked a lot of intelligent questions, and loved to hear the latest scuttlebutt. Whitney, in turn, was delighted with young Wald, who was very sure of himself and had a silver tongue that could be both witty and withering. Possessor of a bachelor's and a master's degree from Columbia, Wald had done advanced work in Cambridge on a fellowship in anticipation of a career as a professor of literature, but the excitement of journalism proved a greater lure. His brightness and cultivation were all too apparent in his early years on the paper, but this phase passed and Wald's undeniable gifts as a writer and thinker tagged him as a comer. His arrival at a top job just seven years after joining the *Tribune* full-time inspired envy; many said Bellows picked him for national editor because he was "Jock's boy" and knew how to drink tea correctly with Betsey Whitney. To city-room veterans, Dick Wald had not paid his dues before being raised to power over them. Perhaps not, but once installed, he proved a huge asset. Bellows found in him a man of calm and reliable news judgment, an excellent liaison with the Washington bureau, and a crack writer who could be thrown into the breach whenever something really important had to be composed—a rewrite on a six-column lead, a particularly tricky "precede," a memo to management. "It wasn't that Jim was incapable of communicating with Jock directly," Wald recounted, "but that he didn't much like explaining himself. He was a doer rather than a justifier . . . most comfortable simply working the paper. By default, I became his interpreter to Jock and Walter."

The arrangement worked because Bellows trusted Wald, and with Weiss they formed a solid triumvirate, their complementary natures smoothly meshing; they radiated energy and dedication that permeated the office. "It was a very healthy place to work," recalled Jane Noakes, Bellows's secretary. "There was a lot of joy there. People weren't looking over their shoulders for the knives."

III

In moderating the excesses of the Densonized *Tribune,* Jim Bellows well understood the virtues of his predecessor's techniques and adapted them whenever possible, especially in framing a big emotional story like the August 28, 1963, march on Washington by black civil rights protesters. In its graphic presentation, it was Denson at his best. Where the *Times* ran two big photos of the marchers as massed clots of humanity seen from a great distance and headlined the story "200,000 MARCH FOR CIVIL RIGHTS / IN ORDERLY WASHINGTON RALLY; / PRESIDENT SEES GAIN FOR NEGRO," the *Tribune* depicted a single black youth in prayer with the great rally reflected in his glasses and bannered the story "Marching Into History" with the subhead "A Triumph With A Clear Meaning." In the age of television everyone in the country knew of the event.

The *Times* recorded it for posterity; the *Tribune* tried to render the poetic feeling of the shared spectacle. Robert Bird's *Tribune* account began:

WASHINGTON.

The Negro march on Washington yesterday turned out to be a profoundly moving demonstration—so big, so orderly, so sweet-singing and good-natured, so boldly confident and at the same time relaxed, so completely right from start to finish, that America was done proud beyond measure.

But Bellows understood better than Denson that the collective human spirit did not soar or plummet every day to meet the editor's need to sell papers, and he did not exploit the format unduly. His restraint somewhat flattened the *Tribune*'s exuberant personality as reinvented by his predecessor, but it made for more honest journalism.

Bellows and his team also moved to strengthen the paper by eliminating features that lacked substance or sparkle—or, as in the case of Hy Gardner's show-business gossip, both. Gardner's daily pieces, they felt, had become a compilation of plugs and name-droppings, not truly gossipy and of scant interest to the younger readership they were seeking for the paper. Judith Crist was offered an opportunity to create a livelier, meatier celebrity column, but when she asked for a real staff to do the job right, the idea was dropped. Gardner was let go a few months later. By then, though, Crist was filling another urgent need that had gone unattended since Whitney took over the paper.

In the late 'Forties and early 'Fifties, Otis Guernsey had functioned with critical integrity as the *Tribune*'s movie reviewer, although he endured hectoring from executive vice president William Robinson for allegedly costing the paper substantial advertising linage from the Hollywood studios because he was too often negative in his opinions. Guernsey was finally asked to switch jobs with drama section editor William Zinsser, who turned out to be even bolder in his naysaying. When Brown Reid had Zinsser retired to the editorial page—an event followed instantly by an increase in the paper's movie advertising by the perpetrators of some of the most ridiculous blockbusters ever committed to film —the new critic, Paul Beckley, took the hint, and the *Tribune*'s historically stringent critical standards in the arts were compromised in the movie department. Then Bellows asked Judith Crist, who had advanced from reporter to arts editor, to take over the job.

An emphatic, unpretentious writer, Crist left readers in no doubt of her opinion of the movies she reviewed. Among her early victims was Warner Bros.' production of *Spencer's Mountain,* which Crist crushed for its "smirking sexuality, its glorification of the vulgar, its patronizing tone toward the humble." To humble Crist—and the *Tribune,* for replacing a bonbon-dispenser with a how-itzer—Warner Bros. took its advertising out of the paper, and Radio City Music Hall, which was showing the "cheap and tasteless" film, as the reviewer called it, heavily cut its space allotment. The *Tribune* editorialized: "We feel sorry for film producers who consider themselves above criticism, and we are amazed that distinguished establishments like Warner and Radio City should stoop to such discredited and ineffectual practices as dropping advertising. They injure their own reputations, and hurt the critic not at all."

Crist was just getting warmed up. In mid-June 1963 she went to see the most trumpeted extravaganza of the age, Walter Wanger's $30 million production of *Cleopatra,* starring Elizabeth Taylor and Richard Burton, whose real-life romance would prove more memorable than the celluloid version. Crist appraised the title performance thus:

> Miss Taylor's costumes are nothing short of sensational and her doing without any at all in a couple of scenes is equally impressive. But the fallacy is, alas, that neither her costumes nor her performance leaves anything to the imagination. We have on hand a rather unsubtle siren, a blatantly ambitious beauty in search of a man to conquer the world for her, with not even the illusion or suggestion of that eternally mysterious woman whose fascination would outlast the centuries.

Her review was headlined "A Monumental Mouse." The morning it appeared, Crist arrived at the paper to find a note on her desk saying, "Call Mr. Whitney's office." Her heart sank. "After all, it was the first $30 million film," she recalled, and she had already cost the paper revenue. She rang Whitney's extension. He was out. But his secretary, Kathryn Ritchie, told Crist that he just wanted her to know how much he had enjoyed her review. Soon afterward, her outspoken opinions won her a moonlighting job on the "Today" show, with its audience in the millions, and between her print and TV outlets, she became perhaps the most influential movie reviewer in the country.

Bellows sustained a serious loss in September 1963 with the defection of his Washington bureau chief, Robert Donovan, to the *Los Angeles Times.* In his place, as part of the youth movement that characterized the *Tribune* under Bellows, went David Wise, thirty-three, just back from a leave of absence after co-authoring a book on covert U.S. intelligence activities, *The Invisible Government,* that was destined to become a bestseller the following year. Wise accepted the job on the condition that he would have a major say in the selection, assignment, and play of stories; that the bureau would not be expected to dance like a puppet at the other end of the telephone lines from New York as it had been required to under Denson; that Wise himself rather than Bellows or Wald would do the hiring for the bureau, which had to be substantially rebuilt with the post-strike departure of veterans Earl Mazo, Don Irwin, Warren Rogers, and Marguerite Higgins;* and that Jock Whitney would provide a bigger budget and larger, more attractive quarters for the Washington operation. Wise's crew of a dozen, now including talented newcomers Douglas Kiker and Dom Bonafede, was raw but energetic, and thanks to the independence granted them by New York, their morale was high and their performance creditable.

---

* Higgins, her star dimmed at the *Tribune,* joined *Newsday* as a syndicated columnist. Covering the war in Vietnam, she contracted a fatal tropical disease and died in 1966 at the age of forty-five. She was buried in Arlington National Cemetery.

Bellows, detecting a case of creeping old-fogeyism in the all-star array of *Tribune*-syndicated Washington columnists, moved to brighten the department by teaming his Capitol Hill correspondent, Rowland Evans, with a transferee from *The Wall Street Journal*—Robert Novak—in a daily column that was more concerned with nuts-and-bolts politics and behind-the-scenes maneuverings than cosmic analyses. They seemed an unlikely pairing: Evans, forty-one, the fair, slender, debonair socialite from the Philadelphia Main Line, who aspired to Joe Alsop's role as the ranking poobah-in-residence of Georgetown; Novak, thirty-two, darker, shorter, rumpled, a graduate of the unstylish University of Illinois, and incurably gloom-ridden. But they worked hard and well together, preferring the right side of the political boulevard, and while their work was sometimes strident, they showed early on that they knew what they were writing about. Their very first "Inside Report," in May 1963, predicted that Barry Goldwater, widely viewed as a political Neanderthal among the Eastern Republicans who read the *Tribune,* had a good chance to win the GOP presidential nomination the following year. Part of their ensuing success and longevity—the Evans-and-Novak byline has lasted nearly a quarter of a century, longer than that of any other syndicated pair in American journalism—stemmed from a brand of liberal-bashing and Soviet-skewering rare among Washington columnists then in vogue.

The *Tribune*'s Washington-based coverage gained still more strength with the transplantation there of the paper's most successful expatriate talent, Art Buchwald. Until 1962, he had been a curiosity, a touch of escapist humor amid a diet of often grim journalistic fare. Now, after fourteen years abroad, having hunted big game in the Congo to prove how yellow he was, having toured the Soviet Union in a chauffeur-driven Chrysler Imperial with a big cigar stuck in his face to prove how capitalistic he was, and having been arrested for wearing swim trunks on the streets of Paris after dark on the way to the Beaux Arts Ball to prove how irreverent he was, Buchwald felt that at thirty-five he had nothing left to prove overseas and wanted to test his skills back home. "All my friends told me I'd go down the tube," he recalled. But it was a risk that his instincts told him he had to take.

The question was where he should install himself. He wanted to deal satirically with real social issues, to be funny about essentially serious stuff—and the only locale that he thought suitable was the nation's capital. The challenge was so daunting that his first act upon settling in Washington was to suffer a nervous breakdown that put him in a hospital for six weeks.

On his recovery, the wisdom of his decision became quickly apparent. Closeness to all that power gave him plenty of subjects to play with; the Washington dateline gave his pieces immediacy. To keep his column fresh he refused to write in advance, preferring to work along the edge of the news and delivering his copy as close to deadline as possible. His overwhelming success—the number of papers carrying his column would climb from 85 when he started in Washington to 450 by the end of the 'Sixties—stemmed from two factors. First, he knew precisely what he was doing: turning out a political cartoon in words, a tight 500 to 550 of them, working with a single idea that he usually carried *ad absurdum.* Second, his satire stung but rarely lacerated. "I try to get the sword in and out before they know they've been savaged," he once told an interviewer. As a result, he was the recipient of a license the nation bestows upon no more than one or two social commentators per generation. Mark Twain and Will Rogers were probably the most successful authorized practitioners of the art before Buchwald, and in his own generation, only television comedian Johnny Carson rivaled him as a popular ribber of the politically mighty. Thus, Buchwald could write, without fear of repercussion, a piece claiming that sacred cow J. Edgar Hoover was actually a fictional character created by *Reader's Digest.* As the civil rights struggle intensified, he lampooned the viciousness of diehard bigotry by writing of how a black Rhodes Scholar with a Ph.D. from MIT, trying to win the right to vote in Bull Whip, Alabama, had to fight his way through a sheriff's posse, penetrate a cloud of tear gas put down by the state police, and o'erleap a hundred cattle prods brandished by jeering rednecks to reach the county registrar's office, which was open only from 11:55 till midnight on the sixth Saturday of the month, and after proving his literacy by reading three pages from a Chinese newspaper, hieroglyphics from the Rosetta Stone, and the first fourteen articles of the Finnish constitution, was finally asked by his examiner, "Would you be so kind as to read to me any two of these Dead Sea Scrolls?" When he stumbles over a word on the second one, the applicant is invited to try again the following year; when the next candidate, a white, is asked to spell "cat" and replies, "K-A-T," Buchwald's examiner says, in the tag line, "Try again. You're getting warm."

Such excoriating satire by Buchwald was occasionally run verbatim in the Soviet press, without any note of explanation, to demonstrate the injustices of life in America. Apprised that his handiwork was being put to such subversive uses by the Russians, Buchwald would look horrified, remove his cigar, and cry, "Stop them!"

IV

Of all James Bellows's efforts to strengthen the *Tribune,* none was more striking than his willingness to take chances on new young writers, whom he encouraged to work in whatever style made them comfortable and who understood, as Dick Wald stated in a memo reflecting the top editors' philosophy, that "there is no mold for a newspaper story." The reporter's chief obligation, wrote Wald, was to tell the truth, "and the truth often lies in the way a man said something, the pitch of his voice, the hidden meaning in his words, the speed of the circumstances"; the real story may be found in "the exact deployment of the characters in the cast" or any of a great many other details that "make up the recognizable graininess of life to the readers." Most of all, the paper was looking for writing with "a strong mixture of the human element," articles that were "readable *stories*, not news reports written to embellish a page of record." Among the newcomers capable of producing such work, three were especially notable.

Gail Sheehy, a slim, red-haired, green-eyed graduate of the University of Vermont with a couple of years of experience in department-store merchandising and two more reporting on fashion in Rochester, joined Eugenia Sheppard's staff in the summer of 1963, drawn by what she felt were the best women's pages of any U.S. newspaper—"they danced with life, energy, and imagination." What they did not do was address serious social problems of women. Sheppard tended to ignore or cosmeticize concerns of the young and the aged, of mothers over childbearing, of tenants driven into rent strikes to obtain minimal household amenities, of Harlem women on drugs. "People with problems were boring to her," Sheehy recalled, while those with money and taste and power captivated her. Their parties and the whole social whirl they generated drew her in and dominated the *Tribune*'s women's pages. Then one day, Gail Sheehy, midway through pregnancy, decided to make the rounds of the city's maternity clinics to see what free services were available to impoverished expectant mothers, of whom she pretended to be one. The results stunned and saddened her, and she wrote them up. Sheppard was not overjoyed, but Bellows backed the initiative of the new reporter, and daily journalism's most potent arbiter of fashion and the high life began to have her social consciousness raised. It was the beginning as well of Sheehy's career as a chronicler of American living patterns and value systems and as a wise instructor in crisis management.

The most exotic figure among the gifted newcomers to the *Tribune* city room was the trim, six-foot, white-suited frame of Thomas Kennerly Wolfe, Jr., whose modish like had not been seen there since the departure of the exquisitely got-up Lucius Beebe a dozen years earlier. And no one quite so literary had performed for the paper since Bayard Taylor a century before. Wolfe was a certified intellectual with a doctorate in American studies from Yale. Besides his wardrobe and his brains, he brought a clinical eye, sardonic sensibility, omnivorous curiosity, and remarkably placid temperament to his work as he helped redefine the permissible limits of American journalism.

The son of an agronomy professor at Virginia Polytechnic Institute, Tom Wolfe was raised in Richmond and graduated from Washington and Lee. After a dreamy five-year immersion in New Haven postgraduate academia, he decided that there was too much fun and angst going on out there in the world to turn himself into a cloistered don. He served his newspapering apprenticeship at the Springfield, Massachusetts, *Union* and moved on to *The Washington Post*, where every time he turned out something fresh and original, he found himself assigned to a story on sewerage in Prince Georges County. It was not long before he presented a carefully composed scrapbook of his clippings to Buddy Weiss, who grabbed him for the *Herald Tribune*'s twilight time of life.

Feature writing used to mean a relaxation of traditional journalistic restraints; features usually involved good news or happy endings or odd characters —in contrast to the preponderantly grim tidings that editors defined as "news" —and reporters were invited to respond playfully. Not many had the creative knack. For Tom Wolfe, all of New York life was a single sublime feature. He did not construct his stories like anyone else. He would plunge into them *in medias res,* drolly painting the scene and happily twirling images to tantalize the reader before doubling back to supply comprehensibility. His stories were not so much about events as their circumstances; the real news he brought seemed to say: look, this is how people are living and behaving now. His first notable piece, about a rent strike by NYU students, ran on the split page on April 13, 1962, and began:

> There have been some tough acts to follow in the field of social protest this season. We have had the sit-in, the sit-down, the hunger strike, the freedom ride, the boycott, the picket line and the marathon march.
>
> But until yesterday in the Bronx when had Americans managed to protest with such stylish fillips as the Hypnotic Hair-Combing Co-ed, the Laugh Bandit, the All-Night Yo-Yo Contest and Great Moments from the Bard?

They'll never go with it, Wolfe told himself. But they did; it was fun, inventive, and most decidedly not *The New York Times*—or any other paper. Used to the tight space requirements of the *Post* in Washington, Wolfe would ask how long he should make his pieces, and day city editor Dan Blum would tell him, "Until it gets boring."

During the inactivity of the long strike, Bellows and his editors recognized Wolfe's extraordinary gifts and resolved to put them on prominent exhibit in the paper whenever possible. And a good thing, for by then he was doing pieces for *Esquire* and being romanced by *Newsweek,* which wanted to give him a column but could not allocate enough space to accommodate his expansive prose. The week the strike ended, a Wolfe story headlined "King Hassan's Bazaar" ran boxed across the entire top of page one—a jaunty account of a buying spree by the playboy ruler of Morocco, in Manhattan with his entourage. Bellows led with Wolfe's romp not merely because it was interesting and fun to read on a relatively slow news day but also because it was a manifestation of a new kind of journalism, one that said that how people lived their lives was as important and meaningful to report on as the official news dispensed by governments and institutions. Wolfe's piece was about how New York retailing worked, about how absolute monarchs lavished wealth, about taste and greed and a few other things that were at least as newsworthy as orthodox front-page fare.

At the end of that summer, Wolfe did his last front-pager before the paper began featuring him in the finally revamped Sunday edition that first appeared in September. The story was trivial on its face, about a bunch of rich kids turned vandals at a debutante party three days earlier; the city desk caught wind of it from a passing reference in a *Mirror* column. Working entirely in the office, Wolfe got the deb party's young hostess, a Wanamaker heiress named Fernanda Wetherill, on the telephone and turned out a piece of revealing social reportage. It began:

> True, all the furniture was on the beach and all the sand was in the living room. And there were holes the size of Harrateen easy chairs and Philadelphia bow-front sidetables in the casement windows on the ocean side. And socially-registered rock throwers had demolished about 1,634 of a possible 1,640 panes from both directions, outside and in—making cotton broker Robert M. Harriss' 40-room mansion at Southampton, L.I., the Ladd House, the most monumental piece of rubble in the history of American debutante party routs.
>
> But what were 100 kids who had come skipping and screaming out of the Social Register for a deb ball weekend in the Hamptons supposed to do after the twist band packed up and went home? Hum "Wipe Out" or "Surf City" to themselves and fake it?

The scene *was* the story to Wolfe, and he took the reader to it instantly, and to enrich it graphically when he had no time to get out to the other end of Long Island and back, he artfully embellished.

Wolfe was at his best dealing with the overprivileged; the other new man to whom Bellows gave extreme stylistic latitude—Jimmy Breslin—excelled at the opposite end of the social spectrum. Breslin's work, while less artful than Wolfe's, had a heavier-duty usefulness because of its elemental emotionalism, generally free of sentimentality. Both could write with wit and color, with an acute ear for speech patterns and a discerning eye for dress and furnishings and eating habits, but it was Breslin, the fat, fierce, self-absorbed swaggerer from the rough Ozone Park section of Queens, who more than any other writer on the staff came to represent the social journalism, with its intensity of feeling and poignant ironies, that the *Herald Tribune* was exploring at the end of its life.

Bellows had been looking for a new kind of columnist when he read a new book called *'Can't Anybody Here Play This Game?'*—a comedy of errors about the first season of the New York Mets, who happened to be owned by Jock Whitney's sister, Joan Payson. It was written by an iconoclastic sportswriter who had worked for Long Island papers, the *Boston Globe,* the Scripps-Howard syndicate, and the *Journal-American* and was now free-lancing. He had done an earlier book on the legendary horse trainer "Sunny Jim" Fitzsimmons; Whitney read both books and shared Bellows's admiration, so they summoned the author, drank with him, laughed with him, and decided they had an authentic primitive on their hands, a rowdy noble savage. Beyond his gritty prose and high bravado, Jimmy Breslin loved New York City—all of it, especially the outer boroughs that Manhattanites scorned—with a chauvinism that prompted him once to dismiss Los Angeles as "two Newarks back to back."

Breslin came to work at the *Tribune* in the middle of 1963. At thirty-three, a year older than Tom Wolfe, he stood five foot ten, weighed 240 pounds, had black hair and dark eyes and the sweet if suety face of an overaged choirboy. His office personality was that of a profane, chain-smoking, volcanic blowhard with a beer belly. Some who were close to him said this persona of an immodest Irish tough was a defense mechanism to cover a sensitive nature and genuine warmth he was too insecure to reveal except to those few he trusted. And trust did not come easily to a man whose father had abandoned the family when Jimmy was six and whose mother was a high school English teacher, an occupation that made her boy suspect in the eyes of his street peers. Taking on the protective coloration of gutter language and bold threats, Jimmy managed to survive high school and attended Long Island University over a three-year period before dropping out for good in 1950, but by then he had learned that he was better at writing than fighting. He married young and had six children, the first two twins born prematurely, so they and their mother had to spend a month in the hospital, and the Breslins were always up against it financially while Jimmy persisted in a profession in which, as he succinctly put it, "they don't pay the fuckin' people." After a year on the *Tribune* they were paying him $20,000 plus $200 a week in expenses, which were considerable because he did not own or drive a car, took taxis everywhere, and obtained no small portion of the raw material for his column in his avocational role as a barfly. Before the decade was over, he would be earning $125,000.

He invented his own literary character, that of a populist who was now and forever on the side of debtors and deadbeats and the impoverished ignorant trapped in criminality. He wrote fondly of those who passed bum checks, who had to transport all their earthly possessions on the subway when they changed residence, who elevated shoplifting to an art form, who burned down buildings under contract, who stole petty cash from their wives. "With working people," he wrote, "there is almost no other kind of marital trouble except money trouble." He could mindlessly taunt a black newsboy at Bleeck's yet turn around and produce the first authentically compassionate coverage of Harlem ever to run in the *Tribune*. Up there, he wrote in a memo to Bellows, they were "bewildered, uncared-about, and angry," mired in apathy as if serving a life sentence in destitution. He wrote with special affinity for the police; he and they, or at least a lot of them, came from the same place. Most of all he was at home with his pals out at Pepe's Bar on Astoria Boulevard in Queens, about whom he fashioned urban parables in an argot at least as authentic as any in Damon Runyon's burlesques. In them he confronted legitimate social issues and captured a mind-set of attitudes he neither condemned nor approved: he understood and reported. His friend Mutchie's idea of a suitable female companion, Breslin wrote, was one built like a municipal statue and just smart enough to answer the telephone.

His prose was simple, obviously indebted in its economy to Hemingway but more various in its rhythms. His sentences were generally terse and declarative, shorn of dependent clauses, but they could also run on and on, repeating words for emphasis or rhythm and gaining power with their length. It was less the richness of the language than the rightness of it for his purposes that distinguished his style, and he used it with emotional control; it could be touching without slopping into bathos—although he was not immune to that—and he could be both funny and serious at the same time, especially in writing of the underworld. "Criminals who talk too much in public," he wrote, "usually wind up among the missing dead."

Essentially he was a storyteller. His technique was generally to approach a story from the standpoint of the least exalted person connected with it or from the most unexpected angle, the one no other reporter had thought of or knew how to do or had been granted the license to attempt. His usefulness to the paper was well illustrated by the work he did following the assassination of John F. Kennedy. While other reporters were concentrating on the fallen President's assassin, theories about his involvement in a plot, and the mood in Dallas before and after the event, Breslin busied himself interviewing the surgeon who had tried to save Kennedy's life, the priest who had administered last rites, and the funeral director who provided the best bronze casket in his stock to bear the President's body to its eternal rest. "A Death in Emergency Room One," the long story he filed for the Sunday paper of November 24, 1963, focused on the surgeon, thirty-four-year-old Dr. Malcolm Perry, whom Breslin pumped gently but thoroughly at a small press conference the day before during which the doctor wondered "about all the questions he asked which seemed not to bear directly on what had happened during the care of the President." Perry's answers to those apparently extraneous questions, of course, allowed Breslin to reconstruct the surgeon's mental state during those horrific moments when Kennedy lay stretched before him, dying "while a huge lamp glared in his face." Breslin's story began:

> The call bothered Malcom Perry. "Dr. Tom Shires, STAT," the girl's voice said over the page in the doctors' cafeteria at Parkland Memorial Hospital. The "STAT" meant emergency. Nobody ever called Tom Shires, the hospital's chief resident in surgery, for an emergency. And Shires, Perry's superior, was out of town for the day. Malcolm Perry looked at the salmon croquettes on the plate in front of him. Then he put down his fork and went over to a telephone.
> "This is Dr. Perry taking Dr. Shires' page," he said.
> "President Kennedy has been shot. STAT," the operator said.

With understated intensity and an attempt at clinical accuracy, Breslin then traced Perry's every move during the next fifteen or so minutes and interposed the doctor's feelings along the way, starting with: "The President, Perry thought. He's larger than I thought he was." Breslin took the reader virtually inside Perry's body and brain as the surgeon "unbuttoned his dark blue glen-plaid jacket and threw it onto the floor" and did his job, always aware of "the tall, dark-haired girl in the plum dress that had her husband's blood all over the front of the skirt" who was standing over there "tearless . . . with a terrible discipline" against the gray tile wall.

Then Malcolm Perry stepped up to the aluminum hospital cart and took charge of the hopeless job of trying to keep the thirty-fifth President of the United States from death. And now, the enormousness came over him.

Here is the most important man in the world, Perry thought.

The chest was not moving. And there was no apparent heartbeat inside it. The wound in the throat was small and neat. Blood was running out of it. It was running out too fast. The occipitoparietal, which is a part of the back of the head, had a huge flap. The damage a .25-caliber bullet does as it comes out of a person's body is unbelievable. Bleeding from the head wound covered the floor.

After desperate efforts to clear Kennedy's chest and restore his breathing and ten minutes trying to massage the still heart back to life, Perry was guided away, dimly conscious of the priest who passed him to attend to the President's soul. Breslin then reconstructed the words that passed in privacy among the priest, the new widow, and the divinity—he managed, by economy of phrasing, not to make it read like sacrilegious voyeurism—and switched the scene to the funeral home when the Secret Service placed its urgent call for a casket befitting the head of state. At the end of his story, Breslin came back to Dr. Perry, following him as he arrived home that grim afternoon and his six-and-a-half-year-old daughter romped up to him, chattering happily and showing him her day's schoolwork. The closing line of the piece quoted Perry as saying at the Saturday press conference, "I never saw a President before."

One of the complaints that would arise over Breslin's work was that he sometimes sacrificed accuracy, consciously or otherwise, to achieve emotional impact in his pieces. His story from Dallas suffered from the defect. The opening paragraphs, quoted above, contained three errors, according to Dr. Perry: Dr. Shires was the chairman of the department of surgery at the hospital, not the chief resident. Dr. Perry did not pick up the page—another doctor did, at Perry's request. The operator did not say the words Breslin attributed to her. The sequence of Kennedy's medical care, moreover, Breslin also got wrong, and the actual procedures followed were "misnamed . . . and inaccurate." And yet, on rereading Breslin's story long after, Dr. Perry thought that "the major focus is correct" and that the mistakes were "to be expected in such circumstances." What he most remembered about Breslin's work was his "concern and kindness" during the interview "and the way he looked when he said goodbye to me, and ended by saying, 'God bless you.' I appreciated all that very much."

Amid the somber pomp of the presidential funeral, Jimmy Breslin, the people's reporter, caught the mood of bereavement by following the activities of the humblest participant connected with the ceremonies—Clifton Pollard, the khaki-overalled digger of Kennedy's grave at Arlington Cemetery. He used a machine called a reverse hoe, not a shovel, for the job. Only Breslin would have noted that Pollard saved a little of the dirt he dug to make room for Kennedy's coffin.

V

When the *Herald Tribune* finally got around to creating a new Sunday paper toward the end of 1963, a dozen years after the need was first perceived, it was such a departure that it lost almost as many old readers as it attracted new ones.

The new Sunday paper was Bellows's main achievement as editor—as exciting in its way as Denson's daring front page had been. The first step was to simplify the package. Instead of the infinite sectionalizing that had become typical of ad-fat Sunday papers, Bellows settled on four standard-sized sections: the main sheet, now incorporating the editorial page, the political columns (which were sprinkled to appear next to the news story or news feature to which each was most closely related in subject), and situation or background pieces that had formerly appeared in the news review section; the women's section, including social news, fashions, gardening, and travel; a section combining financial and real estate news; and the sports section. To these were added a pair of staff-edited new magazines gracefully executed in rotogravure and plainly aimed at what Madison Avenue media buyers called "an upscale readership" —*New York* and *Book Week.* The syndicated supplement, *This Week,* targeted at a less sophisticated readership, was the only holdover from the old Sunday package; if nothing else, it added bulk and color ads.

Far more important than the arrangement of the new paper was its look. Until then, most newspaper editors' idea of page design began and ended with the question "Where shall we put the picture?" The new Sunday *Tribune* was conceived as a graphic totality, rendered with the precision of superior magazine advertising design. Each page reflected what the *Columbia Journalism Review,* in a favorable assessment of the restyled paper, called "painstaking 'packaging.' " Type was massed and set off by white space almost scandalously generous for newsprint pages to create what the newly hired design editor, Peter Palazzo, called "an environment of visibility." Illustrations of unprecedented sizes, shapes, and originality, closely integrated with the text instead of mere window dressing, helped generate visual impact without sacrifice of clarity or dignity. Palazzo, a soft-spoken man with a perpetually brooding mien, set about to re-educate Bellows about what was typographically possible within the framework of a metropolitan newspaper and found the editor blessedly receptive. The collaboration worked because Palazzo, while primarily a designer—trained at Cooper Union, he had worked for such high-fashion advertising accounts as I. Miller and Henri Bendel and magazines as diverse as the State Department's overseas showcase, *Amerika,* and the pocket-sized *Quick*—was also a perceptive reader, skillful at moving beyond the literal into imagery and symbolism to render the often complex ideas behind the news. He had not been impressed with Denson's graphic pyrotechnics, partly because, as he correctly observed, "the tone of the headlines and the style of the articles they applied to were not in consonance." Palazzo was no hype artist.

Bellows cooperated by getting the *Tribune* advertising department to revamp their layouts, doing away with the old stepping-stone arrangement in which the news appeared to be mainly filler on ad-heavy pages. Every page not fully occupied by advertising was arranged so that Palazzo had at least two entire columns to work with, and on most pages the ads were squared off to permit artful treatment of the editorial matter. The composing room had to be retrained to Palazzo's new ways; spacing and proportions had to be precise. Thought went into the location and length of every hairline rule. No longer were there small stories or fillers to plug holes; almost every article in the Sunday main sheet now, except for late-breaking news, was given major treatment as a spread and had to look it without violating Palazzo's canon of visual decorum. Staff photographers now had to give Palazzo a contact sheet instead of a single print of their own preference so the designer could decide what would work best instead of relying on the judgment of the lensmen. And the copy desk had to learn a whole new set of headline counts as Palazzo phased out the *Tribune*'s traditional use of Bodoni type and began using the distinctive Caslon face, with its more subtle proportioning in the weights of the thick and thin parts of the letters and stylishly drawn serifs that he thought gave the news page more character—a classic but not fussy look. For all the openness in his layouts throughout the paper, including the new magazines, Palazzo insisted on keeping the space tight between the elements within a given graphic unit and thereby achieved a kind of binding tension, a coherence of sensibility and substance. His craftsmanship would later be acknowledged throughout the field to have set the pattern for the next generations of newspaper design as photocomposition facilitated many of the techniques Palazzo and the *Tribune* introduced in the waning era of hot type.

The centerpiece of the new Sunday *Tribune*—and one of the two offspring (the Paris edition was the other) that would outlive the parent paper—was *New York*. The visual freshness of the magazine was immediately apparent from its cover, devoted to a full-color panorama or detail of the cityscape that caught its raw energy or unexpected beauty. Its interior set a standard for graphics not seen before in an American newspaper magazine. The look was one of chaste and elegant understatement, achieved within a grid of three columns to a page that played off blocks of gray text, white breathing room, and dark illustration. Headlines were small, hardly more than inviting labels that left the tone-setting to the large, arresting artwork, produced by some of the leading illustrators of the day.

Appearance aside, the contents of *New York* warranted keeping it around for the rest of the week. Its metropolitan orientation, in intentionally sharp contrast to the *Times*'s Sunday magazine, sought to capture the verve and variety of city life in stylish prose that could not be mistaken for the solid *Times* style or the cheap, inflated puffery of the *Daily News*'s Sunday supplement.

Although most of the articles in *New York* were by outsiders, the core of the magazine during its early stages was the work of the paper's prolific new stars —Tom Wolfe, his antennae tuned to the latest from the city's salons, galleries, fashionable boulevards, and expensive playgrounds, and Jimmy Breslin on the town's grubbier precincts and stalwarts. Thus, that first autumn, while Wolfe was writing in *New York* on why Park Avenue doormen hated Volkswagens, how to go celebrity-watching on Madison Avenue Saturday afternoons, the joys of stock-car racing out at Riverhead on eastern Long Island, and what qualified as *le style supermarket* for the chic Manhattan matron, Breslin was covering conditions on skid row, in alimony jail, and along Long Island's public beaches, inventorying New York street action at two in the morning, and lamenting the imminent suburbanization of Staten Island, the city's outermost borough. These were supplemented by pieces from local name writers—such as Langston Hughes on gospel singing in Harlem, Martin Mayer on why New York's public schools were so badly administered, Nat Hentoff on the time-wasting of the jury system, Liz Smith on people-watching at discotheques, and "Pogo" creator Walt Kelly in words and pictures on Greenwich Village types. But for the most part it was not the prominence of the bylines but the subject and treatment of the articles that made them attractive, e.g., the economics of the taxi industry, literacy tests from the Puerto Rican perspective, the fiery personality of transit workers' boss Mike Quill, how the Music Corporation of America was gearing itself to the computer age, why comic books were so violent, the adventures of a cop who moonlighted at midwifery, the agony and the ecstasy of Orson Welles. Each week's lineup was as varied and unpredictable as the city itself. Following the general-interest articles came the *Tribune*'s cultural critics, each given a separate page or more, whose individual appeal—the authority of Walter Kerr on theater, the candor of Judith Crist on the movies, the graceful evocations of Emily Genauer on art, the passion of Walter Terry on the dance, the brightness of new young music critic Alan Rich—seemed to gain in stature and liveliness from being grouped. Behind them *New York* offered a highly readable guide to the city's coming cultural events and most notable entertainment, television listings for the following week, bridge and chess columns, puzzles, and the paper's four best comic strips.

Orchestrating this snappy weekly performance was Sheldon Zalaznick, formerly senior editor at *Forbes* magazine, a smart, broad-gauged, compulsively neat man of thirty-five. A working pencil editor, solid in judging the pace and structure of a magazine story—a different species from the kind most *Tribune* editors were used to dealing with—Zalaznick was the beneficiary from the start of the brainstorming services of Clay Felker, his opposite in temperament and work habits and detectably more ambitious. It was Felker with whom *New York* would shortly become identified as Zalaznick stepped up to editor of the whole Sunday paper in 1964.

Felker, a rapid-fire talker as intense as he was inconstant in his enthusiasms, with an eclectic intellect adept at making connections between ideas and their manifestations, at thirty-eight had recently lost out in a struggle to become the top editor of *Esquire,* where he had been feature editor after working on the *New York Star, Life,* and *Sports Illustrated.* At the time Bellows hired him as a consultant for the new Sunday paper, he was also consulting for the Viking Press and British television personality David Frost and helping manage the film career of his wife, actress Pamela Tiffin. All this well-wired linkage to the world of entertainment and communications made him a uniquely useful idea man. A native of St. Louis, where his father was editor of *The Sporting News,* the definitive journal of organized baseball, Felker graduated from Duke and on his arrival in New York was infected with a Fitzgeraldian fascination for the big city's ephemeral glamour, shifting power bases, and the pecking order of its numerous subcultures. As an editor, he was remarkably good at conceptualizing stories and then putting the idea together with a writer who could fashion it well and on time. He was thought to go off the deep end, sparks flying, with some of his ideas, but that hypercreativity was what made him such a valuable resource—if one was selective in gauging his offerings. Felker's problem on joining the *Tribune* was that he was used to dealing with top-flight free-lance writers, and when he dreamed up story ideas for the new Sunday *Tribune,* most often in the areas of politics and sports, and suggested outside people to execute them, he frequently appeared to be usurping the prerogatives of the paper's editors and writers. "I was poaching on their territory and not doing it very diplomatically," he recalled. Zalaznick, also a magazine man by training, was sympathetic with Felker's problem even as he recognized his gifts. "Clay frightened people," Zalaznick recounted. "He was high-powered, aggressive, and smart as hell. He made second-rate people nervous—and whatever veneer he had wore thin pretty fast."

Soon Felker's services to the *Tribune* were assigned to Zalaznick exclusively, and he used them to complement what he regarded as his own narrower frame of reference. Felker's instincts scouted out who and what was about to be fashionable—"whether it was that the neckline of women's dresses would soon be descending to the nipple," Zalaznick noted, "or that pro football was soon to replace church on Sunday."

New York's companion, *Book Week,* was more than a renamed version of the old *Tribune* book review section, which was retired along with Irita Van Doren, its widely admired editor for nearly four decades.* Produced on newsprint, the old section had become lackluster in both appearance and content and was attracting only a fraction as much advertising as *The New York Times Book Review.* To enhance the new Sunday *Tribune* package, management accepted the proposal of Frederick Shaine, in charge of the paper's book advertising, to publish the section in rotogravure, allowing far cleaner reproduction that would

---

* Van Doren was succeeded by the author, who was heavily dependent upon holdover associate editor Belle Rosenbaum, assistant editors R. Z. Sheppard and Phyllis Larkin, art designer Stanley Mack, and production supervisor Theodore Fratrik.

appeal to vendors of luxury goods like books and records, and to issue it as a nationally syndicated literary supplement. *The Washington Post* and *San Francisco Examiner,* serving two of the best book markets in the United States, signed up for the proposed section sight unseen—the *Chicago Sun-Times* would also take it the following year—and thus guaranteed the new venture a combined circulation of just under the *Times Book Review*'s 1.4 million. Advertising rates were pegged accordingly, and *Book Week* was given an editorial budget that allowed it to pay reviewers as much as the *Times* and a design by Peter Palazzo that made it more appealing graphically than the *Times* section.

Book Week's chief distinction from its predecessor and from its long-dominant rival, the *Times Book Review,* was that it did not conceive of itself as they did—essentially a collection of book reports to consumers on the readability of new titles—but rather as a collection of articles intended to be stimulating in their own right, almost regardless of the merits of the books that prompted them. Indeed, the bylines of the contributors, whose pieces were often more essays than reviews and ran longer than those in any other newspaper book section, were set in far larger type and positioned more prominently than the names of the authors they were assessing. Top literary figures agreed to write on books carefully selected to stimulate their interest—among them, Norman Mailer on a critical biography of President Kennedy that appeared two months before his murder, George Plimpton on Hemingway's *A Moveable Feast,* Ralph Ellison on *The Southern Mystique* by Howard Zinn, Dwight Macdonald on Marshall McLuhan's *Understanding Media* (which the *Times Book Review* chose to ignore), Barbara Tuchman on a biography of Edward VII, A. J. Liebling on a revision of H. L. Mencken's *The American Language,* and Susan Sontag on a study of pop art. *Book Week* was truly a national literary magazine, written by top authors, leading academicians, younger critics eager to show their wares, and knowledgeable journalists, enlisted from all over the country. Besides the caliber of its reviewers, it was notable for paying regular attention to paperbacks, then just beginning to be a major factor in publishing, for running retrospective essay-reviews on reprinted classics (like MIT economist Paul Samuelson discussing John von Neumann's *Theory of Games*), and for applying stringent artistic standards to children's books instead of treating them the way most review media did—as the toy department of literature. Aimed at serious readers, *Book Week* was brightened by clever artwork, catchy headlines, and occasional curiosities, like a joint review of the new Sears, Roebuck and Montgomery Ward catalogues, or spoofs like Lillian Ross's treatise on a serious tennis book (headlined "The Centrality of the Net").

Compared to other newspaper book sections across the country, "*Book Week* must immediately be placed in the first rank," said the *Columbia Journalism Review.* Within a year, *Book Week* had narrowed the *Times Book Review*'s ad-linage lead from nine-to-one to three-to-one. But while it added to the attractiveness of the new Sunday *Tribune,* it did not precisely pay for itself; even with subsidies from its subscribing partners, the book section lost a total of a million dollars in its first two years.

VI

Among older *Tribune* staff members who outlived the paper, the belief was generally held that its golden age, journalistically speaking, occurred between the rise of Stanley Walker at the close of the 'Twenties and the death of Ogden Reid at the beginning of 1947. With regard, however, to one department of the paper—its financial section—no amount of nostalgia can color the judgment that its coverage did not become truly enterprising and its writing lively until the *Tribune*'s last years.

Through World War II and the broad-based prosperity it brought, American financial journalism had been almost notoriously soft on its subject. Among the largest enterprises in their communities, most newspapers were philosophically pro-business to begin with and disinclined, given their dependency on advertising dollars, to bite the hand feeding them. In the case of the *Herald Tribune,* that reluctance was doubly operative because of its historic championing of laissez-faire policies and its own precarious balance sheet. Although it ran the second-largest financial section among U.S. newspapers after its absorption of the *Herald* in 1924, the *Tribune*'s business coverage was, by and large, uncritical—almost an adjunct of industry rather than an objective chronicler of its performance. Press releases were little altered and gladly run, probing inquiries went unmade, news sources were approached with utmost deference, and the prevailing standard of newsworthiness did not depart greatly from that of the trade press—a boosterism that serviced the vested interests of the business community rather than the public at large. The *Tribune*'s financial coverage was defensive, establishmentarian—indeed, blue-chip in its orientation—and journalistically suspect; its longtime financial editor, Norman Stabler, had a reputation as knowledgeable, readable, and something of a stock market tout. James Gordon Bennett would not have approved.

Stabler's successor during the postwar economic boom—Donald I. Rogers, who served as financial editor from 1950 to 1963—continued in the pro-business tradition at a time when elsewhere in journalism a more questioning and irreverent posture was being adopted as proper, even if businessmen had grown no thicker-skinned toward the intrusions of the press; private enterprise still relished its privacy. Don Rogers admired big-businessmen, enjoyed their company and attention, and sought their approval by conducting the financial pages of the *Tribune* in a fashion most likely to win it. A Brown University dropout with little technical training in economics, Rogers worked on the business and editorial pages of New England papers before coming to New York. His specialty was personal finances; the biggest seller among the dozen books he wrote was titled *Teach Your Wife to Be a Widow.* A big, sociable fellow, he was proud to be on the *Tribune* and fought against budget cuts and space reductions affecting his department, which he argued was essential to the paper's well-being. Management made him do double duty as a department head and author of a thrice-weekly column, offered free to subscribers to the paper's wire service—an onerous load for even the most conscientious of workers. But Donald Rogers enjoyed hobnobbing with corporate and Wall Street executives more than the daily grind of newspapering, and as the years went on, his lunches grew longer and boozier, and his columns were ghosted for him by younger staff members.

Casting himself as an eloquent spokesman of the American capitalistic way, Rogers submerged his journalistic impulses in the advocacy of a mutual interest between his newspaper and the business community that he was supposed to be scrutinizing. He was confirmed in this role during the *Tribune* presidency of Brown Reid, whose record for disinterested journalism was spotty at best. Thus, in June 1955, within weeks after Brown's taking power, Rogers noted in a memo to him, "There is a general feeling in the tobacco industry that the Herald Tribune is being unduly harsh in its judgment of cigarette smoking [as a cause of cancer]. . . . The reason I bring this up is obvious: cigarette and tobacco ads produce an important amount of revenue for us each year." Attached were clippings that Rogers thought showed Earl Ubell's reports on the subject to be more injurious to the industry's health than comparable articles in *The Wall Street Journal* and the *Mirror.* In a 1957 memo to Brown, Rogers enclosed a story he had authorized in his Sunday section on the Lane Bryant department store and said he had been advised that it saved the store as an advertising account for the paper. The following year, Brown's last on the paper, Rogers reported to him on the allegedly unfavorable reaction in the business community to a critical mention in a *Tribune* editorial of the late Senator Joseph McCarthy: ". . . [A]n enormous number of people (more than you might suspect) think [he] was right and . . . a much-maligned man."

Rogers was by no means without virtues. He was genial, told jokes, hired able younger reporters, and granted everyone a great deal of freedom. But as the top editor of an important *Tribune* news department, second largest in space and manpower allotment, he was inexcusably deficient. His office hours were short, his supervision lax, his authority largely delegated to subordinates, and in view of his own practices, he looked away from the small favors regularly offered to and not infrequently accepted by his staff—food and drink, gift certificates, the free loan of cars for weekend use, holiday cheer in pinch bottles —and the appearance late in the day on top of the copy desk of a fifth of scotch and paper cups for anyone who was thirsty. A certain fraternal spirit reigned in the department, partly attributable to its physical separation from the rest of the news personnel half a flight below the city room in a low, tin-roofed annex that grew torturously hot four months of the year. More ennobling was the companionable feeling awakened by their competition with the *Times* financial department. "It was like playing in a football game with only four men on your team," recalled Vartanig Vartan, one of Rogers's best young recruits. But the *Tribune* carried almost all the prices and statistical data that the *Times* did, matched it in coverage of the big stories, wrote about business in a somewhat freer and more colorful style, and in some areas, like Ben Weberman's reports on new securities issues, set the pace.

The financial section did not normally attract gifted writers because its subject was abstract and dehumanized; the heroes and villains, especially on Wall Street, were numbers, not people. "You couldn't really say much about the managing partner of Merrill Lynch," Vartan noted. The principal appeal of financial writing among the younger writers was power, stemming from disinterestedness, over people almost totally dedicated to the profit motive. "We felt superior to them," said Warren Berry, another young Rogers recruit, who at the age of twenty-six, when "I knew nothing," was assigned to daily coverage of the New York Stock Exchange. Newcomers like Vartan and Berry brought a more skeptical attitude to the *Tribune*'s financial section. Vartan's vigilance while covering Wall Street took the form of "constant awareness that I was dealing with a selling mechanism. All their attitudes were geared to moving the merchandise and making a commission. It was as if everyone I talked to had 'Get the Order' stamped on his forehead." He was therefore stingy with praise about the successes of brokers and analysts, in part because "no one ever tells you their mistakes on Wall Street." But being negative or critical in print drew antagonism. Every publicly held stock had its own constituency in the financial community and beyond, and there were vested interests scrutinizing everything he wrote about, Vartan discovered, "and the moment you started writing unpleasant things about, say, AT&T, you got a lot of people jumping down your neck. It was a minefield to cover."

For Berry, trying to track down the truth about the daily gyrations of the Big Board was largely a matter of finding out whom to trust. He avoided analysts who were "too touty" and corporate public-relations men artlessly wedded to deception—"The best ones told you the bad stuff as well as the good, even if it was off the record," Berry said. He soon found that if he wanted to learn why a stock was being traded actively, he should start by trying to reach the company's chief executive officer and, if unsuccessful, work his way down the corporate ladder, turning to its official publicists "only as a last resort." Speaking with executives after their office hours was sometimes the most fruitful approach. Berry's colleague and after-work bachelor crony, Dennis Duggan, was a particularly resourceful digger who, as one admirer in the department put it, "practically made love on the telephone" to the secretaries of corporate chiefs to wheedle their bosses' home phone numbers.

The closest approximation to a mentor counseling the largely self-tutored junior echelon of the *Tribune* financial staff in the late 'Fifties and early 'Sixties was Ben Weberman, a no-nonsense type with an advanced degree in business administration from NYU, who had served previously as financial editor of *The Journal of Commerce.* To Berry, Duggan, and some of the other young newsmen, the money beat was fun because they were pure of heart and slender of wallet, in marked contrast to their subjects and sources; for Weberman, as Berry remembered one of his stern precepts, "Money ain't funny."

Weberman had built up a following in the industry as overseer of the recondite but highly lucrative underwriting business. He kept track of the new issues of corporate and government securities coming onto the market and reported on how they sold, in effect passing judgments on relative values and casting light where underwriters and bond traders were often not delighted by the exposure. "They were resistant at first to too much coverage," Weberman said, but his fairness and accuracy won them over and established his usefulness to the maintenance of an orderly and open marketplace. His reportorial technique, though, was hardly confrontational. "I had to know the people I was covering," Weberman felt. "I got much more from them through trust than any adversarial relationship would have yielded." Accordingly, he made a point of socializing with underwriters and bond specialists at their homes and reciprocating at his own in suburban Great Neck; he attended their meetings and conventions, he accepted their occasional gifts—"but never anything I couldn't have afforded to buy myself"—and did not hesitate to trade off his own information (such as telling underwriters how their newest offering was selling at a competing house) for theirs. While the younger breed of financial reporter saw high vulnerability to co-option and exploitation in such fraternizing, Weberman contended, "I could separate professional and social functions, and I didn't hesitate to criticize friends even if they disliked it—as long as I was accurate, they understood. I have never been a patsy for anyone."

He also had no compunctions about running his own bond newsletter on the side, aimed mainly at readers beyond the metropolitan region who could not follow his daily reports in the *Tribune.* Rather than constituting a conflict of interest, Weberman felt, his bond letter gave him greater access to industry sources and government officials and enhanced his stature as an authority. "And I never held anything back from the paper and saved it for the letter." True, this ancillary activity nicely supplemented his income, but if making money had been his prime goal, Weberman said, he would have joined the moneymen instead of serving as their go-between with the investing public. His reward instead of wealth was acting as a principal arbiter of "a big, tough, fast-moving industry with many heartaches—people in it shouted a lot." That he was viewed as an adjunct to the field he covered rather than an outsider was a source of pride and fulfillment to Ben Weberman.

He became the *Tribune* financial editor in 1963 after the largely dysfunctional Donald Rogers had made himself a cause of embarrassment to the paper by openly shilling for it on ideological grounds. At a private gathering in mid-1962 of a group of tory industrial leaders known as the Washington Roundtable, Rogers told his influential listeners, "You are voluntarily paying hundreds of millions of dollars in support of your most vicious and most effective enemies. If I were a top executive of a company, I would quietly lay down a policy that prohibited advertising in any publication or on any TV show which had a predominantly leftish tinge to it." Among the papers he cited as enemies of business were *The New York Times*; among the "influential conservative" papers he urged them to patronize instead were the *Herald Tribune* and *World-Telegram,* which "get very slim pickings from the American business community which they support so effectively in their editorial policies. . . . Is it so foolish to put your money into the hands of your friends instead of your enemies?" Though supposedly off the record, Rogers's remarks had been mimeographed, and a copy reached an aide to Senator Goldwater, who placed them in the *Congressional Record,* and the *Times* wrote them up at length. Apologetic, the *Tribune* explained editorially that Rogers's remarks were his personally and had not been intended for public consumption and that, for its part, the paper was not soliciting political favors and would continue to sell its space "on the strength of the product." Privately, management was sore at being portrayed as the poor little match girl of the New York press, and Rogers's days were numbered.

As his successor, conservative Ben Weberman, who so frankly cast himself as an accessory to the business community, ran a solid enough but unexciting financial section. He dispensed story tips to his reporters, but he was not a vigorous editor or philosophically inclined toward stories that put corporate officials on the spot. After fifteen months in the job, Weberman left for what he said was twice his *Tribune* salary to take charge of the *American Banker,* a trade publication. Recalled from Bonn, where he was doubling as the paper's German and Common Market correspondent, thirty-four-year-old Myron Kandel replaced Weberman and served as the *Tribune*'s last financial editor—and journalistically the best.

Trained on the *Times* for a dozen years, Kandel was of the modern breed of newsmen who believed that the public interest was substantially affected by the activities of private commerce, which ought not to be exempt from the inquiring eye of the press. In contrast to Rogers and Weberman, Kandel exercised hands-on direction of his thirty-five-man department of reporters, editors, and statisticians. With the help of Warren Berry, his imaginative deputy, he opened up the section to more enterprising stories and gave more play to holdover Young Turks like Dennis Duggan and Terry Robards. He brought in knowledgeable, skeptical new reporters like Phil Greer, a former stockbroker who had wearied of the trading game but knew the dynamics of Wall Street, and Dan Dorfman, who had covered retailing for *Women's Wear Daily* and brought with him a driving, untender investigative style that yielded an unusually high number of exclusives. The formerly fixed daily layout that had frozen the stock market report in the lead position was broken, so that newsworthiness rather than tradition dictated the placement of stories. New features were introduced, and suffusing this fresh-spirited performance was an attitude not hostile to business but partial to honesty—an insistence on obtaining what Kandel called "the downside of any story" instead of merely serving as a conduit for sanguine pronouncements of corporate publicists. There were plenty of built-in resources for getting the other side of the story, Kandel taught—competitors, ex-employees, disgruntled current employees, short sellers, analysts, trade authorities willing to talk off the record. The process could work as well to the advantage of companies subjected to false rumors depressing the price of their stock and threatening to stampede the public into unjustified scare selling. "I was always aware that some little old lady somewhere might read us and actually act on what we wrote," said Kandel.

Finally, the *Tribune* had a financial editor who would not do anyone else's bidding. Kandel was even courageously indiscreet enough to run a Sunday cover story on the troubles of CBS, with a big graphic of its new corporate symbol, a large Cyclopean eye, blackened by the blows of the marketplace. That CBS was run by Jock Whitney's brother-in-law was irrelevant to the intrinsic appeal of the story. "Nobody was going to tell me what to do so long as I was in charge," Kandel said.

VII

When the Gallup Poll organization was hired late in 1963 to determine reader reaction to the new Sunday *Tribune* and the paper in general, nobody seemed to have advised the opinion surveyors that the editorial strategy for nearly three years had been to create a newspaper decidedly different from *The New York Times*. The Gallup findings used the *Times* as the frame of reference and reported that while readers appreciated the *Tribune*'s innovations, the *Times* still plainly ranked as the prestige paper in the New York field, based mostly on its completeness. A common reaction to the *Tribune* was "I like your paper, but I've got to read the *Times.*" Gallup suggested that the *Tribune* make more effort to persuade readers that it covered all the important news and adopt a more conservative layout if it wanted to do better in the prestige market.

Walter Thayer seized upon the Gallup report to tell Jock Whitney even more forcefully than he had before that, in his judgment, the paper was inadequate. "We have reached a point where immediate steps, and maybe drastic ones, are required to keep the Herald Tribune's head above water," he wrote Whitney and his top editors in a January 20, 1964, interoffice memo. "These include . . . creating a fresh, new, wholly different approach to the daily paper that will meet the test of our competitive situation . . . [and] cutting costs to the full extent possible—and this means cutting down on people." He called for a freeze on hirings, economies in all departments, and a reduction of white space (i.e., a smaller news hole). "This program should be pursued ruthlessly," he added, said strong leadership was essential, and wound up: "In the absence of whole-hearted, enthusiastic agreement on these points by you and the editorial staff, I would be extremely pessimistic about the future of the paper."

Jim Bellows, who made it a point to keep as much distance between him and Walter Thayer as the geometry of the *Tribune* building permitted, had no choice now but to confront his newspaper's chief operating officer. Thayer seemed to have no positive ideas to offer; he knew only what he did not like. In a low-key, diplomatic, and conciliatory reply two weeks later, Bellows acknowledged that the paper was "far from being what its editors would like it to be" but said he was "deeply concerned" by Thayer's call for drastic changes. "My knowledge of Herald Tribune history is limited, but it's quite clear that this newspaper has flipped and flopped with a variety of approaches in the last 10 years." Reader habits were constantly being broken, Bellows noted, and while it took "extraor-dinary tenacity to stand with what we have, even with the improvements I know we can make, in the face of unimpressive circulation figures and red ink," nothing in the Gallup report proved, or even indicated, that the *Tribune* was headed in the wrong direction. What was needed to save the paper, Bellows told its pessimistic president, was "spirit and enthusiasm . . . to inspire the good talent" on the staff, harder work, and closer cooperation among all departments. "Now I hope we can work together. . . ."

Once more Whitney was being forced to choose between his most trusted financial adviser and the chief editor of his newspaper. In the case of Bob White, the choice had been easy. With John Denson, it had been more difficult, but finally Whitney had become convinced that the paper's fate could not be left in the hands of an irrational, unstable editor, no matter how inspired. In the case of Jim Bellows, Walter Thayer lost. True, the paper was making no financial headway, but Whitney liked the energy and daring of the paper under Bellows, a man as shy as himself, and he was not only comfortable with the editorial team and its handiwork—he was thriving on it.

Jock Whitney had always enjoyed his money and its uses, but it cut him off from a lot of people and life. Never knowing what demands might be made on him, he was understandably cautious about his commitments; the somewhat remote nature of his personality was traceable at least in part to self-defensive-ness. Though he had many connections to the realms of high society, finance, culture, philanthropy, politics, and sport, most of these were at a rarefied level. The *Herald Tribune* was a thing apart. It was his own window on the world, all of it, and it plunged him willy-nilly into a great adventure with a plucky band of younger men who shared his dream and did not defer to him in hushed tones and asked nothing more from him than the chance to practice their considerable skills. He was intrigued by Jimmy Breslin, fresh from the trenches with tales of life's grittier side, and when the pudgy columnist drinking with him one day at Bleeck's tossed a punch toward Whitney's jaw by way of demonstrating the knockout technique of a currently hot boxer, the owner of the *Tribune* did not flinch. Not many fists got aimed his way, even playfully. "He was the only millionaire I ever rooted for," said Breslin. Buddy Weiss, with his happy-go-lucky exuberance, supplied the owner with city-room gossip. "He was really a high-minded guy," said Weiss. "Often he'd say, 'That's not the way I see it, but if you fellows want to go ahead, it's all right with me.' It was like having a resident nobleman." Even the reticent, elusive Bellows touched him—with his modesty, his caring, his manifest exertion to do his best—though the two of them did not exchange a lot of words, either through the door connecting their offices or at the weekly dinners Whitney gave for his top editors in a suite he had had refurbished for the purpose on the fourteenth floor. But what little was said was enough. "He was the nicest man I ever worked for," Bellows recalled twenty years and five jobs later. "I'm only sorry that my own combative nature prevented me from making a real connection with Jock." Whitney, impressed by Bellows's professionalism and privacy, was equally hesitant to break the ice.

Real and lasting connections were made, however, with two younger men on his editorial team who, between them, embodied qualities that would have made the perfect son Jock Whitney never had. Dick Wald was the more outgoing, witty, urbane, unawed by but not indifferent to the Whitney fortune; he explained the paper to Whitney and interpreted Bellows's elliptical phrases and mysterious motions. And on autumn Sundays he would interrupt his dinner to take a call from the boss, who had been out quail-hunting at his Georgia plantation, and read him the afternoon's professional football results. Performing for the emperor was a labor of love for Wald, who found Whitney "a great original—a fascinating man. He knew a lot about politics, about how men behaved in different circumstances, he'd been to a lot of places and seen a lot of things, and he knew everybody. He was fun and easy to talk to—and I liked his wines." The pair of them would get together socially two or three times a week and the younger man would keep the older amused and informed; their rapport grew into an almost filial relationship that endured through the remaining two decades of Whitney's life.

A more subdued and discreet confidant to Whitney was Raymond Kissam Price, Jr., Yale '51, Skull and Bones, politically conservative, distantly related to the Vanderbilts, and so devoted to the paper that he missed his grandfather's funeral rather than not attend a strategy council of *Tribune* brass. After working at *Collier's* and *Life,* Price had come to the paper's editorial-page staff with William Miller, proven himself adept at editorials that wove together discordant elements, served for a time as acting Sunday editor, and made himself so useful to Whitney as a writer of important policy memos, letters, and speeches that he was soon doubling as his assistant. When the editorial-page chief, Dwight Sargent, left in 1964 to head the Nieman Foundation at Harvard, the owner replaced him with the thirty-four-year-old Price, who appealed to the introspective side of Whitney's nature. Despite his intensity, hardworking Ray Price was quick to laughter and more personable than he seemed on short acquaintance; more to the point, his family, schooling, social and political philosophy, and temperament were all congenial to Whitney, who trusted him and turned to him in ways that he could not to Wald, who was caught up in the day-to-day operations of the paper and loyal to his comrades-in-arms. "He was genial, gracious, and considerate," Price said of Whitney, "and when he threw out ideas or suggestions, they were meant to help, not constrict. I liked him fine."

Whitney also enjoyed his broadening but less intimate associations with *Tribune* people knowledgeable about some of his outside interests, like Red Smith, who knew a great deal about horse racing and horse people; the engaging Walter and Jean Kerr, so thoroughly steeped in the theater; and Emily Genauer, the paper's authority on art. While visiting the Whitneys one evening at their East Sixty-third Street townhouse and admiring the masterpieces on every wall, Genauer, never bashful in stating her opinion, told Jock that he ought really to think about adding some twentieth-century modernist work to his collection. "I never thought of it," Whitney replied. "I'll look into it." Soon thereafter Genauer was invited to pass judgment on a composition of interlocking circles in shiny brass by Henry Moore, priced at $90,000, that Whitney was considering buying. Genauer of course approved, but urged Whitney to look at the work of younger, less heralded artists, and when he agreed, she arranged a private showing for him at a communal gallery-studio of avant-gardists in the Bowery, directly across the street from that neighborhood's leading flophouse. Whitney's limousine pulled up to the curb early one morning, and as his chauffeur shooed away winos threatening to settle on its hood, the great art patron emerged and surveyed the five-story walk-up studio with a certain diffidence. Suddenly remembering Whitney's damaged heart, Genauer was all apologies. Whitney said nonsense, popped a glycerin tablet into his mouth, gamely marched skyward, and when he got there bought paintings in volume. That Christmas, though, having decided that the new pictures were discordant companions to his older ones, he gave them all away as presents. Nevertheless, the experience had been worth having, as with so much else in his involvement with the paper.

Whitney's response, therefore, to Thayer's early 1964 memo, all but demanding drastic editorial changes if the *Tribune* was to be kept alive, was sympathetic with Bellows's shrewdly unargumentative reply. The paper had been traveling a bumpy course, Whitney granted, "but Jim has smoothed out most of the bumps," and while there was still considerable room for improvement, the steps Thayer had called for "would be, in effect, a change of editorship and also a public declaration of no confidence . . . in the present editorial product." Anxious to avoid "any appearance of panic" and promising Thayer "a paper we can both be proud of," Whitney listed a ten-point program he had rehearsed with Bellows, including steps "to convince the reader he's getting an extra measure of understanding by reading the *Trib*" and to provide the financial pages with "the authority and substance they still lack"—Myron Kandel had yet to take charge—and the editorial page with "more force and consistency" —which Ray Price would soon supply. The women's pages needed more universal appeal, of the sort Gail Sheehy and some of Eugenia Sheppard's other young freewheeling reporters were beginning to bring to them, and the paper had to get "more intimately and more broadly involved with the life of the city." Most of all, Whitney agreed with Thayer that if the *Tribune* was to survive, "strong leadership is needed, but I think I'm going to have to be the one to provide it."

But he was deceiving himself. Jock Whitney was incapable of leading the *Tribune* with the forcefulness necessary. He was, instead, its chief enthusiast, his role on it symbolic and inspirational. He never worked in his shirt sleeves, but he did at least remove the vest from his diplomat's dark suits shortly after arriving at his office. And he was visible around the place, sometimes just mingling with the staff if the news seemed to justify his presence, like the afternoon of the Kennedy assassination. Richard Schaap, who had just moved over from *Newsweek* to become city editor at the age of thirty, remembered how Whitney "would come around the newsroom with such a sense of innocence. He was so unthreatening—our kindly millionaire owner," the man in whose townhouse Schaap had seen the original of the framed Renoir reproduction that was hanging over his bed at home. Dee Kellett, one of his two secretaries, recalled how Whitney came bursting out of his office one morning, shaking his head over the paper's failure to sell more copies when, as he told her, "there's compelling reading on every page." He seemed to be in love with everything and everybody connected with the paper, which he read thoroughly, even the parts he did not like, and when something struck him as poorly done, he would register his displeasure even if he could not articulate the reason well. "And there was a good chance that whatever it was that bothered him had been done wrong," Dick Wald recalled. That was his chief editorial contribution—setting standards of taste and good writing. "They were not written out," said Bellows, "but you felt them—you knew what they were." The rest of the paper he ceded to Thayer. "He just wasn't interested in the numbers," said the controller, Winslow Maxwell, who would arrive in Whitney's office with carefully prepared tables and charts to report on finances, "all of which bored him stiff. He would sort of doze through the presentation, then rouse himself to ask a couple of questions—to be polite and to let me know that he appreciated my efforts." But the young executives on the business side of the paper had no illusions about Whitney's role. "He gave the news people a helluva shot in the arm from the morale point of view," said Robert MacDonald, Bellows's opposite number on the business side, whose contact with Whitney was almost entirely through Thayer.

Everything that had gone before in Whitney's life seemed to come into play for him now, given the wide range of his activities and the scope of the paper's coverage. The depth of his intelligence and breadth of his acquaintanceships were amply demonstrated during his annual trip to Washington with his top editors to meet with the bureau staff and leading government figures. Wald, newly installed as national editor, remembered his first trip to the capital with Whitney. Their first stop was the office of Secretary of Defense Robert McNamara. "Jock, how are you!" McNamara greeted him ebulliently, to his young colleague's surprise. After brief pleasantries, the conversation turned to substantive matters, like McNamara's theory on "Sears, Roebuck procurement," which held that the last 10 percent or so of sophistication that went into the production of modern weaponry cost a great deal more proportionately than the rest. How did that apply, Whitney wanted to know, to the manufacture of, say, a tank? What could you leave off in the interest of economy—not the safety features that kept the crew from being cooked inside, certainly, or allowed them to be ejected? And with Secretary of Treasury Douglas Dillon the same thing happened: old friends' talk of wines and life in New Jersey's Somerset Hills horse country, where Dillon made his home, then on to serious questioning of the keeper of the federal purse. "He had no hesitancy to engage these statesmen," Wald said, "to test them in fruitful discussions that were much more than ceremonial. He was a good reporter—and goddamn smart."

They admired him, too, for playing it straight. There were no dicta from the office of the editor-in-chief, no sacred cows, no "must use" notes attached to press releases routed through him. The travails of his sister's Mets were not sugarcoated by the sports department nor were space and play in the paper taken away from the racing season at New Jersey's plebeian Monmouth Park to give priority to the socially more prominent session conducted simultaneously at Saratoga, where Whitney was in residence and his horses were entered. When financial editor Kandel joined Whitney and Thayer for a trip down to Wall Street the Monday after the financial section's big Sunday takeout on the problems of CBS—a piece that could not have pleased Bill Paley—Thayer remarked unhappily on the article. Kandel asked him how he liked the striking graphic of CBS's blackened trademark eye that accompanied the piece, and Thayer replied with a glower; Paley's brother-in-law, Jock Whitney, said he thought it was just fine. Similarly, Whitney did nothing to pave the way to prominence at the paper for his son-in-law, William Haddad, who had been a former assistant on the staff of crimebusting Senator Estes Kefauver, a prize-winning reporter on the *New York Post,* and associate director of the Peace Corps before joining the *Tribune* to head an investigative reporting team. Haddad's work did not light any fires with the editors, and not long after he complained about their handling of his copy and threatened to take up the matter with his father-in-law, his *Tribune* career came to an end.

On at least two occasions, when he felt close political allies were about to be unduly maligned by his paper, Whitney did intervene. To review the first volume of Dwight Eisenhower's White House memoirs, Bellows instructed *Book Week*'s editors to enlist conservative columnist and editor William F. Buckley, Jr. Believing the choice to be loaded, *Book Week* counterproposed a quartet of reviewers—Buckley from the political right, Senator Hubert Humphrey from the left, Eisenhower speechwriter Malcolm Moos for an insider's evaluation, and historian Henry Steele Commager for a grand overview. When Buckley's review, the first to arrive and unexpectedly negative, was shown to Whitney, he ordered it killed on the ground that Buckley was irresponsible, but conceded privately that he did not want to insult his—and the paper's—friend

Ike. Despite staff objections, Whitney, with Thayer's strong support, would not relent. Only the Commager review was to run, but when it, too, proved to be negative and *Book Week* headlined it on its front page: "A Reluctance to Reflect: Mr. Eisenhower sheds scant light on the decisions of his era," no sound emerged from Whitney's office. In 1965 Whitney ordered the editors to kill a column by Dick Schaap, who by then had forsaken the city-editorship to write heavily ironic commentary for the split page on the connivances and blunderings of the power elite. Schaap's offending column, noting how Governor Rockefeller's former allies had abandoned him wholesale in the wake of his matrimonial adventures, was intended as a comment on the fickleness of politics, but Whitney, missing the point or not wanting to make it at the expense of his friend Nelson, said, "Why beat a dead horse?" But when Schaap later deftly needled Mayor John V. Lindsay, the great white hope of New York Republicans, whom the *Tribune* had given strong editorial backing—and Whitney and Thayer had supported financially as well—in the mayoral campaign, he was never censored.

Whitney's passion for the paper particularly animated the newcomers on the staff who had been drawn to the *Tribune* by its tradition, their own sense of craft, and the confidence that Jock Whitney would give it every chance to stay alive. "It was one big Whitney Foundation," recalled R. Z. Sheppard, who came to it in his late twenties and served during its last three years as an editor on *Book Week*, "with Jock giving all the young people grants to advance our careers while keeping the older people gainfully employed. What a terrific thing to have done with his money." The *Post* had climbed back past it in circulation after the strike, and the *Tribune* was again the smallest daily in the city, but the numbers did not matter to the staff. "It may not have been a world-shaking enterprise, but it was a pretty darned good paper," Dick Wald observed, "and to those of us who were living inside that bubble, it had a special kind of glory. And there was Walter Thayer, standing over to the side, saying to us, 'Hey, guys, that's a bubble you're inside of.' There was nothing venal about it—and it wasn't related to any need of his for power. All Walter's objections were out in the open and on the record. He never acted in a dishonorable way."

Others, including Bellows, were less generous in their appraisal of Thayer. In his constant carping and implacable demands, they saw less of a loyalty to Jock Whitney's best interests and vigilance against the dissipation of his fortune and more of a reluctant dragon peevish at its entrapment, huffing and puffing for release, mindful mostly of its own lost opportunity for territorial and material enhancement. As Whitney was incapable of whip-cracking leadership, so Thayer's rigidity of manner was viewed as a symptom of some latent insecurity that denied him the capacity for team play. He may have been listed on the masthead as president of the *Tribune,* but everybody knew it was Jock Whitney's paper and after him Jim Bellows's paper, so what was in it for Walter Thayer but frustration and annoyance? When he issued an order prohibiting the editors from charging the paper for restaurant meals taken with one another, it was attributed more to petty jealousy than legitimate monitoring of executive indulgences. There were very occasional glimpses of Thayer's vulnerability, like the time he joined a group of the editors in London for dinner with Si Freidin; afterward they dropped Thayer off at his hotel, and on leaving their taxi he said, sounding as close to plaintive as any of them had ever heard, "I guess you guys are going out now and have a good time." For all his charm, brains, and forthrightness, he could not invite affection and companionship while fulfilling his responsibility as the imminent breaker of their bubble. "And it didn't help," cracked Dick Schaap, "that he looked like Barry Goldwater."

In 1964, the year the *Herald Tribune* turned the back of its hand to Republican presidential nominee Barry Goldwater, Thayer no less than Whitney shared in the anguish of the party's progressive wing over the selection of the Arizona ideologue. "I find these difficult days to be a Republican," Thayer confessed to Clare Boothe Luce, whose strong alliance with Goldwater caused the *Tribune* to drop the column she had begun writing that election year. The paper agreed with the broad principles that Goldwater espoused—unyielding anti-Communism, a strong U.S. military arm, and control of federal power—but the extremes to which he proposed they be carried and his voting record against civil rights made him an unattractive presidential aspirant to the operators of the *Tribune* as well as of many another diehard Republican journal. But the *Tribune* was different from almost all of them. Its founder had been a principal architect of the party. The only time it had deviated from Republican regularity in a presidential election was in 1872, when Greeley himself, in order to reform the party, had run as a renegade with Democratic endorsement. Perhaps as the 1964 campaign went forward, *Tribune* policymakers had hoped, Goldwater would display the dimensions of a statesman equal to the office he sought. Instead, the more he discussed foreign affairs, the greater their conviction grew that he had no grasp of global complexities in the nuclear age.

The task of writing the endorsement editorial fell to Ray Price. "We couldn't fence-sit," he recalled, "because that would have amounted to saying the White House ought to remain vacant the next four years." A choice had to be made between Goldwater and a man to whom the paper conceded manifest competence and broad experience but one "with whom it had many disagreements and whom we did not trust," said Price. "It came down to explaining rather than trying to persuade others to accept our choice." With the help of a double belt of scotch, Price turned out the late-night draft of the historic editorial that ran in the October 4, 1964, *Herald Tribune.* It began:

For the Presidency: Lyndon B. Johnson.

Travail and torment go into these simple words, breaching as they do the political traditions of a long newspaper lifetime. But we find ourselves as Americans, even as Republicans, with no other acceptable course. . . .

Senator Goldwater says he is offering the nation a choice. So far as the two candidates are concerned, our inescapable choice—as a newspaper that was Republican before there was a Republican party, has been Republican ever since and will remain Republican—is Lyndon B. Johnson.

Upon reading those words and jumping a reported three feet in the air, Johnson telephoned his appreciation to Jock Whitney.

The importance of Whitney's paper, out of all proportion to its size, was further corroborated that month by a major spread in *Fortune* titled "The Crisis in New York's Newspaper Row." More than a thousand American dailies had died since 1930, the main story noted, but the net decline in the country was only ninety-eight due to the birth of new papers, mostly in suburbia. Metropolitan papers that survived the erosion of readership on their outskirts by new suburban competitors and the massive impact of television on reading habits in general were doing well, but only a few cities still had more than two newspaper ownerships; New York had six—but, according to *Fortune*'s writer, T. A. Wise, most industry experts expected that no more than three dailies would be left in New York after a shakeout—and one was imminent. His article was an attempt to analyze which three would survive.

The *News* was the only solid moneymaker in the batch. The *Times* was "a great newspaper but a curiously managed business," wrote Wise, which had been hurt by its poorly conceived West Coast adventure and the continuing heavy subsidy of its European edition, selling 32,000 copies daily compared with the *Tribune*'s 49,000 and attracting little advertising. The whole afternoon field was financially very weak: the *World-Telegram,* estimated to be a million in the red, was the loss leader of the Scripps-Howard chain; Hearst's *Journal-American* carried far too little advertising, considering its large, costly circulation, and Dorothy Schiff's *Post,* its revenues down, was walking the tightrope. While Whitney's bright and lively paper remained deep in the red, he was the key player on the New York journalism scene because of his money and his civic-mindedness. For the moment, *Fortune* reported, after discussions about a merger with the *Times* and a new printing plant jointly owned or leased with the *World-Telegram,* Whitney was sitting tight to see what developed. But, as Wise correctly analyzed, "there is little hope that [*Tribune*] management can, without a major capital outlay, modernize a decrepit plant, increase advertising revenue and circulation, and show a profit. The question in newspaper circles is whether Whitney is prepared to make the capital commitment required to do the job." If the prediction proved accurate that only three papers would soon be left in New York, Wise concluded, his crystal ball fogging, "it is fairly obvious that Whitney will be owner or part-owner of one of them. And since Whitney is thinking more and more of a communications complex, he may shake the entire industry from coast to coast."

Such a perception of Whitney as a major figure in one of the most influential of American industries prompted Colby College to invite him that November to deliver the lecture given annually by a ranking journalist in memory of Elijah Parish Lovejoy, who was killed in Alton, Illinois, in 1837, defending the rights of the abolitionist press. At Jim Bellows's urging and in the added light of his grandfather Hay's association with Lincoln, Whitney accepted. Drafted by Dick Wald and repeatedly revised by Whitney, the remarks he made on that occasion were the most memorable of his life, as his efforts to preserve the *Tribune* were the most notable endeavor of his career, and amounted to a soaring explication of what it was that he and his editors were striving to contribute to American journalism. He began with disarming candor: "My predecessors at these lectures have been eminent men who have all worked long at their profession. But I think it is clear that though I have worked at journalism, I am here today primarily because I am a millionaire." His fortune, though, had hardly been enhanced by his journalistic endeavors; indeed, "it may be that there are worse investments in this country than running a competitive morning newspaper in a busy, bitterly competitive, sophisticated town, but I have never run across one." As to the function of the modern daily as perceived by the *Herald Tribune,* he said: "Our task is to cut through the junk in the public mind by seeking the order that underlies the clutter of small events; to winnow out of the apparent what is the real; to cede to television and radio the mere repetition of activities and to look behind the bare event for meanings." He continued:

> Increasingly, those meanings are personal. A newspaper is no longer the only chronicle of events. It is a guide and an interpreter for the reader. It daily grasps the whole cultural kaleidoscope and brings it into focus in terms that will interest him, be meaningful to him—talk to him like a human being talking to another human being.
>
> Fifty years ago our industry fell in love with a convention of objectivity that was to lay a dead hand of pattern on our news pages and freeze us into "good form." But the reporter who writes "objectively" still selects the items he puts into the story, the editor still selects the stories that make up the page and the publisher still selects the men. And in the space between their several objectivities—in what they leave out —may lie the real life of our time, the real color, the grainy detail that mean the difference between the clear ring of life on the printed page and just another newspaper story.

The daily role that a modern paper can try to play, Whitney concluded, is to shape the whole experience of human activity in a form that will interest the reader in his community and give his ideas the excitement they should have. "These are the excellences of our craft. They are produced by men who are truly engaged in producing the poetry of everyday life."

A few weeks after his Colby speech, Whitney joined the top *Tribune* editors on their annual grand tour of Washington, culminating this time with a small White House dinner hosted by a President recently reaffirmed in power. The date was December 3, 1964, shortly after the Tonkin Gulf incident and the major escalation of U.S. involvement in Vietnam. *Tribune* bureau chief David Wise recalled Lyndon Johnson's explanation of his unease over the deepening crisis in Southeast Asia. "I feel just like I'm standing out on a copy of your *Herald Tribune* in the middle of the ocean," said Johnson, at the apex of his power. "If I tilt a little this way or a little that, I'll fall [*expansive Johnsonian falling gesture*], and if I stay right where I am, I'm going to sink [*gestures to show levels of descent*] right to the bottom of the sea."

Jock Whitney, similarly in his prime as a publisher and one of the most powerful citizens in the nation, at that moment faced his own private Vietnam. His choices were to commit vast additional resources to a journalistic war he probably could not win, to stay where he was and sink, or to get out as graciously as possible and take satisfaction in having fought the good fight and lost. None of these choices was acceptable to him.

20

Somewhere a Child Is Burning

I n its last grand civic gesture, the *New York Herald Tribune* bequeathed the city a new mayor. If he was not quite the paper's creature, he was a paragon of its highminded, high-born, blue-eyed, firm-jawed Ivy Protestant Republican progressivism.

That the *Tribune* should take the lead in scouring rascality out of City Hall was first proposed in the strikebound month of March 1963 by editorial-page chief Dwight Sargent, who sent a memo to Jock Whitney saying that the paper would be performing a great public service if it were "to wage a rousing battle" to elect a reform mayor to replace Robert F. Wagner, Jr., then midway through his third torpid term. To accomplish this, Sargent suggested a series of articles on New York's problems: "I think that some old-fashioned, hard-hitting, imaginative journalism could shake the city out of its lethargy and do a lot of good for the Herald Tribune in the mid-sixties." Whitney replied that he favored attacking the city's problems in that fashion, "but I don't *really* believe that going for a new Mayor is the right way. . . . P.S. Walter doubts that we'll get a new Mayor in any case!"

Such skepticism was understandable. The last non-Democrat to serve as mayor was Fiorello La Guardia, who held City Hall from 1934 to 1946 as a maverick Republican with fusion backing and powerful support among several of New York's ethnic subcultures that normally voted overwhelmingly Democratic. Registered Democrats outnumbered Republicans by three-and-a-half to one in New York, and bland Bob Wagner, who bored but did not rile the voters, seemed a shoo-in for a fourth term in the 1965 mayoralty contest. Sargent had not, of course, specified a Republican to champion, but Jock Whitney was not subsidizing the paper with millions of dollars in order to elect Democrats, however noble.

Sargent's idea was given substance eleven months after he broached it by Brooklyn native Barrett McGurn, recalled to the city room after sixteen years as a *Tribune* correspondent and assigned to talk to civic leaders about how the paper might undertake a series diagnosing the city's manifold ills. McGurn delivered a 125-page brief from which probably the longest-running continuous crusade in New York newspaper history was born. His attitude, however, was unsuitably upbeat: McGurn was struck more by what was right with the city than what was wrong with it.

McGurn's treatise passed into the less worshipful hands of the new city editor, Dick Schaap. The series, as Schaap blueprinted it, would have a dual purpose: to improve the city and "to create a favorable Trib image among the so-called leadership community, to get them hooked into reading and advertising in the paper." To succeed, the series had to offer something solid—which would take people, time, and money that could be stolen from the regular staff without crippling the paper—and "specific, workable" solutions to the problems dramatized. It also needed a strong title, Schaap said—"something like 'The City in Crisis: Where Does New York Go from Here?' " A task force that would eventually grow to six, including a black and a Spanish-speaking reporter, was created under Schaap's shepherding, and to head it he brought in Barry Gottehrer, a former sidekick of his from *Newsweek,* who had covered sports and the press but had little to do with urban affairs. To assure some follow-through, Whitney tried to forge a supercouncil of movers and shakers from among the city's business leaders, a select group of whom he invited to lunch at the paper, which, he told them, was not after Mayor Wagner's scalp but wanted only to spotlight the city's monumental problems and help marshal leadership from New York's tremendous pool of resources to combat them. But New York is a cynical city, and the partially self-serving motive behind Whitney's pitch did not escape his listeners. Among them was David Rockefeller, who commended the *Tribune*'s civic-mindedness and pledged spiritual support of its aims but declined to serve under the Whitney aegis in what could not escape turning into an anti-Wagner crusade; Chase Manhattan, Rockefeller's bank, needed every friend it had in City Hall, especially then, in the early stages of the World Trade Center that it was backing. With Rockefeller out, the others also shied away, and with the city's biggest free-enterprisers wary of involvement and its Democratic-run bureaucracy suspicious of the Republican *Tribune*'s purposes, Gottehrer had his work cut out for him.

What ailed New York, Gottehrer soon became convinced, was not so much civic corruption as the massive smugness and indifference of a long-entrenched, one-party machine government. And in its mayor it had the perfect passive magistrate. "He was a very nice man," Gottehrer recalled of his interview with Wagner, who during it revealed the sage advice of his father, a prominent U.S. Senator, that had guided his political career: "When in doubt, don't." Gottehrer's passion was ignited by such civil sluggishness. "It seemed intolerable to me in view of the city's troubles," he said.

Under the title "New York City in Crisis," the series began on January 25, 1965, with the headline "Indictment: Reasons for Outrage and Reasons to Act." Its first sentence, contributed by Schaap, was: "New York is the greatest city in the world—and everything is wrong with it." There followed a list of powerful charges on twenty-two critical counts of the brutalizing conditions of New York, a city where one-fifth of the people lived in poverty, and half a million —more than the total population then of five U.S. states—were on welfare; where the schools were overcrowded and substandard ("You don't worry about teaching these kids here," one principal told the *Tribune* reportorial team, "you just keep them from killing each other and from killing you"); where the courts were so jammed it took four years for a case to come to trial; where the public housing program had "created almost as many problems as it has solved"; and where 80,000 jobs had been lost in the previous five years because of taxes, labor and insurance costs, and municipal red tape that made it a nightmare for small businessmen to operate. And presiding over this infernal mess, a mayor who "seems to be a man almost totally incapable or unwilling to make forceful and meaningful decisions." Lest the charges be dismissed as political partisanship, the blanket indictment was extended to the city's Republican organization, which was criticized for offering complaints about the Democratic stranglehold on power but no program or candidates to improve the situation. With each ensuing installment, Gottehrer and his crew probed more deeply into the appalling conditions on the underside of life in the nation's biggest city. New York had throughout its history been a place where extreme wealth and poverty resided in tight proximity, but the contrast had rarely been brought home to its upper crust with such telling detail and sustained documentation. Asked for Robert Wagner's official response to the "City in Crisis" reports, a City Hall spokesman advised the *Tribune,* "The mayor says to tell Jock to shove it up his ass."

Others were more favorably disposed. The paper had to put on extra operators to handle the phone calls coming in by the hundreds as the daily revelations continued. Gottehrer sifted through a mountain of mail that produced new leads and further evidence of the critical state of New York urban life beyond the glitter and bustle of the center city. But though the series drew praise and prizes, any real hope that it would prompt serious reform efforts failed to materialize until Jock Whitney and Walter Thayer, moved by the paper's monumental indictment, took a major role in sponsoring a candidate to challenge Wagner —an effort they had viewed as fruitless before the series appeared. Now it was essential.

Within twenty-four hours the two of them raised half a million dollars, the bottom layer of a campaign war chest for handsome, liberal Republican Representative John Vliet Lindsay, forty-three, then serving his fourth term in Congress from Manhattan's East Side "silk stocking" district. He was the perfect *Tribune* man: a smooth, socially impeccable white Anglo-Saxon Episcopalian of high probity who had prepped at St. Paul's, graduated from Yale College and Law School, practiced on Wall Street, and served in the Justice Department before entering Congress, where his performance had been vigorous and enlightened. He wanted to be a Senator or Secretary of State. City Hall was a graveyard for ambitious politicians. But Whitney, Thayer, Nelson and David Rockefeller, and a select group of other rich and powerful figures in the party persuaded Lindsay that by running he would perform a noble service to the city and embattled Republicanism, shattered from the Goldwater debacle of the previous year, and assure the ascent of his own star. Fate was with him. Wagner's wife died, and he chose not to stand for re-election. In the Democratic primary, two reform candidates split the ranks of the party's liberal majority, and city controller Abraham Beame, a small, colorless figure who had dutifully served the masters of the party machinery, won the nomination. The Liberal Party, a minor but strategically important local organization, gave Lindsay its backing, qualifying him as a genuine fusion candidate. The picture was further complicated by the candidacy of editor-ideologue-rhetorician William Buckley, running under the Conservative Party label and appealing to voters on the right wing of both major parties. In such a race, anything could happen.

Besides money from the *Tribune*'s owner and president, Lindsay received two other major benefits from the paper. Its "City in Crisis" series gave him a ready-made platform. "The weight of the articles was overwhelming," Lindsay recalled. "It was a gloomy tale of crisis everywhere in the city—and provided a *raison d'être* for me to run." The series was condensed into a book that became his agenda for reform, and its principal author, Barry Gottehrer, his *Tribune* work well done, joined the Lindsay campaign staff. More important, throughout the campaign the paper practiced something close to advocacy journalism—closer than it had come since its habitual prewar hostility toward the New Deal in election years—in forwarding Lindsay's candidacy. He got prominent and favorable play in the news pages whenever it was remotely justified—and sometimes when it wasn't. The *Tribune* ran its own daily poll on the race to make it more dramatic—it showed Beame ten percentage points ahead a month before election day—and eagerly headlined every fractional gain as Lindsay whittled the gap to one point by election eve.

The *Tribune*'s partisanship was especially significant because for two weeks approaching the climactic stage of the fall 1965 campaign it was the only morning newspaper publishing in New York. The *Times* was struck for twenty-five days by the Guild, and the *News* and *Tribune* closed in sympathy; after ten days, though, feeling itself victimized by what Walter Thayer called "the wrong strike by the wrong union at the wrong time," the *Tribune* resumed publishing and sold nearly a million copies daily, plumping hard for Lindsay. Upon the return of the *Times,* which also supported Lindsay, and the *News,* with its own well-respected straw poll showing him doing better than the *Tribune*'s poll did, the *Tribune* seemed to grow almost stridently pro-Lindsay. One morning shortly before the voting, its front-page banner headline, on a television encounter between the candidates that Lindsay had sought, declared, "Beame OKs Debate So He Can Hurl 'Liar' "; Denson's play of the Supreme Court's ruling against prayer in public schools had not been more blatantly biased. Some of those close to Jim Bellows felt the *Tribune*'s Lindsay overplay was the result of heavy pressure from Whitney and especially Thayer, who in the opinion of Bellows's chief administrative assistant, Charles Kiley, was acting "like a power broker and a kingmaker" around the city room. More likely, Bellows was canny enough to understand that Whitney's and Thayer's continued interest in subsidizing the paper would be enhanced by its usefulness to Lindsay's cause, and the story was played accordingly.

On November 2, 1965, election-day morning, the *Tribune* front page carried an editorial where the lead story generally ran. "A Lindsay victory would do more than make possible a beginning of the end of wallowing mis-rule," it asserted. "It would serve notice on every future city administration that the people of New York are no longer to be taken for granted." That day, by three percentage points, the people of New York made John Lindsay their 103rd mayor. "Well, we did it!" an exultant Walter Thayer was heard to proclaim in the *Tribune* city room as the results came in that night.

And if Lindsay had prevailed against very long starting odds, who was to say that the *Herald Tribune* could not yet win its fight for survival?

II

After years of neglect, the Sunday edition of the *Tribune* as redesigned by James Bellows, Peter Palazzo, and Sheldon Zalaznick rapidly attracted so much attention among New York sophisticates that by 1965 the advertising director, Robert Lambert, was gladly seizing on it to project the paper's overall image. Its glossiest, most arresting feature, *New York* magazine, was beginning to win color advertising from department stores and garment manufacturers of the kind that had run exclusively for so long in the *Times* Sunday magazine. With such a promotable vehicle at hand, Lambert campaigned hard on Madison Avenue, arguing that New York was a "top-oriented town" and the *Tribune* readership led the way in education, buying power, and influence.

The freshness and excitement so apparent in *New York* magazine were organically related to the personality of its decidedly top-oriented editor. Clay Felker seemed perpetually overstimulated by the city. "New York is designed for work and accomplishment, not for ease of living," he once wrote. "This city has almost no use for anyone who isn't working and producing well. It's a city for people at their peak. . . . You've got to be the best to survive in New York." People at their peak had a magical lure for Clay Felker. Rarely at ease, his speech a staccato of Midwestern nasality, his mind a buzz saw reducing forests to workable two-by-fours, he practiced a tax-deductible lifestyle—his East Side duplex with its antique silver collection, his parties with the celebrated as a drawing card, the rented limousine and summer place in the fashionable Hamptons—so that people would regard him as a success before he had become much of one. He was an emotional man, one who screamed out his frustrations at the office and could not mask his boredom with people who had no information or talent that might somehow be useful to him. His enthusiasm and intensity, like John Denson's, were contagious, but he was a better-educated man with a much broader-ranging mind and made no secret of the fact that his life was one sustained scouting expedition whereas Denson stole other people's ideas, usually without crediting them. Writers loved Felker or hated him, sometimes both simultaneously. He was on the paper only for its final two and a half years, but Clay Felker, like Denson, must be counted on the short roster of inspired editors of the *Tribune* because he helped reshape New York journalism and redefined what was news.

The understated format of *New York* allowed him to carry a wide range of subject matter and stylistic treatments without risk of discord. Thus, Felker could include both the instructive narratives of onetime *Tribune* reporter George Jerome Waldo Goodman, under the pen name of "Adam Smith," employing the patois of a Wall Street hipster to demythicize the high-rolling gambitry of the money game, and the subdued but equally informative prose of NYU professor Peter Drucker on the latest models of corporate man. Likewise he varied the contents geographically, ethnically, occupationally, and culturally while sticking to a Greater New York frame of reference. One week *New York* might deal with "the New Bohemia" of the East Village or whether commercial success would spoil the offhand personality of *The Village Voice*; the next week, it would be the perils of pampered adolescence in Fairfield County or how Helen Gurley Brown ran *Cosmopolitan.*

The hallmark of the magazine during its life as a *Tribune* Sunday supplement was the work for it by Tom Wolfe, who thrived on the stylistic freedom granted him by Felker. Together, they attacked what each regarded as the greatest untold and uncovered story of the age: the vanities, extravagances, pretensions, and artifice of America two decades after World War II, the wealthiest society the world had ever known.

The first full flowering of Wolfe's technique in exploring this subject matter under Felker's tutelage was "The Girl of the Year" in the December 6, 1964, issue of *New York*. Each year the fashion press seemed to seize on a young, attractive New York woman of at least nominal social standing, investing her with the glamour of a show-business star by way of convincing readers that real people wore designer clothes. The distinction that year was held by twenty-four-year-old "Baby Jane" Holzer, a child of wealth married to a young real estate mogul with a Princeton degree and living in a large Park Avenue apartment with expensive landscapes on the walls. A sometime model and actress in underground movies, Jane Holzer and her world could not have been brought vividly to life under the strictures of traditional journalism, which required the writer to adopt what Wolfe called a "calm, cultivated and in fact genteel voice" with "a pale-beige tone" of understatement that he felt had begun to pall by the 'Sixties. Conventional journalism, Wolfe would argue later, had become "retrograde, lazy, slipshod, superficial, and, above all, incomplete—should I say blind? —in its coverage of American life." To render it adequately, he developed a scenic technique that was the essence of what would shortly become known as the New Journalism: "The idea was to give the full objective description, plus something that readers had always had to go to novels and short stories for: namely, the subjective or emotional life of the characters." To convey this, Wolfe invented a prose style of utter distinctiveness, shifting restlessly back and forth in time and place to gather dimension and perspective as he traveled, absorbing images in multicolored flashes, dialogue in all its often inarticulate inanity, and a surfeit of physical particulars that were both vivifying and inferentially judgmental. His writing indulged in every device the language offered— gratuitous capitalization, insistent italics, dashes and ellipses like traffic signals on the freeway of his thoughts, a picket fence of exclamation points, repetition for emphasis, sometimes no punctuation at all, extended similes, leaping metaphors, somersaulting appositives, mock-heroic invocations, arch interjections, rocketing hyperbole, antic onomatopoeia. Thus, Wolfe opened his portrait of Jane Holzer by peering out of her eye sockets upon the scene of a Rolling Stones concert:

> Bangs manes bouffants beehive Beatle caps butter faces brush-on lashes decal eyes puffy sweaters French thrust bras flailing leather blue jeans stretch pants stretch jeans honey dew bottoms eclair shanks elf boots ballerinas Knight slippers, hundreds of them these flaming little buds, bobbing and screaming, rocketing around inside the Academy of Music Theater underneath that vast old mouldering cherub dome up there—aren't they super-marvelous!
>
> "Aren't they super-marvelous!" says Baby Jane, and then: "Hi, Isabel! You want to sit backstage—with the Stones?"

Then Wolfe moved back and placed his subject in the scene:

> Girls are reeling this way and that way in the aisle and through their huge black decal eyes, sagging with Tiger Tongue Lick Me brush-on eyelashes and black appliqués, sagging like display window Christmas trees, they keep staring at—her— Baby Jane—on the aisle. What the hell is this? She is gorgeous in the most outrageous way. Her hair rises up from her head in a huge hairy corona, a huge tan mane around a narrow face and two eyes opened—swock!—like umbrellas, with all that hair flowing down over a coat made of . . . zebra! Those motherless stripes! Oh, damn! Here she is with her friends, looking like some kind of queen bee for all flaming little buds everywhere. She twists around to shout to one of her friends

and that incredible mane swings around on her shoulders, over the zebra coat. "Isabel!" says Baby Jane, "Isabel, hi! I just saw the Stones! They look super-divine!"

"The Girl of the Year" was not a story at all by any conventional journalistic standard; it was a reportorial collage, the artfully flung debris of a social condition, projected through a lens that distorted by design. Objectivity need not apply. But it was fact upon which Tom Wolfe built his effects. "Style can't carry a story if you haven't done the reporting," he said. "If you're writing non-fiction that you want to read as well as fiction, you've got to have all those details—you can't make it up."

Once at least, when he had not obtained enough details and instead relied on hearsay, indulgent style, and tendentiousness to carry off his performance, Wolfe dishonored himself and the *Tribune.* He and Felker had decided that *The New Yorker* had a grossly inflated reputation and was regarded by all but *derrière-garde* literati as moribund and pretentious; Wolfe would take the magazine—and its august and reclusive editor, William Shawn—down a few pegs in his withering fashion.

Wolfe called Shawn for an interview and was turned down, and everyone else there he tried also refused him, though Shawn later denied Wolfe's claim that the editor had directed his staff to do so. So Wolfe scraped and scrounged for information from former staff members and contributors—no easy trick since the magazine seemed to grant lifetime tenure to its employees and paid its writers the highest rates in Christendom—and anywhere else he could find it, and delivered a two-part, 11,000-word snort intended to be a dose of *The New Yorker*'s own medicine and a disrobing of Shawn. Appearing in *New York* on April 11, 1965, the first part was titled "Tiny Mummies! The True Story of the Ruler of 43rd Street's Land of the Walking Dead!" Shawn obtained a copy before publication, accused Wolfe and the *Tribune* of character assassination, and appealed to Whitney to suppress it.

If he had stuck to literary criticism, Wolfe would have been on defensible ground. In deriding *The New Yorker* as "the most successful suburban women's magazine in the country" and dismissing it for "a strikingly low level of literary achievement" that, save for the contributions of Mary McCarthy, J. D. Salinger, John O'Hara, and John Updike, had taken it "practically out of literary competition altogether" for the past fifteen years, he might have mustered some agreement. *The New Yorker*'s non-fiction did seem to specialize in great, long, limp, meticulously punctuated but unreadable sentences with multiple dependent clauses—"Lost in the Whichy Thicket," Wolfe titled the second article by way of spoofing the magazine's prevailing style. And it was not outlandishly beyond the realm of fair critical comment to suggest that *The New Yorker*'s real value and purpose was what Wolfe characterized as "a national shopping news" with its articles providing "the thin connective tissue" between all the ads for fancy things and ritzy places.

When he went on, however, to mock the fustiness of the magazine's physical surroundings, customs, editorial procedures, and chief editor, Wolfe lacked both factual ammunition and targets worth demolishing. He wrote of how James Thurber's office was maintained as a shrine, of a steady blizzard of multicolored interoffice memos on "rag-fiber" paper of the highest quality, of elaborate editing machinery in which copy went in one end and was eventually extruded in a form often unrecognizable to and unapproved by the author. He pictured the hallways as filled with aged messengers bearing those countless colored memos on paper of the best quality, "caroming off each other—bonk old bison heads . . . transporting these thousands of messages with their kindly old elder bison shuffles shoop-shooping along." But he reserved the full strength of his mockery for Shawn, "the Colorfully Shy Man," whom he portrayed as neurotically diffident, excessively polite, soft-spoken with spastic little pauses between words, draped in layers of sweaters as he went pat-pat-patting through the halls—"The Smiling Embalmer" who ruled with an iron hand over "The Whisper Zone." Shawn's alleged paranoid behavior Wolfe tied by strong intimation to "the story" that it was he rather than Bobby Franks, a fellow pupil at his Chicago private grammar school, who had been the intended victim of the notorious Loeb-Leopold thrill murder. Finally, he reported that Shawn in his shyness failed to attend his magazine's gala fortieth birthday party at the St. Regis Hotel; Wolfe imagined him instead staying home alone with his collection of beloved jazz records and songs of a better, bygone age, listening to the classic version of "I Can't Get Started," which Wolfe attributed to Bix Beiderbecke.

But it was not Bix Beiderbecke who recorded "the real 'I Can't Get Started,' " it was Bunny Berigan—a standard known to most music buffs. James Thurber's old office was not set aside as a shrine but was in regular use. The interoffice memos were on ordinary paper and not systematically colored (and what was funny about old men serving out their years as messengers?). And writers for *The New Yorker* were shown the edited version of their prose and their approval was required. There was no persuasive documentation linking Shawn to the Loeb-Leopold case other than his having attended the same school as the murdered boy. And there were too many other un-facts and wrong details that could not be waved away as literary license. The essence of the charge against Shawn that prompted this elaborate needling was that he was a shy man who ran a dull magazine. The whole business added up to a case of confected overkill. But Whitney would not suppress it, and it raised a storm.

E. B. White wrote Whitney that Wolfe's piece "violated every rule of conduct I know anything about. It is sly, cruel, and to a large extent undocumented, and it has, I think, shocked everyone who knows what sort of person Shawn really is. I can't imagine why you published it—the virtuosity of the writer makes it all the more contemptible. . . ." The *really* reclusive J. D. Salinger wired that Wolfe's "sub-collegiate and gleeful and unrelievedly poisonous article" was so terrible that Whitney's name "will very likely never again stand for anything either respect-worthy or honorable." Richard Rovere, who had written for *The New Yorker* for twenty-one years, added, "In no important respect is the place I have known the one described by Tom Wolfe." *New York Post* columnist Murray Kempton called Wolfe "a ballet dancer whose chief satisfaction from the life of art is the chance it gives to wear spangles."

The uproar appalled Jock Whitney, who knew many of the complainants personally and found Wolfe's pieces gratuitously abusive, done for the sport of it, and overstepping the bounds of propriety—"and propriety was very important to him," recalled Ray Price, Whitney's *Tribune* confidant. But the louder Wolfe's denouncers wailed, the less Whitney was inclined to confess culpability in public. Price's counsel to him was persuasive: "We have every right to dissect The New Yorker, and to do it irreverently, even zestfully, which Tom did. . . . The pieces *were* cruel. They were *not* malicious. . . . Maybe everybody's so protective of Shawn because he needs protection; but dammitall, he *is* a public figure and his magazine *does* dish it out, sometimes with a cruel hand. The crybabies ought to be able to take it, too. . . . Maybe they thought they were, or should be, immune . . ." In the end, Wolfe went unreprimanded, although his editors got a dressing-down from Bellows, and while they would ever after regret the factual errors and distortions, Wolfe and Felker believed the lampoon had captured the figurative truth and accurately lanced the magazine's bloated reputation.

The notoriety of his send-up of *The New Yorker* had the effect unintended by Wolfe's detractors of greatly enhancing his fame. A thoughtful critique by Dwight Macdonald in *The New York Review of Books* animadverted on the Wolfe technique, calling it "parajournalism . . . a bastard form, having it both ways, exploiting the factual authority of journalism and the atmospheric license of fiction." Less hostile was Leonard Lewin, himself a gifted social satirist, who examined the Wolfe–*New Yorker* affair in the *Columbia Journalism Review,* noted that in his more successful efforts Wolfe achieved "an intimacy and a sense of participation rarely possible in conventional non-fiction," but concluded: " 'Fact' and 'fiction,' like 'news' and 'opinion,' must be distinguishable, however interwoven and however great an effort it requires from the reader or the writer. Even when it spoils the fun; it's one of the entrance requirements of the trade."

With Wolfe as its prime attraction, Felker's magazine won increasing attention and admiration. Writing in *Saturday Review* early in 1966 on the proliferation of homegrown Sunday newspaper supplements, John Tebbel said, "Far in the lead is the *New York Herald Tribune*'s New York magazine, whose editor, Clay Felker, is turning out a brilliant, sophisticated product that has broken entirely new ground." Both the magazine and the rest of the Sunday paper, Tebbel feared, might be too far ahead of their time to succeed commercially. He was right. Yet looking back nearly two decades later, *New York Times* publisher Punch Sulzberger remarked, in conceding that his paper had been at least somewhat influenced by the *Tribune*'s stress on lifestyle reportage, "I thought that Clay Felker in particular made an impact on American journalism by what he did with that magazine."

III

Well before March 30, 1965, the common expiration date of the contracts between New York's six daily newspapers and their ten labor unions as a result of the 114-day strike during the 1962–63 winter, Walter Thayer had come to understand fully that the basic issue facing the *Tribune* in the next round of negotiations was not wages but worker productivity. The paper's revenues had been stalled in the $25 to $26 million range for half a dozen years—the strike, of course, had depressed them just when a breakthrough seemed possible, and now it was a struggle to sustain that level—while annual expenses had surpassed $31 million. The only realistic hope for slashing the deficit was to persuade the unions that unless the *Tribune* was permitted to automate and be relieved of featherbedding, it would have to go out of business. Just as the typographical union's president, Bertram Powers, had not been bluffing in 1962 when he talked tough, now Thayer was prepared to be adamant and suspend operations until he got what the paper desperately needed. To do that, though, he would need the cooperation of his competitors.

Bert Powers understood that time was not on his side—that technology was rapidly coming into use that made the basic skills of his Big Six printers obsolescent. But he also understood his adversaries and their divergent motives and was a master at playing them off against one another to buy time and a better deal for his men. Because the printers' contract had remained silent on the publishers' right to introduce new labor-saving equipment, Powers recognized his union's vulnerability; all that had been established earlier was that Big Six personnel had to operate whatever new machines were brought into the shop. Since 1963, the *Tribune* and *Times* had been setting the stock market tables automatically on TTS tape supplied from outside their shops by the AP, but what part, if any, of the resulting savings would be handed over to the printers was left for future negotiations. The *Tribune* was saving $50,000 a year on the TTS stock market setting, the only use of outside tape permitted under the 1963 settlement, and Powers wanted all of it. Not surprisingly, the negotiations were deadlocked and put off for resolution in the 1965 contract.

A far more pressing issue than the use of outside tape was the question of automation within each paper's composing room, and Powers was determined to make the price for yielding on it just as high as he could get—and the longer he could delay it and the more urgent the publishers' need, the better the deal he could eventually swing. By 1965, all the papers were willing to sign contracts with the printers assuring them that if the union gave them the green light to automate fully, the only resulting job losses would come from attrition (i.e., printers who retired, resigned voluntarily, or died). But Powers's price was a good deal higher than that. "We're not trying to hang on to a fixed number of jobs," he told *The Wall Street Journal* a month before the contract was up. "We accept the barrier to job opportunity that attrition means to us; we accept the reduction in newspaper jobs. But we want compensation for this." What he had in mind, Big Six had made known in 1964, was the establishment of an "automation fund," a contribution by the publishers equal to 5 percent of the printers' gross salaries, to be used for retraining them to use the new technology and sustaining their pension and welfare funds, which would be imperiled otherwise as future newspaper jobs dried up.

The *Times,* with by far the biggest payroll and the largest stake in automation among the city papers, hired an outside consultant who, acting independently of the other newspapers, negotiated a formula with Powers in 1964 that might have served as a model for all of them. It projected a fifteen-year agreement under which the printers' union would initially receive 63 percent of the *Times*'s direct payroll savings from automation; the percentage would decline over the life of the agreement until it reached zero. The industrial relations department at the *Daily News* urged its management not to share any savings from automation with Big Six because it felt the amounts were hard to calculate and the union would probably insist on inspecting the paper's books and start fussing about its profit levels. A more prudent plan, it was argued, was a "buyout" arrangement under which a fixed payment would be made to the union for a given number of years as a supplement to a citywide agreement that the printers' payroll would be reduced on an attrition-only basis after the green light for automation. But the *News* industrial relations office's January 20, 1965, recommendation to its negotiating team was that any newspaper employer who offered the attrition-only guarantee without further payment to the union "has met his economic and humane obligations to his employees in addition to his obligation to society." The *News,* in short, was ready to take a hard line against Powers. At the *Tribune,* as the negotiating was about to begin in earnest, Robert MacDonald advised Walter Thayer that if existing automation devices could be introduced into all departments, including the mail room, the savings would amount to between four and five million dollars annually—enough to bring the paper up to the break-even level. Thayer was not eager to lose that chance by giving Powers's union a major portion of such savings.

To prevent a repetition of the 1962–63 negotiations, in which they were outmuscled and impotent, the publishers brought in an outsider, John Gaherin, a labor negotiator with extensive experience in the railroad industry, which had faced automation issues similar to those in the printing trades, to head up their dealings with the unions. While he did not close the door to the principle of an automation fund or other supplementary enticements, Gaherin stated to the unions that their per-worker productivity was 25 percent lower than that of most leading papers in other cities and that TTS was in wide use outside New

York by newspapers that had not been required to pay over a substantial part of the savings in addition to their pledge of attrition-only reductions in the printers' payroll; the time had come for them to give New York's hard-pressed publishers the green light, to end bogus and other obstructionist tactics, and to assure the economic security and well-being of their own rank and file by helping the publishers into the modern age.

But in asking the printers to barter their own future as a union, the publishers showed no willingness to offer Powers the sort of premium he was asking. His price seemed to go up instead of coming down as if to dramatize the gravity of the issue. The publishers were worried about their profits, he said, but his members were worried about their lives. Yes, he would talk automation—*if* all current jobs would be guaranteed, *if* all substitutes on Big Six's rolls were covered as well, *if* the work positions would be assured by the surviving papers in the city in the event any of the six existing ones went out of business. There would have to be an automation fund to cover the effects of what Powers termed the "silent firings," by which he meant the future lost job opportunities in the newspaper trade and the resulting threat to the unemployment and retirement benefits of the current membership. And the rate of automation would have to be approved by the union. Finally, almost as if to convince the publishers they were once again confronted by a wild man across the bargaining table, Powers put down his other inflated contract requests unrelated to the automation issue: a fifteen-dollar weekly pay increase, a reduction in the work week from thirty-five to thirty hours, a fourth week of paid vacation, and a 233 percent increase in the publishers' contribution to the union pension fund. Just in case anyone was not taking him seriously this time, Powers wrote in the president's column of the Big Six monthly bulletin: "The newspaper publishers of New York City would make a fatal error in underestimating the full demands of the [union] membership in these negotiations."

By early February, the contract talks were deadlocked. To dramatize the urgency of the situation, the *Tribune* management sent a letter to all employees stressing that in view of the paper's continuing heavy flow of red ink, money for wage and benefit increases would be forthcoming only if major gains in productivity could be achieved. Management stood ready to make the capital investment in automation because "we have every confidence in the future of the Herald Tribune and we believe the long struggle to put the paper on its feet can be a successful one"—but only if the ownership was granted freedom from the restrictions that had prevented the introduction of new technology or made it prohibitively expensive. The plaintive appeal was like a whisper in a hurricane. On March 3, 1965, Big Six voted 1,978 to 28 to authorize a new strike at the end of the month if the publishers did not accommodate them.

The publishers' only chance to soften Powers's position would have been solidarity within their own ranks. But their degrees of resolve toward the militant printers' leader varied widely. The cash-short afternoon papers were in no position to put up the large sums required both to automate and to meet labor's bill for the privilege to do so. Their vision, as usual, was short-range; their goal, the cheapest settlement obtainable. The morning papers had longer vision and more cash, but their strategies differed with their competitive situations. The *News,* the most prosperous paper in town and free now of competition in the mass market after the 1963 death of the *Mirror,* was ready for an endurance struggle with the unions to win a breakthrough in automation. The *Tribune,* viewing the status quo as ruinous, matched the *News* in determination. But neither paper trusted the *Times* in labor matters. The *News* in particular viewed the *Times* as a weak sister because of its reluctance to shut down to combat union pressure, especially now, after the 114-day interruption of its historic mission in the bargaining two years earlier. From the *Tribune*'s perspective, the *Times*'s vested interest in the 1965 bargaining appeared to be diametrically opposed to its own. The *Times,* still experimenting with the new automated technology, could afford to wait until it was sure the gains in productivity would be worth the price Powers was demanding; the *Tribune* needed immediate relief. More to the point, if automation yielded the promised productivity gains at the *Times,* it would strengthen the *Tribune* as well —and that was not in the interest of the *Times,* which had netted less than 2 percent on its revenues in 1964. If the *Tribune* could not automate and instead had to absorb another costly settlement with the intransigent Powers, Jock Whitney's will to endure his paper's punishing financial performance might be shattered.

With the contract deadline imminent, settlement prospects seemed remote. Five of the newspaper unions, including the Guild, largest of them all, had agreed to a $10.50-a-week package, but Powers's price was higher, and he had given nothing away on the automation issue while still demanding 100 percent of the direct savings on the use of outside TTS tape and control over the rate at which new equipment could be brought in by the papers. Faced with what they considered Powers's exorbitant demands across the board, the publishers decided to avoid a showdown on all the automation issues except one—Big Six's refusal to allow use of outside arbitrators to resolve the dispute over the introduction of the new technology except under circumstances that amounted to a union veto over the publishers' plans. In a second letter to its staff, dated March 22, 1965, with the contract deadline a week away, the *Tribune* management warned that another strike could be "disastrous," then added:

> But, from our point of view, there are limits beyond which we cannot go. The Herald Tribune has been losing money for years. We now are engaged in a massive, determined effort to put the paper on a sound basis financially, and, by doing so, to insure both its survival and its success. We simply cannot do this if, on the one hand, we yield to pressure for higher wages and costly new benefits; and if, on the other hand, we accept a technological freeze which will deny us, perhaps forever, the savings from which these wages and benefits can be paid.
>
> In these negotiations we, and, in our opinion, some of the other newspapers, quite literally are negotiating for survival . . .

But *The New York Times* was not among them, and without the *Times* the other papers were powerless to resist Big Six. When the *Times* declined to be pinned down by the *Tribune* and *News* on a wage settlement figure beyond which it would endure a strike rather than yield to Powers, Thayer and his chief ally in the negotiations, *News* president Jack Flynn, knew the fight was over. The *Times* would not take a strike—not again, not at that time and that price, for doubtful results, which, even if they materialized, would bolster their chief competitor; enfeebled though it was, the *Tribune,* once automated and backed by the Whitney fortune, might become a formidable force. The strike was avoided by the publishers' surrender to Powers. He got a twelve-dollar wage package, 100 percent of the direct savings from the use of outside TTS tape, and, most critical, a veto over the introduction of the new equipment.

After the damage was done, Punch Sulzberger wrote to Whitney, hoping for the restoration of cordiality between them while conceding their "fundamental difference" over whether "this was the year to 'take on' Mr. Powers. Perhaps Walter and I should have talked this one out instead of letting it rest in the background." In *Times Talk,* his paper's house organ, Sulzberger told his staff, "The simple fact of the matter is that the Typographical Union . . . placed a lid on progress. The lid can be removed for money, but to date no one, including the Times, has that much money." To Thayer, the *Times*'s softness in the bargaining was attributable at least in part to its ambition to bring the *Tribune* down. "It was a factor," he charged in retrospect. "There was a certain cordiality between Jock and Punch, but not below that level. Monroe Green and the rest of them [at the *Times*] hated our guts." Sulzberger denied the charge: "It's absolutely wrong to say we took a contract because it was bad for somebody else. We were dictated to by the unions—and there was absolutely nothing we could have done about it."

IV

Far from grieving, the *Tribune* put on a happy face to its advertising clientele in the immediate wake of the labor settlement.

Promotion director Charles Lawliss, with Walter Thayer's blessing, splurged one full quarter of his million-dollar out-of-office budget on a perky musical revue titled "The Saga of the Dingbat" (a reference to the strange ninety-nine-year-old device in the middle of the paper's front-page nameplate) that sang the *Tribune*'s praises. Staged in a small ballroom at the Plaza Hotel and running for thirteen performances beginning at the end of that April of surrender to Bert Powers, the forty-five-minute extravaganza was a slickly professional production with a cast of eight. Some 6,500 members of the New York advertising community were treated to drinks, a meal, and the show, which featured blackout routines needling the competition and songs with lyrics like: "We've got a style / That's versatile / That's what fine writing brings / That's why the Herald Tribune swings."

Meanwhile, Walter Thayer was on the verge of merging the *Tribune* out of existence as an independent entity. Losses for the fiscal year ending that April 30 were over $5 million, and after the collapse of his hopes for progress on the labor front, he saw no other realistic course to keep the paper alive.

Meeting secretly with the chief executives of the *Journal-American* and the *World-Telegram,* which had a combined operating loss even higher than the *Tribune*'s, Thayer took the lead in formulating a proposed equal partnership among the three papers. The new company would issue the *Tribune* in the morning, the *World Journal* in the afternoon, and an amalgam of the *Tribune* and the *Journal-American* on Sunday (since the *World-Telegram* did not publish that day). Through economies realized by combining production and business staffs—the joint payroll would be at least one-third smaller than the total for the three papers separately—a profit in the range of $4 to $5 million annually was projected from the start. And each partner would retain its editorial voice: the *Tribune* management in the morning, the *Telegram* in the afternoon, and the *Journal* on Sunday.

Although Whitney did not find the other papers and their people congenial, under Thayer's prodding he began warming up to the idea. The only real problem appeared to be the tone of the Sunday paper, of which Richard Wald was tentatively selected to serve as the editor. The Sunday *Journal* had a huge sale, 875,000 copies, based heavily on its comics, pocket-sized TV magazine, and some bright features and columnists; the Sunday *Tribune,* far more sophisticated, had shrunk to a circulation of 375,000, but because its readership was far richer and better educated, it carried twice the advertising volume of the *Journal.* Should the combined paper, therefore, be essentially the old *Journal* with the addition from the *Tribune* of *New York, Book Week,* and its galaxy of columnists such as Lippmann, Buchwald, and Red Smith? Or ought it to be essentially the Sunday *Tribune* wrapped inside the *Journal* comics with the top Hearst bylined columnists and the TV magazine added in odd-bedfellowship?

While the Sunday problem and many other loose ends were being played with, in mid-June NBC television reporter Gabe Pressman broke the story of the secret merger talks, causing great alarm among the unions that had not come to terms yet with the city papers and were working without a contract. The publishers' earlier pledge that union jobs would be lost only through attrition if they were allowed to automate no longer applied. Automation was out of the picture under the contract Powers had won, and a merger of the three papers would cost the unions a lot of jobs. Thayer stressed in a public statement that reports of an agreement among the three papers were highly speculative, but he did not miss the chance to use the prospect of the merger as a club to try to get the unions to reverse the Big Six–imposed postponement of the green light for automation. Appearing before the Newspaper Trades Council, Thayer told the union leaders that there was an alternative to the merger. "Our position has deteriorated," the *Tribune* president said. "We are willing to gamble, but not under the present work rules. . . . The *Tribune* could be in the black—and without any job loss—if we were permitted to be. But we're not going to give you savings that don't exist." He added pointedly that "the *News* and the *Times* can sweat it out, until there are fewer papers," and concluded ominously, "Any change will involve [loss of] jobs, but no change will involve more jobs." Some of his listeners were sympathetic, but most of the labor leadership viewed the merger possibility only as a threat to their members' jobs rather than as the act of desperation that it was by the newspapers involved.

As the labor picture grew increasingly snarled, especially over the Guild's insistence on obtaining a veto over automation in workplaces under its jurisdiction similar to the power yielded to the printers, the proposed merger began to come unraveled over the financial impact upon the joint venture of continuing the *Tribune* as a separate morning paper. *Tribune* calculations based on labor savings and other economies in the compacted operation put the morning paper narrowly in the black; the Hearst and Scripps-Howard figures showed a loss on it of about a million a year. Like the good lawyer he was, Thayer sent a brieflike memo in mid-August to his opposite numbers on the other two papers, arguing that the *Tribune* ought not to be abandoned because the morning field was the dominant one in the New York market, with greater growth potential than the evening one, which was suffering badly from competition by suburban papers and television. Without the *Tribune,* moreover, the new venture could not offer a morning-evening combination that would provide advertisers with an attractive alternative to the *Times*; the Sunday paper would lose standing if the *Tribune,* a prestigious national daily, were to disappear; and it was doubtful that the daily *Tribune*'s lucrative financial, media, and travel advertising linage could be readily transferred to the surviving evening paper. But to show the *Tribune*'s confidence in its value to the joint venture as an ongoing morning publication, Thayer was willing to add an "extra chip" to the merger pot: Whitney Communications would make up any loss in excess of $500,000 due to the *Tribune* for the first two years of the joint venture, but if the loss exceeded a million in the first year, the *Tribune* could suspend at that point; and, at any rate, after the second year, the board of directors would be free to discontinue the morning paper by majority vote. The offer was declined.

Before the merger talks could be resuscitated, the Guild, the only union whose contracts called for it to negotiate separately with each publisher, struck the *Times* over the automation issue and two matters that did not affect the other papers—the *Times*'s refusal, on principle, to require its editorial personnel to join the Guild, although some 90 percent of them did, and the paper's contribution to the Guild pension fund, which the union said was inadequate. Admitting it had made a mistake with the printers in granting them a veto on new equipment, the *Times* said it would not compound the error with the Guild and held fast as well on the other issues. Before the Guild walkout, Thayer circulated a memo among the publishers pledging a mutual shutdown if any one of them was struck, provided only that the publishers' association president, John Gaherin, ruled that the struck paper was not acting irresponsibly in its bargaining position. Only the *Times* balked at signing the pledge, refusing to go beyond a statement that it was "almost inconceivable" it would not close down in sympathy with a struck sister paper; the *Times* simply valued its own continuous publication too highly to relinquish to Gaherin or any outsider the power to decide its fate. Thayer, his exasperation peaking, abandoned hope of trying to get the *Times* to play ball with the other publishers. "There comes a limit to trying to pin custard to the wall," he later wrote Flynn of the *News,* "and I gave up."

On September 16, the *Tribune* reluctantly stopped publishing in sympathy with the struck *Times,* as did all the papers except the *Post,* which had never rejoined the publishers' association after breaking with it and resuming publication before the 1963 strike settlement. But after ten days, Thayer and Whitney decided they had had enough—that it was the *Times*'s own ineptness and stubbornness that had caused the Guild walkout and it was suicidal for the *Tribune* to stay down to honor a principle that the *Times* had not absolutely pledged to support. "It was a very close decision for us," Thayer said, meaning for him and Whitney, "and easy for everyone else," meaning the editorial and advertising staffs, which were clamoring for the chance to publish while the *Times* and *News* were off the streets. In his letter to Gaherin resigning from the association, Thayer said the issues in the *Times*-Guild dispute were petty compared to the ones in the "unrealistic" settlement that the *Times* in effect forced in the spring by caving in to Powers; the current shutdown "cannot undo what happened last March. . . . In this critical stage of our history we must, for the future of the Herald Tribune and its employees, be free to follow our own judgment." To *Editor & Publisher,* Thayer explained that the *Tribune* had suffered more than any other paper due to the 1962–63 strike because it had registered circulation gains for eighteen straight months over the year-earlier figures before having to suspend publication. "We had real momentum then," he added, "that we have only just begun to get back."

In order not to appear overly opportunistic, Thayer limited the size of the *Tribune* daily to forty-eight pages but put no lid on the number of copies to be printed. For fourteen days, right in the middle of the hottest mayoral campaign in a generation, and during which the Pope came to the city, the *Tribune* was the only morning newspaper published in New York. Its sales soared past 900,000 copies a day. The mood in the office was euphoric. A lot of readers were being introduced to the paper's liveliness—and perhaps enough of them would stick with it to make a difference.

At the *Times,* they saw only treachery in the *Tribune*'s move. Punch Sulzberger remembered it hotly even after nearly twenty years: "It was a shitty thing to do. If you're in, you stay in; if you want out, you give some warning." At the *Daily News,* Jack Flynn saw betrayal by supposed friends who he had thought would stand firm. He disagreed "strongly and completely" with Thayer, Flynn wrote to him, and bemoaned "the havoc you have wrought." Thayer waited until the *Times* had settled with the Guild before answering Flynn, and when he did he was far from apologetic. Flynn's fury was misdirected at the *Tribune,* Thayer said; it was the *Times* that had failed to stand firm when it counted. He recalled that Flynn had conceded Thayer's surmise at the beginning of the Guild walkout that the *Times* "might not be in a hurry to settle in view of the pressures of the strike on the Herald Tribune." A protracted strike might have hurt the *News,* but "it won't kill you," Thayer argued, as it would have done to the *Tribune.* Actually, Thayer continued, he doubted that the *News* or *Times* had suffered "one little bit" from the *Tribune*'s action, which he felt helped bring the *Times* to its senses and a faster settlement with the Guild. On the other hand, Thayer wrote, "I am extremely conscious of the havoc that the *Times* is trying to bring on us and some of the things they have been doing in an effort to make it impossible for us to publish this newspaper in this city. This is not new. It has been going on for a long time."

No evidence was ever produced, however, to show that the *Times* acted in an illegal or immoral manner toward the *Herald Tribune*; it was, rather, a tough competitor, using its strength to its advantage in a way long accepted as legitimate under American free enterprise. Punch Sulzberger would acknowledge only that the death of the *Tribune* "made a substantial difference in the fortunes of *The New York Times.*" Freed of quality competition in the morning field, the *Times* enjoyed an immediate surge in readership, Sulzberger noted, allowing it to raise its advertising and circulation rates aggressively and to escape from the perilously thin profit margins under which it had long labored while building itself into an invincible institution.

Within a month after the *Times* and *News* resumed publication in mid-October 1965, the *Tribune*'s daily sales were back down to 305,000. It had held none of the huge circulation it had enjoyed when it romped alone in the morning field during the *Times*'s twenty-five-day shutdown. The meaning of these stunning numbers could not be denied.

V

The oldtimers especially knew they were working on a newspaper under a death sentence, but they gave their professional best to the end, even those most resentful of having been bypassed by the Bellows youth movement. None was more loyal—or bitter—than Tom O'Hara.

Among the writers usually cited on a list of those exemplifying the *Tribune* literary tradition was John O'Hara, the prolific author of novels and short stories, whom Stanley Walker hired as a twenty-three-year-old reporter in 1928.

What the legends did not note was that Walker was obliged to fire O'Hara five months later. Often insubordinate to his editors, imperious to his fellow reporters, and hung over, O'Hara was better at flinging inkwells than at turning out copy; he never got a byline or wrote anything of distinction for the *Tribune*. When L. L. Engelking hired O'Hara's brother Tom, eight years younger than John, in 1942, the city editor said he was hoping for an improvement in the family's performance.

As a boy, Tom O'Hara idolized his brother, used to bring his lunch to him at the paper John worked on in their native town of Pottsville, Pennsylvania, followed him into a writing career, mostly on Philadelphia papers before making it to New York, and when John asked him for $900 to help him get married, Tom obliged—and got repaid with $2,000 interest. On the *Tribune*, Tom was a model of dedication as a reporter. With his lilting Irish tongue and outgoing manner, he naturally wound up on the local political beat, which largely meant covering the Democratic machine, not the most rewarding assignment on a devoutly Republican paper. But he cultivated sources expertly, was trusted with confidences he would never break for a mere scoop, learned to distinguish the Throttlebottoms from the back-room powers—a national monument of his acquaintance he described, in one of his often demolishing after-work revelations at Bleeck's, as possessing "the soul of a butler"—and much preferred the adroit manipulations of the sinister-looking Tammany boss Carmine De Sapio to the naïve pieties of the well-scrubbed John Lindsay. "Every day on the paper was an adventure for him," recalled his devoted wife, Rebecca, who raised their family of seven children in a four-room apartment in an East End Avenue walk-up and, knowing Tom's love for the paper and the life of mingling with important people on a daily basis, never pushed him to seek more lucrative work.

A good, accurate reporter, Tom O'Hara was never much of a writer. Listening to him at Bleeck's as he spun out his tales of often wicked politicking, Engel would urge him to put it down on paper with the same bite and brightness, but O'Hara could not. His prose had to be coaxed out of him, and it came slowly, often muddled, the sequence wrong, holes needing to be filled, the entire piece generally requiring a careful editing pencil. And his copy was likely to reach the desk late, close to deadline, when there was little time to refine it, and sometimes it got butchered in haste and a lot of the time wound up in overset. He would rail habitually at the editing he received, yet the more frustrated he grew over his own writing, the more fiercely he seemed to defend his brother John's literary reputation, which for a long while languished despite commercial popularity. In his vocal displays of fraternal loyalty and admiration, Tom never disclosed resentment of John's success—or any sign of being offended when his brother now and then gave him his old suits, which the rumpled reporter had altered to fit him, or because he was never invited to John's fancy house with the swimming pool in Princeton. The brothers stayed in touch by phone and mail. "I don't believe Tom dwelled on it," Rebecca O'Hara said of her brother-in-law's social snubbing of them; she attributed it to John's work habits and need for privacy.

In the *Tribune*'s last five years, after John Denson had placed a much higher premium on condensed and stylish writing than on a reporter's canny inside knowledge of his field, Tom O'Hara was a marginal city-room figure, ignominiously left home even from the team covering the 1964 Democratic convention in nearby Atlantic City and asked to monitor the proceedings on television to be sure the paper did not miss anything important carried on the tube. To the youngsters around him, he was a beaten, degraded man, grubby, overweight, impoverished, his short hair turned iron-gray by then, his role on the paper reduced to serving as a savvy and cynical mentor to newcomers on the New York political beat, young men like Richard Reeves, who admired his shrewdness. "The institution he had wedded himself to," Reeves recalled, "repaid his devotion by doing the same thing to him that his brother had done—it kept him at arm's length." Yet he stayed till the end, extracting what pleasure he could from his nightly hour or two of storytelling at Bleeck's that his wife never resented. "He was entitled to relax a little after work," said Rebecca O'Hara, who did not recall her husband's ever thinking about getting a job elsewhere. "He felt he worked for the best paper. I think he would have worked there for nothing."

VI

Inky Blackman, who joined the staff the same year as Tom O'Hara, was Bob Peck's spiritual and occupational heir as the *Tribune*'s crack rewriteman, speedy, reliable, scholarly, quiet—indeed, so unobtrusive that he never exchanged a word with any of the paper's last three editors, White, Denson, and Bellows. No one had more pride in his craft, though rarely toward the end were *Tribune* rewritemen given something important to handle.

Even the most routine stuff he continued to do with professional care. No matter how many times he wrote up the beginning or the ending of Daylight Saving Time, he always ordered clips from the library to make sure of the direction he would tell readers to move their clocks. Regarding obituaries, of which he was a prime producer, Inky was fond of saying that, as characteristically put to rest in the *Times,* a man had just died; in the *Tribune* account, he had once lived. Inky was an authority on the utility and pomposity of press releases, of which he rewrote an estimated 110,000, most of them of doubtful news value but useful for makeup purposes, during his twenty-four years on the paper. About one in 10,000, he judged, had been suitable for publication as received. Almost all were written to satisfy the clients of public-relations firms rather than the needs of the newspapers to which they were ostensibly directed, and almost none contained the home telephone number of the author-flack, of whom a rewriteman for a morning paper might want to make inquiry in the evening.

Inky was unfailingly kind and helpful toward neophytes, urging them, for example, when writing an obituary to make sure that the subject was in fact completely dead. Usually he kept his own counsel in the office and shared it afterward over a drink or two at Bleeck's with fellow rewriteman Robert W. White, who had worked on a dozen smalltown papers before joining the *Tribune* in 1945. It was White who passed on to Inky his seasoned, all-purpose theory of newsworthiness, which went, in its entirety: "Somewhere a child is burning." Tragedy is in endless supply in this vale of tears called life, and which reports of it made print on any given day depended on the idiosyncratic selections of the editors and the volume of competing news; as a rule of thumb for New York papers, the farther away from Columbus Circle the dateline on a printed story of a child's tragic death, the slower the news day.

Inky Blackman himself never slipped into such cynicism, even as an insulating device. And he kept caring, to the last days of the *Tribune,* when he sent off excoriating memos to copy editors who he felt had fouled up his copy, and dispatched a more tactful note to Jock Whitney, asking why the newsstand nearest his home in Queens invariably ran out of *Tribune*s during the morning rush hour. After the paper died, he bought his old office desk and moved it into his home.

VII

Growing up in the Bay Ridge section of Brooklyn, Barrett McGurn would look out at the great oceangoing vessels passing through the Narrows of New York harbor and dream of the world beyond. The *Tribune* became his ticket to that world and its exciting events, which he covered for the paper for thirty-two years. It was in the last of them that McGurn got his biggest story, a global exclusive.

His only instructions when he was first posted abroad were to send back to the paper whatever was important and interesting—and to try for both in the same story. Rome became his main station. Foreign editor Joe Barnes told him that if he felt he had to spend time on a farm to understand what Italy was about, then he ought to take a week and do that. But the agrarian life of Italy interested McGurn far less than its ecclesiastical one, and he developed close connections with the Vatican, becoming expert on the personalities and policies of the church that had cradled him, the oldest of ten children in a devout family. Eventually, he was elected head of the 400-member association of Vatican correspondents and worked to convince the Holy See that it ought to be more forthcoming in its relations with the press.

A likable man and conscientious worker but a writer of distinct limitations, McGurn was recalled home permanently in 1963 after the great strike and reassigned as a cityside reporter. But he retained his close ties with the Catholic hierarchy in Rome and New York and wrote several books on the church. Toward the end of 1964 he learned from one of his acquaintances high in the New York diocesan office that a papal visit to the Western Hemisphere—the first ever—was being contemplated. It was not a story that could be approached directly, McGurn knew all too well, but he sent out feelers to his Vatican friends and continued to track it quietly through American sources. Gradually, the probable elements of the trip took shape in McGurn's mind, but since he could pin nothing down, he set out early in September 1965 to write a backgrounder for the Sunday paper, speculating on a papal visit. Selecting his sources discreetly, suggesting that the impending papal visit could not remain secret much longer, McGurn broke through one evening over drinks with a well-positioned priest who spilled the details: sometime before October 11, Paul VI would address the UN, meet with President Johnson while in New York, and conduct a mass at Yankee Stadium.

The story was held out of the September 8 city edition so it could remain an exclusive for the main run. No sources were cited—none could be, any more than the Vatican itself could have been asked for confirmation; McGurn had put his whole authority and judgment on the line and went home for a fitful sleep that night. His daughter awakened him at 7 a.m. with the news that the Pope was coming to America—it was on the radio; the Pontiff would arrive October 4, the Vatican told a hastily summoned news conference, corroborating all the other particulars of McGurn's worldwide exclusive. When he reached the office, he found a note on his desk from John Hay Whitney: "I looked for you this morning to say Thanks & Congratulations. We don't often have as big a one as that. Good work."

VIII

Danny Blum of the *Tribune* night desk, with the city room as the playing field, participated in a serious game of whiffleball that lasted until four o'clock one November morning in 1955. The next day he was stricken with severe poliomyelitis, and all the games ended for him at the age of thirty-one.

The stocky, dark-haired son of a German-Jewish father and Irish Protestant mother, Blum had begun working on the paper as a messenger in 1941 while attending Boys High in Brooklyn, after military service earned a degree studying journalism at NYU while holding down his job, and proved an adept night desk technician of cranky disposition and mordant wit. He was married and the father of five by the time the polio hospitalized him for eleven months, and it was doubtful that he could resume his newspaper career or begin any other. The only real movement left in his body was in his left hand; he wrote righthanded. But the *Tribune* did not discard him. They kept him at full salary the whole time he was convalescent and paid for a practical nurse at home so his wife could attend him at the hospital. Science editor Earl Ubell made sure he had the best possible medical attention. "I never felt abandoned," Blum said.

It was decided to try him on the copy desk, where the action was less demanding than on the night desk. When he had recovered enough to stand and hobble a few painful steps on crutches, Dan Blum came back to the city room in a wheelchair, propelled that first day by his wife. He was crying. Everything stopped on the fifth floor. It was in the afternoon, and somebody, day city editor Dick West probably, made a little speech. People tried to shake Dan's hand, but he could not oblige them and was too choked up to talk. It was all he could manage to wipe his tears and blow his runny nose. "It was one of those scenes you see on TV that make you want to upchuck," Blum recalled, "but this was real. And for me terribly sad but for the positive thinkers terribly uplifting. It was a homecoming, not a triumphant one—a devastating icebreaker." A few days later he started to come in regularly to break in on the copy desk. "Everyone was great—solicitous, but not overly. None of that fucking 'You'll walk again if you just keep trying and have faith.' Thank God for the realists."

The staff chipped in $2,000 to help him buy a car with special hand controls, so he could drive to work from his home in Queens. He retrained himself to write lefthanded, to inure himself to the pain of sitting all day in the same position, to edit copy fast enough to be useful and not a charity case. His taskmaster, Norman Digby, the copy desk slotman and a surly sort, showed him no mercy, lashing at him for every little thing. One day, because someone had moved his wheelchair from the stairwell near the elevators where he had left it the day before, Blum had to hobble on crutches all the way from his car, which he was allowed to park in front of the *Tribune* building, to the copy desk— perhaps an hour of excruciating, exhausting effort that left him literally dripping sweat. Panting, trembling, hardly able to talk and fearful he was going to collapse at any second, Blum hovered by his workplace. Slotman Digby looked up finally and said, "You're late. What are you waiting for? Sit down and start working."

"My chair's missing," Blum managed to answer.

"Take any damn chair," Digby said. "They're all the same."

Blum began to explain that he could not sit in just any chair, that it had to be a wheelchair with armrests for lowering and raising himself. Then, for the first time—after seeing him, talking to him, teaching him, scolding him, ridiculing him for months—it dawned on Digby that Blum was handicapped. "I didn't realize you were in a wheelchair," he said, turning white and practically falling over himself as he hurried out of the slot trying to help Blum. "And I don't think he ever got over it," Blum recounted, "not because of pity for me but pity for himself, so tied up with all that lousy copy that he really never made any time to pay attention to what was going on around him." Over the years, Blum came to cherish that apology by Digby as the best compliment he ever received: "I didn't realize you were in a wheelchair."

Through extraordinary will, he became a superior deskman, his thick, strong-looking but inert arms like giant paperweights as his one good extremity speedily improved the stories under his scrutiny. Never the most fastidious of men, he turned into something of a mess, coating the copy beneath him with a fine layer of ash from the cigar that was fixed perpetually in his face and collecting about him bits of Chinese noodles, coffee grounds, packets of sugar, and other remnants of the meals he was forced to eat where he worked; going out was a major production. But his messiness was more than compensated for by the concentration and professional insight his disability instilled. A traditionalist, he scorned the stylistic imperatives of the Denson revolution, which Blum mocked as "Don't let the facts tell the story, jazz it up, color it, back into it, make the reader notice how clever the writing is." He did not regard Bellows any more highly, describing the paper under him as "a lot of flash and fan dancing" instead of solid journalism and referring to the inarticulate editor as "Mr. Sweep" for the vague hand motions he made when he wanted a story opened up in all its cosmic implications. "Polio did not notably improve his disposition," Dick Wald said of Blum. "He was a mean, cranky, stubborn, wonderful bastard," added Don Forst, a baby-faced ex-*New York Post* rewrite ace, who shared the responsibilities of day city editor with Blum in the *Tribune*'s closing era.

Opposed to much of what Bellows stood for but recognizing his skills as a packager of the news and the genuineness of his effort to save the paper, Blum poured himself into the cause. He became the gruff guardian angel of the city room. He was deft at matching reporters to assignments, hounded them with the most reasonable unreasonable questions when their copy came in, and upon receipt of a piece well done in a light vein, would wheel over to the perpetrator's desk, emitting an approving cackle by way of commendation.

So dedicated was Blum to the paper and so warmly was his dedication reciprocated that he often stayed late at the office, until the city edition came up, and by then he was sometimes too drained from his long day's efforts to drag himself down to his car and make the taxing twenty-eight-mile drive to his new home in suburban New Jersey. So he would stay overnight, sleeping on the city desk and growing a bit rank by the following day amid the accumulating debris of his workplace. But no one was offended. Afterward, he worked for eight years at the *Times,* but it was not the same. "There was a camaraderie at the *Trib* like nowhere else," he recalled. "People there had a true affection for it—love might be a better word. It was a second home. *Times* people know how important the paper is and are grateful because that importance rubs off on them— but love it? Never."

IX

New people of talent kept coming to the *Tribune* almost to the very end. But not all were greeted warmly in the last few years, especially when they were awarded prominence, power, and money that the older staff people resented and believed, in a number of cases, to be unmerited. Bellows was said to be operating under a star system that went against the grain of the paper, promoting Jimmy Breslin, Tom Wolfe, and Dick Schaap at the expense of a lot of other gifted writers. No one's elevation generated more grumbling than that of thirty-one-year-old David Laventhol to city editor for the last year and a half of the *Tribune*'s life.

His skills were by no means obvious. A young, cautious, subdued company man with what struck some as a kind of goofy detachment, Laventhol never quite looked people in the eye and seemed ill at ease issuing orders. He knew little about the metropolitan area, relying for guidance on his daytime assistants, New York natives Dan Blum and Don Forst, who good-naturedly patronized him for his outlander's naïveté. His very seriousness invited ribbing, some of it in the form of hardly veiled anti-Semitism. Once inhospitable to Jews in its upper echelons, the paper now numbered among its ranking editors many of that faith, most of them young, who had been jumped over veteran members of the staff. Frank Thorn, a copy editor on the foreign desk and son of the composing-room day foreman, Frank Spinelli, remarked, "There was a feeling that Si Freidin went out and got guys with Jewish names and put them in key spots," and went on to suggest that there was a good deal of cliquishness among those in power "who took care of each other with a lot of money that never got down to us." That Freidin was effectively exiled to London and virtually without a voice in the paper's high council was irrelevant to such grumbling; what mattered was the perception itself, as if Jock Whitney had suddenly mandated an appointment policy based on philosemitism. Laventhol's case particularly rankled because he was not overly personable or as obviously gifted as his predecessor in the city-editorship, Dick Schaap, who could write rings around most of the reporters he edited. During his stint on the foreign desk, Laventhol had not sparkled, in the view of Frank Thorn, who helped him out as the newcomer struggled to compose headlines up to Bellows's exacting standards of liveliness.

But David Laventhol, in his understated fashion, was a highly astute journalist, destined for big things in the profession. He had edited the schoolboy sports section of the *Washington Daily News* as a teenager, was elected managing editor of the *Yale Daily News* at college, underwent thorough training in editing and layout for six years on the *St. Petersburg Times,* one of the best small papers in the country, served on the *Washington Post* national desk, and along the way picked up a master's degree in English at the University of Minnesota.

Though he may have lacked the knack for turning out *Tribune*-style headlines while he was on the foreign desk, Laventhol intently observed cable editor Harry Rosenfeld's skill at selecting, shaping, and compressing the news as he wove together wire-service copy, background from clips, and a precious eight- or ten-paragraph dispatch from one of the paper's remaining four overseas correspondents. Rosenfeld's zeal was contagious, even during the paper's last days; watching him churn out of the wire room with a hot piece of copy, an underling asked, "Was this how it was in Hitler's bunker at the end?"

As city editor, Laventhol had a lot to learn and, characteristically, did so fast. He learned to fight hard for all his people on a paper where every column inch was highly coveted. And he was heeded increasingly as he evidenced a firm grasp of the paper's news values. "The *Times* was like a supermarket where you picked what you wanted from crowded shelves that sprawled off in all directions," he reflected, "while the *Tribune* was a specialty shop that said, 'The stock we've got is limited in range but excellent of its kind.' " In place of "police-blotter news," reports from official sources, in which the *Times* specialized as the newspaper of record, as Laventhol saw it, the *Tribune* was breaking ground in social reporting of "everything that affected readers' lives."

Laventhol's opposite number on the *Times* then was metropolitan editor A. M. Rosenthal, who within a few years succeeded to his paper's executive-editorship, the most powerful position in American daily journalism. Far from disdaining the craftsmanship of his great newspaper's wobbly old rival in its death agony, Rosenthal was generally admiring. He was often in Bleeck's, fraternizing with its best young reporters—like a vulture, some thought, eager to make off with the carrion while it was still warm. "I took the *Tribune* very seriously then—it was something for us to rub up against—the only other show in town," Rosenthal recalled. "It livened things up for us. . . . They had some hellishly good writers. But I thought they overplayed stories, dealt with them promotionally. They had abandoned their old news values in a desperate effort to gain an extra 100,000 readers. What they wound up with was a newspaper that was all dessert and no main course."

Max Frankel, a leading member of the *Times* Washington bureau at the time, who would later take charge of its editorial and op-ed pages, envied the *Tribune* its brightness—"but not its looseness." There was an astringent, formal elegance to the *Times*'s style, Frankel felt, almost like working within the rigid structure of a sonnet yet trying to open it up and energize it. Reporters in his bureau would think long and hard, before filing to New York, about where the word "today" ought to go in the lead and which facts ought to go into the first-page part of the story and which could be held for the jump. "The *Trib* guys couldn't care less about that." Frankel thrived on what he called the *Times*'s "ferocity when it came to accuracy." The *Tribune* men in Washington he found politically astute, and they turned out "good, colloquial, clever copy. But they were not students of their subject."

Patrick Crow, a young Arkansan bored with his job on the national copy desk at the *Times,* noted the *Tribune*'s verve and came over to the *Tribune* city desk for the last nine months of the paper's life. He was pleased by the atmosphere of "a raffish saloon" that he encountered but was struck from the first by the stylistic indulgence extended to *Tribune* reporters. "The tendency was to stretch and color stories that were better told straight," Crow recounted. "Some stories are just more boring than others." He had exchanged the solemnity of the *Times* for the gallows-humor frivolity of the *Tribune,* where the top editors sometimes played basketball with wadded copy paper and a wastebasket during lulls in their editorial conferences.

Such informality was a mixed blessing to Crow's fellow alumnus of *The Arkansas Gazette,* Bill Whitworth, who joined the *Tribune* late in 1963 and was allowed "to follow my own instincts in reporting—they were open and responsive and very good about not pigeonholing you." Moving around the country to report on the early stages of student protest over the war in Vietnam, he was encouraged to probe deeply and quote at length in rendering the students' motives, while on the *Times,* he felt, "they covered the movement as if it were a Thanksgiving Day parade—all you knew [from their coverage] was that a bunch of people had marched, but there was no effort to find out what the point of it all really was." The trouble with the *Tribune*'s approach for Whitworth, a deliberate workman who wrote in a dry, understated way, was that he was expected to produce glittering goods even if his assignment did not warrant it. His announcement, upon returning from a three-day trip to the Miss America pageant in Atlantic City, that he had found no story there worth the paper's precious space became an office joke, his reputation for quality work notwithstanding. And when assistant city editors Blum and Forst got finished operating on Whitworth's story about the Newport Jazz Festival, he threw a tantrum and insisted his byline be removed. "They weren't editing me—they were writing it in their own zippy, corny style," Whitworth recalled, noting the paper's eagerness to appear attuned to the "youthquake" revolution. "It was like a fat lady in a miniskirt. They were trying hard, but it was pitiful when it didn't work."

Red Smith's son, Terence, who came to the staff from the Stamford, Connecticut, *Advocate* after the 1963 strike settlement, was somewhat more receptive than Whitworth to the *Tribune*'s insistent hunger for flair in its young reporters' copy. "They taught you that every piece could be arresting and readable as well as factually right and informative—that nothing really had to be dull if you took the time and got the right angle for it," Smith said. "There was a willingness to be a little outrageous" and to take chances because the paper had nothing to lose by doing so; not to was to hasten its oblivion. Thus, when Smith grew weary cooling his heels outside a session of New York Republican chieftains in a public meeting room at the Biltmore Hotel in March 1965 to discuss the city mayoralty race, he wandered into the adjacent empty room to rest his feet. Through a metal grate in the ceiling he heard familiar voices, one of them with Nelson Rockefeller's inimitable nasal tones, emanating from the closed-door conclave next door. Smith stood up on a chair, scribbled notes madly on the proceedings that he could now clearly overhear, and hurried back to the office, where Dan Blum rejoiced over the eavesdroppings. The resulting story, revealing that John Lindsay was disinclined to yield to his party's prodding that he make the mayoral race but had not definitely ruled out the possibility, was bannered across the top of page one. At the *Times,* where he would work as a reporter and editor for the next twenty years, Terry Smith thought that "a reporter returning with that story would have been met by a sober face and a dutiful decision to give it a one-column head," almost certainly below the front-page fold.

Nothing better exemplified the *Tribune*'s willingness to take risks at the end of its life than the hiring as a reporter—the last one to be taken on and probably the oldest cub in the paper's history—of Seymour Krim, who, at forty-three, was a minor but authentic literary figure of the generation that came of age with World War II. A spirited essayist sympathetic to avant-garde literature, Krim was a passionately serious man in need of work after the folding of *Nugget,* a girlie magazine with literary pretensions on the *Playboy* model, of which he had been the editor. "What a wrench from my little armpit of a world down here," he recalled of his departure from the East Village bohemia where he was a familiar figure. "I had seen myself as a Proustian guy who observes life and then goes back to his well-insulated place in it. I could not retreat at the *Trib.* . . . It was wonderful for an isolate like me." Until then, he had always agonized over his prose; on the paper, he had to deliver his copy by six-thirty every night. The discipline was a release for him: "Instead of pigeon-toeing it and squatting on it and neuroticizing it, I didn't care. . . . I leapt to the rhythm of it." To his surprise, Krim was treated with respect and sensitivity—except for the time Blum set him up to tip the authorities about a nude dancing company on East Eighth Street in the hope of scoring a beat if the police raided the premises. Sickened by his own complicity in undermining a group exercise in authentic artistic expression, especially after his role in alerting the bluenoses had been detected and he got turned away from the theater where the dancers were performing, Krim refused to complete the assignment. But it was the only time. In five months on the *Tribune* just before it died, his copy ran about fifty times.

Krim repaid the paper for providing him with "the most exhilarating time of my life" by writing an elegiac essay in 1970 titled "The Newspaper as Literature / Literature as Leadership" that amounted to a celebration of what the *Herald Tribune* sought to bring to American journalism in its final fling under Bellows & Company. The traditional reporter was not really a writer, Krim suggested, but a subspecies thereof—"a machine, a phone-bully, a sidewalk-buttonholer, a privacy-invader, a freebie-collector," who had to process the information he gathered within strictly formulaic bounds that fell far short of reality. The *Tribune,* as the first newspaper outside the literary underground to promote the New Journalism, significantly reshaped the definition of news "by coverage that made uncommon human sense as well as giving the facts." No longer flat and closed but dimensional and open now, journalism was capable of becoming "the de facto literature of our time." Krim particularly cited Tom Wolfe for his "rhythmic montage of disjointed contemporary phenomena" and Jimmy Breslin for the "novelistic fullness of his re-creation of reality."

It was Breslin more than anyone else on the *Tribune* who drew Krim's attention: "he was the leader." And by far wider testimony than Krim's, it was Breslin who represented the best and the worst of the *Tribune* at its end.

By the force of his talent and an often perverse personality, he dominated the office as he did the paper—its first writer, always on top of the big story, handling it his way, played up in the layout, pampered by his editors until he had become nearly a law unto himself. Breslin seemed incapable of producing his copy until goaded by the deadline; his whole metabolism was synchronized with the day's ebb and flow of news, from the moment he first called in to Danny Blum on the city desk at 10 a.m. to ask, "What's doin'?" He always stayed in touch with the desk, the mark of the professional newspaperman who knows his value.

As a parody of his work in *The New Yorker* suggested, Breslin was not without his sentimental excesses and mannerisms. But at his best, he was capable of conveying more joy or tragedy, or both, than a month of *New Yorkers*. The real trouble with Breslin's journalism was that it was so affecting when it was good that the *Tribune* came to rely on it unduly. When Churchill died and Malcolm X was assassinated, as the civil rights movement came to a boil and Vietnam turned into a full-scale slaughterhouse, it was Breslin they sent to bring back feeling to the paper's reports of the large and increasingly cruel events of the traumatic mid-'Sixties. At the march on Selma, Alabama, he caught the anger, the fear, the courage of the protesters—and the pride of "the high school girls, pin-neat, white socks against their black legs." At the trial for the murder of Detroit civil rights worker Viola Liuzzo, he wrote of an accused Klan leader "with his pointed, red-tipped ears"; of a co-defendant bringing "his Bible-raised little daughter" into court and promising she would behave; of how—after the foregone acquittal—local moderates "have you allowing for things" with their bland contention that backwoods brutalism would be reformed slowly and only from within. On Vietnam, where he did not dwell longer than he needed to for sizing up the dimensions of the unfolding tragedy, he wrote powerfully of the mindless destruction and quiet cruelty he found at every turn.

Few New York newsmen on rival dailies admired Breslin more than metropolitan editor Abe Rosenthal of the *Times*. What struck him most was "how fast Breslin was off the mark—whenever a big story broke, he was there, even in the middle of the night, interviewing the victim or a survivor. He moved his ass." But Rosenthal never considered hiring Breslin for the *Times*: "His very personal kind of journalism would not have fit."

For all his importance to the paper, Breslin was a less than attractive human being; he was Jock's bad boy and relished the license he had won by being a big talent in the owner's eyes. For one thing, he was a bully. A lot of people saw him punch a *Tribune* editorial secretary for daring to attend a farewell party at Gallagher's steakhouse for a prominent editor with whom she was having an affair; the blow was apparently in punishment for her defiling the sacrament of marriage—not by the affair itself but by showing up at the party when the editor's wife was also in attendance. Breslin picked on lesser editors, copyboys, and others powerless to fight back, including the printers, whom he abused for what he regarded as their concerted effort to sabotage the paper in general and him personally by their strikes and militancy. "[A]t the bottom, the people who worked on the production had no regard for the paper at all," he wrote in *Life* after the *Tribune* was gone—as if the printers' stake in and fulfillment from their work could have, or should have, approximated his own.

And although he took editing from those whom he trusted—generally those who admired his work intensely and let him know it—he was badly overindulged, not unlike a temperamental racing stallion. Bellows would get to him by saying, "I don't want you to make yourself look bad by going off here." When he finished a piece for *New York,* Breslin would phone Clay Felker at whatever time of day or night it was and, even if the editor was in the middle of a dinner party or getting ready to go to bed, expect instantaneous attention. He got it, too, usually. "I knew goddamned well I couldn't trust him to leave the piece," Felker said, recalling his fear that Breslin would toss the article out in dissatisfaction or take it away with him to fret it to death. "For a daily journalist, he took himself very seriously and needed that daily feedback." His expense account became so unmanageable that Bellows finally negotiated a lump payment with Breslin's agent and let him settle up with the government at year's end.

Even among fellow reporters who recognized his gifts, the deference paid to Breslin by the editors sometimes rankled, especially when they found themselves pulled from a story so that Breslin could perform. Yet he could be kind to people when he chose to be. Earl Ubell thought a compassionate heart beat beneath the bluster and that Breslin cared about the personal misfortunes of others. And more than one reporter remembered his helping out with a suggested word or turn of phrase when they were stuck, like the time Mickey Carroll asked him for an unclichéd verb to describe the motion of a helicopter, and Breslin promptly said "sidle." For his editors, Dan Blum summarized the consensus: "Jimmy was noisy, aggressive, argumentative, hostile, and obscene—he threw daily tantrums—he was great and he wanted everyone else to know it. He was an immense pain in the butt, the Maria Callas of the city room—but she was worth the trouble, too."

The exalted status awarded Breslin, the preference given to other gifted writers, the apparent capriciousness of some of the editorial appointments, and the shortage of time and incapacity to explain things did not make Jim Bellows a universally admired commander of the news staff, but as David Laventhol suggested in defense of Bellows's conduct of the paper, "You had to throw everything you had into it. Jim couldn't worry if he rubbed some noses the wrong way. He didn't have the luxury of fretting about personnel problems down the road." Despite the seeming arbitrariness and maddening incoherence of his direction of their doomed ship, Bellows had managed, as assistant city editor Don Forst put it, "to appeal to the romance in us to try to save the paper —to a lot of fools like me who didn't want to live their lives in a velvet coffin." All its life the paper had had that effect on its creative staff, and never more so than at the end.

X

During November 1965, after the jolting discovery that the *Tribune*'s circulation had gained no ground at all as a result of the twenty-five-day shutdown of the *Times* and *News* by the Guild strike that fall, Winslow Maxwell, the paper's controller, was told to take a hard look at the numbers. He concluded that in view of the overall decline afflicting the newspaper industry in New York, "the chances of the Trib reaching break-even in the foreseeable future are nonexistent."

Maxwell saw two alternatives besides either continuing to sustain *Tribune* losses in the range of $4 to $5 million a year or killing the paper. The financially more attractive way was to work out the merger with the *Journal-American* and *World-Telegram & Sun*; the new organization would make about $4 million a year, by Maxwell's estimate—but the *Tribune* would of course disappear as a separate institution. Nor could the losses, if any, of the new company be written off by its three owners, none of whom would hold the 80 percent stock interest required by the federal tax code to enjoy such a benefit, as the *Tribune*'s owner, WCC, had been able to do. A second option was to buy the *New York Post*— no mention was made of a price or whether Dorothy Schiff would have sold— and to operate a morning-afternoon combination, attractive to advertisers and benefiting from staff economies, with both papers printed outside of the city, probably in New Jersey, where different union jurisdictions applied and, it was hoped, a better deal could be struck. Assuming that Whitney would have provided the necessary capital, such a *Tribune-Post* venture, Maxwell estimated, would be nearly $3 million in the black by 1969, and the *Tribune* would thus retain its independence. In the final analysis, though, the risk was judged too great, and *Tribune* management decided that New York was too tough a labor town to let the paper get away with such an evasive maneuver as printing outside the city limits. "We thought there was a good chance goon squads would drive off our delivery trucks," Robert MacDonald recalled, "and we'd never get the paper into the city."

Renewed discussions with the Hearst and Scripps-Howard managements, whose New York papers' financial prospects were no brighter than the *Tribune*'s, consumed months but resulted in an agreement under which the three ownerships would contribute a pool of working capital totaling about $6 million to a new venture, to be known as the World Journal Tribune, Inc., and the Whitney interest would add $2 million in marketable securities to help sustain the *Tribune* as a separate morning operation for two years. After that, if it proved a financial drag, the *Tribune* could be closed if two of the three partners so decided.

The official announcement of the merger was made March 21, 1966, after Whitney and Thayer wrote to the staff, conceding that "we enter this new venture with mixed feelings" but insisting the step was "the only sound and possible way" to provide the three papers with "the solid financial backing necessary to their survival." Long afterward, Thayer acknowledged the distastefulness of joining forces with the two chains, hardly ornaments of American journalism, by calling it "an unholy alliance—but it was the next best thing to closing down." In announcing the merger, the *Tribune* said editorially that the three publishers thereby hoped "to meet the inexorable pressures of a communications revolution" that had reduced the number of New York dailies from twenty-five in 1900 to six—and three of those were no longer viable as separate entities.

No sooner was the merger announced than its early doom was foreordained by a declaration from the Guild that there would have to be full agreement between it and the new management on a contract "before the new merger-paper is to go into effect." The Guild's avowed intention was to save all its members' jobs: "It will be up to management, if it wants to reduce staff personnel, to justify even a single reduction." Fighting words, uttered as if the publishers had been contractually or otherwise obliged to perpetuate jobs for their employees on money-losing enterprises. But a large staff reduction—a slated toll of 1,764 out of 4,598 jobholders on the three merging papers—was a key to the financial success of the new company, and it was equally essential that the best people of the three editorial staffs be retained, regardless of seniority. The unions, still insensitive to the last-ditch nature of the merger, viewed it only from a short-term perspective: they wanted as few as possible of their members severed, iron enforcement of the seniority rules (i.e., the last hired were the first to be fired in any staff cuts), and as large an increase in pay scales, severance benefits, and company contributions to pension and welfare funds as could be extracted—even though the financial solidity of the merger had not been demonstrated and their new demands might ensure its never being attained.

Rather than coming hat in hand to the unions, the World Journal Tribune management took the position that it was the ongoing survivor of its merged components and did not need anybody's permission to set the new venture in motion. It would begin operating with the Monday morning, April 25, edition of the *Tribune,* to be issued from the editorial and printing premises of the old *World-Telegram* on Barclay Street in the downtown financial district; the combined *World Journal* would appear that afternoon for the first time, and the three combined as the *World Journal Tribune* the following Sunday. In a letter to the staff on April 13 disclosing the start-up plans, Whitney and Thayer expressed their determination that the new operation had to "stand on its feet financially without subsidy" and that "delay in beginning the operation of our new company will be extremely prejudicial to all concerned. . . ."

The unions, however, responded by saying they would all have to negotiate fresh contracts since the merged company was in effect a new entity. The Guild was especially incensed because it alone among the unions was being asked— told, really, it said—to waive its seniority rules so that the new smaller editorial staffs could be composed as management chose. The April 25 start-up date was "unilateral" and "arbitrary," the Guild asserted, as if management had some nerve in setting its own schedule without first obtaining union approval. Before it would agree to cooperate, the Guild said, there would have to be a written description for every job on the new papers, employees eligible for these positions would have to be classified by name, and the entire staffing process reviewed with a fine-tooth comb—or else the Guild would strike the new company. In short, unless management would accept strict seniority, thereby granting that reporters and editors were all as interchangeable as printers and pressmen, or otherwise justify its staffing decisions to the Guild, the new papers would remain *in utero* indefinitely. Gloom enveloped the *Tribune.*

In his final statement as its owner-operator, Jock Whitney stated in the April 22 edition that he had bought the *Herald Tribune* eight years earlier because he wanted it to continue to be "a lively companion to a wide circle of friends. I did not buy it to make myself wealthy or famous or powerful. You cannot buy the traditions and principles of this newspaper, you can only lend them a hand toward survival. That effort has not been completely successful." The last thing he wanted to do, he went on, was to sell or merge the paper.

> But the Herald Tribune is not a child. It's not a toy or a whim of one man. It is an institution that has something to say to our times . . . and . . . on which many people depend. It must have a stable future independent of my pocketbook.

There were villains on both sides in the labor wrangles of the recent past, he conceded:

> But this is not the past and we are not trying to right those wrongs by fighting the old battles, crying over the money that was lost or the benefits that went unachieved. This is here and now when we are trying to make a new start and we find we can't. The unions won't let us.
>
> . . . We don't even have a clear idea of what they want except that it's a lot more than what has so far been offered, that it's going to cost enough to cripple us before we begin. . . .
>
> We are now at a crucial moment in the history of this newspaper. It is 125 years old [131, actually, starting with the *Herald*] and many men and women have given their best to it. I write this because here and now I want to put on the record how I feel and how I share their pride.

Saturday, April 23, was to be—whatever the outcome of the latest labor negotiation—the final day of operation of the *Tribune* at its West Forty-first

Street location, and the Sunday paper the next day its last as an independent organ. All was melancholy in the newsroom as staffers cleaned out their desks, packed equipment for the move down to Barclay Street, brought in their children to observe the historic occasion, and, here and there, drank scotch out of paper cups for auld lang syne. Engelking, who as city editor had trained a generation of reporters, was still on the premises as an editorial-page writer. Emma Bugbee, wearing a white floral hat, came in to write her last story, about a UN memorial to her good friend Eleanor Roosevelt; she had been on the *Tribune* fifty-six years, and she would not be going down to Barclay Street— it was just too long a subway ride from her apartment on Morningside Heights. As she matter-of-factly dropped her copy on the city desk and headed out, people stood up all over the city room and came to say goodbye to her. In midafternoon the Washington wire from the *Tribune* bureau, where they were certain the paper was done for, began a tattoo of messages:

BELLOWS FROM WASH BUREAU:
 FOR I AM ALREADY BEING OFFERED AND THE TIME OF MY DEPARTURE IS COME. I HAVE FOUGHT THE GOOD FIGHT, I HAVE FINISHED THE COURSE, I HAVE KEPT THE FAITH.
                                                II. TIMOTHY 4:6   4/23 323PM

TO NEW YORK HERALD TRIBUNE, NEW YORK CITY:
 HOW DO I LOVE THEE? LET ME COUNT THE WAYS . . .
 I SHALL BUT LOVE THEE BETTER AFTER DEATH.
  ELIZABETH BARRETT BROWNING
  SONNETS FROM THE PORTUGUESE VI
                                      WASH BUREAU   4/23 332PM

TO EVERYONE IN NEW YORK:
 I WILL INSTRUCT MY SORROWS TO BE PROUD:
 FOR GRIEF IS PROUD, AND MAKES HIS OWNER STOOP.
  WILLIAM SHAKESPEARE
  KING JOHN, ACT II
                                      WASHN BUREAU   4/23 424PM

TO SS NEW YORK FROM SS WASHINGTON BUREAU:
 WE TAKING WATER SLOWLY. POWER ALMOST GONE. LIST INCREASING. UNDERSTAND YOUR SITUATION SIMILAR. MORALE GOOD HERE, CONSIDERING. REPORTS SOME DRINKING BELOW DECKS, BUT CREW STILL LOYAL AND MUTINY UNTHINKABLE. SOME FEAR ABOUT CASTING OFF IN LIFEBOATS ON ICY SEAS, UNKNOWN WATERS. BUT WHAT THE HELL. SHE'S BEEN A GOOD OLD SHIP WHICH KEPT AFLOAT LONG AFTER FINKS ASHORE SAID SHE WAS DOOMED TO SINK. SO DOWN WE GO, LADS, BUT WITH OUR ENSIGNS FLYING AND GUNS FIRING. GO TO HELL, NEW YORK TIMES. DAILY NEWS, YOU DIE. BERT POWERS, BE DAMNED. AND MAY TRUTH IN PRINT, AND HONESTY IN REPORTING, AND INTEGRITY IN PUBLISHING REIGN FOREVERRRRRRRRRRRRRRRRRRRRRRRRRRR . . .
                                                         4/23 510PM

Inky Blackman was the late man on rewrite, doing obits until he knocked off at ten o'clock. His own obituary, he decided, would run twenty lines when his time came and wind up consigned to overset; he would settle, he wrote in an unpublished memoir, for a tombstone with his name, lifespan, and one-word epitaph: Newspaperman.

After the printers had gone home that night, John Bogart, the industrial relations director of the paper, who had been hired out of Yale by Stanley Walker thirty-two years before, made his way into the empty, unlighted composing room, where he knew his way around with his eyes closed. Few on the *Tribune* were more thoroughly steeped in the newspaper trade, and nobody loved the old sheet better than John Bogart did. Threading past the machinery in that vast, slumbering chamber to the composing stone, he flipped a switch that threw a small pool of light over the spot where the front page was nightly assembled from several thousand small pieces of lead. Then he reached for a printer's key, carefully unlocked the form holding the type tightly together, and removed the logotype bearing the paper's proud name and the curious "dingbat" first used one hundred years ago that month. It would not be used again. He took the oblong, heavy piece of metal home with him and kept it. For as much as the paper was Jock Whitney's, it also belonged to John Bogart and all the others who owned none of its stock but had matched or outspent its proprietors in their devotion to an ideal and pride of craft surpassed on no other daily journal ever to issue from an American press.

XI

The Guild pickets came out on Sunday. Monday morning there was no *Tribune*. Downtown, across from City Hall, workmen were rigging scaffolding around Whitelaw Reid's Tall Tower; the still sturdy old *Tribune* building was coming down, as all good sturdy old New York buildings come down before their time, to make way for Pace College's new home. Just as the *Tribune* had not stayed closed the previous fall while the *Times* and *News* were down, so now those morning papers, along with the *Post,* kept publishing as the Guild struck the new company. And every day, as its prosperous rivals remained before the readers, the *Tribune*'s lifeblood was draining away.

None of the other unions would settle until Powers did. Since the new company was not renewing the automation issue that had been at the heart of the labor crisis in 1965, Big Six settled in a relatively statesmanlike twenty-four days. The Guild took another seven weeks to come to terms. By July 13, all but one union had settled, saddling the World Journal Tribune, Inc., with about 250 workers it did not want and some $2 million a year in added payroll it did not need. Then, to prove it knew how to toss a monkeywrench into the machinery as artfully as the rest, the holdout pressmen's union presented the merged ownership with a list of twenty-two demands, including reduction in

the Saturday-night shift from eight hours to six and a half, thereby guarantee-
ing an hour and a half of overtime per man per week. A month later, the
pressmen had still not settled. And by then, half the *Tribune* editorial staff
had drifted off to jobs elsewhere, many at the *Times.* "Percentage loss of
quality is closer to 65–70 per cent," Jim Bellows wrote to Matt Meyer, former
president of the *World-Telegram* and head of the new company. "To put it
bluntly, the Tribune staff has been devastated. I think it almost impossible—
with the present staff—to publish a Herald Tribune I would be proud to be
the editor of, or be able to compete with successfully in the morning field."
The August 13 *Times* carried a report that the three owners of the strikebound World Journal Tribune, Inc., had decided not to resume publication of
the *Tribune*; the story was by Homer Bigart.

Such was the respect and affection that Jock Whitney had attracted from his
editors that, rather than mourning for themselves, they worried far more about
the anguish and emotional strain on the *Tribune* owner, with his cardiac condition, as he prepared to deliver the paper's brief funeral oration. The cortege
drove from WCC headquarters at the Time-Life Building to the now empty
Tribune offices, and at 5 p.m. on Monday, August 15, a hot day, Whitney entered the ninth-floor auditorium, and his face grim and set with sadness, began
to read his remarks into the glare of the television floodlights. "I have
never been involved in a more difficult or painful decision," he said, with
no trace of stammer. "For the years of my ownership, despite the hopes, the
talents and the enormous efforts that were put into it, the paper was never
quite able to stand on its own. The merger, at last, seemed to promise survival in a well-balanced organization." His face was wet with sweat in the
muggy room; only the executive offices had been air-conditioned. "Now that
promise is gone." The toll of the long strike, which had lasted by then as
long as the 1962–63 shutdown, was too great in lost readers, revenues, advertisers, and talent to be overcome in starting up anew, he said, and then
added:

> But though a newspaper must meet the exacting test of profit and loss, it is
> something more than a business. The Herald Tribune had a voice, a presence, a
> liveliness of thought and a distinction of style that many have appreciated. It was
> an attempt I am glad to have made—one that did succeed in bringing together men
> and women of great talent and sensibility. They made it a newspaper to be proud
> of.
> ... I know we gave something good to our city while we published and I know
> it will be a loss to journalism in this country as we cease publication. . . . I am glad
> that we never tried to cheapen it in any way, that we have served as a conscience
> and a valuable opposition. I am sorry that it had to end.

"I guess this is the emptiest day of my life," he wrote to Red Smith in response
to the sports columnist's condolence note, one of dozens he received from an
appreciative staff. At Greentree that night of the interment, that grief-stricken

man of many millions remarked to his wife, Betsey, "This is the first time I've ever really failed at anything in my life."

He did not return to the *Tribune* building after that. But once a week or so for a little while, before the telephones were switched off forever, he called the city room, devoid of life except for Jim Bellows, who was seeking new employment, and Dick Wald, who was slated to edit the new Sunday paper whenever it began. Whitney would ask how they were feeling and what they were doing. They were not feeling very good, and what they were doing was putting together a collection of Jimmy Breslin's best pieces for the paper and linking them with headnotes to fulfill a book contract Breslin had not got around to honoring. In between the cutting and pasting, amid all that battered furniture awaiting the auctioneer's gavel, the last two ranking editors of the *Herald Tribune* amused themselves playing baseball with a bat and ball made from wadded sheets of leftover newsprint. It was not a dignified sight, but nobody was there to watch.

XII

The *World Journal Tribune* finally began to publish September 12, 1966, which was 140 days after its intended start-up date. It was not a bad paper, many talented people worked on it, and the late *Tribune*'s young superstars, Jimmy Breslin, Tom Wolfe, and Dick Schaap, were much in evidence on its pages. Dick Wald ran the Sunday edition for a while with Clay Felker still editing *New York,* a prime feature of the new Sunday package. But it was a misbegotten thing, a patchwork paper, soulless and joyless, trying to blend too many strains and tastes and types of talent without a governing sensibility; it wound up a mishmash, selling a little under 700,000 copies a day, the fourth-largest circulation of any evening paper in the nation, but its overhead was too heavy, its plant too antiquated, and its advertisers too few. It lost $700,000 a month. By the beginning of 1967, the money ran out. Whitney declined to add any more. His two partners kept it going until May 5, when, after hearing Bert Powers assert that there were "no more poor cousins" left among the New York dailies and ask for a 20 percent wage increase, a four-day week, and a cost-of-living escalation clause in the new Big Six contract, they gave up. The *World Journal Tribune* had lasted less than eight months. After severance payments and all other obligations, it cost Whitney Communications Corporation $8.6 million, bringing the total of funds expended to save the *Herald Tribune* and the domestic remnants thereof to $39,476,000 under the regime of John Hay Whitney.

XIII

The Paris edition of the *Herald Tribune,* orphaned by the sad events in New York, became a joint venture owned equally by Whitney Communications, *The New York Times,* and *The Washington Post* as the *Times* gave up its money-losing European effort. Harry Baehr contributed editorials to the paper, now known as the *International Herald Tribune,* that represented the views of Jock Whitney. "I still wake up at night," Whitney once told Baehr, "and wonder whether there was anything more I could have done to keep the *Tribune* functioning."

Whitney's self-questioning suggested a deeper understanding of the factors in the *Tribune*'s death than he had indicated in a letter sent a week after its closing to his friend Dwight Eisenhower, who had so strongly encouraged him to take on the challenge of trying to save it. "Labor is directly to blame, of course, but the leadership in labor relations exercised by the New York Times and the Daily News over the past fifteen years," Jock wrote Ike, "has been so weak that the blame is there, too. It seems almost to have been designed to accomplish what has just happened. Quien sabe?"

But for eight of those "past fifteen years" Whitney had owned the *Tribune,* and what leadership had it shown in labor relations? If the *Times* and *News* had remained financially healthy with antiquated machinery and labor practices while the *Tribune* was running ever deeper into the red, which paper ought to have been in the forefront seeking a formula for relief from the unions? Perhaps it was understandable that an ideologically oriented periodical like *U.S. News & World Report* would headline its account of the *Tribune*'s death "When Unions Killed a Major Newspaper," but the implication that labor was gouging extortionate wages from the New York publishers, out of keeping with the scale paid to comparably skilled workers in other industries, was unfounded. The fact was that the *Tribune*'s rivals in the morning field lived under the same labor contracts as it did and survived the shakeout crisis of the mid-'Sixties while the *Tribune* did not. For Whitney to suggest, as Thayer had also done, sharing the same frustration, that it was their competitors who had driven the *Tribune* to the wall was to beg the question of their own responsibility in the outcome and to understate the plight of the paper when it came into their possession.

Most students of mass media who are familiar with the economic history of New York newspapers are inclined to the belief that Whitney's infusion of cash and spirit served only to delay the inevitable death of the *Tribune* and that nothing he could have done starting in 1958 would have mattered. That standard judgment is no more verifiable than a contrary conclusion, with the full and unfair benefit of hindsight, would be here. What can be ventured safely is that courses of action other than the one he elected to pursue had been open to

Whitney. It is not a political statement, furthermore, to point out that, although he caused nearly forty millions—a lot more money in purchasing power then than it has since become—to be expended in an effort to save the paper, Whitney's personal fortune was in no way reduced nor his personal comforts and grand style of living affected in the slightest as a result. Repeatedly he was told, during the paper's financial travails, that the *Tribune* was draining off profits and thereby deadening the morale of the managers and imperiling the growth of the Corinthian broadcasting network, the prime provider of the profits within the Whitney Communications Corporation. But only five years after the closing of the paper, WCC sold off Corinthian to Dun & Bradstreet for stock then worth $128 million—far more than everything lost on the *Tribune* or invested in WCC, which had been allegedly created in the first place to sustain the paper. In 1973, *Parade* was sold for about three times the price Thayer had bought it for fifteen years earlier in organizing WCC, and other WCC properties were sold off at a high profit in ensuing years, thereby adding to the Whitney fortune. His emotional commitment to the *Tribune* was unquestionably very high, but it cannot be said of Jock Whitney, any more than of the Reids before him, that his connection with it was marked by financial sacrifice. And only that, or at least the willingness to risk that, could have conceivably altered the outcome.

The first course open to Jock Whitney that he did not pursue on taking control of the *Tribune* was to recognize the importance of the newspaper and the severity of its condition by resigning his ambassadorship to Great Britain and returning to New York to oversee its operations. The paper was a greater civic responsibility than his ceremonial service to the Eisenhower administration as its supremely gracious messenger to London, and if he had not so rated it, he should not have taken title to the *Tribune*; having done so, he owed it more than his absentee patronage. And if he had returned, his imposing presence and devotion to the cause might have considerably eased the task of enlisting a dynamic, experienced figure to assume working direction of the paper.

The second course open to Whitney that he did not follow was, on his return from London, to recognize the significance of the grim data assembled for him by Walter Thayer and to take commensurate action. Even before the first major labor crisis arose, the dimensions of the paper's competitive dilemma in hoping to attract new readership were appallingly evident: there were seven major New York dailies then operating within a metropolitan market served by thirty-one other dailies (among them the soaring *Wall Street Journal*), 305 weeklies, nine television and seventy radio stations, and hundreds of general-interest and specialized periodicals, their ranks proliferating annually. All of these were seeking the same advertising dollars the *Tribune* needed for solvency. The city's population was in decline, due mainly to the suburban exodus that was steadily eroding the readership of the New York papers. The pervasive impact of television was the cultural phenomenon of the age, and its deadening effect on the reading habits of Americans was by then apparent. Under such circumstances, the inadequacy of the prescriptive analysis of the *Tribune*'s situation by McKinsey & Co., calling for minor economies in staffing, production, distribution, and the size of the paper while wishfully projecting steady circulation gains, might have been equally apparent. Whitney's real choices were either to give up the ghost then and there, as Thayer might have preferred, or to make a serious commitment of working capital to alter its competitive position. He did neither; instead, he kept paying the bills and hoping against hope that something would turn up.

A massive infusion of capital might have been used in several ways. It could have gone toward the purchase of sufficient talent to reconceptualize the news-paper itself, perhaps along the lines of the news weeklies, as John Denson began to attempt, or perhaps as a more analytical paper written in large part by experts in their fields, and then to promote it exhaustively. Instead, there was Denson, by himself, without the intellect, temperament, editorial budget, or supporting staff a seriously reconceived *Herald Tribune* would require. Or the money might have gone into a major effort to follow the paper's traditional readership in its exodus to suburbia. Perhaps the profitable chain of small Westchester dailies or the quality *Evening Record* in expanding Bergen County, New Jersey, or the *Stamford Advocate, Greenwich Time,* and *Norwalk Hour* in Connecticut, or all of them or some combination of them, could have been bought and merged with the *Tribune,* offering advertisers an attractive city-suburban vehicle conceptu-ally different from the other New York dailies. Perhaps the *Tribune* could then have been printed at one or more of its suburban properties, benefiting from a lower prevailing wage scale and other economies. At the least, the *Tribune* could have devoted several pages every day to sustained, serious suburban coverage, as no other city daily was doing. Or the money might have gone to support a decision to quit the morning field, where the competition was insuperable, and enter the afternoon field as the dominant factor by buying out one or more of the existing entries. Or the money might have gone toward a new plant on the technological frontier of the printing industry with a concomitant outlay to procure the cooperation of labor. Labor might well have remained intransigent, but no serious inducement was put on the table for its consideration.

"What I would have done," said the astute Ivan Veit of the *Times* well after its rival had been buried, would be "to establish the *Tribune* as the best in local coverage, going back to what it was under Stanley Walker, and that would have included financial and cultural affairs, largely New York stories, and let the *Times* go unchallenged as the paper of record with its great strength in national and foreign coverage. I wouldn't have tried to save the *Tribune* by cosmetics and typographical tricks. And then I would have promoted the hell out of it and thereby created a real niche for it. But they never did that, they never supported what they had, either internally with sufficient staff or externally with adequate promotion and personnel to build circulation. Instead, they nickel-and-dimed it to death." The stopgap nature of the Whitney financing was similarly ques-tioned in retrospect by Charles Rees, who rose from assistant treasurer of WCC to Walter Thayer's eventual successor as president. "The investments in the paper might have been more effective if they had been compacted into a much tighter time frame," Rees commented. "The money was dribbled in while people were fiddling with the paper cosmetically. There was an absence of compressed effort."

To take large, decisive steps toward repositioning the *Tribune* in its market would have required boldness and imagination. But Jock Whitney was neither bold nor imaginative; he was cautious and appreciative—a man of taste, tact, civility, and good intentions. He was far too much a gentleman to get tangled up in a street fight of the sort success in the newspaper business in New York then required; possibly, his inherited wealth had muted the aggressiveness in his nature. And he was not a young man when the *Tribune* fell into his hands. "He never took the big, active leadership role in the paper," recalled Jacob Javits, perhaps Whitney's closest political associate. "He didn't bring to it the voice I had hoped he would."

Instead, he relied on Walter Thayer, knowing all the while how dubious and, in the end, negative Thayer was about committing to the paper. Some close to Whitney felt that, in his own lack of self-confidence, he relied excessively on Thayer's counsel. They and others, especially people on the editorial side of the paper, knowing of the close relationship between the two men, were inclined to blame the decision finally to shut the *Tribune* on Thayer's influence. According to Betsey Whitney, Jock agreed to the merger that created the World Journal Tribune, Inc., because of "the strikes, the loss of advertising, and Walter's insistence." Asked in December 1982 whether she thought her husband might have reached a different conclusion if his principal financial adviser had come to him with another recommendation, Mrs. Whitney replied, "I do."

But Thayer was Whitney's employee, however strong the mutual regard between the two men. And as Javits put it, "It's wrong to blame Walter for what happened to the paper. He was just doing his job, which was to help Jock as conservator of his fortune. He was a bottom-line adviser, a cash-flow man." Who finally must be held accountable for the decisions that were made if Whitney vested more confidence in Thayer than he needed to (as Javits and others believed without disparagement of Thayer's sincerity or skill) and in so doing transferred too much of the responsibility for his own affairs to the attorney?

An objective assessment of Thayer's role at the paper may be found in the judgment of Winslow Maxwell, the *Tribune*'s chief numbers man during its final five years. "Every organization needs a naysayer and a son of a bitch," Maxwell said, "especially one like WCC," with its gentlemanly ways. "That's how Walter made his fortune." Maxwell feared Walter Thayer. "He was tougher and smarter than I was, and I saw more of him than I wanted. But he was fair, and he knew what he was talking about. And he was just right for Jock. Walter's real job was making Jock happy with his life." Maxwell never doubted that Thayer was trying as hard as he could to make a success of the *Tribune*, but within the guidelines he had established, which were obviously intended to insulate Whitney's fortune from the paper's fate. And when no hope seemed to remain of saving it under the ground rules he had set down and Whitney had approved, Thayer became its undertaker. "I think Walter did everything right," said Maxwell. In his own defense, Thayer retrospectively viewed his *Tribune* experience as involuntary, if well paid, servitude: "It was an interim assignment that turned into a nightmare. I do not have printer's ink in my blood."

But if Whitney did, or thought he did, there was one last course he might conceivably have followed instead of shutting the *Herald Tribune*—he could have endowed it as a nonprofit institution, the way he helped to endow Yale University and New York Hospital and the Museum of Modern Art. Does not a newspaper serve the well-being of society in as legitimate a way as a college nourishes its mind or a hospital heals its body or a museum delights its soul? Asked just that, Walter Thayer answered with an emphatic no, arguing against the appropriateness of a permanently subsidized newspaper. "It is too likely to become somebody's toy or mouthpiece," he said, "and you can't attract or hold able people on the staff." But even profitable newspapers—perhaps especially profitable ones—have been subverted by their publishers' needs or whims or megalomania. And good people who make major contributions to society by their teaching, writing, and research are attracted to and held by nonprofit universities; why not to and by a newspaper?

Indefinite subsidy of the paper, whether by endowment or some other form, would have been preferable to closing it, in the opinion of William Paley. "I happened to think he could afford to lose the money," Paley said of his brother-in-law. "It was a great paper, and it might have progressed in the future." As to Thayer's argument that the *Tribune*'s losses were negatively affecting the rest of the WCC operation, Paley felt that it could have been met by removing the paper from the holding company and running it independently—even at a loss. "But Jock didn't think it was cricket for the paper to survive on a handout. He thought newspapers were part of the competitive world, and a subsidy was a false way of keeping it going. I pooh-poohed that." Paley paused reflectively, then added, "His life wasn't the same after the paper was gone."

Late Late City Edition:
A Shirttail

The progeny of the *Tribune* survive in apparent financial good health. The *International Herald Tribune,* essentially an assemblage of material taken from two of its three owners—*The New York Times* and *The Washington Post*—and many wire services and syndicates, had a circulation of about 160,000 in 1985 and annual revenues of around $40 million. According to officials at Whitcon Investment Company, the successor to Whitney Communications Corporation, which still owns the other third of the Paris-based paper, the operation is in the black.

In 1967, WCC sold rights to the name *New York* to Clay Felker, who launched it as an independent magazine the following year. He lost control of it, however, in 1977 to Rupert Murdoch, the Australian publisher. *New York*'s circulation stood at 440,000 in 1985.

The New York Times, in a buyout deal assuring lifetime income and benefits to its blue-collar employees, got the green light from its unions in 1974 to automate its production facilities—eight years too late to help the *Tribune.* Editorially, the *Times* became a far more attractive newspaper, with livelier writing and cleaner typography, and its coverage grew still more comprehensive, not only in geopolitical terms but also in its expanded attention to science and technology, the world of ideas, consumer affairs, and recreation. It also grew far more enterprising in investigative reportage and more provocative in its interpretive commentary, and if it seemed disproportionately attentive to the pleasures and luxuries of the conspicuously self-indulgent, the *Times* remained without serious rival as dutiful chronicler of everyday life on earth. The *Tribune*'s death helped it become far more profitable, too, as its daily circulation soared over the million mark in 1985. The *Daily News,* ironically, grew less prosperous the better and more enlightened it became as an editorial product, prominently featuring Jimmy Breslin as its star columnist. Its circulation was victimized by television, which met the limited news needs of an increasing number of its former readers, and the challenge of the *New York Post,* which became a scandal sheet of no observably redeeming social value after its purchase in 1978 by Rupert Murdoch. Despite daily sales of more than 900,000—three-quarters of the *News*'s circulation—the *Post* attracted little advertising and was reportedly operating $10 million in the red in 1985. In the event of the death of either or both of the New York tabloids, the vacuum might be filled by Long Island's *Newsday,* run by former *Tribune* city editor David Laventhol, which was busily in the process of expanding its existing beachhead in Queens to the city's other four boroughs.*

In the two decades since the *Herald Tribune*'s passing, a number of other superior newspapers have died, although none approached the *Tribune* in stature or national influence; among them were *The Washington Star,* the *Chicago Daily News,* the *Philadelphia Evening Bulletin,* the *Detroit Times,* the *Cleveland Press,* and the *Newark News.* A great many cities are now served by a single daily newspaper, others by two papers under a single ownership, and in a few, like St. Louis, Detroit, and San Francisco, formerly fierce competitors share a single plant and supporting business staff. Strong rivals compete on approximate parity in only a handful of cities, among them Chicago, Dallas, and Denver. In a few important cities where the rival paper is economically feeble, the dominant daily has become an editorially outstanding product; among these are *The Washington Post,* the *Boston Globe,* the *Philadelphia Inquirer,* and the *Los Angeles Times.*

As direct competition has dried up within given newspaper markets over the past twenty years, the survivors have tended to become richer, less partisan and more responsible, vastly more powerful institutions, legalized monopolies akin in the communal mind to public utilities—and about as popular, if the opinion polls are to be credited. The special character of the press as the watchdogs of American society, especially its public sector, has been sharply devalued and superseded to a distressing extent by the perception of it as a self-interested, overbearing, impersonal force driven more by profit than principle. These feelings have likely been exacerbated as a result of the steadily increasing control of the daily press by newspaper chains; about 60 percent of daily circulation is

*In April 1986 *News*man Jimmy Breslin became the fourth highly regarded *Tribune* alumnus to win the Pulitzer Prize after the paper's death; the others were Red Smith, Emily Genauer, and Art Buchwald. A month later, David Laventhol was advanced from the chief executive at *Newsday*, with oversight responsibility for the Times-Mirror Company's other Eastern properties as well, to the presidency of the Los Angeles–based chain, one of the nation's most powerful media empires.

now accounted for by chain-owned papers. Salutary effects of this trend are alleged by the chain managements, claiming that they bring economic stability and better resources to newly acquired properties, which are therefore more likely to serve their communities with disinterested professionalism resistant to entrenched vested interests. No doubt in some cases the surrender of local ownership has resulted in an improved paper, but more often the outcome has been a slick, homogenized product, run by outsiders, with a vigilant eye on the balance sheet. For the chains are essentially big businesses and even less inclined to muddy waters and risk profitability than local owners who sometimes managed a show of passionate concern, perhaps misguided, over civic matters. Although most chain managements make a point of stating that news and editorial policies are not centrally dictated but left to the judgment of each paper's staff, such freedom—to the extent it exists—is plainly at the sufferance of corporate managers in whose hands great power has been concentrated and, with it, a fearsome potential for abuse.

The closer that journalism has approached the standing of an authentic profession, oddly enough, the less attractive its individual practitioners appear to have become in the public mind. This irony is traceable in large measure to the distinguished work of the press in its persistent recording of the futility and manifold injustices of the Vietnam War and its disclosures in the Watergate scandal. Those protracted traumas scarred the national psyche, which in turn found solace by blaming the press for battening on the troubles it apparently delighted in reporting. Reporters came to be seen as arrogant in the conduct of their duties, habitually adversarial in posture, often insensitive, and unapologetic about substituting their own right to demand the truth for the public's right not to be stalked ruthlessly like so much grist for the milling of tomorrow's headlines. This impression has been deepened by the coarseness of television news, which is essentially a headline service trading on its emotional graphic appeal and dealing so superficially with events and so rarely with the complex issues behind them that its effect is to divert rather than to inform; TV remains primarily an entertainment medium that has not challenged the role of newspapers as the prime recorders of the community's serious business. But because we *see* television correspondents questioning the President or putting it to the police chief, they become personalities in their own right, far more imposing than a faceless byline over a printed story.

The enhanced power of the news media has surely contributed to the public's heightened suspicion of them, as evidenced in the wide support for President Reagan's decision to keep reporters from witnessing the 1983 invasion of Grenada by U.S. forces and in the epidemic of libel verdicts against the press on findings of excessive investigatory zeal rather than any provable injury to the plaintiff. The intimidating effect of this trend on the willingness of the press to probe for wrongdoing and ventilate it in the public interest has begun to alarm many both within and outside of journalism. Perhaps this anti-press reaction was an overdue corrective to abuses that the news media themselves were unaware of, for they have gone about their business until lately with few restraints upon their capacity to expose and defame, justly or unjustly, absent evidence of blatant malice.

What is most disturbing about the degraded stature of journalism is not the fact of its comeuppance so much as the collateral reactionary judgment that its very purpose, even when functioning at highest competence, is subversive to the public good. Most news, almost by definition, is bad, or at least troubling. For a generation now, America has been convulsed by an overlapping series of social revolutions affecting long-held beliefs and arousing a profound conflict of values: feminism, consumerism, environmentalism, civil rights, the peace movement, the acceptable levels of poverty and profit-making, permissive sexuality, the drug culture, religion as a political force, to cite only the most prominent. If the medium *is* indeed the message, as McLuhan preached, then the media, in reporting all this social upheaval, are indeed undermining the nation's faith in its institutions, leaders, authority itself—never mind the possible therapeutic benefits from constant scrutiny of politicians who lie and distort, of companies that fail to test their products adequately, of nuclear power stations that leak, of policies that are unwise, of courts that are unjust, of defenders of the public safety who brutalize to pacify. The mentality that says "America—love it or leave it" is made unbearably insecure by those who question and criticize and even more so by events that tend to validate the bellyachers. Thus, it has become acceptable to leave the press out of the Grenada invasion, not to maintain tight security during the hostilities, but to prevent condemning revelations in case of disaster; what the people don't know won't hurt them.

But are the authentic patriots those who celebrate the nation's virtues uncritically or those who remain alert to its shortcomings and insist that the people try to measure up to their ideals? Each time a voice in the press is cowed or stilled, democracy in America loses something of its essence. Every time a newspaper dies, even a bad one, the country moves a little closer to authoritarianism; when a great one goes, like the *New York Herald Tribune,* history itself is denied a devoted witness.

Ringoes, New Jersey
May 15, 1986

NOTES ON SOURCES

ACKNOWLEDGMENTS

INDEX

Notes on Sources

Nearly all the material gathered in researching this book has been given to the Manuscripts and Archives Division of the Sterling Memorial Library at Yale University, where it is available for inspection and use under the rules of that institution.

I. PAPERS AND OTHER DOCUMENTS

The most prominent and useful source for this work was, of course, the newspapers themselves. The entire life of both the *Herald* and *Tribune* and their merged survivor of forty-two years is available on microfilm at the New York Public, Yale, and Princeton libraries, where I worked.

(a) *Collected Papers:* The first two generations of Reid family papers pertinent to the *Tribune*—those of Whitelaw and Elisabeth Mills Reid and of Ogden Mills Reid and Helen Rogers Reid—are in the Library of Congress. Helen Reid's papers were most useful. The younger Whitelaw Reid's papers are retained by their owner at his home in Purchase, N.Y., importantly including his mother's letters to her sister cited in Chapter 6. Ogden Rogers (Brown) Reid's papers, which include the most extensive body of material about the *Herald Tribune*'s operations, are at Yale's Sterling Library. The papers of John Hay Whitney are due to be contributed to the Yale library. The papers of the Whitney Communications Corporation and Walter N. Thayer remain in the private possession of the Whitney Communications Company in the Time-Life Building at Rockefeller Center in New York. Of particular usefulness to me among this last collection were the exchanges between Whitney and Thayer and the corporate minute books of the Tribune Association, dating back to 1849 and held by the Whitney company. Other important sources consulted were the papers of: William E. Robinson at the Dwight D. Eisenhower Library, Abilene, Kansas; Joseph F. Barnes, held by his widow, Elizabeth B. Barnes of New York and Warren, Ct. (a fascinating oral memoir of his *Tribune* experience is available through the Oral History Project at Columbia University); James Parton at the Houghton Library, Harvard; and Robert M. White II, retained by him at his residence in Mexico, Mo. Other privately held papers made available to the author and of special value to him were those of

Robert F. Bryan, Barney G. Cameron, Arthur T. Hadley, and John Reagan (Tex) McCrary.

(b) *Unpublished Manuscripts:* Of prime value to me for Part IV of this work was Harry W. Baehr's account of the Whitney years of ownership, undertaken with the assistance of WCC, which sponsored the project. While I was not guided by Baehr's judgments of people and policies and undertook much independent research of my own (see below), I was the grateful beneficiary of his extensive study, which he generously made available to me in its entirety. Any serious student of the subject ought to consult the Baehr manuscript, included among my research materials on file at Yale. Other works in this category were: *Rewrite Man,* a memoir by M. C. Blackman, made available to me by his widow and highly instructive in the craft of a lifelong journalist (a copy is at Yale and the original is with Blackman's other papers at Louisiana State University); chapters from an autobiography by Walter Arm; and a play, *Who Killed the Tribune?,* by Francis Sugrue.

(c) *Miscellaneous Documents:* Uniquely illuminating was the diary of cable editor John M. Price, kept from the time he joined the paper in 1926 until his retirement in 1965, generous portions of which were made available to me by his daughter, Dr. Emily Kennedy. Price also organized a round-robin of correspondence among a number of former *Tribune* staff members, most of them deskmen, that began in April 1965 and continued for a dozen years; these letters are a storehouse of memories by the contributors, who included, in addition to Price: M. C. Blackman, Luke P. Carroll, Richard F. Crandell, Frazier Dickson, Ralph Jules Frantz, Walter Hamshar, Lorimer D. Heywood, Theodore Laymon, Fred Meier, Joe Pihodna, Lewis B. Sebring, Robert Stern, Frank T. Waters, and Richard G. West. The correspondence is at Yale. Frank Waters supplied a substantial number of issues of *The Copyboys' Call* for 1933–34, providing a look at the lighter side of city-room life. E. Douglas Hamilton lent briefs and other legal papers growing out of several cases in which the *Tribune* was sued for libel; most prominent was the 1917 case, *Gimbel Bros. v. The Tribune Association et al.* John Bogart contributed copies of the annual and monthly reports of the industrial relations department at the paper during its last decade. Mrs. L. L. Engelking granted me access to a series of tape-recorded interviews between her husband and his grandson by his first marriage, Bill Teitler, made during 1979, the last year of Engelking's life. Robert Lambert gave a copy of the recorded words and music to "The Saga of the Dingbat," the 1965 promotional revue put on by the paper.

(d) *Extensive Memoranda and Correspondence:* George A. Cornish and Richard G. West, neither of whom the author has met and who between them spent sixty-seven years in the *Tribune* city room, wrote to me at length, answering a long list of specific inquiries; their offerings were invaluable. Others who supplied me with memories on request that were especially helpful were: Dan Blum, Robert J. Donovan, Walter B. Kerr, Al Laney, Barrett McGurn, Robert A. Poteete, Fritz Silber, and Leland Stowe.

II. INTERVIEWS AND CORRESPONDENCE

Unless otherwise indicated, the following were interviewed in person on the date and in the place indicated; where no place is listed, the interview took place in New York City. An asterisk following the date means it was the first of more than one interview session with the subject. The designation (C) means the interview was conducted by correspondence in response to questions sent by the author; the designation +(C) means the personal interview was supplemented by correspondence. The designation (T) indicates that the interview was by telephone, in some cases in addition to the personal interview; (P) means the subject also contributed personal papers to the author's research.

Abel, Elie, August 26, 1981, Stanford, CA (C); Albert, Robert H., December 17, 1981; Allen, George H., July 19, 1982, Darien CT (P); Alsop, Joseph W., November 11, 1981, Washington DC +(C); Andrews, Peter, July 12, 1982, Brewster NY; Arm, Walter, January 11, 1981, North Hollywood CA (C), (P); Attwood, William, October 11, 1981 +(C).

Baehr, Harry W., September 9, 1981* (P); Barnes, Elizabeth B. (Mrs. Joseph F.), February 17,

1982 +(C), (P); Barnet, Sylvan J., October 12, 1982 +(C); Barrett, Laurence I., November 9, 1981, Washington DC +(C); Beech, Keyes, November 10, 1982, Washington DC; Belford, Barbara, December 11, 1981 +(C); Bellows, James G., November 5, 1981 +(C); Berry, Warren, December 8, 1982; Bevans, Margaret Van Doren (Mrs. Tom), July 11, 1982, West Cornwall CT; Bigart, Homer W., August 13, 1981, West Nottingham NH +(C); Bilby, Kenneth W., January 20, 1982; Blass, Bill, November 3, 1982; Blum, Daniel, October 5, 1982*, Atenas, Costa Rica (C); Blum, John A., October 5, 1982; Bogart, John, November 19, 1981* +(C), (P); Boyer, Philip L., August 18, 1982, Clayton NY (C); Bradlee, Benjamin C., November 11, 1982, Washington DC; Braestrup, Peter, August 23, 1983, Washington DC; Braynard, Frank O., January 6, 1982, Kings Point NY (C); Brundage, Howard P., August 30, 1982, Lyme CT; Bryan, Robert F., June 7, 1983, Rye NY (P); Buchwald, Art, May 12, 1982, Washington DC; Bugbee, Emma, July 1, 1981, Cranston RI.

Cameron, Barney G., December 3, 1981 (P); Carroll, Maurice (Mickey), December 22, 1982; Catledge, Turner, November 18, 1982; Clarity, James F., November 29, 1983, Washington DC (T); Cook, Don, December 7, 1982, Paris, France (C); Cornish, George A., December 4, 1981*, Sarasota FL (C), (T); Crist, Judith, November 15, 1981*; Cronkite, Walter, August 4, 1982, Edgartown MA; Crosby, John, May 4, 1982, Esmont VA (C); Crow, C. P. (Pat), January 23, 1983.

Daniels, Judith, November 30, 1982; de Gramont, Sanche (now Ted Morgan), April 4, 1982; Diamond, Edwin, July 27, 1982; Donovan, Robert J., November 10, 1981*, Washington DC +(C), (P); Dougherty, Richard, September 22, 1982; Drummond, Roscoe, October 23, 1981, Princeton NJ.

Eliasberg, Ann (Pringle), December 12, 1982 +(C); Elliott, Osborn, March 10, 1983; Engelking, Hess Houghton (Mrs. Lessing Lanham), September 1, 1982, Cooperstown NY (P).

Farris, Fred, November 8, 1982, Washington DC; Fein, Nat, September 21, 1981, Tappan NY; Felker, Clay S., September 29, 1982; Ferretti, Fred, December 9, 1983 +(T); Flexner, James T., October 23, 1981 (P); Frankel, Max, October 19, 1983; Freidin, Seymour K., August 18, 1982.

Gardner, Hy, June 18, 1982, Miami FL (T); Genauer, Emily, September 24, 1982*; Gillies, Archibald L., December 2, 1981; Glass, Andrew J., November 11, 1982, Washington DC; Goldstein, Nathan W., November 7, 1982, Stamford CT; Gottehrer, Barry, February 6, 1982, New Haven CT; Graham, Katharine, November 10, 1982, Washington DC; Green, Monroe, November 19, 1982, Philadelphia PA; Grynbaum, Joan Brandon (formerly Mrs. Whitelaw Reid), July 6, 1982; Guernsey, Otis L., Jr., August 12, 1982, New Haven CT.

Hadley, Arthur T., July 26, 1982 (P); Hagen, Yvonne Forrest, March 24, 1982; Hamilton, E. Douglas, November 25, 1981 (P); Hamilton, Theresa Alexander, December 3, 1981; Hamshar, Walter, April 14, 1982, Sun City FL (C); Handler, Milton, October 20, 1982; Haxall, Bolling W., September 23, 1982 (C); Heckscher, August V., December 4, 1981; Heiskell, Marian Sulzberger (Mrs. Andrew), November 17, 1982; Hills, Lee, March 30, 1982, Miami FL (T); Hopke, Dorothea, December 2, 1981; Hoving, Walter, October 13, 1982; Huffman, Robert S., January 8, 1982 (C).

Irwin, Don, November 11, 1981, Washington DC.

Javits, Jacob K., March 13, 1983 (T).

Kandel, Myron, September 16, 1982; Kanfer, Stefan, December 17, 1981; Kaselow, Joseph, October 12, 1982; Kehr, Ernest A., December 17, 1981 (C); Kellett, Dee, August 2, 1983; Kelley, Frank, April 19, 1982, Westport CT; Kennan, George F., January 6, 1983, Princeton NJ (C); Kerr, Walter B., September 24, 1982 +(C), (T); Kerr, Walter F., January 11, 1982, Larchmont NY; Kihss, Peter, December 2, 1981 +(C); Kiker, Douglas, May 12, 1982, Washington DC (P); Kiley, Charles F., October 22, 1981*; King, Nicholas, September 30, 1982; Klaw, Barbara Van Doren (Mrs. Spencer), July 11, 1982, West Cornwall CT; Koyen, Kenneth, April 8, 1983 +(C); Krim, Seymour, September 22, 1982 +(C); Kupferberg, Herbert, November 18, 1981*.

Lambert, Robert H., October 22, 1982; Laney, Al, September 21, 1981, Spring Valley NY +(C), (P); Laymon, Theodore, October 8, 1982; Levin, Carl, November 8, 1982, Washington DC +(C); Lewis, Frederick (Bud), February 9, 1982*, Venice FL (C); Lewis, Milton, October 21, 1982; Lindsay, Frank, July 29, 1983, Lexington MA (T); Lindsay, John V., June 22, 1983; Lois, George, August 19, 1982; Loory, Stuart, November 9, 1982, Washington DC; Lynn, James, September 14, 1982, Mineola NY (C).

McAllister, James, December 2, 1982; McCrary, John R. (Tex), April 24, 1982 +(C), (P); MacDonald, Robert T., October 30, 1981, Stamford CT; McGurn, Barrett, May 11, 1982, Washington

DC +(C); Manning, Robert, November 4, 1982; Mapes, Lois, May 4, 1983; Maxwell, Jane Noakes, August 15, 1982, Milbrook NY; Maxwell, Winslow, August 14, 1982, Millbrook NY +(C); Mearns, Jack, February 2, 1983, North Ridgeville OH (C); Midgley, Leslie, October 18, 1981 +(C); Mitchell, Joseph, January 21, 1983; Murphy, Eve Peterson, May 19, 1982.

Newborn, Roy, December 9, 1981*; Newman, Joseph, November 10, 1981, Washington DC.

O'Hara, Mary, September 16, 1982; O'Hara, Rebecca (Mrs. Tom), September 16, 1982; Oliensis, Sheldon, June 22, 1983.

Palazzo, Peter, October 14, 1982*; Paley, William S., October 7, 1982; Parton, James, June 10, 1982 +(C), (P); Perry, Malcolm O., November 21, 1983 (C); Persky, Mort, February 4, 1983; Petersmeyer, C. Wrede, December 22, 1982 (P); Philbrick, Herbert A., October 17, 1982, North Hampton NH +(C); Pinkham, Richard, July 20, 1982, Greenwich CT; Portis, Charles, February 3, 1983, Little Rock AR (C); Poteete, Robert A., November 11, 1981* +(C); Potter, Philip, September 16, 1983, Baltimore MD (C); Powers, Bertram A., September 23, 1982; Price, Raymond K., Jr., November 5, 1981*.

Reed, Roy, February 16, 1983, Fayetteville AR (C); Rees, Charles A., September 8, 1982; Reeves, Richard, November 18, 1982; Reid, Mary Louise Stewart (Mrs. Ogden R.), October 22, 1982, Purchase NY; Reid, Ogden R., April 26, 1982*, Purchase NY (P); Reid, Whitelaw, April 26, 1982* +(C), (P); Reston, James, October 10, 1981, Washington DC; Ritchie, Kathryn, July 20, 1982*; Robinson, Thomas L., April 28, 1983, Stamford CT; Rogers, John, March 10, 1983, Eau Claire WI (C); Rogers, Warren, November 11, 1982, Washington DC; Rosenfeld, Harry M., October 26, 1981, Albany NY; Rosenthal, A. M., November 30, 1982; Rosenthal, Harold, December 16, 1981; Ryan, John F., December 10, 1981.

Safire, William, November 10, 1982, Washington DC +(T); Salisbury, Harrison E., December 1, 1982; Sargent, Dwight, December 18, 1981; Schaap, Richard J. (Dick), December 17, 1981*; Schiff, Dorothy, October 28, 1982; Schmidt, Benno C., October 19, 1983; Schwarz, Ralph G., May 20, 1982; Schwed, Peter, September 15, 1982; See, Arthur, July 6, 1982, Lakewood NJ (C); Sessa, Anthony, October 6, 1982; Seymour, Gerald, October 1, 1982; Shapiro, Henry, September 15, 1983, Madison WI (T); Shaplen, Robert M., August 18, 1982; Sheehy, Gail, March 22, 1983; Sheppard, Eugenia, May 7, 1982*; Sheppard, R. Z., September 23, 1981; Shirer, William L., July 10, 1981, Lenox MA; Silber, Fritz, August 26, 1981, Oakland CA (C); Simon, Maron J., November 6, 1981; Siner, Robert C., November 8, 1982, Washington DC; Smith, Terence, May 13, 1982, Washington DC; Smith, Walter W. (Red), December 14, 1981, New Canaan CT; Spinelli, Frank, April 14, 1982, Fair Lawn NJ; Stanford, Alfred B., June 16, 1982, Milford CT; Steele, Richard C., August 7, 1982, Worcester MA; Stone, Martin, September 26, 1982; Stowe, Leland, March 22, 1982*, Ann Arbor MI and New Haven CT +(C), (P); Straus, Jack I., September 9, 1982; Streeter, Frank, September 9, 1982; Sugrue, Francis, October 14, 1982 (P); Sulzberger, Arthur Ochs (Punch), March 4, 1982; Sulzberger, Iphigene Ochs, July 19, 1982, Stamford CT.

Talbert, Ansel, October 1, 1982; Taylor, Telford, May 26, 1982; Taylor, William E., May 19, 1982; Thalasinos, Gus, September 10, 1982; Thayer, Walter N., October 8, 1981* +(C), (P); Thees, John D. (Jack), March 15, 1982, Pompano Beach FL +(C); Thorn, Frank, April 5, 1982; Tobin, Richard L., August 16, 1982, Southbury CT +(C), (T); Torre, Marie, May 9, 1983; Toth, Robert, December 2, 1982, Washington DC (C).

Ubell, Earl, January 19, 1982*.

Van Horne, Richard W., September 10, 1982*; Vartan, Vartanig S., November 3, 1982; Veit, Ivan, October 5, 1982.

Wade, Betsy, January 3, 1984; Wald, Richard C., September 16, 1981*; Walker, Everett, November 20, 1981 +(C); Warman, Morris, October 28, 1982; Waters, Frank T., March 4, 1982 (P); Weberman, Ben, December 8, 1982; Weiss, Murray M. (Buddy), March 20, 1982*; Wergeles, Ed, January 17, 1983, Sarasota FL (T); West, Richard G., August 10, 1981, Carmel CA (C); White, Robert M., II, June 8, 1982 +(C), (P); White, Stephen, September 21, 1981, New Haven CT +(C); Whitman, Alden, September 12, 1981* +(C); Whitney, Betsey Cushing (Mrs. John Hay), December 12, 1982; Whitney, Kate Roosevelt, April 21, 1983; Whitworth, William, October 17, 1982, Boston MA; Wilder, Roy, Jr., April 20, 1982, Spring Hope NC (C); Wise, David, May 4, 1982*, Washington DC; Wolfe, Tom, October 28, 1982; Wyden, Peter, July 4, 1982, Ridgefield CT (T).

Yerxa, Fendall, July 15, 1983, Seattle WA (C), (T); Yoakum, Robert, August 12, 1982, Lakeville CT.

Zalaznick, Sheldon, November 1, 1981*; Zinsser, William K., October 27, 1982; Zwick, Lester, September 14, 1981, New Haven CT.

III. BIBLIOGRAPHICAL NOTES

Principal sources consulted are listed here by the chapter in which their usefulness was first or most manifest. Part I, dealing with the nineteenth century, was of course drawn almost entirely from secondary sources, except for the newspapers, which in this case represent primary materials. The rest of the work draws heavily on a synthesis of the personal interviews and correspondence cited above. When an individual source is cited, generally for a view or judgment consensual of all those who ventured comment on the subject, I have used the verb "recalled" or "recounted" or "remembered" or merely "said" without stating the context for the remark, which was of course in response to the author's inquiry; thus, the dates of the interviews are provided above. Where sources and events are given and dated in the text, they are not repeated in the notes below.

October 10, 1945: A Prelim

Ogden M. Reid left few revealing papers, in sharp contrast to his wife. A sketchy account of his Pacific tour, from September 25 to November 15, 1945, was written by Wilbur Forrest. "The Trib's Mrs. Reid" ran in *Time*, November 12, 1945. The advertising linage figures cited here and elsewhere were drawn from *Editor & Publisher*, which runs an annual summary and kindly made its library available.

1 The Righteous and the Wrathful

The most valuable contemporary accounts of Greeley's career are James Parton's admiring *The Life of Horace Greeley* (Mason Bros., 1855, expanded and reissued in 1872 to coincide with Greeley's presidential campaign) and Greeley's autobiography, *Recollections of a Busy Life* (J. B. Ford & Co., 1868). The most careful and reliable work on him is *Horace Greeley: Nineteenth-Century Crusader* by Glyndon G. Van Dusen (University of Pennsylvania Press, 1953), but no definitive or masterful life of this fascinating figure has yet been written. Also useful were *Horace Greeley, the Editor* by Francis Nicoll Zabriskie (Funk & Wagnalls, 1890), *The Life of Horace Greeley* by Lurton D. Ingersoll (Union Publishing Co., 1873), and *Horace Greeley and the Republican Party, 1853–1861: A Study of the New York Tribune* by Jeter Allen Isely (Princeton University Press, 1947). The first chapter of Isely's book, the best written of any on Greeley, was especially useful here. The quoted editorial by Greeley attacking the Archbishop ran November 24, 1851.

II. In view of its pervasive influence on the development of democracy in America, journalism has inspired a remarkably scant body of literature about itself. The basic work remains Frank Luther Mott's *American Journalism* (Macmillan, 1941), admirable in scope and venturesome in judgments; no other work approaches his standard. The leading nineteenth-century work is Frederic Hudson's massive, data-jammed, but highly idiosyncratic *Journalism in the United States from 1690 to 1872* (Harper & Bros., 1873). Other leading studies include *The Daily Newspaper in America: The Evolution of a Social Instrument* by Alfred McClung Lee (Macmillan, 1937), *The Disappearing Daily: Chapters in American Newspaper Evolution* by Oswald Garrison Villard (Alfred A. Knopf, 1944), and *Discovering the News: A Social History of American Newspapers* by Michael Schudson (Basic Books, 1978). Schudson's book, too slender for its subject, offers original insights into the nature of news handling by the U.S. press; his chapter notes are also highly useful and suggest a breadth of knowledge only hinted at in the text. *The Newsmongers: Journalism in the Life of the Nation, 1690–1972* by Robert A. Rutland (Dial Press, 1973) is a pleasant gloss on the subject but of limited use to the serious student.

III. Greeley's *The New-Yorker,* available on microfilm at Princeton's Firestone Library, makes for lively reading a century and a half after its short life span; it is packed with social and political data.

IV. No doubt because of his misanthropic and secretive nature, far less literature survives on James Gordon Bennett than on Greeley. The main contemporary source is *Memoirs of James Gordon Bennett and His Times* by "A Journalist" [Isaac C. Pray] (Stringer & Townsend, 1855); the chief modern work is *The Man Who Made News: James Gordon Bennett* by Oliver Carlson (Duell, Sloan & Pearce, 1942). Dan C. Seitz's *The James Gordon Bennetts* (Bobbs-Merrill, 1928) is easy reading but less helpful; it is more informative on Bennett's son, who contributed far less to journalism.

V. Schudson is especially good on the *Herald*'s journalistic innovations; Carlson's account of the Jewett case is detailed. The *Herald*'s March 2, 1840, article on the Brevoort costume ball is a milestone in American social reportage. For an astute discussion of the role of newspapers in the building of a nation, see Chapter 3 of *City People: The Rise of Modern City Culture in Nineteenth-Century America* by Gunther Barth (Oxford University Press, 1980).

2 Instructing the Nation

Van Dusen is instructive on the ironies and contradictions of Greeley's social philosophy. Bennett's anti-Catholic virulence is quoted by Carlson at p. 175; Pray quotes Bennett's defiant rebuttal to his detractors in the Moral War on p. 466.

II. For Greeley's thoughts on starting the *Tribune,* see *Recollections,* pp. 137 ff. The example of the *Tribune*'s political partisanship in covering Tammany Hall ran April 13, 1850. The best source on Greeley's relationship with Raymond is Augustus Maverick's *Henry J. Raymond and the New York Press for Thirty Years* (A. S. Hale & Co., 1870), published soon after Raymond's death.

III. Greeley's socialism is presented extensively in his autobiography, as are the texts and highlights of his six-month debate on the subject with Raymond. The cited rebuke of Greeley's socialism appeared in the *Herald* on October 15, 1845.

IV. Greeley's clash with Cooper is most fully documented in the monograph *The "Effingham" Libels on Cooper* by Ethel R. Outland (University of Wisconsin Press, 1929); it is weak, however, on the legal nuances of the cases. There are many works on Zenger and his landmark trial; Mott's account is an admirable summary.

V. Many works deal with the heroic life of Margaret Fuller, turned into a legendary figure by the women's liberation movement of the 1970s and its literature. Most useful sources to me were *The Writings of Margaret Fuller* selected and edited by Mason Wade (Viking Press, 1941), Perry Miller's article on Fuller in *American Heritage,* February 1957, and James R. Mellows's essay-review in the June 19, 1983, *New York Times Book Review* on the first two volumes of Fuller's letters edited by Robert N. Hudspeth; the letters did not, unfortunately, cover Fuller's years on the *Tribune.* Greeley's warm regard for Fuller and the text of his revealing 1860 debate with Robert Owen on the morality of divorce are in his *Recollections.*

VII. Van Dusen's account of Greeley's performance in the lame-duck 30th Congress is a model study of idealistic impolitics; see also Greeley's detailed account, especially on the mileage expenses, in his autobiography.

3 The Crusader

The leading accounts of the redoubtable Dana are *The Life of Charles A. Dana* by James Harrison Wilson (Harper & Bros., 1907) and *Dana and The Sun* by Candace Stone (Dodd, Mead, 1938). Extensive colorful obituaries appeared in the New York papers of October 18, 1897. Dana's perceptive characterization of American journalism appears in Hudson, p. 680. Most large library collections have ample representation of the prolific travel writings of Bayard Taylor.

II. The immediate urban background against which Greeley wrote his editorials is graphically presented in *Mirror for Gotham: New York as Seen by Contemporaries from Dutch Days to the Present* by Bayrd Still (New York University Press, 1956). Greeley's editorial on street cleaning ran on June 1, 1854.

III. In addition to Maverick's book on Raymond, the beginnings of *The New York Times* are described in *History of the New York Times, 1851–1921* by Elmer Davis (published by the *Times* in 1921) and *The Story of the New York Times, 1851–1951* by Meyer Berger (Simon and Schuster, 1951); both books were sponsored by the *Times* and represent something less than an objective evaluation of the paper. More recent, less reverential, but still highly admiring books about the *Times* are *The Kingdom and the Power* by Gay Talese (World, 1969) and *Without Fear or Favor: The New York Times and Its Times* by Harrison E. Salisbury (Times Books, 1980). A comprehensive critical history of the *Times* remains to be written. Greeley's famous recriminatory letter to Seward was dated November 11, 1854.

IV. Greeley's views on slavery and how to cope with it are best rendered in Isely's book, though Van Dusen's treatment is competent. For details on Representative Rust's assault on Greeley, see the *Tribune* of January 29 and 31, 1856. Financial and other data on the *Tribune*'s second decade and later were found in the corporate minute books, unearthed in a Manhattan warehouse among other records retained by the Whitney Communications Co. and apparently unavailable to earlier writers. Ralph Ray Fahrney's *Horace Greeley and the Tribune in the Civil War* (Torch Press, 1936) is a thin but clear account of the background to the paper's war posture.

4 Trampling Out the Vintage

The North Reports the Civil War by J. Cutler Andrews (University of Pittsburgh Press, 1954) and *Yankee Reporters, 1861–65* by Emmet Crozier (Oxford University Press, 1956) are equally rich and absorbing works. Charles Page's descriptions of his ordeal are cited in Andrews's book on pp. 588 and 644. Hudson includes details on the *Herald*'s elaborate war coverage. Smalley writes about Antietam and its aftermath in the first of his two-volume *Anglo-American Memories* (G. P. Putnam's Sons, 1911).

II. Dana's own speculation about his firing is taken from p. 20 of *Dana and The Sun*. "The Prayer of Twenty Millions" appeared in the August 20, 1862, *Tribune*. Parton's 1872 revision of his Greeley biography has an engaging and friendly account of the editor's behavior during the 1863 draft riots; reports of his craven behavior lack authentication.

IV. Greeley's "Magnanimity in Triumph" editorial appeared April 11, 1865; his defiant letter to the Union League Club over his putting up a bail bond for Jefferson Davis, on May 23, 1867.

V. The best source for information on the paper from 1865 to 1935 is Harry W. Baehr, Jr.'s *The New York Tribune Since the Civil War* (Dodd, Mead, 1936); it is especially good on the editorial policy and politics of the Reids. The most revealing information about the unfortunate *Tribune* career of the precocious John Russell Young came from his diaries in the Library of Congress; his undated *Men and Memories: Personal Reminiscences*, edited by his widow and issued by F. Tennyson Neely, is less illuminating. *The Sun*'s excoriating exposure of Young ran April 27, 1869; a sharp editorial followed by two days. Greeley's careful defense of his editor appeared in the May 1, 1869, *Tribune*. Royal Cortissoz's two-volume *The Life of Whitelaw Reid* (Thornton & Butterworth, 1921) is a family-sponsored, roseate rendering of the man; far more dependable and less effusive is *Whitelaw Reid: Journalist, Politician, Diplomat* by Bingham Duncan (University of Georgia Press, 1975). Cortissoz's brief 1923 study, *The New York Tribune: Incidents and Personalities in Its History*, is a more appealing and honest effort. Raymond's rebuke to Greeley for intemperate editorial language is cited by Hudson on p. 633.

VI. The New York Public Library has an interesting collection of campaign documents from the 1872 presidential election. Among the documents are *Horace Greeley's Jokes*, issued by the Journeymen Printers' Co-operative Association, *From Under the Old White Hat* by "Old-Time

Editors of the Tribune," and the decidedly less friendly *The Life of Horace Greeley: All the "Recollections," Corrections, Deflections, Connections, Reflections, Objections and Elections* by "A Professional Biographer" and published from the "Wild Oats" office on Fulton Street. The *Times*'s misdirected chiding of Greeley for the "Crumbs of Comfort" indiscretion appeared November 8, 1872; the episode was ventilated by *The Sun* as part of its extensive obituary on Greeley on November 30, 1872. The more detailed and damning account, part of the mischievous Dana's war on Reid, ran on July 7, 1877, and was reprinted with relish by *The Boycotter* on January 12, 1884, and alluded to frequently thereafter.

5 Midas Touches

Among the works consulted in trying to unpuzzle the Orton-Colfax-Gould triangle and Reid's takeover of the paper with Gould's backing were: *Life and Achievements of Jay Gould, Wizard of Wall Street* by Henry Davenport Northrop (Ariel Book Co., 1892), *The Life of Jay Gould: How He Made His Millions* by Murat Halstead and J. Frank Beale, Jr. (Edgewood, 1892), *Jay Gould: His Business Career, 1867–1892* by Julius Grodinsky (University of Pennsylvania Press, 1957), *Gould's Millions* by Richard O'Connor (Doubleday, 1962), *The Robber Barons: The Great American Capitalists, 1861–1901* by Matthew Josephson (Harcourt, Brace, 1934), *The Telegraph in America* by James D. Reid (John Polhemus, 1886), and *Life of Schuyler Colfax* by O. J. Hollister (Funk & Wagnalls, 1886). Orton's obituaries in the April 23, 1878, papers, especially the *Sun*, were also intriguing. On the cipher dispatches triumph, Cortissoz is expansive, but the paper itself is the best source, starting with the October 7, 1878, issue. For background on Darius Ogden Mills and his daughter Elisabeth, see their obituaries, the former's in papers of January 4, 1910, the latter's of April 30, 1931.

II. Dana in his heyday is treated in *Dana and The Sun.* The younger Bennett is tolerantly dealt with in Seitz's joint biography and *The Scandalous Mr. Bennett* by Richard O'Connor (Doubleday, 1962); see Seitz, p. 222, for the "black beetles" directive and for the full text of the November 9, 1874, zoo hoax story.

III. *Joseph Pulitzer and the New York World* by George Juergens (Princeton University Press, 1966) is the best work on the subject.

IV. An incomplete file of *The Boycotter* survives on microfilm at the New York Public Library. For examples of the *Tribune*'s lack of editorial compassion for tenement dwellers, see the issues of February 6 and 18, 1884. *Ottmar Mergenthaler and the Printing Revolution* by Willi Mengel, issued in 1954 by the Mergenthaler Company, succinctly describes the inventor's struggle to develop the Linotype; *The Boycotter*'s derogatory report on the invention, "Reid's Rattle-trap!," appeared July 16, 1887.

V. *The Life and Letters of John Hay* by William Roscoe Thayer (Houghton Mifflin, 1915) is the standard source on this attractive personality. Among the works consulted on Riis were: *Jacob A. Riis: Police Reporter, Reformer, Useful Citizen* by Louise Ware (D. Appleton-Century, 1938), the 1970 Belknap Press edition of Riis's 1890 classic, *How the Other Half Lives,* and the 1931 Macmillan edition of Riis's autobiography, *The Making of an American.* Riis deserves a definitive biography.

VI. On the early years of the Paris *Herald*, see Seitz, O'Connor's *The Scandalous Mr. Bennett,* and especially *Paris Herald: The Incredible Newspaper* by Al Laney (D. Appleton-Century, 1946). W. A. Swanberg's *Citizen Hearst* (Charles Scribner's Sons, 1961) is the best work on Hearst; Berger's centennial history of the *Times* deals well with Ochs's career.

6 The Girl with the Goods

The italicized excerpts are direct quotations from Helen Rogers Reid's letters to her sister, Florence Rogers Ferguson, in the possession of and kindly made available by her older son, Whitelaw. *The Atlantic Monthly*'s critical comments about the *Tribune* appeared in the October 1908 issue in an article titled "Is an Honest Newspaper Possible?"

II. Financial data on the *Tribune* are drawn from the corporate minute books; the circulation data are from the *Editor & Publisher* and N. W. Ayer annual directories.

III. See Baehr's mid-life history of the *Tribune* for further details on its revival under Ogden M. Reid. The paper's two most celebrated cartoonists are well covered in *The Best of H. T. Webster* with a preface by Robert E. Sherwood (Simon and Schuster, 1953), *Ding: The Life of Jay Norwood Darling* by David L. Lendt (Iowa State University Press, 1979), and *Ding's Half Century* by J. N. Darling (Duell, Sloan & Pearce, 1962). The Burdick and Curtin cases were argued before the U.S. Supreme Court on December 16, 1914, and decided on January 25, 1915. *Gimbel Bros. v. The Tribune Association et al.* was filed in the New York County section of the New York Supreme Court as #5461-1917 but never reported. Samuel Hopkins Adams's derogation of the Bennett-Hearst-Pulitzer advertising policies appeared in "The Ad-Visor" column of April 5, 1916. Richard Harding Davis's Louvain dispatch was sent August 30, 1914. Simonds's Pulitzer-winning editorial on the first anniversary of the *Lusitania*'s sinking ran May 7, 1916. Baehr discusses the paper's assault on Hearst on pp. 342 ff.

IV. For more on Broun, see Richard O'Connor's *Heywood Broun: A Biography* (G. P. Putnam's Sons, 1975). The cited story on the Giants' game appeared July 4, 1913; the story on the AEF landing in France, on July 1, 1917. Broun's admirable letter of resignation to Ogden Reid, dated January 25, 1921, is in the Reid papers in the Library of Congress.

V. On Garrett, see Carl George Ryant's 1968 doctoral thesis at the University of Wisconsin titled *Garet Garrett's America*; I am also indebted to Richard Cornuelle for a copy of Garrett's journal covering his tenure at the *Times* in 1915 and 1916. Cornuelle edited and wrote an introduction to the journal. The best reference works on Bodoni type and all others are *Printing Types: Their History, Forms and Use* by David Berkeley Updike (Harvard University Press, 1927) and *The Encyclopedia of Type Faces* by W. Pincus Jaspert, W. Turner Berry, and A. F. Johnson (Barnes & Noble, 1970). Abundant evidence of Helen Reid's gritty style as a businesswoman, such as her December 28, 1922, letter to Philip Armour, may be found in her papers in the Library of Congress (LC).

7 Bigger than a Cat Trap

Mott deals in detail with the sad saga of Frank Munsey in *American Journalism*; Stanley Walker offers trenchant comments on Munsey in his autobiography, *Home to Texas* (Harper & Bros., 1956). For the origins of the *Daily News* and its ilk, see *Jazz Journalism: The Story of Tabloid Newspapers* by Simon Michael Bessie (E. P. Dutton, 1938). Helen Reid's letters to her mother-in-law about the *Herald-Tribune* merger are in the Library of Congress; *Editor & Publisher* of March 22, 1924, has an extensive account of the merger. The Reids' Camp Wild Air cheer and Miss Goss's variant on it were supplied by Whitelaw Reid.

II. The Jarrell hoax appeared in the August 16, 1924, issue. *The Morning Telegraph* carried needling comments on it on August 17, 19, and 23.

III. Peck expounded on his craft in a chapter he contributed to *Late City Edition* by Joseph G. Herzberg and members of the New York Herald Tribune Staff (Henry Holt & Co., 1947), one of the few pieces of writing he did outside the columns of the paper; see also *City Editor* by Stanley Walker (Frederick A. Stokes, 1934), pp. 296 ff., for the full text of Peck's piece on the New Jersey tailor.

IV. Stanley Walker deals with Ishbel Ross in *City Editor*, pp. 258 ff., and in an introduction to her *Ladies of the Press* (Harper & Bros., 1936). See also *Women in Media: A Documentary Source Book* by Maurine Beasley and Shelia Silver (Women's Institute for Freedom of the Press, 1977). Ross's story on the pig woman's testimony appeared November 19, 1926. I learned about the experiences of Frances Buss Merrill in a letter from her daughter, Serena M. Mathiasen, and from scrapbooks provided by her family. The Winter 1976 issue of the *Barnard Alumnae Bulletin* carries a profile on Emma Bugbee, who is also treated in *Up from the Footnote: A History of Women Journalists* by Marion Marzolf (Hastings House, 1977); her accounts of the suffragist march on Albany ran January 3–8, 1914. The author interviewed Miss Bugbee three months before her death at the age of ninety-three.

V. E. Douglas Hamilton and Frank Kelley provided vivid memories of M. Jay Racusin; the *Tribune* carried an extensive obituary on him on November 28, 1962, for which Racusin himself supplied some details.

VI. *City Editor* includes Walker's views on McGeehan along with the text of the cited article on the Scopes trial. A detailed biography and tributes from admirers appeared in the November 30, 1933, *Tribune* obituary on McGeehan. Supplementing the April 26, 1937, obituary on Percy Hammond were tributes to him in Franklin Pierce Adams's "The Conning Tower" in the *Tribune* two days later and Brooks Atkinson's appreciation in the May 4, 1937, *Times.* Excerpts of his reviews were taken from *This Atom in the Audience,* a collection of Hammond's best work, privately published as a memorial to him in 1940.

VII. See Helen Reid's LC papers.

VIII. Compare *Behind the Front Page* by Wilbur Forrest (D. Appleton-Century, 1934), pp. 298 ff., with Laney's *Paris Herald,* pp. 218 ff. My interviews with Laney, Stowe, and Shirer added to the conviction that Forrest was piping it in his book. The Lindbergh interview ran May 22, 1927. Stowe elaborated on his reportorial techniques at the 1929 war reparations conference in Paris in interviews for this book.

8 The Sawed-Off Texan and Other High Spirits

In addition to Walker's *City Editor* and *Home to Texas,* see his *Mrs. Astor's Horse* (Blue Ribbon, 1935), obituaries in the November 26, 1962, *Tribune* and *Times, Time* for December 7 and *Newsweek* for December 10, 1962, and, among other tributes, those by Robert Sherrill in the November 30, 1962, *Texas Observer* and J. Frank Dobie in the January 13, 1963, Fort Worth *Star-Telegram.* Other useful articles appeared in *Time,* September 7, 1931, and April 10 and October 22, 1934. Most pertinent of Walker's own magazine writings was his "Heralds of the New Tribune" in *Saturday Review* of August 29, 1959. The most vivid personal memories of Walker were supplied by Joseph Mitchell, Richard West, and Joan Walker Iams, Walker's daughter. Richard Van Horne produced a copy of the 1934 *Tribune Style Book.*

II. Flexner's story on Dreiser and the accompanying editorial ran July 8, 1930.

III. Wolcott Gibbs profiled Beebe in *The New Yorker* of November 27, 1937; the *Tribune* carried an extensive obituary on February 5, 1966.

IV and V. Mitchell's experiences are drawn mostly from his own memories; Alsop's, from his own and many others'.

VI. The merits and failings of the *World* in its last stage are well rendered in *The Best in The World* edited by John K. Hutchens and George Oppenheimer (Viking Press, 1973) and *The World of Swope* by E. J. Kahn, Jr. (Simon and Schuster, 1965). Required reading on Lippmann are Ronald Steel's weighty biography, *Walter Lippmann and the American Century* (Little, Brown–Atlantic Monthly Press, 1980), and *The Essential Lippmann: A Political Philosophy for Liberal Democracy* edited by Clinton Rossiter and James Lare (Vintage, 1965).

VII. Cresswell's memo was sent June 28, 1933.

VIII. Almost every *Tribune* alumnus interviewed had fond memories of Bleeck's; the January 1953 *True* carried a long write-up on the establishment by Richard Gehman, and *Time* had a shorter piece on May 3, 1963. Of the staffers' reflections on the legendary drinking exploits of *Tribune* men, Red Smith's were especially thoughtful. Laymon's and Lewis's memories of the 1939 bachelor party attended by Ogden Reid coincided.

9 Writers of the World, Unite

John Price's diary provided a precise chronology of daily happenings and staff changes in the *Tribune* city room that otherwise would have been impossible to pinpoint. The Reids' Palm Beach lifestyle is documented by their papers in the Library of Congress. Prime sources on the Guild are *A Union of Individualists: The Formation of the American Newspaper Guild, 1933–36* by Daniel J.

Leab (Columbia University Press, 1970), the collection of the *Guild Reporter* on microfilm at the New York Public Library, and *A History of 100 Years of Unions at the New York Tribune,* a pamphlet written by Henry McIlvaine Parsons and privately published on the centennial of the paper. The memories of Fritz Silber, John Ryan, and Parsons were also valuable. The Wilbur Forrest–Laurence Hills correspondence is in Ogden Reid's LC papers; Howard Davis's revealing letter to Julius Ochs Adler of June 27, 1935, is among Helen Reid's LC papers. George A. Cornish is the source of the exchange between Henry Luce and Ogden Reid; he heard it from Forrest, who was on hand.

II. The quoted advisory by Howard Davis to Ogden Reid was dated October 8, 1936. Clementine Paddleford was the subject of articles in *Time,* March 18, 1946, and, more extensively, *The Saturday Evening Post,* April 30, 1949. *Dorothy Thompson: A Legend in Her Time* by Marion K. Sanders (Houghton Mifflin, 1973) is the prime source on the subject. On Helen Reid in her prime, see especially *Time* for October 8, 1934, and "Queen Helen" by Mona Gardner in *The Saturday Evening Post* of May 6 and 13, 1944.

III. Laney's *Paris Herald* and *Hawkins of the Paris Herald* by Eric Hawkins (Simon and Schuster, 1963) were supplemented by interviews with staff members and Hills's correspondence with Forrest et al. "Prelude to War: A Witness from Spain" by John T. Whitaker in the October 1942 *Foreign Affairs* is a greatly affecting antiwar document. A copy of Whitaker's excoriating indictment of Hills in his December 20, 1937, letter to Elliott is among Joseph Barnes's papers, privately held by the family.

IV. Barnes's astute observations on the nature of daily newspaper-making are in his oral memoir at Columbia; details on his experience in Moscow were provided by his widow, who kindly made his Moscow papers available to me. See also Barnes's chapter on foreign correspondence in *Late City Edition* and for general background John Hohenberg's *Foreign Correspondence: The Great Reporters and Their Times* (Columbia University Press, 1964). Kennan's assessment of Barnes was included in his January 6, 1983, response to the author's written inquiry; Shapiro's countervailing view was offered in a telephone conversation on September 15, 1983.

10 The Soul of a Newspaper

Engelking's tape-recorded reminiscences, though fragmented, were invaluable, and dozens of staffers who worked under him were forthcoming with stories that shaped the composite portrait of him. Among written sources were Margaret Parton's autobiography, *Journey Through a Lighted Room* (Viking Press, 1973), pp. 73 ff., and M. C. Blackman's unpublished memoir, *Rewrite Man,* where he recounts the 1944 Hartford fire episode.

II. Many references to Everett (the Count) Kallgren were found in the round-robin correspondence informally directed by John Price; Barbara Belford, now on the Columbia Journalism School faculty, provided a memorandum on Kallgren's peculiar personality.

III. See Barnes's oral history memoir, pp. 140 ff., and Price's diary for March 1, 1939, in his round-robin letter of August 10, 1967.

IV. Woodward's own writings, especially *Sports Page* (Simon and Schuster, 1949) and *Paper Tiger* (Atheneum, 1964), were the prime sources on him; also Al Laney's remarks, "The Coach," delivered at the April 12, 1962, testimonial luncheon to Woodward at Toots Shor's and extensive obituaries, especially in the *Tribune,* on November 30, 1965.

V. Irita Van Doren's papers, at the Library of Congress, include sketches on her by Gerald Carson and Mark Van Doren; see also the twenty-fifth anniversary number of "Books" in the September 25, 1949, *Tribune.* The leading works on Willkie are *Willkie* by Joseph F. Barnes (Simon and Schuster, 1952), *Wendell Willkie: Fighter for Freedom* by Ellsworth Barnard (North Michigan University Press, 1966), and, most recently and more satisfactory than the others, *Dark Horse: A Biography of Wendell Willkie* by Steve Neal (Doubleday, 1984), which deals candidly with the Willkie–Van Doren affair. Willkie's telegrams to Van Doren during the 1940 pre-convention campaign are among her LC papers. Van Doren's daughters, Barbara Klaw and Margaret Bevans, were especially helpful. Roosevelt's knowledge in 1940 of the adulterous relationship was disclosed by R.

J. C. Butow's article on the FDR tapes in the February–March 1982 issue of *American Heritage.*

VI. The Laney and Hawkins books are particularly vivid in dealing with the closing of the Paris paper due to the German invasion. Kerr's delayed dispatches from Paris appeared in the *Tribune* of July 22 and 23, 1940.

VII. Whitelaw Reid was generous with his time and memories. The quoted article on the Channel patrol mission appeared in the paper September 24, 1940; Millis's "Dover Beach" editorial ran December 27, 1940.

VIII. Cornish, who was a reclusive figure to most of his contemporaries, kindly provided extensive written answers to many questions put to him by the author, including background on his formative years. Eve Peterson, Ogden Reid's personal secretary for fifteen years, is the source of Helen Reid's remark to Forrest, who relayed it to Peterson, that Cornish had been the right choice for the managing-editorship.

11 On Higher Ground

Parsons's chapter in *Late City Edition* contains the essence of his beliefs on how to run a civilized editorial page.

II. Thomson discusses his *Tribune* career in some detail in his autobiography, *Virgil Thomson* (Alfred A. Knopf, 1966). William Zinsser kindly called to my attention the chapter dealing with the tutorial relationship between Parsons and Thomson in *Essays After a Dictionary: Music and Culture at the Close of Western Civilization* by John Vinton (Bucknell University Press, 1972). Robert Craft's assessment was offered in his review of *A Virgil Thomson Reader* (Houghton Mifflin, 1981) in the February 2, 1982, *New York Review of Books.* Herbert Kupferberg offered valuable insights into Thomson's work. See also Krehbiel's obituaries in March 21, 1928, papers. Parsons's quoted memo to Thomson on the latter's first slaughter of the New York Philharmonic was sent October 14, 1940.

III. The centennial number of the *Herald Tribune,* April 13, 1941, alluded to here, is a useful gloss on the paper's history, but no more than that; it was, essentially, a self-promotional project. Hoover's accusation of Gannett was made in a June 24, 1942, letter to Mrs. Reid; her admirable answer followed by a week. Gannett's earlier disavowal of Communist Party membership was made in a letter to Mrs. Reid on February 22, 1941. Roosevelt's confidential letter to Mrs. Reid, complaining of Darling's cartoon, was sent August 26, 1942; Darling's letter on Roosevelt's alleged animus toward him and the paper is on p. III of Lendt's biography of him.

IV. Robinson's papers are at the Eisenhower Library in Abilene, Kansas. The standard indictment of the *Tribune*'s wartime policies appears on p. 213 of the 1978 Anchor paperback edition of Talese's *The Kingdom and the Power.* Ivan Veit was instrumental in obtaining data from the *Times* on its financial picture during World War II. The computations in my table comparing the *Tribune* and *Times* in their editorial and advertising contents during the war were based on data in a memorandum from *Tribune* treasurer A. V. Miller to Ogden R. Reid and Frank W. Taylor on January 16, 1956, and found in Reid's papers at Yale.

V. Talese's claim about the virtues of the wartime *Times* is on p. 212 of the Anchor paperback of his book. Data on the *Times*'s wartime editorial budget and subsequent figures on its gross and net income were kindly provided by John Rothman, director of the *Times* archives. O'Reilly's encounter with the circus leopard was reported in the April 5, 1940, paper. Bigart struck me as both highly candid and admirably self-effacing in my interview with him. The abundance of stories told about him, not a few apocryphal in tone and largely unverifiable, indicated his rank as the most admired reporter on the paper. The *Copyboys' Call* carried a sardonic profile of the young Bigart on May 16, 1933. His story on the Wilhelmshaven raid ran in the *Tribune* on February 27, 1943. *Newsweek*'s admiring article on his European coverage appeared in the October 2, 1944, issue. Stories cited from his 1945 Pacific theater coverage, for which he was awarded his first Pulitzer: Luzon rescue raid, February 25; Iwo Jima, March 3; air attack off Okinawa, April 7; last bombing mission of war, August 16; and Hiroshima inspection, September 3. Helen Reid's letter to him urging caution was sent March 15, 1945.

VI. Levin's quoted Patton story ran September 22, 1945.

VII. John Rogers's chapter on newswriting in *Late City Edition* is recommended to any student or practitioner of the craft. The Hitler obituaries appeared in the May 2, 1945, issues.

VIII. Kihss himself, in the author's interview with him, was the principal source for the Empire State Building story; dozens testified to his legendary conscientiousness. Kihss wrote of his reportorial techniques and philosophy in the chapter he contributed to *Late City Edition,* which was the single most useful book to the author in the preparation of this work and is recommended to any serious student of U.S. journalism.

12 Cooking Cabbage

Kihss was especially informative on the circumstances leading up to Engelking's removal as city editor. Mrs. Reid's LC papers reveal her less than enlightened attitude toward Jews; it is ironical that her younger son should have served as U.S. ambassador to Israel upon his involuntary retirement from the paper—and a heightened irony that he should have switched his party allegiance to the Democrats during his six-term career as a U.S. Representative. Herzberg's introduction to his *Late City Edition* is the understated creed of a dedicated newspaperman.

III. Arm's crime reporting is dealt with in *Late City Edition* and at greater length in his unpublished memoir.

IV. This section, along with much of the postwar material, is drawn largely from interviews.

V. The author interviewed Smith a month before his death; when my wife and I left his home, he said "God bless" to us. Among the most useful clips were stories in *Time* of November 22, 1946, March 14, 1949, November 4, 1959, and September 1, 1961, a May 22, 1976, piece in *The Sporting News* by Harold Rosenthal, and "Red, He Juggled for Us" by Jane Leavy in *The Village Voice* of November 28, 1978. The cited examples of Smith's prose were taken from *The Red Smith Reader* edited by Dave Anderson (Random House, 1982).

VI. Fein's Babe Ruth photo appeared in the June 14, 1948, issue.

VII. Washington attorney Milton Freeman was interviewed on the phone September 9, 1983. "Mr. Blank's" name was contained in a November 28, 1947, letter from Andrews to Mrs. Reid and is among her LC papers. For Andrews's role in the Hiss affair, see *A Tragedy of History: A Journalist's Confidential Role in the Hiss-Chambers Case* (Robert B. Luce, 1963), which Andrews began and his son Peter completed; *Perjury: The Hiss-Chambers Case* by Allen Weinstein (Random House, 1978), and *Alger Hiss: The True Story* by John Chabot Smith (Holt, Rinehart and Winston, 1976), who covered the perjury trial for the *Tribune.*

VIII. The essence of Hamilton's considerable wisdom on the subject is contained in *Libel: Rights, Risks, Responsibilities* by Robert H. Phelps and E. Douglas Hamilton (Macmillan, 1966, and revised for the 1978 Dover paperback edition).

IX. The Alsops' quoted first doom-and-gloom column appeared January 29, 1946; see also *Time* of October 27, 1958.

X. The best of Crosby's early work was collected in *Out of the Blue* (Simon and Schuster, 1956). Other useful sources were *Time* of July 19, 1946, and August 20, 1956, and Peter Wyden's article in the *St. Louis Post-Dispatch* of December 2, 1949.

XI. Parton narrated her interview with Gandhi in an October 5, 1947, letter to Helen Reid. Mrs. Reid's letter to Irita Van Doren from Wild Air was sent August 10, 1947. Robinson's lament over the paper's alleged anti-business bias and Mauldin's alleged Red-lining was contained in an August 2, 1947, memo to Mrs. Reid. Robinson's involvement with Eisenhower over *Crusade in Europe* is documented in his papers in the Eisenhower Library. The author interviewed Kenneth McCormick of Doubleday by phone on December 29, 1982.

XII. Pegler's assault on the *Tribune* and Barnes began in the New York *Journal-American* on February 28, 1948; see also that paper on May 18, 19, and 24, 1948, for more of same. Helen Reid's letter to Loeb defending Barnes was sent November 16, 1945. The *Tribune* planning board minutes are among Mrs. Reid's LC papers.

13 'Fifties Follies

William Patterson's letter to Whitie Reid detailing the alleged campaign by *Times* advertising salesman against the *Tribune* was sent March 6, 1950. The New York attorney general at the time, Nathaniel L. Goldstein, issued his statement about the rumor attack on the *Tribune* on April 25, 1950. On McCrary, see the *New York Post* series on him and his wife by Irwin Ross, beginning June 10, 1957.

II. Works consulted on Higgins include her own books, *War in Korea* (Doubleday, 1951) and *News Is a Singular Thing* (Doubleday, 1955); *The American Mass Media and the Coverage of Five Major Foreign Events, 1900–1950*, a doctoral thesis by Michael Charles Emery, submitted to the University of Minnesota in December 1968; *Witness to War: A Biography of Marguerite Higgins* by Antoinette May (Beaufort Books, 1983); and *Tokyo and Points East* by Keyes Beech (Doubleday, 1954), especially pp. 167 ff. The author was also aided by advice and information from Kathleen K. Keeshen, then a doctoral candidate at the University of Maryland. Carl Mydans's article and pictures on Higgins ran in *Life* on October 2, 1950. Bigart's memorable foxhole account ran July 12, 1950. Helen Reid's cable to MacArthur was sent July 17, 1950; his reply was dated the next day. The excerpt on the marines' retreat was taken from Higgins's December 6, 1950, dispatch. Other articles alluded to ran July 6, 9, 15, 19, 21, 28, and 30, 1950.

III. Pinkham's memo urgently calling for changes in the Sunday edition was circulated March 12, 1951. Percival White's letter on the need for legitimate market research to authenticate the *Tribune*'s claims was sent to James Parton on January 27, 1950. The *Tribune* endorsement of Eisenhower for the Republican presidential nomination ran October 25, 1951; Robinson's call for militant Republicanism by the paper was embodied in a June 18, 1951, memo to Whitie Reid. Data on the suburban circulation of the *Tribune* vs. the *Times* were kindly obtained from the archives of the Audit Bureau of Circulation by John D. Stewart while a graduate student at the Medill School of Journalism, Northwestern University. Parton's telling memos are among his papers at Harvard's Houghton Library. Helen Reid's acknowledgment that she wanted to exploit Robinson's relationship with Eisenhower was contained in her letter of May 23, 1953, to Parsons; her views on the aborted *Brooklyn Eagle* purchase were expressed in an October 23, 1953, letter to Brown Reid.

14 Whitie, Brown, and the Reds

The "Talk" piece on Whitie Reid ran in the February 3, 1947, issue of *The New Yorker*.

III. On the *Tribune*'s anti-Communist purity, Whitie Reid made his avowal in a February 16, 1950, letter to David Lawrence, and Helen Reid stressed the point in the February 25, 1950, interview with *Editor & Publisher*. Anyone interested in the American obsession with Communism may benefit from *Joe McCarthy and the Press* by Edwin R. Bayley (University of Wisconsin Press, 1981). The Reid-Bird series "How Strong Is America?" began running August 14, 1950; the Reid-Yerxa series on alleged Red sabotage in the United States appeared November 29 and December 3 and 10, 1950. The commendatory letter from J. Edgar Hoover on the latter series was sent December 21, 1950. I. F. Stone's rebuttal to "The Red Underground" appeared in the *Compass* of November 11, 1951. The article trumpeting Brown Reid's column and anti-Communism was in *Editor & Publisher* of September 15, 1951.

IV. The transcript of the July 5, 1951, executive session of the Internal Security Subcommittee of the U.S. Senate Judiciary Committee, which normally would not have been available for public scrutiny until the year 2001, was kindly made available to me through the courtesy of Senators J. Strom Thurmond and Edward M. Kennedy, the ranking Republican and Democratic members of the committee, with the consent of Joseph Barnes's widow, Elizabeth. The charges made against Barnes, his closed-door testimony to the subcommittee notwithstanding, were reported in the *Tribune* and *Times* of August 1, 3, and 17, 1951.

V. Price's beliefs on the *Tribune*'s anti-Soviet bias in its news presentation were expressed in his diary entry of October 31, 1951.

VI. *I Led Three Lives* by Herbert A. Philbrick (McGraw-Hill, 1952). His speech to the Lumbermen's Association was delivered January 25, 1956.

VII. Among the most useful sources on Buchwald were *Time,* November 23, 1953, and October 3, 1960; *The Wall Street Journal,* November 24, 1969; *Women's Wear Daily,* July 1, 1974; *The Christian Science Monitor,* April 2, 1976; and *People,* November 7, 1977. The best sampling of Buchwald's work is to be found in *Down the Seine and Up the Potomac: Twenty-five Years of Art Buchwald's Best Humor* (G. P. Putnam's Sons, 1977), in which his Venice caper, quoted here, appears on p. 33. Brown Reid expressed his determination to affect the course of the paper on his return from Paris in a March 20, 1954, letter to Philbrick.

IX. Whitie Reid delivered his address to the *Yale Daily News* banquet on March 12, 1954; his memo exhorting the staff to greater editorial effort was sent August 27, 1954. Cameron's quoted memo was submitted May 25, 1954. *Editor & Publisher*'s admiring article on Brown's business-side leadership appeared January 15, 1955.

15 Enter the Perfect Patron

Brown Reid's Sigma Delta Chi speech was delivered May 17, 1955. Parsons's proposal for a new approach to news presentation by the paper was made August 19, 1953; Drummond's, September 29, 1953.

II. The quoted article by May Mann ran March 14, 1956. John Price's distaste for what Brown Reid was doing to the paper was recorded in his diary entry for February 20, 1956.

III. On Brown Reid's personality and performance as *Tribune* president, useful printed sources were the *New York Post* of May 15, 1955; *Newsweek,* May 23, 1955; *Business Week,* January 7, 1956; *The Reporter,* July 11, 1957; *Time,* September 23, 1957; and *Esquire,* January 1958. McCrary's September 21, 1956, letter to Bernard Gimbel is among Brown's Yale papers. Donovan's approval-seeking letter to Brown was sent July 21, 1955; his explanation of why he did not see Eisenhower and other circumstances surrounding his researching *Eisenhower: The Inside Story* are dealt with in Donovan's oral history memoir at Columbia. Nixon's letter of appreciation to Brown was sent August 29, 1956.

IV. The best single source on Whitney is E. J. Kahn, Jr.'s *Jock: The Life and Times of John Hay Whitney* (Doubleday, 1981). See also *Fortune,* October 1964, and Whitney's obituary in the *Times* and editorial obituary in the *International Herald Tribune,* February 9, 1982. Bryan's memo on the difficulties confronting any would-be savior of the *Tribune* was dated August 1, 1957. *Time*'s cautionary assessment of Brown Reid after the Whitney loan appeared September 23, 1957.

V. Compare the write-ups on the Kinsey Report in the *Tribune* and *Times* of August 21, 1953.

VI. Among Hadley's hortatory memos to Brown Reid, the most illuminating were sent August 22, September 5, November 1 and 8, and December 3 and 20, 1957.

VII. The offending article on Garland appeared January 10, 1957. *Garland v. Torre,* No. 325, Second Circuit of the U.S. Court of Appeals for the October 1957 term, was decided September 30, 1958. Reid's statement of softened criticism of the Eisenhower administration was included in his December 23, 1957, letter to Whitney. Reid's conduct of the editorial side of the paper in this period is documented in the minutes of the daily news conferences, supplied by Hadley. Thayer's early conviction that Brown Reid was an impediment to saving the paper was expressed in his December 2, 1957, letter to Whitney.

16 Sick Chicken

Background on Thayer's career was drawn from documents and memorabilia he made available; many others were consulted regarding his personality and character. Details of the Reid-Whitney transaction and financial data covering the Whitney ownership were obtained from the unpublished manuscript of Harry W. Baehr, who had the full cooperation of the Whitney Communications Corporation for his work, and my own inspection of the WCC records. On Lee Hills, the

"New York Closeup" column by Tex and Jinx McCrary in the May 28, 1951, *Tribune* was useful; Hills's advisory memo to Whitney and Thayer was sent February 14, 1958. The chronology for other cited correspondence: Brown Reid to Whitney, expressing confidence that their transaction would be worked out, February 21, 1958; Whitney's bracing letters to Reid, March 25 and April 1, 1958; Reid's counterproposal to Whitney, May 6, 1958; Whitney's tactful rejection of Reid's proposal, May 16, 1958; Reid's ambiguous response, May 23, 1958; Helen Reid's stunning letter to Whitney, June 5, 1958. Details on the Reid-Hills-Whitney meeting at the St. Regis were taken from Chapter 2, pp. 38 ff., of Baehr's manuscript. Thayer's letter to lure Hills back into the deal was sent June 13, 1958.

II. McCrary's unhappy letter to Whitney was sent August 20, 1958; on the Adams affair, see Joseph Kraft's article in *Harper's,* August 1959. Price's tribute to Mrs. Reid was included in his August 29, 1958, entry.

III. Torre's series on her jail stay began running January 25, 1959; her letter of appreciation to Brown was sent January 6, 1959.

IV. Eisenhower's endorsement of Robinson's return to the paper as head of the business side was made in a June 30, 1958, letter to Whitney. The McKinsey & Co. reports are in the WCC files. Thayer's discouragement over the performance of the Brundage-Cornish interim management was contained in a February 14, 1959, letter to Kilgore; his discouragement after the turndown by Duffield, in an April 15, 1959, letter to Whitney. Among clips on White, see especially *Editor & Publisher,* July 8, 1959; *Newsweek,* August 17, 1959; and *Time,* January 18, 1960. Thayer's early enthusiasm for White was in his May 12, 1959, letter to Whitney. The revealing exchange on Whitney's anticipated role in the paper occurred May 25 (Whitney to Thayer) and 29 (Thayer to Whitney), 1959.

V. Kilgore's "no strings attached" advisory was sent to Thayer on August 25, 1958. Hadley's ignored memos on reshaping the paper were dated October 15, 1958, and July 24, 1959. The first McKinsey & Co. report was delivered January 21, 1959.

VI. White's English-Russian editorial directed to Khrushchev ran on September 15, 1959. Whitney's statement of admiration for White's resistance to being stampeded, August 26, 1959. *Editor & Publisher* reported on the establishment of WCC in its October 31, 1959, issue; Thayer's view on WCC's role was spelled out in his October 22, 1959, letter to Whitney, and his misgivings about dependence on White, in his December 6, 1959, letter to Whitney.

17 Who Says a Good Newspaper Has to Be Dull?

Thayer's chastening letter to White on the paper's perceived bias against the TV industry, January 22, 1960; Whitney's still more distraught letter to White on its TV editorials, February 16, 1960. Wise's exclusive on the Doerfer-Storer cruise ran March 3, 1960. Thayer's wire to Whitney urging that he call him if White asked his concurrence with an editorial proposing Doerfer's ouster, March 8, 1960; White's letter to Whitney explaining why he did not contact him in the matter, March 9, 1960.

II. Chronology of correspondence: Thayer to White on why time was now a critical factor, February 8, 1960; Thayer to Whitney on White's "Alice-in-Wonderland air," February 29, 1960; Whitney's memo clarifying the White-Thayer relationship at the end of White's trip to London, April 10, 1960; White's private memo for his files on the visit with Whitney in London and the subsequent meeting with Thayer immediately upon his return, April 15, 1960; Steele's alarming report on the paper's financial status, April 26, 1960; Whitney to White, reversing his earlier affirmation of White's independence and installing Thayer over him, April 21 and May 2, 1960; White's comprehensive progress report to Whitney, May 25, 1960; Whitney to White on his distress over the *Tribune's* criticism of keynoter Judd at the Republican convention, August 9, 1960. The *Tribune's* national ranking of sixth was cited in Bernays's January 26, 1961, letter to *Tribune* promotion director Edward Freeman.

III. Kilgore's memo to Thayer opposing the "shower of gold" effect, January 19, 1961. The *Editor*

& *Publisher* interview with Whitney on his return to take charge of the paper, January 28, 1961. The McKinsey & Co. report establishing definite targets for the paper was delivered April 17, 1961.

IV. Thayer to Denson, presenting him all the reports and proposals to save the paper, March 8, 1961.

V. Denson's touch first revealed in issues of March 19, 29, and 30, 1961. The spoof of Denson's interrogatory style ran in the May 20, 1961, issue of *The New Yorker*. Cameron's memo on missed deadlines due to Denson techniques, May 1, 1961. *Time*'s critical appraisal of the Denson style, July 14, 1961; Shaplen's admiring appraisal, *Saturday Review*, July 8, 1961; *Editor & Publisher* on Denson's credo as expressed on the CBS press show, August 26, 1961.

VI. Whitney's cautionary note to Denson urging grist for serious readers as well as fare for short-order ones was cited in Chapter 5, p. 24, of Baehr's manuscript. Thayer's statement of a five-year plan for the paper on his assuming the *Tribune* presidency was carried in the July 1, 1961, *Editor & Publisher*. Regarding the *Tribune*'s lively new advertising campaign, see *George, Be Careful* by George Lois with Bill Pitts (Saturday Review Press, 1972) and *The Art of Advertising: George Lois on Mass Communications* (Harry N. Abrams, 1977). *Time*'s fonder assessment of Denson ran December 15, 1961.

18 Studies in Stubbornness

Among useful articles on Sheppard were those in *Time*, August 9, 1954, August 12, 1957, April 21, 1961, and April 22, 1966; *Newsweek*, June 15, 1962; *Life*, October 6, 1967; *New York Post*, November 4, 1968; and *Women's Wear Daily*, June 2, 1980.

II. On the RB-47 exclusive-that-wasn't, see *The Politics of Lying: Government Deception, Secrecy and Power* by David Wise (Random House, 1973), pp. 475 ff. On the steel price rise crisis, compare the *Tribune* from April 11 to April 20, 1962, with the *Times* coverage. Whitney's commendation note to Denson over his handling of the White House cancellation of the *Tribune* was dated May 31, 1962.

III. The introduction of *The Forgotten People* by Seymour K. Freidin (Charles Scribner's Sons, 1962) suggests the author's anti-Communism and its origins.

IV. Loory's report from Montgomery ran May 21, 1961. The text of the pothole commercial appears in Lois, *The Art of Advertising*, p. 33.

V. Whitney's unhappiness with Denson's "disastrous indispensability" is cited by Kahn in *Jock*, p. 277; Woodward's view of Denson's fatal misunderstanding of the *Tribune* staff's proprietary concern for the paper is in *Paper Tiger*, p. 280.

VI. Whitney memo to Bellows on the paper's need for consistency and depth, November 5, 1962; Thayer memo to Bellows on need for budgetary restraint, November 19, 1962. The best two sources on the 1962–63 strike are *Union Printers and Controlled Automation* by Harry Kelber and Carl Schlesinger (Free Press, 1962) and A. H. Raskin's two-page account in the *Times* of April 1, 1963. Helpful sources on Powers: *Current Biography; Newsweek*, January 7, 1963; UPI profile, February 28, 1963; *Time*, March 1, 1963; and *The New Yorker*, March 7, 1970. The Powers-Thayer debate on WCBS-TV occurred January 13, 1963; its text and many other documents on the strike are gathered in the WCC papers.

19 The Trail of the Blue Darter

See Talese's *The Kingdom and the Power* for background on Dryfoos and the younger Sulzberger. Robert Bryan's surviving notes of the May 29, 1963, meeting of *Tribune* and *Times* officials were corroborated by my interviews. Mrs. Sulzberger's remarks on the training of her son and the Reid brothers were made during the author's interview with her; see also her autobiographical memoir, *Iphigene*, with her granddaughter, Susan W. Dryfoos (Dodd, Mead, 1981).

II. Whitney's enthusiastic memo on the quality of the paper, July 16, 1963; Thayer's sobering response, July 22, 1963. Among the sources on Bellows: *Time*, March 22, 1948, and July 28, 1975;

Newsweek, August 18, 1958; *Esquire,* August 1, 1978; and the *Columbia Journalism Review,* September–October 1978.

III. Crist's *Cleopatra* review appeared June 13, 1963.

IV. Wald's memo, written in collaboration with Freidin, was undated but its context suggests it was drafted in November 1962. Wolfe's cited articles: NYU rent strike, April 13, 1962; King Hassan's buying spree, April 5, 1963; debutante party, September 4, 1963. On Breslin, see especially *The World of Jimmy Breslin* by Jimmy Breslin and annotated by James G. Bellows and Richard C. Wald (Viking Press, 1967). Dr. Perry's comments on Breslin's coverage of his efforts to save Kennedy were made in letters to the author dated November 21 and December 1, 1983.

V. "Sunday Trib: Middleweight Contender" by James Boylan, *Columbia Journalism Review,* Fall 1963, and "What I Did to Books and Vice Versa" by Richard Kluger, *Harper's,* December 1966, provide details on the revamped Sunday paper.

VI. Rogers's cited memos to Brown Reid were sent June 8, 1955, February 1, 1957, and February 24, 1958.

VII. Bellows's and Whitney's responses to Thayer's call for major changes in the paper were sent the same day, February 4, 1964, strongly suggesting coordination of effort. Commager's negative review of the Eisenhower book appeared in *Book Week* of November 10, 1963. Whitney's Colby speech was delivered November 12, 1964.

20 Somewhere a Child Is Burning

The essence of the paper's crusade was distilled in *New York City in Crisis,* prepared by the staff of the New York Herald Tribune under the direction of Barry Gottehrer (David McKay, 1965). The most grievous example of the paper's partisanship toward Lindsay appeared in the lead headline of the October 29, 1965, edition.

II. Felker's remarks about the nature of New York City appeared in an op-ed piece he contributed to the January 9, 1972, *Times; Time* of January 17, 1977, carried the most extensive material on his talents and personality. Wolfe's thoughts on the so-called New Journalism appeared in *New York* magazine, February 14, 1972, and *The New Journalism* by Tom Wolfe with an anthology edited by Tom Wolfe and E. W. Johnson (Harper & Row, 1972). Wolfe's pieces on *The New Yorker* ran April 11 and 18, 1965. Lewin's balanced assessment appeared in *Columbia Journalism Review,* Winter, 1966.

III. On the 1965 labor crisis: Kelber and Schlesinger, *Union Printers and Controlled Automation; The Wall Street Journal,* February 24, 1965; *Fortune,* March 1965; and the Big Six monthly bulletin for March 1965, Vol. 167, No. 3. Punch Sulzberger's denial that the *Times* accepted a soft settlement to hurt someone else was made during the author's interview with him.

IV. On "The Saga of the Dingbat," see *Editor & Publisher,* May 8, 1965; the revue's music was by Julian Stein and lyrics by Edward Nayor. Gabe Pressman broke the *Tribune-Journal-Telegram* merger story on the air June 15, 1965; papers of the following day had extensive reports on the subject. Flynn's castigating letter to Thayer, October 5, 1965; Thayer's unrepentant response, October 20, 1965. Sulzberger's concession that the *Times* greatly benefited from the *Tribune's* death was made during the author's interview with him.

IX. Terence Smith's eavesdropping exclusive ran on March 6, 1965. *The New Yorker* parodied Breslin in its March 14, 1964, issue. For the most favorable view of the Denson-Bellows *Tribune* and what it was up to, see *Shake It for the World, Smartass* by Seymour Krim (Dial Press, 1970), Part 7.

XIII. Whitney's letter to Eisenhower, largely blaming others for the demise of the paper, was sent August 22, 1966; see Kahn's *Jock,* p. 294. *U.S. News & World Report* blamed the unions in its August 29, 1966, issue. On the short sad life of the *World Journal Tribune,* see *Columbia Journalism Review,* Summer 1967, and "What's Wrong with American Newspapers?" by A. H. Raskin, *The New York Times Magazine,* June 11, 1967.

Late Late City Edition: A Shirttail

Among the more thoughtful pieces on the post-*Tribune* state of newspapering, I found *The Wilson Quarterly*'s 1982 special issue, Vol. 6, No. 5, devoted entirely to "News Media in America"; *Columbia Journalism Review,* January–February 1983, dealing with "On the Libel Front"; *Time*'s cover story on the embattled press in the December 12, 1983, issue; and "The Media Learn a Lesson" by Richard M. Clurman on the op-ed page of the *Times* for December 2, 1983.

Acknowledgments

Nothing is said to be deader than yesterday's newspaper. The effort to bring the *Herald Tribune* back to life in these pages required the sort of massive collaboration of which I have been the glad beneficiary. I had the cooperation during my research and writing of nearly three hundred people, most of whom still harbor a keen fondness for the paper and what it meant to their lives. Indeed, their afterglow of affection cast a collective spell that I have not been entirely able to elude—but it was not for lack of trying to be evenhanded in my judgments. To the best of my powers, the names of all who helped are cited in the foregoing credits and sources, and I am highly appreciative of their assistance. But I must single out five people in particular for their kindness: Walter N. Thayer, for providing full access to the files of Whitney Communications Corporation covering years that were a painful period in his professional life; Harry W. Baehr, for his willingness to share with me the fruits of his labor in the wake of disappointment; Arthur O. Sulzberger, for granting me access to the records, library, and personnel of *The New York Times*; Rutherford D. Rogers, head librarian emeritus at Yale, for access to that university's superb library system; and John Bogart, who never bit a dog or man but on request sternly reviewed my manuscript and offered many suggestions for its improvement. Others deserving of special thanks are Elizabeth Barnes, Pearle Blackman, George Cornish, Robert Donovan, Dorothea Hopke, Emily Kennedy, Jon McKenna, Louis Masotti, Carey Parker, Carol Rinzler, Kathryn Ritchie, Ronald Sheppard, and Richard West. Robert Gottlieb and Charles Elliott at Knopf provided line-by-line scrutiny of the text with a devotion all too rare in American publishing. And finally, my wife's assistance, manifested in many ways during more than four years of research, in justice requires the inclusion of her name on the title page.   R.K.

Index

A NOTE ABOUT THE AUTHOR

Richard Kluger was the last literary editor of the New York Herald Tribune, *on which he worked for the final four years of the paper's life. His esthetic attachment to the* Tribune *was born in his formative years while serving as editor-in-chief of the* Horace Mann Record, *his high school weekly in New York, and chairman of* The Daily Princetonian, *both of which used Bodoni type for their headlines. He worked as a deskman for* The Wall Street Journal, *a reporter for the* New York Post, *and a writer for* Forbes *before joining the* Tribune. *Following eight years as an executive editor in book publishing, he has devoted himself full-time to writing books. He is the author of five novels, the best known of which is* Members of the Tribe, *and one previous work of social history,* Simple Justice, *a widely acclaimed account of the U.S. Supreme Court's 1954 landmark decision outlawing racial segregation in the schools. He and his wife, Phyllis, who assisted him in researching this book, co-authored a novel,* Good Goods.

A NOTE ON THE TYPE

The text of this book was set by CRT in a film version of a typeface called Times Roman, designed by Stanley Morison (1889–1967) for The Times *(London) and first introduced by that newspaper in 1932.*

Among typographers and designers of the twentieth century, Stanley Morison was a strong forming influence as a typographical advisor to The Monotype Corporation, as a director of two distinguished English publishing houses, and as a writer of sensibility, erudition, and keen practical sense.

Composed by The Haddon Craftsmen, Inc.,
Scranton, Pennsylvania
Printed and bound by The Murray Printing Company
Westford, Massachusetts
Designed by Iris Weinstein

Few American newspapers—and perhaps none at all, in the view of some students of the craft—have matched the many excellences of the *New York Herald Tribune*. In the crispness of its writing and editing, the bite of its critics and commentators, the range of its coverage, and the clarity of its typography, "the Trib" (as many of its readers affectionately called it) raised newspapering to an art form. It had an influence and importance out of all proportion to its size. Abraham Lincoln valued its support so highly during the Civil War that he went to great lengths to retain the allegiance of its co-founder Horace Greeley. And President Eisenhower felt it was so significant a national institution and Republican organ that while in the White House he helped broker the sale of the paper to its last owner, John Hay Whitney.

From Karl Marx to Tom Wolfe, its list of staffers and contributors was spectacularly distinguished, including Walter Lippmann, Dorothy Thompson, Virgil Thomson, Eugenia Sheppard, Red Smith, Heywood Broun, and Joseph and Stewart Alsop. At the close of World War II, the *Herald Tribune*, which represented the marriage of two newspapers that, in their early years, had done more than any other to create modern journalism, was at its apex of power and prestige. Yet just twenty-one years later, its influence still palpable in every newsroom across the nation, the *Tribune* was gone. It is this story—of a great American daily's rise to international renown and its doomed fight for survival in the world's media capital—that is the one Richard Kluger tells in this comprehensive and fascinating book.

It begins in pre–Civil War New York with two bitter enemies who, between them, practically invented the newspaper as we know it: the *Herald*'s James Gordon Bennett, a cynic who brought aggressive honesty to reporting for the first time, and the *Tribune*'s Greeley, whose passion for social justice and vision of a national destiny made him an American icon and the most widely read polemicist since Tom Paine. These two giant figures loomed above a colorful, intensely competitive age, and with a novelist's sense of detail and character, Kluger gives us an extraordinary picture of them and their time. Here is Bennett breaking new journalistic ground in 1836 with his extended coverage of the sensational murder of a well-known prostitute near City Hall...the *Tribune* scooping the War Department on the outcome of the battle of Antietam in 1862...Greeley going upstate to testify in a libel suit brought against him by James Fenimore Cooper, then rushing back to the city in time to write a hilarious account of the trial for the morning edition...the birth of investigative journalism as the *Tribune*'s editors cracked the coded messages proving that Tilden's backers tried to fix the presidential election of 1876.

After the two papers and their two traditions—polemical and reportorial—merged early in the twentieth century, the fate of the *Herald Tribune* became intertwined with that of the pride-driven Reid family and its dynastic rule of the paper. In particular, it is the story of Helen Reid, the social secretary who married the owner's son and became the paper's dominant force, and of her two sons, whose fratricidal struggle for control helped bring about its downfall. To try to save it,